W9-CTW-409

Twentieth-Century Literary Criticism

Guide to Gale Literary Criticism Series

For criticism on	Consult these Gale series
Authors now living or who died after December 31, 1959	*CONTEMPORARY LITERARY CRITICISM (CLC)*
Authors who died between 1900 and 1959	*TWENTIETH-CENTURY LITERARY CRITICISM (TCLC)*
Authors who died between 1800 and 1899	*NINETEENTH-CENTURY LITERATURE CRITICISM (NCLC)*
Authors who died between 1400 and 1799	*LITERATURE CRITICISM FROM 1400 TO 1800 (LC)* *SHAKESPEAREAN CRITICISM (SC)*
Authors who died before 1400	*CLASSICAL AND MEDIEVAL LITERATURE CRITICISM (CMLC)*
Black writers of the past two hundred years	*BLACK LITERATURE CRITICISM (BLC)*
Authors of books for children and young adults	*CHILDREN'S LITERATURE REVIEW (CLR)*
Dramatists	*DRAMA CRITICISM (DC)*
Hispanic writers of the late nineteenth and twentieth centuries	*HISPANIC LITERATURE CRITICISM (HLC)*
Native North American writers and orators of the eighteenth, nineteenth, and twentieth centuries	*NATIVE NORTH AMERICAN LITERATURE (NNAL)*
Poets	*POETRY CRITICISM (PC)*
Short story writers	*SHORT STORY CRITICISM (SSC)*
Major authors from the Renaissance to the present	*WORLD LITERATURE CRITICISM, 1500 TO THE PRESENT (WLC)*

ISSN 0276-8178

Volume 63

Twentieth-Century Literary Criticism

**Excerpts from Criticism of the
Works of Novelists, Poets, Playwrights,
Short Story Writers, and Other Creative Writers
Who Lived between 1900 and 1960,
from the First Published Critical
Appraisals to Current Evaluations**

Nancy Dziedzic
Jennifer Gariepy
Scot Peacock
Editors

Pamela Willwerth Aue
Thomas Ligotti
Lynn Spampinato
Brandon Trenz
Associate Editors

GALE

DETROIT • NEW YORK • TORONTO • LONDON

STAFF

er Gariepy, Nancy Dziedzic, Scot Peacock, *Editors*

th Aue, Thomas Ligotti, Lynn Spampinato, Brandon Trenz,
Associate Editors

Marlene S. Hurst, *Permissions Manager*
Margaret A. Chamberlain, Maria Franklin, Kimberly F. Smilay, *Permissions Specialists*

Diane Cooper, Edna Hedblad, Michele Lonoconus, Maureen Puhl, Susan Salas, Shalice Shah,
Barbara A. Wallace, *Permissions Associates*
Sarah Chesney, Margaret McAvoy-Amato, *Permissions Assistants*

Victoria B. Cariappa, *Research Manager*
Alicia Noel Biggers, Julia C. Daniel, Tamara C. Nott, Michele P. Pica,
Tracie A. Richardson, Norma Sawaya, Cheryl L. Warnock, *Research Associates*

Mary Beth Trimper, *Production Director*
Deborah L. Milliken, *Production Assistant*

Sherrell Hobbs, *Macintosh Artist*
Randy Bassett, *Image Database Supervisor*
Robert Duncan, *Imaging Specialist*
Pamela Hayes, *Photography Coordinator*

Library of Congress Catalog Card Number 76-46132
ISBN 0-8103-9308-5
ISSN 0276-8178

Printed in the United States of America
10 9 8 7 6 5 4 3 2 1

Contents

Preface vii

Acknowledgments xi

v

Preface

Since its inception more than fifteen years ago, *Twentieth-Century Literary Criticism* has been purchased and used by nearly 10,000 school, public, and college or university libraries. *TCLC* has covered more than 500 authors, representing 58 nationalities, and over 25,000 titles. No other reference source has surveyed the critical response to twentieth-century authors and literature as thoroughly as *TCLC*. In the words of one reviewer, "there is nothing comparable available." *TCLC* "is a gold mine of information—dates, pseudonyms, biographical information, and criticism from books and periodicals—which many libraries would have difficulty assembling on their own."

Scope of the Series

TCLC is designed to serve as an introduction to authors who died between 1900 and 1960 and to the most significant interpretations of these author's works. The great poets, novelists, short story writers, playwrights, and philosophers of this period are frequently studied in high school and college literature courses. In organizing and excerpting the vast amount of critical material written on these authors, *TCLC* helps students develop valuable insight into literary history, promotes a better understanding of the texts, and sparks ideas for papers and assignments. Each entry in *TCLC* presents a comprehensive survey of an author's career or an individual work of literature and provides the user with a multiplicity of interpretations and assessments. Such variety allows students to pursue their own interests; furthermore, it fosters an awareness that literature is dynamic and responsive to many different opinions.

Every fourth volume of *TCLC* is devoted to literary topics. These topic entries widen the focus of the series from individual authors to such broader subjects as literary movements, prominent themes in twentieth-century literature, literary reaction to political and historical events, significant eras in literary history, prominent literary anniversaries, and the literatures of cultures that are often overlooked by English-speaking readers.

TCLC is designed as a companion series to Gale's *Contemporary Literary Criticism,* which reprints commentary on authors now living or who have died since 1960. Because of the different periods under consideration, there is no duplication of material between *CLC* and *TCLC.* For additional information about *CLC* and Gale's other criticism titles, users should consult the Guide to Gale Literary Criticism Series preceding the title page in this volume.

Coverage

Each volume of *TCLC* is carefully compiled to present:

- criticism of authors, or literary topics, representing a variety of genres and nationalities

- both major and lesser-known writers and literary works of the period

- 8-15 authors or 4-6 topics per volume

- individual entries that survey critical response to each author's work or each topic in literary history, including early criticism to reflect initial reactions; later criticism to represent any rise or decline in reputation; and current retrospective analyses.

Organization of This Book

An author entry consists of the following elements: author heading, biographical and critical introduction, list of principal works, excerpts of criticism (each preceded by an annotation and a bibliographic citation), and a bibliography of further reading.

- The **Author Heading** consists of the name under which the author most commonly wrote, followed by birth and death dates. If an author wrote consistently under a pseudonym, the pseudonym will be listed in the author heading and the real name given in parentheses on the first line of the biographical and critical introduction. Also located at the beginning of the introduction to the author entry are any name variations under which an author wrote, including transliterated forms for authors whose languages use nonroman alphabets.

- The **Biographical and Critical Introduction** outlines the author's life and career, as well as the critical issues surrounding his or her work. References to past volumes of *TCLC* are provided at the beginning of the introduction. Additional sources of information in other biographical and critical reference series published by Gale, including *Short Story Criticism, Children's Literature Review, Contemporary Authors, Dictionary of Literary Biography,* and *Something about the Author,* are listed in a box at the end of the entry.

- Most *TCLC* entries include **Portraits** of the author. Many entries also contain reproductions of materials pertinent to an author's career, including manuscript pages, title pages, dust jackets, letters, and drawings, as well as photographs of important people, places, and events in an author's life.

- The **List of Principal Works** is chronological by date of first book publication and identifies the genre of each work. In the case of foreign authors with both foreign-language publications and English translations, the title and date of the first English-language edition are given in brackets. Unless otherwise indicated, dramas are dated by first performance, not first publication.

- Critical excerpts are prefaced by **Annotations** providing the reader with information about both the critic and the criticism that follows. Included are the critic's reputation, individual approach to literary criticism, and particular expertise in an author's works. Also noted are the relative importance of a work of criticism, the scope of the excerpt, and the growth of critical controversy or changes in critical trends regarding an author. In some cases, these annotations cross-reference excerpts by critics who discuss each other's commentary.

- A complete **Bibliographic Citation** designed to facilitate location of the original essay or book precedes each piece of criticism.

- **Criticism** is arranged chronologically in each author entry to provide a perspective on changes in critical evaluation over the years. All titles of works by the author featured in the entry are printed in boldface type to enable the user to easily locate discussion of particular works. Also for purposes of easier identification, the critic's name and the publication date of the essay are given at the beginning of each piece of criticism. Unsigned criticism is preceded by the title of the journal in which it appeared. Some of the excerpts in *TCLC* also contain translated material. Unless otherwise noted, translations in brackets are by the editors; translations in parentheses or continuous with the text are by the critic. Publication information (such as footnotes or page and line references to specific editions of works) have been deleted at the editor's discretion to provide smoother reading of the text.

- An annotated list of **Further Reading** appearing at the end of each author entry suggests secondary sources on the author. In some cases it includes essays for which the editors could not obtain reprint rights.

Cumulative Indexes

- Each volume of *TCLC* contains a cumulative **Author Index** listing all authors who have appeared in Gale's Literary Criticism Series, along with cross references to such biographical series as *Contemporary Authors* and *Dictionary of Literary Biography*. For readers' convenience, a complete list of Gale titles included appears on the first page of the author index. Useful for locating authors within the various series, this index is particularly valuable for those authors who are identified by a certain period but who, because of their death dates, are placed in another, or for those authors whose careers span two periods. For example, F. Scott Fitzgerald is found in *TCLC*, yet a writer often associated with him, Ernest Hemingway, is found in *CLC*.

- Each *TCLC* volume includes a cumulative **Nationality Index** which lists all authors who have appeared in *TCLC* volumes, arranged alphabetically under their respective nationalities, as well as Topics volume entries devoted to particular national literatures.

- Each new volume in Gale's Literary Criticism Series includes a cumulative **Topic Index,** which lists all literary topics treated in *NCLC, TCLC, LC 1400-1800,* and the *CLC* yearbook.

- Each new volume of *TCLC*, with the exception of the Topics volumes, includes a **Title Index** listing the titles of all literary works discussed in the volume. In response to numerous suggestions from librarians, Gale has also produced a **Special Paperbound Edition** of the *TCLC* title index. This annual cumulation lists all titles discussed in the series since its inception and is issued with the first volume of *TCLC* published each year. Additional copies of the index are available on request. Librarians and patrons will welcome this separate index; it saves shelf space, is easy to use, and is recyclable upon receipt of the following year's cumulation. Titles discussed in the Topics volume entries are not included *TCLC* cumulative index.

Citing *Twentieth-Century Literary Criticism*

When writing papers, students who quote directly from any volume in Gale's literary Criticism Series may use the following general forms to footnote reprinted criticism. The first example pertains to materials drawn from periodicals, the second to material reprinted from books.

[1]William H. Slavick, "Going to School to DuBose Heyward," *The Harlem Renaissance Re-examined,* (AMS Press, 1987); excerpted and reprinted in *Twentieth-Century Literary Criticism,* Vol. 59, ed. Jennifer Gariepy (Detroit: Gale Research, 1995), pp. 94-105.

[2]George Orwell, "Reflections on Gandhi," *Partisan Review,* 6 (Winter 1949), pp. 85-92; excerpted and reprinted in *Twentieth-Century Literary Criticism,* Vol. 59, ed. Jennifer Gariepy (Detroit: Gale Research, 1995), pp. 40-3.

Suggestions Are Welcome

In response to suggestions, several features have been added to *TCLC* since the series began, including annotations to excerpted criticism, a cumulative index to authors in all Gale literary criticism series, entries devoted to criticism on a single work by a major author, more extensive illustrations, and a title index listing all literary works discussed in the series since its inception.

Readers who wish to suggest authors or topics to appear in future volumes, or who have other suggestions, are cordially invited to write the editors.

Acknowledgments

The editors wish to thank the copyright holders of the excerpted criticism included in this volume and the permissions managers of many book and magazine publishing companies for assisting us in securing reprint rights. We are also grateful to the staffs of the Detroit Public Library, the Library of Congress, the University of Detroit Mercy Library, Wayne State University Purdy/Kresge Library Complex, and the University of Michigan Libraries for making their resources available to us. Following is a list of the copyright holders who have granted us permission to reprint material in this volume of *TCLC*. Every effort has been made to trace copyright, but if omissions have been made, please let us know.

COPYRIGHTED EXCERPTS IN *TCLC*, VOLUME 63, WERE REPRINTED FROM THE FOLLOWING PERIODICALS:

The Antioch Review, v. XXVI, Summer, 1966. Copyright © 1966 by the Antioch Review Inc. Reprinted by permission of the Editors.—*Cross Currents,* v. XXII, Winter, 1972. Reprinted by permission of the publisher.—*ELH,* v. 57, Fall, 1990 for "Ruskin's Finale: Vision and Imagination in 'Praeterita' " by Timothy Peltason. Copyright © 1990 by The Johns Hopkins University Press. All rights reserved. Reprinted by permission of the Johns Hopkins University Press.—*Encounter,* June, 1966 for "Rosa Luxemburg" by George Lichtheim. © 1966 by the author. Reprinted by permission of the Literary Estate of George Lichtheim.—*Essays in Criticism,* v. XXXVIII, October, 1988 for "Ruskin's 'Womanly Mind' " by Dinah Birch. Reprinted by permission of the Editors of *Essays in Criticism* and the author.—*Film Comment,* v. 7, Spring, 1971. Copyright © 1971 by Film Comment Publishing Corporation. All rights reserved. Reprinted by permission of the Film Society of Lincoln Center.—*The History Teacher,* v. 19, November, 1985. © The Society for History Education. All rights reserved. Reprinted by permission of the publisher.—*International Philosophical Quarterly,* v. IV, December, 1964 for "Sri Aurobindo's Interpretation of Spiritual Experience: A Critique" by Eliot Deutsch. Reprinted by permission of the publisher and the author./ v. XII, June, 1972. Reprinted by permission of the publisher.—*The Journal of Modern History,* v. XVIII, June, 1946. © 1946 by The University of Chicago. Reprinted by permission of The University of Chicago Press.—*Journal of Popular Culture,* v. 25, Fall, 1991. Copyright © 1991 by Editor. Reprinted by permission of the publisher.—*Journal of the History of Ideas,* v. XLVIII, April-June, 1987. Copyright 1987, Journal of the History of Ideas, Inc. Reprinted by permission of the Johns Hopkins University Press.—*The Massachusetts Review,* v. XVI, Spring, 1975. © 1975. Reprinted from *The Massachusetts Review,* The Massachusetts Review, Inc. by permission.—*Modern Philology,* v. 90, February, 1993. © 1993 by The University of Chicago. Reprinted by permission of the University of Chicago Press.—*The Nation,* New York, v. XCCCVII, December 13, 1933. Copyright 1933 The Nation magazine/The Nation Company, Inc. Reprinted by permission of the publisher.—*Philosophy East and West,* v. 35, July, 1985. Copyright © 1985 by The University of Hawaii Press. Reprinted by permission of the publisher.—*PMLA,* v. 100, May, 1985. Copyright © 1985 by the Modern Language Association of America. Reprinted by permission of the Modern Language Association of America.—*PN Review,* v. 14, 1988 for "Reading Ruskin and Ruskin Readers" by Brian Maidment. Copyright © Poetry National Review 1988. Reprinted by permission of the author.—*Political Science Quarterly,* June, 1957. Reprinted by permission of the publisher.—*Science and Society,* v. XXXI, Fall, 1967. Copyright 1967 by S & S Quarterly, Inc. Reprinted by permission of the publisher.—*Sight and Sound,* v. 45, Autumn, 1976 for "The Road Back" by Jorge Luis Borges. Copyright © 1976 by The British Film Institute. Reprinted by permission of Wylie, Aitken & Stone, Inc.—*Social Research,* v. 40, Spring, 1973 for "Rosa Luxemburg's Theory of Revolution" by Ernst Vollrath. Copyright 1973 by New School for Social Research, New York. Reprinted by permission of the publisher.—*Soviet Studies,* v. XVIII, October, 1966. © 1966 The University of Glasgow. All rights reserved. Reprinted by permission of the publisher.—*The William and Mary Quarterly,* v. IX, July, 1952. Copyright, 1952 by the Institute of Early American History and Culture. Reprinted by permission of the Institute.—*World Literature Written in English,* v. 30, Spring, 1990 for "The Social and Political Vision of Sri Aurobindo" by K. D. Verma. © copyright 1990 WLWE-*World Literature Written in English.* Reprinted by permission of the publisher and the author.—*Yale Law Journal,* v. 42, May, 1933 for "Carl Becker: Historian of the Heavenly City" by Max Lerner. Reprinted by permission of The Yale Law Journal Company, Fred B. Rothman & Company and the Literary Estate of Max Lerner.—*The Yale Review,* v. 74, Summer, 1985. Copyright 1985, by Anthony Hecht. Reprinted by permission of the editors.

COPYRIGHTED EXCERPTS IN *TCLC*, VOLUME 63, WERE REPRINTED FROM THE FOLLOWING BOOKS:

University Press 1982. Reprinted by permission of the author.—Iyengar, K. R. Srinivasa. From "Sri Aurobindo's 'The Life Divine',' in *Perspectives on Indian Prose in English.* Edited by M. K. Naik. Humanities Press, 1982. Copyright © 1982 by Abhinav Publications. Reprinted by permission of Abhinav Publications.—Kazin, Alfred. From an introduction to *Limehouse Nights.* By Thomas Burke. Horizon Press, 1973. Copyright © 1973 by Horizon Press. Reprinted by permission of the author.—Langley, G. H. From *Sri Aurobindo: Indian Poet, Philosopher, and Mystic.* David Marlowe Ltd., 1949.—McNeill, William H. From *Mythistory and Other Essays.* The University of Chicago Press, 1986. © 1986 by The University of Chicago. All rights reserved. Reprinted by permission of The University of Chicago Press.—Nandakumar, Prema. From "Sri Aurobindo: The Prose Canon," in *Perspectives on Indian Prose in English.* Edited by M. K. Naik. Humanities Press, 1982. Copyright © 1982 by Abhinav Publications. Reprinted by permission of Abhinav Publications.—Nettl, J. P. From *Rosa Luxemburg, Vol. 1.* Oxford University Press, London, 1966. © Oxford University Press, 1966. Reprinted by permission of the publisher.—Norden, Martin F. From "Sexual References in James Whale's Bride of Frankenstein," in *Eros in the Mind's Eye: Sexuality and the Fantastic in Art and Film.* Edited by Donald Palumbo. Greenwood Press, 1986. Copyright © 1986 by Donald Palumbo. Reprinted by permission of Greenwood Publishing Group, Inc., Westport, CT.—Peterson, Audrey. From *Victorian Masters of Mystery: From Wilkie Collins to Conan Doyle.* Ungar, 1984. Copyright © 1984 by Frederick Ungar Publishing Co., Inc. Reprinted by permission of the publisher.—Sabine, George H. From an introduction to *Freedom and Responsibility in the American Way of Life.* By Carl Lotus Becker. Knopf, 1945. Copyright 1945 by Alfred A. Knopf, Inc., and the University of Michigan. Renewed 1973 by Carl L. Becker and Alfred A. Knopf, Inc. All rights reserved. Reprinted by permission of Alfred A. Knopf, Inc.—Sawyer, Paul. From "Ruskin and the Matriarchal Logos," in *Victorian Sages and Cultural Discourse: Renegotiating Gender and Power.* Edited by Thais E. Morgan. Rutgers University Press, 1990. Copyright © 1990 by Rutgers, The State University. All rights reserved. Reprinted by permission of Rutgers University Press.—Shell, Marc. From *The Economy of Literature.* Johns Hopkins University Press, 1978. Copyright © 1978 by The Johns Hopkins University Press. All rights reserved. Reprinted by permission of the publisher.—Townsend, Francis G. From "On Reading John Ruskin," in *The Victorian Experience: The Prose Writers.* Edited by Richard A. Levine. Ohio University Press, 1982. © copyright 1982 by Ohio University Press. All rights reserved.—Waters, Mary-Alice. From an introduction to *Rosa Luxemburg Speaks.* Edited by Mary-Alice Waters. Pathfinder Press, 1970. Copyright © 1970 by Pathfinder Press, Inc. All rights reserved. Reprinted by permission of the publisher.—Welsch, Janice R., and Syndy M. Conger. From "The Comic and the Grotesque in James Whale's Frankenstein Films," in *Planks of Reason: Essays on the Horror Film.* Edited by Barry Keith Grant. The Scarecrow Press, Inc., 1984. Copyright © 1984 by Barry Keith Grant. Reprinted by permission of the authors.—Williamson, Audrey. From *Artists and Writers in Revolt: The Pre-Raphaelites.* David & Charles, 1976. © Audrey Williamson 1976. All rights reserved.

PHOTOGRAPHS APPEARING IN *TCLC*, VOLUME 63, WERE RECEIVED FROM THE FOLLOWING SOURCES:

Page of manuscript from Modern Painters, Vol. 4, by John Ruskin. Trustees of The Pierpont Morgan Library. Reproduced by permission: **p.** 252/Voinquel, Raymond. Whale, James, photograph: **p.** 337.

Sri Aurobindo

1872-1950

(Full name Sri Aurobindo Ghose; also transliterated as Arabínda; also Ghosh) Indian philosopher, poet, essayist, critic, historian, translator, journalist, playwright, short story writer, and autobiographer.

INTRODUCTION

One of India's great modern philosophers, Aurobindo was a prolific author who expressed his views on humankind, nature, God, and the cosmos in numerous works of poetry and prose. He believed in the unity of all things material, intellectual, and spiritual, and a central theme that runs throughout all his writings is the divinization of life on earth. As he says in his poetic masterpiece, *Savitri:* "Nature shall live to manifest secret God, / The Spirit shall take up the human play, / The earthly life become the life divine."

Biographical Information

The third of six children, Aurobindo was born in Calcutta into a family with high-caste standing. His father, an eminent physician employed by the civil service, thoroughly embraced the Western way of life, and he attempted to shield Aurobindo from Indian influences from the time he was a baby. Aurobindo had an English nanny, his first formal education took place at a convent school in Darjeeling where all of his classmates were English children, and when he was seven years old he was sent with his two older brothers to study in England. Aurobindo attended St. Paul's School in London and King's College, Cambridge, excelling in English literature, the classics, and languages, including Latin, Greek, French, German, and Italian. Given his upbringing and education, it is not surprising that Aurobindo wrote almost exclusively in English, rather than in Bengali, his native language.

Biographers and critics generally divide Aurobindo's career into two periods, the first dating from 1893, when he returned to India from England, until 1910, when he established an ashram, or spiritual retreat, in Pondicherry, a French settlement in India. During this period Aurobindo worked for the civil service of the state of Baroda for nearly thirteen years, serving first as a professor of English and then as vice-principal at Baroda College. He also embarked on an intensive program of self-directed research into his Indian heritage, learning Sanskrit and Bengali, immersing himself in the Upanishads, the Bhagavad Gita, and other works of ancient Hindu philosophy, and familiarizing himself with various systems of yoga. While Aurobindo wrote and translated poetry during these years and also published articles on literary topics, this phase of his career is most notable for his active involvement in the struggle for Indian independence. Not only did he associate with radical Indian nationalists, he became the leader of the revolutionary movement and edited a newspaper entitled *Bande Mataram,* the organ of the so-called extremists of Indian nationalism. Aurobindo had become interested in Indian nationalism while a student at Cambridge, and his later Hindu studies had added a spiritual dimension to his political ideals, so that he imparted divinity upon his country, "Mother India." Although he did not promote terrorist activities, he justified violence as a last resort to achieving independence on the basis of his belief that the struggle was spiritual as well as political. In 1908, after a series of bombings, Aurobindo was arrested with other suspects on charges of sedition and terrorism. Eventually acquitted, he was imprisoned for nearly a year while awaiting trial. He later reported that while he was in jail he had a deeply moving mystical experience that changed his political and spiritual outlook, causing him to broaden his idea of independence and to attribute the divinity he once vested in the state to humankind in general. Upon his release from prison, Aurobindo founded two weekly papers, one written in Bengali, the *Dharma,* and the other written in English, the *Karmayogin.* Both papers were short-lived, but Aurobindo published several significant series of essays on Indian history and culture in the *Karmayogin* that later appeared in book form, including *The Ideal of the Karmayogin, A System of National Education,* and *The National Value of Art.* In the early months of 1910, Aurobindo retired from active politics and settled with his wife and some of his disciples at Pondicherry to concentrate on developing his spiritual ideas through meditation.

Aurobindo's move to Pondicherry marks the beginning of the second phase of his career. He remained there until his death, acting as guru to an enormous number of devoted followers, writing prolifically on philosophical and religious topics, and translating ancient Hindu scriptures. From 1914 until 1921 he published a monthly journal, the *Arya,* to disseminate his ideas. With the exception of *Savitri,* which he began writing in the 1890s and continually revised until his death, all of Aurobindo's most important works–*The Ideal of Human Unity, The Life Divine, The Human Cycle, Essays on the Gita, The Foundations of Indian Culture, The Future Poetry, On Yoga I,* and *On the Veda*–originally appeared serially in the *Arya.* Many of his other writings were not published until after his death. In 1926 Aurobindo had another profound mystical experience–he claimed to have had a vision of the god Krishna–and he went into isolation for over a decade. However, he kept in close contact with his disciples through letters, many of which were later collected and published as guides to his system of yoga. Aurobindo died in 1950.

1

Major Works

Aurobindo's philosophical beliefs derived from and promoted spiritual experience. The central theme of all his writings–the spiritualization of earthly life–rests on his belief that God exists in all of Nature and that spiritual intuition makes it possible for every individual to become conscious of his own divinity. Because of his emphasis on the unity of existence, Aurobindo's philosophy has been labeled "integralism." Aurobindo's most systematic account of humankind's eventual ascent to a higher level of consciousness is contained in *The Life Divine*, a one-thousand-page treatise in which he develops an evolutionary continuum to explain human and cosmic progress. Aurobindo proposes that the Brahman, the eternal spiritual Being, exists in nature in a seven-phase hierarchical structure that consists of three higher orders of being–Infinite Existence, Consciousness, and Bliss–and three lower orders of being–Matter, Life, and Mind. Mediating between the higher and lower orders of existence is the fourth level of being, Supermind, which is humankind's evolutionary goal. According to Aurobindo, humankind currently languishes at the third level of existence, Mind. Worldwide attainment of the level of the Supermind, Aurobindo believed, will usher in a new world order of peace and harmony. The metaphysical ideas expressed in *The Life Divine* take practical shape in *Essays on the Gita* and *On Yoga I,* in which Aurobindo explains his system of yoga and its role in preparing the soul to accept the Spirit. *Savitri* is Aurobindo's poetic expression of this process of transformation. In this epic poem, which is roughly twenty-four-thousand lines in length, two characters, one human and one divine, dramatize the ascent to divine perfection on earth as it corresponds to Aurobindo's own spiritual progress. *The Human Cycle* explains Aurobindo's philosophy from yet another perspective. In this work he develops his evolutionary theory in historical and psychological terms and states the necessary conditions for the arrival of the next evolutionary stage, the "Age of Spirit": first, there must exist certain individuals capable of absorbing the message of the Spirit and communicating it to the masses (Aurobindo cites Mohandes Gandhi as an example), and second, the masses must be prepared to implement the message of these mystics.

Critical Reception

A turning point in the critical history of Aurobindo's writings occurred with the 1970-72 publication of the *Sri Aurobindo Birth Centenary Library*. Brought out by the Sri Aurobindo Ashram, this thirty-volume collected edition of Aurobindo's works made his writings much more accessible to readers, particularly Westerners, which served to intensify the critical attention prompted by the centenary of Aurobindo's birth in 1972. Prior to this, most of the literature on Aurobindo had been written by his disciples, and while many of these books and articles provided useful summaries of Aurobindo's life and teachings, they were invariably laudatory in tone and rarely approached their subject from a critical perspective. Although Aurobindo studies continue to be dominated by the appreciative commentary of his followers, since the

1970s he has received increasing attention from scholars in the field of Indian and comparative religious thought. Some of Aurobindo's disciples have argued that analyses of Aurobindo's works emerging from the academic community lack the spiritual insight necessary for a sound interpretation of Aurobindo's philosophy. On the other hand, academic critics have charged that Aurobindo's devotees are too personally involved with their subject and his teachings to be objective; for example, they refuse to accept spiritual intuition of the divine as decisive evidence that a new spiritual age is approaching, seeking instead to investigate whether Aurobindo's evolutionary theory can be verified by experience. Similarly, estimations of Aurobindo's status as a literary artist vary. While some critics liken him to John Milton and Dante on the basis of *Savitri,* others contend that such comparisons are evidence of the indiscriminate praise lavished upon Aurobindo by his devotees. Such controversy notwithstanding, critics agree that Aurobindo has had a significant influence on modern Indian history and religious thought in his roles as political revolutionary and philosopher-yogi. He is universally admired for the comprehensiveness of his vision of life and the cosmos and for his devotion to the cause of guiding humankind into a new, more peaceful and productive age.

PRINCIPAL WORKS

Songs to Myrtilla (poetry) 1895
Urvasie (poetry) 1896
Perseus the Deliverer [first publication] (drama) 1907
Ahana, and Other Poems (poetry) 1915
The Ideal of Human Unity (nonfiction) 1919
The Ideal of the Karmayogin (nonfiction) 1919
Ideals and Progress (philosophy) 1920
The Renaissance in India (nonfiction) 1920
War and Self-Determination (nonfiction) 1920
The Brain of India (nonfiction) 1921
Love and Death (poetry) 1921
A System of National Education (nonfiction) 1921
The Yoga and Its Objects (nonfiction) 1921
Baji Prabhou (poetry) 1922
The National Value of Art (nonfiction) 1922
The Mother (letters) 1928
The Riddle of This World (nonfiction and letters) 1933
Lights on Yoga (letters) 1935
Bases of Yoga (letters) 1936
Sri Aurobindo: A Life (autobiography) 1937
The Life Divine. 2 vols. (philosophy) 1939-40
Heraclitus (philosophy) 1941
Poems, Views, and Reviews (poetry, essays, and criticism) 1941
Collective Poems and Plays (poetry and dramas) 1942
Poems: Past and Present (poetry) 1946
Letters of Sri Aurobindo, first series (letters) 1947
More Lights on Yoga (letters) 1948
The Human Cycle (philosophy and history) 1949
Letters of Sri Aurobindo, second series (letters) 1949
Letters of Sri Aurobindo, third series (letters) 1949
Essays on the Gita (essays) 1950

Savitri: A Legend and a Symbol. 2 vols. (poetry) 1950-51

Letters of Sri Aurobindo, fourth series (letters) 1951

Letters of Sri Aurobindo on The Mother (letters) 1951

Last Poems (poetry) 1952

Life–Literature–Yoga: New Letters with Questions (letters) 1952

The Problem of Rebirth (philosophy) 1952

The Supramental Manifestation upon Earth (philosophy) 1952

The Foundations of Indian Culture (essays) 1953

The Future Poetry (criticism) 1953

The Mind of Light (philosophy) 1953

Sri Aurobindo on Himself and on The Mother (letters) 1953

Correspondence with Sri Aurobindo (letters) 1954

On Yoga I: The Synthesis of Yoga (nonfiction) 1955

Bhavani Mandir (nonfiction) 1956

†*On the Veda* (essays and songs) 1956

Illion: An Epic in Quantitative Hexametres (poetry) 1957

On Yoga II (letters) 1958

Thoughts and Aphorisms (philosophy) 1958

The Hour of God (nonfiction) 1959

Thoughts and Glimpses (philosophy) 1964

Sri Aurobindo Birth Centenary Library. 30 vols. (essays, speeches, short stories, poetry, dramas, criticism, letters, autobiography, philosophy, history, notebook entries, and songs) 1970-72

*This work was originally published as *The Psychology of Social Development* in the journal *Arya,* August 1916 to July 1918.

†This work includes *The Secret of the Veda,* which was originally published in the journal *Arya,* August 1914 to July 1916, and translations of selected hymns from ancient Hindu scriptures.

CRITICISM

G. H. Langley (essay date 1949)

SOURCE: "Sri Aurobindo as Poet," in *Sri Aurobindo: Indian Poet, Philosopher, and Mystic,* David Marlowe, Ltd., 1949, pp. 113-33.

[*In the following excerpt, Langley traces the development of Aurobindo's poetry.*]

Sri Aurobindo defines poetry as "rhythmic speech which rises at once from the heart of the seer and from the distant home of truth". It is not by accident that the language is rhythmic, for rhythm gives individuality to the expression and enables the poet naturally to reproduce the creative unity and rhythm of life and spirit.

"The characteristic power of the poet", Aurobindo asserts, "is vision", and he contrasts this with the essentially different powers of the philosopher and scientist, the former of which he describes as "discriminative thought" and the latter as "analytic observation". "The greatest poets", he writes, "are those who have had a large and powerful interpretive and intuitive vision, and whose poetry has arisen out of that in a supreme revelatory utterance of it." Poetry has its source in man's unity with man and with Nature, and the poet's peculiar function is that of revealing what his sensitive spirit discerns with the deep intimacy of truth. Aurobindo makes two reflections regarding the poet's vision that are important. First, vision does not depend exclusively on the individual power of the poet. It depends also on the mind of his age and people, the level of their thought and experience, and the depth of their spiritual attainment. The poet, like other great men, is a product of his age and is representative of his people. Even though he be by nature a rebel, the roots of his personality are in the national spirit and the national mind. Secondly, the greatest poetry, Aurobindo insists, gives expression to the realisation of the Divine in the world and in man; and he explains that by this he means that the great poet discloses something of the divine possibilities for man, as well as the greatness of the power manifest in what man now is. By truer and deeper insight into the nature and meaning of the world he can aid man to bring diviner potentialities and more spiritual values into personal and social life. Aurobindo adds that the nations which most effectively make real these possibilities will produce the creative poets of the future and will lead the world in cultural and spiritual progress.

The dual character of the poet's function is fundamental. As arising from the heart of the seer, poetic expression must reflect the uniqueness and individuality of the personal consciousness of the poet; and, since the poet has his roots in his native soil, such individuality will naturally find expression within the special forms and movements of thought peculiar to his people and age. Hence the expression will be individualised and differentiated by the uniqueness of a people and time, as well as by that of a personal experience. At the same time the vision of the poet penetrates to the distant home of truth and, through expression of deep and significant personal experience, reveals a wider truth that cannot in any other way be attained.

The quotations from Aurobindo's poetic writings are arranged with the purpose of giving some impression of the manner in which he has achieved insight at various stages in the growth of his personal experience. He is convinced that fullness of vision is disclosed only in mystic spiritual experience, but . . . for him the mystic and Divine are integrated with the deeply human.

I

The first selections are from an early period of romantic poetry published between 1890 and 1908. They illustrate the range and penetration of Aurobindo's imagination even at that time. In the poems he employs Greek and Hindu myths and traditions and Greek metrical forms to create poems that were genuinely expressive of the view of life that was then forming in his reflective imagination. They are written in fine and forceful English, of the use of which Aurobindo is undoubtedly a master.

The group illustrates the early growth of conceptions that were later to become central in Aurobindo's outlook on life. They give imaginative expression to his sense of the limitations of sensuous love, however idealised the form of its manifestation, and of how the experience is transformed when integrated with the greater (divine) motives that should inspire human relations. The group includes *Urvasie, Love and Death, The Hero and the Nymph, Perseus the Deliverer,* and other poems.

Urvasie describes the love of King Pururavus for a sea nymph, and is based on a Sanskrit poem by Kalidasa which Aurobindo afterwards translated. The following lines describe how, when the gods had taken Urvasie from sharing Pururavus's earthly kingdom to dwell in their abode, he resolved to follow her whatever the cost:

> Now I
> Endure no more the desolate wide rooms
> And gardens empty of her. I will depart
> And find her under imperishable trees
> Or secret beside streams.

And

> Pururavus went forth
> Through ranks of silent people and gleaming
>   arms,
> With the last cloud of sunset up the fields
> And darkening meadows.
>
> He in that light turned and saw under him
> The mighty city, luminous and vast,
> Colossally up-piled towards the heavens,
> Temple and street and palace, and the sea
> Of sorrowing faces and sad grieving eyes;
> A moment saw, and disappeared from light
> Into forest. Then a loud wail arose
> From Pratisthana, as if barbarous hordes
> Were in the streets and all its temples huge
> Rising towards heaven in disastrous fire,
> But he unlistening into darkness went.

After much painful searching, Pururavus was reunited to Urvasie:

> Glad of his high reward, however dearly
> Purchased, purchased with infinite downfall,
>
> And they were left alone in that clear world.
> Then all his soul towards her leaning, took
> Pururavus into his clasp and felt,
> Seriously glad, the golden bosom on his
> Of Urvasie, his love; so pressing back
> The longed-for sacred face, lingering he kissed.
> Then love in his sweet heaven was satisfied.
> But far below through silent mighty space
> The green and strenuous earth abandoned
>   rolled.

The bliss of sensuous union was gained, but it failed to bring satisfaction:

> Always a sense of imperfection slipped
> Between him and that passionate success.

A similar sense of frustration is expressed by the Brahmin, Manavaka, in Aurobindo's translation of Kalidasa's epic, under the title *Vikramorvasie; or, The Hero and the Nymph*:

> After long pleasuring with Urvasie
> In Nandan and all woodlands of the Gods,

> Our King's at last returned, and he has entered
> His city, by the jubilant people met
> With splendid greetings, and resumed his toils.
> Ah, were he but a father, nothing now
> Were wanting to his fullness.

Love and Death records the love of Ruru, a Brahmin youth, and Priyumvada, the daughter of a nymph. In it the Hellenic story of Orpheus and Eurydice is transformed into a tale of love, Hindu in setting, sentiment, and expression. The poem begins by describing how Priyumvada

> Opened her budded heart of crimson bloom
> To love, to Ruru; Ruru, a happy flood
> Of passion round a lotus dancing thrilled,
> Blinded with his soul's waves Priyumvada.
> To him the earth was a bed for this sole flower,
> To her all the world was filled with his embrace.

It describes how Ruru after wandering from morn till noon through the forest, where everything beautiful reminded him of her:

> Went homeward yearning to Priyumvada,
> And near his home emerging from green leaves
> He laughed towards the sun: "O father Sun",
> He cried, "how good it is to live, to love!
> Surely our joy shall never end, nor we
> Grow old, but like bright rivers or pure winds
> Sweetly continue, or revive with flowers,
> Or live at least as long as senseless trees."

But this was not to be. Priyumvada was bitten by a snake, and while dying:

> Her eyes that clung to sunlight yet, with pain
> Were large and feebly round his neck her arms
> She lifted and, desiring his pale cheek
> Against her bosom, sobbed out piteously,
> "Ah, love!" and stopped heart-broken; then, "O
>   Love!
> Alas the green dear home that I must leave
> So early! I was so glad of love and kisses,
> And thought that centuries would not exhaust
> The deep embrace. And I have had so little
> Of joy and the wild day and throbbing night,
> Laughter, and tenderness, and strife and tears."

Ruru descends to the underworld in his passion to find Priyumvada. There he is warned by Kama, God of desire and love, of the price he would have to pay. The way would be hard, most hard to find, but harder still to tread, and for perishable feet almost impassable. Yet Ruru is not to be deterred:

> But if with price, ah God! what easier! Tears
> Dreadful, innumerable I will absolve,
> Or pay with anguish through the centuries,
> Soul's agony and torture physical,
> So her small hands about my face at last
> I feel.

Kama again urges:

> O ignorant fond lover, not with tears
> Shalt thou persuade immitigable Death.
>
>   A sole thing the Gods
> Demand from all men living, sacrifice:
> Nor without this shall any crown be grasped.

Life the pale ghost requires: with half thy life
Thou may'st protract the thread too early cut
Of that delightful spirit—half sweet life.
O Ruru, lo, thy frail precarious days,
And yet how sweet they are! simply to breathe
How warm and sweet! And ordinary things
How exquisite, thou then shalt learn when lost,
How luminous the daylight was, mere sleep
How soft and friendly clasping tired limbs,
And the deliciousness of common food.
And things indifferent thou then shalt want,
Regret rejected beauty, brightnesses
Bestowed in vain. Wilt thou yield up, O lover,
Half thy sweet portion of this light and gladness,
Thy little insufficient share, and vainly
Give to another? She is not thyself.

Then Yama, God of death, continues with a yet more urgent plea. Would Ruru, in addition, be prepared to sacrifice the wisdom of age?

O mortal, O misled! But sacrifice
Is stronger, nor may law of Hell or Heaven
Its fierce effectual action supersede.
Thy dead I yield. Yet thou bethink thee, mortal,
Not as a tedious evil nor to be
Lightly rejected gave the gods old age,
But tranquil, but august, but making easy
The steep ascent to God. Therefore must Time
Still batter down the glory and form of youth
And animal magnificent strong ease,
To warn the earthly man that he is spirit
Dallying with transience, nor by death he ends,
Nor to the dumb warm mother's arms is bound,
But called unborn into the unborn skies.

But finally love triumphed. Love is transformed by sacrifice, but the experience is bought at the price of much that goes to make up the worth of man's life.

Perseus the Deliverer shows love more fully transformed by the deepening and expansion of human feeling and the insight that comes from the awakening of mind and spirit. The love-story of Perseus and Andromeda is interwoven with the wider action of a play which exhibits the inevitable conflict between brute force and reason or wisdom, the former being represented by the sea monster Poseidon and Polydamon his priest, and the latter by Athene and her messenger Perseus.

While returning from a mission committed to him by Zeus, Perseus arrives in Syria at a time when two Babylonian merchants, who have been wrecked off the promontory on which the temple of Poseidon stands, have been confined within its precincts preparatory to being sacrificed to the sea monster. Moved by pity, the Princess Andromeda has entered the temple and made possible their escape. To her kinsmen who would deter her urging:

What! you will kill yourself, and for two strang-
ers
You never saw?

she replies:

If you must punish me,
Strike home. You should have given me no
heart;
It is too late now to forbid it feeling.

And to the appeal:

You, little princess! Wherefore did you this?

she protests:

Because I would not have their human hearts
Mercilessly uprooted for the bloody
Monster you worship as a god! because
I am capable of pain and so can feel
The pain of others! For which if you I love
Must kill me, do it. I alone am guilty.

Roused by Polydamon and fearing the vengeance of Poseidon, the people cause Andromeda to be stripped and bound to a rock for the monster to come and devour. Yet she meditates:

Heaven looks coldly on.
Yet I repent not. O thou dreadful god!
Yes, thou art dreadful and most mighty; perhaps
This world will always be a world of blood
And smiling cruelty, thou its fit sovereign.
But I have done what my own heart required of
me,
And I repent not. Even if after death
Eternal pain and punishment await me.
And gods and men pursue me with their hate,
I have been true to myself and to my heart,
I have been true to the love it bore for men,
And I repent not.

Andromeda's deep human feeling draws the divine Perseus to her, and, revealing himself, he speaks:

Look up, O sunny-curled Andromeda!
Perseus, the son of Danæ, is with thee
To whom thou now belongest. Fear no more!
Thou art as safe as if they mother's arms
Contained thee.
                    I take into my arms
My own that I have won.
O sweet chained body, chained to love not death.

Perseus slays the monster and, with him, the brute power of Poseidon. The fruits of his union with Andromeda are indicated by the requests they both make of the king, her father. Andromeda pleads: "This I ask",

Let the dire cult
For ever cease and victims bleed no more
On its dark altar. Instead Athene's name
Spread over all the land and in men's hearts.
Then shall a calm and mighty Will prevail
And broader minds and kindlier manners reign
And men grow human, mild and merciful.

And to her wish Perseus adds:

Then let the shrine
That looked out from the earth's breast into the
sunlight,
Be cleansed of its red memory of blood,
And the dread Form that lived within its pre-
cincts
Transfigure into a bright compassionate God.
Whose strength shall aid men tossed upon the
seas.

II

Shortly after the period to which the romantic poems belong Aurobindo left Baroda to immerse himself in the national renaissance of literary and political activity centred in his own province of Bengal. The change led to the publication in weekly periodicals of poems that reflected his political preoccupations. They show how, in the lives of many Indian leaders, national aspiration became fused with moral and religious conviction.

Baji Prabhou is an historical poem published in *Karmayogin* in 1910, and probably written some years earlier. Shivaji, the great Mahratta hero, is retreating towards Raigurh from the Bijapur army and, with the remnant of his army, is obliged to pass through a "tiger-throated gorge":

> Narrowing there
> The hills draw close, and their forbidding cliffs
> Threaten the prone incline.

Shivaji entrusts the defence of the gorge to Baji Prabhou while he goes on to bring up reinforcements. Baji accepts the dangerous task, answering:

> Not in this living net
> Of flesh and nerve, nor in the flickering mind
> Is a man's manhood seated. God within
> Rules us, who in the Brahmin and the dog
> Can, if He will, show equal godhead.

As the enemy approaches, Baji exhorts his men:

> Chosen of Shivaji, Bhavani's swords,
> For you the gods prepare. We die indeed,
> But, let us die with the high-voiced assent
> Of Heaven to our country's claim enforced
> To freedom.

Then:

> They came, they died; still on the previous dead
> New dead fell thickening.
>
> So was the fatal gorge
> Filled with the clamour of the close-locked fight.
> Sword rang on sword, the slogan shout; the cry
> Of guns, the hiss of bullets filled the air,
> And murderous strife heaped up the scanty
> space,
> Rajput and strong Mahratta breathing hard
> In desperate battle.

On and on they came till

> Baji with a gruesome hand
> Wiping the blood from his fierce staring eyes
> Saw round him only fifteen men erect
> Of all his fifty.

Groaning, once more he turned and charged the exultant foe, until

> Eight men alone
> Stood in the gorge's narrow end, not one
> Unwounded.

And Baji

> turned and sought again the war.
> So for few minutes desperately they strove.
> Man after man of the Mahrattas fell
> Till only three were left. Then suddenly
> Baji stood still and sank upon the ground.

> Quenched was the fiery gaze, nerveless the arm:
> Baji lay dead in the unconquered gorge.

But Shivaji, his leader, had arrived, and there by Baji's empty frame he

> Stood silent and his gaze was motionless
> Upon the dead.

Another dramatic poem, **"Vidula",** is based on a tale from the Mahabharata. It tells how the widowed queen, passionate, fiery-souled, resolute, with "tameless heart of storm", is, by fierce eloquence, rousing her son, Sunjoy, to action. Sunjoy had been "hurled down from his lofty throne" by the King of Sindhu, and his mother had come upon him as he lay unnerved and abject. The verse expresses with remarkable power the intensity and rush of Vidula's passion:

> Rise, thou coward, seek not slumber while the
> victors jeer around.
> Out to battle, do thy man's work, falter not in
> high attempt;
> So a man is quit before his God and saved from
> self-contempt.
> For the great heart grieves not though he lose
> the glorious crown of strife,
> But he does the work before him, holding cheap
> his body's life.
> Show thy prowess, be the hero thou wast born,
> with flashing glaive
> Hew thy way with God before thee to the heaven
> of the brave.

Again:

> Shrink not from a noble action, stoop not to un-
> worthy deed!
> Vile are they who stoop, they gain not Heaven's
> doors, nor here succeed.
>
> Man puts forth his manhood, wins and is or dies
> in the attempt.
> All you who are men, awake and rise and strug-
> gle; free and great
> Now resolve to be and shrink not from the dan-
> gerous face of Fate.

Finally Vidula rouses Sunjoy, and he responds:

> O thou strong and resolute speaker, even the fee-
> blest fainting soul
> Would put darkness from him, listening, for thy
> words would make him whole.

In 1909 Aurobindo published a fine translation into English of Bankim Chandra's *Bande Mâtaram* under the title **Hymn to the Mother**. The following extract may give some impression of its beauty:

> Mother, I bow to thee!
> Thou art wisdom, thou art law,
> Thou our heart, our soul, our breath,
> Thou the love divine, the awe
> In our hearts that conquers death.
> Thine the strength that nerves the arm,
> Thine the beauty, thine the charm.
> Every image made divine
> In our temples is but thine.
>
> Loveliest of all earthly lands,

Showering wealth from well-stored hands!
Mother, mother mine!
Mother sweet, I bow to thee,
Mother great and free!

Then in 1941, after Aurobindo had ceased from active participation in politics, he published, under the title of *Mother India,* a translation of another patriotic hymn by Dvyjendralal Roy. The first stanza reads:

India, my India, where first human eyes awoke
to heavenly light,
All Asia's holy place of pilgrimage, great Moth-
erland of might!
World-mother, first giver to humankind of philosophy and sacred lore,
Knowledge thou gav'st to man, God-love,
works, art, religion's open door.

And the last:

O even with all that grandeur dwarfed or turned
to bitter loss and maim,
How shall we mourn who are thy children and
can vaunt thy mighty name?
Before us still there floats the ideal of those
splendid days of gold:
A new world in our vision wakes, Love's India
we shall rise to mould.

India, my India, who dare call thee a thing for
pity's grace today?
Mother of wisdom, worship, works, nurse of the
spirit's inward ray!

III

Between 1909 and 1920 Aurobindo published a number of reflective poems in which he gave imaginative expression to thoughts that had become central in his conception of life, and **"Ahana"**, the Dawn of God, is the longest and perhaps the most important of these. It describes the eternal immanence of the Divine in the Universe, the emergence of consciousness from inconscient nature, and the unfolding of its powers through enjoyment of union with the Divine.

It is only possible to quote a few extracts, but these are selected so as to give some impression of the conception and of the beauty of much of the language in which it is expressed. We are

Children of Time whose spirits came down from
eternity,
seizing
Joys that escape us, yoked by our hearts to a labour unceasing,
Earth-bound, torn with our longings, our life is
a brief incompleteness.

Heaven unchanging, earth with her time-beats
yearn to each other,—
Earth-souls needing the touch of heaven's peace
to recapture,
Heaven needing earth's passion to quiver its
peace into rapture.

Some contemporary thinkers may disagree.

Now have the wise men discovered that all is the
craft of a super-

Magic of Chance and a movement of Void and
inconscient Stupor.

Man who has towered
Out of the plasm and struggled by thought to Divinity's level,
Man, this miniature second creator of good and
of evil,
He too was only a compost of Matter made living, organic,
Forged as her thinking tool by an Energy blind
and mechanic.

Who can believe it?

Naught else is she but the power of the Spirit
who dwells in her ever,
Witness and cause of her workings, lord of her
pauseless endeavour.

Holy
Silences brood in her heart and she feels in her
ardent recesses
Passions too great for her frame, on her body immortal caresses.

Deep in our being inhabits the voiceless invisible
Teacher;
Powers of his godhead we live; the Creator
dwells in the creature.

Man's destiny is to ascend:

That which was mortal shall enter immortality's
golden precincts,
Enter the splendour that broods now unseen on
us, deity invading,
Sight without error, light without shadow, beauty unfading,
Infinite largeness, rapture eternal, love none can
sever,
Life, not this death-play, but a power God-
driven and blissful for ever.

Some single lines are strikingly expressive:

Bliss is her goal, but her road is through whirlwind and death blast and storm-race.

There is a joy behind suffering; pain digs our
road to his pleasance.

Open the barriers of Time, the world with thy
beauty enamour.

In **"Dawn over Ilion"**, which appears to be an experiment in rhymeless hexameters, Aurobindo makes use of the Greek story to express reflections characteristically his own. Of the passage of time he writes:

The moment travels driving the past towards the future,
Only its face and its feet are seen, not the burden
it carries.
Weight of the event and its surface we bear, but
the meaning is hidden.
Earth sees not; life's clamour deafens the ear of
the spirit.

Lights that we think our own, yet they are but
tokens and counters,
Signs of the Forces that flow through us serving
a Power that is secret.

One other quotation I would like to give. It describes the effect of the prolonged siege on the Greek army surrounding Troy. As the years passed the Greeks began to "repose from their toil and incline to the joy of the banquet, filling their hearts with ease". They

> Passed from the wounded earth and its air that
>   is ploughed with men's anguish;
> Calm they reposed and their hearts inclined to
>   the joy and the silence.
> Lifted was the burden laid on our wills by their
>   starry presence:
> Man was restored to his smallness, the world to
>   its inconscient labour.
> Life felt a respite from height, the winds
>   breathed freer delivered;
> Light was released from their blaze and the earth
>   was released from their greatness.

Other poems show the fusion of Aurobindo's thought with Hindu conceptions. The following lines are from **"The Rakshasas"**—supernatural beings symbolising violent strength and self-assertion:

> He takes the brute into himself for man
> Yielding it offerings, while with grandiose
>   thoughts
> And violent aspirations he controls;
> He purifies the demon in the race
> Slaying in wrath not cruelty.
>
>   Were he denied
> His period, man could not progress. But since
> He sees himself as Me [God], not Me in him,
> And takes the life and body for the whole,
> He cannot last.

A similar conception is finely expressed in an imaginative poem of a later period. It is an experiment in free quantitative verse, and is entitled **"The Tiger and the Deer"**:

> Brilliant, crouching, slouching, what crept
>   through the green heart of the forest,
> Gleaming eyes and mighty chest and soft sound-
>   less paws of grandeur and murder?
> The wind slipped through the leaves as if afraid
>   lest its voice
>   and the noise of its steps perturb the pitiless
>   Splendour,
> Hardly daring to breathe. But the great beast
>   crouched and
>   crept, and crept and crouched a last time,
>   noiseless, fatal,
> Till suddenly death leaped on the beautiful wild
>   deer as it drank
> Unsuspecting from the great pool in the forest's
>   coolness and shadow,
> And it fell and, torn, died remembering its mate
>   left sole in the deep woodland,—
> Destroyed, the mild harmless beauty by the
>   strong cruel beauty in Nature.
> But a day may yet come when the tiger crouches
>   and leaps no more in the dangerous heart of
>   the forest,
> As the mammoth shakes no more the plains of
>   Asia;
> Still then shall the beautiful wild deer drink from
>   the coolness of great pools in the leaves' shad-
>   ow.

> The mighty perish in their might;
> The slain survive the slayer.

For the reflective Hindu mind the ocean has always been a symbol of mysterious power, ever revealing its eternal and changeless deeps in the unceasing changes that trouble its surface:

> The Power that moves it is the Ocean's force
>   Invincible, eternal, free,
> And by that impulse it pursues its course
>   Inevitably.

Aurobindo's **Songs of the Sea,** published about 1923, is a magnificent series of translations of short poems on this theme by Chittaranjan Das. The following quotations are from the series:

> I lean to thee a listening ear
> And thy immense refrain I hear,
> O ocean circled with the lights of morn.
> What word is it thou sing'st? What tune
> My heart is filled with, and it soon
> Must overflow? What mystical unborn
> Spirit is singing in thy white foam-caves?
> What voice turns heaven to music from thy
>   waves?
> O vast musician! Take me, all thy mind
> In light, in gloom, by day, by night express.
> Into me, minstrel, breathe thy mightiness.
>
> Evening has fallen upon the world; its fitting
>   tone,
> O sea, thy quiet bosom gives, making dim moan,
> And that wide solemn murmur, passion's ceas-
>   ing flow,
> Becomes a chant of silence for our souls their
>   depths to know.

Later Aurobindo himself, in another metrical experiment, writes:

"Ocean Oneness"

> Silence is around me, wideness ineffable;
> White birds on the ocean diving and wandering;
>   A soundless sea on a voiceless heaven,
>   Azure on azure, is mutely gazing.
>
> Identified with silence and boundlessness
> My spirit widens clasping the universe
>   Till all that seemed becomes the Real,
>   One in a mighty and single vastness.
>
> Someone broods there nameless and bodiless,
> Conscious and lonely, deathless and infinite,
>   And, sole in a still eternal rapture,
>   Gathers all things to his heart for ever.

IV

Finally, it is necessary to give examples of the poems in which Sri Aurobindo endeavours to express his mystic spiritual experience. Many Western readers may be confronted with difficulty when attempting to understand and appreciate these. They may lack the kind of experience Aurobindo is describing and may be unfamiliar with the symbolism employed. At the same time, I feel they will be impressed by the beauty and power of expression and by the depth of insight with which the poems are characterised. These poems were published from 1930 to 1941.

The following quotations from **"The Bird of Fire"** refer to the ascent of the soul to the Divine. The bird of fire represents the divine consciousness, immanent in every man, and tending to impel him upwards towards the light:

> Gold-white wings of the miraculous bird of fire,
>   late and slow have you come from the
> Timeless.
> Angel, here unto me
>   Bring'st thou for travailing earth a spirit si-
> lent and free
>   or His crimson passion of love divine,—
> White-rose-altar the eternal Silence built, make
>   now my nature wide, an intimate guest of His
> solitude.

But the ascent is arduous:

> Rich and red is thy breast, O bird, like blood of
>   a soul climbing the hard crag-teeth world,
> wounded and nude.

Of its goal he writes:

> One strange leap of thy mystic stress breaking
>   the barriers of mind and life, arrives at the lu-
> minous term thy flight;
>   Invading the secret clasp of the Silence and
> crimson Fire thou frontest eyes in a timeless
> Face.

The experience of mystic union is described in the following lines that occur in **"In horis æternum"**. In its unending ascent the soul catches

> A breath, a cry, a glimmer from Eternity's face,
>   in a fragment the mystic Whole.
>
> Moment-mere, yet with all eternity packed,
>   lone, fixed, intense,
> Out of the ring of these hours that dance and die,
>   caught by the spirit in sense,
> In the greatness of a man, in music's outspread
>   wings, in a touch, in a smile, in a sound,
> Something that waits, something that wanders
>   and settles not, a Nothing that was all and is
> found.

In one of the metrical experiments also the following lines occur:

> Wisdom supernal looks down on me, Knowl-
>   edge mind cannot measure;
> Light that no vision can render garments the si-
>   lence with splendour.
> Filled with a rapturous Presence the crowded
>   spaces of being
> Tremble with the Fire that knows, thrill with
>   the might of repose.
> Earth is now girded with trance and Heaven is
>   put round her for vesture.
>   Wings that are brilliant with fate sleep at Eter-
> nity's gate.
> Time waits, vacant, the Lightning that kindles,
>   the Word that transfigures:
> Space is a stillness of God building his earthly
>   abode.
> All waits hushed for the fiat to come and the
>   tread of the Eternal;
>   Passion of a bliss yet to be sweeps from Infini-
> ty's sea.

. . . [In **"Nirvana"**] Sri Aurobindo expresses his sense of the great silence. The following description of the rapture of such experience is from a short poem **"Transformation"**:

> I am no more a vassal of the flesh,
>   A slave to Nature and her leaden rule;
>   I am caught no more in the senses' narrow
> mesh.
> My soul unhorizoned widens to measureless
>   sight,
>   My body is God's happy living tool,
>   My spirit a vast sun of deathless light.

Nevertheless, there is need to pass beyond enjoyment of the mystic experience of oneness with the Divine, for the consummation comes, not with such enjoyment alone, but only as power flows from it and enables man to transform his humanhood after the image of the Divine. In **"The Life Heavens"**, after describing how he had lain

> In the clasp of a Power that enthrals to sheer
>   Bliss and beauty body and rapt soul

Aurobindo proceeds:

> But suddenly there soared a dateless cry,
>   Earth's outcry to the limitless Sublime.
>
> I, Earth, have a deeper power than Heaven;
>   My lonely sorrow surpasses its rose-joys.

He was conscious of the "Earth's heart beating below him still", and calling for the bringing down of divine power into life.

The same belief is again expressed in **"Jivanmukta"**. It opens with:

> There is a silence greater than any known
>   To earth's dumb spirit.

Splendour floods the soul, power descends on it, bliss surrounds it with ecstasy everlasting; and it escapes, rapt, thoughtless, into the Eternal's breast. Then comes the conviction:

> Only to bring God's forces to waiting Nature,
> To help with wide-winged Peace her tormented
>   labour
>   And heal with joy her ancient sorrow,
>   Casting down light on the inconscient dark-
> ness,
> He acts and lives. Vain things are mind's smaller
>   motives
> To one whose soul enjoys for its high possession
>   Infinity and the sempiternal
>   All is his guide and beloved and refuge.

The most impressive and perfect expression of this culminating experience, however, seems to me to be contained in **"Rose of God"**, which, because of the depth of the insight it conveys and the beauty and power of the language in which this is expressed, I quote in full. The third line in each stanza of this poem expresses a cry from the awakened soul for the ingression into our humanhood of the divine attribute referred to in the first and second lines. [The critic explains in a note to the first line of the poem that the word *stain*—defined as a "mark made by a Hindu woman through the parting of her hair as a symbol of marriage"—is used in the poem to symbolize "the union of the soul with the Divine."]

"Rose of God"

Rose of God, vermilion stain on the sapphires of
  heaven,
Rose of Bliss, fire-sweet, seven-tinged with the
  ecstasies seven!'
Leap up in our heart of humanhood, O miracle,
  O flame,
Passion-flower of the Nameless, bud of the mys-
  tical Name.

Rose of God, great wisdom-bloom on the sum-
  mits of being,
Rose of Light, immaculate core of the ultimate
  seeing!
Live in the mind of our earthhood; O golden
  Mystery, flower,
Sun on the head of the Timeless, guest of the
  marvellous Hour.

Rose of God, damask force of Infinity, red icon
  of might,
Rose of Power with thy diamond halo piercing
  the night!
Ablaze in the will of the mortal, design the wonder of thy plan,
Image of Immortality, outbreak of the Godhead
  in man.

Rose of God, smitten purple with the incarnate
  divine Desire,
Rose of Life, crowded with petals, colour's lyre!
Transform the body of the mortal like a sweet
  and magical ryhme;
Bridge our earthhood and heavenhood, make
  deathless the
  children of Time.

Rose of God like a blush of rapture on Eternity's
  face,
Rose of Love, ruby depth of all being, fire-
  passion of Grace!
Arise from the heart of the yearning that sobs in
  Nature's abyss:
Make earth the home of the Wonderful and life
  Beatitude's kiss.

Sisirkumar Ghose   (essay date 1962)

SOURCE: "*The Future Poetry* of Sri Aurobindo," in *Yearbook of Comparative and General Literature,* No. 11, 1962, pp. 149-53.

[*In the following essay on* The Future Poetry, *Ghose discusses Aurobindo's equation of poetry with* mantra.]

Romain Rolland described the contribution of Sri Aurobindo as the greatest synthesis as yet achieved of the genius of the East and the genius of the West. Today Sri Aurobindo is widely known as yogi and thinker, but few have heard of him as a poet, fewer as a literary critic. This in spite of the fact that his writings are characteristic and commanding, and indeed copious. But even more than the scope—which includes [letters] ranging from Aeschylus to the Age of Anxiety—it is the quality of writing which sets him apart, and makes the task of assessment both

mandatory and difficult. Above all, there are the serial essays, *The Future Poetry,* written between 1917 and 1920 but published in book form only in 1953. Here is the pith of the Aurobindean criticism. What is it like?

The Future Poetry is concerned with the now vital question of a civilization on trial, to use Toynbee's phrase, and what poetry, "the rhythmic voice of life," can do about it. It can and must, according to our critic, bring back the possibility of "the discovery of a closer approximation to what we might call the *mantra* in poetry," roughly the poetry of vision, prayer, magic, and incantation: poetry as *mantra* and poetry as the key to the future. Poetry is neither an elevated pastime—"mug's game," as Eliot once informed a bemused Harvard audience—nor is it a matter of technique alone. Its privilege and higher function, its real business is to suggest rhythmically the soul-values of our expanding universe. The nature and essence of poetic speech and the poetic movement comes, he tells us, "from the stress of soul-vision behind the word; it is the spiritual excitement of a rhythmic voyage of self-discovery among the magic islands of form and name in these inner and outer worlds." It holds a mirror to our soul-vision and progressive self-discovery, "the progression of consciousness which conceives, orients and controls life." The possibility of a new and higher evolution of mankind, of which poetry is both an index and instrument, is taken for granted. For to doubting Thomases it can never be *proved.*

Briefly, and in Indian terms, the thematic burden of *The Future Poetry* is poetry as *mantra,* poetry as prayer, invocation, and magic, above all as vision. Let our critic explain: "The *mantra,* poetic expression of the deepest spiritual reality, is only possible when the highest intensities of poetic speech meet and become indissolubly one, the highest intensity of rhythmic movement, of verbal form and thought-substance of style, and of the soul's vision of truth. . . . Or, let us say, it is a supreme rhythmic language which seizes hold upon all that is finite and brings into each the light and voice of its own infinite." This may sound—our author himself is aware of it—a somewhat mystic and Oriental account of the matter, but substantially there could hardly be a more complete description.

Such, then, is the hypothesis or point of view. But it is not a dogma, pronounced *ex cathedra,* though now and then it may sound like that. For, as we shall see, the evolutionary scheme is fundamental to all Sri Aurobindo's writing, analysis, and insight. "Poetry, like everything else, evolves," he says. And since poetry "is a psychological phenomenon, the poetic impulse a highly charged force of expression of the mind and soul of man, therefore, in trying to follow out the line of evolution, it is the development of the psychological motive and power, it is the kind of feeling, vision, mentality which is seeking in it for its word and idea and form and beauty, and it is the power of the soul through which it finds expression or the level of the mind from which it speaks which we must distinguish to get a right idea of the progress of poetry."

So much by way of definition or statement of attitude. There is another, and bigger, surprise in store. He chooses the history of English poetry, from Chaucer to early twentieth century, as illustration to prove the point. He does this because—though few perhaps will agree with him—to him English poetry seems to follow most faithfully the ascending curve of the human spirit in this kind of imaginative rhythmic self-expression. And so, after a glance at the national evolution of poetry, Greek, Latin, and French, he proceeds to sketch the progress of English poetry, which, he says, "began by a quite external, a clear and superficial substance and utterance (that is Chaucer). It proceeded to a deeper vital poetry, a poetry of the power and beauty and wonder and spontaneous thought, the joy and passion and pain, the colour and music of life, in which the external presentation of life and things was taken up, but exceeded and given its full dynamic and imaginative content (the Elizabethans)." From there the attempt was made to master "the secret of the Latins, the secret of a clear, measured and intellectual dealing with life, things and ideas (the Augustans). Then came an attempt, a brilliant and beautiful attempt to get through Nature and thought and mentality in life and Nature and their profounder aesthetic suggestion to certain underlying spiritual truths." The attempt of the Romantics "could not come to perfect fruition, partly because there was not the right intellectual preparation or sufficient basis of spiritual knowledge and experience," and what could be offered depended on the solitary and individual intuition of the poet; partly because after the lapse into an age of reason the spontaneous or the intense language of spiritual poetry could not always be found, or, if found, could not be maintained. "So we get a deviation into another age (the Victorian) of intellectual and representative poetry, with a much wider range, but less profound in its roots, less high in its growth; and partly out of this, partly by a recoil from it has come the turn of recent and contemporary [that is, what was recent and contemporary at the time these essays were written] poetry which seems at least to be approaching the secret of the utterance of profounder truth with its right magic and speech."

Of all the theories and histories of English poetry the sacred or hieratic *ars poetica* put forward by Sri Aurobindo is surely one of the strangest, one to tease us out of thought as doth Eternity.

— *Sisirkumar Ghose*

At the end of the historical survey—the précis does it less than justice—he states his aesthetic ideals once more. The concluding portion is frankly more apocalyptic, and after giving some example of this kind of writing in the past he explains the conditions necessary if poetry is to fulfill its highest promise. In this he notes that "a collapse to the lower levels might bring human civilization to a new corrupted and intellectual barbarism . . . the possibility of such a catastrophe is by no means absent from the present situation." The approaching end of poetry has been announced by many a prophet of doom. But this is to take a small view of its resources, its rationale, and the way out. "Why, in such spiritless times, be a poet at all?" asked Hölderlin. The answer came, strangely, from Nietzsche: "To *affirm, bless* and *deify* existence." The way out, the hope of the race lies, we are told, in an "open realization" of the spirit of man, the infinity of Self and its fit expression in poetry, that is, in *mantra* again. According to Sri Aurobindo, "a larger range of existence made more real to man's experience will be the realm of the future" and it is this which, as Wordsworth had seen earlier if in a slightly different context, "will bind together the vast empire of human society."

This at least is a strong possibility suggested by the newer trends, if we know how to read the signs. (Have not Rimbaud and Eliot and the Symbolists all said the same thing in their own, different ways?) In other words, "the idea of the poet who is also a Rishi (seer-poet) has made again its appearance."

Of all the theories and histories of English poetry—and we have had quite a few during recent years—this sacred or hieratic *ars poetica* put forward by Sri Aurobindo is surely one of the strangest, one to tease us out of thought as doth Eternity. In his own words, "Perhaps no thinking age has been so far removed from any such view of life as the one through which we have recently passed, and even now we are not well out of its shadow. . . . And yet curiously enough it is to some far-off light, at least to the view of ourselves at our greatest . . . that we seem to be returning." The progress of poetry, as he has viewed it, "has been an index of the advance of the cultural mind in humanity, which having increased its scope by a constant expanding of the soul's experience, has now risen to a great height and breadth of intellectual vision and activity, and the present question concerns the next step in the scale of ascension." Differently, "if poetry is a highly-charged power of aesthetic expression of the soul of man, it must follow in its course of evolution the development of that soul. I put it that from this point of view the soul of man like the soul of Nature can be regarded as an unfolding of the spirit in the material world. Our unfolding being has its roots in the soil of the physical life; it shoots up and out in many directions as the stalk and branches of the vital being . . . and from there, nestling in the luxuriant leaves of the mind, and rising from the spirit which was concealed in the whole process, must blossom the free and infinite soul of man, the hundred-petalled rose of God."

> And the beautiful river still flows,
> And flows in time, and makes us
> Part of it, and part of him.
> That, children, is what is called
> A sacramental relationship.
> And that is what a poet
> Is, children, one who creates
> Sacramental relationship.

Granted his hypothesis, the conclusion is not only consistent, but inescapable. He is presenting us not with a fiat but a fulfillment of what has been known and practiced all through history. Even T. E. Hulme talked of an "intuitive language," while some years back Signor Vivante (*English Poetry and Its Contribution to the Knowledge of a Creative Principle*) began by pointing out that "the consciousness of a principle of inward light—an original self-active principle, which characterizes life and spontaneity as contrasted with mechanism—has found in English poetry one of its richest and highest expressions." Sri Aurobindo's commentary only points out the logical finale of such a self-expressive tendency. As in other areas of thought and experience, here too he has seen things in a new and reconciling, fusing vision. He sums up long, lingering, scattered suggestions and turns them, without palpable design, into a rationale of poetry at its purest, poetry of the peak, relating it to the larger laws of human becoming. From Plato's enthusiastic madman, the sublimity of Longinus, the Christian hymns of glory and praise; from Shakespeare's poet, his eye in a fine frenzy rolling, to the romantic visionary, usually an outsider, peering into the life of things; through the symbolist strategy, full of fine sound and refinement often signifying nothing; through Rilke's "terrible angels," and the dislocation ("I hold sacred the disorder of my brains") and dubious illuminations of Rimbaud, through the cults of obscurity and "pure poetry" as some kind of sublimated musical nonsense, then of poetry as prayer (Abbé Bremond) and the poet as a mystic *manqué;* the dry dogmatics of Eliot, most competent verse rather than genuine incantation ("Out of the agony and the imprecision there springs the perfect order of speech, and the beauty of incantation"); the superb rhetoric and the defiant gesture that had become a second nature with William Butler Yeats ("Cast a cold eye / on life, on death. / Horseman, pass by."); the ironic Alexandrian poets of anxiety and the troubled doubtful personalities of the little self ("Alone, alone, about a dreadful wood / of conscious evil runs a lost mankind, / Dreading to find its Father lest it find / The Goodness it has dreaded is not good . . ."); the highly-wrought Canticles of Edith Sitwell; the later apocalyptic writers and the latest of bardic passion in Dylan Thomas ("After the first death, there is no death") . . . in Sri Aurobindo's hands all these broken hints have come together and turned into a certainty. It is his amazing psychological maturity and orchestral oecumenical mind that can unite all these into a single theme—*Mantra.* Instead of the self-inflicted tortures of the "disinherited mind" he can point to a tradition at once more normal and universal and arrive at a far more striking and genuine reconciliation of tradition and individual talent than we have known for some time.

Mantra is not just good, or even great poetry, but poetry *per se.* It is not religious poetry but spiritual poetry that he is talking of. The rest is literature. The theory and practice of *mantra,* Sri Aurobindo's vision of poetry and poetry of vision is surely his most appropriate gift to the life of an evolving humanity. For him it was a daring and simple thing to do. On our part we must try to understand and assimilate—since knowledge is by assimilation, as Aquinas puts it—this emerging truth, unless of course we prefer to be flowers of evil with a short and fierce season in an adolescent hell or wish to suffer the nuances of the *Néant.*

It is only proper to point out here that the early poets of India, the Rishis, were seers and hearers of the suprasensible Truth-Word. They had also the gift of communicating, expressing, or, as the Indian aesthetician would say, "generalizing" (*sadharanikrita*) their experience. "One might almost say that ancient India was created by the Veda and Upanishads, and the visions of inspired seers made a people." They were among the acknowledged legislators of mankind. Obviously poetry such as this was not an entertainment, an intellectual exercise, or a display of "complex sensibility." The poet was something more than a maker of beautiful word and phrase, a favored child of fancy and imagination, a careful fashioner of idea and utterance. The poet was a spokesman of the eternal spirit and beauty and delight, and he shared the highest creative and self-expressive rapture not unlike the original ecstasy that made Existence, the divine *Ananda.* Poetry such as this was a ritual and a remembrance, a purifier and builder of the soul, a means for the culture and integration of personality, *atmasamskriti.* As Robert Graves (*The White Goddess*) says: "The function of poetry is religious invocation of the Muse."

The soul of man and the soul of poetry ("the true creator, the true hearer is the soul") are a reality to Sri Aurobindo, and he can make them real to us as well. Needless to say, he writes throughout as the poet that he is, even if some will demur to his novel annotation of the art of the possible, this pure, divine assault of the ether and fire. He speaks with authority, with full awareness of the foundations of his judgment, a clear and inspiring vision of the destiny of the spirit in man. He is not a doctrinaire nor is he excessively schematic. He is not a "philosopher-aesthetician," a creature against whom Eliot inveighs in his Preface to Vivante's book. He is not trying to choke or force growth and inspiration into a system. Tolerant of a hundred ways of the spirit, he knows that the intensity of the *Mantra* "belongs to no particular style, depends on no conceivable formula." A master of distinctions, of levels of consciousness and levels of poetic adequacy, he is particularly careful not to pay off poetry in terms of "philosophy." What he is not willing to forget is poetry's essential nature and deepest destiny.

The awareness of crisis and emergence—"At present the human mind is occupied in passing the borders of two kingdoms," he says—exposes the vast sweep of an inner, cosmic evolution, which extends almost beyond history. According to this view, "the human intelligence seems on the verge of an attempt to rise through the intellectual into an intuitive mentality." We become part of a greater reality, seeking expression in the poetry of awareness. "Poetry and art are the born mediators between the immaterial and the concrete, the spirit and the life." Sri Aurobindo places poetry, fairly and firmly, at the center of human knowledge and activities, as the leader of our inner progress, the divine *Agni,* the sacred Fire in our creative evolution.

Eliot Deutsch   (essay date 1964)

SOURCE: "Sri Aurobindo's Interpretation of Spiritual Experience: A Critique," in *International Philosophical Quarterly,* Vol. IV, No. 4, December, 1964, pp. 581-94.

[*In the following essay, Deutsch seeks to determine whether the three principle tenets of Aurobindo's theory of spiritual evolution—ascent, integration, and descent—can be verified by experience.*]

OUTLINE OF HIS THOUGHT

Sri Aurobindo's philosophy consists, for the most part, of an organization and interpretation of various types of spiritual experience from the point of view of a "metaphysical" theory of evolution. This theory seeks to answer two fundamental questions: (1) What is the nature of man and the universe which makes spiritual experience possible? and (2) Under what conditions can a sustained, higher mentality and spirituality be effected for mankind?

According to Aurobindo, man is essentially spiritual. He is essentially at-one with an eternal spiritual Being—which is the true self of all beings. Accepting the Upanishad formulae "Thou art that" (*tat tvam asi*) and "I am Brahman" (*aham brahmāsmi*), Sri Aurobindo writes [in *The Life Divine*]: "Our spiritual being is of that substance, is indeed the Brahman." Brahman, or the Absolute, is, for Aurobindo, the One indefinable and ineffable spiritual Reality. It is at once personal and non-personal, immanent and transcendent. Though timeless and spaceless, it manifests itself in the universe as a dynamic becoming and as a pervasive indwelling presence. It is [as Aurobindo says in *The Life Divine*]

> . . . an impersonal Brahman without qualities, a fundamental divine Reality free from all relations or determinates, and a Brahman with infinite qualities, a fundamental divine Reality who is source and container and master of all relations and determinations—Nirguna, Saguna.

The Absolute is personal, then, with respect to its being present in all persons and phenomena; it is impersonal with respect to its transcendence of all forms and categories. Everything, Sri Aurobindo maintains, is, in essence, a "self-expression" of the Absolute: it, however, cannot be circumscribed within, or be limited by, any of these expressions. This dual status of the Absolute, Aurobindo states [in *The Life Divine*], "is indeed one of the most important and fruitful distinctions in Indian philosophy; it is besides a fact of spiritual experience. . . . This distinction arises by a movement of the individual soul from one poise to another, from the poise of Brahman-consciousness in the world . . . to or towards the poise of Brahman-consciousness beyond the world. . . . "

The Absolute, then, subsists as the infinite, eternal silence of the Spirit, as an unconditioned One or pure unity of being, and as the creative energy, the source of the conditioned many. The Absolute cannot be viewed, however, as in any way limited by the fact that it puts forth a world of relations: "The infinite is not limited by building up in itself an infinite series of finite phenomena; rather that is its natural self-expression" [*The Life Divine*]. And further:

> It can be said of it that it would not be the infinite oneness if it were not capable of an infinite multiplicity; but that does not mean that the One is plural or can be limited or described as the sum of the Many: on the contrary, it can be the infinite Many because it exceeds all limitation or

description by multiplicity and exceeds at the same time all limitation by finite conceptual oneness. . . . This is difficult for the mental reason which makes an opposition between the Infinite and the finite and associates finiteness with plurality and infinity with oneness; but in the logic of the Infinite there is no such opposition and the eternity of the Many in the One is a thing that is perfectly natural and possible.

Aurobindo thus affirms the Vedantic designation of Brahman as *saccidānanda,* as an infinite being (*sat*), consciousness (*cit*), and joy of being (*ānanda*), and states that these principles comprise the most fundamental level of Nature: they represent the primal unfolding of the One in the Many. Nature, for Aurobindo, is itself at once uniform and hierarchical. It manifests the ineffable unity of the Absolute and it contains a graduated series of values and existences. [In *The Life Divine*] Aurobindo sums up his vision of Nature as follows:

> The manifestation of the Being in our universe takes the shape of an involution which is the starting point of an evolution,—Matter the nethermost stage, Spirit the summit. In the descent into involution there can be distinguished *seven principles of manifested being,* seven gradations of the manifesting Consciousness of which we can get a perception or a concrete realisation of their presence and immanence. . . . The *first three* are the original and fundamental principles and they form universal states of consciousness to which we can rise; when we do so, we can become aware of supreme planes or levels . . . of the spiritual reality in which is put forth the *unity of the Divine Existence, the power of the Divine Consciousness, the bliss of the Divine Delight of existence. . . . A fourth principle of supramental truth consciousness* is associated with them; manifesting unity in infinite multiplicity, it is the characteristic power of self-determination of the Infinite. . . . The *other three powers* and planes of being, of which we are even at present aware, form a lower hemisphere of *Mind, Life,* and *Matter.* These are in themselves powers of the superior principles; but whenever they manifest in a separation from their spiritual source, they undergo as a result a phenomenal lapse into a divided in place of the true undivided existence. . . . [critic's italics]

Nature, then, in Aurobindo's view, is dynamic: it is involved in an evolution of consciousness, a return of the Spirit to itself.

Aurobindo further holds that man is the basic instrument of, or vehicle for, this evolution. He maintains that man possesses, within the depth of his being, various powers of consciousness which are capable of an unlimited awareness and knowledge, and that in order for spiritual experience, or the spiritual evolution which it reveals, to be fulfilled, these higher powers of consciousness must emerge, develop, and reach completion through the structures of man's actual mental, vital, and physical being. Through a spiritual evolution we are to become greater mental beings: we are to develop a wider and deeper noetic consciousness, a larger capacity for joy in being, and a greater ability to recognize, absorb, and transmit the truth and value that is pervasive throughout being. [In *The Synthesis of Yoga*] Aurobindo sums up his ideal of man as: "A divine perfection of the human being is our aim."

Spiritual experience is thus interpreted by Aurobindo in terms of an evolution of man as this works itself out in intimate relation to an Absolute Being. The subject in experience participates in, and becomes identified with, various objective domains and concentrations of Being as these subsist hierarchically; that is, as they are manifestations, in greater or less degree, of a supreme power and status of Being. Spiritual experience, for Aurobindo, is experience of the Absolute: it is experience of the one spiritual Reality (Brahman) as it is in itself and as it is manifest in the creative becoming of Nature. It requires an ascent of human consciousness to a higher level and status of being, an integration of this higher status with lower principles of mental, vital, and physical being, and a descent of the consciousness of the Absolute into the lower forms that are prepared to receive it. Man is that being in evolutionary nature in whom new powers and capacities of consciousness are being developed. Man has reached the stage, Aurobindo asserts, wherein nature's processes of change may be understood by, and consciously fulfilled within him.

THREE PRIMARY PRINCIPLES: METHOD OF VERIFICATION

It is impossible to criticize an ideal for human nature of the type put forward by Aurobindo without in some way simply judging it by the standard of one's own ideal, and thereby replacing it, or by questioning its very capacity to be realized. Rather than attempt either alternative, in critically appraising his work we will concentrate exclusively upon an examination of the primary principles of his theory of evolution—namely, those of ascent, integration, and descent—and try to determine to what extent these principles are justified.

Referring to the construction of a "physical evolutionary theory," [in *The Life Divine*], Aurobindo states that "the problem of the method of operation is still too full of obscure and unknown factors for any at present possible structure of theory to be definitive." This problem of a lack of factual material is, of course, even greater with respect to a "spiritual evolutionary theory," and hence the question arises: What are the means of verifying such a theory? Sri Aurobindo writes [in *The Life Divine*]:

> The scientific theory is concerned only with the outward and visible machinery and process, with the detail of Nature's execution, with the physical development of things in Matter and the law of development of life and mind in Matter; its account of the process may have to be considerably changed or may be dropped altogether in the light of a new discovery, but that will not affect the self-evident fact of a spiritual evolution, an evolution of consciousness, a progression of the soul's manifestation in material existence.

And further:

> A theory of spiritual evolution is not identical with a scientific theory of form-evolution and physical life-evolution; it must stand on its own inherent justification.

Hence the methods of verifying a spiritual evolutionary theory must be different, in some way, from those used in the physical and social sciences. Controlled conditions, statistical formulations, disinterested observations—in short, the total apparatus of the scientific method as applied to physical nature and social behavior is inapplicable to this other more qualitative sphere: at best it would have to be considerably modified to adjust to the different conditions resident within this value domain. To those inclined to think otherwise, Aurobindo writes [in *The Life Divine*]:

> . . . [It] has been implicitly or explicitly held as an axiom that all truth must be referred to the judgment of the personal mind, reason and experience of every man or else it must be verified or at any rate verifiable by a common or universal experience in order to be valid. But obviously this is a false standard of reality and of knowledge, since this means the sovereignty of the normal or average mind and its limited capacity and experience. . . . Subjective discovery must be pursued by a subjective method of inquiry, observation and verification; research into the supraphysical must evolve, accept and test as appropriate means and methods other than those by which one examines the constituents of physical objects and the processes of Energy in material Nature.

What then are the appropriate means and methods for testing a theory which refers in part to a supersensuous and suprarational domain of being? Sri Aurobindo answers:

> . . . [It] is not every untrained mind that can follow the mathematics of relativity or of other difficult scientific truths or judge of the validity either of their results or their process. *All reality, all experience must indeed, to be held as true, be capable of verification by a same or similar experience;* so, in fact, all men can have a spiritual experience and can follow it out and verify it in themselves, but only when they have acquired the capacity or can follow the inner methods by which that experience and verification are made possible [critic's italics].

It is, then, according to Aurobindo, only through a similarity of experience that a theory of the type put forward by him can be brought to a test and attain verification. If, for purposes of criticism, we accept this criterion as appropriate and assume that in a given case a similarity of experience exists, the problem then becomes: What specific features or tenets of the theory actually can or cannot be brought to experiential confirmation?

IS EXPERIENTIAL VERIFICATION POSSIBLE?

The three central principles in Aurobindo's theory of evolution are, as has been indicated, those of ascent, integration and descent. Nature, for Aurobindo, is a totality of ascending powers which exercise upon each other certain degrees of mutual modification. These ascending powers from the level of "Mind" onward are symbolized as "higher mind," "illumined mind," "intuitive mind," "overmind," and "supermind." They form a line of ascent from man's present status in nature to his life divine. "It is not," however, according to Aurobindo [in *The Life Divine*], "to be supposed that the circumstances and the lines of the transition would be the same for all, for here we enter into the domain of the infinite: but, since there is behind all of them the unity of a fundamental truth, the scrutiny of a given line of ascent may be expected to throw light on the principle of all ascending possibilities. . . . "

Can an ascending gradation as put forward by Aurobindo be tested in someone's direct experience? An examination of the literature of spiritual experience or spiritual philosophy points clearly to an affirmative answer. Plotinus and Meister Eckhart, Philo, St. John of the Cross and St. Bonaventure, Samkara and the seer-sages of the Upanishads all record experiences in which ascent is present. Although there is no uniformity in their symbolic representations of the grades of ascent, and in many of their writings there is less ontological objectification, there does appear to be a unity of vision fundamental to them all. The very possibility of constructing a schema of spiritual experience rests on this principle. There seems to be no reason, therefore, why a principle of ascent cannot be accepted and, by whatever criterion of correspondence, be either verified or rejected by those who have had experiences of higher mental-spiritual states.

With the principle of integration, however, this no longer seems to be the case. Integration is viewed by Aurobindo as a consolidation of preceding evolutionary movements, a preparation of the subject for a further ascent, and a basic transformation of Nature itself as the result of spiritual experience. Whenever any of the higher grades of mind or consciousness are entered into there occurs a transformation of the general status of man and nature.

> A taking up of what has already evolved into each higher grade as it is reached and a transformation more or less complete so as to admit a total changed working of the whole being and nature, an integration, must be also part of the [spiritual] process, if the evolution is to be effective. [*The Life Divine*]

And:

> This can happen because all is fundamentally the same substance, the same consciousness, the same force, but in different forms and powers and degrees of itself: a taking up of the lower by the higher is therefore a possible and . . . a spiritually natural movement; what was put forth from the superior status is enveloped and taken up into its own greater being and essence.

But can this principle of integration be verified in experience? If we again examine the literature of spiritual philosophy we find that a consolidation of preceding experienced states can occur, but not that it necessarily does occur, or that such a consolidation involves a "total changed working of the whole being and nature." This is not to deny its desirability, but rather to note that a return

from spiritual experience may result in a unitive life, a life of wisdom, of freedom, of service or devotion, but that it does not seem to entail a transformation of the basic processes of man and nature. It appears then that the principle of integration is essentially *legislative*. If the ideal of a divine-manhood put forward by Sri Aurobindo is to be attained, a principle of integration, as he describes it, is no doubt indispensable. However, it does not seem to be verified in experience or to be capable of verification as something inherent in the evolutionary structure of nature.

> **Sri Aurobindo, as we have seen, rejects— and no doubt rightly so—the idea of a public, observational, experimental method as applicable to the domain of being with which he is concerned. He demands a subjective experiential method of inquiry. "To refuse," he writes in *The Life Divine*, "to enquire upon any general ground preconceived and *a priori* is an obscurantism as prejudicial to the extension of knowledge as the religious obscurantism which opposed in Europe the extension of scientific discovery."**
>
> **— *Eliot Deutsch***

With the principle of descent, we come upon perhaps the most difficult principle in Aurobindo's theory. Descent, according to him, represents an original involutionary force in the universe and a necessary condition for all future evolutionary transformations. Ascent and integration are themselves ultimately possible only because a principle of descent is operative in Nature. In terms of experience, Aurobindo describes it [in *The Life Divine*] as the "reception and retention of the descending spirit or its powers and elements of consciousness." And further:

> When the powers of any grade descend completely into us, it is not only our thought and knowledge that are affected,—the substance and very grain of our being and consciousness, all its states and activities are touched and penetrated and can be remoulded and wholly transmuted.

In other words, whenever a "level" in Nature evolves (e.g., "Mind"), it is because of a "descent" of a higher level or power in Nature. When applied to a spiritual plane of being, however, this principle becomes quite obviously a rationalizing of a process which, if it exists, is essentially non-rational in so far as causal statements can be meaningfully made about it. Although a feeling of an act of descent might well be present in spiritual experience, the idea of descent in terms of rational expression and objectification can never be more than an "ideogram." "Facts, not causes, lie within the seer's province": to reason, with any degree of certainty, from a feeling of spontaneous movement within an ultimate "Object" to a proximate cause outside that feeling is quite impossible. Hence, by these very limitations there is no way to establish a common framework within which experiential verification could take place: the subject would not know what to verify. He could only compare his feelings in the very broadest terms with those of another, and such feelings, taken by themselves, would indeed provide only a shifting foundation for the objective truth of an evolutionary law in Nature. The principle of descent, we must conclude, is primarily speculative. It is symbolic and suggestive. But Aurobindo formulates the principle dogmatically and in causal terms. And hence the spiritual certitude vouchsafed the seer is translated into an unwarranted intellectual certainty of the philosopher.

Sri Aurobindo, as we have seen, rejects—and no doubt rightly so—the idea of a public, observational, experimental method as applicable to the domain of being with which he is concerned. He demands a subjective experiential method of inquiry. "To refuse," he writes [in *The Life Divine*], "to enquire upon any general ground preconceived and *a priori* is an obscurantism as prejudicial to the extension of knowledge as the religious obscurantism which opposed in Europe the extension of scientific discovery." Our fundamental criticism of his theory is not then directed towards his criterion as such, but towards his own failure to meet it. Certain of the leading tenets of his theory which are formulated as causal principles or laws, and to which he attaches a kind of theoretical certainty, are phenomenologically or experientially unverifiable in the terms in which they are presented. This criticism is not "positivistic," it is not meant to deny that organizing philosophical principles may be formulated in speculative terms which encompass a wide and diversified range of spiritual experience; it is meant to deny only that one can formulate these principles with intellectual certainty as explanatory concepts beyond their symbolic import as "ideograms." Our major criticism, then, is that Aurobindo commits what we might call the "fallacy of misplaced certitude"—the fallacy of translating, without proper qualification, the special kind of certitude obtained *in* spiritual experience to what one theorizes *about* that experience. The confounding of theoretical, explanatory concepts with spiritually grounded symbols is precisely what has brought about to a great extent the "obscurantism prejudicial to the extension of knowledge." The traditions of spiritual experience declare with unanimity that spiritual knowledge is *sui generis*. It illuminates facts, it reveals values, it does not disclose causes. The tendency of Sri Aurobindo to depart from this principle can only be a source for misunderstanding the possible significance and depth of his thought and the supreme value of the infinite spiritual richness of being to which it points.

REQUIREMENTS FOR A PHILOSOPHY OF SPIRITUAL EXPERIENCE

What then are the requirements for a philosophical theory, for a metaphysics, which is grounded in spiritual experience and which seeks to interpret and organize the contents of spiritual experience?

In her work *The Mystics of the Church,* Evelyn Underhill quotes this statement by Jacob Boehme:

O that I had but the pen of a man and were able therewith to write down the spirit of knowledge! I can but stammer of great mysteries like a child that is beginning to speak. . . .

And in her work *Mysticism,* she draws the conclusion that:

Thanks to the spatial imagery inseparable from human thinking and human expression—no direct description of spiritual experience is or can be possible to man. It must always be symbolic, allusive, oblique. . . .

Among interpreters of spiritual experience, as well as among those involved more directly with it, there is common agreement that the "truth" of an Absolute who is beyond all distinction and contingency, though realizable in human experience, cannot be expressed in human words. The human understanding, in "unknowing knowing," recoils from the "abysmal fullness" of the Absolute and has recourse only to symbols. But then what are the symbols symbolic of? Miss Underhill maintains that they are essentially symbolic of, that is they point to, various states of the experiencer. Descriptions of spiritual experience, no matter to what degree they are "objectified," are essentially "allegories." They tell us more about psychological processes than about objective structures of reality. That this is true up to a point can hardly be denied. The "up to a point" qualification needs however to be made for this simple reason, that a description of a state of experience which transcends subject/object distinctions is precisely about it as well as about the way the subject comes to it. The importance of Miss Underhill's observation is not, however, to be overlooked. The vast literature of spiritual experience, in both East and West, is made more readily open to one when it is read not as a series of contending "theologies" or "ontologies," but as records of various attempts, made by men of various temperaments, to speak from out of the fullness of their experience. The ultimate value of these attempts would lie then in their ability to *awaken* one to the realities of which they speak. Rudolph Otto has pointed out [in his *The Idea of the Holy*] that "there is . . . no 'transmission' of [the "numinous"] in the proper sense of the word; it cannot be 'taught,' it must be 'awakened' from the spirit."

A metaphysics based on spiritual experience, then, is an *art* more than a *science*. Its power lies not in explaining the world but in evoking an experience of it. Its primary task is "phenomenological." It must be a clear presentation of, a stimulus to awaken to, the structures and levels of experienced reality. It must be a "map" of the terrain to be crossed over in experience and a presentation of the culmination of that experience—both of which are free from causal, explanatory statements (which cannot be experientially confirmed). A spiritual metaphysics does not, for it cannot, explain natural processes; it does awaken one to values and realities. Second, however, the interpretation needs to be capable of enhancing our philosophical understanding of the world, by showing what the implications of this experience are for the theories and solutions to questions dealt with in specific philosophical disciplines. This is necessary, for otherwise there would be no way to relate this interpreting, this special kind of metaphysics, and what it might have to say, to a philosophical tradition.

A spiritual metaphysics is *like* a work of art—but it is not purely a work of art or a descriptive ontology: it needs to relate to, and if necessary be a source of changing, the contents (the questions and answers) of specialized philosophical disciplines. For example, one of the tasks or requirements of a spiritual metaphysics would be to show how epistemological theories which seek to distinguish the kinds of knowledge available to man, the sources and limits of knowledge, must take into account the special noetic characteristics of spiritual experience; its "knowledge by identity," its "unknowing knowing," and so on; it must show how ordinary structures and patterns of knowledge are transformed by certain kinds of experience, how these transformations may call for alterations in criteria of truth, how different kinds of values ascribed to different kinds of knowledge have their source in experience and how these are changed in the light of spiritual experience. This second requirement, then, is a call not so much for presenting solutions to problems as it is for articulating problems—problems which ordinarily are overlooked or are denied, in an a priori way, as legitimate philosophical problems.

A systematic interpretation of spiritual experience, a spiritual metaphysics, would make no pretension, then, to being a "revelation"; it would not weave a web of explanatory concepts around the infinitely rich content of that experience; rather, together with its phenomenological map-making, it would seek inclusion of the characteristics and qualities of spiritual experience within established philosophical disciplines. It would seek reform of the "known" rather than try to reduce the "unknowable" to the "known." It would, in short, consciously avoid the "fallacy of misplaced certitude." It would leave certitude where it properly belongs—to the spirit.

Grace E. Cairns (essay date 1972)

SOURCE: "Aurobindo's Conception of the Nature and Meaning of History," in *International Philosophical Quarterly,* Vol. XII, No. 2, June, 1972, pp. 205-19.

[*In the following essay, which focuses on* The Human Cycle, *Cairns outlines the five stages in Aurobindo's psychological theory of the development of human civilization, citing examples from Western psychology, theology, scientific thought, and philosophical history that support Aurobindo's system.*]

THE METAPHYSICAL CONTEXT

The philosophy of Aurobindo is so eminently an integrated one that the general pattern of cosmic and human history cannot be discussed apart from his metaphysical system described at length in **The Life Divine.** In this system the Sevenfold Chord of Being is the central concept and provides the framework for the meaning and pattern of history. There are three higher and three lower hemispheres of Being in the Sevenfold Chord, and mediating between the two is the Supermind. The three that belong to the higher hemisphere are aspects of the Eternal Reality or Absolute; they are the *Sat,* the *Cit,* and the *Ānanda* of Upanishadic thought. As Aurobindo interprets them, *Sat* is the Pure Existent, *Cit* is Consciousness-Force and *Ānanda* Delight-in-Existence. Although this is Brahman in its eternal, changeless, infinite aspect—the impersonal Nirguna Brahman—Brahman is pregnant with all creation. Creation is manifested in the three evolutes of the lower hemisphere—Matter, Life, and Mind.

Supermind mediates between the two hemispheres. Its major function is creative activity; it is the manifestation of the Saguna Brahman aspect of the Divine and thus the primal cause of the progressive evolutionary development that is cosmic and human history. The Absolute is infinite, perfect and eternal; why does it choose to manifest itself in creative activity? This activity belongs to the very nature of the Divine; it is the *līlā* (spontaneous play) of Brahman, a familiar view in Indian philosophy. The Saguna Brahman or Supermind, the force behind history, creates in an evolutionary pattern. There is first the involution of the Divine, the descent into Matter, then the ascent to the Life (or Vital) evolute, then to the stage of Mind. The next and final stage to be evolved, the goal towards which all creation aspires, is that of the Supermind (Supramental or Gnostic), a new species of being.

This general pattern of cosmic and human history was inspired not only by modern Western evolutionary theories, but also by Indian traditional thought. We find evolutionary ideas in ancient Indian philosophy in the *Taittīrīya Upanishad* of about 800 B.C. In this *Upanishad* the stages of evolution are related to the sheaths of the Ātman-Brahman, the sheaths of Matter, Life, Mind. These correspond with Aurobindo's evolutionary stages of cosmic history.

These sheaths of the Ātman-Brahman were interpreted by later philosophers of the *Advaita Vedānta,* the dominant school of Indian thought, as *māyā,* i.e., phenomenal appearance and not reality. Man's goal, therefore, was to transcend the temporal space-time universe in an intuitive experience of identity with the eternal Brahman and thereby escape the round of rebirths in this world. In Aurobindo's philosophy the world of nature and history, the space-time universe, is not *māyā,* not a world of appearances, but real, and man's goal is a divine life in this world. Matter is really Matter, the Inconscient level of being; Life the Subconscient, and Mind the Conscious (self-conscious) aspect of the universe. Even when the final stage of evolution is attained, the Supramental, the individual is not one with Brahman in one identity, but remains an individual although he does experience unity, oneness with the higher hemisphere of being, *Sacchidānanda,* as well as unity also with the lower hemisphere. He sees all interfused with the one Divine; yet the individual concrete things, organisms, men are real. Though this integral Supramental consciousness has not yet been reached, human beings, now generally at the Mental level, have individual freedom, though gently inspired by the Divine toward upward progress until all mankind realizes the Supermind.

Aurobindo's view of the pattern of human history directed towards this goal is not a mechanical one, because of the freedom of human individuals. Because of this participation by human beings, Aurobindo thinks that the most adequate approach to an understanding and patterning of human history is a psychological one. He therefore rejects the materialist (both mechanistic and dialectical) and vitalistic (e.g. Bergson's *élan vital*) theories and builds his own philosophy of history around a psychological approach to the development of human civilizations. He finds [Karl] Lamprecht's patterning of this psychological development in a series of five stages a true and useful framework for describing "the human cycle," the pattern of the evolutionary progress of a civilization from its beginnings. Human history is the story of man's civilizations, the group creations that educate mankind for ever higher goals, eventually the goal of Supermind. The five stages (borrowed from Lamprecht) in the development of a civilization [as outlined by Aurobindo in *The Human Cycle*] are the Symbolic, the Typal, the Conventional, the Individualist, and the Subjective. Aurobindo sees these stages manifested in Indian history and elsewhere.

STAGES OF CIVILIZATION

The Symbolic Stage

This is a subjective stage like the fifth, but differs in the kind of subjectivism. The Symbolic stage is a subjectivism at the infrarational level, the Subjective (fifth) state at the suprarational. In a Symbolic age man vaguely intuits the Divine that he feels is everywhere, and expresses his feeling in myth, poetry, and art. In Indian history this epoch is the Vedic Age, a time, Aurobindo comments, when the sacrifice was central and interpreted in mystical symbols. Social institutions also were given a mystical meaning. For example, the Rig Vedic marriage hymn in the Vedic Age was a glorification of the divine marriages of Sūryā, daughter of the Sun—the human was "an inferior figure and image of the divine." Also "the Indian ideal of the relation between man and woman has always been governed by the symbolism of the relation between the Purusha and Prakriti . . . , the male and female divine Principles in the universe." Another key social institution, the organization of society into the four *Varnas* is given a divine origin in the *Vedas* in the *Purusa Sūkta*.

This intuitive, poetic, symbolic age is apparent in the formative stage of all other civilizations, Aurobindo affirms. This is the view, also, of some prominent Western philosophers of history. Among these theorists, Oswald Spengler posits such a symbolic age in the childhood period of a civilization. Pitirim A. Sorokin, the noted sociologist philosopher of history finds religious symbolism dominant in the beginning epoch of a great culture, the "ideational" epoch. In this era the culture is integrated around the Divine as the true reality and value. Religious symbolism has, in fact, played a large part in the early phases of civilizations.

The Typal Stage

This is "predominantly psychological and ethical." Aurobindo again refers to the development of Indian civilization to illustrate the nature of this era. The *varna* system originating in the Symbolic Age develops the notion of psychological human types each with its particular ideal.

In the Symbolic Age the *varnas* were oriented around the idea of the Divine as knowledge in man (the Brahman *varna*); the Divine as power in man (*Ksatriya varna*); the Divine as production in man (*Vaiśya varna*); and the Divine as obedience, service and work (*Sūdra varna*). This orientation of the *varnas* around the Divine changes, in the Typal stage, to one oriented around the human. The focus is now upon the human psychological types and the ethical ideal for each. Religion in this era is mainly the sanction for *Dharma* (ethical ideals) except for a few who develop a more and more other-worldly religion. The finest flower of this stage is the social ideal set for each psychological type, each *varna*. These ideals remain as standards of social honor even in the Conventional Stage that succeeds the Typal.

The Conventional Stage

The Typal stage ends and the Conventional begins when the outward trappings of each *varna* become more important than the inner ethical ideal. A Brahman, for example, is no longer one through observance of the ethical ideal proper to his psychological type, but merely one by birth and honored for similar external circumstances. Religion in the Conventional stage becomes stereotyped, thought subjected to infallible authorities, and education bound to unchangeable forms. The medieval age in Europe illustrates this stage, and in India what orthodox idealists fondly call the Golden Age. Aurobindo thinks that much of the East (including India) is still in a Conventional stage and needs to be awakened to an age of individualism before the fifth, the Subjective Stage, can be possible.

Aurobindo comments on the lack of sincere, profound spirituality in a Conventional epoch:

> Thus at one time the modern litterateur, artist or thinker looked back often with admiration and with something like longing to the medieval age of Europe; he forgot in its distant appearance of poetry, nobility, spirituality the much folly, ignorance, iniquity, cruelty and oppression of those harsh ages, the suffering and revolt that simmered below these fine surfaces, the misery and squalor that was hidden behind that splendid facade. So too the Hindu orthodox idealist looks back to a perfectly regulated society devoutly obedient to the wise yoke of the Shastra, and that is his golden age,—a nobler one than the European in which the apparent gold was mostly hard burnished copper with a thin gold-leaf covering it, but still of an alloyed metal, not the true Satya Yuga.

Aurobindo admits that there is "much indeed that is really fine and sound and helpful to human progress" in such an age, but "always the form prevails and the spirit recedes and diminishes." This becomes most apparent in religion despite the efforts of a few saints and reformers. Ultimately the contradiction between convention and truth becomes so intolerable to men of perceptive intellects that they burst through the walls of convention and begin to use their own individual minds independently in the search for truth in the worlds of religion and nature. This development ushers in the Individualist stage of a civilization.

The Individualist Stage

Aurobindo describes this era as one of Reason, Revolt,

Progress, and Freedom. Reason is essential in freeing man from the sterility of the Conventional epoch. Reason is the stage of self-conscious mind, the human level of existence. In many ways atrophied in the Conventional era, it flourishes forth with its objectivity, its fearless search for truth in the Individualist Stage, and this—the search for truth—is its highest power. (It has, of course, been operative from the first stage, for it is the source of human creativity in the arts and sciences.)

In the Individualist stage, when Reason is dominant, the natural form of social organization is democracy; it stands for the freedom and equality of each member of society to use his individual reason in arranging his life. In practice, however, Aurobindo thinks that it has resulted in party strife, in social classes of rich and poor, and in a kind of competition, often ruthless, in which the most successful and not the best survive. Values deteriorate from the mental level and are mainly those related to man's infrarational nature, his material and vital needs. To satisfy these for the masses of men, socialism comes into being, and to make actual the equality of each member of society in the satisfaction of such material and vital needs, the individual is subjugated more and more to the State. Totalitarianism, either Fascist or Communist is born, the natural outcome of socialism. Only the Scandinavian socialist states, Aurobindo comments, have avoided this thus far and may continue to be successful in maintaining freedom, unless mankind collectively accepts some form of totalitarianism as the form of social organization. If this occurs, there will be an eclipse of Reason and Individualism until, in the human cycle, times grow more favorable for its return. Then the "spiral of human social evolution" may again progress towards its goal, the Age of Spirit, the Subjective Age.

It is important to note here that Aurobindo posits a spiral pattern of progress in history, neither the traditional cyclical one of Indian thought, nor the one-cycle, linear form of the Western tradition. In recent Indian thought, however, Mahadevan argues for a spiral-progress pattern, and in the Western world Toynbee and Sorokin take the same view.

When another and final Individualist stage recurs and Reason again is dominant, there is the obsession characteristic of Reason that all truth can be discovered by objective means, by looking at things from the outside, the "dream that perfection can be determined by machinery," by the computer. Then comes the realization that the deepest, most fundamental, and central truth whence all else springs can be realized only subjectively, through the discovery and recovery of the deeper self. This intuitive knowledge brings in the Subjective Stage of the human cycle of history, the Age of Spirit or Supermind.

The Subjective Stage: The Age of Supermind

The Symbolic stage, the first in the cycle of a civilization, is also a subjective stage, but at the infrarational level; the Supermind era is a subjective one at the suprarational level. At the stage of Supermind man feels strongly the pull of the Divine that inspired him to transcend Intellect itself. He now sees Intellect as mediator between the in-

frarational and suprarational (Supermind) aspects of his being as a microcosm; in the macrocosm Intellect has the same function. In his intuitive unity with the macrocosmic Supermind, he experiences its blissful knowledge as mediator and knower of both the Higher Hemisphere of Being (*Sacchidānanda*) and the Lower (Matter, Life, and Mind). When all men collectively, or at least a majority, attain this kind of subjective, intuitive knowledge-by-identity of the Divine, the everlasting epoch of Supermind, the Age of Spirit, will have arrived. This is the goal of history.

What are the conditions for the advent of this Divine age? Aurobindo names two that must be fulfilled simultaneously. The first is the appearance of individuals "who are able to see, to develop, to re-create themselves in the image of the Spirit and to communicate both their idea and its power to the mass." Such sage-saints, e.g. recently Gandhi, have already appeared. The second condition is the "readiness of the common mind of man" to receive the image. It is the latter condition that is so difficult to bring into being. Mankind at present is preoccupied with the lower self, the Inconscient (Matter) and the Subconscient (Vital) aspects of his being. "If mankind is to be spiritualised," Aurobindo says, "it must first in the mass cease to be the material or the vital man and become the psychic and the true mental being." If this kind of progress is impossible, "then the spiritualisation of mankind as a whole is a chimera." The common man may find an attraction in the spiritual teachings of those rare souls who have attained a supramental consciousness, but because he has not yet become the "psychic and true mental being" he remains unready to receive the Divine image.

To prepare mankind as a whole to receive the Divine image, an age of mental subjectivism is the first condition. There must be a "growth of the subjective idea of life—the idea of the soul, the inner being, its powers, its possibilities, its growth, its expression and the creation of a true, beautiful and helpful environment for it is the one thing of first and last importance." The subjectivism of the mental self of man, a "psychic subjectivism," sees man as a soul developing an "ever-expanding mental existence" that eventually can master all of nature—physical, vital and the mental itself. In art and beauty awesome achievements would be made, and in human relations greater harmony would prevail. Such a full exploration of the mental being to its highest reaches is necessary before mankind is ready for the Age of Spirit. Aurobindo maintains that past efforts to spiritualize mankind were unsuccessful because of the failure to realize that all the intervening levels (the material, the vital, and the mental) must first be completely mastered before the spiritual can find root.

In the age of mental subjectivism the climactic idea must develop that mind is only a secondary power of the Spirit which is the original, eternal, sole reality, *ayam ātmā brahma* (this self is Brahman). When this development occurs, the Era of Supermind comes into being.

The Age of Spirit (or Supermind, or the Supramental Being or the Gnostic Being) would begin with and aim to realize three essential truths of existence: God, freedom, and unity. These three must be realized together; unless God is realized neither can the other two. Possession of

God is possession of one's highest self and the self of all, the foundation for freedom and unity.

Real freedom can only be founded upon freedom from egoism, and possession of God as one with the self and the self of all others means freedom from one's ego. The Divine within each man discovered in self-knowledge is the inner source of freedom in a spiritual age; all external "laws" within societies and among nations will be based upon it. Without man's self-knowledge—without his identification with God and with the self of all—"he cannot escape from the law of external compulsion and all his efforts to do so must be vain." As long as a man is the slave of his own ego, of his lower nature, he will remain the slave of others—his family, caste, church, society, and nation.

The age of the spiritualized society is the age of the Life Divine, the era of finding God within ourselves. As in the Vedic age all knowledge and practice—art, philosophy, science, and the social structure—would be God-centered. The aim of ethics as a branch of philosophy would be the development of the divine nature in all men; the aim of art, to see the Divine symbolized in art-creations; of economics, to work for all according to one's own nature and attain the leisure to develop inwardly in a "simply rich and beautiful life"; of politics, the appreciation of each nation as a group-soul with the freedom to develop its own nature and thereby aid all mankind in the "common work of humanity." The noble work of humanity in this Age of Spirit "would be to find the divine Self in the individual and the collectivity and to realise spiritually, mentally, vitally, materially its greatest, largest, richest and deepest possibilities in the inner life of all and their outer action and nature."

In this era of Spirit the individual will not be swallowed up into a collectivity, but a spiritual anarchy will prevail. There will be no coercive institutions. Each individual will be free to develop his own unique talents and personality. Each will be "*the* law, the Divine law, because he will be a soul living in the Divine and not an ego living mainly if not entirely for its own interest and purpose. His life will be guided by the law of his own divine nature liberated from the ego," and this is real, complete and ultimate freedom.

In Western psychology there is much resemblance to Aurobindo's thought in Carl Jung's view that man's goal is "individuation," a reintegration of the personality around its two poles, the "shadow" (the material and vital aspects of Aurobindo's philosophy) and the "central archetype meaning" (the spiritual pole, the Supermind of Aurobindo's thought).

— *Grace E. Cairns*

But there will be no *isolated* individuals because the era of the Life Divine is characterized also by Unity. The individual knows that the Divine in himself is equally in all others, the same Spirit in all. "The sign and condition of the perfect life" is when the growing inner unity with others becomes perfect unity. Then one seeks the perfection and liberation of all others. Yet this unity with all others does not mean a featureless oneness of all. "The spiritual life is the flower not of a featureless but a conscious and diversified oneness. Each man has to grow into the Divine within himself through his own individual being." Each is a soul free to develop his unique talents, and because he sees God in all he serves men with love; he seeks their freedom and perfection along with his own, and spontaneously because his central allegiance is not to himself, or to the State and society, or to the individual ego or to the collective ego, but to God, the Divine in himself and in the universe.

The new age, then, dawns when the common mind of man begins to be moved by the three: God, Freedom, and Unity. Human history will then cease its "incomplete repetitions" and progress directly upwards towards the perfection of the divine life upon earth. Aurobindo tersely summarizes the "human cycle" thus:

> For having set out, according to our supposition with a symbolic age, an age in which man felt a great Reality behind all life which he sought through symbols, it will reach an age in which it will begin to live in that Reality, not through the symbol, not by the power of the type or of the convention or of the individual reason and intellectual will, but in our own highest nature which will be the nature of that Reality fulfilled in the conditions—not necessarily the same as now—of terrestrial existence.

This will be the actualization of the Kingdom of God on earth which the great religions have for the most part but dimly intuited.

Once the new age begins what will be the nature of this upward progress? Men will not have an other-wordly asceticism as the ideal, but will be integral beings; the material, the vital, and the mental aspects of the self will be integrated with the spiritual or Gnostic self. The Spirit will, however, guide the lower levels of being and divinize them. The desires of the body, e.g., lust for food and for satisfaction of sexual desire, will be sublimated. In an essay published as a book, written at the end of his life with the title *The Mind of Light,* Aurobindo suggests some of the possibilities for divinizing the grosser physico-biological desires. With the growing omniscience to be realized by Gnostic beings, such problems could easily be solved. Aurobindo in his book [*On Yoga*] observes that the occult powers such as clairvoyance that already belong to some yogis will become perfect omniscience in supramental beings, so the kind of knowledge necessary for divinizing the grosser desires of man should pose no problem. The spiritual life in this world in the final age of human history, the Age of Spirit, will fulfill the noblest dreams of the greatest sage-saints for a Kingdom of God on earth.

COMMENTS AND EVALUATION

Aurobindo's argument that cosmic and human history will ultimately achieve the goal of an Age of Spirit, a Kingdom of God on earth, seems pure fantasy, no doubt, to many in the intellectual world both in India and the West. In India where intuitive experience of the Divine is acceptable evidence, perhaps more thinkers are sympathetic with such a philosophy of history than in the scientifically-minded Western intellectual world. Yet there are areas in twentieth century Western thought where we find much that parallels the more significant aspects of Aurobindo's philosophy of history. We shall select examples from Western psychology, from philosophical theology, from scientific thought, and from philosophy of history that support Aurobindo's views or aspects of his system.

In Western psychology there is much resemblance to Aurobindo's thought in Carl Jung's view that man's goal is "individuation," a reintegration of the personality around its two poles, the "shadow" (the material and vital aspects of Aurobindo's philosophy) and the "central archetype meaning" (the spiritual pole, the Supermind of Aurobindo's thought). Jung's concept of the individuation process is similar to Aurobindo's description [in *The Problem of Rebirth*] of the yogic experience on the microcosmic scale of the involution-evolution process which takes place on the grand macrocosmic scale in the vastnesses of time and space that is cosmic and human history. The microcosmic experience of this process is portrayed most graphically in the practice of the Tantric yoga. Involution is represented by the Divine force, *Kundalinī*, asleep in the earth-center, the lowest level of being, the level that corresponds with Matter, the Inconscient. Then Evolution begins. *Kundalinī* is "struck by the freely coursing breath, by the current of Life," the subconscient and "rises flaming up the ladder of the spinal cord and forces open centre after centre of the involved dynamic secrets of consciousness (the conscious and mental) till at the summit she finds, joins and becomes one with the spirit," the ultimate goal. In this experience the yogin has a foretaste and confirmation of the macrocosmic pattern of history. The yogin's reintegration with the Divine resembles, as we said, Jung's individuation process. The essential elements in this process are first the conscious recognition by the individual of his "shadow," his materio-biological self or inconscient and subconscient aspects. Then it is essential that he intuit the spiritual pole of being, "the central archetype meaning," the spiritual experience that transforms him and annihilates his egocentrism. He is now able to control his lower nature, for he sees himself in true perspective in relation to this lower pole of being and the spiritual pole, the ultimate divine meaning which pervades and integrates all selves and the cosmos. This is reintegration, the goal of the individuation process in Jung's psychology. Jung thought that Eastern yogic experience exemplified it. We have seen above in Aurobindo's interpretation of yogic experience that it is a reintegration process on the microcosmic scale that manifests the pattern of cosmic and human history in the macrocosm.

In Western philosophical religion the goal of man in Paul Tillich's theology, the New Being, is similar to man's goal in Aurobindo's thought, the Gnostic Being [see Tillich's *The New Being*]. Tillich's New Being manifests a unity between self and God, between self and humanity and the world, and between self and Self. All elements of egoism, of alienation from man and God are extinguished and replaced with altruistic love. In unity with God the New Being is in unity with the creative ground of being (this corresponds with Aurobindo's Supermind) characterized by Love, Truth, and Beauty, and Love is primary. In participation in the Divine, the New Being is a resurrected soul with the power to create a new life and a new world for himself and all mankind. But Tillich differs from Aurobindo on the question of the perfection of mankind. He does not think that the human individual or human society can ever reach a divine perfection. He maintains that "the Creation and the Fall are one"; therefore "there will never be a state of existence without tragedy" [quoted in Walter Leibrecht, "The Life and Mind of Paul Tillich," in *Religion and Culture: Essays in Honor of Paul Tillich*, edited by Walter Leibrecht]. Although the New Being may be united with the Unconditioned, the Infinite God, he is not one with the Divine. He remains a finite co-creator of a new divinized world that can never attain perfection. This hiatus between God and man, the Infinite and the finite, has been characteristic of the Western tradition in theology from early times. On the other hand, the perfection, the full divinization of man has been a dominant view in Indian thought from the days of the early Upanishads. If Westerners could experience the divine in yogic meditation as practised in the East by Hindus and Buddhists they would be more prone to believe in the probability or even certainty of man's perfection in godlikeness, the view of Aurobindo.

Not only in Western psychology and religion do we find philosophies of history like that of Aurobindo. We find a striking resemblance to Aurobindo's evolutionary description of man's past and future history in the work of a scientist, a paleontologist, Père Teilhard de Chardin [see in particular Teilhard's *The Phenomenon of Man*]. Père Teilhard sees the history of this planet as a cosmogenesis, a progressive evolutionary process from inorganic matter to the biological (the Biosphere) and then to the mental (the Noosphere). These stages obviously parallel Aurobindo's Matter, Life, and Mind spheres. Resembling Aurobindo's thesis of the Supermind pervading all, even Matter, is Teilhard's Within that pervades all things. All entities, even the atom has both a Within and a Without aspect. The Within is the psychic energy aspect; the Without is the physical energy or material aspect. In the evolutionary process as entities become more and more complex at the biological level the Within aspect slowly becomes dominant over the Without until at the human level the psychic energy can control much of the physical. The next and culminating step will be the maximum control of the physical by the psychic energy. This is the Omega point.

Again we notice the likeness to Aurobindo's interpretation of the evolutionary process and its goal. Like Aurobindo's Gnostic Beings, Teilhard's "super-man" will have transcended the present human species of man. In these new ultra-hominized beings there will be complete control over the physical and biological spheres and thus the realization of Divinity and immortality. These new beings will be immortal individual personalities although parts of a hyperpersonal psycho-social spiritual totality, Omega; and each being will be in a completely integrated and harmonious relationship with all his fellow beings. Consciousness will be co-extensive with the universe and space and time will have been transcended for this omniscient ultra-hominised species. This divinization of man into a new species creating a new divinized world is precisely Aurobindo's evolutionary goal. Also, Teilhard agrees that egoless, universal love is a prior condition in reaching point Omega. The evolutionary philosophy of history of Teilhard and of Aurobindo are so much alike that Teilhard may possibly have been influenced by the ideas of his great Indian contemporary. Teilhard has devoted more of his time and writing to the scientific data that, he thinks, strongly support his theories. Aurobindo would have been happy for this kind of evidence that points to the divinizing of man and his world.

In the area of Western philosophies of history two of the most prominent thinkers, Arnold J. Toynbee and Pitirim A. Sorokin, follow Aurobindo's thesis that man's goal and ultimate salvation is the realization in this world of a global society in which egoless love will be the bond among men, or at least a world that would accept the leadership of such saints in the creation of a new society. Toynbee sees the rise and fall of civilizations as the spiral progress of "the chariot of religion" [*Civilization on Trial*], towards the goal of a community of saints on earth—men who will pattern their lives after men like St. Francis of Assisi or the *bodhisattva* ideal of Buddhism [*A Study of History*]. Sorokin, too, sees history as a spiral progress towards this goal. He mentions particularly [in *The Ways and Power of Love*] the intuitive suprarational experience of the great mystics of East and West as evidence that man is capable of attaining the highest kind of spiritual life. When a sufficient number of men can have this kind of experience of intuitive identity with the Divine a new world of altruistic love among men will come into being.

Opposing these glorious views of man's destiny are those historians and philosophers who think that a realistic, scientific, and objective approach to human history inhibits belief in a future age dominated by spiritual values. Besides, say these men, fairly precise predictions about the pattern of future events can be made only in the more exact sciences, those in which experiments can be performed with repeatable phenomena. In the social sciences, and particularly in the area of history, experiments like those common in the physical and biological sciences cannot be performed to verify whether or not a hypothetical pattern is a reality. The best the objective, scientific historian can do is examine segments of past history by collecting documentary evidence; also he must remember that in many studies he has to be selective; he cannot know all the myriad past events that might be related to the area he has chosen for study. Other more subjective factors also enter into his selection. For example, in attempting to ascertain the cause or causes of a significant past event such as the fall of Rome, he can scarcely avoid being influenced in his selection of the most relevant factors by his own personal cultural background and by the general "climate of opinion" of his time.

Granting that a thinker's philosophy, around which he builds his theory of the meaning of history, may have this kind of relativity, there remains as a perennial truth the direct experience of the great Eastern and Western mystics as evidence of humanity's contact with an eternal spiritual reality—a contact which has resulted in a new kind of divine egoless living in this world. Aurobindo, the mystic philosopher of cosmic and human history, Tillich, the renowned theologian, Teilhard de Chardin, the scientist-philosopher, and Toynbee and Sorokin, attempting encyclopaedic empirical philosophies of history—all are convinced that the great mystic saints are forerunners of a new age in history similar to that described by Aurobindo. The very failure of past and present civilizations will, as Toynbee declares, drive humanity forward to the only kind of society that can satisfy his deepest needs and aspirations.

It is true that our world is in a transition stage of global history. The transition may be to a Communist world founded upon a materialist philosophy; or to a spiritual society in which egoless love will be the highest value and a new rich creative integral life for all mankind will flourish. If Communism prevails, perhaps an easier alternative for collective humanity at present, the spiral of history, as Aurobindo thinks, may nevertheless lead eventually to the final epoch, the Age of Spirit. This is the intuitive knowledge of those who have already been infused with the Light Divine, the forerunners of the new species of Gnostic Beings.

Robert A. McDermott   (essay date 1972)

SOURCE: "The Legacy of Sri Aurobindo," in *Cross Currents,* Vol. XXII, No. 1, Winter, 1972, pp. 2-8.

[*In the following excerpt, McDermott compares Aurobindo's career with those of Rabindranath Tagore, Mohandes Gandhi, and others in an effort to determine his place in the modern Indian philosophical tradition.*]

Of the four great exponents of modern Indian ideals, Rabindranath Tagore, Mahatma Gandhi, S. Radhakrishnan, and Sri Aurobindo, the least understood in both India and the West is surely the political revolutionary, poet and philosopher of Pondicherry, Sri Aurobindo (Ghose), 1872-1950. If the first half of the century belonged to the first three of these figures, the last half (dating from his death in 1950)—or, more certainly, the last quarter (dating from the centenary of his birth, August 15, 1972)—will belong to Sri Aurobindo. This belated recognition of Sri Aurobindo's unique importance is not surprising: his radical political activities during the first decade of the century, though pioneering at the time, were overshadowed by the Nationalist Movement of the '20's and '30's; further, his life and writings at Pondicherry appeared to be (and in some respects were) so esoteric and inaccessible that most interpreters of Indian thought and culture have required the perspective of several decades in order to perceive his work coherently.

Part of the problem in approaching Sri Aurobindo is the difficulty of reconciling two seemingly unrelated careers: first, Aurobindo Ghose, leader of the Extremist faction of the Nationalist Movement in Bengal (1905-10) and second, Sri Aurobindo, the philosopher-yogi of Pondicherry, South India. Frequently, those who know one of these two figures fail to know or appreciate the other. This phenomenon is best exemplified by the attitude of one of the great figures of modern India, Jawaharlal Nehru. In his Foreword to Karan Singh's study of Sri Aurobindo's political thought from 1893-1910, [*Prophet of Indian Nationalism*], Nehru wrote as follows:

> It is extraordinary that a person who had spent fourteen of the most formative years of his life, from the age of 7 to 21, cut off from India and steeped in the European classics and the England of his day, should have become, in later years, the brilliant champion of Indian nationalism based on the philosophic and the spiritual background of Indian thought. His whole career in active politics was a very brief one, from 1905 to 1910, when he retired to Pondicherry and devoted himself to spiritual and yogic exercises. During these five years, he shone like a brilliant meteor and created a powerful impression on the youth of India. The great anti-partition movement in Bengal gained much of its philosophy from him and, undoubtedly, prepared the day for the great movement led by Mahatma Gandhi.

> It is significant to note that great political mass movements in India have had a spiritual background behind them. In Sri Aurobindo's case, this was obvious, and his emotional appeals were based on intense nationalism and a concept of Mother India. Mahatma Gandhi's appeal to the people of India, to which they responded in an amazing degree, was essentially spiritual. Though it grew out of the background of India's philosophic heritage, it was addressed to the world.

> Sri Aurobindo retired from politics at the early age of 38. Most of the people of my generation, who were immersed in political aspects of our struggle, did not understand why he did so. Later, when Gandhiji started his non-cooperation movements and convulsed India, we expected Sri Aurobindo to emerge from his retirement and join the great struggle. We were disappointed at his not doing so, though I have no doubt that all his good wishes were with it. During his retirement, he wrote, in his usual brilliant style, a number of books, chiefly dealing with philosophic and religious subjects.

Nehru was not alone in his inability to fathom Sri Aurobindo's precipitous withdrawal from active politics in favor of a life based on yoga. In retrospect, however, the apparently discrete stages of Sri Aurobindo's career evidence a startling continuity (the letters to Mrinalini, 1905, and to Barindra, 1920, are helpful in this respect).

Prominent among those who have understood this continuity is the poet Tagore, Sri Aurobindo's fellow Bengali, who saw in Sri Aurobindo's sadhana (spiritual discipline;

yoga) at Pondicherry not only his personal fulfillment but the forging of an instrument for India's spiritual regeneration. The relationship between Tagore and Sri Aurobindo dates back to 1905 when they were principal figures in the creation of Jadavpur National College, Bengal, a nationalist-inspired institution of which Sri Aurobindo was appointed Principal in 1906. Eventually, this joint effort by Tagore and Aurobindo led to the founding of Tagore's Shantiniketan, the renowned educational center in Calcutta, and the Sri Aurobindo International Center of Education at Pondicherry. When Tagore visited Sri Aurobindo at Pondicherry in 1928 he perceived his friend in the role of prophet and poet of a new India:

> I felt that the utterance of the ancient Hindu Rishi spoke from him of that equanimity which gives the human soul its freedom of entrance into the All. I said to him, "You have the Word and we are waiting to accept it from you. India will speak through your voice to the world, 'Hearken to me.'"

> In her earlier forest home Sakuntala had her awakenment of life in the restlessness of her youth. In the later hermitage she attained the fulfilment of her life. Years ago I saw Aurobindo in the atmosphere of his earlier heroic youth and I sang to him,

> "Aurobindo, accept the salutation from Rabindranath."

> Today I saw him in a deeper atmosphere of a reticent richness of wisdom and again sang to him in silence,

> "Aurobindo, accept the salutation from Rabindranath."

Tagore's line, "Aurobindo, accept the salutation from Rabindranath" (begging comparison with Emerson's salutation to Whitman, whose *Leaves of Grass* established the author as the poet of the American spirit) appears in his five page poem, "Salutation":

> Rabindranath, O Aurobindo, bows to thee!
> O friend, my country's friend, O voice incarnate, free,
> Of India's soul.

While Sri Aurobindo shares with Tagore the poetic expression of the Indian spirit, he shares with Radhakrishnan the philosophic expression of the Indian intellectual tradition and with Gandhi the socio-political expression of Karmayoga or selfless action. Curiously, Radhakrishnan's voluminous writings contain only fleeting and insignificant references to Sri Aurobindo, and Gandhi's career consistently missed Sri Aurobindo's—when Sri Aurobindo returned from England in 1893 Gandhi was sailing for South Africa, and when Gandhi returned to India after twenty years in South Africa, Sri Aurobindo had already settled permanently in Pondicherry. Irrespective of this lack of personal contact, a comparison of Sri Aurobindo with Radhakrishnan and Gandhi should help to locate Sri Aurobindo in the modern Indian tradition.

Tagore, Gandhi and Radhakrishnan were all influenced by Western values, spoke and wrote English with facility, and lived or at least traveled in the West, but only Sri Aurobindo had a thoroughly British education. From age 7 to 21 the young Aurobindo was educated successively by a tutor in Manchester, at St. Paul's School in London and at King's College, Cambridge. Upon his return to India in 1893 he learned Sanskrit and modern Indian languages in order to sink his roots into the Indian cultural soil. He continued to write English poetry, translated and wrote commentaries on classical Indian texts, and gradually became involved in political as well as cultural nationalism.

If one compares his turbulent career before his move to Pondicherry with the rather orthodox early years of Gandhi and Radhakrishnan, it is perhaps not surprising that Aurobindo Ghose developed a profound and radical sense of his own and India's destiny. On the political side, as a student at Cambridge he was a member of two secret societies dedicated to Indian nationalism, and as the leader of the Extremist faction in Calcutta, he advocated complete economic boycott of British goods, armed insurrection, and the goal of complete Independence—steps more radical than those adopted by Gandhi at any time during his leadership. On the religious and philosophical side, Sri Aurobindo not only reinterpreted the Indian intellectual tradition more imaginatively than Radhakrishnan, he based his interpretation on his own intense religious and philosophical experience. Although he worked on the same metaphysical and epistemological problems as run through the Advaita Vedānta tradition from Sankara to Radhakrishnan, his philosophical system is consistently informed by insights derived from yoga. Sri Aurobindo's philosophical system, as developed principally in *The Life Divine,* resembles the processive or qualified monism of Royce, Bradley or Radhakrishnan, but Sri Aurobindo's own experience, primarily the transformation of the intellect by yoga, supports, his contention that his philosophical system, albeit precise and comprehensive, should be understood as one of several mutually dependent ways of progressing toward individual and historical evolution.

Thus, it may not be claiming too much to say that whereas Tagore embodies Rasa-yoga (or the discipline of aesthetic experience), Gandhi embodies Karma-yoga (or the discipline of selfless action), and Radhakrishnan embodies Jnāna-yoga (or the discipline of knowledge), Sri Aurobindo seems to embody all of these disciplines and achievements. In this sense, Sri Aurobindo's yoga system, Purna or Integral Yoga, is not an academic or formal synthesis of competing yogas, but a systematic expression of each of these yogas in his own integrated life experience. The integrality of thought, work and love, of the inner and the outer, and of his aspiration and legacy, all suggest that he will continue to be revered as a paradigmatic individual. As is the function of a paradigm, Sri Aurobindo will continue to generate a legacy of ideals, achievements, activities and institutions. Elements in this legacy will probably be of unequal fidelity to his spirit, but even at this early date it can be claimed with some confidence that the legacy has the scope, depth and fervor to effect a significant transformation. Obviously, the quality of the change depends on the ever-increasing community of disciples in India and throughout the world.

While the quality of discipleship for the philosopher, whether Indian or Western, is frequently significant for that philosopher's place in the philosophical tradition, the stakes are clearly higher when the historical meaning and direction of a great individual's legacy, including the quality of his life, thought, discipline and vision, are dependent on the interpretation and application rendered by the community of disciples. The historical wisdom and self-discipline which Sri Aurobindo exemplified will be equally required of the disciples if they are to succeed where traditional religions, philosophies and social theories have failed.

The Mother of the Sri Aurobindo Ashram, who is presently 94, has been entirely responsible for the material and spiritual welfare of the Ashram and all of its members since 1926, and is well aware of the problems besetting the attempt to create a model society based on Sri Aurobindo's vision and discipline—but she is also uncommonly aware of the extraordinarily positive possibilities of such an attempt.

To find an analogy for this uniquely ambitious enterprise, one has to return to the communities of disciples in the first century after the death of Buddha, Jesus or Mohammed—but unlike the launching of these three great traditions, Sri Aurobindo's legacy is self-consciously and almost aggressively working within the framework of spiritual and historical evolution. In this respect, the work of the Mother, the Ashram and Auroville are distinctly modern.

For a modern analogy, however, one would have to imagine a community built on the vision, philosophy and spiritual discipline of someone like Teilhard de Chardin. By broadening the Christian vision (notably in *The Phenomenon of Man* and *The Future of Man*) and revitalizing the Christian yoga (principally in *The Divine Milieu*), Teilhard clearly embodies some of the same strengths as Sri Aurobindo. Both the similarities and differences are noteworthy: the most striking similarity between Sri Aurobindo and Teilhard is their celebration of human evolution and human unity; both systems argue for the ever increasing spiritualization of man and the world. In short, they share an unqualified confidence in the realization of a global, ultra- or super-humanity. By way of contrast, Sri Aurobindo conceives this evolution in terms of individual and historical discipline (i.e., Integral Yoga), whereas Teilhard, in distinctively Western terms, contends that science and technology is the instrument of this spiritualization. Although some may fault Teilhard for this total confidence in technology (which would seem to be at the expense of the eco-system), it would nevertheless be easy to establish the strength of Teilhard's case for the positive function of technology for social and historical evolution. Although Sri Aurobindo does not share the extreme suspicion of technology typified by Gandhi, neither does he see its enormous significance for the spiritualization and liberation of the material world. On the other hand, there are perhaps two points on which Teilhard's position is less adequate than Sri Aurobindo's: First, despite the many years that he lived in China, Teilhard apparently had so little contact with the mainsprings of Chinese culture and spirituality that his Christian vision remained impervious to Eastern influence; in short, Teilhard lacks the range which Sri Aurobindo, Radhakrishnan and other Indians have developed by virtue of cultural and religious bilingualism. Secondly, Teilhard and the Christian tradition generally are less confident than Sri Aurobindo concerning the value of human action in the dual task of individual and historical perfection.

The purpose of this comparison between Sri Aurobindo and Teilhard is not to criticize Teilhard, but rather to explain in more familiar terms the originality and comprehensiveness of Sri Aurobindo's legacy. Of course, it is possible to interpret any one part of this legacy (e.g., Sri Aurobindo's early political career, his poetry, philosophy, aspects of the Ashram or Auroville) just as one can separate the science and spirituality of Teilhard, but in both cases the coherence of the parts contributes to their significance. If, on the other hand, Sri Aurobindo's legacy were to lose its experimental vitality, then there would be cause to break this cohesiveness in order to save whatever elements retained their viability. While the discipline remains honored and experimental, Sri Aurobindo's legacy may indeed initiate a genuine transformation of man and society. But since the discipline of selflessness, like Christian love, is easier to advocate than to practice, and since disciples are not always effective instruments of their masters' work, Sri Aurobindo's legacy will run perilously close to the kind of religious institutionalization which Sri Aurobindo and the Mother have emphatically rejected. At this time we can only say that Sri Aurobindo's legacy is a uniquely promising attempt to spiritualize human institutions without institutionalizing the spirit.

Prema Nandakumar   (essay date 1982)

SOURCE: "Sri Aurobindo: The Prose Canon," in *Perspectives on Indian Prose in English,* edited by M. K. Naik, Humanities Press, 1982, pp. 72-103.

[*In the following essay, Nandakumar provides a chronological survey of Aurobindo's prose works.*]

During a literary career that spanned almost sixty years, Sri Aurobindo was continuously active with his pen. He left no literary form untouched. Perhaps because of his world-wide fame as a spiritual seer, he is now better known as the author of *Savitri,* but this cosmic epic was but one facet of his total literary achievement.

If poetry was his first love, Sri Aurobindo was an equally tireless practitioner of the 'other harmony' of prose. In fact, the collected prose works of Sri Aurobindo comprise about twenty-five massive volumes in the Centenary Library. In sheer amplitude, depth, richness, and uniform distinction of style, he has not been surpassed—or even equalled—by any other Indian writer of English prose.

Circumstances had conspired to give him in his early years a wholly English education 'untainted' by any knowledge of his native speech. As a child he was carefully insulated from his mother tongue, Bengali, thanks to his English nurse, Miss Pagett. He was presently put to school in the Loretto Convent at Darjeeling where he rapidly mastered

English since almost all his fellow-boarders were English children. Again, Sri Aurobindo was hardly eight years old when he was taken along with his two elder brothers to England and entrusted to the care of an English family, the Drewetts, at Manchester. So fond was his father of the Western way of life that he instructed the Drewetts not to allow his boys to "make the acquaintance of any Indian or undergo any Indian influence."

When Sri Aurobindo entered St. Paul's School at London, he had already received a fair grounding in Latin, French and English, and had been introduced to the pleasures of English literature, especially Keats, Shelley and Shakespeare. Now he began learning Greek as well. He won the Butterworth Prize for Literature and Bedford Prize for History. He assiduously cultivated English literature and also took part in debates on subjects like Swift and Milton.

By winning a Senior Classical Scholarship, Sri Aurobindo was able to move to King's College, Cambridge. Here he could hardly fail to attract the attention of his teachers, and we have on record the words of his senior tutor, G. M. Prothero:

> Besides his classical scholarship, he possessed a knowledge of English literature far beyond the average of undergraduates and wrote much better English than most young Englishmen . . . Moreover, the man has not only ability but character.

And Oscar Browning told Sri Aurobindo himself:

> I have examined papers at thirteen examinations and I have never during that time seen such excellent papers as yours . . . As for your essay, it was wonderful.

The essay was a comparison between Shakespeare and Milton! Such was the well-equipped young scholar who practically rejected a berth in the Civil Service and returned to India only to take up service under the Maharaja of Baroda.

Already Sri Aurobindo had acquired an enviable mastery of the English language apart from a deep knowledge of Greek and Latin. His English translation of a Greek poem on Hecuba had won the praise of Laurence Binyon. Besides, a fairly intimate knowledge of French, German and Italian had widened his understanding and enriched his sensibility. With all these endowments and acquisitions. Sri Aurobindo was now well-set on his ministry as a man of letters.

But, of course, Sri Aurobindo as an artist in prose cannot be explained away by his occidental background alone. During his thirteen years at Baroda he launched upon a programme of intense studies covering Sanskrit, Bengali, Marathi, Gujarati and Hindi, and he continued to be a voracious reader of European literature. In his early years at Baroda, his acquaintance with Swami Vivekananda's English writings had decisively turned Sri Aurobindo to Indian philosophy and yoga. This was partly the reason he learned Sanskrit and Bengali and pored over the *Ramayana,* the *Mahabharata* and the works of Kalidasa and Bankim Chandra Chatterjee. Happily the child of the Ganges was restored to his heritage again. However, the fruits of rigorous self-training in the Western literatures during his impressionable years remained with him, and his new studies were but to impart a polyphonic richness to his linguistic wizardry. On the other hand, although he did achieve a mastery of Bengali and even edited the Bengali weekly, *Dharma,* for some time, he was to feel completely at home only when writing or lecturing in English.

THE FIRST FLASH

Even while all this intense course in self-education was in progress, Sri Aurobindo was invited to contribute to the *Indu Prakash* of Bombay. It was thus that Sri Aurobindo began in 1893 his career in political and literary journalism. As we read today the **New Lamps for Old** series that appeared in 1893-94, we cannot but be astonished by the eruptive incandescence of his English prose. Where was the question of gradual maturation for gifted writers such as he? Sri Aurobindo burst out in a blaze of glory and sounded at once significant and prophetic in the intellectual cast of the essays and the dazzling turn of the phrases.

Sri Aurobindo's theme was the concept and content of national independence, and the key to its realisation. The language breathes fire, and there is a no-nonsense directness and also a fierce impatience in the writing:

> The walls of the Anglo-Indian Jericho stand yet without a breach, and the dark spectacle of Penury draws her robe over the land in greater volume and with an ampler sweep.

Mere political journalism was to be elevated into a study of the bases of freedom, justice and economic well-being. With his seer-wisdom, Sri Aurobindo realised that a mass upsurge was the need of the hour, not a series of closed-door meetings by well-to-do intellectuals. And how Sri Aurobindo lashed at the ruling class:

> If we were not dazzled by the artificial glare of English prestige, we should at once acknowledge that these men are not worth being angry with . . . Our appeal, the appeal of every high-souled and self-respecting nation, ought not to lie to the opinion of the Anglo-Indians, no, nor yet to the British sense of justice, but to our own reviving sense of manhood.

Such bold writing in the first two articles was bound to cause acute embarrassment to the proprietor of the *Indu Prakash* who now requested Sri Aurobindo to be less vitriolic and rather more circumspect in the expression of his views. Accordingly, the remaining seven articles in the **New Lamps for Old** series took a more pedestrian line, and presently he started another series of seven essays on the life and work of Bankim Chandra Chatterjee. But whatever the subject, Sri Aurobindo was tempering and perfecting the instrument of prose, and it is interesting to watch his writing, at first laden with characteristic Western imagery and anecdotage, gradually seasoning itself with Indian thought and sensibility. The Englishmen who came to India were but "types of the middleclass or Philistines"; and Mr. Munro "had the temper of badly educated Hyena". And as for Rishi Bankim, this was Sri Aurobindo's rounded and all-sufficing assessment:

> And when Posterity comes to crown with her

praises the Makers of India, she will place her most splendid laurel, not on the sweating temples of a place-hunting politician nor on the narrow forehead of a noisy social reformer, but on the serene brow of that gracious Bengali (Bankim) who never clamoured for place or power, but did his work in silence for love of his work.

RAINBOW TINTS FROM SANSKRIT

The dawn of the new century seemed to open new horizons to Sri Aurobindo's consciousness. His wide-ranging studies in Indian literature, especially in Sanskrit, and his new-found interest in yoga, gave his writing new depths of meaning and a fresh glow of style. It was during these years that he was busy writing poetry in English or translating from Sanskrit and Bengali into English. To one who had drunk deep in the classical and Romantic springs of the West, Valmiki and Vyasa were exhilarating revelations. Sri Aurobindo's perceptive mind often made a contrastive study of the best of the Occident and of the Orient, and the conclusions flowed with natural ease though in the form of occasional jottings:

> To be fed on the verse of Spenser, Shelley, Keats, Byron and Tennyson is no good preparation for the severe classics. It is, indeed, I believe, the general impression of many 'educated' young Indians that the *Mahabharata* is a mass of old wives' stories without a spark of poetry or imagination. But to those who have bathed even a little in the fountain-head of poetry, and can bear the keenness and purity of these mountain sources, the naked and unadorned poetry of Vyasa is as delightful as to bathe in a chill fountain in the heat of summer. [**Vyasa and Valmiki**]

And the more Sri Aurobindo's mind and sensibility were exposed to the riches of Vyasa, Valmiki and Kalidasa, a qualitative and progressive change appeared in the style as well Sanskrit words and phrases inevitably found their way to the English writings:

> . . . it is that they do not act like common men (*prakrto janah*). They are the great spirits, the *mahajanah,* in whose footsteps the world follows. [**Vyasa and Valmiki**]

Even traditional Indian similes leap into the middle of an argument to prove his point; as when [in the same book] he compares the *adhikara* of the great critic to "the palate of the swan which rejects the water mingled with the milk and takes the milk alone."

Even as Sri Aurobindo was thus steadily enlarging his literary consciousness, he was driven by developing circumstances to take a plunge into nationalist politics in 1905.

His aim in politics was, as later admitted by him [in a letter to Joseph Baptista dated January 5, 1920], "to get into the mind of the people a settled will for freedom and the necessity of a struggle to achieve it, in place of the futile ambling methods till then in vogue."

Writing in English, Sri Aurobindo was no doubt speaking to such of his countrymen as had gained an English education. This was clearly a depressing, if not microscopic, minority. Nevertheless, it was the nuclear minority that held the promise of a wide diffusion of the message among their far-flung illiterate masses. Sri Aurobindo's speeches and writings of the political period were to be permeated with Puranic mythological allusions as also similes and sentiments redolent of the classics of India that they could be immediately translated into the living idiom of Bengali, Gujarati, Hindi, Marathi or Tamil without losing in the least the whole force of the intended message.

Sri Aurobindo's document on *Bhavani Mandir* is a typical example. As India entered the 20th century, Sri Aurobindo seems already to have formulated his plan for revolutionary work.

THE POLITICAL PAMPHLETEER

Of the many power-houses of the spirit that fuelled the upsurge in revolutionary activities in the first decade of this century, *Bhavani Mandir* remains altogether unique. Although it was written for secret circulation, it duly came to the notice of the Government who were alarmed by its stark incendiary fervour and tried to suppress it. It was Surendra Mohan Ghose who discovered it by chance and arranged for its publication in 1956. Sri Aurobindo's sustained studies in English and French literature, his single-minded absorption in the novels of Bankim Chandra and his deep sense of kinship with the Ramakrishna-Vivekananda phenomenon, all went into the making of this packet of "political dynamite". But like Milton's *Areopagitica,* the document transcends the historical context and remains at once a marvel of impassioned literary creation and a perennial plea for noble and heroic endeavour.

> A temple is to be erected and consecrated to Bhavani the Mother, among the hills . . . The Shakti we call India, Bhavani Bharati, is the living unity of the Shaktis of three hundred million people; but she is inactive, imprisoned in the magic circle of tamas, the self-indulgent inertia and ignorance of her sons.

This is not the asseveration of a hard-headed intellectual; nor is it poetic prose with mere decorative imagery. Rather has Sri Aurobindo caught with unerring insight the hoary myth and symbolism that still move a million hearts like a trumpet. The celebrated *Chandi* is a scripture recited daily all over Bengal and India. Sri Aurobindo has invoked the power and personality of Mahalakshmi who springs out of the consciousness of the gods themselves and strides forth to destroy the demon Mahisha. And Mahishasura—the Buffalo-shaped—is not the alien ruler alone. The demon symbolises all darkness, all tamas, and hence that section of Indian humanity as well that compromises with freedom and bars the way to progress. Sri Aurobindo outlines accordingly his plan for an order of monks integrally devoted to Bhavani and her reign of returning Light.

Charged with equal power is his *Hour of God* composed at about the same time:

> In the hour of God cleanse thy soul of all self-deceit and hypocrisy and vain self-flattering that thou mayst look straight into thy spirit and hear which summons it . . . being pure cast

aside all fear; for the hour is often terrible, a fire and a whirlwind and a tempest, a treading of the wine-press of the wrath of God; but he who can stand up in it on the truth of his purpose is he who shall stand.

The years 1905 (the probable date of composition of *Bhavani Mandir*) to 1910 (when he retired from politics) were almost wholly devoted to political journalism though often charged with prophecy. His espousal of the Nationalist Party gave his writings their immediate significance, and a ready forum was opened to him when Bipin Chandra Pal started the daily *Bande Mataram* in 1906.

BANDE MATARAM

Bipin Chandra Pal was certainly inspired by Bankim Chandra's poem to name his paper *Bande Mataram,* for the phrase had become "at once the salvo of defiance of authority and a dedication to the service of the Mother." Sri Aurobindo fostered this double aim with exemplary care. So powerful was Sri Aurobindo's style that the London *Times* began publishing extracts from his unsigned articles and even admitted that *Bande Mataram* was edited with "a literary ability rare in the Anglo-native press!"

Once the issue was joined, Sri Aurobindo withheld no arrow from effective use. Mythology, history, literary allusion, political, economic and social thought were all mobilised and charged with humour, satire, irony or invective as the occasion demanded. As leader-writer or contributor, Sri Aurobindo had always to race against time, and yet there was not let-up, no false note, nor a single faulty construction. He was certainly a lord of language. Consider, for example, the epic simile in which he compares Nationalism to Krishna. The articles scatter with a prodigal hand derisive epithets on the British Government and Indian Moderates, while also delivering a prophetic message to the Indian people:

> As neither the milk of Putana nor the hoofs of the demon could destroy the infant Krishna, so neither Riponism nor Poona prosecutions could check the growth of Nationalism while yet it was an indistinct force; and as neither Kamsa's wiles nor his *visakanyas* nor his mad elephants nor his wrestlers could kill Krishna revealed in Mathura, no, neither a revival of Riponism nor the poison of discord . . . nor Fullerism plus hooliganism . . . can slay Nationalism now that it has entered the arena. Nationalism is an avatar and cannot be slain . . .

But why, it may be asked, this obsession with Nationalism, or political freedom for India? Sri Aurobindo's answer is categorical and uncompromising; our other freedoms lose their sap and savour if Swaraj is denied to us:

> Spiritual freedom the ancient Rishis had already declared to us; social freedom was part of the message of Buddha, Chaitanya, Nanak and Kabir and the saints of Maharashtra; political freedom is the last word of the triune gospel. Without political freedom the soul of man is crippled. [*Bande Mataram,* February 23, 1908]

Whenever the context demanded it, Sri Aurobindo hastened to press for the other freedoms as well. For instance, he was forthright in his stand on caste. He considered it an un-Hindu excrescence which should be firmly rejected by the Nationalists:

> The baser ideas underlying the degenerate per-versions of the original caste system, the mental attitude which bases them on a false foundation of caste, pride and arrogance, of a divinely or-dained superiority depending on the accident of birth, of a fixed and intolerant inequality, are in-consistent with the supreme teaching, basic spir-it of Hinduism which sees the one variable and indivisible divinity in every individual being. Nationalism is simply the passionate aspiration for the realisation of that Divine Unity in the nation . . . [*Bande Mataram,* September 22, 1907]

Again, long, long before the coming of Gandhiji, Sri Auro-bindo castigated the malaise of a lop-sided education that took man away from his rural background. He called for "a system of instruction which will bring the educated Hindu back to the soil", held up as an example Maharash-tra under Shivaji, and hoped that the educated would not play into the hands of the English rulers by rejecting the old way of life *in toto* and aping the West in all things. As for political action, he outlined a scheme of passive resis-tance, but he did not rule out violent resistance either:

> Passive resistance is an attempt to meet such dis-turbances by peaceful and self-contained Brah-matej; but even the greatest Rishis of old could not, when the Rakshasas were fierce and deter-mined, keep up the sacrifice without calling in the bow of the Kshatriya . . .

By now the use of apt Sanskrit words and of Hindu similes had become organic to Sri Aurobindo's style. But now and then there was also the loading of the rift with the ore of Western historical allusion:

> It was the exiled of Italy, it was the men who lan-guished in Austrian and Bourbon dungeons, it was the Poerio and Silvio Pellico and their fellow sufferers whose collected strength reincarnated in Mazzini and Garibaldi and Cavour to free their country. [*Bande Mataram,* May 9, 1907]

But he also warned his readers against being swamped by the new scientific education from the West, which was apt to mistake the lower knowledge of phenomena for the higher knowledge of Reality:

> When we first received a European education, we allowed ourselves to be misled by the light of science. Science is a light within a limited room, not the sun which illumines the world. The *Apara vidya* is the sun of science, but there is a higher Vidya, a mightier knowledge . . . Who-ever has once felt the glory of God within him can never again believe that the intellect is su-preme . . . It is in the heart where God resides. [*Bande Mataram,* February 22, 1908]

A month later he again wrote about the dangers of an un-critical acceptance of Western political ideals, social sys-tems, economic principles, and significantly added:

> India must remain India if she is to fulfil her des-tiny. Nor will Europe profit by grafting her civilisation on India, for if India, who is the dis-tinct physician of Europe's maladies, herself falls into the clutches of the disease, the disease will remain uncured and incurable and Europe-an civilisation will perish as it perished when Rome declined, first by dry rot within itself and last by eruption from without. [*Bande Mataram,* April 14, 1908]

Sri Aurobindo was soon to be arrested and prosecuted for his alleged complicity in the Alipur Bomb outrage. But it was while he was in the Alipur jail that he had the vision of Vasudeva, the omnipresent godhead. Already his mind was unconsciously withdrawing from the political scene, and labouring towards the heights of spiritual fulfilment. His vision of India expanded so as to include the entire world, and in fact there had been clear hints of this shift in his worldview even in some of the *Bande Mataram* arti-cle immediately before his prosecution:

> God has set apart India as the eternal fountain-head of holy spirituality, and He will never suf-fer that fountain to run dry. By our political free-dom we shall once more recover our spiritual freedom. [*Bande Mataram,* February 23, 1908]

EDUCATING A NATION

When Sri Aurobindo came back from jail after acquittal, he found a sad change confronting him. *Bande Mataram* had gone out of publication. Undaunted, Sri Aurobindo started two weekly papers, the *Karmayogin* in English and *Dharma* in Bengali. Although the papers were short-lived, they served an important purpose. Sri Aurobindo's writ-ings in the *Karmayogin* snap the gradual change from po-litical evangelist to spiritual visionary.

The *Karmayogin* was to be a review of "National Religion, Literature, Science, Philosophy, etc." The weekly would emblazon the living Indian heritage in all its facets. Ac-cordingly Sri Aurobindo launched upon a selective pro-gramme of English translations from the Upanishads, Ka-lidasa, Vyasa and Bankim Chandra. Of equal relevance were the series of essays like ***A System of National Educa-tion, The Brain of India, The National Value of Art*** and ***The Ideal of the Karmayogin.*** There were also experi-ments like ***Conversations of the Dead.*** Everywhere the voice of the practical idealist is the bass of the music. The tone of irony and satire that played havoc with proper names and personal predilections in many of the *Bande Mataram* missiles now gives way to a seer's serenity and certainty. Politics is not excluded, but the accent is really on "man-making" in Swami Vivekananda's phrase, or rather on divine man-making:

> Every one has in him something divine, some-thing his own, a chance of perfection and strength in however small a sphere which God offers him to take or refuse. The task is to find it, develop it and use it. [***A System of National Education***]

In the result, Sri Aurobindo sought to educate the aspirant Indian on almost everything including art. His pro-nouncements on this rather neglected subject are worth special attention. A nakedly utilitarian education has tended to obscure the value of art in life. And yet, the satisfaction of the body alone is not enough; one's vital and emotional urges should also find fulfilment. The activities of *buddhi* and the higher spiritual faculties give us the Arts, poetry, music, painting and sculpture, and a study of these helps man to progress as much as, or even more than, the study of sciences and the other utilitarian activities of the *manas*.

The use of art can be aesthetic, intellectual and spiritual in that progressive spiral. The aesthetic appeal—the appreciation of the beautiful in colour and sound—helps man to overcome his savage instincts. Its emotional appeal acts as a *katharsis* or *cittasuddhi*—purging or purifying the soul. It keeps the soul's movements "purified, self-controlled, deep harmonious".

But the national value of Art lies truly in its spiritual appeal, for the greatest Art can transform the mental man and usher in higher consciousness which is the nature of *Anandamaya:*

> To suggest the strength and virile unconquerable force of the divine Nature in man and in the outside world, its energy, its calm, its powerful inspiration, its august enthusiasm, its wildness, its greatness, attractiveness, to breathe that into man's soul and gradually mould the finite into the image of the Infinite is another spiritual utility of Art. This is its loftiest function, its fullest consummation, its most perfect privilege. [*The National Value of Art*]

Not mere man-making but God-making! What a far cry from the Cambridge intellectual who composed the Platonic dialogue on **"The Harmony of Virtue"**? Sri Aurobindo is now wholly committed to the theory and practice of ancient Indian art and sees in their imaginative revival the hope for the future:

> The spirit of old Indian Art must be revived, the inspiration and directness of vision which even now subsists among the possessors of the ancient traditions, the inborn skill and taste of the race, the dexterity of the Indian hand and the intuitive gaze of the Indian eye must be recovered and the whole nation lifted again to the high level of the ancient culture—and higher. [*The National Value of Art*]

THE BIG CHANGE

The first issue of the *Karmayogin* was to come out on 19 June 1909. Twenty days earlier, Sri Aurobindo had delivered the extraordinary **Uttarpara Speech** making a decisive shift in his evangelism, from the political to the spiritual. But of course such things do not happen all at once, but have an aetiology behind. The full story, however, can never be told, for it was an inner history defying recordation. Nevertheless one can piece together a few hints scattered in the writings and speeches.

As a speaker, Sri Aurobindo was no rabble rouser, and purple eloquence was certainly not his forte. And yet he was in great demand during the Nationalist agitation. His personality was of the kind that could convey a sense of infinite energy held back but ready to move mountains

when released. Though he did not give vent to mighty Victorian sweeps of rhetoric, he could always get to the heart of the matter and move his audiences to action. Only a few speeches have now come down to us, and these too are summaries rather than faithful transcripts. There is his brief farewell to the students of the National College when he resigned his Principalship. In his speech, there was no exercise of self-pity or self-glorification; he contented himself with spelling out the alphabet of adoration of the Mother:

> There are times in a nation's history when Providence places before it one work, one aim, to which everything else, however, high and noble in itself, has to be sacrificed. Such a time has now arrived for our Motherland when nothing is dearer than her service, when everything else is to be directed to that end. [*Speeches*]

There was, then, the meeting on 19 January 1908 at Bombay when he "spoke neither like a professional combative politician nor yet like a seasoned statesman. It was more in the tone of the evangelist, the prophet." [K. R. Srinivasa Iyenger, *Sri Aurobindo: A Biography and a History*]. So was it, indeed, for Sri Aurobindo boldly compared Nationalism to a religion:

> What can all these tribunals, what can all the powers of the world do to that which is within you, that Immortal, that Unborn and Undying One, whom the sword cannot pierce, whom the fire cannot burn, and whom the water cannot drown?

Then, a few months later, came the incarceration, the prolonged trial, Chittaranjan's magnificent defence, and the honourable acquittal. Sri Aurobindo seemed to be unmoved throughout the Court proceedings, almost in a trance; always known for his serenity and unflappability, there was now a new tautness and calm suggestive of unknown dimensions of strength. After his release from prison in mid-1909, he was in great demand for public speeches. And the people sensed a big change in the man. Sister Nivedita, for example, noted that "since his imprisonment at Alipur, Aurobindo Ghose was no longer a fighter, but a yogi." Of course he cracked jokes as before and sprayed the Government with the barbed shafts of his irony. But the big change was there all the same, the result of his "Ashramavas" at Alipur, when a blissful realisation had come to him. Sri Aurobindo was to refer to this experience in his Uttarpara speech on 30 May 1909:

> I looked at the jail that secluded me from men and it was no longer by its high walls that I was imprisoned; no, it was Vasudeva who surrounded me. I walked under the branches of the tree in front of my cell but it was not the tree, I knew it was Vasudeva, it was Sri Krishna whom I saw standing there and holding over me his shade. I looked at the bars of my cell, the very grating that did duty for a door and again I saw Vasudeva. It was Narayana who was guarding and standing sentry over me [*Speeches*].

This was no set speech, and Sri Aurobindo was not speaking from notes; there was no effort, no attempt to produce an effect; the words came, the right precise words came, as though someone else was in command, and the speaker was only an instrument. The audience heard him, and watched him spell-bound as it were. The big change had taken place. Even as he had withdrawn from combative politics to devote himself to yoga sadhana, his prose too took a sudden and decisive change. No more a mere spokesman of national politics, Sri Aurobindo was now more like his own Aswapathy, a representative of humanity striving for a new search:

> A voyager upon uncharted routes
> Fronting the danger of the Unknown,
> Adventuring across enormous realms,
> He broke into another Space and Time.
>
> [*Savitri*]

TOWARDS THE HEIGHTS

Sri Aurobindo arrived at Pondicherry in April 1910 and began his silent work with a handful of disciples. In 1914, two French aspirants, Paul and Mirra Richard, persuaded him to launch a philosophical journal to educate people of the world on the problems of self-change and world-transformation. Thus began the publication of *Arya,* a monthly, on 15 August 1914. When the exigencies of the war forced the Richards to return to France early in 1915, most of the writing had to be done by Sri Aurobindo himself, and he kept it going almost single-handed till 1921. Month after month Sri Aurobindo poured out his philosophy of being and becoming, and his views on man, nature and God. Several series of essays were simultaneously published, and several of them have since become famous: **The Life Divine, The Synthesis of Yoga, The Secret of the Veda, Essays on the Gita, The Ideal of Human Unity, The Psychology of Social Development, The Future Poetry, Heraclitus, A Defence of Indian Culture** and **The Renaissance in India**. There were several other important contributions too, including brilliant commentaries on some of the principal Upanishads.

What unified this large body of writing was the two-fold aim behind the *Arya* adventure: "a systematic study of the highest problems of existence . . . (and) . . . the formation of a vast synthesis of knowledge, harmonising the diverse religious traditions of humanity, occidental as well as oriental." One example of this is Sri Aurobindo's essay-sequence on Heraclitus.

Heraclitus began as a review of Professor R. D. Ranade's paper on the subject. Sri Aurobindo's profound intimacy with Greek literature and philosophy encouraged him, even while commending Ranade, "this perfect writer and scholar", to go farther still and present Heraclitus as a mystic in his own right. Heraclitus' symbolic language, like the Veda itself, can be understood with an effort:

> That process (of eternal flux in existence) he sees as a constant change and a changing back, an exchange and an interchange in a constant whole,—managed for the rest by a clash of forces, by a creative and determinative strife, 'war which is the father and king of all things'. Between Fire as the Being and Fire in the Becoming existence describes a downward and upward movement—*pravrtti nivrtti*—which has

been called the 'back-returning road' upon which all travels. These are the master ideas of the thought of Heraclitus.

Sri Aurobindo is particularly struck by the image of Fire in the apophthegms of Heraclitus. It is so Vedic and Upanishadic a symbol! Did Heraclitus who posited the theory of constant exchange think of an Indian notion like *pralaya?* Perhaps he did, if we rightly construe the aphorism "fire will come on all things and judge and convict them." Finally, of what practical use is Heraclitus' philosophy? Indian philosophy percolated to the common man through "its intimate influence on the religion, the social ideas, the daily life of the people." But Greek philosophy was divorced from its religion, and thus Heraclitus and his compeers could influence only "the cultured few". And yet:

> There is the gate of the divine ecstasy. Heraclitus could not see it, and yet his one saying about the kingdom of the child touches, almost reaches the heart of the secret. For this kingdom is evidently spiritual, it is the crown, the mastery to which the perfected man arrives; and the perfect man is a divine child!

Another series that began as a review is now known as **The Foundations of Indian Culture**. The provocation was William Archer's *India and the Future* (1917) wherein he tried to indicate Indian culture with a supercilious smirk of insolence. Suddenly the envenomed sword of *Bande Mataram* days leapt out of the scabbard, and lashed at the egregious Archer:

> That well-known dramatic critic leaving his safe natural sphere for fields in which his chief claim to speak was a sublime and confident ignorance, assailed the whole life and culture of India.

But why blame Archer alone? He was but the symptom, for the malaise ran deeper:

> Why are a certain class of Indians still hypnotised in all fields by European culture and why are we all still hypnotised by it in the field of politics? Because they constantly saw all the power, creation, activity on the side of Europe, all the immobility or weakness of a static inefficient defence on the side of India.

But although Sri Aurobindo embarks upon a massive defence of Indian culture, he also cautions against any overreaction:

> Our sense of the greatness of our past must not be made a fatally hypnotising lure to inertia; it should be rather an inspiration to renewed and greater achievement.

After demolishing Archer's curmudgeonish conclusions which often "verge on the idiotic", Sri Aurobindo fondly unfolds the multi-hued cultural map of India. Nothing escapes his eye, and the four chapters on religion (and spirituality), art, literature and polity achieve a brilliant conspectus. Fullness and wholeness are the marks of India's crown of glory, but where there are flaws Sri Aurobindo doesn't ignore them. For example, India is deficient in recorded reliable history, but even this is not attributable to any deliberate flight from life. The old vitality and zest for life is yet preserved in the art and literature of India, and it is ready for glorious renewal as in spring after winter:

> And in spite of the defect the greatness and activity of the past life of India reveals itself and comes out in bolder relief the more the inquiry into her past unearths the vast amount of material still available.

Indeed, Sri Aurobindo sees resurgent India as

> the ancient immemorable Shakti recovering her deepest self, lifting her head higher towards the supreme source of light and strength and turning to discover the complete meaning and a vaster form of her Dharma.

THE SUMMIT

At the apex of Sri Aurobino's prose works stand *The Life Divine, The Synthesis of Yoga* and *Essays on the Gita*. It is in these—as also in the other *Arya* sequences: *The Ideal of Human Unity, The Future Poetry* and the rest—that what has come to be known as Sri Aurobindo's "global" style is manifest in its meandering rhythms of unfailing opulence. On our first exposure we are no doubt likely to be overwhelmed by the cascades of brilliant, gleaming and fascinating prose, construction piled upon construction, qualification balancing qualification, but the augmented load being carried forward somehow by the charged momentum of the thought. Are we perhaps watching the Kaveri rushing down at Hogenekal, the mist as it rises curtaining off the falls with a sense of brooding mystery? This writing is so distant, so obscure, and yet it is so near, so susceptible to the deeper listening of the soul!

The fertilising power of the *Gita* is unique in the annals of religion and literature. Superbly endowed minds through the centuries have made it yield newer and newer spirals of meaning. Perhaps the Anglo-Saxon idiom isn't quite adequate enough to hold up many-chambered edifices of this kind. But when Sri Aurobindo came to this task, he strengthened Anglo-Saxon with the *Vajra* of Sanskrit and tempered an instrument equal to the demands he might make upon it.

Sri Aurobindo's aim in the *Essays on the Gita* was to fuse the Karma, Jnana and Bhakti facets of the *Gita* into a single blaze. There are two sharp foci to Sri Aurobindo's argument. On the one hand, there is the Avatar, the Redeemer, who is really the Hound of Heaven chasing his devotee, seizing him and pushing him up the spiral of evolutionary consciousness. But the Avatar also comes as one of us, and only helps us to redeem and transform ourselves:

> The Avatar does not come as a thaumaturgic magician, but as the divine leader of humanity and the exemplar of a divine humanity. Even human sorrow and physical suffering he must assume and use so as to show, first, how that suffering may be a means of redemption,—as did Christ,—secondly, to show how, having been assumed by the divine soul in the human nature, it can also be overcome in the same nature,—as did Buddha.

If the Divine descends to the earth and undergoes the sickness of mortality for the sake of man, man too should be prepared to offer a total surrender to the Divine and make himself pliable and ready for being rescued. Indeed total self-surrender is the cardinal teaching of the *Gita*:

> This then is the supreme movement, this complete surrender of your whole self and nature, this abandonment of all dharmas to the Divine who is your highest Self, this absolute aspiration of all your members to the supreme spiritual nature. If you can once achieve it, whether at the outset or much later on the way, then whatever you are or were in your outward nature, your way is sure and your perfection inevitable.

The glossary of Sanskrit words used by Sri Aurobindo in the *Essays* runs to twenty pages of small print. This would give a rough idea of the way Sri Aurobindo's English had been Sanskritised through the years since 1905. The language of *The Synthesis of Yoga* is also of a piece with that of the *Essays,* an English body inhabited by a Sanskrit soul. This was of course inevitable, for Sri Aurobindo's main inspiration had its source in the perennial Vedic springs. While the *Essays on the Gita,* like *The Secret of the Veda,* mined rich spiritual ore from the scriptures, *The Synthesis of Yoga* was more of a comprehensive practical treatise on the classical yogas and the Integral yoga and the Yoga of Perfection.

With a quick backward glance at the history of the East and West, Sri Aurobindo seeks in The Ideal of Human Unity to formulate an ideal of unity that could bring out the best in the constituents, whether it be a family, community, city, state, nation or empire. It is only through the uncongealing of the separative egoistic consciousness that mutual suspicions can end, paving the way for disarmament and human unity.

— *Prema Nandakumar*

If the *Essays* was a cascade, *The Synthesis* is a column of many-tongued fire that dispels the mists of ignorance and shows the way to the goal. Quotation is impossible, analysis unworkable, summary meaningless. *The Synthesis* has to be read in a mood of sustained attention, and in its entirety, if we are to draw close to the heart of the matter. The central argument is simple enough. An Integral Yoga should be undertaken to purify the body, the life-impulses, the mind and the soul. When it is in a condition of alertness, spiritual energy would pour into this mould of man—the "perfectly made man", according to the Aitareya Upanishad—and create a being capable of divine perfection in this life itself.

The Synthesis thus heaves grandly and moves majestically like a King Cobra speeding towards its goal. Finally, unless egoistic separativity cracks and ceases, supermind, the higher consciousness, cannot manifest itself, and man cannot exceed himself and become the superman:

> The Supermind acting through sense
> feels all as God and in God,
> all as the manifested touch, sight, hearing, taste, perfume,
> all as the felt, seen, directly experienced
> substance and power and energy and movement,
> play, penetration, vibration, form, nearness, pressure,
> substantial interchange of the Infinite.

Of the triune summit of Sri Aurobindo's prose, *The Life Divine* is undoubtedly the most elevated. . . . Call it 'prose-epic', 'philosophical tour-de-force' or merely 'supramental manifesto', *The Life Divine* is among the major creations of the modern mind. Understandably enough, Sanskrit words occur less frequently here than in the *Essays* or *The Synthesis,* for although the epigraphs of each chapter are taken from Vedic or Upanishadic sources, the central argument itself flows out of his own mystic experiences or intuitive apprehension of the nature, Law and delight of Existence. *The Life Divine* is also the metaphysical base-plank of the more practical treatise, *The Synthesis of Yoga*.

PROPHET OF HUMAN UNITY

It should not be thought that, in his preoccupations with the emergence of the Superman, Sri Aurobindo has as good as locked himself up in an ivory tower of spiritual speculation. Actually, Sri Aurobindo was very much in close touch with men and events, and thought deeply over the problems before contemporary humanity. Out of these anxious speculations arose these sequences of essays: *The Ideal of Human Unity, The Psychology of Social Development* (later called *The Human Cycle*) and *War and Self-Determination*. 'The Social Philosophy of Sri Aurobindo' is a corollary to his metaphysics and yoga. While an earth governed by the Supermind would doubtless be heaven, what shall we do with the flawed present? We cannot just wish it away! Rather must we learn to understand the evolution of this society and seek to apply the necessary correctives.

The Human Cycle tries to answer these questions. We *can* broadly indicate the stages of social evolution. For example, in the beginning, there was the infrarational stage when men acted as their impulses guided them. Then came the present rational stage. Man is now trying to use his intelligence to control and regulate the social forces. Sri Aurobindo envisages also a future supra-rational stage, when a gnostic consciousness will help usher in a perfect society. Culture would no more be the complex of the mechanical appurtenances of a scientifically or technologically 'civilised' society. Sri Aurobindo examines the possibilities of Communism, but also looks beyond Marx for an answer that would ensure the greatest good of the greatest number. Society can progress and evolve only when the individual feels seraphically free from the taint of ego-consciousness. Supramental consciousness, on the other hand, would usher in the spiritual age:

> It would regard the peoples as group souls . . .

meant like the individual to grow according to their own nature and by that growth to help each other to help the whole race in the one common work of humanity.

The Ideal of Human Unity voices Sri Aurobindo's concern for man's future at the time of dire peril during the First World War. A subsequent global war and the bickerings of the Cold War have but underlined the relevance of Sri Aurobindo's conclusions.

How is one to reconcile individual freedom and collective control? Man by himself is a prey to Nature and his fellowmen. Only in collectivity can he find a measure of safety as well as comfort. But the larger the collectivity, the lesser the chances of harmony. How can we forge a golden poise between individual and collective egoism? With a quick backward glance at the history of the East and West, Sri Aurobindo seeks to formulate an ideal of unity that could bring out the best in the constituents, whether it be a family, community, city, state, nation or empire. It is only through the uncongealing of the separative egoistic consciousness that mutual suspicions can end, paving the way for disarmament and human unity. However, such a unity would still be a unity in diversity, not a regimented and soulless uniformity. Sri Aurobindo gives particular attention to the problem of a nation's language. Verily, a nation's language is its soul, and we should not barter it away Faustus-like, and modern India is a fit subject for study in this context. Sri Aurobindo notes that it was Bengal that first refused to pride in the yoke of a foreign language, and therefore Bengal was also the first to recover its soul, and register superb achievements in spirituality, literature, art and politics:

> Language is the sign of the cultural life of a people, the index of its soul in thought and mind that stands behind and enriches its soul in action.

Sri Aurobindo knew the value of English for Indians, and was himself a master of the language, but he didn't compromise with regard to the role of the mother tongue in shaping the mind and sensibility and soul of the child, and the growing boy or girl, and the full-fledged citizen. And his own Bengali writing—as in Kara-Kahini, for example—is credited to be *sui generis*.

Finally, the question of Internationalism. Sri Aurobindo saw that, notwithstanding the world-conflict, the trend of the times was clearly in the direction of internationalism:

> Even cosmopolitan habits of life are now not uncommon and there are a fair number of persons who are as much or more citizens of the world as citizens of their own nation . . . it might be hoped that the necessary psychological modification will quietly, gradually, but still irresistibly and at last with an increasing force of rapidity take place which can prepare a real and fundamental change in the life of humanity.

The question is whether we can consciously accelerate the pace of this welcome change? "Yes", says Sri Aurobindo, but only when "man in his heart is ready". No unity imposed from outside—political or administrative—can be permanent; the impulse to unity should come from within, and perhaps in the form of a religion of humanity. Then comes the splendid peroration charged with evangelical fire:

> A spiritual religion of humanity is the hope of the future . . . A religion of humanity means the growing realisation that there is a secret Spirit, a divine Reality, in which we are all one; that humanity is its highest present vehicle on earth, that the human race and the human being are the means by which it will progressively reveal itself here.

As for the immediate present and near future, the problem was to end the war and establish the peace, and this subject was discussed in the collection, **War and Self-Determination.**

War is certainly an abomination from a human point of view, although it may be a necessity as viewed by the Time Spirit. Even the Russian Revolution was but "a certain sign that a phase of civilisation is beginning to pass and the Time-Spirit preparing a new phase and a new order." Sri Aurobindo's vision had comprehended the Asiatic resurgence extending from Egypt to China. But any new phase or order can last long and yield maximum benefit only when it is sustained by spiritual energy as it is released when the ego-shell bursts and hearts commingle:

> The recognition of fulfilment of the divine being in oneself and in man, the kingdom of God within and in the race, is the basis on which man must come in the end to the possession of himself as a free self-determining being and of mankind too in a mutually possessing self-expansion as a harmoniously self-determining united existence.

EPISTOLARY ART

After *Arya* ceased publication in 1921, Sri Aurobindo had no pressing reason to write in prose anything with a view to publication. In 1930-40, when he took up the revision of **The Life Divine,** he added a few chapters, and towards the end of his life, he wrote the series of essays since collected as **The Supramental Manifestation upon Earth.** But a great deal of his time between 1926 and 1938 was taken up with correspondence with his disciples in the Ashram. On 24 November 1926, Sri Aurobindo went into complete retirement, and was no more accessible even to his disciples. But when they wrote to him (some daily) explaining their difficulties in Yoga Sadhana or detailing their experiences, invariably he replied to them, often at considerable length. Some of the disciples wrote to him also on problems of poetic composition and interpretation, some on world problems, some on the supramental manifestation. Sri Aurobindo always answered with a divine patience and a divine solicitude and a divine omniscience, and these letters to his disciples were presently to pile up to thousands, if not tens of thousands.

There is a major difference between Sri Aurobindo's *Arya* compositions and the letters. These are written in a simpler style and are garnished with wit and humour as the occasion may demand. However, there is never any banality. Many of these letters that have a direct relevance to

yoga have since been collected as **Bases of Yoga, Lights on Yoga,** [**On Yoga II**] and other volumes.

Aside from yoga, Sri Aurobindo could also be coaxed to writing about literature, psychology, politics, sociology or even science. This makes Sri Aurobindo's letters at once interesting, fascinating and enriching. His all-knowledge strikes awe in us. This, for example, about the Metaphysical poet, Donne:

> He is admired today because the modern mind has become like his—it too is straining for energy and force without having the life-impulse necessary for a true vividness and verve nor that higher vision which would supply another kind of energy—its intellect too is twisted, laboured, not in possession of itself. [**Life-Literature-Yoga**]

Sri Aurobindo's correspondence is the nearest we get to the human face of Sri Aurobindo. Elsewhere he is always on the heights. But there are times when his letters are redolent of the joy of life because of his sheer wit and puckish humour. This is certainly no austere yogi perched high up on the Himalayas! As he himself wrote:

> Sense of humour? It is the salt of existence. Without it the world would have got utterly out of balance—it is unbalanced enough already—and rushed to blazes long ago. [**Letters of Sri Aurobindo, Second Series**]

Nirod had once complained about Madam Doubt and his own lack of progress in yoga: "Kismet, Sir? What to do?" And the Guru wrote back:

> Why out of joint? It ought to strengthen your joints for the journey of Yoga. Not at all, sir. Mind, sir mind. Madam Doubt, sir, Madam Doubt! Miss Material Intellectualism, sir! Aunt Despondency, sir! Uncle Self-distrust, sir! Cousin Self-depreciation, sir! The whole confounded family, sir! [**Correspondence with Sri Aurobindo, Second Series**]

The letters thus tantalisingly mingled instruction with banter, and exhortation with an exhilarating spray of wit and humour. Occasionally a letter became a blazing revelation of indescribable beauty; almost a prose-poem with a mantric potency. Sri Aurobindo's "great little book", **The Mother,** was one such, and grew out of his correspondence with his scholarly disciple, T. V. Kapali Sastriar, himself a devotee of Sri Vidya. (Subsequently, Sastriar was inspired by **The Mother** to compose his own *Matri Upanishad* in Sanskrit.)

The opening sentence of **The Mother** posits with supreme brevity the basis of Aurobindonian yoga:

> There are two powers that alone can effect in their conjunction the great and difficult thing which is the aim of our endeavour, a fixed and unfailing aspiration that calls from below and a supreme Grace from above that answers.

There are unhesitating warnings: "*If* behind your devotion and surrender you make a cover for your desires, egoistic demands and vital insistences . . ."; and there are positive commands: "Reject the false notion that the divine Power will do and is bound to do everything for you at your demand . . . "; and there are nectarean assurances:

> . . . when the grace and protection of the Divine Mother are with you, what is there that can touch you or whom need you fear?

But more important still are the winged descriptions of the Divine Mother. Innumerable are the powers and personalities of the Divine Mother whom we call the Transcendent Divine, the universal Shakti and the visible Avatar. What infinitudes of love for her children assail the Divine Mother as she puts on the cloak of an Avatar to suffer among us, working for our redemption? Is it prose or poetry or scriptural revelation that Sri Aurobindo is inditing here:

> In her deep and great love for her children
> she has consented to put on herself
> the cloak of this obscurity, condescended to bear
> the attacks and torturing influences
> of the powers of the Darkness and the False-
>   hood,
> borne to pass through the portals of the birth
> that is a death,
> taken upon herself
> the pangs and sorrows and sufferings of the cre-
>   ation.

Finally comes the description of the Four Powers of the Mother, and there is a veritable downpour of grace-laden imagery. Only a casual letter? The glow of royal wisdom heralds Maheshwari, the might of electric defiance surrounds Mahakali, and the beauty of a divine harmony radiates from Mahalakshmi. The peak of the evocative prose, however, is reserved for Mahasaraswati the perfect wonder-worker:

> A mother to our wants,
> a friend in our difficulties,
> a persistent and tranquil
>   counsellor and mentor,
> Chasing away with her radiant smile
>   the clouds of gloom.

How is one to anatomise such letters? They are like monologues transmitting spontaneously a great and abiding vision.

OTHER MELODIES

And thus, and in many other ways, did the English language respond to the various demands made upon it by Sri Aurobindo. There was brilliant satire in **The Foundations of Indian Culture**; sparkling wit and purposive conversational ease in the letters; sociological analysis in books like **The Human Cycle**; illuminating exegetics in **The Secret of the Veda** and the **Essays**; the rhetorical sublime in **Speeches**; architectonic amplitude and fullness in **The Life Divine**; and the spiritual ballast in **The Synthesis**. There is an apparent sameness in the style almost everywhere, but this is the sameness of a majestic river that flows unimpeded towards the sea, the same and yet always new. All classes of subjects are seized and presented in a seemingly involved prose which may have had its filiations with the coloured prose of Milton, Browne and other seventeenth century masters, but was firmly transformed into the

Aurobindonian 'global' style. For Milton sometimes loses control over his sentences and descends headlong into artificiality and affectedness.

This never happens in Sri Aurobindo. In this context, we could take up **The Future Poetry,** a collection of essays on the English poets. But although the sweep is wide-ranging, there is nowhere any confusion or uncertainty; he had usually to type out the instalments at terrific speed to meet the deadlines, but the writing is not marred by serious faulty constructions. The work also contains speculations on the past, present and future of the art of poesy itself. This fascinating adventure in creative understanding began as an appreciative review of James H. Cousins's *New Ways in English Literature,* but soon Sri Aurobindo found that he had launched himself upon a journey into seas uncharted ever before.

First, then, about the 'poetic' view of life:

> The poetic vision of life is not a critical or intellectual or philosophic view of it, but a soul-view, a seizing by the inner sense; and the mantra is not in its substance or form poetic enunciation of a philosophic truth, but the rhythmic revelation or intuition arising out of the soul's sight of God and Nature and the world and the inner truth—occult to the outward eye—of all that peoples it, the secrets of their life and being.

Sri Aurobindo then proceeds to trace the history of English poetry. But this is not the usual pedestrian history crammed with chronology and bibliography. He is rather more interested in the inner evolution of English poetry and in making an assessment of the more important poets. Shakespeare's age was the high water-mark of poetic utterance, and Shakespeare was the poet supreme:

> Shakespeare is an exception, a miracle of poetic force; he survives untouched all adverse criticism, not because there are not plenty of fairly large spots in this sun, but because in any complete view of him they disappear in the greatness of his light.

As for Milton, if he failed, it was because, although he had walked in the darknesses and met Satan and Death and Sin, he had not attained the vision of the Divine that alone could have elevated him into a poet of true symbols like the Italian Dante. The Romantics hold Sri Aurobindo's attention for a while. He is gratified by their insistence on "the subjective personality of the man and the artistic personality of the creator." More 'recent' poetry (**The Future Poetry** was written 50 years ago) has shown greater promise, and Sri Aurobindo boldly compares Homer and Whitman, for in Whitman he sees a "giant of poetic thought". Such contrastive studies light up all the essays: Dante and Milton, Byron and Wordsworth, Browning and Tennyson, and Carpenter and Whitman.

What kind of poetry will the 'future poetry' be? The sustaining 'powers' will be five: Truth, Life, Beauty, Delight and the Spirit:

> The voice of poetry comes from a region above us, a plane of our being above and beyond our personal intelligence, a supermind which sees

things in their innermost and largest truth by a spiritual identity and with a lustrous effulgency and rapture and its native language is a revelatory, inspired, intuitive word limpid or subtly vibrant or densely packed with the glory of this ecstasy and lustre.

This brings us back to the Aurobindonian world-view. It is when the supermind takes control of man's whole existence that true poetry can be indited.

> It is in effect a larger cosmic vision,
> a realising of the godhead in the world and in man,
> of his divine possibilities as well of the greatness of the power
> that manifests in what he is,
> a spiritualised uplifting of his thoughts and feeling and sense and action,
> a more developed psychic mind and heart.

Even as Sri Aurobindo who was generally on the heights when he wrote about man, the earth and God did also occasionally stray into wit and humour with natural ease and success, this consummate master of the "global" style threw out also, when the mood came to him, jewelled aphorisms and epigrams. These short jets of scintillating prose deserve particular mention. Aside from the pointed asseverations scattered in his spacious *Arya* sequences, there are also collections like *Thoughts and Glimpses* and *Thoughts and Aphorisms* which directly introduce us to the epigrammatists. *Essays on the Gita* and *The Synthesis of Yoga* cover in sufficient detail the *Jnana, Karma* and *Bhakti* yogas. How the sentences coil and uncoil one after another in those volumes! But the same subjects are explored or x-rayed in *Thoughts and Aphorisms* also, though in the form of racy, crisp, and often paradoxical sentences. The apophthegms on *Jnana* almost tease and exasperate the reader:

> This is a miracle that men can love God, yet fail to love humanity. With whom are they in love then?

Sri Aurobindo would have us see the Divine only as *Anandamaya*:

> To listen to some devout people, one would imagine that God never laughs; Heine was nearer the mark when he found in Him the divine Aristophanes.

It would be wise to read one of these aphorisms, revolve them in the mind in the chamber of silence, forge link after link, make a chain of inferences that may at last comprehend all heaven and earth, and all the realm between.

Sri Aurobindo's prose canon spread over sixty years, and is now available for examination in about 15,000 large packed printed pages, comprising every form of writing, formal and informal, fiction and drama, metaphysical and expository, estimative and exegetic, epistolary and exhortory, poetic and prophetic, aphoristic and epigrammatic; where are the critical measures that can make a definitive assessment of this formidable phenomenon? "In my beginning is my end!" Sri Aurobindo might have said, for in a sense the distinctive stamp of his writing—the quality of the mind, the flavour of the style—may be seen even in the

juvenile Platonic exercise **"The Harmony of Virtue"** and of course in the *Indu Prakash* articles. With his new-born intimacy with Indian (especially Sanskrit) literature and with his deepening contacts with Indian life, he was able to import to his writings in *Bande Mataram* a new edge, a new glow, a new idealism; and his yogic ardours and experiences—at Baroda in January 1908, in the Alipur jail later in the year—effected an emancipation of the spirit, and this in turn was to colour significantly his writing in the *Karmayogin* (1909-10) and the *Arya* (1914-21). Once we have found entrance to this elected Aurobindonian world, we will be kept imprisoned as in a magnificent Chola temple—the Divine's presence and the noble edifice making us forget the merely material and mundane.

K. R. Srinivasa Iyengar   (essay date 1982)

SOURCE: "Sri Aurobindo's *The Life Divine*," in *Perspectives on Indian Prose in English,* edited by M. K. Naik, Humanities Press, 1982, pp. 104-23.

[*In the following essay, Iyengar summarizes Aurobindo's theory of spiritual evolution as it is presented in* The Life Divine, *at the same time responding to critics who charge that the work is overly long and difficult, repetitious, and written in a lackluster style.*]

A senior Professor of English—with a rich background of scholastic training at Madras and Oxford—recently came out with the protentious affirmation: "Surely the message of **The Life Divine** or the beauty of **Savitri** could have been conveyed and better conveyed in a tenth of their enormous length." Thanks for small mercies: the 'message' of the one and the 'beauty' of the other are grudgingly conceded; the objection is only to the length. But, then, the medium *is* the message; and the 'message' is not just the epitome concocted at the behest of the professorial examiner ("Reduce the following to about a tenth of its present length . . ."). A summary, a synopsis, *can* be prepared, and Sri Aurobindo himself attempted such a synopsis for the earlier chapters. But the synopsis is *not* the original, anymore than the skeleton hung in a physiological laboratory is the living man.

Again, one of our younger poets, almost tailor-made in Great Britain, finds **Savitri** "unwinding like an interminable sari through twelve Books and about 24,000 lines in one vast onion of a poem. The layers gradually fade away to reveal nothing." A veritable Duhshasana of a poet-turned-critic foaming at his mouth in impatience, exasperation and discomfiture. Did he take **Savitri** for a striptease cabaret show?

Yet again, a former Union Minister of Education once told me: "See how lucid Vivekananda is! I've been reading his discourses in America and his talks, *From Colombo to Almora;* he is so direct, so simple. But why is **The Life Divine** so unmanageably difficult?" I tried to explain to the Minister that, for a proper comparison, he should read Sri Aurobindo's own talks and letters; but **The Life Divine,** a metaphysical treatise, was on a different footing altogether. The trouble with these clever people is that they would use their own predilections and limitations as measuring rods to judge the work of others cast uncomfortably on rather Olympian proportions. There are lyric intensities, and epic immensities; there are easy clarities, and vast profundities; and we need them both. And while it is natural to have one's own preferences, it is absurd to turn them into critical dogmas.

When one of Sri Aurobindo's disciples complained to him that he was only wasting his time writing unimportant letters, instead of concentrating on the Yoga or on some major work, he answered promptly:

> Each activity is important in its own place; an electron or a molecule or grain may be small in themselves, but in their place they are indispensable to the building up of a world; it cannot be made only of mountains and sunsets and streamings of the aurora borealis—though these have their place there. All depends on the force behind these things and the purpose in their action . . .

In the infinite play of Prakriti, in the universal dance of life, variety and staggering multiplicity are the law, and lifeforms range from the very small and simple to the most colossal and complex, and each has its own logic and inner coherence and circuit of viability. As well dismiss the human anatomy and nervous system because it isn't like a toad's, centipede's or caterpillar's! *The Life Divine,* its great theme, its ample linguistic adequacy, its oceanic sweeps of rhythm and its sheer organisation, all stand together, and the usual comparisons could be worse than misleading.

In the course of his long life, Sri Aurobindo wrote a formidable mass of prose and verse, and most of it is collected in the definitive Centenary Library in thirty large volumes. There are scintillating aphorisms at one end of the spectrum, and there are prose symphonies like *The Life Divine* at the other. There are translations from Sanskrit, Bengali and even Tamil; there are plays and short stories; there are the contributions to the *Indu Prakash,* the *Bande Mataram* and the *Karmayogin;* and there are the letters—whole shoals of them—to the disciples. If the impressive poetic output ranges from the Victorian *Songs to Myrtilla,* the early romantic verse of *Urvasie* and *Love and Death* and the heroic verse of *Baji Prabhou* to the 'overhead'—inspired lyrics like **'Rose of God'** and **'Thought the Paraclete'** of the later period, the quantitative hexameters of the Homeric *Ilion* and the 'Kalidasian' blank verse of *Savitri,* likewise the prose canon ranges from the early Platonic dialogue **'The Harmony of Virtue',** the dialectics and coruscating iridescences of political journalism and the apocalyptic fervour of the *Bhavani Mandir* pamphlet and the *Uttarpara Speech* to the simplicity and candour and immediacy of the letters, the crystalline profundities of the *Thoughts and Glimpses,* and the Himalayan strength, the majestic contours and the fusion of analysis, argument and futuristic projection in *The Life Divine* and its companion treatises. The 'style' is indeed the man, and the style admirably suits the occasion, the aim and the theme, for the 'medium' with Sri Aurobindo was always inseparable from the 'message'.

There is, of course, the distinctive style characteristic of the mighty sequences that appeared in the *Arya* for over

six years month after month from August 1914: *The Life Divine, The Synthesis of Yoga, Essays on the Gita, The Secret of the Veda, The Psychology of Social Development (The Human Cycle), The Ideal of Human Unity, The Foundations of Indian Culture* and *The Future Poetry,* There is undoubtedly such a phenomenon as the 'Arya' style—a "global" style, as J. T. Chadwick ('Arjava') called it. What are the 'marks' of this "global" style? A certain amplitude and fullness of statement, a symphonic elaboration and finish, a suggestion at once of movement and poise, and a total and integral comprehension: all is involved in the word "global". But the 'style' is inseparable from the 'semantics', and the structural organisation from the reverberations of the rhythm.

During the *Arya* period (1914-1921), Sri Aurobindo typed out *The Life Divine* and the other sequences straightaway, and he had to keep them going more or less simultaneously. He had no research assistants, card-indexes, or stenotypists. Besides, since he was writing or typing at white heat, he had hardly the time to apply his conscious mind to the mechanics or the niceties of 'style'. Commenting on his *Arya* writings, the Mother said in 1956:

> It was neither a mental knowledge nor even a mental creation which he transcribed: he silenced his mind and sat at his typewriter, and from above, from the higher places, all that had to be written came down, quite ready, and he had only to move his fingers on the typewriter and it was transcribed. [*Questions and Answers: 1956*]

The Life Divine, however, received some revision and substantial additions in 1939 when the *Arya* articles were shaped into the book that came out during 1939-1940. But the important changes were those dictated by a new assimilation or mastery of consciousness—the Overmental—rather than by what may be called purely 'stylistic' considerations. Thus the main bulk of *The Life Divine* remained as it had streamed out with rhythmic ease and compelling authority during the years of the first world war.

The gravamen of the charge against *The Life Divine* is that, not only it is "too long", but also that it is full of repetitions and that it is "too difficult". Sri Aurobindo doesn't make any secret of the fact that the argument presented by him is "difficult". The *Arya* was launched primarily with a view to outlining in all its amplitude and ramifications a "vast synthesis of knowledge, harmonising the divers religious traditions of humanity, occidental as well as oriental." But with Sri Aurobindo, as with earlier Indian metaphysical thinkers like Yajnavalkya, Sankara and Ramanuja, the basis of real knowledge (Para Vidya) was intuition, inner illumination and authentic spiritual experience. For example, when in the first volume of *The Life Divine,* Sri Aurobindo describes the "vast static and silent Self", the "large dynamic descent of light, knowledge, power, bliss and other supernormal energies into our self of silence", as also of the perception of "a graduality of ascent . . . a scale of intensities", he is but recalling his own Baroda experience of Nirvana and the later experiences in the Alipur jail. But such knowledge had still to be translated into intellectual terms if it was to have a chance of general acceptance. As he wrote in the *Arya* of July 1918:

> The spiritual experience and the general truths on which such an attempt (i.e. a 'synthesis' of knowledge) should be based were already present to us . . . but the complete intellectual statement of them and their results and issues had to be found. This meant a continuous thinking, a high and subtle and difficult thinking on several lines, and this strain, which we had to impose on ourselves, we are obliged to impose also on our readers.

He thus made no secret of the fact that the strain of "a continuous thinking, a high and subtle and difficult thinking" had to be willingly undergone by the would-be reader of the *Arya* sequences, and not least, of its crest-jewel, *The Life Divine*. If one is too tamasic, or too busy otherwise, to face this prolonged strain, well, *The Life Divine* is not just his cup of tea.

Sri Aurobindo's theory of spiritual evolution is not a mimicry of the scientific theory of physical life-evolution. Actually it is an evolution of consciousness with Man the mental being as but the intermediate term opening out to the Supramental being of the future.

— *K. R. Srinivasa Iyengar*

On the other hand, while the argument is admittedly "difficult", it is by no means riddled with obscurity. The title of the book itself—'The Life Divine'—casts a spell on the reader, as if it has a mantric potency of its own. It is not 'the Divine Life', something static and ready-made, but 'the Life Divine', this life on earth itself with all its obscurations, perversions and frustrations, yet divinised as by a native law, as by a compulsive evolutionary process of transformation. The very title thus exercises a magnetic pull, as though one has caught a glimpse from a distance of the *gopura* of a South Indian temple, the spires of the Notre Dame or the lone eminence of the Kutub. As one takes a closer look at *The Life Divine,* as one scans the contents, one is at once struck by the inspiring architectonics of the argument:

> Vol. I. Omnipresent Reality and the Universe (28 chapters)
>
> Vol. II. Part I: The Infinite Consciousness and the Ignorance (14 chapters)
>
> Part II: The Knowledge and the Spiritual Evolution (14 chapters)

What do we know about the phenomenal world, and man's place in it; what can we infer about the Ground of it all, the sustaining and transcendent Reality? How is it that the Infinite Consciousness has sunk into the Igno-rance—death, desire, incapacity—of our phenomenal world? The reign of Ignorance, the rake's progress of Evil and the legacy of suffering are neither an eternal undivine phenomenon nor the progeny of beginningless Maya or Illusion, but a transient siege of dualities at the mental rung of the evolutionary stair. The dualities are also relativities. This poisoned and frustrating life will cease when Ignorance is replaced by Knowledge, mental knowledge by spiritual and supramental Knowledge.

How, then shall we make the ascent, step by step, and triumph over the evils of defeat, self-laceration and death; and how shall we beyond the dualities, enact the spiritual evolution, and establish the Life Divine? To present the structure of the argument more simply still:

> Vol. I. Where we do stand now? What should be our goal?
>
> Vol. II. Part I: What are the impediments on the way?
>
> Part II: How shall we overcome them, and reach our goal?

Even a mere reading of the titles of the 56 chapters in their orderly sequence—and some pondering over the key-words, key-ideas, key-concepts—can unfold the drama of the grand evolutionary thrust from 'The Human Aspiration' (the title of the first chapter) and all the ardours and distractions of the spiralling ascent and pull towards the summit of the Life Divine till the final attainment of the crown of 'The Divine Life' (the title of the last chapter).

Taking courage at last, one starts with the Exordium preceded by two epigraphs from the Rig Veda, the first throwing out seminal hints about "the eternal succession of the dawns that are coming" and the second exhorting us to "become high-uplifted" and pierce the veils to manifest the Divine:

> The earliest preoccupation of man in his awakened thoughts and as it seems his inevitable and ultimate preoccupation,—for it survives the longest periods of scepticism and returns after every banishment,—is also the highest which his thought can envisage. It manifests itself in the divination of Godhead, the impulse towards perfection, the search after pure Truth and unmixed Bliss, the sense of a secret immortality. The ancient dawns of human knowledge have left us their witness to this constant aspiration; today we see a humanity satiated but not satisfied by victorious analysis of the externalities of Nature preparing to return to its primeval longings. The earliest formula of Wisdom promises to be its last,—God, Light, Freedom, Immortality.

With its wide span of comprehension, its sure accents of experiential wisdom and its unerringly captivating prose rhythm, this opening paragraph sets the tone of the whole book. We do not of course "understand" everything at once: it is like the opening note of a great symphony, an invitation to an adventure of consciousness. When young Amrita read this passage on the first page of the inaugural issue of the *Arya,* he felt it was "sweet to read and re-read it. It was as if someone else in me was comprehending all that was read." Presently Sri Aurobindo surprised him in the act of reading the passage aloud, and Amrita admitted rather sheepishly that "the reading was delightful but nothing could be grasped." Sri Aurobindo's reply was: "It is not necessary to understand it all at once. Go on reading. If you find a joy in the reading, you need not stop it." And so indeed it is with all revelatory writing—prose or verse—charged with mantric intensities of connotation:

> The hearer understands a form of words . . .
> He strives to read it with the labouring mind,
> But finds bright hints, not the embodied truth:
> Then, falling silent in himself to know,
> He meets the deeper listening of his soul.
>   [*Savitri*]

"Go on reading" . . . but also give a chance to "the deeper listening" of the soul. A first reading is not enough, a quick reading is worse than useless. Within the first few pages the reader comes across what may be described as the key to the whole book:

> The animal is a living laboratory in which Nature has, it is said, worked out man. Man himself may well be a thinking and living laboratory in whom and with whose conscious cooperation she wills to work out the superman, the god. Or shall we not say, rather, to manifest God?

Animal to man, and man to superman, to the future divinised man! The old dichotomy between Matter and Spirit is fallacious, for in the cosmos as well as in the microcosmos (say, man), there is a teasing and total and transcendent unity of Matter and Spirit. On the one hand, the involutionary descent, and, on the other, the evolutionary ascent; Light above, Darkness below; but together they make a cosmos, with its centre everywhere and the circumference nowhere: "We must accept the many-sidedness of the manifestation even while we assert the unity of the Manifested." What is the secret of this cosmic drama of descent and ascent, involution and evolution, the see-saw between the rhythm of Becoming and the poise of Being? In a single sentence Sri Aurobindo formulates the answer:

> World-existence is the ecstatic dance of Shiva which multiplies the body of the God numberlessly to the view: it leaves that white existence precisely where and what it was, ever is and ever will be; its sole absolute object is the joy of the dancing.

This connects with Ananda Coomaraswamy's classic essay on the Dance of Shiva. If one "understands" the symbolism of the 'Dance of Shiva', one also comes close to the heart of the mystery of 'World-existence'.

If Man is the thinking and living laboratory in whom and with whose cooperation Nature is working out the Superman, the destined change will be effected through mind's self-transcendence into Supermind. One may ask, "What's wrong with the Mind?" The answer would be that Mind is "that which does not know, which tries to know and which never knows except as in a glass darkly." But real knowledge—knowledge doubled with Power—waits "seated beyond mind and intellectual reasoning, throned in the luminous vast of illimitable self-vision."

Is it all that easy, this canter from the Mind to the Supermind? Of course not: there are several intermediate steps of ascent, Higher Mind, Illumined Mind, Intuition, Overmind—

> If we accept the Vedic image of the Sun of Truth,—an image which in this experience becomes a reality,—we may compare the action of the Higher Mind to a composed and steady sunshine, the energy of the Illumined Mind beyond it to an outpouring of massive lightnings of flaming sun-stuff. Still beyond can be met a yet greater power . . . Intuition . . . At the source of this Intuition we discover a superconscient cosmic Mind . . . an Overmind that covers as with the wide wings of some creative Oversoul this whole lower hemisphere of Knowledge-Ignorance . . .

The Overmind is the final occult link between the lower knowledge and the higher Supramental Truth-Consciousness. It may be difficult, it may take long, but the conquest of the Supermind is decreed and inevitable, as affirmed by Sri Aurobindo at the end of the first volume:

> As Life and Mind have been released in Matter, so too must in their time these greater powers of the concealed Godhead emerge from the involution and their supreme Light descend into us from above.

> A divine Life in the manifestation is then not only possible as the high result and ransom of our present life in the Ignorance but, if these things are as we have seen them, it is the inevitable outcome and consummation of Nature's evolutionary endeavour.

It is doubtless a tight argument, which from a more practical point of view is further elaborated in the far more expansive second Volume. In this conspectus of universal knowledge which is at the same time a Manifesto for the Future or a blueprint for the realisation of "a divine Life in the manifestation", naturally enough every cleft is packed with meaning, and there is neither loose thinking nor slipshod writing. The very nature of the argument being what it is, there is need for periodical recapitulations and reiterations. Thus, for instance, at the beginning of Volume II, Part II:

> This then is the origin, this the nature, these the boundaries of the Ignorance. Its origin is a limitation of knowledge, its distinctive character a separation of the being from its own integrality and entire reality; its boundaries are determined by this separative development of the consciousness, for it shuts us to our true self and to the true self and the whole nature of things and obliges us to live in an apparent surface existence. A return or a progress to integrality, a disappearance of the limitation, a breaking down of separateness, an overpassing of boundaries, a recovery of our essential and whole reality must be the sign and opposite character of the inner turn towards Knowledge.

An admirable summing-up of the preceding 14 chapters, and an announcement of the stair of argument to be structured in the 14 chapters to follow (Volume II, Part II). Again, in the key-chapter on 'The Evolutionary Process—

Ascent and Integration', a single sentence formulates with an almost mathematical precision the dialectic of evolutionary advance:

> The principle of the process of evolution is a foundation, from that foundation an ascent, in that ascent a reversal of consciousness and, from the greater height and wideness gained, an action of change and new integration of the whole nature.

Ascent from below, descent of a higher light, and an integration which becomes the new foundation for a fresh ascent—and so on. This evolutionary dialectic must continue till the final attainment of the Supermind and the efflorescence of the Life Divine. Forward, always forward, from Darkness to Light, from the sevenfold Ignorance to the sevenfold Knowledge! After three more chapters of an exploratory nature, the Grand Trunk argument is renewed, and the stage is set for the definitive spurt or lift of the spiritual man, the ascent towards the Supermind, and the conquest of the Life Divine.

But of course Sri Aurobindo's theory of spiritual evolution is not a mimicry of the scientific theory of physical life-evolution. Actually it is an evolution of consciousness with Man the mental being as but the intermediate term opening out to the Supramental being of the future. The heart of the problem is the nature of 'spirituality', its innate infallible power for change and transformation. What, indeed, is 'spirituality'? Sri Aurobindo's answer spans out into a long sentence, but it is broken up below so that its inner logic can stand out clearly:

Spirituality is in its essence

> (1) an awakening to the inner reality of our being,
> to a spirit, self, soul
> which is other than the mind, life and body,
>
> (2) an inner aspiration
> to know, to feel, to be that,
>
> (3) to enter into contact
> with the greater Reality beyond and pervading the
> universe
> which inhabits also our own being,
>
> (4) to be in communion with it and union with It,
>
> (5) and a turning, a conversion, a transformation of our
> whole being as a result of the aspiration, the contact, the union,
> a growth or waking into a new becoming or new being, a new self, a new nature.

Although it is on a first view an involved and heavily weighted sentence, on closer scrutiny it will be seen that the interior stitching is infallible, and there is a trembling life and movement of a piece with its theme of spiritual awakening and growth and realisation. One first wakes up to the deeper truth of one's self (as distinct from the body, life or mind), one henceforth aspires to be that alone, and one responds to the ambience of the Spirit everywhere. From this certitude and puissance, one returns to one's

body, life and mind so as to change and transform them, and achieve a total spiritual rebirth and new life and new power of action. First the inner (or psychic) awakening and change, next the spiritual conversion and transformation of our whole being, and finally the growth or explosion into the new supramental self and nature: such would be the "triple transformation". The third and final or consummating stage—the supramental thrust and transmutation—would itself involve various steps or degrees of ascent "from our mind upwards through a series of dynamic powers by which it can sublimate itself . . . a stairway of four main ascents (Higher mind, Illumined Mind, Intuition, Overmind) . . . a succession of self-transformations at the summit of which lies Supermind or Divine Gnosis."

So much for the change and transformation of individual man into the superman or gnostic being of the future. But an individual change here and there cannot alter the complexion or texture of life upon the earth. The 'Life Divine' must thus involve certainly individual change as the necessary beginning, but also a change integral and total in the environment—"a new perfected collective life in the earth-nature . . . a common consciousness consolidating a common life." Even as there is an inner truth or reality of our individual being, there is likewise an inner truth or reality of a social aggregate, of the human race, of terrestrial life and of the universe itself—and these deeper realities too have to be awakened and brought to the fore and made to participate in the drama of supramental change and transformation. There is here a series of interlinked truths integrating into a total sum of Revelation, and this is conveyed through a set of massive affirmations:

> There is a Reality, a truth of all existence which is greater and more abiding than all its formations and manifestations; to find that truth and Reality and live in it, achieve the most perfect manifestation and formation possible of it, must be the secret of perfection whether of individual or communal being. This Reality is there within each thing and gives to each of its formations its power of being and value of being.
>
> The universe is a manifestation of the Reality, and there is a truth of the universal existence, a Power of cosmic being, an all-self or world-spirit.
>
> Humanity is a formation or manifestation of the Reality in the universe, and there is a truth and self of humanity, a human spirit, a destiny of human life.
>
> The community is a formation of the Reality, a manifestation of the spirit of man, and there is a truth, a self, a power of the collective being.
>
> The individual is a formation of the Reality, and there is a truth of the individual, an individual self, soul or spirit that expresses itself through the individual mind, life and body and can express itself too in something that goes beyond mind, life and body, something even that goes beyond humanity . . .

It is a close paragraph, though the several sentences are shown separately above to facilitate easier reading. There is, according to Sri Aurobindo, the single law of the unity of Spirit and Matter; always the deeper Reality rules the Appearance without, and this is so in the universe—in terrestrial life—in humanity—in the social aggregate—and in individual man. There is a descending stair of decreasing inclusiveness, and there is an ascending stair of increasing inclusiveness, and it is the same stair too, and at every point all else is implied and involved as well. But this phenomenal universe is nothing static; rather is it an evolving universe, and on the earth we are now caught in an "evolutionary crisis", for mankind is today poised between two extreme possibilities: between, on the one hand, a closer and ever closer alliance of Reason and Science, a further aggressive expansion of the individual ego and of various manifestations of the collective ego, and, on the other hand, a life of unity and mutuality and harmony brought about by our awakening and growing into the deeper truth of the Spirit. The former course can only mean a further accentuation of the current malady—

> . . . a chaos of clashing mental ideas,
> urges of individual and collective physical want
>   and need,
> vital claims and desires,
> impulses of an ignorant life-push,
> hungers and calls for life-satisfaction of individ-
>   uals,
>   classes, nations,
> a rich fungus of political and social and econom-
>   ic nostrums
>   and notions,
> a hustling medley of slogans and panaceas for
>   which men
>   are ready to oppress and be oppressed,
>   to kill and be killed,
>   to impose them somehow or other . . .

Here is a synoptic presentation in compellingly vivid and sometimes truly memorable language ("a rich fungus", "a hustling medley"!) of the exponential madman's progress of our present ego-driven technological civilisation. Can there be any doubt that this must necessarily lead, sooner than later, to a world catastrophe and the abrupt end of the human adventure? But the other course, the transcendence and transfiguration of our human nature, is by no means impossibly Utopian:

> . . . What has to be developed is there in our
>   being and
>   not something outside it:
> What evolutionary Nature presses for, is an
>   awakening
>   to the knowledge of self,
>   the discovery of self,
>   the manifestation of the self and spirit with-
>   in us
>   and the release of its self-knowledge, self-
>   power,
>   its native self-instrumentation.

> It is, besides, a step for which the whole of evolu-
>   tion
>   has been a preparation . . .

Through the self-perfection of individual man will issue the gradual movement of perfection of the race, not patterned on the Titan or Asura, or the Nietzschean 'blonde beast', but shaped as the self-realised being governed by the sovereignty of the Spirit over its members and instruments. Beyond the flawed movement of evolution in the Ignorance through the ego's self-enthronement, the evolution can now take a leap towards the "evolution in the knowledge, a self-finding and self-unfolding of the Spirit, a self-revelation of the Divinity in things in that true power of itself in Nature which is to us still a Supernature."

Man to Superman, Nature to Supernature: certainly, it is a plea for a mighty adventure and movement of consciousness, and what is projected in *The Life Divine* is thus a "high and subtle and difficult" thinking, a prophecy sustained by the elect of the race. And yet in all the puissant, leisurely exposition there is no avoidable obscurity. If some terms (say 'subliminal', 'overmind', 'supermind') intrigue us at first, it is because what they are meant to connote is not within the range of our everyday experience; but, then, detailed explanations follow, and the mist duly clears. Thus of the 'subliminal':

> The external forms of our being are those of our
> small egoistic existence; the subliminal are the
> formations of our larger true individuality.
> Therefore are these that concealed part of our
> being in which our individuality is close to our
> universality, touches it, is in constant relation
> and commerce with it. The subliminal mind in
> us is open to the universal knowledge of the cos-
> mic Mind, the subliminal life in us to the univer-
> sal force of the cosmic Life, the subliminal physi-
> cality in us to the universal force-formation of
> cosmic Matter . . . So too is the subliminal soul
> in us open to the universal delight . . .

But always Sri Aurobindo tries to take us from the known to the unknown, and this promotes easy understanding. Again, while the sentences more often than not seem to be weighted and involved with strings of qualifications, on a careful rereading the intricate joinery stands revealed (as illustrated in the passages cited earlier), and there is really no bar to an intellectual understanding of the argument. Considering the grandeur of the theme and the intricacies of the unfolding dialectic, it cannot be said that *The Life Divine* is all that "difficult", that it lacks internal coherence, or that the language or the prose rhythm is undistinguished. On the contrary, what is striking is the grand intellectual architecture of the whole magnificent edifice and the symphonic quality of the prose that generates, in the words of the reviewer in the *Times Literary Supplement*, "wide circles of peace".

> **Too long, too difficult, too repetitive—*The Life Divine* is all this if you will, but only in its outer seeming and on a first casual reading. But the reality about *The Life Divine,* its essential and abiding truth, is far deeper than all this appearance. The length is symbolic of the cosmic amplitude of the subject, the obscurity of difficulty of the nature of the dynamic of transformation, the repetitiveness of the rhythm of the dialectic of change and transfiguration.**
>
> **— *K. R. Srinivasa Iyengar***

But the 'repetitions'! In a work like *The Life Divine,* which aimed at projecting a continuous argument serially month after month over a period of four years, periodical recapitulation was permissible as well as necessary. In a sense, Volume One with its 28 chapters gives us the essence of the argument, but the far more spacious Volume Two— itself divided into two Parts—is by no means a mere repetition or excrescent elaboration, but is wholly relevant to the fullness of the total revelation. To say that we move from theory and the general statement of ends to the theatre of action and the discussion of means would also be too much of an oversimplification. Moreover, although the culminating insights in *The Life Divine* are the concept of the Supermind and the dialectic of spiritual evolution, a lot of ground is covered earlier in recapitulating other philosophical world-views—for example, the Buddhist, the Advaitic and the materialist—and Sri Aurobindo has often first to state in clear terms these earlier philosophical positions before coming forward with his own. In this he follows the classical Indian way of presenting the 'Purvapaksha' first before demolishing or modifying it in his own 'Siddhanta'. As the Mother once explained to her evening congregation in Sri Aurobindo Ashram after reading a para or two from the chapter 'Man and Evolution' (Vol. II, Chapter xxiii):

> It is an argument Sri Aurobindo presents. As he has said, it is one of the ways of looking at the problem and solving it, but that does not mean that this is his point of view. And this is exactly what he does throughout the book, all the time: presenting different arguments, different points of view, different conceptions, and once he has put all these problems before us, then he comes and gives the solution . . . I have heard people who read quite superficially and perhaps also don't read quite continuously (people who consider themselves extremely intelligent and learned) tell me: 'But Sri Aurobindo repeats himself all the time in this book! . . . ' For he presents all the points of view, then gives his own, the conclusion . . . so he 'repeats himself'!
> [*Questions and Answers: 1957 & 1958*]

Again, more penetratingly still next week:

It is as though Sri Aurobindo were putting himself at the centre of a sort of sphere, as at the centre of a wheel the spokes of which ended in a circumference. And he always goes back to his starting-point and comes right up to the surface, and so on every time, which gives the impression that he repeats the same thing several times, but it is simply the exposition of the thought so that one can follow it. One must have a very clear memory of the ideas in order to really understand what he says.

In the first Volume, following the chapters on 'The Materialist Denial' and 'The Refusal of the Ascetic', Sri Aurobindo proposes in the next chapter "to find a truth that can entirely reconcile these antagonists." He is not after a compromise, a bargain, but a true reconciliation emerging out of a mutual comprehension leading to an acceptable "intimate oneness". In a later chapter, almost towards the end of *The Life Divine,* Sri Aurobindo reviews the "four main lines which Nature has followed"— religion, occultism, spiritual thought, and an inner spiritual experience and realisation—to open up the inner being, and while at each stage the description is adequate and the discussion illuminating, yet all lead up to the climactic account of the Gita's insights and revelations, and daring farther still, a suggestion of the possibility of "the supramental ascent or the incommunicable transcendence." Likewise, Sri Aurobindo recapitulates the divers ways of looking at problems like Rebirth, the World Stair and Rebirth, and then puts forward his own definitive views, like a judicial pronouncement but inly lit by the assurance of his own intuition. Also, lest the main steps in the argument be missed, he often reviews and restates his own expositions, as for example in the concluding paragraph of the chapter on 'The Philosophy of Rebirth'

> This then is the rational and philosophical foundation for a belief in rebirth; it is an inevitable logical conclusion if there exists at the same time an evolutionary principle in the Earth-Nature and a reality of the individual soul born into evolutionary Nature. If there is no soul, then there can be a mechanical evolution . . . If the individual is only a temporary formation . . . (rebirth) is not needed as a mechanism of that evolution . . . But if there is an evolution of consciousness in an involutionary body and a soul inhabiting the body . . . rebirth is self-evidently . . . the sole possible machinery of such an evolution . . . It is rebirth that gives to the birth of an incomplete being in a body its promise of completeness and its spiritual significance.

It is a tight argument, and unless one has read carefully the preceding 25 pages, the steps in the concluding summary may seem almost slippery. As in the Upanishadic discussions the Rishis insinuate and bring out their meaning through reiterations, through questions and answers, through suppositions and demolitions, Sri Aurobindo too wields all the arts of the seer-teacher to project the background, weigh conflicting theories and to drive home his own points of view.

Too long, too difficult, too repetitive—*The Life Divine* is all this if you will, but only in its outer seeming and on a first casual reading. But the reality about *The Life Divine,* its essential and abiding truth, is far deeper than all this appearance. The length is symbolic of the cosmic amplitude of the subject, the obscurity of difficulty of the nature of the dynamic of transformation, the repetitiveness of the rhythm of the dialectic of change and transfiguration. Commenting on the superbly organised intellectual content of *The Life Divine,* Charles A. Moore has remarked that "it includes the insights of the East and the insights of the West. It combines their respective unique emphases . . . Sri Aurobindo has thus arrived at a comprehensive . . . all-inclusive view of the universe and life, providing a world philosophy which in effect brings together the East and the West," [*The Integral Philosophy of Sri Aurobindo,* edited by Haridas Chaudhuri and Frederic Spiegelberg]. When it came out in 1939-40 as a divine counterblast to the Asuric war unleashed by Hitler, Sri Francis Younghusband greeted *The Life Divine* as perhaps the "greatest book" published in his life-time. And many years later, having completed a careful reading of *The Life Divine,* the English novelist Dorothy Richardson wrote to me: "Has there ever existed a more synthetic consciousness than that of Sri Aurobindo? Unifying he is to the limit of the term."

What, then, is the last word on the 'prose style' of *The Life Divine*? As in an individual human being, beneath the superfices of the material body, its constituents, its total structure, beneath the vital pulls and balance of desire and disgust, attraction and repulsion, beneath the gyrations and genuflections of the mind, its exercises in analysis, differentiation and integration, behind all this facade of surface life there is also the glassy soul-essence, the spark, the abiding Agni, without which the rest is nothing, less than nothing—so too, in Sri Aurobindo's characteristic prose, the "global" prose of the *Arya* period and more particularly the "other Harmony" of *The Life Divine,* what lights up the massing of all-time human experience, the induction of experiential knowledge and the fitted-in stairway of the evolutionary spiral is the sovereign soul-quality, the Aurobindonian afflatus (to beg the question) which is unmistakable. The 'style' is inseparably the man, and the man is Sri Aurobindo, the Columbus of the Supermind, the prophet of the destined leap of consciousness from the mental to the gnostic, the magician-seer who can generate by the power of words a movement towards Next Future on the wings of "wide circles of peace".

Stephen H. Phillips (essay date 1985)

SOURCE: "The Central Argument of Aurobindo's *The Life Divine,*" in *Philosophy East and West,* Vol. XXXV, No. 3, July, 1985, pp. 271-84.

[*In the following essay, Phillips contests Aurobindo's theory that the incompatibility between evil and the Brahman in the present state of evolution proves that a higher level of evolution—divine life—is inevitable.*]

> . . . because the Non-Existence is a concealed Existence, the Inconscience a concealed Consciousness, the insensibility a masked and dor-

mant Ananda, these secret realities must emerge; the hidden Overmind and Supermind too must in the end fulfill themselves in this apparently opposite organization from a dark Infinite.

Sri Aurobindo, *The Life Divine*

THE ARGUMENT: BRAHMAN AND EVIL

Sri Aurobindo (Ghose), 1872-1950, a mystic in the Indian tradition of yoga, is the formulator of a world view of great originality and breadth, which has now received scholarly attention both in India and the West. Many of the commentators point out that Aurobindo's mysticism motivates his philosophic thought. Clearly the most important of Aurobindo's claims is that he is a mystic, who from his mystical experience has learned of the reality of Brahman (which he also refers to as "the Absolute" and "God"). But none of the commentators, in India or the West, has brought into proper focus the reasoning which leads Aurobindo to make the prediction of "divine life," in honor of which his major philosophical work *The Life Divine* is named.

In that work, Aurobindo argues that evil viewed by the side of the reality of Brahman indicates that the world must be developing to the wonderful state which he calls divine life. He reasons that " . . . struggle and discord cannot be eternal and fundamental principles in His [Brahman's] being but by their very existence imply labour towards a perfect solution and a complete victory [in divine life]." In other words, Aurobindo says that he has arrived at an understanding of Brahman based upon his mystical experience and that this understanding, in turn, is such that human evils, pain, and suffering, for example, would appear impossible. Of course, they are not impossible because they are actual, and Aurobindo acknowledges this: " . . . grief, pain, suffering, error, falsehood, ignorance, weakness, wickedness, incapacity . . . all that makes up the effective figure of what we call evil, are facts of world-consciousness, not fictions and unrealities." Nevertheless, the nature of Brahman as revealed in mystical experience appears to him to be so much in tension with these aspects of our present human reality as to seem to preclude the possibility of our world. This appearance of preclusion and incompatibility forms the philosophic problem-space in *The Life Divine*. Aurobindo calls it a problem of "harmony." He then argues that the appearance of incompatibility between the world and Brahman in the present indicates that the world is evolving to a future harmony in divine life, which would be, he says, "a new heaven and a new earth"—echoing the Romantic conception of a world *telos.*

Now this tension is not all that Aurobindo brings forward in support of his claim that the world is evolving to divine life. Biological evolution and the course of civilization to date are cited as further evidence in support of that prediction. But Aurobindo plainly admits that without mystical experience, by which he claims to know the nature of Brahman, there would be no truly clear indication of an evolution to divine life. Evolutionary theory provides parameters for Aurobindo's theorizing; it may also be counted as a premise in the argument for divine life. The same may be said for Aurobindo's understanding of the course of civilization. He discerns progress along many dimensions, biological, intellectual, moral and spiritual, and claims that the "fact" of progress to the present suggests that there will be further progress and that a "diviner" future will come to be. Thus a number of ideas converge in the prediction of divine life. But the mystical indications of Brahman viewed by the side of evil is where Aurobindo finds the only certain sign of divine life's eventuality. Evolution without those indications might seem "a queer freak in a bit of inanimate Matter." So too human civilization. And without evil, this might be what he calls a "typal" world, whose denizens are content in a fixed world order:

> There is a possibility of self-expression . . . in perfect types fixed and complete in their own nature: that is the principle of becoming in the higher worlds; they are typal and not evolutionary in their life principle; they exist each in its own perfection but within the limits of a stationary world-formula.

Aurobindo views evil as tied to human dissatisfaction and aspiration (as the disease with its symptoms). They are, he says, the clear indication that, assuming the reality of Brahman, ours is not a world having reached the stability and perfection of its type and that there inevitably will be evolution to divine life.

THE ARGUMENT'S PLACE IN AUROBINDO'S PHILOSOPHY

A few words are needed in order to put the argument for divine life into proper perspective within the whole of Aurobindo's philosophical thought. As already indicated, not this argument but rather Aurobindo's "mystic empiricism" is his most crucial claim philosophically, since it is from mystical experience that his concept of Brahman's nature is said to derive. At least half of the force of the argument for divine life depends upon mystical experience— and the controversial half, since we need not dispute the existence of evil. Is Aurobindo's, or anyone's, mystical experience objectively informative? Most commentators have neglected this issue. It is particularly thorny, since Aurobindo, like other famous mystics, declares some of his special experience to be almost unimaginably different from ordinary human experience. The issue of whether mystical experience could provide empirical support for the objective reality of Brahman (or whatever) will not be taken up here, though it is important to keep in mind that Aurobindo claims that his concept of Brahman is an "experience-concept." My intention here is exclusively to lay forth and examine Aurobindo's reasoning from his concept of Brahman, however that concept may have originated, to the prediction of divine life. I aim to elucidate the appearance of "disharmony" between the world and Brahman as it is framed in **The Life Divine,** and thereby to reveal the structure of Aurobindo's world view. Finally, I shall show that the argument fails, and clarify the cognitive status of the theory of divine life.

BRAHMAN'S ESSENTIAL NATURE

What is Aurobindo's concept of Brahman? More precisely, what is it about Brahman in Aurobindo's view that requires the world to develop divine life? In what respect is Brahman in tension with evil? Roughly speaking, Aurobindo's concept of Brahman is like Western monotheistic concepts of God, except that, unlike God in many Western views, Brahman is considered to be in some way everything. Brahman is thought of as the "stuff" of everything that exists, that is, as comprising matter. But while this is so, some things imaginable or logically possible are thought to be in reality impossible because "Brahman-stuff" could not underlie them. According to Aurobindo, Brahman has an essential nature, which he believes is best captured by the traditional Vedāntic term, 'saccidānanda', "Existence-Consciousness-Bliss." This essential nature of Brahman's is deemed such as to make Brahman incompatible with some logical possibilities. Possible worlds, in his conception, are really possible if and only if they are compatible with Brahman's nature, Sachchidananda (his transliteration). Sachchidananda, he says, is Brahman's essential nature or *svarūpa,* "self-form," and thus underlies all that Brahman underlies, namely everything.

In order to see how Aurobindo takes divine life to follow from the nature of Brahman, we shall take up separately each of the three terms in the description of Brahman's *svarūpa* which he champions, beginning with '*sat*', "being." (Through euphonic combination, '*sat*' becomes '*sac*' in the compound '*sac-cidānanda*'; similarly '*cit*' to '*cid*'.) That Brahman is *sat* means for Aurobindo that everything is Brahman, but also that any creation on the part of Brahman has to be "self-manifestation." In his view, Brahman does not create the universe *ex nihilo,* but rather it transforms itself so as to become the universe. Now we can deduce very little about what sort of universe ours must be according to the supposition that Brahman is *sat,* since Brahman for all we know so far could comprise the stuff of any state of affairs whatsoever. Further, just that any actual state of affairs has to be a self-manifestation of Brahman tells us nothing about what in general could be a self-manifestation of Brahman. Only logical impossibilities can be ruled out as candidates for Brahman's self-manifestation on the basis of incompatibility with Brahman in its aspect as *sat* (being). Whatever is imaginable is imaginable as existent (*sat*) in some world or other: this is what it means to say that something is logically possible. Aurobindo's doctrine of divine *sat* postulates Brahman's universal immanence. The doctrine makes a general requirement on self-manifestation, namely, that any universe be in harmony with Brahman. But it is uninformative about the nature of immanent Brahman and consequently about what characteristics our world should have, on the assumption of Brahman's immanence.

That Brahman is essentially *cit,* "Conscious Force" (Aurobindo's preferred translation), means first of all that Brahman is capable of finite self-manifestation. Aurobindo criticizes Advaita Vedānta for reasoning that since Brahman is intrinsically infinite, it could not become in reality finite. He reads Advaita as holding that while Brahman does indeed underlie finite appearance, finite appearance insofar as it appears finite is illusory. Aurobindo believes to the contrary that finite things are real as finite and that Brahman has become finite in reality. Brahman as essentially *cit* has the power to limit itself and become really finite, Aurobindo holds. "This power of self-limitation . . . is precisely one of the powers we should expect . . . of the Infinite." He supposes that Brahman could have refrained from self-manifesting, too. Below, we shall see that this attribution to Brahman of power to self-manifest or not to do so vitiates the inference to divine life.

So far as world or self-manifestation is concerned, Brahman's being essentially *cit* means that everything must be comprised of an energy which is conscious. A very large portion of *The Life Divine* is devoted to elaborating and defending this proposition. One may reasonably object that matter generally does not appear conscious, either in itself or as directly responsive to conscious beings. Aurobindo counters by insisting mystical experience brings occult power over matter and by parading the evidence of evolution. More fundamentally, his rejoinder is *The Life Divine*'s central argument: our world of seemingly inconscient material energy would be impossible were it not in the (evolutionary) process of developing divine life. But while he maintains that a material universe bereft of consciousness could not be Brahman (and thus would not be really possible), he concedes that a very high state of mystical awareness, apparently superseding the powers or *siddhis* of yoga, indicates that the required consciousness might be just that of a disinterested observer. Brahman's consciousness in regard to the world might be that of a witness self, *sāksin,* consenting to a play of material forces without anything at stake. Aurobindo's conception here recalls Sāmkhya's true *purusa,* "conscious being," who is aloof while beholding *prakrti,* "nature," as well as Vedānta's *nirguna-brahman,* Brahman "without qualities," who is *kūtastha,* "transcendent," while beholding the meaningless cosmic activity of *māyā.* That sort of consciousness, Aurobindo says as a kind of admission, might be compatible with almost any world whatsoever, since such a Witness might behold anything whatsoever and *ex hypothesi* it exerts no influence (except for an aboriginal "consent," according to the classical theories) upon that which it beholds. Although Aurobindo is an Indian theist, interpreting divine *cit* as not only consciousness but also power or determining force of consciousness, he does not in the end imply very much about the nature of our world from assuming Brahman is *cit.* Although at least one logical possibility can be ruled out as really impossible from this assumption, namely, an entirely "unwitnessed" universe, not much can be inferred about the nature of our world from the notion that Brahman is *cit.* The central argument of *The Life Divine* rests mainly with Brahman's aspect of *ānanda.*

That Brahman is essentially *ānanda,* "Bliss," means above all that immanent Brahman is so intrinsically *valuable* as to be forcing divine life. Yet Aurobindo does not put forth an explicit theory of value. Nor does he spell out the character of the value which he believes is implicit in Brahman as *ānanda.* It is clear, however, that he believes that a kind of "Ananda" scores high as a hedonic value, as he often repeats traditional claims that mystical experience of Brahman is ecstatic. As will become clear, I read "Ananda" as Aurobindo's ultimate moral and aesthetic value as well, though I do not mean to suggest that he is an ethical

or aesthetic hedonist. He explicitly contrasts divine *ānanda* with just about all that we ordinarily regard as markedly evil. Indeed, it is crucial to his central argument that all prominent forms of evil be repugnant to Brahman's nature. Divine *ānanda* is presumed incompatible with purposeless enjoyment on Brahman's part of any pain, suffering, or evil in general.

Although Aurobindo has no explicit theory of value, he does embrace a means/ends value distinction. He endorses the view that the positive value of an end may compensate and justify the negative value of its necessary means. Further, he holds that pain, suffering, and evil in general could have only this negative and "instrumental" value, not intrinsic value. They are not to be present in divine life, though he believes there could not be development of divine life without them: " . . . if that [Divine] Reality is what we have supposed it to be, there must be some necessity for the appearance of these contrary phenomena [of evil], some significance, some function that they had to serve in the economy of the universe." According to Aurobindo, Brahman as *ānanda* blocks the real possibility of any universe where there would be the slightest evil which was not an indispensable condition for the realization of some great good.

The future good has to be great indeed: not only is future "divine life" conceived as so wonderful that it would match the essential *ānanda* of Brahman, it is also conceived as more wonderful than what Brahman's "bliss" would have been without this self-manifestation. Otherwise, Aurobindo reasons, earthly pain, suffering, and evil in general would be unredeemed, that is, incompatible with Sachchidananda, since, as he says, Brahman as "Ananda" could not undergo a *meaningless* depletion: " . . . nor can they [pain, suffering, and evil in general] be a mere mistake of the Divine Consciousness without any meaning in the divine wisdom, without any purpose of the divine joy . . . to justify their existence. Justification there must be. . . . " Thus it is that *ānanda* is to involve not only "delight" understood hedonically but also the value of a significant process of achievement. Mere delight of play is not Brahman's motive for creation. Brahman wants to accomplish something. There are to be "new riches" from the cosmic adventure as well as a return to awareness of an intrinsic bliss. That Brahman is essentially *ānanda* means that where there is or has been evil there Brahman is itself moving to greater value, in Aurobindo's view.

MATTER AND THE INSTRUMENTALITY OF EVIL

The central argument of *The Life Divine* is that two facts, (1) Brahman's being Sachchidananda, particularly Ananda, and (2) the presence of evil, together indicate the inevitable emergence of divine life through the instrumentality of evil. Now it has to be understood that evil in Aurobindo's view is rooted in our material evolutionary inheritance. I have not included his views of matter and evolution in encapsulating the argument, since the tension which leads to the prediction of divine life centers on (the emergent material phenomena of) human evils, not on matter in general. But in order to understand his account of how precisely evil is necessary to the evolution of divine life, one has to take up his views of the nature of matter and biological evolution. This we cannot do here. My point is that the tension Aurobindo perceives between Brahman and evil is intended to motivate his account of the instrumentality of evil. It is also intended to motivate his account of the root of evil which he identifies as the insentience and other apparently adverse characteristics of matter and of life-forms emergent in matter. The reasoning launched to resolve the tension is that which unites the theological and cosmological portions of his world view.

As I indicated, it is impossible to do justice here to the wealth of detail in Aurobindo's account of the instrumentality of evil for divine life. However the basic point is just this: development of real individuals who would be in part responsible for their own growth and development would not be possible without matter and the evil its insentience entails. Working from this fundamental intuition, Aurobindo tries to make plausible his story of the ways in which such untoward phenomena as aggression, incapacity, and death might be serving indispensably the great good of divine life. This story could prove to be Aurobindo's chief philosophical accomplishment. In general, ends do justify means to an extent, though, as John Dewey insists [in *Reconstruction in Philosophy*], means may also justify ends, that is, when the ends most desirable would require much less favorable means. Still, in general ends do justify means to an extent, and so I feel that the details of the story of evil's instrumentality for divine life are prime candidates for the focus of future criticism.

Through the remainder of this article the focus will remain more metaphysical. I intend to show that despite Aurobindo's ingenuity his account of evil is not motivated in the way he thinks, because his central argument fails. The argument fails for a reason internal to his thought, to wit, that his doctrine of divine *cit* undercuts evil's significance. This failure negates the repeated claim of inevitability for divine life. On the other hand, we should give the philosophic mystic his due: although the argument's premises fail to deliver its conclusion—and that precisely within Aurobindo's own terms—his theory of divine life may be viewed as an explanation of one way in which, on an assumption of the reality of Brahman, evil might be intelligible considered from the human perspective as well as from Brahman's. With a revision of the cognitive status of his "prediction" of divine life, Aurobindo's theory, despite the failure of his central argument, will be seen to have merit. We shall review his theory of the significance of the cosmos in concluding.

THE ARGUMENT'S FAILURE: BRAHMAN (GOD) AS TRANSCENDENT

First let us see why his argument fails. As mentioned before, that Brahman is *cit* means for Aurobindo that Brahman has the power to self-manifest as finite or not to do so. While Brahman is thought to comprise the material of all things finite, Brahman is considered to be Sachchidananda essentially and finite things inessentially. Aurobindo conceives of Brahman as not having to become finite things. Self-manifestation is thought to hinge on Brahman's choice. Brahman is said to have a perspective which is in some way independent of its self-manifestation. It is this independence of perspective attributed to Brahman

which vitiates from the inside Aurobindo's argument for the inevitability of divine life.

In order to see this, let us detour through Western theodicy and its problem of "God's justification in the face of evil." The existence of evil is in tension with viewing God as omnibenevolent and omnipotent: God, it would seem, would create only the best of all possible universes and that, it would seem, would be one without evil. Aurobindo insists that evil presents an entirely different problem for his view. He says that his difficulty lies not in what God does but in what God is: noninstrumental evil in the universe would be meaningless evil in God, and that could not be Sachchidananda. He asserts that a view of God as extrascosmic, creating *ex nihilo,* cannot overcome the difficulty of an apparent divine sadism—God causing others to suffer—a difficulty which is avoided by his view that there are no "others" to Brahman. An extracosmic Creator of our world would be morally inferior to the best of His creatures, Aurobindo says in indictment of the view.

However, despite Aurobindo's insistence that Brahman itself bears all the world's evil, Brahman may be similarly charged with moral inferiority. Brahman may be so charged because of Brahman's independence of perspective. Indeed, sometimes Aurobindo says that essential Brahman does not lose awareness of *ānanda* while it bears suffering and evil. We, on the other hand, do not normally experience "Bliss" when we are in pain, nor are we all aware of pain's presumed cosmic significance. Could not Brahman have borne less evil out of regard for those bits of itself which are not directly aware of *ānanda*? If it could, then it would be just as much a bully as any extracosmic Creator would be.

Aurobindo's response is of course that Brahman could not have borne evil and still realize the great value of divine life. But that would seem to justify "evil" only from Brahman's perspective. We ourselves have values, at least most of us do, and by them we discern very real evil. So even if we grant that the development of divine life truly requires the evils we perceive (an inherently dubious proposition, but one Aurobindo supports with his long and ingenious theory), the existence of these evils, particularly of the "natural" ones not of our own making, such as diseases and death, prompts us to suspect that Brahman would be achieving an "inhuman" goal in its self-manifestation. If our suffering is to be instrumental to Brahman's goal of "divine life," why should not human existence be similarly instrumental and without intrinsic value? Indeed, why should Brahman be bound by human values? Brahman as *cit* is supposed to have an independent perspective on things. Why then should human evil count as compatible with Sachchidananda only by being instrumental to a life that is "divine" according to human standards? By conceiving of Brahman as having an independent perspective on things, Aurobindo leaves room for the speculation that our values do not count in Brahman's goals. The existence of evil would provide support for that view, assuming Aurobindo's Brahman to be a reality. Thus evil cannot be viewed—within Aurobindo's own terms—as the decisive indication he takes it to be that the world is developing to "divine life" as he conceives it. Aurobindo's vision of divine life is one in which human values are fulfilled, not only Brahman's.

THE COGNITIVE STATUS OF THE THEORY OF DIVINE LIFE

Aurobindo's argument for divine life fails because evil need not be considered in tension with his Brahman. As the medieval voluntarists insisted, God may choose God's own purposes; so too Aurobindo's Brahman. But though his argument fails, his story of the instrumentality of evil for divine life may still have value. It may be taken as a theory *explaining* how the cosmic process *might* have meaning and value, to humanity as well as to Brahman, on the assumption of the reality of Brahman. Evil need not be considered in tension with Aurobindo's Brahman, and so he is wrong to suppose that it is evidence, particularly decisive evidence, for the future emergence of divine life. But though Brahman might not intend to manifest a life that is "divine" from the human perspective, there is no reason to rule out such a possibility altogether. Aurobindo's theory would show one possible way the cosmos, despite evil and indeed by means of it, would have meaning and value to us as well as to Brahman. Evil is deemed instrumental to our own arrival in divine life, not only Brahman's. He claims universally to find " . . . a cosmic and *individual* utility in what presents itself to us as adverse and evil" (emphasis mine). Aurobindo's achievement within his own problem-space is a singularly Indian theodicy. He professes that a dual affirmation of the world and Brahman is one of his speculative aims. It is one he may be said to achieve, insofar as the details of his theory of the instrumentality of evil may be judged plausible.

The failure of Aurobindo's central argument means that he should drop his insistence upon the inevitability of divine life. He should claim only that divine life is a plausible eventuality, assuming the reality of Brahman. And at one place he comes very near to such a view:

> All exists here, no doubt, for the delight of existence, all is a game or Lila; but a game too carries within itself an object to be accomplished and without the fulfillment of that object would have no completeness of significance. A drama without denouement may be an artistic possibility,—existing only for the pleasure of watching the characters and the pleasure in problems posed without a solution or with a forever suspended dubious balance of solution; the drama of the earth evolution might conceivably be of that character, but an intended or inherently predetermined denouement is also and more convincingly possible. Ananda is the secret principle of all being and the support of all activity of being: but Ananda does not exclude a delight in the working out of a Truth inherent in being, immanent in the Force or Will of being, upheld in the hidden self-awareness of its Consciousness-Force which is the dynamic and executive agent of all its activities and the knower of their significance.

In this passage, Aurobindo, waffling on the question of the inevitability of divine life, says (or implies) that the problems posed (by our human suffering, dissatisfaction, and aspiration) would have their solution in divine life, that such a solution is "plausible" (as opposed to "certain, given the reality of Brahman beside that of evil," as before), and that it would be significant. With a revision of the cognitive status of his reasoning from that of an argument for divine life to that of an explanation of the significance of the cosmos, Aurobindo's theory would have merit—for one who accepted Brahman—just in that the significance would obtain equally for Brahman and for humanity. Aurobindo's theory of divine life involves a value-anthropomorphism, although Brahman is not otherwise conceived of anthropomorphically. (If God really intended Aurobindo's "divine life," God *would* be worthy of worship.)

DIVINE LIFE AS PROVIDING THE SIGNIFICANCE OF THE COSMOS

That the problems posed (by our human suffering, dissatisfaction, and aspiration) would be truly resolved, in other words, that life would be significant from our perspectives, we may grant in general, because the picture painted is so terribly rosy. (Is Aurobindo's prose style so inordinately rich and roseate because of an inordinate optimism of his vision?) It would be difficult to imagine any more positive conception of the "destiny of the individual" than Aurobindo's. The real question concerns the plausibility of the conception, not whether life would be significant from our perspectives were the conception valid. He tells us we are souls having developed and still developing manifold personality and material form, both individually as well as collectively, through a process of birth and rebirth which preserves our life histories (in individual memory and not only in the "consequent being of God," as with Whitehead). Aurobindo says that each person will share increasingly in the freedom of will and self-determination that is Brahman's essentially, as he grows to be a "gnostic being" who is aware of the "Bliss" of Brahman while participating in ever better forms of earthly society. "Evil" is in the end only apparent or transitional: death guards our perfectibility (we die in order to make further growth possible, our own as well as societal); pain and suffering spur our (yogic) resolve; and apparent material insentience makes possible a real individuality of distinct souls with distinct bodies and minds. Aurobindo provides a theory about how in general divine life might be possible. The question of its plausibility involves that thorny issue of the veridicality of mystical experience, among other complex considerations, including the facticity of the proposed mechanisms of evil's instrumentality and the acceptability of the account of matter. The conceptual question we have still to take up is how this process could be, as he asserts in the quote above, significant for Brahman.

Aurobindo falters at places in his reflection on this question, though the answer lies available in the terms of his view. His trouble is ambivalence over the nature of Brahman's perfection. Given that all manifestation hinges upon Brahman's choice, "Why should Brahman, perfect, absolute, infinite, needing nothing, desiring nothing, at all throw out force of consciousness to create in itself these worlds of form?" Aurobindo's answer is "Delight," and he explains that this "Delight" involves a process of achievement and accomplishment. But why should Brahman want to accomplish anything? Aurobindo does not really believe that the logic of Brahman's perfection precludes Brahman's accomplishing something ("Ananda does not exclude a delight in the working out of a Truth"), but sometimes it appears he believes that this could be no real accomplishment from Brahman's own perspective, as he lapses into viewing Brahman's perfection as "static." Robert Nozick is the first person, to my knowledge, to have resolved this puzzle within the terms of a Brahman philosophy committed to the "perfection" of Brahman. He proposes [in *Philosophical Explanations*]:

> . . . a theory that views Brahman as creating the world to overcome its last limitations as Brahman—the existence of the world becomes a component of Brahman's all-inclusiveness and perfection. The world is part of the process whereby Brahman overcomes the final limits of being infinite existence, consciousness, bliss. Brahman is not limited by even that apparently wonderful nature. We would like a theory that gives us both timeless perfection along with a process of transcending and overcoming, a process of accomplishment. Both are supplied by a view of Brahman (and of people's underlying nature) as Satchitananda and (simultaneously at some level) as casting itself forth into another state so as to overcome the limitations inherent in Satchitananda, then slowly evolving back to an awareness of its true perfect nature as Brahman.

According to an old Aristotelian doctrine, will implies want. Thus Brahman would have to be deficient in its willing divine life. But according to Nozick's view of perfection as dynamic, Brahman's manifestation could be seen as part of its perfection. Brahman would manifest because of the peculiar nature of a perfect delight. So the development of divine life would be significant for Brahman as well as for humanity, assuming that Brahman could accomplish something. With Aurobindo, I see no reason why Brahman could not. The question whether Brahman's attempting to do so would entail imperfection is moot. Either Aurobindo's Brahman is imperfect according to traditional notions, or perhaps perfect according to some dynamic standard such as Nozick's. The point is that in either conception the development of divine life would be significant from Brahman's perspective, as well as our own, just in that Brahman itself is conceived as gaining "new riches" from its cosmic adventure.

In sum, Aurobindo's central argument fails, and he is not entitled to claim that "disharmony" means the inevitability of divine life. But his theory of the instrumentality of evil may be viewed as one possible way that the terrible disharmony he doubtless feels—between what he takes to be the objective indications of his mystical experience and earthly evil—might be both in theory and in fact resolved. However the question remains whether a life that is divine from the human perspective is the *only* way the process could be significant from Brahman's perspective. Could not Brahman fulfill its aim of a perfect delight otherwise than by developing Aurobindo's humanly desirable divine life? Why Brahman would want the cosmic process to be significant from the human perspective is left unclear. Is it to be significant as well for all those species that are or will be extinct?

P. S. Deshpande (essay date 1985)

SOURCE: "Sri Aurobindo's *Savitri*: A Key to Integral Perfection," in *Indian Readings in Commonwealth Literature*, edited by G. S. Amur, and others, Sterling Publishers Private Limited, 1985, pp. 59-70.

[*In the following essay, Deshpande interprets* Savitri *as a guide to transforming mortal nature into divine nature through Aurobindo's system of yoga.*]

Sri Aurobindo's **Savitri** is both a legend and a symbol. Through the legend he tries to convey the most ancient tradition of the realization of the Integral Self and through the symbol all the mystic processes connected thereto. The poem reveals a philosophical wisdom and mystical inspiration and promises the highest kind of life to those who are prepared to sacrifice a limited reward for the blessed promise of fullness.

Sri Aurobindo holds a distinctive view with regard to the place of poetry in the scheme of human evolution, echoed by Satyawan in **Savitri**. Satyawan gropes for the mystery with the lantern of thought. Its glimmerings light with the abstract word a half visible ground, and travelling yard by yard it maps a system of the self and God. He then turns to poetry to find its hints through beauty and art. But he discovers that the form cannot unveil the indwelling power. It only throws its symbols at our hearts. It evokes a mood of self, evokes a sign of all the brooding glory hidden in our sense.

There are always two dimensions to whatever a poet may try to communicate; the outward or instrumental and the inward or spiritual. The outward or instrumental elements, according to Sri Aurobindo, are at a lower level compared to the inward or spiritual.

Our consciousness is always externalised because we live most of the time in the external world. We look at things and happenings from the outer surface of our being. We can see and feel only the results on the material plane. Our senses have a very limited power and they can give us the knowledge of the material things. But Sri Aurobindo reveals in **Savitri** that,

> Our larger being sits behind cryptic walls:
> There are greatnesses hidden in our unseen parts
> That wait their hour to step into life's front.

The key to integral perfection, according to Sri Aurobindo's **Savitri,** lies in turning our consciousness inward. There is a phenomenal determinism in the world of flux in which we dwell. The truth of this world is relative, while the absolute and transcendental truth is the truth of our inner soul.

Integral perfection is possible when we know our entire being. The senses, mind and intellect can know only a surface of our being, a small part of our being:

> The larger part of our being lies hidden behind

the frontal consciousness, behind the veil occult and known only by an occult knowledge.

[*Letters on Yoga*]

Our senses give us the knowledge of the things that are in the external world by directing our consciousness outward. In the same way we can know the things of the inner world which are higher worlds if we direct our consciousness inward and rise into the inner consciousness. We have to take an entirely reverse turn in our consciousness and go beyond the limitations of our physical senses to have the true knowledge of the absolute. There is a correspondence between the inner and the outer and the life within is the same as the life without. The concentration upon our body, life and mind and the realms beyond mind acquaints us with the cosmic character of the forces which govern these elements. Intensive concentration on our different inward elements gives our inward being a poise and a calm and a power to move these forces cosmically, making our soul the artist of our fate. Till then we are slaves of the Matter:

> Here Matter seems to mould the body's life
> And the soul follows where its nature drives;
> Nature and Fate compel his free will's choice.
> But greater spirits this balance can reverse
> And make the soul the artist of its fate.

Sri Aurobindo here draws a distinction between the spirits who are eminently fit, those who are moderately fit and those who are misfit for the spiritual life. The spiritual call does not reach both spiritually fit and unfit alike. Even amongst the fit souls there are degrees of fitness. There are souls who are fit from their birth. They are of the finest type. They do not suffer from the earthly touch; they have their illumination with their nativity and birth. Savitri and Satyawan are such great souls. Then there are seekers after truth who are not in touch with the affairs of the world and those who are in touch with life and life's affairs. Both these types require preparation and have to pass through a period of discipline. It is a period of spiritual instruction and fellowship. The first type respond to the spiritual call immediately and pass into the life of contemplation and silence. The second type take time before they can be in everyway fit for spiritual realization. The way of life in the two cases will be different. The first will be the life of wise passiveness, insight and meditation; the second will be the life of active callings on the path of duty of a house-holder. A house-holder cannot renounce the duties at hand. He will have to pass through darkness and light and he will be finally moulded by life. Close concentration and devotion to the ideal is not possible unless he attains a freedom from the urges of life.

There is a third category of misfits who can never receive a call for spiritual life. Truth remains hidden from them because they are after shadows and appearances. They find what they seek. They are described at great length in the Seventh Book of **Savitri**:

> But only reason and sense he feels as sure,
> They only are his trusted witnesses.

There are also categories below even the level of misfits.

For instance, the man who indulges in evil for the sake of evil:

> I was made for evil, evil is my lot;
> Evil I must be and by evil live.

And the man who clings to his ignorant life:

> But human mind clings to its ignorance,
> And to its littleness the human heart,
> And to its right to grief the earthly life.

The plan of integral perfection is revealed to Savitri by a mighty voice as she sat staring at the dumb tread of time, contemplating in the region above her brows, where will and knowledge meet. Thus contemplating, her body becomes rigid like a golden statue. But there is divine light lit within her. She is asked to—

> Find out thy soul, recover thy hid self
> In silence seek God's meaning in thy depths,
> Then mortal nature change to the divine,
> Open God's door, enter into his trance,
> Cast thought from thee, that nimble ape of light:
> In his tremendous hush stilling thy brain
> His vast truth wake within and know and see.
> Cast from thee sense that veils thy spirit's sight:
> In the enormous emptiness of thy mind
> Then shalt see the eternal's body in the world
> Know him in every voice heard by thy soul:
> In the world's contact meet his single touch;
> All things shall fold thee into his embrace.
> Conquer thy heart's throbs, let thy heart beat in God:
> Thy nature shall be the engine of his works,
> Thy voice shall house the mightiness of his word:
> Then shall thou harbour my force and conquer Death.

The various steps of the plan of integral perfection indicated in the above passage could be spelt out thus:

1. To find out our soul and to recover our hidden self.

2. To seek God's meaning in our inner deep worlds in silence.

3. To transform our mortal nature of triple qualities of *Tamas, Raja* and *Satva* to the divine nature.

4. To open in deep meditation God's door which is hidden in our inner realm.

5. To acquire a lasting peace by freeing our mind from every kind of thought.

6. To acquire the transcendental sight and knowledge by freeing our mind of the tyranny of senses and by awakening the inner vast truth.

7. To recognise the presence of God in all things—animate and inanimate—of the external world, thereby, making it possible to be deeply rooted in Bhakti even while engaged in mundane activities.

8. To banish all seekings, agitations, wishes and desires from the heart and to become an instrument of God's work.

9. The above sadhana will reveal the divine word
and invest it with God's power. With this power
it will be possible to conquer Death.

The divine could be recovered only by the divine. The divine has two aspects—one is static and the other is dynamic. The dynamic aspect of the divine and our soul in its pure form are identical. The soul could be found out if we receive the grace or if we receive spiritual knowledge or if we remain in the company of realised souls or if we read the works of realised souls. *Savitri* has an inexhaustible source of mystical inspiration to arouse our soul if we approach it in a spirit of receptivity. It has enormous possibilities to communicate Truth, Beauty, Light, Power, Knowledge, Wisdom and Consciousness which lead to integral perfection. The wonders of the Deep and the ecstasies of the Height begin to possess us if we open our being to its powerful inrushes. By concentrating on these inrushes, the blissful vibrations in our being, the hidden self can be recovered. The hidden self is static in its nature. This practice of concentration has been called *Abhyas* or spiritual practice by Patanjali: *Abhyas—Vairagyabhyam tannirodhah*. By practice of concentration, contemplation and meditation on the dynamic nature of Purusha in chittam, the material characteristic of mind-stuff is progressively renounced [Rammurti S. Mishra, *The Text-book of Yoga Psychology*].

To seek God's meaning in our inner deep worlds in silence, we have to follow a long drawn programme of meditation. This meditation will disclose to the seeker his cosmic past. It will reveal to him many worlds peopled with seeds of life and the human creature born in time. Also,

> There are occult shadows, there are tenebrous
>   Powers,
> Inhabitants of life's ominous nether rooms,
> A shadowy world's stupendous denizens.

The seeker will have to establish himself firmly in his soul. Firmly to keep attention with all its consciousness is called practice or *Abhyasa*. But this practice will get firmly grounded only when it has been cultivated for a long time, constantly, continuously and uninterruptedly with earnest attention. Which is produced by self-discipline, protected by *ojas,* chemical, bio-chemical and harmonal powers, and energized by self-confidence and self-scrutiny [Mishra, *The Textbook of Yoga Psychology*].

The inner worlds can be broadly divided into the world of inconscience, the world of ignorance and the world of superconscience:

> Above us dwells a superconscient god
> Hidden in the mystery of his own light:
> Around us is a vast ignorance
> Lit by the uncertain ray of human mind,
> Below us sleeps the Inconscient dark and mute.

The poem reveals an adventurous journey in the inner realms. There is no place in it for the conventional ways of thinking about Truth. We have to free ourselves completely of the conventional notions and ideas of the sensuous experiences in poetry and be prepared to receive the blissful light which brings understanding. The poem will unfold the mysteries of silence if we turn our senses and

mind inward. The poem will lead us to the highest beatitude which would free us from the limitations and solicitations of personality.

Individual liberation is not the goal of Sri Aurobindo's yoga. Sri Aurobindo aims at the integral perfection of the entire world.

— *P. S. Deshpande*

The poem gives an account of the journey from consciousness to higher consciousness till it reaches the highest point. The formless and shapeless agencies cast their influence on the course of this journey. They may be baneful or boonful and may either obstruct or help the seeker soul. The worlds through which the soul passes range from the subliminal to supramental. There are valleys of tears and smiles which the soul has to cross before it reaches the realm of supreme light. There he may meet spiritual federations which will help him in his effort to reach the goal. As the *sadhana* increases, the inner radiation of his spirit will become more intense. The transcendent wisdom will bring him a final release from the sense of individuality. He will increasingly feel the inward power and strength of his soul and its subtle spiritual attraction. The constant tension felt because of the apparent limitations of the soul will dissolve. As the soul is anxious to regain its original infinite nature, it will feel subtle attraction for itself. Led by this attraction it will successfully resist all other attractions and tendencies, and be absorbed in itself. The blessed peace that lies in the deep of the soul can be felt and realized when this centripetal movement of the soul itself goes on strengthening. The real tension in the soul which is due to its apparent finitude and its inherent infinitude will no longer be experienced. His heart will be made sufficiently pure and his being will be highly sensitive to the spiritual influences only by the silent contemplation of the dynamic soul. By this the soul will feel a natural attraction for the self and the *sadhana* will become effortless and natural. The greater inrushes of grace and knowledge will suddenly flood the inner chambers of his being with unexpected and unexperienced light. This experience will fill him with peace and plenitude and there will be no agitation in his mind or heart. All other experiences will vanish before the direct experiences of the soul. Since he will become free from all the tensions that are associated with other forms of life, life will appear to him in a different hue, with nobler melody, rhythm, joy and peace. He will discover in this peace God's meaning of life. This is the transcendental meaning:

> Our greater self of knowledge waits for us,
> A supreme light in the truth conscious vast:
> It sees from summits beyond thinking mind,
> It moves in a splendid air transcending life.

The transformation of the mortal nature into the divine is not possible unless 'the Immortal's golden door' is opened and the inner journey started:

> As man disguised the cosmic greatness works
> And finds the mystic inaccessible gate
> And opens the Immortal's golden door.

In the scriptures there is a mention of two doors, the lower, guarded by the Serpent at the *Muladhar* Centre of the *sushumna* and an extremely narrow door in the thousand lotus centre in the crown.

> The Serpent of threshold hissing rose.
> The gate swung wide with a protesting jar,
> The opponent powers withdrew their dreadful
>   guard;
> Her being entered into the inner worlds.

After the gate is opened the being starts to ascend to the higher centres. "These centres are sources of all the dynamic powers of our being. They form an ascending series from the lowest muladhar to the highest thousand-petalled lotus. According to the tantrics, there is the Serpent power at the lowest center *Muladhar* which sleeps in coils. The seeker has to arouse this power and take it through different centres to meet the Brahman in the thousand-petalled centre to liberate oneself into the Divine Being. These centres are closed or half-closed within us and have to be opened before their full power can be manifested in our physical nature: but once they are opened and completely active, no limit can be set to the development of their potencies and the total transformation to be possible" [M. P. Pandit, *Dictionary of Sri Aurobindo's Yoga*].

> Out of Inconscient's soulless mindless Night
> A flaming serpent rose released from sleep

The physical consciousness centre, called *Muladhar*, commands the physical consciousness and the subconscient and governs the physical down to the subconscient. After the *Kundalini* or the Serpent power wakes up, it stands erect and starts climbing on its way. It touches the centres with its flaming mouth and with its fiery kiss breaks their sleep. These centres after being kissed by the Serpent Power bloom surcharged with light and bliss. From the centre of the matter's base the *Kundalini* reaches the centre of the head and joins the Eternal space between these two centres. Then in each divine stronghold and Nature's Knot it holds together the mystic stream which joins the viewless summit of the crown with the unseen depths at the base.

When this Power comes to the second abdominal or *Swadhishthan* Centre, it controls the small vital movements, the little greeds, lusts, desires and the small sense movements. This is the centre of the lower vital.

After reaching the third centre, *Manipur,* which governs the larger vital, the seeker can control the larger life-forces, the passions and larger desire movements.

The fourth centre, *Anahata,* governs the emotions. After the Power touches this centre the seeker acquires power over his emotional and psychic forces.

The fifth centre, *Vishudda,* governs the expressive and externalising mind. When the Serpent power reaches this centre the seeker has control over his expression and all externalisation of the mind movements and mental forces.

The centre between the eyebrows, *Ajnachakra,* when touched by the *Kundalini,* the seeker can control his thoughts, will and vision. He acquires power over dynamic mind, will, vision and mental formation.

When the Power reaches the thousand Petalled centre, the seeker gets many occult powers by controlling the regions beyond mind.

As there is a correspondence between the inner and outer worlds and entities, the seeker with the passage of *Kundalini* through different centres, gets control not only over the powers of his being, but he can also control these powers in the cosmos.

All these centres are situated in the subtle body. In the other yogas like Hata yoga or Ashtang yoga these centres are opened from down upwards. But in Sri Aurobindo's yoga they are opened from up downward, though there is an ascent of the force from Muladhara in his yoga also.

The final union of the individual soul with the cosmic soul becomes possible when the final door is opened by the power and when it enters the mystic cave.

> Onward she passed seeking the soul's mystic
>   cave.

Then through a tunnel dug in the last rock, the individual soul comes out where shines a deathless sun.

> In the last chamber on a golden seat
> One sat whose shape no vision could define,
> Only one felt the world's unattainable fount
> A Power of which she was a straying force,
> An invisible Beauty, goal of the world's desire,
> A Sun of which all knowledge is a beam,
> A Greatness without whom no life could be.

When the individual soul becomes one with this Cosmic Soul, the aspirant is endowed with transcendent wisdom.

After this experience the individual recognises the presence of his own self in every object of the world. Every animate and inanimate being becomes an extension of his own self. The bonds of individual finitude break down. The individual becomes infinite. This is the Bhuma state described in the Upanishads. At this stage the individual is fully liberated. After this stage he does his own Bhakti: *Swa swarupanusandhanam bhaktiritya bhidhiyate.* Among the set of means to bring about liberation, bhakti is the greatest says Shankaracharya. Continuous contemplation of one's essential nature is said to be bhakti [Shankaracharya, *Vivekehudamani*].

Individual liberation is not the goal of Sri Aurobindo's yoga. Sri Aurobindo aims at the integral perfection of the entire world. Also, he was not concerned with the other worlds for themselves. He clearly states the object of his yoga: "It is the object of my yoga to transform life by bringing down into it the Light, Power and Bliss of the Divine Truth and its dynamic certitudes. This yoga is not a yoga of world-shunning asceticism, but of divine life. . . . It aims at a change of life and existence, not as something subordinate or incidental, but as distinct and central object" [*On Himself*].

Sri Aurobindo was pained to see the downfall of the modern civilized world. He saw that the "civilized man lives outwardly the civilized life, possesses all its paraphernalia, but pulls the higher faculties down to the level of his senses, his sensations, his unenlightened emotions, his gross utilitarian practicality" [*The Human Cycle*]. He sincerely felt that "the mere participation in the benefits of civilization is not enough to raise a man into the mental life proper. The philistine is in fact the modern civilised barbarian, he is often the half-civilised physical and vital barbarian, by his unintelligent attachment to the life of the body, the life of the vital needs and impulses and the ideal of the merely domestic and economic human animal" [*The Human Cycle*].

Sri Aurobindo and the Mother through their effort wanted to establish the Divine consciousness on the earth to save the struggling world:

> Even if the struggling world is left outside
> One man's perfection still can save the world.
> A camp of God is pitched in human time.

Savitri made her life a bridge between earth and heaven:

> To aid a blind and suffering mortal race,
> To open the light the eyes that could not see,
> To bring down bliss into the heart of grief.

In the words of the Mother this dream has already been realised:

> The manifestation of the Supramental upon earth is no longer a promise but a living fact, a reality. It is at work here, and one day will come when the most blind, the most unconscious, even the most unwilling shall be obliged to recognise it.

(The Mother's message on April 24, 1956)

K. D. Verma (essay date 1990)

SOURCE: "The Social and Political Vision of Sri Aurobindo," in *World Literature Written in English,* Vol. 30, No. 1, Spring, 1990, pp. 56-71.

[*In the following essay, Verma examines Aurobindo's views on a number of subjects that were integral to his political and social vision, including colonialism, nationalism, evil, freedom, equality, brotherhood, the unity and salvation of humankind, and the human evolutionary process.*]

As a prophet of Indian nationalism, Aurobindo occupies an important place in the history of Indian political thought. When we recall the early Aurobindo, we think of a fiery, aggressive and uncompromising revolutionary who had cast his lot with the larger destiny of India and her people. His active involvement in the struggle against the British empire in general was an expression of his staunch conviction that imperialism and colonialism, whether mercantile or political, are manifestations of repressive egoism or hubris on the part of a nation who simply happened to possess a superiority of means over its relatively less favoured subjects. The Caesars and Napoleons of history have been guilty of exercising this hubris, of perpetuating slavery, tyranny and injustice in the world, of devising and enforcing negative and immoral political,

economic and social systems, and hence, of denying man his basic freedom and individuality. Man, as Aurobindo believed right from the very beginning of his involvement, is entitled to freedom, equality and basic human dignity. He fully shared the ideas of Rousseau, Voltaire and other thinkers of the European enlightenment, and the bases of the French Revolution, although later on, especially as one finds in *The Human Cycle* and *The Ideal of Human Unity,* his ideas of liberty, equality and fraternity assumed a much more metaphysical and philosophical dimension. The early Aurobindo believed quite religiously that nationalism is an immediate and irrevocable necessity, an inevitable phenomenon, much like the powerful thrust of a destined natural cycle of change. He further believed that revolutions in the history of mankind are healthy and fruitful expressions of the creative energy in men, and that they occur and would continue occurring unchecked and uncontrolled at predicated successive intervals of history. The psychology of history of human progress was later fully developed and synthesized by Aurobindo in his evolutionary philosophy of human growth. Readers of Blake may remember the conflict between Orc and Urizen: the revolutionary energy, symbolized in the figure of Orc, manifests itself in the cycle of human destiny as a formidable agent of change against tyranny, oppression, the law, and decay. Himself a fiery Orc of Indian nationalism, Aurobindo was resolutely determined to help the peoples of India not only in getting rid of the foreign yoke but also in achieving for them a happy and honourable condition of existence.

Evil, according to Aurobindo, appears at various periods during the course of evolutionary growth of man, nature and society, but it has no permanent existence of its own. The pattern of evolutionary progress, as envisaged by Aurobindo, is no doubt cyclical, but it does not admit the Spenglerian regression and pessimism [See S. K. Maitra, "Sri Aurobindo and Spengler," in *The Integral Philosophy of Sri Aurobindo,* edited by Haridas Chaudhuri and Frederic Spiegelberg]. The young Aurobindo, as [R. C.] Zaehner notes in *Evolution in Religion* was "a left-wing politician," and had evinced "sympathetic interest in Marxian socialism," perhaps fully sharing the Marxian prophecy of a possible materialization of a new social order "in which the free development of each is the condition for the development of all." Whatever the nature of the obvious similarity between Aurobindo and Marx, we know that Aurobindo's emphasis is on the divinization of man and of this earth and on the ultimate liberation of man. In Aurobindo, the two dreams, one of individual freedom, and the other of collective salvation, are integral parts of the one unified dream; and national independence or nationalism is a preparatory condition to the realization of the larger dream.

For the Indian intelligentsia, especially for men like Aurobindo, Gandhi, Nehru and others who were educated in England and steeped in Western intellectual thought, it was not difficult to comprehend the significance of nationalism. One can argue that modern nationalism is a typical European phenomenon and that it emerged in India mainly as a reaction against British colonialism and racism. In England, of course, nationalism had been imbued with powerful religious feelings: as a result of this amalgam of religion and nationalism, the English have always regarded themselves as God's chosen race, and that monarchy as a divine institution. It is this overpowering sense of nationalism which later grew into colonialism and imperialism. France and England, as [Robert H.] Murray remarks in *Studies in the English Social and Political Thinkers of the Nineteenth Century,* fought the hundred years' war "for a prize of incalculable worth, the leadership of the colonial world." Ironically, Blake thought this inchoate and expedient mixture of politics and religion an infectious perversion and clairvoyantly prophesied the fall of the Empire. But Disraeli, Mill and Carlyle were happy colonialists: underlying their pious convictions was perhaps the paternalistic assumption that God's chosen people had the moral obligation to spread light—to educate and reform the savages and natives, to devise means of introducing European education and civilization and to insure progress and advancement. If this sanctimonious principle had effectively dictated the governance of India, much of the history of the British Raj in India would have been written entirely differently. But the fact remains that the British colonialism—and European colonialism for that matter—was an expression of the powerful urge to gain political and economic supremacy; and it had the blessings of "feudalized Christianity."

As the colonial umbrella grew phenomenally bigger and more unmanageable, the English politicians at home became overly concerned with the problems of unity, homogeneity and consolidation of the imperial power. People like Lord Morley thought that "the empire was united, if it were united, by community of interest, whereas Seeley conceived it as bound together by community of race and religion" [Murray, *Studies in the English Social and Political Thinkers of the Nineteenth Century*]. The phrase "community of interest" is no doubt dubious, but it is pregnant with rich irony: it certainly did not imply uniform interest of people or national units within the Empire. Earlier, of course, Edmund Burke had formulated the clear possibility of forming one commonwealth more expediently and readily by the states of Europe rather than by the racially heterogeneous nations; and for Burke nationalism was the key element in the unification of the European states. Burke, like Coleridge, had accepted the metaphysics of Divine Providence, but he was vehemently opposed to the use of divine authority by England for the gratification of "the lowest of their passions" [See Alfred Cobban, *Edmund Burke and the Revolt Against the Eighteenth Century*]. That is why Burke who was in favour of preserving the integrity of the Indian civilization and maintaining peace in India had proposed a political trusteeship for India. But the questions that intrigued Indian intellectuals like Aurobindo pertained to fundamental humanistic values and moral principles underlying the essential structure of British colonialism. Why is the principle of absolute sovereignty of a people, even if it were the most genuine and authentic expression of their will, not universally and unreservedly acknowledged? If the English as a nation have the absolute right to assert their sovereignty, why should Great Britain deny the same right to Canada, Ireland or India? Why is the Christian ideal, according to which the denial of human rights is supposed to be an of-

fense to God, generally considered to be compatible with the political reality of colonialism? Does colonial politics, especially when its authority and sanction are explicitly derived from religion, have any moral basis?

It is abundantly clear from Aurobindo's early writings that he was distrustful of British justice, for the British, in their injudicious and oppressive governance of India, were essentially led by their boastful pride—"the pride of race, the pride of empire and the pride of colour" [*Sri Aurobindo Birth Centenary Library,* Vol. 1; hereafter cited as *BCL,* with volume number immediately following.] The unpropitious school of toryism and conservatism had made its political views on India too sharply pronounced to incite any feelings of hope and trust, but Aurobindo was equally suspicious of the British liberals. Such parabolic and insensitive vocabulary of colonial consciousness as indubitably defines the incongruous relationship between Prospero and Caliban, the master and the slave, and the ill-conceived obsession of Kurtz ("Exterminate all the brutes") is only reminiscent of the unchaste collective guilt and of the self-destructive political reality that writers like Conrad and Forster were to dramatize in their works. Aurobindo was convinced that the colonial rule, in its lustful intent and approach, was engaged in robbing the subjects of their national and cultural identity and that it had, in the due course of history, firmly established a bureaucratic and despotic system based on fear, repression and tyranny. Because of the rapid debilitation of Indian consciousness prompted by racial bigotry and because of the pervasive colonial hubris, Aurobindo remained vehemently opposed to the idea of India becoming a satellite province or otherwise a confederate state of the Empire.

Metaphysics and religious thought had played a significant role in shaping the political ideas of Dante, Milton and Coleridge. Likewise, in the case of Aurobindo—a poet, a radical, a philosopher—it goes without saying that his political vision of India's nationhood and sovereignty derives its essential outline from his spiritual vision of man's freedom and enlightenment. In fact, both Aurobindo and Gandhi were inspired by Indian spiritual thought, although it is a well-known fact of history that Aurobindo did not share the Mahatma's position on several issues. Aurobindo was an out-and-out revolutionary—he was dubbed as an "extremist"—who did not believe in the policy of mendicancy, appeasement and compromise. His vociferous criticism of the moderate position centered on their psychological vulnerability to the repressive and intimidating measures of the despotic regime and to the self-defeating programs of the Raj. It was practically the same sort of political process that had made people like Sir Syed Ahmed Khan support the colonial regime. "To recover possession of the State," reiterates Aurobindo emphatically, "is therefore the first business of the awakened Indian consciousness" and not "to revive the old dissipation of energies, to put social reform first, education first or moral regeneration first and leave freedom to result from these" (*BCL,* 1, 82). Later, it turned out that the disastrous historical tragedy, the partition of Bengal, not only enabled the radicals to consolidate their own strength, but also forced the moderates to see the truth of Aurobindo's vision. The moderates, it seemed, had followed Burke's exhortation to the Irish of preferring the path of pacific resistance to that of an open rebellion. Aurobindo's spiritual vision had enabled him to invest divinity upon his country, his land and his nation, to see in each man the sleeping divinity that needs to be awakened, and to believe firmly that the solemn and unequivocal affirmation of the will of people can wipe out the stains of slavery. It is this unique vision of divine nationhood or of India as Mother that gave him the inspiration and strength to wage an incessant struggle for the sacred cause of freedom. Aurobindo believed that once India regains its nationhood, the task of strengthening national consciousness and of achieving progress will be much more relevant to the larger goals, for those who have been enslaved and subjugated too long would not otherwise know the meaning of true liberty.

During the period of his active political involvement, Aurobindo advocated the idealistic position—a position which admitted no compromise with the colonial rule on fundamental principles and which called for an equally firm and unequivocal commitment to a comprehensive program of revolutionary action. For Aurobindo, nationalism was a *dharma,* and the revolution was a *yudha.* "Dharma," as Aurobindo explains, "is the Indian conception in which rights and duties lose the artificial antagonism created by a view of the world which makes selfishness the roots of action" . . . (*BCL,* 1). This *dharma,* the selfless act, *nishkam karma* of the *Gita,* is "the basis of democracy which Asia must recognize . . . " (*BCL,* 1). Since the struggle was not merely political but ethical and spiritual, he could, therefore, morally justify the use of violence as a means of achieving the larger ends. In the beginning, however, most of his ideas on freedom, nationalism and revolution were inspired by manifold experiments in the West, especially the long, intrepid struggle of the peoples of Europe to attain basic human dignity. Rousseau and other European thinkers, we may remember, did characterize slavery as immoral. The entire history of the French Revolution and the European Romantic movement, especially in its unswerving commitment to the cause of liberty, had a moral basis. Some of the English Romantic poets, especially Wordsworth, viewed the French Revolution as a fulfillment of the biblical prophecy contained in the Revelation. In the history of European political thought and particularly at the time of the American and the French revolutions clear-cut distinctions had been drawn between political morality which is politically functional and expedient, and ethical morality which has its reference to larger and more fundamental humanistic values. Undoubtedly, Aurobindo considered the latter the only justifiable basis of a revolution which was inspired by a comprehensive vision of liberty.

Liberty for Aurobindo did not mean simply the abolition of the foreign rule and the achievement of self-government based upon the blind imitation of the West. Nor did it mean the attainment of empty and selfish materialistic progress hitherto sought by great nations. Nationalism meant the true awakening of the "Indian proletariate" to a collective vision of such cultural greatness as would enable India to contribute to the progress of human civilization:

> . . . we advocate the struggle for Swaraj, first, because Liberty is in itself a necessity of national life and therefore worth striving for for its own sake; secondly, because Liberty is the first indispensable condition of national development intellectual, moral, industrial, political . . . thirdly, because in the next great stage of human progress it is not a material but a spiritual, moral and physical advance that has to be made and for this a free Asia and in Asia a free India must take the lead, and Liberty is therefore worth striving for for the world's sake. India must have Swaraj in order to live; she must have Swaraj in order to live well and happily; she must have Swaraj in order to live for the world . . . as a free people for the spiritual and intellectual benefit of the human race (*BCL,* 1).

While egoistical nationalism is morally destructive, true nationalism, as is evident from this lucid exposition of the larger responsibilities of freedom, is neither callously selfish nor inherently antagonistic: on the contrary, such nationalism as marks the intellectual and cultural growth of a nation or a group of people is directly and positively related to the welfare of the entire community of mankind. Swaraj (self-rule) is an inner discipline, both at the individual level and the national level, and it cannot be realized without cleansing one's perceptions. "The true source of human liberty, human equality, human brotherhood," maintains Aurobindo, "is in the freedom of man's inner spirit" (*BCL,* 1). Liberty, equality and fraternity are teleological and epistemological concepts, and their place in a social structure is dependent on man's ability to perceive the truth and validity of each of these concepts. In the structure of political reality envisaged by Aurobindo, the recognition of the constitutional or legal rights of liberty and equality is not enough, for the ideal of liberty is not fully achieved without equality and fraternity, and more importantly without fraternity. Teleologically, of course, the term "Swaraj" simultaneously refers to nationalism and liberty.

Aurobindo considered "political Vedantism" to be the basis of the struggle and the strategy: this "political Vedantism," the wisdom of the Vedas, especially of the *Gita,* not only spiritualized the struggle but it gave him a much more profound and authentic political vision of liberty. The kind of swaraj that Aurobindo envisioned was not merely a political liberty; and the kind of struggle that Aurobindo championed was again not merely a political struggle, but a total and endless struggle for true freedom. Generally speaking, most revolutionary struggles are viewed as reactionary insurgences or temporary volcanic eruptions. But for Aurobindo the revolution meant more than a series of sporadic boycotts, fiery protests, and violent demonstrations: it included a large-scale program of political, economic, educational, social and spiritual reconstruction. As a *dharma yudha,* it must be continuously fought simultaneously on several planes.

If man's salvation, as Aurobindo maintains, lies in "a religious or spiritual idealization of a possible future humanity," (*BCL*, 15) then man must continue to evolve, by means of the synthetic discipline of yoga, to the apex of what William Blake would call human form divine.

— *K. D. Verma*

Aurobindo's early political radicalism was motivated by his uncompromising commitment to the ideals of liberty, equality and fraternity and by his optimistic faith in the ability of man to become perfect. Indeed, his early political writings are an important contribution to Indian literature and thought; but, significantly, as he progressed in his self-realization the direct political anxiety and commitment were transformed into a much more universal and comprehensive concern for true human freedom and a new world-order. The later Aurobindo, that is, the Aurobindo of the period following his dramatic exit from the active political scene, has given us not only one of the most subtle analyses of man and society but also a unique vision of human progress and perfection.

One no doubt gathers from *The Human Cycle* and *The Ideal of Human Unity* that Aurobindo is a close student of history, but his philosophic vision is not centered in history, that is, in the past. Aurobindo is essentially an evolutionist, and the evolutionary theory (which, in spite of some of its obvious similarities with scientific and materialistic theories of evolution, is not Darwinian) implies that man, forms of society and other structures must continue evolving. Since man is capable of realizing his true divinity, the form and level of perfection arrived at by man at one particular stage is not absolute. Nor is any one pattern or form of society perfect for that matter. In fact, in *The Human Cycle,* Aurobindo, using [Karl] Lamprecht's phraseology, conceives five physical stages in the evolutionary development of the human race: symbolic, typal, conventional, individualistic and subjective. The movement from the symbolic to the subjective marks a process of divinization of man. However, Aurobindo does not believe that there is a straightforward path which the process of development follows. Nor does he think that man should be overly dependent upon either the past or the future, although for the purpose of immediate development the past and the future most coalesce in the present, such that the point of history absorbed in the present becomes only another point in history. As Aurobindo states:

> It is true that the world's movement is not in a straight line; there are cycles, there are spirals; but still it circles, not round the same point always, but round an ever advancing centre, and therefore it returns exactly upon its old path and never goes really backward. As for standing still, it is an impossibility, a delusion, a fiction (*BCL*).

Since man is capable of becoming perfect, the highest point that he is capable of achieving is the highest point of his divinization only at one particular stage. Similarly, society is not merely a stagnant and abstract political structure; its progress depends upon the degree and nature of perfection achieved by its individual members. In a true sense, an ideal society is a community of mankind, a brotherhood which apprehends the individuality of man. But since none of the political structures so far invented by man allows any one of the two possibilities to be realized in the most ideal sense, a political solution alone is no satisfactory solution of the problem of human existence, individual or collective.

While the movement from the symbolic level to the typal and conventional levels may ordinarily be regarded as symptomatic of man's fall from unity, in Aurobindo it characterizes an essential phase of continuous human advancement without the slightest implication of any pessimistic regression. At these levels, the law is established and enforced strictly according to the dictates of rational and empirical reason. Also, at these levels, the age of scientific advancement has made some of its major claims: our priorities here are confined strictly to the external world of material existence. What is valued more is the shastra (that is, established rules and the logical order), and not Atman, the spirit. The Urizenic government of the shastra (coded morality) is primarily created to safeguard man in his fallen condition of disorder and disunity. No political structure based upon this constrictive reason, however ideal—and be this democracy, communism or socialism—will apprehend the true individuality of man. Under these various political and social systems whatever liberty and equality are granted are given according to the law, the code, and are not consistent with man's fundamental right to be absolutely free and with his evolutionary nature. For example, in a democracy, political liberty or political equality is what is conferred upon an individual at the pleasure of the philistine majority. Therefore, even a democracy is limited in scope and nature; and at best it gives only political freedom. In any political structure, including democracy, absolute freedom breeds egoism; and whether it is individual egoism or national egoism, it will destroy the ideal conception of liberty. As Aurobindo says:

> Freedom, equality, brotherhood are three godheads of the soul; they cannot be really achieved through the external machinery of society or by man so long as he lives only in the individual and the communal ego. When the ego claims liberty, it arrives at competitive individualism. When it asserts equality, it arrives first at strife, then at an attempt to ignore the variations of Nature, and, as the sole way of doing that successfully, it constructs an artificial and machine-made society. A society that pursues liberty as its ideal is unable to achieve equality; a society that aims at equality will be obliged to sacrifice liberty. For the ego to speak of fraternity is for it to speak of something contrary to its nature . . . (*BCL*, 15, 546).

Indeed, Aurobindo's concern with the nature and scope

of liberty is teleological. And he advocates absolute freedom:

> . . . man cannot build greatly whether in art or life, unless he can conceive an idea and form of perfection and, conceiving, believe in his power to achieve it out of however rebellious and unductile a stuff of nature. Deprive him of his faith in his power for perfection and you slay or maim his greatest creative or self-creative faculty (*BCL,* 15).

If man's salvation, as Aurobindo maintains, lies in "a religious or spiritual idealization of a possible future humanity" (*BCL,* 15), then man must continue to evolve, by means of the synthetic discipline of yoga, to the apex of what Blake would call human form divine. Aurobindo, like Blake, is not advocating licentious freedom with which man nourishes his titanic ambitions (asura pravriti) into egoism or hubris, be it Apollonian or Dionysian. But while most political systems are inherently fearful of such egoism, their repressive and sanctimonious laws, paradoxically enough, become a fertile soil for the nefarious perversion of ego as well as for the loss of individuality. After all, political slavery is only one kind of slavery, but the most frightful form of slavery is mental slavery—which is what the passivity of the spirit really means. It hardly needs to be stressed that any amount or degree of political freedom given to an individual whose mind has been conditioned by the language of laws and rights is not only useless but also harmful. That is why Nietzsche, while advocating intellectual anarchism, proposes the annihilation of the stubborn structure of the obsolete system. If absolute freedom implies anarchism, political or intellectual, this kind of freedom, in a sense, is a negation of that divinity which entitles man to seek his freedom and which when realized is in itself true liberty. In the anarchist thought on the whole, we are talking about only partial or one kind of liberty, and not of total and comprehensive freedom. The conception of superman, according to Aurobindo, suggests the fully integrated and realized whole, a heroic consciousness. Therefore, neither the Apollonian man nor the Dionysian man is a whole man; and for the same reason, neither the ethical being nor the aesthetic being is a whole being. Such wholeness and realization as Aurobindo proposes are not anarchial in character, for his conception is based neither on the rejection of history nor on a self-centered alienation from the body of the universe. Rebellion against the yoke of law and its manifest tyranny and general "putrid waste" is a significant step forward towards a program of social reform; but a total rejection of history and of law as generally emphasized by a variety of anarchist thought suggests not only an unnatural discontinuity and disruption in the process of evolution but also a refusal on the part of the systems to recognize man's achievement.

Here we may emphasize a significant difference between a political revolutionary and a karm yogi. In Aurobindo's *Savitri,* King Ashwapathy is a karma yogi, but Savitri is both a karm yogi and a radical. Savitri's heroic consciousness enables her to wage a successful war against the god of death and of a deterministic order of lower nature and to restore to the earth the paradisial vision of life and happiness. The heroic man, according to Aurobindo, is charged by his own consciousness to create paradisial condition on earth: such heroic souls as Plato's men of gold are agents of the Brahman engaged in the redemptive act of regenerating this virile universe. The individual belongs to mankind on the whole, and his true *dharma* is *manav dharma:* the principle and the process which bring him together with his fellowman are summed up by the Sanskrit word *lokasangrah*—which means "the holding together of the race in its cyclic evolution" (*BCL,* 15). Man creates his new higher self by participating in the good of others. He enjoys absolute freedom and equality, but with one imperative—that is, brotherhood. The vision of one consciousness, and of reintegration and wholeness, places Aurobindo in an enviable company of such great figures as Plato, Dante and Shelley. But, most significantly, he shows the practical way of making this earth a paradise.

In Aurobindo's vision of human freedom and unity, as a nation's freedom and progress basically depend upon the nature of individual consciousness, so does the progressive movement towards one-world community depend upon the quality of the "aggregates" of people. Aurobindo maintains that people should be able to organize themselves into nations or "aggregates" in accordance with the principles of free association and unity. As free and equal people are brought together by a communal consciousness, so are free and equal nations brought together not as a conglomeration of "imperial aggregates" that are motivated merely by political and commercial designs of expansion and aggression but as "an ideal aggregate of humanity" that aspire to a vision of spiritualized community. True nationalism will lead, not to antagonism, domination and confrontation, but to understanding, collaboration and cosmopolitanism—and, hence, to creating a better and happier community of mankind. Since Aurobindo's vision of universal humanity is based upon the spiritualization of man, all forms of national and imperial egoism, including such racial egoisms as Europeanism, Asiaticism and Americanism, must be overcome. Man will cooperate with his fellow man, not because he is a *homo economicus* or because he is a political or social animal, but because he has the inner urge to establish a spiritual brotherhood. It is abundantly clear that Aurobindo does not accept the Hobbesian thesis of a basic distrust in man's capacity to become free and of an avowed supremacy of the state. Nor does he regard Utilitarianism, Marxism, and Socialism as sufficiently powerful structures for resolving the problem of human suffering. Most social and political theories of contractual obligation and entitlement are fundamentally inconsistent with the larger vision of human freedom, since all conceptions of contracts and rights are essentially founded on inveterate prejudices, especially fear, distrust and hatred, that in turn provide a basis of human subjugation and exploitation, economic, political and social, and hence, of an invidious social anarchy.

Evidently, Aurobindo's conception of human freedom is bold and radical. Aurobindo tells us that man is the author of social and historical destiny, and that all forms of social, political and religious structures are hindrances to his freedom and creativity. The idealist position, beginning with Plato, recognizes the divinity of state: in *The Repub-*

lic, the soul's liberation from the cycle of existence is ultimately dependent upon social good. Kant, of course, considers individual freedom more important than an unequivocal commitment to the state, although Hegel's belief in the divinity of a nation, which incidentally constitutes the basis of his social ethics, is directly the opposite of the Kantian position. But amongst the English thinkers it is, indeed, Coleridge who emphasizes the divinity of state categorically affirming organicism—not the Spencerian organicism but Romantic organicism—according to which man, nature and society evolve together discovering "the transcendental and divine force of life " [see Ernest Barker, *Political Thought in England, 1848 to 1914,* 2d ed.]. In his conception of the evolution of a new society, Aurobindo, as might be construed, takes a daring leap beyond social morality, rational ethicism, nationalism and statism. In a message delivered on August 15, 1947, Aurobindo says that "Nationalism will then have fulfilled itself; an international spirit and outlook must grow up . . . " (*BCL,* 26). While Burke will still insist upon the need of nationalism as the basis of a European common community or a confederation of nations, Aurobindo envisions the formation of an international brotherhood, a new community of man, where voluntary fusion of cultures takes place, where nationalism and its militancy will have outlived its usefulness, and where narrow national boundaries will eventually become redundant. It is somewhat paradoxical that nationalism or the state as a moral entity carries only a limited value in Aurobindo's vision of the progress of human society: the divinity that was once attributed to the state is now vested in mankind as a whole, the divine humanity. We must note this significant difference between the early Aurobindo—the fiery, youthful and uncompromising radical—and the Aurobindo of the Pondicherry period—the serene, the contemplative and philosophical mind. In his vision of human freedom, Aurobindo may be called a spiritual anarchist, but he is not a nihilist. He is a reconstructionist and a progressive thinker who believes that all precipitous impediments to human progress, whatever their generic form, must be overcome, and that modern socio-economic and scientific progress and spiritual growth are not incompatible with each other. Undoubtedly, behind this vision of affirmation is the hope and belief in the unhindered progress of man to the highest possible point in the human divine image: obviously, on a projected scale of continuous evolution, state, religion and other institutional structures, because of their regressive conservatism and inertia, do not remain compatible with man's progress. That is why Aurobindo stresses the need for newer forms of social and political structures that will eliminate the problem of historical obsolescence and help in the fusion of tradition and modernity.

Since evil belongs to history and the order of nature—and, hence, to the world of Maya, it appears at periodic stages in the evolutionary process of life. In a sense, evil, as Aurobindo would have us believe, is a fortuitous agent of beneficial change, and hence of good, since without evil the redemptive appearance of good will not take place. But moral evil and physical evil are real and not illusory; and Aurobindo deals with the problem of evil with full force in his philosophy of evolution. At the individual level, however, it is egoism that breeds evil. In *The Life Divine,*

Aurobindo's view is clearly monistic: evil and falsehood, according to Aurobindo, result from ignorance (avidya Maya), but there is no absolute evil as there is no absolute ignorance. Evil and falsehood, as Aurobindo observes, "are a by-product of the world movement: the sombre flowers of falsehood and evil have their root in the black soil of the Inconscient" (*BCL,* 18). The world or life as a whole is not evil; nor is man inherently evil. This conception of evil, which essentially comes from Aurobindo's view of human nature, has unmistakably shaped his vision of liberty, equality and brotherhood and of man's salvation—and, hence, of a progressive journey from political freedom to spiritual liberation. One of the most significant elements in Aurobindo's social and political vision is that there is no room for repressive measures and laws based on a system of rewards and punishments. Nor is there any room for negative and punitive religious morality governed by the fear of evil and the self-dissipating bigotry of damnation. Religion that rejects life in preference to the overzealous pursuit of other-worldliness and esoteric goals and rituals, that creates an unwarranted division between life and spirit, and that promotes pain, suffering, fear and retribution is an exercise in spreading ignorance and as such does not hold any hope for man. In *The Human Cycle,* Aurobindo addresses "the historic insufficiency of religion as a guide and control of human society" (*BCL,* 15): while sharply distinguishing between institutional religion and the spiritual religion of humanity, Aurobindo maintains that neither religion nor industrialization should be permitted to thwart human progress and world unity. Hence, it is clear that the way to resolving the problem of evil is not rational and orthodox religion but spirituality. As Aurobindo explains "the idea and spirit of the intellectual religion of humanity":

> Man must be sacred to man regardless of all distinctions of race, creed, colour, nationality, status, political and social advancement. The body of man is to be respected, made immune from violence and outrage, fortified by science against disease and preventable death. The life of man is to be held sacred, preserved, strengthened, ennobled, uplifted. The heart of man is to be held sacred also . . . The mind of man is to be released from all bonds . . . (*BCL,* 15).

Such a cohesive and profound vision of unity and progress of the human race is not utopian: on the contrary, it directly focusses on the intricate muddle of human existence in a comprehensive context and on the ultimate goal of life. Aurobindo's political vision is compatible with his spiritual vision of man's total freedom: political freedom provides the fertile soil needed to pursue the path of spiritual awakening and to discover that intelligent principle which binds men together as a unity and which enables them to evolve into one divine humanity. But politics, education and religion are merely tools for facilitating man's evolutionary progress and his search for Reality and Truth; they are not ends in themselves. An ideal political structure that guarantees such individual freedom as enables man to pursue his search for truth voluntarily, unreservedly and fearlessly is an expression of the most genuine self-assertion and the will of awakened minds, but not of the philistines and the bourgeois. In this sense, Aurobindo is a fearless and astute champion of individual freedom and human dignity: in the struggle between collectivity and the individual, the state, as Aurobindo asserts with Kant, has absolutely no right to force an individual to surrender his freedom, whatever the pretext. The individual has the unquestionable right to strive to achieve the highest form of wisdom, since it is only by awakening divinity in oneself that one would know how to apprehend divinity in another. The recognition of this underlying principle of unity implies that an individual and clusters of people can hope to coexist in the world today in a fraternal trust of love and hope without being trampled, devoured and vitiated. This vision of human freedom and progress and of realizing an ideal condition of human existence on this earth is not a devaluation of the political vision but a fulfillment of the larger and more comprehensive vision of human freedom.

FURTHER READING

Biography

Iyengar, K. R. Srinivasa. *Sri Aurobindo: A Biography and a History.* 4th ed. Pondicherry, India: Sri Aurobindo International Centre of Education, 1985, 812 p.
> The standard biography of Aurobindo, first published in 1945.

Mitra, Sisirkumar. *Sri Aurobindo.* New Delhi: Indian Book Co., 1972, 215 p.
> A biography which relies heavily on Aurobindo's own words to reveal the facts of his life.

Criticism

Basu, Arabinda, ed. *Sri Aurobindo: A Garland of Tributes.* Pondicherry-2, India: Sri Aurobindo Research Academy, 1973, 252 p.
> A collection of twenty-four articles–all of which deal with spiritual thought and many of which address specific components of Aurobindo's philosophy–written to commemorate the centenary of Aurobindo's birth.

Betty, L. Stafford. "Aurobindo's Concept of Lila and the Problem of Evil." *International Philosophical Quarterly* XVI, No. 3 (September 1976): 315-29.
> Seeks a solution to the incompatibility between God and evil in Aurobindo's concept of the "Ananda [Brahman] of becoming," also referred to by Aurobindo as the Lila.

Bruteau, Beatrice. *Worthy Is the World: The Hindu Philosophy of Sri Aurobindo.* Rutherford, N. J.: Fairleigh Dickinson University Press, 1971, 288 p.
> Examines Aurobindo's life and a variety of concepts he discussed in his works, including Brahman, Maya, Mayavada, spiritual evolution, and the Supermind. Bruteau's work also contains a bibliography of Aurobindo's writings that provides original publication information.

Chaudhuri, Haridas. *Sri Aurobindo: The Prophet of Life Divine.* 2d ed. Pondicherry, India: Sri Aurobindo Ashram, 1960, 224 p.
> An introduction to the main principles of Aurobindo's

philosophy and yoga designed for both Eastern and Western readers.

———."The Supermind in Sri Aurobindo's Philosophy." *International Philosophical Quarterly* XII, No. 2 (June 1972): 181-92.
> An interpretation and evaluation of Aurobindo's concept of the Supermind as he developed it in *The Life Divine.*

Chubb, Jehangir N. "Sri Aurobindo as the Fulfillment of Hinduism." *International Philosophical Quarterly* XII, No. 2 (June 1972): 234-42.
> States that Aurobindo's integral spiritual philosophy embodies the guiding principle of Hinduism, unity and wholeness, because it reconciles opposing systems of Hinduism and resolves the apparent contradiction between Matter and the Spirit.

Gandhi, Kishor. *Social Philosophy of Sri Aurobindo and the New Age.* Pondicherry, India: Sri Aurobindo Society, 1965, 274 p.
> A three-part study of Aurobindo's spiritual and philosophical ideas. The first part provides an introduction to Aurobindo's social philosophy; the second part examines the role of yoga in Aurobindo's evolutionary theory; and the third part, in which Gandhi predicts the imminent advent of the new spiritual age, calls upon readers to follow Aurobindo's teachings.

Gokak, Padma Sri Vinayak Krishna. *Sri Aurobindo: Seer and Poet.* New Delhi: Abhinav Publications, 1973, 185 p.
> An examination of the form and substance of Aurobindo's poetry that is largely devoted to *Savitri.*

Koller, John M. "Types of Society: The Social Thought of Sri Aurobindo." *International Philosophical Quarterly* XII, No. 2 (June 1972): 220-33.
> Summarizes the five stages of historical development presented in *The Human Cycle.*

McDermott, Robert A., ed. *Six Pillars: Introductions to the Major Works of Sri Aurobindo.* Chambersburg, Penn.: Wilson Books, 1974, 198 p.
> Essays by six different writers on six of Aurobindo's most important works: *Savitri, The Foundations of Indian Culture, Essays on the Gita, On Yoga I, The Human Cycle,* and *The Life Divine.*

Mishra, D. S. *Poetry and Philosophy in Sri Aurobindo's "Savitri."* New Delhi: Harman Publishing House, 1989, 131 p.
> An in-depth study of numerous aspects of *Savitri,* including its symbolism, sources, leitmotifs, diction, style, and imagery.

Misra, Ram Shankar. *The Integral Advaitism of Sri Aurobindo.* Banaras Hindu University Darśana Series, edited by T. R. V. Murti, no. 2. Banaras, India: Banaras Hindu University, 1957, 410 p.
> An analysis of Aurobindo's integral view of reality in which Misra argues that Aurobindo's most important contribution to philosophy was his concept of "the logic of the infinite," a higher power of reason that he relied upon to reveal the compatibility of seemingly contradictory ideas, especially absolutism and evolutionism.

Nandakumar, Prema. *A Study of "Savitri."* Pondicherry, India: Sri Aurobindo Ashram, 1962, 568 p.

A comprehensive analysis of _Savitri_ in which Nandakumar approaches the poem from three different angles: _Savitri_ on its own, _Savitri_ in relation to Aurobindo's life and other works, and _Savitri_ in relation to the world's greatest poetic epics, especially Dante's _Divine Comedy._

Narasimhaiah, C. D. "Aurobindo: Inaugurator of Modern Indian Criticism, _The Future Poetry._" _The Literary Criterion_ XV, No. 2 (1980): 12-31.

Highly praises Aurobindo as a literary critic on the basis of _The Future Poetry._

Purani, A. B. _Sri Aurobindo's "Life Divine": Lectures Delivered in the U.S.A._ Pondicherry, India: Sri Aurobindo Ashram, 1966, 282 p.

Fourteen essays on Aurobindo's philosophy and yoga derived from lectures Purani delivered during his American tour in 1962.

Reddy, V. Madhusudan. _Sri Aurobindo's Philosophy of Evolution._ Hyderabad-7, India: Institute of Human Study, 1966, 385 p.

A study of Aurobindo's theory of evolution in which Reddy presents him as the "Supramental Avatar."

Satprem. _Sri Aurobindo or The Adventure of Consciousness._ Translated by Luc Venet. New York: Institute for Evolutionary Research, 1984, 384 p.

Follows the changing levels of consciousness Aurobindo experienced through his system of yoga and urges readers to embrace his teachings so that they might discover the meaning of life and learn how to improve the world.

Sethna, K. D. _The Vision and Work of Sri Aurobindo._ Pondicherry-2, India: Mother India, 1968, 217 p.

Explores the role of Aurobindo's philosophy of integral yoga in the practical application of his spiritual ideas.

————. _Sri Aurobindo–The Poet._ Pondicherry, India: Sri Aurobindo International Centre of Education, 1970, 472 p.

Focuses on the strictly artistic qualities of Aurobindo's poetry, as opposed to his thematic and philosophical concerns.

Singh, Karan. _Prophet of Indian Nationalism: A Study of the Political Thought of Sri Aurobindo Ghosh, 1893-1910._ London: George Allen & Unwin, 1963, 163 p.

Examines the historical and biographical circumstances that shaped Aurobindo's political theory and technique and that caused him to retire from active politics.

Varma, Vishwanath Prasad. _The Political Philosophy of Sri Aurobindo._ New York: Asia Publishing House, 1960, 471 p.

An explication and evaluation of Aurobindo's political ideas in which Varma employs a comparative methodology.

Carl Becker

1873-1945

(Full name Carl Lotus Becker) American historian and philosopher.

INTRODUCTION

Becker is known primarily for his ideas concerning the writing of history. He is included prominently among the New or Progressive historians, whose cause he helped further by arguing against the idea of a discernible, objective history. "The past," Becker wrote, "is a kind of screen upon which each generation projects its vision of the future." He maintained that each cultural period possesses a set of examined and unexamined generalizations that are an indication of the greatest aspirations and hopes as well as the weaknesses and fears of the age; this he dubbed the "climate of opinion." Since he considered this climate inescapable, he encouraged historians to recognize their cultural and temporal biases and limitations.

Biographical Information

Becker was born on a farm near Waterloo, Iowa. He was recognized as an exceptional student in high school and in 1892 entered Cornell College, a Methodist school at Mt. Vernon, Iowa. After one year he transferred to the University of Wisconsin, where he studied under Frederick Jackson Turner, historian of the American frontier, and where he earned a bachelor's degree and in 1907 a doctorate. During this time he spent one year at Columbia University on a graduate fellowship. Between 1899 and 1901 Becker taught at several colleges and universities, including the University of Kansas and the University of Minnesota. In 1917 he was invited to Cornell University in Ithaca, New York, where he taught until his retirement in 1941. Becker died in 1945.

Major Works

The first of Becker's works to enjoy wide acclaim was *The Declaration of Independence: A Study in the History of Political Ideas* (1922). Becker's next great success and his best known book was *The Heavenly City of the Eighteenth-Century Philosophers* (1932), in which he put forth the thesis that the *philosophes* of the Englightenment, with their mix of secular rationalism and religious faith, more closely resembled thinkers of the Middle Ages than they did those of modern times. In 1935 he published *Everyman His Own Historian,* his presidential address to the American Historical Association. This work, which amounts to a manifesto in favor of the relativist historical view, is considered seminal to this school of modern historians. Relativist historians reject the idea of an objective, wholly knowable past. Becker was also the author of a well-regarded and very successful high school textbook, *Modern History: The Rise of a Democratic, Scientific, and Industrialized Civilization* (1931).

Critical Reception

Becker is generally praised for his abilities as a prose stylist, while often arousing controversy over his approach to writing about history. Some critics contend that his interpretations often came at the expense of ignoring all the contributing factors to historical events. As Max Lerner has noted: "He leaves out of account the whole play of economic and political forces out of which ideas grow. He is so concerned with giving us the climate of opinion that he forgets about the soil of opinion." According to Richard Nelson, Becker's irony and keen sense of style led some fellow historians to dismisss him as "a clever stylist without serious content." Although he has been accused of inconsistency and of failing to reach a real definition of history, he has also been praised for continuing to grapple with the difficulties of his position of historical relativism throughout his life. As James L. Penick, Jr. has written, Becker avoided "the sop of self-deception; even when most resigned, he never ceased to speculate."

PRINCIPAL WORKS

The History of Political Parties in the Province of New York, 1760-1776 (history) 1909
The Beginnings of the American People (history) 1915
The Eve of the Revolution: A Chronicle of the Breach with England (history) 1918
The United States: An Experiment in Democracy (history) 1920; also published as *Our Great Experiment in Democracy: A History of the United States*
The Declaration of Independence: A Study in the History of Political Ideas (history) 1922
Modern History: The Rise of a Democratic, Scientific, and Industrialized Civilization (textbook) 1931
The Heavenly City of the Eighteenth-Century Philosophers (history) 1932
Everyman His Own Historian (history) 1935
Progress and Power (history) 1936
The Story of Civilization (history) 1938
Modern Democracy (history) 1941
New Liberties for Old (history) 1941
Cornell University: Founders and the Founding (history) 1943
How New Will the Better World Be? (history) 1944
Freedom and Responsibility in the American Way of Life (history) 1945

CRITICISM

Max Lerner   (essay date 1939)

SOURCE: "Carl Becker: Historian of the Heavenly City," in *Ideas Are Weapons,* The Viking Press, 1939, pp. 235-43.

[*In the following essay, Lerner praises* The Heavenly City of the Eighteenth-Century Philosophers *but states that Becker's central argument in this work is weakened by his decision to ignore the economic and social conditions of the period.*]

[*The Heavenly City of the Eighteenth-Century Philosophers*] is a book so simple, so light, so clear, that one feels didactic in pointing out that it is really a scholarly study in the history of ideas, and a bit ponderous in assessing it (as it must none the less be assessed) a classic. It is cast unmistakably in an enduring mold. Into it a lavish scholarship has been poured, but with a hand so deft as to conceal everything except the significant. Those who seek the tortuous in thought and the magisterial in style will do well to avoid this book. They will be cruelly duped by its effortless clarity and will conclude that what is so smooth in the reading cannot have been weighty in the writing. For Mr. Becker has attained here that final simplicity by which the idea and the word are but phases of each other and move to a seemingly inevitable rhythm. In this book he reveals more fully even than in his previous writing a maturity and a wisdom that flow lightly from his experience but for which the rest of us must sweat. He has achieved that most difficult of all victories for the scholar—a knowledge of what to omit as well as what to include. Here is no mere emptying of notebooks but the distillation of a mind.

And since it is a distinctive mind, we may be grateful that through it the author has written his world, his generation, himself into this account of the ideas of the eighteenth-century Philosophers. Reading the book one is impressed with the truth of Maitland's remark that the best history is written backward. The author starts with the preoccupations of his contemporary world; in the light of them he has turned the ideas of the Philosophers about in his mind until they have revealed exactly those facets that hold the greatest interest for our own generation. This brilliant, heroic and slightly ridiculous band of Philosophers—Rousseau, Diderot, Hume, Herder, Gibbon, Voltaire, and the others—who have undoubtedly changed the shape of our thinking and therefore of our history, has been written about copiously and in a variety of ways. Be certain that wherever you have seen some glowing and plentifully capitalized account of the Age of Reason, or the Enlightenment, or the great Humanists, or the growth of Freedom of Thought, or the Increase of Tolerance, or the history of Progress or of Liberty, you have come unavoidably upon their names. And they have been invested therefore with that somewhat unctuous association that comes from always being found on the side of the angels, especially when those angels are nineteenth century and Whig. There was indeed a period in which a slight tang

of scandal still attached to them, the scandal of being atheist and revolutionary and mostly French; but that was before the full effects of the libertarian influence of Auguste Comte and John Stuart Mill had been completely felt. And there has been a period more recently in which we have stipulated a dissent from their theories of natural law before we could quite accept the rest of their doctrine. But in the main our valuations of the Philosophers—have incorporated and expressed nineteenth-century intellectual experience, and have been curiously unreceptive to the tremendous change that has come upon our thought since the World War.

Mr. Becker is far from being an intellectual Whig, although I have read somewhere else his expression of his political faith as a liberal. This is, I take it, one aspect of the importance of his book on such a subject, aside from the sheer delight of it. The detached, remote, slightly acidulous manner in which he inspects the Philosophers and their entire baggage of ideas—their execration of priests and kings, their attempts to become harmonious with Nature, their theories of progress, their eager glances at Posterity—flows not only from the author's shrewd insight into the springs of human conduct; it is the product of our entire present generation, one which has not only learned to question existing institutions but, whether out of philosophy or out of despair, has become skeptical of the very questioning itself. The author's approach to the eighteenth century is not therefore that of the attack direct. He achieves a more telling effect by raillery than he could have achieved by heavy artillery. Instead of blowing the age to smithereens he stands it gaily on its head. His central thesis, expressed also in his title, is a paradox: the Philosophers, who thought that they were using reason to destroy faith, were really constructing a faith of their own, and found finally that they had reared for themselves a new and gleaming City of God.

It is all a little like the two sides of a man's face that are supposed to reveal contrasting aspects of his character: look at one side and it is reason you see, look at the other and it is faith. This dual visage in the system of the Philosophers the author presents with a skill that is at once our admiration and our despair, so subtly has he worked out the logical—or perhaps we should say the psychological—development of their thought.

They are shown as a group of men intent on setting things right; to do this they find it necessary first to remove the obstacles that have stood in the path of human development; they find those obstacles to be chiefly superstition, ignorance, and authority. Accordingly they deliver a frontal attack on Church and State, on priests and kings; they expose to the merciless scrutiny of their intellect institutions which God and man had taken centuries to build up; they find their most effective weapon in the cold power of reason. But in the process the very coldness of their reasoning becomes an enthusiasm with them, their hatred of priests and kings a demonology, their love of humanity and their projects for its reform a religion. They find in the concept of Nature a satisfying mechanistic explanation of life, which makes unnecessary the old theological explanations; they embrace it eagerly, try to come into harmony with it—only to find that they have replaced an old God with a new one. When they try to follow their naturalistic theories to a logical conclusion, they come squarely up against atheism and immorality; trapped, they have recourse to distinctions, and proceed to separate what is essential and noble in Nature from what is base and degraded. They set out on a magnificent research of history, in quest of the something that is essential to human nature, so that on the basis of it they may reconstruct human society. They find in the past certain intervals of lucidity, especially the *quatre âges heureux,* but in the main they find only a wasteland dominated by "the triumph of barbarism and religion," for "in a very real sense they never pass the frontiers of the eighteenth century"; they have only projected their own reformist scale of values into the past, and their "new history" has been "philosophy teaching by example." Having thus ransacked the past for Hell, they turn to the future for Heaven. They find that to fight the Christian religion they must construct a picture of human life as dramatic as the Christian story, for "it is true of ideas as of men that they cannot fight unless they occupy the same ground." Accordingly they evolve the concept of social progress, to which they dedicate themselves; and in the process they discover "the uses of posterity," for the martyrdom suffered in the struggle for refashioning society is rewarded by immortal life in the memory of succeeding generations.

This picture of the eighteenth-century mind as the author draws it before our eyes in vivid strokes is, some will fear, perhaps too brilliant to be fair and too part to be sound. The direct question of its authenticity as an analysis would require a far more immediate acquaintance with eighteenth-century writings and the personalities of the Philosophers than most of us would be able to muster. But more important perhaps than the authenticity of the analysis are its implications. And it is these implications that cut completely across the boundaries of academic specialties, and make this as fitting a volume for the Storrs series of lectures at the Yale Law School as any of the earlier volumes which have confronted directly the problems of legal philosophy. Of the rich mass of these broader issues that the book raises, for law as for other social studies, we may select three groups that seem most significant.

The first has to do with the method that the book presents for the study of the history of ideas. That method is not the traditional one. It has been as we all know, too true in the past that the history of ideas has been written genealogically, in the manner of Deuteronomy. It has been for the most part an exercise in chain-making: link has been added to link in tracing the "development" of some doctrine or theory, each great thinker being represented as having just so much sounder a view than his predecessors and passing on his accumulated advantage to his successors. And the entire development is generally traced within some group of ideas in economics or law or politics. What Mr. Becker succeeds amazingly in doing is to capture the mind and mood of a whole age. He compasses this partly by his skillful use of the concept of the "climate of opinion," partly by his subtle understanding of the anatomy of an entire system of thought and the interplay within it of emotional and intellectual elements. He develops the

idea of the climate of opinion by contrasting the things that seem obvious and the things that seem strange to an ordinary man in the day of Aquinas and Dante, in the day of Voltaire and Hume, and in the day of Einstein and H. G. Wells. The enormous advantage of such an approach in the history of ideas is that it enables the author to deal with things unseen as well as things seen, to discuss for an age those preconceptions which may be more important than its expressed beliefs. Mr. Becker charts not only the things the Philosophers thought and talked about and the ideas they were obsessed with, but also the things they did not talk about, either because they deemed them too obviously true to need discussion or statement, or because they had not yet glimpsed them as separate entities.

Related to this is the chance that such a method offers of studying the entire *Zusammenhang* of an age—the relation of its literature and its law and its religion and its philosophy and its politics. Not in the hands of every writer will this relation be presented as artfully as in this book; there is of course the danger that where the learning is carried less lightly it will lead to the introduction of a horrendous apparatus. But it is a valuable technique, and in the history of legal ideas especially its organic quality will be useful. For legal history is notoriously tortuous, paradoxical, erratic; to try to trace it outside of its integral relations with the rest of the climate of opinion will make it merely whimsical; and to sever the crabbed logic of its development from the rich emotional growths of its time will make it what it was never intended to be—merely a blackletter study.

Mr. Becker's own handling of this method in his book is so effective that it may seem carping to quarrel with it on some scores. But I feel that he would have given his picture of the eighteenth-century-mind a greater air of conviction for us if he had introduced into it some of the roughnesses and loose ends that we see around us in our own age, and had been less insistent in making out of it a paradox within a unity. Such an oversimplification is probably the price we should have under any circumstances to pay for the precision of the analysis. But it is emphasized by several further facts. The system of the Philosophers is, quite rightly, constructed from materials scattered over the century, from Bayle and Fontenelle to Robespierre and Madame Roland. These people span several generations; they were addressing their thought and their words to widely variant situations; and unless these situations are expressly taken into account, the unity of the thought is attained at the cost of some dislocation. Moreover, they were only intellectuals, and the sum of what intellectuals think does not—as some of us have learned to our sorrow—add up to the mind of an age. When you talk of "the age," says Emerson in his essay on "The Times," you mean your own platoon of people. The Philosophers undoubtedly labored under a similar delusion. They were indeed the men of letters, the men of learning, to some extent the "men of sense" of the age. But they represented only themselves, and perhaps also the middle class whose road to power they were smoothing. They did not represent either the classes whom they were seeking to depose or the masses whose plight they could scarcely estimate. And it is here that we reach the gravest criticism that may be made of Mr. Becker's method. He leaves out of account the whole play of economic and political forces out of which ideas grow. He is so concerned with giving us the climate of opinion that he forgets about the soil of opinion.

The second group of issues that the book raises has to do with the theory of natural law. Nature is of course the principal protagonist in the intellectual drama built around the Philosophers: it is in a sense both the hero and the villain of the piece. The Philosophers, says Mr. Becker, were through all those years putting God on trial: "the affair was nothing less than the intellectual *cause célèbre* of the age." In the same way we may say that throughout the book Mr. Becker is putting Nature on trial, and in this he is reflecting the contemporary suspicion of natural law and the whole concept of the natural. From this angle the experience of the Philosophers with "the laws of Nature and of Nature's God" is of real relevance to our own situation. The appeal to natural law by the eighteenth century was an appeal from the positive law of Church and State, which was held to be impeding cultural progress. In the American experience of the last half-century the appeal has also been from the positive law, although it has been made not in the name of cultural progress but in the name of stability, and it has been used by the Supreme Court against the more democratic legislative programs of the states and of Congress.

But Mr. Becker points out an extremely significant progression in the intellectual odyssey of the Philosophers. The natural law that they finally arrived at did not belong to the Nature with which they started. That Nature they took from seventeenth-century science, and its spirit was matter-of-fact and non-ethical, much like our present science. But when they followed up its implications it led either to a complete acceptance of what is, which would have defeated their reformism, or to the denial of morality which would endanger the whole social fabric, including any new one they might construct. They retreated, therefore, to a natural law that was founded upon human nature in its best aspects—something essential to man which they hoped to discover by their historical research. This was, Mr. Becker points out, far from the complete atomism involved in Locke's denial of innate ideas; it was rather the rediscovery of medieval "realism"; and "the innate ideas which Locke had so politely dismissed by way of the hall door had to be surreptitiously brought back again through the kitchen window."

Does this have some relevance to our own situation? The social effects of the application of natural law concepts by the Supreme Court have produced such a revulsion among our jurists and other intellectuals that they have fled to an atomism which would deny that there is anything at all "essential to man" by which positive law must be judged. Can we too rediscover something approaching medieval realism and believe in it? Thus far in our quest for man in general we have had to rely on a psychology no further advanced in this respect than that of Locke and Hartley, and a real natural law must first of all await an adequate psychology. From another direction, the possibilities of the Marxist historical analysis for jurisprudence have not yet

been incorporated into our thinking, but one may read between Mr. Becker's lines the warning that is implied in the fact that in a somewhat similar historical research the eighteenth-century Philosophers never once stirred from the closed-chamber of their own minds.

The book raises finally a group of issues that is tied up with the problem of social change in the eighteenth century and in our own time. The period of the Philosophers was a period remarkably like the present. It was an age of intense disorganization, of changing intellectual horizons, of preparation for a social upheaval. The book, being a study of the minds most active in this context, is therefore most significant as a study in the dynamics of intellectual revolution. And our attempt to appraise the revolutionary thought of an age so like our own, to examine its consistency, to see to what extent these thinkers were gigantic minds and to what extent they were merely deluding themselves with dreams of a heavenly city, is in reality so much more than history: it is an attempt to orient ourselves with regard to our own intellectual instability.

Mr. Becker's scalpel lays bare two principal weaknesses in the anatomy of the Philosophers' thought: the religious, almost messianic, character of their rationalism, and the fact that, although they affected to despise morality and religion, when they found that their fight might lead through the assault on these to the destruction of the social fabric, they pulled their punches. With the first of these the author deals the more effectively. In a very significant section in the last chapter he points to the religious ritualism of the French Revolution as the logical sequel to the heavenly city of the Philosophers, and then turning to the communist movement and the Russian Revolution he shows the fundamentally religious character of Marxist agitation and thought and the religious symbolism involved for example in the apotheosis of Lenin. This is of course entirely true, but it may be pointed out that Mr. Becker's analogy between the Philosophers and the communists is too closely drawn. The enthusiasm of the first was largely *Schwärmerei;* it was the sort of day-dreaming and project-making that intellectuals have always been prone to, and on which incidentally the best of our intellectual achievement has been built. But the religious fervor of the communists has a mass base; it springs, as all of us recognize, from the passion arising out of a desperate economic situation.

It is for that reason that Mr. Becker's second indictment of the Philosophers—that in the crucial moment they pulled their punches—is even less applicable to the present revolutionary movements. The Philosophers were interested enough in an intellectual revolution, so long as it did not involve a real break with the social heritage. But they stopped short of social revolution because they were themselves an integral part of the world that would thus be destroyed. Hume locked his *Dialogues* up in a desk because he shrank from the moral depravity that might flow from his strictly logical theses; Franklin abandoned his youthful atheism because, as Mr. Becker remarks, it was "not very useful to him, a respectable printer and politician living in Philadelphia." For was he not Poor Richard, the best bourgeois of them all, dependent for his career to swim on the rapidly mounting tide of middle-class power? Here again a closer inquiry into the economic soil of eighteenth-century ideas would have clarified and corrected some of the implications of the book. For while communist Russia is keeping a good part of the capitalist social heritage—our entire technological system, our money mechanism, our militarist and international tactics—its driving revolutionary strength is far from the compromises of Hume and Franklin and Diderot. And that strength is, we may guess, derived from an entire economic class, and not from philosophers.

George H. Sabine   (essay date 1945)

SOURCE: An Introduction to *Freedom and Responsibility in the American Way of Life* by Carl Lotus Becker. Alfred A. Knopf, 1945, pp. vii–xlii.

[*In his introduction to* Freedom and Responsibility in the American Way of Life, *Sabine notes that Becker consistently questioned democracy, aiming for an "idealism without illusions and a realism without cynicism."*]

Carl Becker united in a remarkable way the quality of incisive and critical intelligence with humanity of feeling and action. He had experienced in his own thought all the negative influences of modern scientific and philosophical criticism. He had subjected the intellectual framework of the democracy which he loved to the keenest and coolest analysis and had allowed his wit and irony to play over its illusions and its failures. He had found in the framework of the democratic tradition much that was traditional only, much that reflected the religion and the science and the morals of a day gone by, which could no longer endure the light of a maturer science and a new economy. With rare intellectual sensitivity he responded to all the currents of a changing social situation and a changing social thought, in an age when change was rapid and often destructive and when thought was likely to be directionless and conflicting. Yet his life and his thought were at all times molded by the humane ideals of the democratic tradition which he criticized and which his criticism placed among the lasting moral achievements of mankind. He lived and taught and wrote always in the faith that the great and valuable achievements of civilization are the products of intelligence and integrity and good will, to be won only in a society that gives free play to intelligence and good will against the pressure of mass emotion and conformity enforced by authority. For him the test of a civilized society was the degree in which law and public authority rest on free discussion and voluntary consent, and he valued democracy because, with all its faults, it still offered the widest scope for intelligence and good will.

In respect to these fundamental ideas there was little change or development in Becker's writing after he reached maturity. He extended his range and clarified his understanding and polished his style, but the direction of his interests and his native reactions changed little. Already in the brilliant essay on **"Kansas"** which he contributed in 1910 to the *Essays* dedicated to his teacher Turner, he described the frontier as a type of mind to be found in all places, the spirit of adventure and idealism; and "the

Kansas spirit is the American spirit double distilled." Already it is the type of mind—closely related to what he later called the climate of opinion—that interested him: its individualism, idealism, moralism, intolerance, its determination to unite liberty with equality, and its faith in government—all to be understood as the spiritual reactions natural to a mode of living and a set of environing circumstances. His analysis and interpretation of the philosophy of natural rights in *The Declaration of Independence* is essentially identical with that which he gave ten years later in *The Heavenly City:* a new form of worship which "deified nature and denatured God." Again, what fascinated Becker was the transformation of old ideas under the impact of a new situation. His castigation of the triviality and sentimentality and provincialism of American politics, written at the end of the first World War, in *The United States, an Experiment in Democracy,* could easily be paralleled in the essays which he wrote near the close of his life under the spur of the second World War. All of Becker's work moves within a somewhat limited circle of ideas which recur again and again. Always he is interested in these as ideas, and in human beings as the creators and the bearers of ideas. For him the typical and the profoundly interesting and valuable part of human behavior lay in its ideal dimension—in the exercise of intelligence, in the endless effort to conform action to ideal principles, even in the creation of utopias and illusions which are the continual accompaniments of the process. In this he was perhaps as much a philosopher as a historian.

Becker's attitude toward life and his interest in history were profoundly intellectual. He was actuated by the same lively curiosity that fascinated him as a student of Turner when he daily enjoyed "the inestimable privilege of watching an original and penetrating intelligence at work, playing freely with facts and ideas, handling with discrimination the problems of history, problems which so often turned out to be the problems of life itself." There was in Becker himself this combination of seriousness and play which he here attributes to his teacher, the sense that he was dealing with life itself and yet with the detachment that gives to all purely intellectual activity something of the nature of play. Certainly he conveyed the impression of an original and penetrating intelligence always at work. One wonders whether there was not a trace of autobiography in the fine characterization of Thomas Jefferson which he wrote in his chapter on "The Literary Qualities of the Declaration." Jefferson's peculiar felicity of expression, he says, reflects "a nature exquisitely sensitive, and a mind finely tempered," and these are qualities which Becker shared. Perhaps Becker, like Jefferson and most persons of strongly intellectual bent, lacked "a profoundly emotional apprehension of experience. One might say that Jefferson felt with the mind, as some people think with the heart. He had enthusiasm, but it was enthusiasm engendered by an irrepressible intellectual curiosity." But if there was indeed this lack of emotional apprehension, Becker like Jefferson was saved by "his clear, alert intelligence, his insatiable curiosity, his rarely failing candor, his loyalty to ideas, his humane sympathies."

Becker's historical curiosity apparently carried with it little desire to impart what he found; left to himself he would have been satisfied with the pleasures of the chase. As he said of Turner, "He was caught by his friends and set the task of writing." Fortunately, the charm of his style made him an object of pursuit by friends and publishers. Nearly everything that he published was occasioned by some demand other than the inward urge of the author. His first full-length book, *The Beginnings of the American People* (1915), was part of a publisher's series on American history, as was also *The Eve of the Revolution* (1918). *The United States, an Experiment in Democracy* (1920), was written at the suggestion of Guy Stanton Ford, and *The Declaration of Independence* (1922) at the suggestion of Carl Van Doren, though the manner of its publication was not as originally designed. *The Heavenly City* (1932), which will probably be remembered as Becker's maturest work, was written for the Storrs Lectureship at Yale. It was the first of several series of lectures in his later life: *Progress and Power* (1936) at Stanford; *Modern Democracy* (1940) at the University of Virginia; *Cornell University, Founders and the Founding* (1943) at Cornell; and the present volume at the University of Michigan. His connection with the editorial board of the *Yale Review* accounted for most of his later essays, which were collected, as in *New Liberties for Old* (1941), or expanded, as in *How New Will the Better World Be?* (1944), into book form. Throughout his life personal or professional connections accounted for studies like the essays on **"Kansas"** and on **"Frederick Jackson Turner,"** or his Presidential Address before the American Historical Association. The labor of writing was for Becker severe, and the facility of his finished work concealed much careful polishing by which that facility was finally achieved. Some kind of special inducement was necessary to make him write at all.

Improperly understood, however, this fact might be quite misleading, for all of Becker's writing grew very naturally out of his own thought and experience. He hated to be bored, and it is quite certain that even the most persuasive publisher could not have made him write on a subject that did not interest him. His published work probably contained less perfunctory writing and reviewing than that of most professional historians. Even at the very beginning, when he was an undergraduate at Wisconsin, it would probably be false to say that Turner influenced him to study the American frontier and its part in creating the American spirit. That interest was native to Becker, and Turner elicited it from Becker's own experience. In *The United States* Becker tells how he had watched the process of Americanizing the German immigrant in the Iowa farming community in which he was born.

> One of my earliest recollections was the appearance in our neighborhood, it must have been about 1878, of a strange family that came to live in the house across the road. To me, a "typical" American boy, they seemed outlandish folk whom one would naturally avoid as suspicious and yet wish to see from some safe point of vantage as a curiosity. The reason for this primitive attitude of mind toward the new-comers was that they were Germans who could barely speak a word or two of English; and a "typical" little American boy, who was himself descended from English, Irish, Dutch, and German ancestors,

and whose great-grandfather could not speak English, had never in his life seen nor heard of a German, and now learned for the first time this marvelous thing—namely, that there were people in the world who could not talk as he did, but spoke a kind of gibberish which it was alleged they understood, although no one else did.

From this early experience of the making of Americans, and the consciousness of himself as a "typical" American already made by only one or two generations of the same process, it was but a short step to Turner's generalization about the frontier and the westward movement. It was hardly a longer step from this to the idea of the "American spirit double distilled" which had grown up with the frontier and had been intensified as the wave of settlement moved across the country. Here Becker found the roots of his own belief in democracy and individualism. Given his native interest in ideas and the intellectual side of human behavior, it is easy to see why he turned from the crude activity of the frontier to the more sophisticated expression of American ideas in the Revolution and its most characteristic document. It is easy to see also how his historical work should have culminated in the least provincial expression of the revolutionary philosophy in the French eighteenth century. Here, in the faith of the Enlightenment in intelligence and humanity, in its cool ardor for the rights of man, he found his true intellectual affinity.

Becker had no illusions about his methods. He knew that his descriptions ran in terms of abstractions and generalizations which could not even seek to exhaust the embarrassing richness and diversity of human nature.

— *George L. Sabine*

In this process Becker had formed also his conception of the aim of historical writing. As the body of human ideas and ideals moves, as it moves forward in space with the frontier or as it moves forward in time, it encounters new conditions and a new environment by which it is continually transformed and to which it must continually adapt itself. If these new conditions are massive and of long duration, as was the case with the American frontier or as was the case when the ideas of medieval Christianity encountered the commercial and the industrial expansion of modern times, they gradually give to the intellectual and the moral ideas of a nation or an age a characteristic pattern. The age comes to have what an artist would call a style, a manner in which its elements cohere and which expresses its typical reaction to the formative forces that have shaped it. The idea in its general outline was far from new, though there is no reason to doubt that Becker formulated it for himself. He might have encountered it in Montesquieu, and possibly the "American spirit" was an echo of the spirit of the laws. Nor was the idea in any way

Becker's exclusive property, as a host of books on the modern "mind" or the medieval "mind" bears witness. In any case he made it his own and followed it, long before he seized upon Whitehead's apt phrase, "a climate of opinion," to describe it. The idea defined for him the significant purpose of historical writing. That purpose is the imaginative recapture of a past climate of opinion and its accurate description, first in terms of the powerful forces, social or economic, by which the age is shaped and second in terms of the intellectual and moral and ideal adjustments in which the mind of the age consists. Finally, the human individuals come into the picture as the creators and adapters of ideas, often it must be confessed as somewhat recalcitrant illustrations of the ideas for which they stand. For Becker had no illusions about his methods. He knew that his descriptions ran in terms of abstractions and generalizations which could not even seek to exhaust the embarrassing richness and diversity of human nature.

This conception of what history should attempt went far toward determining the nature of Becker's books, both in their weakness and in their strength. It explains his occasional adventures into what might be called fictional history—"a rather free paraphrase of what some imagined spectator or participant might have thought or said"—in *The Eve of the Revolution* and in the Brookings Lecture on "The Spirit of '76," which seemed perhaps not quite serious scholarship to his more academic colleagues. For obviously, as Becker himself said, this kind of imaginative recovery cannot be verified by the checking of references. Perhaps there is no strict way in which it can be verified, for verifying a work of art is nonsense. But this kind of writing gave free scope to Becker's sympathetic and imaginative insight into the past and his remarkable sensitivity to currents of thought and feeling. The attempt to recover and describe a past climate of opinion explains very accurately also Becker's conception of style in historical writing. He disliked the notion that writing of any kind, and history in particular, should be dressed up or decorated for the sake of an extraneous effect. Historians who are read for their style, like Bancroft or Gibbon or Macaulay, were for him to that extent bad stylists and bad historians. For if one wishes to describe, the medium should not obscure the thing described. "Only one thing concerns the writer and that is to find an arrangement of words that will fully and exactly convey the thought or feeling which he wishes to convey."

Finally, Becker's conception of what the historian should attempt determined even the structure of his works. His books were invariably short but they were long enough. An appreciative reader will not wish that even a single chapter had been added to *The Heavenly City*. The very perfection with which he did the thing he did was itself a limitation. No one knew this better than Becker, and he accepted the limitation freely as the price to be paid for what he chose to do. The description of the social forces that work within a period and their interplay must run in terms of general notions and abstract concepts that are timeless. The individual and the march of events are unique. The historian must make the two go together, and in the end a solution is impossible, or at least it is a make-shift that can be maintained only in a book of limited extent.

> Well, the generalization spreads out in space, but how to get the wretched thing to move forward in time! The generalization, being timeless, will not move forward; and so the harassed historian, compelled to get on with the story, must return in some fashion to the individual, the concrete event, the "thin red line of heroes." Employing these two methods, the humane historian will do his best to prevent them from beating each other to death within the covers of his book. But the strain is great. And while any courageous historian may endure it for one volume, or even for two, few there are who can survive ten. [**"Frederick Jackson Turner,"** in *Everyman His Own Historian*]

Becker's view of history was intellectually sophisticated in a high degree. It implied in the historian an extreme form of self-consciousness. The thing that the historian describes is a state of mind induced by a set of conditions which has itself supervened upon an older state of mind. Wherever the historian starts, his material will include the old and the new. It will be a cunning reworking of a tradition already old but now remade in the light of a new human need existent in the historical present. But this is in fact only half the complication, for the historian is himself caught in his own climate of opinion, from which he can no more escape than could the characters in his description. His own writing is part of the process by which his own climate of opinion rewrites the past for a present purpose of which he is the instrument. History seen from Becker's point of view is like a hall of mirrors in which image reflects image until the reality imaged vanishes in a never ending series of images. No point is absolutely fixed, not even that of the historian's own present from which he views the shifting points in his past. Hence it is incumbent on him, more than upon most men, to be aware of his own climate of opinion, since this is the reflecting medium in which he must see whatever past he chooses to describe. This obligation Becker accepted to the full. He sought to re-create imaginatively the social-mind that had first produced the democratic tradition, but to do this he had to be aware of the modern mind which in him was attempting to reconstruct this image of a bygone mind. He was a philosopher whose absolute reference points had been caught in a historian's relativism. And his own predicament, as he conceived it, was essentially that which characterizes the modern mind, produced by the dual factors of science and of history itself. In the opening chapter of *The Heavenly City* he describes the modern mind and the impact upon it of science and history, and contrasts it with the medieval mind, formed by theology and logic.

Becker was always an omnivorous reader, and his reading bridged the past and the present. In his character as a historian he pursued the sources only so far as suited his purposes. The sources that he used he used meticulously and with a fine historical understanding, but he never acknowledged an obligation to have read all that there was to read. He read more than most historians, however, of the literature of his own day and also of the natural science. This he did in part to gratify an unfailing intellectual curiosity, but in part also to fulfill the historian's obligation to understand himself no less than to understand the past that he describes. Since Becker believed that science is the most powerful formative force in the making of the modern mind, it was inevitable that, within the limits set by his own technical competence, he should have sought continually to understand science, more particularly in its larger significance for present-day ways of thinking, as he sought to understand the repercussion of Newton on the eighteenth century. About the details of scientific discovery, its fact and its gadgets, he cared little. It was the constructive effect of science upon the modern climate of opinion that fascinated him.

One consequence of his thinking on this subject can be briefly described as a complete and unqualified acceptance of scientific naturalism. The world as science reveals it is one that cares nothing for man or for his purposes or his values, a world in which he has emerged by a slow and painful process of evolution from brutality and barbarism and in which ultimately man and all his works are doomed to extinction and nothingness.

> Sooner or later there emerges for him [man] the most devastating of all facts, namely, that in an indifferent universe which alone endures, he alone aspires, endeavors to attain, and attains only to be defeated in the end. [***Modern Democracy***]

Becker's own attitude toward this scientific negation of a religious view of nature seems to have been one of simple acceptance. There is nothing to suggest that it had ever cost him a severe moral struggle, as it had William James, and he was never interested in any philosophical attempt to reconstruct religious belief. Probably he regarded such attempts as out of accord with the temper of modern thought. That the change was intellectually devastating he perceived clearly enough. He could not have failed to see this, considering the care with which he showed that the philosophical framework upon which the eighteenth century had built its democratic ideals depended upon convictions rooted in the Christian Middle Ages and upon Newtonian physics only half understood. He had no doubt that a maturer understanding of science, both its methods and its results, had completely undermined the belief that there is any form of intelligence or purposefulness in the system of nature, except of course as properties of human beings. Becker's belief in the moral worth of the democratic ideal depended therefore upon the possibility of detaching a moral conviction from its traditional religious supports and of retaining it in an intellectual setting that gave it no religious support. Possibly he never fully appreciated the gravity of this problem, but for him it was inevitable and there is little doubt that he regarded it as inevitable for the modern mind.

> **It was not the tacit naturalism of modern science that affected Becker most intimately. As compared with the absoluteness which the eighteenth century imputed to Newton's laws of nature, it was rather the hypothetical and tentative nature of modern scientific generalization that impressed him.**
>
> **— *George L. Sabine***

It was not the tacit naturalism of modern science that affected Becker most intimately. As compared with the absoluteness which the eighteenth century imputed to Newton's laws of nature, it was rather the hypothetical and tentative nature of modern scientific generalization that impressed him. Eighteenth-century science, at least in its own understanding of itself, was still rationalist; its laws were imagined to be eternal truths or necessities of thought justified in the last resort by the impossibility of conceiving the opposite. Modern science is consciously empirical and experimental, and its laws are summations of fact justified only in so far as the event, when they are put to trial, confirms them. The importance of this difference Becker found already emphasized for him by American pragmatism, for he was a constant reader of philosophy as he was of science. In James and Dewey he found the idea that the end and purpose of science is practical control, and from his own reading of history he saw that its outcome is an incredible extension of human power over the forces of nature. This power is purchased precisely at the cost of not asking the old questions about their inner essence. The modern understanding is content with knowing the behavior of things, the manner in which they can be controlled and directed to any desired end—in short, the technique of using them.

> So long as we can make efficient use of things, we feel no irresistible need to understand them. No doubt it is for this reason chiefly that the modern mind can be so wonderfully at ease in a mysterious universe. [***The Heavenly City***].

Science, with its naturalism and pragmatism, was only one of the two great forces which Becker saw at work in the making of the modern mind. The other is history itself, and the effect of history is to reinforce the conclusion already suggested by science. For history reveals the world and human experience as an endless process, without beginning and without end. In it there is nothing permanent and nothing timeless; man and his world are forever in the making. In this Becker found the most powerful solvent for the eternal verities, in morals and in politics, as modern science has found a solvent for the axioms of Newtonian mechanics. For moral truths and ideals also are not axioms but hypotheses, pragmatic factors in the experimental business of living. Becker's book on the United States had as its subtitle "an experiment in democracy." The title had perhaps a deeper meaning for Becker than for most of his readers, for in the second edition he reversed title and sub-title, calling the book *Our Great Experiment in Democracy: a History of the United States*. In his preface he explained that he intended to "inject a small question mark" after the assumption that American institutions and American government had "some sacred and sacrosanct quality of the changeless Absolute." Democracy was and remains an experiment, new in its beginning and uncertain in its present, in the face of catastrophic changes in modern economy. "But for the matter of that, what is any human institution, what has it ever been, what can it ever be, but an experiment?" Endless change, endless revision, endless transformation, with at the most only temporary stopping places or relative achievements, were for Becker the lesson of modern history as of modern science. Everything is unstable, he once said, except the idea of instability.

History, however, concerned him far more intimately than science. In science he was, as he well knew, something less than an amateur. It interested him less on its own account than as a force to be reckoned with in assessing its direct effects upon the modern economy and its indirect effects, whether valid or specious, upon the modern mind. History was quite a different matter. It was Becker's life as well as his profession, and he never doubted that the study and writing of history is a work of utmost seriousness. For history as he conceived it is no incidental or extraneous aspect of human experience but something rooted in the nature of consciousness itself. It is therefore in essence not the creation of historians but something which every man must of necessity do for himself, however imperfectly and with whatever mixture of myth and illusion. The historian is important because, by a kind of social division of labor, he does according to a professional standard what the common man is always doing according to the rough and ready standards of his own limited experience. This was the meaning of the title that Becker chose for his Presidential Address before the Historical Association, **"Everyman His Own Historian."** It was a deeper penetration into philosophy than historians are accustomed to or perhaps would have found palatable had it not been enlightened by Becker's wit and his inimitable style. But from his point of view it was no casual excursion. It summed up not only what he had learned from a lifetime of historical study and writing but also his maturest reflections on the philosophy of the art, or, if one prefers, the science, that he practiced. Essentially there was little in it which might not have been gleaned from the asides and the remarks that he had thrown into his earlier writings, if a reader were penetrating enough to catch the implications of those remarks.

What makes human experience inescapably historical is the fact that the present consciousness of every man is but a point poised between the past and the future. Consciousness is a succession of fleeting presents that are always receding into the past and giving place to a new present. The present is as short as you wish, for it can be divided and subdivided until it vanishes in a point. But what is far more curious is the fact that the present may also be as long as you wish, for men speak of the present moment, the present day, the present year, or the present epoch. What holds the present together with the past is the

strange conscious power of memory, and accordingly Becker could say that history, reduced to its lowest terms, is simply "the memory of things said and done." Memory reaches back into the past and pulls together for every man "his little world of endeavor," by co-ordinating the things said and done yesterday with his present perceptions and with the things to be said and done tomorrow. "Without this historical knowledge, this memory of things said and done, his to-day would be aimless and his to-morrow without significance." But equally, the present is held to the future by the no less strange conscious powers of expectation or anticipation, of hope and fear, and memory is no aimless or motiveless recovery of the past but a recovery mainly for the sake of a purpose to be fulfilled in the future. To this present thus united by memory and purpose to the past and the future Becker gives the name, borrowed from William James, of the "specious present." The power of making this union is the peculiar quality of consciousness, and the capacity for having a specious present that can be deliberately and purposefully enlarged and diversified and enriched seemed to Becker to be the peculiar quality of man, the reason why he alone of all animals creates a civilization. Thus understood, history cannot be divorced from life itself.

The theory of mind that Becker thus turned to a better understanding of his own subject had philosophical connections of which he was well aware. It was the conception of consciousness which James had developed in his *Psychology* and which he enlarged in his brilliantly suggestive essays in the eighties and nineties. What it means is that mind—thought, perception, memory, and feeling—is inextricably interwoven with purpose and action; consciousness is "there," as James said, only for the sake of behavior. Its meaning and importance are measured by the degree and the manner in which it affects conduct, or, to put it bluntly, its validity is to be tested by its utility. Far more systematically, and with far more reference to the social questions that interested Becker, James's suggestions were elaborated in the long series of books and essays by which John Dewey made pragmatism the most widely discussed topic in American philosophy. How much of this literature Becker read it is impossible to say. Certainly he cared little for the niceties of philosophical system-making, but he could not fail to be continuously interested in what was so typically the American philosophy of his time. Long before his Presidential Address he had made pragmatism in its general idea his own. In an essay that he wrote in 1913, with an academic title not at all like Becker (**"Some Aspects of the Influence of Social Problems and Ideas upon the Study and Writing of History"**), he said flatly that ideas and beliefs and prepossessions originate in practical interests and "derive validity from the service they render in solving problems which grow out of community life." A bald assertion like this, however, can easily be misleading. It sounds as if Becker were adopting a philosophy when in fact he was merely putting a convenient label on a conclusion of his own. A philosophical doctrine of any kind interested him less on its own account than on account of what he took it to signify. The question he asked about it was not: Is it true? but, as Mill said of Coleridge: What does it mean?

The pragmatic theory that intelligence is interwoven with purpose and behavior attracted Becker because it agreed with his own conclusion about history. It explained why the philosophy and even the science of an age, and in general all its intellectual creations, take on a style that is colored by the social and economic problems of that age. It explained both why there is a climate of opinion for the historian to describe and also why his description must run in terms of interests and prepossessions provided by his own climate of opinion. Historical writing is marked by what Becker, and also some of his critics, called "relativism." By the critics the term was reproachfully intended, but Becker accepted it at its face value. Every historian must of necessity speak from his own specious present. And since consciousness selects its memories in the light of present purposes, the historian like everyone must draw from his documents and sources such facts as appear to him to have a present meaning. Facts are not passively mirrored just as they were, but are selected and interpreted to meet the needs of the present, which in turn depend upon the purposes of the future. Hence history must be continually rewritten and brought down to date, even though no new factual information has come to hand, for at least the present purpose of the historian and his society changes from generation to generation. The historian is played upon, as all men are, by the practical interests and the intellectual forces of the age in which he lives. The least he can do with historical facts is to select them and put them into a pattern which appears to him to be important in the light of what he believes will be done or ought to be done. The historian's imagination, when he attempts to re-create a past climate of opinion, is itself controlled and directed by the climate of opinion in which he works.

> I mean by relativism no more than that old views are always being displaced by new views, that the facts which historians include or omit, the interconnections between the facts given which they stress, depend in no small part upon the "approach" which seems to them a meaningful one, and that the approach which at any given time will seem significant to the historian depends in no small part upon the social situation in which he finds himself—in short, upon the preconceptions and value judgments, the *Weltanschauung,* of the age in which he lives.

The idea that the intellectual creations of an age reflect its temper and practical interests was continually used by Becker to classify and criticize historical writing. The philosophers of the Enlightenment had sought to reform and reconstruct society in the light of what they believed to be manifest principles of justice and right. For them history was "philosophy teaching by example," and they sought in it for the lessons that might enable them to restore to men their just and natural liberties and to avoid or destroy the tyrannical invasions of liberty. Conceiving that the just and right could be made clear by discovering what was natural or essential to men, they looked in history for a core of human nature that might be regarded as the same everywhere and always. After the French Revolution had overturned and destroyed legitimate governments and constitutional traditions over most of continental Europe the temper of the time changed and with it the temper of

the historians. In the nineteenth century it became the fashion to attribute the destructive upheaval of the Revolution to the illusion, as it then seemed, that men could remake society according to their own fancies. The post-revolutionary historians, especially in Germany, came to stress historical continuity and the growth or development of the nation. Man, as Becker said, was safely imprisoned in society. Nation was conceived to succeed nation according to divine plan, or according to the internal development of the Hegelian Idea—the choice of terms made little difference in Becker's estimation. Natural rights gave place to historic rights, and the interest in constitutional history reflected an almost universal need for rebuilding the political structure of every European government. Responding to the temper of an anti-revolutionary age, the temper of the belief in historical continuity was in general conservative and nationalist, as the temper of the belief in the rights of man had been radical and cosmopolitan. In either case Becker's point was that history was interpreted in the patterns to which the prevailing climate of opinion gave significance.

Objective history in Becker's judgment is really condemned by the fact that it runs the risk of being trivial history.

— George L. Sabine

The sharpest shafts of Becker's wit, however, were reserved for so-called objective history, or history for its own sake, against which his own historical writing was a conscious reaction. Such history seemed to him little better than a form of the literature of escape. It corresponded in his estimation to a decline of nationalism from the stage of idealism, in which it had been imagined as the march of God in the world, to a sordid scramble for power and markets and raw materials. The historian disclaimed moral responsibility because his subject no longer enlisted a moral sympathy that he could avow. But in Becker's opinion the disclaimer was largely self-deception, and the notion of history which it produced was illusory. The idea that facts could be made "to speak for themselves," that history could be made scientific by techniques for criticizing documents or by the mere suppression of the historian's more obvious social interests and judgments of value, was contrary to Becker's reading of both philosophy and history. It neglected the psychological relation of emotion to thought, and also the fact that every historian, even the most scientific, is bound to have some kind of preferences which must manifest themselves in his selection and explanation of facts. It is not, he said, the undiscriminated fact that speaks but the perceiving mind of the historian, prompting the fact according to his own judgment of what it ought to say. What passed current as historical detachment seemed to Becker superficial; he described it derisively as "a set of artificially induced and cultivated repressions such as would enable a careful historian to write

. . . an account of the Battle of Cold Harbor without revealing that his father was an ardent admirer of Grant." This kind of detachment is not hard to attain, but it does nothing to insure that the historian will have anything of significance to say.

Objective history in Becker's judgment is really condemned by the fact that it runs the risk of being trivial history. Of it he said in his Presidential Address:

> Hoping to find something without looking for it, expecting to obtain final answers to life's riddle by resolutely refusing to ask questions—it was surely the most romantic species of realism yet invented, the oddest attempt ever made to get something for nothing! ["**Everyman His Own Historian**," in *Everyman His Own Historian*]

Historical detachment as commonly understood Becker described, with more sharpness than his criticism usually displayed, as pernicious because it is "the best substitute for ideas yet invented." Without ideas, and among ideas Becker was convinced that some sort of preferences and moral preconceptions and values must be included, what the historian has to say becomes insignificant, a species of antiquarianism in which, to be sure, ideas of a kind are not avoided but are merely academic and unimportant for any live social interest. Like Charles Beard and other critics of objective history, Becker believed that real historical detachment is produced not by a vain effort to have no interests or prepossessions but by becoming as fully aware as possible of the prepossessions one has. Given intellectual integrity and a consuming intellectual curiosity about the matter to be explained, malicious invention and dishonest selection and distortion are ruled out, because an honest aspiration cannot safely be based upon fabrication. For the rest, as Becker believed, the historian must depend upon a conscious facing of present problems and an explicit awareness of future prospects and ideals. In his literary style this pursuit of self-consciousness was reflected in his habitual use of irony. The ironical description of a prepossession was a vivid way of making his reader realize that a prepossession was there and was affecting the conclusion. Similarly, consciousness of a historian's preconception and of the place of that preconception in the age in which he wrote seemed to Becker the true function of historical criticism. But the critic's own philosophy is an unavoidable factor in his estimate. In a report which he once wrote for the Historical Association on the reviewing of historical books, Becker said: "In seeking to avoid having a philosophy of history, the historian does not succeed in not having one; perhaps after all he succeeds only in having a bad one."

Becker's serious quarrel with objective history was not due to the badness of its philosophy, a fault that he would readily have forgiven if he had found it otherwise enlightening. His final objection was that the historian's avoidance of philosophical and practical commitments was dereliction from his high calling. History for its own sake can never be serious history, just as art for art's sake is the formula not of great art but of æstheticism. Great history is the product of social crisis, an unavoidable aspect of intelligent social action because it is one means by which an age becomes conscious of what it is doing, in the light of

what it has done and what it hopes to do. This belief on Becker's part, for which pragmatism gave him a philosophical formula, was indeed the lesson he had learned from Turner, that history is of a piece with life itself. The key to American history is not the continuity of its institutions with those of Europe from which they came but the transformation of those institutions by the problems set in a new environment, especially of course the frontier. With S. R. Gardiner's dictum that "comparison of the past with the present is altogether destructive of real historical knowledge" Becker contrasted the assertion of Turner that "a just public opinion and a statesmanlike treatment of present problems demand that they be seen in their historical relations, in order that history may hold the lamp for conservative reform." The belief that history may hold the lamp for reform, and must in any case hold the lamp for some kind of change, was an aspect of Becker's deep intellectual affinity with the eighteenth century. He hoped, and on occasion he believed, that the swing of American philosophy away from romanticism and Hegelianism had brought it closer to its point of origin, and the reaction against objective history had for him a similar meaning. This was the reason for his sympathetic reception of the "new history" of James Harvey Robinson and H. G. Wells. When he was in an optimistic mood, such as that perhaps produced in him by the Progressive campaign of 1912, he could hail this change as symbolizing "the arising of a new faith, born of science and democracy"—"the belief that society can, by taking thought, modify the conditions of life, and thereby indefinitely improve the happiness and welfare of all men."

This change in history and philosophy, therefore, which Becker sometimes called relativism and which he often identified with pragmatism, implied for him two things. On its negative side it was a renunciation of the arrogance and sterility, as it seemed to him, of the claim that historians are detached observers of the human scene, able like gods to see the past "as it really was." On its positive side it was a deep conviction of the importance of the historian's work as part of the continual change that is going on in society, and ideally as part of an intelligent effort to reconstruct society in the light of humane and democratic ends. The historical imagination is not a mirroring of the past but a reformulation of it in the interest of present needs and future purposes; once this is admitted, the historian may possibly make his art a factor in a planned and directed reconstruction of society for human welfare. In his Presidential Address Becker summarized his views of the historian's work in his own inimitable fashion as follows:

> It should be a relief to us to renounce omniscience, to recognize that every generation, our own included, will, must inevitably, understand the past and anticipate the future in the light of its own restricted experience, must inevitably play on the dead whatever tricks it finds necessary for its own peace of mind. The appropriate trick for any age is not a malicious invention designed to take anyone in, but an unconscious and necessary effort on the part of "society" to understand what it is doing in the light of what it

has done and what it hopes to do. ["Everyman
His Own Historian"]

It is not surprising that passages like this—and they could
be multiplied in large number—surprised or even shocked
some of Becker's colleagues. The description of history as
a trick played on the dead—a favorite witticism which he
borrowed from Voltaire—was certainly provocative language and intentionally so, for Becker was always "injecting small question marks" after the supposed certainties
of both scholarship and popular belief. Certainly also the
assertion that the trick was played for the sake of peace
of mind might suggest that the desire for a comfortable
conclusion carried more weight than an honest assessment
of the difficulties and the search for a sound and tenable
solution. All this need not be taken too seriously, since it
was not seriously meant. The interesting part of the quotation is rather the contrast between its first and its second
sentence. History, to be sure, is a trick, since it cannot reproduce the past as it was, or even as the dead experienced
it when they were alive. But there are, it appears, tricks
and tricks. Some are malicious and some are appropriate
parts of an effort to understand. But can the historian or
anyone else tell which is which? Malice indeed might be
detected as a moral defect in the historian, but even if he
were malicious, it would not follow that what he said was
untrue. And certainly Becker was not simpleminded
enough to think that non-malicious historians always tell
the truth or even say anything worth listening to. In any
case what the historian says is an invention, even if it is
a part of the necessary effort to understand. In short, if historical interpretation is an imaginative construction, how
are good inventions to be distinguished from bad?

This question, posed by Becker but not answered in the
Presidential Address, was indeed not one of his own making. It was deeply involved in the social philosophy of the
age whose insights and whose puzzlements he reflected so
accurately. With better fortune he might never have had
to face it, but neither Becker nor his age was fortunate.
The question may be stated thus: just what sort of thing
does the social mind invent when it is confronted with the
decay of its institutions and the breaking down of its settled habits and inherited convictions? Consciousness is
there, as James had said, for the sake of will and action,
and it must satisfy the need for peace of mind, for whole-
souled and unimpeded activity. But what does consciousness supply? Two contrary answers run through the social
philosophy of the later nineteenth and twentieth century.
The one conceives of mind as engaged in finding reasonable solutions to social problems, solutions that conserve
and realize the values inherent in the past and move into
the future along a line of moral progress. According to this
understanding of pragmatic philosophy, a new faith in science and democracy, as Becker had paraphrased it, is to
improve indefinitely the happiness and welfare of all men.
Such in general was the hope, so congenial to American
optimism, held out by the pragmatism of John Dewey.
Unfortunately, quite a different answer was possible and
was often given, for American pragmatism was only one
way of reading the general thesis that thought is inter-
meshed in feeling and will. Faced with the shipwreck of
its hopes, the mind can, and often does, seek its peace in

the making of myths and illusions, as Becker himself said,
"by creating ideal worlds of semblance, Utopias of other
time and place." Here it may shelter itself in a quietist's
dream, but equally its dream may be violent and world-
shaking, issuing out in revolutionary action prompted by
its own apocalyptic visions and the need to assert its own
fanatical will. Such was the view of the mind's inventive
power suggested by Schopenhauer and more radically affirmed by Nietzsche. In his later life Becker came to see
this way of subordinating intelligence to will as the philosophical foundation of fascism and the fruitful mother of
social barbarism. The contrast is indeed striking. According to the one view social values evolve in an orderly and
intelligent way along with the means of realizing them,
and the standards of intellectual validity and integrity
guarantee the soundness of both ends and means. About
the fundamental values inherent in human welfare there
is assumed to be a working agreement among all men of
good will. According to the other view social change is dis-
continuous and revolutionary. Its motive power is a Promethean will bent upon bringing down fire from heaven,
a will which has no measure except the strength of its own
desire, and its values are myths created to fortify its own
fanatical self-assertion.

As between these two views of the inventive power of the
mind and the manner of its relation to will and action,
thus set down in naked contrariety, Becker knew perfectly
which he must choose. His conscious affinity for the eighteenth century was due to an instinctive belief that social
intelligence, issuing in the twin faiths of science and democracy, is the root of all the solid achievements of civilization. Yet there was perhaps something a shade paradoxical in his preference for the cool ardors of the philosophers who preceded a revolution and his distrust of the violent emotions without which revolutions cannot be
made. Becker wrote about the eve of two revolutions, but
never about a revolution. It was the Heavenly City and not
the Terror that enlisted his sympathy. But how could he
be certain that human ingenuity extended to having one
without the other, or that Diderot represented the meaning of the rights of man better than Robespierre? So long
as it was merely a question of writing history, the historian
no doubt might begin and end where he pleased. In real
life revolutions run their course without regard for historians' preferences. And it was Becker's fate, and the fate of
his generation, to witness a revolution of which Nietzsche
was a better exponent than John Dewey.

Perhaps there was a paradox too behind Becker's confidence, and the confidence of American pragmatism, that
science and democracy remain twin faiths for the modern
mind. Becker's analysis of the philosophy behind the Declaration of Independence and the French Enlightenment
had demonstrated that the faith in reason and nature had
its roots far back in the ethical tradition of Christianity.
Temporarily it had construed science as a support for its
faith in reason and nature, but Becker was clear that such
a construction was not tenable in the light of the maturer
development of science itself. The belief in natural and inalienable human rights he had described as "a humane
and engaging faith," but it was still a faith. To ask whether
it was true or false, he had said, was "essentially a mean-

ingless question," because its premises to the modern mind had become simply irrelevant. Liberal democracy, as it turned out, like communism and fascism, was an ideology—that faintly disdainful word, suggesting both myth and aspiration, with which the period between the Wars liked to describe social ideals in the mass. Meanwhile science as it advanced separated itself more and more from pronouncements about the value of any human achievement or the intrinsic rightness of any course of action. It brought to men a wonderful access of power over things and indeed over other men, but its recipes for control could be used indifferently for any end whatever whether good or bad, and the farther it went, the less it seemed to have to say about any distinction between good and bad. The chasm between moral ideals and matter-of-fact knowledge became deeper and broader, for Becker knew well that ideologies consist in moral judgments and not in scientifically verifiable propositions. Science and democracy seemed to have no logical relationship to each other. Though the modern mind might be shaped by science, it was hard to see a reason why it must equally be turned toward democracy.

A paradox is not fatal to philosophy, but changing times can make a paradox acute. Without the crisis of the thirties Becker's paradox need never have troubled him. For democracy, despite its failures and the inevitable discrepancies between the ideal and the realization, had, for more than a century, seemed in a fair way to ultimate success. At all events, its fundamental values, both moral and political—civil liberty, constitutional representative government, freedom of thought and discussion, the worth of individual personality—had suffered no frontal attack and had met with no determined denial. Then came the frankly undemocratic philosophies of communism and fascism, the fall of free government, such as it had been, in Italy, the greater fall in Germany, and the success of dictatorship in Russia, all involved with a world-wide depression that shook democracy even in the free countries. Worse followed bad in the futility of democratic diplomacy, the outbreak of the Great War, the successes of Germany, the collapse of France, and the weakness and indecisiveness of American public opinion. With characteristic sensitiveness Becker's thought and feeling followed them all, reflecting the shifting temper of the time, first the pessimism about democracy in the thirties, later the revival and reassertion of a democratic faith in the forties. The last was largely a return to the mood of qualified confidence characteristic of him before the crisis.

It was not the case, of course, that Becker had ever been an unqualified or an uncritical admirer of democracy. From the end of the first World War, possibly from the Progressive campaign of 1912, he had believed that democracy, whatever its political success, was a failure in its traditional economic program. Freedom of speech and thought was one thing; freedom of business enterprise was another. He had closed his study of the American experiment with these words:

> The time for national complacency is past. The sentimentalism that turns away from facts to feed on platitudes, the provincialism which fears ideas and plays at politics in the spirit of the

gambler or the amateur, will no longer serve. The time has come when the people of the United States must bring all their intelligence and all their idealism to the consideration of the subtler realities of human relations, as they have formerly to the much simpler realities of material existence: this at least they must do if America is to be in the future what it has been in the past—a fruitful experiment in democracy. [*The United States, an Experiment in Democracy*]

From this conclusion, once formed, he never departed. In 1944 he said flatly that some form of economic collectivism is inevitable; the only choice is whether it shall be communism or fascism or some form of modernized liberal democracy. Domestic as well as international problems he regarded as basically economic, and he was quite aware that for a century the tendency, in Europe and in the United States and under all forms of government, had been toward an extension of the regulation of business by government. He looked for no reversal of that direction. An international political settlement, however excellent, he said, will not end the present era of war and aggression because political conflict and confusion in the modern world are the results of an underlying economic confusion and conflict. The fundamental problems of the day—the antagonism of social classes at home and the conflict of nations abroad—all presuppose, as Becker always believed, the political regulation of economic relationships. The question is whether the necessary regulation can take place by democratic means within a society that still preserves the democratic civil liberties.

The defects of democracy are one thing and its irrevocable breakdown is quite another, and it was the possibility of the latter that was posed by the events of the thirties. Theoretically this was quite within the gamut of Becker's philosophy. If endless change is the law of history, there is no reason why the ideals of democracy should be permanent. There is always the possibility that democracy is a passing phase, a way-station on the road of human progress, destined like so many others to be by-passed when it has served its turn. Whatever the value of its ultimate ideals, its successful working is dependent upon certain material conditions which democracy did not create and cannot restore if they are once irretrievably lost. This conclusion had been implicit in Becker's philosophy from the start, but the failure of the Weimar Republic made him more keenly aware of it. Surveying history in the large, he was constrained to admit that democracy is a new-comer in the moral world; for untold centuries men had lived mostly by instinct and with only a modicum of intelligence, and the rights of the individual are chiefly conspicuous by their absence. Where they have been recognized and established, this has been chiefly in small countries and for brief times in which a relatively high degree of economic security could be taken for granted. Social problems can be settled by discussion only if the diversity of interests is not too great and the problems are not too complex. The party system, inseparable from any democratic machinery of government, works best when the losing side in a controversy need not surrender what it regards as its vital interests, because the common interest is generally understood and generally conceded to overrule all special interests. In short, government by discussion works best, as Becker said in 1939, "when there is nothing of profound importance to discuss, and when there is plenty of time to discuss it. . . ." Possibly his pessimism about the possibilities of democracy touched bottom when he wrote in 1932, under the stress of the great depression:

> Choose as we will or can, the event is less likely to be decided by our choices than by the dumb pressure of common men and machines. The intellectual liberty we so highly prize is of little moment to the average man, since he rarely uses it, while the liberties he can make use of are just now of diminishing value to him. Of the many liberties which, in our free democratic society, the average man now enjoys (if that is the word), I will mention the one which concerns him most. He is free to take any job that offers, if any offers; if none offers, free to look for one that will pay a bare living wage, or less: if none is found, free to stand in line begging a crust from charity, or from the government that makes him a free man. What the average man wants, more than he wants this kind of liberty, is security; and when the pressure of adverse circumstances becomes adequate he will support those who can and will give it to him. ["Liberalism—a Way Station," *Everyman His Own Historian*.]

It makes a curious contrast to set side by side with this a quotation from Somerset Maugham with which Becker ended an article in 1944 and which he used also when he expanded two or three of his essays into the book entitled *How New Will the Better World Be?*

If a nation values anything more than freedom, it will lose its freedom; and the irony of it is that if it is comfort or money that it values more, it will lose that too.

But in the later thirties and early forties events crowded Becker close, as they did the whole democratic society for which he spoke. He came to see, as who of us did not, that the issue involved more than economic insecurity or the discrepancies between democratic ideals and their inadequate realization in democratic institutions and democratic societies. The devastation of Poland and the downfall of France posed the question whether the humane ideals inherent in the democratic tradition, or even the decencies of civilized society, could survive in a world in which dictatorship had chosen to rest its case on the arbitrament of naked force. The change in Becker's manner of writing about democracy appeared dramatically in the juxtaposition of two essays, one written in 1939 entitled **"When Democratic Virtues Disintegrate,"** the other written in 1940 entitled **"Some Generalities That Still Glitter,"** which were republished side by side in the book *New Liberties for Old*. In the first he was still thinking in terms of the contrast between democratic liberties in the civil and political spheres and what he had long regarded as the false or negative liberty of economic *laissez faire*. "Freedom of the individual in the economic realm has in fact come to mean economic subjection for the many and freedom only for the few." In the second he turned sharply upon "a certain insensitiveness to the moral implications of conduct which characterizes the modern temper" and which he traced to the anti-intellectualism or relativism or

activism of modern thought, issuing at its crudest in the doctrine of Thrasymachus in Plato's *Republic* that "Might makes right; justice is the interest of the stronger." Becker's pragmatism, like that of William James and John Dewey, had always taken for granted—whether it accounted for them or not—the moral certainty of good faith, integrity, humanity, and respect for human personality which, as he had argued in *The Heavenly City,* made democracy continuous with the tradition of Christian civilization. No more than James had he identified utility with a worship of "the bitch goddess success."

From this point on, the main theme of Becker's essays became an explicit and conscious reaffirmation of these moral values. The incredible sophistries of fascism in argument, its cynical disavowal of integrity and good faith in political dealings, and its conscious adoption of cruelty and terrorism in action revolted every fiber of Becker's moral being. What he feared even more—and in this again he reflected a common reaction of the day—was the faltering and flaccid reaction of public opinion in the democracies to these sophistries and barbarities, the willingness to sacrifice even moral ideals in order to avoid war, and the tendency to pitch public discussion at the intellectual and moral level of the "hard-boiled" and the "wise guy." With his native intellectual curiosity, Becker had been willing to explore the ideologies of communism and fascism, to set them beside the ideology of liberal democracy, even to assess at its highest the discrepancies between democratic ideals and practice. But after the fall of France the issue was no longer philosophy; it was war. If this involved some inconsistency with what he had elsewhere said about the relativity of moral values to social circumstances—and Becker was aware that such a charge might be made—he accepted the possibility cheerfully, for minor inconsistencies did not bother him. A difference of emphasis he was ready to admit, but nothing more, for he knew that he had always believed profoundly in the democratic virtues, even when he was engaged in injecting a small question mark after their absoluteness. In the bottom of his heart he had always believed, as he said in 1915 and as he was to say again in 1940, that the democratic values were "basic truths which no criticism can seriously impair," whatever their philosophical basis or lack of it.

> I should like to believe that the essays as a whole are essentially consistent in the premises they start from and the general conclusions they point to. If they are, it is because premises and conclusions derive in the last analysis from certain convictions I entertain—prejudices, if you prefer—prejudgments as to the essential values of life. I believe, without being able to prove but equally without being able to doubt, that the primary valuse of life, upon which in the long run all other values depend, are intelligence, integrity, and good will. Taken separately, any one of these may avail little. Good will, apart from intelligence and integrity, may be a futile or even a vicious thing. Intelligence leads to knowledge, and knowledge confers power, enabling men to transform instead of endlessly to repeat their activities. But knowledge and the power it confers may be used either to degrade or to ennoble the life of man. Only when guided and restrained by

good will and integrity can they be used effectively to achieve the good life. [*New Liberties for Old*]

The emphasis of Becker's last essays is upon the achievements of democracy rather than upon its shortcomings. Hitler and Stalin, he said, "have revealed to us the advantages of democratic institutions and the reality of the humane values that are traditionally associated with them," though he admitted ruefully that Hitler and Stalin were an exorbitant price to pay for a little wisdom. In these essays he tried to ward off in anticipation the reaction which he knew must come with the close of the War. He distrusted alike the moods of exaltation and of depression which arise out of the characteristic sentimentality of American political thought. The generous but ignorant and provincial enthusiasm of the war waged to make the world safe for democracy had ended in the disillusionments of the return to "normalcy," which was equally ignorant and provincial without being generous. Becker dreaded seeing a like reaction of weariness from the exaltation of the present war. War, as he knew, creates more problems than it solves, and of social and political problems he had often said that they are not solved but transformed. The new world, he urged, which was to follow the defeat of Germany, would not be very new, and only by long sustained and intelligent effort could it be made a little better. The sentiment of nationalism and the drive toward imperialism would emerge stronger rather than weaker, and indeed it was the nationalism of the occupied countries that in the end would defeat Germany, as it was the cohesiveness of British imperialism that for a year had stood alone against her after Dunkerque. The notion that some panacea could make politics cease to depend on force now seemed to Becker a fantastic and dangerous illusion which could end only in disillusionment. With all his power he urged the advantages of a piecemeal attack upon limited problems, in international as well as domestic politics, rather than a trust in grandiose schemes of reconstruction. The way of intelligence is neither realism nor idealism, but a clear-sighted grasp of realities patiently controlled in the interest of attainable ideals.

Yet in Becker's last essays there was a note of restrained exaltation, not new exactly, but clearer and more explicit, because after the moral and intellectual confusions of the interwar period it was possible again, as he said, to refer to the Declaration of Independence without apology. In some sense the rights of man had always been for Becker, if not moral absolutes in a cosmic sense, at least the relative absolutes of any truly civilized society. For him as for the Age of Reason intelligence overlapped both the achievements of knowledge and the achievements of moral progress, and in some way which he never professed to understand truth and goodness were inseparably joined. Faith in the ideals of democracy was of a piece with a larger faith, unfolding perhaps through the ages but certainly contained in the moral insight of the saints and sages, which was the clue to all that made life worth living.

> To have faith in the dignity and worth of the individual man as an end in himself, to believe that it is better to be governed by persuasion than by coercion, to believe that fraternal good will is

more worthy than a selfish and contentious spirit, to believe that in the long run all values are inseparable from the love of truth and the distinterested search for it, to believe that knowledge and the power it confers should be used to promote the welfare and happiness of all men rather than to serve the interests of those individuals and classes whom fortune and intelligence endow with temporary advantage—these are the values which are affirmed by the traditional democratic ideology. But they are older and more universal than democracy and do not depend upon it. They have a life of their own apart from any particular social system or type of civilization. They are the values which, since the time of Buddha and Confucius, Solomon and Zoroaster, Plato and Aristotle, Socrates and Jesus, men have commonly employed to measure the advance or the decline of civilization, the values they have celebrated in the saints and sages whom they have agreed to canonize. They are the values that readily lend themselves to rational justification, yet need no justification. [*New Liberties for Old*]

Becker fulfilled in his life and writing his own ideal of the high calling of the historian—to reflect on things said and done in the past of mankind, to see the past as it lives on into the present, to clarify and express for the present those generous impulses which it hopes to achieve in the future. By this work of self-consciousness the generous impulse is transformed into an abiding ideal, never to be realized perhaps in its entirety but giving meaning and direction to human effort. Like a finely sensitized plate Becker's mind caught and recorded the thought and the feeling of his time, sometimes its temporary and passing phases but more generally its deeper and more lasting aspirations. Sharing profoundly the American faith in liberty and equality which had been the guiding light of the Founding Fathers and of the American frontier, he had plumbed the forces, intellectual and social, which had disintegrated the framework of abstract ideas in which that faith had traditionally been enshrined. With complete intellectual honesty he faced the negations which science and criticism and an industrialized economy had brought upon the theology, or the thinly veiled theological philosophy, that the Fathers had imagined to be the immovable foundation of a democratic faith. From the negations he sought to disentangle the more lasting moral affirmations which, in the future as in the past, might still enlighten the struggle for a civilization devoted to democratic ends. In this task there could be for Becker no illusion of permanence. Of him must be said what he said of other historians:

> For my part I do not ask of any historian more than this, that he should have exerted in his generation a notable influence upon many scholars in many branches of humanistic study. ["**Frederick Jackson Turner**," in *Everyman His Own Historian*]

Such influence he did exert, but not upon scholars or study alone, for, as Becker believed, scholars and study are incidents in the adventure of living and in the greater society of which scholars are a part. For the democracy of his time Becker posed the greater problem—perhaps the final problem of emancipated intelligence: an idealism without illusions and a realism without cynicism.

Louis Gottschalk   (essay date 1946)

SOURCE: "Carl Becker, Skeptic or Humanist?," in *The Journal of Modern History*, Vol. XVIII, No. 2, June, 1946, pp. 160-62.

[*In the following essay, Gottschalk argues that* Freedom and Responsibility in the American Way of Life, *Becker's final work, shows his lifelong cynicism to be tempered with optimism.*]

In several ways [Carl Becker's final work, *Freedom and Responsibility in the American Way of Life*] resembles his *How New Will the Better World Be?* (1944). Indeed, as the author's preface indicates, parts of it are borrowed from the earlier work. The essential difference between them is in the focus of attention. Whereas *How New Will the Better World Be?* was concerned with international affairs and world organization, *Freedom and Responsibility in the American Way of Life* deals with United States problems and domestic reform.

In both books Becker, as becomes a historian, reveals a wholesome respect for the principle of continuity in history. Each goes far back into history to trace the roots of contemporary problems. Each seems to say: "The past is both dead and living. It is both an incubus and a source of nourishment. He who forgets the past and thinks that the world can start anew is as unrealistic as he who is blind to the future and thinks that everything must be as it always has been." It is in keeping with this attitude that *The Better World* should end with the well-known quotation from Edmund Burke on society as a partnership: "As the ends of such a partnership cannot be obtained in many generations, it becomes a partnership not only between those who are living, but between those who are living, those who are dead, and those who are to be born."

There is something quite intelligible and yet ironic in the fact that Becker, the outstanding student of Frederick Jackson Turner, who also believed in the principle of continuity in history but owed his reputation chiefly to a thesis that was intended to explain how old cultures are modified by frontier conditions, should owe his reputation so largely to his efforts to show that the new American ideas are inextricably interwoven with European cultures. Turner's writings were a reaction to a generation of historians whose great respect for our European roots was hardly distinguishable from a sense of inferiority. Becker reacted, in turn, to a generation that had leaned so far in the other direction as to run the risk of being provincial. In the modulations of historical interpretation between Herbert Baxter Adams, Turner's teacher, and Carl Becker, Turner's pupil, the so-called "problem of the third generation" propounded by the late Marcus Lee Hansen found an illustration that suggests its appropriateness in the intellectual as well as in the social sphere. Becker was no longer disturbed by conflict between his European and his American background; he wanted only to understand how much he was indebted to each. In both of his two last books, Becker treats the United States as a part of a world cultural pattern—having, to be sure, peculiarities of its own and also being more immediate to both author and reader but sharing a common intellectual tradition with western Europe and common contemporary problems with the rest of the world.

Strikingly similar though the two books are in frame of reference, the reviewer thinks he observes a fundamental difference in attitude between them. That observation, however, may be due only to considerations subjective to the reviewer rather than objective within the works reviewed. Certainly, if the reviewer had not known and been influenced by Becker nearly all of his mature life, he would not have looked for it. Becker, as any reader of his *Everyman His Own Historian* can easily discover and as Professor Sabine's masterful introductory essay to *Freedom and Responsibility* points out, believed that history is an interpretative art, limited though it may be by the obligation to do no violence to documentary evidence and our knowledge of human behavior. Becker would have agreed with the philosopher Schopenhauer's dictum: "Our own experience is the indispensable condition for understanding not only poetry but history as well." In his mild-mannered fashion, he had little patience with those who thought of history as an objective science or of a historical fact as having value and meaning outside a frame of reference. On the other hand, to cull from the infinite past those historical data that explained or made meaningful the "specious present" was a major, if not the best, purpose of the historian. For Becker was not the kind of historian that is "overwhelmed by everything that once existed." It would be quite in keeping with both the character and the philosophy of the man that at different "specious presents" he should find a differing pattern in the historical background, even when the separate "facts" were largely the same.

The "specious present" (1943-44) in which *The Better World* was prepared was one in which liberals nearly everywhere were taking a roseate view of the new order that was to emerge from the war. "The Atlantic Charter," "One world," "Revolution of our time" were phrases repeated over and over again till it was easy to feel persuaded that they were close to realization. Becker, who in certain moods used the word "liberal" as if it were an epithet and who frequently quoted the German definition of a professor as "a man who thinks otherwise," felt that people who mouthed these phrases unthinkingly had forgotten how difficult it is to change the past and that even great cataclysms like the Reformation or the French and Russian revolutions or the great wars had not effected changes that had not previously been prepared by a long historical development. "Hold on!" he says, in effect, in *The Better World*. "It is true that mankind learns from experience, but it learns exasperatingly little and exceedingly slowly. The new world will not be startingly better than the old."

But about a year later (1944-45), his outlook had changed. Victory over Germany and Japan seemed more certain, but callousness and inertia in the press and the schools, stupidity and conservatism in Congress, selfishness and obstruction in economic circles made him now "think otherwise" than those who, faced with the baffling problems of reconversion, dug in their heels and refused to be budged. Becker, with a forbearance that sometimes seems to come quite close to cracking, points out to them that reform, as well as restraint, is a part of the American heritage; that if responsibility is the price paid by those who enjoy freedom, the responsible must also pay by making room for freedom; that certain changes in our constitution, our institutions, and our economic system are not only socially desirable but may be historically invitable. He ends, with an unexpected departure from generalizations and history, in a manner that is unmatched in any of his writings with which the reviewer is familiar—with a plea for a particular proposal before Congress (the Full Employment Bill). In brief, in this essay Becker seems to be saying to his readers, "Look here! Mankind learns but little slowly, but it does learn! And this is the sort of thing it is going to learn regardless of what you may do about it." One is reminded of Tocqueville's pronouncements upon democracy over a century earlier.

There is a significant difference between a book that says, "History moves, but it moves slowly" and another that says, "History moves slowly, but it does move," even when they are both by the same man, use much the same material, and have much the same philosophy of life. Had Becker died without publishing *Freedom and Responsibility,* he would have been remembered by most lay readers as the author of *The Better World*—and his reputation as a gentle cynic and defeatist would perhaps have been fortified. Fortunately, *Freedom and Responsibility* makes it possible to underline another side of his philosophy. "This is the worst of all possible worlds," he once said to me, "but it's also the best of all possible worlds, because it's the only world we have." Cynical, to be sure, but, mixed up with the cynicism, an unmistakable optimism. Surely, hopefulness is a better note with which to end a great career as writer and teacher than disillusionment. And these are (but for one brief paragraph) the last words of Becker's last book:

> When all is said, what is needed for the solution of the difficult national and international problems that confront us, and therefore for the preservation of our institutions and of the liberties they were created to secure, is more intelligence, more integrity, and a heightened sense of responsibility. We need more intelligence—the knowledge required for understanding the situation and for dealing with it effectively. We need more integrity—less dishonesty and less the feeling that, in private and in public life, our conscience is clear if we keep, with whatever slick maneuvering, within the letter of the law. But what we need most of all is a heightened sense of individual and collective responsibility—less insistence on negative rights and the unrestrained pursuit of individual self-interest, and a more united and resolute determination to concern ourselves with the public good and to make the sacrifices that are necessary for it.

Charlotte Watkins Smith (essay date 1952)

SOURCE: "Carl Becker: The Historian as a Literary Craftsman," in *The William and Mary Quarterly,* Vol. IX, July, 1952, pp. 291-316.

[*In the following essay, Smith shows Becker to have been a writer whose concerns were as much literary as they were historical and philosophical.*]

> If it be said that politics has nothing to do with literature, or that the form of a document can be appreciated without reference to its content, I do not agree. On the contrary, it is a favorite notion of mine that in literary discourse form and content are but two aspects of the same thing. [Becker, *The Declaration of Independence*]

If what Becker said about historical method was unpalatable to many other historians, the way he said it could arouse only admiration and envy. His philosophy of history might be heresy, his research dangerously submerged, but his gift for writing was everywhere acknowledged. In a period when historians were beginning to condemn themselves roundly for ruining popular interest in history by their bad writing, and were setting committees to study the problem, a scholar who could also write won rapid recognition. Becker's Wisconsin doctoral dissertation was held up to students at Yale "as an illustration of what may be done" [Max Farrand to Becker, Dec. 22, 1909]. When his first book, *The Beginnings of the American People,* appeared, Professor William E. Dodd wrote to Becker saying, "There is no one now writing history in this country who has written so well." Soon that opinion came to be shared by others in the profession and out of it, as Becker's articles in periodicals like the *Atlantic Monthly* and the *Dial* made him known.

The high literary art of Carl Becker was a source of wonder to his contemporaries as it is to later generations. To ask why a talent amounting to genius appears may be useless, but it is nevertheless interesting, and something may be learned about its development. Perhaps the excellence of his matter could be explained by his intelligence and scientific training, but where did the singular grace of his manner come from? How could a man who never ceased to look like an Iowa farmer write with the urbanity of a Lord Chesterfield, as well as with the pithiness of a Benjamin Franklin? The usual explanation for the polish of the "literary historians" of the nineteenth century will not do for Becker. He did not (like Prescott, Motley, and Parkman) come from a Boston family of wealth and cultivation where he was surrounded by books and literary conversation from his earliest years. Later in his life Becker was able to recall vividly the first time he discovered reading for pleasure. He was eleven years old; he had never previously read a book or had a book read to him.

Moreover he did not, like the "literary historians," enjoy a life of leisurely study in which he could pursue his literary interests without hindrance after his college days were over. Like most twentieth-century historians he had to earn his living by teaching. What was worse, he did all his teaching in small towns far from the stimulation many find in the variegated culture of a big city. His reputation as a sophisticated literary man, an epigrammatist, was made during the fourteen years he taught in that (to Easterners) most unlikely province of Kansas. Whatever it was that made his talent flourish, it was not the background and environment usually thought necessary for the development of humane letters.

What is it then that explains his "peculiar felicity of expression"? Can anything be said beyond what Becker said about Jefferson's writing and Sabine in turn said about Becker's: that it reflects "a nature exquisitely sensitive and a mind finely tempered"? Fortunately, among Becker's papers, there is some evidence about this tempering process, although unhappily it is scanty and cannot always be precisely dated.

First of all Becker had the fundamental requirement of a good writer—he wanted always and overwhelmingly to be a good writer. He had the urge to write, it was dominant over other desires, and it persisted throughout his whole life. It is an index of the enigmatic quality of his character that some who knew him very well indeed believed that he wrote as a result of outside pressures only, that he did not have an inward urge to write. Professor Sabine in his fine and penetrating essay on Becker expressed this opinion strongly, and others have agreed with it. He writes:

> Becker's historical curiosity apparently carried with it little desire to impart what he found; left to himself he would have been satisfied with the pleasures of the chase. As he said of Turner, "He was caught by his friends and set the task of writing." Fortunately, the charm of his style made him an object of pursuit by friends and publishers. Nearly everything that he published was occasioned by some demand other than the inward urge of the author. . . . The labor of writing was for Becker severe, and the facility of his finished work concealed much careful polishing by which that facility was finally achieved. Some kind of special inducement was necessary to make him write at all. ["A Preface" to Carl Becker, *Freedom and Responsibility in the American Way of Life*]

Mr. Sabine substantiated his conclusion by showing that the genesis of most of Becker's books and articles lay in suggestions from friends or in the solicitations of publishers or editors of journals. This evidence can bear another interpretation, however, and another one is now demanded by the evidence of Becker's personal papers, which were not available when Mr. Sabine's essay was written.

Becker's own statements in an unpublished essay called **"The Art of Writing,"** and the less direct testimony of his journals and miscellaneous notes and manuscripts all indicate that whether special inducement was offered or not, Becker had to write. His own statement, written probably in 1941, is unequivocal: "The art of writing has been the most persistent and absorbing interest of my life." And then, noting that the urge to write was something he "endured always as a malady rather than adopted as a racket," he says, "With the writers' malady I was infected at the early age of eleven. . . . From that moment my purpose in life was clear. I would be an author." To others who would write he continued:

> If it be a question of writing really well, of attaining the something more than the correctly written, then it is first of all essential to have, in more

or less acute form, what I have called the writer's malady. . . . For one who has this malady the desire to write will be, not necessarily an exclusive interest, but at least a dominant and persistent one. This is the first essential.

It is, of course, common for people to express an ardent desire to *be* writers who at the same time show little determination actually to write. If, however, a man says it has always been his heart's desire to be a writer, and if he has labored continuously to express himself well in writing, and if he has in fact produced books and articles superlatively well written (particularly when that required him to labor far beyond the demands of his assignment), then there seems to be no reason to doubt his diagnosis of his own case. Particularly is this true of Carl Becker, who was as nearly without illusion about himself as about the world around him.

One further question remains: Did he write continuously, organizing whatever knowledge he had acquired, persistently trying to put in written form what he had to say (as he said a writer should do), or was he "satisfied with the chase," and disinclined to write except when pressed (as he evidently let most people think he was)?

Let us, with the question in mind, follow Becker's own discussion of how he learned to write and so take up the "second essential" before investigating whether or not he had the "third essential" in his list, that is, the habit of writing constantly.

"The second essential is the inveterate habit of reading, reading what is old as well as what is new, what is bad as well as what is good." The habit of reading is irresistible to most writers and usually precedes their desire to write. With Becker it was somewhat different. "A sample copy of *Saturday Night,* a weekly journal devoted exclusively to serials (then called 'continued stories') of the adventure, western, detective type" came into his hands when he was eleven years old. "At that time," he remembered, "I had never read a book or had a book read to me, or heard anyone talk about books or literature or the art of writing." But he was soon breathlessly involved in a story and at once a convert to reading for life. More than that, he found: "Quite apart from the story, there was something in the feel and smell of the cheap, soft, dampish paper—that had for me the essential glamor of romance." He made up his mind on the spot to "be an author, a writer of stories for *Saturday Night.*"

This was the beginning of his career as a reader as well as a writer, but the way was not smooth. His mother, unintimidated by modern psychology, was old-fashioned enough to ban *Saturday Night* because it was "not good reading"; he had to find other fare. He turned to the public library at Waterloo, Iowa, with "its immense collection of perhaps five hundred volumes" and began rapidly to make up for lost time—"ranging from Greek mythology to Eric the Red." When he was about thirteen he read *Anna Karenina,* and Tolstoy came to replace the writers of *Saturday Night* as his literary model.

Although Becker's aim in life became ever more definite and clear, his reading before he reached the University of

Wisconsin was not systematic nor did it give him any notion about how to proceed to become a writer. He set out seriously to seek directions to his goal during his freshman year at the University. He concentrated his full attention upon his rhetoric course, read Genung's *Rhetoric,* his textbook, with great interest, and then, finding himself still without helpful instructions, "took from the library and read with equal care all the other Rhetorics to be found there." Though this was surely reading with system, it availed him little:

> The Rhetorics did not help me much because to the unformulated question I asked them they gave no answer. What I really asked the Rhetorics was, "What must one do in order to learn to write well?" The Rhetorics all, without exception, replied: "Good writing must be clear, forceful, and elegant." I have sometimes wished that I might acquire great wealth and that the authors of all the old Rhetorics would come to me and ask, "What must we do in order to acquire great wealth?" I would reply: "Great wealth consists in a clear title to much money, forcibly secured in banks, and elegantly available for spending."

He came asking for a method and they gave him a definition. Although, at the time, he "took the definition for gospel truth," it budged him not an inch forward. In time he learned from experience what the rhetorics failed to teach him. Finding his way by himself, he decided that there are things that one can do in order to learn to write well and one of these is simply to read. What sort of reading? Wide and constant reading and only partly for information.

> The writer will read for information, but also with an ear always open to catch the meaning and overtones of words and the peculiar pitch and cadence of their arrangement. There will thus be deposited in the mind, in the subconscious if you prefer, an adequate vocabulary, and a sure feeling for the idioms, rhythms, and grammatical forms that are natural to the language. In time these become so much a part of the writer's mentality that he thinks in terms of them, and writes properly by ear, so to speak, rather than by rule. Thinking too precisely on the rule is apt to give one's writing a certain correct rigidity, even a slightly archaic quality, often found in the writing of professors.

It would be hard to find a page in any of Becker's mature writing that does not prove the validity of this advice.

He developed gradually a complete mastery of the art of writing by ear. So literally was this true that he once told some of his students "that he had a feeling for how a sentence should sound even before he wrote it, and did not consider it complete until it sounded the way he thought it ought to have sounded." When it did sound right that was how it stayed. He allowed no prejudice against split infinitives or against ending sentences with prepositions to distort his prose into ambiguous or stilted English. For example, a line in **"Everyman His Own Historian"** reads: "The exact truth of remembered events he has in any case no time, and no need, to curiously question or meticulously verify." Altered to read: "Curiously to question or me-

ticulously to verify," it sounds pedantic and sing-song. "To question curiously or verify meticulously," still sounds a little polysyllabic, and it is impossible because putting "curiously" after instead of before "question" in some mysterious way makes it ambiguous. "To question curiously" could mean "in a strange way" instead of "inquisitively," which is clearly what it means in "to curiously question." Moreover the very sound, the alliteration or the rhythm, of the words as they stand imparts a delicate irony to the sentence which would be lost in any recasting. After the time Becker must have spent on this sentence, after the nice discrimination he had exercised, it would have been no wonder if he had exploded when he discovered his assistant, as yet too young to be free of the tyranny of convention, attempting to "unsplit" his infinitive for him while proofreading the paper. There was no explosion, but the young man did not soon forget his chagrin, nor the fact that split infinitives are not always used by accident or by the uninitiated.

The language of Shakespeare and the King James Bible had been so early deposited in Becker's mind and so completely assimilated that it became part of the very fabric of his prose.

— *Charlotte Watkins Smith*

Another and a more surprising confirmation of the fact that Becker really wrote by ear is that his spelling is shaky. The repeated spelling in his handwritten manuscripts of such a word as "mayhem" as "mahem," or "germane" as "germain" is surely unusual for a constant reader. A more obvious result of his concern with the sounds of words is that his sentences (whether written for lectures or not) seldom have any grating consonants or shaggy sibilants. They want to be read aloud. When so read they slip smoothly off the tongue and into the mind; there are no rough edges, nothing strange and harsh in the rhythms or in the words. The words are honest English of respectable age or the native American of the man in the street, but never synthetic jargon. The abrupt change of pace he achieved by the juxtaposition of rather stately English with the commonest speech gave character and vitality to a passage like this one: "If logic presumes to protest in the name of the law, they know how to square it, so that it complaisantly looks the other way." Although he knew and used the findings of the newer social sciences, anthropology, sociology, and Freudian psychology, he forbore to use their special terms. What is more he learned to avoid ugly compound words like "democratization" and "historiography," awkward alliterations like "procedural postulates," and multisyllable words that are jolting and unrhythmical.

The language of Shakespeare and the King James Bible had been so early deposited in his mind and so completely assimilated that it became part of the very fabric of his prose: "Kansans love each other for the dangers they have passed." "Let not the harmless, necessary word 'myth' put us out of countenance." "I do not present this view of history as one that is stable and must prevail." Often the cadence alone is directly reminiscent of some forgotten classic that can be recalled, but it may be too subtle for that. For example, "It is not possible, it is not essential . . ." brings to mind at once "We cannot consecrate, we cannot hallow this ground. . . ." But another line "Not a life of drudgery, or genius itself shall avoid disaster," is much harder to pin down, though just as haunting. Whether actually familiar in cadence or not, his sentences fall pleasantly on the ear; they are traditional and melodic, never strange and discordant. He kept to the old tonal system, but the tunes are seldom trite.

There is more than the evidence of his writing, though that is sufficient, to prove that Becker saturated himself in literature of all sorts. The twenty-drawer cabinet of research notes which are now in the Cornell University Library prove that he was not only a constant reader of catholic taste, but he was what is much rarer, a participative reader. His reading notes are not so much voluminous as thoughtful. He attended closely; he stayed oriented by any aids he found necessary—often drawing rather clumsy little maps or diagrams; he questioned and reflected upon the author's inferences; he pursued striking ideas out into his own realms of being. All these things he might do whether he was reading a study of the French Revolution, a philosophical essay, or a novel.

Although his reading was broad, it was discriminating and it was not superficial. His reading notes do not indicate that he tried to "read everything," but rather that he read all kinds of things. He was interested in almost all forms of human endeavor and in every type of human behavior. He read with care about them all. Two exceptions should be noted. Music and painting—perhaps the fine arts in general—meant little to Becker. Agreeing as he did with Pascal that "thought makes the dignity of man" he had little comprehension of activities in which emotions and not ideas are the molding force. After a visit to the Louvre he wrote: "The great mass of paintings do not interest me, because I know nothing. It is a language I do not understand. Like music, I don't know enough about what they were driving at, how they tried to get their effects, how far they succeeded and how far failed." A few paintings—especially the "Mona Lisa"—and some of the sculpture—ancient Greek and Roman—did interest him. It was an intellectual, speculative interest in the people represented, however, not primarily an esthetic concern.

His interest in the thoughts of human beings was otherwise unlimited. Mathematical reasoning (if not too technical for him to follow) or even mystical revelations commanded his attention; indeed all the various ways men attempt to understand and come to terms with the universe, whether through science, religion, or simply day-dreams, were of profound interest to him. He believed that great novels, poetry, and drama deal with the fundamental problems of the individual confronting the universe and are therefore a less ephemeral form of literature than history which deals with superficial affairs and temporary institutions. It is not surprising, then, that Shakespeare and Henry James bulk almost as large as Santayana and Bertrand Russell among his miscellaneous notes, and these last two are probably quoted oftener and at greater length than any other modern writers. Bits from Plato's Dialogues stand next to notes on Browning's *The Ring and the Book* or others from T. S. Eliot or Anatole France. These are all notes in the handwriting of his mature years—not remains of his school days.

It is clear that Becker read more fiction than most scholars feel that they have time for. Probably his historical perception as well as his writing was the better for it. His psychological insight—one quality that lifts his biographical studies so far out of the general run—was based partly on the study of Freud and other psychologists, no doubt, but possibly more upon the knowledge of people gained through literature. He was with Santayana, a "literary psychologist." Madame Roland was more understandable in the light of Flaubert's picture of Madame Bovary. The clues are easier to pick up—indeed can only be picked up—if one has the experience to recognize them. Becker's close acquaintance through books with three dimensional people of all social and moral conditions undoubtedly gave life and depth to his historical studies such as no knowledge of "case studies" or "economic man" could have given them.

Yet he did not ignore economic man or any aspect of man which could be discerned and commented upon. All that man had thought or done (including his thoughts about his own thinking) were history in Becker's definition and in his practice, so any clear distinction between his notes on history and those on literature or philosophy or "general reading" is impossible. Yet some classification is possible. Most of his notes are obviously directly related to courses he taught or books he wrote. They contain factual information, interpretation of events and so forth. But one significant part of the notes is of a more unusual description—a category he labeled "Form and Substance."

This group of notes shows that he did not give up finding direct help in learning to write after his disappointment with the rhetorics in his college days. In later years he read and carefully noted such hints as the masters of the craft let fall. Aristotle, Virginia Woolf, Marcel Proust, and Van Wyck Brooks appear among others, but Henry James and Remy de Gourmont seem to have carried more weight with him than any others, except perhaps Pascal whose ideas were peculiarly congenial to Becker. No single author influenced his style noticeably either by precept or example, but he was peculiarly indebted to one period. His aim and his achievement in writing were essentially those of the eighteenth century. "That is best wrote which is best adopted for obtaining the end of the writer," said Benjamin Franklin, and Becker found that definition satisfactory when he discarded the dogma of his nineteenth-century rhetoric books that "good writing must be clear, forceful, and elegant." He read more in and about the eighteenth century than any other; he found it congenial; and eighteenth-century writers must have influenced or at least confirmed his taste for clarity, precision and simplicity in prose.

Hints and standards of excellence were all very well, but Becker early divined that no royal road was to be found and set himself to follow the long and difficult path of self-corrective experience. First, experience through literature: "Abstain and buy books," he peremptorily reminded himself in his college journal! Next, experience through writing.

> The third and most important thing to be done in order to learn to write well is to write. Never let anyone persuade you to refrain from writing until you have something to say—something important is always meant. As well tell the child to refrain from talking until he has learned to speak correctly. It is only by incessant practice in the way of gurgles and noises that he learns to speak at all; and it is only by writing much sad stuff that anyone can learn to write something good enough even, as De Gourmont says, to merit a prize for literary excellence. Whether what one writes is important or not is another matter. That depends upon native intelligence and knowledge. But one thing is certain: there is no better way of developing whatever knowledge one may have acquired, than by persistently trying to put in written form what one has to say, whether important or not. Fortunately those who are infected with the writer's malady will pay no attention to this bad advice. They will write because they must, filling pages and pages, as well aware as any one that what they write isn't important, but always hoping that in time it may be, and at all events determined to say what they find to say, whether important or not, as well as they can.

The question of whether Becker actually did develop his own talent according to these instructions seems to be answered in the affirmative by the papers now in the Cornell University Library. There is much to show that he was always writing as well as he could—and frequently (before he had mastered his craft) just for the practice or in response to an inner urge.

The earliest examples of his writing are the two pocket-sized notebooks which he kept from January, 1894, to May, 1895, during his second and third years at the University of Wisconsin—the "Wild Thoughts Notebooks." After the last dated entries in the second notebook he jotted down all sorts of odds and ends—quotations in English, French, German, and Italian, bits of poetry (some his own), and epigrammatic remarks that bear a close resemblance to his later writings. His characteristic habit of taking a cliché and twisting it in a surprising way is very much in evidence in these early scribblings. He was practicing an art of which he became a master: "A little conscience is a dangerous thing." "Some men are born stupid. And some achieve stupidity." "One man's lust is another's love." Pieces of advice which he was to cleave unto all the days of his life appear: " 'An author should consider how far the art of writing consists in knowing what to leave in the inkstand.' Lowell."

These "Wild Thoughts" are never diaries but the notebooks of an apprentice writer. One day he attempted to record a dialect conversation heard in the street (November 11, 1894). Another time he told a melancholy little tale of the unrequited love of a boy in his rooming house for a ballet dancer who stayed in Madison for a week (March 24, 1894). Several times he tried to describe the audience (and even himself watching the audience!) in the town opera house while he sat in the upper gallery waiting for a play to begin (February 5, 6, 1894). Again he wandered into the park and sat on an iron bench and waited until a man eager to talk about his grievances came along and gave him material for a character sketch with plenty of authentic dialogue (June 12, 1894). Frequently he outlined the life story of a real or imaginary person who had somehow come to a desperate pass; then he left it with a query about whom to blame—society or the individual (March 14, 17, 1894). Not only was he trying hard to say well what he had to say, but also he was trying to develop more important things to say by examining the behavior and motivation of all sorts of people, and by broadening and deepening his own experience. He reflected at length upon the advice of William Dean Howells which he copied into his notebook:

> For this work [realistic fiction] the young writer needs expression and observation not so much of others as of himself, for ultimately his characters will all come out of himself and he will need to know motive and character with such thoroughness and accuracy as he can acquire *only* through his own heart [February 10, 1894].

The "Wild Thoughts Notebooks" throw an interesting light on the mind and thought of Carl Becker during his undergraduate days, but the clearest message in them is that he was then earnestly training himself to be a writer. Moreover the inference is unavoidable that he was already an observer far more than he was a participator in the life around him.

It was not writing history, to be sure, that he had in mind at that time. He wanted to write novels, "as good as *Anna Karenina,*" as he recalled it almost fifty years later. His old notes in their faded ink confirm that it was a deeply felt desire. That he kept some tenderness toward his youthful strivings may be inferred from the fact that he preserved all of his life these records of a day that was gone. Among the files he left to Cornell University, there are no other papers of any kind written during his undergraduate years, unless it be a few undated research notes.

Why Becker turned aside from the pursuit of his first ambition is not entirely clear. There was probably a slow curving of his path rather than an abrupt turn; in any case the new course was not so far from the old as to preclude his reaching the original goal eventually. In **"The Art of Writing"** Becker dropped the autobiographical thread after describing his first year at the university. The thread may be picked up just beyond that point in his earlier article on Frederick Jackson Turner. There he said that he was "infected with the desire to study history" during his junior year (1895) after prolonged exposure to Turner and to Charles Homer Haskins. It is significant, however, that this infection was only his old "writer's malady" in a new form. It was not, he admits, until he ceased to see Turner as a teacher and began to see him as " 'historian' . . . better still 'author' " that he "brought out [his] tiny little wagon and fumblingly hitched it to that bright particular star."

Although the "Wild Thoughts Notebook" of 1895 is the last evidence that Becker was consciously preparing to write fiction, there is much to show that he kept on practicing writing as an art, simply for its own sake, if no immediate purpose offered. He did so during at least one other period of his life by means of a journal. From June 15, 1924 to September, 1924, while making his only trip to Europe, he wrote to his fourteen-year-old son daily accounts of the things he saw and did. This journal served the double purpose of keeping his family informed and of making a record of his trip for himself, as well as giving him practice during a time when he was doing no historical writing. That the last was by no means the least reason for writing the 1924 diary is fairly clear from its contents. It abounds in detailed physical descriptions—of his cabin on shipboard, of Scottish landscapes and castles, of cathedrals in England and France, of Paris streets, of palaces and gardens and trains. It is all quite factual and admirably pitched to the level of interest and understanding of a fourteen-year-old. His descriptions of mechanical gadgets—like the ship's log-line, and the equipment in his cabin on the "S.S. Columbia" are really exercises in clarity and precision of expression. Whether he knew it at the time or not, Becker was laying up for himself experience for the difficult task of writing a textbook for high-school students. Wherever he discussed for his son the history of the places he described, he did it very simply yet without condescension, in the manner of his **Modern History**.

Perhaps more significant than his brief journals was his lifelong habit of making and filing away notes of his ideas and reflections upon books, people and events; these notes testify that he liked to express himself in writing. The kind of vagrant thought that most people would dissipate in conversation and have done with, he would ruminate upon until all its implications came to light and then he would write it out in full and file it away among his research notes. Many of these notes appeared later in clearer form in his published writings; many of them did not, in any recognizable way. A sample of one of his briefer notes is given here:

> "To understand all is to pardon all." This expresses a truth but not exactly. "Understand" is a function of impersonal intelligence. "Pardon" is an expression of a moral judgment. The two have really little or nothing in common. When you understand all, you "pardon" all only in the sense that you understand that things must be as they are and not otherwise. If I knew all about, say a brutal gangster and kidnapper, I might well know that he was not "responsible," that he could not have been otherwise. Yet I might not "pardon" him; I might judge that he should be shot. Just as I would crush a rattlesnake. Then my "understanding" could also understand this, that I should still not pardon him but kill him.— And still I might not "pardon" myself for not "pardoning" the gangster who could not be otherwise: and my understanding would understand this also. To understand all is to understand—among the all, the refusal to pardon

those who cannot do otherwise than they do [Drawer 2].

Notes of this type seem to bespeak a custom of thinking on paper, and so not thinking vaguely but with some form and direction.

Although almost all of Becker's finished work was published, there are more extended writings among his files that were evidently not written in response to any urging but that of his own nature. By the time he reached maturity he had enough to say and had learned how to say it so well, that he was almost never in want of a market. Nevertheless there was one period—a few years immediately after the First World War—when his literary fortunes were at a low ebb. Grave personal cares—his stepdaughter's incurable illness and the beginning of his own painful digestive ailment—must explain it to a large degree, but aside from that the war and even more its aftermath of "normalcy" were profoundly disturbing to him. It was not only his faith in democracy that was blighted by disgust; his faith in himself and in his work suffered as well.

His first postwar book, **The United States: An Experiment in Democracy,** reflects both. It was written at the request of his former colleague, Guy Stanton Ford, for use by the Creel Committee in its overseas information program, but by the time the manuscript was finished the war had ended. The committee ceased all publication and Becker sought a private publisher. It was declined by Scribner's before it was accepted by Harper's in 1920. **The United States** is the only book Becker ever wrote that seldom rises above being, for him, merely competently written. Its flatness is exaggerated by comparison with its immediate predecessor—the sparkling **Eve of the Revolution**. For its original purposes it might have been excellent—it was to have been translated into many different languages and distributed as a sort of handbook of American history and government—but it lacks the characteristic flavor and subtlety of Becker's other books. Perhaps it suffers from the author's blurred or altered purpose. From aiming at a foreign audience, he seems to turn at the end to trying unhappily to jog the American public into a greater sense of responsibility. Evidently Becker felt dissatisfied with his performance. Three years after **The United States** was published Professor Dodd was reassuring him, in effect, that his competence was excellence in anyone else. Dodd added:

> I know you and I both became tremendously concerned in the great drama of 1914-1920. I wrote a book that expressed that concern, a sort of contribution to the cause of democracy. You wrote one. I have not seen that you lost your poise at all, although in some chapters of that book you were not as *gründlich* as you were wont to be.

It is significant of the extent to which ideals of detachment and objectivity were Becker's ideals in historical writing after all, that he did not pour out his intense feelings in a really debunking history, which **The United States: An Experiment in Democracy** is not. Instead, during this time of stress, he tried other literary forms. Writing seems to have been to him a more satisfactory and natural means of expression than talking, although many people testify to his occasional conversational brilliance. Suffering as he was from a temporary discontent with history writing, Becker sought another means of expressing the disillusionment he felt.

It was at this time that he most seriously experimented with writing poetry. Apparently almost all writers (and a surprising number of people in less susceptible professions) are driven to write verse during acute attacks of their malady. Only a very few lines of Becker's verse survived, aside from little jingles to his grandson and other verses for children. But there is no doubt that Becker tried, for a time at least, to write more serious poetry. The whole story, so far as his papers give it, lies in one brief, handwritten letter from Carl Van Doren, dated at Urbana, Illinois:

> Your verses have followed me here, where I have been giving some lectures . . . only after a good deal of delay.
>
> It seems to me that the sonnets suffer from a certain flatness now and then which leaves one questioning a little whether prose would not have been better. They have a vibrant irony, they are correct and strong and they mean a great deal. But they are excellent verse rather than good poetry in my judgment. Perhaps I would put it better to say that I think three paragraphs on this saintly vicar would come nearer to doing his job than three sonnets.
>
> Do I seem very outspoken? It is because I see a pretty genuine satiric gift behind these pieces, which I think you could afford to indulge.

Since the verses have disappeared, one is free either to doubt Van Doren's competence in the matter, and thence to grieve over the loss of the sonnets, or to assume that he was probably right, and to admire Becker for seeing it too. Is there not perhaps too much of clarity, too little of intensity in Becker's writing to indicate a potential poet in the twentieth-century definition? As E. B. White puts it: "A poet dares be just so clear and no clearer; he approaches lucid ground warily, like a mariner who is determined not to scrape his bottom on anything solid. A poet's pleasure is to withhold a little of his meaning, to intensify by mystification." Could anything be further removed from the literary ideal to which Becker had devoted himself for over twenty years? Although he might modify or try to abandon his usual canons of writing when he attempted poetry, it seems likely that his poetic intention would still bear more resemblance to John Gay's than to John Donne's. Van Doren's remarks indicate that his performance was also closer to an eighteenth-century ideal than to a seventeenth- or twentieth-century notion of poetry. Are not the virtues ascribed to Becker's sonnets the very ones allowed the Augustans? And is not its disqualifying defect, the very defect of those virtues? Van Doren thought it was prosaic, and to an age in which "a poem should not mean but be," it probably was.

Still, writing poetry may have been a private emotional outlet for Becker all of his life; on the other hand, he may never have written anything but light verse after 1922. In

either case he evidently accepted Van Doren's judgment that his proper talent lay in prose.

As for the positive part of Van Doren's advice, Becker was already trying satire. He wrote an allegory of contemporary society in all its aspects, with particular attention to the Paris Peace Conference. Ostensibly a story for children somewhat on the A. A. Milne pattern with a good deal of verse incorporated in the stories, it was called *The King of Beasts*. It is Becker's only completed manuscript of book length that remains unpublished. It was rejected by eleven publishers. Again Van Doren wrote frank and direct criticism:

> I read it with steady delight in the satire. At the same time, however, I think the story suffers from a lack of dramatic emphasis. That is the narrative element does not stand out with sufficient conspicuousness to carry the thing through. To put it another way, the satire crouches so close to the path of the story that I found myself always peeping at one side or the other for satirical claws and not being sure where I was going along the path. This quality in the book, it seems to me limits the audience more than was needed in the circumstances. As you see, the book is neither simple enough to be read by children without noticing the satire nor adult enough to be read by adults without making them feel that they are stealing something from the children.

Publishers were undoubtedly right in thinking *The King of Beasts* would not sell in 1922; it would be even less publishable today since many of the contemporary allusions would be missed. Another defect—or perhaps another way of stating what Van Doren points out—is that the satire is both too broad and too deep. Too many of man's ways and institutions are attacked; the force is weakened by being divided among almost innumerable targets. All is folly and wickedness. There is naught to choose between "the Beasts that Prey" and those "that Pray." The creatures who live after the word of the Law are fully as cruel as the Lawless, and none are more contemptible than the Lambs who "mean well," but "have soft hearts and like to live in the blessed hope that some day all will be well."

Becker was perhaps too hard on himself in feeling that he had lost his poise—after all his *Declaration of Independence* was written in 1922 and his teaching at this time was extremely successful—but *The United States,* the vanished sonnets, and *The King of Beasts* do indicate that the course of his writing was considerably less clear and steady than it had been or than it would be again.

Despite the exceptions, the general rule that most of his work was occasioned by someone else's request or suggestion may be true. That is quite different from saying that it arose out of the requests.

If ideas for some of his best work—like the Benjamin Franklin article in the *Dictionary of American Biography,* or the study of the Declaration of Independence—were directly suggested by editors, other things like *The Heavenly City* and *Progress and Power*—seem to have grown naturally out of his own mind, constantly seeded by reading and fertilized by reflection. Possibly he needed the pressure of an obligation to make him put his work into finished form. If so, he undertook enough to keep himself writing steadily. In his early years at Kansas it was constant book reviewing for the *Dial*, the *Nation*, and the *Outlook* that gave him invaluable experience, and which he sought for that reason. Later this was unnecessary and he did reviews only for books of exceptional interest to him. He had standing invitations from the editors of half a dozen journals to write reviews or articles. Toward the end of his life publishers vied for the honor of having a new book of his (or a new collection of old essays) on their lists. He wrote only on what interested him and then only after "exploring with infinite patience every part" of the subject, but he still devoted every morning to writing. He wrote "on demand" only in the sense that everything he wrote was demanded. It is impossible to tell whether books like *Progress and Power* or *The Heavenly City* were written because he was invited to give a series of lectures and had to have something to say, or whether he accepted the invitation because he had something about ready to be said. It is at least plausible to conclude that he simply used some of the many occasions that offered to present lectures or to publish articles that would have been written sooner or later with or without occasion.

These then were the chief rules which Becker found and followed in learning to write—"to have an irrepressible desire to write, to be always reading with discrimination, and to be always writing as well as one can."

There is a tradition at Cornell that Becker once gave another word of advice on writing, and thereby another glimpse of how he wrote himself. A group of graduate students sought him asking what they must do to become good writers. When he told them to go forth and rewrite everything twelve times, they departed sorrowing. It is easy to believe that Becker himself rewrote everything twelve times and more. There are among his papers as many as six or seven typewritten versions of one article and before that there was undoubtedly a handwritten draft much revised. A few original drafts of articles have been kept, although in general only typewritten manuscripts are in the files. Becker did not compose on the typewriter. His habit seems to have been to write a first draft in longhand—doing a good deal of rewriting as he went along—then to type it (seldom revising as he typed). He altered the typewritten copy in longhand, interlining and writing inserts on new sheets or on the back. The corrected copy was then typed again in whole or in part. This process was repeated over and over until the final draft was sent to the printer, Becker doing his own typing by a swift, two-fingered method. And that final copy was full of corrections too. In spite of all his labor over his writing, his manuscripts always needed a great deal of editing because his spelling, punctuation, and references were rather casual. Becker sent his material off in good time—grateful letters from his publishers show that—but so long as it remained in his hands it was under scrutiny. If he did not "wear his soul threadbare in the search for the better word, the happier phrase, the smoother transition," it can only have been because he enjoyed the search.

Good style to Becker was never a "succession of felicitous sounds" but always an appropriate expression of an idea which was interesting, subtle, or universal in appeal.

— *Charlotte Watkins Smith*

This was not quite the whole of his advice nor of his practice, however. For the young writer there are many pitfalls and some of these he pointed out in **"The Art of Writing."** The "misleading, irrelevant word 'style' " was the signpost that pointed directly to the deepest pitfalls in Becker's opinion. He believed: "Good style in writing is like happiness in living—something that comes to you, if it comes at all, only if you are preoccupied with something else: if you deliberately go after it you will probably not get it." Moreover, he disliked the word because "it tends to fix the attention on what is superficial and decorative whereas in reality the foundation of good writing is organic structure." The right path then was "to take care of the thought and let the style take care of itself." Let the writer take thought, decide exactly what it is he wishes to convey, and then look for the words which will fully and exactly convey it. That is all he is concerned with. If he does that the style will be "as good as the quality of the thought permits."

The danger lies in thinking of style as a substitute for ideas, or as a cover-up for trite and uninteresting ones. Good style to Becker was never a "succession of felicitous sounds" but always an appropriate expression of an idea which was interesting, subtle, or universal in appeal. His great care to obtain felicitous rather than unpleasing sounds was not a contradiction of this. Pleasant sounds are simply more appropriate because they aid in conveying the idea, while jarring words, however correct, get in the way.

The last way in the world to write well, Becker thought, is to let some "conventional notion of good writing" determine the arrangement of words. The "shape and pressure of the idea" would determine the form if the writer concentrated on mastering the content—on thinking clearly and logically about the matter rather than the manner. He so far agreed with Henry James, who completely identified form with substance, as to say: "The style, if there is to be any worth mentioning, must wait upon the idea, which is itself form as well as substance." The point of all this, Becker put in a sentence: "Have something of your own to say, and then say it in your own way."

Unlike many who give that advice, he saw fully the difficulties lying in the words "your own."

> We are all under a certain pressure, from the social group or profession to which we belong, to think as the group thinks, and to use the clichés the group understands, so that we easily become habituated to certain conventional patterns of

thought and stereotyped forms of expression. Anyone who wishes to have something of his own to say and to say it in his own way must avoid, as the sin against the Holy Ghost, these conventional patterns of thought and stereotyped forms of expression.

The wry remarks which follow on the academic stereotype must have been more than half serious. The academic style comes naturally to professors, because they know so much, he explained.

> Knowing so much, we cannot easily think of any particular thing without thinking at the same time of everything it is related to in heaven and earth; and so the concrete instance, regarded in this broad way, is a nuisance until, divested of all that makes it vivid and alive, we can subsume it in a generalized statement. Aware that there is much to be said on the one hand, and equally much to be said on the other, we feel the need of safeguarding even the simplest affirmation by triple qualifications, remote historical allusions, and parenthetical cross references.

The dreadful necessity of leaving out everything except what is strictly relevant was one he accepted early and commended to his students, but he saw that the generality of scholars had not screwed their courage up so far.

But more dangerous than any professional stereotype, after all, are the pervasive, inconspicuous literary stereotypes. Every reader has his mind filled with them; they are not in themselves unlovely like the jargon of the lawyer, the business man, or the social scientist, but the predominance of them in anyone's writing gives it "a borrowed excellence" which quite deprives it of character. Avoiding them is difficult; Becker can only say try not to use them. "Try to understand clearly what you yourself . . . know or think or feel about the subject, and then express it in a form of words that is natural to you." If the style is then not very good, it cannot be improved by "borrowed mannerisms" and "tricks of the trade," but only by becoming better yourself through "working, reading, observing, thinking honestly, and becoming absorbed in things more important than oneself."

With that final caution, Becker ended his remarks on the art of writing. Most of the counsel given there could be inferred from scattered comments in his published writings. For example, the major tenet of his creed—be yourself—is implied in his chapter on "The Literary Qualities of the Declaration." The only large defect he saw in the original draft of the Declaration of Independence came from Jefferson's violation of that principle. In the paragraph against slavery, which Congress deleted, Jefferson had tried to adopt a tone that was unnatural to him, Becker believed. The lines rang false because Jefferson himself had not the temperament to sustain "the grand manner" with sincerity. He had not a "profoundly emotional apprehension of experience" and so his "vehement philippic against negro slavery" (as John Adams called it) is not moving as it was meant to be. Becker did not doubt that Jefferson "apprehended the injustice of slavery"; that Jefferson felt it deeply he did doubt. In other parts of the Declaration, the appeal is to the mind and not the heart,

and Jefferson was at his best, but in the slavery charge he felt called upon "to stir the reader's emotions, to make him feel a righteous indignation at the king's acts, a profound contempt for the man and his motives." He could not do it:

> We remain calm in reading it because Jefferson, one cannot but think, remained calm in writing it. For want of phrases charged with deep feeling, he resorts to italics, vainly endeavoring to stir the reader by capitalizing and underlining the words that need to be stressed—a futile device which serves only to accentuate the sense of artifice and effort.

The style must suit the man as well as the subject, for it will inevitably reflect him for better or for worse. This conviction was a fertile theme for Becker, as well as a rule of writing. His comments about George Bancroft's historical writing and far more his brief analysis of Benjamin Franklin's prose illuminate the men as well. But this chapter on the author of the Declaration is surely a supreme example of brilliant literary criticism combined with psychological intuition. Our interest in it is intensified by the peculiar affinity between the minds of Jefferson and Becker. One cannot help thinking that the historian who was no lecturer had felt with the statesman who was no orator that overwhelming desire when speaking to "cross out what he has just said and say it over again in a different way." Becker also clearly felt Jefferson's distress at the "depredations" committed by Congress upon his carefully composed document. Further, Becker's friends saw, and he admitted to one of them, that he examined what he felt to be a limitation of his own writing when he explained Jefferson's inability to achieve the grand manner. Since he was more introspective than Jefferson, he had decided that he lacked a "profoundly passionate nature" and he eschewed any attempt to write in tones of deep emotion. He might have said with Wordsworth:

> The moving accident is not my trade,
> To freeze the blood I have no ready Arts.

Like Wordsworth and Jefferson, he spoke to "thinking hearts." And so he wrote not about manning the barricades, but about revolutions in men's minds.

Becker's literary virtues, although of a lesser order, lay in the same direction as Jefferson's. Like Jefferson's writing Becker's too had "elevation" though it did not have the "massive strength" of the grand manner. Becker's words in defense of democratic virtues, penned during the years when democracy seemed most in peril, resemble the Declaration of Independence far more than they resemble contemporaneous words of Winston Churchill's.

> To have faith in the dignity and worth of the individual man as an end in himself, to believe that it is better to be governed by persuasion than by coercion, to believe that fraternal good will is more worthy than a selfish and contentious spirit, to believe that in the long run all values are inseparable from the love of truth and the disinterested search for it, to believe that knowledge and the power it confers should be used to promote the welfare and happiness of all men rather than to serve the interests of those individuals

and classes whom fortune and intelligence endow with temporary advantage—these are the values which are affirmed by the traditional democratic ideology. But they are older and more universal than democracy and do not depend upon it. . . . They are the values that readily lend themselves to rational justification, yet need no justification.

If these lines fall short of the grand manner, it is because, like the Declaration, they do not have "unsophisticated directness" or the "effect of passion restrained." They carry conviction, but they do not bring the surge of emotion that comes with Churchill's words:

> The battle of Britain is about to begin. Upon this battle depends the survival of Christian civilisation. Upon it depends our own British life and the long continuity of our institutions and our Empire. The whole fury and might of the enemy must very soon be turned on us. Hitler knows that he will have to break us in this island or lose the war. If we can stand up to him all Europe may be free, and the life of the world may move forward into broad, sunlit uplands; but if we fail then the whole world, including the United States, and all that we have known and cared for, will sink into the abyss of a new dark age made more sinister, and perhaps more prolonged, by the lights of perverted science. Let us therefore brace ourselves to our duty and so bear ourselves that if the British Commonwealth and Empire lasts for a thousand years men will still say, "This was their finest hour."

Of course Becker was not, as Churchill was, exhorting a people "to dare and to endure," but he was doing what his talents better fitted him for—persuading a people to think well that they might know their heritage was worth preserving.

For this task of the last five years of his life, Becker wrote the most straightforward, earnest prose that he ever produced. There is little of the delicate irony that pervades *The Heavenly City* in *How New Will the Better World Be?* That was sacrificed, one feels, because it would not help to "obtain the end of the writer"—which was clearly to infuse political concern, judgment, and sophistication into as many people as possible. Once he set out to persuade, Becker could insinuate enlightened views into all sorts of minds—even closed ones—as blandly as ever Benjamin Franklin could. His was not the job of rousing men to fight for democracy, but only to think more clearly about it before it was too late. Still, to do that he had to take his place with the believers, and the skepticism of his days of contemplation, however mellow, had to be put by for less critical times. Sufficient faith for the task he had, and he had it "at the expense of some painful travail of the spirit" after much "reflection upon the enigma of existence." Here the twentieth-century historian parts company with his eighteenth-century model. For Becker, even before 1918, there was none of that "complacent optimism" that Jefferson enjoyed.

Both men put their faith in reason and democracy—Jefferson believing that they had placed all human ills and imperfections in the course of ultimate extinction, Becker believing only that, faulty as they were, their abandonment would bring down the long night of barbarism. Jefferson's optimism was limitless and glowing. Becker's bleak remnant of optimism was almost negative—little more than, with Justice Holmes, *not* believing in sudden ruin.

However strongly Becker's peculiar felicities may remind us of Jefferson's, his mood and tone are anything but Jeffersonian. Although Jefferson's values were Becker's too, their views of how those values fit into the universe were vastly different. Jefferson depicts a world of Newtonian order; Becker a chaos of whirling forces. But both wielded "masterly pens" and both did so by dint of careful labor.

Ralph H. Bowen   (essay date 1958)

SOURCE: "*The Heavenly City*: A Too-ingenious Paradox," in *Carl Becker's Heavenly City Revisited*, edited by Raymond O. Rockwood, Cornell, 1958, pp. 141-55.

[*In the following essay, Bowen criticizes* The Heavenly City *for its assumption that contemporary philosophical fashions establish the final validity of beliefs of an earlier age.*]

Carl Becker's book about the eighteenth-century Philosophers is nearly as difficult to write about as it is easy to read. The odds are, in the first place, that any commentary will be less lively and less persuasive than the original. To praise it seems superfluous, considering the large number who are already convinced that it is a masterpiece. To find fault with it seems, by the same token, presumptuous or—in view of its many merits—ungracious. The book and its thesis must be taken seriously because of Becker's stature as a historian and because of the tremendous influence his book has had, particularly in America, on thinking about the Enlightenment. Yet too much solemnity might well be dangerous, for it is entirely possible that Becker had his tongue in his cheek a good part of the time. One more than half suspects that in a number of places he was mischievously indulging his well-known taste for paradox and that more-than anything else he was trying to stir people up in order to start them thinking.

This ability of Becker's to overcome the inertia of other minds was, of course, one of the qualities that made him such a superb teacher, and it is surely one of the most substantial merits of *The Heavenly City* that it has made a whole generation of students re-examine the *philosophes* in a more critical spirit. The book still retains, after twenty-five years, nearly all of its remarkable power to provoke fruitful controversy. I suppose Becker would regard this fact as ample justification for having written *The Heavenly City*.

But I also believe that the last thing Carl Becker wanted was to have his readers swallow without question the whole thesis of *The Heavenly City*. I think he would be intensely unhappy to see how often his book is taken for a final judgment on the nature and meaning of the Enlightenment—something it most certainly is not and probably was never intended to be. I think he would be especially displeased to know how often college teachers ignorantly or irresponsibly recommend *The Heavenly City* to beginning students as "a splendid short account of eighteenth-century thought."

Becker's Yale lectures, the original version of *The Heavenly City,* were addressed to an audience that could be presumed to be fairly well informed about the eighteenth century. He may well have taken it for granted that he was under no obligation to recite the elementary facts which every schoolboy should—but usually doesn't—know about the *philosophes.* Instead he seems to have tried mainly to suggest new ways of interpreting some of that information. He apparently felt little need to guard against misunderstandings because he assumed that his audience knew what he was doing and would not mistake his frankly tentative suggestions for a balanced treatment of the whole subject. No more would one expect an audience of West Pointers to mistake a series of lectures on the tactics of trench warfare for a definitive military history of the First World War. Yet a mistake of approximately this magnitude resulted from the publication of Becker's lectures in book form.

The new audience was large and miscellaneous and mostly unsophisticated. Becker must have been aware of this, and it is puzzling that he apparently made no special effort to prevent confusion. Perhaps he did not expect the book to have anything like the sensational popularity which it soon achieved and hence did not at first see any need to take precaustions. It almost certainly did not occur to him that his professional colleagues would be the first to fall into the blunder of taking *The Heavenly City* for more than it pretended to be. Yet, beginning with the reviewers for the learned journals, this is precisely what happened. Becker might, of course, have protested in print, although he could hardly have done so at that point without causing embarrassment. One must concede, too, that it is a rare thing for an author to take exception to favorable reviews. Furthermore, there was still no convincing proof that a significant number of persons was relying solely on *The Heavenly City* for elementary knowledge about the *philosophes.* It has taken nearly a quarter of a century for this deplorable state of affairs to become fully evident, though I do not think that even now the average college teacher is aware of the true magnitude of the problem.

These reflections are largely the product of my own experience over the past ten years in assigning *The Heavenly City* as collateral reading in undergraduate courses. No other book is so uniformly misunderstood. Even when they are warned in advance that they may expect to find many debatable judgments in the book, the most able and mature students are often so charmed by its literary perfection that they drop their critical defenses and end by accepting Becker's shakiest hypotheses as a new revelation. I can sympathize with them because the same thing starts to happen to me every time I pick up the book to reread it. Becker had the dangerous gift of being able to make utter nonsense sound completely plausible. The central thesis of *The Heavenly City* is not pure nonsense by any means, but much of it is either wrong or irrelevant.

For when all is said and done, the plain truth of the matter is that the *philosophes* wanted to build an earthly city and not a heavenly one. No amount of wit can in the end ob-scure the momentous difference between the devout rationalism of the thirteenth century and the critical rationalism of the eighteenth. The philosophes accepted nothing on faith except reason itself, while the Schoolmen had found reasons for accepting nearly everything on faith. The eighteenth century's commitment to free inquiry and to free discussion stands in irreducible contrast to the medieval commitment to finality and uniformity of belief. There is a real difference and a very great one between Augustine's view of man's capacities and the view that most eighteenth-century thinkers held. It may be that Becker thought he had taken account of that difference when he inserted the phrase "allowance made for certain important alterations in the bias" in the formal statement of his thesis, but I believe that if *sufficient* allowance is made for these "alterations in the bias," the effect is to cancel out altogether his main assertion that "the underlying preconceptions of eighteenth-century thought were still . . . essentially the same as those of the thirteenth century."

The Heavenly City is often a brilliantly provocative interpretation of eighteenth-century ideas, but it is not always a well-informed one. Becker had certainly read widely in the classics of the Enlightenment, but his knowledge of some of the important European writers was far from encyclopedic and it was sometimes inaccurate. One can find in *The Heavenly City,* along with the perceptive comments that are justly admired, dozens of misconceptions, dubious generalizations, rhetorical exaggerations, erroneous citations, and factual mistakes. Many of these are trivial, but some of them are important. I shall mention only a few of the more serious.

He accepts the thoroughly exploded myth about Galileo's supposed use of the leaning tower of Pisa to measure the acceleration of gravity. His remarks on the status of "enthusiasm" in eighteenth-century discussions betray his unfamiliarity with a whole current of feeling and opinion, the one stemming from Shaftesbury and counting Diderot as its most eminent representative. His assertion that the *philosophes* were "the secular bearers of the Protestant and Jansenist tradition" is doubly unfortunate—first, in implying that there was one tradition rather than two and, second, in ignoring the obvious fact that the only important element common to both Jansenism and Protestantism was the Augustinian idea of original sin: this idea, as Cassirer emphasizes [in his *The Philosophy of the Enlightenment*], was virtually the only one unanimously opposed by "enlightened" thinkers no matter what their tendency or shade of opinion. Becker's appraisal of Raynal's *Philosophical and Political History of European Settlement and Commerce in the Two Indies* is grossly unfair to Raynal in calling his book "half fiction" and in implying that Raynal deliberately twisted facts to suit his beliefs.

Occasionally Becker contrives a bit of startlingly perverse logic like this one: "The Philosophers were, after all, primarily concerned with the present state of things, which they wished to change; and they needed good reasons for their desire to change it." Surely the order of events is here inverted, unless Becker meant to say that the Philosophers' desire for change was in the beginning utterly without reasons, hence completely capricious and irrational, needing to be supported by reasons invented after the event. Perhaps this is his real meaning, but if it is, the point is of sufficient importance to be discussed at length—after all, people do not often set out to change an existing state of things without any good reason. Yet Becker merely goes on to list the reasons which he supposes the Philosophers to have invented *ex post facto*.

> Becker probably did not mean to provide such a spectacular example of Voltaire's saying that "History is a pack of tricks played on the dead," nor did the historians of the Enlightenment deserve to have such a trick played at their expense.
>
> — *Ralph H. Bowen*

There is a small grain of truth and a mountain of exaggeration in the statement that "the eighteenth-century Philosophers held fast to a revealed body of knowledge, and they were unwilling or unable to learn anything from history which could not be reconciled with their faith." The grain of truth is, of course, to be found in the valid but trite observation that the historians of the Enlightenment—like their confrères in other ages—were not always free of unconscious bias. But the remainder of the statement is overdrawn to the point of becoming a caricature. From Bayle and Voltaire through Robertson, Hume, and Gibbon there is—in addition to a candidly avowed and easily discounted point of view—overwhelming evidence of a growing passion for accuracy, completeness, and impartiality, as well as an increasing willingness to hew to the facts, let the philosophical chips fall where they may. Becker probably did not mean to provide such a spectacular example of Voltaire's saying that "History is a pack of tricks played on the dead," nor did the historians of the Enlightenment deserve to have such a trick played at their expense.

Becker correctly emphasizes that the idea of natural law was the most fundamental of the "underlying preconceptions" on which eighteenth-century thought rested. And in his second chapter he rightly makes much of the fact that "in the eighteenth-century climate of opinion, . . . nature is the test, the standard." He has many acute things to say about the religion of nature which enabled the disciples of the Newtonian philosophy to go on worshipping after they had given "another form and a new name to the object of worship: having denatured God, they deified nature." But it is not clear how this point furthers his general argument, for Becker's thesis asserts an identity between the objects of worship of the eighteenth century and those of the thirteenth century. It is not enough for his purpose to show that religious feelings were present and important in both ages, for Becker had undertaken to show that the *philosophes* were really Christians, and medieval Christians at that. Unless he meant to contend that all religions are "essentially" identical, he was obliged to show that nature worship is really the same thing as Christianity and

not a heresy, as Christian theologians have always maintained. Becker does none of these things. His argument marches part way up the hill, proclaims that it has reached the summit, and then marches unobtrusively down again. I do not know whether Becker was aware of this logical hiatus or whether he was taken in by his own verbal pyrotechnics.

A similar confusion, or sleight of hand, appears in his discussion of natural law. Becker is prompt to admit that concepts of nature and natural law antedate both the Enlightenment and Christianity. Then, however, he sweeps all pre-Christian versions of natural law under the rug: "In the earlier centuries the ideal image of nature was, as one may say, too ghostly ever to be mistaken for nature herself." Becker is apparently speaking here only of the medieval image of nature, for the Greeks had not found nature "intractable, even mysterious and dangerous, at best inharmonious to man"; neither had the Stoic philosophers, who transmitted the idea of natural law to Christian thought.

He leaves us to conclude that allegiance to natural law is one of the important "preconceptions" that the eighteenth and the thirteenth centuries had in common. Nowhere does he explicitly draw this conclusion—perhaps he was wise to let it appear only by indirection. At any rate, he was probably aware that it would seriously weaken his argument to point out what is surely an obvious feature of the Enlightenment: that its concept of nature and natural law was sharply opposed to the Christian concept and closely allied to the ancient Stoic notion. Here, as on so many other fundamental issues, Becker adroitly suggests the false while suppressing the true. The *philosophes* must at all costs be proved to be medieval Christians, even if rhetoric has to be substituted for logic in the process.

Detailed criticism of Becker's third chapter would also call attention to a number of serious misstatements, incorrect or misleading references, and erroneous interpretations. These slips are more abundant in this section, for some reason, than in the remainder of the book. The worst distortions occur in the discussions of Montesquieu and Diderot. Space is not available to deal systematically with these distortions, but those which appear in a single paragraph devoted to Diderot may be noted as typical. "Diderot . . . is often classed with the atheists," says Becker; and he goes on to call Diderot "this atheist, convinced against his will." It would be more accurate to describe Diderot as an agnostic, and the weight of specialist opinion supports this interpretation. Becker's next sentence contains a puzzling error of fact: he cites "La Physiologie" as one of Diderot's "speculative works"—but the allusion can only be to some rough notes made by Diderot while reading Haller's treatise on physiology; a few of these notes contain Diderot's own ideas, but by no stretch of the imagination can these notebooks be considered an original "speculative work." The other work cited is presumably *D'Alembert's Dream,* though it is referred to only as "L'Entretien" and Diderot wrote several pieces whose titles begin with that word. In this same sentence there appears a misquotation from *D'Alembert's Dream.* According to Becker's text, Diderot "reached the conclusion that

. . . good will is nothing but 'the last impulse of desire and aversion' "; Diderot's own text is: "The sense of free will . . . is simply the most recent impulse of desire or aversion." I have nowhere found Diderot saying, as Becker would have him say, that "vice and virtue are mere words signifying nothing," though it is easy enough to find him saying the opposite. Finally, the next two sentences contain a misstatement of fact. "Diderot the rationalist wrote these works. But there was another Diderot who refused to publish them." There was never any question of a *refusal* to publish. The notes on Haller were never meant for publication; d'Alembert refused to allow the publication of *D'Alembert's Dream* because the dialogue gave offense to his friend, Julie de Lespinasse. Diderot never had any objection to the limited publication of his dialogue in Grimm's *Correspondance littéraire,* and it did in fact appear there in 1782, two years before Diderot's death. The remainder of the paragraph contains a debatable account of *Rameau's Nephew,* but this is less disturbing than the series of demonstrable mistakes on which the main argument of the paragraph is based.

The concluding chapter on "The Uses of Posterity" is probably the best. Becker here comes closet to being right about the *philosophes.* The trouble is that he also does irreparable damage to his own contention that the *philosophes* were unconscious Christians. We cannot agree with this thesis if we accept Becker's very cogent demonstration that they substituted posterity for the traditional Christian belief in personal immortality. For how many Christians—especially medieval Christians—have thought that worldly reputation is an adequate recompense for the loss of the soul's salvation? Diderot and his friends did indeed believe that "posterity is for the philosopher what the other world is for the religious man," and if it were not for the hypnotic power of Becker's prose, one would think that this fact alone would serve to give some measure of the gulf that divides the eighteenth-century Philosophers from the Christian rationalists of the thirteenth century. The *philosophes* were, no doubt, religious in some senses of the word, and Becker is correct—if somewhat redundant—in insisting on this point. What he fails to take into account is that one can very easily be religious without being a Christian and that one can be Christian without being an Augustinian.

To summarize the foregoing discussion, it seems to me that *The Heavenly City* suffers from two major defects: it often makes irresponsible use of evidence; and it does not always establish a chain of logic between the evidence adduced and the propositions to be demonstrated. The result is that either these propositions stand on a shaky foundation of dubious fact and still more dubious generalization or they are refuted by Becker's own evidence once it is logically construed and evaluated.

This does not mean that *The Heavenly City* is a tissue of error and illogic from start to finish. On the contrary, it is full of telling aphorisms and wonderfully acute observations which, taken singly, can only be enthusiastically applauded. The point is that most of these have no logical bearing on Becker's central paradox. They make *The Heavenly City* a lively, informative, perceptive book—

probably the most provocative ever written about the Enlightenment. It is a pity that it is so often mistaken or irrelevant.

It is a pity, too, that Becker worked so hard in some places to be amusing. He was a master of epigram and of deft characterization. It is all the more regrettable that he so often chose, for rhetorical effect, to adopt a highly objectionable tone of condescending superiority to the men he was writing about. It seems not to have occurred to him that any of his own ideas might be thought naïve; yet the burden of his indictment of the Philosophers is that they were overcredulous:

> These skeptics who eagerly assent to so much strike our sophisticated minds as overcredulous. We feel that they are too easily persuaded, that they are naïve souls after all, duped by their humane sympathies, on every occasion hastening to the gate to meet and welcome platitudes and panaceas. And so our jaded and somewhat morbid modern curiosity is at last aroused. We wish to know the reason for all this fragile optimism. We wish to know what it is that sustains this childlike faith, what unexamined prepossessions enable the Philosophers to see the tangled wilderness of the world in this symmetrical, this obvious and uncomplicated pattern.

What entitles Becker to use this patronizing tone? Evidently some conviction of superior insight, of a more sophisticated mind. If we try to find out where this conviction could have come from, we speedily discover that Becker makes the same gratuitous assumption that he ridicules the Philosophers for having made: he assumes that the philosophical fashions of his own day afford final standards of validity by which to judge the beliefs of all earlier ages. Thus he arrogates to himself and his own contemporaries an infallibility that he thinks ludicrous and pitiable when he finds it claimed by eighteenth-century writers. He is filled with respect for the quantum theory, for Freud, Whitehead, Russell, and—J. H. Jeans! He was at least as awestruck by the quantum theory as Voltaire ever was by Newton's philosophy, and an impartial critic might well conclude that both he and Voltaire were far too eager to draw metaphysical conclusions from current scientific developments.

As an intellectual historian Becker should have been acutely aware of the absurdity of most past attempts to transfer the findings or the methods of physical science to the social or moral realms. Yet he fell headlong into this very trap when he wrote that "the conclusions of modern science" compel us to regard man as "a chance deposit on the surface of the world, carelessly thrown up between two ice ages by the same forces that rust iron and ripen corn." He should have known that the conclusions of science do not compel us to believe anything of the sort any more than the conclusions of Newtonian science compelled the eighteenth-century Philosophers to believe in deism.

I suspect that Carl Becker's real quarrel with the Philosophers arose out of his disappointment at finding that they were not actually such cynics as he had been brought up to believe. He belonged to a generation that was hypersensitive to buncombe and humbug in all its forms, possibly because it was ashamed at having been duped by war propaganda, and it often seemed to delight in parading its disillusionments. To many of Becker's contemporaries, faith of any sort was an unforgivable lapse, the hallmark of H. L. Mencken's boob. Becker, I think, was speaking for and to the nineteen-twenties when he concluded that "we" agree with the Philosophers "more readily when they are witty and cynical than when they are wholly serious. Their negations rather than their affirmations enable us to treat them as kindred spirits."

At any rate, *The Heavenly City* seems to me essentially an expression of Becker's own disillusionment, not to say despair, disguised as an urbane attack on the naïveté of the Philosophers. Simple-mindedness, indeed, forms almost the entire burden of his accusation. They meant well, but they were too credulous—that is, not cynical enough. Voltaire's wit was "too *superficially* cynical to be more than a counterirritant." The Philosophers' aversion to enthusiasm "did not carry them to the high ground of indifference"—one might well ask why indifference should occupy high rather than low ground—and the projects of eighteenth-century reformers are dismissed with a scornful sneer: they are "naïvely simple" or "futile." Later, during the Revolution, their enthusiasm for liberty, justice, truth and humanity "becomes a delirium." By contrast, two thoroughgoing cynics, Frederick II (whom Becker several times refers to as "the great Frederick") and La Rochefoucauld are mentioned with respect because they took a dim, and therefore presumably sophisticated, view of man's prospects.

It is impossible to avoid the suspicion that Becker had a deep-seated animus of some sort against the *philosophes*. The epithets fly thick and fast, the invective is merciless and sustained; innuendo completes the task of demolition wherever logic leaves part of the work undone. We are finally convinced that Becker must have had a heavy score to settle with the Philosophers, for his tone is strikingly like that of the diatribes which some ex-Communists of our own day have directed against Soviet Russia. Had Becker shared the faith of the eighteenth century before twentieth-century developments seemed to make that faith rationally untenable—seemed, indeed, to make faith in reason itself an anachronism? Was Becker taking revenge on the *philosophes* for his own youthful naïveté and subsequent painful disillusionment? Does this account for his emotional intensity? Was Carl Becker unable to do justice to the Enlightenment because for him it was "the god that failed"?

Leo Gershoy   (essay date 1958)

SOURCE: "*The Heavenly City* of Carl Becker," in *Carl Becker's Heavenly City Revisited,* edited by Raymond O. Rockwood, Cornell, 1958, pp. 189-207.

[*In the following essay, Gershoy provides an overview of* The Heavenly City *in the context of Becker's earlier and later work, emphasizing Becker's strong belief in democracy.*]

Of all of Carl Becker's writings, *The Heavenly City of the Eighteenth-Century Philosophers,* if the number of printings is any criterion, is the most admired. Composed rap-

idly, between the late fall of 1930 and the spring of 1931, it was easily written because the subject matter of those lectures had been in the forefront of his thinking for many years. On a stylistic level, it is Becker at his most delightful, maintaining an easy legato, wearing his learning gracefully and unobtrusively, witty and charmingly urbane. Yet, for all their beguiling literary attractiveness these lectures derived their importance from the thesis that they advance. In them Becker posited and elaborated a heterodox view. The debt of the *philosophes* to their thirteenth-century predecessors, he contended, was greater than they were aware of. Despite great differences between eighteenth-century and thirteenth-century modes of thought, there were also many significant similarities. The *philosophes* were less emancipated from the preconceptions of medieval thought than they realized themselves and than we had supposed; in fact, "making allowances for certain important alterations in the bias," their preconceptions were essentially the same as those of the thirteenth century. That similarity went far to explain how, as they demolished the Heavenly City of Thomas Aquinas, they rebuilt it with more up-to-date material.

This startling thesis, engrossing to most readers, he placed in a broader philosophical frame of reference. He maintained that each cultural period had its own distinctive quality, its own set of criticized and more often uncriticized generalizations into which entered, on one level or another of consciousness, the hopes, grievances, inhibitions, and aspirations of the age. This quality or mood, he called, borrowing the phrase from Whitehead, who had already borrowed it from another, "the climate of opinion." In Becker's considered judgment there were notably similar moods or assumptions in the two historical climates of opinion which seemed so utterly different.

As he elaborated his ideas, Becker suggested, rather than expounded in detail, that he, too, knew that the answers which the Enlightenment gave to that "phase of 18 century thought" which interested him differed radically from those put forth earlier. The phase he chose to consider revolved around man's fate and the nature of the universe. We may assume that he was aware of the gap between the other-worldly perspective of Thomas Aquinas and the mundane eighteenth-century conviction which affirmed that man's unsolved problems were soon, that is relatively soon, to be solved on earth. But he was not writing his book to repeat for all what no one disputed, for example, the disparity between the medieval view of nature as a logical concept and the later picture of nature as a neat machine with its own built-in regulator. Almost parenthetically, as though he found it unnecessary to say what everybody knew, he alluded to the difference between the Thomistic view of natural law as a construction of deductive logic and the later doctrine of natural law as the observed harmonious behavior of material things. He chose, deliberately, not to make too much of those differences. His interest lay elsewhere, in the similarities rather than the differences between Christian ethic and cosmology and "the religion of humanity."

What he chose to examine at close range was, first, the fundamental assumptions underlying the different conclusions. In his judgment those assumptions were the same. In both instances, he reminded his listeners, the preconceptions concerning the nature of man and his existence were similar: life was not empty but meaningful; the drama of man's fate was of paramount significance. According to the theologians, man's primitive innocence had been debased into original sin; if the *philosophes* were to be followed, his natural goodness had been vitiated by unnatural custom. Both outlooks postulated the existence of forces or a power greater than man, a God—however differently conceived and called—and both felt a sense of obligation to explain His ways to man. Christianity and *philosophie* were also at one in their common assumption that the dignity of the human person commanded respect; both attributed to man certain natural rights and assigned to the proper authorities the role and the duty of protecting him in the exercise of those rights. Possessed of free will and endowed with responsibility for his action, man could satisfactorily work out his destiny. With either interpretation of the cosmic plan before him as an indispensable reference work, he could adjust thought and deed to the providential scheme and improve his lot.

It was not only the similarity of those preconceptions, which he himself could no longer accept, to which Becker called attention. He gave concrete illustrations of the similarity in the thinking processes which had enabled the two groups of thinkers to accept as valid the preconceptions from which their conclusions followed. In both centuries an awkward dilemma had arisen to confront the thinkers as they began to formulate their views, the inescapable necessity of determining whether man was in fact living in a universe governed by a beneficent mind or in a world ruled by indifferent force. And on both occasions the accredited spokesmen, without intent to deceive of course, indulged in some coercing of reason to have it solve the dilemma to their satisfaction and proclaim that the will of God or the law of the Supreme Being governed the world. They made reason amenable by different devices, such as explaining that things were not what they actually seemed, by insisting that only co-operative facts need apply to answer awkward questions, or by reaffirming that after all the heart did have its reasons. Whether one expedient was employed or another, or a more subtle combination of them, by their deftly guided thinking process they formulated cosmologies which enabled man, sophisticated yet believing man, to live comfortably with himself, while expecting still greater happiness at some future date and place, not precisely specified.

Such, in brief compass, is the theme of *The Heavenly City,* the validity of which several able scholars have subjected to searching re-examination. It transpires from the papers presented at the Sixth Annual Meeting of the New York State Association of European Historians, as well as from the discussion from the floor, that many scholars of the Enlightenment had long, if silently, entertained serious reservations. These reservations ranged from criticism of Becker's style to strictures more or less guarded concerning his scholarship and his seemingly unchallenged status as thinker. In the opinion of one commentator, the ten printings of *The Heavenly City* constituted "an unwarranted success."

The voicing of these evaluations has shaken the equanimity of Becker's faithful admirers, probably more than it would have upset Becker himself. Searching questions concerning the substance of his book would have greatly interested him but without unduly disturbing him. So far as his style was concerned, it is no secret that he recognized with some acuteness the difficulty that a writer experienced in conveying his thoughts through words, a difficulty, he was aware, not peculiar to himself. His comment on the immediate reception of his presidential address to the American Historical Association of the same year (1931) suggests the response he might have made had *The Heavenly City* been criticized in his lifetime as it was twenty-five years later. "Many historians," he wrote, "won't think much of this address ["**Everyman His Own Historian**"]. F. J. Turner was much pleased with it. C. A. Beard and Jameson and Burr also. Of course it isn't up to what I had in mind. But that's an old story."

The criticism, which is expounded in detail in several essays of this symposium, runs somewhat as follows: *The Heavenly City* was deliberately provocative, designed through a willful paradox to stimulate listeners and even shock them. With his customary witty and charming style, playing gaily with words, Becker covered his impatience with his intellectual forebears and veiled a deadly intent to "debunk" the Englightenment. He wished to reveal the naïveté of the *philosophes,* if not also to expose their fraudulence. On a professional level, the critique continues, it would be seen and should be said that Becker showed unsuspected defects as a historian, displaying an ignorance of some facts that he ought to have known and misinterpreting others that everyone knew. In consequence of his failure to grasp what the *philosophes* were trying to do, in the course of trying to prove that they were unwittingly and unwillingly Christians at their most unchristian moment, he ignored the immense differences which set the two centuries apart and so exaggerated the continuity between the thirteenth century and the eighteenth as to give a totally misleading picture of the Enlightenment. In short, *The Heavenly City* had all the virtues save one, that of being right.

The trouble arose, the commentaries go on, because Becker disregarded his own warning not to take the term "Heavenly City" too literally. He did not pay enough heed to his own explanation when he said that the *philosophes* dismantled the Heavenly City of Thomas Aquinas only to rebuild it with more up-to-date materials, that he was only maintaining that the dream of infinite progress of mankind and the attainment of human perfection on earth were Utopian illusions. He fell into a trap of his own making when, first, he took his paradox far more seriously than he should have and, second, did so without seeming to be aware of what he was doing. *The Heavenly City* exposed Becker's feet of clay as a historian, or one foot at least. It showed him up as an innocent, almost ludicrously falling into a trap that he had set for other innocents.

The charges are impressive. What is one to make of them? Certainly, one can appreciate the irritation of professional historians over the spectacle of a distinguished fellow craftsman casting a kind of spell over his readers and persuading them to accept as a comprehensive explanation his highly refracted picture of the eighteenth century. No doubt, also, by his paradoxical insistence upon similarities, he made readers all but forget about the differences. Of course, Preserved Smith and Kingsley Martin were available in English to remind readers of the differences, even if for many years Hazard and Cassirer had still to be read in the original. The historians who point out that Becker was not as familiar with the scientific movement of the Enlightenment as he might have been are certainly right. One wonders, however, how much that scholarly *lapsus* seriously impaired his understanding that such scientific knowledge as the eighteenth century did possess had developed from cumulative efforts and that its belief in progress, at least on a conscious level of thought, was an empirically attained conclusion.

Neither sound, believing Christians nor philosophical skeptics, to employ Hume's ironic juxtaposition as Becker did, are entirely happy over the way in which the latter coupled the modes of thought of the two centuries. Blurring patent dissimilarities and deliberately identifying Thomas' God with Voltaire's Supreme Being, Christian "grace" with philosophical "virtue," and "immortality" with "posterity," was audacious but somewhat less than appealing to men whose strong convictions such intellectual badinage affronted. Conversely, to men of sanguine temperament, less concerned over the dilemmas of philosophy than edified by its consolations, his reminders of the failure of the age to explain the existence of evil in a universe governed in harmony with the laws of nature partook not of irony but of unwarranted, even unnecessary, morbidity.

No one could have been more personally sympathetic than Becker to the aspirations of the followers of the *philosophes;* no one more impersonally convinced that they were never to be realized.

— Leo Gershoy

What the critics overlook was that the conclusions he had reached gave Becker himself slight comfort. The awareness that faith and sentiment had come to the rescue of right reason in the Age of the Enlightenment only superficially gave the impression of affording him ironic amusement. *The Heavenly City,* for all its flashes of wit, was somber not insouciant, not playful but grim. The humor was wry with a clear intimation that the last laugh was on man, on Becker, himself. Like the students whom he had been instructing for many years, he presumably knew that the Enlightenment was both the historical culmination of preceding challenges to Christianity and the point of departure for the credo and the hopes of the two centuries which followed. But the course of human events in those centuries, particularly at the moment that he was writing, had belied hope, and not least the hope that he himself had

once entertained. Like many another thinker, Becker was convinced in 1931 that the perfectibility of man and the progress of the human race was the Great Illusion of modern times. The "religion of humanity" was as little—or as much—tenable as the orthodox Christianity which it had supplanted. It was high time, he was suggesting, that one took a close look at the origins of that illusion.

No one could have been more personally sympathetic than Becker to the aspirations of the followers of the *philosophes;* no one more impersonally convinced that they were never to be realized. He had rejected Christian theology while still a young man. The acids of modernity had destroyed whatever faith he may once have had that human destiny was entrusted to the care of a deity. Science had eliminated the fixed points established by traditional religion and metaphysics to enable man to distinguish between good and evil. But his confidence was also eroded that reason would flood the world with the light of understanding. Here was the crux of his difficulty.

Far from sharing the generous trust that Dewey placed in the capacity of man to be educated, he was dejected by the monumental and seemingly inexhaustible store of human stupidity and cruelty. Like the satirical novelists and publicists of the twenties, he was disheartened and depressed by the intellectual vulgarity of prosperous American democracy, the power drives, complacency, and smugness of the successful, the meanness, envy, and small-mindedness of the masses. As a historian he had not failed to note the widening gap between the ideal of democracy and the nineteenth-century reality. When the great depression fell like a blight upon the lives of his contemporaries, he looked with sadness and with bitterness on the waste land around him and the trail of misery in the wake of prosperity. He could not view with equanimity the gathering of the forces of totalitarianism abroad or, at home, rest unmoved by the spectacle of hungry and angry and bewildered men responding to appeals to their passions and their fears.

Where in all these manifestations of man's weaknesses was the guiding creative force of reason! Did not the plight of mankind, leaders playing cynically upon men's emotions and followers resonding on a primitive level of fears and taboos, give confirmation to Becker's profound beliefs concerning the subjective nature of men's thinking and its purposive and selective character? Was it not evident, as he maintained, that ideas came to the surface of consciousness only for the sake of behavior? Whether he derived that conviction from Dewey or James or from others does not matter. Like Sterne, but without whimsey, Becker also believed that "millions of thoughts are every day swimming in the thin juice of a man's understanding without being carried backwards or forwards till some little gust of passion or interest drives them to one side."

"For good men and bad, ignorant and enlightened," he wrote, "reason and aspiration and emotion—what we call principles, faith, ideals—are without their knowing it, at the service of complex and subtle instinctive reactions and impulses." What was true of the thinking process in general was also specifically true of the thinking process of historians. History, like philosophy, also reflected and dealt with the presuppositions, frustrations, and hopes of its time. Try as he would, the historian could not escape the impress of his epoch. Its assumptions in the main were his assumptions; its frame of reference was his, regarding time and space, man and nature, life on earth and the hereafter. Its values tended to be his values; its truths, his truths.

Becker was writing *The Heavenly City* in 1931, the same year that he composed and delivered his famous address, **"Everyman His Own Historian."** In that resounding manifesto of historical relativism he put forth in its most polished and perfected form the philosophy of history that he had been developing from 1910 on, when he first expressed his views in an essay, **"Detachment and the Writing of History."** And in *The Heavenly City* he was using the Enlightenment as a case study, a specific illustration of his broader theoretical arguments. He also utilized the opportunity of discussing the *philosophes* to intimate that he had as little confidence in the reform projects currently propounded by the twentieth-century descendants of the *philosophes* as he had in the proposals of the earlier apostles of reason.

History, he maintained in **"Everyman,"** was not and could not be actuality. History was written history, and written history was affirmation, a foreshortened and incomplete representation of a reality that once was. To represent all the evidence that ever occurred was clearly impossible, for the historian of necessity had to work with traces. Assuming it were possible to have all the facts, it would still not be desirable. The worth of history as affirmation of a vanished reality consisted, if it possessed any worth at all, precisely in the selectivity exercised by the researcher and the writer. To carry on research without knowing what one was looking for was a waste of the researcher's time; and the published findings of an effort so conceived would be an abuse of the reader's confidence.

The honest researcher prided himself naturally on coming into the court of history with clean hands. It was only his hands and the notepaper they carried which were clean. Whether he knew it or not, his mind and his heart were already smudged. They bore the impress of ideas and emotions—principles if one approved of them, otherwise prejudices—that he had somehow already acquired. Whether the historian knew it or not, it was those ideas and emotions which overwhelmingly inclined him to make the selections of past evidence that he did. It was not a case of his sticking to the facts; it was a case of the facts sticking to him.

Since history was an inside job, an affair of the mind and heart, "historical facts," not vanished realities, were the data with which the historian worked. Those facts, continued Becker, were of course the best possible affirmation of the reality that professional honesty and expert scientific training could give. Nevertheless, they had the defects of their qualities. They were still not the real thing. They were only records of the real thing that had happened once, like Caesar's crossing of the Rubicon or Booth's shooting of Lincoln. With those records, some lengthy, some brief, and all necessarily if unwittingly refracted, since the observer was part of the observed, the historian worked. For all his conscious detachment the historian

too was part of the observed in his procedure of examining reality through the historical facts. In selecting some and excluding others he was guided by his likes and dislikes, by his standards and values. So the historical facts did not speak for themselves. He spoke for them; and through them he expressed what he held to be the truth. Hence the facts were always relatively true, relative to the times and the emotional and philosophical needs of the age. "O History," Becker apostrophized the Muse, "how many truths have been committed in thy name."

The self-evident truths of the eighteenth century were then of a piece with those of the thirteenth; those of the twentieth, with those of the eighteenth. All were variations upon an architectonic model of deception, all illustrations of the persistent and deep desire of men to find a unitary pattern in historical developments, to devise a single mold into which all the facts could be fitted. All those explanations of what had been before and would be again were essentially deterministic, grounded on the premise that history obeyed laws. In consequence all appealed to history, bidding it offer salvation and justice to men and prove to humanity that there was to be a happy ending to present discontent or misery.

For Becker such belief was illusion. It was in the nature of life not to fulfill hopes, of revolutions to be betrayed. After the *philosophes,* there was the French Revolution; after the Marxists, totalitarian Russia. Thinking man, if he were truly wise, would renounce hope. To free himself from the tensions that hope engendered was to escape disappointment, to save himself, if worst came to worst, from the agony of despair. If he followed that counsel, life could not hurt him. Most fittingly Becker ended *The Heavenly City* with a quotation from Marcus Aurelius: "The man of forty years, if he have a grain of sense, in view of this sameness, has seen all that has been and shall be."

To many young readers of the 1930s and 1940s, who had been raised on a rich diet of ironic or cynical explanations of the human scene, his bleak conclusions carried powerful appeal. At the same time those some years older, and of course wiser, felt curiously let down, several of them breaking into print to protest the spectacle of one of America's most thoughtful and admired historians letting his contemporaries down in the great crisis, and either callously or unwittingly refusing to place his uncontested understanding and immense prestige behind the intense yearning of bewildered and unhappy men to enjoy the consolations of history.

Becker himself was far from happy over the conclusions he had then reached. But for several years more he repeated them in his writing, even raising the query in despondent essays whether liberalism after all was not only another way station along the road that humanity had traversed, whether democracy had not played out its role. After plumbing the depths, he was ultimately to regain his buoyancy and reaffirm the credo that his rigorous intellectualism had all but crushed. However, before he could persuade others to believe in those essential values of life in which instinctively and almost reverently he placed his trust, he had first to get out of the dead end to which his thinking had led him. He could not feel justified in trying to bring "spiritual first aid" to humanity, as he wryly re-proached others for attempting to do, until he resolved the paradox of holding that truth exists to be searched for while at the same time asserting that man could attain no more than relative truth. His task, because its emotional implications made it more difficult than a retrospective formulation suggests, was to bring opposites together into a co-ordinated whole. He had to square the conviction that the earth would grow cold and "all the imperishable monuments of man will be as if they had never been" with faith in man.

He had to bring together the view that man was no more than a chance deposit on earth and that "science offered only anesthesia in this life and annihilation in the next" with his predisposition to like people who "went on behaving as if human ideals mattered." He had to reconcile his denial of the possibility of attaining absolute truth with his feeling that the distinction between truth and error never-theless was useful, that the relative truths which the mind of man could attain were still relative to some unknowable but greater reality than their particular needs or desire, truths hence worth living and dying for.

Becker solved his problem in the one way left him. To re-main confidently and innocently wrong with Condorcet and Madame Roland, he could not. He would not, being Becker, make a tragic display of his pain and cry out, with Pascal, that the eternal silence of the infinite spaces terri-fied him. Nor had he any inclination to accept Hume's tart suggestion for philosophical skeptics and "fly back to re-vealed truth with the greatest avidity." Terrified, he was not; believe in revealed truths, he did not. What he could and did do was to join together the two halves of his per-sonality which had never before fitted exactly and put into a single whole the half that was the child of the generous humanitarian Diderot and the other half that was the pupil of the tough-minded-Hume.

The Diderot in him wished to be of service to mankind. To serve was to act. But to act one needed belief in what he was doing. Otherwise the will was paralyzed and one carried on a shadowy existence on the most dreary of le-vels, on the persuasion that effort was futile and achieve-ment empty. So Becker had first to reassert his belief that life in spite of everything was meaningful and man's fate, while tragic, still significant. It was man's destiny, he said, to be crushed by a universe which was unconscious of what he was doing here and offered him only annihilation in the future. Yet insignificant as man was, he alone and no other creature was aware of it. No one else, too, knew what he knew, that the conception of a universe of infinite spaces which crushed him was his creation, "his most in-genious invention, his supreme work of art." If man was weak because he stood alone, he was also most strong when he stood alone, if for no other reason than that there was no other way for him to stand or act. And act, he had to.

The Hume in him, once the hurdle of the problem in epis-temology was cleared, forced him to re-examine more closely what it was he held significant and of value in the meaningful existence of man. He had to define or perhaps redefine what men like himself had to live for. Here, too,

Becker found he could go about his business only by an act of the will. Choosing to believe had to be a precondi-tion of thinking about whatever it was he believed. Having over the course of many years examined and rejected in turn all other social ideologies, he reaffirmed his faith in democracy. Democracy, he knew, did not conform too closely in its earthly form to the ideal pattern laid up in heaven. At least it was an illusion close to the heart's de-sire, more just than any other he knew, more likely than any other to give expression to the dignity and worth of man.

Thus Becker discovered that he too, like the *philosophes,* had no alternative but to reconcile diverse and pragmatic experience with faith. Within five years of the writing of **The Heavenly City,** he was saying in **Progress and Power** that even though today was dreary, tomorrow might be better. Even though history could not justify man's infi-nite perfectibility, the data did show that the power of man's mind and hand had vastly increased. That incredi-ble tapping of new sources of power and relentlessly rapid utilization of new implements might outstrip man's capac-ity to control the power he had released, in which case mankind was embarked on a blind joy ride that could end only in a cosmic smashup. Perhaps, alternatively, the promise that new power held forth was only that of pro-gressive dehumanization of mankind, only a steady ad-vance toward the spiritual automation of a humanity doomed to live the rhythmic group life of happily condi-tioned termites and bees.

He held it likely, when he wrote **Progress and Power,** that a far more cheerful solution impended. He thought it pos-sible, with the rate of technological advance slowing up and the cultural lag narrowing, for man gradually to at-tain a high degree of social stability by "leaving it" to the machines. Leaving it to the machines meant, first, accept-ing life on the terms of a technological, industrialized civi-lization and, then, by social planning, adjusting his needs and many of his ways to it. The long-sought-for material security and social peace could then be attained, perhaps the scourges of war and poverty be abolished. In that hap-pier tomorrow when man's power established the reality of progress, the sustaining idea would become irrelevant and unnecessary, and men could simply and modestly pro-claim the worth of human values and their loyalty to them. With power ensuring material security, they would become free to enjoy as they could not now, in their time of troubles, the miracle of the mind—free to probe and test, learn and err, build and dream, and not cruelly be be-trayed by their hopes.

In 1935, in **Progress and Power,** Becker was like Ulysses, happy in coming home from a long voyage. He was like Candide, after an eternity of disillusionment, finding so-lace in a final illusion—in the better world of tomorrow, better if not altogether new, in which man would at least have a chance to cultivate his garden with dignity, toler-ance, and forebearance. Five years later still, in 1940, when the tide was running hard against the democracies, the reconciliation of stubborn facts and faith was complet-ed. Becker's hesitation lay behind him. Fortunately, he wrote, some generalities still glittered, not least faith in humanity:

> To have faith in the dignity and worth of the individual man as an end in himself, to believe that it is better to be governed by persuasion than by coercion, . . . to believe that in the long run all values are inseparable from the love of truth and the disinterested search for it, to believe that knowledge and the power it confers should be used to promote the welfare and happiness of all men . . . —these are the values which are affirmed by the traditional democratic ideology. But they are older and more universal than democracy and do not depend upon it. They have a life of their own apart from any particular social system or type of civilization.

Condorcet, hiding alas in vain to escape death, found solace for his fate in penning his triumphant *Sketch of the Progress of the Human Mind.* To Becker, with Nazism overrunning the bulwarks of democracy, also were given the consolations of philosophy. In *The Heavenly City* he had reached the conclusion that it was man's fate to seek the thread of justice in the labyrinthine processes of history. That conclusion he reaffirmed in his last years—not with the old ironic disclaimer that hope of salvation was an empty one, but with relief that there were consoling lessons still to be learned from the eternal flux. If faith in infinite progress was not one of them, happily there were other values to defeat despair and imbue men like himself with guarded hope for the future. The wave of the future was the wave of the eternal past, neither the determinism of Thomas nor of Condorcet, but man's freedom to stand or fall, man's responsibility to man for his moment on earth.

Peter Gay   (essay date 1964)

SOURCE: "Carl Becker's *Heavenly City,*" in *The Party of Humanity: Essays in the French Enlightenment,* Alfred A. Knopf, 1964, pp. 188-210.

[*In the following essay, Gay concludes that Becker is ultimately unsuccessful in arguing his central points in* The Heavenly City.]

Carl Becker's *The Heavenly City of the Eighteenth-Century Philosophers* was published more than a quarter of a century ago. Its urbane examination of the *philosophes* has had great and lasting influence; few recent books on European intellectual history have been as widely read and as generously received. It is that rare thing, a work of scholarship that is also a work of literature—a masterpiece of persuasion that has done more to shape the current image of the Enlightenment than any other book. Despite the skepticism of some professional historians, its witty formulations have been accepted by a generation of students and borrowed in textbook after textbook.

When Becker delivered his lectures at the Yale Law School in 1931 and when he slightly revised them for publication, he seems to have thought of them as a *jeu d'esprit,* a collection of aphorisms and paradoxes meant to stimulate and (I suspect) to shock his audience. But, as Terence

warned long ago, the fate of books depends upon the capacities of the reader. And the worldly fate of *The Heavenly City* has been success—unexcelled, uninterrupted, and, I believe, unwarranted success. When it was first published, Charles Beard greeted it as a classic; today *The Heavenly City* is in its tenth printing, it appears prominently in bibliographies on the eighteenth century, and many a student reads no other book on the *philosophes.* It is indeed time that the book be subjected to a careful analysis.

"Before estimating a book it is well to read its title with care," Becker suggests, and the title of this book briefly states its central theme: the *philosophes* destroyed less well than they knew. They were believers in their most skeptical moods, Christians in their most anti-Christian diatribes: "In spite of their rationalism and their humane sympathies, in spite of their aversion to hocus-pocus and enthusiasm and dim perspectives, in spite of their eager skepticism, their engaging cynicism, their brave youthful blasphemies and talk of hanging the last king in the entrails of the last priest—in spite of all of it, there is more of Christian philosophy in the writings of the *Philosophes* than has yet been dreamt of in our histories. . . . I shall attempt to show that the *Philosophes* demolished the Heavenly City of St. Augustine only to rebuild it with more up-to-date materials."

Before launching upon this theme, Becker expounds a general assumption about the relation of change to permanence in history. There is change in history: Thomas Aquinas and David Hume both used the word "reason" but meant very different things by it, so that to compare their philosophies by investigating simply what they said about "reason" would do injustice to both. Words persist, but their meanings change. But also there is permanence in history: no era wholly liberates itself from its antecedents, although its spokesmen may proudly (or perhaps anxiously) proclaim that they have made a complete break. Rhetoric may change while ideas persist. Becker suggests that intellectual historians must reckon with this dialectic of permanence and change and must be misled neither by what I might call spurious novelty nor by spurious persistence.

This historiographical warning is the most valuable idea in *The Heavenly City;* unfortunately, Becker fails to heed it when he elaborates his thesis. He argues that despite the great change in the climate of opinion between the thirteenth and eighteenth centuries the two centuries were far more closely related than would immediately appear or would be admitted by the *philosophes.* The *philosophes'* claim to be modern must therefore be discounted: "I know it is the custom to call the thirteenth century an age of faith, and to contrast it with the eighteenth century, which is thought to be preëminently an age of reason. . . . In a very real sense it may be said of the eighteenth century that it was an age of faith as well as of reason, and of the thirteenth century that it was an age of reason as well as of faith." The overriding fault of the *philosophes* was their naïveté: they "exhibited a naïve faith in the authority of nature and reason."

This is to fall into what I have called the trap of spurious persistence. It is true that the medieval Catholic rationalists, of whom Thomas Aquinas was the most prominent, assigned to reason an important place in their epistemologies. It is also true—and Becker's reminders are valuable—that the *philosophes* depended upon some unexamined premises which, to the extent that they were unexamined, may be called "faith."

But Becker infers far too much from this. Aquinas's rationalism was by no means as characteristic of the thirteenth century as Voltaire's empiricism was of the eighteenth century. Moreover, Becker forgets his own caution that words may be used in many different ways when he argues that "there were, certainly, many differences between Voltaire and St. Thomas, but the two men had much in common for all that. What they had in common was the profound conviction that their beliefs could be reasonably demonstrated." But the point is precisely that the two philosophers differed over what constitutes reasonable demonstration. For Aquinas reasonable demonstration was deductive and definitional; Voltaire derided such demonstrations as "metaphysics," as examples of the despised *esprit de système.*

Aquinas and Voltaire both believed that the powers of reason are limited, but they drew sharply different conclusions from this: for Aquinas, that which is inaccessible to human reason concerns the foundations of Christian theology. Where the light of reason does not shine, the lamp of faith supplies illumination. For Voltaire, on the contrary, that which is inaccessible to reason is chimerical. What can never be found ought not to be sought; it is the realm not of the most sacred, but of the most nonsensical—that is, of "metaphysical" speculation. Where the light of reason does not shine, man must console himself with that philosophical modesty so characteristic of Voltaire's heroes, Newton and Locke. While Aquinas could make categorical statements about the nature of the soul, Voltaire proudly proclaimed his ignorance in such matters. In seeking to show that "the underlying preconceptions of eighteenth-century thought were still, allowance made for certain important alterations in the bias, essentially the same as those of the thirteenth century," Becker thus unjustifiably plays with the word *reason.*

Becker plays the same verbal game in his assertion that both centuries were centuries of faith. The word *faith* usually serves to describe two rather different psychological processes. Thirteenth-century faith (if I may simplify a complex matter) was submission, not necessarily to what was absurd, but to what was beyond proof and, after a certain point, beyond argument. Failure to have faith (as Voltaire put it facetiously) led to burning in this world and in the next. Eighteenth-century faith in reason, while perhaps often naïve, should be designated by the more neutral term *confidence.* Its affirmations were public, open to examination and refutation. "Faith in reason" meant simply that for the *philosophes* the method of reason (strictly speaking the scientific method of such natural philosophers as Newton) was superior to other methods of gaining knowledge; it was superior to revelation, authority, tradition, because it was more reliable. In Diderot's pornographic novel, *Les Bijoux indiscrets,* there is a charming

dream: the dreamer sees himself transported into a building that has no foundations and whose columns rise into the mists. The crowds walking in and around the building are crippled and deformed old men. It is the land of hypotheses, and the cripples are the makers of systems. But there is a vigorous small child, growing into a giant as the dream progresses, who draws near the fantastic building and destroys it with one blow. That giant is Experiment—no dweller of the heavenly city. Did not the *philosophes,* in their reveries, see themselves as that giant? And did they not include thinkers like Aquinas among the lame makers of systems? To denounce the *philosophes* for having faith in reason may be witty, but the paradox solves no problems in intellectual history.

Near the end of the first chapter, Becker adduces evidence to buttress his thesis. But the evidence is unsatisfactory. It is embodied in a dozen-odd generalizations designed to contrast the anti-Christian ideology of the *philosophes* with their real beliefs and premises, which were Christian or at least greatly indebted to Christianity: "If we examine the foundations of their faith, we find that at every turn the *Philosophes* betray their debt to medieval thought without being aware of it." Becker's generalizations are indefensible not because they are too general—most generalizations are—but because some of them are inadequately explored, some are misleading, and others are simply wrong.

"They denounced Christian philosophy," Becker begins, "but rather too much, after the manner of those who are but half emancipated from the 'superstitions' they scorn." This sentence contains an important truth: the *philosophes* were venturing into territory that was largely unexplored, or had not been explored for many centuries, and they were often appalled at their own daring. However, the recurring discussions of the need for a social religion for the masses suggests not that the *philosophes* were "but half emancipated from the 'superstitions' they scorn" but, rather, that they were afraid sometimes of the social consequences of their emancipation. It is the substance of their opposition to Christianity, not the shrillness of their attacks upon it, that matters: much of the *philosophes'* vehemence can be explained by what they considered to be their mission. They were determined to expose *l'infâme* loudly, repeatedly, insistently, unsparingly, until that large public which was tepidly Christian had been won over to the new ideas.

"They ridiculed the idea that the universe had been created in six days, but still believed it to be a beautifully articulated machine designed by the Supreme Being according to a rational plan as an abiding place for mankind." True, but why "but"? There is nothing essentially Christian about this idea of "cosmos"—it had been the foundation of Stoic philosophy. There is nothing essentially Christian about this idea of God as architect—the watchmaker argument for the existence of God, a favorite with the *philosophes,* appears prominently in the discourses of Epictetus. The beautifully articulated machine of the *philosophes* is not a Christian but a pagan machine. What is remarkable is not the supposed resemblance of this machine to Christianity but its always implicit and often explicit repudiation of miracles: God acts through general and uniform laws alone. Here as elsewhere Becker exploits parallels or similarities or correspondences between Christian and *philosophe* thought to claim that the two are identical or that, at the least, the latter is the direct descendant of the former. This has as much logical merit as the assertion that, since Calvin was a determinist and Holbach was a determinist, Holbach was a Calvinist.

"The Garden of Eden was for them a myth, no doubt, but they looked enviously back to the golden age of Roman virtue, or across the waters to the unspoiled innocence of an Arcadian civilization that flourished in Pennsylvania." Becker is doubtless right—a mood of nostalgia for the past or for an unspoiled civilization pervaded Enlightenment thought. But this nostalgia is not merely a substitute for the Christian state of innocence: Roman virtue, Tahitian simplicity, Chinese wisdom, and Quaker pacifism provide worldly standards. They are standards, moreover, which helped the *philosophes* to evade the censorship in the *ancien régime*. Voltaire's England, Diderot's Tahiti, Montesquieu's Persia are not simply utopias; they are indirect indictments of France.

"They scorned metaphysics, but were proud to be called philosophers." True again, but it is hard to see what this sentence proves. A philosopher is a man who loves knowledge, and when he rejects authority, revelation, system making, he may argue that in his empiricism he is the only *true* philosopher, while his forerunners were idle dreamers. This may be a justified or an unjustified claim, but it does not make the *philosophes* Christians.

"They dismantled heaven, somewhat prematurely it seems, since they retained their faith in the immortality of the soul." Damaging if true, but it is largely false. Montesquieu did not believe in the immortality of the soul, nor did Diderot, nor Hume, nor Helvétius, nor Holbach. Voltaire was far from unequivocal about immortality. Rousseau "retained his faith," or rather claimed that he must believe in order to survive: his was a desperate personal need, by no means representative of the *philosophes*.

"They discussed atheism, but not before the servants." This remark is patently derived from an anecdote told about Voltaire: one evening at supper (runs this story of doubtful authenticity) Voltaire interrupted his guests Condorcet and d'Alembert, who were voicing doubts of the existence of God, and sent the servants out of the room. "Continue your attack, gentlemen," Voltaire said after the three *philosophes* were alone. "I do not want my throat cut or my money stolen tonight." Two comments may be made on this anecdote: most of the *philosophes* of the early generation were not atheists, never claimed to be atheists, and only "discussed atheism" in order to refute it. This did not make them Christians, since their deism was a philosophical doctrine more than once removed from Christianity. Moreover, this anecdote does not concern religion as religion but religion as a social policeman. Whether the uneducated masses needed a supernatural religion to keep them under control was much debated in the Enlightenment, but surely this was a most utilitarian, a most un-Christian debate.

In the second chapter of *The Heavenly City*, "The Laws of Nature and of Nature's God," Becker seeks to show that the *philosophes* belonged to the natural law tradition, that natural law is a significant link between the Christian and Enlightenment climates of opinion, but that the *philosophes* failed to recognize this link.

Becker rightly reminds us that the *philosophes* were not cynics; that their negations were far less important than their affirmations; that they were enthusiastic projectors, reformers, moralists; that their confidence in their ability to penetrate into the mysteries of the universe and to prescribe effective remedies for social ills was often exaggerated and sometimes naïve. The *philosophes* might not admit it, but their "childlike faith" was fundamentally Christian: the *philosophes* were the "secular bearers of the Protestant and Jansenist tradition"; their programs for peace and brotherhood were inspired by "the Christian ideal of service"; the words they coined—*bienfaisance, humanité*—were meant to "express in secular terms the Christian ideal of service." And this "childlike faith" was shared by nearly all the *philosophes*: "In the eighteenth century the words without which no enlightened person could reach a restful conclusion were nature, natural law, first cause, reason. . . ." And again: "Nature and natural law—what magic these words held for the philosophic century." This was the *philosophes'* true faith in reason: that they could read God's purposes in the book of nature and that natural law expressed those purposes. "This is the new revelation, and thus at last we enter the secret door to knowledge."

It is difficult to sort out what is true and what is false in this plausible account. I have suggested that the *philosophes* were not free from naïveté, but that is all, I think, that should be conceded. Historians and political theorists know that the natural law tradition is infinitely complex; to draw a map of its growth, its multiple ingredients, its changing modes and varied influence, would be like drawing a map of the Nile Delta. Becker does nothing to clarify and a great deal to confuse the matter by lumping together, in the same paragraph and sometimes even in the same ironic exclamation, natural law and the appeal to nature. The appeal to nature, as Becker himself tells us with engaging candor, has been employed by most schools of thought. He mentions a most miscellaneous crew of thinkers, from Aristotle and Marcus Aurelius to Calvin, Montaigne, and Pascal. He might have added Burke, the great adversary of the *philosophes*. To say, then, that the *philosophes* appealed to nature is to say that they used this word to embody the standard by which they could judge existing institutions, morals, and forms of government. They were doing what most of their predecessors had done, and what most of their successors would do. What is notable about the Enlightenment, as Ernst Cassirer reminds us, is that "it returns again and again to the persistent problems of philosophy."

The natural law tradition is much narrower than this appeal to nature. Becker's rather superficial discussion of natural law is based on two assumptions, neither of which is tenable. He suggests that natural law is essentially Christian. But natural law had originated with the Stoics and, in a less systematic form, with the Greeks. With the writings of Justus Lipsius and Grotius in the early seventeenth century, natural law was beginning to strip off its Christian associations—witness Grotius's celebrated assertion that nature would be orderly even if God did not exist. Christian natural law, even at its most rationalist in Aquinas's systematic theology, is part of a complex of laws (eternal, divine, natural, and human) all of which depend upon the wisdom of God. Modern natural law is secular, "profane," autonomous.

Becker fails to distinguish between natural law as rhetoric and natural law as conviction; while most of the time he does not take the *philosophes* seriously enough, he takes their rhapsodic paeans to natural law too seriously.

— *Peter Gay*

Moreover, Becker neglects the fact that many *philosophes* were reaching beyond even this secular natural law. Diderot still employed the conception of *droit naturel,* Vattel still carried on the seventeenth-century tradition of the natural lawyers, but other *philosophes,* following out the implications of British empiricism, were rejecting the natural law arguments in favor of utilitarianism. Inevitably, there was much ambivalence and uncertainty concerning natural law in this time of transition. But far from being disciples of any natural law doctrine, the *philosophes* were providing a bridge to nineteenth-century utilitarianism and historicism. Bentham and Hegel are the philosophical heirs of Hume and Turgot: it is this real continuity between the eighteenth and nineteenth centuries that Becker neglects in favor of a fancied continuity between the Enlightenment and Christianity.

Finally, Becker fails to distinguish between natural law as rhetoric and natural law as conviction; while most of the time he does not take the *philosophes* seriously enough, he takes their rhapsodic paeans to natural law too seriously. The *philosophes* were, above all, practical social reformers, and through their rhetoric we can sense their impatience to get to work. When Voltaire affirms that some moral rules are universally accepted and that this proves the existence of natural law, when Voltaire says briskly that "a day suffices for a sage to know the duties of man," he seems to be saying to his reader: "You and I know what is wrong in this society; you and I know what evils must be rooted out and what institutions must be changed; to split hairs about the fundamentals of morals is to escape responsibility, to substitute talk for action." Social reform in the first half of the eighteenth century rested on philosophic positions no longer fully convincing even to its most fiery proponents. In overlooking this gap between talk and action, in taking the rhetoric of the *philosophes* as a literal transcription of their deepest convictions, Becker, while claiming to penetrate to fundamentals, only too often confines his analysis to the surface.

What then has become of Becker's thesis that the *philosophes* did not know what they were doing and were rebuilding the old heavenly city, only with new materials? Without wishing to be paradoxical for the sake of paradox, let me suggest that Becker's formulation turns the truth upside down: the *philosophes* knew exactly what they were doing; they were building a new, earthly city. And in building it they used, along with much new material, some of the old Christian bricks. Far from being less modern than they knew, they were even more modern than they claimed.

Becker's analysis of natural law is unphilosophical; his analysis of the relation of the *philosophes* to history is unhistorical. That does not make it any the less delightful: in the last two chapters Becker catches, with superb wit, a certain mood of the *philosophes*. His deft characterization of Madame Roland weeping that she was not born a Roman, of Robespierre apostrophizing posterity; his apt quotation from Diderot, *"La postérité pour le philosophe, c'est l'autre monde de l'homme religieux"*—all these almost convince us that this antienthusiastic century was crowded with enthusiasts. As Becker says, the *philosophes'* aversion to enthusiasm was itself an enthusiasm.

But—like Voltaire's Zadig (and, for that matter, like Becker himself) we are compelled to say "but" once again—while Becker's insights into the character of the *philosophes* are valuable, they are marginal rather than central, and Becker places too heavy a load upon his evidence.

Let me summarize his case: the sensationalism of the *philosophes,* first explored by Locke and extended by his disciples, was at first a heady and later a frightening prospect for them. If Locke was right, there was no total depravity. But if nature was good, whence evil? "How then could Philosophers say that all was somehow good in God's sight unless they could also say that there was no evil to be observed in the world of nature and man?" Pure reason confronted the *philosophes* with "an ugly dilemma, emerging from the beautiful promises of the new philosophy," and in order to escape this dilemma they turned from reason to history. "They found . . . that reason is amenable to treatment. They therefore tempered reason with sentiment, reasons of the heart that reason knows not of; or held in leash by experience, the universal judgment of mankind. . . ." Becker professes to observe a change of temper and ascribes it to fear. "The Philosophers *began* to cold-shoulder abstract reason. . . ." "The age of reason had scarcely run half its course before the Philosophers *were admitting* the feebleness of reason, *putting the ban on* flippancy, and *turning to* the study of useful, that is to say, factual, subjects." And Becker claims to see this historical development in the works of some of the leading *philosophes,* above all in Hume: "Hume's *turning away from* speculation to the study of history, economics, and politics was symptomatic of a certain change in the climate of opinion. . . ."

It is doubtless fruitful to divide the Enlightenment into two periods. In the first half of the century the *philosophes* were an embattled and socially inferior group; in the second half of the century they were confident that they were winning the contest for public opinion and social prestige. In the first half of the century the rhetoric of natural law had still been prevalent; in the second half it was largely supplanted by utilitarianism. But for Becker's division—the shift from pure reason to reason softened by sentiment, from nonhistorical reason to historical reason—there is little convincing evidence. Diderot, in many respects the most representative of the *philosophes,* celebrated the passions in his earliest writings; Vauvenargues, one of Voltaire's favorite writers, warned against separating the intellect from the sentiments; Hume, developing his epistemology in the 1730's, gave the sentiments the precedence over reason.

Similarly, it cannot be shown that the *philosophes* "turned to" history because they were afraid of the implications of their godless rationalism. They wrote history as they wrote everything else: as men of letters they thought of history as a branch of literature. Voltaire wrote history—and very good history—as early as 1727-1728, when he began his *Histoire de Charles XII,* and his other historical masterpieces were conceived and probably begun in the 1730s. Nor is there the slightest evidence that the *philosophes* became more, rather than less, cautious: indeed, their daring grew with their successes. Deism was characteristic of the first half of the eighteenth century; a far bolder atheism was, if not characteristic, prevalent in the second half.

Why should Becker have discovered a shift in the Enlightenment that did not exist? I suspect that he needed the shift to account for the *philosophes*' solution of their moral dilemma—how to explain evil in the face of an all-good nature. But the dilemma is as imaginary as its solution. Becker does well to remind us that the *philosophes*' contribution to theodicy was unimpressive. Perhaps, if God becomes unimportant, it becomes equally unimportant to justify him. The *philosophes* viewed nature as good but not as omnipotent: Rousseau was not the only one who held that human institutions could deprave man, that goodness could be thwarted, and that the original intentions of God could be perverted. The *philosophes*' affirmation that man is by nature good does not mean that they could not account for the existence of evil, and Becker's case (that to the Enlightenment writers history provided a standard which philosophy had destroyed) falls to the ground.

While Becker rightly rejects the nineteenth-century charge that the Enlightenment was unhistorical, he accepts the charge that Enlightenment history was not "real" history but ideology. The Enlightenment historians "start out, under the banner of objectivity and with a flourish of scholarly trumpets, as if on a voyage of discovery in unknown lands. They start out, but in a very real sense they never pass the frontiers of the eighteenth century, never really enter the country of the past or of distant lands. They cannot afford to leave the battlefield of the present where they are so fully engaged in a life-and-death struggle with Christian philosophy and the infamous things that support it—superstition, intolerance, tyranny."

Becker is equally harsh on nineteenth-century historians. The *philosophes,* he argues, wrote history in order to change society; the nineteenth-century historians wrote history in order to keep society as it was. His criticism of historians is therefore not one-sided. But it implies either that to write "objective" history is impossible or that the *philosophes* fell short of writing good history. It was surely the first of these implications that Becker intended to stress, but it is the second that others have stressed in their disparagement of the *philosophes.*

I do not want to enter into the debate on the possibility of objective history here. I only want to point out that the criticism of Enlightenment historians can be overdone. Montesquieu, Voltaire, Hume, Robertson, Gibbon, wrote better histories than their present-day reputations would indicate. Becker quotes two juicy morsels: "Mankind are so much the same, in all times and places, that history informs us of nothing new or strange in this particular. Its chief use is only to discover the constant and universal principles of human nature." Thus David Hume. "History is only a pack of tricks we play on the dead." Thus Voltaire, and it is easy to see why this should have been one of Carl Becker's favorite quotations. But if we look at Hume's history of England instead of this pronouncement on history, if we look at Voltaire's masterpieces instead of this *bon mot* about history, we are impressed by their scrupulous concern for truth, their careful sifting of evidence, their intelligent selection of what is important, their keen sense of drama, their grasp of the fact that a whole civilization is a unit of study. What if Becker had quoted from the opening pages of Voltaire's *Siècle de Louis XIV,* or from some of Voltaire's and Hume's correspondence about their historical works? These quotations might not have been so amusing or so telling as the words Becker actually quoted, but they might have been far more revealing about eighteenth-century historiography.

It is perhaps a reflection of how intent Becker was to debunk Enlightenment historians that he makes a significant mistake. "The Philosophers felt that Montesquieu was too much enamored of facts as such to treat certain facts as harshly as they deserved, and it shocked them to see him dallying lightly with episodes that were no better than they should be. Voltaire (Voltaire of all people!) criticized Montesquieu for his *levity.*" The *Esprit des lois* "left a bad taste in the mouths of the Philosophers because Montesquieu insisted that the 'constant and universal principles of human nature' were after all 'relative.' " The opposite is true: Voltaire and other *philosophes* admired Montesquieu but criticized him because he was a proponent of the *thèse nobiliaire,* a defender of the privileged *parlements.* They criticized him because he was a conservative, and not because he was a relativist. Voltaire criticized Montesquieu, too, for being slipshod in his research, for accepting improbable travelers' tales—not for being "too much enamored of facts as such" but for being too little enamored of facts as such. When Voltaire (and why not Voltaire of all people?) accused Montesquieu of levity, he was referring to Montesquieu's gullibility.

But it is not mistakes such as these that really disappoint the reader in this charming book; the disappointment is, I think, more profound. *The Heavenly City,* as I have said, begins with a significant truth: history is concerned with the dialectical struggle between persistence and change. The eighteenth century is a century in which this struggle becomes peculiarly dramatic and complex, and the opportunities for fruitful research are great. Becker rightly urges the reader to ask searching questions, but he continually suggests the wrong answers He argues for persistence where there was change, and he argues for one kind of persistence when there was really another.

The *philosophes* lived in an epoch in which the vitality of Christianity was waning and in which natural science, the centralized state, the development of industrial capitalism, imposed the need for a new world view. In building their earthly city, the *philosophes* fashioned their materials from the most varied sources: Christianity, a revived Stoicism and Epicureanism, and a pragmatic recognition of the needs of the new state and the new economy. In their battle for liberation from the old standards and in their search for new standards they experienced the difficulties that any individual struggling for autonomy must face. They contradicted themselves; they failed to see all the implications of their ideas; they sometimes used old words to describe new things; they sometimes used rhetoric that was inappropriate to their ideas. All these problems *The Heavenly City* resolves—wrongly, I believe—with the too simple formula of its title.

The failure of the book is all the more paradoxical in view of Becker's own position. His criticisms of the *philosophes* were from the inside; as Leo Gershoy has said, Carl Becker "had always remained a believer at heart. . . . He had rejoined Voltaire and Condorcet and Wells and all the goodly company who wished humanity well." But in his impatience with his intellectual forebears—an impatience which is always so much greater with those whom you admire than with those you detest—he portrayed the *philosophes* as naïve and as a little fraudulent. Becker was no conservative, but the conservative implications of *The Heavenly City* are plain.

And *The Heavenly City* failed in another, and even more paradoxical, way—through its success. Carl Becker dedicated *Everyman His Own Historian* to those who had assisted him in clarifying his ideas, "chiefly by avoiding the error of Hway, a pupil of Confucius. Hway, said Confucius, is of no assistance to me; there is nothing that I say in which he does not delight." In the quarter century that the book has been before the public, the error of Hway has not been avoided. It is time we admitted, borrowing from Lytton Strachey, that Carl Becker's critique of the *philosophes,* like Samuel Johnson's critique of Shakespeare, had every virtue save one, the virtue of being right.

James L. Penick, Jr.   (essay date 1966)

SOURCE: "Carl Becker and the Jewel of Consistency," in *The Antioch Review,* Vol. XXVI, No. 2, Summer, 1966, pp. 235-46.

[*In the following essay, Penick examines ideological inconsistencies and conflicts in Becker's works.*]

Ours is a culture which once placed a high premium on the ideal of spiritual unity. Authority was centralized in institutions which measured social value against an objective standard. The offices of magistrate and priest alike were prescribed within a divinely ordered universe. Time has been unkind to this ideal. While unity dissolved into pluralism, certainty came under the hammer of relativity on the anvil of probability. Today magistrate and priest alike seek to build a foundation of value on the shifting quagmires of history. Doubtless value should emerge from the total civilization, transmitted over a continuum of time and adapted to changing circumstance, but the enhanced importance of history has raised the question whether what was intended as the source of value has not instead become a justification for policy. And what of the fate of the historian? If he could not, like George Bancroft in an earlier age, mold the past to fit a previously conceived notion of the divine plan, he was no less doomed to warp the past, but with what, and to what end? No doubt many have found themselves providing, in the words of Nelson Aldrich, "systematic rationales for the insights of philosophers, poets, and novelists," and still others would evoke value from history itself by incantation and necromancy. But only the fatuous or blind among them have failed to perceive the modern crisis of historical intelligence. This essay deals with an attempt to grapple with the crisis by a man who ranks as one of the most thoughtful among the first generation of American professional historians. The questions he raised remain contemporary, perhaps because his era in headlong rush is our own farther along the same path and proceeding with even greater acceleration.

Carl Becker left Iowa to become a distinguished historian and man of letters and, following his death in 1945, an institution. He was never a prolific writer, and ironically his literary production promises soon to be equaled in quantity by articles and books about him. Whatever else, this astonishing interest in Becker is eloquent testimony to his continued importance in American historiography. Although it is not out of the ordinary for historians to mull over the efforts of notable practitioners of their craft, there is something unusual about the interest in Becker. His few books are certainly evidence of great competence and clarity of style, and at least two are already minor classics, but he wrote no major work on the order of Henry Adams, nor did he offer any overriding hypothesis of historical development comparable to the Frontier Thesis of his teacher, Frederick Jackson Turner. The current interest in Becker seems almost entirely to stem from what he did to history rather than what he did with it. He left it an intellectual shambles, a victim of the modern flight of objective value. All his life he yearned for some standard for judging the past which would not be a mere reflection of the "climate of opinion" of his age—a phrase he borrowed from Alfred North Whitehead and made his own. He defined the concept as "instinctively held preconceptions," but he might well have said intellectual limitations. Becker exercises a strange fascination on historians because his intellectual limitations turned out to be the limitations of history in the modern world.

Becker was always a pragmatist, but less because of the formal philosophy of William James than because of identical influences which operated on both. He made use of

Jamesian psychology, even terminology ("specious present"), when it suited his purposes, but his affinity to the system was not as a disciple but in the broad area of similar approach. Thus in the 1910 essay, **"Detachment and the Writing of History,"** we find him discussing his age as one in which science had reduced the universe to unstable equilibrium, in which inconstancy remained the only constant. In such a world it was only a step to the conclusion that truth too is subject to change; even reality—the facts themselves—was unsafe.

In 1932 Becker dressed his instinctive pragmatism in philosophical raiment, and in *Everyman His Own Historian* he expounded a theory of history embracing the future and the present as well as the past. The present of which men spoke was at best an infinitesimal point in time, a specious present, successive events telescoped into a single instant. Only man had a "specious present that [could] be deliberately and purposefully enlarged and diversified and enriched," because only man was "aware of himself and the universe." Consciousness was the peculiar quality which made possible this union which incessantly changed "in response to our immediate perceptions and the purposes that [arose] therefrom." The past was part of the specious present in the form of memory, the future in the guise of anticipation. History (the past, memory) was thus a living thing, part of the complicated process by which men oriented themselves to their little world of endeavor. Its function was to augment the specious present "to the end that 'society' (the tribe, the nation, or all mankind) may judge of what it is doing in the light of what it has done and what it hopes to do."

Not just any history would serve. Becker had been talking about a new history as early as 1910. In 1913 he listed its attributes (**"Some Aspects of the Influence of Social Problems Upon the Study and Writing of History"**). The new history should emphasize those facts which have an obvious connection with the present, should deal more thoroughly with the recent than with the remote past, and should seek situations in the past analogous to the present. In 1932, the proper function of the historian was not to repeat the past "but to make use of it, to correct and rationalize for common use Mr. Everyman's mythological adaptation of what actually happened."

The role of consciousness, of human intelligence, in this scheme—to make possible a specious present which could be purposefully enlarged and enriched, that enabled man to be prepared for what was coming—was basic to Becker's thought through all of his productive life. Intelligence was above all else an instrument for helping the individual find his way about in a disordered world. But it was a tool with a close interrelationship with the total organism. The mind of a man, like the rest of him, was "at any moment what his biological and cultural inheritance and the conditions of time and place [had] made it." An individual's receptivity to ideas depended upon his past experiences; ideas could take root only in fertile ground. There was no use in a past through which the intellect could not range with a certain sense of security. Yet because "all things, and all principles of things [were] but 'inconstant modes or fashions,' " the ideas that served one age would not

serve another. Not surprisingly, with pragmatism and relativism as the foundation of their thought, not only Becker, but Turner, James Harvey Robinson, Charles A. Beard, and a host of others, declared that history must be rewritten by every generation, because it had meaning only within the context of what Becker called the climate of opinion of the age.

That ideas are instruments, tools, having the practical value of giving idealistic motives to basic, more brutal drives, such as the drive to power, is a logical enough extension of the pragmatic belief that consciousness is "there" for the sake of behavior. Nevertheless, before the Great War Becker seems not to have gone so far. This hesitation is particularly curious since on two occasions, in 1910 and 1913, he preached a kind of philosophical relativism that contained most of the premises for his later conclusions. He held up to contempt the example of an earlier generation naive enough to have believed in the objective reality of historical facts, upon whose subjectivity he insisted to the point of calling them only mental images. Thus the logical end of relativism had moved him beyond science into an area of belief which held that man lived in an ideal world of his own making. It was a relativist world because everyone had his own image of the world. It was also, though not yet explicitly recognized by Becker, a world of lonely egos whose only "truth" was an integration of activities capable of gaining desired ends, whose conscious mind was the agent of the subconscious charged with the responsibility of finding good motives to account for the actions of the driven animal within.

The idea as rationalization first figured prominently in Becker's work with the publication in 1919 of *The Eve of the Revolution*. It received its most extreme development in *The Declaration of Independence* in 1922. The great charm of this latter work scarcely masked the despair which underlay its analysis. The ideas of the eighteenth century, which produced the great expression of human dignity in the Declaration, were mere responses to social, economic, and political conditions. Further, the men who held these highblown ideas of liberty and equality acted from motives of greed and fear—although these motives were translated into high and worthy values which transcended their origins and, eventually, became in themselves worth fighting for. That the mechanism of translation need not result in worthy values became clearer in the nineteen thirties.

A growing tendency to view ideas as phoney trappings for less pretty but more basic drives coincided in time with a gradually weakening faith in progress. In 1912 Becker believed unguardedly that the immediate future would witness "a second attempt to bring to fruition those splendid ideals of social justice which the generous minds of the eighteenth century conceived, and which the men of the Revolution . . . embodied in 'glittering generalities' for the edification of mankind." Yet from a survey in 1936 of 506,000 years of human history, progress ended in a rundown universe which had never had much consideration for man anyway (*Progress and Power*).

In 1913 Becker published an article under the un-Becker-like title: **"Some Aspects of the Influence of Social Prob-**

lems and Ideas upon the Study and Writing of History." He wrote it as a call to arms to historians to join in the battle for social progress. He wrote it also as an attack on historians who would use history to defend the status quo.

The article began by refuting Ranke, who, said Becker, had believed that history was comparable in method to science because it had concrete, verifiable facts. Yet, he said, history was not just a record of tangible and isolated facts. It was equally a record of traditions, values, and ideas, held together in synthesis. "If society is something more than its external manifestations, an adequate description of it must seek to relate those manifestations which, in their concrete setting, seem to have no connection with each other."

The nineteenth-century attitude of objectivity was a renunciation of the present. In its disposition to reconstruct the past as a whole, to know it for itself alone, history became a fetish like art for art's sake. The trouble lay in the historian's belief in "facts" which he inherited from the eighteenth-century faith in science.

> When all the old foundations were crumbling, historians [in the nineteenth century] held firmly to the belief that facts at least could not be denied; and in these days of acrid controversy, the past studied for itself, as a record of facts which undoubtedly happened, was a kind of neutral ground, an excellent refuge for those who wished to sit tight and let the event decide.

But trust in the fact was all that remained of the eighteenth-century faith. The vision of perfectibility flickered and dimmed until the eighteen-sixties when "The evolutionary philosophy fell like a cold douche upon the belief in progress through conscious effort. . . . [T]he biological law of evolution, especially as applied to society by Spencer, indicated that progress . . . could only come through the operation of mechanical forces." Man could not modify or control these forces. "Materialism had its day in science, pessimism in philosophy, naturalism in literature; religion seemed a spent force." Yet, said Becker happily, materialism and pessimism were passing. Science and democracy, which had undermined the faith of the eighteenth century, was in modern times restoring a new faith in progress, in the belief that man can, by taking thought, modify the conditions of life. The new question for historians was, "What light does the past throw on the present and the future?" Of course, since the scientific method provided no safe guide for understanding historical facts, some other guide had to be sought. Facts, said Becker, "must be judged by some standard of value derived from a conception of what it is that constitutes social progress." Thus the modern ideal of history was now inspired by the common motive "to appropriate out of the past something which may serve that ideal of social progress which is the sum and the substance of our modern faith."

In 1932 Carl Becker was obviously less sanguine and more ironic than the historian who had radiated cheery optimism before the Great War.

— *James L. Penick, Jr.*

Where this ideal eventually took Becker can be seen in the *Heavenly City of Eighteenth Century Philosophers*. The world of "objective" fact could not be retained by man, whose attitudes were shaped by an ever shifting environment. The **"Everyman"** essay delivered in the same year, 1932, frankly stated this doubt as a firm proposition. It recognized that men must have values, but they had to come from the subjective imagination within the context of ephemeral social structures. As for our own climate of opinion, Becker said in **"Everyman,"**

> Whatever validity it may claim, it is certain, on its own premises, to be supplanted; for its premises, imposed upon us by the climate of opinion in which we live and think, predispose us to regard all things, and all principles of things, as no more than "inconstant modes or fashions," as but the "concurrence renewed from moment to moment, of forces parting sooner or later on their way."

To predict that the future would throw out the modern climate of opinion because it was a premise of that climate of opinion that all was relative was to make a natural law of something which recognized the existence of no natural law—there was absolutely no absolute. The dilemma was hardly an indictment of Becker. It was the plight of eighteenth-century man to face the suspicion that mankind would have to go it alone without God; faith in reason and purpose sustained them. Even this much was denied Becker.

In 1932 Carl Becker was obviously less sanguine and more ironic than the historian who had radiated cheery optimism before the Great War. There are two explanations for this transition which at least have the virtue of being reasonable. One, naturally enough, focuses upon the impact of the war; the other examines the inner tensions of modern philosophy. If neither answer is entirely satisfactory it is because answers in history seldom are. Becker was fond of Voltaire's aphorism: history is a pack of tricks played on the dead. Equally apt are the words of sometime public servant and eminent social philosopher Charles Wilson: "Looking back is like trying to make birth control retroactive."

The argument that philosophy was at the root of Becker's difficulties seeks for the first break in his optimism a date slightly earlier than America's participation in the war. His 1913 article on social problems and the writing of history was a call to arms for historians to rummage the past for facts which would create the standards by which progress could be judged. Yet only two years later he discovered a flaw in his thought which he was to find irreconcilable with the belief in man's steady advancement. In 1915 he published an article on Diderot which was a watershed in his thought. Diderot had lived in a century in which intelligent men had believed that scientific naturalism could provide positive values. The discovery that Diderot did not accept this basic eighteenth-century belief was a jolt to Becker from which he never recovered.

The problem which he set himself to answer in 1915 was why Diderot ceased to publish at the height of his powers when he had many years of creative life still ahead of him. The answer, which Becker later developed more completely in the *Heavenly City,* had two sides. One side grew out of the realization that each age seemed to have its own peculiar dilemma. In the eighteenth century this was atheism. How did men of the age meet it and, having met, dispose of it? The answer is, that though they were men with one foot in the modern world, the other was firmly planted in the Middle Ages; thus they met atheism with a shudder. They disposed of it by turning away, by eschewing speculation for history, economics, and political science. The other side stemmed from a disconcerting corollary to the eighteenth-century doctrine of Natural Law: if nature is a Grand Design and man is the product of nature, then anything that man does is in accord with Natural Law. Again the philosophers ignored speculation and turned to history for a solution, seeking in Universal Man some measure by which to judge men in relation to Natural Law. A certain epistemological difficulty lay at the root of these tensions. Diderot, for instance, had labored long and hard to destroy the intellectual foundations of the church in order that a new, more beneficial morality could be constructed. In concluding that all is matter, that without matter nothing is comprehensible, that the soul apart from the body is nothing, that nothing can be explained without the body, Diderot took care of the church, but, unfortunately, also of morality. And this was the dilemma. If Diderot the philosopher was right, Diderot the moralist was out in the cold. Why then did he cease to publish? Because he could not, like his colleagues, escape into history; he was too honest to avoid the pressing problem of his age: how to extract moral conviction from its religious context and preserve it in a setting which gave it no religious support; how to avoid the dictum: "Whatever is, is right." Yet because he could not solve the dilemma he would not destroy where he could not rebuild. Therefore he published no more.

Why were the other philosophers not neutralized by the conclusions of Diderot? Because, said Becker, of their climate of opinion. They held certain prepossessions which prevented them from probing so far as Diderot, or protected them, when, like Hume, they did. Those prepossessions were:

> (1) man is not natively depraved; (2) the end of life is life itself, the good life on earth instead of the beatific life after death; (3) man is capable, guided solely by the light of reason and experience, of perfecting the good life on earth; and (4) the first and essential condition of the good life on earth is the freeing of men's minds from the bonds of ignorance and superstition, and of their

bodies from the arbitrary oppression of the constituted social authorities.

There was an obviously embarrassing analogy here for a man who had only recently asked for a new definition of progress to replace the old eighteenth-century faith in science. Was his hope for the future part of the shifting, unstable climate of opinion of his age? To this question he eventually, in *Everyman His Own Historian,* gave a hesitant but unqualified affirmative.

Another argument for the transition in Becker places the burden on the First World War. Although the intellectual community was split sharply in the debate over American intervention in 1917, Becker evidently suffered from few doubts. He swallowed the argument that the struggle was between democracy and autocracy, washed down with ample amounts of Wilsonian idealism.

> [I]t is the part of wisdom as well as highly fitting that we should have our share in making the world safe for democracy. I can not think that in pledging our lives and our fortunes to bring about that fortunate event the people of the United States . . . can be in serious danger of departing from their profoundest traditions.

Poets, philosophers, and historians are of dubious social value when the barbarians invest the city walls; he put aside his critical faculty for the duration and joined Creel's Committee on Public Information.

Yet by 1919 Woodrow Wilson was no longer the hero worthy of quotation, emulation, and unquestioning loyalty. He had revealed "inconsistencies, egoisms and other weaknesses" formerly concealed. He had, in a word, failed at Versailles; the world was not to be safe for democracy, all was fraud, but worse, Wilson persisted in calling it honest. Becker fingered the horns on his head and reflected on the fate of the intellectual cuckold.

> The war and what has come out of it has carried me very rapidly along certain lines of thought which have always been . . . congenial to my temperament. . . . I have always been susceptible to the impression of the futility of life, and always easily persuaded to regard history as no more than the meaningless resolution of blind forces which struggling men—good men and bad—do not understand and cannot control, although they amuse themselves with the pleasing illusion that they do. The war and the peace (God save the mark!) have only deepened this pessimism. . . .

> [I]n itself the war is inexplicable on any ground of reason, or common sense, or decent aspiration, or even of intelligent self-interest; on the contrary it was as a whole the most futile and aimless, the most desolating and repulsive exhibition of human power and cruelty without compensating advantage that has ever been on earth. This is the result of some thousands of years of what men like to speak of as "political, economic, intellectual and moral Progress." If this is Progress, what in Heaven's name would retardation be! The conclusion I draw is not that the world is divided into good men and bad . . . and

that all will be well when the bad men are circumvented. . . . This old eighteenth century view is too naive and simple. . . . The conclusion I draw is that good men and bad, ignorant and enlightened . . . reason and aspiration and emotion—what we call principles, faith, ideals—are without their knowing it at the service of complex and subtle instinctive reactions and impulses.

As hope was put aside as a childish vagary, about all that remained was a weak desire to protest. If he voted at all in 1920, he said, he would vote for Debs.

The ultimate answer to why Becker wrote and thought as he did belongs to a totality of experience in which we are not permitted to share. The fragmentary historical record gives us only an inkling of inner tensions and conflicts. Yet partial understanding is better than no understanding at all. Becker himself adds to the insight. In *The Declaration of Independence* he noted that it is a tearing experience to surrender valued prepossessions. Because of the close connection between experience, *total* experience, and conscious ideas, it is also a slow process. No one does it overnight. In the case of the American Colonists their image of themselves as operating under the British Constitution gave consistency to their struggle, meaning to their lives, and contributed no little to their feeling of self-esteem. When practical difficulties forced them to re-examine this conception, they did so, and eventually relinquished it, very slowly, and very reluctantly. Yet only "practical" difficulties could have led them to such an extreme. The practical difficulty which forced upon Becker the re-evaluation of a cherished prepossession was the disillusionment that stemmed from a philosophical impasse and the events growing out of the Great War. The "revolution" was complete by 1920. But just as we are not really sure what "caused" the American Revolution, so it still remains unclear precisely what changed Becker. Many British officials felt that American Colonists had always been too contentiously concerned with "liberties"; it is well to remember that Becker himself said that he had *"always* been susceptible to the impression of the futility of life." But why was he susceptible? Here truly is a question for the Angels.

The future brought little to check his growing pessimism. The barbarities of the nineteen-thirties presented real problems for a man of his philosophical bent. In *Everyman His Own Historian* he had said:

> We do not impose our version of the human story on Mr. Everyman; in the end it is rather Mr. Everyman who imposes his version on us. . . . Our proper function is not to repeat the past but to make use of it, to correct and rationalize for common use Mr. Everyman's mythological adaptation of what actually happened. We are surely under bond to be as honest and as intelligent as human frailty permits; but the secret of our success in the long run is in conforming to the temper of Mr. Everyman, which we seem to guide only because we are so sure eventually to follow it.

It was difficult to avoid the implication that might makes right, that truth was the decision of the greatest number of votes or the sanction of the largest battalions. Though hard on anyone with aspirations for man as a moral animal, it has proved a difficult conclusion to avoid in the context of modern thought.

The events of these years added urgency to Becker's last writings. The cause of human dignity was now indeed on the firing line. The question of its survival was not only endangered, it seemed to be fast becoming irrelevant to all but a slim minority of mankind. The time for theoretical speculation had ended. In war nothing short of total affirmation and commitment will suffice. Becker had to plump hard; there was, of course, never any question as to where he would plump. The values of Iowa, with all their faults, had at least the virtue of being more familiar than the values of Hitler or Stalin. As for the question of might makes right? Becker remained pessimistic about the "new and better world." He had, after all, been bitten once.

Pragmatism and relativism, taken together as a single system of thought, for Carl Becker proved to be a trap from which there was no exit. It is scarcely surprising that Becker was able to display remarkable insight into the mind of Diderot. The two men had much in common. Both were moral men interested in reform. Both were faced with the ineffaceable conclusion that there could never again be an absolute standard by which to judge the morality of their fellow men. Here the two men moved the closest together. Neither ever succeeded in reconciling themselves to the flight of infallibility. Hard-headed and realistic they undoubtedly were; they nevertheless retained all of their lives a poignant craving for a "lost, and by the wind grieved, ghost," which, though steady was their vigil, never came back again.

There is much good to be said of Carl Becker. He was never comfortable with the conclusion that the data of experience and his opinion of the data were identical, but if Santayana is right, if at "this point the truly courageous empiricist will perhaps say the real past only means the ideas of the past which we shall form in the future," then surely Becker was courageous. If he never ceased to yearn for the absolute, he did not, as did many of his contemporaries, surrender without protest to the crass symbols of naked power which so afflicted his (and our) generation. Unlike his good friends the *philosophes,* he avoided, in so far as it was in his power, the sop of self-deception; even when most resigned he never ceased to speculate. He did not emulate Diderot—he continued to publish. Santayana, the great critic of American pragmatic-idealism, should have the last word: "Consistency is a jewel; and as in the case of other jewels, we may marvel at the price that some people will pay for it."

Milton M. Klein   (essay date 1985)

SOURCE: "Everyman His Own Historian: Carl Becker as Historiographer," in *The History Teacher,* Vol. 19, No. 1, November, 1985, pp. 101-9.

[In the following essay, Klein discusses Becker's skepticism with respect to the possibility of arriving at an objective view of historical events.]

Fifty-three years ago, Carl Becker delivered his presidential address, titled **"Everyman His Own Historian,"** at the Minneapolis meeting of the American Historical Association. It received a standing ovation and created shock waves in the historical profession that have not yet subsided. Becker was pleased with the approval he received from his colleagues. W. Stull Holt, then at Johns Hopkins, hailed the address as grand and glorious treason and a well deserved sacrilege against the goddess of scientific history; Ferdinand Schevill of the University of Chicago was delighted that Becker had exploded the "hokum of scientific method and historical truth"; Frederick Jackson Turner, who received a published version, called it one of Becker's "characteristically fine piece[s] of writing." Preserved Smith, one of Becker's colleagues at Cornell, wrote that **"Everyman"** was the best presidential address within memory, and praise came, too, from Charles A. Beard and J. Franklin Jameson. Outside the profession, Justice Oliver Wendell Holmes, Jr., after reading the essay, wrote Becker: "I have heard you called the finest historian in the country."

Becker himself was not so sure. After he wrote the address, he said "blast the thing," and after it was delivered, he expressed concern that it wasn't up to what he had in mind; but in characteristic Becker fashion, he concluded that since it went over fairly well, while it was not as good as it might have been, it was as good as he could make it.

His ambivalence about what was a major event in American historiography typifies the man, and the man is the key to understanding Becker the historian and the historiographer. He was somewhat of a puzzle to his own students, and he has remained a complex, enigmatic, frustrating, and fascinating subject for biographers and students of American history ever since. His life and work are filled with the strains of irony and paradox. He wrote 15 books, some 75 articles, and almost 200 book reviews on history and current affairs, yet he claimed his chief merit consisted in having thought a good deal about the meaning of history rather than in having achieved any erudition in it. He wrote one of the best and most popular high school history texts, but when he was asked to speak to a session of the American Historical Association in 1928 on the social studies in the schools, he declined on the ground that he had "no ideas on the subject of history teaching in the schools" and had "never thought much about it." He was one of the consulting editors of the Schlesinger-Fox *History of American Life* series, but he blandly informed Schlesinger that he had "no enthusiasm for the kind of thing these books attempt to do." And in 1935, when he had achieved eminence in the profession, he refused nomination for the Harmsworth Professorship of American History at Oxford because he said he had never taught American history and did not think he knew enough of its details to be able to teach it.

Becker seemed intrigued by dualities in history and in life. He spoke of two histories, one real and the other in the imagination; he described two "heavenly cities," one of the Middle Ages and one of the Enlightenment; he wrote about two American revolutions, one external and the other internal. His analysis of that revolution often took the form of opposing personalities, representing its dual nature: John Jay and Peter Van Schaack, the principals in one of his famous essays; Jeremiah Wynkoop and Nicholas Van Schoickendinck in another. The protagonists of his book *The Eve of the Revolution* were Sam Adams and Thomas Hutchinson. His lectures on contemporary affairs all bear the same hallmark of dual forces: progress and power, freedom and responsibility, new liberties and old. The dualities may be seen as those of the perennial seeker and skeptic, at best, or of the constantly uncertain and confused, at worst.

Becker's concern about the nature of history seemed to arise naturally from his own personal insecurities, his diffidence about his scholarly attainments, and his perplexity about the human condition. He seemed never sure of anything, or, at least, seemed not to want to be sure of anything, lest he be disappointed—because he was certain that life was filled with disappointments. He asked searching questions about the nature of history but was never satisfied with the answers he found. He once described a professor as "a man who thinks otherwise," and he admitted that by nature he was a nonconformist. The theory of history he expounded so brilliantly in **"Everyman"** was a perfect mirror of his own unremitting skepticism.

The **"Everyman"** address has been called the fullest expression of the philosophy of historical relativism. The term is not one that Becker particularly welcomed; he decried all labels as confining, saying they told him little that he cared to know about a historian. But he insisted that knowledge derived from historical facts and that the inferences drawn from those facts were relative, not absolute; that facts by themselves were lifeless—they were given meaning by the historian; and that in the process the historian was influenced by his own preconceptions and values and by the social outlook of the age in which he lived. Hence, for the relativist, "old views are always bieng displaced by new views." If subscription to this approach to history made him a relativist, he would accept the designation. But, at the same time, he denied that he was a relativist in not believing that there was a "considerable body of knowledge," indeed, an "increasing body of knowledge," that was "objectively ascertainable."

One reason for the electrifying response to Becker's **"Everyman"** address was its contrast with the dominant theory of historical writing that had controlled the profession from its beginnings in the 1880s as a scholarly discipline and was still in the ascendant. This was the "scientific school," which defined history as a "science of investigation" much like the natural sciences, studied its subject in seminars much as biologists examined insects in laboratories and prepared histories with "as much supreme indifference" as if they were written on another planet. The intrusion of the historian into the process of recovering the past would debase history, it was said, to the level of philosophy and compromise the historian's contact with the integrity of past reality. For Albert Beveridge, "Facts when properly arranged interpret themselves." For George B. Adams, "The field of the historian is . . . the discovery and recording of what actually happened." The goal of scientific history was encapsulated in Henry

Adams's challenge to historians to dream of the immortality that would come to the one who successfully applied Darwin's method to the facts of human history and reduced all history "under a law as clear as the laws which govern the material world."

Becker's rejection of scientific history came earlier than his **"Everyman"** address, and it was built on the work of his teachers, James Harvey Robinson and Frederick Jackson Turner. Robinson's *New History,* published in 1912, proclaimed the need for a past that was useful to the present. "The present," Robinson declared, "has hitherto been the willing victim of the past: the time has now come when it should turn on the past and exploit it in the interests of advance." The New Historians did not reject the old goal of objectivity, but they recognized that the contemporary world would dictate the historian's view of the past. Turner went further in challenging scientific history and in redirecting Becker's thinking. For Turner, history was the "selfconsciousness of humanity," facts were important only as they served to "solve the everlasting riddle of human existence," and "Each age writes the history of the past anew with reference to the conditions uppermost in its own time."

His teachers whetted Becker's curiosity about the historian's craft. He was especially affected by Turner's caution that it was very difficult for a historian not to have a world view. "The question," Turner had advised his students, was "not whether you have a philosophy of history . . . , but whether the one you have is good for anything." Becker himself conceded early in his career that "it is difficult to write history without having any theory about it." Two years later, in 1910, he announced his own full retreat from scientific history in an article in the *Atlantic Monthly.* He boldly asserted that historical reality was the product of the historian's own present, that historical facts were mental images created by the historian—indeed, they did not exist until the historian fabricated them, and that detachment on the part of the historian in reconstructing the past was impossible. Detachment "would produce few histories, and none worthwhile; for the really detached mind is a dead mind."

For the next two decades, Becker mounted a continuing attack on the premises of scientific history, and in book reviews and essays he set forth almost all the ideas that were more felicitously advanced in his **"Everyman"** address. In a review of Robinson's *New History,* he criticized all so-called definitive histories. "Why study a subject about which nothing more can be learned?" he asked playfully? And he dismissed the accounts of the scientific historians with the contemptuous query: "What is the use . . . of so many learned volumes which nobody reads?" An address to the annual meeting of the American Sociological Association in 1912 permitted Becker to reemphasize that historians selected those aspects of the past which reflected their contemporary interests, and that there was always a close connection between the historical writing of a period and "the fundamental prepossessions" of the time during which it was written. Becker went further in defining the function of history: it was a "social instrument, helpful in getting the world's work more effectively done." He short-

ly made clear, however, that he did not expect history to become an active instrument for social reform. Its value, he explained in 1915, lay in "liberalizing the mind, . . . deepening the sympathies, . . . fortifying the will" and thereby enabling us to live more humanely in the present and better prepare for the future.

Three central ideas in Becker's relativism were the subjectivity of historical facts, history as a product of the historian's imagination, and the influence of the contemporary "climate of opinion" in shaping the historian's view of the past. They were all pungently expressed in a book review in 1921 and an address to the American Historical Association in 1926. "The historical fact," he declared, "is in someone's mind"; otherwise it lies inert in the records, lifeless, useless, making no difference in the world. Facts do not speak for themselves: "they don't care what they say; and with a little intelligent prompting they will speak . . . whatever they are commanded to speak." Historical writing, it followed, cannot eliminate the personal equation. Every historian and every age writes history to satisfy a contemporary need. "The past is a kind of screen upon which each generation projects its vision of the future." In this sense, all people have their history, informal and unrefined though it be. Professional history seeks merely to correct the cruder image of the past held by laymen by bringing to it "the test of reliable information."

To those, then, who had read and heard Becker before 1931, his **"Everyman"** address was no surprise; it was merely a richer, more refined, and more elegant restatement of the ideas he had been professing for the past twenty years. To paraphrase **"Everyman"** would do injustice to its beautifully beguiling language. All one can do is quote some of its more luminous passages:

> There are two histories: the actual series of events that once occurred; and the ideal series that we affirm and hold in memory. The first is absolute and unchanged . . .; the second is relative, always changing . . . History conceived as the memory of things said and done . . . enables us . . . to push back the narrow confines of the fleeting present moment so that what we are doing may be judged in the light of what we have done and what we hope to do.

> [Everyman has his own history] which he imaginatively recreates as an artificial extension of his personal experience, . . . an engaging blend of fact and fancy.

> [Professional historians] are . . . of that ancient and honorable company of wise men of the tribe, . . . bards and story-tellers and minstrels, . . . soothsayers and priests, to whom in successive ages has been entrusted the keeping of the useful myths.

> In the history of history a myth is a once valid but now discarded version of the human story, as our now valid versions will in due course be relegated to the category of discarded myths.

> Neither the value nor the dignity of history need suffer by regarding it as a foreshortened and incomplete representation of the reality that once was, an unstable pattern of remembered things

redesigned and newly colored to suit the convenience of those who make use of it.

Becker's resounding repudiation of objective history ushered in an era of relativist historiography that has not yet run its course. If he himself was not the founder of the school, he nevertheless provided it with its fullest theoretical expression. Despite his initial diffidence about the quality of his **"Everyman"** address, he recognized that there was some "dynamite" in its message, and he conceded that it was the best thing he had written on the subject. But for the remainder of his life, he qualified what he had said, sometimes contradicted it, and often departed from his own theories in his writings. He had warned against all final truths, but during the crisis of World War II, he confessed that the "glittering generalities" of the democratic faith were indeed "fundamental realities" worth fighting for. When critics charged him with intellectual nihilism by denying the possibility of objective knowledge, he responded that some facts were indeed truly knowable; but then he quipped to a former student that "all thinking was a falsification for a good purpose," and to Felix Frankfurter he confided that truth was only the most convenient form of error. He said that detachment for a historian was illusory, but in his own writings he seemed to cultivate the art of detachment with literary perfection. Some of his students were awed by his ability to "sit on the moon and unconcerned but interested watch the world go by." His own preference, Becker once tantalizingly remarked, was to sit on the Olympian Heights with the Greek gods, looking down on the human scene with the detachment of one who did not share the fate of Earth Creatures.

Becker was sure that history could enlarge the sphere of human intelligence and fortify individuals for the work of solving the complex problems of an industrial society, but he also expressed his distrust of a "mass intelligence that functions at the level of primitive fears and tabus." He insisted that all historians had a philosophy of history, spoken or unspoken, yet he admitted to a colleague that no philosophy impressed him: "I study what interests me and don't inquire too curiously whether it is worth doing." But in the introduction to his high school textbook, he assured his readers that history was indeed worth knowing because it would permit them the better to manage their affairs.

What, then, shall we make of this perennial skeptic, this bundle of contradictions, who possessed such an acute and imaginative mind? And what did he contribute to American historiography? He surely taught the historical guild to be critically introspective and to constantly reexamine its own premises and purposes. "The trouble with so many contributions to knowledge," he once wrote jocularly, "is that they are made by scholars who know all the right answers but none of the right questions." He himself raised questions of persistent significance. He reminded historians of their fallibility, cautioned them not to expect too much of the historical enterprise, but urged them to pursue it enthusiastically. He asked historians to study the relationship between the rational and irrational, the conscious and subconscious, impersonal forces and human motivations, the social sciences and intellectual thought. He helped to free history from the shackles of scientific de-

terminism and expanded the scope of the historian's craft. He inspired historians to believe that historical study was one of the most important of human activities, intimately connected with the process of improving human intelligence.

Withal, however, he left Clio's image in a state of suspended indecision. If historians today are neither quite relativist nor determinist or partly both, it may be because they have become sensitive to Becker's warning not to be too certain of anything in the business of historical writing. He reminded historians that knowledge alone without some notion of the end to which it could be put was useless, but he never defined those ends to anyone's satisfaction, including his own. Perhaps it is enough that he placed American historiography on the path of intelligent skepticism—although he himself once said that "it is just as vulgar to be parading one's skepticism . . . as to be parading one's fanaticism."

Michael Kammen, who edited a selection of Becker's letters, concluded his introduction to that volume by asking "what more can we ask of any man" than that he should have raised questions of transcendent importance and sought new perspectives on "eternal verities." My own response to this plea was contained in a review of Kammen's book that I wrote ten years ago. Perhaps in a paper on Becker, who so often repeated himself in his own writings, I may be permitted the privilege of doing the same. What I said in 1974 I can say no better now:

> In a world where humanity is struggling for affirmative reassurance even more than in Becker's day, one may well inquire whether skepticism however informed or abdication however erudite is enough to ask of a humane intelligence. As the historian and philosopher of the Holocaust, Elie Wiesel, has so movingly reminded us: 'One may despair at human truth, but despair is not the truth.' Did the gentle Becker recognize the subtle difference?

William H. McNeill   (essay date 1986)

SOURCE: "Carl Becker," in *Mythistory and Other Essays,* The University of Chicago Press, 1986, pp. 147-73.

[*In the following essay, McNeill presents a personal view of Becker as a teacher and historian.*]

Forty-four years have passed since I came here to study history under Carl Becker; and returning to lecture, not to listen, is a little spooky. Memories, filtered and framed by subsequent experience, crowd round; and their vivacity is enhanced by the fact that I chose as my subject three historians who helped to shape my mind and whom I met here at Cornell in three different ways: Becker in the flesh, Toynbee through the first three volumes of *A Study in History;* and Braudel spectrally, through the writings of one of his mentors, Marc Bloch.

Is it an ill omen that Becker comes first? Turning my thoughts to him is perhaps quixotic in this place where his shade still walks and where living members of the faculty have edited his papers and studied his thought professionally, whereas all I have to go on are some spavined recollections and a recent, repentant look at the corpus of his published work. There is further risk in the fact that by a selective reaction to what he had to say, I may merely succeed in cutting Becker down to my own size, misunderstanding him in my own way just as those who have already written about Carl Lotus Becker seem to me to have done.

But once committed to the quest, knights errant need must err I suppose, or at least risk error. So let me proceed, without fear and without research, to tilt at windmills of my own making. Becker as he really was remains, in any case, beyond reach. His own principles make that clear. What I can try to anatomize instead is his meaning for me; a tiny episode in intellectual history, but delicate and difficult enough inasmuch as it involves human interaction across a generation gap and within a now quite vanished climate of opinion framed by the two great wars of this century.

I have no recollection whatever of first meeting Carl Becker. Instead, his name calls two memories to mind, one probably dating from my first year here, 1939-40, and the second dating certainly from the fall of 1940 when I was his teaching assistant.

The first vision takes me back to an afternoon meeting of his seminar. Becker was at the head of the table, and I sat on his immediate left. Perhaps half a dozen other graduate students had gathered to hear what he had to tell us. The announced theme of his seminar that year was historiography; but we seldom met, for Becker was chronically ill and cancelled meetings more often than not. But on this particular afternoon he had made his way to campus with a heavily corrected typescript in hand, and from where I sat I could see how words had been changed, phrases moved back and forth, and whole passages stricken out and rewritten. He read from his text for an hour or more, every so often losing his place amidst the tangled corrections, or pausing to decipher scribbled emendations. I remember nothing about discussion afterwards. Presumably, it was desultory. For Becker's theme that afternoon was the concept of creation and cosmic recurrence as recorded in ancient Hindu and Buddhist texts. Such silly stories did not interest me, and Becker's summary of them remained remote from anything I knew or cared about. He was no expert in these matters, as he freely admitted; and I thought it showed. Altogether, a puzzling performance from a man reputed great.

Callow incomprehension thus prevailed in Mr. Becker's seminar that year—at least as far as I was concerned. Looking back now I much regret that he did not bother to explain what he was up to. Perhaps he assumed that we had read his book review/essay **"What is Historiography?"** published in the *American Historical Review* in the year before I came to Cornell. There Becker described how the history of histories, if conceived with more detachment than Harry Elmer Barnes had brought to the task, might become a "phase of intellectual history" by forgetting "entirely about the contributions of historians to present knowledge" and concentrating instead "upon their role in the cultural pattern of their own time." Such

an approach, Becker had suggested, would reveal the "gradual expansion of the time and space frame of reference which in some fashion conditions the range and quality of human thought." But I had not read that little essay. Others present showed no sign of having done so either; and I certainly lacked the perspicacity to see anything worthwhile in Becker's paraphrase and commentary on Indian myths. It is ironic now for me to realize how utterly I failed to appreciate his effort to transcend the limitation of the European-American world where all his previous work had centered. I was not then ready for such a venture; and the way Becker presented it left me cold.

His obvious difficulty in writing English sentences also surprised me, and may even have been vaguely disquieting. My habit was to write rapidly and correct hastily. The way the words fell onto the page was good enough for me as long as they seemed grammatical on rereading. Yet here was a man who surely wrote well and still couldn't get things right the first time! How odd! I wish I could say that Becker's example inspired me to more careful correction of my own prose; but that is not so. Several years later, in 1952 to be exact, I discovered belatedly that I could improve a manuscript I was readying for the press simply by combing out passive voice constructions. Since then more and more ways of writing badly have come to my attention, and my manuscripts begin to approach the crabbedness of those pages I could see from where I sat at Carl Becker's side in his seminar years ago. But, alas, it is easier to imitate Becker in messing up a manuscript than it is to attain his limpid felicity of phrase.

So much for my first image. The second is even less satisfactory, for in the autumn of 1940, as the Battle of Britain wound down and war visibly approached U.S. shores, Mr. Becker taught his last undergraduate class somewhere in Boardman Hall. I can see him still, a little, balding figure, seated behind a desk, head bent low over his notes, mumbling on and on in a barely audible monotone about the French Revolution and Napoleon. As his assistant, my job was to take daily attendance and each week to distribute a blurred mimeograph sheet, prepared who knows how many years before, that summarized what Becker was about to say in his next few lectures. Each sheet also listed quantities of additional reading, to which no one paid attention.

I found the ritual quite as wearisome as Becker seemed to. Of course, blotted ink and blurred letters did not prevent the weekly precis from remaining beautifully clear—too clear, perhaps, for human affairs are not nearly as tidy as was Becker's mind. But for students looking ahead to an exam, clarity and brevity were a great comfort. Simply memorizing the contents of a slender sheaf of fifteen mimeographed pages provided Becker's students with everything they needed to pass the course. Sitting quietly in class was a price to be paid, but students were biddable then as they are again today. For the really ambitious, there was Gershoy's textbook, which treated everything summarized in the weekly precis at much greater length. Indeed, rumor among Cornell graduate students held that Gershoy had used Becker's mimeographs—the very same I handed out—to write his book, having first checked to make sure that Becker no longer planned on turning his lectures into a book. Whether that is true I cannot say; nothing in Becker's published correspondence seems to support the idea. But that was how we accounted for the resemblance.

Why did he teach so badly? It seemed unpardonable then and it seems so still. Each tattered capsule I distributed to the class was insulated from anything he was thinking about at the time, being no more than a deposit from a then quite distant past, dredged up anew for uncomprehending and indifferent undergraduates; rightly indifferent, I must say, since Becker only expected them to regurgitate scraps from his mimeographed sheets on quizzes afterwards. For someone who held the life of the mind so dear and whose own internal dialogue was so intense, such an abdication seems altogether out of character.

I can only suppose that in a time long before I knew him, institutional constraints required professors to lecture, though Becker's intense shyness made that act terribly painful. Failure to communicate viva voce taught him to rely on written precis of what he was going to say; and once they took form—I presume in his early days at Cornell—duty and convention required him to continue the ritual of meeting classes, whether his lectures served any useful purpose or not. The suggested readings were there for anyone who might by some chance become really interested. What more was there to do?

Perhaps, indeed, the drive to write well that carried him to such heights was tied up with his equally conspicuous failure as a lecturer. Shyness, so inhibiting in public speech, often arises from overweening self-esteem—self-esteem that makes its victim feel unsure of being recognized or accepted by others at anything like his own valuation. As a student, Becker probably did suffer from overdoses both of insecurity and of self-esteem; and as a professor he made up for failure in the lecture hall by more intense effort in his study. So maybe he would never have disciplined himself to write so well if he had not been painfully inadequate in class: who knows?

Nevertheless, Becker's mien in the classroom, however deplorable, was not the only difficulty I faced in reacting positively to his teaching. The fact was that I had heard it all before—from Louis Gottschalk at the University of Chicago, whose version of modern European history was almost as faithful to Becker as Gershoy's textbook was. Nor in listening to Gottschalk was I encountering Becker's thought-world for the first-time. That happened in 1932 when I took modern history in high school, and read Becker's then new-minted textbook from cover to cover.

Anyone seeking to assay Becker's influence in American life ought to begin with that textbook, whose blocky pages and bright green cover remain clearly etched in my memory. *The Heavenly City* and his other famous writings affected professional historians rather than the general public, whereas his textbook was so widely used that it must have gone far to shape my generation's vision of the European past—so far as we have one at all. Moreover, when European history faded out of high schools and become a college subject after World War II, Robert Palmer, an-

other Carl Becker student, wrote the textbook that still reigns supreme in the field. Palmer, to be sure, was no mere carbon copy of Carl Becker, yet it is also true that he reaffirmed and elaborated an architectonic of modern European history that Becker raised initially by searching for a meaningful national past for the United States on *both* sides of the Atlantic. Thus it transpires that ever since 1931, first Becker and then one of his pupils did more than anyone else to introduce Americans to European history. It follows that whatever ideas the American public may have today about Europe's past derive more from Becker than from any other single mind.

Given human aptitude for misunderstanding written and spoken words, such a proposition is probably unverifiable; but were I a scientific historian I would deluge you with statistics of textbook sales since 1931 to back up the suggestion. However, my theme is not Becker as he really was, nor his historical importance, real as that may have been; I confine myself to his meaning for me. And in reflecting on that, I conclude that his high school textbook did indeed provide the principal basis for all I have subsequently thought and written about European history. My negativity in the presence of the great man in 1939-41 drew much of its force from the fact that I had by then already begun the process of modification and amendment to Becker's portrait of Europe's past to which my professional life has been devoted; and being conscious of points of divergence, I was blind to the fundamental continuity. I was the last and probably one of the more intractable of his pupils, quite unable and unwilling at the time to recognize my debt to him because it was against aspects of that heritage that I was in revolt.

Revolt began early, for I recall being shocked at how cavalierly Becker's textbook dismissed the Puritan revolution of the 17th century. The English civil wars got less than a page; the whole Puritan movement became a mere episode in the Age of Kings and Nobles, and marked no fundamental advance of liberty, nor of any other good thing, since Britain remained oligarchic and monarchical. My Scots Presbyterian acculturation in Canada had accorded even English Puritans at least presumptive title to the sainthood they aspired to. So I complained to the teacher about how Cromwell got too short a shrift in the textbook. His response was to invite me to repair the deficiency, so a week or two later I talked to the class about the English civil wars, drawing my information, as I recall, exclusively from a redbound copy of G. M. Trevelyan's *England under the Stuarts* which my father provided from his library. My first lecture; my first revision. Reactionary of course, because I merely reaffirmed views that Becker had rejected when his youthful encounter with puritanical Methodism gave way during his college days to Enlightenment ideals.

During my first year at Cornell, a different kind of revisionism gathered momentum in my mind. Lectures by Philip Mosely and Marc Szeftel introduced me to the history of Russia, Poland, and the Balkans. These lands obviously marched to a different drummer from whatever it was that set the rhythms of historical development in the west. Neo-serfdom came to eastern Europe after serfdom had disappeared from the west; renaissance and reformation were far to seek; and, according to Mosely, the Russian revolution was not a belated and perfected version of the French revolution, as I had been prepared to believe, but had instead set up a heavy-handed police regime, whose xenophobia and wasteful use of human resources were more reminiscent of Ivan the Terrible and Peter the Great than of Marx or even of Robespierre. I can remember quizzing Mosely after class on this point, provoking a brief account of his personal encounters with police in rural Russia during the middle 1930s that was concrete and completely convincing.

Here, then, was a far more important discrepancy between expectation and credible testimony than Becker's brisk dismissal of Cromwell had ever been. The awkward fact was that the version of modern history enshrined in Becker's textbook and therefore in my head in 1939 had no room for countries that did not advance liberty or even contribute to industrialization, save laggardly with Five Year Plans of 1928, 1932, and 1937. Becker had viewed eastern Europe from outside, treating its states simply as military-diplomatic pieces in the age-old game of balance of power. But at Cornell a new perspective opened and with it a new problem of trying to understand how social evolution east and west could follow such different paths. All I have subsequently done in European history revolves around this question; but it was years later, and only after encountering Toynbee and Braudel—among others—that something like a coherent answer took form in my mind.

Mosely and Szeftel had no easy answers to my questions, but what they taught me about eastern Europe quite exploded the snug synthesis of modern European history I carried thither—a synthesis that I now realize had come largely from the way Becker had deftly juxtaposed quite discrepant older traditions in his textbook and in his teaching of my teachers. On rereading that textbook in preparation for this lecture, three different angles of vision upon the European past fairly leaped from its pages, thought when I first read it I was completely unaware of any such thing, still less of the conceptual problem of reconciling one with another. Becker himself surely knew what he was up to, and never ceased to worry about how the diverse heritages of his own age could be combined in a way that would make modern civilization worth preserving, or even trying to preserve.

Becker did his best to understand the world he lived in and argued that the only way to do it was historically. His heirs and successors should do likewise, knowing full well that others elsewhere and in times to come will see things differently.

— *William H. McNeill*

Such worries passed me by in 1932—and subsequently. Instead, I lapped up the textbook's information and rejoiced in the strikingly simple, tidy structure that Becker gave to modern times. First came the Age of Kings and Nobles, when state-building and balance of power prevailed. Then came the Age of Political Revolution, when the advance of liberty and democracy gave new meaning to old forms of political struggle. Finally in the Age of Industrial Revolution, science and machines changed the conditions of human life, provoking social conflict at home and imperialism abroad. The story came to a particularly confusing climax with World War I when Europe was "turned upside down in order to make the world safe for democracy." History as past politics, history as the progress of liberty, and history as the record of changing relations to the means of production thus were combined within the covers of a single book by the simple device of assigning each predominance in a given chronological period. Foreshadowing of the age to come was part of the scheme, for the democratic revolution "was accomplished in men's minds before they made it the work of their hands," to quote the title of one of Becker's chapters; and, of course, the industrial revolution began long before 1871 when Becker started its "Age." Carryover from earlier ages was no less real. Balance of power survived the birth of liberty in 1789, and balance of power *and* liberty both persisted into the industrial age. But the relationship between the old and the newly dominant trends of European history remained profoundly ambiguous. Apparently, that ambiguity remained acute in Becker's mind from 1918, or before, until the day he died. His biographers have already explored the fluctuation of his mood with respect to liberty, class war, and international balance of power more authoritatively than I can hope to do.

Three points seem important in trying to assess the power and persuasiveness of Becker's schematization of modern European history. First, that history, as Becker shaped it, was directly complementary to the national history of the United States. Becker had come to European history in the first place in search of the roots of the American revolution, and he never ceased to search out other relationships that spanned the Atlantic. Not surprisingly he found what he looked for, as we historians usually do.

Moreover, the manner in which Becker's kind of European history complemented that of the United States gave the European past a peculiar significance for Americans. Ideas and techniques that shaped American life came out of Europe; and the fact that they started there implied a longer history from which the wise might hope to profit. Europe, indeed, was like a mirror in which Americans could perhaps glimpse a simulacrum of their own future, or at least of one possible version of it. The view across the Atlantic might conceivably allow the New World to anticipate pitfalls and avoid some of the catastrophes of the Old; but only if we were wise enough, and Becker had little faith in such an eventuality. Nevertheless, Europe as warning against and/or pilot toward the American future was, it seems to me, a very large part of the attraction of European history as Becker presented it to my generation.

Another way of putting this is to say that Becker saw the

United States as part of an Atlantic world whose head-quarters remained on the European side of the ocean. Winds of change in Europe reached America only after a time lag. It therefore behooved us to watch Old Europe closely for early warnings of future dangers to the Republic. Hitler had yet to come to power when Becker's textbook came out; but the ensuing years made this interpretation of European history and its importance no less plausible. Quite the contrary: throughout the prewar decade and especially in 1939-41 when I was at Cornell, Europeans acted and we reacted, moving like sleepwalkers or as though hypnotized by the clash of arms and ideologies coming at us from the other side of the ocean.

A second aspect of Becker's way of presenting modern history was that he made France, not Britain, the protagonist. Britain's industrial revolution he subordinated to the democratic revolution—ruthlessly, just as he buried the Puritan revolution in the Age of Kings and Nobles. In doing this, Becker was presumably reacting against a snooty East coast style of Anglo-American filiopietism and a version of American and world history that made the constitutional adventures of English-speaking peoples the guiding thread of all modern history. Everyone else, in this view, suffered from a regrettable backwardness, to be overcome, if at all, by becoming more and more like virtuous New Englanders or imperial Britons as the case might be. By reaching instead towards Thomas Jefferson and the French, Becker altered the shape of American and European history so as to make more room for the populist mid-America from which he came. Assuredly, Great Britain was quite systematically—almost mischievously—dethroned in his book. After no fewer than four chapters devoted to the work of Napoleon III and Bismarck, for example, Becker spends a chapter tidying up around the margins. It shows, to quote the title, "How Political Liberty Prospered in Two Empires: Russia and Great Britain, 1830-1885"; and as the dates suggest, guess who lagged behind? Great Britain, of course, with manhood suffrage delayed until 1884! And an unsolved Irish problem to boot.

In the third place, I suggest that Becker democratized and broadened access to modern history, by secularizing it. He treated religion as no more than a trivial residue, relegating frictions between Protestants, Catholics and Jews to the back burner—so far back as almost to disappear. Anti-semitism is scarcely referred to and the *Kulturkampf* gets all of twelve lines in his textbook, while the First Vatican Council and Papal infallibility are not mentioned at all! But the resolute secularism of Becker's *Modern History* may have helped Americans of Catholic and Jewish background to feel more fully at home in the "democratic, scientific and industrialized civilization"—to quote the subtitle Becker applied to the whole book—whose rise he chronicled. One can readily see how such a secularized study of modern history, and particularly of the eighteenth century Enlightenment, could act as a solvent to the sectarian stratification of American society in the early twentieth century; and I suppose that this was what attracted Gottschalk and Gershoy so powerfully to Becker's teaching and made them his faithful pupils. If so, this was another secret of Becker's success in shaping my genera-

tion's vision of that newly perceived entity—the transatlantic, European-American past.

If I am right in suggesting that Becker enlarged the geographical and sociological boundaries of the meaningful American past in these two directions, I now can recognize that my own effort to extend the base of European history to embrace Orthodox as well as Latin Christendom, and my even more reckless venture into world history ought to count as no more than a continuation of Becker's own effort to transcend the ethnocentric narrowness he inherited. So in rebelling against perceived inadequacies in Becker's viewpoint I remained in a larger sense true to his example, just as his eighteenth century philosophers, in rebelling against Christianity, remained true to their Christian heritage by finding meaning and pattern in human history.

This brings me to the second level of my interaction with Becker: the professional and fully conscious. For what I have hitherto tried to delineate remained quite hidden from me until a few months ago when I set out to explore the way in which I had actually "known" him. It is quite otherwise with the enthusiastic response provoked by my first reading of *The Heavenly City of the Eighteenth Century Philosophers,* and my no less affirmative reaction to his magnificent essay **"Everyman His Own Historian."** I also read Becker on *The Declaration of Independence* during my undergraduate years, though I cannot now tell in exactly what order nor in what precise context I first encountered these three works.

What I do remember, and believe to be true, is that Becker's pages implanted two key ideas in my consciousness which I have never since found any reason to alter. Others besides Becker undoubtedly played a part in shaping my mind on these matters. But it was his pellucid prose that made everything treacherously clear and thoroughly convincing.

The first of these notions is that absolute, eternal truth in history is unattainable because the historian himself shapes whatever it is that he finds out about the past, whether he wants to or not. Frankly, I cannot see why this proposition is not self-evident to every thinking person. Nor can I understand why we are not willing and ready to admit that a historian's thought, like everybody else's, is governed by the vocabularies he inherits, and by the interplay of experience and interpretive schemes that make up the climate of opinion that happens to surround him. This does not deprive individuals of limited originality. Each of us has some input into our particular climate of opinion which, indeed, consists of nothing more than the totality of messages we exchange with one another, day in and day out. But private and personal innovation can only depart slightly from established norms without surrendering intelligibility and losing relevance to the situation as perceived by others.

To be sure, human beings can and do establish self-consistent conventions that permit us to make perfectly true statements within limits of the conventions that define the meanings of the symbols involved. Two and two will always make four; and the most intricate demonstrations of mathematics remain just as true as that simple proposition so long as the symbolic manipulation involved conforms to the canons of logical consistency. But mathematical self-consistency cannot apply to human affairs. A model of historical truth that disregards the social function of words and the evolution of symbolic meanings across time seems to me—well—silly. But if the world of symbols—what Teilhard de Chardin aptly christened the noosphere—evolves along with the ecosphere; i.e., if there is cultural as well as biological evolution—and again that proposition seems self-evident to me—then how can we reasonably object to finding ourselves immersed in those twin processes?

I must suffer from some sort of mental opaqueness in this matter, for nearly everyone who has written about Becker finds fault with his relativism and thinks him inconsistent in affirming the long-range value of democracy and liberal government during World War II, after having described the limitations of liberalism and the inaccessibility of absolute historical truth in earlier essays. I see no inconsistency at all. Personal choice and preference exist and are entirely legitimate. Becker never doubted that, as far as I can see. Moreover, outlooks change with circumstances, as Becker always insisted. Liberal democracy as practiced in the United States did indeed look different by 1944 or 1945 than it had in 1932 or 1933; and why should a thoughtful historian not say so? Is that inconsistent? I don't see it as such. Quite the contrary. It is the person who maintains unaltered judgments about public affairs under changed circumstances who is inconsistent, for he must either find new reasons for old opinions, or else cut off input from a changing world to keep from having to alter his views.

So far as I can see, therefore, Becker needs no defense against charges of inconsistency or of having exaggerated the force of climates of opinion in shaping historical writing. Instead of apologizing for our limitations—still less denying them—what historians ought to do is to celebrate the grandeur of our calling as mythographers. For myth-making is a high and serious business. It guides public action and is our distinctively human substitute for instinct. Good myths—that is, myths that are credible, because they are compatible with experience, and specific enough to direct behavior—are the greatest and most precious of human achievements. Why should we not aspire to make such myths? No nobler calling exists among human kind.

Once upon a time, people believed that truth was timeless. They therefore relied on poets, priests, and philosophers to explain how the world worked. Of late, evidence of the evolutionary character of the entire physical universe, as well as of human thought and institutions, has become overwhelming. Even the stars are now studied historically, and scientific theories are understood not to be absolute but paradigmatic—approaching truth as a limit perhaps, but never attaining complete adequacy to reality. Thus time has truly become all-devouring. Every intellectual discipline has become historical, and in two senses. First, each discipline evolves internally as new concepts and observations accumulate and interact. Second, its subject matter (whether physical, geological, biological, or human) also changes in *its* behavior across time. Two tra-

jectories, therefore, each of them in motion: one of interacting symbols, the other of interacting entities; and each acting upon the other, time without end!

A complex, confusing picture no doubt; but one that, properly comprehended, is also exhilarating, especially to a historian. For who but he is fitted by training and predilection to comprehend such a scene? Who can better point to the important conjunctures, the main lines, the particular items in the totality of messages available to us that most reward conscious attention?

History has indeed become an imperial discipline in my lifetime. A few economists hold out for universals and stubbornly disregard evidence of temporal and spatial limitations to their equations. But they are becoming a lonely crowd when even astronomers have become historically minded, and compute the evolution of the universe in terms of perhaps no more than three star generations since the "Big Bang."

Simultaneously, specialized historians of science are busy providing a conscious past for all the disciplines, making the contemporary state of each intelligible in a new way. As a result, the social as well as the physical sciences will never be independent of history again, and the notion that truth develops and changes with time and place will be harder and harder to gainsay. This is no small alteration of the intellectual landscape to have occurred in a single lifetime. Moreover this historicizing of knowledge tends to reverse older patterns whereby history and the social "sciences" modeled themselves on physics and other natural sciences. All now tend to become historical, and, being an historical imperialist by temperament, as well as by conviction, I do not see how the trend can be reversed without a deliberate, conscious repudiation of the evidence.

Garden-variety historians have a somewhat less conspicuously imperial role to play, for we traditionally and appropriately confine ourselves to public affairs. But the effort to make group action intelligible is no small task, especially in an age when public identities are in flux, and when personal loyalties heave and crack in response to new patterns of communication and new sensibilities propagated via those communications.

Accordingly, we historians ought to aspire to be the protagonists of twentieth (and twenty-first) century efforts to refine and improve the accuracy and adequacy of one group's reactions to another. Burying ourselves in detail is not the way to achieve that mythopoeic dignity. Thinking carefully about the grand outlines of the human past *is* the way to respond to the needs of our time; and I very much wish that more of my colleagues were bolder in the attempt. Fear of error is craven; serious and sustained effort to take account of available evidence is a moral and intellectual duty; and to know that one's best effort will not suffice for all times and places is the beginning of wisdom.

I for one am glad that we will never so far escape the human condition as to know anything for sure and certain and forever. If we did, there would be nothing to do but repeat the truth—like Becker's undergraduates repeating extracts from those infamous lecture precis. But to make public identities and actions clear and conscious through sensitive study of the human past is a challenge to our best capacities, both intellectual and moral. Becker did his best to understand the world he lived in and argued that the only way to do it was historically. His heirs and successors should do likewise, knowing full well that others elsewhere and in times to come will see things differently. That does not mean the effort is not worth making. Giving up amounts to an abdication of intelligence, and despairs of humanity's future.

So much for point number one. The second idea that I gleaned from Becker's professional writing was similar: to wit, that reformers and revolutionaries retain older patterns of thought even when they are most eager to repudiate the old and affirm something new. As Becker put it, to fight one another, men must find common ground. Common ground is guaranteed by the cultural process itself, since what a rising generation rejects in the inherited wisdom goes a long way to define what it affirms. Even the most violent revolutionaries are, in this sense, prisoners of the past, bound to the climate of opinion created among humans by the communication networks that make us social. Indeed, the only way to escape the past would be to sever contact with everyone else—and that way lies madness.

Our inescapable immersion in a climate of opinion that is both changing and seamless, with no total disjunctions and no perfect continuities, also seems selfevident to me, once the idea had been clearly articulated and persuasively illustrated, as Becker did in his *Heavenly City of the Eighteenth Century Philosophers*. Peter Gay and others who criticized that essay so vigorously in the symposium of 1956, reproduced as *Carl Becker's Heavenly City Revisted,* simply puzzle me. Surely continuity and change are both to be expected in any historical situation. Becker was not the first to affirm *plus ça change, plus c'est la même chose;* and I suspect that the anonymous eighteenth-century Frenchman who first framed these words was not original when *he* said it, either.

Even when I was young, the proposition that Russian revolutionaries had changed human nature by abolishing private property in the means of production seemed unconvincing, though enthusiasts proclaimed it to be true. Today the continuity between old and new in all the great revolutions of modern times seems obvious, whether in France, Russia, or China. Revolutionaries' intentions have little to do with the matter. They, like the rest of us, can be radically mistaken, and sometimes are driven deliberately to disguise continuities that they find embarrassing.

The intentions and self-consciousness of the *philosophes* were no different, and should *not* be taken at face value. Their anti-clericalism was Catholic dogmatism turned inside-out—different, yet also the same. Quite unrevolutionary transmission of completely ordinary tradition—even historiographical tradition—follows the same pattern. My effort, earlier in this lecture, to delineate the difference and continuity between Carl Becker's practice of history and my own is a case in point. My differences with him, great

as they once seemed, were really no more than a ripple in a common stream of discourse—discourse whose basic parameters were all inherited, by him as much as by me, and through great depths of time as well as across the gap of a single generation. That, quite simply, is what human culture *is*—that is how it is transmitted; that is how it shapes our lives by directing attention to some aspects of the world around us, while lumping the rest together as background noise to be disregarded.

In preparing this lecture I read far more widely in Becker's published works than ever before. I am old enough by now and have survived enough blips in our climate of opinion to be able to recognize how broad and deep are the things I share with him and with other Americans. The generational gap between us was not very wide. Continuity was far more significant than I realized before undertaking this probe into the past. Let me in closing, therefore, sum up that continuity, as I am now able to see it.

Becker was interested in big questions: liberty and equality, progress and power, freedom and responsibility; the pattern and meaning of the whole human adventure.

— *William H. McNeill*

First, Becker was interested in big questions: liberty and equality, progress and power, freedom and responsibility; the pattern and meaning of the whole human adventure. Nothing less satisfied him any more than it does me. Historical scholarship that burrowed into detail and lost sight of the big picture distressed and irritated him. I find myself railing against the same penchant among my fellow historians. His professional writing exhibited a persistent widening of horizon in time and space: from the national scene to an Atlantic community, and from that Atlantic community to a global historiography which, of course, he only sketched lightly during the last decade of his life— exactly the time when I knew him and failed to comprehend the task he had set for himself. Alas and alack, that I could have been so blind, but so it was; and only now, some forty-three years too late, do I see how clearly he anticipated the globalism of my own intellectual aspiration.

Second is the conundrum of detachment. Becker was certainly detached, or gave that impression. At the same time, he was firmly committed to liberal values, and cared deeply for the welfare of the Republic. Detachment as an ideal is like truth as an ideal: both remain unattainable, as we can never escape from human limitations. Yet as I just argued, to strive for truth—the best available truth—is a noble calling. And to strive for detachment in the pursuit of truth seems to me no less noble for being persistently just beyond our reach.

Yet awareness of the limits of our powers in seeking truth and in detaching ourselves from personal and collective biases and emotions can have deplorable consequences. Cynics may argue that since historical or any other kind of truth is only self-serving myth, any myth will do as long as it is believed and acted on energetically. Activists will say that since detachment is unattainable, commitment and conscious propaganda are clearly superior since they at least get things done. Either view debases the life of the mind by denying it the dignity of being an end in itself. No man aspires to be a "running dog" of capitalism, after all; nor to fawn on any other sort of interest group, I should suppose. But if we cannot escape limitations of time, place, and cultural heritage, why try? Why not join the interests, whatever they may be, and write our histories accordingly?

It may indeed seem perverse to say Yes, we *are* human and therefore must always be part of a climate of opinion in which special interests play prominent and sometimes dominant roles, and at the same time say that nonetheless it is better to try to escape and rise above the limited perspective imposed by heritage and milieu. It is even more perverse, perhaps, to say so when one also realizes that if everyone became detached, society would collapse. Too many voices loudly proclaiming divergent personal and private views may simply paralyze public action. Becker was aware, more poignantly than most, of this possibility, yet he always held to the path of detachment and exemplified its virtues more fully than most of us ever manage to do.

By now, it seems clear that the risks he recognized were less destructive than he feared. New myths, offering effective guides to public action, emerged in this country during World War II and have served us well for the ensuing thirty years. We face new problems now, not altogether unlike those of the 1930s. But we can perhaps believe more serenely than Becker's generation could, that the survival value of societies that tolerate a more or less free exercise of the life of the mind may turn out to be rather better than the alternative offered by the rigidities of an official ideology imposed by the police power of the state. Having conflicting points of view in circulation may make adaptation to changing circumstances a bit easier than when some rigid orthodoxy has first to be bent or twisted to accommodate the new. Liberalism, in short, may have a future analogous to its not inglorious past. All depends on how well we manage to cultivate detachment *and* insight, so as to repair old myths in the light of new experience, and keep them somehow in workable condition, generation after generation.

I conclude, therefore, that despite the disappointment I felt in 1939-41 when I met Carl Becker on this campus and listened to his voice for a total of, perhaps, fifty to sixty hours, and in spite of the barriers to effective communication between us that then prevailed, I can still lay claim to be his pupil, even if I was so in spite of myself.

Richard Nelson (essay date 1987)

SOURCE: "Carl Becker Revisited: Irony and Progress in History," in *Journal of the History of Ideas,* Vol. XLVIII, No. 2, April-June, 1987, pp. 307-23.

[*In the following essay, Nelson sees Becker's irony as a response to the impossibility of entirely accepting or rejecting the idea of social progress.*]

Carl Becker's lifelong commitment to ambiguity has not served to make him an influential figure among contemporary historians. It has, however, made him one of the more controversial figures within the Guild. Some historians commend him for this quality. They find his writing to be intentionally paradoxical, full of contraries and oppositions, overturned cliches and circular reasoning, designed to "add 'another dimension of thought' to the initiated" [Milton Klein, "Detachment and the Writing of American History: the Dilemma of Carl Becker" in *Perspectives on Early American History,* ed. Alden T. Vaughn and George A. Billias]. Others condemn him for slipping into logical fallacies, demonstrating a lack of respect for historical facts, and escaping from commitment into a disappointed liberal's pessimism, otherwise known as historical relativism. The sense of ambiguity that characterizes nearly all of Becker's work is far too sustained and consistent not to be deliberate, and given the subtlety of his thought, too transparent to be the product of simple evasion. Consequently, this clearest of writers remains the most enigmatic of historians. He has eluded categorization within the major historical schools because, as Gene Wise has shown, he was both a progressive and an anti-progressive, depending upon how he is viewed. Similarly, he was an anti-stylist who was nearly preoccupied with style, and he was a relativist whose writing contained lessons on morality. Becker was a subjectivist who cultivated detachment, a "Historian of Revolutions" who doubted the value of political participation, an anti-elitist who distrusted the masses. If Becker was a liberal progressive, he remained skeptical that liberalism and progress would shape the future. If an anti-progressive, he never ceased to believe planning based on well considered values might create a better world.

Carl Becker would surely have savored the irony of historians puzzling over the incongruities in his writing only to find opposing interpretations reflecting their own predilections concerning knowledge, history and moral responsibility. The author of **"Every Man His Own Historian"** could hardly have overlooked the *double entendre*; for it is irony that is the controlling perspective behind the ambiguities and incongruous juxtapositions throughout his work.

Becker's ironic style has been universally recognized, but little importance has been attached to it for understanding his ideas. Irony, it is assumed, fit his temper, or, as with the Philosophes who so fascinated him, gave his prose a provocative air. But why was his temper ironic in the first place, and what significance did such a disposition serve for interpreting history? These are essential questions because style, for Becker, was always subservient to the higher end of expressing a writer's intention. Appropriateness of form was a principle he adhered to in everything he wrote. For him that meant a marriage between fact, idea or emotion and the kind of expression required to convey one's interpretation.

Why then was Becker's particular marriage consummated

in irony? The answer lies in the dissatisfaction Becker increasingly had with the Idea of Progress in history.

The Idea of Progress had been emotionally tied to faith in a special *American exceptionalism* created even before the American Revolution. The optimism of that American exceptionalism, Sacvan Bercovitch writes, has been such a powerful cultural myth that even critics of American values like Melville, Hawthorne and Mark Twain were unable to reject it though they struggled against it.

As David W. Noble has pointed out American historians have been even more bound to the myth of American exceptionalism than novelists. They have been the secular theologians who have traced the development of American exceptionalism through time. They have mapped the tracks of progress to chart the promise of the future.

Yet, at the zenith of progressive historiography when Becker enrolled at the University of Wisconsin in Frederick Jackson Turner's class in American History the paradigm of progress was already under some strain. Turner's "frontier thesis," published during Becker's freshman year in 1893, retained a progressive American exceptionalism. But the frontier of progress was at an "uneven advance . . . with tongues of settlement pushed forward and with indentations of wilderness" [Frederick Jackson Turner, *Frontier and Section: Selected Essays,* ed. R. A. Billington]. Turner's progress was not the orderly rational progress of a Bancroft following the steady triumph of God's plan. It was more like a brush fire licking at the boundaries of a future that appeared through the smoke to be a fire break. James Harvey Robinson with whom Becker studied at Columbia, similarly reflected the strain in the paradigm of progress. His 'new history' relied on no hand of Providence, saw no steady march of values in time. The historian, he seemed to say, could no longer be content to watch the birth of progress, he must pull the future out of the dead past with the forceps of science.

Becker's interests in European history perhaps helped him to recognize that the intellectual doubts he felt were of larger scope than a crisis of faith in America's special mission. The problem of progress was equally a European one. Since the study of history was so dependent upon the Idea of Progress, the legitimacy of the profession itself was being called into question. Becker's doubt is evident in his essay of 1910, **"Detachment and the Writing of History."** Here his oft repeated quote of Voltaire that "history is only a pack of tricks we play on the dead," makes its appearance. For Becker, at this time, Truth is not located consciously for its use in the present. "Instead of sticking to the facts," the historian discovers "they stick to him," provided he has the necessary ideas to attract them. In a review appearing in *The Dial* in 1915 he says that he "contemplates a new philosophy of history with entire equanimity and some little interest." However, he declines to applaud the attempt under review because the author "merely projects into the future the categories which have been used to classify the facts of the past, in the confident expectation that future events, when they occur, may be pressed, without too much difficulty, into these categories."

The same criticism is leveled against the German historians in a review published in February 1917: "It would be more modest, and more in accord with a safe philosophy of history," Becker wrote, "to let coming events reveal the continued superiority of the German Nation." But, he continues, "without waiting for God to dispose, they have themselves, assuming the task of Fate . . . made tomorrow's programme in the Foreign Office." Becker thought the idea of progress "manifestly important," and complained in a 1920 review of Bury's book on the subject that historians had paid too little attention to it. "Much has been written about 'progress,'" he wrote, "but on the 'idea' of Progress there is little of value. . . ." The ideas of progress and the concept of man in general, he suggested, are intimately tied together. "It is no accident that the belief in Progress and a concern for 'posterity' waxed in proportion as the belief in Providence and a concern for a future life waned"; he argued, "The former belief—illusion if you prefer—is man's compensation for the loss of the latter."

In 1933, the year after the ***Heavenly City*** was published, Becker reviewed a new edition of *The Idea of Progress*. He had been delighted, he wrote, when the book first appeared in 1920 because the subject interested him greatly. In 1932 Becker found himself still delighted and still interested. He appreciated Bury's refusal to deify the 'Idea.' "For him the Idea was not a transcendent force dwelling in the shadowy world of absolute Being; it was no more than a pattern imposed on the factual reality by the minds of actual men." What will happen to the Idea of Progress when the possibilities of invention and technology are exhausted? Becker wondered. Bury did not say, but Becker speculated that Progress, too, would be supplanted by something different. "The price which we must pay for the pleasure of 'escaping from the illusion of finality' is," concluded Becker, "the recognition that nothing, not even the realization that we have escaped from that illusion, is likely to endure." By way of Progress, like the Philosophes before him, Carl Becker had found irony.

The transformation of Becker's ironic temperament, already evident in the 'wild thoughts' notebooks of his college days into a controlling perspective did not occur because of any one event. Early essays like **"Kansas"** and **"Detachment and the Writing of History"** show elements of irony. The First World War must surely have had an effect, but as Becker himself warned it is dangerous to assume cause and effect in history where it seems more apparent. His work does become more ironic after the war, but **"The Dilemma of Diderot,"** published in 1915 captures much of the flavor of his later themes and is as ironic as anything he wrote. Much of that essay reappears in the ***Heavenly City*** which is Becker's most direct confrontation with the ironic dilemma of progress and of its corollary, the problem of objectivity in history. If Becker found the eighteenth century attractive, it was less as a retreat to a simpler time than as a magnet revealing the negative and positive poles of irony and progress within the field of history. The invention of modern history in the eighteenth century was required because, Becker argued, the Philosophes had previously invented progress.

The implications of Becker's interpretation of the Enlightenment conception of history are far reaching. If "Mankind" is a personification, as he suggests, and if progress is built upon that personification, the idea of objective historical truth becomes chimerical.

— *Richard Nelson*

The enlightenment idea of history was made necessary by the Philosophes' realization that in rejecting Providence to create a truly virtuous society they were unavoidably destroying their own basis for virtue. "It was one of the ironies of fate," Becker wrote in the **"Dilemma of Diderot,"** "that the speculative thinking of Diderot, of which the principal purpose was to furnish a firm foundation for natural morality, ended by destroying the foundation of all morality as he understood it." Reason told Diderot as it told the other Philosophes that man is but a speck of dust blown haphazardly through time. All hopes, beliefs, sympathies and virtues are made of "the same purposeless forces that build up crystal or dissolve granite."

Surely, Becker concluded, if the only message provided by the new philosophy could be that no individual can be responsible for his own actions and vice is only social convention to be avoided in so far as it may be found out, then "the religion of philosophy . . . must remain as vain a delusion as the philosophy of religion."

The Philosophes turned away from the barrenness of unaided reason to find a more fruitful basis for morality. They found it, Becker wrote in **The Heavenly City,** in general human experience. Such a foundation could not be built upon the frail and limited perspective of the individual soul which the Medieval Church had linked to the Eternal through revelation. Morality had to be grounded instead in a new Eternal, an Eternal in time; that is, the general experience of Mankind. "History" would provide the source of revelation for reason. It would serve as a standard to discover true virtue, to establish what actually was in accord with human nature.

The "new history" may have been necessary if the Philosophes were to triumph over the **"Dilemma of Diderot."** However, the "new history" was possible only because of two ingenious reformulations of the metaphysics the Philosophes thought they had discredited. The first was the idea of 'Mankind' in general. "Mankind" (and similarly "Posterity"), Becker claimed, is not a reality, not an objective empirical fact. Rather, Mankind like Posterity is a personification that doesn't exist except as a mental construct. Yet it is reified into a thing, a Being, "a divinity . . . invoked in the accents of prayer." Secondly, and closely entwined with the reification of many individuals into Mankind and Posterity, is the idea of "Progress" itself. Becker quoted Pascal's famous statement that "the whole succession of human beings throughout the course of ages must be regarded as a single man, continually living and learning." Present generations, Becker quoted Glanvill as saying, "seek to gather, to observe and examine, and lay up in bank for the ages that are to come." Progress and Posterity are linked together, past and future held together by the "specious present" which compresses the past into consciousness and unavoidably reaches toward the future in anticipation. In Becker's interpretation of the Philosophes, Posterity and Progress as reified ideas, outside of time, become interchangeable. Future generations are continuous with past generations; progress is confirmed by the degradation and unhappiness of the past.

The implications of Becker's interpretation of the Enlightenment conception of history are far reaching. If "Mankind" is a personification, as he suggests, and if progress is built upon that personification, the idea of objective historical truth becomes chimerical. This is so not because all historians have biases and all facts are filtered through individual experience. They do, and they are. But Becker is consistent in his refusal to cynically deny the ability of historians to recognize error, or to separate personal views from evidence. Instead the artificial construction "Mankind" is the source of the instability of historical truth. No matter how many facts are gathered, no matter how detailed the observation, the artificial personification of the experience of separate individuals precludes objectivity. Even if the facts of history could be absorbed without interpretation, which of course Becker denied, objective history would be an illusion. The steady accumulation of knowledge leading from superstition to science can only be the product of "Man in General" because any individual life is too short and too limited to contain evidence for progress.

Historians equally depend upon the increase in knowledge of the profession of "History in General." They rely upon it to make their individual contributions of knowledge significant. As Becker recognized in **"Every Man His Own Historian,"** however, the "Historian in General" is but a reformulation of "Mankind in General." Therefore the attempt to escape the pressures of "Mr. Everyman" finally becomes the dog running away from his own tail. Becker developed this theme in the thirties. His presidential address **"Everyman His Own Historian"** and **The Heavenly City,** appearing respectively in 1931 and 1932, were followed by **Progress and Power** in 1936.

In the later book, Becker made clear a distinction between the "Idea of Progress" and progress itself. It was a distinction that he maintained throughout the rest of his work. He found the Idea of Progress to be built upon a nonempirical basis. Consequently, men can have no objective standard to measure it. Standing detached upon the mountain of Olympus and looking down upon human history, Becker wrote, we see it run from "the Java Man to Mussolini—or Roosevelt." Progress, he said, has been

> raised to the dignity of a noun. . . . [I]t is so heavily loaded with moral and teleological overtones that no scientist with any sense of decency will use it. It implies that there are values in the world. It implies, not only that the world moves forward, but that it moves forward to some good purpose, to some more felicitous state. In short,

the word Progress, like the Cross or the Crescent, is a symbol that stands for a social doctrine, a philosophy of human destiny.

Progress, for Becker, was a word which symbolized "the persistent desire of men (and historians and social theorists are men too—it is perhaps our chief merit) to find something that is and will forever remain good." That is why, he continued, though too sophisticated to believe in infallibility "we still seek, in the half-wrecked doctrine of progress, securities that only infallibility can provide." While historians may not use the word 'progress' the "subtle implications of the idea are in our writings—we contrive to make the facts speak for themselves. . . . "

Becker seems to have pretty well disposed of progress. But the reader of ***Progress and Power*** is surprised to find an apparent contradiction in the last section of the book. Suddenly Becker seems to have rejected his own sound pessimism for the very false doctrine he had been busy debunking:

> . . . we have chosen to observe the progress of mankind in the long time perspective. In the long time perspective, from *Pithecanthropus* to Einstein, the progress of mankind irrespective of the rise and fall of particular civilizations, has been accomplished by the slow, often interrupted, but fairly persistent extension of matter-of-fact knowledge and matter-of-fact apprehension to an ever widening realm of experience. It is only within the last three hundred years that it has been extended to include the entire outer world of Nature and to the forces that are in and behind appearance. Is it then too much to expect that in time to come it will be extended to include the world of human relations.?

Actually, Becker was not guilty of contradiction nor of making a failed effort to transcend his own liberal bias. Nor had he temporarily turned into a technocrat, as Wilkins surmised [in his *Carl Becker*]. Rather, Becker was making a distinction between the Idea of Progress, as discussed earlier, and progress itself. He never denied that progress could occur; only that it could not be affirmed or denied objectively. In a 1919 review, for example, Becker asked if he was expected to teach the progress of democracy "onward and upward to the Seething Caldron" of the World War era. He decided he could not. But on the other hand he would not teach that it was "undergoing degradation with a headlong rapidity towards inevitable death. . . ." Part of the reason that Becker could be neither a doctrinaire liberal nor a committed Marxist was that as a historian he was concerned with the movement of events, "the changes of configuration" in time, not in establishing or debunking objective progress. Becker was definitely unhappy with the idea of progress, but he had no other idea with which to replace it.

Consequently, ***Progress and Power*** must be understood from the perspective of his intense interest in historiography rather than as a Beardian effort to discover a new political faith. From this perspective, Becker's concern with power as mechanical (tools) and intellectual (the pen), establishes that men and women have the ability to transform their world. They do so, Becker argued, by artificial-

ly extending their space/time world. Day follows night. The Sumerians used the flood to divide time on a larger scale. Peoples with kings, which Becker defined as "deified personifications of power," were given a new sense of time—the dynasty.

"As the Time world is ideally extended beyond the range of remembered things, so the Space world is ideally extended beyond the range of known places." Thus, in his example, the kings of Sumer are rulers of "the four regions of the earth" and a Pharaoh becomes "lord of the world."

> Within this enlarged Time and Space world not all that is apprehended is concrete, not all that is known is known with equal certainty. Since the image of such a world can be held together only by the nexus of the general concept, the idea of things is differentiated from the things themselves. . . .

The progress that Becker finally affirmed was, "less an objective world of fact than man's creation of the world in his own image. It is in truth man's most ingenious invention, his supreme work of art."

For Becker, then, Mankind and Progress have become realities in the minds of individual men and women. The physical and social world is transformed by individuals acting together with a common perspective so that the world literally becomes what people think it is. These two tools are exactly like other tools used to extend man's influence over the universe. The personification of 'Mankind' and the 'Idea of Progress' are manifestations of power. As tools, they work in pragmatic fashion. But Becker posits something more than pragmatism when he suggests that such tools actually transform the world into the image they project.

The bleakness of a human world without hope for salvation required Becker to hold fast to a practical belief that progress was possible. It was this impossibility of rejecting progress even as it was impossible to accept it which constituted Becker's ironic dilemma.

— *Richard Nelson*

But Becker could not, during the depression of the 1930s, join an ideological crusade to use this power to build a better political society. He was too much aware of the tendency of historical change to frustrate expectations and make a mockery of individual notions of what "moving forward" may mean. Instead, much to the dismay of his students and committed critics like Louis Hacker, Becker remained aloof from political activity during the 1930s. His continuing interest was the dilemma of the idea of Progress and Power, itself. It was the dilemma of how to build a castle of dreams for the future on a foundation of sand. Becker recognized the dilemma to be one more basic than a debate between liberalism and Marxism. It was not a question of finding the truth in history but a question of whether history itself is true. Historiography absorbed his efforts, not the study of revolutions. In 1938, Becker wrote that "Forty years ago," he was "fascinated by the *study* of history. . . ." But now he was "less interested in the study of history than in history itself." The Subject of History, or, the history of history, he explained

> would have as its main theme the gradual extension of this time and space world (particularly the time world, perhaps, although the two are inseparably connected), the items, whether true or false, which acquired knowledge and accepted beliefs enabled men (and not historians only) to find within it, and the influence of this pattern of true or imagined events upon the development of human thought and conduct. So regarded, historiography would become a history of history rather than a history of historians. A history of history subjectively understood (the "fable agreed upon," the "pack of tricks played on the dead") rather than a history of the gradual emergence of historical truth objectively considered. . . . Nor would he (the historian) be more interested in true than in false ideas about the past. . . .

Carl Becker, therefore, did not believe that history affords solutions to human dilemmas. With J. B. Bury he believed rather that history transforms them. That is precisely what Becker the historian did when confronted with the dilemma of progress. On one hand, he had early doubted the possibility of finding a place to stand sufficiently detached from present anticipations of the future so one could view the past objectively. He could not but see the Idea of Progress as merely a pattern imposed by men trying to create a "refuge from despair" to save their souls "alive out of pessimism," as he wrote in 1921.

On the other hand, the bleakness of a human world without hope for salvation required him to hold fast to a practical belief that progress was possible. It was this impossibility of rejecting progress even as it was impossible to accept it which constituted Becker's ironic dilemma.

That Becker recognized the dilemma of progress to be ironic is central for understanding his response. Had Becker been less steeped in Enlightenment thought, felt less resonance temperamentally with ironists like Hume, Voltaire and Pascal, and had he been less willing to play hooky from his work, reading the fiction of ironists such as James Joyce, Anatole France, Henry James, Virginia Woolf, and Proust; in short, had Becker been less Becker, he might be believed that he had solved the dilemma of progress by separating the Idea from progress itself. On one level, of course, it may be said that he had solved a paralyzing dilemma. Separating the Idea from progress did release him from the ironic dilemma of Buridan's ass, caught between two bales of hay and starving for want of an ability to choose. This dilemma could be overcome. This is the message, for example, of **"Mr. Wells and the New History"**:

> It may be that Mr. Wells has read the past too close to the desire of his heart. But there are

worse things. We may hope at least that the future will be as he thinks. If it should turn out so, Mr. Wells's book will have been more than a history; even if it is not history; it will have been an action that has helped to make history. If it should turn out otherwise, still will the book have been a valiant deed. . . . If you like not the term history for Mr. Wells's book, call it something else—for example, the adventures of a generous soul among catastrophes!

But because Becker looked for transformation in history rather than solutions, he realized that a solution on one level of irony usually leaves one in a more ironic condition than before, precisely because one thinks one has escaped it. To understand why irony operates in this way and how Becker's sense of irony explains the ambiguities, hesitations and incongruities of his writing, it may be useful to consider irony a bit more closely.

Irony is a shadow concept, a kind of *Doppelgänger* to the discovery (or invention) of Progress in the eighteenth century. That is not to say that irony was not to be found earlier, but it was during the Enlightenment that it was consciously recognized as a perspective on the human condition. The Idea of Progress gave a forward direction toward the goal of a world of order, reason, objectivity and virtue. However, in doing so, the perverse, the non-rational, the subjective were made more visible and less explainable. The greater the disparity between the idea of a rational universe moving forward and the contradictions and failures in the lives men and women actually lead, the more ironic the modern vision has become. As a 'double' to progress, irony frustrates yet is dependent upon the Idea of Progress. Because irony is built upon dualism, appearance vs. reality, belief vs. experience, it is a very unstable concept. It can only be recognized in context, so any definition is necessarily partial and therefore subject to irony on another level or seen within another context.

Gene Wise has given a sound basic definition though it is a definition that points more towards specific irony in human affairs than to the general irony of events beyond our control, a form more characteristic of Becker's writing. According to Wise "an ironic situation occurs when the consequences of an act are diametrically opposed to its intentions, and the fundamental cause of the disparity lies in the actor himself and his original purpose."

Becker does write with this kind of irony in several of his essays: **"The Philosophes,"** for example, set out to dismantle the Heavenly City of St. Augustine only to rebuild it with more up-to-date materials. Madame Roland's concern for image leads from an effort to restore her husband's title of nobility to the guillotine as a militant republican. The Germans, Becker prophesies in the 1941 essay with the ironic title **"The Old Disorder in Europe,"** "will be defeated in the end by mounting opposition from without and from within—an opposition generated by the disorder which it creates."

Short sightedness, overconfidence or moral weakness is often the source of the victim's fall. Thus Becker declares Victor Hugo's love affair with an actress to be the result of Hugo's overconfident sense of virtue. In a review Becker suggests to anyone with a clever plan for making a new tomorrow: "I should think he could do nothing better, as a precaution, than to read this book carefully and take another look at his plan."

However, in Becker, the irony is rarely simple. If often doubles back on itself to reveal a second level of irony running in another direction. The actress in Hugo's life, though a kind of victim to his overconfident virtue, does achieve spiritual regeneration. "Such is the strange power of ideals, even the most unpromising." The ideal Marie Jeanne created by the overly romantic imagination of the actual Marie Jeanne, detached Philosophe, "became . . . more and more, and at last altogether, the real Madame Roland." Her transformation completed, Madame Roland is capable of mounting the scaffold with a quite different sense of detachment than that of a Philosophe. Becker takes leave of her as, in high disdain, "she looks down upon the wolfish mob below and lifts unflinching eyes to the poised and relentless knife," revealing a third level of irony running two directions at once. It is as if he sees her as at once the same romantic Marie Jeanne, detached Philosophe, and a new Madame Roland, committed, courageous, revolutionary. Becker seems to suggest that the historian finds both and neither to be true, just as Wilkins notes that personally Becker both fought and joined the "New Historians," and fought and joined "Mr. Everyman."

Because Becker rarely sees simple irony in human affairs but instead discovers levels of irony, often running in opposing directions, the characteristic form of his vision of history is found in the "Irony of Dilemma."

One level on which this kind of irony is expressed is in being confidently unaware that one is caught in a dilemma. This is the perspective from which the fictionalized merchant, Jeremiah Wynkoop in **"The Spirit of '76"** is drawn. He finds himself engaged in revolutionary politics when he thought he was defending social order and conservative values.

But, if an ironic dilemma may be present when one is really in an impossible situation but confident there is a solution, one may conversely think one is in an impossible situation when one is not. This is the case when two alternatives are equally attractive or both are equally unattractive. The victim of this kind of irony remains neutralized by two opposing attractions or repelled by two opposing dissatisfactions. Such a condition is ironic if we, as detached observers, can see a solution the victim is unable to see. Perhaps the best example of this is Becker's view of Henry Adams, who also was preoccupied with transformation in history and consequently was highly ironic. Becker naturally appreciated Adams' perspective. But he was still critical enough of Adams to interpret Adams' ironic work ironically.

Consider the concluding paragraph of **"Henry Adams Once More"**:

> . . . 'his [Adams'] habitual attitude' was that of a man who somehow feels that he has 'missed out,' but does not really *believe* that he *has* missed out, and at the same time cannot quite understand why he should have missed out or should feel that he has. . . . Isn't this precisely the attitude one might expect of a man whose genius for reflection was always at war with his desire for 'power,' and who never knew it? Perhaps then the secret of Henry Adams was simply that he didn't know what was the matter with him. But then again perhaps he did know, but was too proud or perverse to admit it, even to himself.

There is a third mode of irony, however, which operates on a more general level. That is when the detached observer realizes that we all are ultimately frail and shortsighted. We are all caught in dilemmas and therefore we all are victims. "As victims," Douglas Meucke asserts, "we cannot escape irony as long as we believe or assume that we inhabit a rational universe. We can escape only by finding and adopting a detached position from which we can regard the coexistence of contraries with equanimity, that is to say by abandoning the concept of a rational or moral world, but abandoning despair as well as hope."

The Idea of Progress has served to make men and women ever more aware of the contradictions in life because it has served to define the world dynamically. As faith in Science promises to open the realm of objectivity, subjectivity becomes an ever more acute contradiction. This of course is also the dilemma of Diderot, Carl Becker's dilemma and every other historian's dilemma as well. For this reason irony is a historian's concept more fully than it can be that of the philosopher or scientist. The ironist, Meucke points out, is concerned with "the world as men experience it or have experienced it and not with the world as it objectively is or may be." Therefore, while the ironist may use the insights of the philosopher or scientist, the ironist is unable to identify with their ahistorical claim to a logical or empirical objectivity. Rather, the ironist must consider philosophy and science themselves as part of a social context. Consequently the ironist may use philosophy, the laws of physical science or Freudian theory. She or he may apply them to her or his understanding of the aspect of the human condition under study but she or he cannot become a Philosopher, Scientist or Freudian.

For similar reasons Becker was more interested in the personal and social movements of history revealed in the dramatic and accelerated change of revolutionary periods than he was with revolutions themselves. He believed it quite possible that November 1917 would be celebrated in one hundred years as the events of July, 1789 are today. But Robert E. Brown was very wide of the mark [in his *Carl Becker on History and the American Revolution*] when he thought that Becker had skated to the thin edge of communism only to 'retreat' to a safe liberalism in the 1930s. Becker was always far closer to Pascal than Marx or for that matter Adam Smith. He was far too ironic to deny that Marxism could create a better world, but he was equally too ironic to believe that the better world would be all that new.

Becker, by the end of the 1930s had discovered an intellectual and emotional equilibrium that had not been possible earlier. Certainly the anguished uncertainties of **"The Dilemma of Diderot"** can be seen to have been transmuted in the larger vision of *The Heavenly City* and then in the control of creative possibility evoked in *How New Will the Better World Be?* and *Freedom and Responsibility in the American Way of Life,* both published in the last two years of his life. If his sense of irony had filled his earlier years with the uncertainty of progress, that same irony in his later years led him to the discovery of the need to build a world for men and women to find shelter from an unfeeling universe.

Carl Becker's death coincided with the end of World War II, when the contradictions in the modern faith in Progress became increasingly evident to the historians charged with creating a narrative hymn to Mankind's march into the future. Richard Hofstadter and Perry Miller, two of the most influential of Postwar historians, wrote in a consciously ironic mode. For them, however, as for a whole generation of intellectuals, inspiration was not drawn from the work of Carl Becker. Rather, Reinhold Niebuhr's *Irony of American History* summed up the new postwar mood. "Niebuhr," Perry Miller once remarked, "was the father of us all."

But Niebuhr's brand of irony was a far more ethical and limited form than Becker's. For Niebuhr, irony meant that virtue may become vice through some hidden defect in the virtue; strength may turn into weakness if reliance on that strength turns into vanity; wisdom may become folly if it forgets its limits. The ironic situation may be distinguished from the pathetic one because the person involved bears some measure of responsibility for it. It differs from the tragic in that the weakness is unconscious and not the result of a resolution.

The implication of Niebuhr's view of irony is that given a large dose of humility and some serious self-examination, an individual or a nation-may escape the wages of their folly and reaffirm the values from which they have strayed. Consequently, Niebuhrian irony may be seen as a form of the Protestant Jeremiad and therefore an orthodox expression of the American Civil Religion. This ironic perspective was equally open to the critics of consensus history as well as to its defenders. William Appleman William's *Tragedy of American Diplomacy,* for example, paralleled the Niebuhrian view of a flawed vision impairing a realistic appraisal of reality. Like Niebuhr, Williams saw America externalizing evil rather than engaging in self criticism which might have led to a moral foreign policy.

Becker's ironic vision, doubling back upon itself and operating on several levels at once could hardly seem serious from such a perspective. Historians like Hofstadter dismissed Becker as a clever stylist without serious content. With few exceptions that is where the matter has been left. Becker's reputation remains in eclipse.

But, perhaps in the twenty years since historians have taken serious interest in Becker, events have made him and his irony more accessible. The Jeremiad has lost much of its persuasiveness as the present crisis in writing narrative history attests. The inability to unthink nuclear war or to conceive how it might be made less likely may be indicative of a crisis in the very idea of Progress itself. In such time of limited possibilities and massive problems,

Becker's perspective may allow historians to rethink the relation between progress and history. Such a perspective may permit the asking of significant questions of interpretation even as it denies objective progress in history and its study.

FURTHER READING

Biography

Harstad, Peter T. and Gibson, Michael D. "An Iowa-Born Historian and the American Revolution: Carl Becker and the 'Spirit of '76'." *The Palimpsest* 57, No. 6 (November-December 1976): 174-92.
    Examines the effect Becker's early Iowa experiences had on his life and approach to writing history.

Wilkins, Burleigh Taylor. *Carl Becker: A Biographical Study in American Intellectual History.* Cambridge: The M.I.T. Press and Harvard University Press, 1961, 246 p.
    Detailed look at the intellectual and social forces that shaped Becker's relativist view of history.

Criticism

Braeman, John and Rule, John C. "*Carl Becker: 20th Century* Philosophe." *American Quarterly* XIII, No. 1 (Spring 1961): 534-39.
    Assessment of Becker as a biographical subject through a review of three book-length studies of his life and work.

Brown, Robert E. *Carl Becker on History and the American Revolution.* East Lansing: The Spartan Press, 1970, 285 p.
    A study of Becker's interpretation of the American Revolution.

Cairns, John C. "Carl Becker: An American Liberal." *The Journal of Politics* 16, No. 4 (November 1954): 623-44.
    Views Becker's liberalism as having its source in a form of against-all-odds optimism and an incessant questioning of institutions and assumptions.

Carpenter, Ronald H. "Carl Becker and the Epigrammatic Force of Style in History." *Communication Monographs* 48, No. 4 (December 1981): 318-39.
    Attempts to show that Becker's epigrammatic style worked in a persuasive way on readers of his work, particularly in *Modern History.*

Gershoy, Leo. Introduction to *Progress and Power*, by Carl Becker, pp. ix-xxxvii. New York: Alfred A. Knopf, 1949.
    Somewhat anecdotal overview of the place of *Power and Progress* in the context of Becker's previous and later work.

———. "Zagorin's Interpretation of Becker: Some Observations." *The American Historical Review* LXII, No. 1 (October 1956): 12-17.
    Attacks Perez Zagorin's critique of Becker's skepticism and lack of logic.

Gold, Milton. "In Search of a Historian." *The Centennial Review of Arts and Sciences* VII, No. III (Summer 1963): 282-305.

General examination of historiography, with an emphasis on the role played by Becker's relativism and its distinction between facts and the inferences drawn from them.

Klein, Milton M. "Democracy and Politics in Colonial New York." In *Essays in Americal Colonial History*, edited by Paul Goodman, pp. 444-61. New York: Holt, Rinehart and Winston, 1967.

Accuses Becker of exaggeration with regard to his assessment of New York colonial political parties as quasifeudal factions.

———. "Detachment and the Writing of American History: The Dilemma of Carl Becker." In *Perspectives on Early American History*, edited by Alden T. Vaughan and George Athan Billias, pp.120-66. New York: Harper & Row, 1973.

Views efforts to resolve Becker's paradoxes as unprofitable. According to Klein, Becker's strength as a historian lies in his questioning, probing and challenging methodology.

Noble, David W. "Carl Becker: Science, Relativism, and the Dilemma of Diderot." *Ethics* LXVII, No. 4 (July 1957): 233-48.

Notes that Becker's work clarifies the inextricable connection between American and European history.

———. "Carl Becker: Europe and the Roots of the Covenant." In his *Historians Against History: The Frontier Thesis and the National Covenant in American Historical Writing Since 1830,* pp. 76-97. Minneapolis: University of Minnesota Press, 1965.

Portrays Becker as a "spokesman for history as progress."

Rockwood, Raymond O. *Carl Becker's Heavenly City Revisited.* Ithaca: Cornell University Press, 1958, 227 p.

Published papers of a symposium held to commemorate the twenty-fifth anniversary of the publication of *The Heavenly City.*

Skotheim, Robert Allen. "The Progressive Tradition, I: Carl Becker." In his *American Intellectual Histories and Historians,* pp. 109-23. Princeton: Princeton University Press, 1966.

Details Becker's contribution to the rise of "New History."

Snyder, Phil L. "Carl L. Becker and the Great War: A Crisis for Humane Intelligence." *The Western Political Quarterly* IX, No. 1 (March 1956): 1-10.

Maintains that although World War I was not the sole source of Becker's pessimism, it certainly reinforced it.

Strout, Cushing. *The Pragmatic Revolt in American History: Carl Becker and Charles Beard.* Ithaca: Cornell University Press, 1966, 182 p.

Shows Becker's foreshadowing of contemporary scholars who bring "a literary and psychological sensitivity to the subrational meanings of their documents."

Zagorin, Perez. "Carl Becker on History." *The American Historical Review* LXII, No. 1 (October 1956): 1-11.

Takes issue with Becker's notion that there are two histories, one objective and the other subjective.

Additional coverage of Becker's life and works is contained in the following source published by Gale Research: *Dictionary of Literary Biography;* Vol. 17.

Thomas Burke

1886-1945

English short story writer, novelist, and essayist.

INTRODUCTION

Burke is best known for his short stories set in London's Chinatown, the section of docks, warehouses and tenements known as Limehouse. Foremost among these works is the collection *Limehouse Nights*. While Burke also published several well-received novels not associated with Limehouse, as well as many volumes of essays and social history, this collection and its sequels typed him as a purveyor of melodramatic stories of lust and murder among London's lower classes.

Biographical Information

Burke was born in London. His father died when Burke was only a few months old, and he was sent to live with an uncle in Poplar, a district of London near Limehouse. During his childhood Burke enthusiastically gained a familiarity with his dockland surroundings, but his apparent freedom from adult supervision led to his confinement to an orphanage from the time he was nine until he was fourteen. His acquaintance with the Chinese owner of a tea shop inspired him to begin writing, and his first short story collection, *Limehouse Nights*, appeared in 1917. The book was praised by such well-known writers as H. G. Wells and Arnold Bennett. One of its stories, "The Chink and the Child," served as the basis for D. W. Griffith's motion picture *Broken Blossoms; or, The Yellow Man and the Girl* (1919). Another of Burke's stories, "The Hands of Mr. Ottermole" (from the collection *The Pleasantries of Old Quong*), was voted the best mystery story of all time by a panel of critics in 1949. Burke died in London in 1945.

Major Works

Burke first glimpsed what he perceived as the romance of Asia in the establishment of a shopkeeper whom he later fictionalized as "Quong Lee" in *Limehouse Nights* and such subsequent volumes as *The Pleasantries of Old Quong*. These works mark Burke as the voice of London's lower, often immigrant, classes. A concomitant interest in crime runs through much of Burke's fiction and led him to produce *Murder at Elstree*, a novel based on an actual case from the early nineteenth century. Burke also wrote several richly detailed autobiographical novels: *The Wind and the Rain*, *The Sun in Splendour*, and *The Flower of Life*. Another genre in which he excelled was the essay. Burke's many collections dealing with London, its suburbs, and English life in general exhibit the same characteristics that made his fiction popular: a harsh realism derived from firsthand experience, but one tempered by a romantic outlook.

PRINCIPAL WORKS

Verses (poetry) 1910
Pavements and Pastures: A Book of Songs (poetry) 1912
Nights in Town: A London Autobiography (autobiography) 1915; also published as *Nights in London*, 1916
Limehouse Nights: Tales of Chinatown (short stories) 1916
London Lamps: A Book of Songs (poetry) 1917
Twinkletoes: A Tale of Chinatown (novel) 1917
Out and About: A Note-Book of London in War-Time (essays) 1919; also published as *Out and About in London*, 1919
The Song Book of Quong Lee of Limehouse (poetry) 1920
The Outer Circle: Rambles in Remote London (essays) 1921
Whispering Windows: Tales of the Waterside (short stories) 1921; also published as *More Limehouse Nights*, 1921
The London Spy: A Book of Town Travels (essays) 1922
The Wind and the Rain: A Book of Confessions (novel) 1924
The Sun in Splendour (novel) 1926
East of Mansion House (short stories) 1928
Essays of Today and Yesterday (essays) 1928
The Bloomsbury Wonder (short stories) 1929
The Flower of Life (novel) 1929
The English Inn (nonfiction) 1930
The Pleasantries of Old Quong (short stories) 1931; also published as *A Tea-Shop in Limehouse*, 1931
City of Encounters: A London Divertissement (essays) 1932
The Real East End (essays) 1932
The Beauty of England (essays) 1933
London in My Times (essays) 1934
Murder at Elstree: or, Mr. Thurtell and His Gig (novel) 1936
Night Pieces: Eighteen Tales (short stories) 1936
Abduction: A Story of Limehouse (novel) 1939
Living in Bloomsbury (autobiography) 1939
The Streets of London Through the Centuries (nonfiction) 1940
English Night-Life, From Norman Curfew to Present Black-Out (nonfiction) 1941
Travel in England from Pilgrim to Pack-Horse to Light Car and Plane (nonfiction) 1943
Dark Nights (short stories) 1944
The English Townsman As He Was and As He Is (nonfiction) 1946

Son of London (autobiography) 1946
The Best Stories of Thomas Burke (short stories) 1950

CRITICISM

Gilbert Vivian Seldes   (essay date 1917)

SOURCE: "Rediscovery and Romance," in *The Dial,* Chicago, Vol. LXIII, July 19, 1917, pp. 65-7.

[*In the following essay, Seldes offers a favorable assessment of* Limehouse Nights *and* Nights in Town.]

The two substantial books of tales and sketches of London which Mr. Thomas Burke has collected and published since the war began are of a stuff which the world may find outmoded in the unhappy years to come. They are books which might have become only items in the "new literature" of the century's second decade had the revolution of war not prevented, for Mr. Burke is not only one of those who rediscovered romance; he is also of those who taste to the full the romance of their own rediscovery.

Some fifteen tales of Limehouse, the Chinese quarter of London in "the thunderous shadows of the great Dock," and some twenty sketches of London complete Mr. Burke's present contribution. To write about Chinatown is a reporter's holiday; to write about London, giving yourself no limitations but that of the mystic city itself, and to write with love and care and beauty, is a hard and bitter labor, no matter what talents you may have. Mr. Burke's passing repute comes from the tales of terror which the libraries were compelled to bar from their shelves; but to those who have some respect for the English tongue and for whom Walter Pater has not lived in vain, Mr. Burke will always possess an attraction because he has written well his slight sketches of London life. In both of these books one hears the cry of a great joy. At the age of ten the author was taken with the flaring beauty of a fried-fish shop, throwing a warm light and a glamour over the dusky pavement of a London slum; and since then he has been passing from discovery to discovery, rejoicing that these things, these common and tawdry things, are still in existence for him to discover again. He knows well that they were revealed long since, but he makes fresh starts and everything is new and beautiful to him.

Because everything is strange to him, Mr. Burke never quite succeeds in his tales of Chinatown. He writes of Limehouse as Pierre Loti writes of Annam and of Iceland, with the heart of a wanderer who will not be consoled for his separation from home. Lust and wildness, cruelty, perversion and madness, things unclean to the white man's heart, make up the themes of his stories. He has continually to drive his plots with little daggers of exaggeration because he is always impressed with the uncommonness of the people of whom he writes. Will it be the story of a burglar's wife who tries to betray her husband to the police so that she may be free to love his accomplice, or the story of a girl who loses caste by going with a Chinaman in order to pay her mother's funeral expenses? The reality of his events does not satisfy the author; he must try to be convincing by a turn of the plot, so that we get the ten-cent magazine type of sudden and perverse *dénouement.* It is not the husband but the lover who is killed by the police; the girl gets her revenge by a neat trick, revealed in the last line of the story.

These *Limehouse Nights* appeared in three of the most interesting periodicals of England: *The English Review, Colour,* and *The New Witness,* and I can hardly imagine the editor of any one of them insisting that Mr. Burke get more punch or pep into his work. I am afraid he is really to blame for his shortcomings.

He is certainly to be credited with his good things, because he seems a writer with no derivations. Ambrose Bierce might have written some of these tales, but you cannot trace Burke to Bierce, because you are in the presence of a singularly powerful inspiration with which literary affinities have very little to do. Mr. Arthur Machen, the unknown master of the artistic tale of terror, probably returns Mr. Burke's evident admiration. One suggests these names to convey a bit more clearly the quality of Mr. Burke's stories; that is all.

Strange and terrible stories, one hesitates to retell them, not because it would be unjust, for these are good stories and the outline of a good tale will always bear repetition. But they are about things we are none of us too anxious to name, and which Mr. Burke makes tolerable only by the flooding beauty of his telling and the human kindness of his spirit. He knows at least that one must not call down the gods of terror without praying softly to the gods of pity. I take one tale, an artist's story of those famous Sidney Street murders in which the world was once absorbed, those murderers for whose capture the soldiery of England was called out, against whom a street became a barricade and a funeral pyre. Mr. Burke calls it **"Beryl, the Croucher and the Rest of England."** He starts you with the Croucher, a slugging prize-fighter, and Beryl, the girl whom he buys in a fit of drunkenness. He tells you how the Croucher's father broke in upon their assignation with the news that he had killed a man, and how the Croucher, putting lust aside, makes a barricade in the procurer's room and fights to the end. But what an end when, days later, he rushes from the burning room into Beryl's arms.

> There was talk curious talk, the talk of a woman of thirty to the man of her life, monstrous to hear from a child to a boy of nineteen. There were embraces, garrulous silences, kisses, fears and tremblings. In those moments the Croucher awoke to a sense of the bigness of things. He became enveloped in something . . . a kind of . . . well the situation and, oh, everything. The murder, the siege, all London waiting for him, and that sort of thing. It gave him a new emotion; he felt proud and clean all through. He felt, in his own phrase, like as though he was going to find something he had been hunting for years and forgotten. One would like to know more, perhaps, for it might help us to live, and teach us something of pity. . . .

There are other stories, some too terrible for thought, some cheaply startling, one, at least, lovely and lyrical.

Yet if Mr. Burke had written only these stories justice could only say of him that he wrote stories which, in the eyes of English critics, were as good as the stories they imported from America. Our reputation for short-story telling is as marked here as our reputation for telling tall stories. Mr. Burke's authority comes not from the rediscovery of Chinatown; that lay waiting for his step. It comes from the rediscovery of London.

> It is the Call not only of London, but of Beauty, of Life. Beauty calls in many voices; but to me and to six million others she calls in the voice of Cockaigne, and it shall go hard with any man who hears the Call and does not answer.

So Mr. Burke pronounces Cockney. Because it is the call of beauty he can never be a slummer; because it is the call of life he can never be a reformer. Here, in a book which traverses the fastnesses of conventionality in Bayswater, the open streets of hospitality, the commons of sudden friendship, and the mews and alleys of equally sudden violence. Mr. Burke discloses himself. He writes of his early life, the disasters of a Fleet Street apprenticeship, and one understands why he has no harsh words for the beastly and the low. He has too often partaken of their bread and salt. But his precious purity of vision lies in his abnormal ability to write with love and friendship of those whom our novelists are pointedly ignoring, or only dragging forward into shame and ridicule. I mean the real middle classes—those whom Dante rejected and whom Dickens folded to his heart; those who make neither great affirmations nor heroic rejections, but live in placid gentleness, Philistine but not tyrannical, with the good heart and a mind kept in its proper place. He will take his fling at Kensington, "touched with the temper of last night's soda-water" because "there are no girls and no women; they are all young ladies." The gilded haunts of virtue cannot appeal to him. But he will go to Clapham, where mothers keep watchful eyes on daughters, and to a whist-drive at Surbiton and call these happy nights.

The wanderings take him to the Scandinavian quarter and to the Ghetto, to the black Isle of Dogs with its workers, and to Hoxton where gangs of bashers were wont to play with the police. Round the halls or to the promenade concerts, into Soho with its restaurants from France and Italy. But wherever he is, the Cockney remains, rejoicing in his great domain. The Cockney for whom "Tipperary" was false in one thing: "Good-by Piccadilly, farewell Leicester Square." Little did the Cockney care about these show-places of London; he had his little shrine elsewhere, in Seven Sisters Road, in Marylebone, in Walthamstow or Wormwood Scrubs, far beyond the sound of the bells which make him a Cockney in all accuracy, but part of London none the less. Wilde wrote once of a great man's "shrill cockney cry of delight in discovering Italy," and rightly, because there were wonders more fair in London town. To these wonders the new Cockney comes, crying softly and in a likable voice. He has discovered that his home is a place of strange enchantments; he is always finding his way to Paradise by way of Clapham Green.

The Cockney remains in Mr. Burke. Else he might have become a super-guidebook, in the manner of E. V. Lucas.

The Cockney demands population; take Mr. Burke away from human beings and he is lost; he will write you all manner of lovely things about the luminous streets, but it will not last. His ear will hear an organ grinding out "Let's all go down the Strand" and you cannot keep him from beating time. Then he will go down the Strand and swear softly at the despoilers of its Sunday joys.

He writes about everything that is human and he is satisfied with humanity as subject-matter. I am sure that he has been called a stark realist, but since realist has come to mean one who hates humanity enough to lie about it, the name will not pass. Mr. Burke is, I fear, out of class, because the category for him was just being elaborated when the war broke out. He would be with those who have passed through the gray days of pessimism and hatred and even through the soppy days of pity for everything human and divine. He would have been a cheerful companion for the writers who are looking with clear eyes on the world they have discovered for themselves and who know that the essence of romance is that all things are new. We saw the faint beginnings of this romance in such a book as *Carnival* [a popular novel by Compton Mackenzie], and I fear we have seen its end. Our novelists may love the world after the war; but it is questionable whether the world will have time to return the affection for many years. Possibly Mr. Burke's books, at once vigorous and wanton, may be respected afterward; one fears only that they will be found a little purposeless, a little lacking in social direction. It is that lack, of course, which makes them so attractive. For, it may be mentioned, these are wonderfully good things to read.

Milton Bronner (essay date 1917)

SOURCE: "Burke of Limehouse," in *The Bookman,* New York, Vol. XLVI, September, 1917, pp. 15-17.

[*In the following essay, Bronner evaluates the style and themes of* Limehouse Nights *and* London Lamps.]

Violent times seem to beget in those who stay quietly at home a taste for a brutally realistic literature. After the abortive Russian revolution of 1905, when the Czar crushed the rebels with an iron hand and all Russia seemed once more sunk in hopeless and helpless despair, there was an unprecedented production of novels and stories whose realism was unusually frank, even for that country. Strangely enough, it was also pornographic. It was as if by mutual consent of writers and reading public they had said, "Very well, if we cannot have political freedom we will have freedom in our novels. Nay we will go beyond freedom. We will have license."

In Great Britain to-day, confronted always by the terrible lists of her dead and wounded, with signs of mourning and war's wreckage on every hand, the book that has gone speedily into three editions and has already made an English reputation for its author is not of the kind to make sad ones smile and anxious ones forget. It is not light and airy at all. It is one of the most frankly and brutally realistic books that has appeared in our tongue in a long time. Yet it won its audience despite the fact that circulating libraries barred it, and it has been crowned by the high praise of men like Wells and Bennett, themselves masters in the writer's craft.

Thomas Burke is a man of whom little is known. Presumably his *Nights in Town,* a London autobiography, tells of his life and adventures in the world-city, but the book attracted so little attention that its revelations—if there were any—were speedily forgotten. Undaunted by this, he produced the volume that has given him his present standing, *Limehouse Nights*.

Limehouse is a London region of mean shops, low groggeries, humble tenements and small cottages near that part of the Thames where are situated the West and East India docks. In addition to the white people who live there, and the Malays and Lascars who flock from the ships, there is a large permanent and a considerable transient Chinese population. So much is this the case that the section is known as Chinatown, just as are similar territories in New York and San Francisco.

Burke has not sought to prettify his Chinatown. In the main, he has not attempted to become sentimental over it. He has not donned rose-coloured glasses. Whether he is treating of a romantic, a tragic, or a comic theme, he seeks always to be scrupulously truthful. In his wanderings in Limehouse he most often found Chinese whose morals were none too good, English brothel-keepers, thieves and scarlet women. And he takes these people as his *dramatis persona*. For the most part he is realistic in a romantic manner. There is brutal realism, but it appears as if it were wrung from the heart of a man who preferred to be a poet. On the very first page of his book the reader is confronted by this:

> It is a tale of love and lovers that they tell in the low-lit Causeway that slinks from West India Dock Road to the dark Waste of Waters beyond. In Pennyfields, too, you may hear it; and I do not doubt that it is told in far-away Tai-Ping, in Singapore, in Tokio, in Shanghai, and those other gay-lamped haunts of wonder whither the wandering people of Limehouse go and whence they return so casually. It is a tale for tears, and should you hear it in the lilied tongue of the yellow men, it would awaken in you all your pity. In our bald speech it must, unhappily, lose its essential fragrance, that quality that will lift an affair of squalor into the loftier spheres of passion and imagination, beauty and sorrow. It will sound unconvincing, a little . . . you know . . . the kind of thing that is best forgotten. Perhaps . . .

There follows a tale of a Chinaman and a child; of how the Chinaman found her in an unbelievable brothel and took her home with him to love and worship as a fragile thing apart, something too holy to be sullied. The piece has its tragic ending—the child is beaten to death by her prize-fighter step-father, the Chinaman kills himself, and the child's murderer dies from the bite of a poisonous snake left for him by the Chinaman as a "love-gift".

Gaily deceptive, Burke pens lines like these:

> Sweet human hearts—a tale of carnival, moon-haunted nights; a tale of the spring-tide, of the flower and the leaf ripening to fruit: a gossamer thing of dreamy-lanterned streets, told by my friend, Tai Ling, of West India Dock Road. Its scene is not the Hoang Ho or the sun-loved islands of the East, but Limehouse. Nevertheless it is a fairy tale, because so human.

What follows is not keyed up to this pitch of poesy at all. Instead, it is an outrageously frank and comic story of how three Chinamen and one white man disputed as to which was the father of the expected child of Marigold Vassiloff, who, as you may judge, was no saint. Once more turn the pages. Burke begins:

> Memory is a delicate instrument. Like an old musical box, it will lie silent for long years; then a mere nothing, a jerk, a tremor, will start the spring, and from beneath its decent covering of dust it will talk to us of forgotten passion and desire. Some memories are thus moved at sight of a ribbon, a faded violet, a hotel bill; others at the sound of a voice or a bar of music, or at the bite of a flavour on the palate or an arrangement of skies against a well-known background. To me return all the unhappy far-off things when I smell the sharp odour of a little dirty theatre near Blackwall. Then I think upon all those essences of life most fragrant and fresh, and upon . . . Gina Brentano.

There ensues a story of how Gina developed as a child dancer, how she fell, and passed off the stage, both of the theatre and of life. Beware of the Greeks bearing gifts. Beware of Burke charming you with his highly polished, more or less dreamy opening passage. It is a lure, a promise not to be kept. The poet in him sets his trap for the attention of the reader, and, once he is caught, certain grim matters are set down with no respect for feelings. Shocking situations are reported as they might be by a court attaché—if the latter were an artist. The dialogue is set down without an attempt to Bowdlerise it. Ugly words, coarse slang, meaningful phrases are all put in. One reads a Satanic tale of how a man tortured his child into committing a murder he himself was too cowardly to perform and then was trapped; or a nightmare story of the terrible white parrot which, like its master, was a devil incarnate and lived to avenge his death; or a Poe-like story of the gorilla and the girl.

It is a book that, in the main, is concerned with the dark phases of life. Men commit murder or torture children; women avenge great wrongs by arson or by poison; policemen's tools hand over criminals to the waiting constables. All this sounds uninviting enough. But such a description does not convey the whole truth. The fact is that Burke has cast a glamour over his pages that prevents his stories from being merely studies in the sordid and the morbid. He has seen things with sharp vision and he has etched them just as clearly. But somehow also he makes you feel that he has viewed life with pity and tenderness and loving comprehension. He has charity for all because he tries to understand all. These puppets of his are for the most part unlovely, their lives grimy enough, and yet he manages to make one realise there is loveliness amid the crime and the squalor. Bayswater may call some of these things beastly, but Burke shows how Limehouse finds some of these things beautiful. Again and again the reader is adjured to be gentle, to be pitiful, and if he can bring himself to this frame of mind he is apt to see these things as Burke sees them. He sees the high passion, the sudden deep love, the heroism amid the ugly and the criminal. He separates the human gold from the overplentiful human dross.

Burke is decidedly a find. Not since the days when Kipling burst upon the English world has any writer displayed more sheer power and driving force. When he wills it, he has command of fine prose. He has a pen that records things as they are. He has the ability to seize and hold one's attention. He can spin a yarn. And he has the old and invaluable trick of concealing a surprise in the end of his story. He has followed up his success with a slender volume of verse, *London Lamps*. Many of these poems celebrate particular streets in London, just as Arthur Adams and Douglas Goldring have done in recent years. There is nothing very inspired about these pieces. It is only when he sings of his yellow men and of Limehouse that he becomes really interesting. Indeed, some of these pieces sound like a versified appendix to *Limehouse Nights*.

> Yellow man, yellow man, where have you
> been?
> Down the Pacific, where wonders are seen.
> Up the Pacific, so glamourous and gay,
> Where night is of blue, and of silver the
> day.
>
> Yellow man, yellow man, what did you
> there?
> I loved twenty maids who were loving and
> fair.
>
> Their cheeks were of velvet, their kisses
> were fire,
> I looked at them boldly and had my desire.
>
> Yellow man, yellow man, why do you sigh?
> For flowers that are sweet, and for flowers
> that die.
> For days in fair waters and nights in
> strange lands,
> For faces forgotten and little lost hands.

There are many things to be seen and heard down by the West India Dock Road, things that one book of prose and one little sheaf of rhymes have not exhausted. Burke's books may sell and money may come to him, but one visions him slipping away from Fleet Street and Picadilly and going back there where life may be ruder, but where likewise it has sharper savour:

> Black man—white man—brown man—yel-
> low man—
> Pennyfields and Poplar and Chinatown
> for me!
> Stately moving cut-throats and many-col-
> oured mysteries,
> Never were such lusty things for London
> lads to see!
>
> On the evil twilight—rose and star and
> silver—
> Steals a song that long ago in Singapore
> they sang;
> Fragrant of spices, of incense and opium,

> Cinnamon and aconite, the betel and the
> bhang.
>
> Then get you down to Limehouse, by rig-
> ging, wharf and smokestack,
> Glamour, dirt, and perfume, and dusky
> men and gold;
> For down in lurking Limehouse there's the
> blue moon of the Orient—
> Lamps for young Aladdins, and bowies
> for the bold!

Grant Overton (essay date 1922)

SOURCE: "Places to Go," in *When Winter Comes to Main Street,* George H. Doran Company, 1922, pp. 187-95.

[*In the following excerpt, Overton discusses* Whispering Windows *and* The London Spy.]

The book by Thomas Burke called *More Limehouse Nights* was published in England under the title of *Whispering Windows*. At the time of its publication, Mr. Burke wrote the following:

> The most disconcerting question that an author can be asked, and often is asked, is: "Why did you write that book?" The questioners do not want an answer to that immediate question; but to the implied question: "Why don't you write some other kind of book?" To either question there is but one answer: BECAUSE.
>
> Every writer is thus challenged. The writer of comic stories is asked why he doesn't write something really serious. The novelist is asked why he doesn't write short stories, and the short-story writer is asked why he doesn't write a novel. To me people say, impatiently: "Why don't you write happy stories about ordinary people?" And the only answer I can give them is: "Because I can't. I present life as I see it."
>
> I am an ordinary man, but I don't understand ordinary men. I am at a loss with them. But with the people of whom I write I have a fellow-feeling. I know them and their sorrows and their thwarted strivings and I understand their aberrations. I cannot see the romance of the merchant or the glamour of the duke's daughter. They do not permit themselves to be seized and driven by passion and imagination. Instead they are driven by fear, which they have misnamed Common-sense. These people thwart themselves, while my people are thwarted by malign circumstance.
>
> Often I have taken other men to the dire districts about which I write, and they have remained unmoved; they have seen, in their phrase, nothing to get excited about. Well, one cannot help that kind of person. One cannot give understanding to the man who regards the flogging of children as a joke, or to whom a broken love-story is, in low life, a theme for smoking-room anecdotes.
>
> Wherever there are human creatures there are beauty and courage and sacrifice. The stories in *Whispering Windows* deal with human crea-

tures, thieves, drunkards, prostitutes, each of whom is striving for happiness in his or her way, and missing it, as most of us do. Each has hidden away some fine streak of character, some mark below which he will not go. And—they are alive. They have met life in its ugliest phases, and fought it.

My answer, then, to the charge of writing 'loathsome' stories, is that these things happen. To those who say that cruelty and degradation are not fit subjects for fiction, I say that all twists and phases of the human heart are fit subjects for fiction.

The entertainment of hundreds of thousands with "healthy" literature is a great and worthy office; but the author can only give out what is in him. If I write of wretched and strange things, it is because these move me most. Happiness needs no understanding; but these darker things—they are kept too much from sensitive eyes and polite ears; and so are too harshly judged upon the world's report. I am no reformer; I have never "studied" people; and I have no "purpose," unless it be illumination.

What we all need today is illumination; for only through full knowledge can we come to truth—and understanding.

Burke's new book, *The London Spy,* is described by the author as "a book of town travels." Some of the subjects are London street characters, cab shelters, coffee stalls and street entertainers. The range is very wide, for there is a chapter called **"In the Streets of Rich Men,"** which deals with Pall Mall and Piccadilly, as well as a study of a waterside colony, including the results of a first pipe of opium (**"In the Streets of Cyprus"**). Mr. Burke tells a good deal about the film world of Soho and is able to give an intimate sketch of Chaplin. Perhaps the most charming of the titles in the book is the chapter called **"In the Street of Beautiful Children"**. This is a study of a street in Stepney, with observations on orphanages and reformatories and "their oppressions of the children of the poor."

St. John Adcock   (essay date 1928)

SOURCE: "Thomas Burke," in *The Glory That Was Grub Street: Impressions of Contemporary Authors,* Frederick A. Stokes Company, 1928, pp. 13-22.

[*In the following essay, Adcock favorably surveys the early years of Burke's literary career.*]

It used to be a canon of criticism, not so long ago, that all great art is impersonal. We were told (when I was young one distinguished critic told me in most reverent and emphatic terms) that Shakespeare could not be found in his plays or poems; that these were the sublime creations of his intellect and imagination, and that he had kept himself out of them with the perfect reticence of the supreme artist. It was a generally accepted faith. When somebody said that with his sonnets Shakespeare had unlocked his heart, wasn't it Browning who exclaimed, "then so much the less Shakespeare he!"

But this notion that the artist writes in a spirit of serene detachment from his work is only one of the many critical theories we try on from time to time and quietly discard as soon as we find they won't fit. The fact is that every author, especially the novelist, is consciously or unconsciously autobiographical. His personal experiences are naturally, almost inevitably, the raw material with which he makes his stories and his characters. He may not use such experiences literally; he adapts them, adds to them, varies or amplifies them with imaginary details; he joins up incidents that, when they happened to him, had no connection with each other; in the same way, he creates a character by blending in one man or woman the characters of two or three different men or women he has known. The facts about himself are in his books, some disguised closely, some very slightly, and some not disguised at all.

Perhaps no contemporary is more autobiographical than Thomas Burke. You may not always be able to disentangle it and feel sure of where truth ends and fiction comes in to leaven it, but much of his own life-story runs through his *Nights in Town,* through that most personal and poignant of his novels, *The Wind and the Rain,* and you have glimpses of it in his recent volume of *Essays [Old and New],* and here and there in many other of his sketches and stories. When the boy who is telling his tale in *The Wind and the Rain* tells how the reading of a popular semi-literary weekly first woke a love of literature in him, how he began to borrow books from the Public Library, occasionally straining his scanty salary to buy them and, groping his way to the poetry and prose that most appealed to him, found a way of escape out of the poverty and drabness of his surroundings—this is not fiction but Burke going back in remembrance over the road he has travelled himself:

> London was now touched with a new magic—the magic of noble association; and though I couldn't travel with Ariel I could feel the brush of his wings. The hard lines of Poultry became softened because Hood had been born there, and Waterloo Bridge was charged with passion and terror. Oxford Street was no more a busy main street; it was steeped in darkling clouds, not of London, but of bizarre countries of the fancy; and at every corner fluttered the imperial purple of the opium eater. (Him I could understand and I carried him about with me for weeks.) The horrid terra-cotta of the Prudential Building assumed grace as covering the site of Chatterton's last lodging. Tower Hill was lit with Otway, Bankside with Shakespeare and Greene, and the Borough High Street with the Canterbury Pilgrims. Even my own court, Bussell's Grove, took something of the spell. I dramatised it. Perhaps Chalterton or Savage had lived in just such a place as this.

It is Burke again putting his own memories into the narrative when it goes on to picture the boy's bitter sense of the social and other disadvantages against which he had to make headway; his hopelessness of ever being able to emancipate himself from the ill-paid drudgery of office-life; what it was that gave him his first idea for a story; how he wrote it, then "punched it out slowly on the office typewriter" after the staff was gone, and sent it to *T. P.'s Weekly*. It came back, but half a dozen words on the rejection slip encouraged him to go on writing; and the record of his many failures and few successes in the years when he was between seventeen and twenty is true not only of Burke but of all young authors who were

born
Under the starving sign of Capricorn

and have had to work their way through all the length of Grub Street before they could find an outlet to success.

How much of unqualified autobiography there is in **The Wind and the Rain** is more than I can say. There may be some romance in the charming chronicle of his first love—his innocent boyish passion for the little office girl, Gracie Scott, a perfect idyll till it reached its pitiful ending. And there may be some romance in the later story of his love for the tantalising Cicely who will neither accept or definitely reject him, but plunges him into despair at last. Anyhow, it is significant that writing in the first person he gives the narrator no surname, and lets Cicely slip into calling him "Tommy" when they are talking together; and while he is doing all he can to make the best of himself and impress her favourably, "With two pounds that I had received for a story," he writes, "I printed twenty copies of my poems in booklet form for her." In one of his recent essays, with slight variations, incidentally making the girl much younger, he repeats that about his printing the booklet for her, and it happens that before I met Burke I had picked up one of those twenty copies on a second-hand stall for twopence—a thin pamphlet in a grey paper cover, with **Verses** for its modest title. In pursuance of my lawful occasions, reviewing **The Wind and the Rain,** I referred to my possession, and Burke wrote and confessed that it was the booklet of which he had written and lamented that he had lost his copy and never been able to light upon another. As it seemed intolerable that I should keep mine while the author had none, I reluctantly followed the example of Sir Philip Sidney, and when I subsequently told an incurable collector what I had done he used harsh words about me, saying he would have paid me handsomely for it, and making as if he would tear the hair from his head, but I expect he had already suffered too many such disappointments, for he had none left.

Even more than in his novels and stories, I think you may come to a close acquaintance with Burke's history, his personality and idiosyncrasies, in certain of his essays and sketches, particularly those **Nights in Town,** in whose opening essay, **"Nocturne,"** he says,

> As a born Londoner, I cannot remember a time when London was not part of me, and I part of London. . . .

> And always it is London by lamplight which I vision when I think of her, for it was the London of lamplight that first called to me, as a child. She hardly exists for me in any other mood or dress. It was London by night that awoke me to a sense of that terrible spirit which we call Beauty, to be possessed by which is as unsettling and as sweetly frightful as to be possessed by Love. . . . Open your window when you will in the gloating evening, whether you live in town, in the near suburbs, or in the far suburbs—open your window and listen. You will hear London singing to you; and if you are one of her chosen you will have no sleep that night until you have answered her. There is nothing for it but to slip out and be abroad in the grey, furtive streets, or in the streets loud with lamps and loafers, and jostle the gay men and girls, or mingle with the chaste silences.

That love of London and his intense feeling for the beauty and mystery and terror of her streets by night, when they lie naked under the moon, half lost in fog, or lighted and shadowed by lamps and the shine of shop-windows, finds expression in sensitive, graphic impressions and descriptions that are scattered through all his books. When provincials say as they do, in the pride of discovery, that the born Londoner never knows his own city they are talking of what they do not understand. Unless you were born in London, and have wandered about it from childhood to maturity till your past flows through its streets as the blood through your veins, you may acquire an exhaustive acquaintance with it superficially but will never really know the heart and soul of the place as Burke knows them. He reveals the complexities of its character, its various and varying moods, its homeliness, grimness, squalors, loveliness, with an intimacy and sympathetic insight that are instinctive with him, because he did not approach it as an inquiring stranger but is a child of the city, nurtured and moulded by its associations and influences and mystically at one with it. I have marked several passages that illustrate this, but you can turn them up almost anywhere in his books; my space is dwindling and I want to add one more contribution from **"Nocturne"** to my autobiographical fragments:

> When I was a small child I was as other children of our set. I played their games in the street. I talked their language. I shared their ambitions. I worshipped their gods. Life was a business of Board School, breakfast, dinner, tea, struggled for and eaten casually, either at the table or at the door or other convenient spot. I should grow up. I should be, I hoped, a City clerk. I should wear stand-up collars. I might have a moustache. For Sunday I might have a frock coat and silk hat, and, if I were very clever and got on well, a white waistcoat. I should have a house—six rooms and a garden, and I might be able to go to West End theatres sometimes, and sit in the pit instead of the gallery. And some day I might even ride in a hansom cab, though I should have to succeed wonderfully to do that. I hoped I should succeed wonderfully, because then the other boys at the Board School would look up to me.

He has done wonderfully, but not exactly on those lines. He became a City clerk, and possibly wore stand-up collars, but if he grew a moustache he has long since removed it. He can't ride in hansom cabs for there are none. I have seen him in the pit and in the stalls at theatres, and he could wear a top hat if he liked, and possibly has done so in special circumstances, but not when I have been looking.

The City clerk, hampered by all sorts of disadvantages, developed into an author and journalist; the periodicals that had too often rejected his contributions not only began to accept them but to ask for more. Some fifteen years ago his earliest books (not counting the little pamphlet of *Verses*) made their appearance; these were *The Charm of the West Country,* and one or two other anthologies that showed good taste and good judgment in their selections and that he had become a wide and catholic reader. A volume of sketches, *Pavements and Pastures,* was followed in 1915 by *Nights in Town,* which takes you all over London, from Limehouse to Chelsea, from Whitechapel, Stepney, the Isle of Dogs to Surbiton and Clapham Common, and in its general tone and character was as a shadow cast before them by the books that were to come—except that it was more than a shadow, for it established his reputation and there are things in it that for beauty of thought and style and depth of human interest compare with anything he has written. He continued these town travels in *The London Spy,* in 1922, but meanwhile with *Limehouse Nights* (1916) and *Twinkletoes* he had risen into popularity as the laureate of London's Chinatown, of those Limehouse byways in which the wily Celestial furtively runs his gambling hells or opium dens, or, like Quong Lee, of *The Wind and the Rain,* and of that quaint book of verses *The Song Book of Quong Lee,* keeps small gaudily-decorated shops for the sale of tea, jars of ginger, tinned fruit and fish and syrup and such like everyday commodities. One of the *Limehouse Nights* stories, "The Chink and the Child", was turned into a film-play under the title of *Broken Blossom,* and was one of the most moving and artistically produced films I have seen. It had a considerable success, in spite of the fact that one of our leading newspapers made a resolute attack upon its idyllic tale of a Chinaman's devout love of a white girl, on the ground that it threw a sentimental glamour over the relations between white women and yellow men in the East End and might have the harmful effect of encouraging the growth of a tendency that often had disastrous consequences. However that may be, there is no denying the pathos, the power or the humour of these romances of Chinatown. They are the more truthful for being melodramatic, for there is always more melodrama than tragedy in human life, especially the life that Burke depicts in these tales and in *East of Mansion House* (1928). But though his Chinatown tales gave him his popularity and his label and inspired a school of imitators, for his best and most enduring work you must go, I think, to his *Nights in Town* and to his two novels, *The Wind and the Rain* and *The Sun in Splendour* (1927). The Islington publican and his musical friends and the rest of the group of characters in this last are drawn, and the whole quietly realistic story told with the same breadth and depth of understanding, sympathetic humour and mature philosophy that are the distinctive qualities of *The Wind and the Rain,* and would seem to indicate that Burke has not reduced his art to a formula but is still developing it and will presently have left his *Limehouse Nights,* as Dickens left his Boz sketches, behind him—a brilliant background for something bigger.

Edwin Björkman (essay date 1929)

SOURCE: "Thomas Burke: *The Man of Limehouse,* in *Thomas Burke: A Critical Appreciation of the Man of Limehouse,"* George H. Doran Company, 1929, pp. 5-18.

[*Björkman was a Swedish-American novelist, translator, and critic who introduced American readers to the works of such Scandinavian authors as August Strindberg, Biörnstjerne Björnson, and Georg Brandes. In the following essay, Björkman discusses Burke's life, his philosophy, and the sources of his works.*]

Anyone with a love for strong color and brisk action can enjoy the work of Thomas Burke. But to savor it fully, one must bear in mind sympathetically the three main factors that have combined to make his art what it is. The first of these is the soil from which he sprang: the London East End; the life of the slums; the sounds and sights and mysterious doings of the dock district, where, "on the floodtide, floats from Limehouse the bitter-sweet alluring smell of Asia. The second is the metropolis itself, in its vast and protean entirety, which every evening, when the human ebb retires from its heart to the suburbs, "affords an event as full of passion and wonder as any Eastern occasion." The third is his devotion to beauty, to all forms of art that strive genuinely to express it and, above all, to "the secret beauty that lies behind the material beauty of colour and sound" . . . a devotion born and nursed among surroundings and under circumstances so adverse that its triumphant survival seems little short of a miracle. In view of the continued dominance of these factors over his art, there are moments when I wonder whether anyone may grasp the innermost spirit of it, especially in his later and more introspective work, who has not himself been teased by the chimeric dream of perfect beauty; who has not in person felt the appalling sphinx-like lure of the greatest city on the earth; and who has not himself risen from one of those submerged layers of the social structure whence issued so inexplicably the creator of *Limehouse Nights* and *More Limehouse Nights,* of *The London Spy,* of *The Wind and the Rain, East of Mansion House,* and most recently, of *The Sun in Splendour.*

Out of the classes more and more apologetically termed the "lower" are formed the broad basis and main bulk of the social pyramid, which in England tapers to a vanishing apex of nobility and royalty. But Havelock Ellis tells us in his *Study of British Genius* that, in order to visualize the relative distribution of exceptionally gifted men and women among the various strata of the pyramid, we have to turn it upside down. This does not mean that genius may not lie dormant to an unsuspected degree among those doomed to live at the bottom, with all the rest of the social contents pressing down upon them. It means simply that among them the handicap is so great that only a scattered few can fight their way into those realms of beautiful endeavor which seem above all others to require a certain amount of leisure and peace of mind for admission to them. Thomas Burke is one of these rare few, and his success in breaking out of his native environment is the more notable because he started from the undermost surface—from a region lying even lower socially than the miner's cottage which originally sheltered D. H. Lawrence—and because he has never shown any inclination to forget his starting point.

It is not without significance that, in his striking autobiographical novel, *The Wind and the Rain,* Mr. Burke makes no reference to the place of his birth or to his parents. That they were dead at the beginning of the story we may assume from the fact that later he was admitted to an orphanage. But who and what they were we do not know. One might almost think that the author took pride in suggesting that he had sprung out of absolute nothingness . . . and from the viewpoint of the social apex, he might just as well. We become aware of him for the first time as a boy of nine, living with an uncle in the London district of Poplar, adjacent to the great docks and the region particularly favored by Chinamen and all sorts of foreigners. Like other children of that picturesque but morally indifferent region, he was free of the streets, and he used his freedom to the ulmost, though in a manner that would probably have aroused the scorn even of his natural playmates. Where they scoffed and jeered and hated he found friendship and solace and a way to wisdom beyond his years and condition. "Low" as was his own class, judged by the accepted social gauge, there were others still lower, and to these, the unregistered and uncherished classes comprising the criminal and the prostitute, the informer and his victim, the Chink and the oriental flotsam of the docks, his interest and his sympathy went out from the first. Without ever becoming more than a visitor in their strangely self sufficient world, he learned to know its drab byways and suspicious glamours, its occasions of resplendent tragedy.

The uncle of little Tommy, "the boy with the sharp nose," had been an innkeeper and was a gardener when brought on the scene in *The Wind and the Rain*. He was a wise man in his humble way, holding that God might be worshiped as well in the streets or in one's bedroom as in the churches. From him and his chums at "The Barge Aground" must have come some of the gentle and tolerant philosophy that runs like a soothing, harmonious undercurrent beneath all the soul stirring stories later told by his nephew. Among those chums was the "housekeeper," or lock-up guard, of the local police station; when this man began to talk about the outlandish doings in the Causeway, where centers the Chinatown of London, then little Tommy became so "entrapped" that, as he tells us now, "he could recount some of the stories to this day, word for word, pause for pause." How many of those stories are to be found in *Limehouse Nights* and *More Limehouse Nights* we do not know, but we may guess.

The boy's dearest friend during those early years, however, was an old Chinaman, named Quong Lee in *The Wind and the Rain,* whose shop he visited clandestinely and ecstatically, receiving from him bits of ginger, monosyllabic remarks and the incipiency of a mystic dream of beauty that was to pursue him through many purgatorial years, until at last it half goaded him and half guided him into the comparative heaven of artistic self-realization. "In that shop," writes Mr. Burke, "I knew what some people seek in church and others seek in taverns." There, too, he

learned "all the beauty and all the evil of the heart of Asia; its cruelty, its grace and its wisdom."

What would have happened if the Lady of the Big House where the uncle worked as gardener had not begun to "take an interest" in little Tommy, with his "oo's," his "not 'alf's," his dropped "aitches," his Bible "tex" learned by rote, and his shy dreams of something ineffable, who can tell? As it was that interest tore him out of the kindly company of "The Barge Aground" and from the mystically inspiring presence of Quong Lee, giving him instead four years of unspeakable humiliation, oppression, and spiritual mortification in an orphange where, under the guise of Christian Charity, he was brought nearer to hell than he had ever come while still haunting the lanes and back alleys and dark arches of Limehouse. Thence he emerged on the edge of adolescence, a little seared of soul, full of terrifying knowledge, and yet as innocent of heart as any child cradled in Mayfair. His uncle was dead. He was absolutely alone in the world, a queer, uncouth boy of fourteen, and he was held lucky to get a pitifully humble place among the nameless and unnumbered white collar multitudes serving as a foundation for that pyramid of wealth and prosperous enterprise known to all the rest of the world as the City. And once more that boy, so peculiarly immune to poisons that would have killed or eternally warped most other striplings, had to spend years in a purgatory bordering on hell itself . . . four endlessly long years during which, "night after night, he went hungry to bed, actively hungry."

Yet it was during those very years that he began to study London as, before him, under conditions not very dissimilar, it had been studied by the young Dickens and the young Machen—with a passionate love, and an eye for beauty, and a sense for half-hidden mysteries that by and by were to make their possessor one of the most convincing painters of the high lights and dark shadows, the glamour and glory and shame, of what is probably the world's most marvelous city. At seven o'clock he was free of the streets, as he had been years before, and night after night he tramped innumerable miles in "muzzy exaltation," drugging himself with the infinitely variable atmosphere of those streets, and returning at last to his dreary den "hot and dazed." Each night he carried back with him a little parcel of pictures:

> The haze of a fried-fish bar, The tinkle of an organ hidden in a back street. A lamp in an alley giving just light enough to make darkness horrible. The reek and murk of a public house. The massed lights of factories hung, as it were, from the sky. The gleam and gush of drapers' windows. Voices mourning or crying from unseen points. Street corner groupings carven out of shadow. Strange life moving behind curtained windows or half-open doors.

It was that period, too, which brought his discovery of reading and literature and poetry. A paper picked up by chance in a cheap coffee shop flung open doors which until then had been not only closed but unsuspected. Starved already, he stinted himself still further to buy low priced editions of the classic poets. The possibilities of the circulating libraries also became revealed to him, and he read in a fever, omnivorously, but with small realization and scant returns. All he got out of it was a vague desire to write . . . something. More light did not come until he had found what was to be a lifelong love, equalling what he left for the Causeway and the great city itself. Music once encountered in its higher manifestations, became part of himself as much as the underworld of his childhood and the dream of the ineffable started by old Quong Lee's shop. Though he was incapable of musical expression himself, the music that he drank in with open ears and heart seemed to take firm lodging in his mind and gradually come forth again as a curiously stirring melody of words.

He began to write. In fact from the first moment of his authorial start, he was writing all the time, and in conditions that to the overwhelming majority of mankind would have seemed too hideously hopeless for sustained effort of any kind. He wrote reams, on paper when he could get it, otherwise on backs of envelopes, on scraps of wrapping, on anything. And always he wrote with one purpose, one scene in his mind. He wanted to express one moment in a London street . . . the moment when he stood looking into Quong Lee's shop and the old Chinaman for the first time beckoned him to come in. That moment was to him what conversion is to the pious believer. And so, at sixteen, he sold his first story for a fabulous guinea and thought himself made . . . only to find that he had not yet made a real start. It was this writing, however, such as it was, that finally took him out of the City as a rebel to its discipline and flung him back into the streets, a starving, homeless waif more than ever. Then, after a relatively happy period within the grotesquely joyous world of the music halls, he returned briefly to the world of his beginnings, to the Causeway and Quong Lee. It was after meeting the latter once more, a dishonored but philosophic outcast being deported at the completion of his punishment for having conducted an opium den of more than customary disrepute, that young Thomas Burke saw the light fully for the first time, and the stories began to appear which quickly made him famous. It was as if the dream planted in his soul by the old Chinaman could not assume tangible shape until Quong Lee himself had vanished out of the picture for ever. Then the moment of greatest joy merged with that of keenest sorrow, and a writer was born.

The rest of Mr. Burke's story need not be told. *Limehouse Nights* made him. The filming of the first story in that collection under the title of *Broken Blossoms* spread his name across the globe. Since then he has produced many volumes, all eminently readable and worth reading. But the ones that really count are those mentioned in the beginning of this article. He has written poetry, but his verse does not rise to the high level of his prose. His studies of the London scene, though excellent, do not compare in significance with his stories or novels. The first of the novels, *Twinkletoes,* though good as everything he has written, may also be left aside as being in essence an expanded short story. It suggests that its author had not yet found his bearings in that less concentrated medium. *The Wind and The Rain,* on the other hand, and still more his latest work, *The Sun in Splendour,* though the finest, are autobiographical to be sure, yet they are true novels, clearly in-

dicative of a new growth, taking him beyond the highly specialized themes that both carry and limit his short stories.

What is it that catches and holds and charms us in these stories? The pleasingly shocking novelty of the general atmosphere first of all, I suppose. But the appeal of mere novelty wanes with familiarity, and I have read those vibrant tales of Mr. Burke's earlier volumes several times without any slackening of interest. The first startled impression is gone forever. Their subtler appeal remains undiminished. This appeal must touch something that lurks very deep down in my soul. They are full of flamboyant colors, of course . . . colors as tempting and intimidating as those of a tropical jungle . . . colors that glow with the fierceness of living flames when set against the grey background of a modern slum. The life painted with the magic of those colors is remarkably primitive, and for this reason more directly expressive than that to which our daily well regulated existences have accustomed us. Passions and desires otherwise carefully suppressed are there flaunted openly and as openly indulged. The savage in us may be gloating over those stories, but perhaps he is also assuaged and rendered harmless by them. Revenge, of which we civilized creatures hardly dare to dream any longer, stalks unshamed on every page of Mr. Burke's earlier work. There is love, too, brutal or sublime, and there is self sacrifice, and the unwritten law of the jungle. But above all of these revenge thrones supreme, the chief motive of a majority of the stories, and perchance the first sign of an impending exit from savagery . . . for anger is momentary, and well known to brute life, but revenge must wait and plan. It may be held the first specifically human emotion, with a special lure for us who, unwillingly, are persuaded to forget it.

Perhaps, however, the main secret of the appeal exerted by the stories of Mr. Burke may be sought in his attitude toward the life he portrays. He remarks somewhere of Morland's canvases, that "half their charm lies in the fact that he saw his subjects on the level: that he was instinctively of them." This may with equal propriety be said of Mr. Burke's own work. To him may also be applied what he writes of Charlie Chaplin: "Like all men who are born in exile, outside the gracious inclosures of life, he does not forget those early years." Mr. Burke has left behind the underworld where he spent those years, but he is still of it. He has been accepted within "the gracious inclosures," and he despises them both as an artist and a former denizen of Limehouse. He pours scorn on "the land of the half-intellectuals and the bland drivel of drawing-rooms and the sleek grace that lures the impressionable away from beauty." He is not an impressionable of this type. Defiantly he asserts that "low" company is not for "the mean-spirited, who fear its candours and fly from it to their drawing-rooms and dissembling gestures."

Always and in every way he remains mercilously truthful, refusing to falsify or sentimentalize the strange, rough, intense life he shows us. He is frank and outspoken in his references to many things forming an inalienable phase of that life, but not open to discussion in more "refined" gatherings. His very frankness, however, is characterized by an instinctive sense for the right word that should constitute an excuse in itself. Nevertheless he has been called vulgar, and this criticism he resents, pointing out that, in this respect, all great art is vulgar . . . the art of Fielding and Dickens no less than that of Homer and the Old Testament writers. Christ himself, "the greatest of artists," was vulgar, says old Scollard in *The Sun in Splendour,* and on that account Mr. Burke thinks the more of Him. But at the heart this man, graduated from one of England's supposedly most foul spots, is gloriously pagan . . . pagan in the same manner and spirit as his little **"Gina of the Chinatown"** who "opened new doors to the people of Poplar, showing them the old country to which today excursions are almost forbidden; the country of the dear brown earth and the naked flesh, of the wine-cup and flowers and kisses and Homeric laughter." It is, I presume, on all the qualities here suggested, and not solely on any one among them, that his irresistible appeal rests in those stories that will always be primarily associated with his name . . . stories that have brought one more slice of humanity within the ken of literature and of thinking, open minded, beauty-loving readers.

The line of his novels is barely opened. And the autobiographical character of *The Wind and the Rain* makes it a little uncertain as a sample of what may be expected hereafter. It is a beautiful tale exquisitely told, a soul searching and bravely veracious record: tender, poignant, moving, and illumined by an astute understanding of the child as well as of human nature in general. But the story is his own, the child himself, and every man is said to hide one such book in his mental makeup. *The Sun in Splendour* is different . . . his first determined and sustained effort to break away from what theretofore had been his too exclusive setting. Even here Limehouse, with its inevitable crime, its sadistic proclivities, its precarious existence above and beyond the law, may be sensed, though under new forms and new names. Even here one notes a certain tendency to repetition, a willingness to use over again familiar scenes and characters and themes, indicating that the author's imaginative quality may be centered in expression rather than in the actual creation of new life. But the horizons of this work are wider, the superficial movements of life less predominant, the human analysis far more profound. The central figure and his wonderfully attractive old father are quite novel, unlike anything in the stories . . . a foiled dreamer about beauty, and a real creator of it foiled by the nature of his success, both taken out of a life that belongs to no one city or district.

To some extent *The Sun in Splendour* may be described as a book by an artist for artists, but in its wider implications it reaches far beyond that restricted field. It is bursting with sincerity, and with candor of a more sensitive, more spiritual kind. It may not belong with the great novels of all time, but it has a vicelike grip on one's attention and is not easily forgotten when read. Christopher Scollard in *The Sun in Splendour* is more or less identical with Tommy in *The Wind and the Rain,* and both with Mr. Burke himself. Of Christopher we are told toward the end of his story that "he was facing what many a young artist has to face; the knowledge that he was only a skilled craftsman." Yet this latest work of Mr. Burke's, as well

as all else done by him before, gives evidence of an incorruptible striving for genuine artistic values, plus a capacity for recognizing "the secret beauty lying behind the material beauty of colour and sound" that can generally be found in similar measure, with similar intensity, only among writers who possess within themselves at least the possibility of greatness. And Mr. Burke is not yet forty, I understand. His artistic career is merely begun. It will be wise to watch him well, and it will be safe, I think, to place high hopes on whatever he will do hereafter, no matter what form it may take.

Alfred Kazin   (essay date 1973)

SOURCE: An introduction to *Limehouse Nights* by Thomas Burke, Horizon Press, 1973, pp. 12-19.

[*A highly respected American literary critic, Kazin is best known for his essay collections* The Inmost Leaf *(1955),* Contemporaries *(1962), and* On Native Ground *(1942). In the following essay, he discusses the strengths and limitations of* Limehouse Nights.]

Thomas Burke believed that Limehouse, the great grimy port area on the north bank of the Thames, was the most exotic place in the world. When I saw it one day in 1945, wandering about the East India docks, I seemed to see nothing but the most enormous warehouses solidly lining the streets back of the docks. What I remember of that late Saturday afternoon under a cloud of war is pale London urchins playing indecipherable London games in what looked, even in daylight, like some impenetrable shadow cast upon the streets from the warehouses bristling at a stranger from street after street.

The East India docks, to this American investigator, reeked of poverty and toil. It seemed altogether right and fitting to me that Clement Attlee, soon to become Socialist Prime Minister of England, had for many years represented Limehouse in the House of Commons. It would not have occurred to me that Limehouse could be a literary fascination, and that it could stand for Chinatown, opium dens, Lascars, many a stealthy knife (or unspeakably poisonous Indian snake) planted where it would do the most harm—and above all, for the amazing "flower-like" beauty of young London girl-children.

But Thomas Burke did see Limehouse as the most exotic place on earth. Indeed, he never stopped writing about it. He had an all-too-respectable, all-too-genteel, all-too-literary lower-class London clerk's life-long love affair with London—especially, of course, the "disreputable," most "foreign" parts of London. Writing these stories and sketches (and unmistakable fantasies) just as his country was going into the First World War, when "Great" Britain was still the imperial power bestriding the world and London was the financial center of the world, Burke looked away from the official glory to describe, *con amore,* the seamiest, tawdriest side of London, the labyrinth that London's poor and London's foreigners kept secret within the great body of London.

Clearly, Burke saw Limehouse as the greatest possible contrast to the respectable, bristlingly proud self that London (and the English) presented in those days. Indeed, *Limehouse Nights* shows a positive obsession with the exotic street colors of London's Chinatown, the suffocatingly narrow rooms, the hysterical violence between the local English—boxers, bartenders, music-hall "artistes"—and Chinese storekeepers and sailors. Where Clement Attlee, M. P., saw nothing but social statistics (one story, **"The Knight-Errant,"** is a satire on an aristocratic Socialist do-gooder) and where T. S. Eliot in *The Waste Land* refers sorrowfully to parts of Limehouse as blots on the historic landscape of the Thames, Thomas Burke saw what one might well call a silent film. For he saw, as the great film directors did in the era of silent films, that there is a necessary melodrama to the unconscious expressing itself in tawdry surroundings. There is a drama to instinct when the varieties of unconscious emotion are played by "Chinks," drunken and bestial boxers of the slums, precociously voluptuous fourteen-year-old love goddesses out of the gutter—and by such legendary sexual tools as knives and snakes.

Limehouse Nights is saturated in the favorite materials of realism, and it was written at a time when the "handling" of poverty and the poor by such realists as Dreiser, Crane, Gissing, Bennett, had become a truculent literary tradition. But it is a wholly romantic and melodramatic book, saved from absurdity by its cinematic, beautifully eccentric infatuation with the material. It tells the same story in story after story—the coming of love to Limehouse and the sharp sputtering catastrophe that always rounds out the affair in the killing of someone.

It is full of a kind of overwriting that one can find in Crane's *Maggie:* writing about the poor from a distance. And one can tell from the overwriting how much of a tourist Burke remained in Limehouse. There is that too intense "atmosphere" typical of class feelings among English writers who with the best will in the world cannot help writing *down* when they attempt the lower classes. But what makes *Limehouse Nights* fascinating is the fact that Burke's "Limehouse" is not a social problem but a country of people made interesting by their sexual emotions.

It is hard to say how much Thomas Burke, writing half a century ago, recognized that his Limehouse was essentially a sexual landscape. The suspicion and hatred between the Londoners and the Orientals here is conventional stuff. But the race differences, also, come to light as the tremulously shocking relations between people who do not expect to feel what they suddenly feel. Burke was still writing in the late Victorian country of the forbidden, so a "bold," "modern" young writer had to knock things over with a crash. The too elaborate, unmistakably condescending, "picturesque" style of *Limehouse Nights* may remind you of other early twentieth-century romantic novelists "investigating" the seamy side from a literary distance. But the charm of this "picturesque" school is that it described the lower depths always in terms of sex, which still meant love and romance. Poverty, seaminess, tawdriness were the salt of life that would permit a novelist (whether or not he knew why he was so fascinated by

these materials) to describe the violence not of "society" but of individual feeling.

In *Limehouse Nights* the most powerful element is not poverty or the struggle against poverty; it is the violence of people who can express only by violence the amazement of their own tenderness. Indeed, so little is Burke a "social" novelist that his characters are lifted out of the anonymous mass only when they fall in love. Burke is romantic about sex-as-human-expression, for this kind of expressiveness is what holds him to rough characters who are always falling in love, and for whom this is the only possible "revelation" of lives that have no other satisfaction. And, of course, in the pessimistic literary style of the period, these low characters must pay for falling in love by dying in some horrid kind of way. This is the still un-modern world where sex and retribution, sex and fear, go hand in hand.

This is, indeed, the still un-modern world of the silent films where the "expression" on one suddenly gleaming face more than makes up for so much . . . corn. Burke's language, of course, is quite artificial by our standards. In the opening of **"The Cue,"** for example, we read:

> Down Wapping Way, where the streets rush right and left to water-side and depot, life ran high. Tide was at flood, and below the Old Stairs the waters lashed themselves to fury. Against the savage purple of the night rose a few wisps of rigging and some gruff funnels: lyrics in steel and iron, their leaping lines as correct and ecstatic as a rhymed verse.

The literary flavor of this reminds one of the old sub-titles in silent films. " . . . the savage purple of the night . . . lyrics in steel and iron . . . " And Burke, an impetuous writer, just misses when he finds the "leaping lines" of these "gruff funnels" "as correct and ecstatic as a rhymed verse." And I tasted popcorn in my mouth when I read that "Love-mad hands have buried knives in lily white bosoms in Commercial Road, and songs are written by the moon across many a happy garret-window in Cable Street."

But the more I read on, the more I recognized the London where Charlie Chaplin grew up. Indeed, indeed, Burke's love of "lurid" emotions, his extraordinary emphasis on Chaplin's moment of tenderness, on a face suddenly lifted up, all "ecstatic," yea, with the astonishment of feeling love, belongs to the black and white world, the unsubtle but infinitely moving lifting-out-of-everything-else of a woman's face.

There is a lot of sado-masochistic stuff here, too. But what we have, whether to love or to kill, is an art of pantomime, as in the silent films, where a single face—usually a young girl's face—gropes out of the welter of shadowy nighttime streets to display a tenderness as piercing as any of the knives and snakes that finish off—literally—so many of Burke's stories. Revenge is certainly one of the dominant emotions here, and revenge, in all its now old-fashioned colors, is a prime necessity for many of Burke's characters. Nothing like a good solid grudge to keep you going under adverse circumstances.

But as in the great silent movies, these different emotions are lordly powers—they are separate, never in equilibrium, hardly on the same plane. Certain faces stand out, certain emotions rise to the surface, certain people will suddenly die. Out of the dark Limehouse night certain moments of unexpected feeling emerge, for this is a world in which the only human satisfaction is indeed to feel something . . . too strongly.

It all makes up a strangely limited kind of world, a world poorer in every sense than Clement Attlee, M. P.—or Burke himself—could have realized. But its harsh limitations focus its genuineness. Burke was hardly a great writer, but he had the root of all real writing in him. He was hypnotized by his subject. I am sure he kept dreaming of Limehouse long after he had published this book and its sequels.

FURTHER READING

Criticism

Egan, Maurice Francis. "London in Mosaics and Circles." *The New York Times Book Review* (2 October 1921): 7, 23.

Praises Burke's sensitive depiction in *The Outer Circle* of life in London's various suburbs.

Ferguson, Malcolm M. "Thomas Burke of Limehouse." *The Romantist*, No. 2 (1978): 41-2.

An appreciation of Burke's fiction and nonfiction reprinted from *The Fantasy Advertister*, March 1950.

Towne, Charles Hanson. "*The Sun in Splendor.*" In *Thomas Burke: A Critical Appreciation of the Man of Limehouse; With a Note on a Novel, by Charles Hanson Towne*, by Edwin Björkman, pp. 19-20. New York: George H. Doran Company, 1929.

A brief, enthusiastic review.

Additional coverage of Burke's life and career is available in the following source published by Gale Research: *Contemporary Authors,* Vol. 113.

Anna Katharine Green

1846-1935

American novelist, short story writer, poet, and dramatist.

INTRODUCTION

One of the first American women to write mystery and detective fiction, Green is today remembered for her important contributions to the development of this literary genre. Her reputation as the "mother" or "godmother" of the detective story rests on her unprecedented popularity with readers, which helped bring "respectability" to the detective genre, as well as on her many narrative innovations. Green introduced several devices that later became standard in detective fiction, such as the coroner's inquest, expert testimony, and detailed maps or house plans that illustrate the scene of the crime; she firmly established the convention of the recurring detective and the technique of pairing a professional detective with an amateur; and she created two detective prototypes, the elderly spinster sleuth and the young female investigator. Green's best-known detective, however, is the fatherly, endearingly eccentric Inspector Ebenezer Gryce, who is featured in over a dozen of Green's stories. Gryce made his debut in Green's first work, *The Leavenworth Case* (1878). One of the earliest best-selling detective novels, *The Leavenworth Case* preceded the appearance of Sir Arthur Conan Doyle's Sherlock Holmes by almost a decade.

Biographical Information

Green was born in Brooklyn, New York, the youngest daughter of James Wilson Green, a prominent defense lawyer, and Katharine Ann Whitney Green, who died when Green was just three years old. Green attended public schools, first in New York City and then in Buffalo, where the family moved after her father's remarriage. As a young girl, Green aspired to be a poet. She was composing verses by the age of eleven, and while she was a student at Ripley Female College in Poultney, Vermont, she sent samples of her work to Ralph Waldo Emerson. In the mid-1860s, after receiving her B.A., Green returned home to pursue her interest in writing poetry. She also worked on a mystery novel inspired by the detective stories of Edgar Allan Poe and Émile Gaboriau as well as by her father's accounts of his criminal cases. Entitled *The Leavenworth Case,* the novel follows the criminal investigation into the shooting death of a wealthy New York philanthropist. *The Leavenworth Case* enjoyed tremendous popularity upon its publication and for many years afterward. Not only was it reprinted several times, it was also adapted for the stage and filmed in both silent and sound versions. In addition, it was used in a course at Yale University to demonstrate the fallacy of relying on circumstantial evidence. The overnight success of *The Leavenworth Case* made Green's name a household word, and she went on

to write over thirty more novels and several collections of short stories in a career that spanned forty-five years. Ironically, while Green's acclaim as a novelist caused her to abandon her dream of becoming a well-known poet, it did bring some attention to her poetic works, the collection *The Defense of the Bride, and Other Poems* (1882) and the verse drama *Risifi's Daughter* (1887). In 1884 Green married Charles Rohlfs, an actor—he played the lead role in the stage version of *The Leavenworth Case*— who later became a famous furniture designer. The couple settled in Buffalo, where they raised three children, only one of whom was alive at the time of Green's death in 1935.

Major Works

The Leavenworth Case provided a model for most of Green's subsequent works. The basic ingredients of her stories and her methods changed little over the course of her career. Typically, the crime involved is a murder that takes place amid polite New York society, love entanglements provide clues to solving the mystery, and there is a surprise plot twist. Green frequently framed her stories around courtroom scenes or a coroner's inquest to reveal the facts of the case, and she often provided lists of deductions and possibilities as she sketched potential suspects and their motives. Each novel carefully follows the reasoning of the chief detective on the case, who is aided by an eager associate. Green's best-known detective, Inspector Ebenezer Gryce, the hero of *The Leavenworth Case* and such other popular novels as *A Strange Disappearance* (1880), *Hand and Ring* (1884), *A Matter of Millions* (1890), and *The Doctor, His Wife, and the Clock* (1895), has several different assistants, including Horace Byrd, Amelia Butterworth, and his principal protégé, Caleb Sweetwater, who also appears in some of Green's novels as the chief investigator. Gryce collaborates with Butterworth, a nosy but astute spinster from an old New York family, in the novels *That Affair Next Door* (1897), *Lost Man's Lane* (1898), and *The Circular Study* (1900). The feisty and shrewd Butterworth is considered the precursor to Agatha Christie's famous unmarried woman detective, Miss Jane Marple. Green created another important female detective for the short story collection *The Golden Slipper and Other Problems for Violet Strange* (1915). Strange, a young woman who leads a double life as a socialite and an agent for a professional detective agency, is frequently described as an early version of Nancy Drew.

Critical Reception

Contemporary readers and critics marveled at the ingeniousness of Green's plots, remarking that she never told the same story twice. Her appeal derived in large part from the realism of her stories. Unlike much of the detective fiction being written at the time, Green's narratives never exceeded the bounds of probability or relied on fantastic coincidences. Instead, Green constructed plots that usually turned on a piece of medical or scientific evidence, and many of the now-familiar devices she introduced involve legal and police procedures. Green herself commented on her realistic approach in an essay on crime and detective fiction she wrote toward the end of her career: "In writing detective stories, the less one resorts to arbitrary helps in the mystery, the better. I mean that people are not interested in a crime that depends on some imaginary mechanical device, some unknown poison, or some legendary animal. To resort to such expedients for your mystery is a weakness. To employ imagination in making use of *natural* laws, however, is another matter." In her own day, Green was ranked with Poe, Gaboriau, and Doyle among the best writers of detective fiction, and her huge following of devotees included Wilkie Collins and Woodrow Wilson. By the middle of this century, however, Green's name had fallen into obscurity, principally because her strict adherence to Victorian codes of behavior made her books appear dated. Recent critics note that her stories are overly melodramatic and sentimental, her characters forced and unnatural. Yet she is remembered as the first American woman to write a best-selling detective novel and for bringing wider readership to the genre. She is also recognized for her originality. Critics praise her stories as models of plot construction and consistently remark that she anticipated many of the characteristics of modern detective stories, not only with the new devices she introduced but also with old ones she reworked, such as her broadening of the role of the amateur detective to include women.

PRINCIPAL WORKS

The Leavenworth Case: A Lawyer's Story (novel) 1878
A Strange Disappearance (novel) 1880
The Defense of the Bride, and Other Poems (poetry) 1882
Hand and Ring (novel) 1884
Risifi's Daughter: A Drama (drama) 1887
Behind Closed Doors (novel) 1888
A Matter of Millions (novel) 1890
The Doctor, His Wife, and the Clock (novel) 1895
That Affair Next Door (novel) 1897
Lost Man's Lane: A Second Episode in the Life of Amelia Butterworth (novel) 1898
Agatha Webb (novel) 1899
The Circular Study (novel) 1900
One of My Sons (novel) 1901
The Filigree Ball (novel) 1903
The Amethyst Box (novel) 1905
The Chief Legatee (novel) 1906; also published as *A Woman of Mystery*, 1909
The Woman in the Alcove (novel) 1906
The House of the Whispering Pines (novel) 1910
Initials Only (novel) 1911
Masterpieces of Mystery (short stories) 1913; also published as *Room Number 3, and Other Stories*, 1919
Dark Hollow (novel) 1914
The Golden Slipper and Other Problems for Violet Strange (short stories) 1915
The Mystery of the Hasty Arrow (novel) 1917
The Step on the Stair; or, You Are the Man (novel) 1923

CRITICISM

E. F. Harkins and C. H. L. Johnston (essay date 1902)

SOURCE: "Anna Katharine Green (Mrs. Rohlfs)," in *Little Pilgrimages among the Women Who Have Written Famous Books*, L. C. Page & Co., 1902, pp. 91-106.

[*In the following essay, Harkins and Johnston focus on Green's literary beginnings, her role as a trailblazer in the genre of detective fiction, and her strengths as a writer.*]

It is related that when **The Leavenworth Case** was published in 1878, the Pennsylvania Legislature turned from politics to discuss the identity of its author. There was the name on the title-page—Anna Katharine Green—as distinct as the city of Harrisburgh itself. But it must be a *nom de plume,* some protested. A man wrote the story—maybe a man already famous—and signed a woman's name to it.

The story was manifestly beyond a woman's powers. Feminine names were considerably scarcer in the American fiction list then than they are to-day, when girls fresh from the high school take a place among the authors of the "best-selling" books.

A New York lawyer happened to be present at the politicians' discussion. "You are mistaken," he said to the incredulous. "I have seen the author of *The Leavenworth Case* and conversed with her, and her name is really Miss Green."

"Then she must have got some man to help her," retorted the more obstinate theorists. They strongly remind us of the characters whom Miss Green—as we shall call her for the moment—portrays so skillfully, the self-willed characters that aim so well, but do not hit even the target, not to mention the bull's-eye.

The incredulity exemplified by the Pennsylvanians was natural enough. That an American woman in those days should venture into the field of romantic literature was so uncommon as to be noteworthy; but that an American woman should write detective stories—well, that was quite preposterous.

And yet, nowadays, it would seem no more preposterous than a request to Mr. Carnegie to build a library. For the love of a good detective story, of a story interwoven with adventure and mystery, is in most persons a simple manifestation of the instinctive love of excitement. We know a professor—one of the most brilliant men in his profession—who has never lost his juvenile fondness for the pursuit of fire-engines. Similarly, many men and women are never cured of their youthful passion for the literature of the disguises and the handcuffs. Hawkshaw! How the name thrills even to-day! It takes many a man back to the days when the tattered dime-novel was smuggled into the schoolroom. Sometimes the almost breathless attention to syntax or the map of the New England States betrayed the guilt; but we firmly believe that there were teachers who never confiscated those prizes.

But, measuring by the incessant changes in times and in manners, it is not difficult to understand that a quarter of a century ago the still conservative reading public was loth to believe that the author of *The Leavenworth Case* was a woman.

Anna Katharine Green, the woman in question, was born in Brooklyn, N. Y., on Nov. 11, 1846. She was thirty-two, therefore, it will be seen, when the story that made her famous was published. Her father was a well-known lawyer; indeed, the Greens, we have been told, were a family of lawyers. This may account for the skill with which the daughter has tied and cut Gordian knots. It unquestionably accounts for her nimble imagination, her skill in producing subtle hypotheses and her strength in handling the most intricate psychological problems. In 1867 Anna was graduated from the Ripley Female College, in Poultney, Vt., and she may, if she please, write B.A. after her name. She composed verses and stories at the age of eleven. And speaking of verses, how many readers are acquainted with the fact that the author of *The Leavenworth Case* is also the author of a drama in blank verse and of a volume of

ballads and narrative poems? Yet *The Defence of the Bride, and Other Poems* has won encomiums from discreet critics: and in some respects *Risifi's Daughter: A Drama,* is her most ambitious work.

Perhaps, therefore, as we are to consider her poetry as an incidental, it may not be amiss at this point to quote a few characteristic verses. The two stanzas which follow are taken from a poem entitled **"At the Piano"**:

> Play on! Play on! As softly glides
>   The low refrain, I seem, I seem,
> To float, to float on golden tides,
>   By sunlit isles, where life and dream
> Are one, are one; and hope and bliss
> Move hand in hand, and thrilling, kiss
>   'Neath bowery blooms
>   In twilight glooms,
> And love is life, and life is love.
>
> Play on! Play on! As higher rise
>   The lifted strains, I seem, I seem
> To mount, to mount through roseate skies,
>   Through drifted cloud and golden gleam,
> To realms, to realms of thought and fire,
> Where angels walk and souls aspire,
> And sorrow comes but as the night
> That brings a star for our delight.

Some of the criticisms of the book—*The Defence of the Bride, and Other Poems*—were extremely, and, indeed, rather absurdly flattering; a moderately toned opinion was given in *Harper's Monthly:*

> The ballads and narrative poems which form the greater part of this collection are vigorous productions, whose barrenness of redundant words and epithets, and whose directness and straightforwardness of narration, are in strong contrast with the diffuse garrulity of most female writers. She has the true storyteller's faculty for investing what she has to say with interest, and for keeping expectation on the stretch; and she delivers her message with masculine force and brevity.

One of the critics, by the way, compared Miss Green—she was still Miss Green then, in 1882—with Alfred Austin. "Miss Green," says the critic, "seems to be able to say delicate and graceful things as easily as does the English poet." That was before Mr. Austin became Poet Laureate—before comparisons with him were particularly odious.

Risifi's Daughter, we may say, in a word, is notable rather for its well-sustained dramatic strength than for any especial skill or grace of versification. It seems to have convinced its author that her lines might be cast in happier places.

But to return to the main road. We have already seen that as a girl Anna had literary aspirations, but they reached no serious stage of development until after her return from Ripley College. She felt drawn to literature, and yet she was in no hurry either to decide which of the divers literary fields was best suited to her taste and talent, or to see her name in print. At this critical time her father was friend and counsellor. He perceived that there was no fickleness back of his daughter's ambition to adopt literature as a profession; and, what is more important, he perceived that she might successfully qualify as a candidate. So he set about to direct and to encourage her zeal.

He found Anna a docile pupil. When doubts arose, when discouragement appeared, he was nearby to cheer her and to advise. He enlisted her sympathy in different cases that interested him; he sharpened her wits; he discoursed to her on his own interesting experiences; he contributed judicious criticisms; above all, he fostered her confidence in her own powers. In this way she acquired from her father gifts that she had not inherited from him. Hers was a remarkably well-equipped intellect before one of her books had been published.

The Leavenworth Case came to startle the reading public in 1878. The plot of the story had been in the author's mind for some years. The book, therefore, was no inspired or spasmodic effort; rather it was the product of a finely regulated intellect applied to the ever-entertaining theories of cause and effect. What if those legislators had been informed of the fact that the author was a student of criminology!

Mrs. Rohlfs is too adept a psychologist to pretend that instinct led her with the manuscript of *The Leavenworth Case* to Mr. G. P. Putnam's office; it was more likely a simple piece of good fortune to happen upon so wise and liberal an appraiser. It is a tribute to his perspicacity that he introduced to the American reading public one of its most popular writers, and it is a happy commentary on the relationship between author and publisher that, with an exception or two, the Putnam house has issued the periodical output of Anna Katharine Green.

When *A Strange Disappearance* appeared, in 1885 [1880], a critic—or perhaps we should say reviewer—made the comment: "We have a Gaboriau in our own tongue." It must have seemed extremely flattering—assuming that the author of *A Strange Disappearance* is normally susceptible to flattery—to be named favorably in the same sentence with the brilliant Frenchman. Mrs. Rohlfs resembles Gaboriau in so far as her strong point, as his was, is the simple and perspicuous narrative of events; thus, too, she resembles Wilkie Collins, who was called an imitator of Gaboriau. But we doubt that any pen excepting Gaboriau's could write or could have written the first part of *Monsieur Lecocq.* Possibly the English writer thought he saw an imitator in the author of *The Leavenworth Case.* At any rate, while she was enjoying the first fruits of renown, Collins wrote to her publishers that he sincerely admired her stories; and we understand that he conveyed to the young American some "wise practical hints" and "warm expressions of belief in her future." The belief has been abundantly justified.

"It is said"—we quote from an anonymous paper dealing with the career of the New York author—"that she does not herself claim to be a novelist. She is not a novelist in the sense that George Eliot and Hawthorne are novelists." These words remind us of the reflections of Mr. Herbert Paul, the brilliant English essayist, on Collins's *Woman in White* and *Moonstone.* "Are these books and others like them literature?" he asks. "Wilkie Collins deliberately stripped his style of all embellishment. Even epithets are excluded, as they are from John Austin's *Letters on Jurisprudence.* It is strange that a man of letters should try to make his books resemble police reports. But, if he does, he must take the consequences. He cannot serve God and Mammon." The reflections, to some extent, may be applied direct to Mrs. Rohlfs's books, for they, too, are stripped almost bare of epithets. But if, as Mr. Crawford, for example, urges, if the first purpose of a novel is entertainment, then the books bearing the name of Anna Katharine Green are excellent novels. But it is not a point to be insisted upon. Let the statement suffice that the books in question, whatever be their true denomination, give rare pleasure. Fastidious critics, like Professor Bates of Wellesley, may classify them as police-court literature; but even in the police court is revealed the joy and the woe of human passions, the wonderful keenness and the terrible dullness of the human intellect. Mrs. Rohlfs knows her limitations, and is content to be exalted or condemned by her performances.

Her manner of working takes us back to Charles Reade. "The account of any remarkable or strange event that comes to her attention in the reading of the newspapers she cuts out and pastes into a scrapbook . . . When the time comes to write out the plots which she has previously developed in her mind, she takes care to work only when she can work at her best. Sometimes she writes, therefore, two hours a day, sometimes ten; but there is none of that plan of persistent plodding, day in and day out, to produce a prescribed amount, which Anthony Trollope carried on so successfully." Yet in the twenty-three years covering her literary career she has written a score of books. This has been no light task for one with a household to take care of, for in November, 1884, the novelist became Mrs. Charles Rohlfs. Some of the books have been translated into German and Swedish, which circumstance is a notable tribute to their attractiveness.

Technically, Professor Bates was justified in referring to Mrs. Rohlfs as "the foremost representative in America to-day of police-court literature"; yet to us this reference seems unsatisfactory, inadequate. It conveys no hint of the constructive skill, the imaginative power and the perceptive faculties necessary for the praiseworthy writing of police-court literature; and, furthermore, it offers no suggestion of Anna Katharine Green's exquisite sense of humor. How delightfully, for example, that most interesting spinster in *That Affair next Door*—Miss Butterworth, as we remember the name—plays hostess for the Van Burnam girls! What a genuine piece of comedy amid the pathos and terror roundabout! And how much flesh and blood there is in many of these unpretentious tales of mystery. One may not approve that sort of literature, or take any pleasure in it, but it is not to be denied that Mrs. Rohlfs writes artistically. Art concerns the work, not the subject.

We venture the prediction that the stories written by Anna Katharine Green, by virtue not only of their attractive skillfulness but also of their perennially interesting subjects, will be read eagerly and with delight when many of the novels of brighter present fame have accumulated dust.

Grant Overton (essay date 1928)

SOURCE: "Anna Katharine Green," in *The Women Who Make Our Novels,* revised edition, Dodd, Mead & Company, 1928, pp. 167-73.

[*In the following essay, Overton examines* Dark Hollow *in order to illustrate Green's method of writing detective stories.*]

Anna Katharine Green is a remarkable figure among American authors. With almost no literary gift except a power of dramatic emphasis, she possessed an extraordinary skill in the construction of the detective story. At least one of her books, *The Leavenworth Case,* which must have been first published nearly forty years ago, is recalled by everybody familiar with mystery fiction. Others of her books have been republished from time to time or are still, after long lapse of years, kept in print to meet a steady demand. When at the age of seventy she published a book in which could be discerned no lessening of her peculiar skill. Yet her work was always done in the face of a full knowledge of her shortcomings as a writer, under a difficulty of expression that would have conquered almost anybody else, and in spite of a consequent discouragement by which, quite rightly and bravely, she refused to be discouraged to the stopping point.

Anna Katharine Green was born in Brooklyn in 1846, the daughter of James Wilson Green, and was graduated from the Ripley Female College, at Poultney, Vermont, in 1867. In 1884 she was married to Charles Rohlfs, of Buffalo, New York, a designer of furniture. Mr. Rohlfs had been an actor for some years with Booth and other tragedians. We are told that he commenced making furniture to furnish his own home in 1889, "finally developing a new and distinctive style both as to form and ornamental design, with patronage in Europe as well as the United States." Three children were born to the marriage.

Anna Katharine Green's superiority over most writers of detective-mystery fiction lay in her power to ground her story on a single idea and a sufficient motive. Her readers, no doubt, seldom bothered, and in many cases were not able, to analyze so far. But they felt her power, were aware of her excellence if not of its source. Under her spell they not infrequently writhed at trite and cheap expressions, naïve sentences, ludicrous detail; yet the spell bound them.

Her method may be illustrated by some account of her story, *Dark Hollow* (1914), first as it presents itself to the reader and next as he may conceive it to have been fitted together. Lastly "the single idea and sufficient motive" which was the author's starting-point may be stated.

As the Reader Reads: Twelve years before the book opens, Algernon Etheridge had been murdered in Dark Hollow. John Scoville, keeper of a tavern, was tried and executed for the crime, swearing his innocence. Etheridge had been Judge Archibald Ostrander's closest personal friend. Circumstances compelled Judge Ostrander to preside at Scoville's trial. The Judge manifestly favored, so far as possible, the defense. Evidence against Scoville was wholly circumstantial but strong. His presence in Dark Hollow on the night of the crime was proven. Etheridge had been

killed with Scoville's stick. Scoville's reputation was unsavory.

In the twelve years since the death of Etheridge Judge Ostrander has lived shut off from the world, except for his appearance on the bench. He and his son have parted for all time. The grounds are walled off by a high board fence within a high board fence. A negro manservant is the only other person in the house.

When the story begins the negro has gone forth on morning errands, unprecedentedly leaving the gate in the fence ajar. A woman in purple, heavily veiled, has entered the grounds. The gaping neighborhood ventures in after her but does not find her. The crowd comes upon the Judge sitting erect and apparently lifeless in his house. It is, however, a cataleptic seizure. Soon afterward the negro, mortally wounded by an automobile, returns and dies trying to guard the iron door which preserves some secret of his master's.

The woman in purple turns out to be Mrs. Scoville. She sees Judge Ostrander and tells him that his son, Oliver, is in love with her daughter, Reuther. She also tells him that since her husband's execution she has become convinced that he did not kill Etheridge, and, late as it is, she is determined to do what she can to uncover new evidence.

In succeeding chapters, with cumulative and sensational climaxes, we follow Mrs. Scoville's quest. There is the shadow of the man in a peaked cap seen advancing into Dark Hollow at the hour of the crime. There is the picture of Oliver Ostrander secreted in his father's house with a band of black painted across the eyes. There is the point of a knife blade in the stick with which Etheridge was killed, and the blade from which it was broken lies folded in Oliver's desk. A peaked cap hangs in Oliver's closet! When circumstance seems to drive home conviction of Oliver's guilt, Judge Ostrander shows Mrs. Scoville a written statement that establishes the fact of an earlier murder by her husband. But the Judge allows her to look at the document a moment too long; the end has been tampered with, it is a forgery.

Oliver must be found; there is a race between agents of the district attorney and messengers dispatched by the Judge. Tracked to a remote place in the Adirondacks, he takes to further flight. By a desperate drop over a cliff, landing in a tree, he has reached a little railroad station ahead of pursuit. The train is not due for fifteen minutes.

" 'The train south?'

" 'Yes, and the train north. They pass here.' "

Shall he return home at his father's summons or escape to Canada?

As the Reader may conceive the story to have been fitted together: Judge Ostrander has to be the murderer because he is the person least likely; Etheridge was his dearest friend. Oliver has to be put under dire suspicion or it will not be plausible that the Judge should finally confess. By making Judge Ostrander the murderer, his son is put more on a plane with Reuther Scoville—who, after all, as we discover, was not the daughter of a murderer. Oliver must be cleared in order to make his marriage with Reuther admissible.

As the story was actually constructed: The author started with a single striking conception—that of a man who should, in a fit of passion, slay his closest friend and who undertakes his own fit punishment. Judge Ostrander imprisons himself, except when he must appear in public, in a convict's cell in his own home. He sends his son away for all time; that even the eyes of his son's portrait may not look on his father, murderer and coward, a black band is painted across the picture. A double fence is built to guard against intrusion by so much as an eye at a knothole.

On this solid foundation of a single life and this sufficient motive of a single stricken conscience the story spreads out, like an expansive, leafy plant from a tap root. The first step is to get clearly in mind biographies of several people. In particular, every aspect of their relations with each other—whether probably to be used in the telling of the story or not—must be clearly in mind.

It is next necessary to construct the crime. A period of twenty minutes to half an hour, at a given place, is in question. A map (used as an illustration in the book) shows the place with respect to all near-by places. But Etheridge, Scoville, Mrs. Scoville, Judge Ostrander and Oliver were all in or near Dark Hollow during this half hour. Why was each there and what was each doing? Just what could— and did—each say, hear and see? The author must determine *all* these things in order to spare the reader what is irrelevant as well as to control the extent and order of disclosures in the story.

The author, then, has every inch of ground at her fingertips and every instant clear. There is room for improvisation only in the lesser climaxes at the ends of chapters. Most of these are planned in advance but an occasional inspiration may find its place. One has got Oliver to the lonely railroad station, perhaps, when the idea of *two* trains, bound in opposite directions, flashes into the mind. Immediately the dramatic struggle of his mind is substituted for some lesser incident of suspense.

All the nice little expediencies by means of which, in his innocence, the reader may have imagined the story to have been fitted together are easily taken care of if the fundamental building of the story be right. One cannot say: "I will make Judge Ostrander the murderer because he is the least likely person." One must first conceive Judge Ostrander. One must say: "He was the murderer"—and then see to it that he *appears* to be the least likely person.

It will be observed that **Dark Hollow** complies absolutely with the first law of the mystery story—that the unknown agent must be in the tale from the outset. Otherwise he is nothing but a puppet contrived to help the author out of serious difficulty. According to his shrewdness, the reader is given a fair and reasonable chance to identify Judge Ostrander as the criminal. The author, though disclosing clews in a predetermined order, supplies none that are false or misleading.

Without ever creating a character comparable with Sher-lock Holmes, Anna Katharine Green constructed mysteries more baffling than those solved by Conan Doyle's detective. She never resorted to exotic coloring to conceal thinness of story; she did not depend on ciphers or codes; she never found it necessary to carry the reader through generations nor to employ undue coincidences. When pained by the lack of literary quality in her writing, it is possible to recall that she filled all the drawers of a massive bureau with discarded manuscript in the effort to write well a single book, **The Leavenworth Case**. And in the end she wrote it very badly, and it mattered little, so ingenious and satisfying was the story she had to tell.

Kathleen Woodward   (essay date 1929)

SOURCE: "Anna Katharine Green," in *The Bookman*, New York, Vol. LXX, No. 2, October, 1929, pp. 168-70.

[*In the following essay, Woodward recalls her visit with Green in Buffalo, New York, during which the eighty-three-year-old author reflected on the differences between contemporary mystery stories and those written around the time* The Leavenworth Case *was first published.*]

I had not thought to meet a frail and diffident lady, who for the most part would talk to me about the felicities of her home, her husband and her children, when in the city of Buffalo I sought out the author who had given to President Wilson what he called his "most authentic thrills", and was described by Mr. Baldwin, when he was the Prime Minister of England, as the creator of "what I still believe to be the best detective stories ever written".

Mr. Edgar Wallace, lately termed in America "Thrill-maker to the King", I had already met; and there was to me a seemliness in his air of worldly wisdom and spacious opulence. All the ends of the underworld might be revealed to his seeing eye without fluttering his Olympian calm. It was not so with Anna Katharine Green, an established "thriller" of the first rank when Edgar Wallace ran errands up and down the Old Kent Road, and Sir Arthur Conan Doyle was still a medical student in Edinburgh University. She was unlike my most temperate visions of one who had spent her life in a labyrinthine world of hot-footed detectives on the scent of iniquitous crime.

She was gentle, courteous, gracious—even shy. She sat in a high-backed chair surrounded with books and dark oak furniture, distilling mellowness and wisdom. I might have been in the atmosphere of Concord, with Emerson, whose courtly letters to the young mystery writer I had just been reading. I might have been in the company of any one of Barrie's lavender-perfumed ladies of undeniable refinement.

But unlike Barrie's ladies she did not suggest Age; and in spite of tiresomely accurate biographies I still find it difficult to believe that Anna Katharine Green is eighty-three years old. Particularly in her eyes is that expression of eager curiosity which seems more effective than any "treatment" in holding Youth captive. Her interest in life is unquenchable.

Equally alive and active is her memory of the incidents and chapters of her many books—of difficulties surmounted and expediencies resorted to in her efforts to purvey mysteries and puzzles to men who have delighted in such things since before the days when Solomon propounded his puzzles and the Sphinx her mystery.

More than fifty years have passed since Anna Katharine Green published her first mystery story, *The Leavenworth Case,* written during an interval of tedious inactivity after she had graduated from the Ripley Female College at Poultney, Vermont. Her inspiration she traces to Gaboriau who, thirty years after Poe's Dupin, created M. Lecoq, the original begetter of Sherlock Holmes and of every other transcendently infallible detective of the sardonic mood.

She had wanted to be a poet; she had written verse since she was a child; but it was far from the Well of Helicon that she discovered her true vocation. And even now she finds it simpler to trace the source of her inspiration than to understand why a girl brought up in an atmosphere of irreproachable gentility and graduated from the Ripley Female College should at last find herself at home in the dense tangles of crime and passion.

Her literary self she discovered in the conception and execution of *The Leavenworth Case,* born and bred "entirely in my imagination". She ceased to chafe and fret at the triviality of life as it appeared to the graduate fresh from Vermont. Her days, nights, months, years were absorbed in a fever of activity. She filled sheets of odd paper with millions of words—always concealing the masterpiece from her father, who seems to have set his heart upon her being a poet.

As with Fanny Burney—whose first book was composed in circumstances very like those in which the graduate from the Ripley Female College labored—the story secretly written through troubled years was destined for a fate similar to *Evelina,* which moved Johnson to ecstatic praise and which Burke sat up all night to read. Anna Katharine Green at once became famous; and her verse, which had languished in obscurity, now saw the light as the work of "the author of *The Leavenworth Case*".

With what high seriousness the mystery story was approached fifty years ago! In tones of justifiable regret its author talked to me of the decline of the detective story from an art to a process of mass-production; of the degeneration of Mystery to mere surprise:

"We wrote for love of our work," she said. "They, it seems, write only for dollars."

I did not wonder at the sadness in her voice when she described for me the infinite labor, the planning, modelling, the sheer thought and attention to detail that went to the building of a mystery story in those halcyon days. The writer had a conscience which spurred him on through agonizing years to further and yet further effort. It was his high responsibility never to mislead his reader with false devices and puppets designed to involve him in irrelevancies; never to make use of exotic colorings to veil the poverty of his invention; yet on the other hand never to admit a suggestion of the solution by so much as a badly ren-

dered paragraph. His task was dominated and directed by his sense of duty toward his reader.

Alas! how unlike the modern practitioner of the detective story and the cavalier manner in which he treats us: he who leaves his corpse so vaguely accounted for, his ciphers in their pristine hieroglyphic, trusting to luck for the progress and climax of his story—"who thinks that he has done enough if he finds a surprise for the end of his book; for he will not wait for an idea", she said, in gentle reproof. Even the love-interest is "simply lugged in"; it is no indispensable part of the organic whole.

More bitter than gall and wormwood it is to the soul of the spinner of bygone mysteries to survey the hapless writer of today using the machinery of the detective story invented by Poe and Gaboriau.

"I had to wait for an idea before ever I could write my stories—for a vivid, overpowering conception. For years an incident would germinate in my mind. Then suddenly, perhaps in the night, I would wake with my story conceived from the first page to the last."

> Her days, nights, months, years were absorbed in a fever of activity. She filled sheets of odd paper with millions of words—always concealing the masterpiece from her father, who seems to have set his heart upon her being a poet.
>
> — *Kathleen Woodward*

No hasty flinging together of the story was permitted to Anna Katharine Green. Often it took her years to translate her conception—to build detail on detail, to evolve incident from incident, to invent legitimate expediences in tight places—keeping the love-interest always "in its proper place". She never wilfully, playfully or carelessly misled her readers; she only outwitted them with her nicer ingenuity, "so that in the end they had to admit that had they but the eyes to see, the penetration to discover, there, from the start, was the solution of the mystery". In this manner *The Leavenworth Case* was written, chapter succeeding chapter in cumulative dramatic effect until the inevitable end. "Often I would write a chapter ten times over."

Sitting there listening to the history of these past agonies of endeavor I blushed for my prolific compatriot, Edgar Wallace, and for the easy tolerance with which I have looked on while his hero lit a cigarette on one page only to be found on the next page puffing at a pipe. I fear that conscience does not direct his writings. Phrases descriptive of his happy facility have entered the English idiom: "Have you seen today's Edgar Wallace?" Or again: "The latest addition to the Wallace Collection!"

It is said that between a couple of race meetings he casts down the dictaphone a fifty-thousand word "shocker". Moreover, he appears to thrive on this casual fecundity, this trifling with the machinery of mystery so laboriously constructed and used by classic writers. He looks more hale and hearty after each book; while the author of *The Leavenworth Case* so depleted her nervous energy in the creation of that book that she has "never since felt so well".

It is in no querulous, carping, over-critical spirit that Anna Katharine Green discusses contemporary work in mystery and detection. She approaches it as one who cares tremendously for the fate of the medium she has studied and practised so long. She is ever looking for work that is virile in conception and not shoddy in execution, that makes use of legitimate thrills, and shows symptoms of assuming intelligence on the reader's part.

When I think of the disciple of Poe and Gaboriau sitting in her high-backed chair in the company of Dickens and Shakespeare and many various editions of her own work, reflecting pensively on this alien age, I wonder if, forty years from now, any mystery-spinner of today will have the intense interest she has in the fruits of his imagination. I wonder if in his old age he will, like Anna Katharine Green, pore critically over his published work in search of redundancies and superfluities.

I think not! We seem to have lost the attitude of high seriousness toward the mystery story which characterizes the work of Anna Katharine Green and her contemporaries. We are more than tolerant of the efforts of our more than careless generation of mystery writers: we smile at their tenuity, at the inexhaustible strength and faith of their heroines and the infallible, if blundering, perception of their detectives. They have for many of us only one indisputable merit: they move rapidly. And though the swiftness of their action may be the speed of a Jazz age it leaves the author little space for description and strivings after effects; and for this we are glad.

The tributes of statesmen and men of affairs, however, and the revival in her own country and in England of *The Leavenworth Case* are proof that the conscience and quality which distinguish the work of fifty years ago are not entirely unappreciated by this hurried capricious generation.

Howard Haycraft   (essay date 1941)

SOURCE: "America: 1890-1914 (The Romantic Age)," in *Murder for Pleasure: The Life and Times of the Detective Story,* D. Appleton-Century Company, Incorporated, 1941, pp. 83-102.

[*In the following excerpt, Haycraft underscores the historical importance of Green's mysteries, particularly* The Leavenworth Case, *to the detective genre in America.*]

Unless the reader is prepared to admit Nick Carter and his confrères and the semi-fictional Pinkerton reminiscences and their ilk to the dignity of detective novels, it must be said that the American field lay fallow from Poe's "Purloined Letter" (1844) to Anna Katharine Green's *The Leavenworth Case* (1878). Any number of reasons may have contributed to the length of the hiatus, not the least of which was a major internal war, more disrupting

than any upheaval that England or even volatile France underwent during most of the same period. But the silence is of less interest or significance than the circumstances of its breaking.

For there are sufficient aspects of uniqueness about *The Leavenworth Case* to make it, despite some incredibly bad writing, one of the true historical milestones of the genre. It beat Holmes to the post by almost a decade; it sprang full-fledged from its author's head, without traceable antecedents; it contained a sound police detective Ebenezer Gryce, and a remarkably cogent plot; it was one of the all-time best-sellers in the literature; and above all it was written by a woman (the first, in fact, to practice the form in any land or language) at a time and place when feminine literary output was slight at best and confined chiefly to sentimental verse and similar lady-like ephemera.

Anna Katharine Green (1846-1935), variously called the mother, grandmother, and godmother of the detective story, was born in Brooklyn and was educated at Ripley Female College in Vermont. The only explanation she gave in later years for her unprecedented invasion of the detective field was that she made the experiment as preparation for a poetic career! But the fact that her father was a well-known criminal lawyer of the day undoubtedly had something to do with it. In 1884 she married Charles Rohlfs, a furniture designer and manufacturer. Most of her life was spent in Buffalo, where she died in her ninetieth year.

During her long career Anna Katharine Green published between thirty and forty works of fiction. Most of them were mystery or detective stories, but only a handful (contrary to journalistic misstatements at the time of her death) had Gryce for their central character. (Her feminine detective, Violet Strange, is best forgotten.) Aside from *The Leavenworth Case,* perhaps the best of the Gryce stories is the novelette, *The Doctor, His Wife, and the Clock.* Of her other books, Mrs. Rohlfs' own favorite was *The Hand and the Ring,* but connoisseurs prefer *The House of the Whispering Pines* and *The Filigree Ball,* both of which, however, classify as period pieces to-day— as, for that matter, does all her work. For no one can pretend that Anna Katharine Green's stories are distinguished literature: she is best met with, as some one has remarked, at the impressionable age. Her style is unbelievably stilted and melodramatic by modern standards, her characterizations forced and artificial. But her plots are models of careful construction that can still hold their own against to-day's competition. For this quality, and by virtue of precedence and sustained popularity, she occupies an undisputed and honorable place in the development of the American detective story.

John Cornillon   (essay date 1973)

SOURCE: "A Case for Violet Strange," in *Images of Women in Fiction: Feminist Perspectives,* edited by Susan Koppelman Cornillon, revised edition, Bowling Green University Popular Press, 1973, pp. 206-15.

[*In the following excerpt, Cornillon views* The Golden Slipper and Other Problems for Violet Strange *from a feminist perspective, showing how the collection exposes female op- pression and emphasizes sisterhood.*]

As fans of Anna Katherine Green's mysteries picked up her latest book in 1915, **The Golden Slipper and Other Problems for Violet Strange,** they may have asked them- selves as you are asking, "Who is Violet Strange?"

They were familiar with Ebenezer Gryce, the detective hero Ms. Green had created for her first novel, **The Leav- enworth Case,** published in 1878, more than a decade ear- lier than Doyle's Sherlock Holmes; with Amelia Butter- worth of Grammercy Park, Gryce's friend and amateur colleague; Sweetwater, Gryce's youthful companion and ambitious protege; and Jinny, Sweetwater's enthusiastic and energetic assistant. These characters, functioning in- dividually and as a group, had gained an impressive fol- lowing among mystery novel readers as Ms. Green de- tailed their triumphs through a succession of books. But occasionally she veered from the path of sure success to experiment with a new character. Such was the case with **The Golden Slipper**.

Violet is introduced to us right from the beginning of the book as a character about whom seeming belies being. When she is pointed out to a new client, he responds, "That yon silly little chit, whose father I know, whose for- tune I know, who is seen everywhere, and who is called one of the season's belles is an agent of yours!"

The contradiction is too much and the client bursts out, "It's hard to associate intellectuality with such quaintness of expression." She is variously referred to as "inconse- quent," "infantile," and "that airy little being."

This kind of apparent "feminine" personality haunts the work of Green. Again and again we meet see mingly brain- less ninnies, bits of fluff, featherbrains, comic characters, female fools and clowns. Veronica Moore, the victim in **The Filigree Ball,** is just such a character, well-known so- ciety belle who writes of herself, "I was light as Thistle- down and blown by every breeze." The image of mental and emotional lightness and airiness inhabiting a diminu- tive body combine in conveying a picture of insubstantiali- ty and insignificance.

We see in this image a demythologized version of the upper class white woman, so popular in Southern fiction, whose physical insubstantiality signified her spiritual tran- scendence of and disassociation from the world of matter and materialistic motives. But in the works of A. K. G. insubstantiality has come to mean not so much a spiritual transcendence of the material as a social and emotional alienation from what is meaningful and true. It was be- coming increasingly obvious to women of the late nine- teenth and early twentieth century what it really meant to be sequestered away from the material world of economic survival and to be kept pure for the contemplation of "higher things." It often meant social irrelevance, histori- cal invisibility, and economic powerlessness. It meant being intellectually condescended to because the actors in "the man's world" often considered those "higher things" to be nothing more than superstitious and pious dreams on the one hand and sentimental and romantic fancies on the other, just what one would expect of a woman's inferi-

or and undisciplined mind. Excluded from society's eco- nomic and vocational life and given little else to intellectu- ally focus upon other than the realms of religion and art, it was indeed unkind to then turn around and label those religious predilictions as superstitious and those artistic interests as sentimental. For the less well-to-do being saved from the rigors of the workaday world usually meant bearing and raising a number of children, shopping, cooking, cleaning, washing, ironing, sewing, canning, etc., etc., i.e., doing all these tasks of the worker in the domestic factory with no economic control of the means of produc- tion. So the myth of the materially uncorrupted woman was in A. K. G.'s time an outworn, formulaic tool that ex- isted primarily to justify the continued oppression of women. As the myth became increasingly transparent, the nobility with which it once had been imbued became in- creasingly replaced by bitterness, frustration, and self- parody.

It was this vein of malaise pervading female society that A. K. G. was tapping and giving expression to in her cre- ation of Violet Strange. For, although Violet upholds the myth in public by conforming to the role expected of a young woman of her station in life, it is a hollow act, and in secret she lives a life in defiance of those role expecta- tions. "From time immemorial," Allport writes, "slaves have hidden their true feelings behind a facade. . . . Re- bellion and aggression would certainly be met by fierce punishment. . . . By agreeing with her 'adversary' she 'escapes being conspicuous . . . and quietly leads' her 'life in two compartments' " [Gordon Allport, *The Nature of Prejudice*]. But Violet's life is not so quiet. She has gone a step farther than merely surviving an oppressive situa- tion. She is working towards a goal. And her means are as liberating for herself and others as are her ends. The mask that serves to safeguard personal integrity serves in Violet's case to disguise social resistance and noncomfor- mity as well.

A. K. G. represents society generally and fathers specifi- cally, Violet's in particular, as being the repressive factors in Violet's life. When Violet speaks to her employer, we are told by the author that "the extreme carelessness of Miss Strange's tone would have been fatal to her socially; but then she never would have used it socially. This they both knew." Society in the larger sense oppresses by its constant inability to *see* her for who she is, but instead to only see the stereotype she is expected to be: "Who would dream that back of this display of mingled childishness and audacity there lay hidden purpose, intellect, and a keen knowledge of human nature? Not the two men who listened to this seemingly irresponsible chatter. To them she was a child to be humored and humor her they did." There is ironic satisfaction in this last phrase, because Vio- let is capitalizing on their blind objectification of her to pump them for information.

The fathers of three young people are presented in the book. All of them are portrayed as rigid, repressive, and domineering. Violet's own father is presented as follows: "Though she was his favorite child Peter Strange was known to be quite capable of cutting her off with a shilling, once his closed, prejudiced mind conceived it to be his duty. And that he would so interpret the situation, if he ever came to learn the secret of his daughter's fits of abstraction and the sly bank account she was slowly accumulating."

The secret that lies behind the facade of Violet Strange's public image is the fact that she is an agent in the employ of a detective agency. Throughout the book, Violet affects a dislike for her work. She claims she is only working because she needs the money; but the reason for the need is a secret that is not revealed until the last story or "problem" in the collection. In **"Violet's Own"** we learn her story.

In childhood Violet and her brother Arthur were cared for by an elder sister named Theresa. (Their mother died during their infancy.) One night when Violet was about seven, she woke up and heard . . . "My father talking to my sister. . . . She in supplication and he in a tempest of wrath which knew no bounds."

The infuriated father, having discovered Theresa speaking to someone from her window, raves that she has disgraced him, the family, and herself. "Was it not enough that you should refuse to marry the good man I picked out for you, that you should stoop to this low-down scoundrel—this—" (an impoverished, Italian singing master).

Theresa interrupts her father, "I love him! I love him! . . . And I am going to marry him." . . .

The father answers in a paroxysm of frustrated rage which Violet reports as having "left scorched places in my memory that will never be eradicated." The next morning her sister-mother, for so does Violet refer to Theresa, is gone. The children are informed by their father that neither their sister's name nor anything referring to her were to be mentioned in that house again. "Heed me," the father said, "or you go too."

In the days that followed all photographs of Theresa were destroyed, her name was cut out from the leaves of books. Presents she had given the children were surreptitiously taken away. Her piano was removed and her music burnt, until no vestige of her beloved presence remained.

Shortly before the story opens, Violet happens upon her sister by chance. Theresa, however, moves in order to elude her sister and prevent any suffering on her account. Violet goes to the detective who later becomes her employer, and, in the process of tracing her sister, discovers her own remarkable gifts of detection. Theresa's husband has just died, leaving her in the poverty in which they had always lived. Violet wishes to help, but Theresa will not accept anything even indirectly from Peter Strange, preferring impoverished self-sufficiency to charity.

Violet's course of action becomes clear to her however one day when she overhears her sister sing and realizes that Theresa has a "grand voice . . . the voice of a great artist." "All she needed was a year with some great maestro in the foreign atmosphere of art. But this meant money, not hundreds but thousands." Violet ponders the problem and concludes that "if in some way I could earn the money, she might be induced to take it. . . . If she had capabilities in one way, I had them in another." The capa-

bilities to which she refers in herself are the intellectual abilities required by detection, or her powers of "ratiocination." The detective has from the beginning been the symbol of reason and intellect par excellence.

Abstracting the plot from a feminist perspective we see Violet Strange breaking away from absolute dependence upon the patriarch and gaining economic independence by getting a job and starting her own bank account. She is motivated to do this out of a desire to help her sister-mother whom the patriarch has disowned, disinherited, and sought to render invisible in punishment for her refusal to comply with his patriarchal will and for the temerity she displayed by exercising her own will.

In her effort to aid Theresa, Violet performs the following liberating acts: (1) she earns money; (2) she earns the money by using her mind; (3) she helps her sister-mother, a rebel against the patriarch and by extension the patriarchal order, making herself an accomplice to that rebellion; (4) she helps her sister not by finding her a man but by helping her to develop her own artistry and self-sufficiency; and (5) she helps her sister achieve public recognition, putting an end to the obscurity and public invisibility imposed upon her by her father. The book concludes with Violet commenting that Theresa has gained "that place in the world to which her love and genius entitle her."

Anna Katherine Green has used these stories to expose many of the ways women are oppressed by society's laws, conventions, attitudes and institutions.

— *John Cornillon*

It is this sense of, and sensitivity to, sisterhood among women that we see expressed throughout these stories. While it is to help her own blood sister that Violet Strange becomes a detective, in the course of her work she greatly aids those who are her sisters because they share the political condition of women in a patriarchal society. In eight out of nine stories, the principal people she helps are women. In the one exception she meets and helps the man whom she will later marry.

The book opens with the story of five young women who, because of their affection for one another, call themselves the Inseparables. Despite the threats to the existence of the group imposed by a lover and a father, threats of romantic exclusivity and patriarchal possessiveness respectively, the group, with the help of Violet Strange, survives.

In the next story, Violet helps a woman whose husband and child have been killed, leaving the wife penniless, the life insurance company refusing to pay since the coroner has ruled her husband's death a suicide. The woman calls Violet Strange in to prove it was murder. In the course of the investigation the woman reveals she had had an argument with her husband about childcare: "He said there was no need of its crying so; that if I gave it the proper attention it would not keep neighbours and himself awake half the night. And I—I got angry and insisted that I did the best I could; that the child was naturally fretful and that if he wasn't satisfied with my way of looking after it, he might try his." Whereupon he growled at her and she fled the room to sleep in the spare room. The author comments, "It is not difficult to see that she had no very keen regrets for her husband personally. But then he was not a very estimable man nor in any respect her equal."

Violet discovers in the third story who was responsible for committing a particularly brutal murder of a solitary old woman. The case is solved by the testimony of another elderly woman.

Violet Strange meets Roger Upjohn, the man she will marry, in the fourth story. Such a love interest is a firmly entrenched convention in the popular novel of that day and this. But the man she and the author choose, as well as the marital relationship implied by such a choice, is not conventional. He is described as follows: "though a degenerate in some aspects, lacking the domineering presence, the strong mental qualities, and inflexible character of his progenitors . . . , he yet had gifts and attractions of his own." In the course of the story we see that he has overcome his degeneracy, but he does not lose his other qualities. He is neither domineering, inflexible, nor too strongly willed, qualities which mean that he neither has the strength nor inclination to prevent Violet from doing what she wants to do. He is a man who has been married before and has a child for whom he has cared since his wife was murdered. He has been ostracised by high society because of the scandal surrounding her death; he has been humanized by suffering and has few romantic illusions about marriage or parenthood. In marrying him, Violet is not about to give up the freedom she has tasted in stepping outside the prescribed confines of the female social role of her day. She will marry wisely; she has chosen a man of egalitarian temperament, who has experienced and accepted his outcast status, more loyal than he is strong-willed, a good ally in what one assumes will be Violet's continued flouting of feminine convention.

In the fifth story, a woman whom Violet is helping explains her extreme aversion to nicely bound books: "There is a reason for my prejudice. I was not always rich . . . . when I was first married . . . I was so poor then that I frequently went hungry, and what was worse saw my little daughter cry for food. And why? Because my husband was a bibliomaniac. He would spend on fine editions what would have kept the family comfortable."

"O life! life!" the author concludes, "how fast Violet was learning it!"

Both **"The House of Clocks"** and **"The Doctor, His Wife, and the Clock"** deal with the irrational jealousies and hatred born of a possessive and exclusive romantic love. In contrast to this is the conclusion of Violet's own declaration of love to Roger: "Such a union as ours must be hallowed, because we have so many persons to make happy besides ourselves!"

The second to last story, **"Missing Page Thirteen,"** focuses simply on the hatred that the institution of marriage can breed. This hatred is epitomized by a sword duel to the death between a husband and wife for, in the words of one of the partners, "What would either's life be worth with the other alive and happy in the world."

Anna Katherine Green has used these stories to expose many of the ways women are oppressed by society's laws, conventions, attitudes and institutions. Violet Strange, both as a sister and a detective, has struggled against the oppression of women. The collection is liberating in its depiction of both means and ends. Violet becomes independent, self-confident, and triumphant. And Theresa, despite her defiance of the patriarchal order neither repents nor is destroyed, but instead achieves happiness, wealth, fame, and love. The love she finds is the love experienced in the reunited community of sisters and brother from which Pater Peter had sought to have her expelled. Although the popular novels of a later day might have, in a more "liberal" vein, accorded her happiness, it would have been a happiness that resulted from the salvation effected by some heroic Prince Charming. But, to see her come to a happy end with no repentance through the machinations of no man, but by virtue of her own efforts and the aid of her sister is to say the least unusual. It is a pleasure to read in a mass culture novel of sisterhood triumphing over patriarchy. Sisterhood is indeed powerful!

Barrie Hayne   (essay date 1981)

SOURCE: "Anna Katharine Green," in *10 Women of Mystery,* edited by Earl F. Bargainnier, Bowling Green University Popular Press, 1981, pp. 152-78.

[*In the following excerpt, Hayne discusses the historical importance of Green's works in terms of her consolidation of the detective novel and the sensational novel and her contribution to the literary convention of the professional and amateur detective working together to solve a crime.*]

> "It is admirable," said Poirot. "One savours its period atmosphere, its studied and deliberate melodrama. Those rich and lavish descriptions of the golden beauty of Eleanor, the moonlight beauty of Mary!"
>
> "I must read it again," I said. "I'd forgotten the parts about the beautiful girls."
>
> "And there is the maidservant Hannah, so true to type, and the murderer, an excellent psychological study."
>
> I perceived that I had let myself in for a lecture. I composed myself to listen.

Thus Hercule Poirot, in *The Clocks* (1964), expresses his admiration for one of the detective novel landmarks of nearly a hundred years before. And thus a later Queen of Crime salutes the Queen of Crime of the Gilded Age. Three years ago the centenary of *The Leavenworth Case* seems to have passed unnoticed, except for a display in the Buffalo and Erie County Public Library; and despite Agatha Christie's homage, Anna Katherine Green is, in 1981, a writer hailed perfunctorily, if at all, and scarcely read.

Though widely acclaimed as the grandmother, mother, even godmother, of the genre, she dwells in the house of detective fiction as a Victorian cabinet portrait towards the rear of the mantelpiece; the center rear indeed, but rarely taken down and dusted anymore. Howard Haycraft, whose judgments have been copied over into so many subsequent histories, summed her up a generation ago with that very mixture of general acknowledgement and particular depreciation: "Her style is unbelievably stilted and melodramatic by modern standards, her characterizations forced and artificial [*pace Poirot*]. But her plots are models of careful construction that can still hold their own against today's competition. For this quality, and by virtue of precedence and sustained popularity, she occupies an undisputed and honorable place in the development of the American detective story." There are those who would take away that place. Thirty years after Haycraft, Julian Symons gave her a paragraph, dismissing *The Leavenworth Case* as "a drearily sentimental story" "with passages of pious moralizing which are pulled through only with the most dogged persistence." Most recently, in their *Encyclopedia of Mystery and Detection*, Chris Steinbrunner and Otto Penzler, usually scrupulous in describing rather than judging, praise her for her plot construction, but note, with implicit distaste, her "substantial love-story qualities and melodramatic flourishes." In the year before her death, the *New York Times* had headed a story on her "Kept World Awake Half a Century"; forty-five years later, when the Buffalo *Courier-Express* wrote her up on the centenary of her most famous book, the subeditor had to find a more catchy (and local) headline for a writer "now generally forgotten"—"Pioneer Whodunit Author Deduced Them in Buffalo."

Yet *The Leavenworth Case* had sold 150,000 copies down to her death (fifty-seven years after its publication) and, according to her obituary in the *New York Times,* was still much in demand. Eight years before *The Mystery of a Hansom Cab,* and nine years before Sherlock Holmes made his first bow, *The Leavenworth Case* was a best-seller, "one of the all-time best-sellers in the literature," as Haycraft noted. As late as 1926, Norman Hapgood could mention Green with Poe, Doyle, Gaboriau: "we might as well close the list." In 1927, Willard Huntington Wright argued that the very success of *The Leavenworth Case,* rather than any innovations it made in the detective genre, was its importance, for it brought the detective story to a wider reading public. Even Wright, it may be noted, saw Green's novels as "over-documented and as too intimately concerned with strictly romantic material and humanistic considerations," but Wright was speaking for his age, as he admitted, the Golden Age of the detectival cryptogram, and of "the complex, economical and highly rarified technic of detective fiction." Still, *The Leavenworth Case* was in print for most of its first sixty years. G. P. Putnam's Sons, which published it, renewed its copyright in 1906, when the novelist was still writing, with great popularity, in the genre, and the reprint of that year reads "105th thousand" on its titlepage. I myself have seen later, undated reprints with presumed contemporary inscriptions dated 1911 and 1923, as well as a paperback edition of 1937, itself a reprint of a 1934 edition, with introduction by Wright, evidently not ashamed to put the

name and imprimatur of S. S. Van Dine, then at the height of his own popularity, on the old novel. *The Leavenworth Case* was dramatized, enjoyed a long run on the stage, and was also twice filmed: as a silent feature in 1923, which seems to follow the novel fairly closely, though dropping Gryce to leave the lawyer-narrator as the only detective; and in a sound version in 1936 which appears to bear little relation to the original. In the last forty years, however, *The Leavenworth Case* seems to have dropped largely from sight, though a facsimile edition was produced by the Gregg Press in 1970, when a bullish publishing market brought three other titles of Green's back into print.

Attempts have even been made, however, to explain away the great popularity of *The Leavenworth Case*. Julian Symons sees three reasons for that popularity, of which two can be quickly disposed of: that it was written by a woman, aside from the patronizing quality of the statement, is invalidated in any case by the enormous number of popular women writers contemporary with Green—Susan Warner, Elizabeth Wetherell, Miss Braddon and Mrs. Henry Wood (both detective story writers, by the way), not to mention Mrs. Stowe and George Eliot. Symons also attributes the popularity of the novel to the fact that so few detective stories were being written; the refutation of that lies in its evident continuing popularity—and more generally hers—through the Golden Age of detective fiction. Symons' other reason for its popularity, her realistic presentation of legal detail (her father was a famous trial lawyer, Symons is compelled to remind us) is a more cogent reason, though to it might be added her grasp of police procedures generally. Indeed, this takes us to the heart of Anna Katharine Green's continuing claim on our attention—her essential realism.

If Anna Katharine Green is to be reinstated as a figure commanding the attention—the reading attention—of the critic of detective fiction, it must be on two grounds: her consolidation of the detective novel as a *realistic* art form, and her contribution to the development of the detective hero. On the first count, she takes her place as a representative American of her time, a writer writing in the post-Civil War period when the "real" began to replace the "romantic" as the dominant element in American fiction. On the second count, going beyond the partnerships of Dupin and his chronicler, of Sergeant Cuff and Franklin Blake, of even Lecoq and Old Tabaret, she established on firm basis the convention of professional and amateur detective, each supplementing the work of the other to solve the crime. And she claims our attention, too, for presenting the first really credible woman detective.

It will first be as well, then, to place her historically, for what longevity she had! Born while Poe was still writing, she died after Hammett had published his last novel. Her own first novel appeared before Old Sleuth, but when her last appeared, *Black Mask* was already publishing. Her principal predecessors, of course, are Poe, Wilkie Collins, and Gaboriau. A mystifier, who wrote three of the most influential of detective stories for the sake of the puzzle, a sensation novelist whose formula was "make 'em laugh, make 'em cry, make 'em wait," and a hack who spun his *romans policiers* partly from factual narratives, partly from the lurid yellow books of his time. These are the detectival components to which Anna Katharine Green is heir. In representing the dominant realistic strain in post-Civil War fiction, she is also the synthesizer of two subgenres of fiction: the detective novel, for which she established the rules, consolidating the work of Poe, Gaboriau, and the Collins of *The Moonstone;* and the sensation novel, as written by Collins in much of the rest of his *oeuvre,* by Mrs. Henry Wood, by Miss Braddon, and by countless others more obscure. The synthesis she made of these two sub-genres is more realistic than the sensation novel, while maintaining the verisimilitude essential to the detective story.

Green herself, suggestively, preferred the term "criminal romance" for her fiction. . . . In 1902, she said: "Please do not call my books 'detective stories'. . . . I abhor the word detective. It is too often applied to atrocities. I choose crime as a basic subject because from it arise the most dramatic situations, situations which could be produced by nothing else."

— *Barrie Hayne*

It is perhaps not excessively reductive to assume that in the late nineteenth century the sensation novel is the principal repository of what Henry James would later call the "romantic," while the detective novel of the same period embodies what he designates the "real." This assumption carries, of course, a *caveat:* as James's own work amply demonstrates, the real and the romantic are never absolutely to be separated. With that qualification, however, the detective novel is at base realistic, the sensation novel at base romantic, in James's terms: "The real represents to my perception the things we cannot possibly *not* know, sooner or later, in one way or another; it being but one of the accidents of our hampered state, and one of the incidents of their quantity and number, that particular instances have not yet come our way. The romantic stands, on the other hand, for the things that, with all the facilities in the world . . . we never *can* directly know; the things that reach us only through the beautiful circuit and subterfuge of our thought and our desire."

Kathleen Tillotson reminds us that both sensation novel and detective novel spring from the same root: at the centre of each lies a *secret.* But what distinguishes the two sub-genres is the way that secret is treated. Where it is merely sprung upon the reader for the *frisson,* or where the reader is privy to it, his thrill deriving from the ignorance of the other characters and his own consequent superiority, then we are fairly in the realm of the sensation novel. Where the emphasis lies upon a character in the novel unraveling that secret by the exercise of his intellect, with the reader's participation, we have a detective story.

To put the matter in another way, using two terms given currency by Northrop Frye the *eiron,* or self-deprecating, but knowledgeable, character, is represented in detective fiction by the detective and his partner the reader. Such a character is missing in sensational fiction, where all the characters are either in ignorance of the secret, or like the reader himself, in possession of it, but also with an interest in concealing it. They are all, readers and characters of the sensation novel, *alazons:* dupes or impostors. Where all the characters are *alazons,* there must be a notable absence of ultimate moral order unless it be imposed from outside. But moral order is the very goal of the detective novel; it is what is reinstated at the end as a direct result of the detective's ratiocinations.

Because the sensation novel, moreover, is at a further remove from reality, it becomes more than the detective novel a catalyst for the reader's fantasies, allowing him to live for the time being an existence which could never be his in real life; "the things . . . we never *can* directly know" are its staple. The sensation novel is more the product of a class sytem; its middle class readers eavesdrop on the ways of the upper classes who are invariably its dramatic personae (The less marked lines of division between the classes in American society did not make Collins and Wood, Braddon and Ouida, any less popular in America, though the sensation novel *set* in America is a rarity, no doubt because of the absence there of the castled towers and ivied ruins which are so much a part of the genre).

The classic detective novel aims at maintaining a difficult synthesis between formula and reality: the clues must be given to the reader, the broken key, the complicated time scheme, the disposition of the characters at any given time; and all this must be related to familiar and recognizable fact. The hound of the Baskervilles cannot remain, in a detective novel, a specter of supernatural legend; the phosphorous on his snout must eventually return us to reality. Generally speaking, the things we probably never shall directly know—for murder, even in a violent age, is still outside the personal experience of most of us—must be brought into conjunction with the kind of reality we do know. "Wild, and yet domestic"—so Dickens characterized *The Moonstone,* and Henry James commended Collins for "those most mysterious of mysteries, the mysteries which are at our own doors." This is the essence of the classic detective novel. The nineteenth-century sensation novel, on the other hand, deals with a world either necessarily outside the experience of its readers (the supernatural), or practically so (the upper class of life). The detective story is therefore less escapist; it invites the reader's step-by-step participation, with the detective, in the solution of the mystery, and that solution is the final ratification of reality and social and moral order. The end of the sensation novel is more typically the ratification of a middle class ethic, coupled with an ambivalent rejection of aristocratic values. In a sensation novel, moreover, the supernatural may be allowed to stand, as the Ghost's Walk is left unexplained in that magnificent hybrid of detective novel, sensation novel, and so much else, *Bleak House*—I allude to it here only to point to the perils encountered by the formulator of "rules."

In the sensation novel, finally, Fate has a much greater role to play. For Mrs. Henry Wood, or Miss Braddon, character is emphatically not destiny; Fate, usually malign, at best capricious, moves their characters like so many puppets. With Fate, goes her more lowly handmaiden, coincidence. Plot spins the passions. Green, however, partly because of her essentially American concern with the inner lives of her characters, partly because of her adoption of Poe's ratiocinative method, avoids the concept of an outside destiny, and centers her interest in the detective's intellectual pursuit of the criminal. Wilkie Collins, the master of Wood, Braddon, and countless others, is primarily a novelist of "character," though still as guilty of forcing character to conform to plot as his sensational disciples are, even in the best of his sensation novels, such as *The Woman in White* and *Armadale*. It is striking, therefore, that he found "the one weak side" of *The Leavenworth Case,* which he read in a sitting, to be "the want of truth to Nature in some of the characters." But in urging Green to subject plot to character, he was not only welcoming her to his profession of detective story writer, but also giving her advice she did not really need.

To illustrate these generalizations, we may compare Mrs. Henry Wood's *East Lynne* (1861), sensation novel, with *The Leavenworth Case* (1878), detective novel. Both were first novels, both runaway best sellers, both, dramatized, highly popular plays. In *East Lynne*, Lady Isabel is left penniless on the death of her spendthrift father, and shortly afterwards marries the highly respectable and rich lawyer, Archibald Carlyle, who has bought East Lynne, her father's estate. They have three children, before Isabel is seduced by *Captain,* later *Sir,* Francis Levison, who eventually abandons her. She returns, disguised, but also greatly disfigured by her privations, to East Lynne, where Carlyle has married again, and where she becomes governess to her own children. One of them dies in her arms, and shortly afterwards she also dies, still in the house of her former husband, still unrecognized until she herself discloses her identity on her deathbed.

A subplot doubles the chance of coincidence: one of the factors causing Isabel to flee with Levison has been her jealous fears of losing her husband's love to Barbara Hare, a youthful neighbor, whose own love for Carlye is evident to all save Carlyle himself. In fact their relationship is a professional one—he is advising her and her brother, who is a fugitive from a murder charge seeking the real murderer, whom he knows by sight. Much later, that murderer turns out to be Levison.

Of the three secrets of *East Lynne*—that Carlyle and Barbara's relationship is quite innocent, that the governess Madame Vine is actually Lady Isabel, that Levison is a murderer—only one, the last, is a secret from the reader. But all the characters in the novel, sooner or later, are the dupes of one or other of the secrets—Lady Isabel does not know that her husband does not love Barbara Hare, Carlyle does not know his former wife is now his children's governess. All alazons, no eirons. There is *one* eiron, though of the all-knowing rather than the self-deprecating kind, and that is the narrative presence itself of *East Lynne,* from whom the view that the aristocracy are more prone to vice than the middle class, from whom the constant recitation of a series of moral maxims which are punitively ratified in Isabel's intolerably long penance and miserable death. And the same narrative presence manipulates Isabel's malign destiny so as to bring her by coincidence, just as she fears losing her husband's love, into the hands of the supremely attractive Levison.

The Leavenworth Case begins in Leavenworth's lawyer's office as the secretary of the rich retired merchant appears to announce his employer's murder. The senior partner is absent, so the junior, Raymond, returns with the secretary to the Leavenworth house, where a coronial inquiry is about to begin. Leavenworth has two nieces living with him, Mary, to whom he has left the bulk of his fortune, and Eleanore. Mutual suspicion seems to create dissension between the two women, and also has the effect of moving readers' suspicions to and fro between the two. Also suspect is the mysterious figure of Henry Clavering, who has been seen in the Leavenworth mansion both before and after the murder. What finally emerges is that Clavering, an Englishman, is secretly married to Mary—the secrecy has caused the rift between the two women—and has written to Leavenworth, who detests everything English, complaining of her behavior in refusing to see him. Leavenworth is therefore about to disinherit his niece, when he is murdered by his secretary, who loves Mary and, not knowing her married, wishes to marry her himself. The set of secrets, all plausibly connected, is painstakingly uncovered by Gryce's reasoning.

East Lynne, undoubtedly, will live longer than *The Leavenworth Case:* it touches more universal feelings, touching them in a highly sentimental way—mother love, and the sympathy for, yet the reprobation of, the erring woman. It even contains a murder mystery, with Francis Levison, in high retribution, finally unmasked as the murderer. In its kaleidoscope of thrilling incidents, it far overmatches *The Leavenworth Case*. But in that very overmatch is the superior realism of Anna Katharine Green. *The Leavenworth Case* does not strain our credulity as *East Lynne* does. Green adds a second murder, but it follows logically from the first: the secretary has lured away with a promise of marriage a maidservant who has seen him leaving the room of the murder, and then has poisoned her. There is none of Wood's reliance upon fate and coincidence.

Most important of all, whereas *East Lynne* imposes through narrative omniscience a moral unanimity which brooks no contradiction, in *The Leavenworth Case,* through the narration of lawyer Raymond, naive and in love with Eleanore, yet following every step of the reasoning of the great detective Gryce, we get a nice balance of partiality and reasonableness which commands our trust. Raymond, unlike the omniscient persona of Mrs. Henry Wood, is of the same class as the Leavenworths, not peeping up from below stairs, and his initial interest in the Leavenworth mansion is not prurient, but harmlessly voyeuristic—he wants the thrill of seeing the dead body. Even the love interest in *The Leavenworth Case,* which in one of Green's disciples, Mary Roberts Rinehart, becomes a gratuitous convention, is part of its realism, and essential to the tenor of Raymond's narration. There is no moralizing voice in *The Leavenworth Case;* even with Raymond's partiality the approach to the solution of the crime is ratiocinative, and the emotional manipulations of Mrs. Henry Wood's moral attitudes are missing.

Given Mrs. Wood's rather prurient distaste for the aristocracy, one has the sense that she is pulling back the curtain on the elegance and serenity of aristocratic life to reveal the presence—the inevitability, we almost believe—of scandal and crime behind. Green has no such titillatory purpose; though she almost in variably sets her crime not far from a great house, or involves it with the reputation of a great family, the opulence is there to provide a believable contrast with the more pedestrian activities of the police. and it is more believable, for two reasons: it is more fully realized and described that Wood managed to make her presentment of upper class life, and, unlike British upper class life, the American *haut monde* was not hidden behind so many closed doors, but was more familiar, less the subject of prurient interest, to an American public. Both novelists described the upper classes, but the detective novelist described them in truer terms.

If the kind of novel that Green was writing can be distinguished, then by its higher realism, from the sensation novels of Mrs. Henry Wood and her school, Green's novels are still not quite of a piece with those of her predecessors in the detective novel. The realism of Poe's detective stories comes not from minute descriptions of the Rue Morgue or the hotel of the Minister D—, for these locales are scarcely even glimpsed, but from the ratiocinative movement, the pure logic, of Dupin's mind. The realism of *The Moonstone,* which has on analysis a plot quite as sensational as Collins's non-detective novels, comes from the plausibility of the narrators who give us that plot. The realism of Gaboriau comes from his faithful presentation of the streets and alleys of the metropolitan underworld which most of his characters inhabit. Green clearly owes something to Poe's logic, something to Collins's plausible narrators, though she never uses his multiple narrative method, but she owes much more to Gaboriau's descriptive realism—save that her subject is the salon rather than the street. The upper classes, who are always at the centre of Green's mysteries, are offstage in Gaboriau's.

Green herself, suggestively, preferred the term "criminal romance" for her fiction. Interviewed by a journalist in 1902, she said: "Please do not call my books 'detective stories'. . . . I abhor the word detective. It is too often applied to atrocities. I choose crime as a basic subject because from it arise the most dramatic situations, situations which could be produced by nothing else." Even if we forget here to trust the tale rather than the artist, Green's habit of collecting newspaper accounts of actual crimes as the germs for her novels, as well as the fact that a contemporary critic called her "the foremost representative in America to-day of police-court literature" (and that she was asked at least once for her solution to a local Buffalo crime), lay the emphasis upon the "criminal" rather than the "romance." Indeed, her plots never strain the credulity at their most ingenious, and are most often scientifically ballasted: *The Leavenworth Case* itself turns partly on scientific evidence, and one of her last novels, *Initials Only,*

has the victim killed with an ice pellet, which when it melts leaves the investigators with a seemingly supernatural, but actually quite plausible, cause of death. (To take "romance" in a different sense, while her "love" interest has been condemned by modern commentators, it is worth noting that she herself regarded her last novel, in 1923, as "my first love story.")

It is in this understanding of the fundamental realism of her fiction—what Barzun and Taylor see as her presentation of "the tempo and the mores of New York and Washington society in the period 1875-1900"—that it is time to introduce her principal detective, Ebenezer (in some novels spelt "Ebenezar") Gryce. The introduction is made in the first chapter of *The Leavenworth Case:*

> And here let me say that Mr. Gryce, the detective, was not the thin, wiry individual with the piercing eye you are doubtless expecting to see. On the contrary, Mr. Gryce was a portly, comfortable personage with an eye that never pierced, that did not even rest on you. If it rested anywhere, it was always on some insignificant object in the vicinity, some vase, inkstand, book or button. These things he would seem to take into his confidence, make the repositories of his conclusions; but as for you—you might as well be the steeple on Trinity Church, for all connection you appeared to have with him or his thoughts. At present, then, Mr. Gryce was, as I have already suggested, on intimate terms with the door-knob.

So Gryce on his first appearance before the reading public, but actually in mid-career as a detective. The Dickensian touches, not necessarily via Collins, are clear, as is the sense that Green is alluding to, but departing from, a literary stereotype. Noting, in 1903, the vast difference between Old Sleuth and Sherlock Holmes on the one hand, and the real detective on the other, Green observed that all the detectives she had met were "tame and uninteresting." In making Gryce a fairly pedestrian figure, she was determinedly, therefore, moving away from romance to realism.

It will be as well to place beside this passage one from the short story which describes Gryce's earliest case, **"The Staircase at the Heart's Delight,"** set in "the spring of 1840" (late versions say 18—), but published in 1894:

> Fortunately for me, I was in the building at the time, and was able to respond when a man was called up to investigate this matter. Thinking that I saw a connection between it and the various mysterious deaths of which I have previously spoken, I entered into the affair with much spirit . . . Accordingly, I appeared there [in a certain pawnshop], one dull November afternoon, in the garb of a certain Western sporting man, who, for a consideration, allowed me the temporary use of his name and credentials.

> Entering beneath the three golden balls, with the swagger and general air of ownership I thought most likely to impose upon the self-satisfied female who presided over the desk, I asked to see her boss.

Between them, these two passages strike several of the keynotes of Gryce's character: the diffidence in the presence of his social superiors unless he is actually masquerading as one of them; a certain hostility towards women, contained within his patronization of them; his professional ambition which becomes a proper professional vanity as he grows old, older, oldest; his abstraction, sometimes assumed, sometimes despondent at failure, which can spring in a moment to alertness when a new lead is discovered.

Gryce is a member of the official police force of New York, and it is mainly in the metropolis, or its suburbs, where Green grew up, that the novels take place, though there are trips into the countryside, one to Vermont, where Green had her schooling. *Hand and Ring,* her own favorite of her novels, is set in upstate New York, as well as in Buffalo, where she lived for part of her childhood and all of her fifty years of married life. Her detectives do not stray far from those scenes she knew and could realistically describe.

Gryce's career runs through eleven novels and two short stories published between 1878 and 1917, and, within a certain latitude, he ages correspondingly. His career, as it is written, runs in the novels from the Centennial year of Hayes-Tilden to the year of Woodrow Wilson's inauguration, with the two retrospective short stories taking it back to more than a decade before the Civil War. Though not all these events are mentioned, some of them are, and there is a greater sense of the specific kind of larger world that exists beyond Gryce's smaller world than in most detective novels. Above all, there is the sense of Gryce's gradual aging, and the incidental references to telephones, automobiles, and even airships can only enhance that sense, anchoring it in reality. In **"The Staircase at the Heart's Delight,"** looking back, he describes himself as "a young man in those days, and full of ambition." In *The Doctor, His Wife, and the Clock,* set in 1851, published in 1895, he is "a young man of thirty." In *The Leavenworth Case* his age is not specified, though the middle fifties seems about right, and he is laid up through most of the novel with a serious attack of the rheumatism which afflicts him constantly in the still later novels. In two novels in which he plays only a small part, *A Strange Disappearance* (1880) and *Hand and Ring* (1884), his appearance is largely taken for granted, but by the time of *Behind Closed Doors* (1888) his rheumatism has become "proverbial" though he still has a "fine figure," and "when hurry is demanded" the infirmity does not stand in his way. He is by now in his mid-sixties, we presume, and his figure is still "portly."

In *A Matter of Millions* (1890), "he is an old man now, verging on seventy, and both from age and infirmity in no condition to engage in the active exercise of that detective work which has employed his energies for so many years." With age, of course, has come increasing fame: on the first page of *A Strange Disappearance,* the narrator-detective is referred to as "the most astute man . . . in the bureau, always and of course excepting Mr. Gryce." At the beginning of *Hand and Ring,* one of his subordinates calls him "one of New York's ablest detectives." Though in *Behind Closed Doors* he has "passed his prime," he is "the great Gryce yet." And in *A Matter of Millions,* as the authorial voice says, his "record, after all, is chiefly one of triumphs."

In his first collaboration with Amelia Butterworth, *That Affair Next Door* (1897), he looks to her on their first meeting (in 1895) "seventy-five if he was a day"; he later himself says, "I'm seventy-seven, but I'm not too old to learn." In this novel he remains "portly and easy-going in appearance." While her sensitivity about her own "uncertain" age makes her call him "old," she translates "old" in a different way in their second collaboration in *Lost Man's Lane* (1898): " 'You mean old enough to pull the wool over other people's eyes' "; and when he carries a young and attractive woman over an obstacle, she acidly remarks, "Where was his rheumatism now?". In *The Circular Study* (1900), Gryce, the "old reader of human nature," is an "octogenarian," thinking of retiring to his little farm in Westchester (age and fame have their tangible rewards, too), but still drawn to the life of action over mere thought. This case, the authorial voice notes with an authority it may have regretted, was "one of the last to engage the powers of this sagacious old man." Indeed, a year later, in *One of My Sons* (1901), Gryce is now "sagacious but sickly," but he is still "a large, elderly man, with a world of experience in his time-worn but kindly visage." At the end of *That Affair Next Door,* in the wake of failure, he had contemplated retirement, and in *One of My Sons* he relies more heavily upon his assistant Sweetwater, a reliance that becomes more marked still in *Initials Only* (1911), where he has in fact retired; his is the "directing mind," and Sweetwater's the active work. He seems to be losing flesh, even despite the apparent remission of years between 1901 and 1911, for he is now "a tall, angular gentleman," and, though "an old and rheumatic invalid," still "kind-faced, bright-eyed." Though temporary failure brings its sense of uselessness— " 'I've meddled with the old business for the last time, Sweetwater. You'll have to go it alone from now on' "—when the old hound scents the trail he has "an antidote against old age." In this novel, though, he needs a taxicab where before the train had served; the subway is for the young. "I can no longer manage the stairs."

In his last novel, *The Mystery of the Hasty Arrow* (1917), he who had his origins in the world of gas-jets and hansoms makes his appearance in an automobile, from which he has to be helped, and at which he looks rather askance. This novel is set in 1913, presumably to keep its events clear of the war, even in distant Europe (though the principal woman becomes, at the end, a nurse close to the trenches), and presumably also to make more plausible Gryce's continuing longevity; if he was thirty in 1851, he must be beyond ninety by now. So at one moment of despondency in the novel, "the lines came out in Mr. Gryce's face till he looked his eighty-five years and more" (the last two words are conveniently ambiguous—did he have those extra years, or merely look them?). He seems, indeed, "at first blush . . . past the age where experience makes for efficiency," yet "this physically weak but extremely wise old man" dominates the scene with his "mental power." None of his vanity has gone—" 'I have been said to be able to spot a witness with my eyes shut. Let's see what I can do with my eyes open'." Neither has his legendary complaint gone—"An extra twinge or two of rheumatism warned him that he was approaching the point of disablement." As always failure, or in later years the sense that he must arrest a good or likeable man, brings despondency ("If my death here and now . . . would avail to wipe out the evidence I have so laboriously collected against this man, I should welcome it with gratitude"), but with the game afoot, the spirit rekindles—"the almost extinguished spark of early genius had suddenly flared again into full blaze." These words, in fact, are a fair description of Anna Katharine Green's own powers, in this next-to-last of her novels, one of her very best. After it, Gryce goes into the silence. And, after one more novel, so does Anna Katharine Green.

Gryce's principal two social limitations I mentioned in introducing him. He feels his inferior social status, even though his position gives him power; and he has an eye, if at times it is a cold eye, for the ladies. On the first point, he twice notes in *The Leavenworth Case* that he is not a gentleman, and cannot act the part:

> 'Have you any idea of the disadvantages under which a detective labors? For instance, now, you imagine I can insinuate myself into all sorts of society, perhaps, but you are mistaken . . . I can enter a house, bow to the mistress of it, let her be as elegant as she will, so long as I have a writ of arrest in my hand, or some such professional matter upon my mind; but when it comes to visiting in kid gloves, raising a glass of champagne in response to a toast—and such like, I am absolutely good for nothing.'

Though Gryce is "dejected" by, responds "broodingly" to, this deficiency of his, it is later noted that whereas Raymond, the narrator of the novel, is prevented by gentlemanly scruples from intercepting a letter, Gryce the non-gentleman is not so hampered. Raymond, a young lawyer of the same class as the Leavenworth girls whose uncle has been murdered, is eager to solve the crime, for he has fallen in love with one of those girls, who is suspected of the murder. Gryce thus "employs" the younger man to garner information from those rarified social circles while he pursues his own investigation at a lower level of society. The relationship between Gryce and Raymond is thus one of division of labor between the mole and the hound. As Raymond puts it—" 'any hearkening at doors, surprises, unworthy feints or ungentlemanly subterfuges, I herewith disclaim as outside of my province; my task being to find out what I can in an open way, and yours to search into the nooks and corners of this wretched business.' " " 'Just so, I know what belongs to a gentleman,' " Gryce replies.

It has been argued that Gryce's deference to his social superiors is Anna Katharine Green's main breach of realism, taken over from the relationships that exist between Lecoq and his more truly seignurial betters, especially in *M. Lecoq* and its sequel *The Honour of the Name,* where the detective is powerless to bring the ducal criminal to justice in the first part, and in the second part, while he tricks him into a confession, allows him to go free. Earlier, in *The Widow Lerouge,* a woman is murdered for what she

knows of an exchange of babies in the cradle; the murderer, the low-born child, is brought to justice, and one has the distinct impression that were he the aristocrat he would go free. But in democratic America such contemporary documents as Pinkerton's memoirs showed the professional detective as standing at no such disadvantage. It is worth remembering that not only Lecoq, but two more of Gryce's ancestors, Inspector Bucket of *Bleak House* and Sergeant Cuff of *The Moonstone,* are socially the inferiors of those they are investigating: Sir Leicester treats Bucket with aristocratic disdain as he probes for the truth of Lady Dedlock's past; and Lady Verinder summarily dismisses Cuff from the case when his suspicions settle upon Rachel as the thief. But it is unthinkable, as Gryce's own words make clear, that an American Lady Verinder could turn the American Cuff away from her door. The arrest will be made, though it be a social gaffe, and realism is not sacrificed thereby. As the policeman-narrator of *A Strange Disappearance* says: "I felt a certain degree of awe at the thought of invading with police investigation, this house of ancient Knickerbocker respectability. But once in the room of the missing girl, every consideration fled save that of professional pride and curiosity." So Gryce faces down, in his second novel, a man who has been a congressman, and, in his last, unmasks a man who is bidding fair to be a U.S. Senator.

Moreover, Green augments Gaboriau's realism in other ways. His maps of open terrain become in her novels detailed room or house plans, which remind us of their different settings, his the mean streets Maigret would tread fifty and seventy-five years later, hers the parlors of the detective novel's Golden Age (S. S. Van Dine is also a great draughtsman of interiors). Truly, Anna Katharine Green, after Gaboriau, took crime out of the streets, but in doing so she did not make its perpetrators inaccessible to those who still patrolled those streets. Her house plans, too, pin the reader to a greater specificity of detail. And there is a wealth of realistic observation in her frequent use of trial procedures to provide exposition: the knowledge she had from her father *does* give her the authority to use the frame of a trial or inquest to put the reader in convincing possession of the facts of the case.

The way in which Green deals with the inferior status of the policeman, therefore, omnipotent with a writ of arrest in his hand, but hampered in investigating aristocratic guilt as yet unproven, finally brings together realism with significant generic innovation: when the policeman cannot enter freely the great house, he finds an accomplice who can. While the unofficial partnership of Cuff and Franklin Blake is a single earlier example of such an alliance between the street and the salon, the relationship of Gryce and Raymond, between policeman and social habitue, recurs again and again in Green's novels, and adds her own touch to the relationship she may have found in Poe between the thinking detective and his sometimes more active, usually less intelligent, and almost always more narrative, partner—one scarcely needs reminders of those who come after! Much too elementary.

Such a relationship (though the intelligence is more equally balanced) is the stuff of three of Green's best novels, those which describe the partnership between Gryce and a feisty "woman of inborn principle and strict Presbyterian training," with "no faith in premonitions, but once seized by a conviction . . . never . . . mistaken as to its import," with "very few old maid's way or notions," and "none of [her] sex's instinctive reliance upon others which leads it so often to neglect its own resources"—all these are self-descriptions of Amelia Butterworth. One may say that to Ebenezer Gryce this wealthy, fiftyish spinster is always *the* woman (he actually calls her "a woman in a thousand"). She is not of course his adversary, and yet she is, in the way that she elicits the other social limitation I mentioned, his hostility, his attraction, to women, and his patronization of them. For the relationship between Gryce and Miss Butterworth is truly a battle of the sexes, in which the antagonists sound less like Mirabell and Millamant, or even John Tanner and Ann Whitefield, and much more like an older, less uxorious, more acerbic Nick and Nora Charles.

She refers often to her father, "a shrewd man of the old New England type," whose "hauteur" she frequently cultivates. At a triumphant moment in the same novel, she rhapsodizes: "I began to feel my importance in a way that was truly gratifying, and cast my eyes up at the portrait of my father with a secret longing that its original stood by to witness the verification of his prophecy." She doesn't like young men in general, and when she first sees Gryce he strikes her as "paternal-looking." When he acknowledges her detective abilities, "I felt as if my father's daughter had received her first recognition." In Gryce, clearly, she finds a reminder of her father, and their relationship, so established from the beginning, develops as a wrangling, affectionate one, in which each seeks from the other the grudging praise in which neither professes openly to be interested. "Though I have had no adventures," she says at the outset, "I feel capable of them, and as for any peculair acumen he may have shown in his long and eventful career, why that is a quality which others may share with him." And in the second novel, she describes occasional meetings with him of a merely social kind—Gryce is rising in the social scale—"in which he gained much without acknowledging it, and I gave much without appearing conscious of the fact."

Beyond their relationship, certainly, since there is a quarter of a century between their ages, and since Green herself so often sees Gryce as fatherly, it is not fanciful to see the author projecting her own father into her male detective and herself into her female detective. The creative energy so released makes, in my opinion, these three novels the best in all her more than forty; better than *The Leavenworth Case,* where the coadjutor is so pale in character, a mere juvenile lead, and challenged only by *Hand and Ring* and *The Mystery of the Hasty Arrow,* the best two of her many novels that show a figure of high fame and flourishing prosperity stalked by a nemesis from the distant past, more than once an abandoned wife. If, as they do, so many of Green's novels deal with marital tragedy—another mark of her realism, by the way—misalliances which are often corrected by murder, then the Gryce-Butterworth alliance gives the comic obverse of that theme. It is noteworthy that Gryce seems to have no fami-

ly life, until in *The Mystery of the Hasty Arrow* he has a much loved granddaughter who, newly married, has just left him, he complains, "for a man many years my junior." In Miss Butterworth he has a female partner who in her frequent rivalry of his "peculiar acumen" is his comic nemesis, a resurgence of the real family members he has so rigidly excluded from his public life that they do not emerge until the third generation, and then only over his protest.

Moreover, as befits a self-projection, Amelia Butterworth, even more than Gryce, is Green's most human character. Gryce has few sins to soften him; Miss Butterworth has a myriad humanizing touches. She is capable of personal as well as professional vanity, and a certain cattiness: "I am not handsome myself, though there have been persons who have called me so, but neither am I ugly, and in contrast to this woman—well, I will say nothing. I only know that, after seeing her, I felt profoundly grateful to a kind Providence." She is also capable of a disarming brand of self-aware rationalization: "The door to the closet was, as I expected, slightly ajar, a fact for which I was profoundly grateful, for, set it down to breeding or a natural recognition of other people's rights, I would have found it most difficult to turn the knob of a closet door, inspection of which had not been offered me. But finding it open, I gave it just a little pull. . . ."

Whereas Gryce has only his habit of not looking his interlocutor in the eye, his rheumatism, and the portliness which eventually gives way to lanky emaciation, Miss Butterworth has her irrational fear of dogs ("my one weakness"), and her habit of carrying with her extra candles and her own tea, without which she cannot get to sleep. With her own carriage and a house in Gramercy Park, she is a woman of wealth, whose dress is "rather rich than fashionable"; fashion "counts for nothing against convenience." However, in the same novel she explores an old house, full of beetles and spiders, in a "three-dollar-a-yard silk dress." For all her wealth, too, she has an eye for a bargain; at recess during an inquest she "improved the opportunity by going into a restaurant near by where one can get very good buns and coffee at a reasonable price. But I could have done without them." She is rather a snob: when a police official tells a servant, "and this other woman, too," to "stay around" for a coroner's inquest, she remarks, "By other woman he meant *me,* Miss Butterworth, of Colonial ancestry and no inconsiderable importance in the social world." But then her common sense resumes: "But though I did not relish this careless association of myself with this poor scrub-woman, I was careful to show no displeasure, for I reasoned that as witnesses we were equal before the law, and that it was solely in this light he regarded us."

As to her femininity, she uses "no perfumes," but towards one character who eventually proposes marriage and to whom she gives a "reluctant no," she shows a certain flirtatiousness. She is, however, as we have seen, thoroughly down-to-earth, and her response to another suitor is rather more characteristic: " 'I am not easy to suit, so I advise you to turn your attention to some one much more anxious to be married than I am.' " She is as free as she professes to be of feminine foible. She is a thoroughly independent woman, perhaps unliberated only in her deference to Gryce, but of certain kinds of feminine independence her old-fashioned qualities do not allow her to approve. When, not entirely without irony, she curtseys to a group of men, she comments: "It was a proper expression of respect when I was young, and I see no reason why it should not be a proper expression of respect now, except that we have lost our manners in gaining our independence, something which is to be regretted perhaps" (There may be a second thought in the last word). In truth, Amelia Butterworth, christened Araminta, which is what her father has always called her, *is* a dependent woman only in her daughterly "Araminta" role, and overwhelmingly the independent woman denoted by the name she chooses to use; she is scarcely at all "the piece of antiquated sentimentality suggested by the former cognomen." At one of her moments of selfdoubt, with a sense of being led astray by that sentimentality (which she sees as a feminine trait), she looks in a mirror and remarks that she ought to be called Araminta after all. The "stern image" which looks back at her sets her again on the accustomed path.

The particular help Amelia Butterworth is to Gryce, aside from her ease of entre into a society whose doors are closed to him, lies in the insight into feminine behavior of which he is also ignorant. (In *Behind Closed Doors*, it is said of him that he "knew men—he never boasted that he knew women.") In *The Leavenworth Case,* without her aid, he makes a deduction, much ridiculed in recent years, that the murderer was not a woman, for a woman may fire a gun, but would not clean it afterwards. In *That Affair Next Door,* she deduces from the dead woman's bare hands that she has been indoors at least long enough to remove her gloves, for "so well-dressed a woman would not enter a house like this, without gloves." She also deduces that a woman's hat has been worn only once from the single puncture made in it by the hat pin.

In their three collaborations, or rather encounters, Miss Butterworth gets closer to the solution than Gryce in the first, is bested, partly through her feminine vanity, in the second, while the third may be said to be a friendly draw. Their final parting, at the end of *The Circular Study,* as Gryce bows "lower even than his wont," foreshadows a further collaboration: "Was he wondering if a case of similar interest would ever bring them together again in consultation?" But Gryce by the turn of the century was a gentleman himself, with his farm in Westchester, and the need for upper-class coadjutors was behind him. What he still had need for, as from the beginning, was the subordinate alter ego, the man who could do what he, through age, lack of agility, concern for dignity, or even his high degree of recognizability, could not do for himself. So Holmes used his Baker Street Irregulars when he could not take advantage of his penchant for disguise. So Gryce uses a number of auxiliaries, in particular his principal protege, Sweetwater. If Amelia Butterworth looks to him as a daughter, these young men are much more plainly his bequests to the future, his trainees, his surrogate sons.

The earlier avatars of this type, the assistant called "Q," and the detective Horace Byrd, are preliminary sketches of, or searches for, the much more developed Sweetwater. Q makes his appearance in *The Leavenworth Case,* "an agent of mine who is a living interrogation point." Disguised as a woman, crawling across roofs to peep in windows, and with his card inscribed with a single "?", he is a comic character, however serious his function, and he fades out of the story once Gryce is in possession of the information he has acquired. In *A Strange Disappearance,* now a regular member of the police force, he is, after two introductory paragraphs describing him as "the rising young detective," the narrator of the story, still performing the same tasks—he disguises himself as a seedy French artist, and to enter a house climbs a tree with rural expertise ("thanks to fortune I was not brought up in New York"). While the first-person narration works against a primarily comic characterization, the return to the third person in *Behind Closed Doors* again makes Q—"Q the curious", as he calls himself, 417—a figure of fun, a lounger whose main task is to shadow Gryce's suspect. He is not a comic contemptible, however, and one takes seriously enough his statement: "And to be a good detective is meat and drink to me, and more. I have ambition to take Mr. Gryce's place when he is laid up. There are those who say I will."

Before *Behind Closed Doors,* another of Gryce's juniors had appeared, Horace Byrd. That this minor detective is listed in Hagen's *Who Done It?,* while Q is not, is no doubt due to Byrd's presence in *Hand and Ring,* which is one of Green's most popular novels, still in print in the 1920s. Byrd does however have a kind of primacy that Q never attains, and is in fact the principal detective in the novel until his failure causes him to call Gryce from the metropolis to upstate New York. Before that, at least part of the story's interest lies in the duel between Byrd and yet another detective, a private one. But Byrd is a colorless figure, more a functionary than a character. In *A Matter of Millions,* when Byrd is again Gryce's bulldog, it becomes clearer that his principal cachet is his "attractive features, good expression and cultivated manners. He is a detective, too, but neither in speech, look nor action does he show it; hence his usefulness and growing favor with the chief." Byrd is, in fact, a transitional figure between Raymond, persona grata in society, and Q and Sweetwater, who are more like Gryce himself. And the relationship between him and Gryce is not filial: he is more Raymond than Sweetwater.

Sweetwater, Gryce's last and most attractive male auxiliary, appears first in *Agatha Webb* (1899), where he is not a detective, but a musician (" 'a fiddler, a nobody' ", as one character calls him) living in the rural New England town of Sutherlandtown; and much of this novel's interest exists in the conflict between the professional detective, suggestively named Knapp, from the big city (Boston), and this young amateur, like Q a country boy. Sweetwater is early described, self-described, as "not prepossessing to look at," but there his comic potential stops; his confidence, even in the presence of the supercilious Bostonian, is supreme, and carries him through in his "self-imposed role of detective." He is a more authoritative figure than Q. His scruples may be subordinated to his ambition at this stage of his career (he is "not so much high-minded as large-hearted"). But even this early his character is penetratingly possessed by Green, for his ugliness is shown to be the moving principle behind his will to success and fame. At the denouement Knapp is outfoxed, and "Sweetwater was a made man."

In the next novel, *The Circular Study,* is a plethora of riches—not only Gryce and Miss Butterworth, but again Sweetwater, now for six months a member of the New York police force, under Gryce, still supremely confident: his cheer penetrates a mystery as yet impenetrable to the old detective ("But then he was not twenty-three, with only triumphant memories behind him"). Already he demonstrates a greater detective skill than Q or Byrd, and already Gryce's attitude is explicitly paternal for a " 'young man I propose to adopt into my home and heart. . . . Not much to look at, madam, but promising, very promising' ." While Miss Butterworth butters up Gryce by comparing his "genius" with the new pupil's mere "skilfulness," the understudy's role is clearly now taken up with more authority, and approval, than ever before. In *The Circular Study* his primacy yields to the Gryce-Butterworth alliance, but this is the last of Miss Butterworth, and only the next-to-first of him.

In *One of My Sons,* indeed, the balance, of interest shifts from Gryce to Sweetwater. The narrative is a first-person one, told by a young gentleman who is summoned from the street to witness the dying moments of a wealthy patriarch. Sweetwater, while professing to wish for Gryce's help at a crucial juncture, solves the case with a shrewd deduction from a typewritten message from the victim (Shades of Ellery Queen!). Between the narrator and Sweetwater there is something of a reprise of the Raymond-Gryce arrangement of twenty years before; but Sweetwater's pertinacity (one of his emphasized qualities) carries him so much farther, in a less rigid age, that the roles of the two partners are virtually reversed:

> Meantime, Sweetwater, with an air of perfect nonchalance admirably assumed, had stepped past Hewson into the house. Evidently he was accustomed to go in and out of the place at will, and though the old servant did not fail to show his indignation at this palpable infringement upon the family dignity, he did not abate a jot of his usual politeness. . . . But his complaisance did not extend to me.

The next appearance of Sweetwater, after a lapse of five years in which Green was writing a more romantic kind of fiction, though still within our genre, including two serials for Edward Bok's *Ladies' Home Journal,* is a continuation of such regression. *The Woman in the Alcove* (1906) is again a first-person narrative, this time by a society woman, and the romantic element is dominant. Though in *One of My Sons* attention was drawn as usual to Sweetwater's physical grotesqueness—"his lank frame and inharmonious features"—in *The Woman in the Alcove* he is described as "of a commonplace type," and his task of merely shadowing a suspect puts him back into Q's role. The only chapter in which he has any prominence, indeed, is actually entitled "Sweetwater in a New Role."

But four years later, in *The House of the Whispering Pines* (1910), which Haycraft recommends over *The Leavenworth Case* ("connoisseurs prefer. . . ."), Sweetwater, without Gryce, again has pride of place. He calls himself at the denouement "a pupil of Mr. Gryce," however, and the trap that he lays to elicit a sign of guilt from the villain recalls many of Grayce's similar stratagems, from *The Leavenworth Case* on. Sweetwater, who would by now be in his early thirties, has grown in both ugliness and authority. To the male narrator, as usual of the gentlemanly class, he is "no beauty, . . . plain-featured to the point of ugliness," yet "there was a magnetic quality in his voice and manner that affected even one so fastidious as myself." In a court appearance, his "receding chin and far too projecting nose," though matched with "his cheerful, modest, winsome disposition," call forth the suspicion of the presiding coroner, who is mollified only by a letter of recommendation from Gryce, whose fame by now, of course, opens all doors. This letter commends Sweetwater in the same terms that have been so often used for Gryce himself—" 'a man of sagacity and becoming reserve' ": the understudy is moving, with approval, towards the central role.

In *Initials Only,* as we saw, Gryce's age enforces now an even greater reliance on his assistant, and the principal interest in the novel is in the mutual relationship between the two detectives. Sweetwater again carries the case to a successful conclusion, ingeniously identifying an apparent stabbing in which the weapon is missing as in fact a shooting with a bullet of ice, which has melted by the time of the medical examination. As we also saw, the collaboration between Gryce and Sweetwater comes to a suspended end in *The Mystery of the Hasty Arrow.* Here there is a return to the earlier pattern of Gryce as the mental and Sweetwater as the active part. And Sweetwater is again distinctly secondary. When he makes his first appearance at the museum where the murder has just been committed, and notes "the Curator's evident chagrin at his meagre and unsatisfactory appearance," he humorously points out that he is not the principal, that Mr. Gryce will be there presently. Throughout the novel he is Gryce's "recognized factotum." Gryce "was the absolute master of everything, even of Sweetwater, he sometimes thought. For the young fellow loved him—had reason to." Though Gryce's manner to his assistant is more *de haut en bas* than in the previous novel, there is still a strong sense of cooperation, and they spend more time actually conferring. The chapter entitled " 'Write Me His Name' ", in which the two exchange theories and then, on paper, suspects, is a good example of their relation—and it is Gryce who is correct in his choice of culprit.

So Sweetwater remains to the end secondary, never taking over the role of what Carolyn Wells calls "the Transcendent Detective." Though most of Gryce's subordinates, and on two occasions Gryce himself (in *Hand and Ring* and *Lost Man's Lane,* not counting his very first case), carry out the essentially menial side of detective work by disguising themselves, none does this more than Sweetwater. The relationship between a detective writer and his detective—especially if it has lasted long, and both have grown old together (Holmes, Poirot, Miss Marple spring to mind)—is obviously a complex and intimate one. Anna Katharine Green evidently did not wish to see Gryce die, and one of the great successes of *The Mystery of the Hasty Arrow* is its climactic delineation of the coming dissolution of the paternal figure. A weak novel, *The Step on the Stair,* without Gryce, followed tardily six years later, and for the last twelve years of a very long life Anna Katharine Green published no more.

If Anna Katharine Green is to be reinstated as a figure commanding the attention—the reading attention—of the critic of detective fiction, it must be on two grounds: her consolidation of the detective novel as a realistic art form, and her contribution to the development of the detective hero.

— *Barrie Hayne*

But two years before *The Mystery of the Hasty Arrow,* Anna Katharine Green had created her last important detective and a current favorite, Violet Strange, who made her appearance, or series of appearances, in *The Golden Slipper* (1915). The book, with the first of nine "problems for Violet Strange," opens with an exchange between the head of a detective agency and a prospective client, at the theatre: " 'Do you mean to say . . . that you silly little chit, whose father I know, whose future I know, and who is called one of the season's belles is an agent of yours.' " At the end of Green's procession of detectives comes one who is *both* professional and amateur, *both* detective agent and socialite. This "small, slight woman," "vivacity incarnate, . . . and a woman's lofty soul [shining] through her odd, bewildering features," and "of the size of a child of eleven" truly leads a double life, kept secret from her financier father. She is working as a detective for money to train her older sister as an opera singer, the sister her father has disowned for marrying a singing-master, and he would disown Violet too, if he knew. Amid a round of parties, balls and musicales she continues her detective work: "Violet Strange in society was a very different person from Violet Strange under the tension of her secret and peculiar work."

Amelia Butterworth of Gramercy Park at the turn of the century had her carriage; Violet Strange of Seventy-Second Street in 1915 has her limousine. But her habits are much less plain than Miss Butterworth's: she draws her limousine up outside the house of crime on Seventeenth Street ("her entrance was a *coup du theatre*"). The girl is much more stereotypically "feminine" than the older woman, and despite her frequent displays of courage much less truly liberated: *The Golden Slipper* is, in such unity as it has, her love story, as the young Boston aristocrat whose wife's murder is her fourth "problem" returns as an accessory figure in her eighth, and is poised to marry her in her ninth and last. It is difficult to agree with Hay-

craft's view—"Her feminine detective, VIOLET STRANGE, is best forgotten"—but it is clearly wrong, at the other end of the spectrum, to see Violet as engaged in a "positive act of resisting patriarchal domination," for she is very much and always concerned lest her father find out about her secret profession. Somewhat disagreeably she uses her feminine wiles and weaknesses: to gain entrance into the house of crime she plays the flibbertigibbet; it is no excuse to say that "back of this display of mingled childishness and audacity there lay hidden purpose, intellect, and a keen knowledge of human nature." She seems to accept her lover's belief that her mind "has an intuitive faculty more to be relied upon than the reasoning of men"; and when at the end she explains to him her reasons for undertaking detective work, it is an explanation of "why, with all the advantages I possess, I should meddle with matters so repugnant to a woman's natural instincts." Though she with great nerve crawls, as her size allows, into a sealed room which contains—literally—two family skeletons, the room is in the mansion of one of her own class. One cannot see her soiling her three-dollar-a-yard dress (both price and hem would be up by 1915 in any case) in places alien to that class. In fact, Violet tells her employer that she "not be asked to touch the sordid or the bloody"—" 'I have no fancy for handling befouled spider webs." As we saw, Amelia Butterworth had no such scruples.

This then, is the progression over forty years from Ebenezer Gryce to Violet Strange. Conveniently, we can close with one of Green's most famous stories, **"The Doctor, His Wife, and the Clock,"** for this story, written for Gryce in the 1890s, was retailored as Violet Strange's Problem 7 twenty years later. The story, briefly, concerns a midnight shooting in fashionable New York City, in his bed, of a man without enemies; the neighborhood is alerted by a woman's shriek. The inquiry leads to the blind Doctor Zabriskie and his wife, living in a nearby house. The doctor insists he has committed the crime, but the police ignore his confession, because of the accuracy of the killer's aim and the alacrity of his escape. The doctor insists on a test: a clock is to be placed at a distance from him as a target when it strikes the hour. At the last moment his wife, holding another clock, moves into the line of fire and is killed. He shortly thereafter kills himself.

In Gryce's first-person narration the tale is straightforward, a policeman's account, with some interpolated statements. Gryce is early convinced that the doctor committed the crime (though by mistake), and expects him to be able to shatter an audible target. In *The Golden Slipper* the story is enclosed within the author's omniscience: Violet's employer at the detective agency brings her the narrative, largely unaltered from the Gryce version, but now attributed to "an everyday police detective." With its ending, obviously, not yet disclosed, for that is Violet's task, the narrative is given to her at a time when she is "already in a state of secret despondency," either over her sister's plight or her growing love for her young Bostonian (it is not clear which). The narrative is also given to her in two parts, and between the first and the second she wavers as to whether she will undertake the case, being won to do so only "for pity's sake" for "a lovely member of [her] sex." A friendship grows between herself and the doctor's wife, whose "hungry heart opened to the sympathetic little being who clung to her in such evident admiration."

Mrs. Zabriskie is extremely beautiful, and in the earlier version the young Gryce was "much under the dominion of woman's beauty," but not so as to be blinded to the husband's guilt. Violet is convinced of his innocence, and it is she who proposes the test of the blind man's skill with the pistol, for she is sure the test will fail. She is thus, in the result, "overcome by this tragic end to all her hopes." As she says in her next investigation: " 'I have never got over the Zabriskie tragedy. It haunts me continually. . . . I feel guilty. I was responsible—'."

What is most striking in the rewriting of this famous story (invariably anthologized, as far as I know, in its earlier version) is first of all the perceived difference between the male and female detectives. What makes an early triumph for Ebenezer Gryce become a scarifying failure for Violet Strange is that though his susceptibilities could have been involved, his rationality has consistently the upper hand; her emotions and intuition hold sway throughout. In all his stories, Gryce is a thinker, albeit a plodding one, and certainly not an armchair one; Q, Byrd and Sweetwater are primarily doers, and Violet Strange is primarily a feeler. It is one of Amelia Butterworth's most interesting features that she is all three. To go back to an early distinction in this essay, *The Golden Slipper* approaches the novel of sensation; all Gryce's novels are predominantly novels of detection, and Amelia Butterworth's good commonsense keeps her two narratives solidly in that category (There is none but the most superficial resemblance between *That Affair Next Door* and *Lost Man's Lane* on the one hand, and the "Had I But Known" sensation novels of the daughters of Mary Roberts Rinehart on the other). The first version of **"The Doctor, His Wife, and the Clock"** is a short fiction Poe might not have been ashamed to have written; the second version is as though recast by Mrs. Henry Wood.

Audrey Peterson   (essay date 1984)

SOURCE: "Some Minor Voices," in *Victorian Masters of Mystery: From Wilkie Collins to Conan Doyle,* Frederick Ungar Publishing Co., 1984, pp. 155-96.

[*In the following excerpt, Peterson emphasizes Green's influence on later detective writers, and describes three of Green's principal detectives: Ebenezer Gryce, Amelia Butterworth, and Violet Strange.*]

The first thing that strikes the reader of Anna Katharine Green's novels is that they sound like modern mystery stories. Their central purpose is to use a crime as a direct puzzle for the reader to solve and they waste no time in getting on with the plot. Wilkie Collins . . . developed the mystery formula almost by accident, while intent upon writing novels of character and incident. Le Fanu wavered between social comedy and Gothic horror in much of his work. Mary Braddon and James Payn often used sensational crime plots in the manner of Collins, but both engaged in lengthy digressions in order to satisfy serial publication and to fill up the three volumes required by the circulating libraries. As an American, Anna Green was free

to publish her novels directly in one-volume book form, and their comparative brevity and refreshing directness helped to keep the focus on the tightly constructed plots. Her chief models were the detective stories of Edgar Allan Poe and the Monsieur Lecoq tales of Emile Gaboriau. Published in 1878, her first mystery novel, *The Leavenworth Case,* came out nine years before Conan Doyle's Sherlock Holmes made his first appearance and anticipated with remarkable originality many of the characteristics of subsequent mystery fiction.

Born in New York city in 1846, the youngest daughter of a prominent lawyer, Anna Katharine Green lived in the affluent society immortalized by her famous contemporary Edith Wharton. Anna attended Ripley Female College in Poultney, Vermont, and later received a B.A. degree from Green Mountain Junior College (where incidentally she had initiated Ralph Waldo Emerson into a secret society.) For a number of years she wrote poetry without much recognition, finally turning to the writing of mystery fiction, where she met with immediate success, *The Leavenworth Case* alone eventually selling more than 750,000 copies. In 1884 she married Charles Rohlfs, who had been an actor for some years. They settled in Buffalo, where Rohlfs managed a foundry and later became a funiture designer. The couple had three children and were active in community affairs. For more than forty years, Anna Green's mystery fiction continued to sell; her last novel, *The Step on the Stair,* came out in 1923, twelve years before her death in 1935.

A notable feature of Anna Katharine Green's work is that she was able to turn out one ingenious plot after another in more than thirty novels and several volumes of short stories. Of course, some are better than others, but her relative consistency is impressive. Despite her immense popularity, her work fell quickly into obscurity after 1920, no doubt because she remained a Victorian to the last. When the first World War wrought dramatic social change and brought in its wake, on both sides of the Atlantic, the rejection of Victorian and Edwardian codes of behavior, Anna Green was already in her seventies. Her characters had always remained in what was now regarded as the quaintly tiresome society in which men and women talked seriously about Honor and Duty, or made noble self-sacrifices in the cause of Love. Nevertheless, within such limitations, her characters are often charmingly developed and are far from cardboard figures.

Green's first novel, *The Leavenworth Case: A Lawyer's Story* (1878) begins with characteristic briskness. By the end of the first brief chapter, Everett Raymond, the lawyer of the subtitle, has been summoned to the house where the elderly philanthropist, Mr. Leavenworth, has been shot. Raymond is greeted at the door by the detective, Ebenezer Gryce; the coroner's inquest is ready to begin; he is shown the body; and the reader is provided with a diagram of the library and adjoining bedroom which constitute the scene of the crime. There had been no robbery; the doors of the house were locked; in short, as Trueman Harwell, the secretary to Mr. Leavenworth, declares, "The whole affair is a mystery." This could be the opening of an Agatha Christie novel, some forty years before *The Mysterious Affair at*

Styles introduced Hercule Poirot to the world in 1921. Already, Green is using in this novel a number of devices which become familiar in classic detective fiction of the twentieth century. At the inquest, an expert witness identifies the bullet as coming from the murder weapon; later on, the detective, Mr. Gryce, remarks that yellow paper burns differently from white, and traces paper according to the quire from which it came. Even the use of illustrations is modern: in addition to more than one floor plan, there are reproductions of the strips of a letter from which a message is reconstructed, a device later used by Conan Doyle in "The Reigate Squires." Most important, perhaps, is the emphasis upon the medical evidence indicating the position of the victim's head and the distance from which the shot was fired, as well as the approximate time of death.

Green's use of the young lawyer Everett Raymond as the narrator of the story provides an excellent means of sustaining suspense. The characters are seen as he perceives them, from the colorless secretary to the breathtakingly beautiful Leavenworth girls, the nieces of the murdered man. Although Mary's beauty is more dazzling, Raymond is clearly enamored of Eleanore at first sight, giving rise to some ingenious ambiguities as suspicion falls upon each of the characters in turn in a brilliant whodunit pattern. Raymond also becomes a forerunner of Dr. Watson as he admiringly describes Gryce's methods of detection, thus glorifying the figure of the detective.

Although Anna Green struck out in a new direction from her English contemporaries in the tight construction of her mystery plots, her celebrated detective is very much in the tradition of Inspector Bucket and Sergeant Cuff and as unlike Poe's Auguste Dupin as were the detectives of Dickens and Collins. A member of the New York police, Mr. Gryce is even more modest than his prototypes. When he asks Raymond at one point to assist him, it is because Raymond is a "gentleman" who can move with ease in the world of wealth and social distinction of the Leavenworths. Less brash than Inspector Bucket, who did not hesitate to speak his mind to Sir Leicester Dedlock, Gryce nevertheless maintains his own dignity when the occasion requires. Described as "a portly, comfortable personage," Gryce has the endearing eccentricity of rarely looking directly at the person with him. If his eye "rested anywhere, it was always on some insignificant object in the vicinity, some vase, inkstand, book, or button. These things he would seem to take into his confidence, make the repositories of his conclusions." When Raymond remarks that the situation looks dreadful, "Mr. Gryce immediately frowned at the door-knob," but his eyes never miss anything of importance, as Raymond soon learns: "Mr. Gryce was seemingly observant of my glance, though his own was fixed upon the chandelier." In moments of stress, he consults a fly on Raymond's sleeve or holds "a close and confidential confab with his fingertips."

Despite his deceptively casual manner, however, Gryce can become electrified when a series of discoveries seems to lead to a solution of the mystery. He will not give up until he has learned the full truth. "It is a principle which every detective recognizes," he declares, "that if of a hun-

dred leading circumstances connected with a crime, ninety-nine of these are acts pointing to the suspected party with unerring certainty, but the hundredth equally important act is one which that person could not have performed, the whole fabric of suspicion is destroyed." Sherlock Holmes could not have said more.

The Leavenworth Case came out nine years before Conan Doyle's Sherlock Holmes made his first appearance and anticipated with remarkable originality many of the characteristics of subsequent mystery fiction.

— *Audrey Peterson*

Mr. Gryce reappears off and on throughout the course of Green's fiction. Following the pattern introduced by Poe when he used the character of Auguste Dupin in three stories, Green gives the detecting honors to Mr. Gryce in a dozen or so of her novels. Writers of the English school had not as yet used the technique of carrying a detective through a series of stories, probably because the detective was still not the central focus of interest. Today's readers regret, for example, that Sergeant Cuff appears only in *The Moonstone* and that Wilkie Collins did not use him again in subsequent tales of detection. In France, the pattern had been used by Gaboriau in his series of crime stories featuring the detective exploits of Monsieur Lecoq and Père Tabaret. In England, it was Conan Doyle who set the pattern for future generations when he conceived the plan of doing a series of Sherlock Holmes stories for the *Strand Magazine* in 1891, bringing immense popularity to his Great Detective. Anna Green thus anticipated Doyle by several years in the device of the reappearing detective.

One of Anna Green's finest novels is *Hand and Ring* (1883), with its excellent characters and its brilliantly developed mystery plot. The story opens with a group of gentlemen conversing about crime while standing on the courthouse steps in the New York town of Sibley. A stranger in the group, later identified as Mr. Gryce, suggests that the most successful crime is one committed in a place open to view and with many passersby, pointing out a plain little house opposite as an example. A few minutes later, the widow who occupies the house is found dead, and so the plot begins to spin. A number of suspects are provided with motive and opportunity. Imogene Dare—another heroine of dazzling beauty—and her lover each suspect the other of the crime. This device, seeming at first to be fortuitous, becomes stratingly convincing as clue after clue appears indicating that each has good reason for suspicion of the other. There is a coroner's inquest, always well-handled in Green's works, and later on a fine courtroom scene.

The detecting in *Hand and Ring* is done initially by young Mr. Byrd, a "gentleman" detective from New York, aided by a less scrupulous assistant named Hickory. Both are competent enough up to a point, but in the end Mr. Gryce arrives to make the final deductions and wrap up the case. Since **Hand and Ring** was Green's fifth novel and marks the third appearance of Mr. Gryce, her readers were no doubt by this time prepared to recognize him by his eccentricities even before he was named. Thus the heroine, hearing a "bland and fatherly voice over her shoulder," turns and sees a strange gentleman:

> She saw before her a large comfortable-looking personage of middle age, of no great pretensions to elegance or culture, but bearing that within his face which oddly enough baffled her understanding while it encouraged her trust. This was the more peculiar in that he was not looking at her, but stood with his eyes fixed on the fading light of the hall-lamp, which he surveyed with an expression of concern that almost amounted to pity.

Just as Agatha Christie's readers would recognize as Hercule Poirot a dapper little man in pointed shoes who twirled his mustache and spoke of his "little gray cells," Green's readers would know that Mr. Gryce had arrived when the fatherly person bent his gaze of pity not upon Imogene but upon the hall-lamp.

In addition to the lovable Mr. Gryce, Anna Green created another detective figure in the person of Amelia Butterworth, a middle-aged spinster from one of the old families of New York. In **That Affair Next Door** (1897) Miss Butterworth, from her strategically placed window, sees mysterious comings and goings in the Van Burnam mansion next door to her own. When the dead body of a young woman is discovered in the presumably deserted house and Mr. Gryce is sent to investigate, Miss Butterworth discovers her own undeveloped talents for detection. At first Mr. Gryce does not take her seriously, beyond recognizing her superior knowledge in matters of hatpins, bonnets, pincushions, and petticoats, but he soon comes to respect her keen mind and practical good sense. The sparring between them is handled with the deftness of high comedy, as Amelia, who narrates the novel, describes her own persistence in tracking down clues despite Mr. Gryce's gentle hints that she withdraw into ladylike seclusion. In the end, Gryce, with characteristic modesty, admits that he has been mistaken and that Amelia was on the right track. When she tells him of her crucial discoveries, he expresses his delight. "You have saved me from committing a folly, Miss Butterworth," he tells her. "If I had arrested Franklin Van Burnam today, and to-morrow all these facts had come to light, I should never have held up my head again."

Anticipating such famous spinster sleuths as Agatha Christie's Miss Marple and Dorothy Sayers's Miss Climpson, who sometimes assists Lord Peter Wimsey, Amelia Butterworth appears in several other novels, always in conjunction with the inimitable Mr. Gryce. The best of these, in addition to the excellent **That Affair Next Door**, are **Lost Man's Lane** (1898), and **The Circular Study** (1900). In the latter story, incidentally, Green shows a fondness for gadgetry worthy of James Bond, depicting the study as a circular room containing colored electric light signals and a steel door which closes at the touch of a button and cannot be reopened.

Not content with one female detective, Anna Green introduced another in the character of Violet Strange, in **The Golden Slipper** (1915). A young and charming debutante, Violet uses her access to the inner circle of wealthy New York society to solve a series of problems for which she is highly paid by a private agency. Each case is a challenge to Violet's analytical powers and a thread of mystery runs through the series as the reader wonders why this young girl with a wealthy and indulgent father is so desperate for money that she reluctantly and secretly takes the assignments of her employers. In the end, her goal is revealed. Aided by her brother, and ultimately by the man whom she freed from suspicion of murder and whom she eventually marries, Violet has accumulated enough money to rescue a beloved sister who had been disinherited. Despite some improbabilities and some touches of Gothic horror, including a secret passage to a sealed room where dead bodies are interred, the Violet Strange stories are pleasantly entertaining and contain many of the felicitous character studies which adorn Anna Green's work. Moreover, in both of her lady detectives, Green is clearly underscoring the intellectual capabilities of women in an age which was all too ready to relegate the fair sex to the drawing room and the nursery. Amelia Butterworth and Violet Strange are capable, forthright, enterprising women without simper or sentimentality, and while Green is never polemical, the accomplishments of her lady detectives speak for themselves.

Anna Green's influence on writers of mystery fiction may be more extensive than we know. Her work was widely read on both sides of the Atlantic and may well have had its effect upon the "genteel" school of detective fiction which developed rapidly in Great Britain in the early years of the twentieth century. Certainly she must have been the model for writers of the American school such as Mary Roberts Rinehart, whose work resembles that of her predecessor. Green's originality, the tightness of her plots, the attractiveness of her characters, and her astonishing consistency over a forty-five year span make her an author well worth a second look, while the old-fashioned qualities which banished her to obscurity have now, in an age of Victorian revival, taken on a patina of charm.

Cheri L. Ross   (essay date 1991)

SOURCE: "The First Feminist Detective: Anna Katharine Green's Amelia Butterworth," in *Journal of Popular Culture*, Vol. 25, No. 2, Fall, 1991, pp. 77-86.

[*In the following excerpt, Ross calls* That Affair Next Door *a feminist work, arguing that Green challenges conventional notions of female behavior through her portrayal of Amelia Butterworth.*]

Born in Brooklyn in 1846, educated at the Ripley Female Academy in Vermont, and resident of Buffalo, New York, all her adult life, Anna Katharine Green was one of the first American women to write detective fiction. She wrote thirty-five detective novels and four collections of short stories during a career that spanned forty-five years. Her phenomenally successful first novel *The Leavenworth Case* was published in 1878.

Admirers of her work included President Woodrow Wilson, who wrote in a personal letter that he was a voracious reader of detective fiction and that he had gotten "the most authentic thrill out of Anna Katharine Green's books and Gaboriau's." Her contemporary critics consistently ranked her with Poe, Gaboriau, and Sir Arthur Conan Doyle as the premier writers of nineteenth-century detective fiction. One critic, a writer of detective fiction herself, asserted that Green "is far and away the best in our home field [America]. She is entirely conversant with all the rules of detective fiction, and her long list of books stands alone on the top shelf [Carolyn Wells, *The Technique of the Mystery Story*]. Even English critics agreed with Wells' assessment; one anonymous critic believed that "Green herself has certainly as much right as any contemporary writer to claim the mantle of Gaboriau for stories the excellent technique of which should put some popular writers on this side of the Atlantic to shame." Green was known for ingenious touches that made her books interesting and inventive; she never wrote the same book twice.

By the turn of the century, the conventions of detective fiction were clearly defined. These conventions include (1) commission of a baffling crime by an unknown person; (2) a professional male detective who may need assistance in solving the crime from an amateur (also male); (3) the arrest of an innocent person; (4) use of devices such as locked rooms and red herrings; (5) a suspenseful narrative; (6) emphasis on observation and deduction; (7) a visit to the scene of the crime; (8) identification of the criminal, who is usually the least likely suspect; and (9) a credible solution based on information in the fiction itself.

In three novels published between 1897 and 1900—the Amelia Butterworth novels—Green performed subversive activities by undercutting both the conventions of her chosen genre and the assumptions of society to propound a powerful feminist message. In this essay, I will discuss the first of these works, *That Affair Next Door*.

With the publication of *That Affair Next Door*, Green utilized all the conventions she had helped establish in her work since *The Leavenworth Case* (1878), added surprising plot twists, and also extended the boundaries of the genre by transforming the convention of the amateur detective. According to T. J. Binyon [in his *'Murder Will Out': The Detective in Fiction*], such a character—particularly a series amateur—"has no authority to question suspects, no technical knowledge or resources, and is usually impelled by nothing more than insatiable curiosity." Consequently, this character "must establish a close, unlikely relationship with the official investigator as to be privy to all the latter's discoveries." Invariably, the amateur detective was male, until Green created a female one—Miss Amelia Butterworth, thus adding a new dimension to the detective novel while challenging the assumptions of society. Miss Butterworth, fiftyish, upper-middle class, and most respectable, is the first woman detective in American literature to challenge the accepted role of women. To be sure, other women detectives preceded Miss Butterworth, but they were creations of male authors, and by the end of the novels, these women not only find detective work unsuitable for a woman but also are married off by their creators. Totally unlike the previous women detectives, Miss Butterworth is, instead, a precursor of Agatha Christie's Miss Jane Marple, probably the best known example of the amateur unmarried woman detective.

Early in the novel, Miss Butterworth announces her sense of self-worth: she has changed her name from "Araminta" she says, because she is a "sensible woman and not the piece of antiquated sentimentality" suggested by her given name. Dignity, intelligence, and inquisitiveness mark the strength of her self-image. Her inquisitiveness, especially, is presented as an important virtue, though it is marked by irony. She describes herself in the first sentence of the novel with these words: "I am not an inquisitive woman. . . ." She belies her words immediately by arising from her bed to peer out her window in the middle of the night because she has heard the sound of a carriage, and she sees a young man and woman enter the vacant Van Burnam mansion. Again in the second sentence she stresses that "not being inquisitive," she "misses much that would be both interesting and profitable to know." No sooner does she get back to bed than she hears a door open; although she "had to rush for it," she manages to get a glimpse of the young man leaving the mansion alone. The irony is exquisite; clearly, Miss Butterworth does not miss much. As Hanna Charney has observed in discussing the character of Dorothy L. Sayers' Peter Wimsy, "Lord Peter is mocking and mocked—all good detectives tend to be. There is a consistent irony in their presentation" [*The Detective Novel of Manners: Hedonism, Morality, and the Life of Reason*].

The discrepancy between Miss Butterworth's actions and her description of herself seems to include her behavior as a stereotypical "nosy old maid." She asks question after question, and in general "proves to be a thorn in the sides of everyone connected" with the murder. The astute reader, however, soon learns that Miss Butterworth's character goes far beyond this negative stereotype: her inquisitiveness and curiosity are instrumental in bringing the true criminal to justice.

In fact, the strange nocturnal events demonstrate her curiosity, courage, and capacity for leadership. When her curiosity about the young woman next door causes her to summon a policeman early the next morning, she reveals herself as a strong, intelligent woman. The reluctant policeman unlocks the door and, accompanied by a chambermaid and Miss Butterworth, discovers the body, a woman. Only the arms and skirts of the dead woman are visible; otherwise she is obscured by a heavy cabinet and broken crockery that seem to have fallen on her. The chambermaid faints, but Miss Butterworth remains steadfast, knowing that if she is to command respect as a woman, she must maintain her composure: "I felt a sensation of sickness which in another moment might have ended in my fainting also, if I had not realized that it would never do for me to lose my wits in the presence of a man who had none too many of his own."

Her resolve allows her to take charge after the chamber-maid falls into a dead faint and the police officer merely bumbles about. She orders the officer to fetch water with which to revive the maid and instructs him to summon help while she stays with the body. Of course, this arouses the officer's suspicions; clearly, he is unused to women of Miss Butterworth's fortitude. Therefore, he reverts to a standard male role, telling *her* to get the water and call out the window for assistance. Although she finds the officer's attitude foolish, she bows to expediency: "Smiling at a caution so very ill-timed, but abiding by my invariable rule of never arguing with a man unless I see some way of getting the better of him, I did what he bade me. . . ." When the maid revives, she is distraught because the cabinet still rests on the victim. Typically, Miss Butterworth demonstrates both strength of character and diplomacy. "Not being a man, and not judging it wise to irritate the one representative of that sex then present," she refrains from seconding the maid's request, although she does give the maid a sympathetic nod.

To be sure, Miss Butterworth is not intimidated by this policeman, but realizing that this officer will soon be displaced by an official with much more power, she decides to say no more until the real authority in the case arrives. Soon Inspector Gryce, the hero of previous Green novels, appears at the scene. Miss Butterworth's awareness of Inspector Gryce's illustrious reputation brings out her competitive spirit. She believes she has the advantage over him because she, not Gryce, has noticed some peculiarities in the maid's behavior and remarks. Feeling as capable as he is, she seeks to match wits with him, and rather endearingly reports, ". . . for though I have had no adventures, I feel capable of them. . . ."

Her father's faith in her intelligence and ability has fed her confidence. Most fathers of that time held out high hopes for their sons—not their daughters, but evidently Mr. Butterworth was an anomaly in that respect, for he had always believed that somehow she would "live to make her mark." The title of Chapter Three, "Amelia Discovers Herself," reveals that she has finally discerned where her talents lie. She learns she is fascinated with detection, and even before leaving the Van Burnam mansion the tidily organizes her impressions by scribbling on the back of a "disputed grocer's bill" the headings "Accident, Suicide," and "Murder." The recapped evidence is both a strategic device for instructing the reader and a means of demonstrating her acute rationative powers.

The loquacious spinster is another conventional notion that Miss Butterworth overturns through her handling of a young male reporter. She tells him only what she "considered desirable for the general public to know." Her reason for talking with the reporter in the first place is two-fold: she wants to further her own knowledge of the case by developing a source ("one good turn deserves another" she remarks). Expecting that her part in the discovery of the body will likely find its way into print—the public's thirst for sensational details was evidently just as highly developed then as it is now—she hopes the reporter will present her in a favorable light. This loquacious spinster is, in fact, a shrewd and judicious diplomat.

Persistence marks her response to the effort to exclude her from the murder scene. Twice she is aware that her presence there is unwanted, but she perseveres. First, a door is nearly shut in her face; second, Silas Van Burnam, the owner of the house in which the victim is found, remarks, "What the———is she doing here?"

Her handling of Mr. Gryce similarly reveals her determination to question traditional male/female roles. As Barrie Hayne has noted [in "Anna Katharine Green," in *10 Women & Mystery,* ed. Earl F. Bargainnier], their relationship is truly "a battle of the sexes." When Mr. Gryce is available, Miss Butterworth accosts him, hoping to exchange her clues for his knowledge. Gryce is taken aback: "This aged detective is used to women, I have no doubt, but he is not used to *me.*" He is appalled by her idea of their collaboration. As Miss Butterworth remarks, "What to me seemed but the natural proposition of an energetic woman with a special genius for his particular calling, evidently struck him as audacity of the grossest kind." Miss Butterworth will not be deterred. She informs him that the victim's hat had been worn only once because only one prick of a hat pin is evident. Gryce is not unimpressed—"Women's eyes for women's matters"—but he begins to think she may be of some help to him in areas in which only a woman has specialized knowledge. He agrees with her that perhaps the murder weapon was a hat pin and invites her to look for the rest of it. Of course, the room has already been thoroughly searched. In retrospect, Miss Butterworth realizes he was only being sarcastic and "amusing himself." His attitude changes somewhat, however, when she does indeed find the rest of the hat pin: "From that moment onward, he showed . . . suitable deference." Unfortunately, Miss Butterworth has not taken Gryce's measure. It will be a long time before he, in truth, appreciates her ability.

> Anna Katharine Green contributed greatly to the advancement of women's rights by breaking the stereotypical boundaries of acceptable behavior for women in her first Amelia Butterworth novel. She made the first attempt in American literature to create a truly feminist detective.
>
> — *Cheri L. Ross*

Miss Butterworth astutely recognizes the male sense of pride that she confronts. At the inquest, Miss Butterworth is dissatisfied that she is not given the credit she deserves for her contribution, but, as she reflects, "Men are so jealous of any interference in their affairs." She is incensed, moreover, with the conduct of the all male jury. The twelve jurors have no questions even when the coroner encourages them: "A poor lot, I call them! A very poor lot! I would have found plenty of questions to put. . . ." The verdict of the inquest is murder by a person or persons unknown, but shortly afterward, the police arrest Howard

Van Burnam, the younger son of the wealthy family next door, for the death of his wife Louise, who is indeed the victim. Miss Butterworth has already threatened to enter the investigation actively if Howard is arrested because she is convinced that he is innocent. Not excluding intuition, but basing her conclusion principally on logic, she ponders: (1) why would he choose to murder his own wife in his father's house (of all places)?; and (2) if the crime were not premeditated, why use a delicate hat pin; why not just apply brute force in the heat of anger? The inspector denigrates her reasoning even though she has provided important help thus far. Taking his attitude as a personal challenge, she responds, "If I meddle in this matter at all it will not be as your coadjutor, but as your rival." Gryce is both amused and condescending.

Miss Butterworth firmly intends to make Inspector Gryce her rival and compel him to acknowledge her as his equal. Consequently, she exercises all her cunning in her dealings with the police. Thinking Gryce may have put her under surveillance, she takes a convoluted path to interview the chambermaid, Mrs. Boppert, who, she believes, possesses information the police have overlooked. Her suspicion is soon confirmed. After bribing a shopkeeper to lure Mrs. Boppert to a clandestine meeting, she finds out that Mrs. Boppert had admitted another woman, dressed differently from the victim, earlier on the day of the murder. Therefore, there were two women in the "vacant" mansion at the time the crime was committed.

Through Miss Butterworth's persistence and intelligence the other woman's identity is established. For a short while, both Miss Butterworth and Mr. Gryce are convinced of Howard's innocence, but both have alternate candidates for the role of murderer. Miss Butterworth thinks "the other woman" committed the crime, whereas Gryce believes Franklin Van Burnam, Howard's elder brother, is the murderer because Louise tried to blackmail him. Taking the initiative, Miss Butterworth writes to the Van Burnams' landlady to request a photograph of Louise. Then, she realizes the importance of locating the clothes she believed the murderess to be wearing, so she places an advertisement in the newspaper describing them and offering a reward for information. Not content, however, with counting on others to produce results by answering the advertisement, Miss Butterworth takes direct action. Accompanied by her maid, Lena, she retraces the path believed taken by the murderess at exactly the same time—midnight—hoping to discover what has become of the bundle of clothes. She finds the discarded clothes in a Chinese laundry, and they are marked with the initials "O. R."

By this time she is less inclined to be self-effacing. When she receives a reply to her advertisement which was forwarded to her by her attorney, Mr. Alvord, she is not pleased by Alvord's paternalistic attitude:

> Our interview was not an agreeable one. Mr. Alvord is a clever man and an adroit one, or I should not persist in employing him as my lawyer; but he never understood *me*. At this time, and with this letter in his hand, he understood me less than ever, which naturally called out my

powers of self assertion and led to some lively conversation between us.

When Mr. Alvord asks what this letter means, Miss Butterworth puts him in his place. " 'It means,' I retorted with some spirit, for simple dignity was thrown away on this man, 'that I made a mistake in choosing your office as medium for my business correspondence.' "

Miss Butterworth is adamant that she can solve the case without reliance on or intervention by men. Consequently, the next day she and Lena visit the landlady using the ruse that they are searching for one of Lena's relatives, but of course, they are trying to trace the alleged murderess. They learn that she has taken a position as a companion to Ella Althorpe, a very wealthy young friend of Miss Butterworth, who is engaged to marry Randolph Stone, a relative newcomer to New York society. When Miss Butterworth warns Miss Althorpe that her new companion may be involved in something unsavory, Miss Althorpe wants to consult with her fiancé. This idea is vetoed, because Miss Butterworth knows how quickly patriarchal society would unfairly transfer the credit to a man, if one appeared even tangentially to have had a part in the solution. "The work upon which I was engaged could not be shared by one of the male sex without lessening my triumph over Mr. Gryce." Miss Butterworth fully expects to arrive at the solution before Mr. Gryce does; if she can solve it without the help of any male, Mr. Gryce will have to admit her talents.

It is, however, the other woman, Olive Randolph (a.k.a. Ruth Oliver), who eventually identifies the murderer in a melodramatic conclusion categorized by Patricia Craig and Mary Cadogan [in their *The Lady Investigates: Women Detectives and Spies in Fiction*] as the "significant rendezvous" which is "a rudimentary form of the climactic gathering of later detective fiction when the murderer's identity is disclosed." Mr. Gryce has arrested Franklin Van Burnam on the basis of the "blackmail" theory. His theory is just as incorrect as Miss Butterworth's "murderess" theory. Olive tells Mr. Gryce, "Two weeks from tonight as the clock strikes eight. Be wherever I may chance to be at that hour, and see on whose arm I lay my hand." At the appointed time, Olive, dressed in a wedding grown, follows Miss Althorpe down the aisle and asks,

> 'Does he not recognize the only woman with whom he dare face God and man at the altar? Because I am already his wedded wife, and have been so for five long years . . . ' Randolph replies, 'The woman I once called wife is dead . . . ' 'Dead, Olive Randolph? Murderer!' she exclaimed. 'The blow struck in the dark found another victim!' And pulling the veil from her face Olive Randolph advanced to his side and laid her trembling hand with a firm and decisive movement on his arm.

Randolph Stone collapses, and then a complete explanation follows which ties up all loose ends for both characters and readers.

By the end of the novel, Miss Butterworth has not only proved to be Gryce's equal; she has also shown him up. She revels in her success, "I admired him and I was sorry for him, but I never enjoyed myself so much in my whole life." Gryce finally admits that she "is a woman of genius," and according to Miss Butterworth's sources, "he has never been the same since the clearing up of this mystery."

Anna Katharine Green contributed greatly to the advancement of women's rights by breaking the stereotypical boundaries of acceptable behavior for women in her first Amelia Butterworth novel. She made the first attempt in American literature to create a truly feminist detective. In *That Affair Next Door,* Anna Katharine Green sent a strong feminist message about women's possible roles in society. To put it in its simplest form: Intelligent, independent women can succeed at anything, even the most "unsuitable" profession for a woman.

FURTHER READING

Criticism

Green, Anna Katharine. "Why Human Beings Are Interested in Crime." *The American Magazine* LXXXVII, No. 2 (February 1919): 39, 82, 84, 86.

Essay in which Green discusses why people are interested in crime, what types of crimes and what aspects of crime are found most fascinating, and what motivates criminal behavior.

Maida, Patricia D. *Mother of Detective Fiction: The Life and Works of Anna Katharine Green.* Bowling Green, Ohio: Bowling Green University Popular Press, 1989, 120 p.

Scholarly examination of Green's life and writings.

Rosa Luxemburg

1871-1919

(Also wrote under the pseudonym Junius) Polish-born German political activist and journalist.

INTRODUCTION

Luxemburg was a leader of the socialist movement in Europe in the late-nineteenth and early twentieth centuries. In her writings she articulated political viewpoints based on the economic theories central to social thought. Her best known work, *Die Akkumulation des Kapitals, oder Was die Epigonen aus der Marxschen Theorie gemacht haben: Eine Antikritik (The Accumulation of Capital)*, while often questioned for the soundness of its reasoning on economic issues, is nonetheless applauded for confronting such subjects as ethnicity, the expansion of capitalist nations into underdeveloped countries, and the effects of military spending.

Biographical Information

Luxemburg was born into an affluent and well-educated family in Zamosc, Poland, then a part of Russia. She attended secondary school in Warsaw and distinguished herself in her academic studies. She also began to develop a reputation as an independently minded young woman who questioned authority and involved herself in political causes of the day. When she was nineteen Luxemburg left Poland and settled in Switzerland in order to avoid being arrested for her part in anti-czarist activities. At the University of Zürich she earned two doctoral degrees, one in law and the other in philosophy. Her dissertation on the economic history of Poland was published and became a valuable resource for scholars in modern Europe studies. An important element of this work focused on what Luxemburg viewed as the economic threat faced by Poland if it attempted to sever all economic ties with Russia in the name of political self-determination. In 1898 Luxemburg moved to Germany, where she became active in the German Communist party and apprenticed to Karl Kautsky, the founder and editor of the socialist newspaper *Neue Zeit*. Luxemburg wrote a series of newspaper articles and pamphlets and taught economics at a school operated under the authority of the German Communist party. Her writings, often published anonymously or pseudonymously, resulted in both communication and ideological conflict with leading figures in the international communist movement, including Leon Trotsky and V. I. Lenin. Specifically, Luxemburg differed with Lenin in her advocacy of socialism as a political ideal that superseded the integrity and autonomy of individual nations.

On the eve of World War I, Luxemburg and several others organized a communist faction called the Spartacans. The group opposed the war because they perceived it as an attempt on the part of capitalist governments to distract the proletariat from the burdens of capitalism. The Spartacans also condemned parliamentary activities on the part of socialists, as opposed to more radical means of reform, as a surrender to the status quo. Luxemburg was jailed after a failed coup attempt against the German government, although it had been staged by others against her wishes. During this time she wrote her Junius pamphlet, in which she warned that Lenin's nascent Soviet government could easily become dictatorial. In 1919 Luxemburg was assassinated by Prussian soldiers during a period of martial law imposed to suppress rioting by German workers, who had been inspired to violence by the Bolshevik Revolution in Russia.

Major Works

Luxemburg's major work, *The Accumulation of Capital*, developed out of her lectures as a teacher of political economy and economic history. Central to the thesis of this work was a concern with political imperialism, which Luxemburg viewed as having its source in Western industrialism and capitalist economics. Luxemburg argued that it was the nature of capitalist societies to expand their enterprises into less developed areas of the world and that the survival of capitalism depended upon this expansion. While the ideas advanced in *The Accumulation of Capital* were for the most part rejected or ignored by many of the leading figures of the European socialist movement, and continue to be criticized as ill-founded or poorly conceived, Luxemburg remains one of the consummate examples of a brilliant polemicist and political activist whose life was the foremost expression of her convictions.

PRINCIPAL WORKS

Die industrielle Entwicklung Polens [*The Industrial Development of Poland*] (dissertation) 1898

Sozialreform oder Revolution; Mit einem Anhang: Miliz und Militarismus [*Reform or Revolution*] (pamphlet) 1899

"Organisationsfragen der russischen Sozialdemokraten" ["Organizational Questions of the Russian Social Democracy"] (essay) 1904

Massenstreik, Partei und Gewerkschaften [*The Mass Strike, the Political Party, and the Trade Unions*] (essay) 1906

Die Akkumulation des Kapitals: Ein Beitrag zur ökonomischen Erklärung des Imperialismus (nonfiction) 1913

Juniusbroschure [*The Junius Pamphlet*] (pamphlet) 1916

Die Krise der Sozialdemokratie [*The Crisis in the German Social Democracy*] (pamphlet) 1918

Die Akkumulation des Kapitals, oder Was die Epigonen aus der Marxschen Theorie gemacht haben: Eine Antikritik [*The Accumulation of Capital*] (nonfiction) 1921

Die russische Revolution: Eine kritische Würdigung [*The Russian Revolution*] (pamphlet) 1922

Gesammelte Werke. 3 vols. [*Collected Works of Rosa Luxemburg*] (nonfiction) 1923-1928

Einfuhrung in die Nationalokonomie (lectures) 1925

Rosa Luxemburg (speeches) 1928

Leninism or Marxism? The Russian Revolution (essays) 1961

Politische Schriften (nonfiction) 1966-68

Rosa Luxemburg Speaks (speeches) 1970

The Letters of Rosa Luxemburg (letters) 1978

CRITICISM

Paul Frolich   (essay date 1948)

SOURCE: A preface to *Rosa Luxemburg: Her Life and Work,* translated by Johanna Hoornweg, Monthly Review Press, 1972, pp. xiii-xx.

[*In the following essay, Frolich explains how and why he collected material for his survey of Luxemburg's life and work.*]

The first edition of [*Rosa Luxemburg: Her Life and Work*] was published in Paris at the end of August 1939, a few days before the outbreak of the Second World War. The book is a child of the German Emigration and bears the marks of its origins. The author left Germany at the beginning of 1934 after his release from a concentration camp. At the time he thought that the material which he had been gathering for many years to prepare for the **Collected Works (Gesammelte Werke) of Rosa Luxemburg** was in safe hands. Somehow, however, it got lost or fell into hands which would not let go of it. Among these papers were manuscripts and letters of Rosa Luxemburg; almost all of her works published in German, Polish and French; Volume v of the **Gesammelte Werke,** already typeset and ready to be printed, which contained her writings on imperialist politics; political and private letters to Rosa; a number of notes and many other items. Outside Germany only a part of the losses could be made good, and it became necessary to do without many papers which would have been useful in describing background details and personalities.

Despite these unfavourable circumstances, however, the book had to be written. Rosa Luxemburg's name has become a symbol in the international working-class movement. Yet little is known of her work today, and even those who are generally well-versed in socialist literature are acquainted with mere fragments of her writings. The publishing of her literary remains ran into frequent obstacles and—because of the factional fighting within the Communist International—into determined (even if never

openly admitted) opposition. It could therefore not be completed. Thus whole areas of her work, a knowledge of which would have been of great significance in assessing her views, were forgotten. In the disputes of the various parties and tendencies in the working-class movement many teachings of the master were misconstrued, and many maliciously distorted. It seemed that if any socialist literature could be salvaged and brought out of hiding in a post-Nazi period, it would prove to be only rubble. There was a danger that only a faded memory or a deceptive legend of Rosa Luxemburg's historical achievements would be left.

The biographical works published about her either served a limited purpose, such as the one by Luise Kautsky, or they disregarded essential sectors of Rosa's life-work, such as the one by Henriette Roland-Holst. Both authors were very close to Rosa, and depicted her personality with much warmth and understanding. However, because both of them after all advocated views decidedly different from Rosa's, they could not succeed in presenting her ideas correctly and in doing justice to her political work.

One person would have been eminently qualified to revive Rosa Luxemburg's life and work: Clara Zetkin. The two of them had worked together for decades. Each was a strong person in the light of her own development and worth. They came from different backgrounds and each was influenced by other experiences. Nevertheless, in the intellectual disputes and political battles they had arrived at the same views and decisions. Of the leading socialists who survived Rosa, no one knew Luxemburg, the person and the fighter, better than Clara Zetkin; no one was more familiar with the battlefield, the historical circumstances, and with the identity of friend and foe in the skirmishes. Moreover, she knew the specific motives behind many of the decisions, motives which would have remained hidden to a researcher forced to make a judgment based on documents alone. What a biography of Rosa by Clara Zetkin would have provided can be surmised from the essays and pamphlets she wrote to commemorate her friend. Until her death on 20 June 1933, however, Clara Zetkin devoted herself completely to the tasks of the daily struggle, and declared again and again that she was thereby fulfilling the obligation she felt for her fallen comrade-in-arms.

The victory of fascism in Germany and the resulting effort to analyse the causes of the severe defeat of the proletariat led not only German socialists to make a more thorough study of the teachings of Rosa Luxemburg. Indeed, one could speak of a Luxemburg-Renaissance in the international working-class movement. The more the interest in her work grew, the deeper the gaps in the available material were felt to be. However, it was evident that it would not suffice merely to republish the lost writings insofar as they were at all accessible. The attempt now had to be made to provide an overall presentation of her ideas and actions using her own views as a starting-point. To define and work out as clearly as possible the ideas of Rosa Luxemburg was the chief task which the author set for himself. He therefore had carefully to consider his presentation and to let Rosa herself speak whenever the opportunity arose, even if the narrative flow might suffer from the break. He was thereby hoping to serve those readers whom he kept constantly in mind while working on the book—active socialists interested in theoretical and tactical problems.

That the book could be written at all was due above all to the efforts of the distinguished publisher and tireless defender of the deprived and the downtrodden, Victor Gollancz. It was his publishing company which, in the spring of 1940, brought out the English edition of the book in Edward Fitzgerald's excellent translation. It had an astonishing success in wartime England.

The book puts the reader back into a time that is past. In the three decades since Rosa Luxemburg's death the world has undergone cruel changes. Those January days of 1919 when the German Revolution was dealt a decisive blow marked, in fact, the end of an epoch of the working-class movement, a period which had begun with the repeal of the Anti-Socialist Laws and had been characterised by an almost uninterrupted socialist advance. Even in times of serious internal upheaval, such as the years of the First World War, this advance had continued, for, as the new experiences and problems were worked out intellectually, new heights of knowledge and insight were reached, and new moral strengths acquired in the more bitter struggles. Since then the conditions under which socialists have had to work have become increasingly more complicated and more difficult. It is true that working-class organisations everywhere grew impressively in size and that significant successes were obtained in individual struggles. However, the working-class movement remained divided by a deep rift; it became crippled by violent internal struggles, and its fighting morale weakened. The general development went from failure to defeat, finally ending in the terrible catastrophe for the whole proletariat brought on by German fascism. In this period of decline the old comrades-in-arms of Rosa Luxemburg felt more and more keenly how sorely the movement lacked her advice, her leadership, and her example. Today anyone trying to assess the difficulties facing the working class in all countries and particularly in Germany, and to grasp the dangers currently confronting all of mankind, becomes aware of the need of our times for a person with Rosa Luxemburg's clarity and boldness.

An attempt should be made to investigate how, under the cataclysmically changed conditions of today, Rosa Luxemburg's ideas, and particularly her tactical teachings, might be used in a fruitful way. However, this is not possible in a preface, even in bare outline form. The first prerequisite for such an undertaking would be a thorough analysis of all the characteristic social and political phenomena of our times. But it should be emphasised that Rosa Luxemburg never looked upon the results of her theoretical work as ultimate truths or as tactical models to be pressed to fit changed conditions. In a speech delivered to trade-union members in Hagen (October 1910) she herself said:

> The modern proletarian class does not conduct its struggle according to a schema laid down in a book or in a theory. The modern workers' struggle is a fragment of history, a fragment of social development. And it is in the midst of his-

tory, in the midst of struggle, that we learn how we must fight. . . . The first commandment of a political fighter is to go with the development of the times and to account always for any changes in the world as well as for any changes in our fighting strategy.

For her there was no dogma or authority which commanded blind obedience. Even the mere thought that her own ideas should not be subject to criticism would have taken her aback and roused her indignation. Ever alert and critical thinking was for her the lifeblood of the socialist movement, the first prerequisite for common action. Without constant and conscientious examination of the teachings which were handed down, without thorough analysis of the facts, without recognition of the new tendencies of development, it would be impossible for the movement to keep abreast of history and to master the tasks of the present. And, it should be added—because many years of experience have shown its importance—Rosa was well aware of the unavoidability of compromises in both organisational life and practical politics if unanimity in action towards a common aim was to be achieved. Where knowledge and recognition of the facts were concerned, however, she knew no compromise, and especially no submission to alien will. To stand up for her convictions to the bitter end was a moral principle, something she deemed a matter of course for any socialist; behind this was her unbroken urge to get to the bottom of things.

In her work there are enough scientific observations and tactical principles which stand up to every test, as well as conclusions which were not only valid in the particular circumstances of her time but could also stimulate and guide us in the solution of present-day problems. There remain, of course, those views of Rosa which are still the object of intellectual controversy. However, to make a critical evaluation of every word of the master would be to acquire her legacy, to take possession of it.

After the experience of the last decades objections were raised to certain of Rosa Luxemburg's ideas even by Marxists. It is necessary to make a more exact sketch of Rosa's standpoint in these questions and to test its justification. Marxist teaching culminates in the assertion that, in capitalism, production assumes a progressively social character, although private property remains linked to the means of production. Capitalist society must, according to this theory, inevitably perish because of this and other contradictions, i.e. because of the effects of its own laws of development. Rosa Luxemburg was deeply convinced of this historical necessity, and expressed this view in many of her works. Her chief work, ***The Accumulation of Capital,*** was concerned with proving that the decay of the capitalist social order was inevitable. Her conviction has been confirmed by history, for all the things we have been experiencing in the last several decades—this whirlpool of crises, wars, revolutions, and counter-revolutions, with all their frightful effects—are the convulsions of a disintegrating society. Here contradictions are operating which have always been at work in capitalist society, but they have now gelled into an explosive mixture of such force and of such proportions that it seems as if the whole world were being ravaged by a continuous series of earthquakes.

Marxists, including Rosa Luxemburg, have assumed that this process of decay would lead directly to socialism, for the development of the contradictions of capitalism would be accompanied, of course, by the growth of the chief contradiction, the one between the bourgeoisie and the proletariat. As Marx put it, 'As the mass of misery, oppression, servitude, degeneration, and exploitation grows, so, too, does the indignation of the ever swelling working class, trained, united and organised by the mechanism of the capitalist production-process itself'. The fact of the matter was that in the epoch when the capitalist economic mode was developing and bringing the techniques of production to an ever higher level, the working-class movement also grew in size and strength. The generation to which Rosa Luxemburg belonged observed that this process was happening consistently, almost as if it were following certain laws. For this reason Rosa Luxemburg did not doubt that in the coming catastrophes the working class would have the will and the drive to fulfil its historic task.

During the First World War, however, when she experienced the collapse of the International and the crossing of the socialist parties into the imperialist camp, when the working masses were making one sacrifice after the other for the capitalist order, and the German proletarians in uniform were letting themselves be misused even against the Russian Revolution, Rosa repeated the warning more and more loudly: the catastrophes into which capitalist society will be plunged do not by themselves offer the certainty that capitalism will be superseded by socialism. If the working class itself does not find the strength for its own liberation, then the whole of society, including the working class, could be consumed in internecine struggles. Mankind now stands before the alternatives: either socialism or descent into barbarism! And she maintained this either-or view when the Central Powers collapsed and the revolution in Central Europe was making more powerful progress every day. In the *Spartakus* programme she wrote: 'Either the continuation of capitalism, new wars and a very early decline into chaos and anarchy, or the abolition of capitalist exploitation.'

The self-assertion of the Russian Revolution and the long-drawn-out revolutionary tremblings in Europe and in the colonial countries provided new nourishment for the optimism of the most active cadres of the socialist movement. Even if the path of development had to go through violent struggles with occasional reverses, it seemed to be leading inexorably to a socialist transformation of society. Although Rosa Luxemburg's warning of the dangers of sinking into barbarism was often repeated in both speeches and writings, its whole earnestness was not grasped. People had no idea what sinking into barbarism could mean at all—not until the victory of Hitler and his barbarians showed with brutally clear force that Rosa Luxemburg's warning cry had been no mere rhetorical phrase. The destruction of the working-class movement, the atomisation of the different social strata, the book-burnings, the strangulation of intellectual life, the horrors of the concentration camps, the extermination of whole sectors of the population, the total control of society by the state apparatus,

and total war with its inevitable total defeat and terrible consequences—all this was the reality of barbarism.

The socialist working-class movement which had developed so powerfully alongside the capitalist mode of production was drawn into the catastrophe because it was incapable of halting its onset. The overturning of the socialist hopes of the broad masses was perhaps the most dangerous feature of the descent into barbarism. The course of events in Russia, whose revolution would at one time have lent new strength to these hopes, now had an especially shattering effect on the international socialist movement. The stunting of democratic organs in Russia, the control of the people by an almighty bureaucracy, the murder of Lenin's comrades-in-arms, and finally the pact with Hitler, left any remaining faith in the socialist politics of the Russian state only to those who were prepared to sacrifice all their critical faculties. Thus new problems arose for those who clung unswervingly to the aims of socialism. Discussions dealt no longer with the means and ways of achieving socialism, but with the question of whether or not the development towards socialism was at all secure. What is historical necessity? This now became the burning political question.

According to the Marxist analysis of capitalism, the ever greater socialisation of the production process, the growth of cartels and trusts, the development in the direction of state capitalism is historically necessary. This, however, means the formation of the prerequisites for a socialist organisation of the economy. Historical necessity is the dissolution of the capitalist social order in violent economic and political crises in which the class struggle is intensified and the working class obtains the possibility of gaining political power and bringing about socialism. The relative strength of the proletariat in the class struggles is to a great extent historically conditioned. In recent decades certain phenomena have had a disastrous effect on this strength, for example, the strong differentiation within the working class, its political split into different parties, the wearing down of the petit-bourgeoisie by the Great Depression and its swing to fascism, the ruthless use of state power in the class struggle, and finally the general effects of the whole complex of world-political conflicts with its confusing abundance of contradictory phenomena.

The intervention of a class and of its different strata and organisations in the historical process is not only the fruit of knowledge and will. It is heavily conditioned by social and political factors affecting the class from outside. However, classes and parties are themselves factors in the multifarious assortment of forces. Their commissions and omissions react continuously on the conditions under which they themselves have to fight. The knowledge and will of individuals, of the organisations and thereby of the class itself are of weighty significance in this process; they are decisive for the final victory when other conditions have also ripened, and they are decisive for the course taken by history at its turning points. This is part and parcel of the Marxist concept of history, which becomes bowdlerised if viewed as fatalism. Rosa Luxemburg often explained the relation between objective facts and tendencies of development on the one hand and the conscious action of men on the other, as, for example, in the compact sentences of her *Juniusbroschüre:*

> (The) victory of the socialist proletariat . . . is tied to the iron laws of history, to the thousand rungs of the previous tortured and all too slow development. But it can never be brought about unless the igniting spark of the conscious will of the great mass of the people springs up out of all the elements of the material prerequisites collected from this development.

This conscious will arises from a long process of experience, of training and struggle, a development of knowledge and morale. Here the teachings and the example of Rosa Luxemburg should and could be made fruitful. It is not given to everyone to recognise, with her scientific insight and visionary power, the great historic tendencies at work amid the chance phenomena of the day. However, everyone can, as she did, fearlessly and without shirking the consequences, look reality in the eye and strive to recognise the essential features in the events of the day, and thereby find the road that needs to be taken. One would always have to examine one's own views again and again in order to gain the confidence and the strength to stand up for one's own convictions. For Rosa Luxemburg loyalty to oneself was the natural prerequisite for loyalty to the cause of the oppressed. Her whole life bears witness to this.

But what did socialism mean to her? This question is being asked in a period when political concepts have become ambiguous and many have been used deliberately to deceive people. Again and again Rosa Luxemburg emphasised that the strategic aim of the working-class struggle, the aim which was supposed to determine all tactical measures, was the conquest of political power. This is the aim of struggle in class society. But it is only the method of transferring all the means of production into the hands of the general public and of organising production in a socialist way. But even this latter step is only the means to an end. The goal of socialism is man, i.e. a society without class differences in which men working in community, without tutelage, forge their own fate. It is—in Marx's words—'an association where the free development of each individual is the condition for the free development of all.' It is not socialism if the means of production are socialised and set into motion according to a plan, but a class or a social stratum autocratically controls the means of production, regiments and oppresses the working masses, and deprives them of their rights. No socialism can be realised in a country where the state power breaks in and gets rid of the old ruling classes and property relations but at the same time subjects the whole nation to a ruthless dictatorship which prevents the working class from being conscious of its particular role and tasks and acting accordingly. As Rosa Luxemburg expressed it in the *Spartakus* programme: 'The essence of socialist society is in the fact that the great working mass ceases to be a ruled mass, and that it itself lives and directs the whole of political and economic life in free and conscious self-determination.' Socialism is democracy completed, the free unfolding of the individual personality through working together with all for the well-being of all. Wherever state power still has to be applied to suppress the working masses, the socialist struggle has not yet achieved its aim.

The historical process has become more confusing and more cruel than the experiences of earlier times would have led one to expect. Never have the conditions of living and struggle of the German working class been so severe as they are at present, and there is no magic way of avoiding all the convulsions resulting from the greatest social crisis of mankind. However, the socialist movement can shorten the period of decline and of internecine warfare and can direct the course of history to new heights. Rosa Luxemburg's legacy will help the movement to gain the strength, self-confidence, and courage for this task.

F. L. Carsten   (essay date 1962)

SOURCE: "Freedom and Revolution: Rosa Luxemburg," in *Revisionism: Essays on the History of Marxist Ideas,* edited by Leopold Labedz, Frederick A. Praeger, 1962, pp. 55-66.

[*Carsten is a German-born historian. In the following essay, he discusses Luxemburg's pamphlets in relation to the ideals of the German Social-Democratic party.*]

Among the rather unimaginative and pedestrian leaders of the German Social-Democratic Party of the early twentieth century—who were occupied with the task of achieving better living conditions for the workers and passing high-sounding resolutions against the evils of bourgeois society (which did not oblige anybody to take any action)—one was entirely different: a fiery woman of Jewish-Polish origin, small and slender, slightly lame from a childhood disease, an orator who could sway the masses, a professional revolutionary who seemed to belong to the Russian world from which she came rather than to modern Germany. Rosa Luxemburg was born on March 5, 1871, in the small Polish town of Zamosc near Lublin into a fairly prosperous Jewish middle-class family. Her span of life coincided almost exactly with that of the German Empire which Bismarck had founded at Versailles a few weeks before her birth; its collapse in November 1918 she outlived only by some weeks. Her family sympathized with the aspirations of the Polish national movement, and at the age of sixteen Rosa Luxemburg joined an underground revolutionary socialist group called *Proletariat* and participated in its clandestine activities among the workers of Warsaw. In 1889, when threatened with arrest and imprisonment, she was smuggled out of Poland by her comrades and went to Zürich, the centre of the Russian and Polish political émigrés. There she studied at the university and took part in the intense political and intellectual life of her fellow Socialists, in the heated discussion where the battles of the coming Russian revolution were fought out in advance.

Her political activities remained intimately connected with Poland. She was a co-founder of the Social-Democratic Party of the Kingdom of Poland and Lithuania in 1894 and a chief contributor to its paper published in Paris. She was opposed to the slogan of independence for Poland, which was advocated by another Polish Socialist party, the PPS; instead she advocated the overthrow of the Tsarist autocracy in alliance with the Russian working class as the primary task of the Polish revolutionary movement. She aimed at the establishment of a Russian democratic republic within which Poland would merely enjoy cultural autonomy. To Poland she returned during the revolution of 1905 to participate in the revolutionary struggle. There her party had become a mass party which issued papers and leaflets in several languages, organized trade unions and strikes, and co-operated closely with the Russian Social-Democratic Workers' Party. After a few months of great political activity, however, Rosa Luxemburg and her lifelong friend Leo Jogiches were arrested. She was kept in prison for four months, but was then released on account of her German nationality (she had contracted a *pro forma* marriage with a German comrade so as not to be hampered in her political work) and expelled from Poland, never to return.

It was in Germany that she made her home at the end of the nineteenth century; there she worked together with Karl Kautsky, the editor of the theoretical weekly of the German Social-Democrats, *Die Neue Zeit,* and the propounder and popularizer of Marxist theories. In the columns of this paper and at German Party congresses she crossed swords with Eduard Bernstein who had just published his articles on 'Problems of Socialism', emphasizing the evolutionary transition from capitalism to socialism and 'revising' orthodox Marxism in a Fabian sense. In the columns of *Die Neue Zeit* Rosa Luxemburg soon crossed swords with another redoubtable figure of the international socialist movement, V. I. Lenin, on the question of the organization of Russian Social-Democracy and the powers of the central committee of the Party, which showed that she was well aware of the dangers threatening the revolutionary movement from within. There too she commented vigorously on the Russian revolution of 1905 and discovered in it a new weapon of primary importance, the political mass strike, which she attempted to transfer to Germany. Her close association with Kautsky came to an end after some years during which she learned to distrust his Marxist jargon and to doubt the readiness of the Social-Democratic leaders to accompany their revolutionary words by similar deeds.

During the years preceding the outbreak of the First World War Rosa Luxemburg became the acknowledged theoretical leader of a left wing within the German Social-Democratic Party, whose adherents claimed that they were the only true heirs of Marx's revolutionary ardour. She also published her most important theoretical work, **The Accumulation of Capital,** in which she tried to demonstrate that capitalism could expand only so long as it had at its disposal non-capitalist, colonial markets: with their progressive absorption and their conversion to capitalism through the division of the world among the imperialist powers the system was bound to reach its 'final phase':

> Imperialism is simultaneously a historical method of prolonging the existence of capitalism and the most certain means of putting an end to its existence in the shortest possible time. This does not imply that the final goal must be reached inevitably and mechanically. Yet already the ten-

dency towards this final limit of capitalist development expresses itself in forms which will make the last phase of capitalism a period of catastrophes.

She maintained in conclusion that

> the more capital, through militarism, in the world at large as well as at home, liquidates the non-capitalist strata and depresses the living conditions of all working people, the more does the daily history of capital accumulation in the world become a continuous chain of political and social catastrophes and convulsions which, together with the periodic economic catastrophes in the form of crises, will make the continuation of capital accumulation impossible . . . even before capitalism has reached the natural, self-created barriers of its economic development.

In Rosa Luxemburg's opinion capitalism was doomed and its final crisis was inevitable: a point on which she differed from Lenin, whose *Imperialism, the Highest Stage of Capitalism,* written a few years later, contained certain analogies with her analysis of imperialism but avoided any definite pronouncement on the "inevitability" of capitalist collapse.

It is not, however, on economic theories such as these that Rosa Luxemburg's fame as a socialist writer rests. This is, above all, due to her uncompromising stand against war and militarism. In February 1914 she was arrested and sentenced to twelve months imprisonment on a charge of inciting soldiers to mutiny because she had declared publicly: 'if they expect us to murder our French or other foreign brothers, then let us tell them: "No, under no circumstances!" ' At the outbreak of war in August 1914 the German Social-Democratic Party—like most other socialist parties—decided to support the fatherland and to grant the war credits demanded by the government; this decision was opposed only by a small minority in the party caucus and by not a single deputy at the decisive vote in the Reichstag on August 4th. Rosa Luxemburg from the outside hotly attacked this policy and never forgave the party's leaders for their betrayal of the ideals to which they had once subscribed:

> With August 4, 1914, official German Social-Democracy and with it the International have miserably collapsed. Everything that we have preached to the people for fifty years, that we have proclaimed as our most sacred principles, that we have propounded innumerable times in speechds, pamphlets, newspapers, and leaflets, has suddenly become empty talk. The party of the international proletarian class struggle has suddenly been transformed as by an evil spell into a national liberal party; our strong organizations, of which we have been so proud, have proved to be totally powerless; and instead of the esteemed and feared deadly enemies of bourgeois society we are now the rightly despised tools of our mortal enemies, the imperialist bourgeoisie, without a will of our own. In other countries more or less the same breakdown of socialism has occurred, and the proud old cry: 'Working men of all countries, unite!' has been

changed on the battlefields into: 'Working men of all countries, slit each other's throats!'

Never in world history has a political party become bankrupt so miserably, never has a proud ideal been betrayed so shamefully.

She explained why German Social-Democracy was able to change its policy so quickly and successfully, without encountering any major opposition inside the party:

> It was precisely the powerful organization, the much-lauded discipline of German Social-Democracy, which proved their worth in that the whole organism of four millions allowed itself to be turned round within twenty-four hours at the behest of a handful of parliamentarians and let itself be joined to a structure, the storming of which had been its lifelong aim . . . Marx, Engels, and Lassalle, Liebknecht, Bebel, and Singer educated the German working class so that Hindenburg can lead it. The better the education, the organization, the famous discipline, the building-up of trade unions and party press is in Germany than it is in France, the more effective is the war effort of German Social-Democracy in comparison with that of the French.

Soon Rosa Luxemburg and her circle of friends, intellectuals like herself, began to organize opposition to the war and to issue clandestine anti-war leaflets, signed with the pen-name of Spartacus: hence their group came to be known as *Spartakusbund* (Spartacus League). Thus they remained faithful to the resolution that had been voted for the first time by the Congress of the Socialist International at Stuttgart in 1907 at the suggestion of Rosa Luxemburg, Lenin and Martov:

> If the outbreak of war threatens, the workers and their parliamentary deputies in the countries in question are obliged to do everything to prevent the outbreak of war by suitable means. . . . If war should nevertheless break out, they are obliged to work for its speedy termination and to strive with all their might to use the economic and political crisis created by the war for the mobilization of the people and thus to hasten the overthrow of capitalist class rule.

Their underground activities soon landed most of the leaders of the Spartacus League in prison. Rosa Luxemburg was arrested in February 1915 and, with the exception of only a few months, spent the remaining years of the war in various German prisons—until she was freed by the revolution of November 1918. In prison she wrote her most eloquent denunciation of the war, in which she clearly established the responsibility of the German Imperial government because the Austrian ultimatum to Serbia had been issued with its consent, because it had assured Austria in advance of German support in case of war, and because it had given Austria 'an entirely free hand in its action against Serbia'. *The Crisis of Social-Democracy,* written under the pen-name of Junius, bitterly condemned the war and even more bitterly condemned the policy of the German Social-Democrats:

> This world war is a relapse into barbarism. The triumph of imperialism leads to the destruction of civilization—sporadically during a modern war, and finally if the period of world wars which has now started should continue without hindrance to the last sequence. We are today faced with the choice, exactly as Frederick Engels predicted forty years ago: either the triumph of imperialism and decline of all civilization, as in ancient Rome, depopulation, desolation, degeneration, one vast cemetery; or the victory of socialism, that is the conscious fight of the international working class against imperialism and its method: war. . . .

> Yes, the Social-Democrats are obliged to defend their country during a great historical crisis; and this constitutes a grave guilt on the part of the Social-Democratic Reichstag fraction, that it declared solemnly on August 4, 1914: 'We do not desert the fatherland in the hour of danger'; but it denied its own words at the same moment, for it *has* forsaken the fatherland in the hour of its greatest peril. The first duty towards the fatherland in that hour was to show it the real background of this imperialist war; to tear away the tissue of patriotic and diplomatic lies which surrounded this attack on the fatherland; to proclaim loudly and clearly that for the German people victory or defeat in this war is equally disastrous; to resist with all force the muzzling of the fatherland by the state of siege . . . finally, to oppose the imperialist war aims of the preservation of Austria and Turkey—that is of reaction in Europe and in Germany—by the old truly national programme of the patriots and democrats of 1848, the programme of Marx, Engels, and Lassalle: by the slogan of the united, great German republic. That is the banner that should have been raised, a banner that would have been truly national, truly liberal and in conformity with the best traditions of Germany, as well as of the international class policy of the working class.

Rosa Luxemburg's voice became the symbol of opposition to the war, but it remained a cry in the wilderness. Although many Germans became war-weary on account of mounting casualties and increasing hunger, the Spartacus League never mustered more than a few hundred members, and the non-revolutionary, pacifist Independent Social-Democratic Party became the mass opposition party in the later years of the war. Although the Spartacists joined this party, its leaders were men far removed from Rosa Luxemburg's revolutionary idealism, men like her old enemies Eduard Bernstein and Karl Kautsky. Even after the revolution of 1918 it was the Independent Social-Democratic Party which became the mass party of the radicalized section of the German working class; while the newly founded German Communist Party, the successor of the Spartacus League, remained a small sect.

It was in prison, too, that news reached Rosa Luxemburg first of the February and then of the October revolution in Russia; her revolutionary ideals seemed at last to have reached the realm of reality, if not in Germany then at least in Russia. And it was in prison too that she wrote what must remain the most important testimony to her independence of spirit, a trenchant criticism of Lenin's policy after the October revolution. As early as 1904, at the same time and for the same reasons as George Plekhanov, she had criticized Lenin for his advocacy of

> a ruthless centralism, the chief principles of which are on the one hand the sharp distinction and separation of the organized groups of the avowed and active revolutionaries from the surrounding, if unorganized, yet revolutionary active circles, and on the other hand the strict discipline and the direct, decisive intervention of the central authority in all activities of the local party groups. It is sufficient to remark that according to this conception the central committee is authorized to organize all local committees of the party, therefore also empowered to decide upon the personal composition of each Russian local organization, from Geneva and Liége to Tomsk and Irkutsk, to impose upon them its own local rules, to dissolve them altogether by decree and to create them anew, and thus finally to influence indirectly even the composition of the highest party organ, the party congress. Thus the central committee appears as the real active nucleus of the party and all other organizations merely as its executive tools.

Against Lenin's formula that the revolutionary Social-Democrat was nothing but 'a Jacobin who was inseparably linked with the organization of the class-conscious proletariat', Rosa Luxemburg emphasized that it was in a conspiratorial organization of the type created by Blanqui that tactics and activity were worked out in advance, according to a fixed plan, that its active members were but the executive organs of a higher will which was formed outside their sphere of action, and blindly subordinated to a central authority which possessed absolute powers. In her opinion, the conditions of Social-Democratic action were entirely different,

> not based on blind obedience, nor on the mechanical subordination of the party militants to a central authority; and it is equally out of the question to erect an absolute partition between the nucleus of the class-conscious proletariat which is already organized in firm party cadres, and the surrounding sections which are already engaged in the class struggle and are being drawn into the process of class education.

According to her, Lenin's ideas amounted to

> a mechanical transfer of the organizational principles of the Blanquist movement of conspirators into the Social-Democratic movement of the masses of the workers.

Social-Democracy was not 'linked,' with the organization of the class-conscious workers, but was the proper movement of the working class, so that Social-Democratic centralism had to be of an entirely different quality from that of Blanqui. Local organizations had to have sufficient elbow-room so that they could deploy their initiative and make use of the existing opportunities to further the struggle; while the ultra-centralism advocated by Lenin was designed to control, channel, and regiment the activity of the party.

Thus Rosa Luxemburg realized at a very early stage the dangers inherent in the Bolshevik type of organization; but this did not prevent her from co-operating with Lenin during later years and from welcoming the Russian revolution as 'the most tremendous fact of the world war.' Her criticisms of Lenin's policy after the October revolution were above all directed against his agrarian policy and against the anti-democratic, dictatorial tendencies inherent in Bolshevism. Lenin, at the time of the October revolution, had taken over the agrarian programme of a non-Marxist party, the Social Revolutionaries, which sanctioned the division of the expropriated estates of the nobility among the peasants and created a strong class of peasant proprietors. Rosa Luxemburg predicted that this policy would

> create for socialism a new and powerful class of enemies in the countryside, whose opposition will be much more dangerous and tenacious than that of the noble landlords had ever been

and that

> an enormously enlarged and strong mass of peasant proprietors will defend their newly acquired property tooth and nail against all socialist attacks. Now the question of a future socialization of agriculture, and of production in Russia in general, has become an issue and an object of a struggle between the urban workers and the peasants.

How right she was the years of Stalin's forced collectivization were to show; but she did not consider whether, in the conditions of 1917, Lenin, if he wanted to seize and to retain power, had any alternative but to sanction occupation of the land by the peasants, which was proceeding spontaneously and independently of his orders or wishes. On this point she was more orthodox than Lenin.

Far more weighty was Rosa Luxemburg's criticism of the antidemocratic policy of Lenin and Trotsky, of their suppression of free political life, of their establishment of a dictatorship not of the masses, but over the masses. She declared quite unequivocally that

> It is an obvious and indisputable fact that without a free and uncensored press, without the untrammelled activity of associations and meetings, the rule of the broad masses of the people is unthinkable.

And she prophesied correctly that

> with the suppression of political life in the whole country the vitality of the Soviets too is bound to deteriorate progressively. Without general elections, without complete freedom of the press and of meetings, without freedom of discussion, life in every public institution becomes a sham in which bureaucracy alone remains active. Nothing can escape the working of this law. Public life gradually disappears; a few dozen extremely energetic and highly idealistic party leaders direct and govern; among them in reality a dozen outstanding leaders rule, and the élite of the working class is summoned to a meeting from time to time to applaud the speeches of the leaders and to adopt unanimously resolutions

put to them; *au fond* this is the rule of a clique—a dictatorship it is true, but not the dictatorship of the proletariat, but of handful of politicians, that is a dictatorship in the bourgeois sense.

Rosa Luxemburg had not become an adherent of 'bourgeois democracy', nor was she against dictatorship. She stood on the platform on which Marx had stood in 1848; dictatorship of the broad masses of the people was to her the same as revolutionary democracy, a dictatorship against the small minority of capitalists and landlords, but not against the people:

> Dictatorship, certainly! But dictatorship means the way in which democracy is used, not its abolition; it means energetic, resolute interference with the acquired rights and economic conditions of bourgeois society, without which there can be no question of a socialist revolution. But this dictatorship must be the work of the class, and not of a small, leading minority in the name of the class; i.e. it must originate from the continuous active participation of the masses, must be directly influenced by them, must be subordinate to the control of the whole people, and must be borne by the increasing political education of the masses.

These masses must participate actively in the political life and in the shaping of the new order, 'otherwise socialism will be decreed and imposed from above by a dozen intellectuals.'

The masses, however, cannot acquire political education and experience without political freedom: it is here that Rosa Luxemburg realized the deep gulf which separated her libertarian socialism from totalitarian socialism:

> Freedom only for the supporters of the government, only for the members of one party—however numerous they may be—that is not freedom. Freedom is always freedom for the man who thinks differently.

It is proof of her political genius that she could write these words a few months after the inauguration of the Bolshevik dictatorship. The essay was not published in her lifetime, however, but only some years after her death by her pupil Paul Levi (who succeeded her in the leadership of the German Communist Party) after he had broken with Moscow.

The German revolution of November 1918 freed Rosa Luxemburg from prison. She spent the remaining few weeks of her life in feverish activity, exhorting the masses to revolutionary action, pouring scorn over the moderate Social-Democratic leaders who suddenly found themselves in power, writing numerous articles for the communist paper, *Die Rote Fahne,* which she edited together with Karl Liebknecht. In contrast with the majority of communists, she considered it necessary to participate in the elections to the German National Assembly which were to take place in January 1919; but she did so for reasons entirely at variance with those of the large mass of German socialists, who put their faith in the introduction of parliamentary democracy, and not in the continuation of violent

revolution. She wanted to use parliament as a revolutionary platform, as a means of furthering the cause of revolution:

> Now we stand in the midst of the revolution, and the National Assembly is a counter-revolutionary fortress which has been erected against the revolutionary proletariat. It is thus essential to besiege and to reduce this fortress. To mobilize the masses *against* the National Assembly and to summon them to battle, for this the elections and the platform of the National Assembly must be used.

> It is necessary to participate in the elections, not in order to pass laws together with the bourgeoisie and its mercenaries, but to chase the bourgeoisie and its partisans out of the temple, to storm the fortress of the counter-revolution and above it to hoist victoriously the flag of the proletarian revolution. To do this a majority in the National Assembly would be required? That only those believe who render homage to parliamentary cretinism, who want to decide upon revolution and socialism through parliamentary majorities. It is not the parliamentary majority *inside* which decides the fate of the National Assembly itself, but the working masses outside in the factories and in the streets. . . .

> The elections and the platform of this counter-revolutionary parliament must become a means to educate, rally and mobilize the revolutionary masses, a step in the struggle for the establishment of the proletarian dictatorship.

Although the masses of the German workers proved more than reluctant to follow the communist lead, Rosa Luxemburg never lost her faith in them. The day before she was murdered by counter-revolutionary thugs, on January 15, 1919, she wrote in her last article, which contained an appraisal of the attempted seizure of power by the extreme left in Berlin, the so-called Spartacist rising:

> The masses are the decisive element, they are the rock on which will be built the final victory of the revolution. The masses have stood the test; they have made out of this 'defeat' one link in the chain of historical defeats which constitute the pride and the power of international socialism. And this is why out of this 'defeat' victory will be born. . . . Tomorrow already the revolution will arise again in shining armour and will frighten you with her trumpet-call: I was, I am, I shall be!

The course of the German revolution was to show how unjustified her faith in the masses and her revolutionary optimism had been, and when the masses in Germany moved they moved in a direction totally different from that which she had so confidently predicted.

A few weeks before Rosa Luxemburg was murdered, the German Communist Party was founded in Berlin. In its programme, published in December 1918, Rosa Luxemburg once more gave expression to the ideas which had inspired her criticism of Lenin's policy after the October revolution, to her clear refutation of the rule of a minority over the working class and of all putschist tactics (which so tragically came to a head in the Spartacist rising of January 1919):

> The proletarian revolution requires no terror to achieve its aims, it hates and despises murder. . . . It is no desperate attempt of a minority to fashion the world according to its own ideals, but the action of the many millions of the people, which is called upon to fulfil its historical mission and to transform historical necessity into reality. . . . The Spartacus League is not a party which wants to seize power over the working class or through the working class. . . .
>
> The Spartacus League will never seize power unless it be through the clear, positive wish of the large majority of the working masses in Germany, never otherwise than on the basis of their conscious approval of the views, aims and political methods of the Spartacus League. . . . Its victory stands not at the beginning, but at the end of the revolution: it is identical with the victory of the many millions of socialist workers.

It was a tragedy, not only for itself, that the new party did not heed this advice of its founder; throughout its history it remained devoted to putschist tactics, and when it finally came to power it did so as a clique ruling over the workers and maintained in power by the bayonets of a foreign army.

In the new party programme Rosa Luxemburg also emphasized what in her opinion constituted the essential features of socialism:

> The essence of a socialist society consists in this, that the great working mass ceases to be a regimented mass, but lives and directs the whole political and economic life in conscious and free self-determination. . . .
>
> The proletarian masses must learn to become, instead of mere machines employed by the capitalists in the process of production, the thinking, free, and active directors of this process. They must acquire the sense of responsibility of active members of the community which is the sole owner of all social wealth. They must develop zeal without the employer's whip, highest productivity without capitalist drivers, discipline without a yoke, and order without regimentation. Highest idealism in the interest of the community, strictest self-discipline, a true civic spirit of the masses, these constitute the moral basis of a socialist society.

It is in ideas such as these, in her searching criticism of the conceptions of Lenin, in her emphasis on the moral and democratic basis of socialism that the lasting value of Rosa Luxemburg's thought can be found. Her theory of the inevitable collapse of capitalism, her blind faith in the masses and in revolution as such, her vast optimism as to the future of socialism have been disproved by events which she did not live to see. Yet enough remains to make her one of the outstanding exponents of modern socialist thought. It is no accident that she has been classified as a heretic in Eastern Europe and that the only recent edition of her writings omits all that is truly important among them. For Rosa Luxemburg, socialism and freedom were inseparable: those who have abolished freedom have no use for her ideas.

Hannah Arendt   (essay date 1966)

SOURCE: "Rosa Luxemburg: 1871-1919," in *Men In Dark Times,* Harcourt, Brace & Company, 1968, pp. 33-56.

[*A German-born American political philosopher and literary essayist, Arendt was one of the most important political thinkers of the twentieth century. Perceiving the political thinker as a "truth-teller" who counters the lies of politicians, Arendt sought through her writings to expand the realm of human freedom and resist tyranny. In the following essay, which originally appeared in* The New York Review of Books *in 1966, she discusses the value of J. P. Nettl's biography of Luxemburg and the reception of her writings before and after her death.*]

I

The definitive biography, English-style, is among the most admirable genres of historiography. Lengthy, thoroughly documented, heavily annotated, and generously splashed with quotations, it usually comes in two large volumes and tells more, and more vividly, about the historical period in question than all but the most outstanding history books. For unlike other biographies, history is here not treated as the inevitable background of a famous person's life span; it is rather as though the colorless light of historical time were forced through and refracted by the prism of a great character so that in the resulting spectrum a complete unity of life and world is achieved. This may be why it has become the classical genre for the lives of great statesmen but has remained rather unsuitable for those in which the main interest lies in the life story, or for the lives of artists, writers, and, generally, men or women whose genius forced them to keep the world at a certain distance and whose significance lies chiefly in their works, the artifacts they added to the world, not in the role they played in it.

It was a stroke of genius on the part of J. P. Nettl to choose the life of Rosa Luxemburg, the most unlikely candidate, as a proper subject for a genre that seems suitable only for the lives of great statesmen and other persons of the world. She certainly was nothing of the kind. Even in her own world of the European socialist movement she was a rather marginal figure, with relatively brief moments of splendor and great brilliance, whose influence in deed and written word can hardly be compared to that of her contemporaries—to Plekhanov, Trotsky, and Lenin, to Bebel and Kautsky, to Jaurès and Millerand. If success in the world is a prerequisite for success in the genre, how could Mr. Nettl succeed with this woman who when very young had been swept into the German Social Democratic Party from her native Poland; who continued to play a key role in the little-known and neglected history of Polish socialism; and who then for about two decades, although never officially recognized, became the most controversial and least understood figure in the German Left movement? For it was precisely success—success even in her own world of revolutionaries—which was withheld from Rosa

Luxemburg in life, death, and after death. Can it be that the failure of all her efforts as far as official recognition is concerned is somehow connected with the dismal failure of revolution in our century? Will history look different if seen through the prism of her life and work?

However that may be, I know no book that sheds more light on the crucial period of European socialism from the last decades of the nineteenth century to the fateful day in January 1919 when Rosa Luxemburg and Karl Liebknecht, the two leaders of the *Spartakusbund,* the precursor of the German Communist Party, were murdered in Berlin—under the eyes and probably with the connivance of the Socialist regime then in power. The murderers were members of the ultra-nationalist and officially illegal *Freikorps,* a paramilitary organization from which Hitler's storm troopers were soon to recruit their most promising killers. That the government at the time was practically in the hands of the *Freikorps* because they enjoyed "the full support of Noske," the Socialists' expert on national defense, then in charge of military affairs, was confirmed only recently by Captain Pabst, the last surviving participant in the assassination. The Bonn government—in this as in other respects only too eager to revive the more sinister traits of the Weimar Republic—let it be known that it was thanks to the *Freikorps* that Moscow had failed to incorporate all of Germany into a red Empire after the First World War and that the murder of Liebknecht and Luxemburg was entirely legal "an execution in accordance with martial law." This was considerably more than even the Weimar Republic had ever pretended, for it had never admitted publicly that the *Freikorps* actually were an arm of the government and it had "punished" the murderers by meting out a sentence of two years and two weeks to the soldier Runge for "*attempted* manslaughter" (he had hit Rosa Luxemburg over the head in the corridors of the Hotel Eden), and four months to Lieutenant Vogel (he was the officer in charge when she was shot in the head inside a car and thrown into the Landwehr Canal) for "failing to report a corpse and illegally disposing of it." During the trial, a photograph showing Runge and his comrades celebrating the assassination in the same hotel on the following day was introduced as evidence, which caused the defendant great merriment. "Accused Runge, you must behave properly. This is no laughing matter," said the presiding judge. Forty-five years later, during the Auschwitz trial in Frankfurt, a similar scene took place; the same words were spoken.

With the murder of Rosa Luxemburg and Liebknecht, the split of the European Left into Socialist and Communist parties became irrevocable; "the abyss which the Communists had pictured in theory had become . . . the abyss of the grave." And since this early crime had been aided and abetted by the government, it initiated the death dance in postwar Germany: The assassins of the extreme Right started by liquidating prominent leaders of the extreme Left—Hugo Haase and Gustav Landauer, Leo Jogiches and Eugene Leviné—and quickly moved to the center and the right-of-center—to Walther Rathenau and Matthias Erzberger, both members of the government at the time of their murder. Thus Rosa Luxemburg's death became the watershed between two eras in Germany; and it be-

came the point of no return for the German Left. All those who had drifted to the Communists out of bitter disappointment with the Socialist Party were even more disappointed with the swift moral decline and political disintegration of the Communist Party, and yet they felt that to return to the ranks of the Socialists would mean to condone the murder of Rosa. Such personal reactions, which are seldom publicly admitted, are among the small, mosaic-like pieces that fall into place in the large riddle of history. In the case of Rosa Luxemburg they are part of the legend which soon surrounded her name. Legends have a truth of their own, but Mr. Nettl is entirely right to have paid almost no attention to the Rosa myth. It was his task, difficult enough, to restore her to historical life.

Shortly after her death, when all persuasions of the Left had already decided that she had always been "mistaken" (a "really hopeless case," as George Lichtheim, the last in this long line, put it in *Encounter*), a curious shift in her reputation took place. Two small volumes of her letters were published, and these, entirely personal and of a simple, touchingly humane, and often poetic beauty, were enough to destroy the propaganda image of bloodthirsty "Red Rosa," at least in all but the most obstinately anti-Semitic and reactionary circles. However, what then grew up was another legend—the sentimentalized image of the bird watcher and lover of flowers, a woman whose guards said good-by to her with tears in their eyes when she left prison—as if they couldn't go on living without being entertained by this strange prisoner who had insisted on treating them as human beings. Nettl does not mention this story, faithfully handed down to me when I was a child and later confirmed by Kurt Rosenfeld, her friend and lawyer, who claimed to have witnessed the scene. It is probably true enough, and its slightly embarrassing features are somehow offset by the survival of another anecdote, this one mentioned by Nettl. In 1907, she and her friend Clara Zetkin (later the "grand old woman" of German Communism) had gone for a walk, lost count of time, and arrived late for an appointment with August Bebel, who had feared they were lost. Rosa then proposed their epitaph: "Here lie the last two men of German Social Democracy." Seven years later, in February 1914, she had occasion to prove the truth of this cruel joke in a splendid address to the judges of the Criminal Court which had indicted her for "inciting" the masses to civil disobedience in case of war. (Not bad, incidentally, for the woman who "was always wrong" to stand trial on this charge five months before the outbreak of the First World War, which few "serious" people had thought possible.) Mr. Nettl with good sense has reprinted the address in its entirety; its "manliness" is unparalleled in the history of German socialism.

It took a few more years and a few more catastrophes for the legend to turn into a symbol of nostalgia for the good old times of the movement, when hopes were green, the revolution around the corner, and, most important, the faith in the capacities of the masses and in the moral integrity of the Socialist or Communist leadership was still intact. It speaks not only for the person of Rosa Luxemburg, but also for the qualities of this older generation of the Left, that the legend—vague, confused, inaccurate in nearly all details—could spread throughout the world and come to life whenever a "New Left" sprang into being. But side by side with this glamorized image, there survived also the old clichés of the "quarrelsome female," a "romantic" who was neither "realistic" nor scientific (it is true that she was always out of step), and whose works, especially her great book on imperialism (*The Accumulation of Capital,* 1913), were shrugged off. Every New Left movement, when its moment came to change into the Old Left—usually when its members reached the age of forty—promptly buried its early enthusiasm for Rosa Luxemburg together with the dreams of youth; and since they had usually not bothered to read, let alone to understand, what she had to say they found it easy to dismiss her with all the patronizing philistinism of their newly acquired status. "Luxemburgism," invented posthumously by Party hacks for polemical reasons, has never even achieved the honor of being denounced as "treason"; it was treated as a harmless, infantile disease. Nothing Rosa Luxemburg wrote or said survived except her surprisingly accurate criticism of Bolshevik politics during the early stages of the Russian Revolution, and this only because those whom a "god had failed" could use it as a convenient though wholly inadequate weapon against Stalin. ("There is something indecent in the use of Rosa's name and writings as a cold war missile," as the reviewer of Nettl's book pointed out in the *Times Literary Supplement.*) Her new admirers had no more in common with her than her detractors. Her highly developed sense for theoretical differences and her infallible judgment of people, her personal likes and dislikes, would have prevented her lumping Lenin and Stalin together under all circumstances, quite apart from the fact that she had never been a "believer," had never used politics as a substitute for religion, and had been careful, as Mr. Nettl notes, not to attack religion when she opposed the church. In short, while "revolution was as close and real to her as to Lenin," it was no more an article of faith with her than Marxism. Lenin was primarily a man of action and would have gone into politics in any event, but she, who in her half-serious self-estimate was born "to mind the geese," might just as well have buried herself in botany and zoology or history and economics or mathematics, had not the circumstances of the world offended her sense of justice and freedom.

This is of course to admit that she was not an orthodox Marxist, so little orthodox indeed that it might be doubted that she was a Marxist at all. Mr. Nettl rightly states that to her Marx was no more than "the best interpreter of reality of them all," and it is revealing of her lack of personal commitment that she could write, "I now have a horror of the much praised first volume of Marx's *Capital* because of its elaborate rococo ornaments à la Hegel." What mattered most in her view was reality, in all its wonderful and all its frightful aspects, even more than revolution itself. Her unorthodoxy was innocent, non-polemical; she "recommended her friends to read Marx for 'the daring of his thoughts, the refusal to take anything for granted,' rather than for the value of his conclusions. His mistakes . . . were self-evident . . . ; that was why [she] never bothered to engage in any lengthy critique." All this is most obvious in *The Accumulation of Capital,* which only Franz Mehring was unprejudiced enough to call a "truly magnificent,

fascinating achievement without its equal since Marx's death." The central thesis of this "curious work of genius" is simple enough. Since capitalism didn't show any signs of collapse "under the weight of its economic contradictions," she began to look for an outside cause to explain its continued existence and growth. She found it in the so-called third-man theory, that is, in the fact that the process of growth was not merely the consequence of innate laws ruling capitalist production but of the continued existence of pre-capitalist sectors in the country which "capitalism" captured and brought into its sphere of influence. Once this process had spread to the whole national territory, capitalists were forced to look to other parts of the earth, to precapitalist lands, to draw them into the process of capital accumulation, which, as it were, fed on whatever was outside itself. In other words, Marx's "original accumulation of capital" was not, like original sin, a single event, a unique deed of expropriation by the nascent bourgeoisie, setting off a process of accumulation that would then follow "with iron necessity" its own inherent law up to the final collapse. On the contrary, expropriation had to be repeated time and again to keep the system in motion. Hence, capitalism was not a closed system that generated its own contradictions and was "pregnant with revolution"; it fed on outside factors, and its *automatic* collapse could occur, if at all, only when the whole surface of the earth was conquered and had been devoured.

Lenin was quick to see that this description, whatever its merits or flaws, was essentially non-Marxist. It contradicted the very foundations of Marxian and Hegelian dialectics, which hold that every thesis must create its own antithesis—bourgeois society creates the proletariat—so that the movement of the whole process remains bound to the initial factor that caused it. Lenin pointed out that from the viewpoint of materialist dialectics "her thesis that enlarged capitalist reproduction was impossible within a closed economy and needed to cannibalize economies in order to function at all . . . [was] a 'fundamental error.'" The trouble was only that what was an error in abstract Marxian theory was an eminently faithful description of things as they really were. Her careful "description of the torture of Negroes in South Africa" also was clearly "non-Marxist," but who would deny today that it belonged in a book on imperialism?

II

Historically, Mr. Nettl's greatest and most original achievement is the discovery of the Polish-Jewish "peer group" and Rosa Luxemburg's lifelong, close, and carefully hidden attachment to the Polish party which sprang from it. This is indeed a highly significant and totally neglected source, not of the revolutions, but of the revolutionary spirit in the twentieth century. This milieu, which even in the twenties had lost all public relevance, has now completely disappeared. Its nucleus consisted of assimilated Jews from middle-class families whose cultural background was German (Rosa Luxemburg knew Goethe and Mörike by heart, and her literary taste was impeccable, far superior to that of her German friends), whose political formation was Russian, and whose moral standards in both private and public life were uniquely their own.

These Jews, an extremely small minority in the East, an even smaller percentage of assimilated Jewry in the West, stood outside all social ranks, Jewish or non-Jewish, hence had no conventional prejudices whatsoever, and had developed, in this truly splendid isolation, their own code of honor—which then attracted a number of non-Jews, among them Julian Marchlewski and Feliks Dzerzhynski, both of whom later joined the Bolsheviks. It was precisely because of this unique background that Lenin appointed Dzerzhynski as first head of the Cheka, someone, he hoped, no power could corrupt; hadn't he begged to be charged with the department of Children's Education and Welfare?

Nettl rightly stresses Rosa Luxemburg's excellent relations with her family, her parents, brothers, sister, and niece, none of whom ever showed the slightest inclination to socialist convictions or revolutionary activities, yet who did everything they could for her when she had to hide from the police or was in prison. The point is worth making, for it gives us a glimpse of this unique Jewish family background without which the emergence of the ethical code of the peer group would be nearly incomprehensible. The hidden equalizer of those who always treated one another as equals—and hardly anybody else—was the essentially simple experience of a childhood world in which mutual respect and unconditional trust, a universal humanity and a genuine, almost naïve contempt for social and ethnic distinctions were taken for granted. What the members of the peer group had in common was what can only be called moral taste, which is so different from "moral principles"; the authenticity of their morality they owed to having grown up in a world that was not out of joint. This gave them their "rare self-confidence," so unsettling to the world into which they then came, and so bitterly resented as arrogance and conceit. This milieu, and never the German Party, was and remained Rosa Luxemburg's home. The home was movable up to a point, and since it was predominantly Jewish it did not coincide with any "fatherland."

It is of course highly suggestive that the SDKPiL (Social Democracy of the Kingdom of Poland and Lithuania, formerly called SDPK, Social Democracy of the Kingdom of Poland), the party of this predominantly Jewish group, split from the official Socialist Polish Party, the PPS, because of the latter's stand for Polish independence (Pilsudski, the Fascist dictator of Poland after World War I, was its most famous and successful offspring), and that, after the split, the members of the group became ardent defenders of an often doctrinaire internationalism. It is even more suggestive that the national question is the only issue on which one could accuse Rosa Luxemburg of self-deception and unwillingness to face reality. That this had something to do with her Jewishness is undeniable, although it is of course "lamentably absurd" to discover in her anti-nationalism "a peculiarly Jewish quality." Mr. Nettl, while hiding nothing, is rather careful to avoid the "Jewish question," and in view of the usually low level of debates on this issue one can only applaud his decision. Unfortunately, his understandable distaste has blinded him to the few important facts in this matter, which is all the more to be regretted since these facts, though of a sim-

ple, elementary nature, also escaped the otherwise so sensitive and alert mind of Rosa Luxemburg.

The first of these is what only Nietzsche, as far as I know, has ever pointed out, namely, that the position and functions of the Jewish people in Europe predestined them to become the "good Europeans" *par excellence*. The Jewish middle classes of Paris and London, Berlin and Vienna, Warsaw and Moscow, were in fact neither cosmopolitan nor international, though the intellectuals among them thought of themselves in these terms. They were European, something that could be said of no other group. And this was not a matter of conviction; it was an objective fact. In other words, while the self-deception of assimilated Jews usually consisted in the mistaken belief that they were just as German as the Germans, just as French as the French, the self-deception of the intellectual Jews consisted in thinking that they had no "fatherland," for their fatherland actually was Europe. There is, second, the fact that at least the East-European intelligentsia was multilingual—Rosa Luxemburg herself spoke Polish, Russian, German, and French fluently and knew English and Italian very well. They never quite understood the importance of language barriers and why the slogan, "The fatherland of the working class is the Socialist movement," should be so disastrously wrong precisely for the working classes. It is indeed more than a little disturbing that Rosa Luxemburg herself, with her acute sense of reality and strict avoidance of clichés, should not have *heard* what was wrong with the slogan on principle. A fatherland, after all, is first of all a "land"; an organization is not a country, not even metaphorically. There is indeed grim justice in the later transformation of the slogan, "The fatherland of the working class is Soviet Russia"—Russia was at least a "land"—which put an end to the utopian internationalism of this generation.

One could adduce more such facts, and it still would be difficult to claim that Rosa Luxemburg was entirely wrong on the national question. What, after all, has contributed more to the catastrophic decline of Europe than the insane nationalism which accompanied the decline of the nation state in the era of imperialism? Those whom Nietzsche had called the "good Europeans"—a very small minority even among Jews—might well have been the only ones to have a presentiment of the disastrous consequences ahead, although they were unable to gauge correctly the enormous force of nationalist feeling in a decaying body politic.

III

Closely connected with the discovery of the Polish "peer group" and its continued importance for Rosa Luxemburg's public and private life is Mr. Nettl's disclosure of hitherto inaccessible sources, which enabled him to piece together the facts of her life—"the exquisite business of love and living." It is now clear that we knew next to nothing about her private life for the simple reason that she had so carefully protected herself from notoriety. This is no mere matter of sources. It was fortunate indeed that the new material fell into Mr. Nettl's hands, and he has every right to dismiss his few predecessors who were less hampered by lack of access to the facts than by their inability to move, think, and feel on the same level as their subject. The ease with which Nettl handles his biographical material is astounding. His treatment is more than perceptive. His is the first plausible portrait of this extraordinary woman, drawn *con amore,* with tact and great delicacy. It is as though she had found her last admirer, and it is for this reason that one feels like quarreling with some of his judgments.

He is certainly wrong in emphasizing her ambition, and sense of career. Does he think that her violent contempt for the careerists and status seekers in the German Party—their delight in being admitted to the Reichstag— is mere cant? Does he believe that a really "ambitious" person could have afforded to be as generous as she was? (Once, at an international congress, Jaurès finished an eloquent speech in which he "ridiculed the misguided passions of Rosa Luxemburg, [but] there was suddenly no one to translate him. Rosa jumped up and reproduced the moving oratory: from French into equally telling German.") And how can he reconcile this, except by assuming dishonesty or self-deception, with her telling phrase in one of her letters to Jogiches: "I have a cursed longing for happiness and am ready to haggle for my daily portion of happiness with all the stubbornness of a mule." What he mistakes for ambition is the natural force of a temperament capable, in her own laughing words, of "setting a prairie on fire," which propelled her almost willy-nilly into public affairs, and even ruled over most of her purely intellectual enterprises. While he stresses repeatedly the high moral standards of the "peer group," he still seems not to understand that such things as ambition, career, status, and even mere success were under the strictest taboo.

There is another aspect of her personality which Nettl stresses but whose implications he seems not to understand: that she was so "self-consciously a woman." This in itself put certain limitations on whatever her ambitions otherwise might have been—for Nettl does not ascribe to her more than what would have been natural in a man with her gifts and opportunities. Her distaste for the women's emancipation movement, to which all other women of her generation and political convictions were irresistibly drawn, was significant; in the face of suffragette equality, she might have been tempted to reply, *Vive la petite différence.* She was an outsider, not only because she was and remained a Polish Jew in a country she disliked and a party she came soon to despise, but also because she was a woman. Mr. Nettl must, of course, be pardoned for his masculine prejudices; they would not matter much if they had not prevented him from understanding fully the role Leo Jogiches, her husband for all practical purposes and her first, perhaps her only, lover, played in her life. Their deadly serious quarrel, caused by Jogiches' brief affair with another woman and endlessly complicated by Rosa's furious reaction, was typical of their time and milieu, as was the aftermath, his jealousy and her refusal for years to forgive him. This generation still believed firmly that love strikes only once, and its carelessness with marriage certificates should not be mistaken for any belief in free love. Mr. Nettl's evidence shows that she had friends and admirers, and that she enjoyed this, but it hardly indicates that there was ever another man in her life. To be-

lieve in the Party gossip about marriage plans with "Hänschen" Diefenbach, whom she addressed as *Sie* and never dreamed of treating as an equal, strikes me as downright silly. Nettl calls the story of Leo Jogiches and Rosa Luxemburg "one of the great and tragic love stories of Socialism," and there is no need to quarrel with this verdict if one understands that it was not "blind and self-destructive jealousy" which caused the ultimate tragedy in their relations but war and the years in prison, the doomed German revolution and the bloody end.

Leo Jogiches, whose name Nettl also has rescued from oblivion, was a very remarkable and yet typical figure among the professional revolutionists. To Rosa Luxemburg, he was definitely *masculini generis,* which was of considerable importance to her: She preferred Graf Westarp (the leader of the German Conservative Party) to all the German Socialist luminaries "because," she said, "he is a *man.*" There were few people she respected, and Jogiches headed a list on which only the names of Lenin and Franz Mehring could be inscribed with certainty. He definitely was a man of action and passion, he knew how to do and how to suffer. It is tempting to compare him with Lenin, whom he somewhat resembles, except in his passion for anonymity and for pulling strings behind the scenes, and his love of conspiracy and danger, which must have given him an additional erotic charm. He was indeed a Lenin *manqué,* even in his inability to write, "total" in his case (as she observed in a shrewd and actually very loving portrait in one of her letters), and his mediocrity as a public speaker. Both men had great talent for organization and leadership, but for nothing else, so that they felt impotent and superfluous when there was nothing to do and they were left to themselves. This is less noticeable in Lenin's case because he was never completely isolated, but Jogiches had early fallen out with the Russian Party because of a quarrel with Plekhanov—the Pope of the Russian emigration in Switzerland during the nineties—who regarded the self-assured Jewish youth newly arrived from Poland as "a miniature version of Nechaieff." The consequence was that he, according to Rosa Luxemburg, "completely rootless, vegetated" for many years, until the revolution of 1905 gave him his first opportunity: "Quite suddenly he not only achieved the position of leader of the Polish movement, but even in the Russian." (The SDKPiL came into prominence during the Revolution and became more important in the years following. Jogiches, though he himself didn't "write a single line," remained "none the less the very soul" of its publications.) He had his last brief moment when, "completely unknown in the SPD," he organized a clandestine opposition in the German army during the First World War. "Without him there would have been no *Spartakusbund,*" which, unlike any other organized Leftist group in Germany, for a short time became a kind of "ideal peer group." (This, of course, is not to say that Jogiches made the German revolution; like all revolutions, it was made by no one. *Spartakusbund* too was "following rather than making events," and the official notion that the "Spartakus uprising" in January 1918 was caused or inspired by its leaders—Rosa Luxemburg, Liebknecht, Jogiches—is a myth.)

We shall never know how many of Rosa Luxemburg's political ideas derived from Jogiches; in marriage, it is not always easy to tell the partners' thoughts apart. But that he failed where Lenin succeeded was at least as much a consequence of circumstances—he was a Jew and a Pole— as of lesser stature. In any event, Rosa Luxemburg would have been the last to hold this against him. The members of the peer group did not judge one another in these categories. Jogiches himself might have agreed with Eugene Leviné, also a Russian Jew though a younger man, "We are dead men on furlough." This mood is what set him apart from the others; for neither Lenin nor Trotsky nor Rosa Luxemburg herself is likely to have thought along such lines. After her death he refused to leave Berlin for safety: "Somebody has to stay to write all our epitaphs." He was arrested two months after the murder of Liebknecht and Luxemburg and shot in the back in the police station. The name of the murderer was known, but "no attempt to punish him was ever made"; he killed another man in the same way, and then continued his "career with promotion in the Prussian Police." Such were the *mores* of the Weimar Republic.

Reading and remembering these old stories, one becomes painfully aware of the difference between the German comrades and the members of the peer group. During the Russian revolution of 1905 Rosa Luxemburg was arrested in Warsaw, and her friends collected the money for bail (probably provided by the German Party). The payment was supplemented "with an unofficial threat of reprisal; if anything happened to Rosa they would retaliate with action against prominent officials." No such notion of "action" ever entered her German friends' minds either before or after the wave of political murders when the impunity of such deeds had become notorious.

IV

More troubling in retrospect, certainly more painful for herself, than her alleged "errors" are the few crucial instances in which Rosa Luxemburg was not out of step, but appeared instead to be in agreement with the official powers in the German Social Democratic Party. These were her real mistakes, and there was none she did not finally recognize and bitterly regret.

The least harmful among them concerned the national question. She had arrived in Germany in 1898 from Zürich, where she had passed her doctorate "with a first-class dissertation about the industrial development of Poland" (according to Professor Julius Wolf, who in his autobiography still remembered fondly "the ablest of my pupils"), which achieved the unusual "distinction of instant commercial publication" and is still used by students of Polish history. Her thesis was that the economic growth of Poland depended entirely upon the Russian market and that any attempt "to form a national or linguistic state was a negation of all development and progress for the last fifty years." (That she was economically right was more than demonstrated by the chronic malaise of Poland between the wars.) She then became the expert on Poland for the German Party, its propagandist among the Polish population in the Eastern German provinces, and entered an uneasy alliance with people who wished to "Germanize" the Poles out of existence and would "gladly make you a pres-

ent of all and every Pole including Polish Socialism," as an SPD secretary told her. Surely, "the glow of official approval was for Rosa a false glow."

Much more serious was her deceptive agreement with Party authorities in the revisionist controversy in which she played a leading part. This famous debate had been touched off by Eduard Bernstein and has gone down in history as the alternative of reform against revolution. But this battle cry is misleading for two reasons: it makes it appear as though the SPD at the turn of the century still was committed to revolution, which was not the case; and it conceals the objective soundness of much of what Bernstein had to say. His criticism of Marx's economic theories was indeed, as he claimed, in full "agreement with reality." He pointed out that the "enormous increase of social wealth [was] not accompanied by a decreasing number of large capitalists but by an increasing number of capitalists of all degrees," that an "increasing narrowing of the circle of the well-to-do and an increasing misery of the poor" had failed to materialize, that "the modern proletarian [was] indeed poor but that he [was] no pauper," and that Marx's slogan, "The proletarian has no fatherland," was not true. Universal suffrage had given him political rights, the trade unions a place in society, and the new imperialist development a clear stake in the nation's foreign policy. No doubt the reaction of the German Party to these unwelcome truths was chiefly inspired by a deep-seated reluctance to reexamine critically its theoretical foundation, but this reluctance was greatly sharpened by the Party's vested interest in the status quo threatened by Bernstein's analysis. What was at stake was the status of the SPD as a "state within a state": the Party had in fact become a huge and well-organized bureaucracy that stood outside society and had every interest in things as they were. Revisionism à la Bernstein would have led the Party back into German society, and such "integration" was felt to be as dangerous to the Party's interests as a revolution.

Mr. Nettl holds an interesting theory about the "pariah position" of the SPD within German society and its failure to participate in government. It seemed to its members that the Party could "provide within itself a superior alternative to corrupt capitalism." In fact, by keeping the "defenses against society on all fronts intact," it generated that spurious feeling of "togetherness" (as Nettl puts it) which the French Socialists treated with great contempt. In any event, it was obvious that the more the Party increased in numbers, the more surely was its radical élan "organized out of existence." One could live very comfortably in this "state within a state" by avoiding friction with society at large, by enjoying feelings of moral superiority without any consequences. It was not even necessary to pay the price of serious alienation since this pariah society was in fact but a mirror image, a "miniature reflection" of German society at large. This blind alley of the German Socialist movement could be analyzed correctly from opposing points of view—either from the view of Bernstein's revisionism, which recognized the emancipation of the working classes within capitalist society as an accomplished fact and demanded a stop to the talk about a revolution nobody thought of anyhow; or from the viewpoint of those who were not merely "alienated" from bourgeois society but actually wanted to change the world.

The latter was the standpoint of the revolutionists from the East who led the attack against Bernstein—Plekhanov, Parvus, and Rosa Luxemburg—and whom Karl Kautsky, the German Party's most eminent theoretician, supported, although he probably felt much more at ease with Bernstein than in the company of his new allies from abroad. The victory they won was Pyrrhic; it "merely strengthened alienation by pushing reality away." For the real issue was not theoretical and not economic. At stake was Bernstein's conviction, shamefully hidden in a footnote, that "the middle class—not excepting the German—in their bulk [was] still fairly healthy, not only economically but also *morally*" (my italics). This was the reason that Plekhanov called him a "philistine" and that Parvus and Rosa Luxemburg thought the fight so decisive for the future of the Party. For the truth of the matter was that Bernstein and Kautsky had in common their aversion to revolution; the "iron law of necessity" was for Kautsky the best possible excuse for doing nothing. The guests from Eastern Europe were the only ones who not merely "believed" in revolution as a theoretical necessity but wished to do something about it, precisely because they considered society as it was to be unbearable on *moral* grounds, on the grounds of justice. Bernstein and Rosa Luxemburg, on the other hand, had in common that they were both honest (which may explain Bernstein's "secret tenderness" for her), analyzed what they saw, were loyal to reality and critical of Marx; Bernstein was aware of this and shrewdly remarks in his reply to Rosa Luxemburg's attacks that she too had questioned "the whole Marxist predictions of the coming social evolution, so far as this is based on the theory of crises."

Rosa Luxemburg's early triumphs in the German Party rested on a double misunderstanding. At the turn of the century the SPD was "the envy and admiration of Socialists throughout the world." August Bebel, its "grand old man," who from Bismarck's foundation of the German Reich to the outbreak of the First World War "dominated [its] policy and spirit," had always proclaimed, "I am and always will be the mortal enemy of existing society." Didn't that sound like the spirit of the Polish peer group? Couldn't one assume from such proud defiance that the great German Party was somehow the SDKPiL writ large? It took Rosa Luxemburg almost a decade—until she returned from the first Russian revolution—to discover that the secret of this defiance was willful noninvolvement with the world at large and single-minded preoccupation with the growth of the Party organization. Out of this experience she developed, after 1910, her program of constant "friction" with society without which, as she then realized, the very source of the revolutionary spirit was doomed to dry up. She did not intend to spend her life in a sect, no matter how large; her commitment to revolution was primarily a moral matter, and this meant that she remained passionately engaged in public life and civil affairs, in the destinies of the world. Her involvement with European politics outside the immediate interests of the working class, and hence completely beyond the horizon of all Marxists, appears most convincingly in her repeated insistence on a "republican program" for the German and Russian Parties.

This was one of the main points of her famous *Juniusbroschüre*, written in prison during the war and then used as the platform for the *Spartakusbund*. Lenin, who was unaware of its authorship, immediately declared that to proclaim "the program of a republic . . . [means] in practice to proclaim the revolution—with an *incorrect* revolutionary program." Well, a year later the Russian Revolution broke out without any "program" whatsoever, and its first achievement was the abolition of the monarchy and the establishment of a republic, and the same was to happen in Germany and Austria. Which, of course, has never prevented the Russian, Polish, or German comrades from violently disagreeing with her on this point. It is indeed the republican question rather than the national one which separated her most decisively from all others. Here she was completely alone, as she was alone, though less obviously so, in her stress on the absolute necessity of not only individual but public freedom under all circumstances.

A second misunderstanding is directly connected with the revisionist debate. Rosa Luxemburg mistook Kautsky's reluctance to accept Bernstein's analyses for an authentic commitment to revolution. After the first Russian revolution in 1905, for which she had hurried back to Warsaw with false papers, she could no longer deceive herself. To her, these months constituted not only a crucial experience, they were also "the happiest of my life." Upon her return, she tried to discuss the events with her friends in the German Party. She learned quickly that the word "revolution" "had only to come into contact with a real revolutionary situation to break down" into meaningless syllables. The German Socialists were convinced that such things could happen only in distant barbarian lands. This was the first shock, from which she never recovered. The second came in 1914 and brought her near to suicide.

Naturally, her first contact with a real revolution taught her more and better things than disillusion and the fine arts of disdain and mistrust. Out of it came her insight into the nature of political action, which Mr. Nettl rightly calls her most important contribution to political theory. The main point is that she had learned from the revolutionary workers' councils (the latter *soviets*) that "good organization does not precede action but is the product of it," that "the organization of revolutionary action can and must be learnt in revolution itself, as one can only learn swimming in the water," that revolutions are "made" by nobody but break out "spontaneously," and that "the pressure for action" always comes "from below." A revolution is "great and strong as long as the Social Democrats [at the time still the only revolutionary party] don't smash it up."

There were, however, two aspects of the 1905 prelude which entirely escaped her. There was, after all, the surprising fact that the revolution had broken out not only in a non-industrialized, backward country, but in a territory where no strong socialist movement with mass support existed at all. And there was, second, the equally undeniable fact that the revolution had been the consequence of the Russian defeat in the Russo-Japanese War. These were the two facts Lenin never forgot and from which he drew two conclusions. First, one did not need a large organization; a small, tightly organized group with a leader who knew what he wanted was enough to pick up the power once the authority of the old regime had been swept away. Large revolutionary organizations were only a nuisance. And, second, since revolutions were not "made" but were the result of circumstances and events beyond anybody's power, wars were welcome. The second point was the source of her disagreements with Lenin during the First World War; the first of her criticism of Lenin's tactics in the Russian Revolution of 1918. For she refused categorically, from beginning to end, to see in the war anything but the most terrible disaster, no matter what its eventual outcome; the price in human lives, especially in proletarian lives, was too high in any event. Moreover, it would have gone against her grain to look upon revolution as the profiteer of war and massacre—something which didn't bother Lenin in the least. And with respect to the issue of organization, she did not believe in a victory in which the people at large had no part and no voice; so little, indeed, did she believe in holding power at any price that she "was far more afraid of a deformed revolution than an unsuccessful one"—this was, in fact, "the major difference between her" and the Bolsheviks.

And haven't events proved her right? Isn't the history of the Soviet Union one long demonstration of the frightful dangers of "deformed revolutions"? Hasn't the "moral collapse" which she foresaw—without, of course, foreseeing the open criminality of Lenin's successor—done more harm to the cause of revolution as the understood it than "any and every political defeat . . . in honest struggle against superior forces and in the teeth of the historical situation" could possibly have done? Wasn't it true that Lenin was "completely mistaken" in the means he employed, that the only way to salvation was the "school of public life itself, the most unlimited, the broadest democracy and public opinion," and that terror "demoralized" everybody and destroyed everything?

She did not live long enough to see how right she had been and to watch the terrible and terribly swift moral deterioration of the Communist parties, the direct offspring of the Russian Revolution, throughout the world. Nor for that matter did Lenin, who despite all his mistakes still had more in common with the original peer group than with anybody who came after him. This became manifest when Paul Levi, the successor of Leo Jogiches in the leadership of the *Spartakusbund,* three years after Rosa Luxemburg's death, published her remarks on the Russian Revolution just quoted, which she had written in 1918 "only for you"—that is, without intending publication. "It was a moment of considerable embarrassment" for both the German and Russian parties, and Lenin could be forgiven had he answered sharply and immoderately. Instead, he wrote: "We answer with . . . a good old Russian fable: an eagle can sometimes fly lower than a chicken, but a chicken can never rise to the same heights as an eagle. Rosa Luxemburg . . . in spite of [her] mistakes . . . was and is an eagle." He then went on to demand publication of "her biography and the *complete* edition of her works," unpurged of "error," and chided the German comrades for their "incredible" negligence in this duty. This was in

1922. Three years later, Lenin's successors had decided to "Bolshevize" the German Communist Party and therefore ordered a "specific onslaught on Rosa Luxemburg's whole legacy." The task was accepted with joy by a young member named Ruth Fischer, who had just arrived from Vienna. She told the German comrades that Rosa Luxemburg and her influence "were nothing less than a syphilis bacillus."

The gutter had opened, and out of it emerged what Rosa Luxemburg would have called "another zoological species." No "agents of the bourgeoisie" and no "Socialist traitors" were needed any longer to destroy the few survivors of the peer group and to bury in oblivion the last remnants of their spirit. No complete edition of her works, needless to say, was ever published. After World War II, a two-volume edition of selections "with careful annotations underlining her errors" came out in East Berlin and was followed by a "full-length analysis of the Luxemburgist system of errors" by Fred Oelssner, which quickly "lapsed into obscurity" because it became "too 'Stalinist.'" This most certainly was not what Lenin had demanded, nor could it, as he had hoped, serve "in the education of many generations of Communists."

After Stalin's death, things began to change, though not in East Germany, where, characteristically, revision of Stalinist history took the form of a "Bebel cult." (The only one to protest this new nonsense was poor old Hermann Duncker, the last distinguished survivor who still could "recall the most wonderful period of my life, when as a young man I knew and worked with Rosa Luxemburg, Karl Liebknecht, and Franz Mehring.") The Poles, however, although their own two-volume edition of selected works in 1959 is "partly overlapping with the German" one, "took out her reputation almost unaltered from the casket in which it had been stored" ever since Lenin's death, and after 1956 a "flood of Polish publications" on the subject appeared on the market. One would like to believe that there is still hope for a belated recognition of who she was and what she did, as one would like to hope that she will finally find her place in the education of political scientists in the countries of the West. For Mr. Nettl is right: "Her ideas belong wherever the history of political ideas is seriously taught."

J. P. Nettl (essay date 1966)

SOURCE: "Appendix I: Rosa Luxemburg as an Economist," in *Rosa Luxemburg,* Vol. I, Oxford University Press, London, 1966, pp. 828-41.

[*Nettl was a German-born English political scientist and novelist. In the following essay, he surveys the main ideas of Luxemburg's* The Accumulation of Capital.]

Rosa Luxemburg always said that, in so far as her talent lay in the field of the social sciences, it was in economics—and in mathematical economics at that. Mathematics may have been her *violon d'Ingres*—the thing at which she would rather have excelled than those in which she was in fact outstanding. It is quite a common nostalgia. The only evidence for her mathematical claim or wish are the recalculations of Marx's not very complicated compound reproduction formulae in Volume II of *Capital.* And here her calculations are capable both of fairly obvious refinement as well as fairly obvious contradiction. But what is probably true is that the thin end of the wedge of her interest in the problem of accumulation, which gave rise to her remarkable book *The Accumulation of Capital*, was the mathematical difficulty Marx experienced in the 'proof' of accumulation, and which he left unresolved at his death.

Rosa Luxemburg's main talent as a writer and, above all, teacher of economics—the latter was the more important and enduring function—was her capacity to enliven the subject with vivid, unusual, and convincing illustrations. Her textbook on economics—political economy, to use the Marxist phrase for the specific economics of capitalism—was essentially a conducted tour through the historical stages of economic relations, from primitive Communism via the slave economy to feudalism and capitalism. As her friend and editor pointed out, these were lectures, written for oral delivery. They were incomplete; Rosa worked on the manuscript from 1907 to 1912, and again in prison from 1916 to 1918. They were intentionally simple; the fact that most of the theoretical problems (value, surplus value, reproduction) are missing may have been due to her inability to complete the manuscript, but more probably to her reluctance to complicate her lectures with material partially dealt with in *The Accumulation of Capital*. Whatever her preference for mathematical analysis, therefore, she was essentially an economic historian—naturally in a Marxist sense; her facts were chosen to illustrate a fundamental thesis. The fact that she, and in her time she alone, succeeded in enlivening this potentially grey subject is eloquently attested by her students at the party school, and by the many extramural lectures for which friends and party organizations were forever pestering her before the war. Nor was clarity and strong colouring merely a mastered technique. One of the strongest points in her indictment of orthodox academic economics was its dryness, its obscurantism, its persistence in making an important and thrilling subject well-nigh incomprehensible—except to other professors.

It is thus not surprising that Rosa Luxemburg's only piece of original academic research—in the formal sense of the term—was also a piece of economic history. Her doctoral dissertation for the University of Zürich not only gained her the required award of a degree but also achieved the much less usual distinction of instant commercial publication. It was widely reviewed in Germany, as well as in the Polish and Russian émigré press. Its originality lay in two distinct factors. Its thesis—a new one at the time—was Poland's economic integration into the Russian empire since the beginning of the century, resulting in the dependence of the Polish economy on the Russian market, and consequently the logical necessity of this continued integration. Though rigorously dependent on economic evidence, this thesis provided a secure base for the political contest against Polish national independence in the future. Those Socialists who argued for self-determination—no Socialist could play down the primacy of economic evidence—were thus left with arguments that might proliferate frothily on the surface of reality but had no roots in

its economics laws. Try as they might, none of her critics was able to demolish her case. And history, too, proved her right, as the situation of the Polish economy between the wars showed all too clearly; chronic underconsumption and an oversized, unbalanced industry that tottered at the slightest whiff of crisis—with a *laissez-mourir,* not even a *laissez-faire,* government in charge.

The other original aspect of her work was her sources. In the West no one had previously bothered with these (and Polish émigrés were far too politically minded for economics). At home it was not a subject that was encouraged at Russian universities. In the Bibliothèque Nationale and the Czartoryski Library in Paris Rosa dug up hitherto unknown material, and the use to which she put it opened up new lines of investigation into Polish and Russian economic history. Historians can and still do use her work with profit today. In addition, her early researches in 1893 and 1894 unearthed enough material not only for her own thesis, but for Julian Marchlewski's as well; his dissertation on the Polish Physiocrats and subsequent work on the Polish economy were largely due to Rosa's suggestion and indication of sources.

But all Marxists have to know a lot of economics; had it not been for *Accumulation,* Rosa Luxemburg's work would have remained merely a better and brighter-than-most dab at economic history. *The Accumulation of Capital* is a compound work of incidental genius—incidental because it achieved fame and importance in quite a different way from that which the author intended. It was intended to 'clarify' imperialism—but it did not; no more than the theory of relativity 'explains' light (which Einstein did not of course intend it to). It was intended to solve compound reproduction mathematically, but did not succeed—though Rosa Luxemburg admitted that this was not perhaps as vital as she had at first supposed. Finally, it was meant to provide a rational (as well as logical) explanation of capitalist expansion in spite of the severely limiting parameters of Marxist economics, and at the same time identify the theoretical point of inevitable collapse— and though she did provide this, her analysis failed to find favour among contemporary or later economists, whether bourgeois or Communist. Instead it raised and partially answered a question about investment that was entirely new then and is still vital today. Instead of a tenable theory of imperialism Rosa Luxemburg offered a theory of growth which at least some economists today hold to be vital and valid. Her political heirs have relegated the work to the museum of primitive curiosities and have misused her economics to condemn her politically. It is her ancient enemies, on the other hand—the professional bourgeois economists, dressed up with much sophistication and technique since the days of Roscher, Schmoller, and Sombart—who have rediscovered the prophetic quality in her line of economic inquiry.

The mathematics are of secondary importance, and need not be discussed here. Nor do we have to pass judgement on how 'Marxist' a work Rosa Luxemburg's *Accumulation* really is. I would not presume to judge this *in vacuo;* an analysis by way of reference to later authorities is so politically loaded as to subsume the economic arguments completely. We are therefore left, first, with a confrontation of Rosa Luxemburg's intention against her achievement, and secondly with the incidental illuminations. I shall postulate neutrality between Marxist and non-Marxist methods of economic analysis, except to emphasize that Rosa's problems with Marx's own works were not merely technical, but fundamental.

ACCUMULATION

In Marxist analysis of the capitalist economy, production is the primary function, and predominates over consumption and its derivative, demand. Distribution problems are of a technical nature only, and the proper functioning of distribution is assumed (concepts and assumptions which incidentally have been taken over into Soviet economies which in turn are actually rationalized capitalism but without capitalist criteria). Apart from the temporary dislocation caused by crises of boom and slump—from which Rosa Luxemburg deliberately abstracts—all production starts by being 'consumed', either literally by consumers, or as replacement of fixed capital by producers, or by the reinvestment of profits. As long as total production—annual national income, say—is 'consumed' in this way, and the stock of capital remains constant (investment just equals replacement), the economy remains in equilibrium. This is Marx's simple reproduction.

It is only a conceptual basis, however. Production dominates, not consumption; the *point* of capitalist enterprise is the maximization of profit—for reinvestment and further maximization. The stock of capital grows. The central point of Marxist economic analysis is that consumer incomes do not rise proportionately (the iron law of wages); it is the producer who has to absorb the bulk of the increased output as replacement of or addition to his fixed capital. The Marxist model in fact divides the economy into two departments, that of producer's goods and that of consumer goods. The one thus grows faster than the other. Since they are related (consumer goods produced for workers in producer's goods industries, producer's goods produced for the capitalists in consumer goods industries), disequilibrium results. Worse, it is progressive, not circular; it gets worse as accumulation proceeds. Accumulation proportionate to investment is consequently impossible, yet it happens—demonstrably. Accumulation is the capitalist's *raison d'être,* but why does he invest in the first place?

This then was Rosa Luxemburg's problem, as it had been Marx's—one of them. Before his death he had indicated various possible approaches, but no definite or central solution. Initially the mathematics come in here. But neither for Marx nor Rosa Luxemburg was this a question of mere mathematical elegance. What was needed was a function of demand which would furnish, not the need, but the effective means of 'consuming' the cause of the imbalance, the additional output generated by the compulsive quest for profit.

To start with, Rosa Luxemburg examined the various possibilities adumbrated by Marx himself. The most probable one, however, is referred to only in passing, as part of the problem itself and not of its solution. This is the thesis that

the investment criterion is not the starting point of economic causality, but is a derived function of production—derived by that anarchic competition that enforces perpetual technical change, improvement, *and expansion* (to reduce unit cost). Without it a capitalist is forced quickly out of business—and joins the haggard army of the proletariat. Thus profits are still the object of capitalist activity, not by any act of will but from sheer necessity. It is either profits or economic death. Orthodox Marxist economists, both Soviet and anti-Soviet, have accepted this causality, and have developed it into a sophisticated rationality that serves to explain the entire process of capitalist growth.

Why did Rosa Luxemburg bypass this solution, which became and has remained the mainstream of Marxist orthodoxy? For her, it never rises above the level of being a minor constituent part of the problem, an also-ran in the cause of competition and anarchy. Nor is it peculiar to the capitalist system, but has existed in all forms of productive relations from first to last. But if this is so, then it cannot begin to provide a solution to the specific problem of capitalist accumulation. Technological change and economies of scale were merely *additional* complications imposed by real life.

Having searched in Marx, Rosa Luxemburg then looked at the Marxists—or rather at all the important economists from Sismondi and Ricardo to the Russian 'legal' Marxists who were concerned with this problem. In the process of extracting what was relevant they were unceremoniously buffeted about, called to account and then contemptuously dismissed—for none of them provided the answer. It is clear that Rosa never expected that they would. She was much less than fair to many of their ideas. For she thought she had the answer even before she started on them.

The balancing factor is the existence of pre-capitalist economies—and the pre-capitalist enclaves within capitalist economies, mainly agricultural. It is the 'capitalization' of these areas which provides the justified growth drive of capitalists, the expectation of growing profits and continuous investment. The process, and with it the entire capitalist system, can continue just as long as such areas exist. When they have been gobbled up, capitalism will have to rely on its internal resources, accumulation will become self-defeating, capitalism will collapse. Voluntary abstention is impossible by definition; those writers like von Kirchmann who appeared to suggest it are berated most severely by Rosa Luxemburg.

Rosa Luxemburg asserts this solution and describes it—convincingly; she does not prove it in the way she disproves the theories of her opponents. This does not of course invalidate it. Capitalist consumption goods go out to pay for 'cheap' raw materials from colonies. Capital is also exported to exploit 'cheap' labour. The process was then and is now familiar enough—the classic indictment of imperialism, before and since political independence (old *political* as opposed to new *economic* imperialism). The question is whether this is a *feature* of capitalism or the mainspring of its continued existence. And this problem remains open. But curiously enough it remains open only in the non-Communist world, among politicians as well as academic economists. At least it is an arguable case. Among orthodox Marxists, however, the thesis is a manifestation not the cause, and the reasons for this demotion are in the last resort more political than economic.

IMPERIALISM

The only explicit *political* analysis in *The Accumulation of Capital* is the last chapter, which purports to prove the *economic* necessity of militarism—but fails to do so. By this time, the internal logic and beauty of Rosa's analysis made her overreach herself; it began to run wild. But of course imperialism is the necessary consequence of Rosa's whole concept of capitalist accumulation. If one capitalist economy must capture and cannibalize pre-capitalist society in order to survive, then the other capitalist economies must be kept out of 'captured' areas. The whole apparatus of militarism, the sharpened social tensions that were so typical of it, thus had two causes: the need to wrest colonies from their indigenous rulers, and then to keep and if possible extend them at the expense of other people's colonies. As a matter of logical causality, imperialism follows from the moment the problem of accumulation is identified and 'solved' by Rosa Luxemburg.

As already emphasized, the whole political and historical development of imperialism as a specific internal condition of society is absent from the analysis in *The Accumulation of Capital*—implied but not described. In Rosa Luxemburg's political writings of the period it is the effects of imperialism on class relations that are stressed—again not described; the essence of imperialism, *das Ding an sich,* is absent—the missing step already referred to. This leaves an apparent vacuum for followers and critics to fill in as seems best to them. Lenin, at the time unaware of her political writings on this subject, assumed that for psychological reasons Rosa wanted to exorcise the problem of imperialism from home and export it to the colonies, thus belittling its importance among the manifold preoccupations of Social Democracy. This notion is nonsense—though a hostile and isolated reading of *The Accumulation of Capital* makes it conceivable. If anything the opposite is true. Though the location of capitalism's centre of gravity moves to pre-capitalist societies or areas, at least from the theoretical moment of internal repletion of imperialist societies, these are never anything but passive objects. They can neither arrest nor alter the process of their own transformation. The stimulus comes wholly from the colonizers, the imperialists. And though Rosa Luxemburg shared with Lenin the recognition of a need for *political* action to hasten the end of capitalism through revolution, she was much closer to the Mensheviks and Kautsky in her belief that the economic laws of capitalism should not be short-circuited, much less held up. Hence her emphasis on the inevitability of capitalist agrarian relations after the 1905 revolution (which she considered progressive, while Lenin feared they would make revolution in Russia wellnigh impossible). The same reasoning applied to her consistent opposition to tariffs and duties in Germany; these would impede, not assist, full capitalist development.

As with the Russian peasants, Rosa Luxemburg had no vision of eventual colonial independence in a capitalist world. Though she recognized the tendency for industrial investment in colonies, she saw this merely as an extension of 'home' capitalism looking for cheap labour and the procurement of raw materials—without any local response other than misery and suffering. Thus she did not look for any revolutionary potential in the exploitation of colonial peoples—however vividly she described that exploitation. She came very close to laying down the axiom that any colony fighting for independence did so because it had inherent imperialist ambitions of its own—an indictment similar to recent Chinese characterizations of Nehru's 'imperialist' India. The honour of the incorporation of the nationalist-colonial struggle into revolutionary Marxism—and the acquisitive peasant struggle—fell to Lenin. But again it must be said: *The Accumulation of Capital* was intended as an economic theorem, not an analytical text of political revolution. This makes a confrontation between *The Accumulation of Capital* and Lenin's work on imperialism three years later—after the outbreak of the war—not so much impossible as pointless.

And if one wants to extrapolate Rosa's arguments into a political context, as her later critics have done, a more meaningful result than theirs can be achieved. First, an objective case can certainly be made for the pre-eminent importance of colonial 'spheres of influence' for thriving capitalist economies. The classical trade pattern of exports of cheap manufactures to colonial dependencies in return for imports of artificially cheap raw materials is accurate, though not of course complete. Physical domination is not necessary; post-independence control is today called 'economic imperialism'.

Secondly, the classic economic theory that the rationalization of foreign trade which follows this pattern (expanded production of desirable staple exports with all the resultant internal economies of scale) enriches the exporting country is now seriously questioned. In spite of such trade and much aid, the poor countries get poorer and the rich richer, at least comparatively—and this divergence is linked, not discrete. This development (which incidentally is endemic in capitalism, and has only recently been 'discovered') follows from Rosa Luxemburg's *Accumulation* far more naturally than some of the technical criticisms and assumptions made by orthodox Marxist-Leninists like Oelssner, drowning in the minutiae of formal and politically loaded concepts.

Thirdly, once the notion of colonial exploitation becomes central and is brought up to date, the basic confrontation between rich and poor societies—which is today's real dialectic—subsumes the 'old' form of class conflict within society. In this context we are witnessing a curious resurgence of nationalism in ex-colonies; to coin a suitable Leninist formula: 'Neutralism is nationalism in the age of imperialism.' Instead of conflicts *within* colonial societies against imperialist domination, linked to class conflict at home, there is a line-up of poor countries against rich, with the former assuming the role of the international proletariat. This alignment, moreover, cuts across the 'Leninist-Stalinist' division into capitalist and socialist camps; what matters is wealth or poverty and the relative growth of wealth or poverty. This then is an 'international' or 'class' line-up that cuts across national boundaries or rather makes these boundaries into mere markers of autonomy rather than absolute isolation—as Rosa Luxemburg actually advocated. This too follows from her emphasis on colonizers and colonies as basic protagonists in a developing capitalist world. ***Accumulation*** may be an abstract but is by no means a barren work.

Though no reference is made to Rosa Luxemburg's work, modern Soviet writing on imperialism has perforce had to adjust in part to this redefinition of relevance. Imperialism is no longer the highest stage of capitalism, but a specific condition of distortion which cuts across the 'normal' articulation of class relationships. 'Inasmuch as imperialism impeded the development of factory manufacturing, very few of the ruined peasants and artisans became modern workers connected with big, mechanized production . . . they were forced to linger on through the intermediate stages of proletarization and to become not so much capitalist workers as semi-proletarians-semi-paupers . . . an army of hired labour . . . [with] a specific colonial character.' Or 'the European bourgeoisie by no means went into overseas countries in order to implant there the prevailing capitalist production relationships.' 'Normal' capitalism is represented by the domestic 'national bourgeoisie' which thus finds itself in conflict with foreign imperialism. 'The economic interests of the national bourgeoisie are inimical to the interests of imperialism. . . . Everywhere the bourgeoisie tries to attain independent capitalist development, just what imperialism hampers. This is an apparent paradox . . . but imperialism cannot function without colonial or semi-colonial exploitation . . . and will try to keep the exploited countries in a state of rural backwardness; i.e. to preserve that very state of underdevelopment which all nationalist forces, including the bourgeoisie, are trying to remedy. Hence the struggle between them will be sharpened. . . .'

This is no longer either Lenin or Luxemburg. It is Leninist in so far as it relates to current strategy of focusing on American economic imperialism as the main enemy, and thus accepts the very un-Luxemburg notion of (temporarily) better and worse capitalisms. But it is Luxemburgist in so far as it retransfers attention to the 'third world' of underdeveloped or colonial countries, and locates the final struggle of Socialism and capitalism in that arena, thus once more connecting the future of capitalism with the colonial rather than the domestic scene. Soviet writers are making this concession painfully and slowly—under the pressure of Chinese competition.

INVESTMENT AND CAPITALIST EXPANSION

The confinement of Marxist economics has already burst apart in the previous section; we shall now leave it behind altogether in an attempt to identify the mechanism of Rosa Luxemburg's model. If production and profits rather than consumption and income are the prime motives of economic action—this is central to Marxism—then the difficulties of compound reproduction necessarily lead to the question: 'Why do capitalists continue to do something which is incapable of successful achievement?' We have already seen *what* they do (exploit colonies and other pre-capitalist segments of the economy); the problem now is *why*. More specifically, whence do they anticipate a de-

mand which leads them to increase production—in short, to invest?

It is here that orthodox Marxist economics fails us—as it failed Rosa Luxemburg, otherwise she would not have written her book. Marx himself was aware of the problem, though he (and subsequently all orthodox Marxists) dealt with it by assuming that investment was a function of, and limited by, the needs of technology and size which would enable a producer to remain viable, to stay in the game. This minimal viability is not growth. But historically growth has taken place in capitalist economies over the last sixty years—growth, not merely concentration. And, though Rosa Luxemburg nowhere suggests even for a moment that genuine *growth* of capitalist economies (in our sense of that word) is possible or important to analyse, her analysis is in fact close to some modern growth models. It is only necessary to abstract from her two limitations—the lack of an adequate banking system to channel one man's savings to another man's physical investment, and the rather more fundamental assumption that effective demand cannot come from a rise in workers' real wages. Once this is done, the capitalists' search for investment and the whole analysis of cumulative growth of investible savings (surplus) in conditions of technical progress and of a rising rate of capital exploitation, provide the right basis for a modern growth model. Rosa Luxemburg asks—unintentionally—the right question (we can easily alter 'why does he invest' to 'how can he be induced to invest'). She also provides some elements of an answer, by looking for a new and additional source of demand and defining its theoretical quantity. It is better than merely *postulating* investment, however illogical, and then measuring it empirically without explaining it. Instead of starting this problem at the end, Rosa Luxemburg begins at the beginning.

Beyond all doubt, *The Accumulation of Capital* is a work of uneven, flickering genius, ill-confined within the strict limits of the author's self-imposed task. Its explicit quality is considerable, but the real impact comes from the incidentals. Given freer rein than in the immediate political polemics which occupied most of her attention, Rosa Luxemburg's mind plumbed hitherto dark or barely explored depths. The questions asked are more interesting than the solutions offered. But in economics, as in all social sciences, this is the bigger hurdle.

One aspect that is frequently overlooked in discussing Marxist economics—and confronting it with the various economic techniques evolved since classical equilibrium theory began to be demolished—is the very fundamental difference in the ground covered. All too often we assume that we are merely dealing with a different set of techniques, that we shall get answers to what are essentially similar problems. This is not so. For the last 150 years economics has narrowed, like a pyramid, towards increasing specialization—a concentration in depth. Marxist economics was syphoned out of the scientific mainstream of economics at a time when specialization had not passed beyond emphasis—a focus of interest on a particular aspect of the social sciences, but not an abstraction from them as irrelevant or 'different'. It retained this quality of emphasis within totality; all Marxist analysis does. Marxism *means* scientific totality. The Marxist word for over-intensive specializing is 'vulgarization', and bourgeois economics are vulgar economics. Interlocked as they are, the techniques of Marxism have not plumbed any new depths in their particular spheres for many years—however much they may push forward the validity of the whole system.

Rosa Luxemburg subscribed whole-heartedly to the interlocking totality of Marxism; all or nothing. Indeed, she went further in this than most contemporaries. She emphasized that the science of Political Economy—the name itself is a concession to totality—would become extinct when capitalism, its subject of study, disappeared. Probably the same fate would befall all the other tools of Marxist social analysis, originating from and confined as they were to the historical class dialectic they claimed to illuminate. Socialist revolution would wipe away the tools for studying reality when it destroyed that reality itself.

It is this context of the *function* of science that lights up **The Accumulation of Capital** with a luridly nonconformist fire. Intentional or not, the work achieves and (more important still) *demands* a validity for its analysis that has nothing to do with the author's usual acceptance of severe limitations of purpose. In spite of the handicap of loaded and often ill-defined concepts—blunt tools for a precision job—Rosa Luxemburg surrenders herself freely to the search for basic, objective causalities. For the moment revolution and politics hardly matter. Not that this was deliberate. The point is that, given stimulus and the right circumstances, she was capable of thinking in this extended, scientific manner. Marx certainly was. Lenin, for instance, was not. That is why Marx and Rosa Luxemburg (though not of course to the same extent) have provided scientific techniques quite separate from and valid outside their political doctrines, while Lenin and Kautsky and Plekhanov have not. It has nothing to do with ability, but with the depth of mind and analysis.

And this may be ultimately why **The Accumulation of Capital** has been Rosa Luxemburg's *livre maudit*. It is unique among her own writings, in scope even more than in quality. Marxists have dealt with it either by making it subsume all her other writings ('the fount of all her errors') or by treating it as a fascinating deviation—into a blind alley. Among non-Marxists it takes its place in the procession of contributions to scientific analysis. To enable it to do so they have stripped it of its relevance to totality, emphasizing depth rather than breadth. In both cases, however, the book's unquiet spirit continues to haunt a world still inhabited by the obstinate problems with which it deals. That alone is the best measure of its importance.

Rudolf Schlesinger (essay date 1966)

SOURCE: "Marxism Without An Organizing Party: Personal Observations on Rosa Luxemburg's Life," in *Soviet Studies*, Vol. XVIII, No. 2, October, 1966, pp. 225-51.

[*In the following essay, Schlesinger considers the aspects of Luxemburg's writings and activism that pertained to the issue of the military industrial complex.*]

My lack of knowledge of the Polish language and of the source material available in it exclude any claim for this article to be accepted as a comprehensive review of Mr. Nettl's recent biography of Rosa Luxemburg. A picture based primarily upon German and Russian experiences, which is the natural one for me and my contemporaries, is necessarily one-sided. Nettl's emphasis on the Polish aspects, and on the corresponding sides in Rosa's personal life, even if he has exaggerated them, forms the major merit of his book. Its shortcomings are those to be expected from a comparatively young author writing with sympathy, but far away from the intellectual world in which the experience described by him originated, and burdened with the psychological and sociological fashions of our days. The occasional factual mistakes, scarcely avoidable in a work of this size, include, however, some which throw doubt upon the success of the author's efforts to familiarize himself with the whole framework of the drama depicted by him. The following lines are intended as a treatment of a great figure in a specific stage in the development of the Marxist movement, reference to Mr. Nettl's book being made where this may help to make my argument clearer.

. . . . .

On 15 January 1919, the mercenaries who served the Ebert government as instruments for repressing an ill-organized revolt which was more propagandist than power-seeking, led a man and a woman out of the Eden Hotel, which served as a provisional barracks and prison, to shoot them 'while attempting to escape'. The two had been the leaders of the Marxist Left and of the anti-war struggle in Germany; the present author is not the only one whom they, and the Russian October revolution, helped to find his way to revolutionary socialism. (The war, in isolation, would have produced only an indignant pacifism.) Two days before their murder *Vorwärts,* the central organ of the German Social Democrat Party, one of whose editors Rosa Luxemburg had once been, had published verses culminating in the words:

> Many hundred corpses in a row,
> Proletarians.
> Karl, Rosa, Radek and Co.,
> Not one of them is there,
> Proletarians.

It has become the anti-communist fashion to burden Soviet foreign policies with the responsibility for all mistakes committed in German communist policies—but there is that doggerel, which will stay in my mind till I die, and there are the events of those weeks, which occurred before Soviet foreign policies could exercise any influence other than Radek's advice on the formation of German communism. The verses only reflected what Friedrich Ebert, whose memory is honoured by German Social Democracy to this day, had said at the very start of the November revolution of 1918: 'I have revolution like sin. . . . ' No one thought of dismissing the editors in whose paper such a poem could appear, no one in the government camp had thought of disarming the mercenaries and executing the guilty—they were left to the 'justice' of gowned fellow anti-communists; in the Federal Republic they got the official affirmation that their action was 'an execution in accordance with martial law'.

· · · · ·

Rosa Luxemburg had explained Marxism in a way which she regarded, and we accepted, as the orthodox one. For us the rejection by most other Marxists of her theory of accumulation mattered little, for it had helped to make us aware of the inherent inevitability of war so long as its roots, the capitalist mode of production, were preserved. Later, critical consideration of Rosa's work on our part was induced by the obvious contrast between Soviet Russia's triumph and our defeats, which continued even when we had an organized party. (What Rosa had founded at the end of her life was a mere symbol, rent by internal feuds and incapable of comprising more than a minority of those who stood on her platform. A communist mass party originated only in the autumn of 1920.) It was known that Rosa had had disagreements with Lenin on many issues, in particular the organization problem, a wrong solution of which appeared to be the main cause of our defeats. Had the theoretical foundations, so far as they were specifically 'Luxemburgist', been mistaken? From this, and not merely from the Russian interest in controlling potential supports of Trotskyism, followed the 'Bolshevization' of the German party in which the new German leadership of Ruth Fischer and Maslow played a temporary and provocative yet completely unprincipled part.

Even if we leave this episode alone, the need for communism to overcome Rosa Luxemburg's limitations was obvious, and remains obvious, if only because she failed to notice the fact, emphasized by Lenin and even Hilferding, that capitalism had entered a new stage, economically as well as politically. On the other hand, destalinization encourages looking back to those forms of Marxism which *preceded* the system described by Stalin as 'Leninism'. The re-consideration of one of the outstanding non-Russian contemporaries of Lenin (Labriola was another) offers a suitable opportunity for distinguishing the general traits of early twentieth-century revolutionary Marxism from its specific Russian realization.

In order to formulate this problem we must go back to 1892, when Rosa Luxemburg was 22, yet already one of the leaders of a Polish socialist group which tried to oppose the growth of a nationalist conception of Polish socialism. In his article *Socialism in Germany*, Engels tried to develop the prospects of German Social Democracy which, two years before, had emerged triumphant from Bismarck's oppression as the strongest German party. Nearly half a century had passed since Engels, together with his great friend whose name the theory was to bear, had started its elaboration, a mere fifteen years since he had still to fight hard stuggles within the still legal German Socialist party for the publication of its systematization in his *Anti-Dühring,* one year since that very party had adopted a programme, Marxist at least in form, as a symbol of its self-awareness and hope for the future. However, it was only superficially a Marxist party, and Engels was well aware of the basic importance of the periodically recurring disputes on allegedly particular problems. Dr. Nettl suggests that, apart perhaps from the agrarian ques-

tion and from the South German parliamentarians' desire to vote for budgets introduced by Liberal *Land* governments, everything was smooth. This impression, however, merely reflects the party bureaucracy's own self-assuring assertions.

During the first half of the nineties there were various critical developments, in particular in the trade union field to which, when it next became topical, Rosa Luxemburg was to devote so much of her attention. In substance, these developments centred on the question whether the trade unions, which in Germany as distinct from Britain had grown with the party's help, should adapt themselves to existing legislation enough to go on functioning normally but still maintain the spirit that had created them, or aim at ideological as well as organizational independence of the party, perhaps even eventually at the creation of a special trade union party competing with Social Democracy. The second alternative would have imposed a break with the cadres whose socialist convictions had given the unions the strength required to face the initial persecution. This was only one of the adaptations to prosperity within the existing social order, the first germs of which had been noticeable during the last years of the Anti-Socialist law, when repression was losing its strength. A considerable section of the underground workers reacted to these developments with distrust of the parliamentary group which, during the operation of the law, *nolens volens,* had functioned as Central Committee. Some of them (the 'Wild Men') even revived the anarchist attitudes which during the repression period of the eighties had characterized much of the Central and East European labour movement. At the Erfurt Party Congress which followed the restoration of the legal party organization (and which also adopted the first Marxist programme), the 'Wild Men' were expelled from the party. Engels, who was no lover of anarchists, covered the expulsions with his authority, but his distrust of the German party majority caused him to enforce in 1892, against the German leaders' reluctance to interfere with the cult of Lassalle, the publication of Marx's *Critique of the Gotha Programme* of 1875 so as to clarify Marx's and his own opposition to the ideas of Lassalle in which he saw a main source of the tendency of right-wing Social Democracy to adapt itself to the Prusso-German realities. A few years later, immediately before his death, Engels protested against the falsification of his introduction to the new, 1895, edition of Marx's *Class Struggle in France* and demanded, in a letter to Kautsky, the publication of his full original text. The cancer of the oesophagus which Engels was already suffering at the time saved the German party leaders that embarrassment and enabled them to continue—including in their later struggles against Rosa Luxemburg—with his alleged 'last will' which had turned him, as he complained, into 'a peaceful worshipper of legality *quand même*'. In fact he had said, to speak in the terms of his article of 1892, that legality *at this moment* operated in favour of the working class and that no one, except the ruling classes, had an interest in moving the class struggle from peaceful (industrial and parliamentary) methods to street fighting. Engels' favourite model for the transition mechanism was the triumph of Christianity within the Roman empire: the new social organization, inspired by a new outlook which had grown up within a decaying world, would in due course assume responsibility for its estate. (Engels was realistic enough to mention the part played in the eventual triumph of Christianity by the attitude of the army.)

The international socialist movement may return to this approach when acute revolutionary crises, in the sense defined by Engels himself and later by Lenin, are absent as well as in the event (which Engels could not envisage, since his perspectives for a triumph of Western socialism were 'short') of the process being so protracted that the worldwide transformation assumes the character of a competition between those parts of the world where the new order had made its first steps by revolutionary means, and the rest. For this very reason, it may be important to clarify the three basic implications of Engels' approach, the first two of which were fully appreciated by Rosa Luxemburg.

First of all, the social class called to form the basis of the new social cohesion has to be organized and made conscious of its task. (Nettl writes that the SPD was Rosa's fatherland, but what else could it have been? Surely it was not her fatherland to the exclusion of the Polish and Russian parties, nor . . . to the detriment of the best non-socialist achievements of German civilization.) In terms of contemporary sociology—the absence of which in Rosa's days I would not regard as a handicap for her work—this meant the development of a proletarian 'subculture' within West European civilization. Since it has become fashionable to discuss basic problems of socialism in connection with cultural life and in these days, as distinct from those when I was young, we have time for this, I may here formulate the problems arising in this field for Rosa's, and following, generations: the treasures accumulated by the old society had to be assimilated in order to secure their preservation and further development in the new order (Christianity had conspicuously failed in this respect) so as to satisfy the human needs of the emancipated class. Rosa, who conceived revolution as succeeding through a chain of temporary defeats, knew very well that millions of workers would get such satisfaction as they could achieve from the activities of the movement, not from its outcome in the cultural policies of socialist states. Besides, she was too much a Westerner to be satisfied with elementary achievements such as the abolition of illiteracy though she knew very well how many years even Russia—not to speak of the ex-colonial world—would need to satisfy even this elementary requirement. Her, and my, generation of socialist intellectuals who regarded service to the movement as the highest fulfilment of our lives could not and cannot conceive of personal artistic etc. tastes divorced from that standard and obligation. To state that for her it was Goethe, Turgenev, Korolenko, Beethoven, is merely another way of dating her life. People who will be young in the last decades of this century, or in the next, may find something else—provided the artists will succeed in creating something equivalent in a period in which the social incentive for classical art, the preparation of the soil in which lives devoted to the progress of mankind could flourish, may have changed its character. But there is nothing remarkable in the standard as such, as distinct from the encouragement of artistic experiment, which

may be left to the young artists. From Rosa's correspondence, incidentally, it is quite clear that she did *not* regard even the most progressive tendency as a substitute for the spark of genius.

It was not a matter of mere cultural 'superstructure'. As distinct from the young Marx, yet in complete agreement with the mature Marx, who had appreciated trade union struggles as instrumental in the growing consciousness and demands of the masses, Rosa did not believe that mere misery creates class consciousness. Arguing against the widespread conception of a peculiar character of the Russian revolution (of 1905-6) she writes in *Massenstreik, Partei und Gewerkschaft*:

> With paupers one cannot make revolutions of that political maturity and ideological clarity [as she found present in Russia, 1905-6]; from the cultural and intellectual point of view the industrial worker of Petersburg, Moscow or Odessa who stands in the front line of the struggle stands much nearer to the West European type than those who conceive bourgeois parliamentarism and well-ordered trade unionism as the sole and indispensable school of the working class. Even without the external guarantees of the bourgeois legal order the modern development of large-scale industry and fifteen years of social democrat intellectual influences which encouraged and guided the economic struggles have performed a good part of cultural work. The contrast becomes smaller still if, on the other side, the *actual* standard of life of the German working class is subject to a more thorough analysis. . . .

Rosa then proceeds to discuss the conditions of the broadest strata of the German working class which did not justify speaking—if I may use present terminology—of such an 'affluent society' as was claimed by the trade union leaders in order to argue that the 'crude' class struggle was over. It is for us not essential to what extent Rosa may have exaggerated in her desire to show that Russia *was not* an isolated case. My own knowledge of Berlin working-class conditions, fourteen years later, suggests that she was not far off the mark. What matters is the fact that in her concept (and, *a fortiori*, in that of Engels) there was *no* contradiction between improvement in the conditions of the working class and the preparation of that class for the eventual fulfilment of its historical task. The contradiction arises in the Revisionist idealization of the standard of living in opposition to Marx's statement, again and again repeated by Rosa Luxemburg, that reform is the by-product of revolution. And here we are meeting the *second* of the basic problems underlying the approach of Engels, and of the 'classical' type of 'pre-revolutionary' Social Democracy in general.

If the socialist aim is to be taken seriously and, even in the short run, the movement can avoid the splitting up of the working class into a number of possibly conflicting interest groups which can be made use of by the powers-that-be, all partial reforms must be seen as links in a prolonged revolutionary process (at this stage we need not speak of tactics). This concept was attacked by Revisionism, which aimed and still aims at the integration of the industrial workers (more precisely, of their individual groups) as sectional interests in the existing society. Bernstein's *Evolutionary Socialism,* the classical presentation of the outlook in the fight against which Rosa Luxemburg established her authority in Marxist circles, starts quite consistently with a polemic against Dialectics (not just the specific Hegelian terminology). In this he relies on Kant, i.e. he turns socialism from an issue of historical necessity into a demand for moral improvement. The book ends with a chapter on the relationship between the 'final aim' and the actual reform movement, in which the justification of the movement is found in its own existence as distinct from the achievement of a new form of society. The preceding chapters, which deal consistently with armaments and foreign and colonial policies in a spirit of progressive variations within the given framework of national policies, has a motto from Schiller which suggests that Social Democracy 'should dare to appear what it is'. In between stands a series of dissertations of varying relevance and substantiation, starting with the assertion that original Marxism, including the theory of the dictatorship of the proletariat, bears the marks of Blanquism (in the sense of the later discoverers of relationships between Lenin and Tkachev, or even Nechaev). There follows an assessment of the labour theory of value as not superior to the marginal utility theory (quite natural, if one rejects *a priori* the conception of history which gives it sense). Then comes a questioning of Marx's theory of the economic cycle on the sole basis of the two cycles preceding the publication of the book: unhappily for the author, and to Rosa Luxemburg's great satisfaction, the next ('orthodox') depression followed in the interval between the publication of Bernstein's original book and that of her critique. (Similar experiences occurred on the eve of the Great Depression of 1929.) At this point Bernstein expresses quite fantastic wishful thinking on a dispersion of capital ownership by an increase in the number of shareholders—this at the very time when monopoly capitalism was fully developing. He then considers the growing importance of cooperatives and, of all things, Liberalism. Rosa had no difficulty in dealing with his arguments on all these aspects, though she displayed no particular originality. She did not even unearth Engels' statements, made at the end of his life, on monopoly capitalism, a problem which Hilferding was to handle ten years later. As regards liberalism she was clear in stating that democracy, which in her opinion is essential for the triumph of the working class, emerges as a by-product of the successes of the socialist working class, and not from the Liberals. (The First Congress of Russian Social Democracy, not quoted by her, had already said all essentials on the Liberals.) The strength of Rosa's reply lies in the demonstration that militarism, war and domestic reaction, far from being distortions of the normal course of capitalist development, are inherent in modern capitalism.

The remarkable fact about the counter-attack against Bernstein's formulation of Revisionism (the trend in itself was much older and continues up to the present day) was the complete indifference of the intellectual leaders of the German party—who seven years before had formulated the Erfurt Programme—and that the initiative of two young party journalists, Parvus and Rosa Luxemburg, who had come from the western parts of the Tsarist empire, was required to put Acheron into motion. Nettl mentions the pressure exercised from outside by Plekhanov on the German party executive. He might have added that Plekhanov acted in full agreement with all the revolutionary Marxists of his country. Immediately after the appearance of the (Russian) Economists' *Credo,* the authors of which Bernstein eventually referred to as being close to him, the Siberian exiles, headed by Lenin, Martov, Potresov and Dan reacted with a protest, to which Plekhanov referred when his 'Emancipation of Labour' group in Zurich resumed its publications. Reaction against Revisionism stood at the root of *Iskra* which eventually was to shape Russian Social Democracy. There were good historial reasons for this: without its assertion of Marxism, Russian Social Democracy would not only have failed eventually to assume power (the future Mensheviks, who opposed that assumption, shared with Lenin in the protest) but would have dissolved itself in *bourgeois* liberalism, as was explicitly suggested in the *Credo* and was soon pursued by its authors. In Germany this mechanism would not operate since bourgeois liberalism had already fully developed, had a party (or rather two) and was fully compromised in the eyes of the working class by its capitulation to Bismarck's construction of the Empire, in the course of the protest against which German Social Democracy had originated. In Germany rejection of Revisionism by Social Democracy was required not on grounds of self-preservation, for a truly Revisionist party could still fulfil the functions of a Liberal party proper as it does in present-day West Germany, but in order to avoid splitting up the working class into individual interest-groups which would have led to Social Democracy becoming integrated into the framework of Bismarck's empire. As we have seen, party intellectuals who had grown up in the Russian or Polish framework were the first to object. There is no need for Nettl to base explanations on Rosa's alleged urge for a successful party career: such explanations form one of the most unfounded aspects of his book. (However, I realize that the use of the word 'power' ... by him as a sociologist trained to think in terms of machines and 'power' is different from its implications to a Marxist thinking in terms of objective social trends within which the individual has to play his part, within or outside institutional machinery.)

Rosa Luxemburg was in no way suitable for a successful 'career'. Quite apart from her propensity to stick to her views even if these were unpopular at party headquarters there was, for example, her incapacity to keep editorial posts for more than a few months (not all of this due to her status as a woman) and her refusal to work in those very fields of party activities where her sex would have been a definite asset. In her case, and in that of some of our best party workers, this refusal was their specific way of fighting for women's emancipation by demonstrating that they could do other work than that concerned with welfare, family and divorce legislation, the rights of the unmarried mother, etc. They knew well that the days of the Indira Gandhis or even Barbara Castles would not come during their lifetime. In fact, even the government of the Soviet Union has been up to now a *very* male affair, with a few exceptions at the start due to the large part played by women in the technique of underground work and to that played by the Socialist Women's International in the struggle against the war, which also made for Clara Zetkin's importance in the councils of Comintern.

Rosa's views were acceptable to the German party machine only in one point which, however, was of secondary importance to the machine (it is a merit of Nettl's to have emphasized this point), namely her resistance to Polish nationalism and nationlist socialism, as embodied, one should not forget, for example by Pilsudski. This resistance was essential to Rosa from the very start, and formed one of the foundations for her union with Leo Jogiches as well as for her early conflicts with Plekhanov, who in this connection showed no greater capacity for dealing with younger comrades on terms of equality than on other occasions.

Solidarity with the Polish struggle for national independence formed part of the Marxist tradition in general, and in particular in Russia where even the first 'Zemlya i volya', in 1863, had bravely faced isolation from the predominant trends of public opinion in order to express its solidarity with the Polish insurrection. On the other hand, Polish separatism represented a major nuisance for German Social Democracy (the Austrian party kept its Poles happy on a federative basis, while the German party was strictly centralist). From this, notwithstanding Kautsky's insistence on the classical Marxist tradition, originated some interest amongst the German party bureaucracy in Rosa's first activities amongst the Silesian Poles, which promoted her first steps in the German party. But that was all. Her attack against Revisionism made her unpopular with the machine which, like other machines, was not too happy to be pushed forward. With the discussions on the mass-strike (since 1905) begins her differentiation from the party majority. At first hidden, from 1910 explicit, this differentiation turns, with the outbreak of the war, into open and ruthless struggle, to be concluded with the foundation of the German Communist Party and the murder of Rosa.

All this was far in the future when, in answer to Bernstein, she wrote *Social Reform or Revolution?*, attempting to speak for the party. Those parts of the pamphlet which we have discussed above are, indeed, a mere reflection of views supposedly held by the party as a whole. But at the end of the pamphlet Rosa leaves the well-traced path—and Engels' whole concept of a mature fruit falling into the organized workers' grasp. Indeed, she here begins to develop, at the very start of her German party work, twenty years before her death, the specific 'Luxemburgist' attitude. Quoting Marx's statements from *The Eighteenth Brumaire of Louis Bonaparte,* and arguing against all the current statements about the dangers of assuming power before objective conditions have matured, Rosa argues that, since the organization of the socialist society presupposes the assumption of power by a class hitherto removed from current political education and experience, where all the objective conditions for socialist reconstruction are available the assumption of power *cannot* come too early: it will open the series of experiences, including defeats, in which the working class will mature. (I may here recall the last lines from her pen, written at the time when the insur-

rection begun against her advice was defeated and when she could well realize her personal fate. Yet she said of the Revolution: 'I was, I am, and I shall be'.) The first conquest of power by the working class, Rosa writes in 1898, is *bound* to come too early from the standpoint of *retaining it* since a transformation so enormous as the transition from capitalism to socialism cannot proceed otherwise than by a number of steps each unsatisfactory in itself. Only in the course of struggle and partial defeat can the working class become capable of solving that herculean task. The opposite approach, i.e. waiting till all the conditions are fulfilled by some automatic development, amounts to waiting in eternity, and leaving the initiative to opponents who will lead mankind into disaster. (Rosa did not know of atom bombs, but she was one of the first who realized the inevitability of one, or more, all-European wars unless the capitalist control of Europe was broken.) Being in essence a German socialist, Rosa *could not,* like Trotsky, conceive of 'permanent revolution' as an appeal, by the workers of an underdeveloped country, to those of more developed ones. To avoid misunderstandings, she did not even use the term.

As distinct from Lenin, and very much dominated as she was by her local Polish background of struggle against any confusion of socialism with nationalism, Rosa Luxemburg based her analysis strictly on the two main classes of capitalist society. For her, as opposed to the trade unionist ideal of securing material benefits for a skilled and well-organized minority of the working class (the achievements of which, generalized, constituted 'socialism', which was the substance of Bernstein's approach), the maturing process of the working class was a chain of revolutionary mass-movements, economic as well as political in character, which would involve the whole, or nearly the whole, of the class hitherto oppressed and denied the political experience required to build a new world. This, as already noted, was the substance of her **Massenstreik, Partei und Gewerkschaft.** If, in order to draw the lessons from the Russian experience, she may have drawn a picture of the working class at least of Petersburg, Moscow and Odessa slightly nearer to the West than they actually were, it should be added that this lack of precision had enabled her also to foretell, earlier than did anyone else, that 'the future Russia will be the socialist element of fermentation [she did not say more] for the whole of Europe'. On the other hand, her very conviction of a basic identity of Russian and German issues, her conception of the Russian movement as facing tasks not particularly Russian in character, caused her, who knew the bureaucracy of the German labour movement, to use, during the struggle of the Russian Mensheviks (with whom she sided in the organization dispute against the Bolsheviks) expressions such as 'the organization as a process' upon which Lenin, the guardian of the traditions of the revolutionary *Narodniki* and the enthusiastic student of organization problems, poured deserved scorn.

The socialist party of each country was the element of guidance, not more, since Rosa did not believe that revolutions could be organized in the sense of determining their start and practical course, which had to be left to the dynamics of the revolutionary period. Guidance in the revolutionary period meant giving the struggle such slogans and direction that at every moment the maximum of the potential as well as of the actual power of the working class is realized, that the decisiveness and sharpness of the tactics of Social Democracy never lag behind the actual forces but move ahead of them. (No provision is made for retreat. This, presumably, is left to the dynamics of the counter-revolutionary phases: it was in such a one that Rosa was to die.) But Social Democracy is not just identical with the parliamentary party and its electorate. Rosa—and this she had learned from Lenin's *What is to be Done?*—was quite explicit on the existence of two different aspects of the political party: that of fighting for social reforms of all kinds—in *this* respect it was simply another branch of organized labour, equal in rights but not superior to trade unionism; and as the carrier of the long-term interest of the working class in its emancipation. In the latter respect, the trade unions formed only a part of the whole as represented by Social Democracy. Thus, the trade union leaders' claim for a voice equal to that of the party in long-term policy decisions such as calls for revolutionary strikes amounted to a mere indirect way of stating that they could not imagine forms of the class struggle other than that for partial reforms in the framework of the existing society. In all this, however, Rosa lacks one basic element of the Leninist analysis of party, namely his statement in *What is to be Done?* that the insufficiency of the 'trade unionist class-consciousness' (both trade unionist and reformist parliamentary) derives not only from its short view but also from its failure to be based upon the experiences and relationships of *all* classes in society.

With the above observations we have given an explanation of Rosa Luxemburg's failure fully to come to terms with Lenin at any stage of her development. This was not implied in any struggle of hers for abstract 'democracy': in his presentation, Nettl rightly takes issue with the misuse of her attitude for present anti-communist purposes. I may add that, once Rosa had sided with the Mensheviks in the Russian organizational issue, she was bound to use the 'democratic' argument as everyone, including people who apply methods so undemocratic as her companion Jogiches in the Polish disputes from 1911, does in such circumstances. The question was simply why she sided that way. Rosa's attitude to the Russian party might rather be derived from her negative attitude to Polish self-determination. Lenin was quite prepared to regard errors in this respect, if committed *by Poles,* i.e. by members of the oppressed nation, as purely tactical. There was, however, a real fear that, in the event of close collaboration, 'the Russians would soon discover that the SDKPiL [Social Democrat Party of Poland and Lithuania] was in fact like a South American army—all generals and few soldiers'. But all this was subsidiary. Once Rosa saw both the Mensheviks (the Petrograd Soviet, dominated even by the left-wing Mensheviks Trotsky and Parvus as it was) and the Moscow Bolsheviks in action, and had had an opportunity to discuss the actual issues of the revolution with the Bolshevik leaders, her choice would be clear. This, moreover, contradicts the myth that she glorified mass strikes at the expense of armed insurrection, though she would not ascribe to the latter such a central importance as is natural for supporters of 'organizing the revolution'.

Then followed the collaboration with Lenin in the very superficially re-united Russian party, in the struggle for the anti-war platform in the International and (after an interruption due to her and Jogiches' not very democratic manoeuvres in their domestic party split) a loose though never close collaboration during the War, when Rosa, as we shall see later, adopted an attitude similar to that of the 'Left-wing Communists' in Lenin's own party. There is nothing astonishing in this if we keep in mind that within the general framework of revolutionary Marxism, which would assert itself in burning issues of war and revolution, Lenin's specific attitude in the organization issue derived from his concrete analysis of the national and agrarian problems, which forms his world historical merit but which Rosa, enamoured as she was with the classical 'model' of 'pure' capitalism (and with the domestic struggle against the Polish Social Patriots), simply refused to appreciate. Perhaps she chose Germany as her main field of activity precisely because it was closer to the model.

The institutional framework of party life appears, indeed, irrelevant once it is taken for grated that some inherent mechanism of capitalist society will, by its own dynamics, bring about the conditions in which class consciousness and, eventually, the solution of the historical tasks of the working class are generated through a process of mass 'spontaneity'. When Rosa believes that the political level of Social Democracy allows for the expulsion of Bernstein, she suggests it so that he may occupy his true position as a lower-middle-class liberal. When she sees that this is impossible in view of the strength of Bernstein's actual (as distinct from formal) support, she withdraws the suggestion and eliminates the corresponding paragraphs from *Social Reform or Revolution?* What else could she do? By now she had arrived at the conclusion: 'Let us stay at our principle that no one is expelled from our ranks because of theoretical convictions'. This goes of course a good deal further than the view that, since the expulsion of right-wingers is clearly impossible, the party's internal balance should not be disturbed by the expulsion of anarchistic elements, which is a question of tactics. It is clear that for a person capable of making these two statements, at an interval of seven years, it is not just the tactical situation of the intra-party struggle but the concept of party itself which has changed. Now it was no longer the community of socialists inspired by Marxist principles but the place where one could work for those principles, the 'protecting roof over our heads' as Fritz Heckert, the representative of her group, *Spartakus,* frankly enough stated at the foundation congress of the new Independent Socialist Party at Easter 1917. But some ten years before, the feeling that the party bureaucracy, if given a free hand, would purge the party of *all* dissenters was already widespread. From the fear of such developments arose, as Nettl has noticed (though he incorrectly transfers it to the realm of mere 'morality') an occasional united front of right-wing and left-wing Social Democrats. In view of the tendency of the party's executive committee to denounce even such informal Left groupings as *Sonderbünde,* and of the enormous power of the trade unions, which would have backed an expulsion of the Left and even urged it, there can be no doubt that Frölich's retrospective suggestion that the Left might have organized itself in a group, with some journal as the initial centre (as the Right wing had done with the *Sozialistische Monatshefte*), represented, indeed, the maximum of the possible. It should be added that the main purpose of such a journal would have been clarification within the group itself since even Mehring opposed Rosa in the all-important issue of strengthening the mass movement on the Prussian constitutional question. The journal was established, as late as December 1913, in the very elementary form of a *Presse-Korrespondenz,* to be used by sympathetic editors of party papers (there were not many of them) but containing also a lot of articles which Rosa and Marchlewski, the editors, could not expect to be reprinted, and which thus must have been regarded as destined for their sympathizers' information. It still proved useful in the first stage of the war, and formed the basis of the later **Spartakus-Briefe**. As happens in such cases, it had originated from a breakdown of Rosa's earlier tactics, which were to place her articles in widely read Socialist dailies edited by her real or presumed friends.

Wishful thinking in this respect may have been prompted by Rosa's earlier successes during the campaign for mass strikes to enforce democracy in Germany, which began again on the immediate eve of the war. In general, and not only in Petersburg where this was obvious, the war began at a time when a strong radicalization of the labour movement was noticeable. Rosa's position as a member of the International Socialist Bureau and the great authority she enjoyed in it certainly prompted her overestimation of her influence. Her position was in fact strengthened by her intermediate situation between the Germans and the Bolsheviks, the fantastically difficult special problem of the Poles, and her consistent internationalism. She had experienced Kautsky's sudden turn a few months after he wrote, in 1909, the *Weg zur Macht,* to his (if one may use a later communist term) 'struggle on two fronts' against herself and the Revisionists—in fact more against her group, while the Revisionists got away with very formal condemnations. Afterwards she had lost many wavering supporters during the years when it became clear that she was *not* speaking for the party majority. Such experiences were bound to make it clear to her that she and her closest group of friends had to prepare for playing an independent part within the party of the German working class. I can assure Dr. Nettl that the factory workers in her Niederbarnim constituency—young when they attended her classes, experienced shop-stewards when fifteen years later they worked with me—were *not* kept uninformed on basic issues, nor—as he appears to think, on the basis of some correspondence—were they mainly regarded as means of getting mandates to party congresses.

Within hours of learning of the decision of the parliamentary party on 4 August 1914, Rosa did what every intelligent and energetic Marxist is bound to do in similar circumstances, i.e. convened a factional meeting to organize the necessary counter-action. She has proved herself not only a brave (*das moralische versteht sich von selbst*) but also a careful (see her efforts to prevent a premature sacrifice by Liebknecht), intelligent and consistent leader of the anti-war group. That (as Stalin would have said) she concentrated her fire on those who had betrayed *German* socialism was not, as Nettl considers, a matter of pent-up resentment but an application of the principle, formulated in those days by Karl Liebknecht, that 'the enemy stand in one's own country'. Should a German socialist eager to fight the imperialists have joined hands with them to denounce mainly the French and British Social Patriots? Nuances, such as whether one should formulate this attitude in Rosa's terms, or in Lenin's terms of 'defeat of one's own bourgeoisie' while he wrote, to avoid misunderstandings, articles on 'The National Pride of the Great Russians' appear ridiculous in the historical perspective. I am not willing to argue with my two great teachers on such points, after half a century has passed. So far as the Social Patriot right wing was concerned, it was not a matter of arguing against erring comrades but of the class struggle in its most immediate forms. That poem of 1919 and Ebert's observation, with which we have opened this article, forms a mere continuation of earlier statements dating especially from the replacement in October 1905 of the right-wing editors of *Vorwärts* by Rosa Luxemburg and other left wingers. This series of statements carried, at various periods, an intermixture of chauvinistic, anti-feminist and anti-semitic overtones, denunciation of her policies as harmful to the trade union cause and all kinds of attacks against her personal honour.

Her attitude to the Marxist 'centre' logically followed from the resolution of the Stuttgart Congress of the International which she had moved seven years before. If it was correct that in the event of war socialists should use the political and economic crisis created by it as an opportunity to promote the fall of the capitalist regime, no person who took this decision seriously could take anything other than a fighting attitude to a group of which an outstanding leader, Karl Kautsky—once Rosa's supporter in the movement for political mass-strikes—now proclaimed the slogan: 'class-struggle *in peace,* struggle for peace [in alliance with the liberal pacifists] in wartime'. The sharpness of Rosa's critique of the 'Marxist Centre' in no way prevented her from keeping to the principle that 'the worst working-class party is better than none', which she had formulated in 1908, and that

> one can 'leave' sects or conventicles when these no longer suit and one can always found new sects or conventicles; it is nothing but childish fantasy to talk of liberating the whole mass of proletarians from their bitter and terrible fate by simply 'leaving' and in this way setting them a brave example,

as she wrote from prison in early 1917. On such grounds, she opposed even the separation of the Centrist minority of the SPD from the majority party, enforced though it was by the latter's leaders (who had good reasons, for even in my days there were quite a few regions, mainly in Saxony, where most of the 'majority socialist' workers and party activists were far to the left of many of the former 'Independents'). Eventually, those very principles would cause *Spartakus* to participate as an independent faction in the formation of the Independent Socialist Party; as late as 11 November 1918 Rosa's advice would be to remain in that party as long as possible. There was no ground for any different behaviour, unless one took the Leninist position that the party had to *organize* the revolution, a position taken by *none* of the competing left-wing factions in Germany. Even if someone had taken that position, it would have been nonsense to establish an independent party unless one had the potential required at least to *try* it. Lenin had this potential, if only *in nucleo,* when, in Prague in 1912, he rallied a majority of the operating socialist party committees during the start of a revolutionary wave, an obvious aim of which (the establishment of the democratic republic in Russia) was on the cards but in no way assured unless the Russian working class had a party *not* bound to collaboration with, and waiting for, the liberal bourgeoisie.

There follows the Russian revolution. However much use has been made of Rosa's writings of those days to show her allegedly inherent opposition to Bolshevik policies (Nettl . . . is quite sensible on this point), nothing emerges beyond the obvious facts. These were, firstly, that Rosa was a German and hence, according to the principle that 'the enemy stands in one's own country', viewed a separate peace of Soviet Russia with Germany, which was bound at least temporarily to alleviate the latter's position, with eyes different from those of the Bolsheviks (whose obligations to their own revolution she fully recognized). Secondly, she had in general, as we have seen, a tendency to be pessimistic on the prospects of first revolutionary triumphs to be consolidated, and hence to put greater demands on the orthodoxy of practical policies which, in her opinion, would produce lessons for the future rather than consolidated states. This was in principle the position of the Soviet 'left-wing Communists' of the Brest Litovsk period, i.e. that held for a short while by a majority of the Russian party. Finally, Rosa put greater demands than the Bolsheviks could satisfy on the preservation of some kind of proletarian democracy. However, her critique of the dissolution of the Constituent Assembly was only short-lived. At the end she pursued in Germany the same policy, with the difference only that the Bolsheviks were backed by the sympathy of the overwhelming majority of the industrial workers and soldiers while Rosa, in her very last programmatic declaration, had to admit that, in Germany, both kinds of support were conspicuously absent. As regards the terror Rosa, arguing with Radek, now the Russian party representative, is sorry that their old comrade Dzerzhinsky has taken up the job of organizing Cheka, even be it necessary. Leo Jogiches, supporting in the argument their old opponent Radek, says to Rosa: 'If the need arises, you can do it too'. This is the crux of the matter: the Russian revolution has ceased to be a dream, it has become hard reality. If Rosa had survived and become responsible for a real revolution building a new order she, too, would have learned to do hard things. But could she have survived so long?

At the time of that conversation, against Rosa's and Radek's advice, the decision had been taken to leave the Independent Socialists and to establish an independent Communist Party. The programme, drafted by Rosa, concludes with the declaration that Spartakus would never assume power except when called by the workers to do so. But when the revolution started, Spartakus had not more than fifty organized members in Berlin. The decision to establish a party of its own was taken because at a meeting

of the Berlin activists of the Independent Socialist Party Rosa had got less than a third of the votes on her motion to convene an extraordinary party congress. Spartakus did not get a single delegate to the national congress of the German Soviets. Its independent caucus within the Berlin Soviet was established a month after Liebknecht's and Rosa's deaths. But in March 1919, at the National Congress of the Independent Socialists, a motion in favour of participating in parliamentary elections only as a means to promote propaganda for the Soviet system (i.e. the very platform which Rosa had defended at the foundation congress of 'her' party yet been outvoted by the radical anti-parliamentarians) was lost by only one vote. In December 1919 the next congress of the Independents unanimously adopted a resolution in favour of establishing a Soviet government. A motion immediately to join Comintern, which had been established in March of that year, polled 114 votes against 169 in favour of a motion to enter into negotiations with Moscow. When these negotiations had produced Lenin's Twenty-One Conditions, the Leipzig Congress of the Independent Socialists in October 1920 (Zinoviev arguing against Martov) accepted the conditions, which implied expulsion of the right-wing Independents, by 256 to 156 votes. Less than half of the members existing on paper carried out the decision: still, only 50,000 of the 300,000 members of the new communist party had come from Spartakus. Its heroism during the first crises of the revolution and the blood of its founders, who were now regarded as the martyrs of the German socialist movement, had not even been capable of producing the mainstream of German communism. Rosa had been right in opposing the foundation of the party. She was wrong when she gave way to revolutionary enthusiasm, both on that occasion and a few weeks later when the Berlin Independents started an abortive insurrection from which she could not dissociate herself—nor even, though it was disapproved by her central committee, prevent the participation of some of its leaders, because her theory prohibited her from opposing 'mass-initiative', even that of a majority which was only local in a hopeless situation. What further happened to her has been said in the opening of this article.

She would always have been ready to fertilize with her blood the soil for a truly revolutionary party of the German proletariat. In the moral sense she has done so. But she was a theoretician, and her theoretical legacy proved to be a handicap for the development of her party. That she and Karl Liebknecht, the heroes of the anti-war struggle, could be outvoted at the foundation congress in two issues so decisive as the participation in parliamentary elections and in the existing trade unions, was bad enough. That the doomed insurrection could be started against her will was worse. But worst of all was the fact that her theory did not even enable her party to correct mistakes without immediately falling into the opposite extreme. Seven months after her death, under the leadership of her pupil Levi—the same who, when eventually leaving the party, used Rosa's critique of the Bolshevik revolution as an instrument to dissociate his group from it—the party expelled (against Radek's advice) the radical wing, i.e. a near majority of the existing members, including the most important industrial regions. When in the following spring in Germany a situation arose which was analogous to that of the Russian Kornilov coup which had opened to the Bolsheviks the way to power, the Central Committee led by Levi declared, now in a pseudo-orthodox vein, that the working class was not interested in the armed dispute between two factions of the ruling class. In that instance there were no Russians who could be regarded as responsible, as in an analogous case eleven years later. After 1920, there was time to attempt the correction; after 1932, though the correction was attempted, none.

Since I am here concerned with the history not of organizations but of ideologies, I may ask the question to what extent Rosa Luxemburg's failure in every sense other than the moral one was due to weaknesses of theory. Undoubtedly she was to a large extent the heiress of Marx and, with a few exceptions (such as the Accumulation theory) wished it to be so. But though the unquestionable Marxist successes have not been achieved without accommodations, it can hardly be said that Lenin's development of emphasis on Party represents a larger deformation of original Marxism than the opposite one, its virtual negation by Rosa Luxemburg.

The differences in economic theory were almost irrelevant for initial successes or failures. In the period of reconstruction and, *a fortiori* in the post-Keynesian period in the West, it was important to have a theory of imperialism based on full recognition of the phenomenon of monopoly capitalism. But at a time when everything depended on every militant's conviction that the horrors of the First World War were no accident, no consequence of mere faulty politics capable of correction within the framework of capitalist society, the details of theories of imperialism did not matter.

Rosa Luxemburg's negative attitude to national problems has undoubtedly done harm to the communist movement of her home country, Poland, where the political task consisted precisely in finding a combination of the urge for national liberation with the need to prevent a deflection of this urge into chauvinistic if not (in the case of Pilsudski) fascist channels. But this does not hold true of her adopted fatherland, Germany, where the sharpest opposition to aggressive chauvinism was the right one.

One is led to the opinion that her basic weakness lies precisely where also lies her great historic strength: in her function as a transmission belt between the Eastern and the Western developments of Marxism. Her capacity to promote critically creative groups ('peer groups', to use the not very helpful term of modern sociology which Nettl repeatedly employs, perhaps without knowing *how* current the phenomenon was in those days, and thus how little the term explains) combined, in her mind and in her activities, her personal roots in a powerful revolutionary movement which evokes the strongest moral forces in men (yet also, because of the very restricted scene on which its preparation can proceed, makes for all the unavoidable narrowness of groupings) with her operations in a mass party exposed to stagnation and bureaucratization yet also requiring a remedy against those very shortcomings. In the East, Rosa Luxemburg has been a not very successful organizer and a fairly average theoretician; her failure has

been obvious because it contrasted so strongly with Lenin's triumph (though it should not be forgotten that there was only *one* Lenin in the Russian movement; Rosa was not inferior to Trotsky or Bukharin). In the West, she was the greatest Marxist theoretician since Engels' death—outside Italy, which with Labriola and Gramsci had quite a remarkable succession independent of the Russian tradition. Her weaknesses may be explained in terms of a failure of Marxism, as developed in her days, to satisfy the needs of a fully developed Western industrial country.

At this point I wish to return to my observation above that Engels' approach of 1892 has three basic implications. We have hitherto discussed how Rosa Luxemburg handled the first two of these—the need for the new class to be organized and to be made conscious of its task, and the need for it to mature in experience and organization to the demands of that task. There is a third one, which exceeds the framework of Rosa Luxemburg's days, and those of my own youth, when the approach of war, war itself, and in between the wars the Great Depression, appeared to answer the question on our behalf. Indeed, we would then have regarded any application to present-day capitalism of Marx's saying that no social system collapses before it has exhausted all its potential productive capacity as an abandonment of the essentials of Marxism—which it is not, since the correctness of the Marxist analysis does *not* depend upon whether the great transformation takes place in the nineteenth, twentieth or twenty-first centuries, whether there are intermediate stages, etc. By now we have had two decades without major depressions, with an evident raising of the productive resources in both parts of the world, and the hope that the threat of world war may recede. What then?

Rosa Luxemburg has made two contributions to a future tackling of this problem. First, during the years when things appeared to proceed so slowly and the obstacles presented by the German party bureaucracy so overwhelmingly strong, she, living in Germany and realizing the close associations of all aspects of German society with militarism, tried to subsume all of them 'from the poisoning of an old-age pensioner to the pretensions of Prussian officers, from unemployment to taxation' under the general heading of 'imperialism', avoiding both the specific emphasis on the militarist phenomenon that was characteristic of Liebknecht and also a specific economic definition of imperialism, since she had none. Whether this was really such an asset as Nettl asserts is an open question. Certainly it was better than over-specialization, or emphasis on the mere fact of monopoly; both approaches would logically lead to a struggle against purely individual aspects of existing society and thus deprive socialism of its function as an *alternative* to capitalist society (this once taken for granted, the issue of 'reform *vs.* revolution' is an issue of tactics, applicable in definite times and places). Rosa felt that the problem must somehow be tackled. This is the background of her suggestion, made in 1910 and rejected even by Mehring because of the traditional Marxist aversion to emphasis on 'superstructural' aspects, to raise the issue of the monarchy—not quite an irrelevant issue, one would think, in pre-1914 Germany. This line was continued during the war when, in the *Junius* pamphlet, she combined the assertion that no national wars were possible any more (an assertion rejected by Lenin) with the raising of a political, i.e. republican, programme for Germany—as if, to quote Lenin's criticism, the Greater German Republic, if existing, would not also have conducted an imperialist war. Of course, it would—but the question was whether, in the process of bringing it into being in the struggle against a monarchy fully identified with the Army, the latter, and thereby the backbone of the powers-that-be, might have been broken. It is another question whether this could have been achieved with her theory about organization which amounted, in effect, to her rejection of organization. In substance, this is the issue of 'transition slogans in non-revolutionary situations' about which in the late twenties we had so many disputes with our right-wingers, most of them direct pupils of Rosa Luxemburg. It still remains to me more than problematical whether, say, the demand for a transformation of the Reichswehr into a People's Militia, in days where it would have simply amounted to broadening the entrance to the military career, would have amounted to a policy different in substance from that pursued, at present, by West German Social Democracy which supports the so-called national demands of the existing government because it is allegedly unpatriotic to do otherwise.

Secondly, there stands her theory of Accumulation, that is to say her assertion that the part of the surplus value destined for investment cannot be realized by sales to either of the main classes of capitalist society but only outside its framework, to the remaining pre-capitalist classes in the capitalist centres and, in particular, in the colonial countries which, in the process, become capitalist themselves. With the approaching conclusion of the process, and even earlier with a serious reduction of scope for expansion, the viability of capitalism comes to an end and it will fall, presumably in a chain of major depressions with revolutionary consequences. With this theory, which played in her intellectual *corpus* the same role as that of monopoly capitalism for Hilferding and Lenin, Rosa Luxemburg remained amongst Marxist theorists in a minority of one. Her reply to the almost unanimous criticism, including by such unquestionable left wingers as Lenin, under the heading 'What the Epigones have made of the Marxist Theory', albeit from prison, is not one of her best writings. Nevertheless, at a time when stability of the value of money was a basic assumption of all Marxist models, she had a case, and she was one of the few Marxist theorists who seriously approached the problems of the underdeveloped countries. True, she did so with an erroneous concept and from the wrong end, so to speak, as potential yet insufficient markets for the industrialized countries rather than in relation to economic and political processes in the colonial countries themselves. (But may not her approach again be relevant? Will, for example, the effect of the Vietnam war upon South-East Asia be necessarily more important, on the world scale, than that upon the West itself?) However great the temporary impact of Rosa's theory upon the CPG then in formation, it was bound to remain transitory: not because the Russians insisted on Leninist orthodoxy but because it was impossible with its help to handle the problems of real underdevel-

oped countries when they arose, starting with China. The theory has retained a certain influence amongst those non-communist intellectuals who searched for a theory of automatic breakdown of capitalism, the very thing which Rosa rejected in favour of a conception of a series of conflicts and catastrophes, the solution of which by working-class action would demand a maximum of consciousness.

In the last chapter of *The Accumulation of Capital* Rosa Luxemburg describes militarism, at least so far as it is financed by taxes levied from the non-proletarian strata of the population, as an additional field for the realization of the surplus value to be accumulated: only at this point do the activities of the state as a potential regulator of the economic cycle come in. But let us not forget that the book was written in 1912 and that phenomena such as the 'war-industrial complex' are still with us. If her analysis was mistaken then it shows, in any case, points relevant even for our days. Not of all economists and sociologists can this be said after more than half a century.

George Lichtheim (essay date 1966)

SOURCE: "Rosa Luxemburg," in *The Concept of Ideology and Other Essays,* Random House, 1967, pp. 193-203.

[*Lichtheim was a German-born social historian and authority on Karl Marx. In the following essay, which was originally published in* Encounter *in 1966, he considers Nettl's portrait of Luxemburg and her contemporaries, and applauds the moral rigor of Luxemburg's work despite its technical flaws.*]

In the mythology of revolutionary socialism, east and west of the great divide, the name of Rosa Luxemburg (1871-1919) is indissolubly linked with that of Karl Liebknecht: victims of the Spartacist rising in January 1919 whose brutal suppression by soldiers nominally responsible to a Social-Democratic government sealed in blood the wartime split of the German labor movement. Nor is this familiar assessment confined to Communist literature. In Western historiography too, their names invariably appear as though joined together by history's decree. Every study of the Weimar Republic opens perforce with an account of the Berlin insurrection launched by the nascent Communist movement against the government of Ebert and Noske. And while the ceremonial linking of the names Liebknecht and Luxemburg by today's East German regime has long ceased to be anything but a gesture towards a dimly remembered past, the legend persists that German Communism conserves the heritage of this strange pair of martyrs: the solid lawyer and *Reichstag* deputy, suddenly catapulted into fame by his passionate wartime oratory in 1914-1918, and the brilliant Polish-Jewish woman revolutionary who appears in these accounts as his inspirer and companion. The fact that down to 1914 they had virtually nothing in common, that Liebknecht—by philosophical conviction a Kantian—was not even a Marxist, let alone a Communist, and that in 1919 he was merely the popular figurehead of a rebellion not effectively controlled by anyone, is seldom permitted to encroach upon the myth.

It is the great merit of J. P. Nettl's enormously detailed and painstakingly scholarly work that a serious study of

Rosa Luxemburg's actual historical role is now at last available to the public. A biographer by choice and inclination, he is also in effect a historian of the East European socialist movement before 1914; and while his partisanship is never concealed, he has not on the whole allowed it to interfere with the analysis of personalities and events. The comparison with Mr. Isaac Deutscher's biography of Trotsky imposes itself. It works in Mr. Nettl's favor, if only because his intellectual apparatus includes economics and sociology, as well as the standard techniques of the historian. His grasp of Russian and Polish realities is the equal of Mr. Deutscher's, while in relation to Germany his understanding, if not quite flawless, is much superior to that of most writers whose primary background is East European. These are impressive qualifications, and they have resulted in the production of a remarkable work. Readers not put off by its formidable bulk (827 pages of text, plus two lengthy appendices, and 70 pages of bibliography in five languages, including Russian and Polish) can now at last find their way through the maze of political and theoretical conflicts from which in due course the Russian, Polish, Austrian, and German upheavals of 1917-1919 were to derive their shape.

What emerges from Mr. Nettl's analysis of the crucial role played by his heroine in these events is at first glance surprising. Those who had thought of Rosa Luxemburg as primarily a figure in German Socialist history will have to revise what they had gathered from earlier biographers. The familiar and slightly puzzling image—a young woman from Russian Poland who suddenly erupted on the German scene around 1900 and thereafter made a career as a brilliant publicist—is replaced by a far more complex and fascinating picture: that of a woman who was both a gifted theorist and a steel-willed conspirator, the central figure of a small but influential group of Polish revolutionaries who operated simultaneously in the Socialist movements of three countries—Russia, Austria-Hungary, and Germany; an organizer who covered her traces with such skill that even her closest German friends and associates had no real inkling of her true role in neighboring Poland and in the leadership of the conspiratorial Marxist group she had founded with her close personal and political associate Leo Jogiches. Though formally a German citizen (by way of a nominal marriage) since 1898, a prominent member of the German Social-Democratic Party, and a steady contributor to its journals, Rosa Luxemburg—almost down to the eve of war in 1914 when she partly relinquished her Polish ties—remained at heart what she had been since her student days in Zürich in the 1890s: the theorist of a self-appointed "peer group" of revolutionaries with a following among the Polish-speaking masses of the three Eastern Empires, whose simultaneous collapse in 1918 was to restore Poland as a nation, thereby paradoxically inflicting upon Rosa Luxemburg and her group (the SDKPIL—Social-Democracy of the Kingdom of Poland and Lithuania) the most shattering political defeat of her life.

The secret of Rosa Luxemburg's strange personality and career, one may now say with certainty, is to be found in the fact that for twenty years she was the principal link between the German Socialist movement and the totally different world of the conspiratorial and elitist Russo-Polish underground parties and sects. Manipulating her contacts on both sides with remarkable dexterity, she managed to appear in German eyes as an expert on the Russian situation, while representing the German Social-Democratic Party (the SPD) towards the Polish and Russian factions, including Lenin's Bolsheviks, with whom she alternately feuded and cooperated. So great was her operational skill (at least while she had the benefit of Leo Jogiches' advice) that she succeeded in getting her small Marxist group, whose following was limited to a few cities, accepted by the Germans as the official representation of the Polish workers in Germany, as against the more numerous Polish Socialist Party of her rivals, the PPS. This strange configuration in turn she exploited with relentless energy to impose herself on the cautious leadership of German Social-Democracy. To the veteran August Bebel and most of the other leaders she was primarily an ally against Polish nationalism: a growing force among the Polish masses in Silesia of which they stood in mortal terror (as did the Imperial German Government). As long as she was ready to battle the nationalists on their home ground, the SPD Executive forgave her almost anything, even her doctrinaire Marxism and her constant broadsides against their own somnolent passivity. It was for this that Bebel protected her against the South German "revisionists" and against her sworn enemies, the trade union leaders; for this that Kautsky (who liked her personally) opened the pages of his great theoretical organ, the *Neue Zeit,* to her and allowed her to lambaste his old opponent Eduard Bernstein to her heart's content. To the more cynical SPD bureaucrats, indeed, she was hardly more than an unconscious agent of Germanization among the Polish masses in Eastern Germany. The alliance collapsed only when in 1910 she tried of it and turned against Bebel and even against her old friend and protector Kautsky. Only then did she become the leader of the extreme Left in Germany. The whole of this deeply hidden labyrinth of Central and East European politics in the years before the First World War has been illuminated for the first time by Mr. Nettl's truly Herculean labors in the German and Polish archives.

That a degree of secretiveness, and even duplicity, should in consequence have been imposed upon a woman by nature candid, outspoken, and contemptuous of make-believe, must be laid to the peculiar world of Russo-Polish émigré politics from which in 1896 she suddenly emerged, to astound the Congress of the Socialist International with the spectacle of a fiery young woman of twenty-five informing the bearded veterans of a hundred battles that they knew nothing about the East European picture, and that moreover Marx and Engels had been wrong about it. To this point it will be necessary to return. What needs to be retained here is a biographical circumstance to which Mr. Nettl has lent some reluctant prominence: the fact that her deepest loyalties lay in an area which had little to do with her public life as a representative of German Socialism. As her biographer puts it:

> Many of her German friends were totally unaware of the fact that on top of her full-time work in the SPD—and on the problem of Polish

organization on German soil, in Pomerania and Silesia—she was simultaneously one of the main inspirers and leaders of a Polish party whose center of gravity lay in the Russian empire.

Not only were her relations with Jogiches, Marchlewski, and others of her circle more important to her than her German friends she actually disliked Germany and the Germans, though she lived there for twenty years and played a prominent role in the SPD. A self-conscious Easterner, she preferred Russian literature to German (admittedly a judgment shared by many discerning critics), described Russian as "the language of the future," and for the rest reserved her personal affection for the French, the Italians, and other Latins. It is a remarkable story, conceivable perhaps only in an age more liberal than ours, when disregard for national frontiers was thought respectable at least by Socialists. But in large measure it responded also to certain features of her background duly recorded by Mr. Nettl: her early involvement in the conspiratorial world of Polish émigré politics in Zürich and Paris, and her naïve assumption that the moral and intellectual standards of the Jewish intelligentsia in Eastern Europe were natural also to the labor movement, or at least could be implanted in it under the guise of "proletarian internationalism."

This is the key to the story. Mr. Nettl handles it gingerly, though from time to time he summons up courage to remind the reader that the intellectual leadership of Rosa Luxemburg's and Leo Jogiches' private creation, the SDKPIL, was largely (though not wholly) a Jewish affair. Today when this particular story has been played out to its dreadful finale, there is a natural reluctance to dwell upon these circumstances. Mr. Nettl wisely resists the temptation, though he is clearly unhappy with the notion that the emotional spring which fed Rosa Luxemburg's passionate loyalty to the International was a form of Jewish Messianism. He does not wholly repudiate the idea, but leaves it in the air. Her contemporaries were less inhibited. To the majority faction of Polish Socialism, the PPS, she was quite simply a Jewish intellectual who cared nothing for Poland; to the self-consciously Jewish leaders of the *Bund,* the mass movement of the Yiddish-speaking proletariat in Russian Poland, she was a traitor to her people. In her own eyes she was a true internationalist and the only consistent Marxist of the lot: this although her attitude on the Polish question was in flat contradiction to literally everything Marx (and even Engels) had said on the the subject.

It is necessary to pause here. The subject is loaded with passion. It was the central issue of Rosa Luxemburg's political life—far more important to her than the boring quarrels within the German Socialist movement, or even the more fascinating disputations between Lenin and his Menshevik opponents (which she exploited with remarkable skill to promote her own group to a key position inside the *Russian* party). It was the one issue on which she stood ready to break with her closest associates and to fly in the face of every authority, including that of Marx. Poland was dead! It could never be revived! Talk of a Polish nation, of an independent Poland, was not only political and economic lunacy; it was a distraction from the class struggle, a betrayal of Socialism! If Marx had held a different view, then Marx had been mistaken. If the International solemnly went on record affirming the traditional Social-Democratic creed (Poland must be restored as a bastion against Tsarist Russia), then the International was misguided and must be told so, or its resolutions must be tortured to yield a different sense. Above all, the Polish Socialist majority party, the PPS, must be relentlessly pursued, up hill and down dale, and denounced as a nationalist organization falsely parading in Socialist clothing. If the very SDKPIL, her own brainchild, threatened to split and founder on this rock, so much the worse for it. One thing only counted: fidelity to proletarian internationalism as the understood it (and as Marx, poor man, had plainly not understood it). On this point, and on this alone, she was intractable. Even Jogiches at times thought she went too far, though he had originally helped her to evolve this attitude while they were both students in Zürich in the 1890s. Her other Polish associates put up with her fanaticism on the subject, though they did not share it. In the end, the allegedly impossible happened: Poland was restored in 1918, and her veteran friend and colleague Adolf Warszawski, with her reluctant consent, fused the remnant of their following with the left wing of the PPS to form the Polish Communist Party (the right wing under Pilsudski having split off). By then twenty years had been spent, or rather wasted, on one of the strangest aberrations ever to possess a major political intellect.

For the remarkable thing is that on the national question, and specifically on the issue of Poland, Rosa Luxemburg stood entirely alone. Not a single Marxist of her generation, outside her own immediate circle, agreed with her: not even Trotsky, in many respects her equal among the Russians (though they never took to each other); certainly not Lenin, who treated her views on the subject with the good-natured disdain he reserved for the handful of opponents for whom he had a personal liking. Elsewhere the damage was considerable. As time went on, her insanity— there is no other word for it—on the topic of nationalism developed into the gravest of her political handicaps. Her doctrinaire refusal to admit the legitimacy of *any* national movement in Europe was repudiated by Kautsky, by Plekhanov, by the Mensheviks, the Bolsheviks, and virtually every other Socialist group or personality. It angered the verteran leader of Austrian Social-Democracy, Victor Adler, who on this issue became and remained her personal enemy. It embarrassed her old friend and protector Kautsky. It undermined the position of her followers in Poland and her friends among the Russians. It maddened the Polish majority Socialists and drove their less reputable elements into paroxysms of anti-Semitic fury. It very nearly wrecked her own creation, the SDKPIL. It has remained to this day the greatest single obstacle to the revival of a "Luxemburgist" tradition of democratic Socialism in post-Stalinist Poland. And it was totally unnecessary. There never was the smallest justification for it, notwithstanding the pseudo-Marxist sophistries of her Zürich doctoral dissertation of 1898 on the industrial development of Poland: sophistries which her biographer treats with the gravity of a theologian expounding a particularly incomprehensible piece of ecclesiastical doctrine. It was, from start to finish, a display of sheer intellectual perversity, backed up and sustained by the strongest of her emotional commitments: the vision of a proletarian revolution which would institute a new world order. She went so far as to assert that while national self-determination was a farce under capitalism, it would be unnecessary under socialism. Why bother about it if the revolution was going to make all things new?

Her biographer, in general a wholehearted sympathizer with her person and her views, draws the line at this point, though unwillingly. On most other issues he tends to support her and to find fault with her opponents whenever possible, but her calamitous misjudgment of the national problem is too much even for him. He does indeed set out all possible mitigating circumstances at great length, but the effect is not the intended one; for the more earnestly, in his chosen role as counsel for the defense, he addresses the jury on behalf of his client, the clearer it becomes that the case is really hopeless. A more complete misjudgment of a political issue than Rosa Luxemburg's position on the national question was never seen or heard on land or sea. Yet strangely enough, it is this heroic persistence along the wrong track that lends pathos and distinction to her conception of socialism. For her, as for many other East European revolutionaries who had renounced all ties of class and nationality, the only loyalty was to the proletariat, the only true fatherland the International. When in August 1914 the sword broke in her hand, she seriously contemplated suicide.

It is this wholly abstract, totally unrealistic, yet unshakeable commitment to a vision transcending the circumstances of daily existence that sets Rosa Luxemburg apart and lends her the dignity of a tragic figure. As a theorist—*pace* her biographer—she does not take first rank. Her intervention in the German revisionist controversy around 1900 was limited to the political side, if only because she had no understanding of philosophy (a handicap shared by her biographer, to judge from his extremely odd notions about Kant). As an economist she was brilliant and suggestive rather than profound. *The Accumulation of Capital,* her major work, though a truly remarkable tour de force and shot through with extraordinary flashes of prophetic insight into the nature of imperialism, suffers from a fatal flaw: its central theoretical argument is based on a misreading of both Marx and mathematics. (As in the case of Poland she had tried to correct the Master, and predictably come a cropper, the usual fate of Marx's critics, even among Marxists.) Her other theoretical excursions remained fragmentary. She may have anticipated some of Trotsky's notions about the "permanent revolution," though her biographer denies it; but it was Parvus and Radek (both from Eastern Europe) who first developed what was later to become the specifically "Trotskyist" view of the world situation and the function of the coming Russian upheaval within it.

In the factional struggles among the Russian Marxists she wavered uncertainly between the Bolsheviks and their opponents, and in the end reluctantly underwrote the Bolshevik seizure of power in 1917, with qualifications which Lenin's followers have been busy repudiating ever since. She disliked Lenin's organizational concept, but had noth-

ing to put in its place, except a vague faith in "the masses." In general, organizational questions bored her and she never bothered to equip either her Polish party or the German Spartakus League with the kind of effective leadership that might have placed either of them at the head of a mass movement. As a party leader she was effective only when steered by Leo Jogiches (who for years did the organizational work, while she wrote brilliant tracts demolishing their opponents) and promptly lost her bearings when their long-standing personal relationship broke up under the strain of the 1905 revolution and she had to navigate by herself. Her final throw, the Berlin rising of January 1919, led directly to her death, and thereby decapitated the nascent German Communist movement. Nor was this catastrophe accidental, for although the rising had been forced upon her (against her better judgment and that of her experienced Polish associates) by the unwisdom of Liebknecht and the *furor teutonicus* which had seized hold of the German Communists, her decision to participate in what she regarded as an act of madness was in tune with her mystical doctrine of loyalty to the proletariat. For the rest it was an almost literal application of the revolutionary lessons she had been preaching to the Germans since her own participation in the great Russo-Polish upheaval of 1905-1906. The only revolution she had ever wanted or believed in was a spontaneous uprising of the proletariat in the great cities of Central and Eastern Europe. When it came, she was ready for it, though she must have known that defeat was certain.

What then remains of Rosa Luxemburg? Strange to say, that which she least expected: a myth—that of the woman who embodied all the faith and hope of the old pre-1914 revolutionary Socialism, and who paid for it with her life. And something else: a kind of moral heroism. No one who reads her works or studies her career can fail to see that Rosa Luxemburg was above all a moralist. Though tone-deaf in philosophy (she seems never to have understood what the argument over Kantian ethics was about) she was totally serious, and totally committed, where political morality was concerned. For her, every political question had to be argued in ethical terms, though she would have been surprised to hear it said: was not Socialist humanism the most *obvious* thing in the world? Her moral rigorism on matters such as war, colonial exploitation, or the denial of freedom to opponents, lifted her beyond the confines of reformist opportunism and Bolshevist cynicism alike, into a region where she outdistanced her contemporaries. On moral issues her judgment was infallible. Just as in 1914 she saw at once that the International was dead and Social-Democracy, as she put it, "a stinking corpse," so in 1918 she coupled her reluctant acceptance of the October Revolution with an incisive critique of the Bolshevik dictatorship and the beginning of terrorism. Her posthumously published reflections on the Russian Revolution were brushed aside by Lenin. Even the exiled Trotsky refused to accept them. They have nonetheless become the testament of the old humanist Socialism which was shipwrecked in the First World War. In political terms her message was utopian, for a revolution which respects the liberty of *all* is the hardest thing in the world to achieve and perhaps impossible, unless backed from the start by the vast majority of the people. But then a truly democratic revolution was the only kind she had ever wanted. Minority dictatorship and terrorism did not appeal to her. What she stood for was lost in the bloodbath of 1914-1918, which in turn prepared the ground for the ultimate horrors of Stalinism and Fascism: both equally repugnant to the spirit of the woman over whose tormented body victors and vanquished in the first round of Europe's civil war marched into their inheritance.

Paul M. Sweezy (essay date 1967)

SOURCE: "Rosa Luxemburg's *The Accumulation of Capital,*" in *Science and Society,* Vol. XXXI, No. 4, Fall, 1967, pp. 474-85.

[*Sweezy is an American Marxist economist. In the following essay, he describes how Luxemburg's idea of the accumulation of capital grew from her study of Karl Marx's theories.*]

[*The Accumulation of Capital*] was an outgrowth of Rosa Luxemburg's teaching activity at the school of the German Social Democratic Party in the years after 1906. Her main course was a broad survey of political economy, and in connection with it she undertook to write an *Introduction to Political Economy.* The work proceeded slowly, owing to the pressure of other tasks and duties, and there were long periods during which she was obliged to put it aside altogether. In January, 1912, however, she took it up in earnest, hoping to be able to complete at least a first draft of the whole book. It was then that she ran into what she describes in the Foreword to *The Accumulation of Capital* as "an unexpected difficulty."

She was not successful, she tells us, in presenting the overall process of capitalist production "with sufficient clarity." On closer examination, however, she came to the conclusion that the trouble was not one of presentation but rather had to do with "the content of Volume II of Marx's *Capital,* and at the same time with the practice of present-day imperialism and its economic roots." To one of Rosa Luxemburg's temperament and interests, this was a challenge that could not be refused. She liked logically complete and tidy intellectual constructions, and the discovery of what she thought were loose ends in the Marxist system was in itself enough to spur her into action. But perhaps even more important was the belief that she was on the trail of theoretical results that would have great practical importance in the struggle against revisionism on the one hand and imperialism on the other. She immediately broke off work on the *Introduction* and threw herself into this new task that she had set herself. The book was completed and published in 1913. Writing to her friend Diefenbach from prison several years later, she described the composition of the book as follows:

> The period when I was writing the **Accumulation** was one of the happiest of my life. I lived as though in a state of intoxication, saw and heard night and day nothing but this problem which was so beautifully unfolding itself before me, and I hardly know which gave me greater pleasure: the thought processes involved in wrestling with complicated problems as I walked

slowly back and forth across the room, or the putting of results to paper in literary form. Do you know that I wrote the whole thing out in one stretch of four months—an unheard of thing—and sent it direct to the printer without even once reading the draft through?

What was the nature of the gap or weakness which Rosa Luxemburg thought she had discovered in Volume II of *Capital?*

It will be recalled that this volume deals with the circulation of capital, and that it is here that the famous "reproduction schemes," which are in effect Marx's version of the *tableau économique* in numerical form, are presented. According to Marx, the value of every commodity, and hence also the total value of all commodities, is made up of constant capital (raw and auxiliary materials, depreciation of machinery, etc.) plus variable capital (wages) plus surplus value (profit, interest, and rent). At the same time, since all commodities can be classified as either means of production or consumer goods, it follows that production can be divided into two departments, Department I producing means of production and Department II producing consumer goods. Now it is obvious that if the system is to function without hitches, not only must total demand equal total supply but also the demand for the products of each department must equal the output of that department. In the case of what Marx called Simple Reproduction—that is to say, a state of affairs in which everything remains unchanged from one year to the next—these conditions are evidently met if the constant capital used up in both departments equals the output of Department I, and the income of workers and capitalists of both departments (which must be wholly consumed for conditions to remain unchanged) equal the output of Department II. If we designate the components of value by the letters c, v, and s, and use subscripts to designate departments, we can write the output of the two departments in value terms as follows:

$$c_1 + v_1 + s_1$$
$$c_2 + v_2 + s_2$$

The equilibrium conditions then become

$$c_1 + c_2 = c_1 + v_1 + s_1$$
$$v_1 + v_2 + s_1 + s_2 = c_2 + v_2 + s_2$$

And both of these reduce to the simpler form

$$c_2 = v_1 + s_1$$

When we proceed from the case of Simple Reproduction to what Marx called Expanded Reproduction, matters are somewhat more complicated, but the principles involved are essentially the same. The difference between Simple and Expanded Reproduction is that in the latter capitalists do not consume their entire income but instead save a part and invest in additional variable and constant capital. The output of Department I is now greater than the amount of constant capital used up in the two departments, and the new workers employed by the additional variable capital generate a growing need for consumer goods. As surplus value increases, capitalists will also be able to consume more without encroaching on the sources of accumulation. In Expanded Reproduction, therefore, all the magnitudes will increase simultaneously, and there need be no hitches provided only that the proper proportions are maintained. These proper proportions can be expressed in equilibrium conditions analogous to, though of course not identical with, those given above for the case of Simple Reproduction.

Marx's numerical schemes expressed all this clumsily and imperfectly, but the essential logic of the process came through clearly enough and was correctly grasped by Rosa Luxemburg. She did not argue that there was anything wrong with the scheme of Expanded Reproduction as such, and she recognized in a number of passages that in a planned socialist society the course of development would follow more or less closely the pattern depicted in the scheme. But she emphatically denied that the scheme was a faithful reflection of capitalist reality.

This was the heart of Rosa Luxemburg's criticism of the Marxian system, and it is important to understand the nature and grounds of her argument.

According to Rosa Luxemburg, accumulation can take place only *after* capitalists have sold the commodities in which their surplus value is embodied. Just as in the case of the individual capitalist, so for the capitalist class as a whole—she argued—surplus value must be "realized," that is, turned into money, *before* it can be used to buy additional labor power and constant capital. But where are the purchasers? In part, the answer is that the capitalists, in order to satisfy their own consumption requirements, realize each other's surplus value. But if we say that the entire surplus value is realized in this way, we are back in Simple Reproduction. Who, Rosa asks, is to buy the products which comprise "the other, capitalized portion of surplus value"? According to the reproduction scheme, she notes, the answer is "partly the capitalists themselves, to the extent that they invest in new means of production for the purpose of expanding output, and partly the new workers who are needed to put the new means of production into operation." This might seem to be a logical solution to the problem, but Rosa holds that it does not apply to capitalism. "In order to combine new workers with new means of production," she continues, "one must have—capitalistically speaking—a prior purpose for the expansion of production, a new demand for the products which are to be turned out."

The problem, therefore, boils down to this: Where, *within the framework of the capitalist system,* is this new demand to come from? And Rosa Luxemburg finds that there is no answer. The idea that increasing consumption by the capitalists themselves will provide the necessary new demand she regards as too absurd to require refutation. A more plausible answer would be that the new demand comes from the natural increase in population, and Rosa concedes that in a socialist society this would indeed be the starting point for expanded reproduction. Under capitalism, however, babies are not born with money in their pockets and the only kind of demand capitalists care about is a paying demand. This therefore provides no way out. Another possibility is that so-called third persons (doc-

tors, lawyers, civil servants, soldiers, etc.) should provide the demand. But, she argues, their incomes are merely subtractions from wages and surplus value; they add nothing to total demand, nor can they raise it over time. In this fashion she comes to the following conclusion:

> Surplus value must . . . unconditionally pass through the money form; it must shed the form of surplus product before assuming it again for the purposes of accumulation. But who and where are the buyers of the surplus product of Departments I and II? Merely to realize the surplus product of I and II, there must exist, according to the arguments presented above, a market outside I and II. If the realized surplus product is to serve the purpose of expanded reproduction, of accumulation, there must be a prospect of still larger markets in the future which must also lie outside I and II. . . . Accumulation can take place only to the extent that markets outside I and II grow.

Rosa Luxemburg goes over this ground many times and at length, and her line of argument is not always as clear as we have attempted to make it here. But we believe the above accurately presents the gist of her thinking. The difficulty with the Marxian system, she believed, was that Marx never solved the contradiction of the incompatibility of Expanded Reproduction and pure capitalism. He struggled with the problem; at times he saw it more or less clearly; if he had lived to complete *Capital* he doubtless would have discovered the solution. But in fact he did not; the contradiction remains, and it is the responsibility of Marx's followers to solve it. This is the way Rosa Luxemburg saw the problem, and this is the task she set herself.

Seen against this background, the plan of *The Accumulation of Capital* is logical, indeed one might almost say inevitable. Section I, consisting of nine chapters, is entitled "The Problem of Reproduction." An initial chapter dealing with preliminaries is followed by two analyzing Quesnay's *tableau économique* and Adam Smith's theory that the value of all commodities is ultimately reducible to rent, profit, and wages. The remaining six chapters are devoted to the Marxian reproduction schemes, culminating in a lengthy discussion of the "difficulty" that Rosa Luxemburg thought she had uncovered and that has been sketched above. Section II, "Historical Presentation of the Problem," includes fifteen chapters divided into three "Passages at Arms," which are in effect three famous debates over the interrelation of consumption and accumulation in the capitalist economy. In these debates, Rosa Luxemburg saw earlier attempts to grapple with the same problem that she thought had stymied Marx, and she shows why, in her view, none of the protagonists was successful in solving it. The chief authors dealt with are Sismondi, Malthus, Say, Ricardo, and MacCulloch among the classics; Rodbertus and von Kirchman among the pre-Marxian Germans; and Voronzov, Struve, Bulgakov, Tugan-Baranowsky, and Nikolai-on (Danielson) among Rosa's Russian contemporaries. Finally Section III (eight chapters) presents Rosa Luxemburg's own solution of the difficulty under the title "The Historical Conditions of Accumulation."

The title of this last section points to what Rosa Luxemburg regarded as the source of Marx's difficulty. Following in the footsteps of the classical economists before him, he had based his whole theoretical structure on the assumption of what may be called a "pure" capitalist system, that is to say, one consisting exclusively of capitalists and workers. This, according to Rosa, was fully justified in the analysis of individual capitals and also in the analysis of Simple Reproduction. It was natural enough to base the analysis of Expanded Reproduction on the same assumption, and Marx, as well as all the other authors treated by Rosa, did so. But closer examination showed that this was an illegitimate step which led into an impasse. Expanded Reproduction was *impossible* with only capitalists and workers as buyers, and all attempts to find a way out while retaining the assumption of pure capitalism led nowhere. On the basis of this reasoning, the conclusion seemed unavoidable to Rosa that the assumption would have to be dropped and the problem of accumulation would have to be analyzed within a framework defined by the actual historical conditions surrounding the rise and development of capitalism.

Among these historical conditions two seemed to Rosa to be of outstanding importance: First, the existence of noncapitalist countries alongside the capitalist ones; and second, the presence inside even the predominantly capitalist countries of noncapitalist population strata (peasants, handicrafts, etc.). These two conditions defined what she called the noncapitalist milieu or environment of the capitalist system, and it was this environment which provided the needed buyers who, as we have seen, she thought were missing from a pure capitalist system.

This, then, was Rosa Luxemburg's solution to the "difficulty," and she devoted most of Section III to explaining its *modus operandi* and its consequences. Capitalism as a whole, she argued, both lives off its noncapitalist environment and in the process destroys it, that is to say, sucks it into the orbit of capitalism. And each capitalist country fights tooth and nail for the largest possible share of the noncapitalist market. Everywhere she looked, Rosa Luxemburg found confirmation of her theory. The rise of protectionism, for example, which was such a striking feature of the late nineteenth and early twentieth centuries, seemed to reflect the concern of each capitalist country to exclude others from its own internal noncapitalist market. And of course imperialism, with all its grim accompaniments of militarism and war, was the expression of the determination of the leading capitalist powers each to bring under its own control the largest possible share of the noncapitalist world. The chapters in which Rosa Luxemburg describes these phenomena—the aggressions of the strong against the weak and the deadly struggles among the strong for the lion's share of the spoils—constitute the heart of the book. Writing with brilliance and passion, she here leaves far behind the somewhat dry scholasticism of the earlier sections and raises the whole work to the level of a revolutionary classic.

It was not, however, only to an explanation of imperialism that her theory led her. In addition, it pointed to certain definite and extremely important conclusions regarding the future of capitalism and hence also the problems and tasks facing the international socialist movement. If it be true that capitalism depends for its very existence on its noncapitalist environment, but that in the process of living off this environment it also destroys it, then it follows with inexorable logic that the days of capitalism are numbered. When the last of the non-capitalist environment has been used up, the system will break down and its further continuance will be quite literally impossible. In Rosa's view, however, it was unthinkable that the system could live to see the hour of its final and irrevocable doom. As that time approached, the course of capitalist development was found to become increasingly violent and catastrophic and hence to "make necessary the rebellion of the international working class against the domination of capital even before the latter smashes itself against its own self-created economic barriers."

Developed to its logical conclusion, Rosa Luxemburg's theory thus provided an implicit refutation of the revisionist argument that the contradictions of capitalism were becoming milder and the system would continue to expand indefinitely. At the same time, it provided powerful support for the revolutionary view that capitalism must be overthrown, rather than gradually reformed as the revisionists advocated.

There is no doubt that Rosa Luxemburg attached the greatest importance to these political implications of her theory, but she did not spell them out in the book, nor did she attack any of her contemporaries in the German socialist movement. She may have felt that the scholarly form of the book would have been impaired by introducing material of this nature, or perhaps she thought that the book would have wider circulation and greater influence if she did not stress its partisan thesis. In any case she was careful not to give it the appearance of a contribution to the debate between reformists and revolutionaries, and she no doubt expected that the work would be received in the spirit in which it was offered, as a scientific contribution to the clarification and development of Marxian theory.

In this she was doomed to disappointment. Her political opponents were quick to see the political meaning of the book and their reactions were shaped accordingly. Most of the reviews in the German Social Democratic press were hostile, and the few left-wingers who praised it were made to feel the displeasure of the party leadership. The chorus of disapproval included both revisionists and orthodox Marxists: In the latter connection it is significant that Otto Bauer's review in *Die Neue Zeit,* edited by Kautsky, was sharply critical. The truth is that except for a relatively small left wing, of which Rosa Luxemburg herself was the outstanding figure, the entire German movement had by this time adopted a reformist position. It was still acceptable to talk about the revolution as an event which the proletariat would carry through when its moral and political preparation had been perfected. But this was still a long way off, and in the meantime, what was needed was not proof that capitalism must break down but rather proof that capitalism could last until the workers were ready to overthrow it. Very few in the German movement could accept the perspective Rosa Luxemburg offered them, of a crisis-ridden future in which the proletariat would be forced to act in self-defense whether it was ready or not.

Though she had not sought a political battle, Rosa Luxemburg was not one to remain silent in the face of an attack by her opponents. The year 1913 and the first half of 1914 were fully occupied with practical agitation against militarism and the growing war threat, but in the enforced idleness of prison after the war actually broke out, Rosa returned again to the problems of *The Accumulation of Capital* and the bitter controversies it had provoked. It was under these circumstances that she wrote her second book on accumulation. Entitled *The Accumulation of Capital, Or What the Epigones Have Made of Marxian Theory: A Countercriticism,* it was first published in Germany in 1921 and is often referred to in the literature as the *Antikritik*.

There is no necessity to dwell on the contents of the *Antikritik* in this paper. Only two points need to be made for the guidance of the reader. First, the *Antikritik* provides the political element which is lacking from the original volume and in this sense may be regarded as a completion of the earlier work. Second, the *Antikritik* contains a restatement of Rosa Luxemburg's theory of the impossibility of accumulation in a pure capitalist system that is simpler and clearer than any comparable statement of the theory in the original work. It is advisable that the reader who is approaching Rosa Luxemburg's work for the first time begin by reading the first two dozen pages of the *Antikritik* before proceeding to Chapter 1 of *The Accumulation*.

A detailed evaluation of Rosa Luxemburg's theory is, of course, beyond the scope of this paper. A number of critics have subjected it to careful scrutiny and have demonstrated that her contention that accumulation is impossible under pure capitalism is based on a fallacy. Here it will be sufficient to call attention to the nature of her error.

Fundamentally, Rosa's trouble lay in a purely formal confusion. In passing from Simple to Expanded Reproduction she unconsciously retained some of the assumptions of the former. This is the only way to explain her repeated assertion that consumption cannot expand within the framework of the reproduction scheme. Given this assumption, there is no doubt that the rest of her theory follows quite logically. If consumption remains unchanged from one year to the next, there can be no incentive for capitalists to invest their surplus value in additional means of production. Or, to put the matter in Rosa Luxemburg's terms, the idea of capitalists' realizing their surplus value by buying means of production from one another in order to produce more means of production the next year and so on indefinitely without there ever being an increase in the final flow of consumer goods, is an economic fantasy. Accumulation and consumption are linked in such a way that a positive rate of accumulation depends on a rise of consumption; on this point Rosa was absolutely right. Where she was wrong was in assuming that the logic of the reproduction scheme excludes a rise of consumption by either workers or capitalists or both. Actually, Expanded Reproduction typically involves rising incomes for both workers and capitalists, and there is no reason whatever to suppose that both classes will not spend at least some of the increment on consumption. If they do, then at least some accumulation will be justified, and Rosa's impossibility theorem is disproved.

Why did Rosa Luxemburg resist this conclusion with the single-minded determination of which one will find so much evidence throughout this volume? Was it simply and solely intellectual confusion? Or was there something deeper involved? I strongly suspect that the latter was the case. Rosa was afraid that if she admitted the *possibility* of accumulation in a pure capitalist system, she would be forced to admit that the system can expand without limits. If she said *A,* she would have no choice but to say *B*—and it was *B* that she not only refused to say but felt in her bones to be untrue.

The reasons for this fear are not hard to understand. She knew from the history of economic thought that arguments designed to prove the *possibility* of accumulation were usually followed by arguments designed to prove the *impossibility* of too much accumulation. This was after all the message of Say's Law, which, as Keynes was later to point out, exercised such tyranny over the minds of economists for more than a century. But much more important was the fact that essentially the same idea in a Marxian (and much more sophisticated) form had only recently gained currency in the German socialist movement. The Russian economist Tugan-Baranowsky was the first to use the Marxian reproduction schemes in this context. He purported to prove that accumulation can proceed indefinitely provided only that the proper proportions are maintained among the various industries and branches of production. Two things seemed to follow from this: (1) that crises are caused by "disproportionality"; and (2) that crises can be ameliorated and perhaps eventually overcome altogether, by better foresight and planning, even within the framework of capitalism. From this it was but a short step to the conclusion that the trustification of capitalism plus the increasing intervention of the state in economic affairs were ushering in a period of ever smoother capitalist development. This was a conclusion that Bernstein had already reached without benefit of reproduction schemes, but Tugan-Baranowsky's theory seemed to lend it impressive scientific support. Further, the authority of the theory was enormously enhanced when it was taken over in scarcely modified form by Hilferding in *Das Finanzkapital,* which was published in 1910 and was quite the most influential treatise by a Marxian economist since *Das Kapital* itself. By the time Rosa Luxemburg wrote *The Accumulation of Capital,* the disproportionality theory of crises, with all its reformist implications, had for practical purposes become official Social Democratic doctrine.

Rosa Luxemburg was fighting against all this, and she was grimly determined not to concede anything to her opponents. This explains, I believe, why she clung so tenaciously to the theory of the impossibility of accumulation in a pure capitalism and how it happened that she could fail to see that the theory was based on a relatively simple error of reasoning.

Actually, of course, Rosa did a disservice to the position she was trying to uphold by insisting so rigidly on the impossibility thesis. Her critics in the German party tended simply to dismiss her theory as not worth serious examination: After all, didn't the reproduction schemes prove that accumulation could proceed smoothly if only the right proportions were maintained? Why waste time on a theory that flies in the face of well-established principles?

The critics, as not infrequently happens, were throwing out the baby with the bathwater. There certainly *is* a problem of accumulation under capitalism: On this point Rosa Luxemburg's instinct was thoroughly sound. But it is not a question of possibility versus impossibility, nor is it a mere matter of guarding against disproportionalities among the various branches of production. It has to do with the deep-seated, indeed inherent and ineradicable, tendency of capitalism to accumulate too rapidly, that is to say, to add more to the means of production than the rate of increase of consumption can justify or sustain. In a sense, to be sure, this too is a matter of "disproportionality," but it is not a disproportionality that arises from the planlessness of capitalism and can be remedied by this or that reform; it is a disproportionality which is of the very essence of the system. *"The real barrier of capitalist production is capital itself,"* Marx wrote, and he went on to explain:

> It is the fact that capital and its self-expansion appear as the starting and closing point, as the motive and aim of production; that production is merely production of capital, and not vice versa, the means of production mere means for an ever expanding system for the life process for the benefit of the society of producers. The barriers within which the preservation and self-expansion of the value of capital resting on the expropriation and pauperization of the great mass of producers can alone move, these barriers come continually in collision with the methods of production which capital must employ for its purposes and which steer straight toward an unrestricted expansion of production, toward production for its own sake, toward an unconditional development of the productive forces of society. The means, this unconditional development of the productive forces of society, comes continually into conflict with the limited end, the self-expansion of the existing capital. Thus, while the capitalist mode of production is one of the historical means by which the material forces of production are developed and the world market required for them created, it is at the same time in continual conflict with this historical task and the conditions of social production corresponding to it.

There is perhaps no passage in all of Marx's writings which is so successful in distilling the essence of his teaching about the nature of the capitalist system. There was one Marxist contemporary of Rosa Luxemburg who had thoroughly mastered this message and made it his own, and that was Lenin. In his polemics against the *Narodniki* in Russia during the 1890s, Lenin firmly rejected the impossibility thesis—which is precisely what the *Narodnik* writers upheld—and at the same time just as firmly rejected its opposite, the thesis of the indefinite expansibility of capitalism. The conflict between accumulation and con-

sumption, he held, is one of the major contradictions of capitalism, but it does not prove the impossibility of capitalism as the *Narodniki* thought. On the contrary, capitalism can neither exist nor develop without contradictions. What these contradictions prove is not its impossibility but rather its historical-transitional character.

Rosa Luxemburg was familiar with these writings of Lenin, and she referred to or quoted him on several occasions, sometimes critically and sometimes with approval. But she never really came to terms with him, and it is a great pity that she didn't. For Lenin was living proof that it was possible to reject the impossibility thesis without falling into the morass of reformism and revisionism. If Rosa had understood this, **The Accumulation of Capital** might have been both a different and a better book. It would also have been a more influential book.

Nonetheless, despite its faults and weaknesses—which, as we have shown, are not of a minor character—**The Accumulation of Capital** is an important work of a great revolutionary. Much can be learned from it even today—from its excursions into the history of economic thought, from its passionate exposure of the nature and methods of imperialism, from its indomitable Marxist spirit—yes, and even from its mistakes.

Mary-Alice Waters   (essay date 1970)

SOURCE: An introduction to *Rosa Luxemburg Speaks,* edited by Mary-Alice Waters, Pathfinder Press, Inc., 1970, pp. 1-32.

[*Waters is a Philippine-born American author and editor who specializes in feminist-socialist issues. In the following essay, she argues that Luxemburg's criticism of more famous Marxists does not make her anti-communist, as some of her detractors believe.*]

ROSA LUXEMBURG'S PLACE IN HISTORY

Rosa Luxemburg was destined to be one of the most controversial figures in the history of the international socialist movement, and her rightful place of honor among the great revolutionary Marxists has often been denied her. Her detractors have come from every side, and have used virtually every means of slander and distortion to discredit her, to picture her as the opposite of the revolutionary she was.

The ruling class, of course—whether American, German, Japanese, Mexican, or any other stripe—has had no interest in telling the truth about Rosa Luxemburg. They are more than willing to see her revolutionary heritage smeared and buried. But Luxemburg's detractors have come from sources within the traditional left-wing movement as well.

The first major category of her defamers are those who have tried to turn her into an opponent of the Russian Revolution, to make her a proponent of some special school of "democratic" socialism as opposed to the "tyrannical, dictatorial" socialism of Lenin. Perhaps the most widely read modern writer in this category is Bertram D. Wolfe, the virulently anti-Leninist editor of those works by Rosa Luxemburg in which she voiced differences with the Bolsheviks. Also belonging to this category are the various branches of left-wing social democracy (the right wing of social democracy long ago gave up any pretense of being "Red Rosa's" heir).

The left-wing social democrats—unlike Rosa Luxemburg, who understood the basic social and economic transformation that took place in the Soviet Union after the October insurrection—consider the Soviet Union and other degenerated or deformed workers' states to be a form of capitalist state. They thus condemn those countries and find in them nothing that is fundamentally superior to the Western imperialist nations. In their search for some impeccable revolutionary authority to whose reputation they can hitch this un-Marxist analysis, they came up with Rosa Luxemburg, and have since tried to lay claim to her heritage on the fraudulent grounds that she also opposed the Russian Revolution. We will return to her analysis of the Russian Revolution later on, but one need only read her words of praise for the Bolsheviks to see clearly that she was anything but an opponent of the Russian Revolution.

The second major political tendency which has spared no effort in its attempt to slander and distort Rosa Luxemburg's views is Stalinism. During the early years of the Russian Revolution, when Lenin and Trotsky both played central roles in the leadership of the Bolshevik Party and the Third International, Rosa Luxemburg was held in high esteem. She was recognized as a genuine revolutionary—one who made errors to be sure, but, more importantly, a revolutionary woman of action, a fighter whose errors never carried her outside the revolutionary camp.

The fate of her posthumous image was tied to that of the Russian Revolution, however, and as the revolution itself degenerated, and Stalin rose to dominance as the leader of a powerful bureaucracy, she came under attack along with other genuine revolutionaries.

One of the themes that runs throughout Rosa Luxemburg's writings on the Russian Revolution is that without the aid of revolution in Western Europe, especially Germany, the revolutionary regime which had come to power in Russia could not hope to survive. This view was shared by Lenin, Trotsky, and many others. History proved them all correct—but in its own way, in a manner unforeseen by any of the generation of Marxists who helped to make the first socialist revolution. The Soviet regime managed to survive the civil war and invasion of hostile armies. Through incredible sacrifice and effort it managed to maintain its foundation of a nationalized economy and to industrialize the country. With a planned economy free from the built-in anarchy of capitalist production, it was unaffected by the great economic crisis of the 1930s and made tremendous material progress while the capitalist countries stagnated and decayed.

But, while the basic foundations of the Russian Revolution were never destroyed, and while they made possible the economic growth that transformed Russia from the most backward agricultural country in Europe into the second most highly industrialized country in the world,

the revolution did not survive its isolation and initial poverty unscathed. The brutal material conditions in which it was doomed to struggle, unrelieved by the help which would have come from a victorious workers' revolution elsewhere, created the basis for, and nourished the growth of, a huge bureaucratic caste which represented the interests of the middle-class layers of Soviet society. These layers were at first made up of the rich and middle peasantry. Subsequently, Stalin's bureaucratic caste became more and more based on the economically privileged officials, managers, and administrators.

In its rise to power, the wing of the party led by Stalin had to destroy the Leninist, proletarian wing, led by Trotsky. Stalin had to eliminate every last vestige of revolutionary policies and perspectives to be able to carry out his basically nationalist, rather than internationalist, program and his counterrevolutionary, rather than revolutionary, projections. His ruthlessness was total. He was willing and able to use every form of struggle from lies and frame-up to torture, concentration camps, and murder. And while destroying everything Lenin stood for, while eliminating physically the party Lenin had built and wiping out all vestiges of democratic functioning both inside the party and throughout society, Stalin claimed to be wearing Lenin's mantle!

The process taking place within the Soviet Union was reflected in every Communist Party around the world, and in each it meant the destruction of revolutionary tradition.

Along with Trotsky and others who fought uncompromisingly for revolutionary policies nationally and internationally, against the interests of the privileged layers of Soviet society, Rosa Luxemburg became an early target of Stalin and his henchmen. The fact that she was a prime target is, in its own way, a tribute to the revolutionary influence of her heritage.

In 1923, Ruth Fischer and Arkadi Maslow, leaders of the German Communist Party (KPD), launched an attack against Rosa Luxemburg's "right-wing deviations." Her influence was labeled the "syphilis bacillus" of the German Communist movement, her "errors" were "examined" and found to be almost identical to Trotsky's, and thus she was portrayed as the main source of all the defects of German Communism. It was discovered that her theoretical errors in *The Accumulation of Capital* were the source of a full-blown theory of "spontaneity" and all her organizational mistakes flowed from her economic miscalculations.

After the 1925 Congress of the Third International, Communist Parties took a swing to the right. Fischer and Maslow were soon expelled, and Rosa Luxemburg was attacked, no longer for "right-wing deviations" but as an ultraleftist.

During the ultraleft Third Period, 1928-35, when the Communist Party in Germany paved the way for Hitler's rise to power by refusing to work with the SPD to combat fascism, Rosa Luxemburg, along with the rest of the prewar left wing, was accused of differing "only formally from the social-fascist theoreticians." ("Social-fascist" was the Communist Party's designation for social democrats.)

In 1931 Stalin himself entered the debate, rewriting history the way he wanted it read, in an article entitled "Questions Concerning the History of Bolshevism." Here he decreed, contrary to historical fact as well as everything he had previously written, that Rosa Luxemburg was personally responsible for that greatest of all sins, the theory of permanent revolution, and that Trotsky had only picked it up from her. He also decreed, despite the historical record, that Rosa Luxemburg had begun the attack on Kautsky and the German SPD center in 1910 only after she had been persuaded to do so by Lenin, who saw the degeneration of the SPD much more clearly than she.

Trotsky came to Rosa Luxemburg's defense, setting the historical record straight, in the article "Hands Off Rosa Luxemburg," which is printed as an appendix to [*Rosa Luxemburg Speaks*]. But the article by Stalin set the Communist Party line on Rosa Luxemburg for several decades. Since she was never declared an "unperson" and eliminated from the history books altogether, as were so many of her contemporaries, her image has been partially restored with the passage of time. Her anniversaries are commemorated today in Eastern Germany and Poland, but a thoroughly honest evaluation of her role and her ideas has never been and will never be made by the Stalinists. In 1922 Lenin upbraided the German party for its slowness in publishing her collected works; this task has yet to accomplished in either Poland or Germany, almost fifty years later!

The reason is not hard to divine. Rosa Luxemburg's revolutionary spirit breathes through every page she ever wrote. Her internationalism, her call to action, her high standard of truth and honesty, her devotion to the interests of the working class, her concern for freedom and the fullest possible growth of the human spirit: such things are hardly in tune with the thinking of the bureaucratic caste that dominates economic, political, social and artistic life in Eastern Europe! They prefer to ignore her revolutionary politics and leave her in the shadows of hallowed martyrdom.

Historically, Rosa Luxemburg's political record unquestionably places her in the revolutionary camp. On every important political question during her lifetime, she stood foursquare on the side of opposition to the capitalist system and all its evils. She fought tenaciously against every attempt to turn the labor movement away from the fight to abolish capitalism, against every unscientific, utopian, phony scheme to reform the system. She was fond of repeating that the greatness of Marxism was that it placed the socialist movement on a scientific basis, proving from the very laws of capitalism itself the necessity for socialism as the next form of economic organization, if man was to progress and not descend to the depths of barbarism. She remained true to that comprehension of revolutionary Marxism throughout her life.

In the debate with Bernstein and his followers over the possibility of reforming capitalism into socialism, she led the theoretical fight against his revision of Marxism.

When the Frenchman Millerand became the first socialist to enter a bourgeois cabinet, she exposed the illogic of his action and demonstrated why he would have to betray his own socialist principles.

In the fight with the German trade-union leaders she explained the material reasons for their conservatism and their rejection of a revolutionary perspective. She warned against the dangers that pure-and-simple trade unionism posed to the party.

In the debate over the value of using elections as a means of struggle against the capitalist system, she refused to concede to those forces within the SPD that wanted to subordinate everything to parliamentary politicking, and she demanded that the SPD continue to organize the masses in other forms of struggle as well.

In the debates over the character of the 1905 and the 1917 Revolutions in Russia, she stood wholeheartedly with the Bolsheviks and against the Mensheviks, asserting that the working class must lead the struggle, fighting for its own interests. She had nothing but contempt for the Menshevik temporizing and compromising with the liberal, capitalist parties.

She fully understood that in political struggle, program is decisive in the long run. She battled always for programmatic clarity and worked to develop the kind of program that would help advance the class struggle step by step towards socialist revolution.

Living during the first tremendous growth of modern militarism, she was among the first to recognize the importance of military spending as an economic safety valve for capitalism. Faced with the growing realization of the destructive capacities of the imperialist rulers, she neither dismissed the dangers as irrelevant nor surrendered to them in advance.

At the crucial hour of the First World War, one of the fundamental historical dividing lines between revolutionary and non-revolutionary, she and Karl Liebknecht led the small handful of members of the SPD who refused to support the war plans of their own imperialist government.

Years before Lenin or any of the other European revolutionary leaders, she discerned the weaknesses of Kautsky and the German SPD "center," correctly branding them as men without revolutionary principles whose open capitulation to the right wing of the party was doubtless only a matter of time.

While her most enduring contributions are reflected in her writings, she was far from being an armchair revolutionary. She was always in the thick of any action she could find.

Finally, she stood solidly behind the October Revolution, declaring her unconditional support for the direction taken by the Bolsheviks, and proclaiming that the future belonged to bolshevism.

Such a record was matched by only a very few prewar social democrats anywhere in Europe. And Rosa Luxemburg's errors were made within this framework of a totally revolutionary perspective and a genuine search for the swiftest and surest path to a socialist future.

THE NATIONAL QUESTION

Rosa Luxemburg's major errors were centered around three questions: the right of nations to self-determination; the nature of the party and its relationship to the revolutionary masses; and certain Bolshevik policies following the October Revolution. Her theoretical errors in economics, developed in *The Accumulation of Capital,* are also important in the history of Marxism, but as her economic writings are essentially outside the scope of this book, they will be referred to only in passing.

From the beginning of her political life to the very end, Rosa Luxemburg emphatically rejected the basic Marxist position on the revolutionary significance of the struggle of oppressed national minorities and nations for self-determination. Her first writings on this question were published in 1893, and her last were set down only a few months before her death, in her pamphlet on the Russian Revolution. It can be said with certainty that this is one question on which she did not change her mind before she was murdered.

A large part of her writings on national struggles were published in Polish, and unfortunately few have been translated into other languages. Her most important article, for example, **"The Question of Nationality and Autonomy,"** written in 1908, against which Lenin polemicized in his basic work, *The Right of Nations to Self-Determination,* has apparently never been published in any language except the original Polish. However, the *Junius Pamphlet* and the section of *The Russian Revolution* which is devoted to the national struggle contain the essence of her position. . . .

Briefly, without enumerating all the supporting arguments and examples, her position can be summed up as follows: The elimination of all forms of oppression, including the subjugation of one nation by another, was an incontestable goal of socialism. Without the elimination of all forms of oppression one could not even begin to talk of socialism. However, Rosa Luxemburg held that it was incorrect for revolutionary socialists to assert the unconditional right of all nations to self-determination. The demand for self-determination was unrealizable under imperialism. It would always be perverted by one or another of the major capitalist powers. Under socialism it would become largely irrelevant, as socialism would eliminate *all* national boundaries, at least in an economic sense, and the secondary problems of language and culture could be solved without great difficulty.

In a strategic sense, she thought that advocacy of the right of nations to self-determination was extremely dangerous to the international working class since it reinforced nationalist movements which must inevitably come under the domination of their own bourgeoisie. In her opinion, supporting separatist aspirations served only to divide the international working class, not to unite it in common struggle against the ruling classes of all nations. Advocacy of the right of nations to self-determination, which she described as "nothing but hollow, petty bourgeois phraseology and humbug," only corrupts class consciousness and confuses the class struggle. As she says in **The Russian Revolution,** the "utopian, petty bourgeois character of this nationalist slogan" [right to national self-determination] resides in the fact "that in the midst of the crude realities of class society and when class antagonisms are sharpened to the uttermost, it is simply converted into a means of bourgeois class rule."

Lenin and the other defenders of the Marxist position answered her clearly and sharply.

It is not sufficient, they maintained, to say simply that socialists are opposed to all forms of exploitation and oppression. Every capitalist politician in the world would make the exact same assertion. As Rosa Luxemburg herself pointed out so forcefully, the entire First World War was supposedly fought under the banner of assuring self-determination for all nations. Socialists must put their words into action in order to prove to the oppressed and exploited national minorities that their slogans are not hollow and meaningless as are those of the ruling classes.

Theoretically it is incorrect to say that self-determination can *never* be achieved under capitalism. The example of Norway winning independence from Sweden in 1905, with the support of the Swedish workers, is a case in point.

A socialist government, Lenin asserted, can win the allegiance of oppressed minorities only if it is willing and able to prove its unconditional support of their right to form a separate state if they so choose. Any other policy would amount to the forcible retention of diverse nationalities within one state, to a national oppression which would in essence be no different from the national oppression practiced by imperialism. The free association of different nationalities in a single political unit can only be obtained by first guaranteeing each the right to withdraw from that union. Rosa Luxemburg, Lenin charged, tried to avoid the question of political self-determination by shifting the argument to the grounds of economic interdependence.

Paradoxically, while socialists must fight for the unconditional right of self-determination, including the right of separation, the only *party* that can lead such a fight and assure the victory of the socialist revolution is a democratic centralist party, such as the Bolsheviks built, that includes within its ranks and leadership the most conscious sectors of the working class, peasantry, and intellectuals of all the nationalities within the boundaries of the existing capitalist state. As Trotsky explained in the *History of the Russian Revolution,* "A revolutionary organization is not the prototype of the future state, but merely the instrument for its creation. . . . Thus a centralized organization can guarantee the success of revolutionary struggle— even where the task is to destroy the centralized oppression of nationalities."

At the same time, Lenin pointed out, unconditional support for the right of self-determination does not mean that the socialists of the oppressed nation are obliged to fight for separation. Nor does it imply support to the national bourgeoisie of the oppressed nation, except—as Lenin explains in *The Right of Nations to Self-Determination*— insofar as the "bourgeois nationalism of *any* oppressed nation has a general democratic content that is directed *against* oppression, and it is this content that we *unconditionally* support." But only the working class and its allies can lead the struggle to completion, and the oppressed masses must never rely on their own bourgeoisie which, given its ties to the ruling class of the oppressor nation and to international capital, cannot carry the struggle to its conclusion.

Lenin explained numerous times that his disagreement with Rosa Luxemburg and the Polish social democrats was not over their opposition to demanding independence for Poland, but over their attempt to deny the obligation of socialists to support the *right* of self-determination, and particularly their attempt to deny the absolute necessity for the revolutionary socialist party of an oppressor nation to guarantee that right unconditionally. Lenin points out at the end of *The Right of Nations to Self-Determination* that the Polish social democrats had been led "by their struggle against the Polish bourgeoisie, which deceives the people with its nationalist slogans, to the incorrect denial of self-determination."

Finally, he argued that the right of self-determination is one of the basic democratic rights raised by the bourgeois revolution, and socialists are obligated to fight for democratic rights. "In the same way as there can be no victorious socialism that does not practice full democracy, so the proletariat cannot prepare for its victory over the bourgeoisie without an all-around, consistent, and revolutionary struggle for democracy."

Rosa Luxemburg's argument that a demand for self-determination is impractical under capitalism ignores the fact that "not only the right of nations to self-determination, but *all* the fundamental demands of political democracy are only partially 'practicable' under imperialism, and then in a distorted way of exception."

"There is not one of these demands which could not serve and has not served, under certain circumstances, as an instrument in the hands of the bourgeoisie for deceiving the workers." But that in no way relieves socialists of the obligation to struggle for democratic rights, to expose the deceptions of the bourgeoisie, and to prove to the masses that only the socialist revolution can lead to the full realization of the basic democratic rights proclaimed by the bourgeoisie.

Rosa Luxemburg sincerely believed that the Bolshevik policy on national self-determination was disastrous and could only lead to the destruction of the revolution. But she could not have been more wrong.

The February 1917 Revolution which established a liberal republic in Russia brought about a great historical awakening of the oppressed nations within the czarist empire, but the formal equality they received from the revolution served only to emphasize to them the degree of their real oppression. And it was the refusal of the liberal bourgeois government, from February to October, to grant the right of self-determination that cemented the opposition of the oppressed nationalities to the Menshevik government in Petrograd and sealed its doom.

Only by guaranteeing self-determination, up to and including the right of separation did the Bolshevik Party win the indestructible confidence of the small and oppressed nationalities of czarist Russia. This confidence ultimately proved decisive in the battle against the counterrevolution and led, not to the disintegration of the revolutionary forces, as Rosa Luxemburg feared, but to their victory within the oppressed nations as well as among the Great Russians themselves.

She totally underestimated the tremendous force of nationalism which began to awaken in Eastern Europe only in the early twentieth century. She did not comprehend that these movements were destined to explode with full force only *after* the Russian Revolution, not because the Bolsheviks encouraged them but because of the internal dynamic of the struggle generated by the awakening of the oppressed masses.

One of Rosa Luxemburg's most frequently quoted statements from "The Russian Revolution" is her description of Ukrainian nationalism as "a mere whim, a folly of a few dozen petty bourgeois intellectuals without the slightest roots in the economic, political or psychological relationships of the country." Trotsky took her up on this in the chapter on "The Problem of Nationalities" in his *History of the Russian Revolution*.

> When Rosa Luxemburg, in her posthumous polemic against the program of the October Revolution, asserted that Ukrainian nationalism, having been formerly a mere amusement of the commonplace petty bourgeois intelligentsia, had been artificially raised up by the yeast of the Bolshevik formula of self-determination, she fell, notwithstanding her luminous mind, into a very serious historic error. The Ukrainian peasantry had not made national demands in the past for the reason that the Ukrainian peasantry had not in general risen to the height of political being. The chief service of the February Revolution—perhaps its only service, but one amply sufficient—lay exactly in this, that it gave the oppressed classes and nations of Russia at last an opportunity to speak out. This political awakening of the peasantry could not have taken place otherwise, however, than through their own native language—with all the consequences ensuing in regard to schools, courts, self-administration. To oppose this would have been to try to drive the peasants back into nonexistence.

Not a few historians have tried to show that Rosa Luxemburg's position on self-determination and opposition to nationalist movements was actually put into practice in later years by Stalin, with his vicious persecution of the oppressed nations and all the attendant horrors. But, his actions were as much a perversion of Rosa Luxemburg's program as of Lenin's. As an article by the editor in the March 1935 *New International* asked: "Can one imagine Rosa in the company of those who strangled the Chinese Revolution by attributing to Chiang Kai-shek and the Chinese bourgeoisie the leading revolutionary role in 'liberating the nation from the yoke of foreign imperialism'? Can one imagine Rosa in the company of those who hailed the 1926 coup d'etat of Marshal Pilsudski as the 'great national democrat' who was establishing the 'democratic dictatorship of the proletariat and peasantry' in Poland? Can one imagine Rosa in the company of those who for years glorified and canonized every nationalist demagogue who was gracious enough to send a visiting card to the Kremlin . . . ?" [A few years later another question could have been posed: Can one imagine Rosa in the company of those who murdered virtually the entire Central Committee of the Polish Communist Party?]

And the article concludes, "How contemptible are those who dismiss a Rosa Luxemburg with smug disdain as a 'Menshevik,' when they themselves proved unable to rise to the height of her boots!"

Rosa Luxemburg was wrong on the national question, but her opposition to guaranteeing the right of self-determination was not born out of hostility to revolutionary mass action that leads toward struggle to abolish capitalism. Rather she failed to comprehend the complex and contradictory aspects of the revolutionary dynamic of struggles by oppressed nationalities in the age of imperialism.

THE NATURE OF THE REVOLUTIONARY PARTY

Rosa Luxemburg's mistakes concerning the problem of building a revolutionary party, and the parallel problem of the relationship between that party and the working masses, were just as fundamental as her errors on the national question. Within the context of the German revolution they were probably more costly.

Her differences with the Bolsheviks concerning organizational concepts are not as easy to codify as those concerning national self-determination. She never spelled out clearly and completely, in any one place, her thinking on the type of organization needed, although most of the elements of her basic position are clearly discernible in her 1904 article, **"Organizational Questions of Russian Social Democracy."** Following the 1905 Revolution her ideas were further clarified.

The fact is that, despite her dispute with Lenin on the nature of the revolutionary party, she was not deeply concerned with organizational problems, and therein lies one of the clearest indications of the nature of her errors. While she understood that in political struggle, program is ultimately decisive, she did not understand, as did Lenin, that program and tactical positions are always refracted through organizational concepts.

Perhaps one of the most revealing examples of her tendency to dismiss the organizational problems of leadership is the fact that for years she refused to attend the conventions of the SDKPiL or to be elected to its Central Committee. Yet she remained one of the party's principal political leaders and its main public voice. The problem was not her location either, since the Central Committee of the SDKPiL had its headquarters in Berlin. Thus she remained a leader in effect, yet not directly accountable to any specific leading body of which she was a member.

Her attitudes on organizational matters were heavily influenced by her experiences with the SPD. She very early recognized the tremendous conservative weight of the SPD leadership, and pointed, even in her 1904 essay, to their inability to so much as consider any strategy other than continuation of the "grand old tactic" of parliamentary concerns and nothing but parliamentary concerns.

Another aspect of the SPD which greatly influenced her thinking was simply the size and scope of the organization itself, which held within its orbit any and every individual who even vaguely thought in socialist terms.

To mount an effective opposition to a leadership as strongly entrenched and secure as the SPD hierarchy was not an easy matter. It required great tactical flexibility as well as political clarity, and it was a job that Rosa Luxemburg never really tackled. Year after year she maintained a blistering political opposition, but, until the war began, she never tried to draw around her, organize, and lead a group within the SPD.

The clarity of her basic political understanding of the SPD leadership was well expressed in a letter she sent to her close friend Clara Zetkin around the beginning of 1907. This same letter illustrates equally well her inability or unwillingness to give her political comprehension an organizational form. The possibility of trying to be more than a one- or two-woman opposition doesn't seem ever to have received serious thought:

> Since my return from Russia I feel rather isolated . . . I feel the pettiness and the hesitancy of our party regime more clearly and more painfully than ever before. However, I can't get so excited about the situation as you do, because I see with depressing clarity that neither things nor people can be changed—until the whole situation has changed, and even then we shall just have to reckon with inevitable resistance if we want to lead the masses on. I have come to that conclusion after mature reflection. The plain truth is that August [Bebel], and still more so the others, have completely pledged themselves to parliament and parliamentarianism, and whenever anything happens which transcends the limits of parliamentary action they are hopeless—no, worse than hopeless, because they then do their utmost to force the movement back into parliamentary channels, and they will furiously defame as 'an enemy of the people' anyone who dares to venture beyond their own limits. I feel that those of the masses who are organized in the party are tired of parliamentarianism, and would welcome a new line in party tactics, but the party leaders and still more the upper stratum of opportunist editors, deputies, and trade-union leaders are like an incubus. We must protest vigorously against this general stagnation, but it is quite clear that in doing so we shall find ourselves against the opportunists as well as the party leaders and August. As long as it was a question of defending themselves against Bernstein and his friends, August & Co. were glad of our assistance, because they were shaking in their shoes. But when it is a question of launching an offensive against opportunism then August and the rest are with Ede [Bernstein], Vollmar, and David against us. That's how I see matters, but the chief thing is to keep your chin

up and not get too excited about it. Our job will
take years.

Important as the influence of the SPD was, however, it is
not by itself a sufficient explanation for her organizational
attitudes. Not only different objective circumstances but
also different organizational concepts set her apart from
Lenin.

Before discussing what her organizational theories were,
however, it is worth mentioning what they were not. Rosa
Luxemburg has often been credited—by those who think
they agree with her as well as those who disagree—with
holding a full-blown theory of "spontaneity," or even with
advocacy of something akin to an anarchist position.
Nothing could be a greater oversimplification and distortion of her ideas.

As mentioned earlier, the Stalinists at one time even pretended to trace her organizational errors to her theoretical
mistakes in *The Accumulation of Capital*. In this, her principal economic work, Rosa Luxemburg tries to demonstrate that capitalism, considered as a closed or completed
system without precapitalist or noncapitalist markets to
cannibalize, could not continue to expand. Her argument
is basically incorrect on the theoretical level in that she
leaves out of consideration the central factors of competition among different capitals and the unevenness of the
rate of development between different countries, different
sectors of the economy and different enterprises—factors
which constitute the driving force behind the expansion
of capitalist markets. However, the Stalinists accused her
of propagating a crude theory of the "automatic" and
"mechanical" end of capitalism, to occur as soon as the
world's noncapitalist markets were exhausted or absorbed
into capitalist relations. And from this *they* made a leap
into the organizational question, claiming that it followed
that she could not have believed that organizing the struggle for the overthrow of capitalism was an urgent need
since the automatic "breakdown" of capitalism was assured. Her own words, throughout the pages of this book,
speak eloquently enough in her own defense against such
crude distortions.

What was her basic conception?

She disagreed with Lenin that the party should be an organization of professional revolutionaries with deep roots in
and ties to the working class, an organization holding the
perspective of winning the leadership of the masses during
a period of revolutionary upsurge.

On the contrary, in her view the revolutionary party
should come much closer to encompassing the organized
working class in its entirety.

This comes out in her 1904 essay in which she polemicizes
against Lenin's definition of a revolutionary social democrat.

In *One Step Forward, Two Steps Back,* an analytical balance sheet of the Russian party's 1903 Congress at which
there had been a split into "hard" and "soft," that is, Bolshevik and Menshevik factions, over the organizational
question, Lenin had taken up the "dreadful word" Jacobin
(name of the left faction in the French Revolution) which

had been flung at the Bolsheviks. He wrote: "A Jacobin
who maintains an inseparable bond with the *organization*
of the proletariat, a proletariat *conscious* of its class interests, is a *revolutionary social democrat.*"

In objection, Luxemburg wrote: ". . . Lenin defines his
'revolutionary social democrat' as a 'Jacobin joined to the
organization of the proletariat, which has become conscious of its class interests.'

"The fact is that the social democracy is not *joined* to the
organizations of the proletariat. It is itself the
proletariat . . . . Social democratic centralism . . . . can
only be the concentrated will of the individuals and groups
representative of the most class-conscious, militant, advanced sections of the working class. . . ."

In other words, she did not downplay the role of the party
in providing political leadership, but tended to confine the
party to the role of agitator and propagandist and to deny
its central role as a day-to-day organizer of the class struggle, providing leadership for the masses in an organizational and technical sense as well. She did not understand
the Leninist concept of a combat party—a party which
recognizes that capitalism must be defeated in struggle
and understands that the working masses must be led by
an organization capable of standing up under the pressure
of a combat; a party that is deeply rooted in the mass
movement and consciously works to mobilize the combativity of the masses and help give their struggles anticapi-
talist direction; a party that, regardless of its size or stage
of development, bases its conduct on the firm intent to become a mass working-class party capable of leading the
way to victory, a party that prepares over a period of years
for the role it must play in the decisive struggles; a party
that understands the vital, indispensable need for *conscious* organization and leadership.

Instead, Rosa Luxemburg placed great emphasis on the
role of the masses themselves in action, on the steps they
could take without conscious organizational leadership,
on the things which she believed their combativity alone
could accomplish. She assigned to them the task of overwhelming and sweeping away the conservative, backward
working-class leaders, and creating new revolutionary organizations in place of the old. She called on them to perform the task for which she herself was not willing to pave
the way, except in the most general political sense.

In her mass strike pamphlet, for instance, she eloquently
pictures the process: "From the whirlwind and the storm,
out of the fire and flow of the mass strike and the street
fighting, rise again, like Venus from the foam, fresh,
young, powerful, buoyant trade unions." And later she
warns the trade unionists that if they attempt to stand in
the way of real social struggles, "the trade-union leaders,
like the party leaders in the analogous case, will simply be
swept aside by the rush of events, and the economic and
the political struggles of the masses will be fought out
without them."

As against the Bolsheviks' concept that it was necessary
to organize revolution, she came closer to the Menshevik
slogan of 1905—unleash the revolution.

It was Trotsky who put her general concept in an extremely succinct form—and pointed to her central error—in a speech on "Problems of Civil War," in July 1924. Discussing the problems surrounding the timing of an insurrection, he said:

> It must be recognized that the question of the timing of the insurrection acts in many cases like a kind of litmus paper for testing the revolutionary consciousness of very many Western comrades, who have still not rid themselves of their fatalistic and passive manner of dealing with the principal problems of revolution. Rosa Luxemburg remains the most eloquent and talented example. Psychologically, this is fully understandable. She was formed, so to speak, in the struggle against the bureaucratic apparatus of the German social democracy and trade unions. Untiringly, she showed that this apparatus was stifling the initiative of the masses and she saw no alternative but that an irresistible uprising of the masses would sweep away all the barriers and defenses built by the social democratic bureaucracy. The revolutionary general strike, overflowing all the dikes of bourgeois society, became for Rosa Luxemburg synonymous with the proletarian revolution.
>
> However, whatever its power and mass character, the general strike does not settle the problem of power; it only poses it. To seize power, it is necessary, while relying on the general strike, to organize an insurrection. The whole of Rosa Luxemburg's evolution, of course, was going in that direction. But when she was snatched from the struggle, she had not yet spoken her last word, nor even the penultimate one.

Rosa Luxemburg's correct evaluation of the nature of the SPD leadership and her consequent opposition to it led her to question the centralism of a revolutionary organization as well as the centralism of a reformist one—to be skeptical of conscious organizational leadership in general.

It would be a mistake however to accuse her of rejecting any kind of centralized organization. She was concerned primarily with the *degree* of centralization, and the nature of the leadership function of the party. As Trotsky put it in the article "Luxemburg and the Fourth International," . . . "The most that can be said is that in her historical-philosophical evaluation of the labor movement, the preparatory selection of the vanguard, in comparison with the mass actions that were to be expected, fell too short with Rosa; whereas Lenin—without consoling himself with the miracles of future actions—took the advanced workers and constantly and tirelessly welded them together into firm nuclei, illegally or legally, in the mass organizations or underground, by means of a sharply defined program."

The Bolsheviks answered Rosa Luxemburg, in word and deed, over the years. They pointed out that under capitalism the working class as a whole is not in a position to raise itself to the level of consciousness necessary to successfully confront the bourgeoisie in all fields, to destroy bourgeois authority. If it were, capitalism would have perished long ago.

The determination, ruthlessness, and unity of the ruling class demand that the working class create a party that is serious and professional in its concepts, that is disciplined and welded together by common political agreement on the tasks to be performed, that is trained and capable of leading the masses to victory. Such a party cannot be created spontaneously, out of the struggle itself. It is a weapon that must be fashioned before the battle begins.

Lenin labeled Rosa Luxemburg's organizational concepts her "not-to-be-taken-seriously nonsense of organization and tactics as a process." By that he did not, of course, mean that an organization was created in isolation from objective circumstances, or that tactics did not evolve or change, and were not adapted to living reality. To Rosa Luxemburg's view that the historic process itself would create the organizations and tactics of struggle, Lenin counterposed a diametrically opposite relationship between historical developments and the party. As he saw it, the organization and the tactics are created not by the process but by those people who achieve an understanding of the process by means of Marxist theory and who make themselves part of the process through the elaboration of a plan based upon their understanding.

Walter Held, a leader of the German section of the Fourth International prior to the Second World War, once explained the concept by an analogy from natural science: "The power latent in a waterfall may be transformed into electricity. But not every person without more ado is capable of accomplishing this feat. Scientific education and training are indispensable. On the other hand, the scientifically trained engineers are naturally constrained to draft their plans according to the given natural conditions. What can be said, however, of a man, who, because of this, jeers at engineering science and praises instead the 'elementary force of water which produces electricity'? We should be entirely justified in laughing him out of court. Nor is it otherwise with the social process. It was for this and no other reason that Lenin used to jest about the conception of 'organization as process' which was counterposed to his conception."

The differing organizational theories of Lenin and Luxemburg underwent the acid test in the post-World War I revolutionary upsurge. The party Lenin had built was able to lead the masses to power. In Germany, the absence of a similar cohesive, trained, educated and disciplined party and leadership proved fatal to the German revolution and to many of the courageous revolutionaries themselves.

In retrospect the differences now seem obvious; the mistakes of Luxemburg seem underscored by history. But at the time, the issue was certainly not so clear. History itself was uttering the final word on the nature of the revolutionary party, indicating what was necessary to assure victory. And even Lenin did not think he was doing anything so unique. Prior to 1914 he viewed his efforts as being directed toward the creation of a "Bebel-Kautsky" wing in the Russian social democracy. He did not come to understand the political character of that "Bebel-Kautsky" wing of the SPD until several years after Rosa Luxemburg turned her political fire against those vacillating middle-of-the-roaders.

In the years following the Russian Revolution, however—after the lessons of the Russian and German revolutions were drawn and the questions concerning organizational concepts decided by history—many currents within the working-class movement still continue to reject the fundamental concepts of the Bolshevik Party and look to Rosa Luxemburg as the champion of a revolutionary alternative to Leninism. These basically social democratic currents—which also came to equate Leninism with Stalinism rather than recognizing them as irreconcilable opposites—have been fond of pointing out that Trotsky, too, held views similar to Luxemburg's in the years prior to 1917. Trotsky, fortunately, was alive to defend himself.

In 1904 Trotsky wrote a pamphlet, "Our Political Tasks," in which he made a statement that has been quoted by many opponents of Leninism, including Bertram D. Wolfe and Boris Souvarine. Trotsky asserted: "Lenin's methods lead to this: the party organization [the caucus] at first substitutes itself for the party as a whole; then the Central Committee substitutes itself for the organization; and finally a single 'dictator' substitutes himself for the Central Committee. . . ."

In response to all the admiring anti-Leninists who approvingly quoted Trotsky's prognosis and saw his exile by Stalin as confirmation of the warnings he and Rosa Luxemburg had voiced in 1904, Trotsky replied: "All subsequent experience demonstrated to me that Lenin was correct in this question as against Rosa Luxemburg and me. Marceau Pivert counterposes to the 'Trotskyism' of 1939, the 'Trotskyism' of 1904. But after all since that time three revolutions have taken place in Russia alone. Have we really learned nothing during these thirty-five years?"

No one knows what Rosa Luxemburg might have said in the same situation, but she, too, was capable of learning from the course of history.

THE RUSSIAN REVOLUTION

The most serious of Rosa Luxemburg's criticisms of the policies of the Bolsheviks, as expressed in her draft article on the Russian Revolution, have already been dealt with—her longstanding differences on the national question, and her organizational disagreements, which are implicit in the draft. But she raises several other questions that are worth discussing. It would take a book to deal adequately with all of them, and it is in Trotsky's three-volume *History of the Russian Revolution,* in fact, that one finds the most complete answers. But the intention here is simply to indicate the direction in which the reader must search for solutions to the very complex problems of the first socialist revolution in history.

The circumstances surrounding the writing and posthumous publication of Rosa Luxemburg's article on the Russian Revolution are explained in the introductory note to that selection, but some additional comments are in order.

Incarcerated as she was in the Breslau prison, her isolation and extremely limited access to accurate information about what was going on in Russia were important factors. Even outside the jails, the truth was hard to come by. People living in the United States today, for example, can draw a parallel with the difficulties of obtaining anything resembling truthful information on happenings in Vietnam, particularly concerning the areas governed by the Provisional Revolutionary Government.

In Germany following the October Revolution in 1917, the ministry of the interior eschewed any pretense of freedom of the press and ordered "all that explains or praises the proceedings of the revolutionaries in Russia must be suppressed." Anything that the German military thought would discredit the revolutionary government of Russia received wide publicity, while anything that might win sympathy was censored.

Once out of prison, with access to better information, Rosa Luxemburg retained some of her criticisms, and changed her mind about others. And on many questions it is unclear whether she altered her opinion or not, as she never mentioned them again, at least publicly. The tremendous problems facing the revolutionary leadership in Germany between November 1918 and January 1919 became her overriding concern.

What is most striking in her draft article is that she is not really suggesting alternative policies as much as she is describing what would have been the optimum course—if conditions had been different; if the proletarian revolution had occurred almost simultaneously across Europe; if the German, French, and English workers had be able to come to the aid of their Russian comrades. Under such circumstances there would have been no need for the sharp restrictions on democratic freedom. There would have been no strong counterrevolutionary forces backed by all the major capitalist powers.

The leaders of the Russian Revolution recognized this also. Lenin and Trotsky never ceased to point out the isolation of the revolution, the tardiness—and eventually the indefinite postponement—of the German revolution. Such historical facts determined much of the course of the Russian Revolution.

During 1918 Rosa Luxemburg stressed over and over again the decisive importance of the German revolution if the Bolshevik regime was to survive:

> Everything that happens in Russia is comprehensible and represents an inevitable chain of causes and effects, the starting point and end term of which are: the failure of the German proletariat and the occupation of Russia by German imperialism. It would be demanding something superhuman from Lenin and his comrades if we should expect of them that under such circumstances they should conjure forth the finest democracy, the most exemplary dictatorship of the proletariat and a flourishing socialist economy. By their determined revolutionary stand, their exemplary strength in action, and their unbreakable loyalty to international socialism, they have contributed whatever could possibly be contributed under such devilishly hard conditions. . . . The Bolsheviks have shown that they are capable of everything that a genuine

revolutionary party can contribute within the limits of the historical possibilities. They are not supposed to perform miracles. For a model and faultless proletarian revolution in an isolated land, exhausted by world war, strangled by imperialism, betrayed by the international proletariat, would be a miracle.

One could hardly ask for a clearer statement of support for the Russian Revolution or greater comprehension of its difficulties. It is within that framework that she voices her criticisms.

At another time, towards the end of November 1918, after she was released from prison, she wrote to her longtime comrade in the leadership of the SDKPiL, Adolf Warsawski, also known as A. Warski, who was at that time in Warsaw:

> If our party [SDKPiL] is full of enthusiasm for bolshevism and at the same time opposed the Bolshevik peace of Brest-Litovsk, and also opposes their propagation of national self-determination as a solution, then it is no more than enthusiasm coupled with the spirit of criticism—what more can people want from us?
>
> I shared all your reservations and doubts, but have dropped them in the most important questions, and in others I never went as far as you. Terrorism is evidence of grave internal weakness, but it is directed against internal enemies, who . . . get support and encouragement from foreign capitalists outside Russia. Once the European revolution comes, the Russian counterrevolutionaries lose not only this support, but—what is more important—they must lose all courage. Bolshevik terror is above all the expression of the weakness of the European proletariat. Naturally the agrarian circumstances there have created the sorest, most dangerous problem of the Russian Revolution. But here too the saying is valid—even the greatest revolution can only achieve that which has become ripe [through the development of] social circumstances. This sore too can only be healed through the European revolution. And this is coming!

Among Rosa Luxemburg's disagreements with Bolshevik policies it is those criticisms directed against the treaty of Brest-Litovsk, the dissolution of the Constituent Assembly, the distribution of land to the peasants, and the use of revolutionary violence which are most important.

She opposed the decision of the Bolsheviks to sign a separate peace treaty with the German government in early 1918 because she believed it meant surrendering large parts of revolutionary Russia to counterrevolution, to German imperialism. She feared it would only postpone the end of the war, and might possibly lead to the victory of the German armies.

Although her fears proved unfounded, she was certainly not alone in holding the position she did. It was shared by close to a majority of the Bolshevik Central Committee as well. Only after it became clear that the German army intended and had the ability to take even larger sections of Russia by continued military advances, did Lenin con-

vince a majority of the Central Committee that the treaty of Brest-Litovsk must be signed, despite the harsh terms. The cost of continued refusal to sign a separate treaty with the Central powers, Lenin feared, would be the conclusion of a separate peace between Germany and its imperialist enemies, followed by a coalition of all the capitalist powers against revolutionary Russia.

Such fears were eventually to materialize, despite the treaty of Brest-Litovsk, but in the meantime the war-weary Russian masses were able to gain a respite, the revolutionary government was able to begin to consolidate itself, the revolutionary process in the German-occupied territories deepened and the foundations of the Red Army were laid—in short the Brest-Litovsk treaty notwithstanding the fears of all who opposed it, was the only way out for the Bolshevik government and made possible the eventual victory of the revolution. It was not choice, but iron necessity that compelled the Bolsheviks to sign the treaty.

While in prison, Rosa Luxemburg was extremely critical of the Bolshevik dissolution of the Constituent Assembly elected just after the victory of the October Revolution. But she changed her position after being released from jail. During the revolutionary upsurge of November and December 1918 in Germany, the Spartacus League rapidly came to realize that the call for a Constituent Assembly was the rallying cry of the SPD and others who opposed the revolution. To the call for a Constituent Assembly, Spartacus counterposed the demand for the transfer of power to the Workers' and Soldiers' Councils. Thus, compelled by the logic of their own struggle against the counterrevolution, Spartacus developed a position similar to that of the Bolsheviks, and Rosa Luxemburg soon realized the question was not quite so simple as it had seemed from Breslau.

In her prison essay, however, her basic error on the question of democratic practices in the revolution was to ignore the role of the Soviets, which were probably the most democratic institutions of modern times.

The Constituent Assembly was not dissolved because its majority disagreed with the Bolsheviks. If the Bolsheviks and Left Social Revolutionaries had been in the majority they would have dissolved themselves and delegated their authority to the Soviets—which held power anyway. The Constituent Assembly was disbanded because it was totally unrepresentative—as Trotsky explains in the section quoted by Rosa Luxemburg—and far from being simply another organ of workers' democracy subject to pressure from the masses, it would have rapidly become an organizing center of the counterrvolution. Once dissolved, there was no need for a new Constituent Assembly, as the Soviets had assumed the functional role of such a body.

All these things Rosa Luxemburg came to realize very rapidly through her own direct experiences in the German revolution.

Rosa Luxemburg carefully places her criticisms of the Bolsheviks' agrarian policies within the framework of the historical tasks to be accomplished and the tremendous difficulty of assuring the victory of a socialist revolution in one of the most backward capitalist countries.

In the Western European countries the destruction of feudal land relationships had been largely accomplished by the bourgeois revolutions of the nineteenth century; Russia, however, was a country where the vast majority of the peasantry owned no land. For the peasantry the February Revolution meant the opening of the struggle against the landlords, the awakening of political consciousness. At first cautious in its demands, seeking only rent reductions and similar ameliorations of intolerable conditions, the peasant movement rapidly gained in depth, scope, and political intensity. Soon estate after estate was looted, burned, and the land divided up—months before the October Revolution triumphed.

While division of the great estates was the formal program of the Social Revolutionaries, the mass radical peasant party, the SRs opposed the land seizures by the peasants because such actions jeopardized the support of the landed bourgeoisie for the coalition government to which the SRs belonged.

During the summer and fall of 1917, as the Menshevik-SR government began sending troops against the peasants to protect the landlords, the peasantry turned more and more toward the Bolsheviks who promised to support the land seizures.

In other words, the confiscation of the great estates and their division among the peasants was not a policy merely implemented by the Bolsheviks, but a *fact* already accomplished in large measure before the Bolsheviks came to power. To have opposed the division of the great estates would have meant a war against the peasantry and the defeat of the revolution—just as a similar policy by the Mensheviks had assured the downfall of the bourgeois government.

Rosa Luxemburg recognized this when she stated, "Surely the solution of the problem by the direct, immediate seizure and distribution of the land by the peasants was the shortest, simplest, most clear-cut formula to achieve two diverse things: to break down large landownership, and immediately to bind the peasants to the revolutionary government. As a political measure to fortify the proletarian socialist government, it was an excellent tactical move."

She was right, of course, in pointing to the dangers this could ultimately entail for the revolution, if the process could not be reversed, and if a significant layer of rich peasants became more and more powerful. She recognized the absolute necessity of solving the agrarian problem, which had never been accomplished by a bourgeois revolution in the czarist empire; but she did not clearly see how this task combined with the tasks of the proletarian revolution. She favored the nationalization of the large estates, but proposed they be retained intact and operated as large-scale agricultural units. While theoretically correct, such a course would have meant leaping far ahead of the historical possibilities.

The Bolsheviks were able to win the allegiance of the peasantry only by adopting the agrarian policy they did, and only with the peasants as allies was the revolution able to defeat the combined counterrevolutionary forces.

Rosa Luxemburg's final major criticism of Bolshevik policy was directed at the use of violence against the counterrevolution. Her position was basically a moral one, a humanitarian reluctance to use force or violence, to see any life destroyed. But it would be a mistake to put her in the same category as liberal pacifists who hypocritically oppose any kind of violence.

She agreed wholeheartedly that the violence of the oppressed is in no way comparable to the violence of the oppressor. One is justified and the other is not. There was no confusion in her mind concerning the source of the greatest violence and destruction mankind had every known. She wrote in *Rote Fahne,* November 24, 1918:

> [Those] who sent 1.5 million German men and youths to the slaughter without blinking an eyelid, [those] who supported with all the means at their disposal for four years the greatest blood-letting which humanity has ever experienced—they now scream hoarsely about 'terror,' about the alleged 'monstrosities' threatened by the dictatorship of the proletariat. But these gentlemen should look at their own history.

She understood full well that no revolution could consolidate itself without violently putting down the old ruling forces—that no revolution in history had ever succeeded without violence and probably never would. But she fervently wished it could be otherwise, and regretted that the revolutionary forces in the Soviet Union were so weak that they had to resort to violence against the counterrevolution.

At the same time she realized that the revolution's weakness was entirely a function of its international isolation. She realized that a successful German revolution would make violence less necessary in Russia, and that with each additional successful revolution, the forces of counterrevolution would be weaker, and less violence would have to be used against them.

Once again, her criticisms of the Bolsheviks came down to new exhortations to the German workers to come to the aid of their Russian comrades. When she wrote, "There is no doubt either . . . that Lenin and Trotsky . . . have taken many a decisive step only with the greatest inner hesitation and with most violent inner opposition," she was probably referring more than anything else to the use of violence, and reflecting very clearly her own inner revulsion against it, even though she understood it was absolutely necessary. She realized that if counterrevolutionaries were to triumph, the violence they would use would be infinitely more ruthless and barbaric than the revolutionary violence of the class that had history on its side.

Rosa Luxemburg ends her article on the Russian Revolution in the same vein as she begins it: with unequivocal support for the Bolsheviks, proclaiming that the future of the world is in the hands of bolshevism.

Only the most obtuse and hypocritical could take her words and twist them to make her appear an anticommunist. Her own phrases speak more strongly in her own defense than anything which could be added:

> Whatever a party could offer of courage, revolu-

tionary farsightedness and consistency in a historic hour, Lenin, Trotsky and the other comrades have given in good measure. All the revolutionary honor and capacity which Western social democracy lacked was represented by the Bolsheviks. Their October uprising was not only the actual salvation of the Russian Revolution; it was also the salvation of the honor of international socialism.

Ernst Vollrath   (essay date 1973)

SOURCE: "Rosa Luxemburg's Theory of Revolution," translated by E. B. Ashton, in *Social Research,* Vol. 40, No. 1, Spring, 1973, pp. 83-109.

[*In the following essay, Vollrath compares Luxemburg's theory of political action to ideas of Cicero, Robespierre and the American Federalists, as well as her Marxist contemporaries and successors.*]

I

Every political theory contains a theory on the nature of action, whether specifically weighed or tacitly assumed, stated in so many words or lodged in the categorial apparatus. The problem to which every theory of action seeks to give a direct or indirect answer is the problem of the start and of starting—for all action is a beginning, a new beginning of something which previously did not exist. That such a beginning has been made can be established only when that which began is continued; unless the start is carried out, and the beginning is carried on, start and beginning would not come to appear and would not become visible. The structure of action involves (at least) two moments: the start and the continuance, both essentially linked. This dual structure has been noted and registered ever since the Western theory of action, especially of political action, originated in the thinking of Plato and Aristotle. Its classic formula in regard to political theory was stated by Cicero: "For there is nothing in which human faculties come closer to the power of the gods than either founding new states or maintaining those already founded" (*neque enim est ulla res in qua propius ad deorum numen virtus accedat humana, quam civitates aut condere novas aut conservare iam conditas*). Founding start (*condere*) and continuing maintenance (*conservare*) are the two structural moments of human action in general and of political action in particular. To the classic theory of action, above all of political action, this was well known. Political action proper merely shows the structural moments of action pure and unveiled.

Whether political theory to date has been able to do anything with this insight is another question. It indicates the caution with which it should be approached that Cicero, in the line just quoted, is by no means referring to philosophical theory. He expressly stays clear of it, referring instead to men who have done something in politics—in other words, precisely not to the metaphysical theoreticians of practice. Any metaphysically defined theory of action endeavors to make action understandable by the theory's own experiences with itself, i.e., not by the phenomenal fund of action. This is not the place to go into that complex of questionable points. Almost wholly lost sight of in the metaphysical theory of practice is the problem of the start, above all, the fundamental problem of all acting. For when political theory will measure action, not by the phenomenon of action itself, but by its own experiences—and that is what a metaphysically defined theory of politics is doing—there will be no occasion for the problem of start and beginning, and thus of continuance and execution, to be taken any too seriously. Starting is unproblematical to theoretical thought because such thought can posit itself as the start. To the thinker, his thought precedes every beginning and can therefore mediate and posit the beginning at will; there is, and there occurs, no break that would have to be bridged between the thought and the beginning. Needless to say, this is not quite so simple for action, let alone for political action. In real action every start posits a difference from all that has gone before, because every acting start has in itself the element of "not" (not at all, not this way, not as anything like this, etc.) A metaphysically defined theory of practice and politics will vault this chasm by positing itself as the start—that is to say, by understanding itself from the volitive point of view as that in which everything new is anticipated. The immediate consequence is that acting will no longer be understood as acting but as making, or at least as something of the kind. For making, as distinct from acting, the problem of the start has long been solved. The start lies with the maker and with his knowing disposition about the start. All metaphysically defined theory of political action tends to use theory to cover up the problem of the start of action, to make that problem disappear. This means nothing other than that all past theory of political practice has failed to make action an object of its reflections.

II

The premised observations are to serve as a horizon for the following treatment of Rosa Luxemburg's theory of revolution. The duplicity of present political theories—theories of state-authored organizations on the one hand, theories of revolutionary movements on the other—evidently points to the previously stressed dual structure of action with its elements of starting (*condere*) and continuing (*conservare*). True, the task of any political theory is nothing but the solution of the problem of action. Because the problematical part of action is its start, however, the theories of revolution attract more attention today, for what are revolutions other than new starts? They claim, at least, to be new starts—whether rightly or wrongly has been another question since de Tocqueville. In any event, a theory of revolution has to face the problem of the start, of starting to act and of starting by acting.

Rosa Luxemburg's theory of revolution holds a special place among all theories of revolutionary movements. A comparison with Karl Marx's theory of revolution—from which Rosa Luxemburg's differs fundamentally—may make this clear. "Revolution," Marx wrote in 1844, in *Kritische Randglossen,* "the over throw of the existing power and the dissolution of the old conditions in general, is a political act. Yet without revolution socialism cannot be carried out. It needs this political act insofar as it needs destruction and dissolution. But when its organizing activity begins, when its end in itself, its soul, emerges, socialism casts off the political shell." In these early hints lies the core of the orthodox Marxist theory of revolution, basically unchanged until Lenin's work *State and Revolution* of 1917-18 led to its canonization.

According to this common Marxist conviction, revolution is a means to an end that is altogether different from revolution. Yet any means-end relationship takes its bearings from the model of making things, for in making alone is there an unequivocal possibility of assigning means to ends. That Marx and the orthodox Marxists claimed revolution for a mere means to a wholly different end has to do with a distinct view of the nature of politics. Here this view cannot be completely unfolded; even less can its origins in modern political thought be uncovered. The crucial traits may suffice.

To Marx, as to orthodox Marxism, the political realm and all action in it are secondary and derivative in kind. They constitute the alienated form of a true realm and of true doings: of the realm of production by work. Only what is done in this realm is productive, while political action is nothing but an expression of the rule of the unproductive capitalist class. Of the innumerable utterances in which Marx and Engels sought to confirm this thesis we need to cite only one (by Engels, at Marx's grave): "The main purpose of this organization [state] has always been the use of armed force to assure the working majority's economic suppression by the exclusively propertied minority."

It has to be made clear that this appraisal of the political realm and the actions occurring in it is by no means a peculiarity of Marxian and Marxist thinking. Rather, it is the consequence of action being reduced to producing and thus productive work, and we therefore find it also among theoreticians who certainly cannot be suspected of Marxism, such as Adam Smith.

But these are not the only views about action which Marx and Marxism share with a considerable number of bourgeois theoreticians. The concurrence extends to the basic assumptions about the relationship of action and politics, assumptions that are part of the modern concept of the state. According to those, the modern sovereign state monopolizes the realm of politics, and what characterizes it is its simultaneous monopolization of force. Equating politics with the state and identifying this realm with force— this is a legacy which Marx and orthodox Marxism received from the Founding Fathers of the modern state concept—from Thomas Hobbes, for example. These identifications are easy for a way of thinking in which the central category, work, remains characterized by moments of making.

These identifications, so very plausible to modern thought, have considerable consequences for Marx's theory of revolution. They enable us to make that theory completely intelligible. For once the realm of the state and of politics is determined—as a secondary, derivative, and alienated one—by the element of force, revolution can only mean the forcible (i.e., political) seizure of power (i.e., of the realm of politics and the state), in order to use this power so that, by changes in the production context, the realm

of the state will ultimately disappear and politics as well as force will vanish with it. If this is the situation, both revolution and the disappearance of the realm of politics and the state can be planned and "made" according to this revolutionary theory. Lenin's political theory, from *What is to be Done?* to *State and Revolution,* clearly amounts to such a theory of revolutionary planning.

III

It is precisely against this Leninist revolutionary theory with its metaphysical implications that Rosa Luxemburg's theory is directed. She opposes, first, the seemingly so plausible identification of revolution and force: "But revolution is something other, and something more, than bloodshed." The entire question which dominates her political thinking can be understood as a search for this "other" thing, this "more" that distinguishes revolution from pure use of force. In any case, her questioning of the identification of revolution and force lends the total political realm a dimension other than that which determined the classic concept of modern age politics; for in that concept—no matter whether in its bourgeois or its Marxist form—politics is essentially characterized by the element of force. Rosa Luxemburg expressly rejects the theory worked out by Lenin, with its possibility of scheduling the revolution "for a certain calendar day, by way of a central committee decision"—which would mean turning it into a "mere combat technique that might be 'decided upon' or possibly 'forbidden' at will, with the best of science and conscience."

The gist of Rosa Luxemburg's controversy with Lenin's theory of a new type of party—a theory she charges with being a conspiratorial one of the "Jacobin-Blanquist type"—concerns the nature of revolutionary action itself. To Rosa Luxemburg, Lenin's party theory was based upon a wrong view of that action. She characterizes this view as follows: Revolutionary activity issues from an ultracentralistically organized collective will which, in accordance with a plan worked out in advance, in every detail, turns the broad masses of the people into its disciplined tools, to which the strength of the center is mechanically transferable. Such a view of revolutionary action clearly takes its bearings from the model of "making," with the real activity placed entirely into the will of the planning and organizing center, to which the revolutionary act has ceased to be anything but a mere "coup." To Rosa Luxemburg, in other words, Lenin's theory of revolution is alarmingly identical with the "bourgeois" view that sees the essence of revolution in the "battle of the barricades, the open clash with the armed forces of the state," in short, in violent action to take over the power of the state. Rosa Luxemburg has no doubts about the reason behind this Leninist theory of revolution and of action. In fact, Lenin is holding on to the modern identifications of politics and force, of state and force, of political action and force, and in his theory of revolution this appears when his revolutionary tool, the proletariat organized by the central will, is asked for the necessary factory-type discipline—which Rosa Luxemburg proves to him can only be produced "by the *barracks,* also by a modern bureaucracy, in short . . . by the total mechanism of the centralized bourgeois state."

Lenin's concept of politics too is accordingly determined by the modern concept of the state, an essential part of which is the element of force. But since this element makes political action appear as the plannable and makeable fabrication of a "central power which alone thinks, creates, and decides for all," the Leninist theory seems to Rosa Luxemburg to miss the essence of political and revolutionary action.

IV

Rosa Luxemburg's point of departure for all reflections upon revolution is the insight that "there is no separating its economic and its political element." This entwinement suffices to set her political thinking apart from that of Marx and of orthodox Marxists, to whom politics is and remains an estranged derivative of economics. But Rosa Luxemburg's central thesis holds: "Between the two there is complete interaction"—and perhaps it is so in the "mass strike" which is the revolutionary action pure and simple.

Since it is the fundament of Rosa Luxemburg's political thought, this interaction of the economic and political moments calls for closer scrutiny. To understand it, we have to start out from her basic assumption that "the formal side of democracy" differs from its other side, its "real substance." The assumption of such a difference between form and substance is what makes Rosa Luxemburg a socialist thinker—one who holds the conditions of capitalism responsible for formal democracy's failure to be substantially fulfilled. In her writings, therefore, the difference appears in the well-known socialist formulas, principally in that of the class struggle. But Rosa Luxemburg's own crucial idea is her political interpretation of the difference in line with her basic assumption of economic-political interaction. The proletariat, due to its economic situation, is incapable of acting politically to determine its own fate, and it is kept in this state of incapacity, against its will, by the political-economic power of capitalism.

What the difference means politically can be demonstrated with the aid of Kant's definition of the political realm. The formal constitution of this realm as a union of free men takes three moments, according to Kant: "I. *Freedom* of each member of society as a *human being;* 2. *equality* of each member with every other member as a *subject of the state;* 3. *independence* of each member of the community as a *citizen.*" United, these three moments make out the concept, i.e., the form of a state in a political condition, and they must be the criteria for determining whether or not we have to do with that sort of structure. The formality of this concept of politics is the ground of its universality, which entitles each human being as such to claim to belong to the realm of freedom (first moment) and to the realm of law (second moment).

Even more essential to our consideration is the third moment, independence. In that, Kant comprehends man's active self-determination as a citizen, i.e., his claim to be actively engaged in the political realm or, in other words, his claim to political action. Here Kant adds a qualification. Not everyone has such a right of political action; only

he who is "his own master (*suiiuris*)"—that is to say, only he who "has some sort of property." In a footnote to this definition Kant distinguishes two kinds of activity and two corresponding types of actors. The distinction goes back to the ancient European division of all the things men do into "acting" proper (the Greek *prattein,* the Latin *agere*) and "making" (the Greek *poiein,* the Latin *facere*). Kant's resumption of this old distinction—whose ontological interpretation has been demonstrated chiefly by Aristotle in *Nicomachian Ethics*—has two characteristics: first, the distinction is made to bear fruit in a political respect only, and second, the traditional order of rank, in which acting is accorded primacy over making, seems to have been reversed by Kant. For as he expounds the distinction, an active part in the existence of the state can be claimed only by one who knows how to produce a work (*opus*) that he can dispose of by conveying title to another—in other words, only the maker, whom Kant calls an *artifex.* He alone is a self-determining member of the state (*citoyen*). Not entitled to active participation in political existence, on the other hand, is he whose activities do not produce any work that he might dispose of, and who therefore owns nothing but the use of his faculties, which he might grant to another. His sole exclusive property is the activity of living, and in Kantian usage a man engaged in this activity alone is called *operarius.* The term that has since come to prevail as designating such a man is "proletarian." In the horizon of the Kantian distinction, such a man cannot begin to act because he is always already engaged in the pure activity of living—an activity in which there is no such thing as a true start, a new beginning.

The reason why the proletarian *operarii* are excluded from political activity is evident from the following. It does not lie in a mythical power of the property that springs as a work from the producing activity; it lies in its political function. The man whose producing activity can "make" him the owner of a disposable thing is therefore not forced to exhaust himself in the pure use of his faculties, in the sheer activity of "making his living." He is free from the pure activity of keeping himself alive, free for an existence as a political actor. If it did seem initially as though the Kantian distinction of *artifex* and *operarius* implied a revaluation of the primacy of acting over making, an interpretation of the political function of the property produced in making shows that Kant actually preserves that primacy. The making of works that can be turned into property outranks the pure activity of living—but it does not have that supremacy for itself, only with respect to political activity. Freedom of self-determining political action rests upon freedom from the pure activity of living.

What Kant failed to consider in analyzing the formal moments of the concept of politics is the rise in the 19th century of an immense class of *operarii,* i.e., of men for whom active participation in political action was impossible although their active work produced things that were precisely not their property.

This is the problem envisioned by Rosa Luxemburg when she distinguishes the real substance of democracy from its formal side, when she wants the political and economic realms viewed as interacting. Her basic political question is this: How, in a state of formal democracy, can all men—including those barred from acting by the conditions of capitalism—be enabled to participate in political action? This question is to be posed under any system that recognizes the formality of democracy without realizing it substantially, i.e., in action. It is thus to be posed also in the bureaucratic regimes that are formally democratically structured without having a democratic substance. The explosive power of Rosa Luxemburg's ideas for these systems is evident.

At bottom, the cardinal question of Rosa Luxemburg's political thought is how democracy—understood as the self-determining activity of all—can be realized, not only in line with the concept, but by the activity of all. The question arises whenever all men are not capable of and admitted to this activity, when there is democracy only according to the formal concept, but not in what all men really do and are permitted to do. It is worth noting that in this view the problem of the realization of democracy emerges everywhere and in all political systems.

V

What Rosa Luxemburg calls revolution is an activity of those whom the sheer facts of proletarian life—in other words, economic reasons—keep from participating actively in the determination of their fate. It is the activity in which they set out to win this participation. Such a view of the nature of revolution excludes the assumption that revolution is a means to quite another end. And it is equally out of the question, then, to see the essence of revolution in violence or in a pure shift of power according to plans laid by a centralized collective will.

Instead, Rosa Luxemburg's concept—which characterizes revolution as the conquest of a share in self-determining action—corresponds completely to the modern non-Marxist concept. The classic formula for it was found by Maximilien Robespierre. In his speech "On the principles of revolutionary government," delivered before the Convention on 5 Nivôse An II (12-25-1793), Robespierre defined the essence of revolution as follows:

> *Le but du gouvernement constitutionel est de conserver la République; celui du gouvernement révolutionaire de la fonder. . . . Le gouvernement révolutionaire a besoin d'une activitié extraordinaire. . . . Il est soumis à des règles moins uniformes et moins rigoureuses, parce que les circonstances où il se trouve sont orageuses et mobiles, et surtout parce qu'il est forcé à déployer sans cesse des ressources nouvelles et rapides, pour les dangers nouveaux et pressants. Le gouvernement constitutionel s'occupe principalement de la liberté civile; et le gouvernement révolutionaire, de la liberté publique.*

Revolution is here defined with the aid of the two terms used by Cicero to define political action: *fonder,* to found (the Latin *condere*), and *conserver,* to maintain (the Latin *conservare*). The political condition to be brought about by the founding action is what Robespierre calls *République.* In the political language of the eighteenth century, in the *Federalist Papers* as well as in Kant's writings, "Republic" is the word for the realm of the free and public action of

all men. In another speech, "On the principles of political morality," of 17 Pluviôse An II (2-5-1794), in which he celebrates the secular character of revolution, Robespierre identifies that realm with democracy, thereby establishing a revolutionary tradition for the present use of this term.

> *Le . . . gouvernement démocratique ou républicain: ces deux mots sont synonymes, malgré les abus de langage vulgaire. . . . La démocratie est un état où le peuple souverain, guidé par des lois qui sont son ouvrage, fait par lui-même tout ce qu'il peut bien faire, et par des délégués tout ce qu'il ne peut faire lui-même.*

The mission and the goal of revolution is to found the democratic republic as the realm of free action by all men (*fonder la république*); but a republic once founded can do no more than maintain this realm of freedom (*conserver la république*). Liberation to freedom, and being liberated in freedom—this is the nature of political action in its dual form of actively founding and actively maintaining freedom. But Robespierre—wrongly, in my judgment—equates the two moments of political action with a distinction equally essential to the realm of that action. Constrained by the modern concept of the state, he identifies the moment of *fonder* with *liberté politique,* and the moment of *conserver* with (an apolitical) *liberté civile,* thus ignoring the eminently political character which the second moment has also. What this means is that with respect to the second moment he defines freedom only formally, not substantially.

In our context it is important that Robespierre's description of revolutionary action characterizes this as an "extraordinary activity." Revolutionary action is extraordinary because it is the prototype of political action as opposed to all ordinary doings—which are mere behavior. It is therefore rare, because it requires the courageous resolution to start something new. The rules it follows are less uniform and strict than those which govern pure behavior. Unlike, indeed in contrast to, mere behavior—which is subject to norms of behavioral biology, depth psychology, sociology, or economics, is uniform and accordingly fixed and confined—politically revolutionary action is free from these norms and restrictions, is diverse and unlimited. The circumstances it creates and in which it moves are precisely not fixed, confined, and restricted as are the ones of behavior; they are determined by action and counteraction alone. In these circumstances—in the world of acting and speaking human beings, the world that constitutes itself by human action and speech—the individual actor can incessantly, and sometimes with astonishing rapidity, find new fonts of his action in the action of those who join him in counteracting the ever-present danger of a suppression of this free action that has only one goal: to keep restoring its own possibility as free action. This is the *condere* and the *fonder,* the founding and establishing of freedom.

As a matter of fact, revolutionary action and political action are identical. Just as revolutionary action with the characteristics we have shown must be regarded as political action pure and simple, so is political action in itself revolutionary. But if revolutionary action is identical with political action, the consequence for all those concerned with free, public, common, and thus political action can only be to exert every effort to make revolutionary action last, because it is political action. Then the point of revolutionary activity—which is political action—can only be to act in freedom, time and again; or, put another way, to act so that free action will be possible time and again. This is the other moment of free action, the moment of *conservare* and of *conserver*.

VI

In Rosa Luxemburg's theory of revolution we reencounter the two moments stressed by our preceding analysis of revolutionary activity. The revolutionary act of conquering a share in active self-determination, the moment of *condere* and *fonder,* appears—in line with its socialist rudiment—in the phenomenon of the mass strike. The mass strike is that act, that sequence of attitudes, whereby those hitherto not participating in free self-determination conquer that participation (the *metexein* or *koinonein arxus,* as the political realm is defined by Aristotle). Rosa Luxemburg never tires of pointing out that the mass strike is never a one-time operation; it always covers an entire period. Revolutions are not made like things, at one stroke, but over a period of time in which the revolutionary activity must never cease, lest the action vanish in a result that lies outside the action.

The treatise *Massenstreik, Partei und Gewerkschaften* of 1906 is devoted to an analysis of the phenomenon of the mass strike. It seeks to circumscribe the consequences of the Russian revolution of 1905-06 for revolutionary action, i.e., it starts out from real action, not from general theories on revolutionary practice. To Rosa Luxemburg, the mass strike is "the way of motion of the proletarian mass, the phenomenal form of the proletarian struggle in a revolution." For an understanding of her concept of revolution it is important to clarify the real meaning of the term "mass." It has by no means the negative aspect it has assumed in current usage. Quite unlike Lenin—to whose mind the masses are nothing but the remnants of the non-proletarian classes, degraded into means of seizing power after their class structure has been smashed—Rosa Luxemburg uses the term in the original sense of the Roman *populus,* i.e., the political and legal community of men. The state of such a political-legal community of acting individuals has not even been achieved yet by the proletariat, in which Rosa Luxemburg self-evidently sees the overwhelming majority of all men who have become, and have been rendered, incapable of free action by the conditions of capitalism. Rather, it is precisely the mass strike, the revolutionary activity, that lead the proletariat to become a mass.

> Before it can carry out any direct political action as a mass, however, the proletariat must gather itself into a mass, and to this end it must first of all walk out of plants and workshops, out of foundries and shafts; it must overcome the fragmentation and pulverization to which it is condemned under the daily yoke of capital. The mass strike is thus the first, natural, impulsive form of any great revolutionary operation by the proletariat, and the more predominantly industrial the form of the social economy, the more preeminent the proletarian role in the revolu-

tion, the more highly developed the antithesis between labor and capital, the more powerful and decisive are the mass strikes bound to become. In the revolution of today, the previous main form of bourgeois revolution—the battle of the barricades, the open clash with the armed forces of the state—is only an extreme point, only a moment in the entire process of the proletarian mass struggle.

To Rosa Luxemburg, mass strike and revolution are "inseparable."

The community of free men is established by acting in freedom, by the very moment we characterized as *condere* and *fonder.* Hence Rosa Luxemburg's basic thesis: "The revolution produces the mass strike." Revolution means to become active; it is the start of free action on the part of those who were not freely active before, because the conditions of capitalism excluded them from activity. And in accordance with those conditions this onset of activity occurs in an interaction of economic and political moments, i.e., as a mass strike.

> The economic struggle is the guideline from one political node to the other; the political struggle is the periodic fertilization of the soil for the economic struggle. Cause and effect change places here all the time, and so the economic and political moments, far from being neatly parted or even mutually exclusive, as the pedantic schema would have it, are in the mass strike period merely two intertwined sides of the proletarian class struggle in Russia. And *their unity* is the mass strike. When pilpulistic theoreticians try to get at the 'pure political mass strike' by submitting the mass strike to artificial logical dissection, the outcome of this dissection as of any other will simply be the death of the phenomenon, not a knowledge of its living essence.

The characteristics of revolutionary activity which Rosa Luxemburg expounds correspond exactly to the ones attributed to it by Robespierre.

> The mass strike . . . is so protean a phenomenon that all the phases of political and economic struggle, all the stages and moments of the revolution are reflected in it. Its applicability, its effectiveness, the moments of its origin—all are constantly changing. It suddenly opens broad new revolutionary vistas where the revolution seemed already at a dead end, and it fails where you believe you can count on it with assurance. Now it is flooding the empire like a tidal wave, now splitting up into a giant web of rivulets, now welling from the subsoil like a new spring, now draining entirely into the ground. Political and economic strikes, mass strikes and partial strikes, demonstration strikes and combat strikes, general strikes in single industries and general strikes in single cities, quiet wage struggles and street fights on the barricades—all this runs athwart and alongside each other, crisscrossing and intertwining; it is a perpetually mobile, changing sea of phenomena. And the law that governs the motion of these phenomena becomes clear: it does not lie in the mass strike itself, not in its technical peculiarities, but in the

political and social relation of forces in the revolution. The mass strike is merely the form of the
revolutionary struggle, and every shift in the relation of the striking forces, in the evolution of
parties and the division of classes, in the position
of the counter-revolution—all this will instantly
influence the strike action in a thousand invisible, scarcely controllable ways. Yet the strike action itself hardly ever ceases. It changes only its
forms, its extent, its effect. It is the living heart-
beat of the revolution and at the same time its
most powerful driving wheel.

And precisely these characteristics make it impossible for
revolutionary activity to be comprehended technically, as
by Lenin—as something made according to plan and resolved upon by a central will. It is the element of *fonder,*
of the start of action in freedom, that makes out the essence of revolution as conceived by Rosa Luxemburg. It
is to this she gave the name which ever since Kant has
marked all action in freedom: the name of spontaneity.

Kant identifies spontaneity with freedom, since "freedom
is . . . a faculty to start a condition, and thus a series of
the consequences of that condition." He calls this faculty
of free action spontaneity, for what begins by itself (*sponte
sua*) has the character of spontaneity. The element of
starting to establish freedom in and by action is the essential characteristic Rosa Luxemburg underscores in revolution. And it is this characteristic that makes it impossible
to take revolution for the plannable product of a collective
will: "The element of spontaneity plays so preeminent a
role in mass strikes . . . because revolutions will not be
tutored." i.e., because revolution is a course of action, not
a production process to be computerized. What Rosa Luxemburg means by the element of spontaneity—an element
that has always been and will continue to be viewed with
distrust by all the orthodox—is the moment of starting to
act, the *condere* and *fonder* that is the essence of all action.

VII

In her socialist theory of revolution, Rosa Luxemburg has
not only expounded the first moment of revolutionary action, the *condere* and *fonder*; she also preserved the second
moment, the *conservare* and *conserver,* in its political
sense, a sense lost by Robespierre. In her second great controversy with Lenin, in the treatise **The Russian Revolution** of 1918, Rosa Luxemburg—for all her continuing admiration of the Russian Bolsheviki for having started and
advanced the revolution of 1917—sharply condemned the
abolition of democracy by Lenin and Trotsky. This part
of the treatise may be cited as her attempt to present her
principles of the second moment of revolutionary action.
What applies to the first moment must also apply to the
second. Thus Rosa Luxemburg on the connection of both:
Just as free exposure to the rays of the sun is the most effective, cleansing, and healing remedy against infections
and germs of disease, so the only healing and cleansing sun
is the revolution itself and its renovating principle, the intellectual life it evokes, the activity and self-responsibility
of the masses—in other words, the most widespread political freedom as its form.

Just as the realm of a community of free men can be
founded only if they will unite for spontaneous action in

freedom, it can be maintained only if all of them will spontaneously act in freedom. The freedom of action is the sole
determining principle of both moments. One things with
which Rosa Luxemburg reproaches Trotsky (and Lenin)
is to have seen the two moments precisely not as belonging
together:

> Thanks to the open and immediate struggle for
> the power of government, the working masses
> accumulate a great deal of political experience
> in short order and develop swiftly from step to
> step. Here Trotsky refutes himself and his own
> friends in the party. Precisely because this is
> true, their suppression of public life has stopped
> up the font of political experience and the rise in
> development. Or else one would have to assume
> that experience and development were possible
> until the Bolsheviki seized power, had then
> reached their degree, and became superfluous
> thereafter.

In essence, this rebuke shows Rosa Luxemburg's complete
acceptance of the fact that Trotsky and Lenin realized the
first moment of revolution (whether she was right or
wrong in this is quite another question that could be clarified only by analyzing Trotsky's and, above all, Lenin's relation to the Soviets). To her they were revolutionaries
who made a new start. About this moment she can say explicitly: "And *in this sense* the future belongs everywhere
to 'Bolshevism.' " But the second moment of revolutionary activity, the maintenance of the newly established freedom, is perishing under them, due to their wrong course
of action, and that presumably because their views of action came entirely from a theory tied to modern political
philosophy, a theory that never gets down to action itself.
In this context she expressly questions Lenin's basic thesis—taken from Marx, but implied from the outset in the
modern state concept—that the state and the politics identified with the state are nothing but instrumentalities of
oppression and class rule. That her eminent understanding of the nature of action makes such a thesis absolutely
unacceptable to Rosa Luxemburg is a matter of course.

The realm of the freedom of all, founded by the spontaneous action of all and maintained by the active spontaneity
of all—this is what she calls "socialist democracy." It has
none of the pure formality attached to bourgeois democracy. Because her socialist democracy is simply active participation by the masses in political life, it is not something
to be introduced only after a socialist transformation of
the economic structure—a gift, as it were, from a "handful
of socialist dictators." This would mean the abolition of
democracy. "The historic task of the proletariat, when it
comes to power, is to replace bourgeois democracy with
a socialist democracy, not to abolish all democracy." It is
Rosa Luxemburg's view that in a formal, bourgeois democracy the masses of the people remain excluded from
active participation in political action because the conditions of capitalism prevent them from engaging in anything but the satisfaction of their vital needs, i.e., in pure
survival. To her mind, therefore, formal democracy and
capitalism are identical:

> We always distinguish the social core from the
> political form of *bourgeois* democracy; we al-

ways uncovered the bitter core of social inequality and unfreedom under the sweet shell of formal equality and freedom—not in order to reject these, but to spur the working class not to be content with the shell and rather to seize political power so as to fill the shell with a new social content.

The critique of Trotsky and Lenin contains an analysis of the second moment of revolutionary activity, and the analysis is presented under the Marxist formula of the dictatorship of the proletariat. Initially, that idiom—canonized and fetishized by Marx's letter to J. Weydemeyer of March 5, 1852—denotes nothing but the takeover and use of power by the proletarians (presented as the majority) as against the capitalists and their minions (declared to be the minority) for the purpose of establishing the realm of freedom. Marx and Engels (and Lenin) used the concept of the proletarian dictatorship to characterize the interim between the proletariat's conquest of political power and the definitive abolition of the realm of politics and of the state as a stage that is still political, i.e., based on force. More crucial to Rosa Luxemburg, however, is another moment, one also to be found in Marx and Engels. They say in the *Communist Manifesto*: "The proletarian movement is the independent movement of the vast majority in the interest of the vast majority." We are by no means about to analyze the sociological accuracy of that thesis, which Rosa Luxemburg accepts, of course, though with modifications. What concerns us, rather, is its political meaning.

The political relevance of the cliché of the majority dates back to the Abbé Sieyès, although it is unquestionably older (it comes from the medieval election law for such clearly defined electoral bodies as a college of monks, for example). In Sieyès treatise *Qu'est-ce que le Tiers État?* the bourgeoisie's pursuit of political power is led to victory by the compelling argument that the bourgeois far exceed the nobles and clerics in number, and that the nation is accordingly present in the representatives of the bourgeoisie. The principle is stated as follows: "*Il est constant que, dans la représentation nationale ordinaire et extraordinaire, l'influence ne peut être qu'un raison du nombre des têtes qui ont droit à se faire représenter.*" By the way, the man who brought the platitude into the context of socialist thinking was none other than Gracchus Babeuf, who rebuked the Thermidorians for ruling in the name of a million Frenchmen against the twenty-four million plebeians of France.

The political meaning of the commonplace can be interpreted in two ways. The first interpretation—undoubtedly the one of Sieyès, of Babeuf, and also of Marx, starts out from the will, i.e., it is fundamentally Rousseauist even though Rousseau rejects the idea of a majority will (*volonté de tous*). The absolute unfeasibility, noted by Rousseau himself, of really basing the political existence of a state on the pure *volonté générale* led the Abbé Sieyès and all his successors to replace this *volonté* with that of the majority. And since that time it has always been the will of the majority—if only of a future majority—that was retroactively drawn upon to justify political and social action.

But the substitution of majority will for the *volonté générale* as the ultimate ground of political or social legitimacy

could happen only because this retroactive justification corresponds to a political experience in which a principle quite different from the will is posited for political action. That principle is opinion. And if we base political action on opinion, this means from the outset that we are referring to the number of those who share, or can share, an opinion—i.e., to a possible majority opinion. It is startling to see how close Rosa Luxemburg comes here to the ideas of authors of the *Federalist Papers* of 1787, ideas she does not seem to have known at all. The reason for the correspondence is that like Madison, Hamilton, and Jay, Rosa Luxemburg does not start out from a political theory but from the experiences that can be gathered in action.

> Nothing but experience can make corrections and can open new ways. Nothing but the uncurbed effervescence of life hits upon a thousand new forms and improvisations, illuminates creative powers, corrects all mistakes on its own. The public life of states with restricted freedom is so scant, so miserable, so schematical, so barren precisely because by the exclusion of democracy it locks itself off from the living sources of all intellectual wealth and progress.

The point of revolutionary activity is the constitution of the realm of freedom, which can be maintained only by continuing activity in freedom. For this reason, and since she by no means shares Lenin's and Trotsky's view of the derivative character of the realm of state and politics, Rosa Luxemburg clings stubbornly to the idea of "representatives of the people, chosen by the people in general elections," in other words, to representative democracy as the political constitution of those who act in freedom. The formula she found for this—"A backbone of Soviets as well as a constituent assembly and the universal franchise"—does not make her seem far removed from one of the American Founding Fathers, Thomas Jefferson, who tirelessly calls for the institution of Soviet-type councils or "wards."

To Rosa Luxemburg, a representative democracy, one resting on the relationship of "electors and elected," remains the "most important democratic guarantee of a healthy public life and of political activity on the part of the working masses." In this context she makes an impressive presentation of Lenin's and Trotsky's continued adherence to the modern state concept which she considers obsolete, with its identifications of the political realm with violence and domination. She regards the Soviets as conceived to facilitate and to preserve the participation of all men in political freedom. They are to protect the representative body from the danger of detachment from those whose opinions it has to represent, so that "the living fluid of the popular mood will constantly water the representative bodies, permeate them, guide them." Political life remains alive only in the constant practice of public freedom. "The only way to a rebirth is the school of public life itself, the broadest, most unlimited democracy and public opinion." And as a matter of course, this means all those institutions in which alone opinions can make themselves publicly heard, so as to become politically effective. "On the other hand it is an obvious, undeniable fact that rule by broad masses of the people is quite unthinkable without a free and uninhibited press, without a life of unhampered association and assembly."

At bottom, this is exactly what Alexis de Tocqueville in *Democracy in America* describes as "political associations." What is to unfold in the Soviets and in their link with the representative body is that political life "of the broadest publicity, with the most active, unimpeded participation of the masses of the people, in unrestricted democracy," which is "the source of political experiences" as well as "the vital element, the air" from and in which the political existence established by revolutionary action will be preserved and enhanced. Once founded, the freedom of all to act publicly is to be continued and preserved as all act publicly in freedom. Both the foundation and the continuing preservation of the freedom to act are basically identical, going back to one principle: to freedom, to the self-determining action of all. The revolution, conceived as the process of all men coming to be active to establish the freedom of all, is continued and realized as all are active in freedom.

Also part of this context is the famed and controversial formula: "Not to revolutionary tactics by way of a majority, but to a majority by way of revolutionary tactics." The point of this formula is to suggest that an opinion that will be politically relevant must be the product of revolutionary action. This opinion is generated by those who start to act and are joined by others in continuing and finishing what has started. Action, starting and continued, forms the opinion that can become the opinion of a majority; but one cannot wait for the formation from somewhere of a majority of opinions to start action. Rosa Luxemburg is no adherent of a merely formal democracy of majorities because such a democracy does not rest on an opinion produced by revolutionary action, i.e., will not lead all men to act freely at all.

In the *Federalist Papers,* James Madison stated the relation of power and opinion explicitly: "If it be true that all government rests on opinion, it is no less true that the strength of opinion in each individual, and its practical influence on his conduct, depend much on the number which he supposes to have entertained the same opinion." This still leaves open whether a majority opinion leads to the preservation of freedom or to its destruction. The whole political theory of the authors of the *Federalist Papers* serves to maintain a diversity of opinion, because this alone can keep the will of a majority from evolving into an elective despotism. What matters is not to destroy the freedom of minority opinion, because the minority must be preserved for a reconstruction of the political realm by uniting those who can share the same opinion. That is to say: the minority—and in the extreme case this is the individual human being—should be so protected from the threat of rule by the majority will that it remains capable of coalescing in a new majority opinion. In this sense the freedom of opinion, without which there can be no action, takes over the *condere* and the *conservare* of the freedom of political action.

To the authors of the *Federalist Papers,* the only form of government that might be up to the task is representative democracy, to which they—like Kant—give the name "Republic." The point of departure in basing political action on opinion is the fundamental political fact of human plurality, i.e., the fact that the world is not inhabited by man but by men, and that they must try by their actions to make a human world of it. The weakness of basing political action on the will, on the other hand, is that there the plurality of men proves an absolute obstacle to the will—because every will always seeks its realization only in unity with itself, in the "one will" of Thomas Hobbes or in the *volonté générale* of Jean-Jacques Rousseau. A view based on the will as the principle of political action—not as a moment in it, as by Aristotle—will therefore always posit the will of the majority as the only legitimate will. It must try to annihilate the minority's will, whereas the majority of opinion must seek to preserve the other, deviating opinion of the minority. From there alone is a new start of action possible at any time, once the political realm is no longer preserved in action.

The real reason why Rosa Luxemburg holds on to the people's representatives chosen in general elections and to their link with the Soviets is the basic principle she views as governing the entire political and social realm: the freedom of opinion, which she also calls "popular mood." "Freedom is always the dissenter's freedom only. Not because of a fanaticism of 'justice,' but because all the instructive, salutary, and purifying qualities of political freedom hang on this essential side of it, and because their effect fails when freedom becomes a 'privilege.' " The political freedom which the revolution is to found, which is established in the activity for which the masses gather, can be maintained only by this freedom to hold another opinion. Its result is the maintenance of freedom of action, "the active, unhampered, energetic political life of the broad masses of the people."

Nothing makes this clearer than the negation of the established and preserved free public action of all.

> If all this falls by the wayside, what really remains . . . ? With the suppression of political life throughout the country, life in the Soviets too is bound to wane. Without general elections, unhampered freedom of press and assembly, a free struggle of opinions—without all that, life in every public institution withers and becomes a sham life in which the bureaucracy remains the only active element. Public life becomes gradually dormant as a few dozen party leaders of inexhaustible energy and boundless idealism direct and govern; beneath them, the real guidance comes from a dozen eminent brains, and from time to time an elite of labor is summoned to meetings, to applaud the speeches of the leaders and to give unanimous consent to the resolutions submitted—what it all comes down to is cliquism.

If the freedom won in the action of all is not maintained by the free action of all, the established freedom perishes. It is as if its foundation had never occurred. Without the *conservare* and *conserver,* the *condere* and *fonder* has no consequences and becomes null and void. It is as if it had not happened at all.

Sheila Delany   (essay date 1975)

SOURCE: "Red Rosa: Bread and Roses," in *The Massachusetts Review*, Vol. XVI, No. 2, Spring, 1975, pp. 373-86.

[Delany is an American-born Canadian author and educator. In the following essay, she comments on the revival of interest in Luxemburg's ideas and explores what made Luxemburg such a compelling and disturbing figure.]

> Now Red Rosa is also gone,
> Where she lies is quite unknown.
> Because she told the poor the truth,
> The rich have hunted her down.
>   Bertolt Brecht, "Grabschrift 1919."

A woman, a Jew and a Pole—it sounds like the beginning of a bad joke. Rosa Luxemburg was all three, but as a revolutionary communist she transcends definition by sex, religion or nationality.

Franz Mehring, the colleague and first biographer of Marx, called Luxemburg "the best brain after Marx." When Lenin paid homage to Luxemburg in 1922, three years after her death at the hands of German police, he told "a good old Russian fable":

> An eagle can sometimes fly lower than a chicken, but a chicken can never rise to the same heights as an eagle. . . . In spite of her mistakes, Rosa Luxemburg was and is an eagle, and not only will she be dear to the memory of Communists throughout the world, but her biography and the complete edition of her works . . . will be a very useful lesson in the education of many generations of Communists.

Yet six years later, Communist Party stalwarts were denouncing Rosa Luxemburg's work as "opportunist deviation" and even as a "syphilis bacillus" infecting the German proletariat. During Stalin's regime she was linked with Leon Trotsky as a heretic and deviant from "official" Bolshevik doctrine. Today in East Germany Luxemburg's reputation has begun to revive in a limited way, though her antibureaucratic stance and uncompromising rejection of all opportunism still make party bureaucracies uncomfortable. Brecht's "Ballad of Red Rosa" does not appear in his official *Collected Works*.

In the west there has also been a recent revival of interest in Rosa Luxemburg. Several anthologies have appeared, many of her pamphlets are now available in new editions, and the important early biography by Paul Frolich has been reissued. Even this output is far from complete, for Luxemburg was an enormously prolific writer: of pamphlets, newspaper articles, theoretical works, speeches and letters. Much of this material remains unpublished or untranslated, and some was destroyed when Luxemburg's Berlin apartment was ransacked after her murder. Her major work has been taken up by a mixed audience of anarchists, surrealists, spontaneists, feminists, vanguard-party theoreticians, revolutionary groupuscules and disillusioned ex-leftists (I intend no equations here, nor any blanket evaluation). Obviously their motives differ, as consequently does their understanding of Luxemburg's contribution to Marxist theory. Luxemburg's work and her

life are full of apparent paradox—like history itself, or like Marxist theory—and it's in part the inadequate understanding of such paradox that permits such a wide range of interpretation of her ideas. It isn't my purpose here to analyze Luxemburg's contribution to Marxist economics, and I am not convinced that it is primarily as an economist that she should be seen. As Luxemburg herself noted, the reader of her economic work must be

> a master of national economy in general and of Marxism in particular, and that to the nth degree. And how many such mortals are there today? Not a half-dozen. My work is from this standpoint truly a luxury product and might just as well be printed on handmade paper.

Nonetheless I want to try to explore some of the meaning of this immensely powerful figure from our revolutionary past, and perhaps to suggest some of her importance for our revolutionary future.

She was born in 1871, the same year as Lenin and the year of the Paris Commune whose short life did so much to show the world revolutionary movement what proletarian democracy could and ought to be. Her family—like the families of Marx, Engels, Lenin and Trotsky—were cultured and of comfortable means, though far from wealthy. A star pupil in high school, Rosa was denied the traditional gold medal for excellence "because of her oppositional attitude toward authority." In 1889, when Rosa was 19, her involvement in Warsaw with the Proletariat Party and with the new Polish Workers' League was discovered by the Czarist police. It was an offense that carried the punishment of imprisonment or exile to Siberia; so, hidden under straw in a peasant's cart, Rosa Luxemburg left Poland. She escaped to Zurich, a major center of intellectual life and of international socialist activity.

In Zurich Luxemburg made enduring friends and enemies. Among her enemies was Georgii Plekhanov, leader of the Russian exile group and "grand old man" of the revolutionary movement abroad; for personal and political reasons Plekhanov was antagonistic to Luxemburg and her friends. And, most important, Luxemburg met Leo Jogiches, the young Polish revolutionary who was her lover for many years and her lifelong comrade in the Polish socialist movement.

The dissertation with which Rosa Luxemburg earned her doctorate was a study of the industrial development of Poland during the nineteenth century. It was a pioneering effort, still used by modern historians in the field, which became an important part of Luxemburg's argument against the claims of the Polish nationalist movement for independence from Russia. The dissertation demonstrated that Poland's economic growth depended on the Russian market, so that separation would lead to economic chaos. Further, the ideological emphasis on patriotic nationalism would divert the Polish proletariat from class struggle and the struggle for socialism, thus benefiting the bourgeoisie. Luxemburg's position, then, was that Polish communists should lend no support to the movement for national independence in Poland.

This stance was one of the mistakes that Lenin mentioned

in his eulogy of Luxemburg, for the Bolsheviks consistently supported the right of oppressed nations to self-determination, while at the same time recognizing the reactionary nature of nationalism—"national egoism," in Lenin's phrase—and the equally retrograde influence of such mystical trends as pan-Islamism. Luxemburg's mistakes here were several. She confused support for national liberation with capitulation to nationalism. And, in her zeal to avoid the reformist mistake of limitation to democratic demands, she recoiled to the opposite (ultra-left) extreme of rejecting the democratic demand—rather than, as Lenin urged in his writings on the question, taking up the democratic demand for national liberation, supporting it, and combining it with the struggle for socialism. Stalin's analogy to the religion question is helpful: the Bolsheviks will defend freedom of religion, while simultaneously agitating against religion as an ideology hostile to the interests of the proletariat. Similarly, the revolutionary party will support the right of nations to self-determination while agitating for its own program. The Bolshevik position implied neither (as Trotsky put it) "an evangel of separation," nor political support to the bourgeoisie of a colonial country even if that bourgeoisie is waging a struggle for national independence. Here the key principle is the organizational and propagandistic independence of communists within the movement: to support militarily the struggle for national liberation, while simultaneously exposing and opposing the colonial bourgeoisie and pushing the struggle toward socialist revolution.

It was partly through her polemics against Polish independence and her leadership of the Polish group that the young Rosa Luxemburg established her reputation as an important member of the international socialist movement. On completing her degree in 1898, she decided, against the advice of Jogiches, to continue her revolutionary career in Germany. The specific reasons for her decision are not known, but it must have been clear that Germany, with its rapidly growing (though already internally divided) socialist party, its developed capitalist economy, and its well-organized working class, offered the serious prospect of socialist revolution in the near future. It was in Germany that Luxemburg developed into one of the most formidable and creative leaders of world socialism, both a brilliant theoretician and a militant strategist. She sustained that position until she was arrested and murdered by army officers during the abortive German revolution of 1918-19, when working-class militancy made her leadership (and that of her comrade Karl Liebknecht, who died with her) a serious and immediate threat to the government. She and Liebknecht were arrested in Berlin on 15 January 1919, beaten, and shot; Jogiches met the same fate two months later. Rosa's body was dumped into a canal, not to be recovered for another four months. In Goebbels' bookburning of 1933 her works were thrown into the fire along with those of Marx and Engels, Wilhelm Reich and the rest of Europe's greatest artists, scientists and revolutionaries.

The central struggle in Rosa Luxemburg's political life in Germany was the struggle against reformist revisionism; that is, against the abandonment of socialist revolution and class struggle in favor of legal and parliamentary reforms. Until World War I, "social democracy" had been the general name for scientific or Marxian socialism as distinct from such other currents as, say, Fourierist or Owenite utopian socialism. Thus Lenin's party was the Russian Social Democratic Workers' Party. What set scientific socialism apart from other programs for social change was, first, the dialectical and materialist understanding of history and of capitalist social relations (that is, relations of production, together with the class structure and political institutions that followed from these relations of production). Second, the understanding of the revolutionary tendency of the working class because of its position in capitalist society as the productive but exploited class. Third, understanding the necessity of revolution in order to expropriate the capitalist ruling class, smash the bourgeois state, and establish new, genuinely democratic forms of social life.

Reformist revisionism began its major theoretical development in the European socialist movement in the work of the German social-democrat and pacifist Eduard Bernstein who, even while revising the most basic economic and political premises of Marxist theory, continued to pose as a sincere socialist. Briefly Bernstein's argument runs as follows. By means of various adaptive mechanisms such as the credit system, improved communications, and employers' organizations (cartels, trusts), capitalism can avoid the recurrent crises which Marxist economics sees as inevitable. Thus capitalism becomes flexible enough to satisfy everyone, including the proletariat. In addition, the trade union activity of the organized working class will gradually improve its lot to the point where "the trade union struggle . . . will lead to a progressively more extensive control over the conditions of production," while through legislation the capitalist "will be reduced in time to the role of a simple administrator" (the quotations are from Konrad Schmidt, a follower of Bernstein). Class struggle can thus be eliminated by parliamentary reforms, and capitalism can survive indefinitely. The net effect of enough reforms would be socialism—no revolution required.

The best short exposure of this sleight-of-hand is still Rosa Luxemburg's polemic against Bernstein, **"Reform or Revolution,"** first published in 1899. The pamphlet examines the economic assumptions and the practical political consequences of revisionism, counterposing the correct Marxist analysis of the question. It shows, for example, how credit and cartels, far from suppressing the anarchy of capitalism, intensify and precipitate its crises. In particular they "aggravate the antagonism existing between the mode of production and exchange by sharpening the struggle between the producer and the consumer"—a principle whose concrete operation affects us now in the artificially inflated prices of housing, food and other consumer commodities, and in such carefully engineered "shortages" as the recent oil crisis. Nor will the trade union movement lead steadily to a proletarian paradise, for as capitalism proceeds through its decadent phase the demand for labor power will increase more slowly than the supply. Moreover, losses suffered on the world market will be compensated for by reduction of wages. So that unemployment and falling wages (real wages, if not nominal wages) can be expected, and the trade union movement will find its effort to protect the proletariat doubly difficult. Some of these problems are taken up in more detail by Lenin in *Imperialism, the Latest Stage of Capitalism* (1917).

This is not, of course, to say that revolutionary communism minimizes the importance of reform struggles, of safeguarding the gains made by the organized working class, or of defending all democratic rights. Indeed, as Luxemburg notes in her Introduction to **"Reform or Revolution,"** it is only in Bernstein's work that one finds for the first time the opposition between the two indissolubly linked aspects of socialism. In fact, she writes,

> the daily struggle for reforms . . . and for democratic institutions, offers to the Social-Democracy the only means of engaging in the proletarian class war and working in the direction of the final goal—the conquest of political power and the suppression of wage-labor. [For Social-Democracy] the struggle for reforms is its means; the social revolution, its aim.

The difference from revisionism, then, is that revisionism declares the stated aim of socialism to be impossible, unknowable, or unimportant: "The final goal, no matter what it is, is nothing; the movement is everything." Yet since, as Luxemburg notes, "there can be no socialist movement without a socialist aim, [Bernstein] ends by renouncing the movement" as well. It remains painfully familiar; one thinks of Herbert Marcuse's recent advice in *Counter-Revolution and Revolt* to young revolutionaries: to abandon mass action and "labor fetishism" and retreat to the universities.

Perhaps the worst practical consequence of the growing influence of revisionism in the German Social-Democratic Party (SPD) was its inability to deal correctly with the outbreak of World War I. In 1914 the SPD, along with the socialist parties of other countries, went patriotically in support of the national war effort, instead of refusing to participate in a war among imperialist nations. When the SPD voted war credits to the government its theoretical and practical bankruptcy became as obvious to many as they had been for some time already to Rosa Luxemburg. Social-democrat has since remained the term for those who want to reform capitalism rather than destroy it. Such reformists allied with the bourgeoisie to protect interests now their own. Indeed it was with the complicity of an SPD government (to which power had been handed over in November 1918) that Luxemburg and Liebknecht were arrested and killed.

Obviously the collapse of German social-democracy cannot be laid entirely at the feet of Bernstein. In the Introduction to his recent (1972) edition of Luxemburg's political writings, Robert Looker points out that "a stress on the insidious influence of revisionism . . . mistakes symptoms for causes." Looker is surely correct in citing as important contributing factors the history of the German labor movement and the history of the SPD from the nineteenth century on. Still, the 1899 controversy with Bernstein and the 1914 abdication of a proletarian class line were symptoms of the same disease: opportunism. As

Luxemburg wrote in **"Either/Or,"** a Spartacus League pamphlet of 1916, "The proud old cry, 'Proletarians of all countries, unite!' has been transformed on the battlefield into the command, 'Proletarians of all countries, cut each other's throats!' " And the Marxist principle that all written history is the history of the class struggle, now had "except in time of war" added to it (**"Rebuilding the International,"** 1915). This was the demise of the Second International, as Lenin, Luxemburg and other revolutionary socialists recognized. At the Zimmerwald Conference (September, 1915) the foundations of the Third International were laid, though not until 1919 was it officially established.

In spite of their shock and outrage at the party's defection, Luxemburg and other comrades were not paralyzed. Those who were committed to Marxian economics, to dialectical materialism and to revolution formed an opposition faction within the party, the Spartakusbund (Spartacus League), named after the famous leader of a Roman slave revolt. Their tasks were to mount a revolutionary opposition to the party leadership especially around the war issue, to propaganzide among the masses for a correct line, and to organize actions against the war.

In 1916 Rosa Luxemburg was again arrested (taken into "protective custody"), and it was in prison that she heard the news of the Bolshevik revolution in Russia.

> For three years Europe has been like a musty room, almost suffocating those living in it. Now all at once a window has been flung open, a fresh, invigorating gust of air is blowing in, and everyone in the room is breathing deeply of it.

This was her enthusiastic welcome to long-awaited revolution, in the famous essay **"The Old Mole"** (May, 1917). It seemed that the old mole—revolutionary history—having gone underground for the time in Germany, had now surfaced in Russia. Its reappearance there would and must herald similar events in Germany; not only by force of example, but because, as the Bolshevik leaders knew all too well, the success and even survival of their revolution depended on the rapid development of revolutions in other countries. They confronted the dangers of military invasion, economic strangulation, political compromises: these meant either more European revolutions in a fairly short time, or a worldwide setback for the international socialist movement as well as for the Russian revolution itself. Naturally the notion of "socialism in one country," Stalin's invention, was never considered a realistic solution; nor is it dialectically possible, and hence has no basis in the Marxist-Leninist tradition. Rather it represents both an absolute failure to understand the dialectic of revolutionary process, and a most opportunistic attempt to transform the concessions and defeats of the Russian revolution into iron principle and virtue. Without denying that some of these concessions may have been necessary for the survival of the new state, one has nonetheless to call a spade a spade. As Luxemburg acknowledged even while (again incorrectly) denouncing the Treaty of Brest-Litovsk (in **"The Russian Tragedy,"** September, 1918),

> Admittedly Lenin and his friends deluded neither themselves nor others about the facts. They

admitted their capitulation. Unfortunately they did deceive themselves in hoping to purchase a genuine respite at the price of capitulation. . . .

Such a deceptive slogan as "socialism in one country" could not have been and was not seriously entertained by the victorious Bolsheviks in 1917, though the idea (if not the explicit wording) was put forth by some Mensheviks and revisionists. "Imperialism or socialism! War or revolution! There is no third way!" was Luxemburg's battle cry.

The proletarian rising of November 1918-January 1919 seemed to fulfill these hopes. As a participant in what he calls "the German Revolution," Paul Frolich writes, with vividness and pace, of mass risings in Berlin and other major cities, of Workers' Councils, of the revolutionary alliance of sailors and factory workers, of the Kaiser's abdication, and the proclamation by Karl Liebknecht of the Socialist Republic of Germany.

But, having shown its head all too briefly, the old mole disappeared in Germany with the defeat of the November rising. As Luxemburg foresaw it might, it soon went underground in Russia too, after Lenin's death, and it is a favorite speculation among Rosa's biographers what her position might have been had she lived through the periods of the Third (Stalinist) and Fourth (Trotskyist) Internationals.

Luxemburg's criticism of the Bolshevik party has been a thorny question on the left. Her position, and Lenin's too, has often been caricatured and oversimplified, as in Bertram D. Wolfe's introduction to his edition of two Luxemburg tracts. Wolfe goes so far as to publish Luxemburg's 1904 piece **"Organizational Questions of the Russian Social Democracy"** under the theatrical and misleading title given it by a later publisher: **"Leninism or Marxism?"**—as if a revolutionary of Luxemburg's calibre would formulate the problem so mechanically. It seems to me that Luxemburg never understood as profoundly as Lenin did two things: first, the necessity for "iron discipline" within a vanguard party so that the party can be a unified fighting force and avoid the tragic capitulation of the Second International; and, second, the unpleasant necessity to make certain compromises, such as Brest-Litovsk, or NEP, to ensure the immediate survival of the Russian Revolution so that genuine socialism could be built. Lenin, of course, was always painfully aware of the differences between dictatorship of the proletariat as it existed under his leadership, and full socialism: it is a constantly recurrent theme in his writings of the twenties.

It is important to bear in mind and, as far as possible, to duplicate the very finely balanced dialectical sensibility that permits support and criticism to exist simultaneously, in all their complexity, without taking the easy way out by a crudely mechanical solution (whether fanatical enthusiasm or outraged rejection). The Bolsheviks existed, for the moment, "in the center of the gripping whirlpool of domestic and foreign struggle, ringed about by countless foes and opponents." In such circumstances, Luxemburg reiterates time and again, one does not expect perfection. Yet Rosa Luxemburg is also thinking of the long run, always pressing ahead to the long-range implications, the

possibilities. As George Lukacs remarks, "She constantly opposes to the exigencies of the moment the principles of future stages of the revolution." Some may view the idea of perfection as a luxury which few revolutionaries can afford. I suggest that Rosa Luxemburg saw it as a costly necessity and tool of the trade, without which there is no long-range criterion for specific situations—worse, no principled guide to practical action, hence no ability to predict or control events, hence passivity and virtually certain defeat. Is this utopian? Only if we extend the "no place" of *utopia* into "never": it depends on your sense of possibility. At the same time, the vision of perfection can lead, and it sometimes led Luxemburg, into ultra-left, hence incorrect, positions.

Operating, then, from the sense of maximum possibility, Rosa Luxemburg wrote **"The Russian Revolution."** Fourteen years earlier, in 1904, she had published in *Iskra,* the Bolshevik theoretical journal, a review of *One Step Forward, Two Steps Back,* "written by Lenin, an outstanding member of the Iskra group." There she had argued that "the military ultra-centralism" of the Bolshevik tendency would paralyze the party, rendering it "incapable of accomplishing the tremendous tasks of the hour." In 1918, the success of the Russian Revolution forced Luxemburg to revise at least part of her earlier judgment. In **"The Russian Revolution"** (1918) she addressed herself to the Bolsheviks in power. On one hand she eulogized their clear-sightedness and discipline:

> The Bolshevik tendency performs the historic service of having proclaimed from the very beginning, and having followed with iron consistency, those tactics which alone could save democracy and drive the revolution ahead. All power exclusively in the hands of the worker and peasant masses, in the hands of the soviets—this was indeed the only way out of the difficulty into which the revolution had gotten; this was the sword stroke with which they cut the Gordian knot, freed the revolution from a narrow blind-alley and opened up for it an untrammeled path into the free and open fields.
>
> The party of Lenin was thus the only one in Russia which grasped the true interest of the revolution in that first period. It was the element that drove the revolution forward, and thus it was the only party which really carried on a socialist policy.
>
> . . . The "golden mean" cannot be maintained in any revolution. The law of its nature demands a quick decision: either the locomotive drives forward full steam ahead to the most extreme point of the historical ascent, or it rolls back of its own weight again to the starting point at the bottom. . . . This makes clear the miserable role of the Russian Mensheviks . . . etc., who had enormous influence on the masses at the beginning, but, after their prolonged wavering and after they had fought with both hands and feet against taking over power and responsibility, were driven ignobly off the stage.

Now, after the Chilean coup of September 1973, our generation can add to this, that those who hesitate to take full power are driven brutally off the stage, along with thousands of revolutionary workers who sacrifice their lives in the process.

Besides praising, Luxemburg criticized the Bolshevik land-reform as inadequate and tending to create a conservative stratum of land-owning peasants. She also protested the suspension of certain democratic rights, especially for the opponents of soviet rule: such interference with free public life and political debate would certainly, she said, cut the party off from its vital roots in the masses and turn it into an authoritarian bureaucracy. In both cases she was right theoretically but wrong practically—defeated, I would suggest, by that characteristic vision of perfection which enabled her to ignore the exigencies of the particular moment. Indeed one could argue that her criticism is inconsistent, inasmuch as the compromise land-reform did constitute one of Lenin's efforts to halt bureaucratic degeneration by satisfying, through temporary measures, a relatively backward part of the population who would otherwise have to be dealt with by force and bureaucracy.

The bureaucratic degeneration of the Russian revolution after Lenin's death in 1924 does not necessarily prove, as Frolich claims it does, that Rosa Luxemburg was prophetically correct in all her criticism of the Bolsheviks. Such a claim omits the necessary scrupulous analysis of world events, of the Russian situation at any given moment, and of the individuals involved. Certainly to use her work in support of an anti-vanguard or "spontaneist" position, as some groups and individuals have recently done, is dishonest and crude in the extreme. Moreover it ignores the importance of correct leadership which Luxemburg stressed throughout her life and which, after all, provided the impetus for her struggle against revisionism in the party. What was required was a leadership both disciplined enough and flexible enough to work with the spontaneous energies of the masses, to prepare the masses for the assumption of state power, and to direct its spontaneous energies toward that goal. This, like so many other Marxist positions, appears paradoxical to the fragmented or mechanical consciousness; as a dialectical appreciation of reality it is, I believe, correct.

Paul Frolich's book is not new. Originally published in Paris in 1939, London in 1940, and Frankfort in 1967, it appears now in the definitive new edition and retranslation (the translator is Johanna Hoornweg). It is an extremely thorough political biography by a close associate of Rosa Luxemburg, for, with her, Paul Frolich led the revolutionary Spartacus League, participated in the 1918 rising, and helped found the German Communist Party (KPD). With clarity and detail Frolich sets out the historical and political context in which Luxemburg lived and worked.

As a biography, though, Frolich's book presents an almost one-dimensional view of its subject, and that dimension is the political. One gets no sense from Frolich's pages of the passion and inner conflict that emerge from Luxemburg's correspondence. All of the personal material is collected in a single chapter, where Frolich briefly documents Luxemburg's love for music, poetry and botany, her talent for painting, her romantic streak, and the intensity of her personal relations. Yet by confining this material to one chapter, Frolich sets it apart from her political life and makes it seem trivial.

Frolich never alludes to sexual relations, not even the tempestuous long-term union with Leo Jogiches, to whom Rosa wrote nearly a thousand letters over a period of twenty years—intensely personal letters full of passion and wit as well as history in the making. He does not mention Jogiches' extreme possessive jealousy (which had both a sexual and a professionally rivalrous component), nor the breakup of their relationship over Jogiches' friendship with another woman, nor Rosa's romantic rebound affair with Konstantin, the 22-year-old son of her close friend and comrade Clara Zetkin. Her expensive tastes and love of luxury, her sarcasm often at the expense of friends, her craving for privacy and order—all these traits are omitted.

For these reasons it is not Frolich but J. P. Nettl's splendid two-volume biography (1966) that presents the recognizable human being, the political woman rather than the political machine. Partly the lacunae in Frolich's biography can be explained, as the author himself points out in his preface, by the loss or inaccessibility of a good deal of material, particularly correspondence and manuscripts: there is simply a lot that Frolich did not know. Beyond this, though, one senses that Frolich wanted us to concentrate on the important historical and political issues without being distracted by mere curiosity. Though such an approach is not always wrong, it does imply a certain elitism here. It suggests, falsely, that great revolutionaries have easily escaped or transcended the personal difficulties that bourgeois society imposes on all its members. Frolich's presentation suggests further, and equally falsely, that the personal dimension is not really worth the attention of serious political persons.

The tone of Frolich's biography is sustained eulogy—as Nettl remarks, it is "an exercise in formal hagiography," and everywhere Rosa is described in glowing superlatives. Clearly she was an extraordinary person in many respects. Everyone who knew or met her agrees on that, from Lenin to Rosa's housekeeper, and Frolich himself must often have felt the force of her intellect and personality. But Frolich's method tends to undercut his aim, for the exemplary figure instructs not by distance but by closeness to us—not by being without faults, but by overcoming them. Frolich's Rosa Luxemburg is an unattainable ideal. So that it is not in his biography that one finds a clear evaluation of Luxemburg's personal and political limitations (even though he does concede certain errors in her criticism of the Bolsheviks). For such an evaluation Frolich must be supplemented with other sources. Her letters show both the domineering and the sentimental aspects of her nature. Georg Lukacs' 1922 essay "Critical Observations on Rosa Luxemburg's 'Critique of the Russian Revolution' " (in *History and Class Consciousness*) argues that Luxemburg's overestimation of the proletarian character of the Bolshevik revolution resulted in certain errors in judging the Bolsheviks in power. The writings of Lenin and Trotsky are an indispensable guide and an important corrective to her errors. And Nettl sheds light everywhere.

If, as Georg Lukacs declares in the opening sentence of

"The Marxism of Rosa Luxemburg" (1921), "It is not the primacy of economic motives in historical explanation that constitutes the decisive difference between Marxism and bourgeois thought, but the point of view of totality," then certainly Rosa Luxemburg's work remains permanently relevant in demonstrating the dialectical method. Lukacs concludes: "The unity of theory and practice was preserved in her actions with exactly the same consistency and with exactly the same logic as that which earned her the enmity of her murderers: the opportunists of Social Democracy." Thus the essay itself progresses from focus on theory to focus on practice. Yet in his Preface to the new edition (1967) of *History and Class Consciousness* (in which the Luxemburg essay appears), Lukacs performs a self-criticism in which he notes "a—Hegelian—distortion, in which I put the totality in the centre of the system, overriding the priority of economics." The paradox that Lukacs notes here is as relevant today as Luxemburg herself, for his distortion will be repeated by many. Its source, as Lukacs says, is the ongoing conflict in his life between "Marxism and political activism on the one hand, and the constant intensification of my purely idealistic ethical preoccupations on the other." That or similar conflict still describes the condition of many intellectuals today. It is never a waste of time to read Luxemburg. But to read her without the desire to become what she was—a revolutionary communist in theory and in practice—is to read her in bad faith, to approach her merely as a curiosity, to ignore the concrete meaning of her work and her example. The day before Luxemburg died an article of hers appeared in *Die Rote Fahne*. Its last words were:

> Order reigns in Berlin! You stupid lackeys! Your "order" is built on sand. Tomorrow the revolution will rear its head once again, and, to your horror, will proclaim, with trumpets blazing: I was, I am, I will be!

To understand Luxemburg is to understand that those sentences are not mere rhetoric, but a statement about history which lays a claim on anyone who reads it.

Horace B. Davis   (essay date 1976)

SOURCE: An introduction to *The National Question: Selected Writings by Rosa Luxemburg,* edited by Horace B. Davis, Monthly Review Press, 1976, pp. 9-45.

[*Davis is an American author and professor of economics. In the following essay, he discusses how Luxemburg and Lenin differed on the issue of what qualified as nationalism, and how Luxemburg contrasted individual self-determination for the working-class with ethnic group identity.*]

It is perhaps little known that despite Lenin's attacks on her, the philosophical position so ably expounded by Rosa Luxemburg in her articles of 1908-1909 was never refuted; that it was, on the contrary, adopted by a substantial section of the Bolshevik Party, which fought Lenin on the issue, using Rosa Luxemburg's arguments—and eventually, in 1919, defeated him, so that the slogan of the right of self-determination was removed from the platform of the Communist Party of the Soviet Union (CPSU). Later,

when the issue was no longer so acute, the slogan was revived and today represents part of the CPSU's stock in trade. But the basic arguments in its favor are precisely those which were successfully opposed by Rosa Luxemburg and her partisans. The Soviet leadership is working with a blunted tool.

Julius K. Nyerere, President of Tanzania and one of the more subtle theorists of the new nationalism in Africa, has suggested that overemphasis on the slogan of "self-determination" in the campaign for decolonization may make the eventual attainment of socialism more difficult. He says:

> Everyone wants to be free, and the task of the nationalist is simply to rouse the people to a confidence in their own power of protest. But to build the real freedom which socialism represents is a very different thing. It demands a positive understanding and positive actions, not simply a rejection of colonialism and a willingness to cooperate in noncooperation.

It might come as a surprise to Nyerere to learn that just this difficulty with the slogan was pointed out by Rosa Luxemburg sixty years earlier. Surely Marxism has been remiss in neglecting the theory of nationalism for so long.

Western scholars who are aware of this situation have been hampered in their efforts to evaluate the "Great Debate" by the fact that only one side—Lenin's—has been available to them. Lenin, as is known, was an ardent polemicist, and he was not one to present fully an argument of his opponent's which he was unable to answer to his own satisfaction. Thus, some of Luxemburg's most telling points have been neglected or received secondhand, often from the very person engaged in "refuting" them.

We do not intend to imply that either of the antagonists "won" the debate. Certainly Rosa Luxemburg did not. Her estimates of the tendencies of the time were on the whole less accurate than Lenin's, which is one reason for the neglect her views have suffered. She underestimated the force of the nationalist drive (while perfectly appreciating the reasons for it), and her theory was thus unable to cope with the centrifugal tendencies in the modern multinational state. Like Lenin, she wrote for a European audience, so that her presentation lacks generality. But her statement of the case *against* the theory of national self-determination is as relevant today as when it was written in 1908. Indeed, it has never been surpassed in Marxist theory, if at all. The name of Marx is always likely to be drawn into a debate between Marxists, and the present case is no exception. Although Marx was not interested in the principle of self-determination as such, he was still prepared to employ the slogan on occasion.

In 1867 an "Instruction to Delegates" (to the General Council of the First International) included a passage on the "necessity to annihilate the Russian influence on Europe by the application of *the right of peoples to dispose of themselves* and to reconstruct a Poland on a democratic and social basis." This passage was adopted by the General Council and became part of the policy of the First International. Marx probably did not write it but was willing to accept it, although a pamphlet edited by him containing the resolutions of the International Workingmen's Association (IWMA) Congresses of 1866 and 1868 does not include the passage in question.

The differences between Rosa Luxemburg and Lenin may be summarized under several headings as follows:

1. Lenin strongly emphasized the right of self-determination of nations. Rosa Luxemburg said that there was no such right, and putting forward this slogan when the terms were not defined carefully could mean not a contribution to solving the problem but a means of avoiding it.

Luxemburg's point was sound then and it is sound today, but she overstated it. There is a *moral* right of self-determination, when the terms are defined; and she should have so indicated. Her opposition to national oppression shows that she recognized the principle.

2. Lenin emphasized the role of the bourgeoisie in building modern nations. Luxemburg said that there were circumstances when the role of the bourgeoisie in nation-building was minimal, and she was correct, not only with regard to Poland but in relation to precapitalist economic formations, colonies, and so on.

3. Luxemburg allowed a place for federation and autonomy. Lenin's position on federalism was ambiguous. He at first opposed it, then later adopted it for the Soviet Union, at least nominally. Luxemburg's thinking was more flexible on this point, and her criticism of Lenin is receiving renewed attention today. But autonomy may mean little in an undemocratic state.

4. Rosa Luxemburg and her followers interpreted self-determination as meaning the self-determination of the working class. Lenin correctly opposed this formulation, but his statement of the case against it failed to carry conviction and he was overridden by the 1919 CPSU Congress, as we shall see.

5. Rosa Luxemburg opposed nationalism as leading to fragmentation. Lenin stressed the advantages of large national units, but at the same time appreciated the strength of the tendency to fragmentation, to which he was not entirely unsympathetic. Lenin was correct, as anyone today would have to concede.

Our main concern is with the first point above, the question of whether there is a *right* to self-determination of nations. In discussing this and the other points, we shall attempt to show that nationality theory, which heretofore has been treated as lying outside Marxist theory or only distantly related to it, is in fact a central part of Marxist theory; indeed, without a correct nationality theory Marxism cannot solve the most pressing problems of the world today. Hence the importance of a restudy of the whole debate, and especially of Rosa Luxemburg's contributions to it, which have been neglected for so many years.

THE HISTORICAL SETTING

Rosa Luxemburg was born and went to school in what was then Russian Poland. She came of middle-class Jewish parents. She early showed an interest in the revolutionary movement and attracted so much attention from the authorities that she found it advisable to leave Russia. She went first to Switzerland and then to Germany, where she completed her studies while continuing active in the social-democratic movement. She studied Polish history, and was later able to correct Lenin in his exclusive emphasis on the bourgeoisie as the creator of nationalism; for in Poland the nationalist movement was led for many years by the landed nobility (*schlachta*). She always retained her interest in Poland; she worked among the Poles in East Prussia and was the German Social Democratic Party's expert on Poland. At the same time she participated—at a distance most of the time—in the social-democratic movement in Russia, where she usually sympathized with the Bolshevik position. Lenin, although he disagreed with her on a number of points, always had the highest opinion of her ability and sincerity.

The whole 1893-1914 period was characterized by a debate between two parties in Poland on the subject of national self-determination. The Polish Socialist Party (Polska Partia Socialistyczma—PPS) favored the reconstitution of Poland, and its branch parties in each of the partition states (Germany, Austria, and Russia) campaigned among the workers, the peasants, and the middle class on this strictly nationalist basis, hardly mentioning socialism. The Social Democratic Party of Poland—later, after the inclusion of Lithuania in 1899, known as the SDKPiL—was founded by Rosa Luxemburg and others in 1893, and continued an earlier Marxist tradition in opposing self-determination for Poland.

First one and then the other of the parties seemed to have the ear of the workers. The International Socialist Congress at London (1896) heard both sides present their cases and decided, in effect, not to interfere. The SDKPiL seemed to have only a small following in 1903, but when the First Russian Revolution broke out in 1905 the workers in Russian Poland flocked into the SDKPiL and made common cause with the Russian workers. Barricades were erected and there was street fighting in several Polish cities. The PPS split: one faction gravitated toward the position of the SDKPiL and eventually (in December 1918) merged with it; a smaller group, led by Pilsudski, survived and eventually, after the war, took over the leadership in the newly reconstituted country of Poland.

Rosa Luxemburg's position on nationalism was that it was a movement in which the working class had only an indirect interest. She always maintained that the best and quickest way for workers to get rid of the bane of national domination was to bring about the international socialist revolution. In 1903, partisans of Rosa Luxemburg's point of view appeared at the Congress of the Russian Social Democratic Labor Party (RSDLP) and urged that the Congress make no endorsement of self-determination. The RSDLP did come out for self-determination of nations, whereupon the Polish delegates left. Both Bolsheviks and Mensheviks favored self-determination.

The Poles again appeared at the 1906 Congress of the Russian Party, and this time did not press their opposition to self-determination, though they still held the same position as in 1903. They cooperated with Lenin at this Congress, thus indicating the extent of the similarity between their views and his. But the basic philosophical question remained unresolved.

Rosa Luxemburg set forth her position in detail in a series of articles, **"The National Question and Autonomy,"** which were published in 1908-1909 in her Cracow magazine, *Przeglad Sozialdemokratyczny*. Other Marxists also contributed to the discussion, and Lenin commissioned Stalin to write a pamphlet on the subject of nationalism. This appeared early in 1913, and was devoted chiefly to a refutation of the views of Karl Renner and Otto Bauer on national-cultural autonomy.

However, no one had really answered Rosa Luxemburg, and Lenin himself undertook this task. "On the Right of Nations to Self-Determination," written at the beginning of 1914, was directed specifically against her.

THE "RIGHT" OF SELF-DETERMINATION

It is non-Marxist, said Rosa Luxemburg, to talk in terms of absolute rights, or indeed of rights at all, since the dialectic does not recognize the existence of rights in general; the "rights" and "wrongs" of a given situation must be arrived at by an analysis of the given historical circumstances.

Lenin as a Marxist had absolutely no answer to this contention, since he had often expounded this very point. He said both before and after 1908 that the interests of the proletarian revolution were paramount, and he was prepared to sacrifice the right of self-determination to the cause of the revolution at any time. He was also not in favor of self-determination in the abstract, for this might lead to unacceptable conclusions.

Luxemburg denied that there was any "right" to freedom from oppression. Such questions, she maintained, are questions of power and are settled as such. She said that telling the workers that they had the "right" to self-determination was like telling them that they had the right to eat off gold plates.

In a class society, to speak of self-determination for the "people" would ordinarily mean the self-determination of the ruling class; the workers would be left in a subordinate position as before. This was why in her discussions, with Poland very much in mind, she gravitated toward the position that self-determination was the self-determination of the *working* class. This, as we shall see, was a slogan that was used in the Russian Revolution.

Since Luxemburg was specifically opposed to the right of self-determination, it might be supposed that she would also have objected to any special consideration being shown to the minor nationalities as such. But that would not be correct at all. She had a strong feeling for the autonomy of Poland, the smaller nationality in which she was most interested. It is only necessary to read the sixth and last article of the 1908-1909 series in order fully to appreciate how hard she was prepared to work to come up with a plan which, while not based on any general principle of self-determination, still would guarantee the requisite degree of self-government and cultural autonomy to her people. Lenin complained that she limited her demands for autonomy to Poland alone, but that did not necessarily

follow. In the dialectical method Lenin himself advocated, each case has to be considered on its merits, and it is necessary to start somewhere.

Luxemburg took occasion to state why she thought Lithuania and Georgia would *not* be suitable territories in which to apply the principle of autonomy. The reason was quite simply that they were too small—even Georgia with its 1.2 million people was not in her estimation a viable unit. Lenin, by contrast, mentioned a figure as small as 50,000, and indeed some of the nationalities in the Soviet Union are not much larger than that. Since Lenin was prepared to go in for mini-nations, he was also prepared to carve up the administrative units of the old Russian empire where these included more than one nationality.

But did Lenin not realize that a nation with only 50,000 people would not be capable of defending itself, or of developing an internal market large enough to bring the advantages of large-scale production? How could such microscopic nations survive at all? Luxemburg, following in the footsteps of Marx and Engels, emphasized the tendency to form larger and larger national units. Her solution to the problem of popular control was in the Marxist tradition: to have the proletariat of the advanced nations, making common cause with the minor nationalities, overthrow capitalism and bring freedom to the smaller nationalities and to the colonies from the center, under a socialist government. Pending such a solution, it was Luxemburg's view that the smaller nationalities would do better within the larger (imperialist) country. She even criticized Marx for having advocated the independence of Poland. She contended that such a move would have the effect of solidifying the control of the gentry (and, later, the bourgeoisie), and would be of little value to the peasants and workers, who should make common cause with the workers and peasants of the larger country in which they found themselves.

This was indeed a major difference between Lenin and Luxemburg, but it was a difference more of judgment on the practical application of the theory than of theory or method as such. Lenin's attempts to label Luxemburg's theory "abstract" and "metaphysical" come down largely to matters of definition. Lenin asked Luxemburg, rhetorically, why she did not define the nation in accordance with Kautsky's historical-economic analysis and take specific exception to Otto Bauer's psychological definition. Here Lenin was on dangerous ground. In the first place, Stalin, with Lenin's apparent blessing, had just published an article containing a definition of the nation which was based partly on Bauer's "psychological" one. And in the second place, Kautsky, writing incessantly on the nation, had come to define nationality in terms of language, a definition so defective that Lenin himself was presently obliged to attack it. Lenin saved himself the trouble of defining a nation, but that did not give him the license to impose definitions arbitrarily on others. (Incidentally, Kautsky, who had been criticized by Luxemburg for emphasizing the fissiparous tendencies of contemporary capitalism, after the First World War came to the belief that peace could be best assured by a cartel of the leading capitalist nations!)

In calling for the "right of self-determination of nations"

Lenin was endorsing the idea that nations have rights. Luxemburg denied this absolutely; if she was prepared to talk about rights at all, it would be exclusively in terms of the rights of the working class.

Since Lenin was fully aware of the economic advantages of large states—he intended to make a single economic unit of the socialist society of the future, which would be not only as large as the empire of the Tsar but much larger—and since he looked on the "right of self-determination of nations" as a qualified right, subordinate to the aims of the socialist revolution, was he then not seeking to deceive the smaller nationalities about the nature of this "self-determination"? Luxemburg maintained, in effect, that he was, and she proceeded to argue that in a contest involving nationality, the ruling class held all the trump cards. At any given time—short of socialism—any "democratic" determination of the wishes of the "people," even of the proletariat, might be expected to show a majority for the bourgeoisie.

This was a fundamental criticism of Lenin's position. Since Lenin advocated self-determination only up to a point, those who wished for self-determination beyond that point—those who were not interested in social revolution (except to combat it)—would of course charge Lenin with hypocrisy; and this was done, both at the time and later. Luxemburg's position was not any more palatable to the conservatives, but she did escape from the charge of hypocrisy.

By way of defining his position on the separation of small nations from larger, Lenin wrote:

> Never in favor of petty states, or the splitting up of states in general, or the principle of federation, Marx considered the separation of an oppressed nation to be a step towards federation, and consequently, not towards a split, but towards concentration, both political and economic, but concentration on the basis of democracy.

The differences between Luxemburg and Lenin were partly due to a difference in the set of "facts" with which they were operating. This difference emerges most clearly in the discussion of Norway's secession from Sweden in 1905. It is indeed difficult to believe, after reading the two accounts, that the authors are referring to the same incident. Luxemburg's proposition that Sweden was prepared to let Norway go was one that Lenin could not refute. Lenin is less than forthright when he asks Luxemburg: Does the recognition of the equality of nations include the recognition of the right of secession? In the first place, there was no agreed definition of a nation, as already noted. But in the second place, the "right" of secession was a term Luxemburg would have immediately rejected, for the same reason that she rejected the "right" of self-determination.

Lenin did not really anticipate that the "right" of secession would be exercised, but he was prepared to have a small nation secede from Russia (the Soviet Union) because he fully expected that the economic advantages of belonging to a larger economic unit, plus, for the workers,

the advantage of belonging to a workers' state, would bring any such seceding nation back again.

Luxemburg was opposed on principle to the creation of new, small, and as she saw it, nonviable states, even when it could be shown that all classes, including the workers, were in favor. Lenin saw as clearly as she the economic forces that were driving toward creation of larger and larger states. But he saw what she did not see (or chose to overlook), that the contrary forces, making for smaller states, were powerful too and in the short run perhaps determining. Further—and this was the crucial point—Lenin opposed *overruling* the nationalists even when he did not agree with them. They should be brought to see the error of their ways, while at the same time being allowed full *cultural* freedom for their respective nationalities.

Luxemburg was confronted with a particular situation in Poland (which was not necessarily typical, as Lenin pointed out). The Poles in Austria already enjoyed *de facto* autonomy and considerable democratic rights, and the Polish workers there had little to gain and possibly much to lose from being put into a reconstituted Poland dominated by bourgeoisie and landowners. Much the same could be said of the Poles in East Prussia with whom Rosa Luxemburg worked, and in Russia it was plain that the days of tsarist absolutism were numbered, so that the Poles in "Kingdom Poland" could reasonably hope for autonomy and/or democracy within the foreseeable future.

It was the analysis of the concrete situation that divided Luxemburg and Lenin, not the method of analysis or the starting point, both of which were nearly identical. Lenin, as a Russian internationalist, was fighting against Great Russian chauvinism. Luxemburg, as a Polish (German) internationalist, was fighting against Polish social patriotism (chauvinism). Paradoxically, they arrived at exactly contrary positions on self-determination. But Lowy finds that Lenin's position was superior in that it applied elsewhere too; it recognized the constructive aspects of nationalist movements in a way that Luxemburg's did not.

Is "freedom from national oppression" (a freedom which Luxemburg favored) the same as "self-determination of nations"? Her strong and continuing objections to the latter phrase make it seem as if she thought there was a difference. But if so, what? Or was she merely opposed to the idea that self-determination was a *right*?

Phrases like "national liberation" and "freedom from national oppression" are, to be sure, vague and general, but less so than "national self-determination." In either case, we have to define what the nation is supposed to include—that is, its territorial boundaries. There is also the question of who is to do the determining, or, alternatively, just what the nation is supposed to be liberated from. But the phrase self-determination is hopelessly vague on the question whether what is meant is independence or some status short of independence. The anticolonial movements of recent years have been in favor of independence, and when they called themselves "national liberation" movements no one has doubted what was meant.

FREEDOM FROM OPPRESSION AS A MORAL RIGHT

Perhaps Social Democrats do not have the duty to protest against national oppression. Rosa Luxemburg said that on the contrary, Social Democrats have the duty to raise such a protest, not because it is *national* oppression but simply because it is oppression. Luxemburg insisted that to be a socialist one had to protest against *all* kinds of oppression, and to this point Lenin had no real answer either.

When Luxemburg spoke of the *duty* of Marxists to protest against oppression, was she reintroducing, by the back door, the concept of morality and ethics which she had just thrown out the front door? Some have been misled by Marx's repeated attacks on "bourgeois" morality into thinking that Marxism recognizes no morality at all, that it is a philosophy of power pure and simple, one in which the "workers are always right." But the larger morality, for which Marx was contending, does not dispense with rights and duties; it redefines them, gives them a new content. So it is not a contradiction to speak in terms of socialist morality, and that is the concept that Luxemburg had in mind.

Did Lenin believe in the idea of (socialist) morality? Definitely. To the Young Communist League, in October 1920, he said: "Is there such a thing as communist morality? Of course there is." Lenin continued, arguing that "our morality is subordinated to the class struggle of the proletariat. . . . Communist morality is the morality . . . which unites the working people against all exploitation."

Let us pause a moment at the phrase "all exploitation." Against exploitation of women? Clearly. Against national oppression? Obviously. Lenin showed by his actions all through his life that he was prepared to fight against exploitation wherever it was found. What is the difference between him and Luxemburg? None at all on this point, unless it might be in the manner of phrasing and the priority given to economic (class) exploitation in Lenin's writings. Lenin thought that the class question was of overshadowing importance. But he was broad-minded enough to admit that under certain circumstances the national question might assume prior emphasis. Thus, the national question takes its proper place in the hierarchy of social values, and a rounded socialist ethic becomes possible.

We find then that for Marxists to use phrases like the "right of self-determination" invites misunderstanding. Luxemburg's "freedom from national oppression" is superior on all counts.

In her basic theoretical articles, Luxemburg especially stressed the economic aspects of nationalism and understated the importance of the political aspects. Her theory of nationalism thus lacks generality, and Lenin was right in criticizing her on this ground; further, the political aspects are of the greatest importance in the wars for national liberation which have dominated the scene since World War II. She also underestimated the importance, for the revolutionary struggle, of the allies of the proletariat, including both the minor nationalities and the peasants. However, we cannot accept a point that is sometimes made, namely that she overlooked the effect of national oppression on the working class. We interpret her eloquent denunciation of national oppression as such, and

her insistence that resistance to such oppression has more emotional content than mere economic exploitation could evoke, as indicating a realization on her part that national movements affect the working classes profoundly. We cite here in proof a passage from a work heretofore not translated from the Polish, a preface to a compendium on the national question which she edited in 1905:

> To the credit of mankind, history has universally established that even the most inhumane *material* oppression is not able to provoke such wrathful, fanatical rebellion and rage as the suppression of intellectual life in general, or as religious or national oppression.

The debate on self-determination continued up to and during World War I. When Luxemburg was in and out of prison in Germany, her point of view was argued in Bolshevik circles by Piatakov ("Kievsky") and Bukharin.

THE FIRST WORLD WAR

In the *Junius* pamphlet, written anonymously from her prison cell in 1916, Rosa Luxemburg again discussed the question of self-determination. The phrasing is more moderate, but the point of view has not changed. "Socialism," she then said, "recognizes for every people the right of independence and the freedom of independent control of its own destinies." But at the same time she argued that self-determination was impossible to attain under capitalism, and added: "Today the nation is but a cloak that covers imperialistic desires, a battle cry for imperialistic rivalries." National wars, said *Junius,* are no longer possible. Lenin pointed out in the friendliest spirit (he did not at first know who had written the pamphlet) that, on the contrary, national wars *of liberation* were quite possible in the imperialist epoch and indeed were the order of the day. He also did not altogether accept Luxemburg's contention that self-determination was impossible under capitalism.

Poles holding Luxemburg's point of view submitted theses on the national question to the Zimmerwald Conference; these were published in 1916. They opposed the independence of Poland. Lenin drafted theses in opposition, and wrote a special article to answer the Polish theses ("The Discussion on Self-Determination Summed Up").

In this "answer," Lenin conceded Luxemburg's main point, namely that Poland would not be a viable state under existing conditions. He therefore advised the Polish Social Democrats not to press for Polish independence. At the same time, he tried to stick to his former advice to the Social Democrats of Germany, Austria, and Russia that they should recognize the *right* of Poland *to* secede. The result was a hybrid policy which cleared up nothing. According to Lenin:

> People who have not thought out the question find it "contradictory" that Social Democrats of oppressing nations should insist on "freedom to *secede*" and Social Democrats of oppressed nations on "freedom to *unite*." But a little reflection shows that there is not and cannot be any *other* road to internationalization and to the fusion of nations, any other road from *the present position* to that goal.

Professor Carr calls this a "somewhat nebulous" foundation for Bolshevik nationality policy, a restrained judgment indeed. Lenin's position had become very difficult to grasp.

However, Lenin's platform on the national question had other planks, and it was for these quite as much as for the rather meaningless demand for "self-determination" that Lenin was fighting in his battles on the nationality question. The principles which he succeeded in impressing on his followers were primarily two: (1) equality of nations; and (2) the right of nationalities to a cultural existence of their own. There were also other aspects. It was Lenin who led the fight for the legal protection of national minorities against discrimination, for the right to schools and court proceedings in the vernacular, for writing down languages that had never been written down before, and for directing new investment precisely into backward areas with the avowed aim of bringing their standards up to those of the most advanced areas.

Lenin did not invent these principles, which were in general circulation at the time. They had been developed in struggle, on the initiative of the minority peoples themselves. It was to Lenin's lasting credit that he perceived that a general principle was involved, the right—which Marxists could not deny—for the working class to be free of *national as well as class* oppression. Lenin believed in this principle and acted on it; Luxemburg made it the cornerstone of her position.

Lenin's "Theses on the Right of Nations to Self-Determination" (March 1916) emphasized the "politically conditional nature and the class content of all demands of political democracy, including this demand." He specifically denied that the right of self-determination was in a separate category from the other democratic demands. He also emphasized a point that was to be of increasing importance: "The necessity of drawing a distinction between the concrete tasks of the Social Democrats [then including the Communists] in the oppressing nations and those in the oppressed nations." These qualifications differentiated his theory of self-determination from certain unqualified statements then current in liberal political theory.

SELF-DETERMINATION IN THE RUSSIAN REVOLUTION

The Seventh Conference of the Bolshevik Party was held in April 1917. A major discussion on the national question resulted in the adoption of the Lenin-Stalin proposals. The Conference called for "broad regional autonomy" but not national cultural autonomy, for protection of national minorities, and for annulling all privileges enjoyed by any nationality whatever.

The year 1918 found the Bolshevik Revolution victorious but beset on all sides. The attitude that the border nationalities would take became of crucial importance to its survival. Luxemburg was at this time in prison in Germany. She was full of misgivings. In a pamphlet written in 1918 and published after her death the next year (**"The Russian Revolution"**), she found that the slogan of national self-determination was a liability, indeed the source of the revolution's severest headaches. It was of course true that the border republics had become separated from the central

government in the early stages of the October Revolution, and that they were brought back only with some difficulty. But was their separation due to the slogan of self-determination? Rosa Luxemburg was in no position to prove that it was; she merely stated that she believed this to be the fact.

To illustrate the difficulty of applying the principle of self-determination, she noted that the bourgeoisie in the border republics (meaning, no doubt, the Mensheviks in Georgia) had preferred the violent rule of Germany to making common cause with the Bolsheviks. But was this government really representative of the people, the workers? She emphasized that there was no machinery available to test the sentiment of the masses of the population, where this was different from that of their (unrepresentative) government.

This rather legalistic approach was inconsistent with two points in Luxemburg's other writings. In the first place, as a revolutionary socialist she never thought that the revolution could be made peacefully; the sentiment of the workers would be expressed on the barricades and not in the ballot box. The question of self-determination would be settled as a matter of force, not of right. In the second place, she fully endorsed Lenin's effort to bring back into the new socialist state as many as possible of the peoples who had been subject to the rule of the tsar of Russia.

With this parting shot, the debate between Luxemburg and Lenin may be said to have concluded. But the issues she had raised were debated for some time after 1918.

A group around Bukharin and Piatakov had campaigned against the idea of self-determination during the war. In November 1915 they spelled out their position in a set of "Theses on Self-Determination and a Fifteen-Point Program" which they submitted to the Central Committee of the Party. They argued as follows:

> In the epoch of imperialism, the tendency is for large capitalist states to become larger. This tendency is in the nature of the case and cannot be fought piecemeal; the only solution is to abolish capitalism. The Bolsheviks should not advise the proletariat to spend its forces campaigning for national "self-determination" within the capitalist orbit; this would be utopian, and would create illusions. It is no different from calling for "arbitration" or "disarmament" as a means of combating militarism. The task of the workers is to mobilize the proletariat of both the oppressing nation and the oppressed, under the slogan of a civil, class war for socialism. In colonial countries we can support the uprising of the popular masses as an event which weakens the imperialist countries; in such areas we can work with the national bourgeoisie. The question has to be reached not by stressing abstract rights, which have no meaning in this connection, but by an analysis of the situation of the given nation at a particular time.

In 1919, at the Eighth Party Congress of the Bolsheviks, Bukharin took the point of view that the interests of the international revolution were paramount, and in this matter he was strongly seconded by Piatakov, then in actual charge of the Ukraine, who urged centralized control of all proletarian movements by the newly established Communist International. Piatakov condemned the slogan of the right of nations to self-determination as reactionary. The slogan of the hour was self-determination for the *working class* of each nationality, but this did not satisfy Piatakov, who said that Soviet Russia must keep control of the Ukraine, even against the wishes of the Ukrainian proletariat. He thus pushed Luxemburg's point of view to its logical conclusion (Lenin called Piatakov a Great Russian chauvinist).

The slogan of "self-determination for the working class" seems at first blush to incorporate the bourgeois ideal of self-determination for a nation into the revolutionary theory of the Bolsheviks, which is based on the working class. Lenin had used the slogan himself in 1903. The Armenian Social Democrats had taken a position in favor of self-determination for Armenia. Lenin wrote then: "We on our part concern ourselves with the self-determination of the *proletariat* in each nationality rather than with the self-determination of peoples or nations." He was to repeat the same idea in "The National Question in Our Program" (July 1903). He objected to the emphasis on the right of self-determination because it obscured the class point of view.

By 1919 Lenin had come to realize that "self-determination of the working class" was an unacceptable formulation. A close analysis will show that the slogan is not realistic. The working class that won independence for a national unit and set up a state would thereby have constituted a nation, actual or potential. If that state was free of class oppression, there would still remain the question of abolishing or guarding against other kinds of oppression. A social class may control a state, or (in Marxist theory at least) it may constitute a state, but it cannot exist independent of and outside of a state. The classless state, which has existed so far only as a theoretical concept, does not by its existence solve all problems of nationality. The Bolsheviks conducted a victorious revolution under the slogans of internationalism and the ending of class domination; but if they had not been guided, to the extent they were, by Lenin's principles of the freedom of nationalities, the "classless" state would hardly have survived. And Russian nationalism was not held in abeyance for long. "Self-determination for the working class," taken in context, meant "all power to the working class," to the Bolsheviks, and down with the bourgeois nationalists, the bourgeoisie. The utilization of a slogan from the field of nationalism in what was essentially a class struggle may have been legitimate as a revolutionary tactic, but it made no sense as a logical proposition; it was no contribution to the argument on self-determination.

The Congress actually did remove the phrase "self-determination" from the Bolshevik program. However, it left in the right of secession, so that Stalin was later able to describe the change as having made no difference.

Those who took Lenin's theory of self-determination seriously and attempted to apply it to concrete situations were faced with insuperable difficulties. In the Ukraine, for example, people were unable to find out just how self-

determination was supposed to be applied. This problem was discussed at the time (1919) by two writers who professed to be loyal Communists but who were also interested in the freedom of the Ukraine. They said: Show us how self-determination should be applied, and we will. "openly and publicly renounce the independence of the Ukraine and become the sincerest supporters of unification." We do not have any means of checking up on these authors, but the point is that the dilemma they cite could have occurred. So Lenin laid himself open to an attack that was not long in coming. His "self-determination" was later called a "tactical propaganda trick to deceive [the non-Russians] and to bring about the 'speedy extinction of their national feelings.' "

The situation in the Ukraine was not as bad for the Bolsheviks as Piatakov made it sound. The masses of the workers and peasants were, by and large, *for* the Bolsheviks, even if there was no possibility of testing the point by a plebiscite. The witness whose testimony has usually been accepted on this point is V. Vinnichenko, who headed the (bourgeois) Central Rada General Secretariat and the Directorate, and who was among those forced out of power when the Rada collapsed. He freely admitted that by the time of the Brest negotiations the Rada, whose representatives were admitted to the conference, had ceased to command the support of the people. By that time, he said, the "vast majority of the Ukrainian population was against us." And again: "If our own peasants and working class had not risen, the Russian Soviet government would have been unable to do anything against us. . . . We were driven out of the Ukraine not by the Russian government but by our own people."

LENIN'S TWO-PRONGED POLICY

The "official" Bolshevik version of this phase of Russian history is that Lenin's policy of self-determination for the border republics was a major reason for the success of the revolution. This contention calls for some discussion.

Lenin's policy toward the border peoples was two-pronged. On the one hand, the central Bolshevik government went to great lengths to recognize the desire of these peoples for freedom if they desired it. One of the first acts of the new government was to grant independence to Finland, and this was confirmed in an elaborate ceremony in which Stalin represented the Bolshevik government. The Baltic republics were also recognized.

The Georgian Mensheviks called themselves Georgian nationalists. They had never demanded secession from the tsar's empire, and did not seek to secede from the Kerensky government. When the Bolsheviks seized power, the Menshevik leaders proclaimed the independence of Georgia and organized a federation of Transcaucasian governments. Within a mouth, the Georgian authorities had invited the Germans to come in, and 3,000 German troops landed.

With the defeat of the Germans in 1918, the Transcaucasian federation broke down. The British replaced the Germans in Georgia, at the invitation of the Menshevik government. In Azerbaijan, however, a Soviet republic was set up. On May 7, 1920, the Bolshevik government signed a treaty with the Georgian Menshevik government. According to this treaty, Georgia was required to break all contacts with the Russian counter-revolution, to have all foreign military forces withdrawn from Georgia, to grant legality to Bolshevik organizations, and to recognize the Soviet Republic of Azerbaijan.

Nationalist Armenia was given a kind of *de facto* recognition. Turkey was fighting the Greeks in Asia Minor, and the Bolsheviks wished to assist the Turks: "The Armenian delegates in Moscow in May 1920 were offered assistance if Armenia allowed transport of Russian troops over the Kars Railway to go to the rescue of the Turks." The American government rejected the Russian offer.

Later Armenia, Azerbaijan, and Georgia were all brought into the USSR on a basis of formal equality with the RSFSR.

The Far Eastern Republic, which had been set up in eastern Siberia, faded out after the Bolsheviks established military control over the area. As a French newspaper headline put it at the time, the Far Eastern Republic "committed suicide for the beautiful eyes of Moscow."

The other prong of Lenin's policy toward the border peoples was to mobilize in each territory the friends of the revolution, to have them set up a revolutionary government, and to insure the accession of this government to power, with the aid of Red Army troops if necessary (as it was). This policy is defended as not inconsistent with self-determination, since any other policy would have endangered the revolution without benefiting the masses.

Eventually most of the former tsarist colonies were reincorporated into the USSR. But where the Western powers had established their military occupation, as in Finland and the Baltic republics, or where the Red Army was defeated, as in Poland, it was the self-determination of the bourgeoisie that won out.

The case of Finland is instructive in this connection. The newly recognized government of Finland asked to have the Red Army units then stationed in Finland withdrawn. Lenin did not do this. The intention had been to stage an uprising of the Finnish Communists, who would be aided by the Red Army in setting up a new government sympathetic to reunion with the Russians. But an expeditionary force of Germans under von der Goltz arrived in Finland in time to upset this plan.

In Poland it was the Luxemburgists, known as the "internationalists," who would have set up a government if the Red Army had won the war with the Polish army. The failure of the Polish workers and peasants to support the Russians was of course a major disappointment to Lenin. With regard to the peasants, the nationality question furnished part of the explanation. In the Ukraine the peasants supported the Bolsheviks, but in Poland they did not. Carr points out that the landlords in the western Ukraine were mostly of Polish extraction, so that there was an element of national antagonism between them and the Ukrainian peasants: "The national problem became acute when it acquired a social and economic content." But in Poland, both peasants and landlords were by and large Poles. Also,

the Polish Communist Party's land policy did not have sufficient appeal to attract many peasants.

The issue was settled finally, in the way that Rosa Luxemburg had predicted, by force of arms, although the outcome was as unpalatable to her as to Lenin. The idea that the theory of self-determination was responsible for the breakup of the Russian empire was just as badly overdrawn as the opposite proposition, that the adherence of the border republics to the Bolsheviks was due to the same theory. Concrete evidence is lacking that the theory of self-determination had much to do with the outcome one way or the other.

The other points in Lenin's nationality program—equality of nations, freedom for national cultures to develop—were of very great importance. These were not issues between Lenin and Luxemburg. But they almost became an issue between Lenin and Stalin.

With the victory of the Russian Revolution, Lenin perceived that national oppression had not been abolished "as it were automatically," and he rose passionately to the defense of the minority peoples. In the summer of 1922, when his health was failing, Lenin learned of a proposal made by Stalin to limit the rights of the several republics in a plan that went by the name of "autonomization." Stalin's "autonomization" project would have had the national republics accede to the Soviet Union on a basis that would have led to a considerable paring of their rights. Lenin insisted that all of the nationalities should be equal: "We consider ourselves, the Ukrainian SSR and others, equal, and enter with them, on an equal basis, into a new union, a new federation." The debate between Lenin and Stalin ended, as such debates always did, with the victory of Lenin, whose ideas were made the basis of the draft that was adopted.

LATER HISTORY OF SELF-DETERMINATION

What has been the practice of Lenin's disciples, inside and outside the Soviet Union, with regard to the according of self-determination?

The Soviet Union will not countenance secessionist movements in its constituent republics. A recent article states specifically: "While giving every encouragement to the development of all genuinely national values, the Communist Party does not tolerate manifestations of nationalism and chauvinism, or anything that fosters national discord and isolation." Plain enough, it would seem.

But perhaps some other socialist nation, confronted with the same problem, takes a more lenient line? It seemed for a while that Yugoslavia, with its excellent record on the national question, might fail to crack down on secession movements even as developed as that in Croatia in 1972. But the central party and the central government, with Tito acting as spokesman, did eventually clamp down on secessionist talk. The Croatian party officials who had sponsored secession were asked to resign, and while they were not purged like the Ukrainian nationalists in the 1930s, it was made quite clear that nationalism would not be tolerated if it meant splitting the Yugoslav state. The socialist governments have continued to give lip-service to the general principle of self-determination of nations while deciding each question in practice in a way that accorded with their own national interests. This generalization is just as true of China and Cuba as of the older socialist nations. It was of course not to be expected that China would accede to the demand for self-determination for Tibet, but its opposition to self-determination for Bangladesh (East Bengal) is more difficult to explain. Fidel Castro's defense of the Soviet occupation of Czechoslovakia in 1968 was hardly a principled stand.

A Communist Party which is not in the government may be swept up in a nationalist psychology to the point where it forgets about self-determination. Thus it is hard to understand the position of the Communist Party of India on the Kashmiris, the Mizos, the Nagas, and other minor nationalities. On the other hand, the position of the party in the 1940s favoring the independence of Pakistan has been attacked as "totally opportunist." The Communists of India have been slow in working out a consistent revolutionary strategy. Lenin does not offer specific guidance in cases like this; each one has to be considered on its merits.

The proposition advanced by Lowy and others, that denial of the right to form an independent state constitutes national oppression, is now generally accepted as far as colonies are concerned, but there are still arguments about what constitutes a colony. When the Algerians became insistent in their demand for independence, the stock answer of the French establishment was that Algeria was a constituent part of the French nation. The response failed to carry conviction, but that did not prevent the prerevolutionary government in Portugal from using it with regard to Portugal's African colonies. Spokesmen for the U.S. government deny that Puerto Rico is a colony.

Article 17 of the Soviet Union's constitution specifies that the national republics have the right of self-determination (secession), but that of the People's Republic of China does not. This provision has been in the Yugoslav constitution at times. But no state, capitalist or socialist, has spelled out in its basic law the modalities for bringing about such separation; nor can any be expected to do so. As Abraham Lincoln remarked, no state makes provision for its own dissolution.

The degree of freedom allowed to national dissidents in campaigning for independence has varied greatly among countries, and within particular countries at different periods. It may still be possible, even under capitalism, and presumably therefore under socialism, for an amicable separation arrangement to be worked out—Lenin never ceased to refer to the separation of Norway from Sweden in 1905. It may also be true that in the "last stage" of communism national rivalries will disappear, as contemplated by Marx and Lenin. But for the moment, socialist states are just as conscious of their national interests as capitalist states, and not any more likely to permit separatist propaganda—perhaps even less so. So, the multinational socialist states that include disaffected national groups are oppressing them, in Lowy's view. This was also the point of view of a substantial section of the Croatian Communist Party in 1971, as we noted above.

Before accepting this proposition, we need answers to certain questions. We need to know whether the demand for separation genuinely represents the sentiment of the proletarians, and is not the idea of some clique. We need information on whether the grievances complained of are demonstrably traceable to nationality discrimination, or whether they arise from other causes, or from the conjuncture as a whole. (This was the weak spot in the Croatians' argument.) Lenin always insisted on an analysis of the whole situation, "and then, perhaps, we shall not regard the rebellion of the Southern States of America in 1863 [sic] as a 'national rebellion.'"

If we ask who is to make such an assessment, the answer of course is that the separationists and the central governments make their respective assessments, and there is no impartial arbiter to reconcile the conflicting claims. But Marxists have a duty to make their own judgments on such matters, and the "opinion of mankind" is not always devoid of influence, as we have noted above.

The traditional Marxist remedy for national grievances is more democracy in the country in question. This was the remedy offered by the French revolutionaries to the dissident national minorities in 1789, a solution retrospectively approved by Engels. The same solution was advanced before World War I by Lenin, and very strongly by Stalin in his 1913 essay. The bloodbath that accompanied the formation of Pakistan in 1947 was blamed, with some justice, on the traditional suppression of free speech by the British in colonial India. The Soviet Union cannot claim to be following a Leninist nationality policy when it suppresses nationalist agitation in the national republics as consistently and ferociously as has been customary.

But it is also true that in a condition of economic crisis, such as that which gripped Yugoslavia in 1971, the inflammation of national hatreds might cause a repetition of the bloodbaths of the period of World War I, when Croats slaughtered Serbs and vice-versa. For the central government to continue to follow a hands-off policy in such a situation would have been to risk disaster. National hatreds, like race hatreds, are sometimes more easily aroused than curbed.

Rosa Luxemburg's solution to the Polish problem was for "Kingdom Poland" to be reorganized as an autonomous province within a democratized Russia. Recent history has shown the limitations to this type of solution.

Eritrea is located between Ethiopia and the Red Sea, and has a certain strategic importance because it controls the entrance to the sea. It came under Italian colonial rule in 1890; in World War II it passed into the hands of the British. After the war it was proposed that Eritrea be annexed by Ethiopia, but an independence movement objected to this. In 1952 the United Nations sponsored an arrangement whereby Eritrea was to be a federative state under the Ethiopian crown, with full local autonomy, for a ten-year period, after which it was to exercise its right of self-determination. From the time the Ethiopian army marched in, Eritrean autonomy was a mirage. In 1962 Eritrea was formally annexed by Ethiopia. The Eritrean national liberation movement began guerrilla warfare, which was still continuing when the rule of Haile Selassie was ended in 1974.

Or take the case of the Kurds, who campaigned all through the 1960s for freedom from the arbitrary rule of Iraq. The more extreme Kurdish nationalists favored an independent Kurdistan, to include parts of neighboring Iran and Turkey. The fighting ended in a stalemate, and in 1970 the Kurds were granted autonomy within Iraq and laid down their arms. The Communist Party of Iraq favored this arrangement, provided that all of Iraq was democratized. Five years later, as part of a general settlement of differences between Iraq and Iran, the latter agreed to withdraw support from the Kurds in Iraq. The Iraqi army promptly marched into "autonomous" Kurdistan, and the Kurd national leader Mustapha al-Barzani took refuge abroad.

No movement for national liberation should campaign for autonomy within the larger unit. Autonomy is like religious toleration; it can be terminated at any time, as the French Protestants learned when Louis XIV revoked the Edict of Nantes in 1685.

It is not enough to dump this whole issue in the lap of the United Nations, for this body is not constituted to deal with the problem. At most it can pass a resolution, and it does not do even that with any consistency. The United Nations is not set up to enforce any standard of behavior on the large states, which are the worst offenders against the principle of self-determination. But even if it had the power, it would not know how to proceed. The principles that would be applicable have not been developed. The General Assembly's "Declaration on Strengthening Internal Security," adopted in 1970 on Soviet initiative, envisages an end to repression and to the use of force against nations fighting for liberation from colonial rule, and urges aid for their legitimate struggle. Much more important than this, however, was the furnishing of arms to Guinea-Bissau during its struggle with the Portuguese, and to the other Portuguese colonies since. (The Soviet Union, to its credit, did furnish arms to the liberation movements in Guinea-Bissau and Angola.)

"RIGHT OF SELF-DETERMINATION" RECEIVES ONLY LIP-SERVICE

Soviet international lawyers have never accepted the idea that national self-determination is a principle that is valid regardless of the interests of the socialist revolution—nor, we should say, the interests of the Soviet Union. Since other nations cannot be expected to accept the principle of self-determination in cases where it contravenes principles—or interests—that *they* consider important, the operation of the general principle of self-determination would appear to be limited to cases not considered vital by any party, and this is indeed what we observe.

Amilcar Cabral, the late leader of the national liberation movement in Guinea-Bissau, raised the question of whether the slogan of self-determination was not after all one invented by the imperialists as a means of covering their retreat. He pointed out that it was precisely the imperialist powers that had introduced national liberation as an objective:

I would even go so far as to ask whether, given the advance of socialism in the world, the national liberation movement is not an imperialist initiative. Is the judicial institution which serves as a reference for the right of all peoples who are trying to liberate themselves a product of the peoples who are trying to liberate themselves? Was it created by the socialist countries who are our historical associates? It is signed by the imperialist countries, it is the imperialist countries who have recognized the right of all peoples to national independence, so I ask myself whether we may not be considering as an initiative of our people what is in fact an initiative of the enemy? Even Portugal, which is using napalm bombs against our people in Guiné, signed the declaration of the right of all peoples to independence. . . . The objective of the imperialist countries was to prevent the enlargement of the socialist camp, to liberate the reactionary forces in our countries which were being stifled by colonialism and to enable these forces to ally themselves with the international bourgeoisie. The fundamental objective was to create a bourgeoisie where one did not exist, in order specifically to strengthen the imperialist and the capitalist camp.

A good example of the way the shibboleth of "self-determination" is used to gloss over differences without really settling anything is furnished by the recent experience of Portugal. When the Armed Forces Movement took power in 1974, the question of the future of the colonies was of key importance, but full agreement had not been reached within the government itself on the form that their liberation should take. If we are to believe an American who was on the spot, the first statements said that the colonies would have self-determination, this being intended as a kind of compromise. Later, the pro-independence element gained the upper hand and "self-determination" was forgotten.

It is still true, as it was before World War I, that a consistent Marxist puts the interests of the international socialist revolution ahead of the interests of any one country. So any head of state, be it socialist or neutral, any spokesperson for a state, socialist or other, cannot be a consistent Marxist. He or she is obligated in the nature of the case to consider the interests of his or her country ahead of any other interests. This is just as true now as it was when Molotov signed the pact with von Ribbentrop in 1939.

Yet the truth of this proposition is challenged on every side. Is it not true (people say) that the interests of the international socialist revolution are best served by having strong socialist states, to help the weaker ones toward socialism? Would the long-run interests of socialism be served if China (or, the Soviet Union, or Vietnam) were to become a prey to capitalist imperialism?

A moment's thought will dispel any illusions on this head. All the successful socialist revolutions from 1917 to 1960 were made not only without the active assistance of the Soviet Union, but actually against its advice. Powerful socialist states may lead weaker ones toward socialism or away from it.

Those who look to the socialist chiefs of state for guidance on particular problems as they come up may find themselves failing to condemn Yahya Khan in his attempt to liquidate the intelligentsia of East Pakistan (Bangladesh). Or they may justify the invasion of a peaceful smaller state. The truth is that neither Mao, nor Tito, nor Castro, nor any spokesperson for any of the socialist countries, can afford to take positions that conflict with the national diplomatic policies.

Marxism is not a philosophy of power, of the strong and mighty; it is a philosophy of the poor, the downtrodden, the proletarians and the outcasts. Marxism is a philosophy of equality, of communism. And this philosophy can be advocated by anyone, at any time; only not when his or her point of view is warped and predetermined by considerations of national power.

The device of the plebiscite, in which high hopes were once placed, is still occasionally used, as in setting the boundaries of the Cameroons in 1961. One assumes that the areas in question in that case were not well enough endowed with natural resources to be of special concern to any major economic interest. There cannot have been much oil in the Cameroons. The use of the plebiscite requires the cooperation of both disputing parties, together with their willingness to accept the results; and where such agreement cannot be secured, as in Kashmir, no plebiscite can be held.

The ascendance of the doctrine of the right of self-determination at the time of World War I, and especially its implementation with regard to certain East European states (succession states), is seen by the historian Cobban as a happy accident—happy, that is, for the Polish, Czech, and other nationalists. The moral doctrine happened to coincide to a degree with the perceived interest of the Great Powers who made the Versailles treaty. The moral doctrine is even more widespread now than it was then, but the adoption of machinery to implement it has lagged.

As used today, the "right of self-determination" means that the political unit concerned—and we have to assume that it has been defined—may choose any status within its purview as far as the people according that right are concerned. Thus when the Federal Republic of Germany (West Germany) signs a treaty with the German Democratic Republic (East Germany), in which each accords the other the "right of self-determination," that means that each recognizes the existence of the other and is prepared to do business with it. When North Vietnam, the DRV, recognized that South Vietnam had the right of self-determination, it was saying that South Vietnam was independent as far as it, North Vietnam, was concerned. Of course, later events caused this declaration to be reconsidered.

Rosa Luxemburg was after all correct in one of her main points about self-determination. When the term is not defined with exactitude, adoption of the slogan may not be a solution of the problem but a means of avoiding it. The world is still waiting for Marxists to live up to the implications of this discovery.

FURTHER READING

Biography

Cliff, Tony. *Rosa Luxemburg*. London: Socialist Review Publishing Co. Ltd., 1959, 96 p.

Cliff provides a biographical sketch, an overview of Luxemburg's teachings, and an essay on her place in history.

Dombrowski, Eric. "Rosa Luxemburg." In *German Leaders of Yesterday and Today*, pp. 271-76. New York: D. Appleton and Company, 1920.

Dombrowski eulogizes Luxemburg.

Ettinger, Elzbieta. *Rosa Luxemburg: A Life*. Boston: Beacon Press, 1986, 286 p.

The biographer draws from multilingual source material housed in Poland, Switzerland, Sweden, and other countries.

Nettl, J. P. *Rosa Luxemburg*. 2 Vols. London: Oxford University Press, 1966.

Considered the definitive Luxemburg biography.

Wolfe, Bertram D. "The Last Man in the German Social Democratic Party." In *Strange Communists I Have Known*, pp. 117-37. New York: Stein and Day, 1965.

Wolfe offers a biographical sketch and compares the views of Luxemburg and Lenin.

Criticism

Ascher, Abraham. "A Marxist Heroine." *Problems of Communism* XV, (November-December 1966): 78-80.

The reviewer finds Nettl's biography an able inventory of Luxemburg's strengths and weaknesses.

Ascherson, Neal. "Love and Revolution." *The New York Review of Books* XXVII, No. 3 (6 March 1980): 14-16.

Favorably reviews *Comrade and Lover: Rosa Luxemburg's Letters to Leo Jogiches*.

Lenin, V. I. "On the Junius Pamphlet." *Labor Monthly* 17, No. 7 (January 1935): 114-19.

This reprint is part two of Lenin's article, first published in 1916, refuting Luxemburg's arguments in the *Junius Pamphlet*.

"Rosa Luxemburg." *Times Literary Supplement*, No. 3349 (5 May 1966): 377-78.

Favorably reviews J. P. Nettl's biography, but considers the two volumes to be too heavily detailed.

Sweezy, Paul M. "Three Works on Imperialism" and "Rosa Luxemburg and the Theory of Capitalism." In *The Present as History: Essays and Reviews on Capitalism and Socialism*, pp. 93-107, 291-94. New York: Monthly Review Press, 1953.

The first is a review of Luxemburg's *The Accumulation of Capital*, Hallgarten's *Imperialismus vor 1914*, and Sternberg's *Capitalism and Socialism on Trial*; the second regrets that the *Antikritik* was not included in the reviewed edition of *The Accumulation of Capital*.

Additional coverage of Luxemburg's life and career is contained in the following source published by Gale Research: *Contemporary Authors,* Vol. 118.

John Ruskin

1819-1900

English critic, essayist, historian, nonfiction writer, poet, novella writer, autobiographer, and diarist. The following entry provides an overview of Ruskin's career. For further information on Ruskin's life and works, see *TCLC*, Volume 20.

INTRODUCTION

Endowed with a passion for reforming what he considered his "blind and wandering fellow-men" and convinced that he had "perfect judgment" in aesthetic matters, Ruskin was the author of over forty books and several hundred essays and lectures that expounded his theories of aesthetics, morality, history, economics, and social reform. Although his views were often controversial and critical reception of his works was frequently hostile, Ruskin became one of the Victorian era's most prominent and influential critics of art and society, and his admirers have included such figures as Leo Tolstoy and Mohandas K. Gandhi. Ruskin is also considered one of the greatest prose stylists in the English language and is perhaps as well known today for the eloquence of his prose as for its substance.

Biographical Information

Ruskin was the only child of a wealthy London wine merchant and his wife. From an early age he was dominated by his mother, a devout Puritan and strict disciplinarian who was responsible for much of his early education. Her emphasis on Bible study played a prominent role in the formation of Ruskin's prose style as well as his moral thought. A precocious child, Ruskin began studying Latin at the age of seven and Greek shortly thereafter in preparation for what his parents hoped would be a career in the ministry. The elder Ruskins were excessively protective of their son's moral and physical well-being and demanded much of him. According to biographers, Ruskin's interest in art dates from his thirteenth birthday, when he was given a copy of Samuel Rogers's poem "Italy," with illustrations by J. M. W. Turner. Captivated by Turner's depictions of nature, Ruskin conceived what became a lifelong fascination for both landscape painting and Turner's art. Four years later, in 1836, a vicious review of Turner's latest works prompted Ruskin to write an eloquent defense of the artist, but at Turner's request the manuscript was not submitted for publication.

In the fall of 1836 Ruskin left home and entered Oxford University. He graduated in 1842, and in that same year a further attack on Turner's work prompted Ruskin to compose a second defense of the artist. Although he envisioned the work as a brief pamphlet similar to the essay of 1836, Ruskin found himself unable to limit his argument and the pamphlet gradually developed into a lengthy

treatise on art and taste. Published in 1843 as *Modern Painters: Their Superiority in the Art of Landscape Painting to the Ancient Masters,* the work sold slowly but received praise from such prominent literary figures as Elizabeth Browning, Charlotte Brontë, Walt Whitman, and William Wordsworth, and launched Ruskin's career as an art critic. In order to elaborate the argument begun in *Modern Painters,* he published *Modern Painters II* in 1846, followed in rapid succession by five volumes of architectural studies, two more volumes of *Modern Painters,* and numerous minor works. According to R. H. Wilenski, Ruskin's works of the 1840s and 1850s were generally disparaged by leading artists and architects, who considered Ruskin a pretentious dilettante whose enthusiasm and eloquence were insufficient to offset the amateurish quality of his aesthetic judgments. Undaunted by their criticism, however, Ruskin continued to write prolifically on aesthetic subjects, and his works gained a small following among the cultured public.

During the late 1850s the focus of Ruskin's works gradually shifted from aesthetics to social problems. According to biographers, the sense of mission instilled in Ruskin as a child endowed even his aesthetic studies with an overriding moral purpose, and led him to question the justifiability of the study of art "while the earth is failing under our feet, and our fellows are departing every instant into eternal pain." His writings of the late 1850s and the 1860s are dominated by the problems of the underprivileged, the elderly, and the working class, and by proposals for the amelioration of social and economic inequities. During this period he also taught at Frederick D. Maurice's Working Men's College, became a popular public lecturer, and wrote prolifically on numerous subjects, including art, mythology, education, war, law, geology, botany, and ornithology.

Commentators have observed in Ruskin's writings of the 1860s an increasing diffuseness, which they attribute to emotional distress resulting from failures and frustrations in his personal life. Although married in 1848, Ruskin remained under the domination of his parents, and his inability to assert his independence from them contributed to the discord that beset his marriage. At his wife's request the marriage was annulled in 1854 on the grounds of Ruskin's impotence, causing a minor public scandal. Five years later Ruskin fell in love with eleven-year-old Rose La Touche, a physically weak, mentally unstable, and fanatically devout child who repeatedly rejected Ruskin as a suitor over the course of the next sixteen years, but for whom Ruskin harbored an obsessive passion long after her death at the age of twenty-seven. As Ruskin's emotional distress intensified, his writings and lectures became more personal, fragmented, and at times nearly incoherent, and by the end of the 1860s he had begun to fear insanity.

In 1870, through the intervention of friends, Ruskin was elected Slade Professor of Fine Art at Oxford University. Although pleased with the position, which he felt elevated him from amateur to official status in the art world, Ruskin continued to question the social and moral value of the study of art. In what he considered atonement for his continued work in aesthetics, Ruskin began *Fors Clavigera: Letters to the Workmen and Labourers of Great Britain,* a series of monthly "letters" through which he sought to instigate social action and which he used to publicize his Guild of St. George, a utopian organization devoted to "the health, wealth, and long life of the British nation." Although few reforms were effected by the group, both the Guild and *Fors Clavigera* attracted a great deal of attention, and the increasing eccentricity of Ruskin's behavior established an image in the public mind of a mad prophet and literary genius. During the last decades of his life Ruskin acquired a large following. In 1878 he suffered a severe mental breakdown, followed by a series of delusions and obsessions that plagued him until his death. According to biographers his remaining years constituted a struggle to write during periods of lucidity, which alternated with bouts of madness. After spending the last decade of his life in seclusion, Ruskin died in 1900.

Major Works

The dominant tone of Ruskin's writings on art and architecture was established in *The Poetry of Architecture,* a series of articles published while he was a student at Oxford, in which he wrote: "Our object, let it always be remem-

bered, is not the attainment of architectural data, but the formation of taste." *The Poetry of Architecture* also introduced Ruskin's concept of an intrinsic relationship between art and morality, which formed the basis of the doctrines developed in his most important study of aesthetics, *Modern Painters.* In Ruskin's view, moral virtue and beauty were inseparable, and the success of a work of art was at least partially a reflection of the integrity of the artist. Critics often cite *Modern Painters* for intentional digressions from the subject of Turner's artwork to such topics as the nature of truth and beauty and for the internal contradictions arising from the evolution of author's thought during the work's eighteen-year composition. Critics also object to contradictions in the work resulting from Ruskin's apparent compulsion to legitimize his personal aesthetic prejudices through elaborate theoretical justifications. At the same time, at least one critic attributes the strength of Ruskin's works to the apparent chaos other critics find so repellent in *Modern Painters.* Robert Hewisohn asserts that "it is precisely his refusal to distinguish between the normally accepted divisions of thought—aesthetic, ethical, social, economic, philosophical and personal—that is the source of his most important insights."

Like *Modern Painters,* Ruskin's architectural writings are primarily moralistic in nature, arguing that a structure is not only a reflection of the architect's moral state but also of the morality of the era in which it was built. His most famous study of architecture, *The Stones of Venice,* traces the history of the city in order to demonstrate the effect of national morality on the evolution of art. According to Ruskin, the book had "no other aim than to show that the Gothic architecture of Venice had arisen out of. . .a state of pure national faith, and of domestic virtue, and that its Renaissance architecture had arisen out of . . . a state of concealed national infidelity, and of domestic corruption." Commentators observe that Ruskin's architectural writings are almost exclusively concerned with areas of his particular interest or expertise. As a result, some scholars criticize these works for their excessive preoccupation with such architectural styles as Venetian Gothic and such elements as ornamentation. Others, however, applaud Ruskin's attempt to relate a society's art to its beliefs and values, and consider *The Stones of Venice* both Ruskin's greatest work and one of the most significant studies of architecture written during the Victorian era.

Ruskin's writings on economics are similarly valued for their moral force, rather than for their importance to the study of political economy. Unschooled in economics Ruskin based his economic theories on the same moral principles as those on which he based his aesthetic theories. Ruskin's economic works are often criticized for their basis in untenable analogies between the economics of an estate and those of a nation, as well as for the same disorder and illogic that mar his aesthetic writings. Critical reception of these works at the time of their publication was universally hostile and initial sales were poor; however, Ruskin's writings on economics gradually gained popularity and eventually came to exert a strong influence on public thought. Today critics credit these works with helping to raise the social consciousness of Victorian readers and economists.

Although his social, aesthetic, and economic theories were oftencriticized by experts in those fields, Ruskin was the most widely read art and social critic of the Victorian era. His ideas influenced some of the most prominent figures of his time, including Bernard Shaw, William Morris, and Gandhi, who asserted that *Unto This Last* "brought about an instantaneous and practical transformation in my life." Critics today consider Ruskin one of the most perceptive social and cultural observers of his era, and praise his organic vision of art and life. According to Kirchhoff, Ruskin "teaches a way of thinking that not only bridges intellectual disciplines, but fuses intellect with perception and feeling." The conflicting characteristics of Ruskin's works—which have been lauded and disparaged with equal enthusiasm by critics for over a century—have been accurately summarized by Marcel Proust, who wrote that although Ruskin's writings are "often stupid, fanatical, exasperating, false, and irritating," they are also "always praiseworthy and always great."

PRINCIPAL WORKS

Modern Painters: Their Superiority in the Art of Landscape Painting to the Ancient Masters (criticism) 1843
Modern Painters II (criticism) 1846
The Seven Lamps of Architecture (criticism) 1849
Poems (poetry) 1850
The King of the Golden River (novella) 1851
Pre-Raphaelism (essay) 1851
The Stones of Venice I (criticism) 1851
The Stones of Venice II (criticism) 1853
The Stones of Venice III (criticism) 1853
Lectures on Architecture and Painting (lectures) 1854
Modern Painters III (criticism) 1856
Modern Painters IV (criticism) 1856
The Political Economy of Art (essays) 1857; also published as *A Joy For Ever* [revised and enlarged edition], 1880
The Two Paths (lectures) 1859
Modern Painters V (criticism) 1860
Unto This Last (essays) 1862
Sesame and Lilies (lectures) 1865
The Crown of Wild Olive (lectures) 1866
The Ethics of Dust (dialogues) 1866
Time and Tide (essays) 1868
The Queen of the Air (criticism) 1869
Lectures on Art (lectures) 1870
*Fors Clavigera: Letters to the Workmen and Labourers of Great Britain (letters) 1871-1874
The Eagle's Nest (lectures) 1872
Munera Pulveris (essays) 1872
Val d' Arno (lectures) 1874
*Proserpina (nonfiction) 1875-1886
*St. Mark's Rest (history) 1877-1884
The Art of England (lectures) 1883
*Praeterita (unfinished autobiography) 1885-1889

**The Poetry of Architecture (criticism) 1893
The Works of John Ruskin. 39 vols. (criticism, lectures, essays, history, poetry, novella, dialogues, textbooks, catalogues, letters, and diaries) 1903-1912
Ruskin's Letters from Venice (letters) 1955
The Diaries of John Ruskin. 3 vols. (diaries) 1956-1959

*These works were issued in periodical installments.

**The essays in this collection were originally published in the *Magazine of Architecture* in 1837 and 1838.

CRITICISM

Audrey Williamson (essay date 1976)

SOURCE: "Ruskin: Art and the Critic," in *Artists and Writers in Revolt: The Pre-Raphaelites,* David & Charles, 1976, pp. 16-34.

[*In the following essay, Williamson examines Ruskin's conflicted relationship to the social and artistic status quo of Victorian England.*]

Described as 'the most eloquent and original of all writers upon art', John Ruskin was the fountain-head of the most vital developments of painting up to the time of the Impressionists. He was born on 8 February 1819, the son of a wealthy Edinburgh wine merchant settled in London. There was a possible dark psychological legacy from his grandfather, John Thomas Ruskin, who committed suicide at Bowerswell in 1817, after the death of his wife; and it was the fact that Bowerswell ten years later was bought by George Gray, Writer of the Signet in Perth, that set the scene for one of the great disasters of Ruskin's life, his marriage to George Gray's daughter Effie.

John Ruskin was an only and idolized son, whom both parents, strictly religious, were prepared to indulge in every whim of taste; and this too had its effect in forming the man. He was privately educated but entered Christ Church, Oxford, as a 'gentleman commoner', gaining the Newdigate prize for English poetry in 1839 and taking his degree in 1842.

Ruskin wrote in later life that as a boy he had 'vialfuls, as it were, of Wordsworth's reverence, Shelley's sensitiveness and Turner's accuracy all in one', and it is interesting that he showed in this no apparent knowledge of Shelley's politics, although his own social outlook was eventually to be similar. Shelley, disciple of Thomas Paine, by the mid-nineteenth century had already become a legend of romanticism, his best political writing still unpublished and his radicalism swept out of sight by the busy brooms of his conformist family and baronet son. Ruskin, a dutiful son, only towards the end of a long life acknowledged, with bitterness, the stultifying effect of his parents' hold over his life, and religious beliefs.

In artistic matters, however, they left him free and gave him every encouragement. He studied painting under Copley Fielding and Harding, but acknowledged as his real masters Rubens and Rembrandt. His independency of taste was shown more originally in a passion for Turner, an aged recluse whom he enthusiastically courted and of whose will he became an executor. In 1843 the first volume of his *Modern Painters* was designed to protect Turner, then still alive, from an attack in *Blackwood's Magazine,* and to proclaim the superiority of modern landscape painters, especially Turner, to the Old Masters. In four later volumes, the last published in 1860, this design was expanded into a great treatise on the principles of art, 'interspersed with artistic and symbolical descriptions of nature, more elaborate and imaginative than any writer, prose or poetic, had ever before attempted'. It was in its time a revolutionary work, which helped to inspire a whole generation of young artists; and it set a pattern for descriptive and imaginative criticism, in all branches of the arts, until World War II changed and streamlined literary style into a kind of skeleton of word and image.

It is significant in assessing *Modern Painters* to realize that Ruskin was not only a scholar and linguist of wide classical range, he was also a student of geology, knowledge of which he had deepened on early foreign tours. In 1834 he had published, as a result of one of these tours, a paper in the magazine *Natural History,* **'On the Causes of the Colour of the Water in the Rhine and Facts and Considerations on the Strata of Mont Blanc'**. During his second tour the following year he sent geological papers again to the same magazine, this time relative to stone and its changes due to exposure. In the *Architectural Magazine* he published articles on perspective. He was thus equipped in more than one direction to react with sympathetic understanding to the Turner Exhibition of 1836, which aroused critical abuse on a wide scale, not the least in *Blackwood's Magazine* which categorized Turner's use of sunset-flame and white gamboge as 'all blood and chalk'.

'I was first driven into literature', wrote Ruskin long afterwards in *Fors Clavigera,* 'that I might defend the fame of Turner.' In essence, Part I of *Modern Painters* was this defence. It took him seven years from the time of the Turner Exhibition, and it rocketed him into fame. And this fame was not undeserved, for whatever its misjudgements upon other and especially classic painters, which Ruskin in subsequent tours of Italy came himself to acknowledge, *Modern Painters* was a panegyric of England's greatest and at the time most underrated painter, which drew on an immense range of knowledge and language. This knowledge was drawn on to analyse the very structure and variations of stone and cloud, mountain and valley, sky and chiaroscuro. It enables him to characterize 'Turner's use of one of the facts of nature not hitherto noticed, that the edge of a partially transparent body is often darker than its central surface, because at the edge the light penetrates and passes through, which from the centre is reflected to the eye. The sharp, cutting edge of a wave, if not broken into foam, frequently appears for an instant almost black; and the outlines of these massy clouds, where their projecting forms rise in relief against the light of their bodies, are almost always marked clearly and firmly by very dark edges.'

He is able to perceive with both the geologist's and artist's eye. 'All mountains, in some degree, but especially those which are composed of soft or decomposing substance, are delicately and symmetrically furrowed by the descent of streams. The traces of their action commence at the very summits, fine as threads, and multitudinous, like the uppermost branches of a delicate tree. They unite in groups as they descend, concentrating gradually into dark undulating ravines . . . ' He can notice 'the grey passages about the horizon' unperceived by the old masters, and point to the daring of Turner in a still unsurpassed description of The Fighting Temeraire.

> Take the evening effect with the Temeraire. That picture will not, at the first glance, deceive as a piece of actual sunlight; but this is because there is in it more than sunlight, because under the blazing veil of vaulted fire which lights the vessel on her last path, there is a blue, deep, desolate hollow of darkness, out of which you can hear the voice of the night wind, and the dull boom of the disturbed sea; because the cold, deadly shadows of the twilight are gathering through every sunbeam, and moment by moment as you look, you will fancy some new film and faintness of the night has risen over the vastness of the departing form.

It was a new voice in writing, just as Turner's was a new brushstroke in painting. Charlotte Brontë on reading *Modern Painters* wrote that she felt as if she had hitherto been walking blindfold, that the book seemed to give her eyes. George Eliot later referred to Ruskin as 'one of the great teachers of the day'. And Holman Hunt sat up reading the book all night, feeling as if it had been written expressly for him. It was, in the end, a bell which tolled in the whole Pre-Raphaelite movement.

In 1849 *The Seven Lamps of Architecture,* and in 1853-4 *The Stones of Venice,* extended Ruskin's reputation and influence and posed new conceptions of architecture. Both works were illustrated by Ruskin himself. A chapter in *The Stones of Venice,* 'Of the Nature of the Gothic', was to influence William Morris in his whole attitude to art and craftsmanship, based on Ruskin's belief that the vital roughness of the work of medieval sculptors and carvers was a sign of 'the life and liberty of every workman who struck the stone'—that the splendour of medieval craftsmanship derived from the pleasure of the workman in his work, and his status as an instrument in the creative process. And *The Seven Lamps* equally inspired Morris in his attacks on the artistically disastrous attempts of his time to restore ancient buildings, and indeed reached down to similar resistance to building desecration or destruction in our own age. Ruskin himself in the preface to a later edition of *The Seven Lamps of Architecture* wrote that the book had become 'the most useless I ever wrote: the buildings it describes with so much delight being now either knocked down or scraped and patched up into smugness and smoothness more tragic than uttermost ruin'. The progress from this to Morris' later Society for the Protection of Ancient Buildings is clear.

In the development and success of another artistic revolution, into which Morris was also drawn, Ruskin had an equally decisive part: and it was a part which was to involve a profound and cathartic experience in his personal life. In 1848, 'the year of revolutions' in a more political sense, several young men, led by the painter-poet Dante Gabriel Rossetti, banded together in a brotherhood which they called 'Pre-Raphaelite', because it was based on a rejection of the now stultified 'classical' school of painting exemplified by the Royal Academy, and supposedly deriving from the Raphael tradition, and turned back to the artists who preceded Raphael in Renaissance Italy. It involved at once a 'return to nature' and a romantic medievalism: a renewed freshness and brightness of colouring achieved partly by abandoning the dark brown base of the current Royal Academy 'antique' school of painting, and the use of a white canvas, or white painted ground. Turner's white gamboge had already to some extent anticipated this, but the Pre-Raphaelites carried the lighter backgrounds to new and dangerous lengths. For the fumes of the white lead they used caused headaches, and perhaps some of the symptoms of psychosomatic illness later shown by so many of the practitioners.

The three young painters who led this new 'school' were Rossetti, William Holman Hunt and Hunt's passionately devoted friend, John Everett Millais, and the members agreed to sign their pictures only with the initials 'PR-B', in an enthusiastic and romantic emulation of the world of secret societies, so much a part of Rossetti's Italian inheritance (his father was a follower of the Italian freedom movement, the Carbonari, and had fled to exile in London). But by the time of the 1850 Academy Exhibition the secret of identity had been leaked, and a storm of critical abuse broke over the heads of the now desperate young revolutionaries. *The Times* described Hunt's "Fugitive Druids" as 'a deplorable example of perverted taste' and the influential *Athenæum* referred to the same picture and Millais' "Christ in the House of his Parents" as 'pictorial blasphemy'. Even Charles Dickens, for reasons rather obscure (but probably connected with his Academy friends), joined in the attack with a savage misrepresentation of Millais' work in *Household Words*.

Hunt and Millais tended to blame the leak on Rossetti, who had missed the worst brunt of the attack by showing his main picture, not at the Academy, but at the Free Exhibition. It was therefore into a distracted and slightly dissident group that Ruskin, his attention attracted to the young painters and their plight by a friend, the next year plunged with characteristic generosity. The 1851 Pre-Raphaelite entries to the Academy had provoked even greater savagery of response, what Hunt called a 'hurricane' of attacks. Ruskin went to see the pictures, and in two letters to *The Times* came out in support of a new artistic force which he felt to be of infinite promise. He did not know the artists personally, he wrote, but considered they had shown high fidelity to 'a certain order of truth and should be taken seriously'. He did more: he secured a buyer for Hunt's picture, "The Two Gentlemen of Verona," made a personal offer for Millais' "Return of the Dove" (which had, however, already been sold), and later added a footnote to a new edition of *Modern Painters* commending the high finish of their work. More fatally to himself, he made a personal call on Millais with his young wife, Effie.

Ruskin at this time was thirty-two years of age, Effie twenty-three. She was certainly not his first love, and it was his parents' fear of a recurrence of the grave depression he had suffered over a previous disappointment in love that had induced them not to oppose his marriage to a young girl whose sociable instincts, and lightness of character, they distrusted. (Their attitude, which Ruskin Senior was unwise enough to pass on to Effie's parents, did not help Effie to settle peacefully into matrimony. And it could not have helped Ruskin, either, if it were true, as he wrote in a letter, that Effie 'does not care for pictures'.) Ruskin was entirely dependent on his father, as his writing did not yet provide him with a living, and Mr Ruskin settled on Effie, at the time of the marriage, £10,000, the interest on which provided their basic income. He also provided an allowance and travelling expenses, on which the young couple had spent a long time in Venice, where Effie sparkled in society while Ruskin collected material for his book, *The Stones of Venice*.

There is no reason at this time to question the genuine affection of the pair; but it was a marriage in name only, some curious inhibition in Ruskin having decided him not to consummate the marriage. There are, in fact, various theories and stories as to his reason for this. One, spread by Mrs George Allen, who had been old Mrs Ruskin's maid, was that Effie had told her mother that she feared she would die if she had children, and Ruskin, hearing of this, vowed he would never be the death of any woman. It was not inconsistent with his basically gentle nature, but its source makes it suspect as a kind of post-divorce 'vindication' (Effie swiftly had a family by Millais). Another story, also not inconsistent with Ruskin's curious vein of romanticism, was that his image of women was innocently founded on the nude paintings of past and present artists, and his discovery of Effie's natural differences physically revolted him (Manet's most famous and reviled nude had not yet burst the bubble of artistic decencies). Effie herself, when passionately seeking her freedom and the annulment of the marriage, claimed that Ruskin had promised that he would 'marry' her in the full sense six years after the wedding: if so, the promise was not met, and by that time Millais' love for her had evoked in her a response that made her need for divorce doubly urgent.

This did not happen by any means at once, although soon after the visit Millais was using Effie as a willing model for several pictures. As for Ruskin, most deeply attached to his work, he was absorbed utterly in writing *The Stones of Venice,* and travelling every morning from his and Effie's new home in Camberwell to the study he still retained in his parents' house at Denmark Hill. The study was lined with the works of his beloved Turner: a collection which was to enrich the nation on his death.

He was still proud of Effie's success in society, which he himself hated, and curiously naïve, in the circumstances, about the type of temptations to which his young wife might be exposed. He seemed also unaware of his wife's critical correspondence with her own parents, concealing of course the sexual situation but showing already an irritation with Ruskin's general attitudes and character. It was based in part on a sense of daily neglect that she did not appear to realize was the lot of every young wife left at home by her working husband, and in part on a blank insensitivity to her husband's fundamental nature. Ruskin's religious questioning (on forms of religion, not yet its basic truth) was the subject of Effie's almost hysterical interpretation. He was, he patiently wrote to Mrs Gray, not contemplating Catholicism but felt he could not write more against Catholics, 'for as I have received my impressions of them from Protestant writers, I have no right to act upon these impressions until I have at least heard the other side'. 'He has a number of ideas of this kind which I think most dangerous', wrote Effie, 'as his mind is naturally so imaginative.'

She complained about John's extravagance in buying '£160 of Liber Studiorum' (a now immensely valuable Turner collection) as compared with her own attempts at household economy. And she was completely out of key with her husband's tolerant and already slightly socialistic leanings. He had accepted with unsnobbish kindness her uncle's misalliance with his housekeeper, bitterly resented, with typical Victorian parvenu snobbishness, by herself and the Gray family. 'I have been much less shocked than anybody else by the whole affair:' wrote John to her mother: 'but I have long held it for a fixed law of human nature that the best and wisest of men may lose their heads as well as their hearts—and what is worst their consciences—to a woman . . .'

Was John Ruskin already weighing up the consequences of losing his own heart, if not his head? Effie in her neurotic later letters, at the climax of the incipient break, was definitely to accuse him of deliberately throwing Millais and herself together in the hope of getting rid of her; but the accusation is at best unproven, and Ruskin not unnaturally denied it. But the initial base of [the collapse of the Ruskin marriage] was in Ruskin's character and the marriage itself. He was, he had written to Mrs Gray, 'as cool headed as most men in religion—rather too much so', but this was far more deeply, though not ineradicably, applicable to his general temperament at this time. Millais, before the Scottish episode reached its climax, and perhaps even before he was fully aware of his feelings for Effie, wrote to Holman Hunt: 'Her husband is a good fellow but not of our kind, his soul is always with the clouds and out of reach of ordinary mortals.' How much Ruskin's literary soul was enmeshed in the clouds we know from *Modern Painters*. Millais may have been obliquely referring to this.

That Ruskin was impervious to emotional involvements his later ill-starred passion for Rose La Touche was to disprove; but they were volcanic eruptions in a nature often more akin to a placid, even a little snow-touched, green field in a temperate climate. His truest passion was his work, his world of ideas: 'I have hardly any real warmth of feeling, except for pictures and mountains', he wrote to his father. ' . . . I have no love of gaiety as people call it . . . whatever I do love I have indulged myself in.'

It was hardly an uncritical self-estimate. In a remarkably candid letter to Rossetti later, Ruskin was to write: 'I am very self-indulgent, very proud, very obstinate, and very resentful; on the other side, I am very upright—nearly as just I suppose as it is possible for a man to be in this world—exceedingly fond of making people happy . . .' And he added: 'It seems to me that one man is made one way, and one another—the measure of effort and self-denial can never be known, except by each conscience to itself.' It was a balanced and uncensorious comment on the variations of human nature that not all—least of all, all critics—are capable of making.

His reasoning on the breakdown of his marriage at the time was clear enough:

> Looking back on myself—I find no change in myself from a boy . . . from a child except the natural changes wrought by age. I am exactly the same creature . . . in temper—in likings—in weaknesses: much wiser—knowing more and thinking more: but in character precisely the same—so is Effie. When we married, I expected to change her . . . she expected to change me. Neither have succeeded, and both are displeased.

Yet Ruskin was not cold: all (including even Millais) stressed his gentleness. His warmth was for pictures as he said, but it was also for a wider spectrum of humanity than the closely personal. It led him in the end to socialism: a caring for humanity as a whole, the nature of social justice and the betterment of conditions: something that, in spite of his own self-indulgences, was of wider benefit to people in the aggregate than any personal sexual attachment could have been. His detachment and apparent frigidity in this were not unlike those of two other humanitarian writers, Thomas Paine and Bernard Shaw, both of whom also appear to have had unconsummated marriages. 'The more I see of the world the more I find the warm-feeling people liable to go wrong in a hundred ways that quiet people don't', he wrote to his father. It was extraordinarily close to a sentiment expressed by Shaw's Dick Dudgeon, in his play *The Devil's Disciple,* when he said he had always been suspicious of the self-sacrifice that sprang from a red-hot emotion.

Whatever the psychological inhibitions or hidden stresses that dictated Ruskin's attitude in his marriage, he showed himself singularly free from the neurotic resentments that wracked Millais and Effie over the affair (could this have been unconscious guilt complex on their part?). Remarkably in a critic, he never apparently allowed personal feelings to influence his artistic judgement, at least with regard to Millais. He had the curious naïvety of the naturally kind, showing hurt and surprise even when Millais, after Effie's divorce and remarriage, refused to renew the friendship. He continued to admire Millais' work and praise his pictures. It was only in later life, when the whole affair over Effie had receded, that Ruskin attacked Millais' work—the work of a revolutionary artist who had toed the line of success and least resistance, and become an honoured Academician. If he had artistic enthusiasm, the crusading spirit which is behind all the greatest criticism, he also had artistic honesty and detachment, which are among the critic's rarer qualities. His judgements could be unsound: but they were not unsound for the wrong reasons, at least for the major part of his life. In age, with its darkening mental pressures, it was sometimes a different story.

In old age, in spite of this recurring mental breakdown, he kept his passion for his work, and indeed for that of many others, intact. He had one great later love for a woman, Rose La Touche, in which for the first time he showed in his letters real and bitter appreciation of the damage Effie's proclamation of his failure as a husband had done to his chances of happiness. What he may not have known was that Rose's mother had written to Effie and received in reply a letter of such deliberately damaging content to Ruskin that all hope of his marriage to Rose was ended. He denied impotence strenuously, although how much to protect his reputation and how much from real knowledge of his capacity it is difficult, on the evidence, to say.

His reaction to Effie's unexpected flight to her parents and plea for annulment was one of slight shock but greater courage. To Effie's baffled fury (she seemed to take it as a personal affront) he made a point of being seen in society and at exhibitions, and wrote a letter to *The Times* as calmly as if his name were not being bandied about in quite a different context. He left a little later for a Swiss tour with his parents only because this had, in fact, been arranged long before the marital crisis. The even tenor of his life, a life of dedicated work for art and social philosophy, resumed on his return. Whatever Ruskin locked within the recesses of his heart, was never revealed: he threw away the key. Like Swinburne, he turned to the inaccessible Elizabeth Siddal, Rossetti's red-haired, mysterious model, now his ailing wife, for the feminine friendship some dim corner of his nature required. It was a companionship totally without emotional demands, safe and soothing to both sides (Lizzie, too, had her marital problems). Ruskin's gratitude was generous and uncomplaining, even when Lizzie, provided by Ruskin with money to go to Italy for her health, and indulge there in the painting he admired and encouraged, lingered instead in Paris, where she was joined by Rossetti until Ruskin's 'tin' (as Rossetti always called the elusive means of subsistence) ran out.

The story of his violent and all-consuming infatuation with Rose La Touche is strictly outside his involvement in Pre-Raphaelite history; but like his earliest emotional attachment, to Adèle Domecq, it shows a deep and inconsolable self-abandonment that makes clear how little, in comparison, his original affection for Effie Gray meant to him. 'The worst of it for me has long been passed' he wrote as early as 1854, when the undertow of the break with Effie had hardly subsided. His immediate reaction, as always, was the basically natural one for him of seeking gentle and entirely asexual female society: Liz Siddal, so soon to die, was only the first of his 'platonics', as Mary Shelley called her husband's more questionable Italian devotions.

In a sense, this was Rose's rôle at first. She was a precocious child of only ten years when Ruskin first became enamoured of her. But it was no ordinary and idle child-complex, for unlike the little-girl friendships of, for example, Lewis Carroll, it continued and indeed grew into an exclusive obsession until the child was a woman in her twenties, herself torn between a growing love for Ruskin

and the barriers which Victorian sex morality and religious conformity placed between the two. Parental disapproval, rumours of the Ruskin divorce, a kind of sexual petrification and something which grew, in the end, into religious mania destroyed Rose, burdened with a sense of Ruskin's nameless guilt in the matter of his divorce and his loss of faith: divisions which he became too inhibited and over-sensitive to dispel or justify.

The torment of this luckless pair in the self-inflicted inferno of Victorian puritanism and religiosity makes clear the inevitability of the reaction to permissiveness in our own society. Ruskin himself, unable either to deny his religious doubts or to live with them, was almost equally shattered. He could at once see clearly Rose's dilemma, and be appalled by it, while becoming powerless to fight the mental darkness that fitfully accompanied his loss of faith. 'The sky is covered with grey cloud; not rain cloud, but a dry black veil, which no ray of sun can pierce.' Shelley put it another way:

> When the lamp is shattered
> The light in the dust lies dead—
> When the cloud is scattered
> The rainbow's glory is shed.

In the end, this was Ruskin's tragedy, even although he was, nearly to the end of a long life, able to gather together the shattered fragments and for periods light once again the almost burnt-out wick.

To classify him as a psychiatric lover of little girls, as has sometimes been done, does not actually fit Ruskin's case. This was in the end an adult passion, and an adult tragedy. The progressive girls' school, Winnington Hall, Cheshire, run by one of his sturdy admirers, Miss Bell, which Ruskin often visited (as did many others, sometimes with him), was really a part of his educational enthusiasms. He also took an interest in boys' schools. Certainly he was charmed by the girls and gravely danced with the older ones at school balls; but there is no evidence that he looked on them with anything more than the aesthetic pleasure with which he would regard a Cumberland cloud formation or a group of butterflies. His heart remained with Rose. The preference for young girls was and is in any case not a Ruskinian but an English male characteristic. Old men traditionally married (and still marry, in this age of divorce) very young wives, and the Victorian vice (which was also a self-protective device against disease) of seeking little girls of twelve or thirteen years in brothels was something the idealistic Ruskin would have looked on (if indeed he was aware of it) with revulsion.

In the end, although he travelled with her letters in a rosewood box for many years after her death, he came to some kind of resignation, even about Rose. 'There is no use in trying to keep with us those who are not of this world', he was able to write; 'one might as well try to keep a rainbow.' Essentially, in his socialism as well as his love for at least two women, he was a romantic and an idealist. And like other humanitarians, romantic and the opposite (Shelley, Bernard Shaw, Albert Schweitzer), his reverence for life extended to the animal world. 'I would rather watch a seagull fly than shoot it, and rather hear a thrush sing than eat it . . . ' ('Reverence for life' was his own phrase, used first in *The Eagle's Nest* and later adopted by Dr Schweitzer.) In the end, he resigned from the University when it endowed the study of vivisection.

Art has many facets, and Ruskin's interests spread wide. His was the type of wide-ranging mind that was a feature of the eighteenth-century Enlightenment, and still lapped over into the following century, before the division of what C. P. Snow has called 'the two cultures'. But his scientific awareness took a different course: surrounded by the growing, blackening evidences of the Industrial Revolution, with the search for material wealth on the one hand, and appalling squalor and heaviness of labour on the other, Ruskin fought all his life these aspects of political economy and attacked them in particular in *Munera Pulveris*.

True political economy, in his creed, was neither an art nor a science; it was a moral and legislative system, intended to provide happiness and ample provision for the population, the 'multiplication of human life at the highest standard'. By this Ruskin meant beauty, intelligence and moral character, in the rather smug and restrictive moral terms of the Victorian age; but he carried the theme much further than that. It was with him a political philosophy which should deal, as one historian put it, 'with the relation of master to servant, employer to workman, of the state to its subjects, with the province of sanitary and commercial legislation, and with the duty of the state in promoting education, suppressing luxury, regulating the hours and wages of labour'.

It may be a strange ambivalency that some of this should come from a man who had never thought to question his right to live on his parents, so that he could fulfil himself as a writer. Probably Ruskin's crusading instincts, as well as a degree of personal egoism, were far too strong for him to question the means. He committed himself absolutely to the Working Men's College, at which he lectured regularly for the furthering of education and technical skills, and in the middle of his Scottish tour had given a course of four lectures at Edinburgh covering Architecture, Decoration, Turner and his Works, and Pre-Raphaelitism. In one of his most forward-looking if abortive experiments, he devoted much of his inherited fortune to founding the St George's Guild, intended as a form of agricultural community in which we read hints of 'hippie' communities, and the Israeli communes, later.

He continued to pour out books and articles on every aspect of art, architecture, sculpture and social ideas, and although his work was not directly political it formed a kind of yeast in the rise of more committed ideas of social reform and revolution later. His socialism and its influence (particularly on Morris) . . . flowed alongside his wider aesthetic interests and never superseded them. These extended to a remarkable range of studies, often originally delivered in lecture form. His lecture on "Modern Manufacture and Design," given at Bradford in 1859, was an historical spur to Morris and the famous Pre-Raphaelite 'Firm'. 'We have at present no good ornamental design', said Ruskin. His hopes lay in the schools of art then hardly envisaged outside London, and which Burne-Jones among others was very prominently, later, to support.

Even in lecturing, his feeling for the fine phrase did not desert him: 'the names of great painters are like passing bells' is a sentence which rings out from this lecture given among the 'satanic mills' of the north. The year before, he had astonished Tunbridge Wells, in the heart of rural Kent, with an exposition, *The Work of Iron, in Nature, Art and Policy,* in which his geological resources were used as a base for a study of post-industrial uses of iron and the advocacy, again, of improvements in design of everything from iron railings to gates and balconies. It pointed out the beauties of Swiss and Italian balconies and referred to 'a rich naturalist school at Fribourg, where a few bell-handles are still left, consisting of rods branched into laurel and other leafage'. It went on, indefatigably, to discuss fetters and ploughs, with a sideline on social policy: 'We buy our liveries, and gild our prayer-books, with pilfered pence out of children's and sick men's wages . . . this is only one form of common oppression of the poor— only one way of taking our hands off the plough-handle, and binding another's upon it.' Cheap labour, and speculation, were already themes which to Ruskin were ineradicably involved with the artistic product. In this he was an heir to the Lunar Society idealists at the birth of the Industrial Revolution.

Unlike many prophets (and especially revolutionary prophets), he was not only honoured in his own country in his lifetime, but honoured on an extensive scale. From 1869 to 1879 he was Slade Professor of Art at Oxford; and in 1871 he was given the degree of LL.D. by Cambridge University. The same year he donated £5,000 for the endowment of a master of drawing at Oxford, and subsequently founded a museum at Walkley, near Sheffield, which in 1890 was transferred to Sheffield itself. Part of his great library and art collection was housed there, and the rest still enrich many galleries and museums.

He died on 20 January 1900, on the very edge of a century which was to reverse many of his artistic ideals and bring others into new and startling focus: a world which was to abandon his gift of literary description for a visual outlook he almost certainly would not have understood, as he failed to understand either Whistler or the French Impressionists—hardly seeming to notice their echo of the experiments with light and image first indulged in by his idol Turner.

In some ways this was not surprising, for in spite of his long and devoted hours cataloguing Turner's works, and his youthful idolization of the painter, Ruskin, like the rest of his world, never understood Turner's ultimate period; the explosions of sunlight on indefinable objects which so haunted the dying painter's mind that his last words reputedly were 'The sun is God'. Turner himself must have realized this; he accepted the idolatry but never entirely the idolizer, as Ruskin admitted: showing, in fact, very much the same reaction as Rossetti to the critic as at best only a partial evaluer of the artist. In later life, Ruskin's clash with Whistler in a libel action merely emphasized the widening gap between the critical amateur, with a marvellous gift for words, and the artist as creator and innovator, thrusting his brush through the canvas of current taste.

In spite of his sexual neutrality and Protestant morality, and his inability to accept his own atheism without being mentally disturbed by it, Ruskin was, nevertheless, the first link in the chain-reaction that brought together so many of the artistically-inclined young men of his century, in a revolt against Victorianism in its more crushing aspects of art and society.

Marc Shell (essay date 1978)

SOURCE: "John Ruskin and the Political Economy of Literature," in *The Economy of Literature,* The Johns Hopkins University Press, 1978, pp. 129-51.

[*In the following essay, Shell explores Ruskin's belief that aesthetic taste is inseparable from political and economic realities.*]

John Ruskin attempted to hold in a single vision the theoretical and practical problems of esthetics and economics. In works such as *The Political Economy of Art* (1857), *Munera Pulveris* (1862-63), and *Sesame and Lilies* (1865), he sought to explain the economic value of art and the relation of esthetic taste to economic organization. For Ruskin, esthetics and politics are finally inseparable. The special considerations by which he binds them together are the most original aspects of his critical theory.

Many students have not understood the need for and significance of a political economy of art and literature. They have misunderstood Ruskin's economic and political theory and criticism of art and have almost entirely ignored the special "economy of literature." Even Marcel Proust, one of the most careful and sympathetic of his readers, refused to follow Ruskin's attempt to understand the relation between the arts and economy. Ruskin, wrote Proust, "chercha la vérité, il trouva la beauté jusque dans les tableaux chronologiques et dans les lois sociales. Mais les logiciens ayant donné des 'Beaux Arts' une définition qui l'exclut aussi bien la minéralogie que l'économie politique, c'est seulement de la partie de l'oeuvre de Ruskin qui concerne les 'Beaux Arts' tels qu'on les entend généralement, de Ruskin esthéticien et critique d'art que j'aurai à parler." Ruskin did not use the term Beaux Arts "tels qu'on les entend généralement." Unlike the logicians (to whom Proust seems to defer), Ruskin explicitly rejected the definition of Beaux Arts that excludes économie politique. Proust, in fact, does consider the economic implications of Ruskin's esthetics. The easy separation of art from political economy, however, has helped many critics to avoid serious consideration of *The Political Economy of Art* and other political and economic works by Ruskin. Although they recognize Ruskin's attempt to join economic and literary studies, they make no real effort to follow him closely in this exciting experiment.

Even the chronologies of Ruskin's interest in art and political economy have been inaccurate because his biographers (like his critics) have not understood exactly what he meant by the "political economy of art." Ruskin's consideration of this economy predates both *The Seven Lamps of Architecture* (1849) and the chapter entitled "The Nature of the Gothic" in *The Stones of Venice* (1853). According to Ruskin, this most important interest began in 1828, when he was only nine years old. In *The Queen of the Air* he cites a curious poem written in his youth.

> Those trees that stand waving upon the rock's side,
> And men, that, like spectres, among them glide.
> And waterfalls that are heard from far,
> And come in sight when very near.
> And the water-wheel that turns slowly round,
> Grinding the corn that—requires to be ground,—
>   ("Political Economy of the Future!") . . .

As Ruskin comments, this poem foretells *The Stones of Venice* and *The Queen of the Air.* The poet hears the sound of a water wheel, built by human specters and turned slowly by natural waterfalls, grinding the corn that men require. By the sudden interjection, "Political Economy of the Future," Ruskin, however ironically, interprets his early poetic art as a literary attempt to illustrate the "political economy" of man. Such an attempt is different from, but related to, the attempt to locate art itself within the whole economy.

In his first major publication, *The Poetry of Architecture* (1837-38), Ruskin analyzes architectural decoration (which he elsewhere calls "the costliness or richness of a building") as an example of art within the whole economy. "We can always do without decoration; but if we have it, it must be well done. It is not of the slightest use to economise; every farthing improperly saved does a shilling's worth of damage: and that is getting a bargain the wrong way." Ruskin argued that the economy of decoration in architecture should be like that in nature. (*The Poetry of Architecture* is pseudonymously signed kata physin, or "according to nature.") "We have several times alluded to the extreme richness and variety of hill foreground [in nature], as an internal energy to which there must be no contrast. Rawness of colour is to be especially avoided, but so also is poverty of affect. It will therefore add much to the beauty of building, if in any conspicuous and harsh angle, or shadowy moulding, we introduce a wreath of carved leaf-work,—in stone, of course. This sounds startlingly expensive; but we are not thinking of expense: *what ought to be,* and not *what can be afforded,* is the question" (Italics mine). The architect should carefully imitate nature's economy and mode of decorating. In *The Elements of Drawing* (1857), Ruskin similarly advises the painter to imitate nature's husbandry of colors. "Nature is just as economical of her fine colours as I have told you to be with yours." The addendum to this advice, entitled "Nature's Economy of Colours," is a foreshadowing of the "Economy of Literature," in which Ruskin advises writers about the proper economy of the verbal art. Although he sometimes pretends to ignore the related economic problem of "what can be afforded," he knows that he must justify the expense of his recommendations to artists and statesmen. In the *Poetry of Architecture,* Ruskin raises the problem that is to dominate his thinking for the rest of his life: What value of art justifies its cost and locates it in the economy of a nation? In its fullest form this problem is at the center of the practical decisions about art in a free or planned market economy.

The expense of art and the unpleasantness of discussing the matter are factors that led Ruskin to begin to study art systematically in terms of its economy. This study of the economy of art is closely related to Ruskin's great argument that the quality of work produced by manual laborers is directly related to their conditions of labor. Indeed, in *The Stones of Venice* he tries to show that the society in which the worker lives is the most serious factor to consider when studying the reasons why the work of one period is great and that of another mediocre. This way of relating art and economic conditions was not original with Ruskin, but he does make strange and exciting applications of the principle to both painter- and poet-laborers. In *Modern Painters* (1843-60), for example, he seems to protest that poetic production differs from that of other craftsmen: "A poet, or creator, is therefore a person who puts things together, not as a watchmaker steel or a shoemaker leather, but who puts life into them." However, in other works he is less certain about the differences between poetic and other labor. In *The Political Economy of Art,* as we shall see, he relies heavily on the metaphor that the labor of the poet is like that of a particular craftsman: the goldsmith. Ruskin's study of the political economy of art, however wide in focus, is never so diffuse that there disappears the significant and frequently ignored concept of the poet as a laborer who is or who produces some kind of economic value.

A work of literature may attempt to establish its own value for society by establishing the supposedly parallel value of a smaller literary unit within itself. For example, one critic has suggested that Balzac's *Sarrasine* seems to establish its own value by establishing the "exchange value" of the *récit* within itself; and as we shall see, Ruskin himself argues that Shakespeare's *A Midsummer Night's Dream* seems to establish its own special value by establishing the lack of "use value" in the tradesmen's play-within-the-play. The economic relations of the *récit* to *Sarrasine* or of the tradesmen's play to *A Midsummer Night's Dream* are, however, not necessarily identical or even mimetically faithful to the economic relations of *Sarrasine* or *A Midsummer Night's Dream* to society. It is possible, then, that literature cannot truly establish its own esthetic or economic value. Therefore a friend to art and literature may wish (if only for rhetorical reasons) to write an apparently nonliterary work about the economics and value of literature. In such a work, literature itself would play a role similar to that of the *récit* in *Sarrasine* or the tradesmen's play in *A Midsummer Night's Dream.* This is one of the explicit goals in most of Ruskin's later works: to locate the work of literature within the actual world of production and exchange and to establish the true value of literature in that world. A reviewer of *The Political Economy of Art* wrote that it was Ruskin's "chief purpose to treat the artist's power, and the Art work itself, as items of the world's wealth, and to show how these may be best evolved, produced, accumulated and distributed."

The economy of art, as understood by Ruskin, has two bases: first, that art is a value in a national economy, and second, that taste in esthetics and morality in society are identical. He argues that the products of the "Fine Arts" are a valuable part of national wealth and that economists who do not understand the value of these products must necessarily be mistaken in their analysis of the laws of political economy. In the preface to *Munera Pulveris,* Ruskin insists that his works were the first to present the problems of political economy from this (proper) perspective. An "accurate analysis of the laws of Political Economy," he begins, cannot be made by "any person unacquainted with the value of the products of the highest industries, commonly called the 'Fine Arts. . . .'" Ruskin believes that his main thesis is original because it centers on the importance of artistic value. In *Munera Pulveris* he notes five principal groups of economically valuable things: "land, with its associated air, water and organisms; houses, furniture, and instruments; stored or prepared food, medicine, and articles of bodily luxury, including clothing; books; works of Art." The correct economic organization of these five valuable items differs, but their values are qualitatively identical. From this difference and yet identity arises the need for the specialized economies of art and books.

In his list of valuable items Ruskin omits gold. This is strange for two reasons. First, Ruskin states, in the chapter entitled "Commerce" of *Munera Pulveris,* that uncoined gold is a commodity with value like any other. Second, he frequently compares the value of art and books to that of gold. Indeed, he believes that not only art but also the artist or his talent is a kind of golden natural resource. The talents of the artist, like Ruskin's own innate "art-gift," cannot be manufactured any more than can gold. In the chapter entitled "Discovery" of *The Political Economy of Art,* Ruskin writes that "you have always to find your artist, not to make him; you can't manufacture him any more than you can manufacture gold. You can find him, and refine him: you dig him out as he lies nugget-fashion in the mountain stream; you bring him home; and you fashion him into current coin or household plate, but not one grain of him you originally produce." Ruskin argues that art or the artist is like gold because both are rare natural resources, "limited in use." Throughout "Discovery," gold is the artist or art object on which the statesman works.

In *The Political Economy of Art* as a whole, however, the metaphor of gold seems to play multiple, even contradictory, roles. In the chapter entitled "Application" (about the necessity not to waste the gold that is art), gold becomes, by a significant transformation, the natural resource on which the artist works, and the artist himself is discussed as if he were a goldsmith. As the particular material with which the artisan works, gold is both a commodity and a medium of exchange. Ruskin maintains that if gold has a higher exchange value than artistic talent, then art is impossible. The goldsmith will never be truly artistic until such time as he can be confident that his golden plates will not be melted down and recast to suit the fashions of some future decade. The metaphorical identity of art and gold, which Ruskin asserted in "Discovery," is thus undermined by the argument in "Application": art can be destroyed by melting, but gold is not destroyed even when exchanging its old (possibly artistically superior) shape for a new (possibly inferior) one. The implication is that gold, not art, is a heavenly treasure that neither rust nor moths can destroy and that art depends upon. As we shall see, this dependency of the art of the goldsmith on gold is, for Ruskin, not unlike the dependency of the art of the writer on wisdom.

The Political Economy of Art is about architecture, painting, and sculpture. The value of literature is identical to that of these other arts, but its laws of production and distribution differ. In *Munera Pulveris* Ruskin considers "the economical and educational value" of books, which consists "first, in their power of preserving and communicating the knowledge of facts" (which corresponds to the negative power of "disguising and effacing the memory of facts"), and "second, in their power of exciting vital or noble emotions and intellectual vision" (which corresponds to the negative power of "killing the noble emotions, or exciting base ones"). Under these two headings Ruskin discusses briefly "the means of producing and educating good authors, and the means and advisability of rendering good books generally accessible, and directing the reader's choice to them." Moreover, he promises the reader an entire lecture devoted to the economy of literature. He did not keep his promise. One lecture in *Sesame and Lilies,* however, is intended to open the doors to the treasures of books. In this lecture, entitled "Of King's Treasure," Ruskin does not use literature to illustrate his economic ideas about society; rather, he considers the special economic role of literature itself within society.

Throughout *Sesame and Lilies* Ruskin compares and contrasts the treasures of books and those of wisdom. In "Of King's Treasures" it is not clear whether Ruskin intends books or wisdom to be the real treasure of kings, "gold to be mined in the very sun's red heart." Sometimes Ruskin implies fearfully that art, artist, book, and writer are not valuable in themselves. Only wisdom (which "positive" literature may or may not contain and which "negative" literature does not contain) is truly valuable. The implication is that books are merely storehouses of easily accessible capital, containers of wisdom that can be extracted only by a terrific effort on the part of the reader who—like the critic seeking Ruskin's own economy of literature—must dig for it as for an especially valuable vein of gold. The difference between books and wisdom is not clear because Ruskin tries to dissolve the very distinction between container and contained (or imitator and imitated) that he himself established. This conflation of books (as golden capital) and wisdom (as the gold that books contain and that the reader must mine) is like the conflation in *The Political Economy of Art* of art or artist (as the golden material upon which the statesman works) and the material upon which the artist works (such as gold or wisdom). Both conflations derive from an almost purposeful confusion of the differences between the value of gold as a commodity and its value as a medium of exchange. Ruskin seems to distinguish clearly between these two values, but actually he obscures their differences. He fears that art is not really like wisdom or gold insofar as art is not a real commodity. He fears that art—and literature in particular—is like gold only insofar as it is a medium of exchange. As we have seen, one of the values that Ruskin ascribes to books is their "power of preserving and communicating the knowledge of facts." This power of exchange is identical to that of money, a medium of exchange that Ruskin defines as "documentary expression of legal claim." But gold, as both medium of exchange and commodity, deceives many into believing that medium of exchange and commodity are identical; it is a documentary expression of legal claim that lays claim to itself as commodity. Similarly, literature is a medium of exchange insofar as it may hide or contain wisdom. When it pretends to be wisdom, it too conflates medium and commodity.

Sometimes Ruskin seems to believe that not only literature but all written language is a representation or documentary expression of a claim to wisdom. Throughout his later works he suggests that literature, like money, is only "the written or coined sign of relative wealth." Money, however, is "the transferable acknowledgment of debt," of which there are two kinds: "The acknowledgment of debts which will be paid and of debts which will not." If literature is valuable, then it must have good credit. The reader expects wisdom from a book as the owner of a bank note expects it to be transferable for gold. Ultimately Ruskin fears that all literature is necessarily misleading, false, or counterfeit; that it is only foolishness in artful disguise, pretending to a wisdom that only the best literature admits it does not contain; that the lie of literature is ignoble. If this fear were justified, as Ruskin knew, it would entirely destroy his theory of the value of literature, which depends largely on the "economic and educational value" of books to make men good. It is, then, "in defense of art" as he sees it that Ruskin confuses commodity value and exchange value.

Perhaps, as Proust suggested in the brilliant introduction to his translation of *Sesame and Lilies,* Ruskin does not pay enough attention to the act of reading. Although frequently he does stress the importance of educated readers, Ruskin does not analyze closely enough *la lecture,* or the mining of wisdom from books. Nevertheless, he is able to question both the possibility of *la lecture* within the confines of his understanding of reading and the very concepts of literary value that inform that understanding. This questioning is most apparent within the context of Ruskin's more conventional literary criticism, such as the famous passage about avarice and prodigality in *Munera Pulveris*.

In a remarkable note to the second edition of *Munera Pulveris,* Ruskin explains that paragraphs eighty-seven to ninety-four are "of more value than any other part of this book." He integrates these paragraphs into the second edition as the second part of the chapter entitled "Coin-Keeping," to which they were a mere addendum in the first edition. Usually this section of Ruskin's treatise on economics is read out of context, without considering the whole of *Munera Pulveris,* to which it has a relation justifying Ruskin's high regard for it. It should be read in the light of the whole book, in which literature, supposed to be one of the five values in political economy, itself illustrates principles of political economy. In "Coin-Keeping," literature illustrates its own value.

Ruskin begins "Coin-Keeping" by considering various problems of monetary currency. Currency is used to exchange equivalents in wealth—in any place, in any time, of any kind. It is the great metaphor. The special power of gold in Victorian society (where it was the medium of exchange) is even greater than this exchange value because gold is also a valuable commodity. According to Ruskin (himself a coin collector), this double existence of golden currency leads many citizens to imagine its value as even greater than it actually is. Such citizens avariciously hoard their idolized gold. Money has the power of quantitative comparison, which appeals to those whose minds cannot conceive of other media of comparison, such as the linguistic or moral. Ruskin argues that both hoarding and prodigality have the bad effect on the economy of stopping the free or natural current stream of wealth. In paragraph eighty-six (the last paragraph of the original version of "Coin-Keeping"), he tries to bolster this argument with an illustration from Dante's *Inferno* and its interpretation of the Homeric Charybdis: "The *mal tener* and *mal dare* are as correlative as complementary colours; and the circulation of wealth, which ought to be soft, steady, far-sweeping, and full of warmth, like the Gulf stream, being narrowed into an eddy, and concentrated on a point, changes into the alternate suction and surrender [associated with hoarding and prodigality] of Charybdis." The metaphors throughout "Coin-Keeping" center on such words as *currents, streams, flows,* and *fluctuations.* Ruskin takes these metaphors seriously, so that, without accepting the protection of poetic license, he makes an easy transition from *currency* as the topic of a supposedly systematic economic investigation to *currency* with all its aquatic and literary associations.

In the second part of "Coin-Keeping" Ruskin illustrates his conclusions about monetary currency with passages from great works of literature. Moreover, he considers the currency of literature itself in terms of a substantial golden truth on which he implies it is based. "It is a strange habit of wise humanity to speak in enigmas only, so that the highest truths and usefullest laws must be hunted for through whole picture-galleries of dreams, which to the vulgar seem dreams only." The enigmatic habit of speaking enigmatically is useless to the multitude and therefore its products can have no true currency for them. Plato argued that all works of literature, and the Homeric epics in particular, do not hide truths useful to anyone. But Ruskin asserts that literature may be useful to those who know how to seek out esoteric truths. He defends his position by attacking Plato's imaginative capability. "Plato's logical power quenched his imagination, and he became incapable of understanding the purely imaginative element either in poetry or painting: he therefore somewhat overrates the pure discipline of passionate art in song and music, and misses that of meditative art." Ruskin seems to be siding with Homer against Plato. He admits, however, that there is a deeper reason for Plato's distrust, which cannot be so easily dismissed, namely, "his love of justice, and reverently religious nature [that] made him fear, as death, every form of fallacy." Finally, Ruskin only appears to agree with Plato that literature is merely the coining of idle imaginations. He admits that "Homer and Dante (and in an inferior sphere, Milton) . . . have permitted themselves, though full of all nobleness and wisdom, to coin idle imaginations of the mysteries of eternity, and guide the faiths of the families of the earth by the

courses of their own vague and visionary arts." In this sentence, significantly, Ruskin is trying to soften Plato's austere and utterly devastating argument against art and artists. Plato was not convinced that the poets were "full of all nobleness and wisdom" or that truth lies behind the "fallacies" of art. Ruskin, however, insists that "the indisputable truths of human life and duty, respecting which [all works of art] have but one voice, lie hidden behind these veils of phantasy ['idle imaginations'], unsought, and often unsuspected." These truths Ruskin himself would hunt in "picture-galleries of dreams." "I will gather carefully, out of Dante and Homer," he promises us, "what in this kind [the 'indisputable truths'] bear on our subject [currency], in its due place." The goal of interpretation, as he understands it, is to find the truth hidden in the fallacies of art. If Ruskin can do this, he will have shown either that Plato was mistaken in his harsh judgment of art or that the Platonic judgment was itself an esoteric enigma needing Ruskin's interpretation. He would take gifts of dust, show that they are potentially valuable, and transform them into the truth that is wealth.

The section of "Coin-Keeping" that follows this brief but significant "theory of interpretation" examines the possibility of the worthy uses of material riches and illustrates its examination with passages from many writers. At the same time, however, this section purports to be an example of the worthy uses of bibliothecal riches. Ruskin digs into the "gold mines" of many writers (Plato, Dante, Homer, Spenser, Goethe, Herbert, Macé, and the authors of the Bible) in order to seek out the indisputable truths that he, an educated bibliolater, believes are hidden in books. Because Ruskin is not fully certain of the justice of his "idolatry of books," however, he integrates with his interpretation of these books an enigmatic critique of bibliothecal riches that questions their value and ability to illustrate accurately the problems of avarice and prodigality in the currency of material riches.

The Divine Comedy is one of the books Ruskin uses to illustrate his ideas about currency. In *Inferno,* a place of bad economy, the *mal tener* and *mal dare* "meet in contrary . . . currents as the waves of Charybdis." In *Paradiso,* the opposite place of perfect economy, there is a correspondingly perfect currency. In *Purgatorio* there occurs the wonderful transformation of those who have been prodigal and avaricious, but (unlike the sinners in hell) for love of earth. *Purgatorio,* then, is a kind of translation from false to true economy. It is a place where the apparently total falseness of sinners is purged until they can participate in the truth of heaven. As we have seen, Ruskin considers interpretation itself to be such a purgation of the apparent falseness of literature. Apparent falseness can become truth only if truth and that falseness have something in common (for example, love in *Purgatorio*) through which the metaphor from one to the other can happen.

In this section of ***Munera Pulveris*** the connection between the falsehood of literature and the truth of philosophy is a series of verbal juxtapositions by which Ruskin hopes to prove that Dante (the exemplar of literature) and Plato (the exemplar of philosophy) both agree with George Herbert about the nature of truth and economic value. Ruskin begins with a purposefully mistaken translation of a line from the *Purgatorio*: "Dante's precept for the deliverance of the souls in purgatory is: 'Turn thine eyes to the lucre (lure) which the Exernal King rolls with mighty wheels.' " The Italian *logore,* however, is properly translated only by the English "lure," which Ruskin places between parentheses. He pretends that the English "lucre" has an etymological connection with either the English "lure" or the Italian *logore.* On the basis of a supposedly common etymon, then, he uses "lucre" (meaning money) as the principal English word to translate *logore* in Dante's precept for purgatorial deliverance.

Ruskin cites George Herbert as one who agrees with Dante about the relation of money (lucre) to stars (true wealth).

> Lift up thy head;
> Take stars for money; stars, not to be told
> By any art, yet to be purchased.

Herbert opposes money to stars. Similarly, Dante (according to Ruskin) opposes lucre to the lure of the mighty wheels of the "Greater Fortune," whose constellation (of stars) is ascending in the *Purgatorio.* Herbert makes the further point, however, that stars cannot be told (meaning "related" or "counted out") by any art. Ruskin seems to take no note of Herbert's artful questioning of the ability of art to "purchase" stars. He simply uses the passage from Herbert to make a slippery connection between Dante (to whom he compared Herbert by "false" translation and etymology) and Plato, from whose *Republic* (416e) he cites: "Tell them they have divine gold and silver in their souls for ever; that they need no money stamped of men—neither may they otherwise than impiously mingle the gathering of the divine with the mortal treasure, for through that which the laws of the multitude have coined, endless crimes have been done and suffered; but in theirs is neither pollution nor sorrow." The implication in paragraph eighty-nine (in which this series of passages from Dante, Herbert, and Plato occurs) is that Dante (a producer of "veils of phantasy") and Plato (a sharp critic of all art) are somehow in agreement about the nature of real or "stellar" value. In fact, however, Plato includes art as a species of "money stamped of men." Art is not to be trusted, as Ruskin would trust the art of Dante and Herbert and his own artful conflation of "lucre" and "lure." For Plato there is only the noble philosophical lie, not the potentially truthful artistic lie. All art is guileful and counterfeit.

In considering the economy of literature, Ruskin wonders whether literary currency is necessarily misleading, false, or counterfeit. He distrusts his own artful pose or noble lie, not in defense of philosophy but in defense of and for the sake of art. By the end of the chapter "Coin-Keeping," the reader's credulity about the value of art has been stretched—purposefully and frequently—almost to the breaking point. Ruskin is in the painful position of defending literature while knowing that philosophers (such as Plato) and poets (such as Herbert) suggest that it is useless. At one and the same time, he tries to defend literature from the point of view of political economy and to attack it vehemently from the point of view of literature itself.

Ruskin's elegant attack is also strange praise of literature. In one of the lectures in *Sesame and Lilies,* entitled "Mystery of Life and Its Arts," Ruskin argues that the most significant characteristic of great art is its distrust of itself. Great writers differ from lesser ones in that great ones know they write nothing truthful. Whatever claim to truth is made by Plato (or Ruskin) is a rhetorical pose. Beauty, therefore, has to do with the knowledge of wrongness. The first principle of esthetics is "that the more beautiful the art, the more it is essentially the work of people who felt themselves to be wrong. . . . The very sense of inevitable error from their purpose marks the perfectness of that purpose, and the continued sense of failure arises from the continued opening of the eyes more clearly to all the sacredest truths." Yet sensing "invitable error" with the partly closed eyes of the artist is not the same as knowing it, as Ruskin wishes to know it, with eyes wide open to the inevitability and degree of error. That some writers see "more clearly" than others does not mean that any one of them sees perfectly clearly, and that some works of literature are "more beautiful" than others does not mean that any work is able to be at all valuable to society by exciting noble actions and teaching wisdom.

Ruskin finds it useful to compare the relative clarity, or closeness to value, of three groups of thinkers: Christian writers, naïve writers, and capitalists. He finds the Christian writers to be unclear and wrong. Milton's account of the loss of paradise he supposes to be unbelievable even to Milton himself. Dante's *Divine Comedy,* to which Ruskin seems to refer seriously in "Coin-Keeping," is judged "a vision, but a vision only." According to Ruskin, the great Christian writers "do but play sweetly upon modulated pipes; with pompous nomenclature adorn the councils of hell." In "Coin-Keeping" Ruskin expressed his wonder at the arrogance with which writers such as Dante and Milton "coin[ed] idle imaginations." In "Mystery of Life and its Arts" he pretends amazement that the Christian writers have "filled the openings of eternity, before which the prophets have veiled their faces, and which the angels desire to look into, with idle puppets of their scholastic imagination."

Ruskin prefers the naïve poets such as Homer and Shakespeare, who show a greater truthfulness than the Christian writers in their relative silence about the greatest mysteries. In *Eagle's Nest,* he praises the "faultless and complete epitome of the laws of mimetic art" that is "Shakespeare's judgment of his own art" in *A Midsummer Night's Dream*: "The best in this kind are but shadows: and the worst are no worse, if imagination amend them." Ruskin interprets this sentence of Theseus, "spoken of the poor tradesmen's kindly offered art," to be a warning about the deceitfulness or counterfeitness of mimēsis. Ruskin chooses to describe the dangers of preferring art and shadows to the simplicity of truth by using not a truthful argument but merely a skillful, pleasant illustration from Prodicus. Writers who question or mock their own mimēsis are more to be trusted than those who claim direct access to and reproduction of the truth.

Ruskin's distrust of literature sometimes takes the extreme form of questioning language itself. Proust, a most sophisticated critic, cites Ruskin's sentence on the necessary fallibility of human language: "Il n'y a pas de forme de langage humain où l'erreur n'ait pu se glisser." As Proust suggests, Ruskin's argument invites us to question the works of Ruskin himself. "Ruskin aurait d'ailleurs été le premier à nous approuver de ne pas accorder à ses écrits une autorité infaillible, puisqu'il la refusait même aux Ecritures Saintes." All written works are *mensonges* slipping forth from the intellectual sincerity of the writer "sous . . . formes touchantes et tentatrices." It is impossible for a writer to be truthful or to clarify completely any mystery. As Proust maintains, however, Ruskin was pleased to affect in his writings " 'une attitude de la révérencé qui croit ínsolent d'éclaircir un mystère.' " Ruskin adopts the *mensonge* that he can clarify a mystery, in order to defend the concept of the value of literature. That defense lacks the obvious humility of the writers whom Ruskin professes to admire and instead resembles that of the capitalist class Ruskin professes to dislike.

Capitalists constitute the third group of thinkers whose access to truth Ruskin considers in the "Mystery of Life and Its Arts." They are the avowed enemies of art and the Economy of Life. Ruskin sarcastically gives them the power to know all things: "These kings—these councillors—these statemen and builders of kingdoms—these capitalists and men of business who weigh the earth, and the dust in it, in a balance. They know the world surely." Ruskin is ironic in suggesting that the self-assured capitalists know the world more surely than the Christian and naïve writers, but he has been able to assign to these latter writers no sure knowledge. His own uncertainty about the value of beautiful art and his dislike of capitalist esthetics and morality combine to form a powerful invective against the capitalist economy of art. What is most strange in this invective is that it is a defense of art not merely on the basis of the value of art (which we have already seen is a kind of noble lie) but also on the basis of a supposed identity between esthetic taste and economic morality.

The ambiguities of the value of literature constitute one large problem in Ruskin's economy of literature. A second and corresponding problem is that of the relationship of taste in esthetics to morality in society. Ruskin pretends that this relationship is one of identity and that esthetics is ultimately an economic matter. His sociology of art assumes not only the Marxist formula that social conditions give rise to certain forms of art but also the non-Marxist formula that a morally good society gives rise to and corresponds to esthetically good art. He sometimes even judges or prejudges the morality of an age by the good or bad taste manifested in its art. For example, on the basis of his high regard for ancient Greek and Christian Gothic art, Ruskin concludes that the societies that gave rise to such art must have operated according to the laws of his "Economy of Life." Other writers, including Marx, argue that Greek art was good but that Greek society (which gave rise to it) was slave-based and, from the perspective of history, immature. Some writers, such as Plato, suggest that the best society would not produce the best art, but rather no art. The positions of these latter thinkers, whereby a bad society (for instance, bourgeois France) can produce a good art (for instance, Balzac's novels), is not without

difficulties. Ruskin's assertion that only a good society can produce great art is politically dubious and finally self-contradictory.

Proust argues that Ruskin's *mensonge* about the identity of esthetic taste and economic morality (like his *mensonge* about the value of literature) was motivated by the desire to defend art. "Les doctrines qu'il [Ruskin] professait étaient des doctrines morales et non des doctrines esthétiques, et pourtant il les choisissait pour leur beauté. Et comme il ne voulait pas les présenter comme belles mais comme vraies, il était obligé de se mentir à lui-même sur la nature des raisons qui les lui faisaient adopter." Ruskin renders politics esthetic, but he pretends that he is politicizing art. As Proust knew, the greatest problem in interpreting Ruskin is that he exhibits "sans cesse [cette] attitude mensongère." One of the clearest indications that Ruskin "insincerely" confused the relationship between art and politics is the famous treatment of architecture and society in *The Stones of Venice*. "Or, si Ruskin avait été entièrement sincère avec lui-même, il n'aurait pas pensé que les crimes Vénitiens avaient été plus inexcusables et plus sévèrement punis que ceux des autres hommes parce qu'ils possédaient une eglise en marbre de toutes couleurs au lieu d'une cathédrale en calcaire." Proust concludes properly that Ruskin virtually idolized art, to the point of blinding himself to historical politics and its real relation to esthetics.

Both the theory of the economic value of art and the theory of the identity of morality and esthetics, however, fortified Ruskin in his battle to reform the arts and finally society. He stresses the importance of reforming the arts, arguing (like Wagner on opera and Morris on architecture) that art can transform society. When Wagner lost faith in the social power of art, he turned ever more strongly to reactionary opera and simple idolization of medieval Christianity. Ruskin, too, has his idols, but he looks to social reform to make the good society that could give rise to good art. He questions the possibility of reforming the political economy of art without first forming a planned, nonsocialist economy. Although his understanding of society and economics was (as Proust argues) distinctively esthetic, Ruskin finally argues that great art is impossible without economic reforms. His famous desire for reforms, then, arises not only from moral indignation at the horrid conditions of the working class, but also from the fear that a society producing such conditions could never produce great art. In *Sesame and Lilies,* Ruskin fears that in Victorian England even "reading well" is impossible. The desperate conclusion he draws from this state of affairs is that literature cannot have an educative value in Victorian England, where good, self-evaluating literature cannot be produced and the works of past masters cannot be read properly. Such a conclusion may have pleased Ruskin, who was notoriously dissatisfied with his own literary production, but the supposed impossibility of good and therefore valuable art in his own time drove him to ever more bitter invective against his society and its false self-assuredness.

The most famous example of Ruskin's invective is his lecture "Traffic," delivered in Bradford. He addressed leaders of England's capitalist class who had invited him to advise them on how to build a beautiful building to house their Exchange. They wanted architectural, not moral, advice. However, Ruskin argued that good taste in architecture is (like all esthetic taste) "not only a part and an index of morality; it is the ONLY morality." Beauty, therefore, must be moral truth. Good buildings cannot be had by asking the advice of an expert in architecture, but by following the advice of an expert in morality and truth. Here Ruskin, pretending for rhetorical reasons to be an expert in both architecture and economic morality, claims no interest in the construction of the Bradford Exchange, which must be as ugly as capitalism is immoral. He does "not care about this Exchange of [theirs]." Instead, he focuses his attention on the conceivable Exchanges of more moral societies.

One such society, argues Ruskin, was that of the Gothic Christians, in which there could have existed an esthetic theory for the construction of beautiful Exchanges. He suggests that the decorations for his proposed medieval Exchange would represent the morally admirable economic exchanges that took place in the medieval era: "On his houses and temples alike, the Christian put carvings of angels conquering devils; or of hero-martyrs exchanging this world for another." Only by its admirable moral heroism does Ruskin judge the worthiness of an action—such as exchanging—to give rise to imitation in the form of architectural decoration. The practice of supplying poor people with food (for example, Jesus' miracle of loaves and fishes) is such an exchange. Because the audience is not interested in this "good" kind of exchange, however, Ruskin concludes that he is unable to "carve [as decoration for the Bradford Exchange] something worth looking at." He states that Christian or beautiful subjects are "inappropriate to the manner of exchange" to be represented by the decorations for the un-Christian Bradford Exchange, whose actions are more insidious and "cunning than any of Tetzel's trading." He describes the worthless decorations he deems most appropriate to the Bradford Exchange, and he makes an ironic suggestion that "in the innermost chambers of [the Exchange] there might be a statue of Britannia of the Market," his detailed and bitter description of which is an indictment of modern economic exchange.

The lecture "Traffic" is rhetorically powerful because Ruskin argues for the identity of architectural Exchange and monetary exchange and insists that the first cannot be good unless the second is also good. He conflates Exchange (as work of art) and exchange (as economic organization) and opposes one bad society to two good societies. To the morality and art of Bradford capitalism Ruskin contrasts first those of the Gothic Christians and then those of the ancient Greeks. To the thought of Victorian capitalism, he opposes the *Republic* and *Laws* of Plato, who was one of the greatest enemies of "this idol of yours" and who taught men "to bear lightly the burden of gold." Ruskin is deceived (or wishes to deceive others) in judging the whole of Greek society by the art and philosophical writings it produced. The philosopher-king, so necessary to the Platonic "economy," exists only at the extreme margins of possibility in Greek society. Plato was able to produce great writing within and even define his philoso-

phy against the conventions of classical Athens, just as Ruskin (a disciple of Plato and the prophets) lectures to an assembly with which he believes he is in some disagreement. The writing of "Traffic," and even the possible construction of the temple to Britannia of the Market, are proof that "good" critical art is possible in "bad" society.

Not all thinkers in Victorian England came to Ruskin's conclusion about the ineffectiveness or impossibility of good art in the society in which they lived. In a lecture entitled "Ruskin's Politics," George Bernard Shaw compares Ruskin's extraordinary power of invective with that of Karl Marx. Shaw argues perversely that Ruskin's skill is greater because, unlike Marx, he was a "Tory-Socialist" in his attitude to society: "When you read [the] invectives of Marx and Cobbett, and read Ruskin's invectives afterwards, somehow or other you feel that Ruskin beats them hollow. Perhaps the reason was that they hated their enemy so thoroughly. Ruskin does it without hatred, and therefore he does it with a magnificent thoroughness. You may say that his strength in invective is as the strength of ten thousand because his heart is pure. And the only consequence of his denunciation of society was that people said, 'Well, he can't possibly be talking about us, the respectable people;' and so they did not take any notice." We have already seen, however, that Ruskin's heart was anything but "pure." His falsification of the economic value of art and the identity of taste and morality are, as Proust knew, signs of a certain intellectual evasiveness that he employed in the "noble" lie that is his defense of art. The power of Ruskin's invective derives from these falsifications. A biographer might even argue that Ruskin was so bitter because he believed that his own "art-talent" had been wasted in a bad society in which it could not flourish.

Marx had a different understanding of the roles of art and intellectual discourse in society, and of the solution to the ills of society itself. Like Ruskin, he attacked capitalism on the level of abstract political economy, but his principal goal was to understand not artistic reproduction in particular, but economic production in general. In "Traffic," Ruskin is strangely satisfied with his too-much-protesting opposition of the Victorian "Goddess of Getting-On" to the Greek "Goddess of Wisdom," comparing the mythology of his own age with that of the heroic Greeks. In an essay written in London in 1857 (when Ruskin was delivering his lectures on *The Political Economy of Art* in Manchester), Marx made a similar comparison. For him the *Crédit mobilier* is the symbol of modern economic exchange, just as Printing House Square is the symbol of modern linguistic exchange:

> We know that Greek mythology is not only the arsenal of Greek art, but also its basis. Is the conception of nature and of social relations which underlies Greek imagination and therefore Greek [art] possible when there are self-acting mules, railways, locomotives and electric telegraphs? What is . . . Hermes compared with the *Crédit mobilier*? All mythology subdues, controls and fashions the forces of nature in the imagination and through imagination; it disappears therefore when real control over these

forces is established. What becomes of Fama
side by side with Printing House Square?

This passage is both elegy for the mythology of Greece
and eulogy of the capitalist technology of France and England. Hermes—whether thief or messenger of the gods—
is impossible in the Promethean age of the *Crédit mobilier.*
Ancient art (the technological and material basis of which
have been transcended) can nevertheless give "esthetic
pleasure" and in certain respects can be regarded as "a
standard and unattainable ideal." Marx explains this
power of Greek art not by arguing (as does the *menteur*
Ruskin) that it contains some sort of golden eternal truths,
but rather by arguing that "the charm [that Greek] art has
for us . . . is a consequence of [the immature stage of the
society where it originated], and is inseparably linked with
the fact that the immature social conditions which gave
rise, and which alone could give rise, to this art cannot
recur." Artistic production, perhaps, is a superstructure,
and material production a substructure. If so, however,
they correspond to each other not mimetically but dialectically. Unlike Ruskin, Marx does not need to argue that
ancient Greece was morally superior to modern England
and France because Hermes and the Goddess of Wisdom
seem esthetically superior to the *Crédit mobilier* and the
Goddess of Getting-On. Indeed, Marx sometimes admits
to a grudging admiration of the heroic accomplishments
of Promethean capitalism. The "Tory-Socialist" Ruskin,
on the other hand, feared that if capitalist exchange were
heroic, then good decoration would be conceivable for the
Bradford Exchange. "There might indeed, on some theories, be a conceivably good architecture for Exchanges—
that is to say *if* there were any heroism in the fact or deed
of exchange, which might be typically carved on the outside of your building" (Italics mine). But Ruskin pretends
that there is nothing serviceable or heroic about capitalism, just as he pretends that Greek society was somehow
"good." Such pretence, of course, differs from the curious
recognition of capitalist serviceability and heroism in the
writings of Shaw and also from the Marxist recognition of
the heroism of the working class and of capitalist technology.

This respect for capitalism enabled Marx to offer his
scathing critique of it. His theory of a dialectical relationship between esthetic taste and economic morality enabled
him to understand how a work of art could be of a period
yet also in opposition to that period. It was unnecessary
for Marx, as it was necessary for Ruskin, to estheticize
politics by arguing that the societies that give rise to great
artists must be good societies. Because of this understanding, perhaps, Marx did not feel the debilitating despera-
tion that haunted Ruskin.

The great danger to literature is not the argument that literature subverts citizens by teaching them falsehoods; it
is the argument, implicit or explicit, that literature has no
real value or potential to affect either good or evil, that it
has no real role in human affairs and ought not to be taken
seriously. Although the student and lover of literature
may find his most theoretically exciting enemy in the arguments of those attackers of literature who (like Plato) take
it seriously, he finds his most threatening and politically
insidious enemy in the ignorance of those who do not

bother to consider the economic and political significance
of literature. Assuming the social value of literature, they
are unable or unwilling to define precisely the exact nature
of that value and trust hopefully that such things do not
matter. These enemies of the serious consideration of literature would shield it from the significant and interesting
analysis to which John Ruskin attempted to subject it in
his theoretical and practical writings.

Ruskin's attempt to write an "economy of literature" corresponding to his economies of the other arts was not totally successful. His theoretical writings are mirror reflections, albeit unwilling, of capitalist ideology transferred
from the realm of economics to the realm of art. They do
not completely transcend the capitalist ideology from
which they arise and against which they constantly inveigh with rhetorical ammunition. Ruskin protests against
the abstract theories of classical political economy and
only pretends to substitute for its concept of economic
value a new understanding of Life. He knew the errors and
dangerous implications of some of the theories he proposed in the economic defense of literature. He knew how
unsuccessful were his attempts to treat literature and wisdom as commodity and as medium of exchange, and to
identify esthetic taste and economic morality. Ruskin
himself felt the wrongness of these theories. Most interesting, he felt a certain necessity to continue in that wrongness in order to defend what he believed to be the proper
place of art in a national economy. His pose of certainty
(what Proust calls an "attitude mensongère") was like the
very capitalist self-assuredness that he mocked sarcastically throughout his lectures. Both capitalist and his own
ideological defenses are too-much-protesting assertions
without rigorous argument. Fortified with such assertions,
however, Ruskin suggested and supervised many excellent
reforms in the arts, some of which surpass in vision many
of his theoretical writings.

John Ruskin's economy of literature is much more than
a self-contradicting attempt to apply a special variation of
classical political economy to the economy of art. To the
extent that Ruskin did analyze his own thinking, he found
it inadequate. He recognized the hidden capitalist ideology of his theory of literary value and the politically dangerous implications of his theory of the identity of taste
and morality. That he recognized and criticized implicitly
his own theoretical *mensonges* is a great example and contribution to the sociology of literature. That he persevered
in these *mensonges* is the sign not of his intellectual dishonesty, but of his tremendous desire to understand and
interpret the relation between art and economics in his
own time.

John Dixon Hunt   (essay date 1982)

SOURCE: "Oeuvre and Footnote," in *The Ruskin Poly-
gon: Essays on the Imagination of John Ruskin,* edited by
John Dixon Hunt and Faith M. Holland, Manchester
University Press, 1982, pp. 1-20.

[*In the following essay, Hunt examines Ruskin's tendency
to footnote, cross-reference, and recast aspects of his own
work.*]

My theme is simply how we should read Ruskin. There is, first of all, the sheer bulk of the oeuvre—not only the thirty-nine volumes of *The Works,* but close on as many more volumes of subsequently edited diaries, letters and other 'primary materials'. Then there is the problem of how to use all the material that Ruskin's editors, Cook and Wedderburn, crowded into their edition of the *Works*. Against the advice of Charles Eliot Norton, another of Ruskin's literary executors, Wedderburn argued that the Library Edition should be *all* Ruskin, and he and Cook accordingly included all books then available in other editions, all those out of print or available only in private printings; gathered all Ruskin's occasional articles, letters to newspapers and other scattered writings; collated the different editions published by Ruskin; reproduced not only all the illustrations which Ruskin had inserted in his works but also large numbers of his drawings as well as portraits, facsimiles of letters and manuscripts and photographs of Ruskin's 'haunts'; and, finally, for their introductions, footnotes and bibliographical annotations drew upon unpublished MSS, holographs of published books and letters and diaries. The result was and remains probably the richest mine of materials for the study of an English author ever established—yet a mine in parts largely unquarried, for who has not come across uncut pages in any 'Cook and Wedderburn' they have used?

'All Ruskin is in his work,' wrote Robert Furneaux Jordan. 'One must take him whole or not at all.' It is a law for the serious study of any writer, surely, but it would not be special pleading, I think, to claim that Ruskin above all must be taken 'whole'. There are special considerations, which will be more fully explored later, why Ruskin's *oeuvre* requires some overall scrutiny before any part of it is studied and why this is so in a different fashion from other writers—one must be his omnivorous, polymathic mind, which inevitably forged connections between its individual operations; another, less frequently argued but equally crucial, would be the enormous importance of Ruskin's youth, which provided him with all the major concerns of his subsequent career, which has consequently to be read as a continuous elaboration of early ideas and experience.

But even if it were readily acknowledged that Ruskin constitutes a special case, there would still remain the problem of how we are to take him whole. As usual, Ruskin himself somehow registered the difficulty. Not only his revisions, by themselves no more unusual than for other self-conscious authors, but his deletions from and additions to the corpus of his work represent his own adjudication of what he wished to establish as the core and therefore the structure of his writings: thus in the New Year of 1871:

> Being now fifty-one years old, and little likely to change my mind hereafter on any important subject of thought (unless through weakness of age), I wish to publish a connected series of such parts of my works as now seem to me right. . . .

> The first book of which a new edition is required chances to be *Sesame and Lilies,* from which I now detach the old preface, about the Alps, for use elsewhere; and to which I add a lecture given in Ireland on a subject closely connected with that of the book itself. . . .

Of his two major works, *Modern Painters* he came to feel should never be republished 'as a whole', but he allowed some selections to be issued in 1875 as *Frondes Agrestes,* to which, however, he added thirty-four notes, and in 1884-85 as *In Montibus Sanctis* and *Coeli Enarrant* he planned to reissue the 'scientific portions' of *Modern Painters* 'on the origin of forms in clouds [and] mountains,' to which he also added new material as well as cross-references to *Deucalion* and *Proserpina*. With his other great work, *The Stones of Venice,* he was equally if not as radically revisionist: in the 1870s, at the instigation of Prince Leopold, he determined to revise his Venetian study, a project which gave rise immediately to a *Guide to the Principal Pictures in the Academy* (1877), between 1877 and 1884 to the parts of *St Mark's Rest,* subtitled *The History of Venice, written for the help of the few travellers who still care for her monuments,* and to the 'Travellers' Edition' of *Stones*. And if these suggest only the indecisions and 'weaknesses of age', it must be remembered that the pattern of his earliest works was similarly composed of determined directions, then chance indirections, of writing himself into situations where he found he did not know enough to continue, then submitting himself to further research and travel. Thus the first volume of *Modern Painters* was reissued with a new preface before even the second appeared, its lengthy reconsideration of Ruskin's ambitions for the project seeking to accommodate new directions in his reading and thinking, while in the third edition of volume one many modifications were made to the original text; after the second volume of *Modern Painters* he diverted his energies into work that emerged first as *Seven Lamps of Architecture* and then *The Stones of Venice;* his return to the 'main' project with the third and fourth volumes of *Modern Painters* was inevitably a resumption of directions no longer as distinct as they had appeared ten years before with volume two, and indeed before the fifth and final volume could appear in 1860 Ruskin had announced fresh territories for his mind in *The Political Economy of Art* in 1857.

Such a pattern of thinking and writing might be seen to exemplify the idea he announced in a letter to Carlyle on the eve of the New Year, 1853: 'It is the worst of the minor incapacities of human life that one's opinions ought, by rights, to be tested and refitted every five years. They are the soul's clothes—and a healthy soul is always growing too big for its opinions and wanting them to be let out.' The Teufelsdröckhan metaphor, apt enough homage to his correspondent, does not really suit the problem. It does not provide much critical purchase upon the phenomena of Ruskin's intellectual career, I suggest, simply to see him preparing to 'let out' the third and fourth volumes of *Modern Painters* now that the end of *The Stones of Venice* in 1853 is in sight. He himself considered that 'All *Modern Painters* together will be the explanation of a parenthesis in *The Stones of Venice*'. This moves closer to what I would like to suggest as a more profitable approach to Ruskin's mind and writings—the notion of the footnote.

It was Hillis Miller who recognised in passing that Ruskin was 'one of the great masters in English of the footnote'. The perception may be extended: for not only does Ruskin use the footnote and—by extension—the appendix most

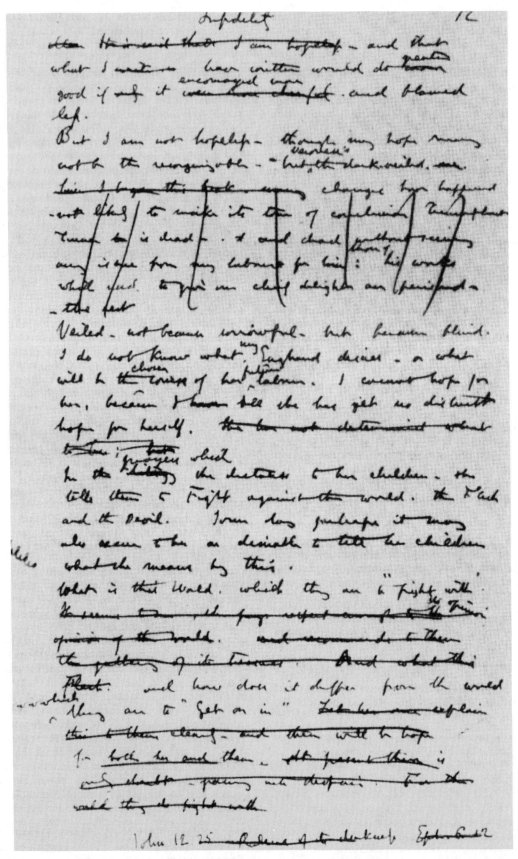

Page from the manuscript for the final chapter of Modern Painters.

creatively, but the best model perhaps for describing his *oeuvre* is—paradoxically—the footnote, together with its more magisterial ancestor, the marginal gloss, and its maverick cousins, marginalia. Though Ruskin's own marginalia are not particularly striking, his own exploitation of the footnote is thoroughly creative. A footnote on kingship in *Unto this Last,* for instance, blossoms into larger considerations of that theme in *Munera Pulveris* and *Sesame and Lilies,* while the third chapter of *Munera Pulveris* was almost undermined by its notes, one of which got elevated into the main text when the essays from *Fraser's Magazine* were issued in book form.

Now there is much to stimulate a reader of Ruskin in Lawrence Lipking's witty and perceptive essay 'The Marginal Gloss'. He reminds us that Burnet's marginal commentary in *Telluris Theoria Sacra* of 1681 was printed as footnotes in eighteenth-century editions, and that such a revision of the habitual spaces of a page signals important intellectual changes. No longer did the Bible and God's other book, of Nature, constitute parallel authorities; a rival relationship of hard or literal fact, established in the main block of text, was set over against legend, myth, conjecture, hearsay, even gloss, which were now relegated sceptically to the notes below. But that in the version of 'The Ancient Mariner' which appeared in *Sibylline Leaves* of 1817 Coleridge recovers something of Burnet's original typography in order to harmonise the parts of his poem; for between the mysterious and gnomic verses and the gloss which knows the world makes sense and is not in thrall to the other's perspective there emerges—as the reader 'snakes' back and forth between text and margin—a larger whole.

Now Ruskin seems to me to occupy an interesting position in this history of the gloss and the footnote. Belonging to the scientific age which placed its 'hard facts' in the text above notes which either simply provided sources or inveighed against earlier myth, conjecture and gloss, Ruskin also subscribed to the convictions of a Thomas Burnet that the natural world and the word of the Bible were parallel texts and to Coleridge's confidence in multiple perspectives. It is a vision that at least in the first place was inherited with his Scottish evangelicalism. Its typological structure did not ever really recover the typographical form of Burnet's page, but the strong conviction that Nature is God's book and is to be read side-by-side with the Bible inevitably affected the mode of Ruskin's writing. Furthermore, Bible and natural world are text and gloss (or gloss and text), and Ruskin invoked both as a gloss upon Turner's painting, which was in its turn a gloss upon the divine texts. This multiplicity of 'texts' in *Modern Painters,* texts which are also glosses, makes for difficult reading, no easier for the absence of any typographical help on the printed page; yet it is part of Ruskin's own difficulty that no satisfactory form offers itself to accommodate his vision—the addition of brief explanatory marginal glosses in a later edition of *Modern Painters* was rather a clue to the sequence of thought than a proper recovery of Burnet's layout. Similarly, in the 1880 edition of *Seven Lamps of Architecture* (hardly the dizziest of Ruskin's works to fathom) crucial passages were printed in thick type—

glosses on, from, and in the text; Ruskin's first thought had been to issue some notes on the text separately.

A more interesting mode of gloss/note also associated with the *Seven Lamps* was Ruskin's provision of illustrations for its first edition, an aspect of his books that became a permanent feature after 1848. 'There was never a writer before,' he told his father proudly, 'who could illustrate his own writings.' Among the various manifestations of text-and-gloss/gloss-and-text which Ruskin's life and works afford, that of word-and-image/image-and-word is central; even his division of the beauty perceived by the theoretic faculty seems to cater to his verbal and visual skills—'Typical Beauty' requiring the literary text as its commentary, 'Vital Beauty' needing largely the draughtsman's skills. From an early age he was composing works where visual and verbal languages collaborate, creating facsimile 'books' after the manner of Rogers's *Italy;* his picturesque tastes which necessarily brought word and image into some conjunction were extended in both *Modern Painters* and the interpolated architectural books by his writing about visual materials. The provision of illustrations in 1848 for the *Seven Lamps* gave the illusion of being the provision of objective facts, upon which Ruskin's prose then served as gloss. Since he always prided himself upon the accuracy of his drawings, the use of 'illusion' may seem unfair; but it is odd, and not a little begs a central question in such a book, to offer his own drawings and engravings of natural and architectural forms as proof of his *analyses* of their originals. And this method of providing his arguments with illustrations—even to the extent of his own reworking of details from paintings of Claude or Turner—has never been discussed: it is, I suggest, properly a question of text and gloss—are the illustrations in Ruskin's books simply the 'citation' of sources (as in conventional footnotes), are they glosses upon his verbal text, or are they the essential visual text upon which the author writes his commentary? The answer is that sometimes they are each in turn, sometimes and more importantly, all together.

This *oeuvre* made up of an incremental series of notes must have an original 'text' upon which to begin. With Ruskin, as it had been with Montaigne, this was his own life. His first important publication, the essays which formed *The Poetry of Architecture,* though they assume a studied air of impersonality, were largely a commentary upon his own travel experiences; where these were insufficient Ruskin merely indulged in some undergraduate bluffing. The essays are made up of glosses upon his favourite landscapes and their indigenous buildings—the word 'gloss', Lipking reminds us, comes from the Greek for tongue, and in *The Poetry of Architecture* we first find the distinctive Ruskinian strategy of setting himself up as the interpreter of the voices or languages of things:

> A mountain . . . does not tell this fact to our feelings, or, rather . . . tells us of no time at which it came into existence . . . But a very old forest tree . . . is always telling us about the past. . . .

But the essays also give tongue to his experiences of scenery and architecture. It is also worth observing that as the essays proceed they steadily lose their careful control of the rigorous enquiry and acquire another characteristic Ruskinian habit of always needing more space than had been envisaged for them: and as the subjects grow and flourish in Ruskin's imagination, so long footnotes are introduced to accommodate what we may register as central ideas, but which for the author at that point are too important to waste and yet not apt for the main text. One of these, by a publishing accident, actually got itself printed separately.

The remainder of Ruskin's works after *The Poetry of Architecture* all derive from the need to give tongue to his own life and contacts. We in our turn—for no critic of Ruskin has ever escaped being his biographer as well—are then forced to provide his works with marginal glosses from his life: many opinions and arguments in *Modern Painters* and *The Stones of Venice* depended entirely on the accidents of where Ruskin had travelled and what he chose to annotate at that time. It became an ineluctable mode of his imagination at a very early age to seize anything that lay to hand as stimulus; in some of his youthful stories, written so evidently out of personal experience, we get glimpses of this habit:

> such a fine day that they all got out and walked a good way they had intended to walk very quick but they did not for they were attracted by such a variety of objects such as the white major convolvulus in the hedges the black & white broad beans the butterfly like pea's the sparkling rivulets and winding rivers all combined their forces to make them walk slowly'

It is, in miniature, a model of both single works and his *oeuvre;* examples from his adult life would include his discovery of Tintoretto in 1845 or of some Veroneses in 1858—'I unexpectedly found some good Paul Veroneses at Turin.' The texts of books he wrote are composed out of these often random encounters. And then they are recomposed, as he discovers fresh materials and earns new insights.

Thus his own experiences acquire an ambiguous status as both text and gloss for his ideas (some examples will be examined later). In early books his own experience may be adduced to document his views; later books increasingly refer their readers for further documentation back to previous Ruskin works—professed autodidacts, Lipking suggests, habitually give references to their own writings: his example is Vico, but Ruskin would be another. He can give in one letter to his father a cross-reference to another four years before! The first footnote of *Praeterita,* significantly, uses his late work for the St George's Guild as a gloss upon his early visits as a boy to country houses, galleries and gardens. *Deucalion* resumed ideas first entertained and even written about in 1833 in Chamounix, while *Proserpina* took up some notions first canvassed in a footnote to *The Poetry of Architecture* on the treatment of flowers by Shelley and Shakespeare; both, according to Ruskin, had their source in his youthful poem 'Eudosia'.

This strategy by which his *oeuvre* aspires to the condition of footnote and gloss has at least two distinct causes, though they are also closely related. The first is his lifelong determination to write about things that were for him more important than his own writings—mountains, Turner, Venetian and other Gothic architecture, social and economic health, botany, mineralogy; this sense of priority always meant that he was writing notes upon them. He was driven, he says, 'into literature that I might defend the power of painting' and, if we think of *Modern Painters,* into geology and natural history that he might be able to write that literature. The second cause of the note-like structure of his works is that, as the first implies, all his major interests as an adult writer were somehow initiated before he was twenty-one; the result is that many of the mature works are explicitly offered as extensions to, elaborate glosses upon, juvenile texts and his own early life.

Much of this is acknowledged by Ruskin, though the full significance of his tendency to cross-reference has, I think, been neglected. But there is also a hidden, implicit structure of glossing that is also crucial to his imagination, and it revolves around his lifelong determination to create some working relationship between his living self and his writing self. His career, from this perspective, may be seen as a constant effort to establish some liaison between two competing modes of existence: on the one hand, the world of myriad facts, to be carefully gathered and annotated in countless memoranda, an empirical world without end; on the other, the need to organise coherent, general principles. The most widely known version of this competition is *Praeterita,* a recollection of first things, undertaken among the last things that he did and in lucid moments of a steadily encroaching darkness. These *Outlines of Scenes and Thoughts perhaps Worthy of Memory in my Past Life,* as its subtitle glossed the distancing and lapidary tones of the Latin title, reveal his instinct for myth and fiction and for salvaging some sustaining and healing visions from the world of experience.

An autobiography holds out, especially to a writer, the promise of some congruence between his life and his art. Ruskin was always obsessed by this: in 1852 he wrote to tell his father that 'I shall some day—if I live—write a great essay on Man's work, which will be the work of my life'; thirty years later he confessed to Kate Greenaway that 'the truth is my *Life* never went into my books at all. Only my time.' At that point he was indeed putting his life into a book, namely *Praeterita.* Published in twenty-eight instalments, these essays in autobiography have, as we have come to realise, a problematical relationship to the facts of his biography. Ruskin writes them not simply to disclose his early years, but to use these 'first things' as a commentary upon his subsequent career. Yet since, on his own admission, they avoid anything 'disagreeable or querulous', they are also an attempt to invent a version of himself that he can live and die with.

Above all, *Praeterita* involves yet another adjudication between accumulation of facts and their glosses. Ruskin had at his disposal a vast archive of family papers. Yet he chose largely to ignore them. In *Praeterita* he told his readers that he knew very little about his parents; yet he had in his house at Brantwood 'all' the material that would establish their story. Furthermore, he actually looked at it—the diary records in February 1885 'a terrible day of chagrins and difficulties; finding my Croydon Grandmothers last letters to my mother. . . . ' It is obvious that he simply could not bring himself to review the necessary documents—too painful, but also too formidable a bulk of materials—that would have provided the true basis for his autobiographical work. And, indeed, the pictures that *Praeterita* offers of his childhood—toyless and often joyless, without 'companionable beasts'—and the dismissive version of his time at Oxford ('I learned four dialogues of Plato—of Theology, the Thirty-Nine Articles;—of myself—or the world I was to live in—nothing')—these and much more of *Praeterita* are quite specifically qualified, even contradicted, by the family letters and his own diaries which he could have consulted at Brantwood.

What he did, in fact, was to cannibalise sections of *Fors Clavigera,* re-using them with only minor changes as the initial chapters of *Praeterita*. He had chosen to write such passages in *Fors* because he felt that his wide-ranging coverage of social, economic and spiritual topics needed footnoting with references to his own background. Re-used in *Praeterita,* they had in their turn to be glossed and expanded: 'I fear the sequel may be more trivial, because much is concentrated in the foregoing broad statement, which I have now to continue by slower steps'; it was partly the changed context, above all its altered tone, that necessitated this extended commentary upon the condensed fragments of autobiography. In *Fors* they had been notes to a larger text; but even supplied with their own gloss in *Praeterita* they could not, in the end, stand by themselves. In 1886, when sixteen chapters of the autobiography had been issued, Ruskin began to publish selections of 'primary materials'—'Correspondence, Diary Notes, and Extracts from Books'—to illustrate and gloss the autobiography in its turn. The completion of both *Praeterita* and *Dilecta* (as this second compendium was called) was never achieved by Ruskin himself; his biographers and critics continue to add, as it were, to both volumes, but material for *Dilecta*—unpublished and published—seems (at least to some of us) infinite. If a *Dilecta* were ever to be completed, it would, as foot-notes, overwhelm the text of a finished *Praeterita*; indeed, it would probably become the text, with the chapters of autobiography its glosses.

These rivalries between text and footnote, life and autobiography, which I would suggest are an ineluctable dialogue of Ruskin's career, may be illustrated by one, more local, example. In April 1833, during the family's first major tour on the Continent, Ruskin saw the Alps from Schaffhausen. It had been perhaps a rather desultory Sunday, for the Ruskins on principle never travelled on the sabbath; so that towards sunset they found themselves, almost by accident, walking upon the terrace promenade above the Rhine. From there, for the first time, he saw the Alps, to which, as *Praeterita* put it half a century later, 'my heart and faith return to this day'. Now we have five ingredients of this crucial experience: the actual moment of sighting the Alps themselves—unrecoverable to Ruskin, let alone to us; a prose account written some time, maybe soon, afterwards; a versification of that, probably written the following winter when the family were back in England; then, many visits to the Alps over many years,

recorded in various forms from an early scientific paper on **'Facts and Considerations on the Strata of Mont Blanc'**, published when Ruskin was fifteen, to sections of later books like *Modern Painters* and *Ethics of the Dust*; finally, *Praeterita's* version of the original event in the light of Ruskin's subsequent career.

In 1833 the Alps offered themselves as a paradise; in the 1880s they were 'the seen walls of lost Eden. In 1833 at Schaffhausen it was a Sunday, much insisted upon in both prose and verse accounts of the immediately succeeding months, and the sabbath aptly provided a 'revelation of the beauty of the earth, the opening of the first page of its volume'. But the end of his life required a less explicitly theological gloss upon that divine page and so the Alps in *Praeterita* become 'beautiful in their snow, and their humanity'. The text which they had opened for the fourteen-year-old Ruskin on his day of rest needed annotation for years afterwards, filling his days and even spilling over into Sundays that had before been sacrosanct. The poem he wrote in 1833 rather flaccidly announced:

> The Alps! the Alps!—Full far away
> The long successive ranges lay.
> Their fixed solidity of size
> Told that they were not of the skies.

That 'told' is among the first of innumerable acknowledgements of a language in things, a gloss or tongue within a text that needs translation: 'not a leaflet', he would write about Gothic ornament, 'but speaks, and speaks far off too'.

For Ruskin in the late 1830s there were, he thought, two available languages in which to gloss, analogous to the two modes of diary-keeping he noted on 31 March 1840—'I have determined to keep one part of diary for intellect and another for feeling.' During the winter of 1833-34 he tried a studiedly scientific one for his first published paper, on **'The Causes of the Colour of the Water of the Rhone'**, which appeared in J. C. Loudon's *Magazine of Natural History* in September 1834. This note upon another 'epiphany' of that summer of 1833 is carefully objective—even similes, for there are no metaphors, invoke scientific analogies. It is simply an 'Enquiry' as to why the Rhone, as it flows out of Lac Léman through the city of Geneva, is 'so transparent, that the bottom can be seen twenty feet below the surface, yet so blue, that you might imagine it to be a solution of indigo'. Ruskin seems to be submitting his fascination with the rush of water, at once headlong in its speed but seemingly a stationary mass, to the need for scientific explanation, though he himself provides no answers. Although he did not apparently treat of the Rhone in any alternative language, from his verses at the time it is obvious that a sub-Byronic effusion in the manner of *Childe Harold's Pilgrimage*—we have seen four verses of this sort on the Alps from Schaffhausen—would have served to accommodate the 'feeling' as opposed to 'intellectual' response.

Years later he returned in *Praeterita* to the topic he had so narrowly treated in the *Magazine of Natural History*. There is still some suggestion of 'technical work', the careful discrimination of optical and physical effects. But there is also a passionate refusal to be limited by the language of such considerations—at one point the autobiography actually uses the idea, specifically rejected in 1834, that the Rhone is blue because it obtains the colours of the glaciers whence it flows. That covert allusion makes the famous *Praeterita* passage an intricate gloss upon fifty years of 'text'; its opening implies a crucial contrast between natural jewels, like the river, and the work of the jeweller Bautte, in whose shop 'twenty steps' from the water Ruskin had bought his wife a bracelet in 1849:

> For all other rivers there is a surface, and an underneath, and a vaguely displeasing idea of the bottom. But the Rhone flows like one lambent jewel; its surface is nowhere, its ethereal self is everywhere, the iridescent rush and translucent strength of it blue to the shore, and radiant to the depth.

> Fifteen feet thick, of not flowing, but flying water; not water, neither,—melted glacier, rather, one should call it; the force of the ice is with it, and the wreathing of the clouds, the gladness of the sky, and the continuance of Time.

> Waves of clear sea are, indeed, lovely to watch, but they are always coming or gone, never in any taken shape to be seen for a second. But here was one mighty wave that was always itself, and every fluted swirl of it, constant as the wreathing of a shell. No wasting away of the fallen foam, no pause for gathering of power, no helpless ebb of discouraged recoil; but alike through bright day and lulling night, the never-pausing plunge, and never-fading flash, and never-hushing whisper, and, while the sun was up, the ever-answering glow of unearthly aquamarine, ultramarine, violet-blue, gentian-blue, peacock-blue, river-of-paradise blue, glass of a painted window melted in the sun and the witch of the Alps flinging the spun tresses of it for ever from her snow.

If we respond to that visionary passage of water and prose, it is not because it is 'fine writing', but because we register in its language a tongue or gloss that articulates Ruskin's mind. It is partly that such careful apprehensions of the natural world are somehow cognate with self-apprehension; as *Praeterita* puts it some pages later, 'minute knowledge and acute sensation throw us back into ourselves'.

Both the larger example of *Praeterita*'s composition, intricately related to other works like *Fors* and *Dilecta,* and the smaller instance of his commentaries upon two important events of the 1833 Continental tour (themselves, in fact, linked—as alp and river are one) may serve as paradigms of Ruskin's mind and method of work. The dependence of all subsequent texts upon a first, usually the 'text' of himself, initiated a sequence of writings the status of which was always ambiguous.

At the centre of this complexity of *oeuvre,* I think, is the 'digression' into architectural work for *Seven Lamps,* which in its turn led to *Stones*. Something of Ruskin's scope is emblemised in the advertisement in the first edition of *Seven Lamps* for the next book: it tells us that there is 'In preparation' (though nothing is said of three volumes, nor of publication over two years) *The Stones of*

Venice, which is 'uniform' with *The Seven Lamps of Architecture* and by the author of *Modern Painters*. One of the 'uniformities', of course, is Ruskin's conviction of the 'brotherhood between the cathedral and the alp' and that the Gothic craftsman looked to other stones and natural things for inspiration. The stones of Chamounix and the stones of Venice were parallel texts. From an early age, owing partly to his picturesque tastes which endorsed his scrutiny of particulars and partly to his mineralising, Ruskin had attended to details, whether of mountains or of buildings; so that the ornaments of Venetian buildings, to which he devotes the majority of his space in *Stones* and which we might think of as something like marginalia on a building, become the main text for him, which he reads and glosses as he did natural phenomena in *Modern Painters I*.

At the stage in his son's work when *Modern Painters* was losing ground to the architectural work for *Seven Lamps* John James Ruskin wrote (on 25 May 1846) to his old friend and literary advisor, W. H. Harrison, from Venice:

> He is cultivating art at present, searching for real knowledge, but to you and me this is at present a sealed book. It will neither take the shape of picture nor poetry. It is gathered in scraps hardly wrought, for he is drawing perpetually, but no drawing such as in former days you or I might compliment in the usual way by saying it deserved a frame; but fragments of everything from a Cupola to a Cart-wheel, but in such bits that it is to the common eye a mass of Hieroglyphics—all true—truth itself, but Truth in mosaic.

And some eight years later, writing and still researching the second and third volumes of *The Stones,* Ruskin himself wrote to his father twice on the same day (18 January 1852) to confess his own frustration, even panic, with what his work entailed. First, he simply laid out the problem—that he had had only twelve months 'to examine piece by piece—buildings covering five square miles of ground—to read—or glance at—some forty volumes of history and chronicles—to make elaborate drawings . . . and to compose *my own book*'. But then in the second letter he announced more revealingly:

> There is something burdensome in the vast breadth of the subject at present—It is all weighing on my brains at once, and I cannot devote my full mind to any part of it. As soon as I have it all down on paper—out of *danger* as it were—and well in sight, I can take up any part and finish it as highly as I like, but as soon as I begin to dwell on any bit carefully, thoughts come into my head about other parts—unfinished—which I am afraid of losing and then I go away and touch upon them.

What is written down is, significantly, 'out of danger' and somehow controllable. What is as yet only projected threatens with its details and ramifications as yet uncoded and unrelated, one bit tempting the writer from another in an endless series of fragmentary rushes and *essais*. In 1877 he was still involved in the same problems, issuing the first supplement to *St. Mark's Rest* with the prefatory advice that 'The following (too imperfect) account of the pictures by Carpaccio in the chapel of San Giorgio de' Schiavoni, is properly a supplement to the part of "St. Mark's Rest" in which I propose to examine the religious mind of Venice in the fifteenth century'. Supplements to work in progress but as yet unavailable are entirely typical of a temperament that in the 1830s was accurately described by Margaret Ruskin as spoiling 'a good beginning from not taking the trouble to think and concluding in a hurry'. Hurried conclusions, in their turn, would often necessitate clarifications, either public or private, though by the time of *Fors* such distinctions seem to have been deliberately blurred. Indeed, *Fors Clavigera* as a whole should perhaps be read as Ruskin's last attempt to establish a form flexible enough to accommodate the writings of his life and mind. Its very title acknowledges the chances that direct his writing.

Something of Ruskin's imaginative skill at shaping his various texts can be examined best at the point where he brings *Modern Painters* to a conclusion. He had interrupted this work after two volumes, letting his architectural books—*Seven Lamps* and *The Stones of Venice*—expand upon the consideration of early Christian art in *Modern Painters II*. But when he resumed *Modern Painters* those architectural writings seemed (increasingly to Ruskin) to be metamorphosed from gloss to crucial text, to which later volumes of what started as the defence of Turner assume the status of notes in their turn. As he brings *Modern Painters* to its conclusion with lengthy expositions of Turner's 'Garden of the Hesperides' and 'The Python Slain by Apollo' and their coda, the very last chapter entitled 'Peace', Ruskin strives to draw all his experience and work into their pages. Despite the cumbersome segment of text involved, it is worth examining its structures more carefully.

In the first place, we may notice how the footnotes proliferate as Ruskin tries to gather in the work of seventeen years: they refer readers to other works, to 'various statements made respecting colour in different parts of my works' now collected into a 'system' in one huge footnote to the second painting discussed, to Ruskin's redrawing of Turner details, to now altered facts of European topography ('the railroad bridge over the Falls of Schaffhausen') which have been crucial to him, to *projected* work on 'benevolent and helpful action towards the lower classes', or to work on Turner 'being as yet impossible'. Then the second painting is invoked to serve as a commentary upon the first: 'The [second] picture is at once the type, and the first expression of a great change which was passing in Turner's mind' (one of the many places here when I feel that what Ruskin writes about Turner is covertly or unconsciously a gloss upon his own history). Further, and most important, the defence of Turner that has been the ostensible *raison d'être* of *Modern Painters* is intertwined with the cultural history of Venice that was narrated in *The Stones* so that each text may serve as gloss upon the other. This intertwining bears unravelling.

The titles of the two chapters devoted to Turner paintings ('The Nereid's Guard' and 'The Hesperid Aeglé') announce only gnomically how Ruskin will gloss their im-

ages; thus they are a type of the pictures themselves. He refers the reader first to his *Notes on the Turner Collection* and singles out his emphasis there on Turner's 'generally gloomy tendency of mind', with which he is 'only' concerned in the following sixty pages. Turner's temperament is a gloss on (tongue for) the condition of England, but to understand the full implications of this Ruskin must first invoke the Greek myths which Turner is said to paint (though it soon becomes unclear whether picture or myth is text or gloss):

> How far he had really found out for himself the collateral bearings of the Hesperid tradition I know not; but that he had got the main clue of it, and knew who the Dragon was, there can be no doubt; the strange thing is, that his conception of it throughout, down to the minutest detail, fits every one of the circumstances of the Greek tradition.

To elucidate these traditions requires a text from Hesiod, which Ruskin translates and footnotes—he is, as Hillis Miller observed, an 'interrogator of origins', which explains his determination to 'look to the precise meaning of Hesiod's words'. Collateral texts from Dante and Spenser, equally in need of glossing, threaten to extend the materials indefinitely (but 'We must yet keep to Dante, however'), The typologies that Ruskin establishes are, of course, a series of parallel texts, each as authoritative as the others; this structure of meaning authorises further parallels—the dragon's body in Turner's 'Hesperides' is a nearly perfect representation of glacier movement; the mythologies of sea recall Venetian history; the sea dragon parallels the serpent in Eden (Ruskin refers us to his earlier genealogies of dragons) and thus is a type of all corruptions of paradise; this sea dragon, Geryon, is the 'evil spirit of wealth', and the implied comparison with Venetian history then surfaces clearly when the Goddess of Discord, present in Turner's 'Hesperides,' is glossed by Ruskin's allusion to his own discussion of the Ducal Place—'remember the inscription there, *Discordia sum, discordans*'. And so via evil wealth and disharmony in the Venetian paradise we begin to see how Turner's England ('a paradise of smoke . . . the Assumption of the Dragon') and the early Christian worlds of which Venice was a type are connected; both feature St George, and Turner, contrary to *Modern Painters III,* is now acknowledged to have been 'educated under the influence of Gothic art'.

The following chapter extends and ultimately clarifies that connection; the destinies of England and Venice are once again compared, as they had been at the very start of *The Stones* (' . . . the thrones of Tyre, Venice and England'). Turner's second painting images the 'worm of decay'; his vision is increasingly, we are told, of 'Ruin, and twilight'—a long passage on Turner's attraction to English ruins distantly recalls the 'ruin' of Venice, also adumbrated at the very start of *Stones*. And via Turner's own obsession with the fate of Tyre we arrive, finally, at Turner's intense imaginative response to Venice herself, the type of that 'death which attends the vain pursuit of beauty':

> How strangely significant, thus understood, those last Venetian dreams of his become, them-

selves so beautiful and so frail; wrecks of all that they were once—twilights of twilight!

The scarlet colour which Turner 'dared' to paint and a discussion of which rather inexplicably filled the opening pages of this chapter is now glossed by Giorgione's scarlet frescoes on the Fondaco dei Tedeschi ('sanguigna e fiammeggiante, per cui le pitture cominciarono con dolce violenza a rapire il cuore delli genti'); seen by Ruskin ten years before, and already fading then, the frescoes are an emblem of Venice—decaying; yet by the Sea Sybil, Deiphobe, who has twice appeared in preceeding pages, Venice's 'enchanted voice' will for ever tell of 'faithful light and truth'. Now, in a footnote to his very last paragraph, Ruskin explains the engraving of a Giorgione woman, placed without explanation at the start of the chapter:

> My impression is that the ground of the flesh in these Giorgione frescoes had been pure vermilion; little else was left in the figure I saw. Therefore, not knowing what power the painter intended to personify by the figure at the commencement of this chapter, I have called her, from her glowing colour, Hesperid Aeglé.

As prose explication of Turner's visual images Ruskin's chapters are hardly lucid. But his verbal imagination—this is, significantly, juxtaposed to Turner's 'silence'—subsumes the paintings into a larger mediation, difficult in its allusions and intricate patterns of analogy and gloss, on the histories of England and Venice, Turner and Giorgione. We are dealing, in fact, with a verbal fabric that has all the density and elliptic structures of poetry, in much the way that Ruskin himself expatiates on 'the Real Nature of Greatness of Style' in *Modern Painters III*:

> Let us therefore look into the facts of the thing, not with any metaphysical, or otherwise vain and troublesome effort at acuteness, but in a plain way; for the facts themselves are plain enough, and may be plainly stated, only the difficulty is, that out of these facts, right and left, the different forms of misapprehension branch into grievous complexity, and branch so far and wide, that if once we try to follow them, they will lead us quite from our mark into other separate, though not less interesting, discussions.

That the misapprehensions ('not less interesting') are connected to the plain facts by some organic growth makes the task of distinguishing them problematical for Ruskin and for the reader. It ensures, too, as Hillis Miller remarked, that any one of Ruskin's books is in fact potentially endless. One end to which these final sections of *Modern Painters* that I have been examining gesture is Ruskin himself; they have often the strength of personal identification, not only by involvement in their topic, but by a sub-stratum of personal metaphor discovered in other materials. This is initiated in the reader's mind, first, by the cross-references Ruskin supplies to his other writings and by the allusions to other obsessions like geology, climate and marriage; then, by his stress upon Turner's 'Education amidst country possessing architectural remains of some noble kind', which so evidently accounts for Ruskin's own work from *The Poetry of Architecture* to *The Stones of Venice*. Finally, when he treats of 'Rose and

cankerworm', I hear in his celebration of the former his awareness that its 'loveliness and kindness' have already found their embodiment in Rose La Touche, first encountered in the autumn of 1858.

The last chapter, 'Peace', is Ruskin's exorcism of the daemon that has kept him at work on *Modern Painters* through seventeen years and five other collateral volumes: 'Looking back over what I have written, I find that I have only now the power of ending this work,—it being time that it should end, but not of "concluding" it; for it has led me into fields of infinite inquiry, where it is only possible to break off with such imperfect result as may, at any given moment, have been attained.' To which might be added—and which at any moment may be resumed. For this is exactly the difficulty of reading Ruskin 'whole': that even as he ends he is aware both of beginnings and of future work; that he realises nothing can stand alone (this partly because he was such a polymath) and that each text requires and represents the notation of others, finished or yet unbegun.

By now it is perhaps clear how singularly inappropriate are the conventional criticisms of Ruskin's propensity to be led away from 'one' topic by 'digressions'; yet from his mother onwards commentators have looked askance at what Townsend, for example, calls Ruskin's 'inability to avoid digressions' or his being 'constitutionally unfitted to avoid digressions'. As early as *The Poetry of Architecture* 'digressions' and footnotes announced his typical absorption in many things simultaneously or at random—footnotes at least evade writing's usual insistence upon sequence and permit two texts almost equal status on the same page. Ruskin was even encouraged by his editor, J. C. Loudon, who said he could not be too diffusive!

But it is important to insist that this tendency was creative rather than just pathological. When he excuses his modes of proceeding in *Modern Painters*—'they will lead us quite from our mark into other separate, though not less interesting, discussions'—he is in fact attempting to establish connections between things generally considered to be different. His later writings especially have this tendency to synthesise 'separate branches of knowledge into "grammars" for the schools of the Guild of St George'. Indeed, a perfect emblem of Ruskin's imaginative energy in relating the disparate objects of his study would be the museum that he started to establish for the Guild, which had its prototypes in his collections for the Oxford Drawing Schools, his dream in 1852 of an ideal Turner Gallery, and the Oxford Museum ('my habits of system could only be of use if I took the thing wholly in hand'). But, like everything else in Ruskin's career, this idea of a museum in which wide-ranging interests might be accommodated without needing to give priority to any one was encountered very early in his life, at the famous Crosthwaite's Museum in Keswick during the family tour of the Lakes in 1830. In this bewilderingly eclectic display were presented, *inter alia*, 'several old manuscript books, written before printing', 'the rib of a man, 21 feet high!!' and some 'musical stones' of the sort that Ruskin was to have made for himself in the 1880s. Faced with such an indiscriminate profusion of objects collected and displayed by one man and received with the same spread of interest by the Ruskins, it is difficult to talk of incoherence, irrelevance or digression. The same dedication to a seemingly inchoate mass of items, ideas and pursuits never ceased to enthral Ruskin. He was a true, old-fashioned virtuoso, the keeper certainly in spirit and often in fact of one of those cabinets of curiosities where each item has equal authority with any other, where coherence lies simply in the *tout ensemble*. Thus it is, I suggest, that the Ruskin Museum at Coniston, with its early Ruskin manuscripts 'written before printing', its mineral cases, stone harmonicum, local history display, model of Ruskin's boat and so on, is an absolutely authentic memorial of him. It lacks only his own imaginative framework, a coherence in which text and note are one—and the other.

Robert Hewison   (essay date 1982)

SOURCE: "Notes on the Construction of *The Stones of Venice*," in *Studies in Ruskin: Essays in Honor of Van Akin Burd,* edited by Robert Rhodes and Del Ivan Janick, Ohio University Press, 1982, pp. 131-50.

[*In the following essay, Hewison analyzes* The Stones of Venice *in terms of the politics, economics, and religious beliefs of the mid-1800s.*]

The Stones of Venice is arguably Ruskin's most successful work. It is also arguably his most important. It is the only one of his books for which he had a predetermined plan, a plan that he largely carried out. It is the only major work in which he began by saying what he was going to say and then, with minor qualifications, said it. Anyone reading Chapter 1 of Volume I, "The Quarry," cannot, if he or she is at all familiar with the works of Ruskin, fail to be struck by the way in which he firmly states his purpose and makes his propositions plain. And anyone at all familiar with the works of John Ruskin will of course expect him neither to carry out his stated purpose nor to demonstrate the propositions he has laid down.

There are many reasons for the unity of *The Stones of Venice*: unity of place, the concentrated location in which the unity of drama, the tragedy of rise and fall, is set. Unity of place and time also for Ruskin, for his work was concentrated over two intense periods, the winters of 1849-1850 and 1851-1852; and rarely for Ruskin, unity of study, since he had already done a great deal of research before writing his first volume, and he knew where he was going. This paper, however, concentrates on one further reason for the unity of *The Stones of Venice*—the contemporary political references that underlie it.

The first of these references, and the most important, comes in the opening paragraph of the book.

> Since first the dominion of men was asserted over the ocean, three thrones, of mark beyond all others, have been set upon its sands: the thrones of Tyre, Venice, and England. Of the First of these great powers only the memory remains; of the Second, the ruin; the Third, which inherits their greatness, if it forget their example, may be led through prouder eminence to less pitied destruction.

Ruskin set out to write *The Stones of Venice* as a warning for his own times. That it is a warning is implicit in the sonorities of his opening sentences as they were published and explicit in his earlier manuscript draft, where the second sentence reads, "Of the first of these great powers only the memory remains; of the Second the Ruins—and the Third will in like destruction have inherited their Greatness, if it will not take warning from their example."

The opening lines of *The Stones of Venice* are intended, then, as a warning—but what is the warning against? Further, what made the circumstances of 3 March 1851, when Volume I appeared, so urgent? Here the opening chapter is less explicit, or rather, less explicit to anyone not reading it on 3 March 1851. There are, however, some clues, some contemporary references, possibly so obvious in Ruskin's own day that they needed to be no more than allusions. Over 125 years later we have a right to be puzzled by the passing comments on the "temper of our present English legislature," or even to miss them altogether.

Contemporary reference was not a new thing for Ruskin; the political upheavals of 1848 made their influence felt on the text of *The Seven Lamps of Architecture,* in particular in "The Lamp of Obedience," and indeed Ruskin refers to this passage in the third volume of *The Stones of Venice*. The references serve as a reminder of the severe shock the political system of Europe had so recently experienced at the time he came to write his studies of architecture, the "distinctively political art."

Ruskin's contemporary references in the opening of *The Stones of Venice* are, in the main text, somewhat cryptic. Writing of the collateral decline of Venice's prosperity with the decline of private religion, he comments:

> The stopping short of this religious faith when it appears likely to influence national action, correspondent as it is, and that most strikingly, with several characteristics of the temper of our present English legislature, is a subject, morally and politically, of the most curious interest and complicated difficulty; one, however, which the range of my present inquiry will not permit me to approach[,]

and readers at all familiar with the works of Ruskin will know that he will probably not respect this restriction.

The reference to the Parliament of 1851 becomes a little clearer when shortly afterwards Ruskin discusses the traditional Venetian resistance to the power of Rome: "To this exclusion of Papal influence from her councils, the Romanist will attribute their irreligion, and the Protestant their success." In the main text he continues:

> The first may be silenced by a reference to the character of the policy of the Vatican itself; and the second by his own shame, when he reflects that the English legislature sacrificed their principles to expose themselves to the very danger which the Venetian senate sacrificed theirs to avoid.

But meanwhile, a footnote leads to a seemingly innocuous appendix, number 5, "The Papal Power in Venice."

And, in turning to the back of the book, we discover another reason for the particular coherence of this introductory chapter: a great deal of less-well-shaped material has been thrust into the appendices. Indeed, of the twenty-five appendices to the first volume of *The Stones of Venice,* twelve hang from the first chapter. Appendix 5 begins, as it describes itself, as a study of the Papal power in Venice, but gradually it turns into an attack on Catholic Emancipation in England. Venice excluded priests from the Senate, but England, since 1829, had allowed Roman Catholics to sit in Parliament.

> If they [the Venetians] were to blame, in yielding to their fear of the ambitious spirit of Rome so far as to deprive their councils of all religious element, what excuse are we to offer for the state, which, with Lords Spiritual of her own faith already in her senate, permits the policy of Rome to be represented by lay members? To have sacrificed religion to mistaken policy, or purchased security with ignominy, would have been no new thing in the world's history; but to be at once impious and impolitic, and seek for danger through dishonour, was reserved for the English parliament of 1829.

So strongly does Ruskin feel about the growing threat from Catholicism that he proceeds to reprint part of an article on the disturbed condition of Ireland, written not by himself, but by his father, John James Ruskin. According to Ruskin it had been published in a "journal" in 1839. As far as the son is concerned, it contained "truths to which the mind of England seems but now, and that slowly, to be awakening."

The fuel for John James's article is hatred of Roman Catholicism, "the cause of darkness and ignorance", but his case is that there is a constitutional conflict between Catholicism and Protestantism, which means that they should not be allowed to exist side by side in the relatively democratic—at least not despotic—government of England. "So entirely is Protestantism interwoven with the whole frame of our constitution and laws," writes John James, "that I take my stand on this, against all agitators in existence, that the Roman religion is totally incompatible with the British constitution. We have, in trying to combine them, got into a maze of difficulties; we are the worse, and Ireland none the better."

Now, it might seem a little odd that in 1851 John Ruskin should be reprinting an article written in 1839 about an event of 1829, namely the decision to permit Catholics to be elected to the House of Commons. Catholic Emancipation would surely be a dying issue—but not if you were John James Ruskin; nor, I suggest, if you were his son. To discover why, we must consider just what was going on in "the present English legislature" of 1851.

In terms of party politics, England had been going through a period of instability ever since Sir Robert Peel had broken the unity of his own Tory party in order to force the passage of the abolition of the Corn Laws in 1846. A weak Whig administration under Lord John Russell had come to power in 1847 but was under pressure both from the radicals demanding further parliamentary reform and the extension of the franchise and from the Tories who wanted to reintroduce trade protection (except,

that is, followers of Sir Robert Peel). Even though the economy was recovering from the crisis of the 1840s, there was still considerable agricultural distress, and Ireland continued to be a problem. The forces in Parliament were so divided that when, in February 1851, Lord Russell's administration resigned, no one could be found to form a government to take over; and after a week Lord Russell's government returned to office. During this crisis Lord Russell stated that there were three issues that had placed his government in difficulties: free trade, demands for extension of the franchise, and the Ecclesiastical Titles Bill. Ruskin had something to say in 1851 on all these issues, but the last was the most important.

Catholic Emancipation was a live issue in 1851 because of what was seen as a highly provocative act performed by Pope Pius IX the previous year. In October 1850, the Pope had decided to establish an Episcopal hierarchy in England. This meant that there would be Roman Catholic dioceses in England; and since they would follow the same main geographical areas as the sees of the Church of England, the Roman Catholic bishops would have the same titles as the English bishops. Protestants in the established Church immediately detected a constitutional threat since the Roman Catholic bishops would be loyal, not to the Queen, but to Rome. Further provocation came from the new Roman Catholic Archbishop of Westminster, Cardinal Wiseman, who published a pastoral letter announcing that "Catholic England has been restored to its orbit in the Ecclesiastical firmament." On the enthronement of the Roman Catholic Bishop of Birmingham, Father Newman, a recent convert from the Church of England and thus perceived as a renegade who proved the dangers of High Church practice, preached a sermon that appeared to assert that the whole of England, and not just the Roman Catholics, were once more in the power of Rome.

The Pope's action became familiarly known as "The Papal Aggression," and Guy Fawkes night was celebrated with particular vehemence in 1850. Lord Russell's reply was to bring in the Ecclesiastical Titles Bill, which intended to make it illegal for the new Catholic bishops to use their titles; but the measure, introduced in February 1851 ran into considerable difficulties with both the Irish and Roman Catholic members of the House of Commons and the Peelite Tories (Peel had died in 1850), who were unhappy about details of the bill in relation to Catholic Emancipation. While the issue was still in balance, Disraeli brought in an anti-free-trade measure, which was only narrowly defeated; and when a radical reform measure was passed against the government's wishes, Lord Russell resigned—though, as we have seen, no one could be found to replace him. Following the advice of the Duke of Wellington, Russell returned to office on 3 March 1851, which, quite by coincidence, was the date of the publication of the first volume of *The Stones of Venice*.

It would be too much to expect this particular crisis to be referred to in *The Stones of Venice,* but three days later, on 6 March, Ruskin published his pamphlet, **"Notes on the Construction of Sheepfolds."** And there, in a footnote, we read that "an Oxford friend" had advised him against compromising himself with his blunt opinions.

I think we are most of us compromised to some extent already, when England has sent a Roman Catholic minister to the second city in Italy, and remains herself for a week without any government, because her chief men cannot agree upon the position which a Popish cardinal is to have leave to occupy in London.

I hope that it will now be becoming clear that there is a serious as well as a humorous intention in the title of this paper, for **"Notes on the Construction of Sheepfolds"** began life as an appendix to the first chapter of *The Stones of Venice*.

Ruskin makes this clear in his pamphlet, pointing to its origins in a passage on the suppression of the political power of the Venetian clergy. From there he goes on to attack the High Church or Tractarian movement in the Church of England and the fact that "infidels and Papists, gamblers and debtors" made up such a large proportion of the membership of the House of Commons. The sheepfold in question is the Church. The problem is what constitutes the Church—the priesthood alone, or priesthood and laity. Ruskin decides on the latter and concludes with a call for not just the Evangelical and High Church parties to unite, but also the English and Scottish Churches, in order to make a stand against the Papacy.

"Notes on the Construction of Sheepfolds" shows more than a lively interest in contemporary politics on Ruskin's part—so lively that he inserts a comment on a political crisis almost as soon as it has occurred. It helps to place Ruskin within a particular political tradition and, if we realize this, the political tradition has far-reaching implications for the interpretation of Ruskin's thought.

No one, of course, is surprised that Ruskin at this stage in his life should be anti-Catholic. To a strict and as yet unconverted Evangelical, the Pope was in league with the Devil. But if we look at the political as opposed to the strictly theological stance of Evangelicals such as Ruskin and his father—and indeed that of their favorite Evangelical preachers—then we will see that it was not simply blind prejudice, because hostility toward Catholicism was part of a coherent political philosophy.

When Sir Robert Peel broke the unity of the Tory party on the wheel of Corn Law repeal, this was the second, not the first, great betrayal of Tory principles. The first had been with the introduction of Catholic Emancipation and the Great Reform Act of 1832. Those most fiercely resistant to these changes, who were known to themselves and others as the Ultra-Tories, are the subject of a doctoral thesis for Oxford University by Dr. G. S. Simes, "The Ultra-Tories in British Politics 1824-1834," and I must acknowledge this work as a major source for the case I am about to make.

Popular ultra-right-wingers in British politics are commonly treated as something of a joke, presented by their enemies as diehard, elderly, reactionary, and irascible bigots. It is Dr. Simes's argument that in fact the Ultra-Tories constituted a vigorous parliamentary grouping with a coherent ideal of constitutional government and society, an ideal firmly based on religion and the Anglican Church. Support for the Anglican Church was central to the Ultra-

Tory view of society as a balance of forces: the democratic power of Parliament limiting and limited by the aristocracy; aristocracy and the enfranchised classes in turn limiting the power of the crown. The Anglican Church, unlike the Catholics, whose extranational allegiance to the Pope was a permanent threat to the royal prerogative, set the seal on this particular social contract. It was logical, therefore, that those who governed should be members of the national church, and only those. Thus it was not a question of "toleration" at all; there was no obligation to be an Anglican, but if one wished to participate in government, then he had to be a member of the only church that upheld it. We see this argument influencing the article by John James which Ruskin reprinted.

The Ultra-Tory ideal of a balance or harmony of forces extended to the economic and social fields. Both rested on the national virtue of sound agriculture, which led to protectionism, both positively as a guarantee of the landed interest and negatively, in doing down foreigners. The Liberal doctrine of free trade was anathema in that it encouraged divisive competition and weakened the state. In 1829 and 1830 *Blackwood's,* the leading Ultra-Tory journal, published a series of articles on "Political Economy" by David Robinson. In these he argued that England needed a managed economy designed to maintain the highest national income available for distribution among the classes, as opposed to an unmanaged one in which the national income was reduced by competition from foreigners and between the classes. Robinson attacked Ricardo and Malthus and criticized the degeneracy of the aristocracy. (Tories were particularly worried by the political consequences of the failings of the Anglo-Irish aristocracy.) He recommended education and high living standards as an antidote to social distress and advocated a policy of reclaiming wasteland and the encouragement of cottage gardens. If any of these proposals sound at all familiar to those interested in Ruskin's economic ideas, then note further that Robinson signed himself "One of the Old School."

Resistance to Liberal mammonism was part of a general social ideal that Dr. Simes has described as

existing English society rid of its more manifest imperfections. Their ideal was of an harmonious and unified society with a due subordination of ranks, and an equitable balance of economic interests. Diffusion of religious sentiment would keep each man in his place, and each class and interest from attacking his neighbour. Religion would persuade the poor to do their duty, and to leave the existing hierarchy unchallenged—it would also persuade the rich to perform their social duty towards the poor. Obligation to God would ensure that the hierarchical society was also a just society.

And, Dr. Simes says later, "Agriculture was the base upon which an idyllic society might be constructed." To readers of *Fors Clavigera,* I suggest that this program is very familiar indeed.

These are only general parallels between the Ultra-Tories and Ruskin's thought. There are, however, direct links. The Ultra-Tory party had not only a political philosophy;

it had political philosophers. I note especially the posthumous influence of Edmund Burke and the current influence of Ultra-Tory intellectuals, among whom Dr. Simes names William Wordsworth, Robert Southey, De Quincy, Coleridge (though with some reservations), and the historian Archibald Alison. These are names familiar to Ruskin scholars but not, perhaps, in an Ultra-Tory context.

The Ruskinian connection becomes even stronger when we consider the role played in the Ultra-Tory party by Evangelical divines, among them the Reverend Thomas Dale and the Reverend Henry Melvill, who were regular guests at the Ruskin dinner table. This is how James Grant describes the Reverend Melvill's sermons in his account of popular preachers in *The Metropolitan Pulpit*:

> Mr Melvill is not only a violent politician, but occasionally carries his politics into the pulpit. I have heard him deliver sermons in which there were passages of so ultra-political a character, that had a stranger been conducted blindfolded into the place in which he was preaching, and it had been a time when Parliament was sitting, he would have been in danger of mistaking the sermon of the reverend gentleman for a speech of the Earl of Winchelsea in the Lords, or of Sir Robert Inglis in the Commons.

These two gentlemen were, respectively, leading Ultra-Tories in the 1850s in the Upper and Lower Houses.

Finally, a third Evangelical and Ultra-Tory preacher, Dr. George Croly, had an even closer connection with the Ruskin household, besides dining regularly with the Ruskins. His daughter, Helen-Louisa-Mary Croly was John Ruskin's godchild.

What, then, has the Ultra-Tory tradition to do with the construction of *The Stones of Venice?* I believe that it has great significance for the interpretation of all three volumes; but before I suggest some applications, we must consider one further source of Ultra-Tory influence on Ruskin—that "violent Tory of the old school," his father, John James.

In a sense John James's influence on *The Stones of Venice* was so close that he actually wrote some of it for his son— the passage in Appendix 5 referred to earlier. But that is only a type, one might say, for the editorial control he exercised.

We are able to follow the construction of *The Stones of Venice,* at least as far as the second and third volumes are concerned, through the correspondence between father and son. One side of the letters has been edited and published by John Lewis Bradley as *Ruskin's Letters from Venice: 1851-1852*; that is to say, they cover Ruskin's second long stay in Venice after the publication of Volume I, when he was drafting the chapters of the following volumes. Unfortunately, when Professor Bradley's edition was published in 1955, John James's letters in reply were not available to him. They did, however, exist and are available now, being part of the collection of the Bembridge Education Trust, Bembridge School; and I am very grateful to the Ruskin Gallery's curator, James Dearden, for allowing me to consult the manuscripts. It is greatly

to be regretted that Distinguished Professor Van Akin Burd's masterly editing of the Ruskin family correspondence has not yet reached the Venetian letters of 1851-1852.

The John James side of the correspondence is vital because it enables us to see the pressure John James was putting on his son. And lest there be any doubts about the tenor of John James's views, this is his response to Napoleon III's coup d'état at the end of 1851:

> Pretty work in Paris—a Kingdom to be scrambled for or played for or battled for—I have a taste for Despotism & see no way in which a Country torn into fragments—can be again united but under an Iron Despotism—but civil War is feared—I am so partial to Despotism that I am tired of Radicals Socialists & Communists & mobs & equality & fraternity private liberty I find may be enjoyed & very delightfully a la John Lewis at Grand Cairo

—a reference, I presume, to the painter John Lewis's portrayal of the sultans of Cairo.

The first of Ruskin's two winters in Venice, that of 1849-1850, had been spent in historical and topographical research, a process that can be followed in Ruskin's MS notebooks (again, these form part of the collection of the Bembridge Education Trust). The text of the first volume of *The Stones of Venice* was subsequently written on his return to London. During the second winter visit, in 1850-1851, Ruskin was actually writing sections of Volumes II and III and sending them back to his father for comment, usually in the form of fair copies by his servant "George," John Hobbs. Thus we can trace the process of composition of the key passages of *The Stones of Venice*—for Ruskin did not write them in sequence—in his daily and sometimes twice-daily letters to John James.

Two factors dominate John James's view of the material he was receiving: his obsession with getting *The Stones of Venice* completed so that his son would in turn at last complete *Modern Painters* (then scheduled as three volumes); and the fact that in contrast to the wild success of *Modern Painters* I and II, the first volume of *The Stones of Venice* (1851) and the accompanying edition of large plates available through subscription, *Examples of the Architecture of Venice,* were not selling. Nor, for that matter, did he like his son dissipating his energies in pamphlets like **"Pre-Raphaelitism,"** which had appeared just after he went back to Venice in the autumn of 1851. The first volume of *The Stones of Venice* is, after the first two chapters, a dry and theoretical work. George Smith, its publisher, backed John James in wanting something richer. Here is the father's response to receiving material for the chapter on Murano:

> The fact is I was in the act of reading *Seven Lamps* to Mama every morning which is a magnificent Book—eloquent from first word to last—now in your yet received portion of 2nd Vol. Stones you have a vast deal of plain matter of fact & very minute details to give—as I have past [sic] the age of Enthusiasm & I know too little of Architecture to enter into the technicalities—& do not see what however the end will

certainly show—how every little thing is a link in a long & important chain the Reading is as compared with your M.P. & *Seven Lamps*—a little tedious & heavy & in some parts reads as if after Dickens—whom you are generally so much above & before—I judge as a mere general Reader seeking Delight & Entertainment[.]

Later in the letter he tries to reassure his son that he "shall no doubt change my Opinion when you come to the Eloquent passages—when you, in fact, retire from Business & get to sea or up in the clouds." That was a letter of 6-7 January 1852; on 11 February things are no better.

> You can only be an author of the present day by studying public taste—& for the future by writing what is durable—publishers Know—Smith says the public expected a more pictorial Illust[rated] Book—full pictures—not fragments—then as to Books no technical works are popular or sell—*Modern Painters* is the selling Book—the fairy Tale will continue—The pamphlets Smith considers done with—*The Seven Lamps* sells slowly being Technical—but surely—*The Stones of Venice* being more so goes very slowly & you must not expect 2nd Volume to sell (he says) unless it is a Book like the 2 first Chapters in Vol 1st—a Book continued in that stile [sic] would go like Wildfire.

The first casualty of this editorial policy was the *Examples of the Architecture of Venice,* which was abandoned after completion of only three of the twelve projected issues. At one point John James calculated that he would lose £1,200 on the publication. Needless to say, he was paying Smith and Elder for publishing *The Stones of Venice,* so his editorial interest had a certain edge. His son did not protest a great deal at the project's cessation. Another victim was what was planned as a long chapter on funeral monuments, only portions of which were eventually used. It was in vain for John to protest to his father:

> You know I promised them no Romance—I promised them Stones. Not even Bread. I do not feel any Romance in Venice. It is simply a heap of ruins, trodden under foot by such men as Ezekiel describes 21, 31: and this is the great fact which I want to teach: to give Turneresque descriptions of the thing would not have needed ten day's study—or residence.

John James would press on with his policy of getting what he called "the Spirit of too minute Antiquarian discussion" out of the main text and into the notes:

> I am interested in Foscari Tomb Huge Curtains & very generally interesting I speak as one of the public—all your figures & small minute grave Business details we, the public pass over and desire greatly to have in small print & note,—I have however taken no opinion—shown none to publishers[.]

The effect of this editorial policy was to produce not one, but two versions of *The Stones of Venice*—Ruskin's and his father's, which exist uncomfortably side by side within the same covers. At one moment Ruskin's spirit of antiquarianism is counting capitals and measuring volutes; at the next he is dutifully producing a purple passage. Hence

the use of appendices in all three volumes and the existence of the Venetian Index, which acts as a repository for undigested material.

I do not wish to exaggerate this point (John James may even have been right). The very first piece that Ruskin sent back was the description of the journey through the alleys of Venice to St. Mark's, and this delighted his father—but even here there is evidence of censorship.

> These St Mark pieces are very lovely & as poetical as Broken Chain—The finer objects marvellously described & the truth as marvellous tho from my sympathies held only by the Beautiful or sublime in nature, or the noble things of human nature—or among the low only by humour—I cannot enjoy the truth or rather the very truth of your description deprives me of pleasure by making me actually see what I so heartily feel to be decidedly unpleasant—from the Jars of pickles all the way past Vinegar Cruets—stale apple Fritters—sausages—crumbs etc distresses me—yet I see that you put them as foils—I cannot help my fastidious taste & feelings[.]

Search the published text of the chapter on St. Mark's and you will find no jars of pickles or stale apple fritters.

The manuscript, however, is more revealing. The section in question is written in Ruskin's hand on four sheets of paper which have been cut and then stuck together with sealing wax in a primitive paste-up for the printer, who used the result as the setting copy for the final text. The printed text reads:

> Here, at the fruiterer's, where the dark-green watermelons are heaped upon the counter like cannon balls, the Madonna has a tabernacle of fresh laurel leaves; but the pewterer next door has let his lamp out, and there is nothing to be seen in his shop but the dull gleam of the studded patterns on the copper pans, hanging from his roof in the darkness. Next comes a "Vendita Frittole e Liquori," where the Virgin, enthroned in a very humble manner beside a tallow candle on a back shelf, presides over certain ambrosial morsels of a nature too ambiguous to be defined or enumerated. But a few steps farther on, at the regular wine-shop of the calle, where we are offered "Vino Nostrani a Soldi 28.32," the Madonna is in great glory, enthroned above ten or a dozen large red casks of three-year-old vintage, and flanked by goodly ranks of bottles of Maraschino, and two crimson lamps.

Compare this with the original manuscript. I have used [parentheses "("] to indicate passages crossed out, and rows of dots to suggest the joins in the separate sheets of paper.

> the dark green water melons are heaped upon the counter like cannonballs, the madonna has a tabernacle of (some) fresh laurel leaves, (on each side of her frame: and some jars of pickles to support her on each side)—but the pewterer next door has let his lamp out—and there is nothing to be seen in his shop but the dull gleam of the studded patterns of the copper pans, hang-

ing from his roof in the darkness: Next comes a "Vendita Frittole e liquori"; (and of many other things besides)—where the Virgin—enthroned in a very humble manner beside a tallow candle on a back shelf—presides over Frittole—crumbs (of everything very ambiguous nature) of nature too ambiguous to be defined or enumerated.

. . . . .

pepperbox—some lucifer matches—some sausages and a few (and various) strings of onions hung up against the wall—a portable furnace choked with ashes, on a table under the onions—and finally a series of vials and bottles of (various) indescribable shades of yellow and green looking like a number of disbanded vinegar cruets. [All the above passage to the dotted line was obscured by the bottom of the previous sheet.]

But a few steps farther on: however at the regular wineshop of the calle, where we (may have) are offered Vino Nostrani a Soldi 28.32 the Madonna is in great glory; (presiding over) enthroned above ten or a dozen large red casks of three year old vintage, and flanked by a

. . . . .

In other words, the jars of pickles and vinegar cruets have been crossed out and the stale apple fritters cut away entirely; striking, but to John James offensive, images have been reduced to the phrase "certain ambrosial morsels of a nature too ambiguous to be defined or enumerated," which is written in over the top.

This is just one example of John James's editorial control of the text, and there are other passages with comments by John James in pencil in the margin and with strikings-out in the text. Some of these Ruskin obeyed; others he ignored. An example of John James's censorial, as opposed to merely textual, influence is the occasion in 1852 when Ruskin, stirred by political events at home, wrote three letters to *The Times,* on representation, taxation, and education. As is well known, Ruskin submitted them to his father first, and his father decided that they should not be published.

John James's letters to his son explaining the reasons for this censorship give a full picture of his political views and comment on the political figures of the day. John James disapproved of his son's remarks about Disraeli and his son's advocacy of higher income tax, but in one area there was surprising agreement between father and son. Ruskin's liberal belief in the virtues of free trade might be taken as an example of Ruskin's independence from his father. Quite the contrary, for it appears that John James was not totally orthodox in his Tory principles either. In a letter of 22 March 1852, he writes, "Though a moderate Free Trader and anti-Corn Law man—as I dislike the Whigs & have all whom I respect in the present Ministry [at the moment a Tory one]—it would throw me into a nervous fever to see my name to anything Whiggish and radical." Although in sympathy with the free traders, John James believed that his sherry business would be hurt if such controversial documents as these letters should appear in *The Times* above the name Ruskin. Al-

ready, he writes in the same letter, he has lost clients in Ireland because of his and his son's anti-Catholic views.

However, just as material from Appendix 12 of Volume I was extruded to become **"Notes on the Construction of Sheepfolds,"** so a little of these letters appears to have squeezed its way into Appendix 7 of Volume III, the appendix on "Modern Education." Nor should we be surprised, for John James approved of his son's ideas on education and suggested that they should be used in an appendix to *The Stones of Venice*.

Having glanced at these two examples of John James's close editorial influence, we must move on to consider how the particular political philosophy I have described may be said to have influenced *The Stones of Venice,* in particular the second and third volumes, published in 1853, when the Ecclesiastical Titles Bill had become law (though in fact so modified as to become a dead letter) and the immediate controversy over the "Papal Aggression" had subsided.

Pursuing the policy of staying alert to contemporary references, we shall note the sudden, startling, and effective description of contemporary Venice which appears in the chapter on the cathedral of St. Mark's. There, a military band of the occupying Austrian army is playing on the piazza, obscuring, as it were, the religious message of the architectural Bible of St. Mark's:

> The march drowning the miserere, and the sullen crowd thickening round them,—a crowd, which, if it had its will, would stilletto every soldier that pipes to it. And in the recesses of the porches, all day long, knots of men of the lowest classes, unemployed and listless, lie basking in the sun like lizards.

Here is a contemporary reference if ever there was one. Effie Ruskin's letters from Venice record a number of stabbings along dark canals. However, although Ruskin complains that he cannot examine the twenty-fourth pillar of the Ducal Palace because it is "encumbered by the railing which surrounds the two guns set before the Austrian guard-house," these references, though reminding us of Ruskin's awareness of current events, may be less important in themselves than for the part they play in the structure of the St. Mark's chapter. At this stage Ruskin approved of the Austrian occupation, and he and especially Effie moved in high garrison society. Both were highly embarrassed by the activities of the Hungarian radical Kossuth, who made a visit to Britain in 1851 while they were in Venice. Kossuth was rapturously received by the British radicals, much to the fury of John James as we can see from his letters. Napoleon III's *coup d'état* was the only bright news to offer any consolation to father and son.

The Venetian crowd, so powerfully described, has a different function. The chapter is built around contrasts, between a quiet, empty, ordered but rather grim English cathedral close, and the noise and smells of the Calle Lungha San Moisé, between the Austrian band on the piazza and the quiet within St. Mark's. These contrasts use contemporary reference in a particular way in order to move continually between the locations and time scales of past and present—and *Past and Present* is precisely what I have in mind, for I suggest that the St. Mark's chapter is Ruskin's first exercise in Carlylese.

That Ruskin was beginning to take a serious interest in Carlyle's views—as opposed to the earlier opinion that they were "bombast"—is established by the direct reference to his phrase "human beavers" in the first volume of *The Stones of Venice*—an echo of either *Past and Present* or *Latter-Day Pamphlets;* there are references in Ruskin's manuscript diary of 1851 to *Latter-Day Pamphlets* and to *Sartor Resartus,* and interestingly, Ruskin refers to Carlyle's attitude to faith in one of the crucial letters describing his religious difficulties at Easter 1851.

The significance of Carlyle's thought for Ruskin has been most usefully analyzed in a D.Phil. thesis for Oxford University by Nicholas Shrimpton. Dr. Shrimpton describes the tradition of "critical medievalism" which used the Middle Ages as an ideal to be favorably contrasted with the present day, and he mentions in particular two books that preceded what must be considered the high points of this tradition—Ruskin's own *Seven Lamps of Architecture* and *Stones of Venice*. The first of these is Robert Southey's *Sir Thomas Moore: or, Colloquies on the Progress and Prospects of Society,* published in 1829. Ruskin knew the work well, and Southey we have already met as a Tory intellectual. The date 1829 is significant, for Southey argues against Catholic Emancipation. The second work is Carlyle's *Past and Present* of 1843; add to this the deliberately topical note of Carlyle's *Latter-Day Pamphlets* of 1850, and I suggest we have found another reason for the particular voice of the second and third volumes of *The Stones of Venice*.

I am arguing here for more than a stylistic influence from Carlyle on the construction of *The Stones of Venice*. Carlyle might not be classed as an orthodox Ultra-Tory, but we can see a parallel system of ideas. Carlyle was anti-Catholic and he was antidemocratic, but he was also deeply concerned about the condition of the masses, attributing their misery both to the failure of a true aristocracy to emerge and to the activities of Liberal economists who encouraged reliance on the cash nexus as the sole moral authority.

And the one thing that can be said with certainty about both Carlyle and the Ultra-Tories is that they were not by any stretch of the imagination socialists—which brings us to the nature of "The Nature of Gothic."

There is a myth about Ruskin's attitude to the worker as expressed in his chapter on the nature of Gothic, a myth which began when Dr. Furnivall reprinted the chapter in 1854 as a pamphlet for the Working Men's College, which was encouraged by William Morris when he reprinted the pamphlet for the Kelmscott Press in 1892 and which has flourished mightily in recent years. It is a myth stimulated by works such as one published in 1976 which makes great play with a comparison between Ruskin and Karl Marx—I refer to my own *John Ruskin: The Argument of the Eye*. James Sherburne in *The Ambiguities of Abundance* has also noted the similarities between Ruskin and Marx and, if something may be said in mitigation, I do at

least say that Ruskin was a conservative, and I do not go so far as Dr. Sherburne, who says that "the chapter is a liberal tract." Much as we would like to associate Ruskin's philosophy with the radical tendencies of our own times, it is nothing of the sort.

In all respects, the passage on the conditions of labor and their political consequences is in line with the Ultra-Tory social ideal as Dr. Simes has described it. The attack on the division of labor, which is an attack on Adam Smith in that it uses the same reference to pin making as in *The Wealth of Nations,* is exactly the criticism of the Liberal economists the Ultra-Tories were making. It was the Liberal system that had introduced division and competition where an organic interrelationship of classes should be. It was the Liberal system that had reduced the working man to the status of a slave. It was the Ultra-Tories who wanted each man to fulfill himself within an ordered and harmonized hierarchy in which the ruling classes earned their position by justly caring for the interests of those below them, and the lower classes rewarded their rulers for the care they showed by giving them loyalty and respect. This is the contemporary reference of "The Nature of Gothic":

> Never had the upper classes so much sympathy with the lower, or charity for them, as they have at this day, and yet never were they so much hated by them: for, of old, the separation between the noble and the poor was merely a wall built by law; now it is a veritable difference in level of standing, a precipice between upper and lower grounds in the field of humanity, and there is pestilential air at the bottom of it. I know not if a day is ever to come when the nature of right freedom will be understood, and when men will see that to obey another man, to labour for him, yield reverence to him or to his place, is not slavery. It is often the best kind of liberty,—liberty from care.

And the way this "right freedom" would be taught would be through the education of the worker and the return of the social system to an ordered hierarchy based on agriculture and craft—the sort of society the Guild of St. George was intended to be.

There may be something unfashionable about presenting Ruskin as the product of a dying and reactionary philosophy rather than as the precursor of a new and revolutionary one, but if we understand that the main thrust of Ruskin's argument is coming not from the Left but the Right and that the warning contained in the first paragraph of *The Stones of Venice* is that England must return to former (and much idealized) ways, then a great deal of Ruskin's later writings, especially on economic matters, falls into place. Indeed, the later writings show Ruskin to have been even more coherent and consistent than recent writings have tried to show, for there is no shift from art criticism to social criticism. It was all part of the same philosophical drive.

Finally, we must conclude that when Ruskin began his autobiography with the words, "I am, and my father was before me, a violent Tory of the old school," he was not, as I have mistakenly written in *The Argument of the Eye,* joking; he meant exactly what he said.

Francis G. Townsend   (essay date 1982)

SOURCE: "On Reading John Ruskin," in *The Victorian Experience: The Prose Writers,* edited by Richard A. Levine, Ohio University Press, 1982, pp. 150-73.

[*In the following essay, Townsend discusses the inspiration for and logical inconsistencies in Ruskin's work, particularly* Time and Tide.]

I first made the acquaintance of John Ruskin in January, 1946, about a month after I had been honorably discharged from the United States Marine Corps. Ruth and I had chosen Ohio State because we had heard of its general strength in nineteenth-century literature. On the first day of class at my new institution, I found myself in a Victorian seminar conducted by one Charles Frederick Harrold, who was a stranger to me. The first day he gave a long lecture, in which he outlined all of Victorian literature, and told the five of us that from then on we would read books and report to one another in class.

Inspired by the tremendous knowledge of Professor Harrold, I went home to our basement apartment in downtown Columbus, a block from the Public Library, and that afternoon checked out a book by one of the writers Harrold had mentioned, Thomas Carlyle. It was a book called *Sartor Resartus,* which I had heard of. That night I read it, and the next day in the seminar Harrold asked what books we had been reading. I spoke up and said I had read *Sartor Resartus* the night before, so he asked me to report on it. I held forth for an hour on the subject with the help of occasional questions from Harrold. At the end he asked what edition I had used. With sublime ignorance I said it was some old text, dated about 1905, and edited by no one in particular. Harrold assimilated this information, said I had made a good report, and neither of us ever talked about the incident again.

In that first week another student, Jack Heidi, began reporting on the life and work of John Ruskin, who was connected in some way with Cook and Wedderburn. I was mildly interested and since I had decided to sample his works anyway, I went to the library and checked out the first Ruskin book which was handy, an odd collection of twenty-five letters to a working man, entitled *Time and Tide*. It was one of the wildest, most undisciplined books I had ever read, and yet it was this first reading that led to my lifelong connection with Ruskin.

On this first acquaintance with Ruskin I was not nearly so impressed by him as a writer as I was by the others we were studying in Harrold's seminar. Arnold was far more artistic; *Culture and Anarchy,* on first reading, seemed far superior to anything Ruskin ever managed. Newman's prose was far more sensitive, and Carlyle, initially at least, was more stimulating, but my fascination with Ruskin grew. As a prose stylist he was an unparalleled virtuoso. He had a magnificent power to go straight to the heart of the issue, unrivalled, as I believe now, by any nineteenth-century critic, and an incredible way of losing the train of his own argument and descending from the sublime to the ridiculous from one page to the next. Even his folly was fascinating.

Why did this strange, sometimes deranged, writer make such an impression on me in January, 1946? I had been born during World War I, had been a child during the Roaring Twenties, and had grown to manhood in the Great Depression. By rights I should have been a member of the Democratic party, like nearly everyone around me, because from 1929 to 1939 no one in my family managed to hold any job for more than about two years. We survived in the way of the poor, circa 1933, by pooling the resources of two or more interrelated families, two or three members of which might be working at any one time. We were never quite sure of who owed what to whom. Now in those ten years, to the best of my recollection, the total amount of financial aid my family got from the government was ridiculously small, perhaps as much as four hundred dollars. It was fairly clear, however, that the adherents of the Pendergast machine in Missouri were feeling little pain.

When I emerged from World War II, my faithful Penelope and I were plunged into the most striking of the postwar anomalies, which we found no one was particularly interested in, except the GIs who were working for college degrees in cities like Columbus, Ohio. The people who had not been called up for service during the preceding years had lived in rent-controlled apartments; the veterans returning from places like the South Pacific, flush with cash saved during the years spent on islands where spending was impossible, descended by the thousands on Columbus and tried to find places to live. The landlord who owned a rent-controlled apartment could do nothing, unless he also owned a dilapidated building, in which case he could slap a coat of paint on the outside, tack up a plywood partition or two on the inside, install a second-hand privy and stove, and charge whatever he pleased, because according to the rationale he was bringing new rental units into the market.

Thus in the winter and spring of 1946, graduate students at Ohio State faced the economic problem of A and B: if you went into A's apartment and it was clean and nicely furnished, with French doors between the parlor and the dining areas, a foyer, and a tiled bathroom with tub, sink, and stool, you could safely estimate the rent at $35.00 a month; if you went into B's apartment and found a dirtencrusted floor, wallpaper hanging from the walls, water stains on the ceiling, and a bath on the next floor up, you were reasonably sure the rent was between $45.00 and $65.00 a month, depending on the benevolence of the landlord. The reason was rent control. It was infuriating to spend money on high rent and find other people with far better quarters for a fraction of the rent, simply because they had been there the preceding two or three years while you had been otherwise occupied. The explanation, of course, was that you had to look out for the poor people: if you took off rent controls, their rents might go up. To be sure, the rents had gone up, right through the ceiling, but that was beside the point, whatever the point was—to help the poor, I suppose, as rent controls preserved the good life in the South Bronx and Manhattan.

Here was a case of flagrant, palpable injustice which anyone could see. All that was needed was a pair of eyes. No intelligence was required, nor any subtle analysis, only a pair of eyes, yet people did not see it. I did not know what to call this perversity, but the advancement of knowledge has given us blessed folk of the late twentieth century a word for it. My friends had perceptions; they knew what they wanted to see and were expected to see, and they saw it. If I pointed out the obvious inequities involved, they answered, "But we can't have increases in rent!" They simply could not see that there had already been monumental increases, even when the fact was right before their eyes.

The rest of the price controls imposed by the government during World War II were equally well intentioned and led to equally anomalous ends. Just before the war I had worked for the F. W. Woolworth Company as an assistant manager. In those days Woolworth stocked nearly everything that could be sold for a dollar or less, and in 1940 almost everything in the American home except fixtures and furnishings could be acquired for that price, from hardware, dry goods, bathroom sundries, and assorted picture frames (each with a glossy photo of a movie star), to Hershey's Arcadia (ten-pound slabs of milk chocolate broken into fragments before your eyes with a wooden mallet and a chisel, and sold at twenty cents a pound). Few archeologists of the future will know the size and shape of a ruby iridescent cuspidor in 1940, much less the price, but in addition to those bits of information I also knew the cost and selling prices of more than ten thousand items of daily use in the United States, if you count sizes and colors separately.

In the South Pacific, 1943-1945, I read the overseas edition of *Time* and followed with interest the debate over the effect of price controls. The pundits of the left pointed with pride to the government statistics, showing how well the line had been held: the pundits of the right viewed with alarm governmental interference with freedom of the marketplace. In June, 1945, I came back from overseas and took the first opportunity to wander down the aisles of a nearby Woolworth store and check retail prices. What had happened was obvious. A sizable number of the best-selling items had disappeared; in some cases there was a substitution, almost the same but modified ever so slightly and priced about fifty per cent more, a price which represented, one supposes, the value of the new brand name. The facade of price control concealed an inflation of roughly fifty per cent.

But my friends, who were nearly all good liberals of the New Deal variety, had all arrived independently at identical conclusions. They knew that price controls were good for the poor and they did not want to be bothered by evidence, which always confuses the issue. Between rent controls and price controls I lost respect for the liberal Establishment. Since I had already been disillusioned with the business mentality—after all, I was a child of the Great Depression—I was neither left nor right, and then I read *Time and Tide*.

These twenty-five letters addressed to Thomas Dixon struck my mood in the winter of 1946. Things that I was to read shortly thereafter confirmed me in my esteem for Ruskin. "For, indeed, I am myself a communist of the old school—reddest of the red;" and a little later, "I am, and

my father was before me, a violent Tory of the old school;—Walter Scott's school, that is to say, and Homer's." Here, in John Ruskin, was the exemplar of Wordsworth's "eye that cannot choose but see." He was impervious to the weight of opinion, informed or otherwise, in the society around him. He was not a reed shaken by the wind. Neither the intellectual world nor professional opinion nor social prejudice could move him. He was impervious to the demands of fashion; he refused to be, in one of his marvelous phrases, a respectable architectural man-milliner. Matthew Arnold warned us of the difficulty of thinking for ourselves when everyone around us is talking like a steam engine, but Arnold was not immune to this particular disease. Ruskin could see, and he could not turn away from his vision. This fidelity to the evidence of the eye, this devotion to the obvious has, in recent times, been one of the marks of distinction that have established Ruskin's continuing value as a writer of critical prose.

It is fascinating to watch him in action. As an illustration of why Ruskin is so provocative, why it is easy to refute him, and why in the long run he defies refutation, consider his letter to the *Daily Telegraph*, Christmas Eve, 1868, in which he poses a problem. Citizen A of Town X takes a train to Y to take business away from Citizen B, while at the same time Citizen B of Town Y takes a train to Town X to take business away from Citizen A. Is the national wealth increased thereby? Of course any economist can justify the activity with talk about diversifying products, establishing prices in the marketplace, the mechanics of distribution, and so forth. Ruskin was not so naive about such matters as he sometimes liked to pretend; he knew the conventional arguments. But after all the arguments have been made, there is still a question to be answered. Does it really make sense? To which, in a world of essences and absolutes, the only conceivable answer is no.

The trouble is, Ruskin was living in Victorian England and his foes were Gradgrind and McChoakumchild who lived in a different kind of world, or perhaps the same world with a different set of absolutes. And in 1946 the trouble with me was that I had no idea whatsoever of the kind of economist Ruskin was fighting against, and my only guide was R. H. Wilenski, who knew Marx and Keynes, presumably, but almost nothing about the economic orthodoxy of 1860. I was in the same position as an English graduate student in 1980 who brings to reading **Unto This Last** and **Munera Pulveris** all the rich background of an elementary Economics course, or even less.

Such a student faces the same kind of problem reading Milton on the subject of archangels, if, like most graduate students nowadays, she has scant faith in archangels, but she can avoid serious difficulty by thinking of Raphael in Eden as a charming Cupid come to dinner at Dido's court. Since she believes in neither Cupid nor Raphael, she can accept both as pleasant fictions. She faces a similar problem with a novelist like Hardy, whose handling of moral issues is as questionable today as it ever was, but Hardy was using a genre which, to employ Newman's phrase, does not run immediately into argument. Critical prose does just that: it is a literature of confrontation. There is little mediation between the writer's mind and the reader's; in fact, the more nearly perfect the prose, the sharper the clash. When a Victorian critic like Ruskin confronts issues which are within the province of a modern social science, the immediate reaction of a modern student is to discount everything he says, thus reducing Ruskin's possible literary significance to a bag of rhetorical devices. Why bother with somebody who is out of date?

I sought to answer the question by accepting Wilenski's estimate of Ruskin as an economist, namely that he had made important contributions to modern thought on the subject; thus the substance of what he said would have permanent value, at least as a historical document. Very early in my study of Ruskin, therefore, I found it necessary to read Adam Smith, David Ricardo, Parson Thomas Malthus, John Stuart Mill, and lesser lights like Henry Fawcett. Certainly Ruskin was unjust to them; I would agree with John T. Fain that at times Ruskin deliberately misrepresented them. Even more damaging to my opinion of his importance was my dawning realization that to any historian of economic thought it is fairly obvious that the men he opposed contributed to the advancement of the science, and he did not.

Yet, paradoxically, it is they who have gone out of style, and not Ruskin. He was not writing about Economics as they understood the term: he was establishing the limits of Economics as a science. As he said in **Munera Pulveris,** "Political Economy is neither an art nor a science; but a system of conduct and legislature, founded on the sciences, directing the arts, and impossible, except under certain conditions of moral culture."

In my opinion, there is a single idea which undergirds everything he wrote on the subject. In any society, given a certain amount of money, people will always spend it one way or another. The problem is that the choices men make when they do spend will determine the quality of the society. There is no way an economy can avoid making moral choices, for instance, whether to produce grapes or grapeshot, to use one of Ruskin's examples. In the case of a building, to have or have not is a relatively simple question to answer. But when we have it, will it be a monstrosity, like a false Gothic ("send down a gross of angels from Kensington") in the nineteenth century, or, in the twentieth, a childish arrangement of steel and glass blocks signifying nothing? Ultimately the decision of the capitalist or the commissar is of little moment compared with the decision of the Beaux Arts Committee. In Ruskin there is a deadly insistence on pursuing every issue back to its roots in Western culture. Sin resides in the will, in the free choice between opposed courses. Mores, the manners and the customs of the nation, are the record of its past choices. Taste is the only morality.

Yet as I reread **Time and Tide** more than thirty years later, I wonder how my interest survived the perplexity anyone would feel on first looking into Ruskin. Of the "twenty-five letters addressed to a working man of Sunderland on the laws of work," the first three are on the subject. The fourth letter, however, expresses his reaction to the national budget and its relative expenditures on the arts and on preparations for war, a slight digression, perhaps, except that it is followed by a fifth letter, in which he tells

about the pantomime at Covent Garden, *Ali Baba and the Forty Thieves.*

> The forty thieves were girls. The forty thieves had forty companions, who were girls. The forty thieves and their forty companions were in some way mixed up with about four hundred and forty fairies, who were girls. There was an Oxford and Cambridge boat-race, in which the Oxford and Cambridge men were girls. There was a transformation scene, with a forest, in which the flowers were girls, and a chandelier, in which the lamps were girls, and a great rainbow which was all of girls.

In all this nonsense Ruskin found only one saving grace. Mr. W. H. Payne and Mr. Frederick Payne came on stage costumed as the fore and hind parts of a donkey, and performed a pleasant little dance with an innocent little girl of eight or nine, who danced with a natural ease and charm which put the rest of the show to shame. In all the audience only Ruskin applauded.

> Presently, after this, came on the forty thieves, who, as I told you, were girls; and, there being no thieving to be presently done, and time hanging heavy on their hands, arms, and legs, the forty-thief girls proceeded to light forty cigars. Whereupon the British public gave them a round of applause. Whereupon I fell a thinking; and saw little more of the piece, except as an ugly and disturbing dream.

Indeed disturbing, but now certainly Ruskin will pick up the thread of his argument. Unfortunately the sixth letter is about the Japanese jugglers whom Ruskin had paid to see on Thursday night, just before the Friday night when he saw the pantomime *Ali Baba.* The Japanese jugglers explode into a dithyramb on such disparate themes as Balzac's *Contes Drôlatiques,* the illustrations of M. Gustave Doré, Evangelicals and the Bible with animadversions on the authorship thereof, the function of dancing in Exodus, Judges, and Jeremiah, together with the Cancan in the Paris of Napoleon III, and lastly, Satanism in the nineteenth century, this in Letter XI, curiously entitled "The Golden Bough."

It was absurd, and I loved it, but in those days we had to be orderly about these things, and so I accepted Wilenski's way of distinguishing between the Jekyll and Hyde in Ruskin. My aim was to make straight the ways of the lord in **Fors Clavigera** and elsewhere. Before I could get to that point, however, it was necessary to know something about **Modern Painters,** which seemed to have been his principal work before 1860.

Here in these five volumes the confusion was worse confounded, because to all outward appearance the book was thoroughly rational and organized down to the last detail, yet when I had finished the five volumes I did not know what they had said. Like a well-trained lad of the twentieth century I consulted the best commentary so that I would know what to think. The best at the time was Henry Ladd's *The Victorian Morality of Art* a systematic, orderly, rational analysis of the esthetics of a man who was none of these. A graduate student pricks up his ears when he comes upon the term imagination: he knows good fodder by instinct. Ruskin must have been writing about imagination; a sizable part of the second volume is devoted to an analysis of it. There are three forms of it—associative, penetrative, and contemplative, each with its own proper function. He also wrote about Truth and Beauty, exhaustively, to say the least. Ladd traced the ramifications of these terms in the British esthetics of the eighteenth and nineteenth centuries, and did it about as well as it could be done at the time. I tried without very much success to keep the terms separate in my mind, but I still could make no sense of the argument of *Modern Painters*.

In the meantime, however, my Penelope noticed a change in me. I had never cared particularly about the visible world around me, but now I observed the shapes of the clouds and their colors and the way a rain cloud drew a veil of mist across the Illinois prairie. I watched how the marigolds grew beside our beloved crackerbox house, and knew the thrill of catching the first hint of green as the grass broke the soil of what we fondly hoped would be a lovely lawn. In the darkness of a late October night, when a light rain was falling, we went out into the side yard and planted "our stick," a sycamore tree. Every day we made the grand tour of our estate and followed every change in the vegetation, as winter gave way to spring, and one year to the next. The last time we were in Champaign we went back; the sycamore shaded that side of the house.

After reading the first volume of *Modern Painters,* Charlotte Brontë said that Ruskin had given her a "new sense": ". . . this book seems to give me eyes." Nothing more profound has ever been said of him, not by Marcel Proust, not by Lord Kenneth Clark. Ruskin forces us to attend to the world outside ourselves. One who has the patience to read *Modern Painters* is never quite the same afterward; it is impossible to read even the first volume without seeing the world and J. M. W. Turner in a different light.

To learn to look on nature with a wise passiveness is no mean achievement, especially when there are so many quondam artists who explore nature as if they were on a scavenger hunt for usable symbols, a common occupation in the middle of our century. I remember a television drama with high aspirations, a life of Billy the Kid, in which Billy comes to the bailiwick of Pat Garrett, has a drink in the saloon, strides to the swinging doors, and peers into the west. "There's a red sun a'settin'," he says. Perhaps it is better to watch the sunset for its own sake. Too many artists are like Wordsworth's philosophers, who prize

> the transcendent universe
> No more than as a mirror that reflects
> The proud Self-love her own intelligence.

But to learn to look at art as Ruskin did is quite another matter. What he had to say about "The Old Shepherd's Chief Mourner" leaves one with mixed emotions, to put it mildly, with a smile certainly, with tears possibly, though not of grief but embarrassment. Yet even here there is something to be learned from Ruskin. In 1950 it was all too easy to dismiss a Victorian painter as an illustrator; who ever heard of putting a literary idea on canvas? Quattrocento and cinquecento painters to be sure, but in their best efforts we can descry an abstract design struggling to break the chains of representation and soar upward into the unsullied purity of contemporary art. Giotto, my masters? Murillo serves his need! As a critic Ruskin had no monopoly on the ridiculous. More recent critics have come to a saner estimate of him, namely, that he was often wrongheaded but seldom trivial.

Thirty years ago the problem with Ruskin was to find a way to read his works intelligently and thus to secure a sympathetic hearing for him. Even at the nadir of his reputation it was obvious to Victorian scholars that some knowledge of him was essential to an understanding of the age, and even a small acquaintance with him is an introduction to some of the finest passages in English prose, like the first half of "The Nature of Gothic," the comparison between Giorgione and Turner in *Modern Painters V,* the approach to St. Mark's in *The Stones of Venice II,* the brief analyses of Milton's "Lycidas" and of Byron's "The Prisoner of Chillon." He has not lacked for distinguished art critics and historians who know and respect his work, like Joan Evans and Lord Kenneth Clark, who began his television series on the Humanities with a quotation from Ruskin. Both concede, however, that despite his brilliant insights, and the marvelously acute observation of external fact on which those insights are based, his books will never again be widely read. The question is, can John Ruskin's books be read as anything more than aperçus? Can they be read as coherent essays?

Probably, for the common reader the answer is still no. But for a reader well versed in the nineteenth century that answer no longer holds true, at least for Ruskin's early work, down to 1860, or for his last book, his autobiography *Praeterita,* written in the lucid intervals of his madness, 1885-1889. The middle years, however, still present a problem. Fortunately, however, in the process of learning to read Ruskin's early work and his autobiography better than we could a generation ago, we may have learned a few things about how to study what he wrote in those middle years, 1860-1885.

The Sphinx riddle of the early works was the baffling existence of *Modern Painters,* a major critical essay of roughly the length of *War and Peace,* which set out in 1843 to prove a thesis, namely, that art and art education could be a potent force for the moral improvement of man, and thus of society. Seventeen years later, in 1860, in the fifth and final volume, after innumerable lengthy digressions and in spite of huge gaps in the argument, *Modern Painters* ended by asserting that art is a reflection of society and that the way to improve art is to reform society. Somewhere in the voyage the pilot had shifted course one hundred and eighty degrees.

Until about 1950 conventional criticism was quick to point out the inconsistencies, the lapses, the downright self-contradiction in *Modern Painters*. But it is not a conventional treatise, with an intellectual position neatly staked out, fertilized, and cultivated, ending with all the plants in neat little rows, and it cannot be read intelligently as such. Instead it must be read as the exploration of a proposition, to which in the end a negative answer is given. Once *Modern Painters* is seen, not as the defense of an intellectual position, but as the record of an intellectual process, criticism of its inconsistency seems irrelevant.

As for the gaps in the argument, the most obvious and the most important coincides with the gap between the second and third volumes. *Modern Painters I* was published in 1843, *Modern Painters II* in 1846, *Modern Painters III* not until 1856, after a ten-year interval. In 1846 Ruskin was still in the first flush of success, confident of his ability and his thesis. By 1856 he had known defeat, and he had radically altered his thesis, for reasons unexplained in the text of *Modern Painters,* but understandable when we know that he was doing between 1846 and 1856.

Seeking an answer to his main question—namely, whether or not the arts could be an effective instrument of moral improvement—he had turned to architecture, the most social of the arts because the most closely connected with the basic facts of human existence, and he had recorded his research in two architectural treatises, *The Seven Lamps of Architecture,* 1849, and *The Stones of Venice* in three volumes, the first in 1851 and the second and third in 1853. In them his original position was abandoned and his new position established. In a sense the two architectural treatises constitute a footnote to *Modern Painters,* the longest footnote in literary history, and absolutely indispensable to the reading of the main text, since the treatises are the turning point of the whole argument. These three books . . . should be read as a unit.

I suggested this reading of *Modern Painters* in 1951. Admittedly it was oversimplified and my use of evidence was highly selective, but it has served its purpose, most recently in Robert Hewison's *John Ruskin: The Argument of the Eye,* which pieces out my impoverished frieze, and adds a vizor and a term. It is now clear that Ruskin must be read with due regard for chronology. Listen to Jay Fellows, a scholar whose critical approach is psychological: "Although my instincts are to view a body of literature—Ruskin's more than most—in its 'collective aspect,' as if, removed from serial progression, it were alive, autonomous, all portions occurring simultaneously, I have attempted, though with few references to dates, to proceed with what I hope to be a tactful regard to sequence, beginning close to the beginning, ending at the end, . . ." He adopted this procedure because in Ruskin's case it becomes "perhaps necessary." The result was *The Failing Distance: The Autobiographical Impulse in John Ruskin,* the most controversial study of Ruskin in almost fifty years.

Some of Fellows' interpretations are questionable, but he does tell us much about Ruskin's autobiography. Since 1972 when James Olney wrote the first full-length, truly scholarly study of this genre, the idea that the autobiographic impulse lies near the source of creative activity has gained increasing acceptance, it seems to me. The experience of any human being is unique, in the absolute sense of that word, since an individual's precise genetic heritage and environmental experience are never duplicated. The urge to express oneself is almost universal: it is also impossible to satisfy. The best anyone can do is to create a metaphor acceptable as an expression of his/her life as it really was.

Fellows argues that in John Ruskin the autobiographical impulse was extraordinarily insistent almost from the beginning, for what reason is not clear. Fellows speculates that possibly Ruskin had a fear of introspection, a typically Victorian literary reaction to the excesses of Romantic subjectivism, or that possibly he suffered from a fear of his own emptiness, of the deep uncertainty which he compensated for by an ugly habit of dogmatic assertion. He was forever seeking a window with a view of vast distances, forever avoiding a mirror which would force him to confront himself. And just as he sought distance in space, so he sought remoteness in time, preferring the future and the past over the present. He could use his eyes, no one better, but close contact, touching, was perilous. Consider the startling clarity of two images he selected to express his childhood. In one image he is a child, seated behind a table in an alcove, reading and writing, looking out into the fullness of the drawing-room, observing the life of his parents—he has no life of his own, except for his eyes. In the other image he is a child, alone in a room, with nothing to occupy his mind but the pattern in the carpet, which he studies avidly. From what we know of the external facts of his life, he was not really that lonely, but from what we know of his inner life, his loneliness must have been terrifying. What emerges from these two images is the portrait of a child isolated from his kind, unable to find himself, acted upon, not acting, a voyeur of life, not a participant in it.

Hence the necessity to create a self. All through his life John Ruskin was writing his autobiography in various forms. At times it took the shape of his diaries and notebooks, addressed to a later self who would employ the observations in his research or, perchance, in an autobiography. This is an escape from the present to the future. At times it took the shape of a history of his own thought, disguised as an analysis of art, of economics, of cultural phenomena, or whatever came to hand. The most obvious is the history of the landscape feeling in *Modern Painters III,* in which he used his own experience as representative of the European mind. This is an escape from the present to the past.

And then as he goes through middle age the distance closes in on him, the future vanishes, and he is forced to live in the here and now. These are the years when his work reflects the tensions that tear him apart. There is no longer any escape, and in the collection of letters known as *Fors Clavigera* he must confront the oppressive evils in the foreground, immediately before his eyes, and finally, himself. He begins to compose fragments of an autobiography—loose, disjointed, like pieces of a puzzle. Then a man who had dominated his youth begins to fascinate him; the letters keep returning to this figure. Fitted together, these bits resemble an incomplete portrait of Sir Walter Scott. Were they experiments in the creation of an alter ego?

The confrontation ended in Ruskin's first mental breakdown. When he recovered enough to work, he had to be very careful to control what he called "his daily maddening rage," and in his last years of effective life he turned to the composition of *Praeterita,* but now he was no longer an old man indulging his emotions. He was an artist creating a character, a fictional person in the past, safely removed in distance and time. Cook and Wedderburn, Ruskin's editors, tried as a matter of policy to interpret *Praeterita* as the literal truth: it seems reasonably clear that the John Ruskin of *Praeterita* never existed. The real John Ruskin was not that lonely, nor was he that ineffectual. As Fellows says, *Praeterita* is a book by an old man about a young man whom he dislikes; it is more biography than autobiography.

Fellows' interpretation is highly speculative, but it has already borne fruit. Elizabeth Helsinger calls *Praeterita* "strangely self-destructive," and notes that it has no principles of inclusion. It is apparently formless, like the young protagonist, whom the old writer compares to a number of formless animals, a tadpole, for example, or an insect with a chrysalid stage, such as a caterpillar. In Helsinger's words: "*Praeterita* is hardly adequate as personal history or apology. It is an apparently perverse undertaking, almost a sabotage of the self."

Helsinger sees it as a rejection of conventional autobiography. In a conventional autobiography there is a progression along a definite track, with events given order and precedence by their part in the metamorphosis of the child into the man. Instead, in *Praeterita* there is a series of views, paintings if you wish, in which a place is summoned up with all of the attendant emotions associated with it during a lifetime. The surface arrangement is deceptively chronological, while the real arrangement is that of a portfolio of Turner engravings. The chapter headings are the titles of pictures, which are metaphors of Ruskin's existence.

Here, as in *Modern Painters,* the problem for the reader is that the composition is so massive that one has to move far away from the picture in order to see it. Close up it seems chaotic although beautiful in detail. There is a complicating factor: *Praeterita* is incomplete. The last paragraph, which is probably the most powerful paragraph that Ruskin ever wrote, is also his last moment of conscious life. What he intended to write is clear because we have his prospectus for the work, which was to consist of three volumes, each in turn consisting of twelve chapters. The last two chapters were to echo the opening two. The very last chapter was to be entitled "Calais Pier," where Ruskin first left the enclosure of his life in England and ventured into the world of Western civilization, or, seen in another irrational way, the place of embarkation for a journey into a new life. In the middle of the second volume, in the fifth, sixth, and seventh chapters, he wrote in his marvelously haphazard way about Geneva, and about Lucca, the Campo Santo in Pisa, and Florence, which those expert in such matters might mistake for the Protestant and Catholic centers of Western Europe.

There is more in Elizabeth Helsinger's article but that is enough to show its bent. To it I have added a few thoughts of my own about the "Calais Pier" and the Campo Santo, without, I hope, distorting it. Is it too fanciful? In 1969, eight years before Helsinger's article, Pierre Fontaney analyzed in detail one of the most famous purple passages in all of Ruskin's work, the description of the Rhone at Geneva, in that fifth chapter of the second volume of *Praeterita*.

> But the Rhone flows like one lambent jewel;
> its surface is nowhere, its ethereal self
> is everywhere, the iridescent rush and
> translucent strength of it blue to the
> shore, and radiant to the depth. . . .
> No wasting away of the fallen foam, no
> pause for gathering of power, no helpless
> ebb of discouraged recoil; but alike
> through bright day and lulling night, the
> never pausing-plunge, and never-fading
> flash, and never-hushing whisper, and,
> while the sun was up, the ever-answering
> glow of unearthly aquamarine, ultramarine,
> violet-blue, gentian-blue, peacock-blue,
> river-of-paradise blue, glass of a painted
> window melted in the sun, and the witch
> of the Alps flinging the spun tresses of
> it for ever from her snow.

Ruskin proceeds to infuse a spirit into the Rhone, as if the fluminal deities had returned, and the river is personified in a magnificent pathetic fallacy extended to almost inordinate length, which returns at last to the jewel simile with which the whole passage began, ". . . and the dear old decrepit town as safe in the embracing sweep of it as if it were set in a brooch of sapphire."

The passage is an example of his consummate mastery of prose style, but also of his characteristic failure to subordinate his rhetorical powers to the whole composition, or so it seems. Although the passage is brilliant, it is a digression. It has attracted the attention of Joan Evans, Lord Kenneth Clark, and John D. Rosenberg, none of whom, however, adequately accounts for its peculiar incandescence. Pierre Fontaney sets the passage in the whole context of Ruskin's description of the approach to Geneva, in this fifth chapter entitled "The Simplon." The features Ruskin chooses to describe "may be identified with a small number of archetypal motifs. These motifs recur under different forms, appearing first in a readily identifiable guise and then in a more cryptic fashion." The images have a personal significance; he uses them often in his works. Eventually, according to Fontaney, the motifs and the images converge.

Geneva is the city at the center of the world, with the mountain rising beyond it, the axis mundi. The old city is a paradise, a "bird's nest," a place of security. The path to it must have its ritual obstacle, so Ruskin does not follow the highroad across the moat—he takes the precarious suspension bridge which can accommodate only a few people at a time, the Bridge Perilous. And then, of course, there must be a trial before the hero can unlock the mystery. He must choose an article of jewelry which is what he really most desires. He goes to the shop of Mr. Bautte, the jeweler, passing through a "narrow arched door," a "secluded alley," a "monastic courtyard," ascending a "winding stair," and coming at last to a "green door." And now, having made his journey to the Underworld, he faces the moment of trial, presided over by a clerk, or "Ruling power," as Ruskin calls him. The hero makes his choice, steps outside, and before him lies the Rhone, like a jewel, its blue the color of the sky, the sea, the virgin, and the peacock; and the river dances "as if Perdita were looking on to learn." Shades of the underworld and Winnington!

Having analyzed the passage in detail, Fontaney pronounced it a subtle and complex set of variations on a few archetypal themes. Fontaney concluded, however:

> There is no doubt that Ruskin was not aware of the imaginative structure of these pages as I have reconstructed it, and that he did not know that his relaxed, rambling narrative ran in the time-honoured grooves of ancient motifs and myths.

In other words, Ruskin, of all people, did not know enough about mythology to have planned such an intricate effect in English prose. Who could have thought the old man had so much blood in him?

Ruskin happened to comment on this problematical passage in a letter to one of his female correspondents: ". . . I've written a nice little bit of *Praeterita* before I went out, trying to describe the Rhone at Geneva." His tone suggests that although he was pleased by his day's work, he did not take it seriously, so Fontaney may be right in arguing that the passage was unconscious, or then again he may be wrong, because Ruskin could be playful about such matters. Criticizing Ruskin is like playing with Montaigne's cat.

From these successful studies of Ruskin's early work and of his autobiography we have learned what traps to avoid and what strategies to pursue in reading the works of his middle years. There is a Ruskin who is deceptive because his organization is too massive to be readily comprehensible, a sort of macro-Ruskin. I have pointed out why it is hard to grasp the overall pattern of *Modern Painters* and *Praeterita*. To give another example, there is the matter of the epiphanies in *Praeterita*. Most autobiographies trace the development of a child into an important, powerful personality; and of course in such a book there is a place where a single incident unifies the protagonist's experience and gives it meaning and direction, like the epiphany vouchsafed a certain Irishman at the beach, in the persons of certain bathers sacred and profane. Helsinger points out that Ruskin describes in his letters and diaries no less than seven religious conversions, and in his autobiography he experiences eight moments of esthetic revelation: ". . . these passages span a period of seventeen years and refer to eight different occasions on which Ruskin says his 'true,' . . . 'best,' . . . or 'new' life began." For example, describing his first view of the Alps, 1833, he says:

> . . . I went down that evening from the garden-terrace at Schaffhausen with my destiny fixed in all of it that was to be sacred and useful. To that terrace, and the shore of the Lake of Geneva, my heart and faith return to this day, in every impulse that is yet nobly alive in them, and every thought that has in it help or peace.

For a second example, in 1835 at the Col de la Faucille, he received what he called the "confirming sequel" of his first view of the Alps.

> But the Col de la Faucille, on that day of 1835,

opened to me in distinct vision the Holy Land of my future work and true home in this world. My eyes had been opened, and my heart with them, to see and to possess royally such a kingdom!

For a third example, in May, 1842, at Norwood he discovered that if he drew ivy as he saw it, his drawing was better composed than if he had consciously worked at it. Later in 1842 at Fontainebleau, he drew an aspen tree outlined against a blue sky, and saw that the lines were composed "by finer laws than any known of men."

> The woods, which I had only looked on as wilderness, fulfilled I then saw, in their beauty, the same laws which guided the clouds, divided the light, and balanced the wave. "He hath made everything beautiful, in his time," became for me thenceforward the interpretation of the bond between the human mind and all visible things; and I returned along the wood-road feeling that it had led me far;—Farther than ever fancy had reached, or theodolite measured.

For a final example, on first visiting Lucca in 1845, he was overwhelmed by the tomb of Ilaria de Caretto.

> . . . here suddenly, in the sleeping Ilaria, was the perfectness of these, expressed with harmonies of line which I saw in an instant were under the same laws as the river wave, and the aspen branch, and the stars' rising and setting; but treated with a modesty and severity which read the laws of nature by the light of virtue.

To say the least, one epiphany is understandable, but eight seems careless of him, except that they stress the essential timelessness of his life, the failure of the young man to change and develop, and the way the old man scorned him for it. But then again, there is a logical sequence in these four examples, from the inanimate to the animate to the human, each order in turn submitting to the laws of nature, and owing its beauty to that submission. There is progress, just as there is in the amorphous animals to which Ruskin compared himself, from the tadpole to the frog, from the caterpillar to the butterfly; nevertheless through all its changes the animal retains its identity.

But just when we begin to expect patterns everywhere in Ruskin, we discover that there is another Ruskin who is highly deceptive because, like a wayward freshman, he cannot follow an outline but must continually deliver asides to his audience, a sort of micro-Ruskin. Jay Fellows points out that in Ruskin's middle years all tenses are condensed into one, where everything is present to his mind, and his prose becomes parenthetical. Parentheses appear within sentences, as sentences within paragraphs, as paragraphs within chapters. His passages become reflections of everything in his mind at the moment without regard to time or sequential logic. They are solipsistic, but then solipsism has not met with unmixed condemnation recently. And at times, just when we are forced to admit that a digression is a digression, we begin to notice that considered in isolation from its context it is superb. Lord Kenneth Clark observes that the apparent digressions in Ruskin should be read with special care.

Everyone who has studied Shakespeare for a number of years has had the experience of reading a play which on first acquaintance seems confusing, but which after repeated readings has a clear outline, marred by occasional digressions. Then one day we know in a flash the reason for a digression and its relation to the whole. We come to assume that in Shakespeare everything contributes to the total effect,—but wait; there is still Peter's scene with the musicians in *Romeo and Juliet,* and perhaps Borachio speaks for Shakespeare when he says, "I tell this tale vilely," as indeed he does. The experience of reading Ruskin has the same puzzling quality.

In addition to the marco-Ruskin and the micro-Ruskin there are other obstacles to the reading of Ruskin, but these are more easily set aside. It is a mistake to search for conformity between Ruskin and social science. Carlyle spoke derisively about determining moral issues by a count of heads; it would be a mistake to expect Ruskin to put much stock in behavioral criteria arrived at by questionnaires, any more than Moses or Mohammed would. His interests lay in other directions, where quantification goes galumphing into infinity. The money supply is not ultimately important: how people choose to spend the supply of money is the real question. A nation which engages in titanic efforts to clutter its threshold with garbage will indeed generate impressive statistics, mostly worthless.

It is a mistake to be distracted by Ruskin's preoccupation with St. George's Guild. It is not just graduate students who are misled by it: the impracticality of it is occasionally cited as indicative of the general incompetence of Ruskin as a thinker. To suggest that to Ruskin St. George's Guild was not very important catches even serious scholars by surprise. There is nothing novel about the suggestion; his editors, Cook and Wedderburn, advanced it in their introduction to *Fors Clavigera*. They felt that what he wrote about St. George's Guild should be read as utopian literature, a happy thought since both Thomas More and John Ruskin were celestial idealists with hard heads for business. After all, one of the most interesting tributes to Ruskin came from a Liverpool journal which, after observing his lucrative operations in the publishing field with his protegé George Allen, pronounced him "a great tradesman." Ruskin felt a kinship with Jonathan Swift; does anyone criticize Swift for implying that horses are smarter than people? St. George's Guild was Ruskin's equivalent of Houyhnhmmland.

It is a mistake to be disconcerted by Ruskin's self-contradictions. To think in terms of polarities was characteristic of Ruskin from the beginning. For him, to think of one side of a proposition led him to think of the other; thesis begot antithesis and self-contradiction became a way of life, until the only consistency in his work lies in its anticipated inconsistency. In Ruskin's words, "the more I see of useful truths, the more I find that, like human beings, they are eminently biped; . . ." The dominant opposition in his entire literary output is between good and evil. In his early work it appears as light and dark, in the works of his middle years as life and death, in his apocalyptic moments as heaven and hell, in one

guise or another, as for example St. George's Guild and the goddess Britannia of the Marketplace.

But despite all that we have learned about reading John Ruskin, the works of his middle years, 1860-1885, are still puzzles. That they have great merits no one doubts; these, however, all too often lie buried in a context which cannot sustain interest. That is why there are so many selections from Ruskin, by John D. Rosenberg, by Joan Evans, by Lord Kenneth Clark, by Harold Bloom, by Robert L. Herbert. They are impressed by Ruskin, but they feel that his virtues must be disengaged from his vices. It would seem, however, that his vices and his virtues are well-nigh inseparable. Our gains have come from exploring the complex and highly deceptive patterns in his essays.

Let us turn one last time to that little-known book published in 1867, *Time and Tide,* where for me it all began. Why do the Japanese jugglers appear in Letter VI and how can the ensuing explosion of diverse subjects be fitted into any recognizable pattern?

The subject of *Time and Tide* is the laws of work, and the first three letters are logical and orderly. The digressions begin in Letter IV, because Ruskin has been reading the account in the *Pall Mall Gazette* of the doings of the House of Commons, including the projected budget for the Army and Navy (25 millions) and for "science and art" (164 thousands). It is a matter of choice and the values of the nation are clear.

After that instructive comparison Ruskin returns in Letter V to the laws of work, specifically to how much constitutes a "modest competence." Certainly the worker is entitled to a small sum for entertainment, but that raises an interesting question, and with a bound Ruskin is off on a false scent, describing his night at the pantomime *Ali Baba.* When the British workers pay for entertainment, this, or worse, is what they buy, a splendid story burlesqued by a bevy of cigar-smoking girls. Then in Letter VI enter the Japanese jugglers.

> Sir Toby Belch.   O, ay, make up that! He is now at a cold scent . . .
> Fabian.   Did not I say he would work it out? The cur is excellent at faults.

Their manual dexterity is marvelous, but one of them wears masks which in the Japanese fashion are well made but "inventively frightful," suggesting as they do mankind's kinship with the lower animals.

At the beginning of Letter VII, *Time and Tide* simply falls apart. The second paragraph consists of a single sentence which would be embarrassing in a freshman theme.

> I had intended to return to those Japanese jugglers, after a visit to a theatre in Paris; but I had better, perhaps, at once tell you the piece of the performance which, in connection with the scene in the English pantomime, bears most on matters in hand.

In the next paragraph he describes a dance by a girl of about thirteen, whose motions were a series of contractions and jerks, like those of a puppet. Watching her, he thinks of Exodus 15:20. "And Miriam, the prophetess, the sister of Aaron, took a timbrel in her hand, and all the women went out after her with timbrels and with dances." And with that Ruskin's mind leaps to Paris.

> Not at once, however, to the theatre, but to a bookseller's shop, No. 4, Rue Voltaire, where, in the year 1858, was published the fifth edition of Balzac's *Contes Drôlatiques,* illustrated by 425 designs by Gustave Doré.

Ruskin is like the Homeric hero who leaped on his horse and fled in all directions. Transitions are supposed to signal a logical progress, not a digression, except that in this case the digression is worth the confusion. Balzac's text is full of blasphemies, and the illustrations revel in "loathsome and monstrous aspects of death and sin," reaching a climax in a picture of a man cut in half by a downward sweep of the sword, with full anatomical detail. The letter ends with a swift return to the British public and the way it chooses to spend its money. Just then the Evangelicals were buying a new edition of *The Holy Bible, with Illustrations by Gustav Doré,* in cheap monthly parts.

All of which supposedly leads to Letter VIII, entitled "The Four Possible Theories Respecting the Authorship of the Bible," which does not sound like a law of work, but wait: perhaps there is method in his madness.

> Celia.   How prove you that in the great
>   heap of your knowledge?
> Rosalind. Ay, marry, now unmuzzle your
>   wisdom.

In this particular letter he feels it necessary to justify his use of the Bible as a moral authority, because he, as well as much of his audience, no longer believes it is the inspired world of God. His position is much the same as Matthew Arnold's in 1867. The Bible represents the best moral judgment that western civilization has been capable of arriving at, that judgment which is best supported by the experience of men and nations. What the Bible condemns is what has proved destructive to men and nations.

By now we know for sure only that what follows will be surprising. Letter IX is headed "The Use of Music and Dancing under the Jewish Theocracy, Compared with Their Use by the Modern French." The ancient notion of singing and dancing as a prayer of thanksgiving for man's deliverance from evil has yielded to the new dispensation, such as in Geneva, once a center of Christianity, where the Sabbath is now a time for drunken brawling to the rhythm of horse pistols fired aimlessly into the air, or in Paris, where the supreme choreographic expression of the nineteenth century is the Cancan, which is not exactly what Miriam performed. Ruskin's use of the touchstone method is gargantuan.

The dance theme was introduced in Letter V with the girl who danced with the donkey. It was continued in Letter VII with the puppet-girl whose dance consisted mostly of contractions and jerks. Her dance set Ruskin to thinking of Miriam the prophetess, sister of Aaron, and what dancing meant then and now (Letter IX). That this is the structure of the five letters is clear from the transitional passages, but the bewildering profusion of images, together

with the ad hoc remarks which they generate, tends to obscure the line of the argument.

If such is the structure of Ruskin's sermon, then we should expect what follows to be the homilist's interpretation and his exhortation. This time we are not disappointed. Letter X is headed "The Meaning and Actual Operation of Satanic or Demoniacal Influence." Ruskin believes in Satan, though not in "the gramnivorous form of him, with horn and tail," but rather as that force, whether within or without, that reduces the powers and the virtues of men to whatever "corruption is possible to them." The Satanic Power rides with us on our way, as the Fiend rode behind Albert Dürer's Knight, but that is not to be feared so much as the state of mind in which we do not know the Fiend when we see him, just as men live in modern society without recognizing its power to corrupt. Letter XI tells us how to recognize the Adversary: he is the Lord of Lies and the Lord of Pain. Ruskin concludes by admitting that he has been led away from his subject, the laws of work, to which he will return in Letter XII, and he does, although not for long.

So this long section of *Time and Tide,* Letters IV through XI, is not a series of digressions. It is rather one enormous digression, nearly one-third of the whole book, ostensibly organized around the dance theme, but actually a complex arrangement of juxtapositions on a larger theme, the corruption of modern society. The whole digression is triggered by the annual appropriations for war and for science and art, and what this budget tells about the nation. "By their fruits ye shall know them."

Here in embryo are the later works of John Ruskin, both the ideas and the rhetoric. Here, within a few pages, Ruskin has brought together as wildly unlikely a set of elements as can easily be imagined, and yes, in a way it is about the laws of work, as the subtitle promised. Yet something is wrong. Therefore, since brevity is the soul of wit, perhaps here, as elsewhere in Ruskin's work, our verdict must be brief: "Your noble son is mad." Let us remember, however, that he who pronounced that judgment was not himself a paragon of wisdom.

Richard L. Stein   (essay date 1985)

SOURCE: "Milk, Mud, and Mountain Cottages: Ruskin's *Poetry of Architecture,*" in *PMLA,* Vol. 100, No, 3, May, 1985, pp. 328-41.

[*In the following essay, Stein offers a critique of Ruskin's idealized view of nature and of rural life as expressed in* The Poetry of Architecture.]

Ruskin teaches us how to see, Charlotte Brontë remarked. He also teaches us how to read, particularly his own works and certainly the forbidding collection of early essays called *The Poetry of Architecture*. The standard approach to this series follows a path laid out in Ruskin's autobiography, which scans the past for the dawning of his genius. "Now, looking back from 1886 to that brook shore of 1837, whence I could see the whole of my youth, I find myself in nothing whatsoever changed." In the shimmering haze of biographical hindsight, those early essays glow with promise: "though deformed by assumption, and shallow in contents, they are curiously right up to the points they reach; and already distinguished above most of the literature of the time, for the skill of language which the public at once felt for a pleasant gift in me." No matter that the series was discontinued when Loudon's *Architectural Magazine* closed or that the "literature of the time" included the writing of Carlyle, Dickens, Tennyson, and Wordsworth. Ruskin would have us regard his first extended prose works as an intimation of his future literary immortality. Indeed, most readers have done just that and have treated *The Poetry of Architecture* primarily in terms of its successors in the Ruskin canon. As a result, it is known for a few splendid passages or for the scattered insights that might have come from other books. It is known, that is, in a kind of anthologized version of itself. We need other ways of seeing this book, not so much because it anticipates Ruskin's maturity as because in many respects it does not, because, despite its fairly straightforward argument, it rests on a fundamental paradox—one blazoned in the title and therefore easily overlooked. In proposing an alternative view, I focus on that title and the problem embedded in it: What does it mean to term architecture poetic?

I

Ruskin's title invites two sorts of readings. It may refer to all architecture as poetic or to a distinction between two aspects of the art—the poetry of architecture as opposed to its prose. The opening paragraph confidently addresses these questions, though instead of settling them it recasts them, substituting some new and equally troublesome terms:

> The Science of Architecture, followed out to its full extent, is one of the noblest of those which have reference only to the creations of human minds. It is not merely a science of rule and compass, it does not consist only in the observation of just rule, or of fair proportion: it is, or ought to be, a science of feeling more than rule, a ministry to the mind, more than to the eye. If we consider how much less the beauty and majesty of a building depend upon its pleasing certain prejudices of the eye, than upon its rousing certain trains of meditation in the mind, it will show in a moment how many intricate questions of feeling are involved in the raising of an edifice; it will convince us of the truth of a proposition, which might at first have appeared startling, that no man can be an architect, who is not a metaphysician.

Between them, science and metaphysics make large claims for this subject—but make them in curiously negative and exclusionary terms. Architecture is "not merely" one sort of activity; certain kinds of persons cannot be architects. Before Ruskin can explain what he has in mind, he must disqualify the most common connotations of the words he uses.

He first cautions us not to associate architecture exclusively with "rule and compass" or allow "prejudices of the eye" to warp our view. Here we have not simply what Ruskin called his "pert little Protestant mind" at work but the voice of a representative of a particular social class for which buildings become undignified when linked too closely with physical bulk, or specific functions, or the labor of construction. A later essay in *The Poetry of Architecture* satirizes the conversation of an architect and his patron, who commissions a design incorporating Egyptian, Grecian, Gothic, and American Indian motifs. Yet the most acid tones are reserved not for the befuddled "proprietor" but for the quiescent architect, who "sits calmly down to draw his elevations; as if he were a stonemason, or his employer an architect." One must not mistake an architect for a laborer or, equally important, for an employee. This thinking helps explain the reference to science as well, for even amid rapidly increasing intellectual specialization, science in the early nineteenth century remained the domain of the gentleman. I discuss science in its own right later on; here I am stressing its relation to a larger "class" of intellectual activities. Poetry, science, metaphysics—all things one did not "do" for money. Associating architecture with poetry, then, is one way of insisting on its genteel status.

Poetry requires readers. Ruskin defines architecture similarly in relation to the right kind of audience. Once again, he is not thinking of the ordinary experience of architecture—the insider's or user's experience. Ruskin stands outside the buildings he speaks about, distinguishing the object of contemplation from the article of use. That those buildings are houses emphasizes this distinction. The two parts of *The Poetry of Architecture* treat cottages and villas, the respective dwellings of the lower and upper classes. But we are not taken inside, for Ruskin has a "pictorial view" of architecture, one rooted in the traditions of eighteenth-century associationist psychology. Elizabeth Helsinger defines this approach more specifically as an exercise in "excursive sight." Ruskin moves among buildings like a refined and perceptive tourist, consistently viewing them with cultivated detachment. In fact, his original scheme for the essays—curtailed by the demise of the *Architectural Magazine*—was to begin with "the lower class of edifices, proceeding from the roadside to the village, and from the village to the city." But if such a grand perceptual tour draws on traditions of meditative poetry and psychological theory, it also depends on the social and economic status of the traveler. The philosophical tourist requires both the leisure and the capital to sustain research; and it may turn out that the research itself offers ways to increase that capital, even if only in the form of poetic gems.

To some extent, any collection of touristic views implies an appropriation; even cameras, as Susan Sontag has pointed out, enable us to "take" pictures. This acquisitiveness is all the more prominent in the tradition of hunting picturesque views, of reducing a living world to a series of portable, dead scenes. As it happens, the final volume of *Modern Painters* attacks this practice. Ruskin grimly exposes the difference between a rhapsodic prose account of Highland scenery and the realities obscured by picturesque distance: rough landscape, a violent stream, and the carcass of a ewe supply the background to "a man fishing, with a boy and a dog—a picturesque and pretty group enough certainly, if they had not been there all day starving." Yet, as John Rosenberg has remarked, such passages are self-admonitory (*Darkening Glass*). Indeed, *The Poetry of Architecture* offers many examples of enthusiastic but illusioned prose, a picturesque not simply detached from reality by the absence of sympathy but depicting objects according to a social myth that only heightens this distance. The habit is reflected in the first description of a specific building, an English lowland cottage. Ruskin stresses its "finished neatness." Thatch is pegged down firmly, whitewash is stainless, and "the luxuriant rose is trained gracefully over the window." A glance among the sweetbriar leaves reveals a diamond-latticed window opened to admit the breeze "that, as it passes over the flowers, becomes full of their fragrance":

> A few square feet of garden, and a latched wicket, persuading the weary and dusty pedestrian, with expressive eloquence, to lean upon it for an instant, and request a drink of water or milk, complete a picture, which, if it be far enough from London to be unspoiled by town sophistications, is a very perfect thing in its way. The ideas it awakens are agreeable, and the architecture is all that we want in such a situation. It is pretty and appropriate; and if it boasted of any other perfection, it would be at the expense of its propriety.

Here distance seems to increase with every period. As John Rosenberg observes, *The Poetry of Architecture* "usurps a tone of authority which age of knowledge alone could not confer." The "acuity of vision" belongs to Ruskin, "but the idiom is stiff and fits him like an oversized costume" ("Style"). *Costume* is the right word here, because Ruskin is speaking in a class idiom that appropriates the visual details of a particular setting to clothe a traditional myth in modern dress. The drink of milk suggests a harmonious feudal world. The picture is completed, according to Ruskin, only when we imagine ourselves incorporated into it, receiving both refreshment and reassurance that our presence is normal and welcome.

Ruskin's iconography of class harmony is not unique, nor is his implication that such idealized scenes actually exist. Carlyle's 1832 essay "Biography" cites a passage from Clarendon's *History of the Rebellion* describing Charles I receiving shelter and "a great pot of buttermilk" from a loyal farmer. The vogue for such images is also evident in two popular paintings by William Collins, Rustic Civility (1832) and Cottage Hospitality (1834), the latter depicting a child taking broth to a poor traveler. Ruskin's essay on Swiss mountain cottages refers to an even older tradition, inviting us to indulge in "Sweet ideas . . . of such passages of peasant life as the gentle Walton so loved; of the full milkpail, and the mantling cream-bow."

It is difficult not to love such pictures, unless one happens to be a peasant. The picturesque translates real country life into the formal structure of pastoral, a mode that William Empson and Raymond Williams have traced to an idealized conception of class relations. We can understand this vision more fully if once again we notice its negations and exclusions: the realities of rural poverty are carefully hidden in what John Barrell has termed the dark side of the landscape. Yet, as Ruskin himself acknowledges, this scene might take other forms. Its perfection could be

spoiled by London sophistications; further improvements would only lessen its propriety. He insists, in other words, that it must remain fixed: untouched by the city, unaffected by change. A perfect cottage is picturesque, then, insofar as it exists apart from history, subtly persuading spectators that they can even view themselves outside any specific social context.

"The architecture is all that we want in such a situation." What else might we find? For one thing, cottagers. These essays mention them only occasionally, usually referring to their "ideal character" rather than to their actual conditions. When the discussion of lowland Italian cottages forces Ruskin to confront the fact of poverty, he at first dismisses, then excuses, then finally praises the architectural dilapidation that symbolizes it. After all, we are told, "the filthy habits of the Italian prevent him from suffering from the state to which he is reduced." If this state creates "a picture which, seen too near, is sometimes revolting to the eye, always melancholy to the mind. . . . even this many would not wish to be otherwise." For the observer, the tokens of human misery compose a moral tableau, an instructive spectacle of mortality:

> adversity and ruin point to the sepulchre, and it is not trodden on; to the chronicle, and it doth not decay. Who would substitute the rush of a new nation, the struggle of an awakening power, for the dreamy sleep of Italy's desolation, for her sweet silence of melancholy thought, her twilight time of everlasting memories?

The Italians would, one is tempted to answer. But of course Ruskin is addressing British readers, and members of a class unfettered by place and time. The opening remarks on villas explain that "Man, the peasant, is a being of more marked national character, than man, the educated and refined." It is the latter who is "led into general views of things," the "things" apparently including human beings. To the practiced eye of the genteel spectator, poverty will seem as permanent, as inevitable, and perhaps even as moving as the forms of nature themselves.

The subtitle of these essays, "The Architecture of the Nations of Europe Considered in Its Association with Natural Scenery and National Character," could be taken as the subtitle for most of Ruskin's later socioarchitectural writings, but his examination of these terms in 1837-38 has little of the complexity or critical sophistication of *The Stones of Venice,* written fifteen years later. Ruskin is not yet prepared to stand apart from and criticize the institutions of his society; this lack of distance is probably what he was referring to in writing later that the essays are "deformed by assumption." In another sense, however, he stands too far outside, not so much outside his society as outside all human relations, ignoring them as if they did not exist. He integrates architecture into a dead landscape, uninhabited by anyone except the spectator and the occasional figure of a statuesque peasant, who helps compose the countryside into a picture. This sort of distortion is hardly what Charlotte Brontë had in mind when she praised Ruskin for giving her the sense of sight. *The Poetry of Architecture* (which was not, after all, the book she had in mind) both bestows and denies that sense, teaching us to see some things by not seeing others. It is a lesson in looking and overlooking, so that architecture's poetry becomes a way to distract us from the prose of ordinary life.

Books like E. H. Gombrich's *Art and Illusion* tell us that all vision is selective, constitutive. A number of writers were advancing remarkably similar arguments when Ruskin was producing these essays. Of course, the literary attention to vision is even older, and almost all Ruskin's works can be seen as outgrowths of a Romantic stress on the transformative power of the poetic eye. But the writings of the late 1830s I have in mind emphasize not so much the visionary as the reportorial, the need to observe social realities that were so familiar as to become invisible. The best-known example of this interest is *Oliver Twist*, not simply because the book rests on close observation of London life but also because it dramatizes various characters' attempts at observation; in Dickens the processes and problems of seeing become thematic. Harriet Martineau's *How to Observe* (1838) takes an even more self-conscious approach to perception. Subtitled "Morals and Manners," it proposes a socially conscious observation in the service of broadly utilitarian principles. Martineau's first "philosophical requisite" for seeing clearly is an awareness that the only true measure of particular conditions is their effect on "the general happiness of the section of the race among whom they exist." Architecture thus becomes a means rather than an end, symbolic of social conditions in much the same way that it is in *The Stones of Venice*. "The Records of any society," she writes, "be they what they may, whether architectural remains, epitaphs, civic registers, national music, or any other of the thousand manifestations of the common mind which may be found among every people, afford more information on Morals in a day than converse with individuals in a year." Buildings lose their privileged status in this account; indeed, as "manifestations of the common mind," they become part of the prose of the world. But Martineau's main point is that architecture gives physical form to otherwise imperceptible moral conditions. In that way, it helps observers objectify their own responses: they do not assume the necessity of the institutions the buildings represent but rather can examine those institutions critically.

Similar remarks on the art of observation appear in another book of 1838, William Howitt's *Rural Life of England*. As the title suggests, this book is much closer than Martineau's to Ruskin's subject, and it reads, far more than hers, like the journal of a genteel, picturesque tourist. Nevertheless, it achieves a social and epistemological self-consciousness Ruskin never attains in *The Poetry of Architecture*. The opening pages, for instance, warn us against allowing our admiration for the beauties of the countryside to distract us from the facts of rural poverty:

> I say, let every man gratefully rejoice, who has the means of commanding the full blessings of English life,—for alas! there are thousands and millions of our countrymen who possesses but a scanty portion of these; whose lives are too long and continuous a course of toil and anxiety to permit them even to look round them and see how vast are the powers of enjoyment in this country, and how few of those sources of ease,

comfort, and refined pleasures are within their reach.

Howitt stresses that both what we see and our ability to see it are determined by social and economic conditions. And like Martineau, he insists above all that we pay careful attention to differences. "What a mighty space," he exclaims, "lies between the palace and the cottage in the country! Ay, what a mighty space between the mansion of the private gentleman and the hut of the labourer on his estate!"

Differences of this sort are naturalized in Ruskin, transformed poetically into inevitable features of a landscape far more important than the lives of its inhabitants. Indeed, part of the charm of the most beautiful places he describes is the absence of human activity. Thus the power of Italian picturesque is directly proportional to its distance from the realities of a peopled world:

> Every part of the landscape is in unison; . . . the pale cities, temple and tower, lie gleaming along the champaign; but how calmly! no hum of men; no motion of multitude in the midst of them: they are voiceless as the city of ashes.

As that final phrase suggests, picturesque beauty is associated with the fixity of death and of the past. Ruskin treats Italy like "one wide sepulchre, and all her present life . . . like a shadow or a memory." He creates, in John Dixon Hunt's phrase, a poetry of distance, in which the fixity of an artifact is counterposed to the confusion of the present (Hunt). In these early essays, Ruskin invites us to see the world not only through architecture but as architecture—as a series of iconic structures manifesting a higher Platonic reality. Insofar as we can focus on that ideal, the present is conceived only as an absence, "a shadow or a memory."

The few references to "present life" concern deviations from these high standards. But although Ruskin's vocabulary is ostensibly aesthetic, his concerns are broader: the yearning for architectural purity is closely related to a desire for more orderly social conditions. He glances at "the streets of our cities," for instance, to document the "clashing of our different tastes." There buildings are "either remarkable for the utter absence of all attempt at embellishment, or disgraced by every variety of abomination." The connotations of that final word make us suspect that Ruskin is thinking, too, of nonaesthetic clashes. Underlying his condemnation of vulgar taste, here and elsewhere, is a fear of social conflict. Poetic architecture pacifies such threats and even transforms them into their mythic opposites. Indeed, when Ruskin finally brings us to his ideal cottage, in Westmoreland, he seems to recognize the difference between his conception and an ordinary response to such a building. Some observers might find it disappointing, or even disturbing. "Is this all?" they might object—"a hovel?" Yes, he insists, this is all; and it is "enough." In the *locus amoenus* of Westmoreland, "nothing is required but humility and gentleness." There we come upon actual examples of the abstract ideal presented in the opening chapter: "the cottage always gives the idea of a thing to be beloved; a quiet life-giving voice, that is as peaceful as silence itself." This architecture, in other words, never addresses us at all unless we approach it first, and even then it never obtrudes: "it can never lie too humbly in the pastures of the valley, nor shrink too submissively into the hollows of the hills. . . ." It is poetry secured by distance, pleasing largely because it never threatens to emerge from the background to force itself into the lives of its observers.

Such thinking helps explain why *The Poetry of Architecture* begins with an examination of cottages. Ruskin's ideology would be shattered by the facts of rural poverty. A poetic depiction of cottages—a transformation, in other words, of the prosaic realities of cottage life—is the necessary first step toward reasserting a traditional pastoral myth. Such pastoralism took on added importance in England after the passage of the Reform Bill. But, as the example of William Howitt suggests, it was not always invoked uncritically. Five years after Ruskin's essays appeared, Carlyle introduced the same myth, with greater urgency, in *Past and Present* (vol. 10). Only there, even more than in *The Rural Life of England,* the myth is condemned. Arguing for a new, viable mythology rooted in actual conditions, Carlyle juxtaposes his own panoramic grasp of history with various distorted perceptions and false ideals. Indeed, his very first description of a real place could have been addressed to the young author of *The Poetry of Architecture,* although there is no evidence that Carlyle knew of that book. The subject is not a thatched cottage but a workhouse, the home of the modern rural poor. To stress the difference between his account and the sort usually supplied by chroniclers of country life, he ascribes the passage ironically to a "picturesque Tourist." Nor do the parallels end here. Ruskin grows especially rhapsodic over the stillness of Westmoreland; Carlyle also emphasizes the silent fixity of the St. Ives Workhouse and its inhabitants, but here it signals a deadly torpor, reminding him of Dante's Hell. Yet in a curious way this passage also resembles the social criticism of the mature Ruskin, who calls Carlyle his "master"; it seems to anticipate directly the grim account of starvation in the Highlands discovered by the picturesque tourist in the last volume of *Modern Painters*. Perhaps the pointed attack on attitudes so close to his own initiated the growth of his political consciousness. Or perhaps the St. Ives passage, and similar ones, helped Ruskin discover latent and contradictory strains within his own thought, elements of *The Poetry of Architecture* itself that required him to reexamine the mythologies he invoked.

II

The frequency of pious social clichés in Ruskin's account of cottage life should not surprise us. The author has barely emerged from his comfortable middle-class home, and he writes as a "gentleman-commoner" of Christ Church, Oxford. What is more surprising is that he should move beyond the platitudes of his class at all and that he should do so as his architectural focus shifts from the cottage to the villa. We would, of course, expect that shift to produce a heightened social conscience in the last half of *The Poetry of Architecture*: what better time for a demonstration of noblesse oblige? Even William Howitt appeals to this instinct: "Is it not in these noble ancestral houses, amid their ancestral woods and lands, that the spirit of our gen-

try is most likely to acquire its right tone?" Ruskin is engaging in the monied class's most traditional form of self-criticism, raising the classical question of the proper use of riches. But though his answers sometimes merely reassert conventional platitudes, they sometimes go beyond or begin to subject those platitudes to critical scrutiny. At some points he becomes entangled in the contradictions between myths and realities; at others he measures those myths and realities against one another. The argument is hardly consistent, or mature. That is what makes it exciting. The tortuous journey down the road from cottage to villa and finally to the city eventually leads to Venice and London. As he sets out, he begins to discover his critical vocation.

Ruskin defines the subject of the concluding essays, the villa, as the "ruralized domicile of the gentleman." His critical task begins in the ambiguities of that phrase. "Ruralized" suggests the artifice of naturalness in an urban patron's construction of an appropriate country seat. It is a "domicile" (as distinguished from the "rural dwelling of the peasant"), a term that in legal usage refers to the mobility of the owner; the *OED* describes it as the "place where one has his home or permanent residence, to which, if absent, he has the intention of returning." One might argue that the villa is the country residence of the cultured traveler who contemplates the cottage in the earlier essays. Certainly the possibility of absence implies not only travel but absenteeism, so that the very existence of this domicile determines some of the essential conditions of those left behind. Peasants are as rooted and narrowly national as the gentry are mobile and cosmopolitan. The former are confined by their labor as well as by the small circle of their lives and contacts. The latter, the villa builders, are what the British call holiday makers; and "man, in his hours of relaxation, when he is engaged in the pursuit of mere pleasure, is less national" than in "the business of his life." But genteel travelers, as this remark suggests, are divided beings, occupying different roles as well as different homes. Ruskin's strictures on villa architecture become a vehicle for examining the contradictions between those roles. The second half of *The Poetry of Architecture* reads in places like a critique of a monied class, in others like a handbook for those who want to belong; the essays consistently warn against the poor taste that often betrays the pretensions of wealth. Real gentility requires a delicate balance. The last essay, citing Juvenal and Molière's *Bourgeois gentilhomme,* chides those "who are setting all English feeling and all natural principles at defiance."

I do not claim, as Charles T. Dougherty does, that the last group of essays in *The Poetry of Architecture* ought to be read as satire, though I do agree that Ruskin's argument begins "to come apart" when he attempts to apply it to villas. The problem results not from playfulness but from the emerging contradictions of a point of view advanced with great seriousness—that it is possible to build a house uncontaminated by associations with work. To some extent, Ruskin is concerned about the reminders of business that new classes of proprietors import to the supposed vacation ground of the villa. Here traces of satire do emerge: "the rich stock-jobber calculates his percentages among the soft dingles and woody shores of Westmoreland." But

Ruskin is addressing a larger issue. If a villa is to be associated with leisure, how can it be built without reminding us of the physical labor it is supposed to transcend? Ruskin almost seems to imagine an idealized dwelling in a prelapsarian world, where idleness will be universal and wholly natural:

> For the very chiefest part of the character of the edifice of pleasure is, and must be, its perfect ease, its appearance of felicitous repose. This it can never have where the nature and expression of the land near it reminds us of the necessity of labour, and where the earth is niggardly of all that constitutes its beauty and our pleasure; this it can only have, where the presence of man seems the natural consequence of an ample provision for his enjoyment, not the continuous struggle of suffering existence with a rude heaven and rugged soil. There is nobility in such a struggle, but not when it is maintained by the inhabitant of the villa. . . .

This passage continues tortuously to its end half a page later; and Ruskin is at pains to acknowledge that some labor is heroic. But in insisting that it be kept at a distance from the role of the country proprietor, Ruskin shows how precarious that role necessarily is. "The residence which in the end is found altogether delightful, will be found to have been placed where it has committed no injury." Apparently, then, there are other sites and other proprietary roles. Here, however, we are not to be reminded that the proprietor either works somewhere else or employs others to do work. The intellectual cultivation of the villa dweller can only be imagined in an uncultivated landscape; only an unproductive setting can persuade us that the villa itself has not been produced. This fiction is not easy to maintain. Any country house potentially belies the myth it was erected to perpetuate. Ruskin struggles to establish conditions that would sustain that myth.

Yet we are also allowed to glimpse a reality behind the myth and for brief moments even compelled to question reality and myth together. For although Ruskin treats the thing of beauty, he calls attention to circumstances under which it might cease to be a joy. A villa, after all, is "the dwelling of wealth and power," an architectural form made possible by particular social, economic, and historical conditions. Such homes could not have existed in warring Greece. They appeared in Rome because the state "secured tranquility, and . . . distributed its authority among a great number of individuals," without giving them enough power to build palaces or fortresses. The creation of villas thus presupposes a delicate balance between the centralization of authority and the distribution of wealth, presupposes, that is, a powerful class that is still subject to limits. The arrangement Ruskin describes sounds vaguely like the bourgeois capitalism of the early nineteenth century—but only vaguely. That ideal of balanced, stable power was increasingly threatened, not only by popular discontent but by the very expansion of bourgeois wealth. Ruskin almost seems to grasp the Marxist conception of capitalism as class warfare, although his model is classical rather than modern. Will the British villa extend its power beyond the Roman limits? Does the existence of monied houses threaten pastoral harmony? Is the British villa a contradiction in terms?

That such questions are not asked directly distinguishes Ruskin's architectural writing of the 1830s from that of the 1850s and 1860s; yet it is important to recognize that they are implied. Ruskin discovers a threat in modern capitalism, although he sees it as a threat to things rather than to people—to tasteful buildings and especially to the harmony of the landscape. In the emergence of rich individuals asserting their power, he fears a modern version of the warring classical city-states. And it is the individuality as well as the power that concerns him: capitalism enables individuals to appropriate a landscape that ought to remain common property. Though *The Poetry of Architecture* does not advocate nationalization of the land, or of anything else, it does insist on the privileged status of countryside as a symbolic property. The very beauty of the landscape, the necessary backdrop to Ruskin's idyllic vision of class relations, makes it a "national possession" not to be appropriated or defiled by any individual or class:

> The nobler scenery of the earth is the inheritance of all her inhabitants: it is not merely for the few to whom it temporarily belongs, to feed from like swine, or to stable upon like horses, but it has been appointed to be the school of the minds which are kingly among their fellows, to excite the highest energies of humanity, to furnish strength to the lordliest intellect, and food for the holiest emotions of the human soul.

Here a "natural" standard begins to undermine a social one: "The minds which are kingly among their fellows . . . the lordliest intellect." The claims of class and property suddenly shrink beside those of the land, the school of the soul. From this premise, Ruskin moves to a simple but radical conclusion: ownership of the land is temporary and must remain so. The landscape cannot become capital. Suddenly, this architectural brand of natural philosophy is legislating rather than justifying the behavior of the monied classes. The beauty of the landscape must be preserved from forms of life "not congenial with its character," and

> that life is not congenial which thrusts presumptuously forward, amidst the calmness of the universe, the confusion of its own petty interests and grovelling imaginations, and stands up with the insolence of a moment, amid the majesty of all time, to build baby fortifications upon the bones of the world, or to sweep the copse from the corries, and the shadow from the shore, that fools may risk, and gamblers gather, the spoil of a thousand summers.

Ruskin is moving toward the concept of a "national store," which is at the heart of his later communal projects, including the Guild of St. George. Here, though, the argument is as much negative as positive—aimed not just at a certain class of intruders but at certain "uncongenial" notions of the earth itself. Indeed, the self-righteousness of the passage suggests an almost religious sense of mission in preserving "the bones of the world" from desecration, a mission that eventually carries Ruskin beyond political economy as well as beyond architecture.

III

In *The Poetry of Architecture,* and in almost all Ruskin's other writings on art and architecture, the underlying subject is landscape, as we are reminded by both the subtitle, ". . . Considered in Its Association with Natural Scenery . . . ," and his nom de plume, Kata Phusin, or "according to nature." "According to nature," of course, really means "according to Ruskin," but the author establishes his authority by invoking the landscape as arbiter of architectural taste. He shows us that certain forms derive from specific geographical conditions and others conflict with them; that beauty depends on a harmonious relation between architectural lines and natural ones, between building materials and the materials of the environment. Such discourse easily becomes quasi-scientific, and, although Ruskin does not demonstrate the structural origins of fundamental architectural forms until the first volume of *The Stones of Venice,* in 1851 (see Stein, *Ritual*), he does classify major building types according to the subdivisions of landscape. Describing four sorts of countryside—woody, or green; cultivated, or blue; wild, or gray; hilly, or brown—he associates each with a set of normal psychological or behavioral responses and, hence, with a set of appropriate architectural responses and specific structural forms. Before long, he reduces this four-part division to a simple opposition, parallel to that between the cottage and the villa: "Nature has set aside her sublime bits for us to feel and think in; she has pointed out her productive bits for us to sleep and eat in; and, if we sleep and eat amongst the sublimity, we are brutal; if we poetize amongst the cultivation, we are absurd." Ruskin is writing, in effect, to enforce the distinctions between the landscapes of poetry and prose, and as the tone of urgency suggests, he senses that the rigid separation has begun to break down. It is not simply that architectural decorum has been neglected but that the very rules of nature have been violated. And nature can include human beings. Ruskin's use of the word *brutality* suggests how readily he can turn an argument about architectural practice into one about human nature, our status as members of a species.

This dimension of his argument is one of the least developed, that is, one of the least explicit and possibly one of the least conscious. If Ruskin becomes uneasy and self-contradictory on the subject of wealth—where he treads dangerously close to his father's upper-middle-class position—he understandably becomes even more restless on the question of brutality. For the word in its literal sense refers to "the state or condition of the brutes," or animals. The first definition in the *OED* adds, "Wanting in reason or understanding; chiefly in phrases *brute beasts, the brute creation,* the 'lower animals.' " Thus brutality is bound up in other issues: the relations between lower and higher forms of life and ultimately between different species. The evidence of vocabulary alone (and there is more) suggests that, while writing about the "Science of Architecture," Ruskin was aware of some of the burning issues other sciences were addressing. In exploring architectural poetry, he is led to question the most poetic claims about human beings: to what extent are they to be defined by their own "highest" faculties? To what extent are they merely "pro-

saic," merely creatures, another biological species building functional shelters dressed up as "architecture"?

Such questions were hardly neutral in the late 1830s. In the years that Ruskin was writing *The Poetry of Architecture,* Tennyson was reading Lyell's *Principles of Geology* and experiencing the anguished religious doubts he records in the darkest sections of *In Memoriam.* They are doubts, in fact, about the "higher" nature of humankind. The image of a "monster" replaces that of the spiritual creature whom the poet had thought of as nature's "last work," an idealist, an architect:

> Man, her last work, who seem'd so fair,
> Such splendid purpose in his eyes,
> Who roll'd the psalm to wintry skies,
> Who built him fanes of fruitless prayer. . . .

Ruskin would undergo a similar crisis over the findings of modern geology in the 1850s, but in the 1830s he found the new science more fascinating than dangerous. As he prepared to enter Oxford in December 1836, his "light reading" included "Saussure—Numboldt—and other works of natural philosophy, geological works, &c, &c . . . " (Burd). A month later he attended a meeting of the Geological Society at which a young naturalist named Charles Darwin presented a paper entitled "Recent Elevations on the Coast of Chile" (Burd); and in October 1837 he dined with "two celebrated geologists" and Darwin, with whom he "talked all evening" (Burd). Ruskin does not say what they talked about. Darwin was then developing the hypotheses about evolution through natural selection that eventually led to *The Origin of Species,* in 1859. But in 1837 these speculations were confined to his private "Transmutation Notebooks," so that Darwin probably would not have shared them with his dinner companion. Nevertheless, the word *species* turns up unexpectedly in Ruskin's "Concluding Remarks" on cottages, published in May 1838 (and hence probably written shortly after that dinner). It is one of several places that biological undercurrents appear in the architectural argument, undercurrents it is difficult but necessary to follow.

The first appears after Ruskin summarizes his four-part division of landscape. He has been restating his Wordsworthian insistence on the inherent relation between human feelings and certain fundamental "forms" in nature (see Stein, *Ritual*):

> Thus it is evident that the chief feeling induced by woody country is one of reverence for its antiquity. There is a quiet melancholy about the decay of the patriarchal trunks, which is enhanced by the green and elastic vigour of the young saplings; the noble form of the forest aisles, and the subdued light which penetrates their entangled boughs, combine to add to the impression; and the whole character of the scene is calculated to excite a conservative feeling. The man who could remain a radical in a wood country is a disgrace to his species.

What makes the remark curious is that the final biological term merges into a political argument. Somehow Ruskin finds a connection between apparently disparate categories: the perception of landscape, architectural taste, political conventions, and our dignity as members of a biological or social group. Ruskin's final word may refer to class rather than to species in the scientific sense; but what matters is that one word can serve for both, as if social position is somehow caught up in biological identity. The failure to venerate nature, we are told, is partly social and political, partly a failure to rise above our own potentially animal nature. Indeed, the closing flash of conservative fire is blinding enough to distract us from asking exactly how we might fail, or what it means to "disgrace" a species. The passage is vague, I believe, because Ruskin is touching on a profoundly disturbing issue, although he is only dimly aware of it himself. It is the question that unsettled Tennyson, although it is merely alluded to here in the word *species* or in the image of those decaying patriarchal trunks. Architecture has led Ruskin to consider life and death—the succession of generations, the decay of the body, the fundamentally physical character of existence. The question raised is implied in a word not mentioned here, although it does appear at other points in Ruskin's essays. Buried at the base of those venerable trunks is a reality so simple that it cannot be avoided and yet so unpleasant—so dirty—that it cannot be named: it is mud.

I introduce this word partly because Ruskin defines his various architectural countries by their soils but more particularly because it suggests the many issues underlying, beneath, the architectural argument. In the passage I have been discussing, Ruskin's language almost compulsively returns to these unpleasant, buried elements, alluding to mud in both a geological and a psychoanalytic sense. Psychoanalytic, because those "decaying patriarchal trunks," like his analysis of the use of riches, suggest his father's world. If his tentative argument about wealth were developed further, it might begin to dismantle the architecture of bourgeois ideology to reveal the ground on which class relations, like villas and cottages, are built. Ruskin had this intention in his major economic writings of the 1860s, **Unto This Last** and **Munera pulveris**—and he concludes the second of those books, whose title refers to the "gifts of the dust," by exhorting readers not to "take dust for deity, spectre for possession. . . ." His arguments were radical enough to lead his father, who regularly scrutinized and sometimes censored his son's work, to attempt to modify and even suppress the most alarming sections. In 1838, though, I believe that Ruskin truncated the argument for other reasons. I have called them geological because that term, in the 1830s, applied to the study of both the earth and what was found within it, to rocks and fossils. Geology thus became a science of origins, especially of the origins of life—and hence a danger to theologians. A believer in Genesis who spoke of life originating in mud might mean only that God created men and women from the earth. The same statement by a geologist might imply a belief in the evolution of human beings from lower forms, a wholly material architecture of the organic world—perhaps even an architecture without an architect. Ruskin could not have moved in the scientific circles he did without being aware of such views. Indeed, as I have been suggesting, he had difficulty speaking of architecture without also alluding to geology.

He was not the only one to make the connection. In his

monumental *History of the Inductive Sciences,* published in 1837, William Whewell defines geology in the largest possible terms, classifying it, along with the subdivision of paleontology, within the larger category he calls palaetiology, the sciences of causes of past events. But he views geology as particularly inclusive, comparing it to architectural and cultural history:

> The organic fossils which occur in the rock, and the medals which we find in the ruins of ancient cities, are to be studied in a similar spirit and for a similar purpose. Indeed, it is not always easy to know where the task of the geologist ends, and that of the antiquary begins.

This science, however, is not limited to the past, for it also deals with the "physical history of the *present* population of the globe." Whewell himself stresses that presentness, but he also takes pains to qualify his use of the word *physical*. Although geology is a physical science, it cannot be valid if it is merely that, if its findings do not accord with the truths of metaphysics. The *History* continually warns us against such a split, and Whewell probably treats geology at the end of his survey because it poses this threat.

Whewell's last sections, "Geological Dynamics," deal with fossils, the question of transmutation (i.e., the evolution of the species), and hypotheses about the creation and extinction of species; his final chapter, "The Two Antagonist Doctrines of Geology," discusses catastrophism and uniformitarianism. All these issues are linked to one another and to larger theological questions: if we grant the doctrine of transmutation, he warns, we must then "abandon the belief in the adaptation of the structure of every creature to its destined mode of being." This view "has constantly and irresistibly impressed itself on the minds of the best naturalists," and "most persons would give [it] up with repugnance." All truths, he adds, "must be consistent with all other truths, and therefore the results of true geology or astronomy cannot be irreconcileable with the statements of true theology." A footnote refers us to Whewell's *Bridgewater Treatise,* part of the series initiated to demonstrate the "Power, Wisdom, and Goodness of God, as manifested in the Creation" (*Astronomy*). It is a project that expresses perfectly Whewell's own ideal of science. Yet, as he admits, we do not always know enough to attain this ideal, to achieve a "true" physical science that accords with theology. How, then, is one to express uncertainties or to deal with data that seem to contradict received truths? Whewell urges patience—and Ruskin shows how difficult it is to achieve. Ruskin's speculations on architecture carry him toward a momentary recognition of the sorts of contradictions Whewell prefers to ignore, "anomalies" of the kind Thomas Kuhn associates with the period of crisis leading to the emergence of new scientific paradigms. Sensing this crisis of traditional beliefs, Ruskin retreats.

His reference to "species" is the first and smallest example of an impulse we see elsewhere. Ruskin is on the verge of unmasking, in the same stroke, two fundamental truths concealed beneath prevailing contemporary ideologies: the existence of *Homo economicus* and that of *Homo biologicus,* the latter the more formidable for being wholly physical, without economic or social identity. What is disturbing in this view, then, is materialism: not just a recognition that human beings have bodies, or economic motives, but the notion that they may have nothing else. Such creatures are not the sort Ruskin wishes to see, not the sort he projects in the mythology I discussed earlier. Indeed, the abruptness with which the word *species* intrudes suggests that Ruskin regards the issue of biology as out of place and feels uneasy about raising it. One should not experience such thoughts in the country, he is saying; to do so is to be less than human, to become a mere animal. In beautiful buildings, however, aesthetics keep such possibilities at bay. The architectural argument, after all, is designed (like architecture itself) to elevate: poetry serves both to distance and to raise. This function is made clear (as if it were not clear from the start) when Ruskin changes his focus from cottages to villas. He says he makes the shift regretfully—but only in part: "not that we have any idea of living in a cottage, as a comfortable thing; not that we prefer mud to marble, or deal to mahogany. . . . But we are going into higher walks of architecture. . . ." The loftier subject seems to rise out of the simpler, more humble one, just as every "ideal" form is defined by contrast to some reality, or "abomination." The wish to ennoble, as Freud would add, always depends on its opposite, the potential for (perhaps secretly a desire for) degradation. Thus the beautiful harmony of ideal human architecture in the landscape is at best precarious, always implying the possibility of other, less perfect relations.

Ruskin would persuade us—and himself—that this harmony remains complete. He takes pains to show that those dwelling in the "higher walks of architecture" are in no way soiled by the earth, by their physical surroundings. He takes equal pains to convince us that those "higher walks" rise above a conception of architecture as "merely" useful. The "Chapter on Chimneys," which anticipates some of Ruskin's later functionalist strictures, may seem contradictory: "what is most adapted to its purpose is most beautiful"; yet we must not be made aware of this purpose by chimneys that obtrude, "interrupting all repose, annihilating all dignity," and substituting the sort of mock picturesque that appeals "to the mind of master-sweeps." And if emphasis on function links us to the wrong social class, it can bring us into a disturbing proximity with the wrong biological class as well. The chapter on Italian villas considers the implications of building houses "*merely* to be lived in" (Ruskin's italics are significant), so that "the whole bent of our invention, in raising the edifice, is to be directed to the provision of comfort for the life to be spent therein. . . ." After describing such a project at length, Ruskin asks what it represents: in using "great knowledge and various skill" in this way, what have we done?

> Exactly as much as bees and beavers, moles and magpies, ants and earwigs, do every day of their lives, without the slightest effort of reason; we have made ourselves superior as architects to the most degraded animation of the universe, only insomuch as we have lavished the highest efforts of intellect, to do what they have done with the most limited sensations that can constitute life.

Without the poetry of architecture, it seems, the poetry of humanity is also lost, as is what Keats termed "the poetry of earth." In spite of himself, Ruskin cannot avoid returning to the notion of a wholly material world, for it is one of the dark possibilities that his architectural-poetic edifice is designed to refute. The passage is a classic instance of Freudian denial, but it results only in a return of the repressed. No other moment in these essays indicates so clearly how much he feels is at stake: the dignity of the human species itself, its distinction from the rest of the animal kingdom. Architecture enshrines that difference.

In 1860, in *Unto This Last,* Ruskin argued that contemporary political economy, in trying to account for human behavior without referring to a soul, was like a science of gymnastics founded on the assumption that bodies have no skeletons. *The Poetry of Architecture* never identifies any opposing philosophy explicitly, yet many of its most powerful passages are directed against the "soullessness" of other forms of dismal science, including, but not limited to, the "Science of Architecture." Ruskin's contemptuous reference to "degraded" ants and earwigs reveals how closely he associates a materialist conception of architecture with the materialist views of life that were beginning to emerge, amid intense debate, from the work of contemporary naturalists. Earlier writers had also expressed such views. Erasmus Darwin (to mention the best known) described the evolutionary links between organic beings, originating in primordial slime:

> ORGANIC LIFE beneath the shoreless waves
> Was born and nurs'd in Ocean's pearly caves;
> First forms minute, unseen by spheric glass,
> Move on the mud, or pierce the watery mass;
> These, as successive generations bloom,
> New powers acquire, and larger limbs assume;
> Whence countless groups of vegetation spring,
> And breathing realms of fin, and feet, and wing.

Darwin is describing a process that begins with the "GREAT FIRST CAUSE," but as Whewell's remarks indicate, such views were often regarded as the harbingers of an atheistical materialism. Darwin's grandson Charles was sensitive enough to such hostility to caution himself to suppress his own thoughts on these matters—one reason the *Origin* did not appear for twenty years after he first arrived at his conclusions on evolution by means of natural selection. In 1838, as he was shaping those conclusions, he reminded himself in his notebooks "To avoid stating how far, I believe, in Materialism. . . ."

Of course Ruskin needs no such warning; his antipathy to materialism can never be stated strongly enough. But the very intensity of that feeling tells us something about its motive, about his fears for what science might become. He is concerned that the emerging materialist party will appropriate science, that the split Whewell warns against is beginning to take place. Hence, Ruskin's scientific writing is invariably conservative. It sets out to restore the spiritual element to modern naturalistic research. In a characteristic example, in his **"Remarks on the Present State of Meteorological Science"** (1839), Ruskin applies the language of art to meteorology, as he would to geology, zoology, and finally to all science: "It is indeed a knowledge which must be felt to be, in its very essence, full of the soul of the beautiful."

Ruskin seeks to mythologize science as well as social relations, a project to which he remained committed for another half century, even in the writings that seem least scientific. *Modern Painters,* which appeared in 1843, opens with an epigraph from Wordsworth's *Excursion,* a passage in which the Wanderer angrily dissociates his own poetic approach to nature from the work of materialist "Philosophers," "Viewing all objects unremittingly / In disconnection dead and spiritless." Shall they, he asks,

> . . . who rather dive than soar, whose pains
> Have solved the elements, or analysed
> The thinking principle—shall they in fact
> Prove a degraded Race?

Ruskin, who was already a Wordsworthian in 1837, fears that degradation could extend from scientists to the entire world. Indeed, it becomes clear that modern science and modern political economy pose identical threats, for both propose, in Ruskin's view, to reduce humanity to a "barbaric," purely creatural existence. The poetry of architecture resists this assault, enabling all civilization to claim that "we have made ourselves superior as architects to the most degraded animation of the universe. . . ." The politics of these scientific questions are illuminated when we contrast Ruskin's position with an opposing one, like William Howitt's in *The Rural Life of England.* Howitt also brings political and biological terms together, but he does so ironically: "If the peasant can be satisfied with his establishment, and the gentleman could not tell how to live without his, one would be almost persuaded that they could not be of the same class of animals. . . ." He is, of course, attacking the use of supposedly scientific categories to enforce artificial social distinctions. But for Ruskin such distinctions are real and inevitable: without a separation into higher and lower forms, all architectural, social, and biological dignity would be lost.

Ruskin's only direct comment on this issue emerges almost accidentally, but it is no less forceful for that. He is weighing the merits of building with brick, itself compounded of the earth, of mud. Not surprisingly, he insists that this material violates the highest architectural decorum. But there are conditions in which it does belong. Ruskin endorses the use of brick in "the Simple Blue Country"; like that phrase itself, his description of this region seems partly (perhaps unconsciously) ironic. It is a productive countryside, including agricultural lands and manufacturing districts, a world of "temporary wealth" and "matter-of-fact business-like activity" that is dizzying in its instability. And the ambiguity of the tone matches the ambiguous approval of brick itself: a lower form of architecture is justified by a lower form of life. Thus brick, Ruskin says, is

> admirably suited for that country where all is change, and all activity; where the working and money-making members of the community are perpetually succeeding and overpowering each other; enjoying, each in his turn, the reward of his industry; yielding up the field, the pasture, and the mine, to his successor, and leaving no

more memory behind him, no farther evidence of his individual existence, than is left by a working bee, in the honey for which we thank his class, forgetting the individual.

This passage reads like a post-Darwinian nightmare vision of industrial competition. But in fact Ruskin's imagery derives from some of the same sources Darwin knew, and ultimately from Malthus. It is as close as Ruskin comes to fully amalgamating *Homo economicus* and *Homo biologicus* or to openly acknowledging what makes their presence so foreboding. The figure of the drone, caught up in an endless Malthusian struggle, incorporates them both, suggesting that our membership in a class—whether a social or a scientific classification—robs us of individuality, that is, of identity itself. Ruskin did not articulate this issue, or its aesthetic alternative, until he wrote *The Stones of Venice,* where he praises Gothic for affirming "the individual value of every soul."

The Poetry of Architecture is only groping toward a definition of such ideals and of the problems they address, but the basic outlines of Ruskin's mature conceptions of architecture and society are already faintly present. Ruskin is aware that the problems of architecture are problems of history and that an aesthetic critic must help others discover—or rediscover—something essential that has been lost. At one point he recalls the "ancient name of 'merry' England; a name which, in this age of steam and iron, it will have some difficulty in keeping." Architecture, then, is poetic insofar as it is an art of renaming, resymbolizing, rebuilding (or else preserving what was built before) so that ancient names still apply. It is a poetry that alters the way we see, or read, everything around it and that alters us as well. For at the heart of architecture's poetry we can discern a capacity to supply a new ordering ritual for the whole of life (see Stein, *Ritual*), what Yeats would call a "ceremony of innocence." Ruskin senses a need, amid all the social and intellectual changes of 1838, for forms that can exhibit and exercise the highest faculties of the mind (he would say soul), that can sustain humanity itself in an increasingly materialized world. The social history of the following decades makes it difficult not to sympathize with the concerns that motivate his project. Yet the project remains vague—how vague the history of Ruskin's own work in those decades makes clear. It is a sign of his immaturity that in the 1830s he has no more precise word for his goals than poetry. Much of the rest of his life would be devoted to the search for more accurate terms. But here at the outset he shows the direction that search will take, for he associates poetry with architecture, the discipline that unifies all his aesthetic and social writing. Perhaps it was that initial, essential choice—to write about architecture—that enabled him to look back fifty years later and find nothing changed.

Anthony Hecht (essay date 1985)

SOURCE: "The Pathetic Fallacy," in *The Yale Review,* Vol. 74, No. 4, Summer, 1985, pp. 481-99.

[*In the following essay, Hecht explores the meaning of "pathetic fallacy," a term coined by Ruskin.*]

Un paysage quelconque est un état de l'âme.

—Henri-Frédéric Amiel

The world is a fair field fresh with the odor of Christ's name.

—St. Augustine

My title is a famous coinage of John Ruskin's, and comes from his five-volume study called *Modern Painters*. I want to begin by quoting Ruskin at some length, intruding an occasional impertinent interruption, as a way of recalling to you his original and provocative formulation, while permitting myself an obbligato of comment. I begin with a sentence of his full of high disdain and mockery.

> German dulness, and English affectation, have of late much multiplied among us the use of two of the most objectionable words that were ever coined by the troublesomeness of metaphysicians—namely, "Objective," and "Subjective."

A promising beginning, and Ruskin proceeds with a brisk and touching confidence that these philosophic muddles can be laid to rest once and for all.

> Now, therefore, putting these tiresome and absurd words quite out of our way, we may go on at our ease to examine the point in question,—namely, the difference between the ordinary, proper, and true appearances of things to us; and the extraordinary, or false appearances, when we are under the influence of emotion, or contemplative fancy; false appearances, I say, as being entirely unconnected with any real power or character in an object, and only imputed to it by us . . . what is more, if we think over our favorite poetry, we shall find it full of this kind of fallacy, and that we like it all the more for being so.

> It will appear also, on consideration of the matter, that this fallacy is of two principal kinds. Either . . . it is the fallacy of wilful fancy, which involves no real expectation that it will be believed; or else it is a fallacy caused by an excited state of the feelings, making us, for the time, more or less irrational.

I interrupt here to remark that Ruskin was no slouch at employing the fallacy when he cared to. Here, for example, is a fragment of description from *Modern Painters*:

> Such precipices are . . . dark in color, robed with everlasting mourning, for ever tottering like a great fortress shaken by war, fearful as much in their weakness as in their strength, and yet gathered after every fall into darker frowns and unhumiliated threatening. . . .

That sentence continues for another two hundred and eight words. Of the two kinds of fallacy he distinguishes, the first (that of the "wilful fancy, which involves no real expectation that it will be believed") is characteristic of the poetry of wit both of the Renaissance and of the eighteenth century, and of poetry that adopts conventions meant to be recognized as conventional and tradition that is consciously traditional. It is this kind for which Ruskin feels the easiest and most derisive contempt. The other

kind (the fallacy caused by excited and irrational feelings) enlists his deeper and more serious consideration.

> All violent feelings have the same effect. They produce in us a falseness in our impressions of external things, which I would generally characterize as the "pathetic fallacy."

> Now we are in the habit of considering this fallacy as eminently a character of poetic description, and the temper of mind in which we allow it, as one eminently poetical, because passionate. But I believe, if we look well into the matter, that we shall find the greatest poets do not often admit this kind of falseness,—that it is only the second order of poets who much delight in it.

And by way of explaining this distinction, he adds an important footnote:

> I admit two orders of poets, but no third; and by these two orders I mean the creative (Shakespeare, Homer, Dante), and the Reflective or Perceptive (Wordsworth, Keats, Tennyson). But both of these must be first-rate in their range, though their range is different; and with poetry second-rate in quality no one ought to be allowed to trouble mankind.

There is enough in that note to make almost any modern poet tremble; but I ask you please to observe, before Ruskin proceeds, that he has neatly arrogated the three poets of the first rank to his side as being virtually guiltless of the fallacy. Having divided all poets conveniently into two ranks, only a moment later he adds another:

> So, then, we have the three ranks: the man who perceives rightly, because he does not feel, and to whom the primrose is very accurately the primrose, because he does not love it. Then, secondly, the man who perceives wrongly, because he feels, and to whom the primrose is anything else than a primrose: a star, or a sun, or a fairy's shield, or a forsaken maiden.

I interrupt to intrude as an example D. H. Lawrence's statement, "The perfect rose is only a running flame," the sort of statement that in all likelihood prompted Gertrude Stein's famous reflection, "A rose is a rose is a rose." But to return to Ruskin's third rank:

> And then, lastly, there is the man who perceives rightly in spite of his feelings, and to whom the primrose is forever nothing else than itself—a little flower apprehended in the very plain and leafy fact of it, whatever and how many soever the associations and passions may be that crowd around it. And in general, these three classes may be rated in comparative order, as the men who are not poets at all, and the poets of the second order, and the poets of the first; only however great a man may be, there are always some subjects that ought to throw him off his balance . . . .

So, having begun with two ranks, and moved onward to three, Ruskin now advances to four, though only two, properly speaking, are poets:

> And thus, in full, there are four classes: the men

who feel nothing, and therefore see truly; the men who feel strongly, think weakly, and see untruly (the second order of poets); the men who feel strongly, think strongly, and see truly (the first order of poets); and the men who, strong as human creatures can be, are yet submitted to influences stronger than they, and see in a sort untruly, because what they see is inconceivably above them. This last is the usual condition of prophetic inspiration.

You will not have failed to notice how central is the notion of strength to Ruskin's formulation and how for him the ideal poet of the first rank enjoys a neatly symmetrical balance of strong mind and strong feeling perfectly matched. There is, in any case, no question in his mind (nor, he assumes, in the reader's) that strong feeling, all other considerations apart, is essential to poetry. He declares quite flatly:

A poet is great, first in proportion to the strength of his passion, and then, that strength being granted, in proportion to his government of it; there being, however, always a point beyond which it would be inhuman and monstrous if he pushed this government, and, therefore, a point at which all feverish and wild fancy becomes just and true.

That point, for Ruskin, is the acknowledgment of the divine order and divinity itself, which, according to him, would seem to permit any kind of rant and raving whatever. For him, the forces of mind and of feeling are pitted against each other in exhausting contest, the mind obliged to govern the feelings, but the feelings determined to make it as difficult as possible for the mind to do so; and the quality of the poetry, according to this combative metaphor, will be determined by the ferocity, the persistence, and inconclusiveness of the antagonism. It is, quite clearly, a distinctly romantic description of the problem, and it should come to us as no surprise that Ruskin is as loftily dismissive of Alexander Pope as he is of Claude Lorrain. He exhorts us sneeringly to "hear the coldhearted Pope say to a shepherd girl—" and then quotes the lovely lines that Handel set so beautifully to music:

Where'er you walk, cool gales shall fan the glade;
Trees, where you sit, shall crowd into a shade;
Your praise the birds shall chant in every grove,
And winds shall waft it to the powers above.

Of these lines Ruskin writes contemptuously, "This is not, nor could it for a moment be mistaken for, the language of passion. It is simple falsehood, uttered by hypocrisy," and one cannot help feeling that there speaks the voice of the complete prig. The entire genre of the pastoral, which presupposes a sympathetic relationship between nature and rustic humanity, is here dismissed. So much for "Lycidas." Falsehood is charged, we may suppose, because we don't for a minute believe Pope (in eighteenth-century London) is really addressing a genuine shepherdess; and hypocrisy because a compliment involving the universal obeisance of nature to the young lady presents us with a pathetic fallacy so hyperbolic, so extravagant and beyond the limits of credence, that it ceases to be a compliment,

and proves itself mere artifice and empty flattery. But Pope and his century ought not to be spurned quite so easily. Paul Fussell has observed that even when poetry of this period

has not been specifically dismissed on charges of artifice and conventionality, it has been benignly neglected in favor of the sort which seems to reflect back onto us those extreme emotional states made peculiarly our own by modern history—strain, personal and collective guilt, hysteria, madness.

He proceeds to remind us that "any kind of art, just because of its conspicuous distinction from the natural and the accidental, is much more conventional and institutionalized than we may have imagined."

Ruskin, however, turns from what he regards as the coldheartedness of Pope to the ungoverned passion of a poem by Wordsworth and concludes:

I believe these instances are enough to illustrate the main point I insist upon respecting the pathetic fallacy,—that so far as it is a fallacy, it is always the sign of a morbid state of mind, and comparatively of a weak one.

And he adds that it is "eminently characteristic of the modern mind."

His eagerness to find this morbidity distinctly modern may perhaps be an attempt to protect a badly exposed flank. You will recall that he numbered among his poets of the first order both Homer and Shakespeare. And Ruskin is eager to forestall the charge that the earliest of the great poets was liberal in his use of the fallacy. So to anticipate our objections, he himself raises the question in regard to the famous passage in the *Iliad* in which Achilles and the river Scamander argue and fight with one another. One would suppose this was the *locus classicus* of the pathetic fallacy. But Ruskin is concerned to claim all the Greeks, and Homer as their representative, for the camp of clear-sighted realism, and he insists that the deification or personification of the river—which allows it to remonstrate and petition and express all manner of feeling in human language—is not to impute human feelings to the world of nature but is the Greeks' pious deification, not of the river itself, but of the power behind and within it. There is something unnervingly question-begging about how he makes this obscure and not-altogether-convincing distinction, but I had best let him make it in his own words.

With us, observe, the idea of the Divinity is apt to get separated from the life of nature; and imagining our God upon a cloudy throne, far above the earth, and not in the flowers or waters, we approach those visible things with a theory that they are dead; governed by physical laws, and so forth. But coming to them, we find the theory fail; that they are not dead; that, say what we choose about them, the instinctive sense of their being alive is too strong for us; and in scorn of all physical law, the wilful fountain sings, and the kindly flowers rejoice. And then, puzzled, and yet happy; pleased, and yet ashamed of being so; accepting sympathy from nature, which we do not believe it gives, and giving sympathy to nature, which we do not believe it receives,—mixing, besides, all manner of purposeful play and conceit with these involuntary fellowships,—we fall necessarily into the curious web of hesitant sentiment, pathetic fallacy, and wandering fancy, which form a great part of our modern view of nature. But the Greek never removed his god out of nature at all; never attempted for a moment to contradict his instinctive sense that God was everywhere. "The tree is glad," he said, "I know it is; I can cut it down: no matter, there is a nymph in it. The water *does* sing," said he; "I can dry it up; but no matter, there was a naiad in it."

Ruskin's position here is predicated on what he seems to posit as the incontestable sincerity of Hellenic pantheism, a very doubtful and certainly unprovable ground. But Homer is not as neat in his distinctions as Ruskin, and he not only exhibits to us the deity that animates the river but presents a Trojan named Asteropaeus, a valiant mortal, whose mortality is put beyond question when Achilles kills him, but who identifies himself as the son of a river. So the genetics of divinity begin to thin out a little. But Homer carries the matter further still. When Asteropaeus and Achilles were engaged in their duel, the Trojan let fly one of his spears, which grazed Achilles, drawing blood. Homer then declares, "the spear passed over him and stuck in the ground, still hungering for flesh." This locution of the hunger of the spear for flesh comes up again and again in the *Iliad,* and it has no bearing upon Greek piety or pantheism. It is a straightforward imputation of human feelings to an inanimate object. As for Shakespeare, another of Ruskin's poets of the first order, he elects to put into the mouth of Hotspur, a professed hater of poetry, what amounts to a very deliberate imitation of these very passages from the twenty-first book of the *Iliad,* when Hotspur commends Mortimer and rises hotly to his defense before King Henry IV.

> He never did fall off, my sovereign liege,
> But by the chance of war. To prove that true
> Needs no more but one tongue for all those
>   wounds,
> Those mouthed wounds, which valiantly he took
> When on the gentle Severn's sedgy bank,
> He did confound the best part of an hour
> In changing hardiment with great Glendower.
> Three times they breathed, and three times they
>   did drink,
> Upon agreement, of swift Severn's flood;
> Who then, affrighted with their bloody looks,
> Ran fearfully among the trembling reeds
> And hid his crisp head in the hollow bank,
> Bloodstained with these valiant combatants.
>   (1 *Henry IV,* 1.3)

Shakespeare, of course, *pace* Ruskin, is a mine and fund of instances of the fallacy, of which Duke Senior's famous speech in the Forest of Arden is a useful example.

> Now, my co-mates and brothers in exile,
> Hath not old custom made this life more sweet
> Than that of painted pomp? Are not these woods
> More free from peril than the envious court?
> Here feel we but the penalty of Adam;

> The seasons' difference, as the icy fang
> And churlish chiding of the winter's wind,
> Which, when it bites and blows upon my body
> Even till I shrink with cold, I smile and say
> "This is no flattery"; these are counsellors
> That feelingly persuade me what I am.
> Sweet are the uses of adversity,
> Which, like the toad, ugly and venomous,
> Wears yet a precious jewel in his head;
> And this our life, exempt from public haunt,
> Finds tongues in trees, books in the running
>   brooks,
> Sermons in stones, and good in everything.
>   (*As You Like It,* 2.1)

This speech may be taken as representing the anagogic or emblematic mode of viewing nature that was nearly a commonplace from the Middle Ages up to at least the seventeenth century. It is a mode characteristically religious, beautifully stated in the epigraph I have used from St. Augustine, and premised on the conviction that the whole purpose and majesty of God is made legible in the most minute, as well as the most stunning and conspicuous, parts of his creation; that attentive contemplation of any single part will reveal in code but with clarity the whole glory and intent of the Creator. This conviction is based on biblical texts as well as theological argument, and one of the best known of the texts is the Nineteenth Psalm.

> The heavens declare the glory of God; and the
>   firmament sheweth his handiwork.
> Day unto day uttereth speech, and night unto
>   night sheweth knowledge.
> There is no speech nor language where their
>   voice is not heard.

This eloquence of the physical universe, this demonstration on the part of the natural world, amounts to a revelation to all who are not blind and deaf. "He that hath ears to hear, let him hear; and who hath eyes to see, let him see." The world as holy cipher and mute articulator can be found not only in medieval texts and Shakespeare but in those emblematic or symbolic poems by Herbert and Donne and Herrick that are among the great achievements of their age, and for which I will let the less well-known poem by Henry King, called "Contemplation Upon Flowers," stand as an instance.

> Brave flowers, that I could gallant it like you
> And be as little vain;
> You come abroad, and make a harmless shew,
> And to your beds of earth again;
> You are not proud, you know your birth,
> For your embroidered garments are from earth.
>
> You do obey your months, and times, but I
> Would have it ever spring;
> My fate would know no winter, never die
> Nor think of such a thing;
> Oh, that I could my bed of earth but view
> And smile, and look as cheerfully as you.
>
> Oh, teach me to see death, and not to fear,
> But rather to take truce;
> How often have I seen you at a bier,
> And there look fresh and spruce;
> You fragrant flowers, then teach me that my
>   breath

Like yours may sweeten, and perfume my death.

From such grave counselors as these let me ask you to shift your attention abruptly to the world of fiction. Novelists were not slow to make use of strategies that Ruskin discovers in the works of poets and painters. Merely to propose to you such diverse authors as Dickens, Conrad, Dostoevski, Hawthorne, Joyce, and Mann may suggest without further elaboration the various ways in which a setting is made to bear a significant burden of meaning and a virtual role in a story. But let me use Hardy's *Return of the Native* as an example. The first chapter of that novel is given over entirely to the description of a landscape, a landscape not only bleak in itself but here, in its initial appearance, devoid of human life and habitation.

> A Saturday afternoon in November was approaching the time of twilight, and the vast tract of unenclosed wild known as Egdon Heath embrowned itself moment by moment.

That's Hardy's first sentence, and I invite you to notice that his chief verb, *embrowned,* is not only active, suggesting that the landscape is purposively engaged in its own transmutations, but that the word is richly Miltonic, coming straight from a landscape in *Paradise Lost*:

> Both where the morning sun first warmly smote
> The open field and where the unpierced shade
> Embrowned the noontide bowers. . . .

And it bears, in consequence, the omen of a landscape shadowed by doom. I continue to quote selectively from Hardy's chapter.

> The face of the heath by its mere complexion added half an hour to the evening; it could in like manner retard the dawn, sadden noon, anticipate the frowning of storms scarcely generated, and intensify the opacity of a moonless midnight to a cause of shaking and dread. . . . The spot was, indeed, a near relation of night. . . . The sombre stretch of rounds and hollows seemed to rise and meet the evening gloom in pure sympathy, the heath exhaling darkness as the heavens precipitated it. And so the obscurity of the air and the obscurity of the land closed together in a black fraternization towards which each advanced half-way. . . . It was at present a place perfectly accordant with man's nature—neither ghastly, hateful, not ugly: neither commonplace, unmeaning, nor tame; but, like man, slighted and enduring; and withal singularly colossal and mysterious in its swarthy monotony. As with some persons who have lived long apart, solitude seemed to look out of its countenance. It had a lonely face, suggesting tragical possibilities.

The point is not merely that Hardy gives a countenance and human quality to his landscape, as might the composer of a *paysage moralisé,* but that he gives to it a dimension we may call superhuman: as mise en scène it becomes the destiny and fate, tragic in character, of all those who there inhabit. Hardy, of course, did much the same thing in his best lyrics, but I should like to give you instead another poetic example, one that when I was a college student in the 1940s was still able to confound, bewilder, and even enrage a large number of readers. By now, of course, most of you will know these lines by heart.

> Let us go then, you and I,
> When the evening is spread out against the sky
> Like a patient etherized upon a table; . . .

There was in those days a certain splenetic sort of reader who never got beyond this point in the poem. Red-faced and apoplectic, he would ask explosively, "How can an evening be like a patient? How can similes be used with so little regard for visual accuracy or plain intelligibility? This is just modern hokum." But Eliot is doing pretty much the same thing Hardy did in the passage I quoted; instead of a landscape, he presents a skyscape that shall serve as the presiding fate and destiny of the chief characters who inhabit beneath its crepuscular dimness.

Let me retain my splenetic reader in the witness box for yet a moment longer. There is so much in modern poetry that sends him into paroxysms of fury. Think of the fulminations engendered by his reading of William Carlos Williams's "The Red Wheelbarrow."

> so much depends
> upon
>
> a red wheel
> barrow
>
> glazed with rain
> water
>
> beside the white
> chickens

If I may be allowed to eliminate my witness's characteristic expletives, expressions of repugnance at omissions of capitalization, and his blank incomprehension about the division of lines (though syllabically they form a handsome and symmetrical pattern), his central complaint comes to this: What is the thing that so much depends; and how much is "so much"? To which we may respond that the "so much" does not require measurement, being part of what is an exclamatory statement, implying astonishment at how very much indeed is concerned in this dependency. And what, finally, is the dependency but the intimate and indissoluble relationship of the inner and outer worlds, the "subjective" and "objective" states that Ruskin was so eager to eliminate. The objective is straightforward, factual, visual; the subjective is evaluative, secret, and interior. The objective world is nothing but random data without the governing subjective selection and evaluation; the two are halves of a single act of cognition. So there is mystery to the poem, but it is the common mystery of our moment-to-moment existence. Thus stated, it would seem that the pathetic fallacy was almost unavoidable, however condemnatory Ruskin felt about it. And, indeed, as a puzzle, it has fascinated modern poets, who have even written about the possibility of trying to avoid it. Can it be avoided? The topic was famously addressed by Ortega y Gasset in his essay "The Dehumanization of Art," from which I want to quote selectively:

> What is it the majority of people call aesthetic pleasure? What happens in their minds when they "like" a work of art; for instance, a theatri-

cal performance? The answer is easy. A man likes a play when he has become interested in the human destinies presented to him, when the love and hatred, the joys and sorrows of the personages so move his heart that he participates in it as though it were happening in real life. And he calls a work "good" if it succeeds in creating the illusion necessary to make the imaginary personages appear like living persons. In poetry he seeks the passion and pain of the man behind the poet. Paintings attract him if he finds in them figures of men and women whom it would be interesting to meet. A landscape is pronounced "pretty" if the country it represents deserves for its loveliness or its grandeur to be visited on a trip. . . . Now . . . not only is grieving and rejoicing at such human destinies as a work of art presents or narrates a very different thing from true artistic pleasure, but preoccupation with the human content of a work of art is in principle incompatible with aesthetic enjoyment proper. . . . I will not now discuss whether pure art is possible. Perhaps it is not; but as the reasons that make me inclined to think so are somewhat long and difficult the subject better be dropped. Besides, it is not of major importance for the matter in hand. Even though pure art may be impossible, there doubtless can prevail a tendency toward a purification of art. Such a tendency would effect a progressive elimination of the human, all too human, elements predominant in romantic and naturalistic production. And in this process a point can be reached in which the human content has grown so thin that it is negligible. We then have an art which can be comprehended only by people possessed of the peculiar gift of artistic sensibility—an art for artists and not for the masses, for "quality" and not for hoi polloi.

The masses, who would include my splenetic commentator of a moment ago, can point contemptuously to what they regard as elitist paintings wherein, in Ortega's words, "the human content has grown so thin that it is negligible." In Mondrian, for example. And they are not likely to be persuaded otherwise even by so eloquent a spokesman for the opposition as is Meyer Schapiro in his fine essay "On The Humanity of Abstract Painting." But is such purity possible in a poem? Is it even imaginable? The puzzle lies at the center of Wallace Steven's celebrated poem "The Snow Man."

> One must have a mind of winter
> To regard the frost and the boughs
> Of the pine-trees crusted with snow;
>
> And have been cold a long time
> To behold the junipers shagged with ice,
> The spruces rough in the distant glitter
>
> Of the January sun; and not to think
> Of any misery in the sound of the wind,
> In the sound of a few leaves,
>
> Which is the sound of the land
> Full of the same wind
> That is blowing in the same bare place
>
> For the listener, who listens in the snow,

> And, nothing himself, beholds
> Nothing that is not there and the nothing that
> is.

The poem projects a kind of mind that out of either numbness or a gritty and stoical courage can set itself apart from every chilling fact of its existence, a chill which is thermal and metaphysical at once, accepting both the coldness and the nothingness for what they are and apart from any human valuation. As a poem it is wonderful and harrowing; as a strategy to circumvent the pathetic fallacy it almost works. Almost, except that it claims of the wind that it blows "in the same bare place / For the listener," thereby attributing a motive and purpose, a curiously human attribute, either to the wind or to some fateful agency that presides over wind and listener. But in any case the poem suggests that objectivity is a condition that can be approached only by canceling our humanity and by advancing toward a state that strongly resembles insensibility or death. Stevens is continuously concerned in his work with the peculiar relations between subjective and objective reality and returns to the puzzle again and again in such poems as "Esthétique du Mal" and "Extracts from Addresses to the Academy of Fine Ideas."

Though Stevens and Frost used to taunt one another about being antipodal and polar opposites in their poetic concerns (Stevens said that Frost's poetry was full of "subjects," by which he seemed to mean the sort of human-interest topics that belonged to a classroom assignment, while Frost said that Stevens's poems were "full of bric-a-brac"), Frost nevertheless addressed the same puzzle so continuously in successive poems that the two poets seem curiously allied. I have had some difficulty deciding which poem of Frost's I could best employ here, having given serious consideration to "Directive," "The Need of Being Versed in Country Things," "For Once, Then, Something," and "The Most of It," and I've settled on "The Wood-Pile."

> Out walking in the frozen swamp one gray day
> I paused and said, "I will turn back from here.
> No, I will go on farther—and we shall see."
> The hard snow held me, save where now and
>   then
> One foot went through. The view was all in lines
> Straight up and down of tall slim trees
> Too much alike to mark or name a place by
> So as to say for certain I was here
> Or somewhere else: I was just far from home.
> A small bird flew before me. He was careful
> To put a tree between us when he lighted,
> And say no word to tell me who he was
> Who was so foolish as to think what he thought.
> He thought that I was after him for a feather—
> The white one in his tail; like one who takes
> Everything said as personal to himself.
> One flight out sideways would have undeceived
>   him.
> And then there was a pile of wood for which
> I forgot him and let his little fear
> Carry him off the way I might have gone,
> Without so much as wishing him good-night.
> He went behind it to make his last stand.
> It was a cord of maple, cut and split
> And piled—and measured, four by four by eight.

And not another like it could I see.
No runner tracks in this year's snow looped near
 it.
And it was older sure than this year's cutting,
Or even last year's or the year's before.
The wood was gray and the bark warping off it
And the pile somewhat shrunken. Clematis
Had wound strings round and round it like a
 bundle.
What held it though on one side was a tree
Still growing, and on one a stake and prop,
These latter about to fall. I thought that only
Someone who lived in turning to fresh tasks
Could so forget his handiwork on which
He spent himself, the labor of his axe,
And leave it there far from a useful fireplace
To warm the frozen swamp as best it could
With the slow smokeless burning of decay.

Like countless other Frost poems, this one insists upon the solitariness and isolation of the speaker, involved in some sort of quest or pilgrimage, and the opening lines cannot fail to remind us of

Nel mezzo del cammin di nostra vita
mi ritrovai per una selva oscura
ché la diritta via era smarrita.

(When I had journeyed half of our life's way,
I found myself within a shadowed forest,
for I had lost the path that does not stray.)

The journey is perilous, over unstable and uncharted terrain, by one so lonely and uncertain that he talks to himself, as the lonely do, positing an alter ego, a companion and dialectical double, with whom to debate the wisdom of going on, and with whom to join ranks in "we shall see." The role of doppelgänger is then taken over by the bird, onto which the speaker projects thoughts, fears, all manner of human attitudes, not least of them paranoia, which is itself an illness consisting of projecting baseless feelings upon others. It is an illness from which Frost himself was not immune, and here he is trying to make light of it with a jest that has its deeply touching aspect. That bird is clearly part of his own psyche, and, though troubled, he is also wise enough to acknowledge this. The bird may be governed chiefly by fear; the man seems directed wholly by chance (as are most of us in the main matters of our lives), and it is chance that brings him to the woodpile. As in many another Frost poem, like "After Apple Picking," "Two Tramps in Mud Time," or "The Tuft of Flowers," in which well-and-patiently performed manual labor symbolizes the craft of writing poetry, the woodpile is the symbol once again of accomplished craftsmanship, a human opus, a body of work, here inexplicably lost from common sight or practical utility, a carefully composed effort that has come to nothing. And what do most of our lives come to after all? Dante, of course, attained Paradise within his poem, and even worldly immortality by means of it. In this pilgrimage poem the poet, who is still as lost at the end of the poem as at the beginning, tries to put a cheerful face on a situation that looked bleak right from the start by saying, "I thought that only / Someone who lived in turning to fresh tasks / Could so forget his handiwork on which / He spent himself." But surely we are allowed to consider the possibility that the speaker is trying

to cheer himself up, since other possibilities present themselves to explain the odd abandonment of that woodpile, only the most obvious of which is that the man who cut and stacked it has died. And if his labor decays unnoticed, how much more likely is this to be the case with the work of poets, whose audiences are not inclined to be large, whose work is quickly forgotten after their deaths, if it was ever noticed in their lifetimes, unless it were to be stumbled upon by some total and unexpected stranger. The poet composes his world in solitude and anxiety, for which Frost has here found what Eliot called an "objective correlative," and he has done this, as I think, with stunning success. The poem appeared in 1914, when the poet was by no means confident he would ever be famous or remembered and was much inclined to question his entire goal and purpose.

The poet's digression into paranoia and related psychic states, the critic's coinage of "objective correlative," invite further inspection. George Steiner has remarked that "the primary thrust of all libido is towards injection of all realities into the self," and in *Crime and Punishment* we are witness to a dream of Svidrigailov's in which he cunningly transforms his lust for a child by turning her into a six-year-old prostitute and making himself her helpless victim. As for the strategies of the critic, things have come a long way since the comparative critical innocence of Mr. Eliot. Here, from an essay that appeared in the Winter 1983 issue of *Daedalus,* is Eugene Goodheart commenting upon and quoting from the work of Roland Barthes.

> For Roland Barthes, the pleasure of the text is in the making of one's own text at the expense of another's. "Thus begins at the heart of the critical work the dialogue of two histories and two subjectivities, the author's and the critic's. But this dialogue is egotistically shifted toward the present: criticism is not an homage to the truth of the past or to the truth of 'others'—it is a construction of the intelligibility of our own time." In shamelessly confessing the egotism of the critical act, Barthes casts doubt upon the objective existence of "others." . . . His motive is to make the "other" vulnerable and defenseless, so that he can appropriate the text to his own purpose: Barthes speaks of the critical act as theft. Interpretation, in this transvalued sense, is not obliged to represent the text, which is, rather, broken up so that it can fill the critic's subjectivity. In declaring "the death of the author," Barthes eliminates interference from an author's intention. The critical reader's access to the text is immediate, dominant, and impermanent. The critic's text is always provisional, his relationship to the text of the other in constant change. The critic need be faithful only to his own changing, desiring subjectivity.

It was not Eliot, of course, but W. K. Wimsatt who long ago pointed out the dangers of the "intentional fallacy," i.e., limiting the meaning of a text to what either the author thought it meant (since, as Freud has told us, we can often mean more than we are aware of) or what the critic posits as the author's intention. But it is a giant step, a seven-league stride, from Wimsatt to Barthes and others of the current French School of Decomposition so favored these days in certain circles. And so, by an easy exchange of critic for lover, the modern reader, paraphrasing Theseus, may conclude that "The lunatic, the critic and the poet / Are of imagination all compact." But might not the reader also assume that however screwy the literary types might be, however lost in their subjective mists, their solipsisms, their blind self-absorption, at least the scientist, the physicist, could be appealed to as clear-headed defender of "Objectivity"? This would be rash. Listen to Werner Heisenberg: "What we observe is not nature itself but nature exposed to our method of questioning." So much for Ruskin's easy dismissal of the terms "subjective" and "objective." But I dare not end my lecture in a celebration of chaos and confusion. And by way of rescuing myself from that peril, I turn with pleasure to one more poem, this one by Richard Wilbur, called "Advice to a Prophet."

> When you come, as you soon must, to the streets
> of our city,
> Mad-eyed from stating the obvious,
> Not proclaiming our fall but begging us
> In God's name to have self-pity,
>
> Spare us all word of the weapons, their force and
> range,
> The long numbers that rocket the mind;
> Our slow, unreckoning hearts will be left behind,
> Unable to fear what is too strange.
>
> Nor shall you scare us with talk of the death of
> the race.
> How could we dream of this place without us?—
> The sun mere fire, the leaves untroubled about
> us,
> A stone look on the stone's face?
>
> Speak of the world's own change. Though we
> cannot conceive
> Of an undreamt thing, we know to our cost
> How the dreamt cloud crumbles, the vines are
> blackened by frost,
> How the view alters. We could believe,
>
> If you told us so, that the white-tailed deer will
> slip
> Into perfect shade, grown perfectly shy,
> The lark avoid the reaches of our eye,
> The jack-pine lose its knuckled grip
>
> On the cold ledge, and every torrent burn
> As Xanthus once, its gliding trout
> Stunned in a twinkling. What should we be without
> The dolphin's arc, the dove's return,
>
> These things in which we have seen ourselves
> and spoken?
> Ask us, prophet, how we shall call
> Our natures forth when that live tongue is all
> Dispelled, that glass obscured and broken
>
> In which we have said the rose of our love and
> the clean
> Horse of our courage, in which beheld
> The singing locust of the soul unshelled,
> And all we mean or wish to mean.
>
> Ask us, ask us whether with the worldless rose
> Our hearts shall fail us; come demanding
> Whether there shall be lofty or long standing

> When the bronze annals of the oak-tree close.

My motives in reading that poem here in Washington are by no means confined to their pertinence to my topic, though that pertinence is of a rich and complex kind. In his reference to Xanthus, another name for the River Scamander, Wilbur returns me to my beginnings with the *Iliad,* and in his beautiful and intricate weavings of the imagery of speech and sight, his protracted braiding of "These things in which we have seen ourselves and spoken," he recapitulates the very means and methods of the Nineteenth Psalm: "The heavens declare the glory of God; and the firmament sheweth his handiwork. Day unto day uttereth speech, and night unto night sheweth knowledge." But in addition to all these important resonances, there is the beautiful and undoubted fact that metaphor is not merely our mode of expressing ourselves but of expressing the world, or what we are able to know of it. And metaphor is not merely the gadget of poets; it is virtually unavoidable as an instrument of thought. Here is Ruskin himself upon the topic.

> Will you undertake to convey to another person a perfectly distinct idea of any single emotion passing in your own heart? You cannot—you cannot fathom it yourself—you have no actual expression for the simple idea, and are compelled to have instant recourse to metaphor.

The very act of description is in some degree metaphoric, and when Socrates tries to say what the Good is, the nearest he can come is to say that it is like light. In Wilbur's rich intertwining of voice and image, of sight and sound, he asks,

>   . . . how shall we call
> Our natures forth when that live tongue is all
> Dispelled, that glass obscured or broken
>
> In which we have said the rose of our love . . .
>   . . . in which beheld
> The singing locust of the soul. . . .

That glass of Wilbur's is not only the lens or prism of the sciences but also the infinitely lavish hall of mirrors, the Versailles of facets and reflections, in which wherever we look we see, as we must, unfailingly, some unexpected aspect of ourselves.

Dinah Birch   (essay date 1988)

SOURCE: "Ruskin's 'Womanly Mind,' " in *Essays in Criticism,* Vol. XXXVIII, No. 4, October, 1988, pp. 308-24.

[*In the following essay, Birch argues that while Ruskin's work has enraged feminists, his thinking was often "womanly" and not antagonistic to some of the tenets of modern feminism.*]

Ruskin's reputation survives, but in a fragmented form. His writings are voluminous, demanding, and often out of print. The books, lectures, or passages that do retain currency are usually studied in specific contexts. For students of Victorian literature, **'The Nature of Gothic'** and, more recently, **'Traffic'** have gained solid status as classics of social thought. *Unto This Last* has comparable prestige for those concerned with political history, while contemporary interest in forms of autobiography has guaranteed a readership for *Praeterita*. Art historians may have a more or less respectful acquaintance with *Modern Painters* and *The Stones of Venice*. The rest has nearly disappeared from view. Perceptions of Ruskin have accordingly diverged as they have crystallized. But there is at least one other work by Ruskin, his 1864 lecture 'Of Queens' Gardens', which has long been widely read. *Sesame and Lilies,* the volume in which 'Of Queens' Gardens' was first published, was for decades a favoured choice as a prize for schoolgirls. As such it found a place, as a sign of success in the established order, on the shelves of countless young women. Perhaps that gave Ruskin a bad start among feminists. For many women, *Sesame and Lilies* has become familiar as the supreme expression of all we need to know and despise about Victorian culture.

This current of contempt can be traced to a powerful source. Kate Millett's *Sexual Politics* (1969) set 'Of Queens' Gardens' against John Stuart Mill's robust piece of progressive humanism, *The Subjection of Women* (1869)—an encounter in which Ruskin comes off spectacularly badly. Millett is unrelenting in her analysis of the various ways in which Ruskin's lecture 'recommends itself as one of the most complete insights obtainable into that compulsive masculine fantasy one might call the official Victorian attitude'. She describes how Ruskin, with 'bland disingenuousness', adopts an ingratiatingly chivalrous attitude to women that flatters their bourgeois pretensions while denying them access to real political or economic power. Ruskin is advocating a pernicious kind of sexual apartheid, in which equality is speciously claimed for separate social spheres which are in fact monstrously and oppressively unequal—as John Stuart Mill's political and historical analysis makes painfully clear. Kate Millett is particularly devastating about the claim with which Ruskin ends his lecture—the allegation that women, despite the crippling disabilities imposed on them by men, are nevertheless peculiarly responsible for the moral welfare of society. 'There is a certain humour', Millett grimly reminds us, 'in Ruskin's proclamation that women, confined through history to a vicarious and indirect existence, without a deciding voice in any event, with so much of the burden of military, economic and technological events visited upon her, and so little of their glories, is nevertheless solely accountable for morality on the planet.'

Though Millett's influential work has, inevitably, been challenged and revised, some of the implications of her polemic have remained unquestioned—including the still prevalent view that a historically-minded feminist can read Ruskin only with the worthy but depressing ambition of familiarizing herself with some of the murkier sources of patriarchy. However, as feminist criticism has grown in maturity and scope, it has begun to establish ways in which reading Ruskin from the perspective of gender can reaffirm his significance and value. We do not need to abandon Millett's fierce insights in order to reclaim Ruskin's work as a rewarding rather than simply enraging matter for women's study.

Ruskin's writing grows out of his life. Sympathetically or not, various biographers have shown us how extraordinary that life was. Among its many contradictions is a disparity between the arguments advanced in 'Of Queens' Gardens' and the way in which Ruskin actually lived and behaved. Despite his dismal structures about the proper limitations of women's education in that lecture, Ruskin was for much of his life actively concerned with the furtherance of education for women. He was keenly interested in the foundation of the first women's colleges in Oxford, particularly Somerville, and endowed them with valuable pictures and artifacts. He also lent his support to Whitelands, a new women's college in London, and to a women's college in Cork. On becoming Oxford's first Slade Professor of Fine Art, he often gave his lectures twice—first to members of the University, and then in open session, so that interested members of the public, including women, could attend. He gave time and money to Winnington Hall, a girls' school in Cheshire founded on the conviction that girls could and should be given educational opportunities at least comparable with those provided for boys. He spent many hours writing careful letters of instruction to the many girls who wrote to him asking for help—patronizingly, perhaps, but his advice paid them the rare compliment of taking their aspirations seriously. More usefully still, and more unexpectedly, he gave economic support to women who were trying to establish self-sufficient professional lives. Kate Greenaway is probably the most famous of the women painters whose careers were furthered by Ruskin's practical and financial help. There were many others. It was Ruskin, not the equivocal Rossetti, who encouraged Lizzie Siddal to try to become an artist in her own right. By agreeing to buy all the pictures she could produce, he offered her a degree of self-respect and autonomy that marriage to Rossetti notably failed to provide. Women writers, too, earned his praise—especially women poets, such as Elizabeth Barrett Browning or Jean Ingelow, who were after all attempting to work within a literary tradition that, unlike the novel, had always been dominated by men. His assistance was often overbearing. Nevertheless, he did enable women to do genuinely independent creative work. Here he differed from William Morris, whose notion of what women could most appropriately contribute to the arts was more or less confined to their filling in the boring background of tapestries designed by himself or Burne-Jones, while he stitched the more interesting bits. It is to Ruskin's credit that he had little interest in decorative needlework.

A still more surprising aspect of Ruskin's life is the fact that he consistently found it easier to relate to and communicate with women than men. This did not mean that he found sexual relations easy, or even possible, as the embarrassing collapse of his marriage testifies. But his closest friends were always women—usually married women, who represented no sexual threat. His friendships with men were by comparison stiff, defensive, and constrained. It was to women such as Pauline Trevelyan, Georgiana Cowper-Temple, Margaret Talbot, Margaret Bell, Jane Simon, Joan Severn, among many others, that Ruskin freely confided his hopes and worries, as thousands of surviving letters prove. This seems less odd when we recognize the extent to which Ruskin himself, despite his ener-

getically public presence as a writer on art, nature, and social justice, was often seen by his contemporaries as in
some way feminine, or unmanly. F. J. Furnivall met Ruskin for the first time in 1848, the year of the disastrous
marriage: 'I never met any man whose charm of manner
at all approached Ruskin's. Partly feminine it was, no
doubt; but the delicacy, the sympathy, the gentleness and
affectionateness of his way, the fresh and penetrating
things he said . . . combined to make a whole which I
have never seen equalled.' Such terms as 'charm', 'delicacy', 'sympathy', 'gentleness', 'affectionateness' were not
usually chosen to praise powerful Victorian men. It was
at about this time that Thomas Carlyle, the thinker to
whom Ruskin owes most, met him for the first time. He
shared Furnivall's view, though he put it differently and
less admiringly. He was later to describe Ruskin as a
'small but rather dainty dilettante soul', speaking of his
'sensitive, flighty nature', which disqualified him for 'serious conversation' despite his 'celestial brightness' 'Dainty', 'sensitive', 'flighty'—again, the implications are clear.
Indeed, the combination of flightiness with celestial radi-
ance almost makes Ruskin sound like a version of the
angel in the house. Those who stopped short of calling him
'feminine' often called him 'boyish', as did Furnivall and
many others. The American critic Charles Eliot Norton,
for instance, was one of those incisive and confident men
who always made Ruskin nervous. Norton, who was forever urging Ruskin to be more of a man, spoke half scorn-
fully of his 'boyish gaiety of spirit and liveliness of humour'. Clearly, Ruskin was by no means a man's man.

There is nothing new in the suggestion that there was
something strange about Ruskin's sexual nature, and there
is not much point in speculating about the personal problems to which this led. What matters is that Ruskin's
womanliness did find an intellectual expression with momentous consequences for his work. It was more than a
matter of his acting the bully in order to compensate for
his own inadequacies. Obliquely, it dictated what he had
to say about the powers of men and women in **'Of Queens'
Gardens'**. The paradoxes of his femininity become clearer
in this passage, one of those which women find most exasperating:

> The man's power is active, progressive, defen-
> sive. He is eminently the doer, the creator, the
> discoverer, the defender. His intellect is for spec-
> ulation and invention; his energy for adventure,
> for war, and for conquest, wherever war is just,
> wherever conquest necessary. But the woman's
> power is for rule, not for battle,—and her intel-
> lect is not for invention or creation, but for sweet
> ordering, arrangement, and decision. She sees
> the qualities of things, their claims, and their
> places. Her great function is Praise; she enters
> into no contest, but infallibly adjudges the crown
> of contest. By her office, and place, she is pro-
> tected from all danger and temptation. The man,
> in his rough work in open world, must encounter
> all peril and trial;—to him, therefore, the failure,
> the offence, the inevitable error: often he must
> be wounded, or subdued; often misled; and al-
> ways hardened. But he guards the woman from
> all this; within his house, as ruled by her, unless

> she herself has sought it, need enter no danger,
> no temptation, no cause of error or offence.

This passage is primarily autobiographical. Ruskin is writing across gender, and he is writing of himself. He had insistently claimed, in **Modern Painters** and **The Stones of
Venice,** his great works of the 1840s and 1850s, that the
vital purpose of all great art is praise. This was a function
that he had made his own. The great Gothic buildings of
medieval Europe, the paintings of Fra Angelico, Perugino,
or above all Turner, the richly moral significance of nature: Ruskin's business as a writer had been to 'enter into
no contest, but infallibly a judge the crown of contest'. In
choosing to be a critic, rather than a poet or painter, he
had not, in his own terms, opted for creativity. He was a
judge, a celebrator, a praiser. And in going about this business, Ruskin had not gone independently into the world.
He had lived submissively with his parents, economically
and emotionally subservient to them, protected from danger and temptation in very much the way that he ascribes
to women here.

But in 1865, the year in which **Sesame and Lilies** was published, Ruskin's life was undergoing troubling change. He
was no longer content to write about art, the subject on
which an appreciative audience had granted him authority
to speak. It had become his conviction that art was so involved with the social and economic circumstances of the
culture which produced it that it was necessary for him
to write about politics before anything he had to say about
painting could be justified. This is what he had begun to
do—most famously in **Unto this Last,** the measured denunciation of Victorian capitalism published in the *Cornhill* in 1860. His public had been much less grateful for this
new venture into political economy—the deferential or
even enthusiastic reviews which had greeted **Modern
Painters** and **The Stones of Venice** gave way to indignation. 'The world is not going to be preached to death by
a mad governess', proclaimed *The Saturday Review,* always Ruskin's most outspoken enemy. The sexual insult
in that response is revealing. In turning from the graceful
celebration of mountains and pictures in order to assert
the claims of charity and justice, Ruskin has forgotten his
place. To teach an appreciation of art was, after all, one
of the permitted tasks of the governess. Governesses traditionally scold: equally traditionally, they are heeded only
by nicely brought up girls of the kind who had always been
Ruskin's most dedicated readers. Having made his name
in what could be identified as a woman's province, Ruskin
had not entitled himself to deal with more weighty social
issues. To talk about anything that really mattered, like
money, with any hope of getting yourself heard, you had
to be more of a man than it seemed Ruskin was.

In **Sesame and Lilies,** Ruskin is both stating his claim to
be a man in the eyes of the world, and, at a deeper level,
brooding on the nature of his own work in terms of a complicated sexual identity. There is a sense in which it had
been 'woman's work', and he is now asserting the right to
move beyond that vocation. But there is also a sense, as
Ruskin's argument develops, in which he lays down for
himself a task which is still defined as that of a woman.
This is what he had to say about the woman's 'public work
or duty':

There is not a war in the world, no, nor an injustice, but you women are answerable for it; not in that you have provoked, but in that you have not hindered. Men, by their nature, are prone to fight; they will fight for any cause, or for none. It is for you to choose their cause for them, and to forbid them when there is no cause. There is no suffering, no injustice, no misery in the earth, but the guilt of it lies with you. Men can bear the sight of it, but you should not be able to bear it. Men may tread it down without sympathy in their own struggle; but men are feeble in sympathy, and contracted in hope; it is you only who can feel the depths of pain, and conceive the way of its healing. Instead of trying to do this, you turn away from it; you shut yourselves within your park walls and garden gates; and you are content to know that there is beyond them a whole world in wilderness—a world of secrets which you dare not penetrate; and of suffering which you dare not conceive.

It is not hard to see why this incensed Kate Millett. But Ruskin's sermons are always at their most censorious when he is admonishing himself, and this is the case here. Ruskin had come to feel encumbered with guilt at the way in which he had shut himself up in his parents' safe and comfortable home, shrinking from engagement with the injustices of the world. He now defines moral responsibility in a way which includes both male and female reference. Secrets are to be penetrated, suffering conceived. In **'Of Queens' Gardens'** Ruskin is publicly talking himself into manhood, without relinquishing the perspective of the woman. It was a process that led to the social campaigning of the 1870s, his most erratic and fruitful decade—the decade in which he published the first provocative numbers of ***Fors Clavigera,*** established the utopian Guild of St George, and claimed the right to call himself its Master.

1864, the year in which the ***Sesame and Lilies*** lectures had been written, was a crucial year in this development, for it was the year in which Ruskin's father died. John James Ruskin had been an industrious and remarkably successful wine merchant, along the lines approved by Samuel Smiles. But he had also been a frustrated artist, and Ruskin's career up to 1864 had been to a large extent a vicarious fulfillment of the blocked ambitions of his father. Now he was on his own, the new male head of the Ruskin family. It was a role that perturbed him. In **'Of Queens' Gardens'** we are confronted with a good deal of transposed anxiety. Defining the perfect woman, Ruskin is again talking about himself:

> But do not you see that, to fulfil this, she must—as far as one can use such terms of a human creature—be incapable of error? So far as she rules, all must be right, or nothing is. She must be enduringly, incorruptibly good; instinctively, infallibly wise—wise, not for self-development, but for self-renunciation: wise, not that she may set herself above her husband, but that she may never fail from his side.

This is the uncomfortable model Ruskin proposes for himself. Taking on a mantle of infallibility, he will make himself incorruptible through self-renunciation. In setting out

a moral agenda for women, he describes his own calling—while apparently speaking from an emphatically male platform. Ruskin presents this exemplary self-denial as an act of service to the higher wisdom of the husband. Here too he is finding a way of both voicing and displacing a sense of his own authorial function. The wish for self-development had never been a principle of his critical ideal. He had begun his career in the belief that the higher truth which it was his duty to express was that of the Christian faith. Ruskin was no longer a Christian in 1865. Yet he was as convinced as he had ever been that his work as a writer should be religious, devoted to the interpretation of insights which were not his own. He would continue to honour and obey the godhead, as he had always done, just as the wife in a Christian marriage honours and obeys the husband.

To see Ruskin's argument in **'Of Queens' Gardens'** as a matter of strange cross-gender movements of thought, movements at once self-protective and self-expressive, makes his lecture a good deal more intelligible, though hardly more attractive. Other writings of the period, however, make it clear that his reasoning in this notorious lecture is not characteristic of what he says about women elsewhere in his work of the 1860s. One thing he had learnt from his experience of long devotion and service to his parents, and especially to his father, is that self-sacrifice is a dubious blessing. In the year in which ***Sesame and Lilies*** was published, he also brought out ***The Ethics of the Dust,*** a textbook about crystallography. This strange book has as much to do with the moral as with the scientific education of women. In writing about self-renunciation in ***The Ethics of the Dust,*** Ruskin is again thinking of his own situation. But here he turns to a rueful recognition of the cost of obedience, rather than giving voice to the unforgiving self-censure that motivated **'Of Queens' Gardens'**. The book takes the unlikely form of a series of dramatic dialogues. Ruskin casts himself in an accustomed role—that of 'Lecturer', or simply 'L':

> L. The self-sacrifice of a human being is not a lovely thing, Violet. It is often a necessary and a noble thing; but no form nor degree of suicide can ever be lovely.
>
> VIOLET. But self-sacrifice is not suicide!
>
> L. What is it then?
>
> VIOLET. Giving up one's self for another.
>
> L. Well, and what do you mean by 'giving up one's self'?
>
> VIOLET. Giving up one's tastes, one's feelings, one's time, one's happiness, and so on, to make others happy.
>
> L. I hope you will never marry anybody, Violet, who expects you to make him happy in that way . . . the will of God respecting us is that we shall live by each other's happiness, and life; not by each other's misery, or death . . . A child may have to die for its parents; but the purpose of Heaven is that it shall rather live for them;—that not by sacrifice, but by its strength, its joy, its force of being, it shall be to them renewal of

strength; and as the arrow in the hand of the giant. So it is in all other right relations. Men help each other by their joy, not by their sorrow. They are not intended to slay themselves for each other, but to strengthen themselves for each other.

Such a position is closer to John Stuart Mill's point of view than anything reasonably to be expected from the author of *Sesame and Lilies*. No-one, however, could mistake this for Mill's writing. The rhetorically Biblical resonances of Ruskin's language are utterly alien from the bases of debate in *The Subjection of Women*. Here, as in **'Of Queens' Gardens'**, Ruskin puts forward his argument as a matter of religious belief.

Ruskin differs radically from the tenets of liberal humanism in the persistently religious framework of his thinking. His work throughout the 1860s demonstrates that the loss of Christian certainty did not lead him to lose the conviction that his writing could only be an interpretation of wisdom more certain than his own. *Sesame and Lilies* was one of his earliest attempts to define a new and non-Christian form for the fixed spiritual truths to be discerned in nature and art. Seeking authority, he looked back to the myths of pre-Christian peoples—the ancient Egyptians and Greeks. What he found was a female divinity. Ruskin explains how 'that great Egyptian people, wisest then of nations, gave to their Spirit of Wisdom the form of a Woman; and into her hand, for a symbol, the weaver's shuttle; and how the name and form of that spirit, adopted, believed, and obeyed by the Greeks, became that Athena of the olive-helm, and cloudy shield, to faith in whom you owe, down to this date, whatever you hold most precious in art, in literature, or in types of national virtue'. This is an extraordinary claim for Ruskin to have made. It is not that he was alone in looking to ancient mythologies for codes of belief that might replace a Christianity that seemed to be failing. Many were doing something similar, and the upsurge in new scholarly interpretations of myth is one of the characteristic features of the age. But it is odd to find him, in a book that is in many ways a paradigmatic statement of patriarchal religious control, suggesting an alternative religion that is in some ways matriarchal. Although Ruskin did not develop the idea very fully in *Sesame and Lilies,* it is one of the most significant of the contradictions and transferences that make up the substance of his text.

Ruskin's religion of Athena cannot, however, be described as wholly matriarchal. Athena, born fully armed from the head of her father Zeus, had no mother; nor did she become one. Though she carried the female attribute of a weaver's shuttle, and was considered by the Greeks as the deity of women's work, she was also a goddess of war, often represented with helmet and spear. Chaste and unforgivingly stern, she combined male and female qualities in her defence of order, control, and reverence. She could be protective and calmly loyal, but she was also more given to violent anger than any other Greek deity. Ruskin found in her a deeply attractive emblem. She was an authoritative expression of the sexual ambivalence in his own work, translated into power, and removed into the distant

and culturally prestigious world of Greek literature and art.

In *The Ethics of the Dust* he develops a more assertive concept of this formidable female divinity. Athena is now defined, not only in opposition to the maleness of patriarchal Christianity, but also against the maleness of patriarchal science. Ruskin saw that the dominance of Christian religion and of progressive materialistic science are two aspects of the same phenomenon. The goddess he creates for himself out of the old images of Athena is opposed to both. She is a goddess of natural fact rather than abstract theory, of quick-tempered emotion rather than cool reason, and her function is to sustain life. Modern philosophy, or modern science, cuts things up, dissects, compartmentalises human experience. So too does Christian religion. Ruskin's discourse, following the female ideal of Athena, attempts to put things back together, seeing the physical world as an ethical phenomenon. The essential impulse of *The Ethics of the Dust* is formulated by Ruskin in female terms, a process of celebrating what he describes as 'the ideas of Life, as the power of putting things together, or "making" them; and of Death, as the power of pushing things separate, or "unmaking" them'.

Ruskin's attack on the apparently unquestionable cultural prestige of science has had more to do with the decline in his standing than any other aspect of his late work. Now that feminists are beginning to assemble a cogent critique of scientific methodology, however, much of what has seemed simply eccentric in Ruskin's repudiation of contemporary science falls into place. Evelyn Fox Keller's work as a theorist of feminist science marshalls the arguments concisely:

> The most immediate issue for a feminist perspective on the natural sciences is the deeply rooted popular mythology that casts objectivity, reason, and mind as male, and subjectivity, feeling, and nature as female. In this division of emotional and intellectual labour, women have been the guarantors and protectors of the personal, the emotional, the particular, whereas science—the province par excellence of the impersonal, the rational, and the general—has been the preserve of men.

> The consequence of such a division is not simply the exclusion of women from the practice of science. That exclusion itself is a symptom of a wider and deeper rift between feminine and masculine, subjective and objective, indeed between love and power—a rending of the human fabric that affects all of us, as women and men, as members of a society, and even as scientists.

As Keller remarks, orthodox perceptions of gender also have their basis in mythology, a 'popular mythology' quite different from the one proposed in *The Ethics of the Dust*. Ruskin's thinking is by no means free from the divisive structures of this common mythology. Nevertheless, his reverence for the synthesizing power of Athena is an attempt to repair that rent in the human fabric which Keller describes.

One of the controlling metaphors in Ruskin's writing of the period is that of sewing, or weaving, supervised by

Athena and her symbolic shuttle. This is not a matter of the superficial embellishment of embroidery, but the kind of needlework that sews things together, making and mending the garments we all need. It is a housewifely activity, and Ruskin calls the girls to whom he dedicates his crystallographic lectures 'little housewives'—a feature of the book which has done little to endear it to feminist readers. Ruskin interprets the act of sewing, like that of writing, as essentially one of service. It is creative, but never independent. In a goddess's hands, it might touch the dignity of representative art, or painting. It is, Ruskin knew, possible to weave a picture. But Athena's mythical contest with the insubordinate Arachne demonstrates what Ruskin saw as the proper function of such illustrative needlework. Athena's loom produces an image of orderly celebration and homage to the gods, finished with a border of the trim and useful olive, which was sacred to herself. Arachne's work is as rebellious as Athena's is reverential. She figures the crimes of the immortal gods; their rapes and deceptions of mortal women. Her web is completed with a border of the unruly ivy, sacred to Dionysus, another sexually ambiguous deity who, in contrast with Athena's austere discipline, fosters wild disruption and subversion in his female followers. Athena punishes her audacious rival by turning her into a spider, the enemy of housewives—whose weaving, as Ruskin puts it, 'instead of being an honour to the palaces of kings, is to be a disgrace to the room of the simplest cottager'.

Sempstresses, housewives, and weavers, like governesses, were not much respected in Ruskin's lifetime. It is nevertheless a literary counterpart of their labour that Ruskin undertakes. His work was, as he saw it, a loving duty to Athena, and a refusal of Arachne's proud infidelity. Instead of confining himself to writing about the pleasures of painting and poetry, with sumptuous descriptions of trees and mountains and flowers thrown in, his works after 1865 are concerned with politics and pollution, crime, vivisection, botany, history, education, geology, ornithology, music, cookery, and a great deal more. He writes about these things in serviceable relation to each other, claiming that you cannot study a geological specimen rightly unless you are alert to its ethical meaning, or that the understanding of modern political economy bears a vital relation to the history of Venice in the middle ages. It is not surprising that it is at this point in his career, after the success of **Sesame and Lilies,** that Ruskin's public image as a harmless, or not so harmless, lunatic began to take shape. His continual interweaving of matters kept separate by the dominant ideology meant that the was not taken seriously.

Ruskin's fading influence in the late 1860s and 1870s cannot be simply attributed to his writing like a woman. There are, clearly, many ways in which he does not write like a woman. But there are some ways, in the most ambitious of his late works, in which he does. He was not oblivious of the effect that this had on his reputation. As he aged he acquired a bitter sense of the standards by which he was judged. Ruskin, like Athena, was not slow to express his anger. In 1874, he published a monumental grumble in **Fors Clavigera**. He thinks back over his life:

> . . . because I have passed it in almsgiving, not in fortune-hunting; because I have laboured always for the honour of others, not my own, and have chosen rather to make men look to Turner and Luini, than to form or exhibit the skill of my own hand; because I have lowered my rents, and assured the comfortable life of my poor tenants, instead of taking from them all I could force for the roofs they needed; because I love a wood walk better than a London street, and would rather watch a seagull fly, than shoot it, and rather hear a thrush sing, than eat it; finally, because I never disobeyed my mother, because I have honoured all women with solemn worship, and have been kind even to the unthankful and the evil; therefore the hacks of English art and literature wag their heads at me, and the poor wretch who pawns the dirty linen of his soul daily for a bottle of sour wine and a cigar, talks of the effeminate sentimentality of Ruskin'.

There is an element of self-pity in that, and of self-aggrandisement. It could be argued that its unshakeable assurance of moral righteousness marks it as a piece of very male apology. But there is also truth in Ruskin's complaint: he did depart from the norms of male discourse, and this did eventually cause his work to be set aside in ways comparable with the marginalisation of generations of women's voices.

One of the sharpest controversies in the school of feminist theory which has arisen from the work of Derrida and Kristeva has revolved round the concept of a specifically female discourse, or écriture féminine. Hélène Cixous is among those who have both used and questioned the concept of écriture féminine, arguing that the idea of a discourse specific to women maintains division, perpetuating the tyrannical opposition in thinking about gender that feminists ought to wish to challenge. Cixous suggests that while there there may indeed be male and female kinds of writing, each may be appropriated by either male or female writers. She describes the possibility of a difference between the sex of the writer and the sex of the writing he or she produces. The masculine and the feminine need not be endlessly locked in destructive combat; nor need they obliterate each other. Cixous maintains a buoyant vision of bisexual writing:

> To admit that writing is precisely working in the inbetween, inspecting the process of the same and of the other without which nothing can live, undoing the work of death—to admit this is first to want the two, as well as both, the ensemble of one and the other, not fixed in sequence of struggle and expulsion or some other form of death but infinitely dynamized by an incessant process of exchange from one subject to another.

This is as far from the confidence of Victorian discourse as from the vehemence of Kate Millett's confrontations. Nevertheless, Cixous's tentative prose could be seen as a definition of Ruskin's distinctive intelligence.

Among the unforeseen consequences of Cixous's radicalism is a return to the values on which Ruskin built his work. Cixous, like Ruskin, champions the idea of an unchanging body of truth, constantly expressed through the infinite flux of human development and variation. It is a truth to be discovered, or rediscovered, through memory and love. Cixous's literary heroes—Rilke, Kafka, Clarice Lispector—might not have earned Ruskin's veneration; nor is she interested in Ruskin's myths. But what Hélène Cixous has to say about her work is startlingly close to Ruskin's deepest convictions:

> One thing I've discovered just by being alive is that there is truth, and that it's that same everywhere. This might seem obvious, but it's essential. Life has its secrets and they are always the same, but they have to be rediscovered. Truth has to be worked for. Everyone has to rediscover truth and this truth tells itself differently. It tells itself according to each individual biography, each memory and experience.

Ruskin's cultural analysis is turning out to be less antagonistic to the changing work of feminism than we had supposed.

Brian Maidment   (essay date 1988)

SOURCE: "Reading Ruskin and Ruskin Readers," in *PN Review*, Vol. 14, No. 5, 1988, pp. 50-3.

[*In the following essay, Maidment suggests that Ruskin's importance lies in how his ideas have been understood, as well as in his large—but largely unread—oeuvre.*]

Reading books about Ruskin always makes me wonder if anyone ever reads, or ever read, Ruskin's own books. His cultural presence has always been something more than that of a producer of texts. Beyond being an author he has always been a rallying place for a whole variety of heterodox social views, many of them unsanctioned by any conceivable reading of his works, and the owner of a proud and sad biography which is only just becoming available for a relatively fair interpretation. So Ruskin the cultural icon constantly obtrudes on Ruskin the writer and Ruskin the man.

Even the evidence of precisely how and where Ruskin has been read provides contradictions. On the one hand there is a long history of fervent attention to his texts, underscored by a series of claims for Ruskin's work as life-changing, and revelatory, an author whose words continually spill over into people's lives. Even consideration of Ruskin's most ambitious readers offers a curious exercise in social history. That staggering memorial to Victorian deification (and reification) of the book as presence, the thirty-nine volumes of the Cook and Wedderburn edition of Ruskin, contains a wealth of stories of men and women like a Glasgow shipyard worker copying out *Unto This Last* by hand, or writing to Ruskin to complain about the way in which reading his works represented a new version of the pursuit of knowledge under difficulties. To the constant question that Ruskin could not have intended his works to be 'scarce, dear, and difficult to obtain' (as a pamphlet issued by the Manchester Ruskin Society in 1880 put it), the sage would only respond by lengthy and apparently heartless polemics on his theory of value. It cannot have consoled a Glasgow artisan to be told that copying out

Unto This Last was something that the author had had to do twice, so what was his grievance?

In the 1880s and 1890s there were Ruskin Reading Groups, Ruskin extension courses with detailed exegetical handbooks, Ruskin magazines, and books interpreting Ruskin's works line by line. In addition to the development of such communal or collective reading practices, many individual readers of Ruskin have left detailed marks of their precise attention to his printed texts. Many volumes in my own Ruskin collection are extensively annotated, and one edition of *Ethics of the Dust* includes a letter Ruskin wrote to its sixteen-year-old reader over a detailed point in the argument. This was one birthday present which seems to have been taken extremely seriously, as the whole volume is annotated with great care and intelligence. As well as such an extensive history of textual attention, there is also an elaborate anecdotal history of Ruskin's influence over, or even transformation of, individual lives. Beginning with the Oxford undergraduates who laboured for Ruskin on the Hincksey Road (Oscar Wilde and Cecil Rhodes included), Ruskin's presence through discipleship has always been asserted. *Unto This Last,* so the story goes, was cited by the new Labour MPs of 1906 as the single book which had most determined their political life. Such visions of reading as a form of self-transformation are still persistently associated with Ruskin. A recent Principal of the polytechnic where I work, a research scientist by training, introduced himself to me through an account of the crucial effects which *Unto This Last* had had on his social vision. Just the other month, the women's magazine *She* printed a piece under its 'New Man' headline about a man in a cycle shop who thrust 'into my hands a copy of Ruskin's 1862 (sic) tract on men and work called *Unto This Last,* wondering what I thought of his ideas. Fond of riding Christmas gift horses, I said yes, yes, and yes.' The columnist, Phillip Hodson, goes on to describe the man in the cycle shop as one who 'used to be in local government until *Unto This Last* got to him.' Without wanting to be pompous over a space-filling column, the linking of Ruskin to emergent masculine analysis of differing versions of self-realization published in a mass circulation, middle-brow magazine is an interesting one, and satisfyingly within the traditional reading of Ruskin as the sponsor of individual epiphanies and transformations. At one level Ruskin has had, and evidently still has, readers who are prepared to invest astonishing amounts of personal and emotional energy in the close reading of his texts, and who are willing to make the transition from reading to conduct, or at least from reading to belief, without anxiety or self-doubt.

Yet, at another level, years of scholarly work on Ruskin have left me with a persistent feeling that Ruskin had no real readers at all beyond the few heroic individuals immortalized by stories such as I have cited. Much of Ruskin's work was not in book form, but produced occasionally as lectures, letters to the press, pamphlets. His publishing policies certainly frustrated his late Victorian readers, and when his works came out of copyright in 1907, his day was nearly past. Many of his books were given (and marketed accordingly) as prizes and presents—a notoriously unread genre. The Ruskin reading groups soon lost their particular focus, and moved on to a whole range of alternative social visionaries. The working men's libraries of course stocked Ruskin, but a book on a shelf does not mean readers, as the librarian of one such institution clearly recognized—'only one man, so far as I could see, cared for Ruskin's *Fors,* and I was not that man. Well read as I certainly was, I was certainly a philistine in regard to Ruskin, and saw nothing then in what he said, and in this I undoubtedly expressed the feelings of the few—the very few—workmen who read his books.' Even if Ruskin did have his readers among the members of the polite world of letters, it is open to doubt whether he ever substantially managed to change the nature of the discourse in which his books were read, and, despite large sales figures between 1890 and 1914, it seems likely that his books were used as much as cultural tokens as revelatory texts. The novels of H. G. Wells are full of clerks and shop assistants whose cultural pretensions are metonymically revealed in unopened volumes of Ruskin with purple calf bindings. If Ruskin was read at all in Edwardian Britain, the feeling was that he was read wrongly—Lucy Honeychurch's panic at being unable to find the 'tomb so admired by Mr. Ruskin in *Mornings in Florence* causes her to ignore the mysterious beauty of the whole church, and McTurk in Kipling's *Stalky & Co* uses his copies of *Fors Clavigera* as an emblem of his idiosyncratic and even subversive individuality.

And now we have the academic readers of Ruskin, the professional explicators and evaluators, who perhaps read with the intensity of Ruskin's early devotees but with the cultural aspirations of his later admiring non-readers. The critical energy being expanded on Ruskin is quite prodigious, perhaps even prodigal. Yet for all the resources of intelligence, manuscripts, and critical theories being brought to bear on Ruskin, it is interesting to see that the problems of reading him have not been at all resolved. Ruskin himself, obsessed with the relationship between perception, language, and action, recognized the dangerous way in which ideas were reified into commodities by print. His growing worry over 'Ruskinism' as a phenomenon was a major source for his persistent attack on the book as a representative commodity within the cash nexus, an attack which transformed the generic construction of his later work. Ruskin believed that discourse and dialogue (of a limited kind) were denied by the lapidary nature of books. So he lectured, wrote to the press with magnificent stylistic vigour, invented the self-lacerating, half ludicrous, but ultimately profoundly moving form of polemic which he called, with typical apparent disregard for his readers, *Fors Clavigera,* and set up a publishing house 'in the middle of a field in Kent'. These were all calculated polemical gestures, all the more disturbing for his audience ('readers' is too limiting a definition) because the calculations obviously had to include some personal evaluation of his own sanity. Ruskin wanted his audience to do and not just to read, even if his own movement from literature into public life—'Fors in deed, not word' as he put it—exposed him to public ridicule, and even to an increased threat to his own stability.

The model I have drawn here is a crude one—that of a minority of committed, attentive Ruskin readers, who Ro-

mantically seek to link Ruskin with their self-myth, with the epiphanies and 'spots of time' by which the self is made consistent, and a majority of 'readers' for whom Ruskin is more a cultural presence, a set of assumptions, with which to extend or validate cultural prejudices, an open text to be re-written by the act of 'reading' itself. What is interesting is that the most important recent books on Ruskin persist in basing their assumptions about Ruskin on the kind of close personal commitment which characterized his earliest, most earnest readers. Such work has been primarily biographical, though it includes a novel and several critical studies, and has properly sought to clear away the biographical and cultural constructions which Ruskin's disciples carefully built in the last years of his life and the decades which followed his death in 1900. Ruskin's presence in Victorian England should not be understood as a genial one. He was not a lovable eccentric, or an engaging sage. Nor ought Ruskin, in my view, to be understood solely in terms of his domestic and personal tragedies, moving as these are. Yet it has to be acknowledged that the best criticism of Ruskin has been biographical and psychological in its emphasis, in a line running from R.H. Wilenski's 1933 biography, through J.D. Rosenberg's *The Darkening Glass* (1961), to the recent work of Van Akin Burd and Tim Hilton. In dealing with all these difficulties, both Burd's important reassessment of Rose La Touche, the young religious melancholic whose presence, and absence, obsessed the ageing Ruskin, and the first volume of Tim Hilton's long awaited biography, are important moments. In insisting that there must be a return to original sources, to letters and diaries in particular, Burd and Hilton condemn themselves to a long and difficult preoccupation with Ruskin which challenges the scholarly wish to situate Ruskin clearly within the Victorian landscape. Such pursuit of Ruskin as an individual would make a good subject for a novel—indeed it has done so, for Peter Hoyle's *Brantwood* offers a brilliantly realized account not just of the search for Ruskin beyond his own myth, but also of how the researcher's own identity is threatened by the search. Within a similar tradition of research which draws the searcher on into a version of his or her own consciousness is Malcolm Hardman's *Ruskin and Bradford,* a book which attempts to reconstruct a set of social, intellectual, and personal relationships in a Victorian provincial city as a way of approaching many of Ruskin's preoccupations with community, industrialism, and design. The result is a remarkable demonstration of how research matters to the individual researcher, though the resultant reconstruction of Victorian community is open to all kinds of scholarly challenge. To find individuals still engaging with Ruskin at this level of seriousness and ambition is rather frightening for a student confronting a syllabus, or, indeed, for any reader trying to find a way into Ruskin's work.

There is a price to be paid for defining Ruskin largely through the texts he produced, including letters and diaries, rather than by the ways in which he has been understood, however unfaithful these may be to the texts. Hilton in particular, following out the work of other Oxford-educated Ruskin scholars like Robert Hewison, reads the development of Ruskin's social philosophy largely in terms of family dynamics: the debts, anxieties, and pieties of the Ruskin clan and its intellectual circle. Hilton recently, and brilliantly argued in a public lecture that the source of *Unto This Last* was not Ruskin's evolving social analysis but his attempt to avert an insult offered to art criticism by Thomas Carlyle ('Papa Carlyle' as Ruskin sometimes called him) in the last of *The Latter-Day Pamphlets*. It is, of course, necessary to recognize the authoritarian and paternalistic thrust of Ruskin's social thought, and to acknowledge his High Tory family background. But to see Ruskin's social critique as essentially an act of devotion, acknowledged by rejection, to his mother and particularly his father, is to use biographical scholarship, however scrupulously written, as the essentially conservative form of perception described by post-structuralism. The internal logic of the continuous, autonomous self revealed by letters and diaries, may not be the best way of understanding Ruskin. Reading his written texts may only help a little, if you regard 'Ruskin' as existing largely as a set of cultural assumptions held by his readers rather than as a coherent intellectual developing his ideas by successive and cumulative perceptions. What Ruskin said is largely independent of how he has been understood. Thus the pertinent question is how far his writing acknowledges the possibility of an 'open' text of this kind, and how far his radical literary method and mode of literary production does move his work into a different form of social discourse than that of most major Victorian social critics. Understanding Ruskin remains a challenging but entirely implausible project. Understanding how Ruskin has been read or understood seems a more possible line of study. But perhaps we should be content with a simple sense of how we understand Ruskin not as a personality or a historical force but as an aspect of ourselves and our own industrial world.

These themes—the return of biography as a way of making Ruskin a coherent and explicable thinker, the idiosyncracy and complexity of the discourse constructed in and by his late work, the baffling allusiveness and diffuseness of his work which to some extent forces modern readers to find 'themselves' as the subject articulated in Ruskin's works—have haunted my recent reading of books about Ruskin. I stopped reading a densely argued five-hundred-page book on Ruskin's use of myth when the author commented that as most of his readers would not have read Ruskin's minor works, he would summarize them as part of his argument. The author, in all apparent innocence, felt it perfectly proper for his readers to observe at some cost of time and effort his quest for meaning in Ruskin's patterns of allusion, without necessarily pursuing Ruskin's similar quest. I say this in genuine bewilderment, with no disrespect to Professor Fitch's well received study. Yet secondary commentary must not be used as a mode of avoiding Ruskin, nor as a way of bypassing confrontation with ourselves as we read Ruskin. Clearly Ruskin must be reclaimed for the ordinary reader.

In this task there are clear signs of hope, indications that Ruskin might be read without a lifetime's commitment, without even the alarming prospect of a necessary link between reading Ruskin and personal transformation. Clive Wilmer's Penguin selection, *Unto This Last and Other Writings,* at last replaces the selections or editions of Rus-

kin built on his art criticism, his wonderful autobiography *Praeterita,* and his overwhelming rhapsodic prose style. Wilmer's selections is really an extension of a recent critical orthodoxy in accounts of Ruskin which perceives a coherent development within his social critique. This coherence runs from an early analysis of the social preconditions for good art (Protestant, Gothic, no division of labour) in 'The Nature of Gothic' chapter of *The Stones of Venice* (II) through attacks on laissez-faire and developing theories of 'value' in the curtailed *Cornhill* and *Fraser's* essays (reprinted as *Unto This Last* and *Munera Pulveris*), through the educational and social debates on patriarchy and family in *The Crown of Wild Olive* and *Sesame and Lilies,* to the autobiographical allusiveness and violent rhetoric of *Fors Clavigera*. This line of thought may be a critical assumption open to various challenges, an attempt to find intellectual pattern where something more complex and less consistent exists, but up to now it has been impossible for even strenuous and committed students to find any route through Ruskin's works, let alone to find a context for his intervention in a crucial series of Victorian debates about gender, authority, and education. Using this anthology, together with Jeffrey Spear's recent *Dreams of an English Eden* (an excellent, if ungenerous, recent account of Ruskin between Carlyle and Morris), students can at last get some sense of Ruskin as a social thinker without an unreasonable commitment of personal energy. A. Dwight Culler's *The Victorian Mirror of History* too offers a clear account of Ruskin's historical analogies without the agonized immersion in Ruskin of, say, Fitch's *Poison Sky*. Other useful introductory accounts are now available, notably George Landow's valuable *John Ruskin* in the Past Masters Series. Ruskin would have both relished and feared the ambiguities of being called a Past Master. Is a past master merely an adept, or one who speak solely in the past, or one who speaks from the past, or one who is past speaking? Ruskin found himself tragically in the last condition during his long illness, although in a moment of rare lucidity and communicativeness he told a visitor that he felt the world cared more for his books than he did. Perhaps, then, Ruskin speaks primarily from the past to the present; though this should be understood more as an invitation to understand ourselves than an order to understand Ruskin.

My plea for an accessible, even if not fully realized or accurate, version of Ruskin against which to construct our own preoccupations should not be read as an attack on scholarship. I have read and enjoyed much good recent work on Ruskin, especially the work of Elizabeth Helsinger and Gary Wihl. I much admire Hilton's biography. But I feel less and less willing to pursue Ruskin beyond a sense of him within a tradition of social analysis and dissent which dominates our own reading of an industrial society. In giving less and less time to Ruskin, I hope I do him no dishonour. There are many other scholars who are prepared to run the risks of pursuing him further.

Timothy Peltason   (essay date 1990)

SOURCE: "Ruskin's Finale: Vision and Imagination in

Praeterita," in *ELH,* Vol. 57, No. 3, Fall, 1990, pp. 665-83.

[*In the following essay, Peltason examines Ruskin's last work,* Praeterita, *which he wrote after he had suffered several bouts of mental illness.*]

Like the "Mutabilitie Cantos" or the last awkward bow of Keats's letters, the final paragraphs of John Ruskin's *Praeterita* have a conclusive rightness that cannot easily be ascribed either to chance or to design. The book stops well short of its projected length, just four chapters into a third volume, but at a moment in Ruskin's troubled history when he knew that any words he wrote might be his last. To follow closely the rise and fall and associative flow of these two remarkable paragraphs is to be drawn backward into the rest of *Praeterita* and into the whole tangled discussion in Ruskin's writings of the familiar mystery that combines chance and design and obviates the necessity to choose between them.

Ruskin is a maddeningly willful writer who nevertheless distrusts his will and its creations and who would like to receive from the world much more than he imagines himself capable of giving. It was both a deep pleasure and a spiritual necessity for him to discover in experience meaningful patterns that he had not himself created. *Praeterita* offers, in its account of Ruskin's childhood, a rich psychological explanation of this habit of deference to external authorities. But I am less interested in origins than in effects, and *Praeterita* also offers a sequence of achieved memories and visions, passages in which Ruskin and the reader come together on meaningful emblems of his life.

Perhaps the greatest of such passages is the book's finale, which gains at least part of its power from the unexpectedness with which it emerges out of the chapter it concludes, called "Joanna's Care." The chapters of *Praeterita* had been appearing at longer and longer intervals and "Joanna's Care" was delayed for nine months. Ruskin wrote the last of it in July, 1889 at Seascale, a resort on the Coventry coast. Just recovering from one in a long series of debilitating attacks of madness, soon to succumb to the worst and the last, he seemed to visitors to be "lost among the papers scattered on his table," as he "turned from one subject to another in despair" and struggled to complete his tribute to Joan Severn, the young cousin and caretaker of his final years.

The resulting account is as digressive and miscellaneous as one would expect, but these words alone will hardly distinguish it from the rest of Ruskin's writing. The exhaustion of his will appears less in the variety of subjects than in the transitional formulae that freely acknowledge a loss of direction and control. He gives over several pages to Joan's narration, as he has given over more than a third of the preceding chapter to a letter from Rose La Touche, and then takes his next direction readily from what she has written. "I am so glad to be led back by Joanie to the thoughts of Carlyle." Where Ruskin has earlier—in *Praeterita* and in his career—moved from subject to subject with the self-assurance of inspiration, he pauses frequently here to signal to the reader the unplanned arbitrariness of his transitions: "I interrupt myself for a moment to ex-press, at this latter time of life . . ."; "The thoughts come too fast upon me, for before Joanie said this, I was trying to recollect . . ."; "I must pause again to tell the modern reader . . ."; "I pause again to distinguish this noble pride of a man of unerring genius . . ."; "I must pause again, to crowd together one or two explanations . . ."; "I do not know how often I have already vainly dwelt on . . ."; "I may forget, unless I speak of it here. . . ." Buffeted by memories and fleeting urgencies, Ruskin writes memorable paragraphs about a variety of pet subjects, but without any sense of inevitability or control.

Of course, the surrender of control may be empowering as well as enfeebling if there is an appropriate higher power to surrender to—a parent, or God, or Nature, or, for Ruskin, the final and most inclusive form of all these, *Fors*. As if to confirm his faith in Fors—his term from the 1860s onward for the power both beyond and within the self that makes things what they are—Ruskin has given over much of the composition of *Praeterita* to chance and impulse, following not just the promptings of his nature, but of the world of things about him. The result is a sense of immediate, spontaneous transcription, which seems less calculated in Ruskin's sentences than in the blank verse of the Romantic lyrics that were his likely model. He tells us, for instance, in an account of his childhood training, that "I have just opened my oldest (in use) Bible" and, then, that a list of chapters "has just fallen out of it" and that he will reproduce for us "the list thus accidentally occurrent." This seems at once authentic and suspiciously convenient, a version in small of the reconciliation that Ruskin was always trying to effect between contingency and significance.

For long stretches, though, this grace is denied him, and for most of "Joanna's Care," Ruskin seems to wander free. Then, at the very close of *Praeterita,* the reconciliation is achieved, and Ruskin is delivered from his ramblings into an extraordinary and emblematic sequence of memories and visions. I quote the penultimate paragraph in its entirety.

> I draw back to my own home, twenty years ago, permitted to thank Heaven once more for the peace, and hope, and loveliness of it, and the Elysian walks with Joanie, and Paradisiacal with Rosie, under the peach-blossom branches by the little glittering stream which I had paved with crystal for them. I had built behind the highest cluster of laurels a reservoir, from which, on sunny afternoons, I could let a quite rippling film of water run for a couple of hours down behind the hayfield, where the grass in spring still grew fresh and deep. There used to be always a corncrake or two in it. Twilight after twilight I have hunted that bird, and never once got glimpse of it: the voice was always at the other side of the field, or in the inscrutable air or earth. And the little stream had its falls, and pools, and imaginary lakes. Here and there it laid for itself lines of graceful sand; there and here it lost itself under beads of chalcedony. It wasn't the Liffey, nor the Nith, nor the Wandel; but the two girls were surely a little cruel to call it "The Gutter"! Happiest times, for all of us, that ever were to be; not but that Joanie and her Arthur are giddy

enough, both of them yet, with their five little ones, but they have been sorely anxious about me, and I have been sorrowful enough for myself, since ever I lost sight of that peach-blossom avenue. "Eden-land" Rosie calls it sometimes in her letters. Whether its tiny river were of the waters of Abana, or Euphrates, or Thamesis, I know not, but they were sweeter to my thirst than the fountains of Trevi or Branda.

Ruskin returns, in this wistful meditation on origins, to a garden that he does not hesitate to mythologize into the garden, thus conflating momentarily the garden at Denmark Hill, where he entertained Joan Severn and Rose La Touche, with the garden of his childhood at Herne Hill, an Eden in which "all the fruit was forbidden; and there were no companionable beasts," but which "answered every purpose of Paradise to me" even so. Chapter 1 of *Praeterita* is called "The Springs of Wandel," and Ruskin is still thinking here about those springs and others, still prey to the ceaseless, mysterious fascination of flowing waters and still in search of the sources of things. Even before Herne Hill, Ruskin's first memories are of the stream that ran by his aunt's house in Perth, "swif-eddying,—an infinite thing for a child to look down into"; and, outside the Hunter Street home of his first four years, of the filling of the water carts "through beautiful little trap-doors, by pipes like boa-constrictors; and I was never weary of contemplating that mystery, and the delicious dripping consequent." The past is an infinite thing for an old man to look down into, and, for the space of this paragraph, Ruskin's pleasure in memory contains the frustration of all his projects—with the little cruelty of "The Gutter" standing in discreetly for Rose's crushing refusal to re-create Paradise with him—and earns for him the radiant present tense in which the twenty-years dead Rosie "calls" the garden by its mythologically right name.

Ruskin has, in fact, returned to Herne Hill for much of the writing of *Praeterita,* occupying his old nursery as the guest of Joan and Arthur Severn. "I write these few prefatory words on my father's birthday," he announces at the beginning of the book, "in what was once my nursery in his old house." The anniversary is the temporal emblem of return, and Ruskin is a compulsive keeper of anniversaries. Recalling in the earliest pages of *Praeterita* a love of kings that blends naturally in Ruskin's case with a love of parents, Ruskin recalls his punctilious childhood observance of the 29th of May, and, in so doing, strikes off a neat psychological profile: "Deep yearning took hold of me for a kind of 'Restoration,' which I began slowly to feel that Charles the Second had not altogether effected." Returning to the garden, and bringing back the dead to a more satisfactory life, Ruskin indulges, at the end of his book, the longing for every kind of restoration and return that is one of the animating impulses of both the book and the life.

The pleasures of the garden are not just the pleasures of return, but also the pleasures of enclosure. When he enumerates in the first chapters of *Praeterita* the advantages and disadvantages of his remarkable childhood, Ruskin claims to regret the chaste and cloistered character of his childhood virtue. But he is everywhere the celebrant of a clearly bounded existence and of the clarity and intensity that a rigorous system of exclusions makes possible. *Praeterita* itself, in the metaphor of its preface, is an enclosed garden, a place to gather "visionary flowers in fields of youth," while fencing out all those "things which I have no pleasure in reviewing."

In one after another of his happiest memories of childhood, Ruskin places the stress on containment and limitation. Many of his favorite enclosures are observation posts, serving the fantasy, later the aesthetic principle, of being the unwatched watcher, the observer who has no warping effect on what he observes. "My entire delight was in observing without being myself noticed," Ruskin recalls, and he loves to think back on the "little recess" in the drawing room from which he silently observed his parents' evening activities, like "an Idol in a niche." He loves even more the specially outfitted carriage in which the family rode out on their summer holidays, dwelling happily on its simple and solid construction and on its perfect, contained sufficiency.

> The four large, admirably fitting and sliding windows, admitting no drop of rain when they were up, and never sticking as they were let down, formed one large moving oriel, out of which one saw the country round, to the full half of the horizon. My own prospect was more extended still, for my seat was the little box containing my clothes, strongly made, with a cushion on one end of it; set upright in front (and well forward), between my father and mother. I was thus not the least in their way, and my horizon of sight the widest possible.

A few well-made things. A place for everything and everything in its place. Whether Ruskin is describing his family's carriage, or cuisine, his mother's system of household management or his father's conduct of his business, he strikes again and again these same notes and founds a whole aesthetic on the virtues of order, simplicity, and self-suppression. To the austerity of his childhood diet he ascribes "an extreme perfection in palate and all other bodily senses." To the discipline of sitting for long hours with nothing to observe but the patterns in the carpet and the household furnishings, he ascribes the fineness and accuracy of observation that he prizes as the highest of human qualities, thus making a virtue out of the necessities of an austere household.

Recent biographers argue convincingly that Ruskin exaggerated these austerities. An inward reading of *Praeterita* suggests that he exaggerated them not to provoke sympathy or interest, but because he loved them. When Ruskin describes the toys that he could not have, his regret yields quickly to the satisfactions of describing the few toys he could have, the good workmanship of his "well-cut wooden bricks," which, along with a cart and ball and keys, formed the right little sum of his "modest, but, I still think, entirely sufficient possessions." He loves as well the temporal equivalent of these careful constraints, the rigorously scheduled days whose perfect order made paradoxically possible a perfect freedom. Both when travelling and at home, the Ruskins followed a schedule that protected their son from any sense of hurry or fret, a schedule that mastered time not just by using it efficiently, but by guaranteeing the intervals in which nothing was scheduled and in which the young Ruskin found his freedom. "My mother never gave me more to learn than she knew I could easily get learnt, if I set myself honestly to work, by twelve o'clock. She never allowed anything to disturb me when my task was set . . . and in general . . . I was my own master for at least an hour before half-past one dinner, and for the rest of the afternoon." In a later chapter, "Schaffhausen and Milan," Ruskin's account of a typical day's continental travel is even more sensuously exact, and his pleasure in the perfect order of the schedule blends naturally into an account of the clean, fine rooms and the good, simple dinners that were another feature of his family's right living.

But *Praeterita* is hardly the record of simplicity and sufficiency that this would suggest. Ruskin's aesthetic of limitation is vulnerable to irony on several grounds: first, because it relies on the idealizing exclusions and oversimplifications of memory; second, and coming from another angle, because it has everything to do with a power of purchase that Ruskin does not subject to analysis, except to see it as the rightful reward of his father's virtues. Finally, Ruskin's urgent endorsement of order and simplicity must be challenged by the counter-example of his own crammed, various, limitlessly exfoliating art. Again and again in his writings, Ruskin tries to speak out the few plain and simple truths about the subject at hand, and again and again he is driven to multiply and qualify and complicate those truths until his systems are no longer systematic, and his few simple truths are a thousand minute particulars of observation and opinion.

This takes the special form in *Praeterita* of an awkward profusion of myths of origin. When Ruskin returns to the garden and the stream at the end of *Praeterita,* he cannot stop the flow of recollection and association until he has invoked several gardens and half a dozen rivers. Even then the flow is not stopped, but diverted. This multiplication of primal rivers and fountains is paralleled elsewhere in the book by the multiplication of decisive moments and simplifying explanations of his character and life's work. His parents, of course, and his childhood training were the foundation of all that he later became. But so, too, was his first sight of the Alps: "I went down that evening from the garden-terrace of Schaffhausen with my destiny fixed in all of it that was to be sacred and useful. To that terrace, and the shore of the Lake of Geneva, my heart and faith return to this day, in every impulse that is yet nobly alive in them, and every thought that has in it help or peace." And later: "I must here, in advance, tell the general reader that there have been, in sum, three centres of my life's thought: Rouen, Geneva, and Pisa. All that I did at Venice was bye-work. . . ." And later still: "But the Col de la Faucille, on that day of 1835, opened to me in distinct vision the Holy Land of my future work and true home in this world." But then he is embarrassed to discover a journal entry from Venice declaring that "this, and Chamouni are my two bournes of Earth." He has an explanation—"But then, I knew neither Rouen nor Pisa, though I had seen both. (Geneva, when I spoke of it with them, is meant to include Chamouni)"—but the explanation only empha-

sizes the persistent problem, which is the unreconciled breach between Ruskin's reverence for the power and beauty of a few simple truths and his still more exacting reverence for the accuracy and fullness of observation that can exclude nothing that he sees or feels.

Just as simple truths are always subject to complication, perfect enclosures are always subject to violation, if only to the violations of time. If Ruskin manages, in the penultimate paragraph of *Praeterita,* to contain the frustrations of experience and to recover lost time, this recovery is itself only temporary. Streams refer back to sources, and sources to other sources, backwards and outward into other regions of myth and memory. Denmark Hill is not Herne Hill, and the stream in the garden is neither a river of Paradise nor the Wandel. Even the song of the corn-crake refers backward to a source that cannot be found, and the elusive bird becomes an emblem of frustrated effort and inscrutability. Like flowing waters, the past is endlessly fascinating at least partly because it is upgraspable, and Ruskin's fascination with origins is necessarily a fascination with loss and unfulfillment.

Longing for restoration, Ruskin is notoriously a subscriber to the twin myths of decline and fall. Often in his later writings, he is the inspired curmudgeon who sees that everything is worse than it used to be—art, commerce, travel, and even the weather. Although *Praeterita* rarely shifts into the high denunciatory mode of **"The Storm Cloud of the Nineteenth Century,"** it seems to share with that late, angry sermon the conviction that the world is now literally a darker, colder place than in the days of Ruskin's childhood. Not only was the Herne Hill garden a Paradise, but "the climate, in that cycle of our years, allowed me to pass most of my life in it."

More, though, than the gradually worsening weather has doomed Ruskin to spend his adult life in exile from that garden. There can be no Eden without a Fall, and in many passages throughout the book, Ruskin divides time and space more sharply, into innocence and experience, Eden and exile. Even the exchange of one garden for another is registered as a decisive rupture, as in this passage describing the family move from Herne Hill to Denmark Hill:

> But at last the lease of the larger house was bought: and everybody said how wise and proper; and my mother did like arranging the rows of pots in the big greenhouse; and the view from the breakfast-room into the field was really very lovely. And we bought three cows, and skimmed our own cream, and churned our own butter. And there was a stable, and a farmyard, and a haystack, and a pigstye, and a porter's lodge, where undesirable visitors could be stopped before startling us with a knock. But, for all these things, we never were so happy again. Never any more "at home."

Not all the reasonable persuasions and comfortable presences of this thing-filled description can hold off for long the recognition that time is a field of loss, of things gone by. *Praeterita* is the book of "things gone by," and, as such, it rehearses again and again, and in a wide variety of moods and registers, this oscillating movement of paradises lost and ambivalently, sometimes triumphantly, re-found. The sense of an ambivalent re-finding in the passage above springs partly from our knowledge that this Denmark Hill garden will become, in the penultimate paragraph of *Praeterita,* Ruskin's "own home" to draw back to. The two passages hold each other in suspension, and this uncertainty whether Denmark Hill is truly "home" is neatly framed by the fact that Ruskin has returned for much of the writing of *Praeterita* to the Herne Hill where he was never "at home," whatever that might mean, again. Even staying within this passage about the move, there is the palpable pleasure of objects enumerated and re-grasped that makes it difficult to associate Denmark Hill with absence, and that fulfills the avowed intention of the book to "summon . . . long past scenes for present scrutiny." Last, and most important, there is the immediately registered qualification of the next paragraph, the sign of Ruskin's characteristic inability to conclude on the conclusive note of "never any more 'at home.' "

"At Champagnole, yes; and in Chamouni,—" Ruskin goes on to list a half-dozen of the Continental destinations of which *Praeterita* is also the story and that serve him as points of renewal and reorigination. When Ruskin says earlier of his first sight of the Alps that "the seen walls of lost Eden could not have been more beautiful to us," he makes what is only the most explicit of many such claims to find in travel what has been lost in childhood. The scenes of Europe, to which the penultimate paragraph in its last sentence conducts us, are essential to Ruskin's effort in *Praeterita* to rediscover his origins and to discover the saving design of his life. Both destinations and origins, these scenes serve the double purpose of seeming to suggest an alternate, redemptive image of temporal progression and of explaining to Ruskin and to his reader the sources of his character. Just a page or two after lamenting his exile from Herne Hill, Ruskin offers this strikingly different account of the effects of passing time:

> Of my early joy in Milan, I have already told; of Geneva, there is no telling, though I must now give what poor picture I may of the days we spent there, happy to young and old alike, again and again, in '33, '35, '42, and now, with full deliberation, in '44, knowing, and, in their repetitions twice, and thrice, and four times, magnifying, the well-remembered joys. And still I am more thankful, through every year of added life, that I was born in London, near enough to Geneva for me to reach it easily;—and yet a city so contrary to everything Genevoise as best to teach me what the wonders of the little canton were.

Ruskin describes here a process of intensification through repetition and thus a new time-sense to be set over against the elegiac and fallen sense of time that so dominates the book. Whatever the particular forms of fulfillment that Geneva offers, the mere possibility of worthy destinations in life is redemptive and matches a stylistic and structural feature of *Praeterita* that we have already remarked. If the sense of time-as-loss is everywhere present in the sorrowful backward-gazing attitude of the whole, another sense of time is witnessed by the staging in the book of a memorable sequence of grand arrivals. Faithfully recording his "real first sights" of things, Ruskin deliberately dramatizes the moment of arrival and revelation, the moment when the Ruskin family first sees the Alps—"suddenly—behold—beyond!"—or, just a few pages after the paragraph above, when the walker of Geneva's streets comes suddenly and satisfyingly upon the Rhone. And this moment is replicated for the reader, and for Ruskin himself, by the special processes of writing, in a book whose great unit of composition is the paragraph and whose greatest rewards are the embedded prose poems that Ruskin keeps bringing us upon with the artful artlessness of inspiration.

Ruskin prepares for the revelation of the Rhone by a trip to Bautte's jewelers in Geneva, described in a paragraph which is itself a dense confluence of Ruskinian positives. The "entirely sound workmanship" of the merchandise, the perfect fitness of every aspect of the transaction combine to create "a figure of fulfillment," in Pierre Fontaney's apt phrase. And then "you returned into the light of the open street with a blissful sense" and "went usually to watch the Rhone." After a few glimpses from the main street, a simple turn, and "with twenty steps you were beside it."

> For all other rivers there is a surface, and an underneath, and a vaguely displeasing idea of the bottom. But the Rhone flows like one lambent jewel; its surface is nowhere, its ethereal self is everywhere, the iridescent rush and translucent strength of it blue to the shore, and radiant to the depth.
>
> Fifteen feet thick, of not flowing, but flying water; not water, neither,—melted glacier, rather, one should call it; the force of the ice is with it, and the wreathing of the clouds, the gladness of the sky, and the continuance of Time.
>
> Waves of clear sea are, indeed, lovely to watch, but they are always coming or gone, never in any taken shape to be seen for a second. But here was one mighty wave that was always itself, and every fluted swirl of it, constant as the wreathing of a shell.

The description goes on. It is almost too much, a tour-de-force whose closest analogues and probable sources are the central evocations in Romantic and Victorian poetry of a condensed moment in which all times are one. This chapter, entitled "The Simplon," recalls such a moment in Wordsworth's account of the Simplon Pass in *The Prelude,* with its "immeasurable height/Of woods decaying, never to be decayed, / The stationary blast of waterfalls." Still closer is Robert Browning's "Thamyris Marching," from *Aristophanes' Apology,* an extraordinary lyric burst that represents a sublimely extended moment of condensed time and "fulfilled imaginings" at least partly through a hallucinatory exchange of functions and properties like that in which the waters of Rhone fly rather than flow and are at once ice and water.

The spatial equivalent in the Ruskin passage of a time that does not gather or fade is the visual field that has neither surface nor depth, no separations or distances, nothing to be irritably reached after, nothing either—to give brief play to the psycho-sexual vibrations of the first sentence—

to recoil from in horror. This is a scene before which the observing self can empty itself of all interfering anxieties or desires and simply receive the offered fulfillment.

A repeatable joy is the redemption of time, and Geneva is pre-eminently the scene of successful repetitions. The description of the Rhone is introduced by a series of habitual verbs which make clear that the excitement of first arrival was freshly there on each returning trip. And it was there again for Ruskin in the exercise of memory and imagination that constituted the writing of *Praeterita*. Writing is thus allied with memory, and in the first passage above about Geneva, with the possibility of adequate, even ecstatic, repetition. When Ruskin refers to the "well-remembered" joys of Geneva, he describes not just a vivid object of consciousness, but a skillful and successful operation of consciousness, a virtually creative act. He says earlier that the preparation for travel, particularly the outfitting of the carriage, was "an imaginary journey in itself, with every pleasure, and none of the discomfort, of practical travelling." *Praeterita* itself is such an imaginary journey, both a record and a witness of the compensatory powers of imaginative activity. The distinction between a repeated activity and a remembered one dissolves in the act of writing, for Ruskin has reached an age and condition in which remembering is the only form of repetition available to him, and the two activities are allied as stays against time.

A system of compensations is thus set in place, in which travel becomes the redeemed form of exile and imaginary travel the redeemed form of absence and unfulfillment. If Geneva was the great, good place, then not living there was the great fact about it, a fact for which Ruskin grows "more thankful, through every year of added life," in another example of intensification through repetition. Like the earlier moment in which Ruskin, telling of his love for kings and castles, concludes "that it was probably much happier to live in a small house, and have Warwick Castle to be astonished at, than to live in Warwick Castle and have nothing to be astonished at," this goes beyond a need to keep open the distance between reach and grasp and expresses as well Ruskin's lifelong need to stand second to some power greater than himself. Clearly, this need is the result of Ruskin's preternaturally submissive relationship to his parents. Just as clearly, though, Ruskin has once again turned limitation to account, and this childhood habit of submission reappears, transformed, as a central tenet of Ruskin's mature theory of the creative imagination.

For all his emphasis on the redemptive powers of physical and imaginative activity, Ruskin hardly acknowledges in *Praeterita* his own agency in the making either of his life or of the book. He rather casts himself as the object of influences and the recipient of visions, the beneficiary and not the creator of meaningful designs. This is nearly pathological, an extension of the solitary child's fantasy of invisibility, and it is sometimes disingenuous and self-deceptive, a willful form of delusion. But it is also perfectly consistent with the many assertions in *Praeterita* and throughout Ruskin's writings that identify the rightful functioning of the imagination with a curious form of pas-

sivity, a passivity that blurs the distinction between spectatorship and creation, between seeing and doing.

Take first this celebrated passage from volume 3 of **Modern Painters**. "The greatest thing a human soul ever does in this world is to see something, and tell what it saw in a plain way. Hundreds of people can talk for one who can think, but thousands can think for one who can see. To see clearly is poetry, prophecy, and religion,—all in one." The mechanics of "telling" are slighted here in the emphasis on an apparently effortless clarity of vision. In the previous paragraph Ruskin has explicitly named "the appearance of Ease," the sense given by the work of Scott and Turner that "they have honestly and unaffectedly done it with no effort," as a test of greatness in execution. Earlier in volume 3, Ruskin offers what is perhaps the most memorably explicit of a variety of earlier comments on "this awful, this inspired unconsciousness."

> Herein is the chief practical difference between the higher and lower artists; a difference which I feel more and more every day that I give to the study of art. All the great men see what they paint before they paint it,—see it in a perfectly passive manner,—cannot help seeing it if they would; whether in their mind's eye, or in bodily fact, does not matter; very often the mental vision is, I believe, in men of imagination, clearer than the bodily one; but vision it is, of one kind or another,—the whole scene, character, or incident passing before them as in second sight, whether they will or no, and requiring them to paint it as they see it; they not daring, under the might of its presence, to alter one jot or tittle of it as they write it down or paint it down; it being to them in its own kind and degree always a true vision or Apocalypse, and invariably accompanied in their hearts by a feeling correspondent to the words,—"Write the things which thou hast seen, and the things which are."

Several features of this remarkable passage compel our attention. The refusal to distinguish between mental and physical vision, like the refusal in *Praeterita* to distinguish between the efficacy of remembered and repeated events, may seem at first a descent into the abyss of idealism. But it is also a form of liberation, from the issueless, repetitive, "Is it in here or out there?" alternations of epistemology. If truth and falsehood are no longer matched up with "real," physical vision and illusory, mental vision, then both the definition of realism and the criteria for truth of vision are enablingly enlarged.

Several chapters later, Ruskin opens his discussion of the pathetic fallacy with a vexed dismissal of "subjective" and "objective" as useful categories, and a firm rejection of the idealism that would claim "that it does not much matter what things are in themselves, but only what they are to us." The third and highest rank of poet, according to this chapter, is the one "who perceives rightly in spite of his feelings, and to whom the primrose is for ever nothing else than itself—a little flower apprehended in the very plain and leafy fact of it." But then, as so often, Ruskin corrects and complicates himself a paragraph later, driven by his own compulsion to tell the whole truth to name a fourth and still higher rank of poets, the rank of those who leave the clear outlines of the material world behind in the grip of "prophetic inspiration." Ruskin will neither abandon truth of vision as an ideal, nor submit it to the test of any lesser realism.

Ruskin's passionate advocacy of seeing things as they are also anticipates the argument of Matthew Arnold's "The Function of Criticism at the Present Time," written and published eight years later. Arnold's critic, seeing "the object as in itself it really is," makes common cause with Ruskin's inspired artist (and with Arnold's artist, too, I would claim, but that is a separate argument). The passage from *Revelation* that closes Ruskin's paragraph and suggests the divine compulsion under which the truly inspired artist works, finds its parallel in Arnold's discussion of Burke, who is likened to Balaam in being "unable to speak anything but what the Lord has put in [his] mouth."

But the most striking feature of Ruskin's paragraph is its emphasis on the passivity of all true creation. The actual labors of painting or writing melt away in the heat of inspiration, and the highest human accomplishment is a form of submission to something higher still. The difficulty, of course, is to distinguish between true and false visions, between the following of true inspirations and of mere "wandering fires," to borrow a phrase from Tennyson's "The Holy Grail." One distinguishing feature of true inspirations, looked at from without, is the "almost unmistakable" character of authenticity, an authenticity whose emblems, quoting further from *Modern Painters,* are the "pieces of sudden familiarity, and close specific painting which never would have been admitted or even thought of, had not the painter drawn either from the bodily life or from the life of faith." This is a distinctively Victorian doctrine of realism, but one that hearkens back to the Aristotelian conundrum of probable impossibilities. The measure of realism is not the object, but the mode, of representation, as Ruskin's engaging illustration makes clear. "For instance, Dante's centaur, Chiron, dividing his beard with his arrow before he can speak, is a thing that no mortal would ever have thought of, if he had not actually seen the centaur do it. They might have composed handsome bodies of men and horses in all possible ways, through a whole life of pseudo-idealism, and yet never dreamed of any such thing. But the real living centaur actually trotted across Dante's brain, and he saw him do it."

The close, specific touches of many of Ruskin's own evocations of the past in *Praeterita* firmly establish their reality and their value for the reader. His carriage, his toys, one room and place and event after another are called up with a pleased and pleasing clarity of recollection. Persons, too, particularly Ruskin's mother and father, are drawn with a sharpness of anecdotal detail that triumphantly passes the Centaur test, and the reader does not doubt that the real, living objects, events, and persons of Ruskin's past have trotted across his brain in the course of writing. But there are other tests to apply, and the attentive reader of Ruskin will hardly need reminding of the ways that an inclusive accuracy of observation and a submission to the forms of one's own vision can fray out into digressive miscellany. A reader can love *Praeterita* and still find it neither a surprise nor a scandal that it is read most often in

excerpt or abridgement, for the narrative of Ruskin's early childhood or for the many charmed fragments and heightened moments throughout the text in which Ruskin strikes a sudden and rich vein of inspiration. Ruskin, as much as Robert Browning, whom he admired, is a quester after the good moment, and his reader is necessarily engaged upon the same quest. This is to return, by way of the pathetic fallacy, to our opening emphasis upon the relations between chance and design in Ruskin's writing and upon the ambiguous issue of a surrender of control.

At one of the many decisive, founding moments in *Praeterita,* Ruskin describes his drawing of an aspen tree, and, in so doing, reproduces in substance his critique of the pathetic fallacy from *Modern Painters*. He has just completed his degree at Oxford and is traveling with his parents towards the Alps. After passing a feverish night at Fontainebleau, he awakes in a dull and heavy state, familiar from narratives of conversion and clearly preparatory to some revelation. He goes out walking until he can walk no further, and is left "with no prospect whatever but [a] small aspen tree against the blue sky."

> Languidly, but not idly, I began to draw it; and as I drew, the languor passed away: the beautiful lines insisted on being traced,—without weariness. More and more beautiful they became, as each rose out of the rest, and took its place in the air. With wonder increasing every instant, I saw that they "composed" themselves, by finer laws than any known of men. At last, the tree was there, and everything that I had thought before about trees, nowhere.

Things in themselves take charge here, and the tree displaces all ideas about the tree in the perfectly receptive mind of the beholder. Such moments are rare, and they are marked for Ruskin by the inward assurance that, though he himself is not in control, something is. The lines that rise and take their place in the air are like the melodic lines of Browning's "Abt Vogler," a witness and tribute to the powers of inspiration. As at other of Ruskin's good moments, there is also a saving, counter-entropic feeling of intensifying joy—"with wonder increasing every instant." Like the artists he most admires, Ruskin has given himself to something larger and better, and he revels in the possession.

At such a moment, "Nature" or "Reality" can be invoked as the guiding force to which the creative imagination has rightly deferred. Harder to place and to judge are the moments when the mind defers to itself and where the test of strength and rightness is the ability not to commit the pathetic fallacy upon the materials of one's own surging memory. In the last paragraph of *Praeterita,* Ruskin gives way ecstatically to the process of free association that has taken the penultimate paragraph from the Wandel to Trevi and Branda.

> How things bind and blend themselves together! The last time I saw the Fountain of Trevi, it was from Arthur's father's room—Joseph Severn's, where we both took Joanie to see him in 1872, and the old man made a sweet drawing of his pretty daughter-in-law, now in her schoolroom; he himself then eager in finishing his last picture

of the Marriage in Cana, which he had caused to take place under a vine trellis, and delighted himself by painting the crystal and ruby glittering of the changing rivulet of water out of the Greek vase, glowing into wine. Fonte Branda I last saw with Charles Norton, under the same arches where Dante saw it. We drank of it together, and walked together that evening on the hills above, where the fireflies among the scented thickets shone fitfully in the still undarkened air. *How* they shone! moving like fine-broken starlight through the purple leaves. How they shone! through the sunset that faded into thunderous night as I entered Siena three days before, the white edges of the mountainous clouds still lighted from the west, and the openly golden sky calm behind the Gate of Siena's heart, with its still golden words, "Cor magis tibi Sena pandit," and the fireflies everywhere in sky and cloud rising and falling, mixed with the lightning and more intense than the stars.

After the purposeful beginning of the previous paragraph—"I draw back"—Ruskin has found a better way, and he lets things bind and blend themselves together. Just as the lines of the aspen tree " 'composed' themselves, by finer laws than any known of men," Ruskin's memories here compose themselves into a vision finer and more gratifying than any deliberate evocation of a primal happiness. Rivers have given way to fountains, progress to simultaneity, and the only flowing waters of this vision are more than natural, made over by art into the manipulable representation of the miracle of real presence. But Ruskin himself engages in no manipulations and seems rather to follow than to lead this train of images and recollections. At least, this is the sense effectively given, a sense only reinforced by the likelihood that Ruskin dictated this passage, like most of "Joanna's Care," to Joan Severn. If the hesitancy and waywardness of the earlier sections of the chapter seem the authentic expression of an old man's wandering fancy, the rapt intensity of this last paragraph seems equally the product of a loss of self-possession, a loss that is now and at last a release into inspiration. Always a fluent and copious writer, the Ruskin of "Joanna's Care" can speak out his mind without the encumbrance of pen and paper, thus minimizing the mechanics of production (though the manuscript page reproduced in the Cook and Wedderburn edition does show this last page recopied and lightly edited in Ruskin's hand) and approximating, in his last paragraphs, the condition of inspired, effortless seeing and telling that he identifies in *Modern Painters* as the greatest accomplishment of art and humanity.

Passing easily from Trevi to Branda, Ruskin comes upon the last, great image of the night sky of Siena, lit at once by the fading sunlight, the lightning, and the fireflies. William Arrowsmith has traced the filiations and documented the ubiquity of the image of the fireflies in Ruskin. He has also identified this extraordinary night-scene as the redeemed form of the Storm-cloud that haunted Ruskin's later writings, and thus of the thunder cloud in which God will come to judge the world. We might press further to see in this night-scene the redeemed form of all randomness and disorder, a chaos of appearances that nevertheless "means intensely and means good," in the phrase that

Browning's Fra Lippo uses to describe and to vindicate the created, fallen world. An image of broken lights against the night sky might easily not have meant good to Ruskin. It is an image of fragmentation—"They are but broken lights of Thee," says Tennyson in the prologue to *In Memoriam,* denigrating all merely human efforts to understand the creation. And it was another image of broken lights against the night sky, "the Nocturne in Black and Gold" of Whistler, a painting of the fireworks at Cremorne, that compelled from Ruskin the disgusted criticism for which Whistler took him to court. But these last sentences of *Praeterita,* like the great line from Nashe's "Litany in Time of Plague," take an image of potential destruction and render it sublime in representation: "Brightness falls from the air."

Holding out against chaos and impending darkness, the passage also holds time in suspension, maintaining the precarious balance of rising and falling against the pulsing background of the fireflies. With the repetition of "how they shone!" the passage freezes time, levers itself from one memorable evening to another, three days earlier, as if the firefly-lit sky were fixed in its shining, a single spectacle that effectively binds together all the different times at which it was viewed.

It is, furthermore, an act of pure, self-abnegating spectatorship that Ruskin evokes, the analogue to the passive, inspired remembering that has led him here. Near and far, like present and past, are indistinguishable, as the ideally receptive spectator refuses to interpret the visual field, to sort out surface and depth or to read the difference between fireflies and stars. The Rhone was also a depthless field, another of many occasions for the interpretive passivity that is Ruskin's ideal. "There is something peculiarly delightful," Ruskin says much earlier ". . . in passing through the streets of a foreign city without understanding a word that anybody says! One's ear for all sound of voices then becomes entirely impartial; one is not diverted by the meaning of syllables from recognizing the absolute guttural, liquid, or honeyed quality of them: while the gesture of the body and the expression of the face have the same value for you that they have in a pantomime; every scene becomes a melodious opera to you, or a picturesquely inarticulate Punch." And much earlier still, he remembers learning to read not by syllables, but by recognizing the patterns of whole words, much "assisted by my real admiration of the look of printed type, which I began to copy for my pleasure, as other children draw dogs and horses." Reading and looking, properly managed, have none of the vulnerability to error or frustration that would be involved in a working backward from surfaces to depths, signs to meanings, or present to past.

For Ruskin, the best meanings of things come unbidden. The last paragraph of *Praeterita* abandons the quest for origins and brings the past into the present in the form of a scene supersaturated with allusion and memories. The effect is of an unreduced complexity that is nevertheless a meaningful design. In the first sentence of the preface to *Praeterita,* Ruskin introduces the book as "these sketches of effort and incident," a matched set that divides experience at the outset into the categories of the made and the given. What Ruskin is given in closing is an experience of true seeing that unites him with the artists he most admires.

He had to make this conclusion, too, of course. He is the author as well as the subject of his book, the sponsor as well as the spectator of the vast theatrical display that is taking place not in Siena, but in an old man's busy imagination and, for us, in the pages of a book. This is not vision, but language, and it is thus subject to our ironic awareness of its own contradictions, not least among them the fact that Ruskin was often querulous, desirous, willful—nothing like the passive and satisfied remembrancer of this conclusion. Just as Ruskin's aesthetic of simplicity is violated by his own baroque practice, his aesthetic of passivity is violated both by his own particular willfulness and by what we know of the conditions of any act of making. But it is a false superiority to illusion that can come to rest in this demystification, as if there were no triumphs to be won over the will, and no differences worth knowing between the human and aesthetic failures of Ruskin's life and the sublime successes of which the conclusion to *Praeterita* is the last and perhaps the greatest.

Richard Dellamora   (essay date 1990)

SOURCE: "John Ruskin and the Character of Male Genius," in *Masculine Desire: The Sexual Politics of Victorian Aestheticism,* University of North Carolina Press, 1990, pp. 117-29.

[*In the following essay, Dellamora explores Ruskin's changing views of sexuality as reflected in his writings about art history.*]

Thus far I have said little about John Ruskin, England's leading critic of the visual arts at midcentury and a presence unavoidable for a young man beginning a career as a critic of art in the 1860s. The following chapter considers the contribution that Ruskin made almost despite himself to the reflections on the character of artistic genius that culminate in Pater's essay of 1869 on Leonardo da Vinci. Pater's decision to present a self-consciously perverse model of aesthetic creativity in that essay brings to a coherent conclusion the debate that Ruskin wages with himself and others on the place of desire in artistic production.

Starting with his self-styled religious unconversion in 1858, Ruskin's art criticism begins to converge with the classicizing and humanistic tendencies that characterize advanced art and criticism, especially in the work of the Pre-Raphaelites, during the following decade. Beginning with his reflections on genius in a book that Pater read, *Modern Painters V,* Ruskin attempts to devise a secular artistic norm capable of harmonizing the different, and at times competing, claims of body and spirit. The achievement of such harmony becomes the telos of a new, secular ideal of art. In contrast to Arnold's antagonism to this ideal, expressed in his assault on Heine in "Pagan and Mediaeval Religious Sentiment," Ruskin identifies himself with the aspirations of younger artists and writers, with whom he associated during these years. That he does so against the odds and ultimately to his grief indicates yet more clearly his courage. Moreover, the inclusiveness of

his humanism lends light and warmth to the effort on behalf of rural and industrial laborers that he likewise undertakes in the 1860s and later.

Although these tendencies in fact predate 1858, Ruskin's willingness to abandon claims of a divine telos in cultural production exposed him to a combination of acute pressures from which he increasingly came to suffer during the decade. For one thing, there were continuing debates with family and friends over the validity of Christian belief. For another, he found himself no longer able to ignore his needs for personal intimacy, needs that focused, inappropriately, on a young girl named Rose La Touche. Ruskin's infatuation with her spelled unhappiness and illness for both. Most significantly for the present discussion, he had occasion to be reminded in 1858 that the lives of artists, including his exemplar, J. M. W. Turner, showed not harmony but disharmony and that they produced works of art marred by sensuality and bearing the marks of moral and mental disease. Accordingly, Ruskin's ideal of artistic harmony carries with it a parasitical counterideal in which genius is almost inevitably linked with sexual irregularity and mental aberration.

The character of genius is not simply an academic matter for Ruskin, who worried with reason about his own physical and mental health during these years. By 1870 he even found himself charged with "madness" in a letter that his former wife sent to Rose's mother. Yet the argument that he wages with himself reflects views being articulated in the general culture. At this point, the fact that for Ruskin what counts is *male* genius becomes a relevant factor. As Elaine Showalter has pointed out in *The Female Malady,* during the nineteenth century the meaning of insanity was strongly coded in terms of gender. In women, insanity was regarded as a product of bodily difference originating in the peculiarities of the reproductive system; in men, however, insanity was regarded as a product of the increasing demands that modern progress exacts on the nervous system. As a doctor writes in 1857: "In this rapid pace of time, increasing with each revolving century, a higher pressure is engendered on the minds of men and with this, there appears a tendency among all classes constantly to demand higher standards of intellectual attainment, a faster speed of intellectual travelling, greater fancies, greater forces, larger means than are commensurate with health."

In the 1860s, however, the assurance that insanity was a sign of modernity was undermined by the advent of psychiatric Darwinism, which "viewed insanity as the product of organic defect, poor heredity, and an evil environment." The leader of the new group, Henry Maudsley, who published his first book, *The Physiology and Pathology of Mind,* in 1867, argued that insanity was both symptom and effect of degeneration of the species. Although one could use Darwinist arguments in a contrary way by arguing that geniuses exemplify variations necessary if the species is successfully to adapt, the implications of psychiatric Darwinism were not positive either for men generally or for artists in particular. Since writers also argued that sexual vice, especially masturbation, was both a cause and an effect of mental degeneracy, signs of sexual nonconformity on the part of artists were especially ominous.

Ruskin, alas, discovered such signs in himself as well as in Turner and other artists. As for Pater, by deciding to celebrate Leonardo's perversity, he attempts on the one hand to convert the perceived disabilities of sexual nonconformity into sources of cultural growth. Simultaneously, he counters the climate of opinion established by Maudsley and other medical experts. Psychiatric Darwinism could be and was used to aggrandize a new profession while enforcing demands for social conformity. By 1896, the year following the Wilde trials, Maudsley himself realized that things had gone too far. "The concept of degeneracy . . . had become an ideological weapon, a 'metaphysical something' stretched to 'cover all sorts and degrees of deviation from an ideal standard of feeling and thinking, deviations that range actually from wrong habits of thought and feeling to the worst idiocy, and some of . . . which are no more serious marks of morbid degeneracy than long legs or short legs, long noses or short noses." Because French writers on Leonardo had already detected sexual irregularity in his work, he provided an especially good instance for Pater to consider.

During the Long Vacation of 1869, during which Pater wrote "Notes on Leonardo da Vinci," Ruskin was appointed Slade Professor of Fine Art at Oxford. In London on March 9 and 15 of the same year, he had delivered the lectures on Athena in Greek mythology that were published in June in revised form under the title *The Queen of the Air*. The highly personal approach that he takes in these lectures demonstrates "that myths must discover an answering sensibility in their interpreter as he constructs, deconstructs and reconstructs the matrix of their hieroglyphs." Although other Victorian writers respond similarly to Greek myth, both Ruskin's text and Pater's, published in November in *The Fortnightly Review,* share a common concern with the myth of Medusa, a figure that has special appeal to a number of the Pre-Raphaelites and their associates: to Swinburne, for instance, whose serpentine women may have been a major influence on *The Queen of the Air*; to D. G. Rossetti; to Simeon Solomon; and to Hopkins, among others. Ruskin himself had helped to prompt this attention by his discussions of Medusa in *Modern Painters V* (1860). And Swinburne, in turn, admired *The Queen of the Air* (1869).

Ruskin's study of Athena brings to an end a decade in which he emerges as a social and political prophet, in which despite his continuing use of biblical language, he publicly moves away from orthodox Christian belief, and in which he promotes a body-centered and aestheticized version of humanism. This process takes as point of departure 1858, the year in which he met Rose, then aged ten, and in which he experienced the shock of discovering Turner's erotic drawings, drawings that Ruskin took to be signs of mental derangement. To his later regret, he agreed to witness the destruction of these works. Since Ruskin had based his early career on celebrating Turner as the greatest of modern painters, the discovery had major implications for his thinking about the character of artistic imagination, reflections that issued two years later in the

statement in *Modern Painters V* that "his [i.e., man's] nature is nobly animal, nobly spiritual—coherently and irrevocably so. . . . All great art confesses and worships both." During summer of 1858 Ruskin also underwent what he later referred as his unconversion. Standing before Veronese's painting *The Queen of Sheba before Solomon* in the Royal Gallery at Turin, Ruskin was struck by the contrast between Evangelical asceticism and, as he says in his diary, "the Gorgeousness of life which the world seems to be constituted to develop." By advocating social and economic reform; by associating himself with younger members of the Pre-Raphaelites, including Swinburne, whom Ruskin met, read, and corresponded with; and by his ill-advised preoccupation with Rose, to whom he proposed marriage in 1866, Ruskin attempted to put his new ideal into effect.

During the 1860s, Ruskin's relationship with Rose, whose mental health deteriorated over a number of years, beginning with attacks in October 1861, was something of an "'open secret.'" As Van Akin Burd points out, Ruskin discussed and wrote about the matter to a number of friends and acquaintances. For him, the relation was connected both with his ambivalent rejection of dogmatic Christianity and his likewise ambivalent acceptance of physical delight. As he remarks to Charles Norton in December 1862: "I've become a Pagan, too; and am trying hard to get some substantial hope of seeing Diana in the pure glades." Ruskin quarreled about religion both with Rose's parents and with Rose herself, for whose benefit he includes attacks on Christianity in *The Queen of the Air*. As he writes in April 1869, to one correspondent: "There's a word or two here and there which only ρ [= Rose] will understand." This text, which is particularly rich in its representation of feminine figures, is also remarkable for its display of masculine gender anxieties, evident in the contradictory, shifting, and overdetermined interpretations of figures like Athena and Medusa.

In the chapter on rain clouds in *Modern Painters V,* Ruskin explains Medusa as the personification of the towering cumulus cloud seen in approaching thunderstorms: "'Medusa' (the dominant), the most terrible. She is essentially the highest storm-cloud; therefore the hail-cloud, of cold, her countenance turning all who behold it to stone. ('He casteth forth His ice like morsels. Who can stand before His cold?') The serpents about her head are the fringes of the hail, the idea of coldness being connected by the Greeks with the bite of the serpent, as with the hemlock." In this context Ruskin celebrates Medusa, associating her with the immanent presence of a divine masculine principle as imaged in the words of the psalm. Associating her later in the chapter with the "noblest thoughts" of Turner, he finds the painter portraying "the Medusa cloud in blood" (7:18) in an angrily prophetic work that Ruskin owned for a number of years, *Slavers Throwing Overboard the Dead and Dying—Typhon Coming On.* Medusa haunts Ruskin's imagination during the decade. In 1862 he writes in a state of depression to Charles Eliot Norton: "I . . . try to feel that life is worth having—unsuccessfully enough. . . . I sometimes wish I could see Medusa." Subliminally recalling both Medusa and Turner's painting, a year later he writes again: "I am still . . . tormented between the longing for rest and for lovely life, and the sense of the terrific call of human crime for resistance and of human misery for help—though it seems to me as the voice of a river of blood which can but sweep me down in the midst of its black clots, helpless. What I shall do I know not—or if dying is the only thing possible."

The reference to Medusa occurs within the tradition of nineteenth-century poetic representations of her that I examine in greater detail in the following chapter. In the poem by Shelley, "On the Medusa of Leonardo da Vinci in the Florentine Gallery," that stands at the head of that line, Medusa is conceived in a positive way as a trope of political and social revolution. Ruskin's identification of Medusa with the storm clouds suggests an affinity with, even an influence from the poem by Shelley, whose work Ruskin often cites and whom he praises at the end of *Modern Painters V*. Shelley wrote the Leonardo poem concurrently with a poem that Ruskin cites, the "Ode to the West Wind," in which the storm-bearing west wind carries with it the seeds of social and political revolution. In the letter to Norton, the driving winter rains, Shelley's "Wild Spirit," is metamorphosed into a menstrual flood in which Ruskin himself may drown.

Despite the fact that he identifies himself with her justified anger, Ruskin's Medusa also signifies the almost-wished-for extinction of a gendered self, gendered because Ruskin, already dispirited by his romantic entanglement with Rose, mingles with it a specifically male bourgeois fear of social disorder. In this secondary context, Medusa, contaminated by the image of the bloody river of popular revolt and revenge, becomes the negative trope that Catherine Gallagher has argued Medusa is for nineteenth-century men overcome by fears of an uncontrollable female generative power. In the aftermath of the French Revolution, "the sexually uncontrolled woman . . . becomes a threat to all forms of property and established power. Her fierce independence is viewed, even by revolutionaries, as an attack on the Rights of Man."

Although there is no direct evidence that Pater knew about Ruskin and Rose, Ruskin's talkativeness about the subject suggests that gossip is likely to have reached his younger contemporary. Moreover, autobiographical allusiveness is evident in a number of Ruskin's texts during the 1860s. Pater had means of access to Ruskin's psychological state through conversation with Swinburne and Solomon. Ruskin, who shared the details of his private life with Sir Henry Acland, Regius Professor of Medicine at Oxford, asked him to arrange a meeting with Swinburne as early as 1858. In 1866 and 1867, Ruskin also confided in the young Pre-Raphaelite painter, Edward Burne-Jones, who was a friend of both Swinburne and Solomon. Ruskin even hired Swinburne's friend, the sexually "ambiguous" Charles Augustus Howell, as a clandestine go-between with the La Touches in 1866.

Ruskin's connection with Swinburne in the 1860s is an important one. Having read a draft manuscript of *Poems and Ballads* as early as 1863, he wrote gleefully to Lady Trevelyan in December 1865: "I went to see Swinburne yesterday and heard some of the wickedest and splendidest verses ever written by a human creature. He drank three bottles of porter while I was there. I don't know what to do with him or for him—but he must not publish these things." Obtaining possession later of the manuscript of the anti-Christian "Hymn to Proserpine," Ruskin regarded Swinburne as a valuable ally in the battle against Evangelical Christianity. When *Poems and Ballads* came under attack in 1866, Ruskin wrote on Swinburne's behalf to his father. He also refused to support the efforts of those who wished to have Swinburne's publisher prosecuted for obscenity. There is evidence, moreover, that Ruskin also drew Swinburne's poetry into his own growing obsession. He took Atalanta, "the maiden rose" of *Atalanta in Calydon,* to be a type of Rose La Touche. As well, chillingly and even before Rose's early death, Ruskin "greatly admired" Swinburne's "Before the Mirror," in which a suicidal, female Narcissus-figure "is repeatedly described as—and sees herself in the reflection as—a rose"; the poem ends with her "metaphorical drowning." Even the words with which Ruskin defends Swinburne's poetry to his father suggest that the critic has conflated Swinburne's female personae with Rose: Swinburne's poetry, says Ruskin, "is diseased—no question—but—as the blight is . . . on the moss-rose—and does not touch—however terrible—the nature of the flower."

Ruskin acknowledges that genius, including implicitly his own, is also a diseased thing. At the end of the letter he urges: "There are sick men—and whole men; and there are Bad men, and Good. We must not confuse any of these characters with each other." Unfortunately, however, for Ruskin the terms were confused. In the public, hence reserved, reply that he sent Swinburne in return for a presentation copy of *Poems and Ballads,* Ruskin gives himself away more than he would like: "There is assuredly something wrong with you—awful in proportion to the great power it affects and renders (nationally) at present useless. . . . So it was with Turner, so with Byron. It seems to be the peculiar judgment-curse of modern days that all their greatest men shall be plague-struck." The artistic analogues—Turner, Byron, and Swinburne himself—to whom Ruskin refers connote a plague that is venereal in type.

These thoughts suggest an underside to the humanistic credo of *Modern Painters V*:

> All art which involves no reference to man is inferior or nugatory. And all art which involves misconception of man, or base thought of him, is in that degree false and base.

> Now the basest thought possible concerning him is, that he has no spiritual nature; and the foolishest misunderstanding of him possible is, that he has or should have, no animal nature. For his nature is nobly animal, nobly spiritual—coherently and irrevocably so; neither part of it may, but at its peril, expel, despise, or defy the other. All great art confesses and worships both.

In notes that Ruskin made in Turin and sent to his father, he indicates the need to accept sexual nonconformity as an aspect of "nobly animal" male artists:

> Titian and Veronese are always noble; and the curious point is that both of these are sensual

painters, working apparently with no high motive, and Titian perpetually with definitely sensual aim, and yet invariably noble. . . . And Michael Angelo goes even greater lengths, or to lower depths, than Titian; and the lower he stoops, the more his inalienable nobleness shows itself. Certainly it seems intended that strong and frank animality, rejecting all tendency to asceticism, monachism, pietism, and so on, should be connected with the strongest intellects. Dante, indeed, is severe, at least, of all nameable great men; he is the severest I know. But Homer, Shakespeare, Tintoret, Veronese, Titian, Michael Angelo, Sir Joshua, Rubens, Velasquez, Corregio, Turner, are all of them boldly Animal. Francia and Angelico, and all the purists, however beautiful, are poor weak creatures in comparison. I don't understand it; one would have thought purity gave strength, but it doesn't. A good, stout, self-commanding, magnificent Animality is the make for poets and artists, it seems to me.

Ruskin is prepared to acknowledge a necessary "animality" even in an artist like Michelangelo, whose sexual interests, insofar as they are declared by his sculpture, appear to focus on a variety of male body-types. To Ruskin, Michelangelo, in moral terms the most extreme and base of artistic types, is still of "inalienable nobleness." Moreover, Ruskin is prepared to take this view despite the fact that he perceives the eroticism of Michelangelo's portrayals of the male nude. In a phantasmagoric evocation of the artist, written while Ruskin was still in his twenties, he notes "the earth of the Sistine Adam that begins to burn" and "the white lassitude of joyous limbs," of the Bacchus, "panther-like, yet passive, fainting with their own delight, that gleam among the Pagan formalisms of the Uffizii, far away, separating themselves in their lustrous lightness as the waves of an Alpine torrent do by their dancing from the dead stones, though the stones be as white as they."

Despite Ruskin's ability to share erotic responses beyond conventional ones, in the 1860s he mainly associates himself with the Venetian masters of the female nude. In *Modern Painters V,* for instance, he makes Giorgione the type of the healthy artist. One would be mistaken, however, to infer that erotic aspects of Ruskin's aesthetic responses change basically between the 1840s and the 1860s. Already in *Modern Painters II* (1846), he shows himself charmed with Giorgione's nudes, even if at that date his delight is filtered by biblical and natural imagery: "There is no need nor desire of concealment any more, but his naked figures move among the trees like fiery pillars, and lie on the grass like flakes of sunshine". In the early 1850s and under pressure of an unconsummated marriage that ended in annulment, anxiety about his relation to images of the female body helps to inflate the negative rhetoric of works like *The Stones of Venice III,* in which he takes pleasure in abusing both the Renaissance, figured as a female prostitute, and Raphael, an artist closely associated with amorous power and images of beautiful women.

Ruskin's avowed conversion to the norms of Venetian art at the end of the 1850s belies a continuing anxiety. In *Modern Painters V* he may oppose Giorgione to Turner as the modern, morbid artist, in part because he still found

disturbing Turner's erotic drawings. In that text, Ruskin discloses his fear of female touch in the image of Venus/death that he sees haunting Turner's art: "Death. . . . The unconquerable spectre still flitting among the forest trees at twilight; rising ribbed out of the sea-sand;—white, a strange Aphrodite;—out of the sea-foam; stretching its gray, cloven wings among the clouds; turning the light of their sunsets into blood."

Ruskin's double attitude to the female body shows as well in the contrast between his description of a Giorgionesque nude and its illustration in the same volume. Just as with the blighted moss-rose, Ruskin in writing can delight in the decay of the original image of a female nude, the Hesperid Aeglé, that Giorgione painted in frescoes on the external wall of a Venetian palace. Ruskin speaks of "the last traces of " the image, which he had seen ten years earlier "glowing like a scarlet cloud, on the Fondaco de' Tedeschi." When he comes to reproduce the image, however, he excludes precisely the conflated signs of sensuousness, temporality, and nature that he registers in the prose. Instead and because of the wreck of the fresco, . . . the body below the waist is missing. At the same time, the upper portion, based on an engraving, is decorporealized.

The Hesperid Aeglé personifies the rosy western skies that both Giorgione and Turner loved. In the latter part of *Modern Painters V,* Ruskin identifies her with the virtues of domestic life among humble folk: "—the life of domestic affection and domestic peace, full of sensitiveness to all elements of costless and kind pleasure;—therefore, chiefly to the loveliness of the natural world." In this chapter, too, he identifies her with the color (and, in a private code, the person) Rose. In all these respects, Hesperid Aeglé is a positive manifestation of the shifting formation of clouds that at other moments is Medusa herself. In "The Hesperid Aeglé," however, he portrays Medusa as well in her negative manifestation as the Dragon of the Hesperides or as Python in the myth of Apollo and Python. And in a presentation in which Turner appears to be a virtually transparent surrogate of Ruskin himself, he sees both aspects of Medusa locked in struggle in Turner's divided self:

> He is distinctively, as he rises into his own peculiar strength, separating himself from all men who had painted forms of the physical world before,—the painter of the loveliness of nature, with the worm at its root; Rose and canker-worm,—both with his utmost strength; the one never separate from the other.
>
> In which his work was the true image of his own mind.

This final pair of images, one phallic and one vaginal, is hermaphroditic. Moreover, in a bodily code, the struggle of Apollo and Python that Ruskin describes in the preceding pages may well refer not only to Ruskin's checkered view of Turner's sexuality but to Ruskin's own youthful struggle to overcome the practice of masturbation, a struggle that came to mind as he became involved with Rose. At any rate, the climactic description of Apollo and Python, though it refers in context to the struggle against the industrial and commercial disfigurement of England, sounds like a description of struggle with bodily desires: "I believe this great battle stood, in the Greek mind, for the type of the struggle of youth and manhood with deadly sin—venomous, infectious, irrecoverable sin. In virtue of his victory over this corruption, Apollo becomes thenceforward the guide; the witness; the purifying and helpful God. The other gods help waywardly, whom they choose. But Apollo helps always: he is by name, not only Pythian, the conqueror of death; but Paean—the healer of the people."

In the passage cited above, hermaphrodeity is a symbol of the "mind" of male genius. Ruskin, however, projects the image onto female figures as well, onto Medusa, for instance, whom he associates both with Athena and with the retributive power both of Turner-as-prophet and of the male deity of Christian dispensation. Ruskin further expresses a disturbed sense of female difference in the imagery of hermaphrodeity that recurs in his dreams in 1869. "In November he dreamed of a serpent with a woman's breasts which entered his room under a door; and another which fastened itself on his neck like a leech." And in **The Queen of the Air** he had included similar images in a cruel assault on Rose. The nickname of Rose's mother was Lacerta, Latin for lizard. "Ruskin, writing of the serpent with which Athena was associated, had moved to the serpentine corruption of Christianity. 'And truly, it seems to me, as I gather in my mind the evidences of insane religion, degraded art, merciless war, sullen toil, detestable pleasure, and vain or vile hope . . . —it means to me, I say, as if the race itself were still half-serpent, not extricated yet from its clay; a lacertine breed of bitterness.' " As Burd comments: "Rose did not miss the sting, writing in the margin: '?Poor green lizards! they are not bitter: Why not say serpentine?' "

As I mentioned earlier, Pater could not help situating his work in relation to that of Ruskin. When Pater in "Diaphaneitè" praises Raphael, "who in the midst of the Reformation and the Renaissance, himself lighted up by them, yielded himself to neither" [*Miscellaneous Studies*], he responds to Ruskin's highly publicized condemnation of the same artist in **The Stones of Venice III** (1853) and **"Pre-Raphaelitism"** (1853). Taking as his example the frecoes of the Stanza della Segnatura, in which Raphael placed a Christian subject on one wall and Apollo presiding over poets and the muses on another, Ruskin avers: "From that spot, and from that hour, the intellect and the art of Italy date their degradation. . . . He elevated the creations of fancy on the one wall, to the same rank as the objects of faith upon the other. . . . In deliberate, balanced opposition to the Rock of the Mount Zion, he reared the rock of Parnassus, and the rock of the Acropolis. . . . The doom of the arts of Europe went forth from that chamber." In contrast to Ruskin's tendentious claim, Pater praises the "deliberate, balanced opposition" of Christian and Classical elements in Raphael's art and outlook. As Donald Hill has pointed out, Pater contests Ruskin on the point again in "Winckelmann." And in the preface to *Studies in the History of the Renaissance* (1873), Pater remarks: "Christian art is often falsely opposed to the Renaissance." Ruskin appears to have received the message, since in 1876 he writes: "Raphael, painting the

Parnassus and the Theology on equal walls of the same chamber of the Vatican, so wrote, under the Throne of the Apostolic power, the harmony of the angelic teaching from the rocks of Sinai and Delphi."

By representing Leonardo in a private but accessible code, Pater participates in the hieroglyphic presentation of self that the Victorian sages often engage in but that Ruskin especially indulges in the late 1860s and in the 1870s. In "Notes on Leonardo da Vinci," Pater too reads classical and Christian icons as though they are hieroglyphs of cultural experience and takes signs of psychological and sexual instability as indices of a troubled greatness. What he adds to the approach, however, is an acceptance of sickness in the artist and culture that permits Leonardo to negotiate the anxieties about women, about the body, about genital activities, that confound Ruskin. Pater does so by acknowledging and embracing perversity, both Leonardo's and implicitly his own, a solution that has a remarkably contemporary ring to it. In his preface to *Homosexualities and French Literature*, Richard Howard remarks: "It was Freud who first taught us that a perversion is the opposite of a neurosis, that homosexuality, for instance, is not a problem but the solution to a problem." Although Howard may be overly sanguine as to whether or not Freud found homosexuality to be "a problem," the next point is one that Pater might have made, indeed that he does make in his study of Leonardo. Howard writes: "When we are troubled—bored, provoked, offended—by characteristic features of a writer's work (and might one not say, by characteristic behavior of a person's sexuality?), it is precisely those features (and that behavior) which, if we yield to them, if we treat them as significance rather than as defect, will turn out to be that writer's (and that person's) solution to what we mistakenly regarded as problems of composition and utterance (and character and consciousness)." Pater turns to the recherché aspects of Leonardo to arrive at a similar solution to the enigmas of his art, personality, and method of work.

As J. B. Bullen has pointed out, when Pater contends that the "beauty" of the Mona Lisa is of a kind "into which the soul, with all its maladies has passed," he affiliates himself and Leonardo with an art that is both romantic and modern. As Goethe had said: "Das Klassische nenne ich das Gesunde und das Romantische das Kranke. . . . Das meiste Neure ist nicht romantische, weil es neu, sondern weil es schwach, kranklich und krank ist"; Sainte-Beuve, whom Pater read, concurs: "J'appelle le classique le sain, et le romantique le malade. Les ouvrages du jour ne sont pas romantiques parce qu'ils sont nouveaux, mais parce qu'ils sont faibles, maladifs ou malade." With reference to Leonardo, Pater draws upon major French revaluations of the artist in order to portray both an artist who subverts Christian orthodoxy and one who, in the suggestion of the French, is sexually perverse. Picking up Gautier's comment of 1857 that Leonardo's figures portray "les désires réprimés, les espérances qui désespèraient" and Hippolyte Taine's remark of 1865 concerning the Louvre Saint John, "c'est une femme, un corps de femme, ou tout au plus un corps de bel adolescent ambigu, semblable aux androgynes de l'époque impériale," Pater bases his view of Leonardo's creativity on the painter's sexual and emotional attraction to members of his own sex. Like Taine's, Pater's Leonardo is much like that of Winckelmann, who in the *History of Ancient Art* singles out the artist for having portrayed Christ as a divine hermaphrodite.

Pater may also have sensed an affinity between his Leonardo and Ruskin's Turner. Both artists were great landscapists and analysts of the structure of optical perception. Both were fascinated by the powers of nature, imaged in "the motion of great waters" (*Studies in the History of The Renaissance*). And both associate flowing water with feminine power, in Turner by way of the yonic structure of many of his paintings. Pater himself, moreover, shares Ruskin's fascination with feminine experience, with hermaphrodeity, with Medusa herself. However, Pater's cool, analytic approach, though appropriate both in view of his fastidiousness and his exposed public position, was reinforced by the contrasting display of Ruskin's embarrassments. In discussing the Victorian sages, David DeLaura has argued their "continuous, or at least intermittent, readiness for self-exploration and self-manifestation and the manipulation of one's own personal presence for highly diverse ends." DeLaura regards Arnold's "apparent paean to Oxford" in the preface to *Essays in Criticism* (1865), first series, as a signal instance of such use of the self. At Oxford between 1865 and 1870, Pater drew on both "self-exploration and self-manifestation" in fashioning a novel subject-position in criticism. Given the delicacy and risks of the venture, he is liable to have been appalled at the confessional outpourings of that other great figure, John Ruskin. In view of possible analogies between Turner and Leonardo, the prominence of Medusa in the myth making of both Pater and Ruskin, and Ruskin's visibility at Oxford after he became Slade Professor of Fine Art there in 1870, Pater is likely to have regarded his precursor and rival as a leading example of how not to interfuse cultural critique with personal self-revelation. In this regard, the Leonardo essay, even more so in revised form in the 1877 edition of *The Renaissance,* makes sense as an attempt to bring under conscious control elements that remain evidently contradictory in Ruskin's life and work after his public conversion to humanism. Pater's emphasis on the self-conscious exploration of sexual perversity indicates a less alienated sense of sexual difference than Ruskin's, together with a will to analyze and govern experience. In the study of Leonardo's perversity, Pater resolves the sort of antinomies that in the 1870s were to undo Ruskin. This positive evaluation of perversity shows a way out of an impasse like Ruskin's and at the same time provides Pater with an opportunity to distance himself from the older man's antithetical frame of mind and disabling moralism. From 1871 to 1878, Ruskin in the letters of *Fors Clavigera* attempts to take the lead in a movement of social reform and experimentation called the Guild of Saint George. In the letters too he refers to Rose, openly and covertly, again and again. Pater likely discloses his sympathetic recoil, in light both of these texts and of gossip at Oxford, in a passage that he adds to the essay in the second edition of *The Renaissance* (1877). There he describes Ludovico Sforza, Leonardo's former patron and sometime ruler of Milan, inscribing Infelix sum ("I am unfortunate") in arabesques on the walls of his prison cell. Ludovico traces these words along with images of "vast hel-

mets and faces and pieces of armour" (*The Renaissance*). Pater speculates that the images may recall Leonardo's drawings for a colossal statue of Ludovico's father. They suggest an outsized masculine ambition, which Pater also divined in the author of *Fors Clavigera* and in the critic who celebrated the sexual vigor of artists like Rubens and Titian, yet whose writings often write large an acknowledged unhappiness.

Paul Sawyer (essay date 1990)

SOURCE: "Ruskin and the Matriarchal Logos," in *Victorian Sages and Cultural Discourse: Renegotiating Gender and Power,* edited by Thais E. Morgan, Rutgers University Press, 1990, pp. 129-41.

[*In the following essay, Sawyer discusses Ruskin's view of girls and women in* The Ethics of the Dust, *"Of Queens' Gardens,"* and The Queen of the Air.]

To define Victorian nonfiction prose as a discourse is almost invariably to think of it as masculine discourse—at least so long as we accept the customary description of the sages as a group of secular prophets. At the very beginning of the Judeo-Christian tradition, the Hebrew prophets marked all sacred human speech as masculine by virtue of their roles as oracles of a patriarchal deity, a gender distinction repeated through the centuries by male clergy who have preached the law. In general, the figure of the Victorian sage as a prophet underscores the notion of discursive authority itself as patriarchal—which was perhaps the chief reason for the figure in the first place. Attempts to define sage writing as a prose genre have been valid and useful. Yet the gender-marking of the notion of a prophet, if unexamined, subtly influences our sense of who really counts among Victorian nonfiction prose writers, of who belongs to that visionary company and who begets them. Most studies of the sages, for example, name Carlyle as prime progenitor, the virtual inventor of Victorian nonfiction prose, but since few Victorians tried to write in Carlylese, Carlyle's "invention" must be rather the prophetic stance itself, a pose or assertion that required the support of personal temperament. In this context, Carlyle's toughness, his rages, his hints of silent suffering, his exaggerated manliness in general, made lively theater for his reading audience.

Carlyle's radical suppression of the feminine, in both his works and his personality, was anomalous in the group of Victorian sages that he supposedly fathered. Such disparate figures as Mill, Newman, Arnold, Ruskin, and Pater, if they share anything at all, share an interest in the power of the aesthetic sensibility to uplift and ennoble, to soften, refine, humanize, and harmonize—the power of what Arnold called the Hellenic as opposed to the Hebraic. All of them were in some way apostles of culture. In terms of gender this label is mildly paradoxical, since the notion of cultivation and refinement, like the notion of gentility, was associated with the feminine sphere of the domestic as opposed to the masculine sphere of economic competition. Arnold's famous description of Newman ("Who could resist the charm of that spiritual apparition . . . rising into the pulpit, and then, in the most entrancing of voices, breaking the silence with words and thoughts which were a religious music—subtle, sweet, mournful?") defined an androgynous charisma more appealing to a mid-century audience than the Carlylean warrior-hero—a charisma powerful precisely in its mingling of feminine sweetness and masculine authority. Arnold's Newman is an Angel in the house of God.

Of all the sages, John Ruskin—the product of both a sternly "masculine" Evangelicalism and an affluent, "feminized" childhood—most fully embodied the complex interplay of gender and writerly authority in Victorian times and the cultural tensions this interplay symbolized. His first published book, the opening volume of *Modern Painters* (1843), presents an extended portrait of a male deity, who is most awesome when He displays His power and most powerful when He reveals His wrath. Twenty years later, Ruskin delivered his honey-tongued defense of the subjection of women in **"Of Queens' Gardens"**—the most widely-read of his works in his lifetime (and perhaps again today, though for opposite reasons). Yet, in these same years, he positioned himself amid a wide network of women, ranging from distant correspondents to enraptured disciples: aristocratic patronesses, philanthropists, artists, drawing pupils, elderly neighbors, enraptured readers, and of course schoolchildren. In 1868 he wrote the gendered reverse of *Modern Painters, The Queen of the Air,* an extended portrait of a female deity who, as the Logos, inspires her creatures with the breath of life and sustains them with her presence.

Gracious yet autocratic, utopian and reactionary, patron of women and advocate of their suppression, Ruskin attracts or repels readers today in equal measure. His chief interest for intellectual history resides not in any single one of his positions but in the degree to which he internalized the conflicts of his culture, including the Victorian male's ambivalence toward female authority. In what follows, I consider the figure of the Ruskinian woman and her distinctive power: the moral force he called "wisdom." My texts will be some books of the 1860s—*The Ethics of the Dust, Sesame and Lilies,* and *The Queen of the Air*—which touch on the most scandalous of Ruskin's interests, his obsession with girls and their pedagogy. I want to show why this obsession, however eccentric or aberrant, nevertheless expressed an essential feature of the Victorian construction of womanhood, specifically, the tendency to view the pure maiden as a symbol of social order itself. When he sings the praises of girls, housewives, and the goddess Athena, Ruskin slips on the mantle of Carlylean prophet, embodying in his gentler manner a social ideal based not on masculine force of will but upon feminine sweetness and light—the ideal, in short, of a hegemonic order. I will argue, ultimately, that there is no such thing in the Victorian period as a Woman Question that is not also a question about bourgeois hegemony.

In 1858 Ruskin met Margaret Bell, headmistress of a girls' academy in Cheshire, and in the following decade he paid sixteen visits to the school as an unofficial benefactor and resident man of letters. Winnington Hall is a spacious sixteenth-century manor house twenty-two miles south of Manchester, with an excellent view of rural Cheshire; Bell leased it in 1851, knowing that an aristocratic residence would attract the daughters of the local gentry, the clergy, and the Manchester "Cottentots" (as the owners of the house called them). Though she was the daughter of a Methodist clergyman, Bell had imbibed the Broad Church opinions and progressive pedagogy of F. D. Maurice and his associate, Alexander Scott of Manchester. (On his first visit, Ruskin saw four portraits on the drawing room wall: Maurice, Samuel Wllberforce, Archbishop Hare, and himself.) Female education in England had usually been a matter of rote learning, often administered by overworked and underpaid governesses in a cramped environment, resulting in a superficial smattering of facts and a few elegant "accomplishments." In his influential lectures on female education, Maurice banished frivolous pursuits and rote learning, proposing instead serious subjects and an emphasis on experience, self-expression, and respect for individual differences. Girls were to be made aware of themselves as "spiritual creatures" and of the divine presence in all things, so that education would not be simply subservient to commerce or politics. Winnington put these precepts into practice. In addition to the serious subjects—mathematics, natural history, reading—the girls drew, sang, and danced. Above all, they kept healthy through athletics: they played cricket, bowled hoops, and swung ten or fifteen feet off a high bank in a rope swing.

Ruskin's descriptions, characteristically, convert Winnington into a paradise of girls: "the drawing room is a huge octagon . . . like the tower of a castle (hung . . . with large and beautiful Turner & Raphael engravings)—& with a baronial fireplace,—and in the evening, brightly lighted, with a group of girls scattered round it, it is a quite beautiful scene in its way." The choral parts of the Sunday service remind him of Rome; the light and shade of the table cloth and the girls' dresses at dinner of a Venetian painting—"a 'marriage in Cana' or some such thing." These words are from Ruskin's letters to his father, and no doubt he saw in Winnington Hall the image of a gentlemanly ideal—the kind of estate his father, a wine-merchant, showed him as a boy when on visits to wealthy clients. He would also have seen an image of his own suburban education, except that at Winnington he was part playmate, part tutor and always in charge: he conducted the girls' drawing lessons and supervised their Bible readings, while Bell, who worshiped him, moved in the background as a facilitator.

But if Ruskin was vicariously recapturing his own childhood at Winnington, he was also rewriting it, for this charmed place was free of the faults of his own upbringing: its harsh rigidities, its seclusion, its neglect of physical culture. And of course the Winnington world was free from the faults of adulthood. He wrote to Bell, "You can't conceive how few people I know with whom I can be myself. . . . My Father & Mother themselves, much as they love me—have no sympathy with what I am trying to do . . . sometimes I get very sulky—so that it really is no wonder that the feeling of being made a pet of as I was—at Winnington, made me wonderfully happy."

The book based on the Winnington visits is one of Ruskin's most eccentric, yet it conveys precisely the cultural significance of Bell's pedagogy. *The Ethics of the Dust* (1865) is a set of feminized Socratic dialogues featuring an amiable, "ageless" Lecturer and a group of adoring girls with names like Lily, Florrie, and Iris. The children clamor to learn the elements of mineralogy, and the Lecturer manages to incite their wonder and curiosity, partly by showing them crystals and precious stones, partly by telling them miniature creation myths that are also moral allegories. At one point, he has the children dance quadrilles so that they can visualize the molecular structure of crystals. When at last they grasp the analogy between themselves and crystals—that they are themselves "vital" or organic structures, the crowning link in the chain of being that begins with crystals—the book's lesson has been achieved and its religious meaning revealed: "You may at least earnestly believe, that the presence of the spirit which culminates in your own life, shows itself in dawning, wherever the dust of the earth begins to assume any orderly and lovely state."

The Ethics of the Dust is a child's view of romantic nature philosophy, but even more, it is an allegory of romantic pedagogy. By grasping that they are the very subject they are studying, the girls do not memorize precepts, they internalize a sense of "Life." The quadrille, strictly ordered but seemingly free, like a work of art, is the emblem of Ruskin's (and Bell's) pedagogy, and of the beautiful, perfectly-bred child who is its end product. Subject and object are one, since Life, the force pervading organic structures, is the objective manifestation of an instinctive will to good. Puritanism had depended on an ethics of earnestness that required breaking the child's will and forging a conscience stern enough to do battle with temptation; the new liberalism constructed a pedagogy requiring the gentle training of instincts, now represented (somewhat inconsistently) as both natural and regulated. A similar argument appears in Ruskin's essay on fairy tales (1866), which advocates the reading of tales that will awaken a child's love and reverence for the created world rather than the teaching of didactic tracts that will threaten and stifle her. Imagination replaces conscience, and romantic vitalism replaces Christian dogma. In effect, this idealized pedagogy constituted a new religion for Ruskin, succeeding to the collapse of his biblical faith and requiring as the central figure of its mythology a young girl—a suburban version of the romantic doctrine of innocence. Moreover, as Ruskin makes clear, internalizing a sensibility controls a child more efficiently than inculcating maxims; if anything, the "natural" purity of Ruskinian liberalism imposes a more stringent discipline than the old: "A child should not need to choose between right and wrong. It should not be capable of wrong; it should not conceive of wrong. Obedient, as bark to helm, not by sudden strain of effort, but in the freedom of its bright course of constant life." No child, of course, can live up to such a standard. Presumably, the after effect of such a failure would be a perpetual nostalgia of the sort that Ruskin experienced at Winnington.

What are the implications of this myth of innocent childhood for adult relationships? *Sesame and Lilies* (1864), the collection containing his most famous lecture, was Ruskin's most popular book. Its burden is that gentility carefully nurtured and internalized is the first principle of social cohesion. **"Of Queens' Gardens"** (like its masculine companion piece, **"Of Kings' Treasuries"**) was delivered in December 1864 at Manchester to the very "Cottontots" and their wives who might have sent their daughters to Bell's school. This now-classic (and, for some, classically repulsive) statement of the ideology of separate spheres uses a sweet tone and a stock of pseudochivalric images, presenting to the mind both a sermon and a sentimental genre painting. The "true place and power" of women, Ruskin says, are not inferior to those of men but different: the man encounters "all peril and trial" in his "rough work in the world," whereas the home is "the place of Peace; the shelter, not only from all injury, but from all terror, doubt, and division." Women are not excluded from all political power: for example as Ruskin argues, the Circassians had been driven recently from their homeland, yet this could not have happened had English ladies cared about it and wept over it. Nor are women excluded from all knowledge: they ought to learn just enough to sympathize with their husbands' pursuits. Within their spheres, women must be the moral guide of men and "incapable of error . . . instinctively, infallibly wise—wise, not for self-development, but for self-renunciation: wise, not that she may set herself above her husband, but that she may never fall from his side; wise, not with the narrowness of insolent and loveless pride, but with the passionate gentleness of an infinitely variable, because infinitely applicable, modesty of service—the true changefulness of women." It turns out that the woman's sphere is not only the home and garden per se but that greater "home" and "garden," the English nation, bound together in a spirit of benevolence and wisdom. Over that nation the virtuous wife is the true "Queen."

The wifely children of *The Ethics of the Dust* and the childish wife of **"Of Queens' Gardens"** share a predominant feature: the paradoxical combination (caught in the queen metaphor) of submissiveness and economic power. As Plato's philosopher starts his spiritual ascent with the contemplation of physical beauty, so Ruskin's bourgeois children begin their spiritual ascent with the right acquisition of clothing, books, and healthy looks. The very rhetoric that circumscribes the bourgeois wife in her activities and subordinates her to her husband serves to elevate the bourgeoisie, legitimizing its rule by prescribing a moral education in which the feminine virtue of sensibility (which Ruskin calls wisdom) is paramount.

Feminist critics have provided major insights into this linkage of bourgeois hegemony with the doctrine of separate spheres. Nancy Armstrong, for example, has suggested that women's writing—conduct books and novels in particular—created the bourgeois domestic woman, a refined, cultured subject who was a necessary prerequisite to the triumph of the bourgeoisie as a class: "such writing provided people from diverse social groups with a basis for imagining economic interests in common. Thus it was the new domestic woman rather than her counterpart, the new economic man, who first encroached upon aristocratic culture and seized authority from it." According to Armstrong, the new domestic woman could become the ideal wife for men in different walks of life, and she was able to compete with the aristocratic woman because her virtues were inherent elements of character, not surface shows. If this analysis is correct, the Ruskinian woman is a close descendant of the late eighteenth-century domestic woman, belonging to a now-dominant bourgeoisie that seeks to legitimize its claims. In a similar vein, Catherine Gallagher has argued that the ideal Victorian housewife contained the moral contradictions of capitalism by acting as a subordinate helpmate to her husband. She occupied a region—the home and family—that represented the antithesis of capitalist society while imitating its structure:

> If the family were to function as a normative model of industrial society, it had to be both hierarchical and harmonious. It had to be uncontaminated by the competitive spirit of the as yet unregenerated society. In short, it had to be a protected enclave where women and children gave voluntary and loving submission to a benign patriarch. . . . if the family itself were divided by a consciousness of separate and antagonistic interests, it could not serve as a model for countering the competitive ethos in the sphere of production and commerce.

In Ruskin's books, the girl-woman is the emblem of an organic society because she exemplifies sympathy, the first virtue binding that society together; yet in submitting herself to her husband she exemplifies obedience, the other virtue binding that society together. In **"Of Queens' Gardens"** Ruskin suppresses the possibility of separate and conflicting interests by means of a metaphor: the housewife "rules" the nation that is also her home.

Ruskin's career as a domestic ideologue is ironic, but the irony lies more in his audience than in himself. His own wife's elopement and the ensuing annulment formed the prime topic of society talk in 1854, yet by the end of the century *Sesame and Lilies* had sold 160,000 copies, in addition to countless separate issues of **"Of Queens' Gardens."** Ruskin's difference from his countrymen seems to have been the literalness by which he defined a wife as child, servant, and spirit of perfection. A marriage founded on such definitions resulted in scandal, but a lecture founded on them sold well. For the same reasons, his desperate love for Rose LaTouche—a child some thirty years his junior—carries the logic of separate spheres to its extreme. He seems to have craved Rose narcissistically, as an innocent child-other who would satisfy both his need to be indulged and his need to dominate. I have argued elsewhere that by marrying Rose (or any child-wife), Ruskin could use the doctrine of separate spheres to "marry" two inner contradictions: the split between the independent, aggressive adult and the perfectly obedient son; and guilt over a life of leisure built on the backs of those who toiled and starved. Ruskin's contradictions mirror those in the culture as a whole. The industrial middle classes could reconcile the conflict between capitalist greed and Christian charity by dividing competitiveness and piety between the two sexes. In Ruskin's construction, Rose becomes on the one hand the obedient child and on the other the savior of suffering humanity. He himself becomes the sufferer at the end of **"Of Queens' Gardens"**: "Oh—you queens—you queens! among the hills and happy greenwood of this land of yours, shall the foxes have holes, and the birds of the air have nests, and in your cities, shall the

stones cry out against you, that they are the only pillow where the Son of Man can lay His head?" Thus, although Ruskin's "queen" is an abstraction, she is visually concrete and so becomes, as Rose, the sign of male desire. She also becomes a figure for the social order as a whole.

In his recent, important study, *The Ideology of the Aesthetic,* Terry Eagleton offers a historical explanation for the rise of figures like Ruskin's queen. This book ambitiously links notions of the aesthetic in Western thought with the rise of an autonomous bourgeois subject and a social order governed by hegemonic persuasion rather than by autocratic coercion. Eagleton's complex argument appears most concisely in his remarks on Rousseau:

> The ultimate binding force of the bourgeois social order, in contrast to the coercive apparatus of absolutism, will be habits, pieties, sentiments and affections. And this is equivalent to saying that power in such an order has become *aestheticized*. It is at one with the body's spontaneous impulses, entwined with sensibility and the affections, lived out in unreflective custom. . . . To dissolve the law to custom, to sheer unthinking habit, is to identify it with the human subject's own pleasurable well-being, so that to transgress that law would signify a deep self-violation. The new subject, which bestows on itself self-referentially a law at one with its immediate experience, finding its freedom in its necessity, is modelled on the aesthetic artefact.

Just as an aesthetic artefact is an autonomous system of self-regulating, harmonious interrelationships, so the new bourgeois subject, obeying what seems to be the law of one's own nature, functions as part of what seems to be a harmoniously self-regulated whole. To explore another feature of this ideology, Eagleton turns to Burke's gendered distinction between the sublime (masculine) and the beautiful (feminine). If the sublime is felt to be coercive, then the beautiful—the thing one loves but does not fear or respect—is hegemonic: "The Law is male, but hegemony is a woman. . . . The woman, the aesthetic and political hegemony are now in effect synonymous." It is important to note, though, that if beauty must be included "within the sublimity of the masculine law, in order to soften its rigours," the reverse is not true: "Beauty is necessary for power, but does not itself contain it; authority has need of the very feminine it places beyond its bounds."

Eagleton's reading of Burke most obviously resembles the bourgeois gentleman of sentimental fiction, with his characteristic blend of sweetness and strength—strength humanized by a feminine sensibility and sensibility emboldened by a masculine power to govern and direct. In Victorian times this union of traits reinforced the doctrine of separate spheres by negating the contradiction between Christian ethics (the female part) and competitive capitalist practice (the male part); it also ensured that actual governance, however well-counseled by female "wisdom," remained in the hands of men. In more general terms, the ideology of the aesthetic provides a powerful means of rethinking what has elsewhere been called, in relation to nineteenth-century England and America, the "feminization of culture." Conversely, the notion of a feminized culture suggests that the ideology of the aesthetic is also an ideology of the feminine—that since bourgeois hegemony intimately involves the subordination of bourgeois (and other) women, the aesthetic philosophers that support that system will be patriarchal as well.

The career of Ruskin—the major Victorian aesthetic theorist—offers evidence for this broader claim. I have argued that Ruskin's increasing interest in young women and their education was not merely a personal eccentricity but a logical extension of his thinking about art and society. By describing the natural and social order in powerfully sensuous terms, he feminized beauty at the very time that he was aestheticizing women through a similar technique of sensuous description. By the 1860s, his writings about women's place in society developed the figure of the pure woman as a symbolic expression of hegemonic control. In *The Ethics of the Dust* the girls are patterns of hegemonic subjectivity, introjecting the Law as a principle of spontaneous consensus; in **"Of Queens' Gardens,"** wives are simultaneously hegemonic subjects and symbols of hegemony as a whole—they rule, one might say, in a Pickwickian sense. As I have suggested, Ruskin uses the half-disguised narrative of his own erotic desire to lend enormous affective power to hegemonic persuasion. But the opposite of hegemonic control—anarchy, insurrection, the resort to tyranny—is similarly feminized. The Ruskinian woman seems capable of radically unsettling the balance of forces she supposedly also contains. Might she in fact represent the very site at which those forces are generated?

By settling on the girl as an emblem of purity, Ruskin seems almost to acknowledge the impossibility of his vision of social unity. In one of the lessons of *The Ethics of the Dust,* the girls mistake a piece of gold for an ugly brown stone; in another, he allegorizes capitalist society as a dangerous valley where serpents sing in the trees; in a third, he tells the tales of "male" crystals that do fearful battle against evil in the "after life"; in yet another, the girls pretend he has dozed at the fire and lost track of time. Like the Red King in *Through the Looking-Glass,* Ruskin is sleeping through the dream he has created, a child-world of memory in which neither greed nor struggle nor suffering nor death can yet be thought. But that child-world will end and the unthinkable will become thinkable when the children reach maturity. For the moment, they are but "little housewives," whom Ruskin endows with the names of deities and compares playfully with dragons. The girl is the creature who has the seed of her own opposite almost ripe within her—that is to say, the breakdown of social control.

Three years after this book Ruskin published his fullest portrait of female power, *The Queen of the Air*. First delivered as a set of lectures on Greek mythology, it sets forth the cosmology of Winnington in Greek terms for Christian (or post-Christian) adults. But if the "little housewives" are figuratively goddesses, Ruskin's goddess-queen is only figuratively a housewife: her "home" is all of nature, and the contradictions willfully denied in the figure of the child reappear as the several natures of a manichean deity. Ruskin's Athena blends certain Greek myths and the idea of a universal generative goddess with the Old

Testament figure of Wisdom, said to be God's helpmate at the Creation. Ruskin's concluding hymn to her is a Universal Prayer to a kind of *natura naturans* which is also the objectivized form of moral virtue inscribed in the physical order. But in her other manifestation, Athena is not a maiden but a war-goddess; as the mark of an old victory, she bears the emblem of the gorgon on her sleeve, and in the frantic third lecture, Ruskin's vision of her is direful and apocalyptic: "her wrath is of irresistible tempest: once roused it is blind and deaf—rabies—madness of anger—darkness of the Dies Irae . . . Wisdom never forgives."

Wisdom is Ruskin's name for what Eagleton calls the "ideology of the aesthetic," the introjection of the social law experienced as spontaneous consensus. In *The Queen of the Air,* Ruskin now inscribes a hegemonic order in the cosmos itself, which is governed by an indwelling feminine divinity combining sweetness and strength. That divinity is lovely and graceful, the object of devotion and affection, with some sign upon her of the strength of Law—a Law having obvious relations to the Victorian woman's domestic responsibility for supervision, ordering, and surveillance, but whose ultimate sanction, though hidden, is nevertheless absolute. For Ruskin the mark of that sanction is the gorgon head, emblem of the woman's presumed castration and, therefore, in Athena, the emblem of her castrating power, her power to condemn, to cast off, to darken, never to forgive. In contemplating the extremities of that power, Ruskin's text becomes disturbed and disjointed.

What does it means for a Victorian patriarch to have written a book that freely revises the deity of the Judeo-Christian tradition, envisioning the Logos as present, full, and female? The answer is an acute paradox. *The Queen of the Air,* the one text which of all writings by Victorian men seems most pervaded by an apprehension of female power may also be read as a full-scale allegory of the patriarchal social order, an order that maintains its control (in times of relative calm) by appeals to the feminine virtues and to feminine images of domestic harmony. Literary representations of strong women no doubt could have had a utopian, transforming power, inspiring their women readers and opening up subversive possibilities. As a mythological abstraction, however, Ruskin's goddess-queen, like his queenly housewives, inhabits the looking-glass world of hegemonic ideology—an ideal region that reflects in reverse the power relationships maintained by the sexes in the actual social world in order to perpetuate them. In that mirror of the bourgeois order, women rule and guide and uplift: it is a "kinder, gentler nation" there.

This is not to argue that Ruskin's political thought is merely an elaborate mystification of the status quo—that is untrue. What was generally at stake for the men known as Victorian sages was less the status quo than the question of who should control the necessary changes. For Ruskin, Arnold, and many others, the regulators should be men of culture and sensibility (and perhaps also, on application, women) who could perceive the "ideal": the dynamic and flexible harmony of a system of unequals, where each unequal developed to the limits of her or his capability. Because this system lacks the possibility of internal conflict, it should not be disrupted, for example, by feminist or trade union agitators. It should also not be disrupted by an unregulated industrial system, the usual metaphor for which in sage writing was the machine, but which was also seen as the active producer of filth and disorder.

Probably all representations of female power produced by these writers are bivalent, confirming patriarchal hegemony but also making new roles for women thinkable: in this sense, one might say that the "feminine" contests or subverts patriarchy. But we must also remember that Victorian patriarchal culture used the "feminine" to legitimize itself from the start. Obviously, femininity so conceived was a very different matter from granting actual rights to actual women: the Victorian ideology of womanhood became a polemical weapon not only against working class aspirations but also against the woman's movement itself. For these reasons, I have preferred not to speak of the "feminine" as something that acts on its own to subvert or to contest. Ultimately, texts have no invariant political meaning divorced from the history of their social interpretations. Only when women are able to demonstrate their power concretely and to speak in their own voices can the lives of both women and men be understood in their true relations to the hegemonic structures that seek to define them. And only then can we give adequate readings of the books written about them.

Sheila Emerson   (essay date 1991)

SOURCE: "The Authorization of Form: Ruskin and the Science of Chaos," in *Chaos and Order. Complex Dynamics in Literature and Science,* edited by N. Katherine Hayles, The University of Chicago Press, 1991, pp. 149-66.

[*In the following essay, Emerson examines how order and chaos function in Ruskin's theories of artistic composition and in his autobiographical writings.*]

Ruskin's relentless discriminations between order and disorder seem to leave no intervening space for what is now named the science of chaos. Yet he would not have been the least bit surprised to learn that in 1984 one of the world's leading physicists would be reported to

> have begun going to museums, to look at how artists handle complicated subjects, especially subjects with interesting texture, like Turner's water, painted with small swirls atop large swirls, and then even smaller swirls atop those. "It's abundantly obvious that one doesn't know the world around us in detail," he says. "What artists have accomplished is realizing that there's only a small amount of stuff that's important, and then seeing what it was. So they can do some of my research for me. (Gleick, "Solving")

In fact Mitchell Feigenbaum's method, as described here and in [James] Gleick's *Chaos: Making a New Science* (1987), is anticipated by Ruskin in the first volume of *Modern Painters* (1843). Defending Turner's drawings against charges that they are chaotic, meaningless, Ruskin

discovers in them an order so scientifically accurate that they "afford" viewers

> the capability . . . of reasoning on past and future phenomena, just as if we had the actual rocks before us; for this indicates not that one truth is given, or an other . . . but that the whole truth has been given, with all the relations of its parts; so that we can . . . reason upon the whole with the same certainty which we should after having climbed and hammered over the rocks bit by bit. With this drawing before him, a geologist could give a lecture upon the whole system of aqueous erosion, and speculate as safely upon the past and future states of this very spot, as if he were standing and getting wet with the spray.

Whether for the nineteenth-century geologist or the twentieth-century scientist of chaos, what makes "reasoning on past and future" possible is the representation of "phenomena" in a differently visible medium. The transitions from a subject in nature, to Turner's picture of it, to Ruskin's reasoning back from that account to nature and definitions of composition—these changes might with qualification be compared to those involved in computer experimentation, suggesting the complexity of the work of representation as information becomes pattern, as data become design. Of course Ruskin's modes of representation were developed to contend with problems faced on different disciplinary terms by the scientists of chaos; and a great deal might be said about the inadequacy of any model—whether on canvas or a computer screen—to the flow of a "real system." But there is an important connection to be made between Feigenbaum's dependence on images which display "the way one function could be scaled to match another" (Gleick), and the premise in *Modern Painters* that the revelation of "the whole truth" comes only through images expressing "the relation of its parts."

We can approach this connection by recalling that Ruskin studied science as well as art all his life, and that both he and Feigenbaum worked towards order in apparent disorder by rethinking some of the same paradigms—in Plato, in Goethe's holism, in British romantic notions of organic form. In fact some of Ruskin's formulations were probably mixed up in what Feigenbaum rethought. More to the point, like other nineteenth-century scientists and writers, Ruskin was able to move back and forth between the natural world, pictures, and writing by virtue of inherited convictions that the physical creation and art are both inherently languages, the one of God and the other of men. But it is Ruskin's brilliantly innovative substantiation of the familiar assumption that art is a language which forms the crucial link in his work between the order of nature and the order of visual or verbal designs. In *Modern Painters* I and IV, as George Landow has remarked, Ruskin shows how painting displays "structures of relationships"—whether among forms, colors, or tones—which repeat the proportions, though not the scale or intensity, of "the visual structures of the natural world." These "proportionate relationships" are the "basic element of vocabulary" in Turner's "visual language." Art's capacity to create systems of proportionate relationships parallel to those of nature is what "allows the artist to make statements of visual fact" (Landow, "Nature's Infinite Variety").

In the long passage from *Modern Painters* I quoted above, Ruskin seems not only to read what Landow calls a "language of relationships" but to write one as well. By paragraph's end, it is difficult to tell whether the reference to "exquisite and finished marking" is Ruskin's response to the scene or to Turner's painting of it. But by that time, the language of the observer—whether he is Ruskin or a hypothetical geologist whom we might as well call Ruskin—has been segregated from that of the painter and his subject, as if the image could persist in the reader's mind without Ruskin's words.

> But neither [the geologist] nor I could tell you with what exquisite and finished marking of every fragment and particle of soil or rock, both in its own structure and the evidence it bears of these great influences, the whole of this is confirmed and carried out.

Ruskin's disclaimer about his own language has the effect of authenticating Turner's. The sense of a personal, or personified, competition or collabration between the two individuals was further diminished in the fifth edition of *Modern Painters* I, when Ruskin erased the comparison that had appeared earlier in the same paragraph, in which the geology of the scene is said to be "treated with the same simplicity of light and shade, which a great portrait painter adopts in treating the features of the human face."

But such a face-to-face meeting is exactly what Ruskin requires of his reader in a previous chapter. In this case, though, he is not making claims for a particular artifact but establishing the authority of his own perception of scenes such as those Turner painted.

> Observe your friend's face as he is coming up to you. First it is nothing more than a white spot; now it is a face, but you cannot see the two eyes, nor the mouth, even as spots; you see a confusion of lines, a something which you know from experience to be indicative of a face, and yet you cannot tell how it is so. Now he is nearer, and you can see the spots for the eyes and mouth, but they are not blank spots neither; there is detail in them; . . . there is light and sparkle and expression in them, but nothing distinct. Now he is nearer still, and you can see that he is like your friend, but . . . there is a vagueness and indecision of line still. Now you are sure, but even yet there are a thousand things in his face . . . which you cannot see so as to know what they are. . . . And thus nature is never distinct and never vacant, she is always mysterious, but always abundant; you always see something, but you never see all.

From a private perception of the indefinite, Ruskin renders a public definition of nature. The differentiation of order from disorder is a problem posed by and in terms of human perception.

In subsequent volumes Ruskin will repeatedly return to the difficult contradictions about perception that are incipient in *Modern Painters* I: contradictions in criteria whereby distorted representation is distinguished from au-

thoritatively imaginative accuracy, or whereby his own acts of representation are distinguished from Turner's. Some of the resolutions he works towards might be compared to a beginning made by Feigenbaum at about the same age as Ruskin was when he started *Modern Painters*. Feigenbaum's experience, like those Ruskin uses in his demonstrations, gains credence by being ordinary. But the two observers approach their destinations from opposite directions. Out on one of the long walks he took during graduate school, Feigenbaum passed a group of picnickers and began to puzzle about why their sounds and gestures suddenly seemed incomprehensible as he moved away from them. Questions about how the brain makes sense of all this apparently random noise and movement led him to ask "what sort of mathematical formalisms might correspond to human perception, particularly a perception that sifted the messy multiplicity of experience and found universal qualities" (Gleick). In the case of Ruskin's experiment, the "resultant truth" is the same whether the object under scrutiny is a simple geometric form or a landscape; that the aspect of a person may also be a proof of nature's character suggests that Ruskin, like Feigenbaum, seeks a congruence between the workings of human faculties and the ordering of what those faculties work on.

It was while reminiscing about this early stage in his thinking that Ruskin located, in his autobiography, his own discovery of "the bond between the human mind and all visible things": "the same laws which guided the clouds, divided the light, and balanced the wave." He made these laws out in the face of nature's "palpitating, various infinity." No one has ever loathed chaotic deviation more eloquently than Ruskin, but neither has anyone celebrated more powerfully the variety of nature. And no one, not even Darwin, has so vividly evoked the labor of attending to nature's fluctuant multiplicity. In fact to Ruskin, the capacity to preserve and oversee this multiplicity is an indubitable sign of genius:

> Imagine all that any of these . . . [great inventors . . . Dante, Scott, Turner, and Tintoret] had seen or heard in the whole course of their lives, laid up accurately in their memories as in vast storehouses, extending, with the poets, even to the slightest intonations of syllables heard in the beginning of their lives, and with the painters, down to minute folds of drapery, and shapes of leaves or stones; and over all this unindexed and immeasurable mass of treasure, the imagination brooding and wandering, but dream-gifted, so as to summon at any moment exactly such groups of ideas as shall justly fit each other: this I conceive to be the real nature of the imaginative mind. . . .

Ruskin's insistence on the vast information necessary to the discernment of order may seem less daunting to those who depend on the memory of computers. But this very dependency makes it easier to recognize that Ruskin's great delineations are presented as pictures derived from a disorderly welter of data he has remembered, and made memoranda of, in drawings and in prose. These pictures are not mere limitations but—to use a favorite phrase for chapter titles in *Modern Painters*—"the truth of" the things he recalls. He is concerned not simply with distinguishing finite pattern from infinite variety but also with the definition of each of them in a variety of media. As in chaos theory, where the same pattern of order is discernible in the movements of diverse phenomena, so in Ruskin's renderings of miscellaneous subjects, the crucial "transition is the same in every member . . . and its importance can hardly be understood, unless we take the pains to trace it in [its] universality."

For Ruskin, the perception of "universality" begins with the individual. The problem for physicists—that a system of representation inevitably registers the involvement of the perceiver and may repeat his or her definition of order and disorder—is for Ruskin the advantage of art as an expressive medium. For it requires the expressiveness of the greatest artists to make others see that the present aspect of a thing, whether in nature or on canvas, expresses its own past. Ruskin's diary continually registers his grasp of the relationship between formal design and developmental history. "I was struck in looking over the Shells at [the] Brit[ish] Mus[eum] yesterday," he begins in 1848, going on to present a theory he will soon develop in *The Seven Lamps of Architecture*:

> Now I think that Form, properly so called, may be considered as a function or exponent either of Growth or of Force, inherent or impressed; and that one of the steps to admiring it or understanding it must be a comprehension of the laws of formation and of the forces to be resisted; that all forms are thus either indicative of lines of energy, or pressure, or motion, variously impressed or resisted, and are therefore exquisitely abstract and precise. . . . The same principles apply to the patterns and forms of G[ree]k vases and to mosaics and frescoes, &c. (*Diaries*)

The lesson of the shells prefigures what he sees among Alpine peaks eight years later in *Modern Painters* IV:

> The hollow in the heart of the aiguille is as smooth and sweeping in curve as the cavity of a vast bivalve shell.

> I call these the governing or leading lines, not because they are the first which strike the eye, but because, like those of the grain of the wood in a tree-trunk, they rule the swell and fall and change of all the mass. In Nature, or in a photograph, a careless observer will by no means be struck by them, any more than he would by the curves of the trees; and an ordinary artist would draw rather the cragginess and granulation of the surfaces, just as he would rather draw the bark and moss of the trunk. Nor can any one be more steadfastly averse than I to every substitution of anatomical knowledge for outward and apparent fact; but so it is, that, as an artist increases in acuteness of perception, the facts which *become* outward and apparent to him are those which bear upon the growth or make of the thing.

The leading line inscribes form in the flux of its own creation. History—whether of nations or architecture or Turner's mastery of the "science of *Aspects*"—is legible in an image. "You need not be in the least afraid of pushing

these analogies too far," as Ruskin says elsewhere; "They cannot be pushed too far."

But in fact they can be pushed too far for comfort when it comes to Ruskin's realization that the composition not only of his subjects but also of his writing about them is a function or exponent of growth or force, inherent or impressed. Whereas in the 1830s Ruskin was delighted to take his own art as the basis for conclusions about how art takes shape, over the seventeen-year course of *Modern Painters* he struggled to represent himself as a critic rather than an artist, so that it would be his Turner and not himself who would be viewed as "the master of this science of *Aspects*." As we observed in *Modern Painters I,* it is precisely when his own representation of Turner enables him to discern aesthetic and geological patterns that Ruskin insists that he cannot represent what he sees in words. And it is in the midst of his intensely imaginative representation of the imaginative mind that Ruskin distinguishes that mind from his own—again, precisely when he is exercising the power which he implies he lacks. As both of these instances suggest, Ruskin conceals his creativity during, and by means of, his creative renderings from one medium to another.

In the next two parts of this essay, I will be looking at the history of Ruskin's verbal and visual renderings of the physical world, particularly as it develops in *Fors Clavigera* and *Praeterita*. For this history raises telling questions about the discernment of pattern in disorder, and about the relationship of pattern to what Ruskin calls "the movements of his own mind." If thinking about twentieth-century science conduces to thinking about Ruskin, the reverse is also true. Ruskin forces the reader of chaos theory to pursue the connection between definitions of order and definitions of the mind's composition: both the mind's acts of composition, and the way that mind is composed.

In *Chaos: Making a New Science,* Gleick repeatedly dramatizes the unconventionality of his chosen characters, whom he finds incongruous or even adversarial in relation to teachers and institutions. As in other disciplines, the formation of new ideas of order is generally redolent of a child's transgression against parental authority. But what Gleick discloses is not finally a series of transgressively isolated accomplishments. A passage from perceptions of disorder to perceptions of order is in a sense personified in the book, as disjunct individuals sometimes form themselves into collectives, and always produce work that eventually coheres in an implication of order. Comparison to Ruskin suggests why it is a "technique" that becomes the key in this transformation from disorder to order, and also why the means of representation are generally at the center of a contest between old and new definitions of order.

The fullest account of Ruskin's pictorializing—of his seeing the act of composition in imagery drawn from physical objects, and his finding in such imagery a warrant for personal authority—emerges over the long course of *Fors Clavigera,* which is surely one of the most monumental assertions in English of both coherence and incoherence. In these ninety-six "Letters" addressed between 1871 and 1884 "To the Workmen and Labourers of Great Britain," Ruskin originates a comprehensive design for living in St.

George's Company and reluctantly assumes the role of "Master." In fact he writes with such breathtaking mastery of his incapacity to master, that what seems "thrust and compelled" on him—"utterly against my will, utterly to my distress, utterly, in many things, to my shame"—is not authority over the tiny Company but rather his enormous power and ambition as a writer. The three massive volumes set themselves against what Ruskin regards as the world's horrifying disorder; and they do it in an "irregular," "desultory," "fragmentary" manner which he repeatedly deplores. Yet this very way of writing—this means of representation—comes to work as a justification both of Ruskin's attack on society and of his designs for its reorganization. So I will concentrate on Ruskin's explanation of how he reads and writes, as that becomes a crucial basis of the authority he claims in *Fors.*

Most people remember that he calls his bible reading with his mother "the one essential part . . . of all my education," but they forget his exclusion of any record of her teaching him to write—although she was his only teacher during those early years when he was regularly sending his prodigious poems and letters to the places where his father was traveling on business. What the history of his reading with his mother does include is a telling disagreement about his memorizing the visible pattern of words on a page.

> [T]he mode of my introduction to literature appears to me questionable, and I am not prepared to carry it out in . . . [the schools I propose] without much modification. I absolutely declined to learn to read by syllables; but would get an entire sentence by heart with great facility, and point with accuracy to every word in the page as I repeated it. As, however, when the words were once displaced, I had no more to say, my mother gave up, for the time, the endeavour to teach me to read, hoping only that I might consent, in process of years, to adopt the popular system of syllabic study. But I went on, to amuse myself, in my own way, learnt whole words at a time, as I did patterns; and at five years old was sending for my "second volumes" to the circulating library.
>
> This effort to learn the words in their collective aspect, was assisted by my real admiration of the look of printed type, which I began to copy for my pleasure, as other children draw dogs and horses.

The word "aspect" draws attention to his responding to words less as representations of sound or signifiers of ideas, than as visible objects, pictures. Like the reading which accumulates what he calls its "flow" by following the "flow" of what is read, writing assembles its own "aspect" in dutifully retracing the aspect of what was previously written. The self-questioning with which he began the passage has come to coexist with "resolute self-complacency": Ruskin promises that he will "have much to say on some other occasion" about "the advantage, in many respects, of learning to write and read . . . in the above pictorial manner." That writing, which he says he taught himself, precedes reading in this sentence anticipates Ruskin's explicit conviction that children learn best

what they teach themselves. Nine years later, he argues that

> nothing could be more conducive to the progress of general scholarship and taste than that the first natural instincts of clever children for the imitation, or often, the invention of picture writing, should be guided and stimulated by perfect models in their own kind.

Here, only paragraphs before he announces that he is closing *Fors* in order to write an autobiography proving that "I had not the slightest power of invention," Ruskin is admiring the "invention" of a manner of writing which he brilliantly mastered in his childhood, and which he considers worthy of use as a model in the education of thousands of other children. When he wants the reader, no less than the children, to understand what he means by "symmetry," "grace," "harmony," he points to picture writing to illustrate that capacity for "composition" which he says he entirely lacked. The most notoriously dutiful of all Victorian sons, Ruskin so describes his being out of order that it issues in a vision of that obedience to higher laws which is the defining characteristic of artists like Turner and Walter Scott. His insistence on learning words "in their collective aspect" evolves into an education for the reader of *Fors,* an education which resolves his double sense of transgression and obedience into a program which implies that his readers must obey their teacher, because he did not.

The importance of his having learned in a "pictorial" manner may begin as a rationale for accounts of his childhood lessons, but it ends as the justification for the lessons in writing, and then reading, which he proceeds to give his reader. Ruskin offers as a model a facsimile of a Greek sentence that begins with an illuminated letter "A." While copying this instance of "pure writing, not painting or drawing," the reader is instructed that "the best writing for practical purposes is that which most resembles print, connected only, for speed, by the current line," and that beautiful writing can be produced only by the hand that is "in the true and virtuous sense, free; that is to say, able to move in any direction it is ordered." Writing is "ordered" both by the aspect of print and by the impulse of the person who writes. Ruskin's moralization throughout *Fors* of the implications of handwriting recalls his argument in *The Stones of Venice* and elsewhere that all handwork expresses the moral state of those who produce it. Ruskin's analysis of handwriting is the most fundamental deconstruction of this idea in any of his books. For writing is the work of Ruskin's own hand, and the exfoliation of his self-knowledge substantiates the view that handwriting does not simply register the moral condition of the subject and the self; it also has the "aspect" of them.

The bond between the composition of one's words and one's subject is made graphic in Ruskin's next lesson on the writing of the letter "B." Noting that the model "A" instances no "spring or evidence of nervous force in the hand," Ruskin promises (but never delivers) a "B" from the Northern Schools that has so much "spring and power" that the reader cannot hope to imitate it all at once, but must be prepared "by copying a mere incipient fragment or flourish." What Ruskin does present is the outline of a shell—insisting that "This line has been drawn for you" not by himself but with "wholly consistent energy" by a snail. The "free hand" required to draw this line will thus be retracing not only a portion of a Gothic letter "B" but also, simultaneously, a picture of a living thing: in Ruskin's case, the hand has traced the living thing itself. Or rather, no longer a living thing but the visible creation and record of one—for the line incarnates and memorializes the "strong procession and growth" of the animal. In the next four Letters of *Fors,* Ruskin's fascination with the snail's record of growth—with the implications of the form of its shell—returns amidst discussions of many other historical subjects, including himself. So that the most interesting implication of the fact that Greek writers illuminated "the letter into the picture" after the Egyptians had lost "the picture in the letter," is that the public history of writing is recapitulated in Ruskin's own. His guiding his student's hand as it follows the form, or picture, of its subject is the most basic, and ultimate, demonstration of an identity between his "winding way" of composition and the composition of his favorite subjects. This identity was formed when Ruskin first fused letters and pictures, words and things, in his childhood. Maybe not while he was making the flourishes in his poems and letters to his father, but surely on the basis of them, Ruskin was helped "to understand that the word 'flourish' itself, as applied to writing, means the springing of its lines into floral exuberance,—therefore, strong procession and growth, which must be in a spiral line, for the stems of plants are always spirals."

In fact the leading line in Ruskin's earliest writing is arguably the serpentine or "winding way"—which he celebrates not only as an enactment of a subject that is not himself but also as a sign of his own invention (*Ruskin Family Letters*). The recurrence of the serpentine in Ruskin's work calls to mind the prominence of curves within recent chaos studies, of spiraling or scrolling forms like sea shells or waves. Ruskin's avowedly ethical preference for such organic forms anticipates the preference of scientists attracted to fractal geometry. Their assessments of the bond between nature and architecture, their valorization of forms that "resonate with the way nature organizes itself or with the way human perception sees the world" (Gleick), are already resonant with values given currency in *The Seven Lamps of Architecture* (1849) and *The Stones of Venice* (1851-53).

In one of his latest works, a lecture on the motion of snakes called **"Living Waves,"** (1880), Ruskin begins by making a connection between "undulatory" geological movement and his own "curiously serpentine mode of advance towards the fulfillment of my promise"—between his proposed revisions of his text and "one colubrine chain of consistent strength." But the energy of this beginning winds up in a venomous passage about paternal ambition, which breaks down the will and breaks up the designs of the sons of England: "fathers love the lads all the time, but yet, in every word they speak to them, prick the poison of the asp into their young blood, and sicken their eyes with blindness to all the true joys, the true aims, and the true praises of science and literature." As this language sug-

gests, the moralization of form allows sinister as well as righteous plots to bear on, or emerge from, representative designs. Thus it is that the shape of Ruskin's writing expresses not only the beauty of organic form and the obedience that issues from perfect freedom, but also the dangers of self-assertion. Like the quintessential Gothic in *The Stones of Venice*—"subtle and flexible like a fiery serpent, but ever attentive to the voice of the charmer"—even the very best handwriting records a sinister association. For the serpent not only has but is a tongue, an "inner language" Ruskin deciphers in *The Queen of the Air* (1869).

> In the Psalter of S. Louis itself, half of its letters are twisted snakes; there is scarcely a wreathed ornament, employed in Christian dress, or architecture, which cannot be traced back to the serpent's coil.

Ruskin catches in this coil the involvement of order with disorder. The continuity between serpents and the devil is spelled out in the disorder of language; so that language is powerless to dispel it. In *The Queen of the Air,* words designed to demystify the creature assemble a mysterious new creation instead: representation meant to redeem the art Ruskin loves is doomed to display its own damnation.

It is because of this taint that he seeks to distinguish different kinds of handwriting in *Fors*. Displayed by Ruskin's editors in a two-page facsimile, the manuscript of Scott's *The Fortunes of Nigel* is said to illustrate "the same heavenly involuntariness in which a bird builds her nest," or in which "the great classic masters" of art produce an "enchanted Design." The instance of "incurably desultory" handwriting which Ruskin facsimiles is, not surprisingly, his own—"distinct evidence . . . of the . . . character which has brought on me the curse of Reuben, 'Unstable as water, thou shalt not excel." Once again, Ruskin's authority as a teacher develops from his having been a disobedient student. As in the lecture on **"Living Waves,"** it is his own superior capacity to decipher, to follow, and to reproduce the true form of geological forces, of snakes' movements, and of sons' lives that underwrites his assault on fathers, while it is the congruence of these forms with each other which redeems the apparent disjunction of his writing into an approximation of organic design. But in these later works, nature's order is already poisoned by man's disorder, the son's authority by the father's authoritarianism. For all his buttressing of the patriarchal order of things, the aspects of "brightly serpentine perfection" can only lead Ruskin to an act of filial disobedience. And filial disobedience of an explicitly phallic kind is just what led Reuben's father to deliver upon his son the biblical curse Ruskin claims as his own blight in *Fors*: " 'Unstable as water, thou shalt not excel."

Yet the sign of the serpent—"A wave, but without wind! a current, but with no fall"—remains a reminder of the "advantage" of the "pictorial manner." For if writing reflects the "flow" of one's own mental movements, it has a more than personal aspect as it cleaves to the flow of its subject. Nine months after he writes about the instability of his writing and his character, Ruskin says that he composes *Fors*

> by letting myself follow any thread of thought or

point of inquiry that chances to occur first, and writing as the thoughts come,—whatever their disorder; all their connection and cooperation being dependent on the real harmony of my purpose, and the consistency of the ascertainable facts, which are the only ones I teach. . . .

Ruskin's title emblematizes the nexus of values implied or asserted in his writing about writing. Among its other meanings, "Fors" is both the fate that acts upon him from without, and the forces within that work themselves out in his life. In every moment, *Fors* bears the form of those forces in action. It is not simply that Fors will lead to form, but that it already, inherently, has a form, no matter how formless it may seem. The Fors, or force, of the writing reveals a pattern of order in the welter of data, for the interval between flow and form is only the time within which growth and force do their work, the time it takes for them to show themselves as *Fors*—which is the design of a person's life, the picture of a self and writing as "Unstable as water."

What may seem like the book's waywardness with regard to one set of forces turns out to be its lawfulness with regard to another. This is ultimately because Ruskin derives his authority from his denial of having any authority over himself—from his having been absolutely obedient not to his mother or father, but to the forces he could not resist as a boy, including the force exerted by the look of print on a page. Here more than ever the vocabulary of chaos studies seems apt. Like natural objects constrained to take certain shapes, like chaotic activities constrained to repeat certain patterns, Ruskin's writing is, in his account, constrained to assume the forms that it does in *Fors*. The result is a book at once private and public, intimate and estranged. *Fors* is Ruskin's own idiosyncratic signature; and it is a design by whose emergence he was as much astonished as were those twentieth-century scientists, when they first beheld a "strange attractor" taking shape on the screen before them.

Ruskin's discovery of a pattern at once within and without receives its last display in *Praeterita* (1885-89), the autobiography which began in passages transferred from *Fors*. Transferred and sometimes transposed, for *Praeterita* "has taken, as I wrote, the nobler aspect of a dutiful offering at the grave of parents." It is this changing "aspect" that I want to consider in closing, for it bears the weight of a lifetime's representations of order and disorder.

Coming at the center of the book, the chapter called "Fontainebleau" is centrally about Ruskin's discovery of the laws of composition during the summer before he began *Modern Painters*. The diverse materials assembled in the chapter have elsewhere passed through a number of versions whose evolution constitutes an instance of those laws. The whole story is too long to lay out here. But it should be borne in mind that Ruskin's revisions tend to create a more "dutiful" context for two assertions in particular: that in his sketches of 1842, "Nature herself was composing with" Turner; and that in his own attempts, Ruskin proved, once again, that "I can no more write a story than compose a picture." The connection latent between these two discoveries first emerges just after he re-

calls his recognition that Turner's "sketches were straight impressions from nature,—not artificial designs." While thinking this over on a road near his house, Ruskin has a foretaste of what he will describe as a momentous experience.

> . . . one day on the road to Norwood, I noticed a bit of ivy round a thorn stem, which seemed, even to my critical judgment, not ill 'composed'; and proceeded to make a light and shade pencil study of it in my grey paper pocket-book, carefully, as if it had been a bit of sculpture, liking it more and more as I drew. When it was done, I saw that I had virtually lost all my time since I was twelve years old, because no one had ever told me to draw what was really there!

Ruskin's self-reproach that he "was neither so crushed nor so elated by the discovery as I ought to have been" deflects attention from the way his discovery elevates him above his teachers (who forced him to regard nature in terms of previous paintings and principles), and above his father (whose fault in not buying a supreme Turner landscape is transferred to his son in the *Praeterita* version of the story).

The full force of what has happened is postponed until a few paragraphs (and a month or so) later, when Ruskin finds himself "in an extremely languid and woe-begone condition" in a cart-road at Fontainebleau. He begins only to interrupt himself with miscellaneous quotations and reminiscences of other journeys. But the pieces of the account cohere all the more dramatically for the detours.

> . . . getting into a cart-road among some young trees, where there was nothing to see but the blue sky through thin branches, [I] lay down on the bank by the roadside to see if I could sleep. But I couldn't, and the branches against the blue sky began to interest me, motionless as the branches of a tree of Jesse on a painted window.
>
> Feeling gradually somewhat livelier . . . I took out my book, and began to draw a little aspen tree, on the other side of the cart-road, carefully. . . .
>
> Languidly, but not idly, I began to draw it; and as I drew, the languor passed away: the beautiful lines insisted on being traced,—without weariness. More and more beautiful they became, as each rose out of the rest, and took its place in the air. With wonder increasing every instant, I saw that they "composed" themselves, by finer laws than any known of men. At last the tree was there, and everything that I had thought before about trees, nowhere. . . . The woods, which I had only looked at as wilderness, fulfilled I then saw, in their beauty, the same laws which guided the clouds, divided the light, and balanced the wave. "He hath made everything beautiful, in his time," became for me thenceforward the interpretation of the bond between the human mind and all visible things. . . .

Ruskin's critics have made a great deal of the differences between this account and what does or does not appear in his diary of the summer of 1842. But what is more interesting for the purposes of this essay is the fact that Ruskin derives the law he declares from the movements of his own hand. It is entirely characteristic of his prose that in the course of putting his own compositional capacities "nowhere," Ruskin composes one of the most powerful narratives in all his work—a narrative that shows how one can learn what one most inalienably and importantly understands from the process of composition itself. Much as Feigenbaum sees that artists like Turner "can do some of my research for me," Ruskin sees that a person who has devoted years to drawing Turners, and Turner's subjects, can do some of his work for himself.

But Ruskin does not acknowledge that the image of the tree is his own, that it records the movements of his own mind. The translation from tree to image encodes Ruskin's language of relationships—much as Feigenbaum's "inspiration came . . . in the form of a picture," a "wavy image" in the mind (Gleick). Ruskin's picture of a tree is in fact a picture of the laws of composition, a picture of relations between mind and its objects. The picture is a statement about, not a mere imitation of, two things at once: about how a tree is composed, and about how an artist composes. Both statements express order as a visual record of movement, change. This order is an abstraction from the growth of his own compositions, verbal or pictorial, through time—it is the comprehensive grasp of form as an inscription of flux.

The drawing of the tree is not there in *Praeterita*. Instead there is an account of a tree that completes the genealogy begun when Ruskin likened the seventeen-year development of *Modern Painters* to the changes "of a tree—not of a cloud," and continued in the image of a wind-and-flood-swept "birch-tree," that has no more control over the arrangement of its boughs than Ruskin does over the shape of *Fors*. The account of the aspen in *Praeterita* becomes the evidence that "nature" has broken through the "heavy," "languid" dullness induced explicitly by Ruskin's schooling, and implicitly by parenting that was at once "too formal and too luxurious." Yet for all his exaltation of the natural, Ruskin is interested in the aspen (as he was in the ivy he drew "as if it had been . . . sculpture") because it is composed as an artifact is composed, because it looks like something "painted." Where there is no Turner to bear responsibility, Ruskin comes to nature as if it already looked like an artifact.

Against the vision of his elders, Ruskin sets not nature but a representation of it—a representation which involves him in a competition that could bear as bitter a fruit as the tree forbidden to Adam. When he wrote about fathers in **"Living Waves,"** it was in sorrow, not in fear of those who "prick the poison of the asp" into their sons, and "sicken their eyes with blindness to all the true joys, the true aims, and the true praises of science and literature." But he senses danger for the son who gains his sight in *Praeterita*. This is one of the most pressing reasons for his affirmations of order in apparent disorderliness, for his reliance on metaphors of organic form, for his recurrent assertions that "I was without power of design." But none of this is enough. By the end of the chapter, father, mother, and son are all removed from what Ruskin regards as the "Eden" of their home—the home they shared before the achievement of *Modern Painters*, the home to which he returned alone to write the preface of *Praeterita*. Not only parental but also filial ambition is punished in this removal; for "in this hour of all our weaknesses," Ruskin succumbed to his "temptation" to occupy a scene where he might make an artifice. His original idea of building a canal was only realized twenty years later in "water-works, on the model of Fontainebleau"—the place where he both experienced and denied the power of his invention. It is the punishable implication of invention, of a competition with the father, that Ruskin seeks to displace by introducing the tree of Jesse—another inscription of genealogy which composes moving development into "motionless" pattern. The asp may lurk in Ruskin's words about the aspen that opened his eyes, but the root of Jesse is there to identify his composition, and his ideas of composition, with God's design for his own true son.

In disguising the role of the will, the chapter called "Fontainebleau" ironically demonstrates the artist's will to compose himself, to grant himself composure. It takes art to redeem the impulse to make art. At the very moment when a pattern materializes out of Ruskin's own mental and physical movements, he devotes all his force to showing that the pattern certifies a force beyond his own. If there is an "attractor" shaping the design of his "dutiful offering," then it must be God, not the chance of *Fors Clavigera*. And the only thing he finds "strange" in "Fontainebleau" is that he had never before seen the divine design according to which the order of the human mind is fitted to the order of all visible things.

It required years of revisions to work out the will that authorizes form in *Praeterita*. But the self behind the moment of inspiration is not lost as a tree becomes a drawing, and a drawing becomes print on the page. The process by which this is disclosed may seem to be light-years away from the experiments of contemporary physics. But there is a connection between Ruskin's way of thinking about representation and the comments made by the men who made the science of chaos:

> It's an experience like no other experience I can describe, the best thing that can happen to a scientist, realizing that something that's happened in his or her mind exactly corresponds to something that happens in nature. It's startling every time it occurs. One is surprised that a construct of one's own mind can actually be realized in the honest-to-goodness world out there. A great shock, and a great, great joy. (Leo Kadanoff in Gleick)

The "shock" and the "joy" are different for Kadanoff and for Ruskin, no doubt. But both of them achieve the exciting correspondence by translating mental "construct[s]" and the "world out there" into other media. Just how "honest-to-goodness," just how far outside the mind, are the operations that produce this correspondence? Like the work of Ruskin, the work of twentieth-century scientists suggests that a shift in the definition of order may be based on an interaction between the thoughts of an individual and patterns that are rendered for others to see. The science of chaos and Ruskin's science of aspects both investigate and finally deny the barrier between private mental movements and the design of the world that is not oneself.

E. H. Gombrich   (essay date 1991)

SOURCE: "The Conservation of Our Cities: Ruskin's Message for Today," in *Topics of Our Time: Twentieth-Century Issues in Learning and in Art,* University of California Press, 1991, pp. 74-91.

[*In the following essay, Gombrich uses quotations and excerpts from Ruskin's* The Seven Lamps of Architecture *to argue for conserving buildings from earlier times.*]

> Be it heard or not, I must not leave the truth unstated, that it is again no question of expediency or feeling whether we shall preserve the buildings of past times or not. We have no right whatever to touch them. They are not ours. They belong partly to those who built them, and partly to all the generations of mankind who are to follow us.

I know of no clearer or more uncompromising answer to the question 'Why preserve historic buildings?' than these defiant words, which John Ruskin wrote in 1849. They are taken from *The Seven Lamps of Architecture,* to be exact, from the sixth chapter, which bears the title 'The Lamp of Memory'. As a historian I feel bound to commemorate Ruskin at this hour, because it may well be that without the rousing words of this prophet this Congress would never have taken place.

I intend to come back to Ruskin several times in the course of this address to provide evidence for that assertion, but first the historian must also ask, how did Ruskin himself arrive at this position, unparalleled in this extreme form? We have seen that he bases his categorical ban against the least kind of interference with old buildings on a twofold argument: they belong not to us but, in the first place, to our ancestors who built them, and, in the second place, to our heirs. So, placed between past and future, we are not their owners but merely their trustees. What is so novel about Ruskin's contention is, above all, the extension of the idea of a monument to the whole of our architectural heritage, and I shall have more to say about that, too.

A monument, in the original sense of the term, is destined for future generations which, for their part, should respond to its message and take it to heart. Very often this message to posterity is contained in an inscription, which sometimes outlives the monument itself. Think of the famous lines from the grave at Thermopylae:

> Go, tell the Spartans, thou who passest by,
> That here obedient to their laws we lie.

The gravestone itself has long since disappeared, the burial place cannot be found, and there are no Lacedaemonians left in the world, but the message has come down to us over centuries and with it the fame of the three hundred Spartans who sacrificed their lives. It is posthumous fame which is the purpose of a monument and, to ensure its continuance, rulers and conquerors have seen to it that its construction is as massive and permanent as possible. Ad-

mittedly, this has occasionally provoked posterity to cast down the statues of detested figures and efface the inscriptions. Roman law even knew the sentence of *damnatio memoriae,* the eradicating of memory, and, properly considered, it also shows that Ruskin was not so wrong when he denied us the right to deprive the future of the monuments of the past. Our emotions tell us that there is still something like a right to an afterlife, which expresses itself in the conservation of monuments. What our ancestors achieved and suffered should not be surrendered to oblivion.

This right is, perhaps, independent of whether the past addresses us direct, as is the case with an actual monument, or whether we have a reason for commemorating it in connection with some historic event. In the latter case we say that memory sanctifies a place, and here the Swiss will think of Rütli, the clearing in the woods where their Confederation was founded, the English of the little island of Runnymede, where the Magna Carta was signed, and Americans of Gettysburg. This sense of sanctification corresponds to what we call piety. The Latin word *pietas,* from which the English word originates, means not merely devoutness; it includes loyalty to parents, to family and to the homeland. But, above all, piety manifests itself in the attitude towards religious traditions. Sacred shrines, the graves of martyrs, and indeed relics and ancient customs, are the object of piety. And yet I know of only one religion which imposes on its believers the pious duty of maintaining architectural monuments; I am thinking of Shintoism in Japan, and in particular of its greatest sanctuary at Ise, with its devotional shrines constructed of timber. As early as AD 690, a decree ordained that these buildings had to be wholly rebuilt every twenty years, without alteration. Except for very brief interruptions during periods of internal strife, boards and beams have been transported there in solemn procession every twentieth year, before the old ones rotted. And it is almost certain that at least some of these dwellings of the Gods confront us today precisely in the form in which they were erected more than one thousand five hundred years ago.

However, since Western civilizations hoped to secure the durability of monuments through stone and mortar, that solution was not available to them. Age renders buildings venerable in the West, but it does not preserve them from the pious zeal of restorers. As Professor Alfred Schmid has demonstrated in his contribution to this Congress, it was not the sacred but the pagan edifices, whose might and size seemed to defy the centuries, which were first regarded as monuments. Because Rome, the metropolis, fell into ruin in the Middle Ages, the derelict fragments of antiquity became silent witnesses to a vanished splendour: *Roma quanta fuit ipsa ruina docet* ('How great Rome once was, is still shown even by the ruins'). In the Renaissance, when cattle grazed on the Forum, the contrast between the miserable present and the glorious past became a commonplace of humanist rhetoric, and the Popes of Rome strove not to allow the evidence of the past to disappear. After several abortive beginnings Raphael was commissioned by Pope Leo X to arrest the destruction of antique remains, meaning mainly inscriptions and sculptures; but at least the claims of *sacrosancta antiquitas* to the care of posterity were thus recognized in principle.

It is significant that the enthusiasm for the might and splendour of ancient Rome devalued Christian buildings. If it had not been for the ambition of Pope Julius II to build a new Rome, it would never have been possible to come to the decision to demolish the most venerable church in the Papal capital, the Basilica of St Peter, which dated from the time of Constantine the Great, and to have a new church built by Bramante, which would rival the Hagia Sophia in Constantinople. What concerns us in this episode is the fact that this bold disregard of piety led to a protest, which for the first time, perhaps, attempted to uphold the rights of the past. In 1517, the year of Luther's public protest against the sale of indulgences to finance the rebuilding of the basilica, a little satirical pamphlet appeared in Rome under the title *Simia* ('Ape'). It was directed against Bramante, who had died three years previously, and describes a dialogue with Saint Peter, who, as we know, guards the Gates of Heaven. When the architect arrives, the saint asks him: 'Aren't you the man who destroyed my church?', whereupon a third person not only confirms this but also adds: 'He would have destroyed all of Rome, if only he could.' After all, Bramante had been given the sobriquet *Il Rovinante*, ('The Destroyer'). Saint Peter then asks the architect direct: 'Why did you destroy my church in Rome, which by its age alone reminded even the worst unbelievers of God?' Note the form in which the question is put. The highly venerable monument itself, not just its dedication to the saint, bids us to be reverent. Its destruction is an impiety in every sense.

But Bramante does not allow himself to be intimidated. On the contrary, he refuses to enter Heaven unless he is permitted to take charge of its architecture. To begin with, the steep path from Earth to Heaven must disappear. He wants to build a new convenient road, so that the souls of the weak and old can ride up on horseback. Then he wants to build a new Paradise, with beautiful, cheerful dwellings for the blessed. As Saint Peter will not hear of this, Bramante declares he will go to the Mansion of Pluto and there build a new Hell in place of the old dilapidated one, which has almost been destroyed by the flames.

Here, possibly for the first time, a theme is touched upon which continues to echo through the centuries, the lament about the pride of architects, their irreverence and arrogance. Who knows, perhaps in those days we would have joined in this condemnation. And yet, I do not need to stress that there are two sides to the matter. However much we deplore the ruthless demolition of the old basilica of St Peter's, we would not gladly forgo Michelangelo's dome, which Friedrich Schiller, for his part, was able to celebrate as the symbol of Rome's greatness:

> Any beggar in the eternal city
> Can regard us Northerners with pity
> As he looks upon the monuments of Rome
> Naught but beauty meets his dazzled eyes
> When he sees a second heaven rise
> In St Peter's awe-inspiring dome.

Yet Schiller wrote that poem 'To My Friends' not as a laudator temporis acti. On the contrary, his message is:

> We, we live, these times belong to us
> For the right is ever with the living.

How and when, you may ask, did the loss of this proud self-confidence come about, which alone can explain Ruskin's injunction for a standstill in building?

One might adduce social and psychological reasons, but I think that as far as architecture is concerned, the self-confidence was well founded. After all, many generations benefited from dominant architectural idioms, recognized styles, which, in a way, reduced the risk of putting up new buildings. Except for such men as Julius II and Bramante, no one troubled himself about innovation. On the contrary, an architect who received a commission to build a new house or renovate an old one was able to consult prevailing customs. Indeed, most beautiful old towns, whether Solothurn or Amsterdam, Rothenburg or Bath, owe their unity and harmony precisely to the absence of any striving for originality. This adherence to tradition did not of course exclude the possibility of improvements. Where a type of house or façade was established, it was easier to introduce practical or aesthetic variations, which themselves became traditional. This steady development gives the buildings of these epochs the character which we like to describe as 'organic'. When we speak so confidently of things which are organically rooted in the locality, we are certainly resorting to metaphors, to figurative expressions; but there must be reasons why this comparison with natural growth continually forces itself upon us. Probably it is because, as the old saying goes, Nature, too, does not act by fits and starts: new forms of life have arisen gradually from the variations which have particularly proved themselves in the struggle for existence. It is this adaptation to the environment which distinguishes the development of building—think, for example, of those farmhouses which accord so naturally with their surroundings that they seem like part of the landscape. Something of this unplanned balance is expressed in the traditional townscapes, and about this, too, Ruskin has written what is, to my knowledge, the most beautiful and convincing statement of its kind, in which he indicates the reasons which make these buildings so precious. For us today, admittedly, Ruskin's excited prose is a shade too rhetorical; nevertheless, listen to him once more:

> A fair building is necessarily worth the ground it stands upon, and will be so until Central Africa and America shall have become as populous as Middlesex: nor is any cause whatever valid as a ground for its destruction. If ever valid, certainly not now, when the place both of the past and future is too much usurped in our minds by the restless and discontented present. The very quietness of nature is gradually withdrawn from us; thousands who once in their necessarily prolonged travel were subjected to an influence, from the silent sky and slumbering fields, more effectual than known or confessed, now bear with them even there the ceaseless fever of their life; and along the iron veins that traverse the frame of our country, beat and flow the fiery pulses of its exertion, hotter and faster every hour. All vitality is concentrated through those throbbing arteries into the central cities; the

country is passed over like a green sea by narrow bridges, and we are thrown back in continually closer crowds upon the city gates. The only influence which can in any wise there take the place of that of the woods and fields, is the power of ancient Architecture. Do not part with it for the sake of the formal square, or of the fenced and planted walk, nor of the goodly street nor opened quay. The pride of a city is not in these. Leave them to the crowd; but remember that there will surely be some within the circuit of the disquieted walls who would ask for some other spots than these herein to walk; for some other forms to meet their sight familiarly.

It seems to me that here Ruskin has put a finger on a decisive point, which is certainly essential to answer the question 'Why preserve historic buildings?' Technical progress and the rapid change in our environment make the past all the more precious to us. It almost seems as if there was a kind of law, which I would like to call the Law of Compensation. The faster the transformation, the greater the desire for permanence. Without the impressions, which 'meet [our] sight familiarly', a feeling of alienation takes hold of us, indeed of fear, which threatens our mental balance: and not only in modern times; no one has spoken more forcefully about this feeling than the great lyric poet of the Middle Ages, Walther von der Vogelweide (c. 1170-1230), in his 'Lament for Lost Youth':

> The people and the land where I have spent my
>   youth
> Have become strange to me, as if it weren't the
>   truth.
> Those who my playmates were, are sluggish, old
>   and sore:
> The fields are lying waste, the forest is no more.
> But for the rippling waters which still flow, as
>   of late,
> Indeed I feel my misery would have become too
>   great.

The stream, the sole childhood memory which he can greet as familiar, preserves the poet from extreme spiritual distress. Today it would probably also have fallen victim to drainage.

I am not one of those people who nowadays prefer to write the word progress between quotation marks. Even the landscape of Walther's youth had long been a cultivated landscape. For generations it had been cleared, ploughed and planted and had so to continue if field and wood were to offer the population shelter and food. We are ever more painfully conscious that there is no progress without a price. If meadow and field are to go on flourishing, we must protect them from the exploitation which can so easily transform whole regions into deserts. Even the greatest boons, such as the advances in medicine, present us with the grave problems of overpopulation and an ageing population. And yet, who would really like to be transplanted to one of the European towns as they were two hundred years ago, without street-lighting, refuse disposal, or hygenic water supplies?

Listen to the musicologist Charles Burney, reporting thoughtfully in 1773 on his visit to Potsdam:

> In visiting the principal streets and squares of this beautiful city, which is well-built, well-paved, magnificent, and new, I could not help observing, that foot passengers were here, as well as in every other city of Europe, except London, exposed to accidents from being mixed with horses and carriages, as well as from the insolence and brutality of their riders and drivers, for want of a foot-path . . . perhaps, England is the only country, at present, where the common people are sufficiently respected, for their lives and limbs to be thought worth preserving.

No wonder the desire for improvements was at the fore then. This mood between resignation and hope is tellingly reflected in the words of the Hungarian count Fekete de Galantha, published anonymously in Vienna in 1787:

> An infallible means of making Vienna rank with Paris and London, indeed, of raising her above these two magnificent rivals, would be to execute the following plan, the realisation of which, perhaps, the year 2400 will see, if the ever-active and extraordinary intellect of the Emperor [Joseph II] leaves it to others to carry out. . . .

> One would have to knock down the fortifications and join the suburbs to the actual city, by which means a significantly greater number of inhabitants could be accommodated. Then, in order to widen the side streets, numerous buildings could be pulled down, so that the crowds which now flood the public places could distribute themselves in the city more easily.

> The progress of taste, for which the sovereign has given more than one example . . . would impart a less old-fashioned aspect to the buildings. Then one would no longer lay eyes on the shapeless colossi, in whose piled up storeys the owner takes much more satisfaction than the eye of the indignant beholder.

In those days, as we perceive, the accusation of greed applied not to the land speculators who pulled down the old buildings, but to the landlords who wanted to keep their tenement blocks.

Well, Vienna did not have to wait until the year 2400 before the walls and the glacis had to yield to the Ringstrasse, and even the most zealous architectural preservationist will not wish this step quite undone. Yet there can be no doubt that what I call the Law of Compensation makes an appearance at the same time as the desire for progress, that is to say, the growing demand not only for preservation of historic buildings but also for their statutory protection. The radicalism of the Enlightenment, which reached a climax in the French Revolution, led, as we know, to the destruction of the royal tombs in St-Denis and the profanation of Notre-Dame Cathedral, which was transformed into a Temple of Liberty. No wonder that a sense of offended piety, in which, naturally, national sensitivity, political interest and intellectual currents were interwoven, made itself felt ever more urgently. On both sides of the Rhine there were efforts to turn that feeling into action: in 1810 the French minister responsible for venerable monuments ordered a census of such buildings, and nine years later he approved a budget 'pour la conservation des anciens monuments', which was soon followed by legislation and a Commission for Historic Monuments. In Germany in 1815, the architect Carl Friedrich Schinkel composed a memorandum to the Prussian Ministry of the Interior 'on the preservation of ancient monuments and antiquities in our country'; at the same time the Boisserée brothers campaigned for the recording and completion of Cologne Cathedral; and in 1818 the Grand Duke of Hesse promulgated a law according to which the old monuments of his territory had to be inventoried.

Admittedly it seems to us now, in retrospect, that the romantic longing for the vanished past often had devastating consequences for our architectural inheritance. Wherever there were the means, medieval cathedrals, castles and secular buildings were sacrificed to an academic ideal of supposed stylistic purity, through which the traces of the past were erased cosmetically and the genuine monuments transformed into false theatre architecture. Soon, however, clear-sighted connoisseurs began to oppose this activity. As early as 1839 Montalembert said that antiquities had two enemies, vandals and restorers, but in his own country the almost superhuman energy and conviction of Viollet-le-Duc triumphed over the doubters and his hand still weighs heavily on the medieval monuments of France.

In pursuit of an answer to this problem the historian is again led back to Ruskin; it was he who lent his considerable authority to putting a stop to this activity. But it would be better to let him speak for himself:

> Neither by the public, nor by those who have the care of public monuments, is the true meaning of the word restoration understood. It means the most total destruction which a building can suffer: a destruction out of which no remnants can be gathered: a destruction accompanied with false description of the thing destroyed. Do not let us deceive ourselves in this important matter; it is impossible, as impossible as to raise the dead, to restore anything that has ever been great or beautiful in architecture.

Ruskin, who attached so much importance to manual work, stressed repeatedly that the spirit of the dead craftsman cannot be conjured up again, and that even the most careful copy must be a counterfeit. 'There was yet in the old some life', he says,

> some more mysterious suggestion of what it had been, and of what it had lost, some sweetness in the gentle lines which rain and sun had wrought. There can be none in the brute hardness of the new carving. . . .

> Watch an old building with an anxious care; guard it as best as you may, and at any cost, from every influence of dilapidation. Count its stones as you would jewels of a crown; set watches about it as if at the gates of a besieged city; bind it together with iron where it loosens; stay it with timbers where it declines; do not care about the unsightliness of the aid: better a crutch than a lost limb; and do this tenderly, and reverently, and continually, and many a generation will still be born and pass away beneath its shadow.

When *The Seven Lamps* was reprinted thirty-one years

later, Ruskin wrote a bitter and angry preface. He called it the most useless work he had ever written; the buildings which he had described with so much delight had in the meantime been torn down 'or scraped and patched up into smugness and smoothness more tragic than uttermost ruin'. Ruskin was too pessimistic. Admittedly it took a long time for his conviction—that the ideal of 'purist restoration' had and has fatal results—to gain widespread support. But we read with relief in the Charter of Venice of 1966 that according to its Article 11 the valuable contributions of all epochs must be respected, for purism is not the aim of restoration. Satisfactory though it is that the fight against the purist restorers has finally been won, it was a relatively easy victory. One had only to persuade the well-meaning Romantics that this costly practice did more harm than good. The fight against the destruction of old buildings was another matter. It had to reckon with quite different forces and powers and, properly speaking, it could never be completely won, for the standstill which Ruskin desired was neither possible nor really desirable. As so often in life, there is a real moral conflict here, which cannot be talked away. To quote Friedrich Schiller once more:

> Ideas can dwell together easily
> But solid things will clash in real space.

I can hardly imagine a space where 'solid things' clash more against each other than our towns. If that were not so, there would be no discussion or debate such as engages us today.

Here I must make a confession. When I was honoured with the invitation to give this lecture I had no idea how much had been written on the subject and how much there would be to read: not only the continuously changing laws and ordinances in all European countries on the care of monuments, which certainly fill many volumes; not only the countless books, periodicals and articles which have dealt with this question over more than one hundred years; but above all the meetings, conferences and international symposiums whose collected papers, as I realized with trepidation, frequently comprised a thousand closely printed pages. I had to content myself with considering the full bookshelves which I found under the classification 'conservation' in the library of the Royal Institute of British Architects as an expression of that psychological law which I have called the Law of Compensation. Precisely because the last hundred years have brought such decisive changes, because new modes of transport, new materials, new social attitudes and, above all, a new density of population have confronted the guardians of the architectural heritage with ever graver problems, our heritage—which year by year is increasingly threatened—year by year becomes more precious. I am not talking merely of academics or of high-minded aesthetes; I was delighted in the course of my unsystematic reading when I came across a local example: some twelve years ago there was a disagreement in Basle about the preservation of the Schmiedzunfthaus, which was finally saved from demolition by a referendum with a majority of 1400 votes. These votes were assuredly not all cast by art historians.

We often ask ourselves how much the individual can do

to remedy a growing evil. Here, too, Ruskin is a shining example. In spite of his depression, he did not give up and in an essay which he wrote four years after the publication of *The Seven Lamps,* on the occasion of the opening of the Crystal Palace, he put forward a concrete plan:

> Something might yet be done, if it were but possible thoroughly to awaken and alarm the men. . . . If every man, who has the interest of Art and of History at heart, would at once devote himself earnestly—not to enrich his own collection—not even to enlighten his own neighbours or investigate his own parish-territory—but to far-sighted and fore-sighted endeavour in the great field of Europe, there is yet time to do much. An association might be formed, thoroughly organized so as to maintain active watchers and agents in every town of importance, who, in the first place, should furnish the society with a perfect account of every monument of interest in its neighbourhood, and then with a yearly or half-yearly report of the state of such monuments, and of the changes proposed to be made upon them; the society then furnishing funds, either to buy, freehold, such buildings or other works of untransferable art as at any time might be offered for sale, or to assist their proprietors, whether private individuals or public bodies, in the maintenance of such guardianship as was really necessary for their safety; and exerting itself, with all the influence which such an association would rapidly command, to prevent unwise restoration and unnecessary destruction.

Ruskin closes with the observation that a task of this kind contained its own reward; it would also require sacrifices and yet, as he says, 'is it absurd to believe that men are capable of doing this?'

It was not absurd. Success did not come overnight, but this conference is only one of many proofs that it did come. Twenty-three years after Ruskin's apparently utopian suggestion, his admirer William Morris founded the Society for the Protection of Old Buildings, later popularly known as 'the anti-scrape society'. I do not wish to give the impression that the conservation and protection of monuments had been waiting for this initiative alone. I have already directed attention to the origins of the relevant legislation which reach much further back. But it is just the history of this legislation which proves how much the pressure of public opinion during the last hundred years has contributed to the widening of the concept of a monument to embrace the whole architectonic heritage, including our familiar streets and squares, even if they can claim no kind of historic significance. Let me illustrate this process by the British example.

In 1882 the Ancient Monuments Protection Act was concerned with sixty-eight monuments; these were almost all prehistoric. In 1900 more medieval buildings were included, and in 1907 even medieval half-timbered houses; in 1931 the statute also covered protection of the surroundings of ancient monuments, and by the next year the directive speaks of the protection of buildings, or groups of buildings, which are not ancient monuments in the original sense of the term. In 1937 the efforts to save the beauty

of Bath made it easier for the Georgian Group to inventory all other buildings from before 1830, when different degrees of need for protection were introduced. Here I feel I must mention the contribution of Lord Duncan-Sandys who, as founder of the Civic Trust in 1957, bore the main responsibility for extending conservation from individual buildings to areas—the so-called conservation areas; whereupon, in the following year, the Victorian Society upheld the right of Victorian architecture to respect and consideration. Lord Duncan-Sandys piloted the Civic Amenities Act to victory in Parliament in 1967. In 1972 there were 170,000 buildings and 2,000 conservation areas under some kind of protection, though of course this protection was not and could not necessarily be made effective.

'Could not', because in these questions there are and must be at least two sides. Let me mention a little example drawn from London: on the road between Hampstead and Highgate stands an old and popular public house, the Spaniards Inn, and opposite that is a little toll-house, before which conveyances once had to halt in order to obtain passage. The toll has long been done away with and the narrowing of the road between the public house and the toll-house has been a thorn in the flesh for many car drivers. The demolition of this modest monument of a vanished era had been decided upon, when one of the protesting citizens wrote to *The Times* saying that he appreciated that with the road widening the trip between the two suburbs might be reduced by five minutes—but what would people do with these five minutes? It seems that his argument struck home, for the toll-house was reprieved and I, too, am happy about this. But although these minutes may not matter in 9.999 cases, you could easily imagine a situation when a life depended on them. If that is so, then we bear the responsibility; but at the same time we can console ourselves with the thought that the slowing down of traffic would also avert accidents.

However that may be, one thing is certain: among the public at large, planners are increasingly regarded as meddlers, and whether they want to be Bramantes or only Rovinantes they have now been forced on to the defensive. This reversal originates to some extent from the widespread disillusionment which has made itself felt in recent years—from the disappointed rejection of the modern movement in architecture, the growing suspicion of all planning, and genuine fear of what the future may bring. Books such as *The Death and Life of American Cities* by Jane Jacobs in 1961, which has the subtitle 'The Failure of Town Planning', and Rachel Carson's *Silent Spring*—an attack on the indiscriminate use of pesticides and weed-killers—from the following year, have translated Ruskin's message into the language of the twentieth century and initiated a whole political movement, the 'Greens', whose members are not always mindful how much easier ideas live together than objects.

We may sometimes feel that this movement has succumbed to the same immoderation as Ruskin. On 17 January 1983 I read in *The Times* of the astonishing fate of a nineteenth-century barn in a Lincolnshire village: the limestone-and-slate structure had recently been made a protected building, but the local authority declared it to be dilapidated and had it pulled down. They had the express permission of the planning department for this, but it was apparently based on a misunderstanding, which came to light when the local population promptly protested that the village had been deprived of an old landmark, whereupon the barn was re-erected.

I do not know the village or the barn and I do not in the least wish to pillory the villagers, but their action shows how far the idea of a monument has been extended. The newspaper article says expressly that the barn was a landmark, a word which probably derives from marine navigation and indicates an aid to orientation, enabling the captain to find his way near a coast. Such a landmark sometimes turns into an emblem or symbol which remains, and is intended to remain, connected with a person, a family or a town.

I do not think I shall go wrong if I connect the increasing significance which the landmark has assumed in our minds with the ever-growing flood of tourism. Year in, year out, millions of our fellow citizens leave the comfort of their homes and crowd abroad for the sake of just such landmarks, which are considered 'sights'. If we can draw conclusions about the demand from the supply, then the monument becomes a 'souvenir' which we can take home on a postcard, or on an ashtray or, best of all, in our own photographs. It hardly matters whether the landmark reminds us of the past, like the pyramids, or of the present, like the Sydney Opera House. What does matter is its uniqueness; the Leaning Tower of Pisa, the Eiffel Tower, but also the Matterhorn, fulfil this function. To me the behaviour of the tourist taking photographs in front of these sights is enormously instructive: whether he wants to snap a spectacle of nature or a monument, the visitor searches assiduously for a viewpoint from which the intrusive evidence of the commonplace is as little visible as possible. He avoids the telephone wires, the cars and the posters. He is after the uniqueness, after what gives the area its character. 'That could be anywhere', the photographer says, meaning the standardized mass products of our civilization, such as petrol stations and garages, factories and tenement blocks. But here, too, new categories arise, which become new landmarks and monuments of a vanished age, like that barn and the disused railway stations in America, of which a certain cult is being made.

What stirs the traveller's imagination is an ideal. He is a refugee from the levelling tendency of our civilization. He is looking for what is called local colour. He would be happier if all the 'natives' still wore traditional costumes, always danced folk dances and, of course, served only their local dishes and drinks. As an Austrian by birth, I could tell you a thing or two about these bogus attractions. The native population no longer want to be extras in a performance which they cannot take seriously. What we can take seriously is our landscape and our architectural heritage, and we want to keep these landmarks for our sake and for the sake of posterity.

For the last time I want to let Ruskin speak. In his article on the Crystal Palace he addresses us direct on the subject of travel:

> What do men travel for, in this Europe of ours? Is it only to gamble with French dies—to drink coffee out of French porcelain—to dance to the beat of German drums, and sleep in the soft air of Italy? Are the ballroom, the billiard-room, and the Boulevard, the only attractions that win us into wandering, or tempt us to repose? And when the time is come, as come it will, and that shortly, when the parsimony—or lassitude—which, for the most part, are the only protectors of the remnants of elder time, shall be scattered by the advance of civilization—when all the monuments, preserved only because it was too costly to destroy them, shall have been crushed by the energies of the new world, will the proud nations of the twentieth century, looking round on the plains of Europe, disencumbered of their memorial marbles—will those nations indeed stand up with no other feeling than one of triumph, freed from the paralysis of precedent and the entanglement of memory?

The nations of the twentieth century have answered Ruskin's call; I am thinking not only of this Congress and the organizations which called it into existence, but of the sacrifices those countries have made which have seen their monuments and cities totally destroyed, such as the ravished cities in Eastern Europe, above all Warsaw, which suffered so grievously in the Second World War, as if they had been subjected to *damnatio memoriae*. In their worst time of suffering and deprivation the people rebuilt their houses and streets from the rubble, as if to prove that Ruskin's answer to the question 'Why preserve historic buildings?' was basically the right one.

David C. Hanson   (essay date 1993)

SOURCE: " 'Out of the Same Mouth Proceedeth Blessing and Cursing': Ruskin as the 'Strange Disciple'," in *Modern Philology*, Vol. 90, No. 3, February, 1993, pp. 360-380.

[*In the following excerpt, Hanson examines Ruskin's idealized version of his own childhood from the perspective of a God who is capable of condemning as well as blessing.*]

I

In his childhood conception of a sacred covenant, John Ruskin exulted in the exchange of a child's obedience for the Father's blessing. He was reluctant, however, to confront the Lord's cursing, which, inescapable in Scripture, left him silent and incapacitated. He abruptly ended his childhood sermons, the Sermons on the Pentateuch, with an unfinished account of the cursing in Deuteronomy. Thirty years later, on the verge of a religious crisis, he cut short his epistolary sermons to the children at Winnington Hall, a girls' academy, and retracted his discussion of cursing the Lord's enemies in what he called the "Hostile Psalms." A year after that, when Mrs. La Touche exacted a ten-year public silence about his religious doubt, Ruskin accepted a ban that merely formalized a long-standing pattern of impotent speechlessness.

This pattern is broken by an episode in letter 20 of *Fors Clavigera* that may record Ruskin's victory over helpless silence in the face of cursing. As he struggles to write amid a Dantean vision of an accursed Venice, its people capable only of cursing, the steamboats in the Lido shriek so "that I could not make any one hear me speak in this room without an effort," and their repeated and quickening whistles threaten to splinter his letter into incoherent fragments. But Ruskin appears able to cope with the cursing. Earlier in the letter, he hears a boy vendor's cry, "Fighiaie!" (Figs!), rise above the confused quarreling of gondoliers, and Ruskin reads this as emblematic of cursing—a curse shot from between the boy's legs, grotesque and latently obscene in its complex allusions to "making the figs," the gesture that scandalizes Dante in the *malbolgia* of thieves. Ruskin not only discerns in the curse the prophetic sign of God's anger that the boy unconsciously bears, the untimely fallen figs of Revelation and the evil fruit of Jeremiah and Amos, but also overcomes his past paralysis to counter the boy's accursedness with a few coins of blessing.

Yet this positive response also repeats another pattern that had always accompanied Ruskin's past silences: a regression to a childhood myth in which there is no cursing. His three-halfpence blessing too cheaply purchases a blessing from the boy that, unlike Ruskin's, arises from unconsciousness of the accursedness in which he is caught up: "His face brought the tears into my eyes, so open, and sweet, and capable it was; and so sad. . . . He little thought how cheap the sight of him and his basket was to me, at the money." In the Winnington letters, a similarly sentimental image of childhood had offset the children's lessons on the Hostile Psalms; to counter those lessons, Ruskin recalled his audience to their "child character" of open trust, like the fig boy's, and their role of keeping ignorant of sin rather than cursing the enemies of God. This impulse to nullify cursing in a child's world can be traced back as far as Ruskin's own childhood Sermons, where the formulaic language of judgment conflicts with a more earnest desire for childlike trust in a kindly Father.

Ruskin's persistence in regressing to and cherishing a childhood paradise is well known. However, it has not been remarked how such regressions evade a contradiction that had paralyzed him from childhood: a blessing Father could become a cursing Judge. Once we see Ruskin's later religious teaching as overcoming his attachment to a blessed childhood free of contradiction, his later prose appears remarkable in exorcizing paralysis and dwelling on destruction and redemption simultaneously. Letter 20 of *Fors,* which presents one such confrontation (as well as nostalgia for the body's sweet trust), is aptly explicated by John Rosenberg in terms of its opening quotation from James 3:10, "out of the same mouth proceedeth blessing and cursing." But Rosenberg mistakes Ruskin's achievement as that of controlling his sanity by releasing his own need to curse. The letter is more courageous than therapeutic, declining Saint James's childlike hope "that there should be no cursing at all" and instead exchanging silence for the psalmist's speech "in which the blessing and cursing are inlaid as closely as the black and white in a mosaic floor."

In this essay, I shall first examine Ruskin's unpublished Sermons on the Pentateuch (juvenilia dating from about

1832-33) to ground my claim that he created his first myth of childhood to escape the contradiction between the Father and the Judge. Next, I will compare these Sermons to Ruskin's Winnington "Sunday letters," arguing that his purpose here was to challenge his earlier myth by urging the Winnington girls to curse as well as bless, to bear witness to God's wrath as well as to God's kind providence. Seeking to remake his own childhood education vicariously and recover an adolescence better prepared to face the Lord's cursing, Ruskin ultimately fails in this confrontation, and the Sunday letters revert to the patterns of the Sermons. Nevertheless, the letters anticipate and illuminate the rhetorical structures of such later works as *Fors* in which Ruskin relays the complexity of judgment and blessing through a harsher myth. Overcoming paralysis, he repudiates his childhood faith, which had assumed his own elect blessedness, and adopts a persona that opens him to judgment: he identifies with the "strange disciple" of Mark 9, who, casting out devils in Christ's name, neither opposes Christ nor follows him. Such estrangement means in part that Ruskin conceals the extent of his religious doubt from audiences of childlike purity—children and women—whom he fears to mislead and on whom he continues to rely for comfort. At the same time, however, strange discipleship calls on an ethical and religious energy that eschews the platitudes of ordinary evangelical Calvinism and works in the world without self-assurance of reward and blessing. Such energy is characterized as intense in both joy and vengeance, even when it emits from the mouth of babes.

II

Ruskin's childhood Sermons on the Pentateuch follow a plan conventional in evangelical Calvinism. A portion of Scripture, in this case the first five books of the Old Testament, is interpreted as revealing the process of conversion: conviction of sin, justification by faith, and sanctification of the justified sinner. At each stage in the plan, Ruskin lays particular stress on obedience since evangelicals during this period characteristically advocated severe childhood discipline. The child is to rely on his parents (an analogy for and intermediate step toward reliance on the Heavenly Father) for help in withdrawing from the world; this docility preserves him or her for the conversion that can be worked only by the grace of the Holy Spirit and never by the sinner's own efforts. Ruskin's self-consciousness about the child's part in this doctrinal mode is evident in the considerable attention he devotes to the Fifth Commandment.

In what may reflect a larger contradiction in Victorian evangelical approaches to children, the Sermons also insist on reverencing a wholly kind and providential Father in contrast with their Calvinist stress on judgment. In rehearsing the maxim that a child learns to obey God by obeying parents, Ruskin is careful to argue that both the earthly and the divine parent can be reverenced without fear because they are kind. God is "not a despotic and tyrannical monarch who forms laws merely for the purpose of gratifying his pride"; just so, the injunction to "fear" earthly parents "must be understood as meaning, reverence" since "the child ought rather to trust in his father and his mother, than to fear them." Ruskin again illustrates his rejection of filial fear with the story of Joseph's testing of his brothers. He revises the usual reconciliatory motive ascribed to Joseph, for "instead of producting . . . the object which I think erroneously he is said to have had in view, namely to soften his brethren and cause them to repent, he only made them fear him." Such a result, in Ruskin's mind, is so reprehensible that he reads the story as an example of "Pride . . . Joseph's bane."

To obviate this conflict between orthodox Calvinism and joyful, unfearing obedience, Ruskin resorts to special pleading. The Sermons raise the usual sharp distinction in evangelicalism between the children of God and the children of "the world," who deserve God's wrath. Paradoxically, while Ruskin energetically condemns the world, he also makes the child's joyful obedience form the basis of the entire social order, accursed "world" and all. The social instinct, he believes, must be based on a "universal" desire for "pure, and honest intercourse." Since he believes that "society would be the cause of its own annihilation, if it were impure," he conceives of it as a household maintaining perfect order and joyful peace by adherence to the Fifth Commandment. Accordingly, with honor for parents postulated as "the basis of all government," his ideal society, like the home of *Sesame and Lilies,* must remain untroubled by the world's battles, lest conflict imply "impure" contradiction in children and their earthly or divine parents. The actualities of "impure" authority and compliance are glossed over. "No shepherd was ever placed over . . . flocks, who was unable to guide and protect them, no judge was ever placed upon the bench, who was not endued with powers to [do] justice impartially although he might punish unwillingly, no sovereign has ever attained to the throne, who might not have been the protector, the governor, the Father of his people; I do not say these faculties have never been abused, I only say that The Almighty has always given them, in order to promote this pure, and honest society." Having staved off contradiction by special pleading, Ruskin proceeds to offer a myth of a millennial kingdom of the heavenly Father. A nation that obeys parents "would go down in its prosperity to the conflagration of the earth" without need of enforcement measures because its "children would gradually rise up into a nation possessing such a healthiness of morals, & purity of principle, as even to do away with the necessity of magistracy, and handing those morals and principles down from generation to generation, and watching the convulsions and revolutions of all other nations on the earth, itself unchanged, and unchangeable."

In due course of this commentary on the Pentateuch, however, the Judge reemerges when Ruskin arrives at Deuteronomy. Since the cursing in this book challenges Ruskin's wholly beneficent providence, the Sermons collapse into rough draft. In effect, the Sermons do conclude by celebrating spiritual love when, in the last completed sermon (the nineteenth), a peroration connects the Decalogue with Paul's spiritual gifts. Perhaps uncertain about the orthodoxy of such a conclusion yet unwilling to change direction, Ruskin allows the Sermons to peter out with a draft on Deut. 30:19, a text that would force on him precisely the contradiction he has avoided: "I . . . set before you life and death, blessing and cursing."

The charmed circle projected in Ruskin's childhood myth, its covenant of unmixed paternal blessings on perfect filial obedience, anticipates his illustration of the "law of help" in *Modern Painters V.* There, warring elements, if left "quiet," will purge themselves of "impurity" and compose themselves into adamant and pure color. Unlike the law of help, however, which functions through energy, the earlier myth is static: perfectly obedient children revere perfectly honest rulers, who were once (and fundamentally remain) perfectly obedient children. Power can only be kindly and providential since there is no need for cursing. This passivity and serenity of obedience will be the first feature of his childhood myth to be critiqued in Ruskin's Sunday letters to Winnington.

III

In the bulk of correspondence between Ruskin, Winnington Hall's headmistress Margaret Bell, and "the birds" (as he called the girls), the connected group of Sunday letters (1859-60) reintroduces the theology presented by the Sermons as appropriate for children. The letters start by establishing obedience as a keynote from Matthew to Revelation. The Gospels' "primary" and "conclusive" teachings are "first the subduing of the heart to obedience" in the Beatitudes, then "fulfillment of obedience" in the Commandments, and, finally, the "Reward of obedience" in Revelation's water of life. Ruskin insists, however, that these texts demand "obedience by *action.*" In keeping with the law of help, which he is formulating at this time, he demands purposive, positive activity from the children.

To obtain this active form of obedience, Ruskin assaults the 'purity' that, in the Sermons, justifies the child's passiveness. Refusing to allow the children to substitute the "metaphorical term" of 'purity' for 'holiness,' as he himself had done, he revises the etymology of 'sanctification': "If you mean by sanctus—'set apart,' " he tells the girls, "you might think it meant you were all to go into convents. If you mean by sanctus—pure—you might think it meant that you were to *know* nothing of evil." In Ruskin's meaning of 'holiness' as "Helpfulness, Healing, or Sustaining," etymology points to engagement with the world and knowledge of its evil. Thus, Ruskin enjoins an obedience through action that, by the standards of his childhood, would appear "impure" in its dual potential for joy or fear, for showering blessings in the name of the Father or hailing curses in the name of the Judge.

This obedience to both Father and Judge entails no return to the orthodox Calvinist evangelicalism that Ruskin avoided in childhood. He expressly repudiates evangelical doctrine, which he finds so rooted in justification by faith that it approaches justice in this world neither terribly nor joyfully enough. His profound quarrel with evangelicals, pursued in much of his later work, is that they fail to both bless and curse, love and fear, with sufficient intensity and energy.

According to Ruskin, insofar as evangelicals conceive of man's righteousness as imputed by faith, their outlook on the "world" is too removed. Emphasizing man's social duty, he distinguishes between human righteousness, the mercy Christ orders us to perform in the world, and God's punitive role. Man's righteousness is "a *power*," not merely "a submission," and should therefore be intensely joyous when exercised as constructive action: "No Dreadful justice this—no sworded & blinded justice. But all Joyful—Because, the only Justice which man *can* do is to Undo the misery he has made.—That's *his* equity—In God's Equity there is also the 'Vengeance is Mine'—But Man's Equity is Mercy." Ruskin asked the children to copy this teaching of his for Rose La Touche but then dared not show it to her because her father, "staunch Evangelical of the old school, . . . might not like . . . speaking mercifully of Error."

At the same time, if evangelical faith is too dour in its understanding of man's duty, it is not severe enough, Ruskin thinks, in understanding God's equity, the "Vengeance is Mine." Again, Ruskin counters what he perceives as the evangelicals' preoccupation with justifying faith as opposed to obeying moral law: the doctrine "that men may go on knowingly contending with God all their lives & be forgiven at last" is "the invention of the great Adversary"; "neither in the Levitical Law nor in the Gospel is there . . . such a notion." Whatever a sinner professes, we must be prepared to condemn sin as vigorously as we work to save. God will not forgive, and we must not forgive, sins that prevent humans from fulfilling their active part in this world. These are sins against the law of help or, as Ruskin says in **Unto This Last,** against "justice": "sins which in their very nature separate one Being from another."

Thus, if even the joyful vigor of "man's equity" cannot offset the fact of transgressions against the law of help, childhood religion must sacrifice its preoccupation with joy as well as purity. Here, Ruskin leads the children away from the Gospels, draining platitudinous comfort out of the injunction to love one's enemies—"You are to love all, but not to treat them as your friends; that would be unjust to your friends"—and introduces them to the "Hostile Psalms," David's invective against his enemies. If the children have understood that holiness means helpfulness, they must recognize—at whatever cost to their complacency—that the opposite, separation and competition, cannot be forgiven. "The justice of man is mercy," he reminds them, quoting himself from earlier in the letters, but he adds, "What is mercy? The Spear through the throat may sometimes be the only mercy Possible." The implicit image of a slain dragon was much on Ruskin's mind, having recently read Turner's dragon in the Garden of the Hesperides as a fearful sign of England's Mammon worship (*Works*). Such sins that defile by causing separations "are unforgiveable—because," he sees, "the gulfs cannot close." Charity in such cases mistakes the meaning of purity, which Ruskin now defines not as the negation of sin but as social harmony achieved through active help. But Ruskin finds that he cannot advocate active help without also embroiling the children in the conflict that he had expelled from his childhood myth.

This threat to joy is clearly what most disturbs Ruskin in his revision of childhood religion. His habitual teasing of the girls becomes sardonic in the letters on the Hostile

Psalms ("You should *fight* against the World. Do you suppose . . . that phrase only means . . . not to buy strings to your bonnets at too much the yard?"). These letters are also the most guarded, warning the children that merely to think about God's vengeance against his enemies is "very terrible" and that, "for petted little birds who live in a park . . . and are locked in it, it is quite intolerable that they should have to sing about being delivered from . . . the fear of their enemies"—"people have gone mad in thinking of that." The threat, in fact, becomes so disturbing that Ruskin abruptly ends his discussion of the Hostile Psalms and instead recommends to his audience "two main conditions of child character" that exactly reverse the ethos of wariness and retribution he has been inculcating in them. First, with faces open and sweet (like the fig boy's), the children are to exhibit "trustfulness": "An ordinarily right minded child thinks everyone about it is its friend—believes what everyone about it says. . . . Therefore the child-voice is against all distrust—all strangeness—all enmity." Second, the children are to eschew vengeance on injustices. The strain is manifest in Ruskin's commentary as he reverses himself: "Well, you know, I've told you before there are some injuries which can't be forgiven—But if you are child enough—even some of those may be forgotten—And generally the child voice is for submission—for patience—for Forgetfulness. 'That thou mightest still the Avenger.'" Thus, with that adaptation of Psalm 8, the vengeance of the Hostile Psalms is stilled by inducing limitless forgiveness "out of the mouth of babes and sucklings." After this drastic reversal, the Sunday letters become intermittent as well as disconnected from a clear plan.

In this reenactment of the Sermons' paralysis and retreat, Ruskin shuns an added peril in cursing that he never imagined in childhood: he fears judgment on his personal loss of faith. He has kept this loss hidden from the children, but his revision of their education has in effect brought their curses down on his own head. Needing their consolation, as well as worrying that a revised education might lead them likewise to skeptical questioning, he restores the children's capacity to forgive and forget. Yet, prior to this reversal, Ruskin uses the Sunday letters to respond constructively to doubt by evolving a new persona for bearing and withstanding the onus of cursing and blessing. Here and in the public letters of **Fors,** Ruskin figures as an exiled prophet who is possibly accursed himself, or at least edging near doubtful margins of faith where he himself fears to tread, much less lead children.

IV

Ruskin's criticism of modern evangelicals for failing to bless and curse with sufficient energy sounds evangelical in itself, but he is trying to imagine for himself religious obedience without faith. At their most daring, the Sunday letters not only urge a more active and confrontational "holiness" beyond the Winnington park gates but also suggest that helpfulness may be rendered from outside the conventional community of the faithful. To illustrate, Ruskin repeatedly cites Mark 9, the unlikely example of the disciple who casts out devils in Christ's name but does not follow Christ. The earlier Sermons on the Pentateuch had illustrated unquestioning faith and obedience by concentrating on Abraham. The example of Mark 9 in the Winnington sermons, by contrast, depicts action from the very margins of faith. As Ruskin explains the text, "You cannot indeed in the separated—doubting state of his—be sure that he is right, yet," he immediately adds, "forbid him not—he is not against us."

Identifying himself with the strange, increasingly estranged disciple, Ruskin reveals in his reading of Mark 9 both sympathy and discomfort with such equivocal authority. On the one hand, since an estranged disciple seeks the witness of a following to cast out devils—that is, transgressors against the law of help—Ruskin revises childhood religion to form an alternative community with himself as its teacher. From the start of the Winnington correspondence, he proclaims the children "progressive," thrilling them with heresy ("I think you are not quite shocked enough by some things I have said") and flattering them with intimacy ("You can't conceive how few people I know with whom I can be myself—They are all half doubters. . . . My Father & Mother themselves, much as they love me—have no sympathy with what I am trying to do," and "I've no sisters." Complementing this role of "separated-doubting" yet authoritative prophet is Ruskin's role as a child among frank and advanced children, who will approach the Bible with him so as not "to bring out anything" predetermined, as his doctrinaire mother did, "nor to be *afraid* of *finding* out anything," but "only to make sure that whatever [they] read, [they] either *do*—or *don't* understand." Thus, the sentimental Victorian notion of becoming like a child to accept a simple faith transmutes, in Ruskin's progressive pedagogy, to a fearless innocence. Because children remain unpracticed in their elders' doctrinaire readings, which (in Ruskin's view) encourage otherworldliness over a holy worldliness, they will heed Christ's commandments to social duty. These paired roles of militant child and marginalized prophet no doubt arose from Ruskin's belated rite of passage to adolescence, usually documented by an 1863 letter to his father, written from Winnington, in which he unleashed his frustration with his parents' effeminizing overprotection.

On the other hand, uncertain of his authority despite his demands for his own followers' belief, the strange disciple needs reassurance and comfort, so he clings to the skirts of orthodoxy by cutting short the Hostile Psalms and reinvesting childhood with the spiritual capacities of trust and obliviousness to sin. Fearful lest he taint that comforting purity with doubt, Ruskin must have been acutely aware that the gospel verses on the strange disciple climax in the pertinent warning, "Whosoever shall offend one of these little ones that believe in me, it is better for him that a millstone were hanged about his neck, and he were cast into the seá." (Mark 9:42). Accordingly, Ruskin's roles as child and father doubly change aspect as he becomes a child subservient to the girls' authority ("The time has come for you to teach me") and a parent solicitous of their purity ("I should be very sorry that any of you should share in some of my feelings").

In this at once tentative and deliberate heterodoxy, Rus-

kin keeps the comforting image of childish trust and forgiveness safely in reserve while exploring the limits of his own apostasy through loss of faith: How far dare he withdraw himself and his following from the faithful without falling away from God in his "separated-doubting state" or harming the children? His discussion of unforgivable sin seems reassuringly couched in a conventional evangelical rhetoric, yet it reveals how far he has departed from traditional faith. Conventionally, the children are to understand unforgivable sins as arising from the failure of merely "formal" Christians to realize what evangelicals called the experiential "religion of the heart": "There are Sins against the 'Helpful Spirit.' Not against the *Law*, But the Spirit; Against all the inner teaching—all the instinctive kindly impulses—all the plainly written characters of the will of God in the heart. Not against a known law, not against a scheme of redemption, but against a spirit that strives with man. They shall not for they cannot be forgiven neither in this world nor in the world to come." This definition resembles arguments in the Sermons on the Pentateuch that law must be felt in the hearts of the justified but differs in discriminating between the failure to achieve an experimental faith and sin against "known law" and the "scheme of redemption." According to the earlier Ruskin, law and the experience of faith are one and the same: the unity binding ceremonial sacrificial law, the New Testament scheme of redemption, and the moral law enforcing holy purity of mind and conduct proves the divinity of the Bible. Holiness of mind and conduct is taught through the sacrificial law of Leviticus as a typological shadow of the Atonement. The whole rationale for this older law, as the Reformers had held, is to impress man with his inability to fulfill it and thus throw him on the redemptive mercy of Christ that the old law foreshadows. In a transitional passage between his sermons on the Levitical law and the following sermons on the moral law, Ruskin articulates the cohesion of these parts of Scripture in forming a foundation for faith:

> We . . . examine how far this economy [of Mosaic law] unites the necessity for moral purity, & holiness, with the doctrine of atonement for sin, by sacrifice. For, could it be supposed, that throughout the whole bible, there could be found one single sentence which inculcated the principle, that there was no necessity for purity of conduct, . . . [sin being] atoned for when committed, it would be so entirely out of keeping with the doctrine of God, as to afford us sufficient ground for the entire rejection of the Bible,—at least as a book of divine origin; but when on the other hand, we find a directly contrary principle held up to us, it is as strong a confirmation of the divinity, as the contrary would have been of the nondivinity, of the Bible.

At Winnington, Ruskin similarly unifies the Bible on the basis of deeds, not creeds, and asserts that it contains not a single antinomian sentence; however, by enjoining obedience to a mysterious "Helpful Spirit" who can be understood apart from a "scheme of redemption," he also tests his own apostasy. "He that is not against us is on our part," he repeats from Mark. Read as a gloss on Ruskin's preceding sentence, "You need never fear falling into [willful sin] so long as you love God ever so little," the verse implies Ruskin's salvation through his good works and perhaps through his reverence for the children's faith. Read with Ruskin's following sentence, however, the verse is countered by a check on his alienation: "But I believe no doctrine was ever so entirely the invention of the great Adversary himself as the doctrine that men may go on knowingly contending with God all their lives & be forgiven at last." I interpreted this assertion earlier as Ruskin's exhortation to an active obedience as opposed to the otherworldly antinomianism that he associates with evangelical worship, but his assertion can also be read as a judgment on his own contention with God—on his inability to believe in a scheme of redemption. Ruskin had ventured to affirm earlier that "God will look with most love on those who have the hardest & least—(here) rewarded battles with themselves," but now his assurance may well be faltering.

At this point, as he comes close to turning the Hostile Psalms against himself, Ruskin reverses the children's lessons in recognizing and redressing evil and instead asks them to "still the Avenger." The estranged disciple puts to rest both his self-appointed vengeance on social injustice and his fears of vengeance on his own possible apostasy; now, addressing the children as "babies," he switches to a playfully domestic persona. The request to still the Avenger is presented in the form of a poem composed as a "singing dance" for the children, anticipating the inventions of the self-indulgent "Old Lecturer" of *The Ethics of the Dust*—dialogues with "young housewives" that grow out of the Winnington experience.

This retreat serves to locate the barrier that Ruskin must overcome if he is to bear the onus of cursing as well as blessing: he must be open to bringing cursing on himself. The persona that he has begun to prepare for this confrontation is that of the estranged prophet who accuses an accursed people while remaining full of doubt and uncertain of his own grace as well. In the sardonic public letters of *Fors,* this figure wanders in a wilderness, and gardens like Winnington appear only as threatened visions.

V

In letters 18-20 of *Fors* (1871), a group on blessing and cursing that includes the apocalyptic vision with which I began, Ruskin specifies St. George's Company as "outcasts and Samaritans" who give alms. What has estranged discipleship come to mean to him in the decade since Mrs. La Touche silenced his doubt?

First, while Ruskin adopts a persona of estrangement in *Fors,* he does still rely on the consoling myths and the guarded teachings of the Sermons and Sunday letters. Carried over from both is the general method of defining the key to an entire text as obedience and then, within those confines, cradling blessed landscapes that blossom from obedience. In *Fors* 18-20, the method is applied to the "not unblest" peasant life in the Val di Niévole. Ruskin surveys the valley from a tower whose bell is embossed with the covenant that the people will reap the fat of the land if they obey the voice of the Lord; the covenant is fulfilled by the peasant children, Adam and Eve, whose hon-

esty, Ruskin implies, is rewarded by the scene's exquisite fullness. Again, just as the child of the Sermons kept himself pure and apart from the world, the Val di Niévole has survived by remaining separate from the "curse of your modern life." Hence Ruskin admonishes St. George's Company to create more such mythic vales by rejecting the world's wisdom of personal profit and working communally to capture waters on barren land. His advice on these hydraulics, "one strong impression" remembered from childhood, would re-create conditions in the kingdom of the heavenly Father: "*If you will educate* [mountain streams] *young,*" they will behave with "*utter docility and passiveness.*"

Fors does not rest with the formulations of the Sermons, however, for letters 18-20, like the Sunday letters, stress an active faith. They reiterate criticisms of "polite" clergy who, in failing to curse idlers and wrongdoers, contribute to the modern spectacle of a wholly accursed people who no longer know how to bring about blessing. More significantly, the *Fors* letters break with both the Sermons and the Sunday letters by moving from blessed vales to accursed modern cityscapes, a process in which the estranged prophet shows himself willing to bear a share of the cursing on his own head.

At the exact center of letter 20, Ruskin places neither the Val di Niévole nor the fig boy episode with its slighter suggestion of escape to comforting childhood but the exegesis of texts on blessing fragmented by the cursing of the steamboats—a moment-by-moment interruption of blessing by cursing enacted in the prose itself. This grotesquerie is keenly explicated by Rosenberg as an antiphony between Ruskin's " 'blessed,' episcopal self " and his " 'accursed' self," a controlled expression of divided consciousness arising from "the 'accursedness' of modern civilization and its assault upon [Ruskin's] own sanity. I would argue, however, that Ruskin's achievement lies in confronting the transmutation itself of blessing and cursing, not just in portraying his own divided consciousness. Such a confrontation, judging by the aborted attempt in the Sunday letters, must have arisen from his acceptance of some part in the curse—not just a succumbing to the curse of madness. The fig boy episode is saved from sentimental escapism by the suggestion that both the boy and his benefactor stand in need of blessing. In the middle of the letter, Ruskin's movement toward the experience of blessing and cursing resists the pull to childish forgiveness that had comforted him at the abrupt end of the Sunday letters.

As Paul Sawyer remarks, the biblical model for this persona of penitence and movement into the "wilderness of this modern world" is John the Baptist. "Bred in luxury, which I perceive to have been unjust to others, and destructive to myself; vacillating, foolish, and miserably failing in all my own conduct in life—and blown about hopelessly by storms of passion—I, a man clothed in soft raiment,—I, a reed shaken with the wind, have yet this Message to all men again entrusted to me: 'Behold, the axe is laid to the root of the trees. Whatsoever tree therefore bringeth not forth good fruit, shall be hewn down and cast into the fire.' " Ruskin has become capable of adopting this persona by explicitly exorcising both his incapacity in the face of cursing and his penchant for retrogression to blessed childhood. In a passage from "Traffic" (1866) that remains obscure without reference to this past paralysis, he overcomes the Gorgon's stare and accepts a harsher myth, an acceptance that he labels coming of age. The myth is that of Athena, whose

> aegis, the mantle with the serpent fringes, . . . and the Gorgon, on her shield, are both representative mainly of the chilling horror and sadness (turning men to stone, as it were,) of the outmost and superficial spheres of knowledge—that knowledge which separates, in bitterness, hardness, and sorrow, the heart of the full-grown man from the heart of the child. For out of imperfect knowledge spring terror, dissension, danger, and disdain; but from perfect knowledge, given by the full-revealed Athena, strength and peace, in sign of which she is crowned with the olive spray, and bears the resistless spear.

A more complete rejection of Ruskin's past pattern of silence and retrogession is unimaginable. The mature Ruskin does not achieve peace by the child's "stilling the Avenger," a mere postponement of the recoil of cursing; rather, peace lies in a chastened acceptance of the double truths of Greek myth, emblemized in Athena's olive crown and spear. The Greeks acted in Athena's name, Ruskin emphasizes, without "ardent affection or ultimate hope [in an afterlife]; but with a resolute and continent energy of will, as knowing that for failure there was no consolation, and for sin there was no remission."

Ruskin's mastery of paralysis and refusal to escape to a myth of blessed childhood are figured in his choices of feminine deities as his objects of contemplation and of flesh-and-blood women as his allies in activism. In an 1863 letter to his father from Winnington (written shortly before the rite-of-passage letter), he abandons children as icons and allies ("It is especially the young ones between whom & me I now feel so infinite a distance,—and they are so beautiful and so good, and I am not good. . . . The weary longing to begin life over again, and the sense of fate forever forbidding it—here or hereafter—is terrible"), while only a few months earlier he referred for the first time to the "young women," not children, at Winnington, who would now provide his strength: "I am quite certain no man can be in a healthy or strong state of mind or body unless he is in proper relations with women."

Ruskin's feminine mythology overcomes the thwarting desires and fears of a disjointed mind because it is structured, as Sawyer remarks, like Blake's 'contraries': as oppositions that remain related in that, "in both worlds, there can be no real forgiveness." Sawyer is misleading; however, in identifying one of those worlds as that of children and women (i.e., innocence). Ruskin has exchanged the child's world for the woman's, imagining gardens tended by women whose righteousness arises not from oblivion, as does children's purity in the kingdom of the heavenly Father, but from an aesthetic of order and design, like the measures of dance and song created for Winnington. Design characterizes human justice actively at

work in the world; it is distinguished from but responsive to the inscrutable justice of Ruskin's opposing myth, the divine wrath of destructive storm that he attributes to Athena. This juxtaposition was apparent to Ruskin in Psalm 85 on sowing righteousness and reaping peace, which he explicated for the Winnington children: "When Justice is wild—it is cruel—loses its fruit. When ordered and tamed and grown into full ear, it is merciful"—"ordered Righteousness—Grain set opposite grain."

Suggestive of Ruskin's juxtaposed worlds of blessedness and accursedness, one always transmutable into the other, is the myth by which Nina Auerbach explains Victorian representations of women—a myth of transfiguration. Auerbach, however, sees Ruskin's good women merely as his "defensive response" against their transformation into demonic power. To Auerbach, Ruskin is the "pristine" example of simultaneously doing homage to and shielding himself against self-transforming female power: his child-women cutting down to size, as it were, his own massive goddesses of cursings. It is true that Ruskin often conflates women with children as naive interpreters and spiritual agents, like Tennyson's Elaine, to whom he can turn to escape enigma. Thus, at the time he sought to restore "child character" to the Winnington girls, he praised the "consolation" in the fictional domestic "conversations," *Friends in Council,* by his friend Arthur Helps, because its new series (1859) included women as interlocutors. Ruskin adopted the dialogue genre in *The Ethics of the Dust* (1866), the first book to exhibit his preoccupation with the child-woman Rose La Touche as both audience and object of contemplation. Similarly, the queens of *Sesame and Lilies* must retain a "majestic childishness," their education limited to sympathetic support of men, not independent mastery, because otherwise men could not rely on them for comfort. Even in letter 20 of *Fors,* if Ruskin pivots the letter on the transformation of blessing into cursing in the steamboat passage, he flees from its agitating immediacy to the enclosed dreamworld of the child-woman Saint Ursula.

Despite the consolations of these dreaming and timeless child-women—in fact, as a critique of Rose's intense religious purity—Ruskin imagines more active women who bless in full knowledge of evil. Thus, attention to women's role in Ruskin's later mythmaking does not result in the "equal plausibility" that Auerbach finds in arguing for his antifeminism and for his feminism (or, in the most recent formulation, arguing for his patriarchal ethos and for his womanliness); his good women simply are not assigned the demeaning and sheltered "child character" of the Sunday letters. Far from protecting their ignorance, in *Sesame* Ruskin foists on women the agony beyond the garden wall. Lest they ignore this in seeking the next world, his bitter invective against women who occupy themselves with theology is meant to attack not "female interference . . . [with] the interests of a patriarchal religion" but evangelicals who emphasize the Atonement and speculate about the afterlife to the exclusion of practical justice here and now—an invective he directs with equal fury against male clergymen.

In his persona of the domestic Old Lecturer of *Ethics,* it

is true, Ruskin does move to preserve the purity of his "housewives," even as he lays out their feminine duties, by invoking a masculine "brotherhood, to enforce, by strength of heart and hand, the doing of human justice among all who [come] within their sphere." Similarly, in *Fors* he enumerates the duties of Guild members (resembling the girls' creed in *Ethics*) as if "for the great Monastery of the Servants of God." No doubt Ruskin resisted exposing a feminine following to trial as outcasts and Samaritans "whom the world hates" since he continued to believe that only men must become "hardened" by battle. Finally, the Old Lecturer suppresses the strange disciple as he ends *Ethics* with the assurance that the earth is providentially advancing to "animated Rest". Unlike his childhood myth, however, Ruskin's gendering of duties does not constitute a retreat from action and complexity of vision. In his persona of the Old Lecturer, as in his persona of the strange disciple, Ruskin elicits radical support along with comfort. Dismissing the forgetfulness of sin that would win himself easy grace, he refuses to allow the women to excuse wrong as the product of good intentions. Rejecting conventional tenets of faith, he tells the young women (having sent the younger girls out of hearing) never to meditate on heavenly reward since otherworldliness weakens duty. His meditation in *Fors* 18-20 on modern work inlays blessing and cursing "as closely as the black and white in a mosaic floor." In *Fors*—written, unlike *Ethics,* in the apprehension of a world laid under a curse, where even the speech of children forebodes apocalypse—the strange disciple does not merely inveigh against the accursedness to seek alternative blessedness in the Father but resolves to bring blessing out of accursedness by humane effort. Such effort relies on no facile forgiveness, neither for himself nor for the spectacle of lost souls he contemplates.

FURTHER READING

Biography

Bradley, Alexander. "Ruskin at Oxford: Pupil and Master." *Studies in English Literature 1500-1900* 32, No. 4 (Autumn 1992): 747-64.
    Explores Ruskin's years at Oxford and his disinclination to accept instruction from others.

Hilton, Tim. *John Ruskin: The Early Years 1819-1859.* New Haven: Yale University Press, 1985, 301 p.
    The first volume of Hilton's projected two-volume biography of Ruskin, focusing on Ruskin's childhood, his early education, and his travels through Europe.

Criticism

Austin, Linda M. "*Praeterita*: In the Act of Rebellion." *Modern Language Quarterly* 48, No. 1 (March 1987): 42-58.
    Argues that in the autobiographical *Praeterita*, Ruskin rebels against prevailing notions about himself.

———. "Labor, Money, and the Currency of Words in *Fors Clavigera*." *ELH* 56, No. 1 (Spring 1989): 209-27.
    An exploration of labor theory in the narratives of Ruskin.

———. "Reading and the Romantics: Ruskin's *Fiction Fair and Foul.*" *Studies in Romanticism* 29, No. 4 (Winter 1990): 583-601.
    Discusses Ruskin's proclivity for quoting and paraphrasing the Romantics, especially Wordsworth, in his work.

Bradley, Alexander. *Ruskin and Italy.* Ann Arbor: UMI Research Press, 1987, 123 p.
    Examines the significance of Italy in Ruskin's life and work.

Casillo, Robert. "Parasitism and Capital Punishment in Ruskin's *Fors Clavigera.*" *Victorian Studies* 29, No. 4 (Summer 1986): 537-67.
    Explores Ruskin's support of capital punishment and his belief in public hangings during the 1870s, when he wrote *Fors Clavigera.*

Casteras, Susan P. "Ruskin, His Champions, and His Challengers: William James Stillman, James Jackson Jarves, and Charles Eliot Norton." In *English Pre-Raphaelitism and Its Reception in America in the Nineteenth Century,* pp. 19-30. Cranbury, NJ: Associated University Presses, 1990.
    A discussion of the influence that Ruskin's blend of art, morality, and nature had on audiences in the United States.

———. "Ruskin's Rage and Ours: The Dramatic Style." *Browning Institute Studies* 18 (1990): 33-53.
    Examines both the "passion" and the "frigidity" of Ruskin's works.

Caws, Mary Ann. "Against Completion: Ruskin's Drama of Dream, Lateness and Loss." In *Sex and Death in Victorian Literature,* edited by Regina Barreca, pp. 107-19. Bloomington and Indianapolis: Indiana University Press, 1990.
    Considers the "immense sorrow" that seems to haunt Ruskin's writing and his life.

Cosgrove, Denis and John E. Thornes. "Of Truth of Clouds: John Ruskin and the Moral Order in Landscape." In *Humanistic Geography and Literature,* edited by Douglas C. D. Pocock, pp. 20-46. London: Croom Helm, 1981.
    An examination of Ruskin's studies of landscape.

Finley, C. Stephen. "Scott, Ruskin, and the Landscape of Autobiography." *Studies in Romanticism* 26, No. 4 (Winter 1987): 549-72.
    An exploration of Sir Walter Scott's influence on Ruskin, especially in Ruskin's autobiographical works.

Johnson, Alan P. "The 'Scarlet Cloud': Ruskin's Revaluation of the Sixteenth-Century Venetian Masters, 1858-60." *CLIO* 17, No. 2 (Winter 1988): 151-72.
    Analysis of Ruskin's changing views of Tintoretto and the other Venetian masters.

Nord, Deborah Epstein. "Mill and Ruskin on the Woman Question Revisited." In *Teaching Literature: What Is Needed Now,* edited by James Engell and David Perkins, pp. 73-83. Cambridge, MA: Harvard University Press, 1988.
    Explanation of how Nord teaches such Victorians as Ruskin and John Stuart Mill through an analysis of their very different perpectives on the same issue–the role of women in society.

Sawyer, Paul. *Ruskin's Poetic Argument.* Ithaca: Cornell University Press, 1985, 336 p.

Compares and contrasts aspects of Ruskin's personal and public life in order to illuminate his writings.

Wihl, Gary. *Ruskin and the Rhetoric of Infallibility.* New Haven: Yale University Press, 1985, 234 p.

Contends that Ruskin creates a "mosaic of truth" when his theoretical and figurative texts are read together.

Williamson, Audrey. "Ruskin and Morris: The Socialist Legacy." In *Artists and Writers in Revolt,* pp. 103-31. Newton Abbot: David & Charles, 1976.

A discussion of how Ruskin and William Morris rebelled against what they viewed as the destruction of human values and justice under nineteenth-century capitalism.

Additional coverage of Ruskin's life and career is available in the following sources published by Gale Research: *Contemporary Authors,* Vols. 114, 129; *Concise Dictionary of British Literary Biography,* 1832-1890; *Dictionary of Literary Biography,* Vol. 55; *Something about the Author,* Vol. 24; *Twentieth-Century Literary Criticism,* Vol. 20.

James Whale

1896-1957

English filmmaker and stage director.

INTRODUCTION

Whale is best known as the director of several classic horror films released by Universal in the 1930s. These films, including *Frankenstein* and *The Invisible Man,* have been widely praised for their inventive adaptation of classic literary works to the relatively new artistic medium of film. *Frankenstein* and its sequel *Bride of Frankenstein* are considered quintessential horror films of the early sound era, breaking ground both technically and thematically.

Biographical Information

Whale was born in Dudley, England, to working-class parents. He had taken art classes in his youth and was working as a cartoonist when he joined the British army at the outbreak of World War I. Captured by the Germans, Whale became involved with amateur theatrical productions put on by his fellow prisoners in the POW camp. After the war he joined a number of British repertory companies, serving backstage as a scenery designer and stage manager and onstage as an actor. It was his staging of the play *Journey's End* by R. C. Sheriff, a hit first in London, then New York, which led to Whale's Hollywood career. Adapting *Journey's End* to film in 1930, Whale scored a success with his well-received directorial debut and was offered other projects by the studio, most notably *Frankenstein.* Whale resisted making a sequel to *Frankenstein* until 1935, when he was assured of complete control over all aspects of the film's production. The resulting *Bride of Frankenstein* left both audiences and studio executives unimpressed. While he continued to make more films after *Bride,* including successes like *Showboat,* Whale never directed another horror feature. With the exception of the long-shelved *Hello Out There,* made in 1949, Whale walked away from the movie business in 1941 to concentrate on painting and set design. After a decade of directing feature films, he had been able to retire comfortably, having made strong investments in the real estate market. Mystery surrounded Whale's death in 1957, when he was found drowned in his swimming pool. Rumors circulated suggesting that Whale, who was a homosexual, was murdered by one of his companions. However, biographers have pointed out that Whale had been recovering from a minor stroke at the time of his death and may have simply fallen.

Major Works

Casting a virtually unknown actor named Boris Karloff as the monster, Whale approached the story of Frankenstein with an artist's eye for the visual. Through the use of low

camera angles, dramatic lighting, and macabre sets, he achieved an effectively creepy atmosphere. The commercial success of *Frankenstein* soon established Whale as Universal's top horror director during the early 1930s, despite the filmmaker's reluctance to be pigeon-holed within a single genre. Among his other films from this period are *The Old Dark House* and *The Invisible Man,* the latter of which amazed audiences with its innovative special effects. In *Bride of Frankenstein,* which is generally considered superior to the original film, the director indulged his subversive sense of humor by introducing eccentric characters and bizarre subplots.

Critical Reception

Critics who first viewed Whale's horror films during the 1930s were divided over the director's talent. Some viewed the acting method he summoned from his performers as too stagy and not fluid enough for sound film. Since his death, Whale's stature as a filmmaker has grown considerably. Film scholars have praised his ability to balance literary themes with cinematic and theatrical techniques. His version of Frankenstein's monster, portrayed with equal measures of gruesomeness and pathos by Boris Karloff, has become an instantly recognizable icon in American popular culture.

PRINCIPAL WORKS

Journey's End   (film)   1930
Frankenstein   (film)   1931
Waterloo Bridge   (film)   1931
Impatient Maiden   (film)   1932
The Old Dark House   (film)   1932
The Invisible Man   (film)   1933
The Kiss before the Mirror   (film)   1933
By Candlelight   (film)   1934
One More River   (film)   1934
Bride of Frankenstein   (film)   1935
Remember Last Night?   (film)   1935
Showboat   (film)   1936
The Great Garrick   (film)   1937
The Road Back   (film)   1937
Port of Seven Seas   (film)   1938
Sinners in Paradise   (film)   1938
Wives under Suspicion   (film)   1938
The Man in the Iron Mask   (film)   1939
Green Hell   (film)   1940
They Dare Not Love   (film)   1941
Hello Out There   (film)   1949

CRITICISM

William Troy   (essay date 1933)

SOURCE: "Films: 'The Invisible Man'," in *The Nation*, New York, Vol. CXXXVII, No. 3571, Dec. 13, 1933, p. 688.

[*In the following essay, Troy praises Whale for his direction of* The Invisible Man.]

There are two very good reasons why the version of H. G. Wells's *Invisible Man* at the old Roxy is so much better than this sort of thing usually turns out to be on the screen. The first is that James Whale, who is responsible for the direction, has taken a great deal of pains with something that is usually either reduced to a minimum or altogether ignored in these attempts to dramatize the more farfetched hypotheses of science—namely, setting. Ordinarily we are precipitated abruptly and without warning into the strange and violent world of the scientific romancer's imagination. We are given no time to make our adjustment to the logic of this new world which is so different from the world to which we are accustomed. The result is of course that we never truly believe in this new world: it is too abstract, too intellectually conceived, to take us in very successfully through our feelings. For this reason one is always tempted to lay down as a first principle for writers and directors dealing with the extraordinary the

principle that to respond to the unusual we must first be reminded of the commonplace. And James Whale's success in observing the principle makes one more convinced than ever that it should be regarded as a general one. He begins with a carefully documented picture of a small country inn in England: the people, the furnishings, the whole atmosphere are not only instantly recognizable but also so particularized as to have an interest in and for themselves. The background is solidly blocked in so that we can have no uncertainty as to the reality of the people and the places with whom we have to deal. Everything is made ready for the invisible man to step in and perform his marvels.

Now the only problem for the director was to make the best possible use of his idea—an idea which happens to be ideally suited to the talking screen in so far as it is impossible to imagine it being equally well treated in any other medium. For the wretched scientist who has made himself invisible still has a voice. A body without a voice we have had on the silent screen, but not until this picture have we had a voice without a body. And in Wells's novel the sight of the printed words on the page cannot be so disturbingly eerie as the actual sound of Claude Rains's voice issuing from empty chairs and unoccupied rooms. The problem for Mr. Whale, then, was to miss none of the opportunities for humor, pathos, and metaphysical horror which this rare notion opened up to the sound-camera. How admirably he has succeeded it is impossible to indicate without reference to the numerous instances in which his ingenuity surprises our habitual sense-patterns. It will be enough to mention the books hurled through space by an invisible hand, the cigarette smoked by invisible lips, the indentation in the snow of the shattered but still invisible body. Also one must point to the effectiveness of not showing the visible features of the scientist until, in the last few feet of the film, death restores them to him. Of Claude Rains's richly suggestive voice it is not too much to say that it is hardly less responsible than the direction for the peculiar quality of the picture as a whole. The preternatural compound of Olympian merriment and human desolation which are its overtones lends a seriousness that would otherwise be lacking. But taken either as a technical exercise or as a sometimes profoundly moving retelling of the Frankenstein fable, *The Invisible Man* is one of the most rewarding of the recent films.

Jorge Luis Borges   (essay date 1937)

SOURCE: "The Road Back," in *Sight and Sound*, Vol. 45, No. 4, Autumn, 1976, p. 233.

[*An Argentine short story writer, poet, and essayist, Borges was one of the leading figures in modern literature. His writing is often used by critics to illustrate the contemporary view of literature as a highly sophisticated game. Justifying this interpretation of Borges's works are his admitted respect for stories that are artificial inventions of art rather than realistic representations of life, his use of philosophical conceptions as a means of achieving literary effects, and his frequent variations on the writings of other authors. In the following essay, which was first published in the Argentine journal* Sur *in 1937, Borges examines* The Road Back.]

In the winter of 1872, among the jacaranda furniture of a hotel whose balconies faced the treeless Victoria Plaza, don José Hernández—enemy of Sarmiento and of Mitre—wanted to expose the degradation that the disastrous military regime had produced in the natives of Buenos Aires and wrote the anti-war poem *The Gaucho Martin Fierro.* The hero—who is not aware of it?—was a deserter from the army; his companion a deserter from the police. We are familiar with the consequences. Around 1894, Unamuno discovered that Hernández' book 'was the song of the Spanish fighter who, after having planted the cross in Granada, went to America to serve the progress of civilisation and to open the road into the desert.' In 1916, Lugones stated, 'And for that reason—because it personifies the heroic life of the people with their language and their most genuine feelings, embodying it in a champion or, rather, in the most perfect symbol of justice and liberation—*Martin Fierro* is an epic poem.'

I have recalled the case of *Martin Fierro* because it is not unusual. Works denouncing the indignities or the horrors of war always run the risk of seeming to be a vindication of war. In effect, the more horrible the war, the greater its satanic prestige, the greater the virtue of those men who look it in the face. That stubborn Dr. Johnson once declared that patriotism is the last refuge of a scoundrel. Around 1778 he also said that the profession of sailors and soldiers has the dignity of danger. Of the acclaimed pacifist film, *All Quiet on the Western Front,* what remains now in our memory? A fierce and enviable bayonet charge, exactly like the ones shown in any war movie.

The Road Back is undeniably inferior to *All Quiet on the Western Front.* Its climactic moment is also one of battle. The peculiar pathos of the scene comes from its being absolutely clear to us that the soldiers' fears and agonies are useless: Germany had already surrendered. The other scenes seem to me very forgettable. The thesis (I think) is the unadaptability of the military to civilian life, the conflicts of city ethics with trench ethics. Fear of rendering the protagonists disagreeable has dulled or cancelled out the demonstration of the thesis. It is true that one of the veterans winds up a murderer, but his victim is such an execrable, such an oily, such a minutely Jewish Schieber that his destruction is in every light a meritorious act. Another of the veteran fighters ends up in a marriage of convenience; another improvising speeches; another coveting (and stealing) other people's chickens.

On seeing *The Road Back,* I felt that mere pacifism is not enough. War is an ancient passion that tempts men with ascetic and mortal charms. In order to abolish it, you have to confront it with another passion. Maybe that of the good European—Leibnitz, Voltaire, Goethe, Arnold, Renan, Shaw, Russell, Unamuno, T. S. Eliot—who recognises himself as the heir and the perpetuator of all the countries. Unfortunately, Europe is teeming with mere Germans and mere Irishmen. Europeans are scarce.

Paul Jensen (essay date 1971)

SOURCE: "James Whale," in *Film Comment,* Vol. 7, No. 1, Spring, 1971, pp. 52-7

[*In the following essay, Jensen discusses Whale as an early example of an auteur film director.*]

It certainly is becoming harder and harder to keep track of the auteurs, especially now that more and more lost films are reaching present-day screens. Directors who once existed solely as names without identity now must be evaluated on the basis of a body of work long unknown. James Whale is one such filmmaker. Even though a few of his films—*Frankenstein, The Invisible Man, Bride of Frankenstein*—show up fairly often on television, these works are only a fraction of his output; and the fact that they are all horror films causes him to be typed as an effective but limited genre specialist. Some of his films are still out of reach and others are rarely screened (this writer is particularly indebted to William K. Everson for privileges in this area), but many are now available and enough is known about the others to warrant educated guesses.

Actually, Whale's decade-long career encompassed an impressive variety of styles and subjects. He has viewed war from the trenches (*Journey's End*) and from London during an air raid (*Waterloo Bridge*), and he has followed some youthful German soldiers home when the war ended (*The Road Back,* Erich Maria Remarque's sequel to *All Quiet on the Western Front*). He made the second version of Kern's and Hammerstein's *Show Boat,* a biography of actor David Garrick (*The Great Garrick*), a feature based on Marcel Pagnol's *Fanny* trilogy (*Port of Seven Seas*), an adaptation of Dumas' *The Man in the Iron Mask,* and a version of John Galsworthy's last novel (*One More River*). To these can be added a jungle picture (*Green Hell*), a Lubitsch-style sophisticated comedy (*By Candlelight*), a comedy-romance set in a hospital (*Impatient Maiden*), a comedy-mystery (*Remember Last Night?*), a courtroom drama (*The Kiss before the Mirror,* which he also remade as *Wives under Suspicion*), and a shipwrecked-on-an-island story (*Sinners in Paradise*). Clearly, Whale's career is quite a bit more varied than might at first be assumed.

But a wide variety of subjects does not assure a director of individuality; indeed, it could easily be a sign of an eclectic personality with no real interests of his own. Yet despite considerable differences, Whale's films do contain consistencies of content and technique that should encourage any auteur-seeking critic. Other difficulties may arise because Whale, though an Englishman, directed all his films within the Hollywood studio system and never received a screen-writing credit. Yet there is considerable evidence that he at least "conferred" a great deal with his writers, and since he entered the field a successful stage director whose first movie was also successful, he no doubt had considerable say as to what projects he would undertake. (One need only recall Whale's winning of *Frankenstein* from Robert Florey to realize the extent of his influence.)

One indication that Whale exerted substantial creative control over his films is the fact that he tended to work with the same people more than once. He didn't have a stock company in the Ingmar Bergman sense, and he didn't work with any single writer as closely as Frank Capra did with Robert Riskin, but there is enough overlap to confirm that when he found someone with whom he could work he made it a point to keep him around. The best illustration is that of R.C. Sherriff, the playwright for whom Whale directed the stage and screen versions of *Journey's End*. Later, Sherriff worked on the scripts of *The Old Dark House, The Invisible Man, One More River,* and *The Road Back,* as well as a few unfilmed projects. While Whale was working on Howard Hughes's *Hell's Angels,* he met Joseph Moncure March, the dialogue writer on that air epic. Deciding that March knew his job, Whale and production supervisor George Pearson went out of their way to obtain his services in adapting *Journey's End* to the screen. Similarly, playwright Benn Levy worked on the scripts of both *Waterloo Bridge* and *The Old Dark House.* Arthur Edeson photographed five Whale films, John Mescall five, and Karl Freund three.

As for performers, certain ones turn up with interesting frequency. Colin Clive was leading man in four films, and E.E. Clive provided comedy relief for four. Mae Clarke, Gloria Stuart, and Lionel Atwill appeared in three films each, while quite a few others can be seen in at least two: John Boles, Frederick Kerr, Paul Lukas, Ernest Thesiger, Reginald Denny, Frank Morgan, Warren William, Joan Bennett, Andy Devine, and (unfortunately) Una O'Connor. From a look at other Universal films of the period, it seems that this consistency is less a case of studio contract players being injected into films than of a director making as many personal choices in casting as he could.

Perhaps the most difficult kind of auteur to be is one whose films rely a great deal on their scripts, which are written by others. Whale's career in particular has an unabashed literary tone to it: his films are almost always adaptations of plays or novels by respected authors like Robert E. Sherwood, H.G. Wells, Mary Shelley, Sherriff, Galsworthy, Remarque, and Pagnol; and when a man like Sherriff provides a script it is usually equipped with adroit and witty dialogue. What, then, makes Whale's handling of these scripts different from or better than anyone else's?

For one thing, the mere fact that he could select this sort of script, and could film it with a sensitivity to its virtues, sets Whale apart from many of the other directors working in Hollywood. His British restraint produces a style best described as refined, graceful, well-bred; his directorial technique refuses to draw attention to itself, yet is extremely confident and competent. All the mechanical devices of cinema are used—cutting, moving camera, composition—yet with a civilized discretion and an emphasis on subtle character revelation.

One review of *Journey's End* expresses this quality:

> The man who directed the stage productions in England and in this country also directed the picture—James Whale. With almost the first shot you get the feeling that he knew just what he was doing and just how to do it: you can surrender yourself without any fear that fumbling and uncertainty and inadequacy are going to bob up and spoil things. He has not done anything revolutionary or even novel in technique—in fact the production may easily be made a theme for argument among those who like to discuss the relative merits of stage and screen. For myself I find that the screen brings the characters closer to me . . .

Even though *Journey's End* was officially Whale's first film, and that should be soon enough to expect this kind of praise, his skill was actually illustrated even earlier. In 1929 Whale had been hired by Howard Hughes to supervise the numerous dialogue scenes of *Hell's Angels,* and supposedly it was he who had the story changed and who directed these parts. (His credit line reads: "Dialogue staged by James Whale.") These scenes, viewed today, have a surprising quality of conciseness which is consistent with Whale's handling of *Frankenstein* and *One More River* Many scenes last for little more than a minute and contain very little dialogue; overtly, not much seems to happen, but a great deal is revealed nonetheless. The direction is fluid, with a considerable number of long, medium, and close shots—with the latter two dominant. There is even counterpoint between sound and image, and some tracking shots during delivery of lines. Among sequences shot in 1929, these stand out as not microphone-inhibited, as looking like "normal" scenes or even somewhat better, as lacking self-conscious speaking and pausing.

In one such vignette, from *Hell's Angels* a hand in close-up delivers a letter to one of the main characters, a German youth named Karl. This is followed by a medium shot of three boys standing around a lamp as one of them, Karl, reads the letter to himself. One of the others asks, "Someone ill?" The now-drafted Karl hands him the letter; the friend reads it, then exclaims, "Karl!" Fade out.

An earlier scene introduces the two British heroes, still students at Oxford; it gives us needed information about the personalities and social situation in a natural, casually indirect way. Two young men in a room are prompted by a newspaper headline to discuss the war. A third, Monte, sits reading on a couch, occasionally interrupting to tell the others to be quiet. The first two continue talking. Eventually, Monte interrupts to ask how to spell "ecstatic." Fade out.

Probably the shortest, most concise episode has Roy rush excitedly into the students' room. "I've enlisted, Monte—Royal Flying Corps!" Monte replies, "You're a fool, Roy." Fade out, and on to the next scene.

In this fashion Whale goes to the heart of a narrative without wasting time or space. And yet, this ability is combined with his obvious pleasure in a leisurely pace, and a fondness for observing the small details of person and place that might not be needed to tell the story, but which do give social and psychological texture to it. By saving time on the narrative, Whale is able to provide these "extras" while still making an efficient, short film that encompasses a great deal of character interaction.

Probably the best example of this is *One More River,* which brings in a governmental crisis, the gold standard, an election, comments on British divorce laws, a trial, and numerous characters the relationships between whom must be clearly established. In the midst of all this, Whale is still able to digress by showing how a cloakroom attendant remembers which hat belongs to which customer, or by having the stiffly polite Reginald Denny get slightly (unspokenly) irritated at the many women who stop at his restaurant table to greet the recently returned Diana Whynyard, since he has to stand up each time. At their best, Whale's films offer many such bonuses.

Apparently Whale was quite aware of this aspect of his work, and consciously aimed to achieve it. Speaking of *Journey's End* in one interview, he noted that

> the suspense was made up of very small things. But the audience cared so much about the actors in it; whether one of them drank tea or wanted coffee mattered enormously.

Earlier he had said:

> When it comes to human emotions people are the same . . . and the simpler a big situation is presented to them the harder it strikes. The whole foundation of *Journey's End,* to my mind, is that it presents an unusual situation in a most appealing way. Some critics have said that it violates the ethics of the drama. It does not, because the essential element in all drama is truth . . .

The feeling that truth is most convincingly presented through simplicity might be seen as a guiding principle in Whale's work. Recall, for example, that the success of Henry Frankenstein's original experiment is presented solely by showing the Monster's hand moving. This in itself is unimpressive, but because the characters are people we believe in and care about it functions as a dramatically charged moment, whereas having the Monster get up and stumble about would be pushing credibility too far.

Whale's commitment to truth and to good humored British restraint also robs his films of the impure and simple villain, since even characters who do bad things are rounded and human enough to be somehow sympathetic. This is obviously true of the Monster and scientist in *Frankenstein*. In *Bride of Frankenstein,* the satanic Pretorious has charm, wit, and some justification for his bitterness. The inhabitants of *The Old Dark House* are quaintly eccentric, and even the homicidal maniac is helpless-looking and ingratiating, while Karloff's butler only gets violent when he is drunk. Arrogant and dangerous individuals like Griffin in *The Invisible Man* or the husband in *One More River* usually have other sides to their personalities to make them fuller figures, and the personal dignity and charm of their actors (Claude Rains and Colin Clive, respectively) aid in creating this effect.

These virtues no doubt originated, or at least found support, in the theatrical milieu of which Whale was a part before (and after) entering films, and other aspects of his work also indicate a sense of "theatricality" that gives the films a distinctive tone. His occasionally perverse sense of humor is seen in bits of business that are straightforward, unexpected coups de théâtre. Fritz's pause on the stairs to pull up his sock (in *Frankenstein*) and Horace Femm's tossing of his sister's flowers into the fireplace (*The Old Dark House*) fall into this category.

A penchant for pointing out the roles and poses of characters also indicates a sensitivity to the "phoneyness" of performing. The clearest example of this is in *Frankenstein,*

when the scientist explains to his visitors what he is about to do. In Whale's own words:

> He deliberately tells his plan of action. By this time the audience [in the laboratory and in the movie theatre] must at least believe something is going to happen; it might be disaster, but at least they will settle down to see the show. Frankenstein puts the spectators in their positions, he gives final orders to Fritz, he turns the levers and sends the diabolic machine soaring upward to the roof, into the storm. He is now in a state of feverish excitement calculated to carry both the spectators in the windmill and the spectators in the theatre with him.

Clearly, Whale viewed Henry Frankenstein as a director-performer manipulating his dual audiences. In a letter to Colin Clive about the character, he notes that "in the first scene in his laboratory he becomes very conscious of the theatrical drama." Frankenstein is even given the following dialogue, "Quite a good scene, isn't it? One man, crazy; three very sane spectators," and the scene is staged to emphasize this performer-audience division.

Other illustrations of this side of Whale are less obvious, but grouped with the above they do seem consistent. Ernest Thesiger must have aroused Whale's interest, because after directing him in *The Old Dark House* he put him in *Bride of Frankenstein,* thus establishing the film's overall outré tone. Yet Thesiger's style is totally mannered and quite unrealistic; he is obviously acting, with this exaggeration partially justified by making it the character who is speaking in this artificial, ironic style. Interestingly, the "eccentric" aunt played by Mrs. Patrick Campbell in *One More River* is an only slightly less extreme female version of Thesiger, which points up the stage origin of this entertaining style. Similar is Whale's fondness for the broad playing of British character actors like Frederick Kerr and E.E. Clive (and the fatal fascination with Una O'Connor), as well as Americans like Andy Devine. Conveniently, Whale's discrete and gentle handling of these performers often managers to blend them smoothly into the rest of the film.

Other elements of Whale's films deserve a closer look for what they might reveal about the director's awareness of artificiality and poses, and occasionally of the things they cover up. A "truth game" is played in *The Old Dark House,* forcing the visiting characters to be honest about themselves, and there is a considerable contrast between the weak and gentle appearance of the Femms and their very real, and quite dangerous, insanity. *The Kiss before the Mirror* and its remake *Wives under Suspicion* hinge on whether or not a seemingly "normal" man might be driven to commit murder; and the appearance-reality contrast of the Frankenstein Monster is well known. Reflections, usually in mirrors but occasionally, as in *Bride,* in a pool of water, keep turning up to emphasize someone's external "image."

Whale's ability to handle the visual side of his films is often taken for granted, because it isn't flamboyant, yet it should be discussed since it is totally under control and unusually expressive. His background as a newspaper cartoonist, and as a theatrical set and costume designer, equipped Whale for supervising the appearance of whatever he planned to photograph, and helps to explain his fondness for a semi-expressionistic vision of characters silhouetted against a stark sky, as though standing on a hilltop with no visible land in the background. This is of course important to Whale's Frankenstein films, but it also can be seen in the laborer shots in *Showboat*'s "Old Man River" number. Whale also had a well-developed sense of camera movement, yet he was never so fond of a tracking shot that he wouldn't cut away from it before completion if it seemed to have served its purpose.

It is the editing that gives Whale's best pictures their quite special flow and grace. However, his cutting is not noticeable unless a viewer is looking for it, since its purpose is to support and reveal the content rather than to distract from it. Whale's secret is simply that he is willing to go to the extra trouble of securing multiple camera set-ups—not from different angles, necessarily, but from different distances. As a result, he will cut from a medium shot (mid-groin to top-of-head) to a medium-close shot (mid-chest to top-of-head) during a character's speech; the shots are similar enough to each other that the cut goes unnoticed, but they are not so similar that a jump-cut results.

Whale often used this cutting when introducing a character, as in the long shot-medium shot-close shot-extra close shot series as the Monster backs into the laboratory and turns around in *Frankenstein*. A variation on this occurs when the butler (Karloff) in *The Old Dark House* gets dangerous and Whale cuts from a close-up of the face to tight close-ups of just the eyes and the mouth. Other examples are Griffin's entrance into the pub in *The Invisible Man* and the deserted husband's arrival in *One More River*. The agony of the Monster's semi-crucified position when captured by the mob in *Bride* is emphasized by this style of editing, while a conversation between Dr. Pretorious and Henry Frankenstein in that film cuts between several different but very similar camera angles.

The opening thirty shots Mary Wollstonecraft-Percy Shelley-Lord Byron episode of *Bride* is a lengthy illustration of how this technique can be used in a dialogue scene as a cinematic equivalent of a stage director's attempt to analyze a line and "point up" the more significant parts, and direct the audience's attention to the subject of the line when appropriate.

> 1 long shot of building; camera tracks in.
>
> 2 dissolve to exterior of window: Byron is seen looking out, the other two sitting within.
>
> 3 dissolve to long shot of interior: characters are in same positions, but seen from the side. Camera tracks in.
>
> 4 dissolve to right side of room: Byron in center, Shelley on left, window on right.
>
> 5 dissolve to medium long shot of Byron as he says: "How beautifully dramatic! The crudest, savage exhibition of Nature, at her worst without, and we three, we elegant three, within."

While talking Byron walks to the left; camera pans to follow, and final shot includes all three.

> 6 cut to medium shot of Byron: "I should like to think that an irate Jehovah was pointing those arrows of lightning directly at my head—"
>
> 7 cut to close-up of Byron: "—the unbowed head of George Gordon, Lord Byron, England's greatest sinner."
>
> 8 cut to medium long shot of Byron standing on the left, Shelley sitting on the right: "But I cannot flatter myself to that extent. Possibly those thunders are for our dear Shelley—"
>
> 9 cut to medium close shot of Shelley: "—Heaven's applause for England's greatest poet."
>
> 10 cut to slightly different medium close up as Shelley replies: "What of my Mary?"
>
> 11 cut to medium close up of Mary, sewing. Byron's voice: "She is an angel." Mary: "You think so?"
>
> 12 cut to medium long shot of Byron and Shelley. Byron: "You hear? Come Mary, come and watch the storm."
>
> 13 cut to medium close up of Mary: "You know how lightning alarms me—"
>
> 14 cut to close-up of Mary: "—Shelley darling, will you please light these candles for me?"
>
> 15 cut to long shot of the three as Shelley crosses in the background. Byron: "Astonishing creature!"
>
> 16 cut to close-up of Mary: "Aye, Lord Byron?"
>
> 17 cut to medium shot of Byron: "Frightened of thunder, fearful of the dark, and yet you have written a tale—"
>
> 18 cut to close-up of Mary. Byron's voice: "—that sent my blood into icy creeps." Mary looks up and laughs.
>
> 19 cut to medium shot of Mary on the left, Byron on the right. Byron continues: "Can you believe that bland and lovely brow conceived of Frankenstein—"
>
> 20 cut to medium shot of Byron: "—a monster created from cadavers out of rifled graves?"
>
> 21 cut to long shot of the three, as Shelley returns to his original position. Byron continues: "Isn't it astonishing?"
>
> 22 cut to medium shot of Mary: "I don't know why you should think so."
>
> 23 cut to medium shot of Byron. Mary continues: "What do you expect?"
>
> 24 cut to close-up of Mary. Mary continues: "Such an audience needs something stronger than a pretty little—"
>
> 25 cut to close-up of Shelley. Mary continues: "—love story."

26 cut to close-up of Mary. She continues: "So why shouldn't I write of monsters?"

27 cut to long shot of the three. Byron: "No wonder Murray's refused to publish the book; he says his reading public would be—"

28 cut to close-up of Mary. Byron: "—too shocked." Mary: "It will be published, I think."

29 cut to medium shot of Shelley. Shelley: "Then, darling, you will have much to answer for."

30 cut to close-up of Mary in profile: "The publishers did not see that my purpose was to write a moral lesson, of the punishment that befell a mortal man who dared to emulate God."

Byron then recalls certain parts of the story, as we are shown short sections of the first film. Soon after, Mary starts to tell the rest and we are into the main body of the film.

This complicated but smooth editing technique is something that only the director could have imposed on the film; there is no indication of it in the original shooting script. It is in this way, as well as in the others already described, that Whale deserves to be classified as a director of personal films, despite the fact that he used scripts credited to others. As for his career as a whole, it is still impossible to say for sure just how many of his films are good, and how many reveal his individuality. It is enough, for the moment, to conclude that in general he reveals a maturity and sensitivity of content and style that should assure him of our continued respect.

Donald F. Glut (excerpt date 1973)

SOURCE: "Karloff Sets the Standard," in *The Frankenstein Legend: A Tribute to Mary Shelley and Boris Karloff*, The Scarecrow Press, Inc., 1973, pp. 90-150.

[*In the following excerpt, Glut describes the making of Whale's two Frankenstein films, including the director's casting of Karloff and Lanchester as the monsters.*]

Universal Pictures in 1931 announced that it was planning to film *Frankenstein*. The first talkie version of Mary Shelley's novel would be based on the stage play by Peggy Webling, adapted to the screen by John L. Balderston. *Dracula,* the first sound version of Bram Stoker's immortal vampire novel, had been made by the studio earlier that same year. The film was so successful that Universal immediately recognized the beginning of a trend toward horror films and again turned to the classics for a follow-up. *Frankenstein* had been filmed three times during the silent era of movies, three times more than *Dracula*. There was obviously an audience appeal for the story of the man-made man. Thus *Frankenstein* seemed to be the logical selection for a horror film intended to be greater than *Dracula*.

The executives at Universal Pictures, wasting no time, began selecting the tentative cast and list of technicians that would hopefully bring *Frankenstein* to theatres before the end of the year. Directing was to be assigned to

Robert Florey, surely one of the studio's most capable directors. The cast would include such performers as Edward Van Sloan, identifiable to those who had seen *Dracula* as the elderly Professor Van Helsing and who would be typecast at Universal in this type of role (being considerably younger than these characters), and a youthful, up-coming actress named Bette Davis. Van Sloan was to virtually recreate his Van Helsing portrayal as Professor Waldman in *Frankenstein,* while Miss Davis was to play Elizabeth, the fiancée of the infamous scientist who created the Monster. The role of Henry Frankenstein was intended for the noted English actor Leslie Howard.

The casting for the Frankenstein Monster was the result of logic. *Dracula* had made an immediate star of the macabre out of a Hungarian actor, who though a veteran to the European and American stage and a performer in earlier movies of both continents, was a new face to American horror films. The actor was Bela Lugosi, who was intrigued with the idea of leaving his vampire role to star as this entirely different fantasy character. Having just acted in the Fox Charlie Chan film *The Black Camel* and eager to give more variety to his roles, Lugosi heartily accepted the part of the Monster.

Without first devising the make-up of the creature and still not entirely sure of the treatment *Frankenstein* would be given, Universal's advertising department rushed out a color, full-page magazine spread which heralded their upcoming production. The Monster was shown in the advertisement as a green giant of King Kong proportions, lumbering through a panic-stricken city, walking off with screaming victims in his enormous hands, and shooting powerful deathrays (in the style of many future Frankenstein-like robots) from his eyes. The Monster's face bore no hints as to how the make-up would look. The countenance of the skyscraping brute was barely more frightening than a frowning man who growled under a head of mussed hair. (Many smaller versions of this man walk the streets today.)

Catchlines such as these accompanied the artwork: ". . . no man has ever seen his like . . . no woman ever felt his white-hot kiss . . . . Surpasses in THRILLS even DRACULA . . . world's greatest hold-over picture for 1930 . . . with BELA LUGOSI (Dracula himself) . . . as the leading spine-chiller . . . as a story it has thrilled the world for years."

Bela Lugosi was quite enthusiastic in his regarding the part. He was so enthusiatic that he eagerly saved and pasted all the publicity clippings he could find about *Frankenstein* in a large scrapbook, in which the film received two full pages. These were the days of less strict union regulations. Actors could assist with or do their own make-up. Lugosi, whose stage career had trained him in the art of make-up, was still trying to decide on the appearance of the Monster when the following item appeared in the Hollywood, California *News* for 20 June 1931: "Bela Lugosi begins work soon on 'Frankenstein,' playing the name role at Universal. He is now studying makeup for the part." The actor finally decided upon a suitable make-up for the test film that would be made before the actual production of *Frankenstein*. Recalling the silent *Golem* movies, legitimate predecessors of the Frankenstein movies, and the Golem-like make-up Hamilton Deane wore in the play from which this film was taken, the make-up was designed appropriately.

Press releases, which may or may not be accurate since such items were written to promote the star at the moment and not to give scholarly data, further described the make-up Lugosi would wear as the Monster. One of these, appearing in the 7 June 1931 Los Angeles *Record* related:

> Something has got to be done for Bela Lugosi. Lugosi has been trying for weeks to make a screen test for *Frankenstein*. He has to wear weird make-up, with two or three different colors, stripes, streaks, and striations. But after a few blasts of hot air, the makeup all fuses together, making him a clown instead of a menace.

A later report in the 27 June 1931 edition of another publication stated:

> What probably will be one of the trickiest jobs in makeup since *The Hunchback of Notre Dame* will be seen when the picture *Frankenstein* is released. Bela Lugosi, in the starring role, will be built up with makeup and padding, to resemble the eight foot superman Mary Shelley, wife of poet Percy Shelley, wrote about in 1817.

> When Lugosi is made up only his chin and eyes will be visible, greasepaint and putty completely hiding the rest of his face. Shoes to which nearly 12 inches have been added will complete the illusion.

Since actual photographs of Lugosi as the Monster apparently no longer exist, to image the make-up he was to wear in the feature we can only incorporate these descriptions, always remembering the appearance of the Golem.

Finally the day arrived to shoot the test scenes of Lugosi and various members of the proposed cast of *Frankenstein*. The Hungarian actor came onto the Universal set wearing the Monster make-up. Also on the set were director Robert Florey, cinematographer Paul Ivano, Edward Van Sloan who was probably photographed in the scene, and possibly Bette Davis. (It is not known if Miss Davis actually appeared in the test footage. Although she was originally scheduled to play Elizabeth, Carl Laemmle, the head of Universal Pictures, saw in her a star potential that he thought would be hampered by her appearing in a horror film. Therefore he removed her from the cast of *Frankenstein*. Just when this removal took place is unknown. We can only say that Bette Davis might have been photographed in the *Frankenstein* test.)

Paul Ivano shot the test footage, an entirely different concept than what finally was accepted by Universal. Unfortunately this short reel of film appears to have been lost to the decades. Even authorized personnel searching through the storage vaults at Universal have failed to rediscover the priceless film. It is hoped that the footage still exists on some forgotten shelf. Although Ivano followed Florey's direction in shooting the Lugosi-*Frankenstein* test film, changes were about to happen, based on several factors, that would abandon this initial interpretation. The first of these involved Bela Lugosi himself.

Lugosi had been an actor on the European stage since he graduated from elementary school in his home town of Lugos, Hungary (where he was born Bela Blasko on 29 October 1882 and from which he adopted his professional name) and studied drama at Budapest's Academy of Theatrical Arts. He had gone on to be acclaimed as one of the country's finest actors, achieving star status in such distinguished plays as William Shakespeare's *Romeo and Juliet*. The actor's motion picture career began in 1914 in an Hungarian silent feature, followed by a number of starring roles in the German cinema. By the time Lugosi became an American star in the film *Dracula* he had already enjoyed the fame and fringe benefits that accompanied stardom. To the American screen Lugosi was a new—albeit handsomely terrifying—face, although he had starred in many American films and stage plays. To Lugosi that face which cast no reflection in mirrors in his vampire role was established, and that of a star.

The actor, with the professional conceit understandable to a star of so many years, was told that the Frankenstein Monster would not speak, save for a few growls and groans in the manner of an animal. Immediately the actor's pride was shattered. He had made women swoon with his elegant mannerisms and rich voice. Even his horror role in *Dracula* was designed more to make women want his teeth to pierce their jugular veins than, as in the novel by Bram Stoker, to convey total revulsion with a breath that reeked of the grave. Bela Lugosi's interpretation of Count Dracula was more than of a blood-sucking Rudolph Valentino, a romantic character that his female victims would anticipate rather than flee. The heavy make-up of the Frankenstein Monster would have been accepted by Lugosi had the creature been played as Mary Shelley had intended—a warm, intelligent, verbose artificial man, going on for long pages with rich monologue. Such a part would have been welcomed by Lugosi, whose acting style played all the way to the back rows of crowded theatres. Examination of the test scenes of Lugosi made Universal's executives agree that the whole concept of the Monster, make-up and performance, was not correct for what they really wanted to convey. They were not too disappointed when Lugosi later responded to the role with a heavily-accented "no."

The original concept was abandoned in which the following description of the Monster's characterization, related in the 13 June 1931 issue of *Television,* would have been quite different from what was finally accepted:

> The story deals with a scientist who creates a weird creature resembling a man of the neanderthal age whose mentality is astounding in some respects but whose heart is that of a monster. Devoid of sentiment, *Frankenstein* keeps things active wherever and whenever he contacts human beings.

As Lugosi left the production of *Frankenstein,* so went director Robert Florey. Together Lugosi and Florey would create new terror in Universal's 1932 adaptation of Edgar Allan Poe's *Murders in the Rue Morgue*. Before leaving

Frankenstein, Florey had given the plot many of his own ideas, blocking out most of the story. He conceived the placement of a criminal brain in the Monster's skull, thus giving the brute somewhat of an excuse to kill. This change from Mary Shelley's conception of a brilliant mind in a grotesque body pleased the Universal executives. The climax of the eventual film, set in a windmill, came from the imagination of Florey who, staring out of his hotel window, spotted a Van de Kamp's bakery across the street, with its windmill trademark. The production already had a basic plot when it changed to the directorial hands of James Whale, formerly of the British stage.

At the time he accepted the job of directing *Frankenstein,* Whale, an extremely talented Englishman with a yen toward bizarre characterization, had directed few films, including *Journey's End* and *Waterloo Bridge*. He was a genius at presenting the macabre on the screen through characters and settings that could only exist in a parallel nightmare world. Whale began working on *Frankenstein* with a cast change. Edward Van Sloan was retained as Henry Frankenstein's medical school dean, Professor Waldman. Whale did not favor Leslie Howard as Young Henry. He substituted Colin Clive, whom he had directed as the star of *Journey's End,* and who was adept at protraying the neurotic creator of soulless life. The selection of a new actor to play the Monster was another matter altogether.

Since Bela Lugosi was already a horror films star and unquestionably out of the role, Whale thought it better to go the opposite route and use an actor with no star status. Then the Monster would be even more mysterious, with viewers unable to associate him as really a made-up actor. A number of considerations were made, all unsatisfactory. (The notable actor John Carradine, whose performances ranged from parts in the worst of the "poverty row" horror films to distinguished roles in such film classics as *The Grapes of Wrath,* states that he was considered for the Monster in 1931, made-up, and tested. Since the actor has always been extremely thin, the visual strength of a Carradine version of the Monster is questionable.)

At last Whale remembered a cultured English actor (he delighted in using English performers) with a particularly menacing countenance, that he had seen in several films. The actor, though virtually unknown and lacking any real name value as far as luring people into theatres was concerned, had already appeared in sixty-five feature length films and serials. Soon, to the detriment of Bela Lugosi's career, the star echelon of the horror film would undergo a significant change.

CREATION OF A MASTERPIECE

Boris Karloff was seated in the commissary at the Universal studios one afternoon in 1931. He was eating lunch and sipping his traditional cup of tea when he was summoned by a man who told him that Mr. James Whale, at a nearby table, would like to speak to him. Karloff was immediately impressed, since Whale was Universal's most respected director.

The British actor walked to Whale's table and introduced himself with his slightly lisping voice. Whale commented

that he was aware of Karloff's excellent performances in the Los Angeles stage presentation of *The Criminal Code* (with Karloff portraying Ned Galloway, an imprisoned murderer), its filmed version made by Columbia (with Karloff in the same role), and in Universal's *Graft* (with Karloff as a murderous gangster named Terry), all in 1931. The director was impressed by Karloff's six-foot height, his lean, sullen features, and his ability to evoke sympathy through acts of villainy. "We're getting ready to shoot the Mary Shelley classic, *Frankenstein,*" Whale said, probably anticipating the actor's refusal of the part, "and I'd like you to test—for the part of the Monster."

Karloff's sinister features expanded with surprise. "A monster indeed!" he exclaimed. But then he indulged in a bit of recalling of his past. He had already been in a long list of films, acting on the screen for a dozen years. He was forty-four years old. Straight dramatic roles failed to bring stardom to Karloff. Perhaps his luck would change in the portrayal of the Monster. "But I didn't look a gift horse in the mouth," Karloff later told an interviewer. "I needed to eat and I took it."

The actor was not always known as Boris Karloff. He was born on 23 November 1887 with the less menacing name of William Henry Pratt at Forest Hill Road in Dulwich, a suburb of London. He was the son of James Pratt, an official in the British Indian Civil Service. His seven brothers mostly followed in their father's line of work, except an elder brother who became a stage actor under the name George Marlowe. William, the youngest of the family that also included a sister, admired George and, to the chagrin of the others whose work took them to such places as China and India, he vowed to become an actor.

William Pratt's acting career suffered through a long beginning. Before appearing on any professional stage he moved to Canada, where he labored digging ditches, selling real estate, driving trucks, chopping trees, and performing various other mundane jobs. Finally his break came in 1910 with an offer to join the Jean Russell Stock Company in Kamloops, British Columbia. Without second thoughts Pratt left his lumberjack position and took a train bound for Kamloops. While anticipating the start of a fabulous career, he dwelled upon his own name, believing that no one would pay money to see an actor billed as William Henry Pratt. He needed a name that rang with individuality. William's mother's family name was Karloff. That name had a certain sound that would be difficult for people to forget. The name Boris was merely snatched from air, sounding Russian, which made it the more sinister. Together the two names became Boris Karloff, which sounded right.

Boris Karloff bluffed his way through the stage manager's questioning, supplying a fabricated list of acting credits, and acquired a part in a theatrical presentation of *The Devil*. This was the start for Karloff, who continued to act on the stage. In 1919, realizing the potential in the rising art of motion pictures, the Englishman secured the part of a Mexican bandit in United Artists' silent film *His Majesty, the American,* in which he menaced Douglas Fairbanks. More screen roles followed, fluctuating between featured player and extra, and quite often featuring Karloff as a French-Canadian, a half-breed Indian, or an Arab sheik. This typecasting was premature.

James Whale, impressed with Karloff as both an actor and a man of presence and culture, was most anxious to give him a screen test as the Frankenstein Monster. Unlike Florey's intention to allow Bela Lugosi to decide upon his own make-up, Whale had the entire task given to a real genius of greasepaint and nose putty—Jack Pierce, Universal's top artist of disguise. Pierce, who had previously worked as a semi-professional baseball shortstop, a theatre manager for Harry Culver, and an independent film producer, created his first "monster" make-up on Jacques Lerner in the 1926 Twentieth Century-Fox film *The Monkey Talks.* His knowledge of anatomy made him almost as capable of creating the Monster as Frankenstein himself. Completely ignoring the Lugosi concept, Pierce sat down in deep contemplation, leaving his mind open to the suggestions of Boris Karloff, who displayed an unexpected ability to assist, and of the boss, James Whale.

It was first decided to keep the Monster's features as simple as possible, allowing the human to show through the inhuman. Horror film characters that are at least partially human are always more terrifying than a bug-man from outer space or a lumbering Godzilla smashing its way through the world's cities. Lon Chaney's pathetic creature in *The Hunchback of Notre Dame* (1923) and his living face of Death in *The Phantom of the Opera* (1925) proved that the distorted human visage can produce true fear, while the rampagings of a dinosaur through a modern metropolis can be ludicrous. Karloff's Frankenstein Monster would be horrible, yet human allowing for identification by an audience haunted by the feeling that such a face could exist in real life.

The make-up master regarded the Monster from the viewpoint of the scientist. "If the monster looks like something I dreamt after something I ate, don't blame me, blame science," Pierce told an interviewer for the *New York Times* during the filming of *Son of Frankenstein* eight years later. "I made him the way the textbooks said he should look. I didn't depend on imagination. In 1931, before I did a bit of designing I spent three months of research in anatomy, surgery, medicine, criminology, ancient and modern burial customs, and electro-dynamics."

Frankenstein, Pierce said, was a practical scientist and not an artist. His artificially-created man would appear as if he were made to function rather than please the eyes. The description of the humanoid given by Mary Shelley was vague, allowing Pierce to incorporate his own theories and knowledge in the Monster's features.

The head was given an overall squareness, flat on top. Pierce had read that a surgeon could cut the skull to get at the brain in six different ways. The simplest way would be to saw through the top of the skull, straight across, leaving it hinged at one side. The brain would then be transplanted into the host skull and the "lid" replaced, joined with metal clamps circumventing the top of the head. The forehead was high, with a surgical scar running upward from the right eye; a remnant of the brain operation. To give the Monster a primitive, Neanderthal appearance that would stress his low intellect, Pierce sloped the brow over the eyes in a pronounced ape-like ridge of bone. (During the creation of the make-up other versions, some subtly different, were tested on Karloff. One of these, suggested by Whale, ignored the forehead scar and replaced it with two tubular masses of malformed flesh, one over each eye and running up to the hairline, and each fastened by an unsightly ring of metal.) The high forehead was shaped from uncomfortable tin and blended with the actor's own features with layers of putty. Covering the top of the head was a black mass of straight hair, which hung long at the sides and dropped over the metal clamps in bangs. Two hollow metallic caps were placed on Karloff's neck, one on each side, to simulate the electrodes which Henry Frankenstein would charge with electricity, the life current that would spark the spine of the Monster. The left cheek was given a long red scar to further attest the workings of a surgeon. Several of Karloff's teeth in the right side of his mouth were false. The actor consented to remove them so that the side of his face naturally caved in to accentuate the impression of a thin corpse. Pierce heightened the effect by darkening the area with shadow. (In later films, with the Monster played by different actors, this hollow was indicated by a black "beauty spot." In *Abbott and Costello Meet Frankenstein,* seventeen years later, the traditional mark was shown only in the earlier scenes. Later in the film the spot was either intentionally omitted—or, more likely, forgotten.)

The hands of the Monster also told of its unnatural creation. The right arm was stitched to show where the alien hand was attached. A strip of sewn metal braced the left arm to reinforce the creature's strength. The fingernails on both hands were discolored with black shoe polish.

The color of the Monster's corpse-like flesh, which had to photograph on black and white film as close to dead white as possible, was a bluish gray (a color developed by Pierce for the cosmetics industry). Pierce contrasted the Monster's pallor by darkening the lips with brownish greasepaint. The make-up was always open for alterations, made in between scenes, dependent on variations in lighting and mood. (When the Monster screamed in terror, subtle changes were made so that his face seemed to function naturally and appear different from scenes in which he smiled with innocent delight. Such care was lacking in later films of the series.)

As Pierce finished applying the make-up for the first time to Karloff's face, the actor looked into the workshop mirror from his place in the regulation barber chair and noticed that something still was not right. There was a look about his eyes that failed to give the impression of a newly-awakened being spawned from graves. Somehow the Monster looked too aware. Karloff considered the matter for a while, then suggested that his eyelids be heavily caked with putty, giving the creature a look of only partial awareness. Pierce liked the idea and fashioned two heavy eyelids from mortician's wax and joined them to the rest of the make-up. The thoroughly satisfying effect was retained.

The make-up of Frankenstein's Monster was complete and would be re-applied every morning before shooting in four-hour sessions including Karloff, Pierce, and one assistant. The guise, however, was still not finished. There was yet the body of the Monster, which would appear as realistically mismatched as the head and hands. Jack Pierce had read that ancient Egyptian criminals were buried with their hands and feet tightly bound. When their blood changed to water and flowed into the limbs, the arms lengthened, and their faces, hands, and feet swelled to hideous proportions. The make-up artist thought of applying this idea to the Monster, since some of the parts used by Henry Frankenstein would come from criminals. To get the effect he desired, Pierce ordered an ill-fitting black suit made by Universal's costuming department with shortened sleeves to make the arms seem longer.

Finally Pierce gave Karloff a five-pound brace to wear on his spine to keep his movements impaired and stiff, and a pair of raised boots that further hampered his walking, weighing an uncomfortable twelve and one-half pounds each. The entire outfit came to forty-eight pounds. (Wearing the guise proved almost as unbearable to Karloff as actually being sewn together by Henry Frankenstein. The film was shot during the hot California summer. Sound stages were not yet convenienced by air conditioning. To make the Monster appear larger, Karloff wore a doubly quilted suit under the black clothes. After an hour's work under the hot studio lights, Karloff would be soaking wet and was forced to change his underclothes or risk catching pneumonia. His own perspiration caused the make-up to crumble. Minute particles of make-up material fell into his eyes, causing tremendous pain. But Karloff endured the agony aided by Pierce, who was always nearby to remove the particles with eyewash.)

After three weeks had been spent developing the guise, Karloff was finally given a screen test, wearing the make-up of the Frankenstein Monster, standing nearly eight feet tall in the raised boots. During the test the actor performed his best, trying to emote as realistically as possible without the use of dialogue. The make-up photographed superbly. There was no doubting that a true masterpiece of make-up artistry had been created. It was not, however, merely the work of Jack Pierce, but the emoting of Boris Karloff that made it a true masterpiece.

James Whale viewed the test scenes enthusiastically and immediately knew that Karloff was the right man for the role. For Jack Pierce the make-up was the beginning of many years of creating Universal's most famous creatures. For Karloff it was the beginning of stardom. And for both Pierce and Karloff it was the start of a lasting friendship and a mutual respect. In countless interviews Boris Karloff, when asked about the Frankenstein Monster, credited Jack Pierce as the real genius behind the compelling make-up.

The sound stage had been set; the cast selected. Then one day in August of 1931, Universal Pictures' *Frankenstein* went before the cameras.

"FRANKENSTEIN"—1931

The black screen of the movie theatre faded-in to reveal a simple stage and curtain. A man dressed in a fine suit stepped onto the stage with a personal message to the audience.

"How do you do," Edward Van Sloan addressed the people waiting anxiously for *Frankenstein* to begin.

> Mr. Carl Laemmle feels it would be a little unkind to present this picture without a word of warning. We are about to unfold the story of Frankenstein, a man of science who sought to create life after his own image, without reckoning on God. It is one of the strangest tales ever told. It deals with the two great mysteries of creation—life and death. I think it will thrill you. It may shock you. It may even . . . horrify . . . you. So, if any of you feel you'd not care to subject your nerves to such a strain, now's your chance to . . . er . . . well, we warned you.

Besides the theatrics in the introduction to *Frankenstein*, Edward Van Sloan's speech served another purpose. Most horror films of the silent era explained away fantastic and supernatural occurrences as nightmares or the narratives of madmen. But like its predecessor *Dracula*, *Frankenstein* was, within the context of the plot, a real happening. This introduction helped attune the viewers' minds to the fact that what they were about to see would be, as far as the characters in the film were concerned, real.

The action in *Frankenstein* began with a funeral in a bleak graveyard. The grim ceremony was observed by two sinister figures—one sophisticated, determined, handsome; the other boorish, dwarfed and hunchbacked, with an ugly face locked into a seemingly sadistic mask. The first man was Henry Frankenstein, a young former medical student, played by Colin Clive. The hunchback was his assistant Fritz, portrayed by Dwight Frye, who relished such roles. (Frye was best cast as a psychopath. In *Dracula* he played Renfield, a wide-eyed lunatic with a particular appetite for flies and spiders.) Henry Frankenstein and Fritz waited until the funeral procession left the graveyard. Then hurrying through the shadows, the two ghouls of the night disinterred the newly buried corpse. The scientist spoke profoundly while patting the casket: "He's just resting . . . waiting for new life to come!"

More bodies were needed for the project Henry Frankenstein had been nurturing in his over-ambitious mind for so many years. Another corpse was secured from the gallows. Henry had hoped to use the brain from the hanging body, but expressed disappointment when he learned that the neck had been broken and the brain was useless. He needed another; a perfect brain.

While Henry Frankenstein was the scientific genius, most of the manual work was done by the hunchback. Managing, surprisingly, to avoid notice, Fritz peered through the window of the Goldstadt Medical College, while the white-haired Professor Waldman lectured to his students about the differences between the normal and criminal brain. He left specimens of both types for his class to inspect at the end of the period. After the classroom had been evacuated, Fritz stole his way through the window and toward the two bottled brains. Uneasy in this room of death with its hanging skeleton, the hunchback was on the verge of collapse. He grabbed the bottle labeled "Normal Brain." As he began to leave with his prize he was startled by the sound of a loud gong and dropped the brain with a shattering of glass. (The nature of the gong was never established. It was probably a contrived excuse to let Fritz make his blunder.) There was but one alternative—stealing the other container marked "Abnormal Brain." (The present writer wonders how a man of Henry's standing could fail to notice the conspicuous label, as Fritz was never shown tearing it off.)

Concern for the young Henry aroused the suspicions of his lovely fiancée Elizabeth (played by blonde Mae Clarke) and their mutual friend Victor Moritz (played by handsome matinee idol John Boles). Knowing the respect Henry always had for Professor Waldman, they visited the dean at the university and told him about his former student, who was now in self exile in an old watchtower. The elderly professor shocked his two visitors, telling them that Henry dreamt of creating human life from the remnants of the dead. After listening to the pleas of Elizabeth, Waldman agreed to accompany them to Henry Frankenstein's tower laboratory.

Seen from the outside, Henry's watchtower was in fact a studio miniature. The interior was one of the cinema's most impressive laboratory sets. Designed by Herman Rosse, the set was massive, reaching skyward where a transom would open to receive the lifeless form Frankenstein had assembled. The walls of the tower were realistically set in crudely arranged bricks. There were barred windows and a winding stairway to complete the illusion. The laboratory apparatus used by Frankenstein was designed by Kenneth Strickfaden, who created some weird devices that actually sparked and flashed with believable electric life. In the center of the laboratory was the horizontal platform which would lift the dormant body to the transom.

The watchtower was in the middle of a violent electrical storm in an upheaval of nature ideally suited to the needs of Henry Frankenstein. The scientist looked proudly at the gigantic human form on the platform, covered with a white sheet. "There's nothing to fear," Henry assured Fritz, who was recoiling in terror from the stitched limp hand. "Look. No blood, no decay. Just a few stitches." Then Frankenstein pulled the sheet to reveal the top of the creature's head, with the black bangs and pieces of adjoining metal. "And look! Here's the final touch . . . the brain you stole. Fritz. Think of it! The brain of a dead man, waiting to live again in a body I made! With my own hands . . . my own hands. Let's have one final test. Throw the switches!"

Fritz did as he was told and, aided by Henry who worked the other controls, brought the furies of electricity into the laboratory machines. The test showed that all the equipment was in perfect working order. The storm would be at its peak within fifteen minutes. Frankenstein was thrilled, for the world's greatest scientific experiment was about to begin.

Professor Waldman, Elizabeth, and Victor arrived at the watchtower at precisely the worst time. Forced to give them entrance because of the storm, Henry announced his extraordinary plan to the small gathering:

> Dr. Waldman, I learned a great deal from you at the University . . . about the violet ray, the ultra-violet ray, which you said is the highest color in the spectrum. You were wrong. Here in this machinery I have gone beyond that. I have discovered the great ray that first brought life into the world.

The professor was skeptical; demanded proof. "Tonight you shall have your proof," Frankenstein retorted. "At first I experimented only with dead animals. And then a human heart which I kept beating for three weeks. But now, I am going to turn that ray on that body, and endow it with life!"

"And you really believe that you can bring life to the dead?"

"That body is not dead," Henry replied to his former superior. "It has never lived. I created it. I made it with my own hands from the bodies I took from the graves, the gallows, anywhere!"

After Waldman examined the sheeted creation, Henry began the experiment. The platform holding the patchwork corpse was raised to the thundering storm—to the lightning, while the laboratory erupted with the splendors of electricity. No longer was the creation of the Monster left open to speculation as far as procedure was concerned, as Mary had written of it. Electricity had been established as the Mother of the Frankenstein Monster; thus it would remain.

Karloff himself regarded the creation scene in *Frankenstein* with remembered fear.

> The scene where the monster was created, amid booming thunder and flashing lightning, made me as uneasy as anyone. For while I lay half-naked and strapped to Doctor Frankenstein's table, I could see directly above me the special-effects men brandishing the white-hot scissors-like carbons that made the lightning. I hoped that no one up there had butterfingers.

At last the electrically-charged body was lowered to the laboratory floor. Slowly the fingers of the creature moved. "It's alive! It's alive!" Henry shouted again and again. He was seized by unholy emotion, so violently that Waldman and Victor were forced to exert all their combined strength in restraining him. (The Hayes Office, that seemingly omnipotent board which dictated what could and could not be publicly screened in those days of moviemaking, was worried about *Frankenstein*. It dealt with the objectionable theme of a man trying to play God. James Whale was careful not to treat the story in an offensive way. The Hayes Office even allowed actor Colin Clive's next line to be spoken in 1931. "In the name of God," Henry emoted, "now I know what it feels like to be God!" The line was, however, deleted by the censor in a later re-release of *Frankenstein* leaving a jump cut where it had been.)

Days later, Henry Frankenstein and Dr. Waldman were seated in one of the tower rooms. The professor warned the young scientist, "Here we have a fiend whose brain. . . ."

"His brain must be given time to develop," said Henry. "It's a perfectly good brain, doctor. Well . . . you ought to know. It came from your own laboratory." Waldman's words were grim: "The brain that was stolen from my laboratory was a criminal brain!"

Frankenstein tried to dismiss the issue, arguing that the brain would develop normally given ample time. But Waldman insisted that he had created a monster, one that would destroy its creator. Then heavy footsteps could be heard approaching the closed door of the room. It was the Monster. The two men extinguished their candles, throwing the room into darkness. The footsteps stopped and the door began to open. Seen only from behind the Frankenstein creature lumbered into the room.

The first shots of the Monster's face were expertly directed. It was first seen in a full shot. There was an abrupt cut to a medium close-up, then a quick shift to an extreme close shot. The effect was thoroughly terrifying in 1931 (before the make-up became familiar from overexposure) as if the Monster and the audience were nearing each other. The absence of music in this scene (as well as the rest of the picture) heightened the horror. The Monster and the viewer had met, face to face with the impact their meeting would have had in reality in such a setting as the old tower.

Henry then showed Waldman the effect light had upon the creature that had so recently been "born." He opened the overhead transom, allowing the warm rays of the sun to streak into the chamber. As if recalling the crackling light from the sky and machinery which spawned him, the Monster futilely tried grasping it, unable to touch the intangible. Then light in another form confronted the creature. Fritz rushed into the room holding a blazing torch. This light could burn, eating away the flesh with excrutiating agony (establishing the beast's fear of fire). The hunchback continued torturing the creature. Later he paid for his repeated sadism. Henry and Waldman heard a scream and found Fritz hanging lifelessly from the ceiling, a rope entwined about his neck. Censorship again attacked *Frankenstein*. The scene in which the Monster actually killed Fritz for his cruelty, understandable for a creature with an imperfect brain, was cut from the final release prints. What remained was a shot revealing only the shadow of the hunchback, his corpse dangling from the rope.

Henry now realized that the Monster had to be destroyed, reversing the process of creation. Leaving Dr. Waldman alone in the laboratory to dissect the pathetic being, Frankenstein returned to his family estate to relax and marry Elizabeth. This made old Baron Frankenstein (played by hefty Frederick Kerr), Henry's stubborn father, happy since he had suspected another woman was taking up his son's time. The villagers had long been preparing for the celebration.

At the watch tower things were not so lax. Dr. Waldman was about to end the Monster's unnatural life. As the creature lay drugged on an operating table, the professor took notes. "Increased resistance is necessitating stronger and more frequent injections," Waldman wrote. "However, will perform the dissection." As the professor prepared to begin taking the Monster apart piece by piece, the creature moved unnoticed. The enormous hand seized the old man's neck and squeezed with fatal result.

While the wedding feast began getting underway, Hans (Michael Mark), a woodsman, left his little daughter Maria (Marylin Harris) to watch their property while he looked at his animal traps. During his absence the Monster lumbered out of the woods and encountered the child. She had been tossing flowers into the lake and watching them float. Dropping to his knees the creature was delighted. "Would you like one of my flowers?" she asked, totally unaffected by the creature's bizarre appearance. He accepted the flowers with a gutteral vocal sound and smiled for the first time in his short life. "I can make a boat," the girl continued, showing the Monster how nicely the flowers floated upon the water's surface. "See how mine floats."

The Monster mimicked her actions with his own flowers. When there were no more left he looked innocently at the child, then moved forward. . . . Most existing prints of *Frankenstein* do not have the succeeding action. It was excised from all American versions of the picture during the original release but shown in selected foreign countries. . . .

The scene was cut from American prints before the film was released at Karloff's request (although it did appear in selected prints during a re-release in the Forties). James Whale had tremendous respect for the actor and heeded his explanation:

> My conception of the scene was that he would look up at the little girl in bewilderment, and, in his mind, she would become a flower. Without moving, he would pick her up gently and put her in the water exactly as he had done to the flower—and, to his horror, she would sink. Well, Jimmy made me pick her up and do THAT (motioning violently) over my head which became a brutal and deliberate act. By no stretch of the imagination could you make that innocent. The whole pathos of the scene, to my mind, should have been—and I'm sure that's the way it was written—completely innocent and unaware. But the moment you do THAT it's a deliberate thing . . . and I insisted on that part being removed.

An interesting point concerning the scene with little Maria was made by Ivan Butler in his book *The Horror Film*. Butler observed that James Whale's selection of an "ugly [sic] little girl" with an even uglier manner of speaking heightened the pathos of the scene. Such touches were characteristic of Whale. He often attributed offbeat traits and habits to his characters, giving them true and yet strange individuality. (When Fritz stopped his hobbling walk to pull up his sock he demonstrated a true bit of Whale characterization.)

The omission of the scene accomplished what Karloff intended, while at the same time bringing a new and more terrible element into the story. The next time we saw the little girl she was a bloody corpse, carried by her father through the streets of the village. Now judging from the girl's disheveled state, there is the blacker suspicion that she was raped by the Monster. Hans' entry into town bearing the dead body of his daughter naturally brought the wedding festivities to an end. The pompous burgomaster Herr Vogel (Lionel Belmore) organized three search parties to find the murderous fiend. Realizing his own responsibility for Maria's death, Henry led one of the three groups.

The Monster had already been in Elizabeth's room, creeping silently through the window, surprising Henry's bride-to-be while she made ready to appear before the crowd in her wedding gown, a scene inspired by Mary Shelley's novel. But as the Monster could not speak and demand a mate as in the book, he had no real motivation to kill Elizabeth. Instead he merely frightened her.

The search of the countryside for the Monster with irate villagers storming about brandishing clubs and flaming torches became an established ingredient in the Frankenstein legend. Finally in the hills (obviously an interior set, but so atmospheric that it was most acceptable) Henry Frankenstein encountered his Monster face to unsightly face. For several moments the living horror looked with hatred upon his maker. Then braving Henry's torch he lunged out, knocking down the scientist. The Monster picked up Frankenstein in his mighty arm, then stomped off toward a deserted windmill, which he then entered and ascended.

Down below, the villagers were using the Monster's most dreaded enemy. They were burning down the windmill. Enraged, screaming with terror and from the pains of the biting fire, Frankenstein's Monster hurled his creator from the top of the burning mill. Henry's wounded and weakened body smacked hard against one of the windmill vanes, breaking his fall. The villagers rushed to his assistance, taking him off the vane and back to his home.

The Monster was trapped. The flames were increasing and the very structure of the windmill crumbling all around him. The creature that had been formed from the dead was still screaming hideously when the mill collapsed into the remnants of the inferno.

Henry Frankenstein lay in his bedroom recuperating from one of the most terrifying ordeals ever faced by a man. His servants would attend to him and soon there would be a wedding in the house of Frankenstein.

Frankenstein is undoubtedly the most famous, and one of the greatest, horror films ever made. The three factors which made the film a classic were the direction of James Whale, whose camera was remarkably fluid for a film made in 1931 and whose shadowy atmosphere completely devoid of comedy and music has never been equaled in such a motion picture; the make-up masterpiece of Jack Pierce which remained believable even under the closest scrutiny; and the performance of Boris Karloff as the Monster. Karloff's Monster was never a wanton engine of destruction. It was a pathetic character, begging with speechless lips and a distorted brain for understanding, receiving only hatred and burning torches from the people.

Without the genius of Karloff in the role, *Frankenstein* could have been just another horror film.

Before the picture was officially released, Karloff was not regarded by Universal as anything more than a living prop. The premiere of the film was in early December of 1931 in Santa Barbara, California. When the cast credits flashed on the screen the part of the Monster was attributed to "?" Only in the final title after the film had ended, boasting "A good cast is worth repeating," was Karloff given credit for portraying the Monster. "I was not even invited," Karloff remarked about the premiere, "and had never seen it. I was just an unimportant free-lance actor, the animation for the monster costume."

When *Frankenstein* opened the publicity sometimes was sensational. Registered nurses were stationed in theatre lobbies in case viewers should need their services. Although the picture was terrifying in 1931 it is doubtful that anyone actually required such help. During the picture's initial release in Chicago at the State Lake Theatre there was even more sensationalism. An actor named Jack Kelly wore a Frankenstein Monster costume, his face being sprayed with purple make-up. Kelly's wife stood several feet behind him clutching a string which was connected to a buzzer on his outfit, apparently making him "work." Together they paraded about the streets near the theatre, she guiding him around as if via remote control. As they turned a street corner in downtown Chicago the couple encountered an unsuspecting woman who immediately fainted. When she revived she wasted no time in suing the theatre.

As the reviews hit the trade papers Universal knew that the picture was going to be a success. After *Frankenstein* opened on December 4th it was praised in the 8 December 1931 issue of *Variety:*

> Looks like a 'Dracula' plus, touching a new peak in horror plays, and handled in production with supreme craftsmanship. Maximum of stimulating shock in there, but the thing is handled with subtle change of pace and shift of tempo that keeps attention absorbed to a high voltage climax, tricked out with spectacle and dramatic crescendo, after holding the smash shiver of a hair trigger for more than an hour.

> Finish is a change from the first one tried, when the scientist was also destroyed. The climax with the surviving Frankenstein (Frankenstein is the creator, not the monster itself) relieves the tension somewhat, but that may not be the effect most to be desired.

> The figure of the monster is a triumph of effect. It has a face and head of exactly the right distortions to convey a sense of the diabolical, but not enough to destroy the essential touch of monstrous human evil. Playing is perfectly paced. . . . Boris Karloff enacts the monster and makes a memorable figure of the bizarre figure with its indescribably terrifying face of demoniacal calm, a fascinating acting bit of mesmerism.

> Photography is splendid and the lighting the last word in ingenuity, since much of the footage

calls for night effect and manipulation of shadows to intensify the ghostly atmosphere. The audience for this type of film is probably the detective story readers and the mystery yarn radio listeners. Sufficient to insure success if these pictures are well made.

Indeed *Frankenstein* was successful. The film cost only $250,000 to make, yet it grossed over $12,000,000, starting a cycle of horror films and a countless list of imitations. It has enjoyed numerous re-releases. As late as 1969 the motion picture was given considerable distribution on a double bill with the original *Dracula*. The picture, like its Monster, seems to be indestructible. More remarkable as far as Universal was concerned was the immediate stardom achieved by the actor not "important" enough to attend the premiere. Karloff was getting fan mail in the extreme. Much of this mail came from children who were able to see through his greasepaint and electrodes to discern the true sincerity inherent in his portrayal of the Monster.

Finally recognizing that Boris Karloff was a "name star," the studio rushed him into *The Old Dark House,* directed by James Whale in 1932. Karloff played Morgan, the butler of a weird household. He was made-up by Jack Pierce with a heavy beard, scars, and a broken nose. The part was again that of a non-speaking brute who groped around much in the fashion of the Frankenstein Monster. There was a big difference between *The Old Dark House* and *Frankenstein*. Despite his lack of dialogue and his minimal scenes, Karloff was given top billing. A title introducing the film announced that, to dispel all rumors to the contrary, the actor under the guise of Morgan was indeed the very same Boris Karloff who played the Monster in *Frankenstein*. Boris Karloff had been transformed into a star. Unlike many stars who are manufactured in the studio publicity department—as was the Monster in Frankenstein's laboratory—Karloff was a tremendous acting talent. A movie actor since 1919, his career was just beginning.

For the Frankenstein Monster, a stitched and burned creature, was stirring at the base of the old windmill.

FRANKENSTEIN TAKES A BRIDE

As early as 1933 Universal Pictures had planned to film a sequel to the extremely successful *Frankenstein*. The second sound Frankenstein movie was to surpass the original in greatness and feature in the role of a mad doctor the actor who had turned down the part of the Monster in 1931—Bela Lugosi. The Hungarian actor was to emote alongside Boris Karloff, who was signed to recreate his role of Frankenstein's Monster.

A press notice of 1933 reported Lugosi's plans: "His current role is opposite Karloff in *The Black Cat*. Following this it was planned to co-star the two in Robert Louis Stevenson's *The Suicide Club* and *The Return of Frankenstein*."

Neither *The Suicide Club* nor *The Return of Frankenstein* saw production that year. Lugosi had again changed his mind by dropping out of the mad doctor part in the Frankenstein movie. *The Return* remained on the studio's planned production lists until 1935, when James Whale picked up the script and began casting the picture. Karloff was naturally the Monster again. The studio's publicity department had dropped the "Boris," despite its sounding Russian, in the belief that the simple "Karloff" appearing on advertising posters and in a film's credits seemed more foreboding.

Colin Clive was back as Henry Frankenstein. His wife Elizabeth, who had changed her hair color to brunette, was now played by beautiful Valerie Hobson, who years later would be involved in the infamous Profumo (her husband) scandal. The part of Dr. Pretorius, the role rejected by Lugosi, was given to English Ernest Thesiger, whose face was like a human hawk's and whose expression always indicated that he detected a foul odor somewhere. Dwight Frye, Fritz in the first movie, was cast as Karl, a demented killer and body snatcher. Comedy relief, absent from the first film, was given by the beloved English lady Una O'Connor as Minnie, the screeching housekeeper of the Frankenstein estate. Others in the cast included a very young John Carradine as a woodsman, an infant Billy Barty (later to become a famous television and movie personality) tyepcast as a baby, and eternally old Walter Brennan, who in this early phase of his career had a bit part—as noted in the 9 March 1935 "Call Bureau Cast Service" sheet for *The Return of Frankenstein*—"a Neighbor."

The film was to return to the original novel, picking up where the 1931 movie had ended, and in many ways be closer to the Mary Shelley story than its predecessor had been. In the novel the real conflict between creator and creature began when Frankenstein refused to build the Monster a mate. The mate was never finished in the book but would come alive on the screen. This was the premise of the sequel to *Frankenstein*.

There was still deliberation about the title. For a while it was decided to call the film *Bride of Frankenstein*. Again the decision went back to *Return,* as the Universal executives feared that confusion would result since the "Bride" would be that of the Monster. For a while, according to a 1935 movie fan magazine, the film was going to be called *Frankenstein Lives Again!* After much consideration it was settled on the better title, *Bride of Frankenstein*.

In the role of the Bride was the delightful wife of actor Charles Laughton, the very British Elsa Lanchester. Whale's own selection of British performers in his casts made one think that his Frankenstein stories were taking place in England, although the costumes worn by his actors were Germanic. Miss Lanchester also played the part of Mary Shelley in the film's prologue: "James Whale in his production of *Bride of Frankenstein* did deliberately use me to play both 'Mary Shelley' and the monster's bride," wrote Elsa Lanchester in a letter to *Life* magazine for 5 April 1968, "because he wanted to tell that Mary Shelley indeed had something in common with the dreadful creature of her imagination."

Elsa Lanchester was turned over to make-up artist Jack Pierce for her transformation into a female creature composed of parts of corpses. Pierce did not give her the same trappings as he had given Karloff. Apparently since Frankenstein had gained some experience in creating life, and since he would be aided in assembling the Monster's mate by sinister Dr. Pretorius, the Bride would not appear so grotesque. Miss Lanchester was too short to be a worthy mate for the gigantic Frankenstein Monster. Pierce gave her shoe lifts, then wrapped her hands and arms in mummy-like bandages and had her wear a floor-length gown that hid her true height. This gown was indeed a macabre article of clothing, for it resembled both a wedding dress and a burial shroud.

Pierce's own readings in the subject of Egyptology entered into his creating the Bride's make-up. Remembering statues of Queen Nefertiti, Pierce gave the Bride a similar appearance by making her thick mass of hair, streaked with lightning-like silver, stand out from her head. This matched the gauze on her arms for effect. The eyebrows shot up like those of a movie vampire. The Bride's neck showed stitched scars where the head had been attached. The "Bride of Frankenstein" stood seven feet tall in the disguise. She was a veritable monster, a suitable mate for Henry Frankenstein's first attempt at creating a human being. Yet despite her terrible appearance, there was something weirdly attractive about the Bride that made her even more bizarre.

The appearance of the original Monster was changed by Pierce to conform with the incidents in the script by William Hurlbut and again John L. Balderston. One hand and arm, the hair, and right side of the face, had been severely burned by the windmill fire. The head was nearly bald (although a short crop of hair grew back by the end of the picture), and for the first time we could see the stitches and healed wound that ran about the top of the head and down the left side to the ear. (The top wound did in fact lie beneath *all* of Universal's Frankenstein Monster make-ups—including the later Herman Munster—although it was covered by hair.) The Monster's clothing had also shown damage done by the flames.

Press releases said that the creature's make-up was now a pale green. (Similar statements were printed concerning the Monster's color in *Son of Frankenstein* in 1939.) Green seemed a more suitable color for a being made from dead limbs. It is possible that Pierce changed the color from bluish gray to green for the sake of experimentation. But he later stated that his Frankenstein Monster had always been gray, leaving the inconsistency more credible if conceived by the publicity department. ***Bride of Frankenstein*** was filmed in black and white. What photographed best mattered; not what looked best when seen on the live set.

Bride of Frankenstein opened with Mary Shelley in the early nineteenth century speaking about her brainchild *Frankenstein* to foppish Lord Byron (Garin Gordon) and her husband Percy (Douglas Walton). This was the role credited to Miss Lanchester in the film's titles. Like Karloff in the first film her name became a question mark to identify the actress playing the Bride. Mrs. Shelley explained that the Monster did not die in the flames of the mill and that the story was just beginning. The scenes of Mary Shelley presented an almost ludicrous anachronism in ***Bride of Frankenstein***. The setting for the prologue was

Mary's own era of the 1800s. When her flashback narration dissolved onto the screen with her fading words, the picture miraculously jumped into the *future* by almost a hundred years.

The curious villagers watched until the last burst of fire sent the wreckage of the windmill into crumbling ashes. Hans, the father of the poor child drowned by the Monster, waited after the other spectators had left. He wanted to see the charred bones of the Monster before he would be satisfied and return home. Despite the pleas of his wife (who was not written into the first film) Hans entered the wreckage. Then the floor collapsed, tossing the man into the stagnant cistern below the structure. A pale hand moved out of the shadows. The burned, hate-filled face of the Frankenstein Monster followed. In another moment Hans met the same fate as did his Maria. The brutal killing of Hans was witnessed by a passively blinking owl, beginning the story with a decisively James Whale touch of the macabre.

The set in which the Monster drowned Hans was only one of many elaborate and often bizarre sets created for the film by Charles D. Hall. Often his sets included little absurdities like steps leading nowhere. Some enormous sets representing forests and hillsides were constructed indoors, with countless naked trees filling the area like staggering prison bars. These were more than obviously manufactured. Yet they were photographed with the sweeping camera work of John D. Mescall in such a way that the artificiality was almost welcomed.

When Karloff worked on the scene in which the Monster killed Hans he was subjected to some rather unpleasant inconveniences. He wore a rubber suit under his regular clothing to keep out the coldness of the water. Unfortunately it did not keep out everything. The suit accidentally filled with air. Karloff then proceeded with the scene, lurching toward his victim. As he moved, his outfit inflated like a balloon. To the laughter of the crew he floated. He had done what the Monster had envisioned for Maria. Karloff was injured during that scene. His left side was bruised to the extent that he needed massage and infra-red ray treatments to relieve the pain and stimulate blood circulation. (A stand-in was spared the hardships of waiting around under the studio lights in the uncomfortable costume between takes. Instead of a living double the prop department literally built a stand-in. The prop Frankenstein Monster was made from a seven-foot high pole of one half inch piping and moved on rubber tires. The makeshift double was given a plaster face in the image of Karloff as the Monster.) The Frankenstein Monster climbed out of what was believed to be his grave and hurled Hans' wife into the watery basin. He was free again to obtain mercy and understanding or deal out a grim revenge.

Young Henry had finally married Elizabeth, making her the first of the film's two "brides," this one *really* the bride of Frankenstein. Henry's father had passed away, leaving him to be the new Baron Frankenstein. During one particularly windy night the Frankenstein household was visited by the spectral Dr. Pretorius who had been expelled from his teaching position at Henry's former medical school. Pretorius had his own theories concerning the secrets of death and the creation of life. Henry did not want to discuss his own experiments with the doctor. But when he was told that the older scientist had also created humanoid life, the Frankenstein curiosity made him decide to get involved.

Henry followed Pretorius to his tiny apartment where the latter showed him the results of his own experimenting. From a casket-like chest (purposely designed in that form by Whale) Dr. Pretorius removed six glass jars, each containing a tiny, living homunculus. Henry gasped at this "black magic," seeing the miniature archbishop, ballet dancer, king (in the likeness of Henry VIII), queen, mermaid (from an experiment involving seaweed), and devil who, Pretorius boasted, resembled himself. The king's habit was to climb from his jar to get to the queen. Frankenstein was startled to learn that the doctor did not work from the scraps of the dead but literally grew his homunculi from seeds.

Pretorius approached Henry with the idea of collaborating on a new living being, combining their techniques. Frankenstein, recalling the ecstacy of his last excursion at usurping the rights of God, accepted the weird invitation. Together they would create a woman. "That," said Pretorius, "should be really interesting."

(The following scenes were cut from the final release prints of **Bride of Frankenstein**: Dr. Pretorius had introduced Henry to Karl, a homicidal maniac working as a resurrection man—one who dug up bodies for dissection by doctors and medical students. Karl had once brought Pretorius the body of a woman known to suffer from catalepsy. Observing that the "corpse" was still warm he proceeded to dissect her. The doctor had cut up much of the woman before she screamed and he killed her out of mercy. Pretorius finished his story telling Henry that Karl feared him. As long as that fear existed Karl would be the perfect servant. Meanwhile in the village, the burgomaster tried to convince the townspeople that there never was a Monster made from the parts of deadmen; that he was just a large but otherwise normal human being.)

The Frankenstein Monster was roaming the countryside. His hulking form was seen by a young shepherdess who, terrified, lost her balance and toppled into a lake. Reversing what he did to Maria, the Monster rescued the girl from the water. She began to scream repeatedly. Two hunters, thinking the Monster was attacking the girl, shot and wounded him.

Prowling through the forest, his arm aching from the pain of the bullets, the man-made man entered the hut of a blind hermit (played by bearded O. P. Heggie). The hermit immediately convinced the Monster that he was a friend. In a truly beautiful and moving scene, the blind man soothed him with a sentimental number played on his violin—Ave Maria. Hearing the sightless man thank God for his new-found friend, the Monster, for the first time in his artificially given life, shed tears.

In the days that followed the hermit taught the Monster to speak simple sentences. "Bread . . . good," is a classic example of the creature's dialogue. Karloff disliked the idea of letting the Monster speak since he claimed it broke

the illusion established in the first film. However, the speaking Monster gave new insights to his character and closer approached Mary Shelley's concept.

The Monster had finally found a true friend. But his happiness was not to last. Two hunters (one played by gaunt John Carradine) entered the hut and tried to shoot the giant, who retaliated and in the confusion and congestion, accidentally started the hut on fire. The Monster rushed out of the burning structure.

The villagers declared that the Monster was a vampire and had to be disposed of in the traditional ways. Bearing their torches they pursued the creature through the forest, descending upon him en masse, and binding him to a crude cross (symbolically identifying him with the crucified Christ). The trapped Monster was dumped into a wagon and imprisoned, chained to a throne-like seat in another macabre contrast. Chains could not hold the Frankenstein Monster. After a few tugs at his metal bonds and after overpowering his guards, he tore off the jail door and escaped. Panic seized the town as the Monster attacked all who stood in his way. (There were scenes filmed of Karl at the same time creeping through windows of homes robbing and wantonly killing his own victims, taking advantage of the confusion. These scenes were excised from the film, probably for the sake of better pacing.) As the Monster rampaged through the village to freedom, pursued by torch-wielding townsmen, the vibrant march composed for the picture by Franz Waxman sounded over the action.

The Monster was chased to a graveyard, where he disappeared through a hidden entrance to an underground crypt. In that subterranean vault Dr. Pretorius had just disinterred the skeleton of a young girl. Alone, he was confronted by the Monster, who was delighted to learn that he would soon have a wife.

Later Henry Frankenstein began regretting his decision to make a second living creature. When he refused to go on with the experiment Dr. Pretorius revealed the card he had up his surgical smock—the living, demanding Monster. To insure that Baron Frankenstein would not desert him in this great work of mad science, Pretorius told the Monster to kidnap Elizabeth and take her to a secluded cave.

Forced to go on with the project Henry Frankenstein took Dr. Pretorius to the tower laboratory in which the original beast had been brought to life. There the two scientists began assembling the female body. The brain was grown by Pretorius' own process. But Frankenstein required a new female heart—a relatively *fresh* one. Dr. Pretorius squinted menacingly and told Karl to get him a new heart. In the original conception of the story, mad Karl apparently crept into the cave, killed Elizabeth, and sliced out her heart, presumably offscreen, for the Monster's mate. This was later considered too gruesome for the picture. Instead Karl killed an unidentified woman on the street and returned with his trophy which, he told Henry, had come from a recent accident victim now lying heartless in the morgue.

The sequence in which the Bride was given her artificial life was even more spectacular than that of the original

Monster. Huge bolts of lightning zigzagged across the dark, stormy heavens. The top of the watch tower was bombarded with sprays of white-hot sparks. Great kites rose into the sky to attract the natural electricity. Then the Bride, secured to a horizontal platform, was charged by a vibrant, phallic electrical device which descended from the ceiling to instill the beginnings of life into her on this bizarre wedding night. The form was raised to the ceiling to receive the full power of the electrical storm, while in a series of quick editorial cuts the weird devices of Frankenstein were shown to spark, hum, light up, and spin. Over all this turbulence blared the climactic music of Franz Waxman.

After the female body was lowered, Baron Frankenstein and Dr. Pretorius heard a low gasp from beneath the bandages which completely wrapped the body. The eyes were staring wide open. Again Henry spoke the lines of power: "She's alive! Alive!" The living woman, created by two mortals, was unwrapped. The head of the being, with its upstanding electrified hair, snapped unnaturally from side to side. Dr. Pretorius, with his own brand of James Whale humor, stepped back and said with the poise of an ordained minister, "The Bride of Frankenstein!" The scene was even more bizarre as reverant music, accompanied by wedding bells, came over the soundtrack of the film. This was James Whale at his best.

When the Monster was called in to meet the woman with whom he was to spend the rest of his life, she did not rush to his titanic arms so that he could carry her over the threshold of their bridal crypt. Instead she recoiled in horror from her "husband's" monstrous appearance (not taking the time to first see *herself* in a mirror) and moved toward Henry. Her motivation was really the result of Elizabeth's heart, which had almost found its way into the Bride's body before script changes were made. Again the Monster tried to attain the lanky woman's love. With a wide grin contoring his pathetic face, Frankenstein's original creature stroked her hands with delight. The Bride screeched again with a voice that reverberated through the laboratory. "She hate me," the Monster said, "like others!" Unable to endure more pain in his heart, the Monster lumbered forward. Pretorius looked in horror as the beast's gigantic hand reached for a lever protruding from the wall. "The lever!" Pretorius shouted, holding out his hands. "Look out for that lever! You'll blow us all to atoms!"

The Monster told his creator to leave with Elizabeth, who was now standing in the doorway of the laboratory. The creature forced Pretorius to stay. "We belong dead!" he growled. Then with a tear streaking his cheek the Monster pulled down the lever, which (like so many levers installed in laboratories in horror films to inevitably get rid of incriminating evidence) ignited a chain reaction of explosives that erupted in a violent cataclysm of flames, falling bricks, and searing death, destroying himself, Pretorius, and the Bride of Frankenstein.

The master scene in which the laboratory exploded showed not only the Monster, the Bride, and Dr. Pretorius, but also Henry Frankenstein. The scene was quick, expansive, barely giving the viewer time to see both Fran-

kenstein and the older scientist. Nevertheless both scientists were present, indicating that the scene was filmed prior to that showing Henry's escape with Elizabeth. (One version of the script had Elizabeth die in the explosion.) The final shooting script, still titled *The Return of Frankenstein,* gave Henry the suspicion that Elizabeth's heart was in the Bride. At the last moment Elizabeth, alive and well, banged on the door of the laboratory, but was inadvertently killed with the others in the explosion. Had Elizabeth's heart been stolen, Henry would have had even more reason to perish with his two creations. The storyline was changed to that of the typical Hollywood happy ending. Since the costly scene had already been filmed, wrecking the set, it was retained with the hope that no one would notice the inconsistency. Hardly anyone did as their eyes naturally watched the explosions.

The reviews of **Bride of Frankenstein** were favorable, as in the following clipping from the 15 May 1935 issue of *Variety*:

> Perhaps a bit too much time is taken up by the monster and too little by the woman created to be his bride. Karloff (the Boris is shelved) is, of course, at top form as the monster using the same bizarre makeup as in the first Frankie film. He nevertheless manages to invest the character with some subtleties of emotion that are surprisingly real and touching. Especially is this true in the scene where he meets a blind man who, not knowing he's talking to a monster, makes a friend of him.
>
> When the film was previewed in Hollywood it ran 90 minutes, but seems to have been clipped 17 minutes since, oke since the footage is not missed.

Bride of Frankenstein, surprisingly unlike most sequels to great films, was even better than its predecessor. With its more impressive sets and photography, its excellent music score, its humorous flavor and caricatures of human beings, and the performances of a superb cast headed by Karloff, the film was James Whale's masterpiece and the best of its type ever produced. For Whale there would be no more horror films. Universal executives tended to shy away from his new version of the Monster which, they contended, made him more human and less monstrous. (The Monster was actually one of the most "human" characters in the movie.) A controversial character himself, Whale was found mysteriously drowned in his own swimming pool in 1957.

The Frankenstein Monster had survived a burning windmill. An exploding watchtower should not be much worse for a creature infused with artificial life. Perhaps in the rubble of charred brick and crumbling ash a son could be born with the name of Frankenstein.

William K. Everson   (excerpt date 1974)

SOURCE: "Frankenstein—and Successors" and "The Old Dark House," in *Classics of the Horror Film,* The Citadel Press, 1974, pp. 36-61 and 80-3.

[*In the following excerpt, Everson studies the style and*

structure of three Whale films, Frankenstein, Bride of Frankenstein *and* The Old Dark House.]

FRANKENSTEIN

Although blazing a trail for horror films, and indeed made before the descriptive phrase "horror film" came into usage, *Frankenstein* was carefully thought out as a morality play, designed to provide food for thought as well as enjoyable shudders. The hard to read, but even more bizarre original novel merely provided a point of departure for the film. Moreover, the filmed concept was itself changed by James Whale from a reputedly equally original treatment, conceived by another notable director, Robert Florey. Never dreaming that it would spawn a whole genre of much stronger chillers, reviewers were generally impressed by its artistry and the way it almost ripped a kind of raw poetry out of a charnel house of horrors, but wondered whether viewers were ready for such nightmarish stuff, and indeed, whether the screen had a moral responsibility to avoid such frightening material.

Its leisurely developed story of Dr. Frankenstein's creation of a Monster from the bodies and tissues of the dead—quite literally, and with no pun intended—now seems like the bare bones of the many imitations and sequels that followed. In some ways, its relative crudities, including the total lack of a musical score and the obvious use of studio "exteriors," give it a kind of rough hewn realism, which the later, slicker ones lacked. And the word "relative" crudities should be stressed; for its day, it was an extremely well done and stylish film. Only its lack of music dated it, in a technical sense, and it held up so well (both artistically and commercially) in endless reissues that it is surprising that Universal did not see fit to modernize it by the addition of a score.

Colin Clive, fresh from his Stanhope in James Whale's earlier *Journey's End* (still a powerful if theatrical film, and by no means a lesser Whale, despite being his first), made a perfect dedicated, frenzied, tortured Frankenstein. In key, supporting roles, Edward Van Sloan and Dwight Frye were towers of strength in the kind of roles they were to specialize in throughout their careers. But it was the dynamic presence of Karloff, launched into his first major role after more than a decade of bits, extras, villains, and only very occasional worth-while parts, that of course commanded—and rightly so—the major attention.

Two key cuts have plagued *Frankenstein* ever since its release. One is the removal of Clive's line—"Now I know what it feels like to be God"—after the Monster has been successfully brought to life, the removal of the line and the accompanying footage resulting in an awkward jump cut that weakens Clive's near hysteria. The other is the more notorious scene: Karloff's happy dalliance with the child by the lake, and how he unwittingly throws her into the lake, expecting her to float like the daisies that she has thrown in. Initially, audiences were either shocked by its apparent callousness, or amused by its incongruity; the result, in either case, was laughter—and destruction of the mood. The scene was cut, although the sudden appearance of the father, holding his child's mudcaked body, unfortu-

nately suggests a crime of bestiality rather than one of lack of comprehension.

Frankenstein not only shows that Whale had studied the silent and specifically, the German cinema well—there are obvious echoes from *The Cabinet of Dr. Caligari* and *The Golem*—but it also stresses the theatricality that was always to be a cornerstone of Whale's work.

Mordant humor was equally present, although in this initial film, more serious in concept than most of its successors, it is largely absent, and the jovial Baron Frankenstein—inexplicably stage English, despite his name and ancestry, complete with monocle and stereotyped "aristocratic" accent—is used as an antidote to the generally downbeat atmosphere. The theatricality could hardly be more pronounced than in the scene of the Monster's creation, which Dr. Frankenstein literally stages for his guests, by seating them in chairs while he performs his experiment. When the Monster is unveiled to the audience, the confontation is first delayed, and then developed slowly. The Monster is seen in several varied closeups, the action freezing until we have had a good look at him, much as a noted actor will pause on stage for his initial appearance, accept the applause, and then go into his performance. This gradual revelation of his principal menace is a device that Whale repeated profitably in other films: *The Old Dark House,* in particular, and twice in *The Bride of Frankenstein*.

Bravura exits and entrances punctuated all of Whale's films, as did his use of huge windows as a backdrop to form a logical, if not totally realistic proscenium arch. Frequently too, Whale would track his always mobile cameras through the walls of multi-roomed sets, as if to remind us that none of this was real, but an exercise in theatrical style. Perhaps most of all, he knew exactly how to pinpoint editing (long shot cutting to closeup), camera movement, and lighting, to get the most out of a given line of dialogue. Interviewed in the New York *Post* in August of 1973, actress Susan Clark commented on the necessity of having "in depth" roles and writing for an actor to make an impression. She asked: "How can anyone make a dramatic impact on audiences with the line, 'Please pass the potato salad'?" Obviously, she had never seen James Whale direct Ernest Thesiger in a classic reading of an even simpler line—"Have a potato"—one of the thespian joys and highlights of *The Old Dark House*!

THE BRIDE OF FRANKENSTEIN

Beginning with a crackling thunderstorm, in the midst of which Mary Shelley, in a spacious chamber and accompanied by a charming minuet, tells of the further adventures of Dr. Frankenstein and his Monster, we are immediately taken back to the burning ruins of the old mill which saw the climax of the first film. Cheating a little, the sequel implies Frankenstein's death at the hands of the Monster, and has him regain his senses only after being brought home in a stately funeral procession. By far the best of Universal's eight *Frankenstein* films, *The Bride of Frankenstein* is probably also the best of the entire man-made-monster genre from any period. If one judges a horror film only by the genuine fright that it inspires, then *Bride* might perhaps have to take a secondary position, but in terms of style, visual design, literate scripting, performance, music, and just about every other individual ingredient, it is virtually unsurpassed. As an essay in Gothic Grand Guignol, it overtakes its predecessor and yet, despite its care and lavish budget, it still manages to retain much of the rough-edged quality of the original, which the later ones failed to achieve or, more probably, deliberately avoided.

There are admitted flaws. It tries a little too hard to become the absolute peak of its genre, and while it succeeded (so well, that it was not only the peak but also the climax of its particular cycle), its constant succession of shocks and sensations from the first sequence on, work against, rather than for, it. One is never again as afraid of the Monster as in his first scene in the charred mill; with less shock and a subtler handling of the character, Murnau's Nosferatu, and Mamoulian's Mr. Hyde became more horrendous as their films progressed. Too, the occasional mixture of sex and religions is sometimes close to being offensive, rescued only by James Whale's innate good taste, or the genuine poignancy that Karloff generates. Few other actors could carry off the scenes in which Karloff, trussed up by the mob on a form of crucifix, is photographed almost as a Christ figure; or the delicate and oddly moving scene (it has a Frank Borzage-like sensitivity to it) in which Karloff accidentally stumbles across the cobweb-covered body of the girl who is to be turned into his mate, and hums happily to himself as he strokes her face. (Removal of this scene by British censors lessened the impact of the later scene in which the mate is shown to have emerged as a monstrosity in his own likeness.)

Just as the original *Frankenstein* drew much inspiration from the silent German film, so does *The Bride of Frankenstein*, originally made and publicized as *The Return of Frankenstein*, draw on it too. The movements of Elsa Lanchester's head, the framing of her closeups, are quite clearly patterned on those of Brigitte Helm, as the robot in Fritz Lang's *Metropolis*. Indeed, Brigitte Helm, as well as Louise Brooks, was among the players that Whale had in mind at one time for the role of the Monster's mate. Originally, and briefly roadshown at a 90-minutes-plus length, the film shows signs of having been reshaped, with sequences transposed after completion, and one cut (after the Monster has kidnapped Frankenstein's bride), rendering inexplicable one of Ernest Thesiger's lines. Continuity is a bit vague. It seems as though the redoubtable Dr. Frankenstein has been living in sin, since he and his beloved are sharing the same quarters before their marriage. The period is somewhat in doubt, too, with Thesiger beating Alexander Graham Bell to the invention of the telephone (herein called just "an electrical device"), yet using a great deal of post-Bell equipment in his laboratory work. The post-Production Code moralities of the 30s come through quite plainly, however, in the Burgomaster's admonition that "it is high time every man and *wife* was home in bed."

But it seems churlish to quibble over such a lavish and enjoyable fairy tale, which has genuine pathos to offer along with all its thrills. Karloff's performance remains one of his best, although not surprisingly, Ernest Thesiger steals the whole show with a marvelously written and played bravura performance as the mad Dr. Praetorius, who enjoys a light snack of bread and cheese, toasting a skull atop a pile of bones, before getting down to his graveyard endeavors. Dwight Frye, too, gets some of the best and juiciest lines of his career in this film.

Entirely studio made (unlike *Frankenstein,* which did use one or two actual exteriors and deliberately contrasted the serenity of the real world with the nightmare world of laboratories, gibbets, and graveyards), *The Bride* is never at too many pains to make its sets convincing, but since they are consistent, with a grey twilight predominating, they work. The trick work—especially involving Thesiger's miniature people in bottles, an episode played largely for comedy—is always ingenious, and the long laboratory scenes are the best and most elaborate ever created for this kind of film. (The laboratory set itself, with its stress on height, accented by tilted camerawork, is a beauty.) Franz Waxman's score, ranging from the march theme, as the dimwitted villagers take to their torches yet again, to the peals of church bells when the bride is presented, is likewise superb. The interior sets, making good use of painted shadows and also of such standing sets as the crypt, used earlier in *Dracula,* and later in *The Mystery of Edwin Drood,* are all beautifully designed—though one does wonder what kind of oversized delinquents ran wild through the countryside with such regularity as to justify the presence of that huge stone throne with chains and neck-clamps, all conveniently exactly the Monster's size.

The plot humanized the Monster somewhat this time, bringing him in contact with a blind hermit, introducing him to the pleasures of drink and music, and allowing him to learn a little English—a sequence suggested by, though hardly copied from, a like episode in the original novel. His new found wisdom persuades him to return Dr. Frankenstein and his bride to freedom and life in the last sequence, while (presumably) killing himself, his mate, and the colorful Dr. Praetorius (who, after all, had been a genuine friend to him) with one of those convenient all-purpose levers that exist in most horror-movie laboratories as a handy last-reel tidy-upper. "Don't touch that lever—you'll blow us all to atoms!" cautions Dr. Praetorius. No more explanation is offered for its existence than is vouchsafed for why the Monster survives the ensuing holocaust (in the sequel), but his mate does not.

THE OLD DARK HOUSE

The Old Dark House, last seen theatrically in the early 1950s, after which it was withdrawn to make way for William Castle's practically blasphemous "remake," is a film that almost invariably disappoints on its first viewing. In England, it made its first reappearance after a long absence during the later years of World War Two, when the censors had banned the release of new horror films, and older chillers were being reissued to fill the void. In the United States, it became available again—in a very limited way, via archives and film museums—only in the early 1970s.

Whole generations grew up, and knowing only its title,

and tantalized by wonderfully atmospheric stills and the reputations of Karloff and James Whale, assumed it was one of the greatest of all horror films. In many ways it is; it is certainly the apotheosis of all "Old House" chillers, and a virtual climax to such works as *The Bat, The Cat and the Canary, The Gorilla, Seven Footprints to Satan,* and other silents and early talkies. Nothing better in this vein has been done before or since. However, on the basis of its name, stars, and reputation, expectations run high—and when one first sees it, those expectations are not altogether fulfilled. Nothing really seems to happen, despite the predicament of five travelers, cut off by floods and landslides and forced to spend a night at the most mysterious of old houses, presided over by the most bizarre of households!

The disappointment was compounded for British audiences. The distributors jazzed up their set of stills by including a genuinely gruesome scene from the old, and then quite forgotten Columbia thriller *Night of Terror,* giving the impression that meaty scenes had been cut from the reissue. But, fortunately, **The Old Dark House** is the kind of film one wants to see more than once, and from the second viewing on, it gains tremendously. One has time then to forget about its lack of spectacular thrill set-pieces, and just sit back and admire its mood, its style, and its wit. James Whale, a former stage actor and director, handles the film much like a play: it is a series of dramatic entrances and exits; Karloff crashing through a heavily timbered door, a hand appearing on the bannister at the top of the stairs, staying there until it is almost forgotten, then its owner making a dramatic appearance on a near-empty stage; moments of genuine shock providing a form of "curtain," to be followed by a "buffer" scene of tranquility before the next thrill sequence develops. But if the methods are those of the stage, the execution is pure cinema, with a wonderfully mobile camera, Whale's typically effective use of short, sudden closeups, and beautiful lighting. (Arthur Edeson was one of Hollywood's best cameramen, and he did some of his finest work for James Whale.)

Priestley's original novel was rather uneven; he was generally much more at home with his "social," semi-political books and plays—or with his simple, regional comedies of manners, like *When We Are Married,* which dealt with the people and class-distinctions of Yorkshire that he knew so well. Elements of both schools of writing seem to be forced into *Benighted,* and get in the way of the melodrama too often. The one major difference between novel and film was that Priestley killed off his hero, Penderell, whereas the film lets him live—although there are definite indications in the film that this might have been a last minute decision. The well-knit scenario is carefully balanced, pitting the five inhabitants of the house against the five guests. In a very rough kind of way, each has an opposing counterpart, and the night of terror brings out the best (or worst) in all of them, solving all their problems, just as dawn automatically banishes the insoluble fears and dangers of a nightmare. (Somehow, it is a little difficult to consider oneself free of problems with Karloff's semi-mad butler still lumbering around!)

More than just a delightful example of its genre, **The Old**

Dark House is a prototype in reverse; a belated blueprint and summing up of all that had gone before in this kind of film, distilling the best from all of them, yet adding so much that was uniquely James Whale's. Despite the many colorful ingredients, it works best when it eschews the grim exterior set and the fearsome Karloff figure. The plot is really just a basic situation, and the highlights bear little relation to what plot line it does have. There's a marvelous sequence in Eva Moore's cluttered, claustrophobic Victorian room, in which she talks about the sin and debauchery of an earlier day, and makes the baleful influence of the past far more menacing than the bogeymen of the present. Later, there's a lovely little vignette (predating many similar Val Lewton scenes) in which the scared Gloria Stuart tries to cheer herself up by making shadows on the wall, and is interrupted by the unexplained shadow of Eva Moore. James Whale's always sardonic sense of humor is very cunningly employed. A "shock" closeup of the principal menace on his initial introduction was always an unwritten law in this kind of film, and Whale dutifully supplies it for Karloff's introduction. But then he follows it up with a comedy line of dialogue which squashes the Karloff menace, and suggests that a tongue-in-cheek approach is under way. To an extent it is. The audience is nicely lulled into a sense of false security, heightened by a deliberate anti-climax near the end, only to be outsmarted when Whale plays his final act completely straight.

Unlike *Dracula,* and so many other early horror films, **The Old Dark House** does not suffer from a lack of music. Apart from a few notes of highly evocative music in the main titles, there is no music, but the constant sounds of wind, rain, thunder, flapping shutters, billowing curtains, forms its own kind of symphony. Moreover, the film is so tightly paced (it runs a little less than 70 minutes) that there are none of those awkward pauses where one becomes aware of the absence of music.

Photographically, it is superb; the first glimpse of the House, seen through mud and lightning flashes, is one of the most effectively ominous establishing shots ever created. (Again, Whale deliberately downplays it by having Raymond Massey deliver a beautifully underplayed line, "It might be wiser to push on!" a piece of understatement that he exceeds later on, when he tries to soothe his wife's fears about "this awful house" and agrees, "It isn't very nice, is it?")

The sets are splendid, yet they still need a man of Whale's taste and imagination to get the best out of them. Universal later rented the same sets to small independent companies for their cheap thrillers, and yet they were almost unrecognizable since so little was done to exploit them in terms of camera placement and lighting. A few shots are superbly designed miniatures, and Whale wisely never gives us a really good look at the exterior of the House in daylight. Thus, even though the human menaces are explained away, the House itself, as a kind of baleful embodiment of evil, can remain undiluted in our memories.

Notwithstanding the pictorial splendor of the film, or the Karloff diversions, perhaps the greatest joy of the film lies in the teamwork of Eva Moore and Ernest Thesiger as the Femms, owners of the House, and in their beautifully written and delivered dialogue. It's unquestionably Thesiger's best role, and I'm not forgetting his colorful Dr. Praetorius in *The Bride of Frankenstein.* There's just the right mixture of fear, pride, potential insanity, and mordant humor in everything he does. While the camerawork and specific angles stress his thin, bird-like body and features as he walks into the camera, his contempt for the characters surrounding him seems to extend to the film crew and theatre audience as well! "My sister was on the point of arranging these flowers!" he remarks cheerfully, at one point, immediately transforming his benign smile into a sneer as he tosses the bouquet into the fire. On another occasion, as bluff, hearty Charles Laughton tries to add some merriment to the occasion by getting everybody to talk about themselves, pointing out that they're all together, all friendly, yet know nothing about each other, Thesiger promptly dumps them back into a spirit of gloom again by sniffing "How reassuring!" However, none of his marvelous lines match the combination of contempt, miserliness, and distrust that he manages to inject into the simple line, "Have a potato," as he hosts his uninvited guests to a singularly frugal meal.

The casting of Eva Moore as his sister was almost an accident. A familiar character actress in minor roles in British and American films of the 30s and 40s, she had come to Hollywood the year before, not really seeking work, but accompanying her daughter, actress Jill Esmond, then married to Laurence Olivier, and looking (quite successfully) for Hollywood work herself. Her casting by Whale was a stroke of fortuitous genius. She is perfection itself as the kind of aging hangover from Victorian days that was a surprisingly common national type in England of the 30s. Whale knew and understood such people, and one finds them turning up quite frequently in his films—in *One More River,* for example, although more warmly there, and with no sinister undertones. I still remember the feelings of mixed awe and mild fear I had when, in the mid-30s, I was (frequently) taken to visit such an old lady, who apparently never emerged from a parlor that contained gaslight fixtures, who kept the thick velvet curtains permanently closed against the sunlight, refused a radio or other modern contraptions, and filled her room to overflowing with stuffed birds and butterflies in glass containers.

To further complete the image that Whale recreated so accurately in *The Old Dark House,* a large solemn portrait of Queen Victoria hung on the wall, together with one of the daughter of the house who had been forced into a life as Captain in the Salvation Army. In all probability they're still there, with a horrid secret hidden in the upstairs attic, awaiting the rising waters of a James Whale storm to sweep them away.

Radu Florescu   (excerpt date 1975)

SOURCE: "The Frankenstein Films," in *In Search of Frankenstein,* Warner Books, 1975, pp. 257-62.

[*In the following excerpt, Florescu compares Whale's* Frankenstein *to his sequel* Bride of Frankenstein.]

In 1931 Universal had scored a spectacular film triumph with Bela Lugosi in *Dracula.* Anxious to capitalize on their new-found star, the studio sought an equally impressive story to use as a follow-up. Director Robert Florey suggested *Frankenstein* and the studio assigned him to fashion a screenplay loosely based on Shelley's novel (but with a creature more horrible than she had described). In the finished script that Florey and Garrett Fort wrote, Lugosi was visualized as portraying "Henry" (rather than "Victor") Frankenstein. The only link to the novel was the premise of a man creating life from parts of dead bodies. Universal, however, felt that the public associated their new star with pure horror and wanted him to play the creation rather than the creator. Carl Laemmle, then head of Universal, persisted and Florey and Lugosi capitulated. Florey shot a two-reel test of the creation sequence on one of the still-standing *Dracula* sets. Jack P. Pierce, the head of Universal's make-up department, monster-wise, created a grotesque hairy make-up that Lugosi loathed putting on. In the meantime, director James Whale, new to the Universal fold, had read the script of *Frankenstein* and decided that HE had to direct it. Universal, coddling its new man, pulled Florey and Lugosi off *Frankenstein* and put them to work on *The Murders in the Rue Morgue.* Lugosi was not unhappy with the switch, but it turned out to be a mistake on his part. After *Dracula* his career was to turn to increasingly more trivial vehicles. Florey's script for *Frankenstein* was revised and a rather obscure actor by the name of Boris Karloff was brought in to portray "The Monster." (It is interesting to note that even though Karloff was scarcely known, on the opening credits of the film the role of the monster was listed simply as "The Monster . . . ?", although Karloff's name did appear in the repeat of the cast at film's end.)

Karloff's performance makes *Frankenstein* a notable cinematic event, but the film itself is a rather creaky vehicle. Based on Peggy Webling's 1927 play, the revised screenplay credited to Garrett Fort and Francis Edwards Faragoh frequently unspools more like a photographed stage play (as was even more true in the screen version of *Dracula*) than an original film concept. The feeling of "stage" rather than "film" is set for the audience almost immediately when Edward Van Sloan, who played "Doctor Waldman" in the film, steps in front of the curtains of a stage and warns the audience that what they are about to see "may shock you . . . it might even horrify you!" Adding to the artificiality was an extremely un-restrained performance by Colin Clive as "Henry Frankenstein," posturing and gesticulating as though he were playing to a Saturday matinee theatre crowd.

As to the plot itself, the story began immediately with Frankenstein gathering up the mutilated body parts he would ultimately incorporate into his masterpiece. Anticipating that a creature with a normal brain (like Shelley's) would not be hideous enough to create screen mayhem, this script had Dwight Frye, as Clive's assistant "Fritz" (in a marvelous supporting role that often had unique touches of humor), steal an abnormal brain. This damaged brain accounted for the monster's lack of speech and predilection toward violence. The creation sequence was visually exciting, with electrical pyrotechnics setting a fine example for future film versions, and Karloff's first appearance as the monster was truly a shocker for the unsophisticated viewers of the day. We see a door slowly opening and the creature backs in. As he slowly turns, the camera cuts in to a full close-up of the now well-established famous make-up. The only missing ingredient was the sudden burst of music for emphasis. (One of the film's main flaws is a lack of background music). Also established in this first Universal feature was the scene most filmgoers always associate with horror films: the mob of villagers pursuing their monstrous quarry with flaming torches. It has been suggested that the idea for the monster's fiery death in the blazing windmill came about because Robert Florey lived in an apartment over a Van de Kamp Bakery in Los Angeles whose trademark was a small turning windmill. Of such trivialities are great endings made!

Whatever shortcomings may have been exhibited by James Whale in directing *Frankenstein,* and they must be considered minor, for he certainly possessed great cinematic skill, all was forgiven four years later when he gave the world the best of all the Frankenstein sagas, *The Bride of Frankenstein* (originally the working title was *The Return of Frankenstein*). Here was a case where all the elements of filmmaking meshed together to form a nearly perfect feature. The original screenplay was fashioned by William Hurlbut based upon his and John L. Balderston's adaptation from "events in the 1818 novel by Mary Wollstonecraft Shelley." Actually, the only idea to come from the novel was the idea of creating a bride for the monster. Shelley's creature wanted the mate for companionship, and when he was denied, fearful consequences ensued. In *Bride,* Henry Frankenstein is forced to create the grisly mate when the sardonic Doctor Praetorius uses the monster to abduct his bride, Elizabeth. *Bride* was impressively photographed, utilizing huge macabre Gothic-like interior settings that tended to dwarf the human participants. Frank Waxman, one of Hollywood's most illustrious film composers, created a background score so dynamically different that Universal re-used his compositions countless times in the late thirties and forties to supply the accompaniment for a wide assortment of features and serials. Whereas in *Frankenstein* the camera tended to be stationary a great deal of the time, now Whale utilized its vast potential in huge panning and traveling shots. The viewer is literally caught up in the chase as Karloff moves swiftly through the stylized cemetery with the incensed villagers hotly in pursuit. The creation sequence becomes infinitely more expansive as we witness long overhead crane shots and pan along with the bride's cadaver as it is elevated skyward to receive its jolt of life-giving electricity.

The original *Frankenstein* ended on a happy note with Henry's father toasting the recovery of his son after having been thrown from the fiery windmill. So as to tie the new version together with the old and not confuse audiences, this ending was excised from all prints of the first film that were still in circulation at the time. The scriptwriters on *Bride* then came up with a fascinating gimmick to tie the two together. In a long establishing shot we find Elsa Lanchester, who also portrayed the "Bride," essaying the role of Mary Shelley, and telling her husband and Lord Byron that the story of the monster had not ended with the creature's fiery death at the windmill. Instead, the monster had fallen to an underground cistern and was still alive. The pivotal role in *Bride,* however, was not that of Karloff's monster, but rather that of Dr. Praetorius, played by Ernest Thesiger. Whale, in his cunning, has given us the maddest of all mad scientists. Praetorius's sardonic soliloquies lend a style and flavor to the film that tends to elevate it from horror films in general and place it more in the macabre-fantasy vein.

If there is a serious flaw in this gem, it is in trying to humanize Karloff's characterization. In a scene in which the monster goes to a blind man's cottage and learns to grunt words and smoke a cigar, the creature is reduced to engaging in a kind of buffoonery that Karloff and most audiences found totally out-of-place within the framework of the entire piece. Whale's final touch of irony—that of having the reconstructed bride repel in horror upon gazing at her mate—was a superbly cunning slice of macabre comedy. It can seldom be said of sequels that they are superior to the original, but in the case of *The Bride of Frankenstein* that is exactly what has occurred.

R. H. W. Dillard   (excerpt date 1976)

SOURCE: "Frankenstein: 'What Changes Darkness Into Light?'," in *Horror Films,* Monarch Press, 1976, pp. 11-32.

[In the following excerpt, Dillard explores the symbolism of light and fire in Whale's Frankenstein.*]*

Frankenstein is, according to the horror-film historian Carlos Clarens, "the most famous horror movie of all time," and, as John Baxter says in *Hollywood in the Thirties,* "deservedly so." Frances Marion in her autobiographical *Off With Their Heads!* recalls the "curious fact" that even in Hollywood "scarcely anyone old or young in the audience viewed the picture without some nerve-tingling reaction" when it was first shown in 1931. And the film still retains most of its impact, despite the familiarity of the monster's features even to those who are seeing it for the first time. Ivan Butler reports that the "first sight of Karloff . . . still manages to shock," and it has been my experience with recent showings of the film that it can still hold its own with an initially uninterested or even hostile audience—which cannot be said for Tod Browning's *Dracula,* Karl Freund's *The Mummy* or Victor Halperin's *White Zombie.*

The source of *Frankenstein*'s continuing popular strength does not really lie in its shock value, for audiences don't scream at it the way they used to do, or the way they still do at *Night of the Living Dead* or *The Texas Chain Saw Massacre.* It appears to lie rather in the slow transformation of that initial shock and horror into a sympathy, both for Henry Frankenstein, whose dreams have gone fatally awry, and for the monster himself. Ivan Butler has noted the depth of this sympathy and described it as "more than sympathy—a tragic sense of human potentiality wasted, destroyed by a lack of understanding which leads so quickly to panic and disaster." He attributes that sympathy to Boris Karloff's skill as an actor and to James Whale's "dignity of treatment; a respect, not only for the 'normal' people, not only for the monster, but for the whole inherent significance of his subject." When he continues by ascribing to the film "a largeness of purpose, a hint of the grandeur of mysteries beyond our knowledge," he has certainly touched the source of the film's success, and he offers a starting point for an examination of *Frankenstein*'s nature.

However, to attempt to explain the film's largeness by examining its technical virtues is really a futile exercise. For example, most of the film's horrific quality is usually ascribed to Jack Pierce's makeup, and certainly that is true, and to Karloff's gaining sympathy for the monster despite the makeup. But an examination of photographs of earlier versions of the monster reveals that the makeup was toned down, was made more human—in an earlier version, the monster's forehead was marred by two metal rings with ropes of flesh twisted through them. For all of Karloff's genius as an actor, some of his later success must, then, be ascribed to Pierce's makeup and its remarkably subtle fusion of the grotesque and horrific with the recognizably human. And to say that the film's sense of dignity is solely the work of Whale is to deny the soundness of the screenplay by Garrett Fort and Francis Edward Faragoh or the suggestions of the first director on the picture, Robert Florey. Whale's direction is impeccable, but it is not stamped with Whale's identity to anything like the degree that his later films *The Old Dark House, The Invisible Man* or *Bride of Frankenstein* are. And certainly Arthur Edeson's photography, Clarence Kolster's editing and the sets themselves deserve proper credit, to say nothing of the acting of Colin Clive, Dwight Frye and Frederick Kerr.

The only effective approach to the film is to disregard the efforts of its makers and look directly at the thing they made, the film as an esthetic entity with its own life and qualities and values. The film is problematic as any genuine work of art must be, but it is its own solution. It has an integrity and wholeness which offers itself up, not only to emotion or even to imagination, but to understanding.

The initial problem which confronts the understanding of any horror film is that one which is involved in the approach to any work of fantasy or fable. The theme appears too readily available; a simple allegorical reading seems to milk the work of its substance all too quickly. And certainly such is the case with most horror films—an evil invades the lives of a group of people, and they repel or destroy it by their resourcefulness, their caring for each other and their faith in the general rightness of the nature of the world. A viewer may expand that allegorical reading as far as he likes, but the film itself has little more to offer. He may see a film like Robert Siodmak's *Son of Dracula* more than once, but only for the pleasure of re-covering familiar narrative ground or perhaps for the imaginative frisson which may be gained from, say, the image of Count Alucard floating across the dark swamp water, standing on his coffin. The film will offer his understanding very little more than it did on a first viewing. Its matter is drained by a simple rational and allegorical reading of its symbols and events; it remains as essentially abstract experience with minimal existential concretion, an experience which does not bear thorough and continuing acquaintance.

The temptation is to read *Frankenstein* in that way, alle-

gorically and quickly. It is a temptation compounded by the Edward van Sloan introductory remarks, in which he says that it is "the story of Frankenstein, a man of science, who sought to create a man after his own image without reckoning upon God," or by Mary Shelley's explication of the film in the opening scene of *Bride of Frankenstein* when she describes it as an account of "the punishment that may befall a mortal man who dares to emulate God." That is a tidy explanation, one that would reduce the film to a retelling of the medieval Faust legend as if Goethe or the passage of several centuries had not occurred. And since James Whale did direct both pictures, that must have been what he had in mind, or so the argument goes. But van Sloan's preface is scarcely appropriate to the film and its values, and *Bride of Frankenstein,* for all its virtues, is not *Frankenstein,* and the temptation to identify them must be avoided in order to arrive at the genuine substance of Frankenstein.

Frankenstein does have to do with a man's overreaching himself, but the failure lies not so much in the daring or in the act, but in his inability to cope with the product of his actions. The real Mary Shelley puts it much better than her later film avatar when she has her monster point out to his creator that he has not fulfilled the duties of a creator: "Remember that I am thy creature; I ought to be thy Adam, but I am rather the fallen angel, whom thou drivest from joy for no misdeed." The film has much to show us about the nature of creation and its moral consequences, but even an examination of that thematic element will not exhaust the film, for it has as much to show us about the fact of death and the resiliency and strength of life in its face, about the very nature of human experience and of life itself. Frankenstein's experience and his moral pilgrimage can only be fully understood in the context of the larger texture and motion of the film itself; the form gives the matter of the film its value and meaning, just as that matter fills out and gives substance to the abstract idea of the form. The film's complex texture of physical and mental fact not only explains its thematic specifics but is actually its "meaning."

The symbols in the film are not static, nor are they exterior to the texture of the film itself. Fire, for example, carries its traditional meanings in the film, but it never appears except when it is a functional element in the narrative. It is not imposed on the film; the film creates and recreates its own symbolic levels as it goes. This narrative activity of the film's symbols is one of the major reasons why it is in this respect superior even to so fine a film as Carl Dreyer's *Vampyr. Vampyr* is a book film; its symbols are drawn directly from a European literary heritage (a book even serves as one of those symbols in the film). The static shots of weathervanes and still water are striking, but they are essentially extraneous to the remarkably poetic moving texture of the film itself. Only the reversal of traditional black-white symbology which reaches its functional climax with the doctor's death in the white flour of the mill develops into a fully cinematic and organic use of symbol in the film. Even so fluid a film as Rouben Mamoulian's *Dr. Jekyll and Mr. Hyde,* with its brilliant and completely integral metamorphosis scenes in which physical motion and moral change are identified as fully as they ever have been in any work of art, is nevertheless marred by the interposition of static and exterior symbols such as the statuette of Cupid and Psyche offering ironic commentary on Hyde's murder of Ivy.

Frankenstein is an interpretation of Mary Shelley's novel, but it is no book film. It is a thoroughly cinematic film, drawing its symbolic texture and meaning out of its own narrative movement. That the monster's life begins in lightning and ends in fire, for example, is a simple enough observation and a rewarding one, but it would be a misleading one if the whole complex pattern of fire, light and darkness were not also taken into consideration.

Frankenstein opens in darkness in a graveyard. The first shot is of a gravedigger's hands pulling up the rope with which he has lowered a coffin into a grave. The grave is seen in the context of the graveyard with its leaning crosses and an effigy of skeletal Death (who at first seems almost to be one of the graveside mourners), but those are not the vital and ongoing symbols in the scene. Rather the fact of death and the literal darkness become symbolic when the gravedigger strikes a match to light his pipe, introducing fire in the film to darkness and death. By the light of the moon, a dim and reflected natural light partially obscured by night clouds, Henry Frankenstein and Fritz set about robbing the grave and then cutting down a hanging corpse from a gallows. During these activities, Fritz carries a lantern. His clothes are also much darker than those of Frankenstein, and Fritz is thus texturally more closely involved with fire, darkness and death than is Frankenstein. This initial context establishes a pattern which develops throughout the rest of the picture. Elizabeth, Victor and Doctor Waldman are introduced by lamplight, fire tamed to civilized uses, and their symbolic context in the film is one of ordinary light rather than darkness and fire. When Henry reveals that he has been searching for a ray beyond the ultraviolet, "the great ray that first brought light into the world," his ambiguous relation to fire and darkness is explained; he moves through a context of fire and darkness seeking a light beyond seeing, the answer to the very question, "What changes darkness into light?" The movement of the first part of the film is that of Henry's search through darkness for the source of light and life, against the advice of Doctor Waldman, Elizabeth and Victor, none of whom can really see into that darkness because of their civilized vision of tamed light, with the assistance of the hunchbacked Fritz who is integrally a part of that darkness. In this part of the film, only Henry is a free agent, moving purposefully through a dark context; it is Henry who literally flings dirt in Death's face in the cemetery. Fritz merely does his bidding, unencumbered by either higher vision or normal daylight vision, and Doctor Waldman, Elizabeth and Victor merely react to Henry's actions which they cannot properly see or understand.

The actual creation scene is literally an explosion of the higher light into the darkness, guided by Henry Frankenstein (in white clothes) with the aid of Fritz (dressed in black). The shrill electricality of the scene is certainly appropriate to its content. Light and dark tangle and crackle in the atmosphere and dance wildly down into the labora-

tory. The monster's inert form with its skin noticeably dark and dead is raised into the night to the light—the lightning, that most active and meaningful fusion of light and fire. When it is lowered back into the room, the rigid dark hand has now relaxed. And when that hand moves with a wondrous grace, Henry cries out, "It's moving! It's alive!" At that moment, he has achieved a triumph that enlarges the scale by which humanity must be measured. He has joined the light and the dark (and, despite his lack of awareness, the fire) into an electrical tension which is life itself. He has repeated in small the original creation of man by joining earth and air (flesh and spirit) together—a joining made symbolically specific by the infusion of the lightning's life into a body pieced together from dead bodies dug up from the earth. He has become what Mary Shelley wished him to be, "The Modern Prometheus."

Henry Frankenstein is, then, in the first part of the film an heroic figure, the moral free agent who can see that the apparently fixed distinctions between light and darkness, life and death are not unalterable. And he acts upon his vision. But his triumph is, like his creation, inextricably involved with his defeat. The end is in the beginning. After the harnessing of the great ray and its gift of movement and life to his creature, Henry relaxes under a bright light, dressed in light clothes, speaking lyrically of doing the dangerous and pressing beyond. When Doctor Waldman warns him that "You have created a monster, and it will destroy you," Henry replies calmly, "Wait until I bring him into the light." Even the revelation that the monster's brain is a criminal brain gives him only a moment's pause. But he is smoking a cigar, and fire is present in the relaxed scene, however tamed and harmless. When he hears of the brain, he abruptly removes the cigar and puts it down. Then the monster makes his first full appearance, and light, darkness and fire, earth and air, come actively together, not to be successfully parted until the final scene of the film.

Henry darkens the room. The monster backs through the door and then turns to face his creator, moving from shadows into a lighter context. Frankenstein shows no revulsion or dismay towards what he has created—the first irrefutable proof of his blindness to certain essential values of the light, for his creature is huge and ugly, an emblem of death in life. As Ivan Butler puts it, "His gaunt features and dark-socketed eyes have a true charnel-house appearance." But when the monster is shown sunlight for the first time, spilling down onto him from a skylight, his appealing innocence, his yearning for the light and his confused hurt when it is withdrawn reveal to the viewer the beauty that Frankenstein alone has been able to see in this monstrous figure. The monster, sewn together from dead bodies and with a criminal brain, does nevertheless yearn for air and the light like a flower. The life that animates him is the life we all share, created though he was by a fellow man. Paul Jensen reads this scene as "a small-scale allegory of man's efforts to grasp the intangible unknown, and of his bewilderment at a creator who keeps him from it." But then Fritz runs into the room with a torch, and the monster's innocent struggle to regain the lost light turns into something much uglier as darkness, earth and fire assert their ascendancy in his nature. As John Baxter points out in *Sixty Years of Hollywood,* the light for which he yearns is "a symbol of reason and grace from which he is forever barred." And, as he might have added, the monster himself is an emblem of fallen and unredeemed man. After he is subdued, he is chained in the cellar below earth level like a wild beast, tormented by Fritz with a whip and with the fire of his torch. Frankenstein turns away from his creation, betraying its potential, and he reveals his dangerous flaw.

Henry, in his idealism, has become a half man. By yearning for the light beyond seeing, he has forgotten that he is a mortal man, susceptible to error and to sin. While venturing out into the dark, he has forgotten the darkness in himself; while reaching into the air, he has forgotten the earthiness of his nature. He and Fritz have become two halves of one man—not allegorically but actually. Henry has become all brain and nerve, idealistic, daring, able to think and to do the impossible, and he uses Fritz as his body—fearful, ignorant, crippled, dark Fritz, whom Henry called "fool" in his first line in the film. They have become like Aylmer and Aminadab in Hawthorne's "The Birthmark," and Henry, like Aylmer, is striving to be more than man while forgetting what it is to be a man. In the film, Henry's forgetting is more than symbolic or even psychological; it is experientially active. He has not only forgotten his own lower self, he has also ceased to think of Fritz as a separate entity.

When Henry is forced to allow Doctor Waldman, Elizabeth and Victor to observe the act of creation, he scorns their imputation that he has gone mad. He says to them, "One man crazy, and three very sane spectators." And, of course, there are five people in the room. He has forgotten to include Fritz. In strictly narrative terms, he has forgotten the man who will teach the monster fear and hatred, who will introduce him to fire and pain, who will transform him from an innocent seeker of the light into a murderer. Fritz, whose fear and trembling give the monster his criminal brain, is the agency by which the new Adam will be transformed into the new Cain. And in the symbolic terms flowing out of the narrative, Henry has forgotten what it is to be human and to be limited and, therefore, who and what he is. The future should be a quickening of what now is, but Henry's imagined future grows out of a false present, and cannot then be what he dreamed. Henry as a creator and an artist has forgotten that the imagination feeds upon the real and paradoxically causes the real to fulfill itself by that feeding. He has forgotten that his new creation is composed of dead flesh. "That body is not dead," he brags to Waldman, "It has never lived." The statement is true in the sense that any work of art or any earthly creation is something new. But, as Poe reminds us, that same work of art is the product of "multiform combinations among the things and thoughts of Time." It is this latter truth which Henry earlier expressed when he spoke of the freshly exhumed corpse in the first scene as "just resting, waiting for a new life to come," and that he has now forgotten. Henry's imagination has come to feed only upon dreams, and when the real reasserts its primacy, he cannot face what he sees. "Oh, come away, Fritz," he says, aware again of who he is and who Fritz is, "Leave it

alone." But in his shocked recovery of his own identity, he blinds himself to the nature of his creation—the "him" has become again an "it"—and he betrays even the potential life his imagined future might have in a real world.

When Frankenstein loses sight of his creation's reality, he also loses his moral force and his control over Fritz. He allows Fritz to torment the monster, and when the monster turns on Fritz and kills him, Henry loses heart completely. He is able to recognize his moral responsibility for what has happened as he says of the monster (granting him again the dignity of a personal pronoun), "He hated Fritz. Fritz always tormented him," and later when he mumbles, "Oh, poor Fritz! Oh, my poor Fritz! All my fault!" But this recognition does not give him renewed vitality. He collapses, surrenders his belief in his work and passes his responsibility on to Doctor Waldman, beginning thereby a new cycle of death and darkness and forcing the dark of his creation to escape into the very light of day. He allows himself to be taken home by his father, back to a childhood dependence on a man who, by Henry's own confession, "never believes in anyone."

The Baron Frankenstein, an irascible, comic figure, represents the whole world Henry has been struggling to transcend, a world in which men are creatures of material comfort—tamed light and tamed fire—with fixed positions in an unchanging social order, a world of unalterable facts and unalterable values. The Baron cannot imagine what Henry could be doing in his laboratory, for what more could he want than a home, food and a beautiful girl? He is a kindly but utterly condescending local ruler. The good wine, he tells us, would be wasted on the servants, and the full extent of his knowledge of human nature would seem to reside in his observation that the villagers are happy on Henry's wedding day as they are drinking beer, but that tomorrow they will be fighting. He is by his own lights a good man, but his is a mundane and static goodness, stifling the possibility of genuine moral growth. His sole wish is for Henry to settle down and produce an heir—"A son to the House of Frankenstein!"—which will assure the preservation of his orderly world. The wine with which he toasts Henry's wedding was his grandmother's, as are the carefully preserved orange blossoms which have served for the weddings of the Frankensteins for decades.

It is at his father's house that we see Henry and Elizabeth for the first time in bright sunlight, sitting in comfortable ease on a terrace. Henry tells Elizabeth, "It's like heaven being with you again," and she replies, "Heaven wasn't so far away all the time, you know." The scene is the most brightly lit and romantic one in the film with one exception—the parallel scene between the monster and little Maria, a scene that proves that even in heavenly surroundings, hell is never very far away. Henry is smoking on the terrace, so that fire is present even in that romantic context, its smoke literally dividing Henry and Elizabeth while he promises not to think of "those horrible days and nights" any more, the time when he "couldn't think of anything else." And, of course, the idyllic quality of the scene has already been undercut by the preceding scene in which the monster and the darkness have entered the open air.

Frankenstein's monster, introduced so suddenly to life and light, to fire and death, gains strength as rapidly. Doctor Waldman reports in his journal as he prepares to vivisect him that he requires increasingly stronger injections to remain inert. Waldman, also a good man and the father of Henry's intellect, cannot cope with the living force that Henry has created, and shortly after sunset (after 7:30 in the evening) he prepares to kill the monster but is killed himself. The gracefully beautiful first movement of the monster's hand in the creation scene is repeated in this scene, but it has now become an expression of menace and strength. The monster raises his hand and strangles Doctor Waldman. He then stumbles clumsily downstairs in the tower, rejects the cellar of pain and death, and wanders out into the night.

The monster continues to grow in strength and skill as the film proceeds. He opens the door of the tower only accidentally, but by the time he arrives at Frankenstein's home, he is able to move silently and to open a French window. His growth into life is, however, always ironically a movement toward death—the deaths of others at his hands and finally his own. without the guidance of his creator, he is forced to be only a creature of his senses. He leaves the tower mainly to escape the awful cellar room below the ground. He meets the little girl Maria in the sunlight by a lake, and her kindness and innocence rouse the yearning for light in him again. The two children, both left alone by their fathers, play together, tossing flowers into the lake to watch them float. But the monster cannot differentiate between Maria and a flower, so he drowns her while only hoping to see her float. Light, air and water have become as deadly for the monster as darkness, earth and fire. These elements continue to mingle dangerously for the rest of his life. After the discovery of Maria's death and the monster's attack on Elizabeth, he is tracked down by the villagers bearing torches. Fire offers the only illumination under a blurred and cloudy sky of dimly mingled light and dark, and in one striking and significant shot, fire even enters its natural antagonist, water, as the villagers' torches are shown burning in the night air and reflected beneath them in the lake. The hitherto controlled camera moves freely from high to low, moving over the water and into the barren hills as it tracks the villagers and their prey through the dark and elemental landscape.

Henry Frankenstein reassumes the moral responsibility for his creation after the attack on Elizabeth. He first attempts to protect her by locking her in her room, just as he had earlier locked his visitors in the tower and then locked his monster away. But he realizes that a man cannot simply lock up his values and his life and expect them to be safe from the dangers of day and night. He rejects the Baron's world and its preserved flowers once again when he sees the necessity to face his creation directly and handle it with his own hands (not Fritz's or Doctor Waldman's). He thinks of Elizabeth, as he had not done in his laboratory, when he places her in Victor's care—a selfless act, for Victor loves her. (Earlier Elizabeth had said lightly to Victor, "I'm far too fond of you," and Victor had re-

plied, "I wish you were.") His home responsibilities in relative order, Henry ventures out, dressed in a light suit, to face his dark creation. But now too late, the damage of his earlier failure beyond undoing, Henry vows not to create further (nor to redeem his creation), but to destroy: "I made him with these hands and with these hands I will destroy him." Henry is acting now in full consciousness. He admits the manhood of his creature (he calls him "him"), but his moral reactions to that man are dark ones, those of justice and vengeance.

The monster meets his maker in the mountains, and Henry meets darkness, earth and fire as he meets his creature. The monster knocks Henry's torch away, and as they struggle Henry rolls on the ground into the fire. The monster then carries him to a windmill, and there the two face each other—alone but surrounded by an angry humanity, their faces given to the audience identically as they stare at each other through a turning wooden gear in the mill, two living faces in a context of motion beyond either's control, not creator and creation now, but fellow creatures, victims each to each.

The monster was born in an abandoned watch tower, given life by the fire and light of the lightning and the great ray, the light beyond seeing. He dies, trapped and in a frenzy of fear, by fire in another tower, a windmill; Paul Jensen says that "Frankenstein's laboratory was originally to have been located in the old mill, so when the monster returns there at the film's end, it is because that is the only refuge he knows," and the Baron still refers to Henry's tower as "an old ruined windmill." The elements gave him birth, and they now conspire to give his life back to the air and him to death. He hurls his creator from him like a broken doll, almost as if the life of them both were contained solely in the monster. But it is the creator who survives, saved by the vanes of the windmill and dropped back safely to the ground. Earth and fire, joined by the gravedigger in the initial scene, separate again, as Henry comes finally to earth and his creation is destroyed by fire, the only light which was ever given him without denial.

The final scene in the film takes place in the light. Henry is restored to a comforting Elizabeth, but he is a figure in the distance, seen through a doorway. The Baron is in the foreground, talking to the maids about his grandmother's wine again. The door is closed, and the Baron repeats his toast. "Here's . . . Here's to a son to the House of Frankenstein." but it is his toast; it is not shared by Elizabeth and Henry. There may well be a son, but the order of the Baron's world has been forever shattered, for all the appearances to the contrary. The Baron gets the last word, but the last real scene in the film was at the burning windmill, the last real shot a descent away from that windmill, itself a torch now against a dark sky. It is no wonder that Orson Welles copied this shot so scrupulously at the end of *Citizen Kane,* for both films close with the burning of a great man's dream and the camera's appropriate withdrawal down and away from the ruins. The last time we see Henry's face clearly is there, by firelight, the face of a broken hero but of a man who has dared look himself and his actions directly in the face.

The texture of the film will not allow an easy triumph of

the tamed light of the Baron's house. The Baron's preserved orange blossoms are no longer in evidence, but there are fresh flowers in Henry's room by his bed. The light which finally shapes the film is the whole pattern of light and shadow and fire. We first see Henry's face in a domestic context at Elizabeth's home, where her framed picture of Henry shares the frame with a burning candle. The whole movement of the film indicates that for Henry, the man who dared to be free, the light will never be free of the flame, or of the night.

If the pattern of light and dark in the film helps enrich the moral and thematic ambiguity of the conclusion, another structural pattern certainly helps to shape that ending. The movement in the film is not primarily horizontal, but vertical—a movement which the film shares with much Romantic art. Henry Frankenstein strives to transcend his earthbound mortality; he wants to discover just one answer, "what eternity is, for example," and he dares ask that question and act to answer it. He reaches to the heavens for his answer, just as his monster reaches upward for the light and was raised to the lightning for his birth. The film is an elaborate structure of vertical movements to match and give esthetic substance to Henry's striving (and that of his creation), but for all the striving and movement upward, the general movement of the film is downward.

The clearest vertical movement in the film's structure is the plot's. From a hillside graveyard up to the tower, the narrative then moves down into the village as the monster and Henry descend to the depths of what they are. The film rises again to the windmill and those two characters' mutual recognition of themselves and of each other. But that movement is halted by fire. The monster dies in the collapsing windmill, pressed to the floor by a fallen beam, and Henry falls to the earth and is taken back down to his home. (The Burgomaster says, "Take him down to the village, and let's get him home.")

All of the upward movements in the film are concluded by a movement down. The coffin is buried and then dug up, but the body in it returns to earth in the dying monster's form. Fritz climbs the gallows, but only to cut down the corpse and leap after it himself. Frankenstein's first command to Fritz, his first words in the film, are, "Down, down, you fool!" His commands later to Victor and then to the monster echo those first words; he tells them both to "Sit down!" All of Fritz's journeys up and down the stairs in the tower end in his death by hanging (a last small up and down) in the cellar room. Henry comes down from the tower to the village himself in defeat. And the monster's first journey as a free man is to come down the tower steps and on down into the village.

The camera moves into the village and up to the Burgomaster's door on Henry's wedding day—an upward movement that reveals the town at its most cheerily innocent and happiest. But Ludwig follows that exact journey carrying little Maria's dead body, and the music that escorted the camera on its trip is stilled by Ludwig's movement over the same way. (Even the sock that Fritz tugs up over his skinny shanks on the steps in the tower reappears in reverse on the pulled-down sock on Maria's swinging dead leg.) And finally the men of the village retrace that journey

in reverse with burning torches as they go out to hunt down the murderer.

The chase moves up into the mountains, but that movement is also a reversal of an earlier movement rather than a new positive one. Frankenstein and his monster move back up to a windmill, only this time the creature brings his creator to the heights. The death reverses the birth, and the spent Henry is finally brought down again to his ordinary life.

What goes up, in *Frankenstein,* does finally come down. The Baron does have the last word. But the gained awareness, earned by violence and pain and death, of the necessity of the descent as well as the ascent is itself perhaps the final ascent in the film. Henry will never be able to ignore the real or the fallen again, and the audience, because of the complexity and integrity of the film's textural structure, will never itself be able to ignore either the power of the yearning for the ascent and the light, nor the awesome necessity for the descent and the darkness as well. The source of the film's largeness and of its sympathy and dignity is in that gained awareness. Mary Shelley's monster claims that human sympathy is all that he requires to become a moral man: "If any being felt emotions of benevolence towards me, I should return them a hundred and a hundredfold; for that one creature's sake I would make peace with the whole kind!" No one offers *Frankenstein*'s monster that sympathy except for an innocent child, with the possible exception of Frankenstein himself for that one moment in the windmill when he faces the monster through the turning gear. And the monster does not die at peace with humankind.

The texture of the film seems to indicate that Henry has grown morally in the course of the film, perhaps not to the heights of which he dreamed at the beginning, but to heights of perception that most men (the Baron and the villagers) never reach. But the film itself demands another ascent, the development of a genuine sympathy for the monster, the figure of horror and fear, by the audience itself. Karloff said that "Whale and I both saw the character as an innocent one" and that "What astonished us was the fantastic number of ordinary people that got this general air of sympathy." Give the credit to Karloff's astonishing performance or to Whale's direction or to the film as a whole, but that sympathy is gained and the film's ultimate moral structure finds its resolution in the individuals in the audience. That sympathy is finally the film's "meaning." Its narrative and symbolic and thematic texture is the necessary medium for that meaning's creation, its flowering in actual experience.

This discussion has by no means exhausted *Frankenstein*. If it had, it would have been its own refutation. The film's conscious and expressionistic artificiality in setting and costume, its use of flowers and of dogs, its emphasis upon the ceilings of its rooms as well as the walls and floors, the camera's movement and rhythm, the sparse and extraordinarily effective use of music, the use of numerous sets of paired characters, the film's social implications (the evil's flowing down from the upper class to the ordinary villagers), the contrasts of the solid earth with the fragility and hollowness of man's structures and even with water—all of these approaches to the film will add much more to what I have suggested here. *Frankenstein* is a genuinely vital work of art in which matter and form are actively one. It expresses the human need for growth and largeness, and it also expresses the limitations which hamper that growth and give to life both its tragic possibilities and its heroic potentialities.

Lester D. Friedman (essay date 1981)

SOURCE: "The Blasted Tree," in The *English Novel and the Movies,* edited by Michael Klein and Gillian Parker, Frederick Ungar Publishing Co., 1981, pp. 52-66.

[*In the following essay, Friedman compares Whale's adaptation of* Frankenstein *to the original novel by Mary Shelley.*]

In the "wet, ungenial summer" of 1816, a season filled with incessant rain that often confined her for days on end to her house in Geneva, Mary Shelley found herself in almost constant contact with one uncommon and two extraordinary men. However bad the weather may have been that year, it was nonetheless a period of unusual creative productivity for these four people. During the days in Switzerland Byron worked on "Canto Three" of *Childe Harold,* wrote *Prometheus,* and began Manfred. His friend Percy Shelley completed "Hymn to Intellectual Beauty" and "Mont Blanc" and undoubtedly began thinking about what would eventually become his masterful epic poem, *Prometheus Unbound.* Even the least accomplished of the quartet, the young physician John Polidari, wrote a tale entitled *The Vampyre,* which was eventually published (though wrongly attributed to Lord Byron).

Yet it was also a time of harrowing personal tragedy for the Shelleys. Mary still lamented the loss of her premature, two-week-old baby in February of the previous year, and the suicide of her half-sister, Fanny Imlay, in October was closely followed by that of Shelley's first wife, Harriet Westbrook, in December. It was within this churning cauldron of creativity and personal grief from June of 1816 to July of 1817, both in Switzerland and England, that the daughter of feminist Mary Wollstonecraft and radical philosopher Willam Godwin wrote her now famous tale of Dr. Frankenstein and his immortal monster.

But none of those huddled around the fire telling ghost stories in Byron's Villa Diodati could possibly have imagined the success young Mary's story would have in the world. For thirty years of the nineteenth century, *Frankenstein* would reign as the most popular novel in the English-speaking world, would eventually be translated into at least twenty-nine foreign languages, and would remain in print from the day of its publication. Indeed, *Frankenstein* provided Mary with much more popular acclaim in her own lifetime than Shelley was accorded in his, and for over twenty-five years the public regarded her as a major novelist who had been married to a rather minor poet; the revenues from her work brought more in each month than her husband's writings did in a year. The novel inspired at least nine different plays while Mary was still alive, several twentieth-century productions (such as that by the Living Theater), as well as some loosely related parodies

like *Frank In Steam or the Modern Promise To Pay* (1833). Generations of films based on her story, ranging from the Edison Company's lost silent version of 1910, to James Whale's classic of 1931, to the Andy Warhol/Paul Morrisey modern interpretation (*Andy Warhol's Frankenstein,* 1975), to the Mel Brooks comedy (*Young Frankenstein,* 1975), keep Mary and her monster alive today. It would seem that whatever Mary Shelley discovered "with shut eyes and acute mental vision" that rainy summer in Switzerland struck a responsive chord in her own day that continues to reverberate even more strongly in our own.

Most traditional *Frankenstein* criticism, whether of the book or of Whale's film, centers around the notion that Victor (Henry in the movie) has somehow transgressed God's moral and natural laws by attempting to create life from dead matter. Yet a close reading of the novel reveals that this position represents, at best, a simplistic view, and at worst, a total misreading of the work. Mary Shelley specifically refuses to make value judgments in *Frankenstein,* allowing both the doctor and his creation to state their cases with equal eloquence and effectiveness. Throughout the work she remains much more interested in presenting the tensions between the man of genius and his world, and between a creator and his creation, than she is in assigning good or evil to either one. It is precisely these points of greatest tension, never fully resolved in the book, that James Whale captures so brilliantly in his film; he, better than anyone else who adapted the story to a different medium, understood the tragic majesty of *Frankenstein.*

To understand the method by which Mary Shelley carefully develops the seemingly opposing sides of her fictive world—society versus the genius, creator versus creation—one must first admit something that seems very basic, but inevitably fails to be mentioned by most commentators: Frankenstein is successful. He has literally done the miraculous. Whatever deaths may occur in the rest of the novel, whatever grief his experiments occasion, nothing should blind us to his truly spectacular achievement. He has duplicated the "first principle of life . . . the cause of generation," and the desire to do so is in and of itself neither evil nor inglorious. Where Frankenstein fails miserably is not in the dream, but in his inability to integrate the dream with his social obligations. Even more importantly, it is his refusal to provide the parental responsibility due his "offspring" that seals his fate.

Frankenstein's isolation becomes a major reason for the tragedy that follows. In relying upon no one but himself, Frankenstein becomes concerned only with how the events will affect him, and not with how it may possibly affect the world beyond the sheltered boundaries of his laboratory. What Mary Shelley suggests to be positive forces are the very things Victor in his isolation rejects: manly friendship represented by Henry Clervel, and feminine love represented by Elizabeth. Victor's isolation inevitably leads him to blind egoism, ultimately dooming his family and closest friends; a union with a like spirit on either the sexual or nonsexual level is the only potential salvation offered in the novel.

One need not look very far for the sources of Mary's notion of the need to combine intellectual goals with human interaction, for both of her intellectual idols—her father William Godwin and her husband Percy Shelley—stressed the need for even the man of genius to integrate his personal quest for knowledge with the concerns of the outside world. In his *Enquiry Concerning Political Justice,* Godwin wrote:

> No being can be either virtuous, or vicious, who has no opportunity of influencing the happiness of others. . . . Even knowledge, and the enlargement of intellect, are poor, when unmixed with sentiments of benevolence and sympathy . . . and science and abstraction will soon become cold unless they derive new attractions from ideas of society.

Shelley's long poem *Alastor,* published a scant six months before Mary began *Frankenstein,* contains an even more profound vision of the relationship between one "who seeks strange truths in undiscovered lands" and the society he rejects. Even more to the point, the poet in *Alastor,* much like Dr. Frankenstein, makes his bed "in charnels and on coffins" as he obstinately searches for "what we are." Though Shelley is poet enough to express deep admiration for the doomed protagonist of his work, he remains man enough to make his position clear in the preface:

> The intellectual faculties, the imagination, the functions of sense, have their respective requisitions on the sympathy of corresponding powers in other human beings. . . . Those who love not their fellow-beings live unfruitful lives and prepare for their old age a miserable grave.

Though perhaps overstating his case in the heat of despair, Victor's warning to young Walton comes as no surprise to anyone familiar with Godwin and Shelley: "If the study to which you apply yourself has a tendency to weaken your affections and to destroy your taste for those simple pleasures in which no alloy can possibly mix, then that study is certainly unlawful, that is to say, not befitting the human mind."

Frankenstein also stands as a good example of what Harold Bloom labels "the internalization of Quest-Romance," in that it presents a turning away from an outward union of man with nature and a turning inward toward an internalization of the imagination that becomes overly self-conscious and destructive of the social self. Bloom notes that at the same time the Romantics strove to widen their consciousnesses, to intensify their intellectual awarenesses, they ran the inevitable risk of narrowing themselves to an acute over-preoccupation with the self. Frankenstein mistakenly substitutes cold, abstract logic for the warmth of human friendship and love. Almost all the great works of the Romantic Age cry out for some sort of completion, for a union of like beings, and *Frankenstein* is no exception; Walton, Frankenstein, and the monster all long for companionship. If Frankenstein deserves punishment for his actions, it is not for mocking God but rather for ignoring the social order. Any endeavor carried out in such isolation can lead to nothing good for society; and the duties one owes to society, Mary argues, are as strong and as binding as that owed to any abstract principle.

Obviously, Mary is not saying that Promethean man must

exchange his glorious dreams for the mundane pleasures of hearth and home, but the novel does yearn for a compromise between the two. To fail to achieve this compromise is to become a robot incapable of discerning right from wrong. Thus, Frankenstein becomes an irresponsible researcher, for he fails to take human consequences into account. His original dream was oriented toward humanity's good ("to render man invulnerable to any but violent death"), a natural outgrowth of his upbringing among a loving community of family and friends, but his vision becomes perverted by his isolation and denial of the very impulses that first motivated him. In his solitude, a new and more selfish desire arises:

> A new species would bless me as its creator and source; many happy and excellent natures would owe their being to me. No father could claim the gratitude of his child so completely as I should deserve theirs.

Thus, ambition overtakes humanitarianism; the dream becomes an obsession.

Victor Frankenstein errs, therefore, not in his dream, but in the method he selects to achieve it. But his blindness extends even further, to the very nature of knowledge itself, for he fails to grasp its essential paradox. It is precisely in relation to the entire question of the price of gaining knowledge that Mary reaches her highest tension point and, not coincidentally, when she speaks most directly to our own age. With its vast Miltonic framework, it comes as no surprise that *Frankenstein* presents knowledge and sorrow as inextricably bound up with each other because Edenic knowledge must inevitably contain cosmic sorrow. All the characters in the novel come to realize that "increase of knowledge" makes them wretched outcasts. Every step upward is an "increase in despair," as it further alienates the learner from those who do not possess his knowledge. Can the individual genius accede to the natural demands of society, thus avoiding the risk of dissipating his wisdom in an unproductive void of sterile solipsism and perpetual alienation, and still progress upward along the path of knowledge? Within *Frankenstein* there is no answer to this crucial question.

Though Mary presents no answer to this question, she does show that Victor's rejection of the heterosexual love offered by Elizabeth and the friendship offered by Henry lead directly to his most crucial error: the failure to take moral responsibility and provide parental guidance for his creation. Again, this idea has a contemporary ring to it. Given Mary's position in the novel, she might well have argued that those who worked on the Manhattan project must bear as much responsibility as those who decided to drop the bombs on Japan. Responsibility begins, not ends, with creation.

In the very act of the monster's "birth," we witness the ever-widening gap between Frankenstein's original dream and the reality with which he is forced to deal. Because the "minuteness of the parts formed a great hindrance to [his] speed," the doctor resolves to make the creature of gigantic stature. The resulting misshapen and hideously ugly creature appears so twisted and bizarre that he is forever doomed as an outsider. When Victor beholds his creature's "dull, yellow eye," he is "unable to endure the aspect of his being" and is filled with "breathless horror and disgust." The dream vanishes, but the creature remains, a harmless, love-starved being called to life by a creator who now rejects and abandons him. Victor assumes his one act of supreme creativity will be his final one, only to discover it occasions a dependence he cannot tolerate.

The monster's drive to revenge and murder results from his intense desire to obtain what Victor has so carelessly rejected: friendship and love. He tells his creator:

> Unfeeling, heartless, creator! You had endowed me with perceptions and passions, and then cast me abroad an object for the scorn and horror of mankind. . . . I am alone, and miserable; man will not associate with me; but one as deformed and horrible as myself would not deny herself to me.

Whether or not Frankenstein errs by not creating a female counterpart for the monster remains, at least for me, an issue open to question, but surely his very refusal to do so is evidence of a lesson learned; in the past he gave no heed to the consequences of creative actions. Yet the failure of love at this point is not the creature's; it is the creator's, who rejects his own creation solely on outward appearances. The monster's initial crime is merely his physical repulsiveness, something over which he had no control. Indeed, at one point, the monster rises to a level of moral understanding unsurpassed by any other figure in the novel, lecturing his maker on the responsibilities of creation: "How dare you sport thus with life? Do your duty towards me, and I will do mine toward you and the rest of mankind."

Though Frankenstein may not have performed the required duties toward his creature, James Whale certainly recognized his responsibilities toward Mary Shelley's "hideous progeny." And, like the novel, the film attained a great level of success. Critics like Paul Jensen label it "the most prestigious horror film ever made," while Carlos Clarens calls it "the most famous horror movie of all time." In the collection of essays entitled *Focus on the Horror Film,* the editors begin their chronology with the publication of *Frankenstein* in 1818 and end with the death of Karloff in 1969. The film catapulted Karloff from minor roles to overnight stardom, and it is no wonder he always cited it as his best horror film while affectionately calling the monster "my best friend."

Not only did Whale understand the elements needed to make a financially successful and critically well-respected film, but he intuitively grasped the significance and meaning of Mary Shelley's work in such a modern way that the film retains its power for successive generations of moviegoers. Furthermore, he comprehended something about the film/literature relationship that is gaining only slow acceptance even today. The best film adaptations seek the spirit rather than the letter of their original source, and in fact, transferring that spirit to the screen sometimes demands violating the letter of the work. Lewis Milestone stated the situation correctly when he observed:

> If you want to produce a rose, you will not take the flower and put it into the earth. This would not result in another rose. Instead, you will take the seed and stick it into the soil. From it will grow a rose. It's the same with film adaptation.

So, for example, if one judges Akira Kurosawa's *Throne of Blood* by how well it reproduces the outer events in Shakespeare's *Macbeth,* he might well conclude it is a rather poor adaptation. But once we examine the themes and moods of Shakespeare's drama and then analyze how Kurosawa uses cinematic devices to recreate those ideas and feelings visually, we can see that, far from being a weak adaptation, *Throne of Blood* (1957) remains extremely faithful to the spirit and meaning of *Macbeth.* Thus, a director can become not only an illustrator of the written text, but an artist in his own right, one who draws inspiration from original sources as Shakespeare himself drew inspiration from the Holinshed Chronicles. It is precisely in terms of his visual constructions, particularly image motifs and a sophisticated mise-en-scene, that Whale communicates the essential tension points in Mary Shelley's novel, giving us a work that rivals its source in complexity while conveying its essential themes.

Whale's sophistication is conspicuously evident in the intricate pattern of light and dark, both natural and man-made, that he weaves throughout the film, never subverting organic, contextual unity for a strained or baroque effect. The inspiration for this image pattern probably comes from the novel itself, for lightning in darkness first draws the young Victor to the power of electricity, and he later comes to view himself in terms similar to the "blasted stump" that first so overwhelmed him: "But I am a blasted tree; the bolt has entered my soul". Whatever its source, the light/dark imagery dominates the film, functioning both as basic *mise-en-scene* environment via its almost perpetual contextual presence and as symbolic metaphor via its role in the overall abstract theme of knowledge versus ignorance.

Immediately after Van Sloan's theatrical and readily dismissible prologue, the film proper begins with a medium shot of a pair of hands lowering something into the ground. From here, and as a good example of Whale's fluid visual style, the camera starts a long pan rightward past a young boy, an old woman dressed in black, an old man with his arm around her, a man fixing his glasses, a priest holding a banner, another man, a large tilted cross, another priest, another mourner, a skeleton symbolizing death and leaning on a cross or sword, and finally to the ghoulish face trapped between the posts of an iron railing (Fritz). Immediately, another more aristocratic man yanks him down. Whale then cuts to a medium long short of this man (Dr. Frankenstein) along with the skeleton of death in the same frame, intimately linking the two together as they will be throughout the film. At this point an old gravedigger finishes his chores and searches around in his pockets for a pipe and some matches. Lighting the pipe, he gives us the first of numerous images of fire surrounded by darkness, or darkness penetrated by light, that the film offers as its central motif. Here, however, the fire is small and under control, harnessed by man to aid his fellow creatures.

The film's second fire image is similar to the first in that it represents the tremendous forces of natural light and energy controlled to aid rather than injure man. The lantern that Fritz (Dwight Frye) carries on his pole cuts out patches of light in the night so that he and Dr. Frankenstein (Colin Clive) can see the convict, whose brain they need, hanging on the post. Fritz gives the lantern to Frankenstein, who holds it aloft so that his assistant can see to cut the man down. The light proves insufficient, however, since the man's broken neck has rendered the brain useless.

Up to this point, the entire film possesses a dark, nightmarish quality illuminated only by the tiny lights of matches and lantern. With the next scene we are thrust into a brightly lit hall at Goldstadt Medical College, a room dominated by high-powered electric lights over an operating table. In fact, several shots illustrate the predominance and power of the lights in the frame, particularly when Whale positions the camera for low angle shots beneath the feet of the cadaver, making the ring of lights on the wheellike fixture seem like a protective circle. Of course, when Fritz enters the school to steal the brain, the bright lights have been extinguished; he is a creature of darkness and of night.

The fade-out on the now dark and empty medical school is matched by a fade-in on a portrait of Henry (Victor in the novel) illuminated by candlelight; in fact, candles glow from all over the Frankenstein manor: on the piano, on chandeliers, to Elizabeth's (Mae Clark) right as she reads Henry's letter to Victor Moritz (John Boles). Troubled by the letter, Moritz and Elizabeth visit Dr. Waldman (Edward Van Sloan), Frankenstein's tutor at school, who warns them of the "mad dreams and insane ambitions" that have driven him from formal medical study. This scene takes place in a potentially eerie environment. Human skulls on Waldman's desk and bookcase surround the trio. Yet the scene's frightfulness is almost totally mitigated by the electric light gleaming over the doctor's desk. Here, Whale demonstrates Mary's idea that the study of human life and death is not in itself evil, and when carried out under the proper conditions—lighted, in the open, and surrounded by colleagues and friends—can contribute to the betterment of mankind.

The next use of lighting, and one of the most famous in movie history, brings us to the dark and isolated castle (it was originally to have been the same windmill where the last scene between Frankenstein and the monster occurs) lit only by a fierce lightning storm. No longer is light under human control. It remains beyond the realm of human knowledge. Frankenstein's outlandish *hubris* in these scenes, such as when he exults that "the brain of a dead man is waiting to live again in a body *I* made with my own hands," is not to be seen as research similar to that of Dr. Waldman's. The buzzing, flashing, sputtering lights in the laboratory seem under his control, but of course this later proves to be a scientific illusion. Fritz's comic parody of the porter scene in *Macbeth,* accompanied by a lantern, sets the stage for the film's most famous scene. Frankenstein sends up his being's body like some

ancient, votive offering to the creative forces in the universe as symbolized by the lightning.

It would be possible, of course, to continue listing and interpreting all the various sources of light in the film, but this opening description should provide sufficient insight into the feeling of the film's images. Three different, major sources of light exist: the untamed natural light formed by lightning, the sun, and the moon; the light made subservient to man such as lamps, candles, and matches; and the light that exists somewhere in between, like torches, that can either illuminate or destroy. Throughout the entire film, Whale makes us aware that light in various contexts presents various meanings. Like the knowledge it comes to symbolize in the film, light is a double-edged sword that is capable of great harm or great good. Again, it is not a matter of rejecting fire (light), but of realizing its potential for both evil and goodness.

In addition to the pattern of darkness and light that infuses the film on both an imagistic and symbolic level, Whale is also clearly aware of the other two sins committed by Dr. Frankenstein which form the tension points of greatest interest in the novel: Frankenstein's isolation, both moral and physical, from the community of men, and his refusal to accept proper responsibility or provide sufficient parental guidance for his creature. Like Mary, Whale refuses simply to censure Frankenstein as a mad lunatic, making him an incredibly vulnerable figure in the person of Colin Clive and giving him the least mundane speech in the entire film:

> Have you never wanted to do anything that was dangerous? Where should we be if nobody tried to find out what lies beyond? Have you never wanted to look beyond the clouds and the stars or to know what causes the trees to bud? And what changes the darkness into light? Well, if I could discover just one of those things, what eternity is for example, I wouldn't care if they did think I was crazy.

Clearly this is no deranged, stereotypically mad scientist, but a man whose dream is no less great and no less valid than that of his literary precursor.

But how does Henry go about accomplishing his dream? First, he secludes himself from the positive forces of love, friendship, and familial affection and replaces them with Fritz (a character not present in the book), who represents some sort of middle stage between human being and monster. Even though the actual "birth" is witnessed by a friend, a loved one, and a father-figure, none of these people have any influence in the process or before it. As in the novel, Frankenstein's dream becomes an obsession, and his concern is not for his creature but for his own experience of bringing life out of dead matter.

Frankenstein's rejection of his creation is strongly presented in the film. When informed that he has mistakenly used a criminal brain, Frankenstein puts out his cigarette (tamed fire) and tells Waldman the creature is "only a few days old . . . wait till I bring him into the light." And in the astonishing and poignant scene that follows he does just that, but in a way that forever seals his fate. He reaches up and turns out the lamp (man-made light) and watches as the monster appears in what must rank as one of the greatest entrances in film history. First Karloff backs into the room, then we see him in a medium shot profile, then a full front medium shot that changes to a close-up, that changes to an extreme close-up from the middle of his forehead to his chin. Frankenstein seats the monster in a harsh-looking wooden chair, reaches over for a chain that slides back the hatch in the ceiling, and allows the sun to enter the darkened room. In a tender moment, the monster glances upward toward this new sensation, stands, looking directly up into the sun, and slowly reaches out with his oversized arms to capture it. "Shut the light!" screams Waldman unexplainably, and Frankenstein, for no apparent reason, obeys him. In the moving moment that follows, Karloff holds out his hands to his creator, mutely begging for more light, more knowledge, more love. It is, of course, refused, and when Fritz slams into the room with his brightly burning torch, symbolizing the harsh light that can destroy with its painful heat, the monster reacts in terror. This is too much light at one time, and this combination of the refusal of natural light and the harsh imposition of man-made light enrages the monster and causes his imprisonment in the cellar below.

From this point until the film's conclusion, Frankenstein refuses to accept responsibility for his creative actions. Telling Fritz to "come away . . . just leave it alone," he abandons the being to the demented Fritz's inhuman tortures. He even allows Dr. Waldman to deal with the disastrous results of his experiments. The scenes with Henry and Elizabeth sitting lovingly on the patio of his father's house contrast in image, brightness, and feeling, to the dark and foreboding isolation of the laboratory. But the doctor's hiatus from terror is short-lived. Hearing his father toast to "a son of the House of Frankenstein," Victor embarrassingly recognizes the irony, that the House of Frankenstein already has a "son" who will soon make his presence felt throughout the countryside.

It is only after this "son" makes an overt attack on his creator's intended bride (his rival?) that Henry can once more find the moral courage to assert his position of ethical leadership by helping a search party, equipped with torches, to find the creature. "I made him with these hands," he tells Victor, "and with these hands I will destroy him." The parade of torchbearers sets off in three directions, with Victor leading those assigned to the mountains. There, protected by a sole torch which the monster unfearingly knocks to the ground, Henry confronts his beast amid the mountains of Universal's soundstage, and after being knocked unconscious, awakens in the windmill for one last battle. Here again Whale's visual sensibility becomes evident as the monster and his maker confront each other around a large gear mechanism that turns the windmill. Each is shot in an identical way through the mechanism, visually emphasizing that there is as much of the monster in Frankenstein as there is Frankenstein in the monster. The shot further underlines the inevitability of their fates being forever linked together, round and round each other. This shared entrapment and identity is highlighted when the Burgomaster (Lionel Belmore) screams and points to the windmill's platform where the creator and his creation grapple with each other, "There he is.

There's the monster." At that point, we understand that Whale means us to take that remark as referring to both combatants.

Two actions occur then that conclude the film's major image patterns of circular shapes and light and dark. The monster throws Frankenstein from the top of the windmill. He catches on one of the blades (which have been moving clockwise), changes its direction (counterclockwise) for a moment, then falls lifelessly to the ground, while the wheel returns to its original rotation. The townspeople plunge their torches into the windmill, trapping the monster by the flames. Finally, after a huge beam falls on him, the monster perishes (in the original version) amid the fire he has both sought and avoided throughout the film. For the monster, light is both death and enlightenment. As in the novel, the more knowledge he gains, the more despair he feels; the more torture he receives, the more crazed he becomes.

As this analysis of the film demonstrates, Whale viewed the *Frankenstein* story much in the same way as did Mary Shelley. Of course, the novel/film comparison cries out for additional study in various areas: the doppelgänger motif, the political overtones, the sexual tensions, the role of parental figures, specific biographical relationships in the novel, the allegory of the artist and his creation, to name just the most obvious. Furthermore, if Paul Jensen is right in saying that the scientist is the last potential tragic hero, since the grandeur of his aims makes possible the greatest of falls, then it is not too much to claim that we all live in a Frankensteinian age. Certainly, we have to deal with forces man has unleashed that now range out of his control. The potential destructibility of nuclear power, the possible uses and misuses of DNA, and the wonder and fear created by the space exploration program—just to cite some clear examples—give us all pause to contemplate the ramifications of scientific endeavors made in the name of mankind, yet having the potential to destroy it. Both Mary Shelley's novel and James Whale's film are crucial to thinking about these issues, for if Mary Shelley wrote the word, James Whale made it flesh. Within this context, *Frankenstein* raises problems that strike at the very heart of our culture, become central to our values, and speak to the very survival of our species.

Janice R. Welsch and Syndy M. Conger (essay date 1984)

SOURCE: "The Comic and the Grotesque in James Whale's Frankenstein Films," in *Planks of Reason: Essays on the Horror Film,* edited by Barry Keith Grant, The Scarecrow Press, 1984, pp. 290-306.

[*In the following essay, Welsch and Conger discuss Whale's use of the comic and grotesque in* Frankenstein *and* Bride of Frankenstein.]

Both the grotesque and the comic are much discussed terms, and for much the same reason: their discovery in art or life is largely a subjective matter; both depend for their intensity, and even for their existence, on the perceiver. If we find something comical, it is largely because we temporarily become disinterested, spectators whose hearts are momentarily "anesthetized." We distance it by concentrating our attention on the presence of incongruity, eccentricity, infirmity, or illogicality. Similarly, if we find something grotesque, it is because we temporarily become alienated, spectators who feel threatened: we distance it by perceiving it, labeling it an unnatural, even satanic, fusion, distortion, or fragmentation. "The grotesque," as Wolfgang Kayser suggests, "is the estranged world," and one we find quite appalling: it is "an attempt to invoke and subdue the demonic aspects of the world." Students of the grotesque as well as the comic point out the close alliance between the two: both surprise us and both underline life's absurdity. The comic inspires surprise by juxtaposing things seemingly incongruous; the grotesque evokes shock by fusing the seemingly incompatible, by creating a world "in which the realm of inanimate things is no longer separated from those of plants, animals, and human beings, and where the laws of statics, symmetry, and proportion are no longer valid." A descriptive equivalent for the grotesque current in the sixteenth century emphasizes the unsettling dreamlike quality of the grotesque—*"sogni del pittori"* (dreams of painters). The comic, according to Freud, also bears resemblance to the dreamlike.

Although the response to both juxtaposition and fusion may be laughter, the laughter inspired by the grotesque is quite distinct from that produced by the purely comic; the latter may be liberating or therapeutic, but the former is "involuntary and abysmal." The grotesque evokes the realization of a world at once "playful" or "fantastic" and "ominous and sinister," "a world totally different from the familiar one" of the comic muse. Yet because of their close proximity, and because of the subjective factor that frustrates definition, the grotesque and the comic constantly threaten to collapse into one another, the sinister into the silly. Gargoyles may produce shudders or giggles or both; so may Gothic novels or horror films. A major task of the serious artist of the Gothic, then, is to prevent an unplanned comic escape from the chamber of horrors.

Critics intent upon underscoring the serious implications of the novel *Frankenstein, or The Modern Prometheus* have not been particularly eager to explore the presence of the comic and the grotesque in the text. They have concentrated instead on reading the novel as religious allegory, or as political, philosophical, or feminist protest. Recently, however, Maximilian Novak has explored the relationship between the grotesque and the Gothic and used *Frankenstein* as one example, and Philip Stevick, in his analysis of the novel, has ventured to assert that it is profoundly comical. Novak finds the " 'straight black lips' of Frankenstein's monster" reminiscent of the Renaissance woodcut "skeleton with its combination of deathly terror and horrible grin." This, concludes Novak, is "the essence of the grotesque and the essence of the Gothic." In seeming contradistinction to Novak, Stevick believes that the novel *Frankenstein* stands in a great literary tradition, headed by *The Odyssey,* which combines "mythic seriousness . . . and laughter." He focuses, in a sense, on the "horrible grin." As he reads the work, he is caught up in its linguistic claim to high seriousness, but in retrospect its dreamlike qualities—its ineffectual hero, its fragmentary and illogical plot—seem absurd to him.

If Mary Shelley was at all aware of the potential dreamlike absurdity of the Gothic tale, however, she certainly made no visible attempt in her masterpiece to exploit it. The only laughter in the novel is the satanic laughter of the monster mocking Victor's midnight oath to avenge the death of Elizabeth and others: "I was answered through the stillness of night by a loud and fiendish laugh. It rung on my ears long and heavily; the mountains re-echoed it, and I felt as if all hell surrounded me with mockery. . . ." Moreover, the clearest admission of the presence of the grotesque in the novel is Victor's initial description of the monster as "deformed," "ugly," "a mummy," as "a thing such as even Dante could not have conceived". After this scene, the novel employs a number of traditional techniques to counterbalance, if not to erase, this grotesque surface. The monster is seen in half light, darkness, or from a great distance. Walton first glimpses him through the arctic mist "at the distance of half a mile; a being which had the shape of a man, but apparently of gigantic stature, sat in the sledge and guided the dogs".

If here we are encouraged to grant the creature epic stature, we are elsewhere invited to admire and even to sympathize with him; and sympathy, according to Bergson, co-exists uneasily with the comic. The gigantic creature is given eloquence, intelligence, noble aspirations, and a keen sensitivity to his outcast status; and when his story inspires the pity even of Victor, who has hitherto hated him, the reader can almost forget that the creature is an absurdly grotesque fusion of life and death, a motley collection of disparate parts ("yellow skin," "lustrous black" hair, "pearly" teeth, "watery eyes," "dun white sockets," "shrivelled complexion," and "straight black lips"). The novel's close is most effective in diverting attention from the monster's surface absurdity.

> 'But soon,' he cried . . . 'Soon these burning miseries will be extinct. I shall ascend my funeral pile triumphantly, and exult in the agony of the torturing flames. The light of that conflagration will fade away; my ashes will be swept into the sea by winds. My spirit will sleep in peace. . . .

His closing remarks allow the monster rhetorically to erase his monstrosity and bestow on himself a death of a hero.

Seen in this context, the 1931 and 1935 Frankenstein films of James Whale are full of surprises, especially if we come to them from a recent reading of the novel. We expect the grotesque to center on the creature; but instead, we gradually come to realize that the grotesque surrounds the creator and his associates, particularly his satanic partner Praetorius, and the laboratory scenes. We may not expect to laugh at all since "there is no doubt that the book is as utterly serious in intent as it is serious in execution," or we may expect to laugh only at minor characters "specifically designed as comic relief" because we have learned that "terror and laughter are near neighbours in our reaction to the iconography of the cinematic tale of terror." We do laugh at Baron Frankenstein, the burgomaster, and a village gossip, but later, with considerable unease, we also find ourselves laughing at the monster himself, and *with* the amoral, manipulative Praetorius. Instead of insisting on the story's high seriousness, then, as the novel does, Whale's films openly acknowledge its comic and grotesque potentialities. Whale's striking response invites the viewer, on one level, to reflect on the absurdities and grotesqueries of modern technological society. This level of appeal, of course, Whale shares with such fellow Expressionists as Georg Kaiser, Franz Kafka, Edvard Munch, and F. W. Murnau. On another level, however, the films invite the viewer to reflect, in a way that Mary Shelley's novel does not, on the danger any artist encounters who dares to tell Gothic tales, the danger of having one's tales dismissed as ludicrous. With increasing audacity, and primarily through the character of Praetorius, Whale successfully faces that danger. This level of appeal ties Whale's films into another, older literary tradition of sophisticated and self-conscious Gothic tale-telling, one which begins with Ann Radcliffe and has among its greatest representatives Charles Robert Maturin, Herman Melville, Edgar Allan Poe, and Henry James.

Whale's *Frankenstein* plunges its viewer abruptly into a world of traditional grotesquerie. The graveyard is a visual catalog of objects which Kayser identifies as inherently grotesque: the *skeletal* figure of *death* with its *scythe,* the *vertiginous* angle shot of *hunchback* Fritz's *mad* stare through fence *stakes,* the barren, *twisted* branches behind him. The spectator is confronted immediately with a world at once distorted and sinister which fuses life and death, sanity and madness, and which accentuates fragmentation and dizzying distortions. Moreover, the viewer is frequently reminded of that world thereafter: by the jagged rocks and by the visual juxtaposition of hunchback and hanged man; by the distorted shadows in the crowded medical classroom, and by a skeleton's shadow and a death's head which guard the foot of the classroom stairs; and by the skulls that decorate Dr. Waldman's desk and bookshelf. The one skull on the desk seems to be a fourth partner to the conversation Waldman has with Victor and Elizabeth, and behind them is a row of macabre spectators, death's heads all slightly tilted to one side.

The workshop of the grotesque in *Frankenstein* is, of course, the laboratory of Henry. There mind, machine, and nature's lightning conjoin to animate inert matter in the form of a creature constructed by Henry "from the bodies I took from the graves, from the gallows, anywhere!" to be a walking emblem of the grotesque: unnatural in origin, body, and brain, and despite its initial gentle behavior, too deformed, enormous, and powerful not to seem threatening and sinister. The appearance of the laboratory, its giant instruments reminiscent of Bosch's implements of torture, encourages the conclusion that Henry's creation is actually a satanic parody of the divine creation. The *mise-en-scène* suggests that Henry, despite his protests to the contrary, is involved in "an attempt to invoke and subdue the demonic aspects of the world." Waldman guides viewers towards precisely this conclusion with his repeated warnings: "Mark my words, he will prove dangerous!"

Caught between his absurdly idealistic dream ("Have you never wanted to know what causes the trees to bud? And what changes darkness into light?") and his grotesque realization of that dream (a fusion of dead limbs, abnormal brain, and electrified heart), Henry becomes the embodiment of the mad scientist, a type which has often been the nexus of comedy, and which was for Shelley a cause for sympathy, but which can, as Kayser suggests, be an experience of the grotesque in one of its most alarming forms: "In the insane person, human nature itself seems to have taken on ominous overtones. Once more it is as if an impersonal force, an alien and inhuman spirit, had entered the soul." The novel does not deny Victor Frankenstein's madness; but it does romanticize it. Walton reports that Victor's "eyes have generally an expression of wildness, and even madness; but there are moments when . . . his whole countenance is lighted up . . . with . . . benevolence and sweetness"; and he concludes, "How can I see so noble a creature destroyed by misery without feeling the most poignant grief?" Even on the night of the creation, at the height of Victor's "enthusiastic madness," his terror, his remorse, his disgust, and his painful dreams all work to evoke our sympathy for, rather than alienation from, this misguided student. Whale, in contrast, seems interested in compelling his viewer to an alienating recognition of Henry's instability. Henry taunts Waldman, his fiancée, and Victor as they interrupt his experiment; he acknowledges his madness, but with a sarcasm that attempts to belie it: "A moment ago you said I was crazy. Tomorrow we'll see about that." We catch no glimpse of melancholy benevolence in his cold stare, and just after his monster begins to move, we must witness Henry's disconcerting ecstasy as he shouts, over and over, "It's alive—it's alive! . . . IT'S ALIVE!" If Whale does not leave us witnesses to this alarming frenzy for long, he has made it grotesque enough to imprint it on our memories.

He rescues us temporarily by immediately cutting to the sunny, flower-filled parlor of Henry's father; Henry's grotesquerie is thus displaced by the comic—but only for a time. Only after the creation scene does Whale introduce the comic. Its deliberate avoidance seems quite apparent in the initial gravedigger's scene—traditionally a comic interlude, like the Yorick scene in *Hamlet,* but in *Frankenstein* the humor is left unexploited. The viewer watches the pudgy, slightly fatuous-looking gravedigger intently but is given little open invitation to laugh. The comic reigns, however, in the house of the Baron Frankenstein. The Baron, and his mundane conclusions—"I understand perfectly well . . . huh . . . there is another woman"— also seem reductive, hence comical, in this world thus far so consumed by the grotesque. The burgomaster, whose name Vogel ("bird") might bring a smile to the lips of any German speaker, is his comic foil: he is as formal as the Baron is informal, as conservative as the Baron is outlandish in dress, and equally preoccupied with the comic festival of marriage. Where the comic prevails in *Frankenstein,* the grotesque, although not altogether banished, is subdued. The Baron's dress and his taste in interior decoration (tasseled fez, polka-dotted tie, oversized pipe, baroque chair, the mixture of living and artificial flowers) strike us as at least mildly grotesque, as do the blossoms under glass the Baron presents on the wedding day. But his is the fanciful grotesque of seventeenth-century illustrations. The grotesque is temporarily domesticated by the world of the comic.

Once the father leaves his comfortable sitting room and pounds on the door of the castle laboratory with his walking stick, he seems to carry this comic spirit with him. He mocks the negligence of those in the castle for leaving a burning torch on the floor, he forces Victor to rally his spirits with a fatherly insult, and he declares to Waldman his conviction that the whole situation is "tommyrot." He does not know the gravity of his son's experience—Fritz has just been murdered, the monster subdued with an injection—and he administers brandy and vows to take him home and cure his woes as if he believed he were a modern *deus ex machina*.

The grotesque reasserts itself, however, once the monster murders Waldman and escapes the castle of his birth. He invades the world of the pastoral Maria, inferring by his own macabre, unspoken logic (a logic that fails tragically to distinguish between plant and human) that a girl can be tossed into a lake. (Remarkably, Whale conveys the logic—flower, soft and pretty, floats; girl, soft and pretty; therefore, girl will float—solely through the visuals.) Thereafter, he enters the Baron's castle, until now the stronghold of the comic, and leaves Elizabeth flung across her bed in Fuseli's memorable nightmare pose. Once the monster overpowers Henry, dragging him to the windmill and hurling him from the balcony, the comic spirit seems permanently banished from the tale. This final scene, with its unabashed apocalyptic resolution, is not simply a reassertion of the traditional grotesque of the graveyard where the story began. With its visual allusion to a Cervantic windmill, it is also a subtle infusion of the comical into the ominous, a new intertwining, and as such looks forward to the complex fusion Whale will achieve in *The Bride of Frankenstein*.

In his sequel to *Frankenstein,* Whale initially treats the comic and the grotesque much as he had in the earlier film. Gothic arches, flickering shadows, open fires, ornate furniture, coffin-like bureaus, stone lions, wooden cupids, and flowers in the Frankenstein castle remind us of Henry and his monster's grotesque world even while Henry seems to be integrating himself into a more socially acceptable relationship. Other settings—the cemetery, the crypt, Henry's laboratory, and the cottage of the hermit who befriends the monster—also suggest this strange, alienated world through the distorting diagonals and shadows of wooden beams, iron grilles, statues, skeletons, and scientific apparatus and the unsettling juxtaposition of nature and religion and the worlds of the living and the dead. Only one brief scene involving a shepherdess visually suggests another world, the pastoral world Henry and Elizabeth retreat to in *Frankenstein* for Henry's recovery after his monster kills Fritz. In *The Bride of Frankenstein* this bright idyllic setting is immediately shattered by the monster's intrusion, and we are returned to the dark, deformed world of the grotesque.

Emphasis on an ominous, fragmented world does not prevent Whale from a traditional use of comic relief and he quickly introduces two characters who, as S. S. Prawer would say, "drain off our laughter." As in *Frankenstein,* one of those characters is a good-natured but self-important and patronizing burgomaster; the other is the opinionated, gossipy and excitable Minnie, a servant within the Frankenstein household. The burgomaster ceremoniously dismisses the crowd after the burning of the windmill while reminding the villagers of their good fortune in having him to keep them safe—certainly an ironic reminder, given the mob action leading to the monster's entrapment as well as the audience's anticipation of his reemergence. The burgomaster's age and size compared to the monster's underscore the comic overtones of his claims and reassurances as he wishes the townspeople pleasant dreams, or, in later scenes, unrealistically declares that he is in control.

Minnie is the burgomaster's most vocal challenger, demanding the satisfaction of seeing the monster's roasted remains. Her age seems at odds with her strident and childish petulance. She obstinately stays behind while the burgomaster ushers the other villagers home and is, therefore, one of the first to meet the resurrected monster. She reacts with an unbalancing double-take before running hysterically back to town shouting, "He's alive! The monster is alive!" thus echoing Henry's earlier frenzied exclamation. Though we know she should be believed we are not surprised when Albert the butler dismisses her as an "old fool," her extravagant theatricality provoking laughter as well as easy dismissal. Since she reacts with the exaggeration and abruptness of a mindless marionette, she is difficult to take seriously even when she is responding to a genuine threat. The frilly cap perched precariously atop her head only adds to her comic oddity.

Whale's invitation to laugh at several of his minor characters may not be surprising given the tradition of comic relief within horror works, but what is surprising is the opportunity he gives us to laugh at his monster. We might laugh involuntarily at him in *Frankenstein* because of our unease at seeing such a stiff, mechanical and oversized creature identified with man, but he is so quickly and unjustly thrust into the role of criminal by Waldman and Frankenstein that we tend to view him primarily with sympathy and pity. His attempts to communicate with Henry and Maria evoke the same response. But in *The Bride of Frankenstein,* during the hermit sequence, Whale presents Henry's ungainly creation as laughable as well as sympathetic. Drawn to the hermit's cottage by his music, the monster is apparently so moved by his host's hospitality that he sheds his first tears. The hermit quickly perceives the monster's needs and gives him food, a place to rest, and most importantly, friendship. The monster responds enthusiastically, and given only minimal encouragement and coaching, he attempts his first words. Spoken with great effort by the awkward man-monster-child, the words are at once funny and poignant since he categorizes food, wine, and cigars "good" with as much ardor as he designates the hermit ("friend") "good." While he does so he wolfs his food, gulps his wine, and puffs so energetically on his cigar that, although we acknowledge his growing identification with what is human, we are reminded too of his grotesquerie. When he sits and listens to the hermit play violin, his huge frame dwarfs the stool that supports him and his arms move awkwardly in time to the music.

Although this image is comical, Whale's juxtaposition of

the monster's ugly hulk and visceral reactions with his childlike innocence and his delight in the music elicits more than laughter. Because of the low intelligence of the monster we cannot laugh with him; our laughter is directed at him here, but his importance within the narrative and our sympathy for him make laughter at his expense uncomfortable. Whale's incorporation of religious symbolism further complicates our response. Earlier, when captured by the villagers, the monster was tied to a large pole and dropped onto a wagon, his position as he was raised above the crowd absurdly recalling Christ's crucifixion. In the scene with the hermit, a crucifix is frequently prominent and the hermit repeatedly expresses his gratitude to God for sending him a companion. Whale seems to ask us to take the budding friendship between monster and hermit seriously, while reminding us at the same time of the impossibility of doing so. He tries simultaneously to draw us closer to the monster with his growing capacity and desire for human identification and contact, and to distance us from him by inviting mockery. Since the "comic and the caricatural fringe of the grotesque" to which Whale brings us conflicts with the sympathy and seriousness evoked, we feel disconcerted, unable to juggle our contrary responses.

Ultimately, the monster's identification with human desire and this association with Christian symbolism make him more grotesque. He is physically disproportioned and unnatural, and his growing consciousness and human activity only accentuate the "fusion of realms" he embodies. He becomes more threatening, more estranged, since he fits nowhere within the natural order. His physical abnormality may no longer seem sinister because of our growing familiarity with it and because of the sympathy the monster elicits, but in *The Bride of Frankenstein* the monster is actually more hideously deformed than in *Frankenstein*. The burns he has suffered intensify his monstrosity. When he resurrects himself from the well of the burnt windmill, he immediately kills the first people he sees, a solitary owl the appropriate witness to the ominous events. Later he is captured and shackled to a throne-like chair on a raised platform within the village prison, further isolating him from society. He frees himself through rage and brute strength and resumes his search for a haven, finding it briefly with the hermit. When his bond with the hermit is shattered, the monster aligns himself with the dead and strikes his own fatal bargain with the demonic Praetorius.

Introduced in an early sequence, Praetorius controls the monster and the hero, the events and the unsettling comico-grotesque tone of the *The Bride of Frankenstein*. His first appearance is heralded by an hallucinatory image of death that Elizabeth sees as she tries to dissuade Henry from looking further for the "secret God is so jealous of . . . the secret of eternal life." Praetorius's knock mingles with Elizabeth's hysterical laughter just when she collapses in fear after recounting a dream, a dream so powerful she relives it. She sees "a figure like death . . . reaching out for" Henry and points in the direction from which Praetorius will soon make his entry. She screams, "It's coming for you here! Henry! Henry! Henry." Whale cuts to Praetorius, his dark, sinister figure framed by bare, twisted branches and animated by his wildly blown black

cape, before showing Minnie reluctantly scurrying to the door in answer to his knock. Praetorius's imposing presence and hypnotizing stare gain him entry despite Minnie's protests. As the door opens the doctor's gaunt face with its piercing eyes gradually emerges from the darkness and continues to compel Minnie. Shadows underscore both figures as Praetorius follows the maid to Henry's room. Disregarding Minnie's injunction to remain at the end of the hall, Praetorius instantly appears when Minnie announces him, a huge shadow of his figure and a musical crescendo effectively punctuating his sinister appearance. He promptly apologizes for his intrusion, bows to Elizabeth, and helps Henry complete his introduction by volunteering the information that he "was booted out" of the university for "knowing too much." When Elizabeth reminds him that Henry has been ill and should not be disturbed, Praetorius assures her he is a doctor. Despite their gentility, the exchange presages the opposition between them, an opposition based on Elizabeth's concern for Henry's health and her desire that he return to his traditional role within society and Praetorius's disregard of the established social order.

After effecting Elizabeth's dismissal and ignoring Henry's anguish and anger, Praetorius skillfully rekindles Henry's interest in the act of creation. Praetorius's coolness and persistence in the face of Henry's moral and physical distress, coupled with the rigidity and disdain apparent beneath his barely civil response to Elizabeth, intimate Praetorius's estrangement from society as well as his unswerving determination. The intelligence and calculation with which he pursues his goals make him particularly dangerous, especially since he is not hampered by a conscience. He makes this clear again and again, sometimes with great seriousness, at other times with levity, as when he toasts a "new world of gods and monsters" before taking his homunculi from their coffin-like box and displaying them for Henry.

The viewer is suspended between laughter and alarm as a grim-faced Praetorius opens his miniature coffin and unveils and then wryly introduces his creatures one by one: a king gnawing on a drumstick, a chattering queen, a disgruntled archbishop, a ballerina who dances to Mendelsohn's "Spring Song," a preening mermaid, and a devil with whom Praetorius particularly identifies. Charming as these miniatures may seem, Kayser would quickly remind us that they are all technically grotesques: they break the laws of proportion; they fuse the realms of human and animal, land and sea, life and death; they link together the natural (human body) and the unnatural (existence under glass); and two specifically invoke the demonic, the replica of a Mephistophelean satan and the figure of the king, unmistakably reminiscent of Henry VIII who beheaded his discarded wives.

Frankenstein is properly repelled by Praetorius's show, accusing him of black magic, but the elder scientist is determined to force Henry to see his creations in a more playful light. His introductions are made with aplomb, relish, and wit; and he stresses—indeed, he has himself literally created—the comically infatuated king, the ridiculously disapproving archbishop, and the mundanely conventional mermaid and ballerina. Only in his commentary on the devil do the sinister implications of his experiment begin to surface:

> The next one is the very devil. Very bizarre, this little chap. There's a certain resemblance to me, don't you think? Or do I flatter myself? I took very great pains with him. Sometimes I wonder if life would not be much more amusing if we were all devils and no nonsense about angels and being good.

These darkly satanic reflections are muffled, however, by Whale's deliberate focus on the lovesick mini-king climbing out of his glass enclosure and comically storming the queen's bell jar. When the king is rather unceremoniously picked up by the scruff of his collar and plopped back into his glass cage, the spectator is reminded that all this is Praetorius's show. He is a puppeteer; these are his puppets, as Henry and others will be soon. He is the master artisan and the machinator of these comico-grotesques. They, especially the lovely female creatures, all prefigure the final creation of Praetorius in the film, the bride of the monster: stunning yet repelling in her wooden gestures and expressions and in her electrifying coiffure.

Praetorius again suggests that he and Henry collaborate. They could "leave the charnal house and follow the lead of nature" to create a race. In doing so they would be following the scriptural admonition to "be fruitful and multiply." Praetorius's sophistical advice echoes to some degree Henry's remarks when thinking of his dream to create life: ". . . What a wonderful vision it was. Think of the power—to create man!" The intensity and passion of Henry's articulation bring him to the brink of madness, his mania contrasting dramatically with Praetorius's wry intelligence and humor when speaking of the same desire. Henry's frenzied outburst and his absurd egocentrism, alarming as they are, are ultimately less threatening, less grotesque than Praetorius's because they reflect the seriousness of Henry's presumption and at the same time are readily identified with the ultimately ineffectual ravings of other fictional mad scientists. Praetorius's witty irreverence belies the gravity of his proposal. His casualness in identifying with Satan and death and in asserting his will while nimbly turning scripture to his own use is far more unsettling because of the unexpected mingling of serious matters and cavalier approach.

Praetorius's jocose irreverence is apparent in later scenes, especially when he meets Frankenstein's monster while enjoying a drink and a cigar beside an open coffin in a crypt. Again Whale brings together traditional images of the grotesque: the crypt, coffins, shadows, and dead bodies juxtaposed with religious symbols, the monster, and Praetorius's gallows humor. While the monster hides in the shadows, Praetorius dismisses two murderers hired to help open a coffin and then relaxes as though in the most natural setting. He graces the coffin with candelabra and a skull before unwrapping some food and pouring himself a glass of wine. As he salutes the skull and drinks a toast to "the monster," he laughs the "mocking, cynical . . . involuntary and abysmal laughter" Kayser associates with connoisseurs of the grotesque. If we are appalled by Praetorius's continuing cynical disregard for what society holds sacred, here demonstrated by his studied necrophilia, we nevertheless admire his temerity in greeting the monster when he unexpectedly reveals himself. Soon the two are sharing a smoke while Praetorius amiably and adroitly questions the monster and wins his confidence.

The facility with which Praetorius masters Henry's creature recalls the ease with which he gained entry into Frankenstein's home, secured Elizabeth's dismissal, and aroused Henry's interest in the homunculi. Authoritative and self-assured, Praetorius proceeds with his plan to create a woman, even though Henry is hesitant. With the monster ready to back his genteel requests with force, Praetorius reappears at the Castle Frankenstein and again demands to see Henry alone. He enters on a level above Henry and Elizabeth, asserting himself both through his position and his words. He assumes agreement but is ready for Henry's refusal. Summoning the monster, Praetorius unscrupulously terrorizes Elizabeth and forces Henry to cooperate. When the monster kidnaps Elizabeth, Praetorius leaves no one in doubt about his authority, dramatically smashing a vase to gain attention and then charging Henry's servants "to do nothing and to say nothing of this episode."

Once at work on the second monster, Praetorius, with his cool, dispassionate demeanor, functions on the sidelines and in the background, allowing the more emotional, excitable Henry center stage. Praetorius facilitates Henry's work by sanctioning Ludwig to commit murder in order to provide the fresh heart that Henry needs, by helping to cover up the murder when Henry questions the source of the heart, and by controlling the first monster when he pressures Henry to work harder. Praetorius controls events up to the moment the Frankenstein monster, rejected by his newly fashioned bride, places his hand on the lever through which he subsequently destroys himself, his bride, and Praetorius. Thus Praetorius, master manipulator and appropriator of supernatural powers, inadvertently brings about his own demise.

That Praetorius is destroyed along with the two manmade monsters is fitting, considering his own monstrousness. His demonic coldness isolates him from normal human relationships and from human values and emotions. Beneath his suave, authoritative manner, his precise logic, and his crisp, clever dialogue is "the very devil," a man apparently bent on revenge and self-vindication through the usurpation of godlike power. In blending the comic with the grotesque in the character and creations of Praetorius, Whale challenges viewers with a complex presentation of the serious amid satanic comedy. That blend is potentially far more unsettling than Henry's mad desire; and therefore, what dictates Henry and Elizabeth's escape and Praetorius's and the monsters' deaths may not simply be Hollywood's penchant for a happy ending. With those deaths audiences can relax in the knowledge that the grotesque, with its threatening nihilism and absurdity, is once more contained, while Henry is reclaimed by the community, its traditional values and sense of order intact.

The faces of Henry and Elizabeth as they embrace and watch the castle crumble and burn, however, suggest that theirs is far from a fairy-tale happy ending. They, and the spectator with them, have gazed into the grotesqueries of the human imagination, and have come away from the experience subdued, reflective. Whale exerts himself, particularly in his sequel, to allow the viewer the chance to think repeatedly about the thematic implications of this Shelleyan myth. From the film's prologue, with Mary's assertion that her publishers did not understand the moral of her story, to the monster's words in the laboratory just before he pulls the lever, "You stay. You belong dead . . . ," Whale clearly allegorizes the literal and transforms surface absurdity into serious commentary on human ambition, madness, and modern science. Whale's bold exploitation of the comic and the grotesque deftly guides viewer responses, occasionally allowing for well-directed laughter, more often insisting on revulsion. That the film sports with the myth, then, or seems to, should not mislead us. In doing so, it reaffirms its belief not only in the power of this Promethean myth but also in the capacity of the Gothic mode to communicate that power.

Martin F. Norden   (essay date 1986)

SOURCE: "Sexual References in James Whale's 'Bride of Frankenstein'," in *Eros in the Mind's Eye: Sexuality and the Fantastic in Art and Film,* edited by Donald Palumbo, Greenwood Press, 1986, pp. 141-50.

[*In the following essay, Norden discusses sexual themes and motifs in* Bride of Frankenstein.]

The few critical evaluations of the cult favorite *Bride of Frankenstein* (1935), directed by James Whale, have largely been limited to explorations of the film's horrific and humorous qualities. Critics have commonly observed that *Bride,* an early example of the American horror film, is a worthy successor to the original *Frankenstein* (1931), also directed by Whale. *New York Times* film critic Frank Nugent, one of the earliest to recognize the importance of the film to the genre, termed it "a first-rate horror film" in a 1935 review. *Bride's* reputation as a masterpiece of horror remains undiminished, as is indicated by Michael G. Fitzgerald's late-1970s classification of it as "one of the best films of the genre." The alternative perspective is to examine the film as a parody that satirized the horror genre. As James Curtis notes of *Bride* in his biography of Whale, "Those looking for an exciting, well-paced monster movie are not disappointed. But adults and the more sophisticated can enjoy *Bride* as not so much a horror show as a whimsical fantasy and an exciting piece of cinema. *Bride* is frequently hilariously funny. What distinguishes it from a lot of other such films is that the humor is entirely intentional."

A third, relatively unexplored quality is the film's presentation of sexual issues. This lack of attention is surprising, since *Bride's* status as a cult classic depends in no small way on the sexual themes and motifs that run rampant through it. In addition to offering a depiction of "normal" heterosexual love, the film is replete with veiled references to bisexuality, homosexuality, necrophilia, incest, the Oedipus complex, and the Virgin Birth, and also features a prominent sperm-egg metaphor.

The genesis of *Bride of Frankenstein* is itself a strange story. The original *Frankenstein,* featuring Boris Karloff as the Monster, proved so successful at the box office that Carl Laemmle, Jr., the film's producer, immediately made plans for a sequel. Whale, however, initially wanted nothing to do with the new project, tentatively titled *The Return of Frankenstein.* Said he of Laemmle and producers in general:

> They're always like that. If they score a hit with a picture they always want to do it again. They've got a perfectly sound commercial reason. *Frankenstein* was a gold-mine at the box office, and a sequel is bound to win, however rotten it is. They've had a script made for a sequel, and it stinks to heaven. In any case, I squeezed the idea dry on the original picture, and I never want to work on it again.

Nevertheless, Whale eventually relented and agreed to direct the film. He decided to treat the project as a "hoot," however, and had "no intention of making a straight sequel to *Frankenstein.*"

One of the first tasks facing Whale and scenarists William Hurlbut and John L. Balderston was to build a new story from the literal ashes of *Frankenstein's* conclusion: the Monster's fiery end in an old windmill. Despite the seeming definitiveness of this scene, the filmmakers managed to continue the story in the now-retitled *Bride of Frankenstein* by showing that the Monster (again played by Karloff) had avoided a barbecued fate by falling into the mill's conveniently flooded cellar. The filmmakers gave this explanation more credibility by framing the new film with a short prologue that features *Frankenstein* author Mary Shelley (Elsa Lanchester) weaving a sequel to her famous novel for an enraptured Lord Byron and Percy Bysshe Shelley. The story she spins is indeed bizarre.

As the Monster lays waste to the countryside once again, the loving Elizabeth nurses her fiancé, Baron Henry Frankenstein, back to health from the ravages of his frightening ordeal. Their tender moments are shattered in short order by the arrival of Dr. Pretorius, an eccentric old scientist who, like Frankenstein, engages in grave-robbing to meet an obsessive end: the artificial creation of life. He proposes to Frankenstein that they work together to create a woman, but the younger scientist, still shaken from the heinous results of his previous experiment, will have none of it. Undaunted, Pretorius enlists the aid of the Monster to convince Frankenstein of his proposed project's worthiness. The Monster obliges by abducting Elizabeth and holding her captive until Frankenstein and Pretorius make a woman for him. The scientists eventually create a Monstress (Elsa Lanchester, in a dual role) stitched together from corpse bits and animated by lightning bolts, but the Monstress rejects the Monster and develops an attraction to Dr. Frankenstein. In response to this unanticipated turn of events, a deeply wounded Monster blows the laboratory, himself, the Monstress, and Pretorius to smithereens after allowing Frankenstein and Elizabeth to escape.

With aberrant procreation and "love among the dead" as its main foci, *Bride* cannot help but raise questions concerning sexuality. The answers do not coalesce into any single, neat, unambiguous interpretation, however; though they overlap, they often conflict. Since *Bride's* sexual themes and motifs are considerably varied, they are best discussed in terms of a series of love triangles that structure the film.

Elizabeth, Pretorius, and Henry, who respectively exemplify heterosexuality, homosexuality, and bisexuality, constitute the first love triangle. Without question, the premiere heterosexual in the film is Elizabeth, technically the "Bride" of the title (though there are a number of other contenders for this titular honor). She is engaged to Henry, and her love for him seems genuine if not downright obsessive. Indeed, neither her dogged devotion to the troubled Henry nor her love for him ever wavers. If anything, they grow even stronger when it appears as if the Monster has permanently deferred their wedding by nearly killing Henry on the day it was to have occurred. The filmmakers not only endow Elizabeth with the "mainstream" sexual orientation, but also made her the sanest and least "hung up" of all the characters. Hers is the only voice of reason, of common sense, in the entire film. Indeed, next to such unquestionably fey characters as Henry, Pretorius, their squirrelly grave-robbing assistant Karl, and Henry's paroxysmal housekeeper Minnie, Elizabeth is a bedrock of normalcy. The filmmakers do allow her one flight of fancy, however; on the night of their would-be wedding, she tells Henry with mounting hysteria that she has seen a strange apparition: "It comes, a figure like Death, and each time he comes more clearly . . . nearer. It seems to be reaching out for you, as if it would take you away from me."

Her words are prescient, for within moments her rival for Henry appears at the door. Dr. Pretorius, described by critic Carlos Clarnes as exuding a "waspish effeminacy," represents the homosexual in the love triangle formed by the three principal characters. He is a threat to Elizabeth and Henry's relationship; his attempts to convince Henry to work with him to create artificial life constitute nothing less than a seduction, and threaten to pull the couple apart. Arriving at the Frankenstein manor late at night "on a secret matter of grave importance" (tongue securely in cheek, no doubt), Pretorius tells Henry his business with him is private and insists on their being alone. The first thing Pretorius says to Henry after Elizabeth has withdrawn is, "We must work together" to create new life, but Henry vehemently rejects this proposal. In discussing their past experiments, Pretorius claims he and Henry "have gone too far to stop, nor can it be stopped so easily." After Pretorius tells Henry that he too has created life, Henry suddenly drops his opposition and becomes very interested. That very evening, when Henry and Elizabeth would otherwise have shared their first honeymoon night, Henry and Pretorius run off to the latter's laboratory and leave Elizabeth behind. In a sense, Pretorius is as much a claimant to the title "Bride of Frankenstein" as Elizabeth.

Pretorius needs Henry's assistance to create a new race. He is so desperate to create life—but without female participation—that he has already grown miniature human

beings from seed, beings he eagerly shows to Henry as proof of his "fertility." Pretorius observes to his would-be consort, "My experiments did not turn out quite like yours, Henry, but science, like love, has her little surprises." He invokes the first chapter of Genesis in describing his plan:

> Pretorius: Leave the charnel house and follow the lead of Nature, or of God if you like your Bible stories. "Male and female created he them. Be fruitful and multiply." Create a race, a man-made race, upon the face of the earth. Why not?
>
> Henry: I daren't. I daren't even think of such a thing.
>
> Pretorius: Our mad dream is only half realized. Alone you have created a man. Now, together, we will create his mate.
>
> Henry: (leaning forward): You mean . . . ?
>
> Pretorius: Yes. A woman. That should be really interesting.

Representing the bisexual caught between the advances of Elizabeth and Pretorius, Henry is easily the most troubled of all the characters. He desires a normal relationship with a woman, yet is quite amenable to Pretorius's seductive powers. His resultant behavior—frequent and agonized vacillations between Elizabeth and Pretorius—borders on the schizophrenic. He is secretly relieved that he must work with Pretorius to create a mate for the Monster to save Elizabeth; he is thus able to serve both "brides" simultaneously—while, ironically, creating a third.

A number of critics, most notably Roy Huss, have paid special attention to the pyrotechnics that suffuse the creation scene in *Bride of Frankenstein*. With its rapid editing, dramatic high-contrast lighting, flashing lights, flying sparks, smoke, fire, pulsing buzz of electrical equipment, frequent explosions, and throbbing musical score, the scene unmistakably resembles an extended orgasm. Its climax—lighting striking the inert female body raised on a platform high above the laboratory floor—thus takes on a new meaning; the body, consisting of corpse bits that Henry and Pretorius have stitched together, may be likened to an egg, while the lightning may symbolize the sperm that penetrates it. A line of Karl's dialogue early in the creation scene—"The storm is rising!"—reinforces this association with its suggestion that nature is experiencing a tumescence. Metaphorically, then, the doctors are linked with the female principle, the ovum, while nature, in the form of the lightning, is associated with the male principle, the sperm. Natural and unnatural forces, in the respective forms of lightning and the sutured body, thus combine to create life. It is as if Henry and Pretorius, knowing they cannot between them bring a child into being through sexual union, create instead the female contribution to the embryo-to-be; having thus "ovulated," the doctors then arrange for their egg to be fertilized.

Critics have discovered a number of Christian allegories in *Bride,* most notably in the scene in which the Monster is shackled to a crosslike structure by angry villagers. Conspicuously absent from this discussion is any consideration of the creation of the Monstress, which is a Virgin

Birth. By equating Nature with God, Pretorius invites the film's audience to find in *Bride of Frankenstein* references to the nativity; just as Jesus was born of Mary and God in the form of the Holy Ghost, the Monstress is conceived (and thoroughly maculated) by two human "mothers" and Nature in the form of the lightning. The strange triangle formed by Henry, Pretorius, and Elizabeth is superseded by an even stranger *ménage à trois* consisting of Henry, Pretorius, and a decidedly potent Nature.

A third love triangle, formed by Elizabeth, Henry, and the Monster, resembles nothing so much as a manifestation of the Oedipal complex. Tania Modleski has echoed a number of modern critics in opining that "all traditional narratives re-enact the male Oedipal crisis." While this assertion is no doubt moot, the Oedipal complex does act as a major structuring element in *Bride of Frankenstein*. The Monster's awkward movements and halting speech (he actually learns a few words in this film) reinforce the natural inclination to accept him as Henry's metaphorical child, and his smoldering hatred for Henry suggests he has entered the phallic stage of development. The Monster's feelings toward Henry, his clear father figure, contrast sharply with his feelings toward many others in the film. Despite the townspeople's xenophobia, the Monster craves friendship and eagerly seeks it in almost every individual he meets: a blind hermit, Pretorius, the Monstress. "Alone—bad. Friend—good!" he rumbles at one point. In a most pathetic scene, he ironically queries "Friend?" of a beautiful female corpse he has stumbled upon inside a crypt. Yet he immediately grows sullen when his newfound friend Pretorius asks him if he knows Henry. Bitterly, he responds, "Yes, I know. Made me, from dead. I love dead. Hate living." The Monster has his gentle moments in this film, but virtually all his scenes with Henry are marked by expressions of enmity that range from glowering at the mere thought of his "father," to ordering the poor scientist about, to threatening him with violence. In a distinctly Oedipal act of hostility, the Monster abducts Elizabeth and holds her captive in a cave while Henry and Pretorius work together to create his mate. The Monster's demand for a wife represents a possible resolution of his Oedipal crisis. He definitively resolves it at the end of the film in telling Henry to go back to Elizabeth before obliterating himself, Pretorius, and the Monstress.

The Monster, the Monstress, and Henry form a tenuous love triangle that hinges on one of the movie's ambiguities: the real identity of the "Bride of Frankenstein." The official title of the film, *Bride of Frankenstein* (not *The Bride of Frankenstein,* as some sources list it), underscores this uncertainty. The absence of the definite article suggests the possibility of more than one bride: Elizabeth, Pretorius, even the Monstress. The Monstress would not normally be listed among Henry's potential mates were it not for a conspicuous deletion from the screenplay and a troublesome line of dialogue that is retained. The script originally called for Karl to murder Elizabeth and bring her body back to the laboratory after the doctors summon him to find a fresh female corpse. Had this scene been included in the final film, two contenders for the title role would have been combined into one.

The troublesome line of dialogue occurs immediately after the Monstress is brought to life and unveiled; Pretorius delightedly proclaims her "the Bride of Frankenstein" as a wedding-bell motif plays in the background. Over the years, audiences have associated the name "Frankenstein" with the Monster, but it actually refers only to Henry Frankenstein, the hapless young doctor played in the movies by Colin Clive. Throughout both *Frankenstein* and *Bride of Frankenstein,* the filmmakers scrupulously adhered to the correct usage, with this one possible exception. If it is not a mistake, then Pretorius may view the new creature as Henry's bride, not the Monster's, and thus suggest a symbolically incestuous relationship, as Henry is a parental figure for her just as he is for the original Monster. This potential relationship is suggested further by the fact that the Monstress, after registering her disgust for the Monster with an ear-splitting shriek, is unmistakably drawn to her creator. Protective of her new "mate," she even shields Henry with her body from the others in the room. The movie in any case suggests an incestuous relationship between the Monstress and the Monster, Henry's other metaphorical offspring whose "sister"—or, perhaps, "half sister," considering Pretorius' involvement—humiliatingly rebuffs his romantic advances.

Incest is only one of several dark aspects of human sexuality suggested by the Monster/Monstress/Henry triangle; necrophilia is another. If this term refers not only to an erotic attraction to corpses but also to an abnormal fascination with the dead in general, then *Bride of Frankenstein* is a veritable necrophilic love-in. The Monster's utterance, "I love dead," is only the most overt of the many references to a necrophilic fascination lurking at the heart of this film, which is based on the bizarre premise that two entities constructed from pieces of previously dead bodies are about to be united in holy matrimony. Universal was quick to exploit this grotesque "love story" angle—and at the same time to satirize the conventional Hollywood love story—in its promotion of the film, which featured images of the Karloff and Lanchester characters gazing tenderly into each other's eyes. The interests of the scientists and their body-snatching helpers, particularly as revealed in the grave-robbing scene, further illustrate the film's flirtation with necrophilia. When Pretorius and his assistants come across the remains of a young woman in a crypt, Karl remarks, "Pretty little thing in her way, wasn't she?" Pretorius responds, "I hope her bones are firm." Later, Pretorius is enjoying a candlelight dinner in the crypt, his only "companion" the skeletal detritus of a woman, when the Monster interrupts him (or them, perhaps). Hinting at a fifth love triangle (Pretorius/Monstress-to-be/Monster), the scene concludes with a reiteration of the movie's aberrant love theme; after Pretorius promises that a woman will be made for him, the Monster gently examines the disconnected skull of his "betrothed" and slowly intones, "Woman, friend, wife."

In summation, the many sexual references in *Bride of Frankenstein* may be seen as elaborations of several love triangles: Pretorius/Henry/Elizabeth, who represent hetero-, homo-, and bisexuality; Pretorius/Henry/ Nature, through which the mystery of conception takes on a preternatural, mock-religious quality; Henry/

Elizabeth/Monster, which embodies the Oedipal triangle; and Henry/Monstress/Monster and Pretorius/Monstress-to-be/Monster, which reverberate with the unsavory suggestions of incest and necrophilia. With Henry a conspicuous component of each *ménage à trois* save the last, the film might well have been subtitled "The Many Loves of Henry Frankenstein." More importantly, *Bride* has taken such archetypal subject matter as the mysteries of birth, death, sexuality, love, marriage, and religion, turned them upside down, turned them inside out, and intermingled them in such unexpected ways as to subvert or defile them all.

The most disturbing aspect of *Bride of Frankenstein* is its understated degradation of women and indictment of their role in reproduction. Ordinarily, of course, men cannot give birth, yet they manage to do so (albeit with disastrous results) in this film. Moreover, the scientists seem shockingly unconcerned when they sense that Karl, whom they have commissioned to retrieve the body of a recently deceased young female, plans to commit murder; when Henry feebly notes that "There are always accidental deaths occurring," Pretorius replies laconically, "Always." Mesmerized by the promises of a huge reward, Karl does murder an anonymous young woman, an act only one step removed from the filmmakers' original plan to have him kill Elizabeth. There is also the bondage imagery associated with the Monstress, whom the doctors initially immobilize with metal bonds and the bandages that cover her, mummylike, from head to foot. Even after she is free of these restraints, she remains figuratively (and sometimes literally) in the grip of the scientists. And while Elizabeth is the most sympathetically treated of the female characters, she too is victimized by men; most notably, she is abducted and held hostage by the Monster. On a more subtle level, she lacks any "personhood" apart from her relationship to Henry; her identity is presented solely in terms of the man to whom she is engaged. Her background, her interests apart from Henry, even her prenuptial surname remain enigmatic.

Since Whale was a known homosexual, one might assume that his sexual preference contributed to some extent to the aura of misogyny that lurks beneath the humor and horror of the film, although no particularly dark or bitter tone tinges its superficial depiction of women. The film's many sexual references, quirky humor, and overall kinkiness may have been responsible for its initially limited appeal to the moviegoing public. As Curtis has suggested, "The problem with the film was that it was a little too much toward Whale's own peculiar tastes to relate fully to the mass audiences of the period." These same qualities, however, enabled Whale to give birth to something significantly his own: one of the film world's first camp classics.

Dennis Fischer (essay date 1991)

SOURCE: "James Whale (1889-1957)," in *Horror Film Directors, 1931-1990,* McFarland & Company, Inc., 1991, pp. 710-35.

[*In the following essay, Fischer provides a survey of Whale's career, focusing on his horror films.*]

Although James Whale is best known for his four famous horror features—films which practically defined the genre for several decades—he was a talented and versatile director who worked with many genres. In fact, before embarking on his horror period, he had been typed as a director of war films due to his work on *Hell's Angels, Journey's End* and *Waterloo Bridge.* While they do not fall within the scope of this work, these films are noteworthy along with *One More River,* an adaptation of John Galsworthy's last novel about an overbearing husband (Colin Clive in his fourth great performance for Whale) who accuses his wife (Diana Wynyard) of having an affair; the 1936 (and best) version of *Show Boat,* the Jerome Kern-Oscar Hammerstein musical with a magnificent performance by the great Paul Robeson; the overlooked gem *The Great Garrick* in which a French acting troupe, having heard that the famous English actor David Garrick (Brian Aherne) has boasted of the superiority of English actors to French, decides to pull a hoax on the egotistical thespian by impersonating the inhabitants of an inn along Garrick's way; and the highly entertaining swashbuckler *The Man in the Iron Mask* based on Alexandre Dumas' classic novel. These films demonstrate that Whale was one of the most talented directors in the Hollywood of the '30s and is long overdue for a major reevaluation.

However, Whale was initially ignored by auteur-ist critics for much the same reasons that John Huston was. Rather than concentrating over and over again on a particular theme or type of story, Whale dedicated his skills to bringing the best he could out of various literary and stage properties which he selected with care. At the height of his films' popularity, Whale was considered the top director at Universal Studios and had a good deal of power. Unfortunately for his career, he was also a homosexual when such behavior was not socially acceptable and his parties were considered minor scandals. When the box office takes of his films declined, he was virtually shut out of the film industry, and his last film, *Hello Out There,* a 41-minute adaptation of William Saroyan's play, was never released. (It might have been intended to be combined with the two other shorts that comprised the Huntington Hartford production *Face to Face.* For the record, that film contained an adaptation of Joseph Conrad's "The Secret Sharer" by the talented John Brahm and a memorable version of "The Bride Comes to Yellow Sky" by Stephen Crane directed by Bretaigne Windust.)

Whale was born in the English Midlands on July 22, 1889, to relatively poor parents. He disdained the idea of a life of manual labor and delighted in drawing and painting. After the outbreak of World War I, he was a volunteer and enrolled in the Cadet Corps to become an officer. Commissioned a second lieutenant, he fought in France and was captured by the Germans in Belgium. To keep himself occupied, he drew and he also organized a theatrical company.

While in a POW camp, Whale gambled a lot with young men from wealthy families, winning checks and promissory notes by wagering nonexistent wealth. After the war was over, he quickly returned to England and cashed the checks before payment could be stopped and proceeded to get a job as a staff cartoonist with *The Bystander*. Now solvent, Whale devoted more time to theater, occasionally undertaking to perform spear-carrier roles. It was while performing in Shakespeare's *The Merry Wives of Windsor* that Whale first met Ernest Thesiger, who would perform so memorably for him in **The Old Dark House** and **The Bride of Frankenstein**. When working on *The Insect Play*, he met Elsa Lanchester, who was to be the title character in **Bride** as well as Mary Shelley, while she was making her stage debut.

Working in English theater, Whale became more and more involved in designing the scenery for various productions. Reportedly, Whale was very conscious of his lower class accent at the time and worked very hard to eradicate it, developing the manners and speech of a gentleman. Whale also began taking larger acting roles in Oxford and London, managing to make a decent living for himself on the stage. By about 1927, Whale started actively seeking directing assignments, having gained skill and confidence from performing and designing other shows as well as assisting various directors. Whale finally landed a chance to act in and direct the Spanish play *Fortunato* by Serafin and Joaquin Alvarez Quintero. However, Whale suffered a blow to his ego when Harley Granville-Barker, the translator of the play, came in and removed Whale from the lead and changed around much of the staging.

Fortunato, cobilled with *The Lady from Alfaqueque*, was not a great success, nor was the next play Whale directed, *The Dreamers*, which Whale directed while concurrently appearing in another play. However, the next production offered him was ideally suited to the World War I veteran and proved his big chance, R. C. Sheriff's *Journey End*.

Journey's End is a play about the difficulties and pressures of living in the trenches in World War I. It centers around the character of Captain Stanhope, an alcoholic commander whose best friend is Lt. Osborne. When Second Lt. Raleigh, an old school chum, arrives, it throws Stanhope into a tizzy because it reminds him that he has fallen short of his own dreams of glory and he fears that Raleigh will report his inadequacies back to the woman he loves— Raleigh's sister. The original play production starred a then unknown Laurence Olivier as Stanhope with Maurice Evans as Raleigh and George Zucco as Osborne, Stanhope's good friend who dies on the battlefield.

Olivier only stayed with the production for its initial test dates and then landed a part in *Beau Geste* and left the play. Whale and Sheriff, who worked together on the final version of the script in an effort to keep it from getting too sentimental, decided to take a chance on another unknown, Colin Clive, despite Clive's initially bad audition and rehearsals. Clive carried with him the right ragged and agonized air that they wanted Stanhope to have, and after getting over his case of nerves with a stiff drink, Clive proved that their instincts were right.

Despite the fact that plays about the wars were considered uncommercial, Whale and Sheriff were able to find a backer for a longer production. The play connected with both audiences and critics and enjoyed a spectacular run. A deal was cut to take the play to Broadway where it enjoyed a similar success, despite fears that it might be considered too British. Film rights to the play were purchased by two small British companies as a joint venture; however, talkies had just come in and neither company had the facilities for making a sound picture. A deal was cut in America with the small independent company Tiffany-Stahl to produce the film and distribute it in the United States.

Whale's associates stuck up for him as the only man who should be allowed to direct **Journey's End**. Whale was taken out to Paramount to see how picturemaking was done and received his first screen credit as "Dialogue Director" on the Richard Dix vehicle *The Love Doctor*. While he was out there, his name was brought to the attention of Howard Hughes as a hot, new British director.

Hughes had sunk over $600,000 of his money into making a silent picture called *Hell's Angels* about World War I flying aces. Unfortunately, despite some highly impressive aerial photography directed by Hughes, the film was considered unreleaseable. Hughes hit on the plan of scrapping the ground footage and shooting a new story incorporating the aerial footage which would be dubbed for sound. Though he took full directing credit himself, Hughes hired Whale to direct these ground scenes concocted by writer Joseph March.

This erratic and fragmented footage unfortunately remained dull and Whale found the eccentric Hughes a trial to work for, though Hughes was pleased enough with Whale's work to give him a $5,000 bonus. The Whale footage is notable for the screen debut of Jean Harlow and for the snappy and quick way many of the scenes are edited. Whale wanted to go for naturalism and not waste a moment in establishing the point of a scene, which ran contrary to the more theatrical sense of most '30s directors. One brief scene consists of nothing more than Roy running in to tell his best friend, "I've enlisted, Monte— Royal Flying Corps!" To which Monte curtly replies, "You're a fool, Roy." Snap, end of scene, personalities established, emotional point made, on to the next scene. As Paul Jensen puts it in *Film Comment:*

> In this fashion Whale goes to the heart of a narrative without wasting time or space. And yet, this ability is combined with his obvious pleasure in a leisurely pace, and a fondness for observing the small details of person and place that might not be needed to tell a story, but which do give social and psychological texture to it. By saving time on the narrative, Whale is able to provide these "extras" while still making an efficient, short film that encompasses a great deal of character interaction.

Far more significant than Hell's Angels was the film version of **Journey's End**. While nowhere as well known as *The Big Parade* or *All Quiet on the Western Front,* I believe **Journey's End** has dated better and stands up today as the best World War I film ever (with the exception of Kubrick's *Paths of Glory* which was filmed much later). Unfortunately, coming from a small company, the film did not get a big push. It came out the same month as *All Quiet on the Western Front,* which went on to win the Best Picture Oscar, and was left forgotten in its wake. Nowadays it is seldom revived and a hard film to get to see, but well worth the effort for Clive's magnificent performance and for the feelings of pressure and despair that Whale brings to bear on these characters, most of them trapped in a war they no longer wish to fight.

Whale returned to England to direct more plays while Tiffany hoped to get him involved on another project, but soon the studio was dead. Meanwhile, Carl Laemmle, Jr., had bought the rights to a Robert Sherwood play, *Waterloo Bridge,* about how a chance encounter between a soldier and a prostitute develops into a failed relationship, each going to his separate fate. Laemmel wanted John Stahl, who was busy, but was persuaded to talk with Whale and the two hit it off well. Whale was still under contract for two pictures to Tiffany, but when he threatened to sue them for additional post-production time on *Journey's End* for which he had not been paid, they agreed to let him go.

Waterloo Bridge was not as good as *Journey's End,* but it did make some improvements on the Sherwood play. Its reputation has been eclipsed by the more frequently seen Mervyn LeRoy version (1940) in which the prostitute was changed to a ballet dancer when Vivien Leigh took the lead. Bette Davis, under contract to Universal, had a small part in *Waterloo Bridge* and was considered to play the female lead in Whale's next production, *Frankenstein,* but was passed over in favor of *Waterloo Bridge*'s star, Mae Clarke. *Bridge* also united Whale with Arthur Edeson as cinematographer, Clarence Kolster as editor, and Joe McDonough as assistant editor, and Whale took these people with him to work on *Frankenstein.*

There can be no question that the original *Frankenstein* is one of the most important horror films ever made and was for its time a fantastic success. The director Robert Florey remained bitter for the rest of his life that the project was taken away from him . . . , but I'm convinced that Whale's peculiar touches were what made the film as great as it is. This is not to downplay the superb performance of Boris Karloff which made that actor's career, but that performance would not have existed had not Whale decided to give the Monster a personality, one that suggests an innocent alternately hurt by and attacking a cruel, uncaring world.

The simple idea of providing the character with pathos and sympathy was somehow overlooked by many of the film's imitators who often would treat their Frankensteinian creations as unreasoning brutes, and the difference is enormous. But there are other touches as well that make Whale's film particularly memorable.

Universal got interested in the property when they purchased the rights to the Peggy Webling stage adaptation of Mary Shelley's classic novel (the novel itself was in the public domain, but there is no evidence that anyone went back to consult it). The play switched the monster creator's name, Victor Frankenstein, with the name of his best friend, Henry, and the film does likewise. The play had been performed in Great Britain, along with Dracula, which Universal had had a success with, but was never performed in the United States. Screenwriter John Balder-

ston managed to sell an adaptation of the play and rights for $20,000 plus 1 percent of the gross of the film. A number of different hands labored on different screenplays with Robert Florey conceiving of the criminal brain episode and the burning windmill at the end. Garrett Fort came up with Frankenstein being thrown off the windmill. When Florey was forced off the project, Francis Edward Faragoh took over as Fort's collaborator. Faragoh, who had written *Little Caesar,* changed Fritz from a mute into a character with dialogue, and Frankenstein's laboratory was switched from an old windmill to an old watchtower. (However, in a continuity gaffe, there is still a scene in the film where Baron Frankenstein, Henry Frankenstein's father, wonders what his son is doing messing around in an old windmill when he has a pretty fiancée.)

Obvious cinematic influences on the film include *The Magician,* the 1926 Rex Ingram film, and *The Cabinet of Dr. Caligari,* a film that Whale specifically sought out. *The Magician* contained a similar tower and also involved the creation of human life by lightning by a sorceror and his dwarfish assistant. *The Cabinet of Dr. Caligari* has an abduction scene similar to the one in which the monster attacks Elizabeth and then leaves her behind, plus the film has a toned-down expressionistic look.

Colin Clive's angular face was particularly exploited to give the film some expressionist shots. Universal originally considered the low-key Leslie Howard for the role, but Whale insisted on and got Clive, who was equally good projecting warmth and hysteria. Clive's performance as Frankenstein is one of the anchors of the film, suggesting an intelligent man who is frantically driving himself to the breaking point in the search for his ideal. It is significant that both he and his creation remain sympathetic throughout the course of the film.

After seeing Boris Karloff in Howard Hawks' *The Criminal Code,* David Lewis suggested that Whale check the actor out for the part of the Monster. In the Hawks film, Karloff plays a kind of angel of death who stalks and kills a prison stoolie with the kind of silent menace and power that Whale was looking for in his Monster. Karloff was on the Universal lot working on *Graft* when he was approached by Whale in the studio commissary. Karloff gave interviews saying that he worked as a truck driver when he was not working as an actor, and so some publicity was released which suggested that Whale cast Karloff after seeing him as a truck driver, but this is pure fiction. Karloff had been acting in films since 1919, mostly in bit roles.

Of course, a key part of making the Frankenstein Monster the unforgettable horror icon that it is the makeup of Jack Pierce. In preparing for the film, a number of sketches of what the Monster should look like were prepared, but none of them resemble the final result. Pierce worked for some time with Karloff on a way to best accentuate his features while allowing the highest latitude of expressions and emotions. The result is a far cry from the rubber-and-latex monsters of later, more technically advanced pictures, evincing the painstaking care that Pierce put into his work. Making Karloff up was a daily four-hour task.

In a rare interview with the *New York Times* around the time of making *Son of Frankenstein* (Rowland Lee, 1939), Pierce explained his design:

> My anatomical studies taught me that there are six ways a surgeon can cut the skull in order to take out or put in a brain. I figured Frankenstein, who was a scientist but no practical surgeon, would take the simplest surgical way. We would cut the top of the skull off straight across like a pot-lid, hinge it, pop the brain in and then clamp it on tight. That is the reason I decided to make the Monster's head square and flat like a shoe box and dig that big scar across his forehead with the metal clamps holding it together. . . .
>
> Here's another thing. I read that the Egyptians used to bindsome criminals hand and foot and bury them alive. When their blood turned to water after death, it flowed to their extremities, stretched their arms to gorilla length and swelled their hands, feet and faces to abnormal proportions. I thought this would make a nice touch for the Monster, since he was supposed to be made from the corpses of executed felons. So I fixed Karloff up that way. Those lizard eyes of his are rubber, like his false head, I made his arms look longer by shortening the sleeves of his coat, stiffened his legs with two pairs of pants over steel struts.

A blue-green greasepaint was applied so that the Monster would have a deathly gray pallor, with black shoe polish applied to its nails to further the impression of something dead. The shambling walk was necessitated by a pair of asphalt spreader's boots which weighed a total of 25 pounds. Pierce inserted bolts into the sides of the neck to further suggest the Monster's electrical origin. The whole thing weighed a staggering 48 pounds, and under hot studio lights, it is not hard to imagine the suffering Karloff put in for his art. Karloff claimed he requested mortician's wax on the Monster's eyelids because otherwise he looked too aware and awake, while what they wanted was a puzzled and confused creature.

Like many early '30s films, *Frankenstein* has no underscoring music, just a strange "mysterioso" theme (composed by David Broekman) under the odd opening credits which show a face and a swirl of staring eyes in the background. There is no other music until the closing credits. An added measure of suspense was built up by not listing Karloff in the opening credits, which read "The Monster?" However, Karloff 's name does appear in the closing credits and on the film's poster.

Whale sets the mood right off with a clanking bell accompanying a funeral that Frankenstein and his hunchbacked assistant, Fritz (a memorably wigged-out performance from Dwight Frye), are observing. The story wastes no time in getting under way, but Whale still takes time out for the quick character bits which help distinguish his work. Though afraid, Fritz does his master's bidding, whether it is cutting down hanged men or ascending the laboratory's electrical equipment in a storm. When Victor, his fiancée, and Dr. Waldman show up, Fritz is dispatched to get rid of them. His hobbling gait down the steps, sup-

ported by a too-small cane, encapsules his pathetic nature, and he seems to delight in having the power to turn the visitors away. However, his frailty is instantly suggested as he stops while returning up the stairs to pull up his garterless socks.

Fritz does not get much screen time, being the Monster's first victim, but in a very short amount of time his character has been established. We understand why he sadistically delights in torturing the Monster with a whip or a flaming torch, finally having found a creature more pathetic than himself. When Frankenstein sets up the creation scene, he says, "Quite a good scene, isn't it? One man, crazy; three very sane spectators," omitting reference to Fritz, also present, entirely. In Frankenstein's view of things, Fritz simply does not count, and Fritz longs to assert himself, though he is so nervous that a simple gong sound causes him to drop the normal brain he originally snatched from Waldman's laboratory.

Some people have criticized the fact that the Monster is given a criminal brain, explaining his propensity towards rage, violence, and murder, and that Frankenstein does not recognize that Fritz has given him an abnormal brain. However, what if the brilliant Dr. Waldman's theory about criminal brains is just so much poppycock? There is little medically to support it, nor does the film itself support that as the reason for the Monster's actions, giving him different motivations. It could be considered a device to build up dread in the audience and yet another example of Waldman being wrong. (Waldman is also incorrect about Frankenstein's ambition, thinking Henry wanted to murder people and then revive them, and ignorant of the secret light "above ultraviolet" that Frankenstein has discovered.)

The creation scene shows that Whale had a clear understanding of showmanship. Paul Jensen quotes Whale in his *Film Comment* article:

> [Frankenstein] deliberately tells his plan of action. By this time the audience [in the laboratory and in the movie theatre] must at least believe something is going to happen; it might be disaster, but at least they will settle down to see the show. Frankenstein puts the spectators in their position, he gives final orders to Fritz, he turns levers and sends the diabolic machine soaring upward to the roof, into the storm. He is now in a state of feverish excitement calculated to carry both the spectators in the windmill and the spectators in the theatre with him.

Thus economically Whale sets up the required exposition and builds interest in what is happening in the scene. Adding to the interest are Herman Rosse's set designs and Kenneth Strickfaden's odd electrical devices which arc, clack and spark all over the lab. (These devices were put in storage and successfully rescued for the film *Young Frankenstein,* Mel Brooks' loving tribute to the series and his funniest and most artistically successful film.) There is even a parallel setup, with Henry commanding Victor to sit down several times, just as he will later do to the Monster. Throughout the scene he is in command and commands our attention until the final discovery where the Monster's hand moves and he ecstatically proclaims it alive.

It is at this point that one of the most famous excisions from *Frankenstein* was made. Originally, after Henry shouted "It's alive!" several times, Victor responded, "Henry, in the name of God!" However, this was later considered too blasphemous as Hollywood tightened its moral code in the mid-'30s and so was replaced by an obvious jumpcut with the sound being covered over by a peal of thunder just as the scene fades out and Henry collapses.

Some have criticized that the moving hand does not make much of a climax to the scene, but the focus here is on Frankenstein's reactions, not the Monster. Certainly, there have been enough subsequent movies where the Monster gets off the slab to show that perhaps Whale was right in not showing this action, just as Browning did not show Dracula leaving his coffin. Instead, the Monster's entrance is given a beautiful buildup and development.

But first there is an excellent scene where Henry, talking to Dr. Waldman (Edward Van Sloan), is questioned about doing something so dangerous and explains what it is that drives him: "Dangerous? Poor old Waldman! Have you never wanted to do anything that was dangerous? Have you never wanted to look beyond the cloud and stars, or to know what causes the trees to bud and what changes the darkness into light? But if you talk like that, people call you crazy. Well, if I could discover just one of these things—what eternity is, for example—I wouldn't care if they did think I was crazy." Clive's quiet delivery of this scene is a marked contrast to the frenzy of his previous one. Suddenly Frankenstein is not a mad scientist, but a fevered seeker of knowledge revealing both his motivations and his human side.

The Monster too is portrayed as a seeker of knowledge, symbolized by light, which is cruelly denied him by his creator. Whale builds the Monster's entrance beautifully, beginning with shambling footsteps, a slowly turning dark figure in a doorway, and a series of increasingly closer shock cuts to Karloff's face. This is simply one of the loveliest scenes in the film.

Frankenstein explains that his creation has been kept in darkness. By a commanding tone and gestures, he makes clear to the Monster that he wants it to sit down, which it does. Frankenstein then pulls open a skylight, revealing light to the Monster for the first time. We see the character as a total innocent, a tabula rasa on which anything can be written. The Monster slowly stands up and reaches out, trying to touch the light. When Frankenstein arbitrarily shuts it out again, the Monster's face conveys a questioning and pleading expression. He reaches out to his creator for understanding. It is clear that the Monster is a child in a man's body.

And like a child, it learns from the environment around it. When Fritz carelessly arrives and sends his torch in the Monster's direction, we see it experiencing unwarranted cruelty. Fritz then torments it whenever Frankenstein, now disappointed in his creation, keeps himself occupied elsewhere. In retaliation, the Monster hangs his tormentor, earning a death sentence from Dr. Waldman. Fran-

kenstein and Waldman successfully drug the uncomprehending creature, but it wakes up as Waldman is about to dissect it, strangling the good surgeon and achieving his freedom.

Whale effectively contrasts the village of Goldstadt celebrating the coming nuptials of Victor and Elizabeth with the later scenes of the angry mob pouring through the village (a set that remained standing from *All Quiet on the Western Front*) in search of the Monster. For years, fans have sought the missing footage of Frankenstein tossing the little girl into the pond after he runs out of flowers to throw, and recently MCA has released some videocassettes and discs with the long-sought footage. Despite Karloff's expressed misgivings, the scene remains a touching one.

In it we see two innocents meeting. The child is not afraid of the Monster and immediately treats him as a playmate, evoking a smile on the Monster's visage. However, only moments after discovering joy, the Monster experiences loss when he tosses his newfound friend into the water and she unexpectedly drowns. We see that the event at first perplexes the Monster—he slaps at the water as if scolding it or summoning his playmate back, and as the realization dawns on him, he leaves the scene emotionally devastated.

However, with the last part of this scene cut, there is the unwanted suggestion that the Monster molested the child when we see her father carrying her drowned body through the midst of the village celebration.

Regarding the classic scene where the Monster starts to abduct Elizabeth on her wedding night, Mae Clarke told me the following story:

> I . . . had known Boris because we'd all been together, more or less, like a play, rehearsing and meeting each other and becoming familiar with each other. Mr. Whale managed all of this in his own wonderful way, so that we all knew each other almost like a family excepting it wasn't a gooey family, it was a professional understanding of each other's motivations, etc. So we had a very pleasant association that way.

> When it came to the day . . . I'd been watching as we all had—taken little trips down to see how Jack Pierce was creating this marvelous make-up, and they spent hours and hours and weeks. They spent hours doing it every day; in getting it created, they worked for many hours, and we'd all go down and watch the progression, so I should have been familiar with it. I knew that it was gray, and I knew that this went on, and then the hat, which was his head—there was this hat like a pillbox with hair coming down, and then his knob things which they pasted on, well, I knew they weren't coming through his neck. I knew all these things. I knew this enormous thing in the corner was what he would put his arms into . . . and these enormous shoes that not only added to his height but were so heavy he could lean his weight against them, you see, because he always walked forward.

> So when the day came for the scene and I knew he was going to come in that window, we didn't

have a playing scene, but I saw a visual effect of him coming in through the window. I said, "Boris, I can't do it. I'm not going to be able to control myself. When you're that far away, I know it's the Monster, I don't know it's you." He said, "I'll tell you what I'll do. You know the camera will be over there, I'll be coming in there, and you're standing here. My left hand is my up-camera hand, and I'll just take my little finger and wiggle it, so when you turn and see me coming, don't look at me at all. Just look right for my hand, and when you see that wiggling, I just hope you don't laugh." And that's what happened. I remember it distinctly. Here's this incongruous little finger going, and there's this whole body and head and everything else. I nearly laughed.

The mountain chase and windmill fight proved less happy occasions. Carrying Clive up the hill and through the windmill several times resulted in a painful back injury for Karloff, while the increasing aggressiveness that Whale asked for in their fight scene resulted in Clive dislocating his shoulder. The film was budgeted for $262,000 and given a 30-day shooting schedule, but it went five days and $30,000 over budget.

For the time period, it was an adequate budget but not an overly large one. Whale seems to have liked the control he could get in a studio and filmed many of the outdoor locations on a stage. He was also fond of vistas where the horizon disappears quickly as if the participants in the scene were framed on on the top of the hilltop. This can be seen in the opening funeral scene and the later mountain chase scenes, including some scenes where the background is particularly phony, and appeared in some of Whale's other films as well.

One final peculiarity about the film is that it was originally intended that the Monster and his creator both be destroyed at the end, but Frankenstein was given a last-second reprieve after a disastrous preview that alarmed Universal executives with a large number of walk-outs. Throughout the film, Victor is set up in traditional Hollywood fashion to take Henry's place with Elizabeth after Henry's death, and Henry even gives a speech to that effect before undertaking his pursuit of the monster in the mountains. However, after he is thrown off the windmill, a voice was dubbed in saying, "He's alive," just before the burgomaster calls his name, gets no response, and says, "Take him to the village." Finally, a scene was tacked on with Baron Frankenstein drinking a toast outside his son's sickroom to "a son to the house of Frankenstein."

Additionally, Edward Van Sloan, who played Dr. Waldman, was recalled to provide a curtain speech at the start of the film warning the audience that the subsequent film would thrill, might shock, and might even horrify them. The advertisements played up how horrifying the film was, unlike *Dracula*, which promoted itself as a "strange love story." This led to even greater receipts than the Browning film and so a new sound genre was born: the horror film.

Whale was quickly assigned to a floundering comedy, *The Impatient Maiden*, which he directed in a perfunctory

manner and which has become deservedly obscure. Meanwhile, Whale developed an interest in J.B. Priestley's short novel *Benighted*, which was titled **The Old Dark House** in America. Universal acquired it for him while assigning him to tackle Eric Remarque's sequel to *All Quiet on the Western Front*, **The Road Back**. Benn Levy was assigned to write the script for **The Old Dark House**.

The Old Dark House is an odd film in many respects. The Priestley novel was largely an allegory about the precarious position of post-war England with disillusionment running rampant. The character of Roger Penderel (played by Melvyn Douglas) has been battered by the war but puts on a cheerful facade. He cannot see much point in doing anything until he falls in love with Gladys Du-Cane (nee Perkins, played by Lillian Bond), an inebriated chorus girl who is the weekend companion of Sir William Porterhouse (Charles Laughton in his first American film performance). Porterhouse is a hard-working industrialist who is driven to destroy his competitors and earn money after his late wife died of a broken heart when society had snubbed them for being too poor.

Much of this introspection remains in the film, but mostly it concentrates on the eccentric characters and a kind of black comedy. The story is also a parody of a series of Broadway mystery plays in which characters would enter an old dark house on a rainy night and find a family full of murderers and dark secrets. Despite the horror scene setting, **The Old Dark House** is a film where something keeps threatening to happen but very little does.

The film begins with Penderel riding with Mr. and Mrs. Waverton (Raymond Massey and Gloria Stuart), who are lost in the Welsh countryside during a storm. They trade amusing banter and seek shelter in a convenient nearby mansion belonging to the Femm family. They are met at the door by Morgan (Boris Karloff), the family's mad mute butler, who growls at them and lets them in.

After achieving stardom with *Frankenstein*, Karloff was used as a major draw by Universal, though he has one of the least interesting characters in this film and is primarily used to provide the few action scenes that exist. Because his makeup here is so different from the one in *Frankenstein*, a prefatory note assures the audience that the Karloff in the film is the same one who "played the mechanical monster in *Frankenstein*."

The real star of the film is Ernest Thesiger, whom Whale had specially imported from England to perform the role of Horace Femm. Horace is a delightfully eccentric character who is at once civilized, fearful, greedy, haughty, and pathetic. His hatred for his sister Rebecca (Eva Moore) is peculiarly established in one of Whale's most offbeat touches. Horace picks up a bouquet of flowers, says, "My sister was on the point of arranging these flowers," and then unceremoniously dumps them on top of the fire in the fireplace.

Rebecca proves a little deaf, chanting over and over again that there are no beds available for the guests to sleep in. She is a religious fanatic and head of the household; it is apparent that Femm is afraid of her. One of the most effective scenes in the film has Rebecca describing the family history to Mrs. Waverton in her bedroom, talking about her late sister's screams while being oddly reflected in a distorted mirror, climaxing with her gesturing to Waverton's dress and saying, "That's fine stuff, but it'll rot," and then touching Waverton's breast and adding, "This is fine stuff, too, but it'll rot too in time." After this lecture on the evils of vanity, she stops to check her hair in the mirror on the way out.

Whale did not evince much humor in *Frankenstein,* though there is an odd touch near the beginning where Frankenstein's first shovelful of grave dirt gets tossed in the face of a cemetery idol. There were a few scenes with a pompous Frederick Kerr as Baron Frankenstein that were designed to relieve tension but which were not too amusing. In contrast, *The Old Dark House* shows Whale a master of the humor of the unexpected.

One of the best examples comes during the dinner scene where Horace explains that his sister is about to embark on one of her "strange tribal rights," as she is about to say grace. When she chastises him for it, he explains to the guests that she feels that the food will be better if she prays "to her gods" first and gives thanks for all the many blessings that have been bestowed upon the family. This last statement drips with sarcasm.

The guests watch Horace cutting into some roast beef and expectantly wait for their portion, which never arrives. Instead, Horace turns to each and says, "Have a po-ta-to," which apart from some vinegar and pickled onions is all they are offered. It is at this point that Porterhouse and DuCane arrive and are reluctantly let in. Porterhouse sees the roast beef and sings about roast beef in expectation only to have Femm's peculiar rite and offer of a potato repeated. When Porterhouse tries to lighten the mood, observing that they are all together, friendly, and yet know nothing about each other, Horace immediately dampens their spirits with a quick, "How reassuring!"

Throughout, Whale develops a mood of menace. The house is in danger of being swept away by a flood; it makes its own electricity, but Horace observes, "We aren't very good at it"; Morgan is described as dangerous when he is drunk and he starts getting drunk; and finally Rebecca goads her brother into going upstairs to get the lamp, though clearly he is afraid of what is up there.

Mr. Waverton is finally persuaded to go in his stead. Upstairs the Wavertons meet the other members of the Femm household. Sir Roderick Femm, the elderly invalid father, believes himself the only sane member of the family in between mad cackles, and warns against Saul (Brember Wills). Roderick is played by the oldest female actress that Whale could find, Elspeth Dudgeon, in chin whiskers. She is credited as John Dudgeon.

Saul is the last and most dangerous member of the family, a pyromaniac who is dedicated to killing. In a drunken rage, Morgan frees him and he is introduced as a hand on the stairwell, but at first Morgan unexpectedly appears instead of him. He feigns timidity at first, but Saul develops an evil leer when Penderel is not looking. Finding a carving knife, Saul threatens Penderel and compares fire to knives. He makes an unsuccessful knife attack and proceeds to start setting fire to the house, but he is stopped by Penderel, and both of them tumble over a stairwell railing.

The result is that Saul is killed, cradled in Morgan's arms (the claim that Morgan used to beat him adds an odd touch to their relationship) and carried away never to be seen again. The surviving Penderel waits for an ambulance and proposes to DuCane, having found in love a reason for striving again.

Arthur Edeson in photographing *The Old Dark House* took the "dark" part very seriously, and the film does indeed have a dark look with heavy shadows. Unfortunately, many copies of the film today are not too clear for that reason. Ownership fell into private hands which has kept the film off television and videocassette for years, making it a hard film to find. Those who do see it and expect an exciting, Karlovian horrorfest like *Frankenstein* are inevitably disappointed, as were audiences when the film was first released.

As in *Frankenstein,* there is an introduction of the dangerously drunken Morgan in a series of three jump cuts, each coming closer to his face, but Whale's direction here is not as effective as it was in *Frankenstein.* The film acknowledges the implication of DuCane's relationship with Porterhouse, but then skirts around it by indicating that they are just good friends and he is still in love with his dead wife, leaving DuCane virginal enough to go away and marry Penderel at the end.

The comedy is not broad here, but subtle and offbeat. No doubt it left many audiences perplexed, though Whale does evince a good scene sense. Highlights include Thesiger's performance throughout, stealing the film from his better known fellow cast members; the oddball scene in Rebecca's bedroom, at once atmospheric, comic and unnerving; and the development of the genuinely dangerous Saul's madness into a crescendo. Following this film, peculiar characters became the main delight and focus of many subsequent Whale films.

The Road Back was temporarily shelved and numerous other projects were discussed, especially as Universal wanted to develop some new properties for their new star, Karloff. In keeping with his reputation for working on play adaptations, Whale was given *The Kiss Before the Mirror* to complete in the interim. He obviously enjoyed developing the irony of the film, which concerns a defense attorney with an unfaithful wife defending a friend who murdered his wife for being unfaithful.

Like *Frankenstein, The Invisible Man* started off as a proposed project for Robert Florey, but with *Murders in the Rue Morgue's* lack of success, the project was taken away from him and eventually fell into the hands of James Whale. Both Garrett Fort and Preston Sturges took a whack at a screenplay adaptation of Wells' famous science fiction novel, with the Sturges version being set in Russia, but these attempts got further and further away from the book.

Whale suggested that his old friend R. C. Sherriff be given a chance. Meanwhile, Universal also bought the rights to

Philip Wylie's *The Murderer Invisible,* a variation on the idea of the Wells novel, to plumb for ideas and to protect themselves against any possible lawsuit. Sherriff, however, insisted on sticking solely to the Wells original.

The project was originally developed for Boris Karloff to star in, but the actor had just temporarily left the studio when, after he had agreed to one salary reduction, the studio balked at paying him the agreed-upon salary increase when it came time to renew his option. Initially, Whale approached his old friend Colin Clive to take over the role, but Clive turned down the part in favor of returning to England.

Whale then saw possibilities in a screen test for Claude Rains for *A Bill of Divorcement.* Rains was a prominent actor on the London and New York stages, but he had never appeared in films. After performing a test involving the scene where Griffin outlines his plan for taking over the world, Whale was convinced he had his man. Now all he had to do was convince the studio.

Given that it was the leading role, Rains insisted on star billing, which caused costar Chester Morris, a one-time box office idol, to leave the cast. Universal agreed to have Rains head the cast when Whale convinced them that the real draw of the film would be its spectacular special effects.

These effects would be accomplished by the new head of Universal's special effects department, John P. Fulton, who assured Whale that the shots could be done. Shooting on the film took two months, a long time for a '30s film only 70 minutes in length, and the final lab work took even longer.

In the June 1934 issue of *American Cinematographer,* Fulton explained how the effects of ***The Invisible Man*** were accomplished:

> We used a completely black set—walled and floored with black velvet to be as nearly non-reflective as possible. Our actor was garbed from head to foot in black velvet tights, with black gloves, and a black headpiece rather like a diver's helmet. Over this, he wore whatever clothes might be required. This gave us a picture of the unsupported clothes moving around on a dead black field. From this negative, we made a print and a duplicate negative, which we then intensified to serve as mattes for printing. Then, with an ordinary printer, we proceeded to make our composite: first we printed from the positive of the background and normal action, using the intensified, negative matte to mask off the area where our invisible man's clothing was to move. Then we printed again, using the positive matte to shield the already printed area, and printing in the moving clothes from our "trick" negative. This printing operation made our duplicate, composite negative to be used in printing the final master prints of the picture.
>
> The chief difficulty we encountered in these scenes was not primarily photographic, but had to do with acting and direction—getting the player to move naturally, yet in a manner which did not present, for example, an open sleeve end

to the camera. This required endless rehearsal, endless patience—and many "takes." In many scenes, too, we had to figure out ways of getting natural-looking movement without having our "invisible" actor pass his hands in front of himself.

> In several sequences, the player had to be shown unwrapping the concealing bandages from about his head; and in another, pulling off a false nose, revealing the absolute emptiness of the head-swatchings, the back of which showed through when the nose was removed. This latter scene was made by using a dummy, an exact replica of the player's makeup, and with a chest ingeniously contrived to move as though breathing. The unwrapping action was handled in the same fashion as the other half-clad scenes—that is, by multiple printing with travelling mattes. . . .

Fulton's effects have stood the test of time superbly, largely due to the inordinate amount of detail and time he spent on the project. To cover up any imperfections (e.g. hidden eyeholes that should not be seen), Fulton had the negative retouched on 4,000 feet of film in which each frame was individually worked on by hand. The most difficult effects shot in the film had the invisible man unwrapping his head in front of a mirror, which required four separate takes to be perfectly matched and combined so that one simultaneously sees his head unwrapped from front and back in the mirror.

But while ***The Invisible Man*** remains an effects marvel, there is more to the picture than that. Whale wanted Griffin, the man who is invisible throughout the film, to remain sympathetic, though he does some rather horrific things, so a bit was added to the script in which the drug that makes him invisible also renders him partially insane. (Actually, without anything to reflect light off the retina, an invisible man would also be blind, but this problem has been ignored in virtually every movie involving invisibility.)

One way Whale kept the film fresh during the effects scenes was by frequent cutting, rather than locking down the camera in one or two positions for a given effects sequence. The movie is shot as if the special effects could be taken for granted, and the number of different angles from which we can see them adds to their believability.

Another important aspect is the lively characters that have been injected throughout the storyline. For the first time, Whale used Irish actress Una O'Connor to be an oddball innkeeper's wife, and she gives a broad and amusing performance that builds up interest and tension in the opening scenes of the film.

The film begins like Wells' novel with a stranger wrapped in bandages checking into a snow-covered country inn. The innkeeper's wife continually gets more suspicious of and interested in her alarming new guest, who hides his features and speaks to everyone in a contemptuous manner. She finally badgers her husband into turning him out for cursing, spilling chemicals and being a week behind in the rent, which unleashes Griffin's fury.

The humor is sometimes broad but nonetheless funny. The

atmosphere in the inn is established by a character taking bows for his piano playing only to have his compatriot insert another coin in what proves to be a player piano. The astonished constable (E. E. Clive) tells patrons of the bar, "'E's invisible, that's what the matter with him is," before leading them on back to the room. In a bit of risqué humor, Griffin turns his back and unzips his fly just as he delivers the line, "Now they'll see something really shocking!" My favorite bit of oddball humor comes near the end of the film as Griffin frightens a woman by donning only a pair of pants and singing gaily, "Here we go gathering nuts in May, nuts in May, nuts in May, on a chill and frosty morning."

The film has interesting small turns by people such as Walter Brennan (who gets his bicycle stolen), John Carradine (who calls the police with a suggestion on how they might capture the invisible man) and Dwight Frye (as a newspaper reporter asking the police what techniques they thought of). Gloria Stuart does not have a large part as Flora, the love interest, but she is appealingly sympathetic.

The largest role other than Rains' is William Harrigan's as Dr. Kemp, who wants to take Griffin's place in Flora's affections. When Griffin reappears at his house Kemp is utterly terrified and his pusillanimous behavior quickly loses him any sympathy from the audience as he deceives and betrays his former, though admittedly mad, friend.

Rains' physical gestures are a trifle overly theatrical, though some of this is for the benefit of frightening his spectators, putting on a mad act. The film allows the audience to live out prankish fantasies vicariously, and it is obvious that Griffin enjoys his invisible antics, and the audience does with him.

Rains' voice is quite commanding though, switching from feverish arrogance to frantic pleading to gentle wooing of Flora that builds as madness replaces Flora in his mind. The best speech amply demonstrates the horror and Griffin's growing megalomania:

> Just a scientific experiment at first. That's all— to do something no other man in the world had done. Kemp, I know now! It came to me suddenly. The drugs I took seemed to light up my brain, suddenly I realized the power I held—the power to rule, to make the world grovel at my feet. Ha, ha! We'll soon put the world to right now, Kemp. . . . We'll begin with a reign of terror. A few murders, here and there. Murders of great men, murders of little men, just to show we make no distinction. We might even wreck a train or two. Just these fingers 'round a signalman's throat.

In a departure from the book, Griffin succeeds in killing Kemp, which becomes the dramatic climax of the movie. (Griffin's eventual shooting and capture seem perfunctory by comparison, given little in the way of buildup by Whale.) Kemp performs the function of an antagonist, with the police being a secondary force opposed to Griffin. Additionally, Griffin is given some murders and a train derailment which allow him to relish his powers, as well as

outwitting the police who are trying to protect Kemp through elaborate measures.

Whale's seemingly simple style is actually quite meticulous. He knows when to use a series of quick cuts to imply a broad range of action (people locking their doors after being warned about an invisible man; the police searching everywhere). There are smooth tracking shots that focus the audience's attention. One of his most effective techniques is to provide a slightly different angle when cutting from a close-up to a two-shot and then back again, moving his camera fractionally closer as if the audience is bending forward with interest to catch every syllable that a character utters. He also shoots Rains from a low angle when he wants him to appear more commanding, and while deprived of facial expression for obvious reasons, Rains commutes his character's feelings through inflection and body language quite effectively.

There may have been something more elaborate intended for the climax; Fulton revealed that he had been instructed to devise a method for producing footprints in the snow that was not stop-motion—that is, taking some frames without a footprint, then adding one, taking some more frames, then adding another and so on—because the shot would have people in it. However, no such shot appears in the film with the footprints appearing by themselves. Fulton's technique involved laying a trench under the snow with secret wooden doors. When a footprint needed to appear, the door was pulled away and the snow fell into a pit in the shape of a footprint.

As Griffin dies, he slowly becomes visible again, allowing us our only look at Claude Rains. To accomplish this effect, Rains lay under some sheets made of papier-mâché (to keep their shape and not move from shot to shot). In a slow dissolve, the invisible figure becomes a skeleton, which was then replaced by a sculpted figure resembling Rains and finally by the actor himself before the camera pulls away to end the film.

Universal needed a big success and it got one in *The Invisible Man,* which helped Rains become established in Hollywood. While primarily designed as an entertainment, the film also touches on wish fulfillment, power fantasies, brutal violence, arrogance, aspirations and some humorous absurdities. It helped establish that big horror cliché of "there are some things in which mankind was not meant to meddle" by stating it overtly (but unselfconsciously). It shows the wisdom of the old Chinese proverb, "Be careful what you wish for, you might get it." All told, *The Invisible Man* remains one of horror's greatest classics.

However, Whale's greatest horror film would prove to be his next and last one, *The Bride of Frankenstein,* a film he had long resisted doing, feeling he had used up his ideas on the initial film. Following *The Invisible Man,* he planned to make *A Trip to Mars,* with Boris Karloff, who had been loaned to John Ford and RKO for *The Lost Patrol.* Instead, he was asked to assume direction of *By Candlelight,* which had been started by Robert Wyler, William Wyler's brother. The film is a typical romantic comedy about a butler who is mistaken for a prince falling in love with a maid whom he mistakes for a grand dame.

A Trip to Mars was eventually canceled because Carl Laemmle, Jr., decided it would be too costly for the financially strapped studio to film and because he did not like the script. Meanwhile, Whale, concerned over the financial situation at the studio and receiving offers from others, considered getting out of his contract. But as he left for his vacation, he did find a property which interested him, John Galsworthy's novel *Over the River.*

This led to the film *One More River,* one of Whale's better efforts, though it ignores half of the novel it is based on, concentrating on the story of a woman, Diana Wynyard, who, having been beaten by her husband (Colin Clive in one of his best performances), finds herself named as correspondent in a court case in which Clive accuses her of having an affair with Frank Lawton. The film also featured the debut of Jane Wyatt as Wynyard's sister and such delightful English actors as C. Aubrey Smith, Mrs. Patrick Campbell, Alan Mowbray, Lionel Atwill and E. E. Clive.

Given Whale's insistence that he did not want to do *The Return of Frankenstein,* the studio temporarily handed *Bride of Frankenstein* over to Kurt Neumann, but it languished until Whale agreed to make the film if guaranteed complete artistic freedom. Desperately in need of more hits, Universal readily agreed.

Whale consulted with writers John L. Balderston and William Hurlbut on working out a treatment for the sequel. Several ideas from the original novel were incorporated: the Monster trying to save a drowning girl, meeting with a blind man in the woods, learning to speak and demanding a mate. Balderston reportedly grew unhappy with the amount of horror injected into the story and so the final screenplay was the work of Hurlbut alone.

Most of the original cast returned along with some regular Whale performers with the exception of Mae Clarke, who had departed Universal and was replaced by Universal contract player Valerie Hobson. Frederick Kerr, the original Baron Frankenstein, had died and so was not included in the script, while E. E. Clive took over the officious role of burgomaster, proving more amusing than Lionel Belmore. To the lamentation of some critics who considered her role an injection of camp, Una O'Connor was given a major supporting part as Minnie, the Frankenstein's housekeeper and general village busybody.

For the key role of Dr. Septimus Pretorius, who persuades Henry Frankenstein to resume his work and build a mate, Whale wanted to use Claude Rains again. However, Rains proved unavailable, so Whale substituted Ernest Thesiger, who once more practically stole the show whenever he was onscreen with his odd personification of a demented doctor.

As in *The Invisible Man,* both John Carradine and Walter Brennan were given bit parts, while Dwight Frye was given the role of Karl, combining two characters from the script—Pretorius' assistant and a village idiot who takes advantage of the Monster's rampage to murder his miserly

uncle, a subplot that was eliminated after initial previews of the film because it turned attention away from major characters to minor ones. All told, 15 minutes were removed from *Bride of Frankenstein* before general release.

Some of the missing footage expanded the prologue that Whale insisted on and that film editor Ted Kent recommended be cut entirely. In the prologue, we are introduced to Mary Shelley, author of the tale, and her companions Percy Shelley and Lord Byron. Whale agreed to some cuts but was very insistent on retaining this opening as being important to his conception.

One can see that he took a great deal of effort in crafting it, setting up a separate angle for each line of dialogue, showing the speaker or what is being spoken of or simply reaction shots. Gavin Gordon makes a delightful Lord Byron, who loves horror and delights in shocks. Whale wanted this sequence for a number of reasons. First, it obviously made it easy to show flashbacks and encapsulate the plot of the preceding film to prepare audiences for the current one (though note one quick shot of the Monster strangling E. E. Clive as the burgomaster among the flashbacks, a sequence cut out of *Bride of Frankenstein* rather than the original film). Second, it takes the tale from being "real" to being a story that Mary Shelley is telling her friends (and us). Finally, it allows Whale to contrast the seemingly innocent and demure Mary Shelley with the monster that Elsa Lanchester will later play in the film, demonstrating a proposition that terrible things can spring from the most seemingly ordinary people.

Some have been bothered that the characters in *Bride of Frankenstein* largely wear modern dress and that it contains such devices as a telephone. Originally, this was explained in the script by giving Mary Shelley the line: "I've taken the rest of the story into the future—and made use of developments which science will someday know—a hundred years to come. I think you will find the new horrors far more entertaining, Lord Byron." However, this line was excised and we must suppose that either Pretorius or Frankenstein invented the telephone, called an electrical device, far ahead of Alexander Graham Bell.

The film itself is suffused with cinematic references and oddball humor. However, the story itself begins on a properly horrific note. Having fallen through the floor of the mill and into a pit of water below it (providing the only plausible survival of the Monster from one film into the next in the entire series), the Monster waits angrily below for the villagers to depart. A relative of Maria, Hans (Reginald Barlow), insists on seeing the charred remains for himself so that he can sleep at night. (Maria's father was Ludwig, played by Michael Mark in the original film.) Falling into the underground pond himself, he encounters the Monster, who quickly kills him and then climbs up the stairs to the top where Hans' wife (Mary Gordon) waits to give him a hand up. In a bit of macabre humor, she helps rescue the Monster only to be thrown to her death for her pains. The ubiquitous Minnie sees the Monster, gives a shriek and runs off while the perplexed Monster looks on in bewilderment, making no attempt to harm her.

In carting away Henry, a reference is made to taking him

to his father. In a scene cut from release, it is revealed that the Baron died of shock after hearing what happened to his son, making Henry the new Baron Frankenstein (and so he is addressed when Dr. Pretorius pays a call). In order to accommodate the new continuity, Universal cut the sequence of the Baron toasting a son to the house of Frankenstein from the re-release prints of the original film, and said scene was not shown again until the film's television sale in the late '50s.

In **Bride of Frankenstein,** the Monster and the creator switch places in many ways. While the first film concentrated on Frankenstein's dream and its dissolution and consequences (his crime being not so much creating the Monster but ignoring him and not raising him properly), **Bride** concerns itself more with the Monster and his development. While Henry is a divinely created human soul who rejects the company of others, the Monster is portrayed as a humanly created being who seeks the company of others but is continually rejected.

Henry is presumed dead until, in a parody of the original creation scene, he moves his hand and Elizabeth screams, "He's alive!" When the Monster and Henry first meet again late in the film, the Monster has taken over Henry's role, instructing Frankenstein to sit down, and he uses the same hand gestures that Frankenstein used.

Whale gives a big buildup to the entrance of Dr. Pretorius into the story, beginning with Elizabeth trying to comfort Henry after his delirium and then going into a kind of delirium herself as she proclaims that there is a figure of death coming to take Henry away from her. Indeed, with his swirling cloak, Dr. Pretorius could easily be a death figure as he knocks at the door, his face fully revealed only when the light from inside hits it as Minnie opens the door to this unexpected guest. He explains that he has come "on a secret matter of grave importance."

Frankenstein and Pretorius are left alone as Pretorius alternately tries to intrigue, cajole and threaten Frankenstein. He has been booted out of the university in which he had once taught Henry but proclaims he has succeeded in creating artificial life on his own. He threatens to expose Henry as the creator of the Monster and lay the blame for the deaths the Monster has caused at his door. (While it is not clear in the first film if the villagers connect Frankenstein with the Monster, later in this film when the huntsmen come upon the Monster in the blind man's hut, they obviously know all about who the Monster is and who made him, making Pretorius' threat here seem rather empty.) Somehow he has knowledge that the Monster did not die in the mill fire but still lives, and he desires that Henry become partners with him to create a female Monster and hence start an artificial race. "A woman," he leers, "that should be really interesting."

Rather than reanimating dead corpses, Pretorius has been growing miniature human beings from cultures, and in a delightful effects sequence, he displays the results of his work. Originally, there were to have been seven bottles, the last with Billy Barty portraying a baby in monster makeup pulling a flower apart while Pretorius promises, "I think this baby will grow into something worth watch-ing," but the last bottle was cut and only a brief glimpse of it remains in long shot and in a publicity still.

Echoing his line from **The Old Dark House,** Pretorius proclaims that gin is his only weakness before drinking a toast, "To a new world of gods and monsters." (Later, Pretorius offers the Monster a cigar, proclaiming them his only weakness.) One of his creations is a little king, patterned after Henry VIII from the film *The Private Life of King Henry VIII* which won an Academy Award for Elsa Lanchester's husband, Charles Laughton.

Pretorius proclaims himself a doctor of philosophy and his personal philosophy seems to be based on the Marquis de Sade's. He wants to eliminate the concept of good and evil, and thinks it would be so much more "amusing" if everyone did what he or she wanted to. However, as the film develops, we find Pretorius is unscrupulous and is only interested in getting people to do what he wants them to. One of his figures is of the devil (played by Peter Shaw, Thesiger's double), in whom Pretorius sees a certain resemblance to himself—"Or do I flatter myself?"

With the mechanics of the plot set up, the film then concentrates on the chronicle of the Monster. Espying a young shepherdess who screams and falls into a stream at the sight of him, the Monster tries to rescue her (apparently learning from his experience with Maria the danger of water). Here the Monster is humanized, even heroic. But when his visage still provokes screams, despite his overtures of tenderness, he simply waves his arms above her, indicating "no."

The screams attract the attention of nearby villagers, who shoot at him, wounding him in the arm. While he rolls a boulder on a pair of his pursuers, he is soon overpowered and trussed up in a parody of Christ imagery. (A bit cut from the script had the Monster trying to rescue a figure of Christ from its cross.) The angry villagers throw rocks and pillory him, placing him in a chair in the town jail that is peculiarly just the right size and shape.

The comic character of the burgomaster proclaims the Monster an escaped lunatic ("Monster, indeed," he repeatedly sniffs) but with his great strength the Monster almost immediately breaks his chains and goes on the rampage through town. Whale shows an anxious mother looking for her missing child, who is found dead in a graveyard, and a married couple are found dead in their beds but never shown. By not showing us the victims themselves, Whale is able to keep the audience's sympathies with the much-persecuted Monster.

Additional scenes were shot here but later removed in which the burgomaster conducts an inquiry, dismissing the charges of a Monster because of a lack of eyewitnesses—though he himself has seen the Monster, having had it helpfully pointed out to him by Karl in the earlier forest scene. (Whale provides a suitably bleak atmosphere for the forest scene by showing only the bare trunks of trees and leafless or needleless trees in the background, giving the impression of desolation.) The burgomaster is subsequently strangled by the Monster he has declared nonexistent. Observing this, Karl then murders his uncle in the previously mentioned subplot, exclaiming, "Very convenient to have a Monster around. This is quite a nice cottage—I shouldn't be surprised if he visited auntie too!"

However, these scenes take too much time away from the story of the Monster and make the Monster more unsympathetic, particularly in an unprovoked attack on a comic character. The Karl bit makes a worthwhile point about copycat murderers, but it fails to provide a coherent portrait of his character, later shown to be nervous following Dr. Pretorius into a crypt ("If there's much more like this, what you say, pal, we give ourselves up and let'em hang us? This is no life for murderers!") though subsequently he murders a young girl for her heart under instructions from Dr. Pretorius and the promise of 1000 crowns from Frankenstein, who assumes he acquired it from an accident victim.

An additional bit of filming was ordered, showing the monster stumbling on some gypsies in an effort to get food. This connects up well with the scenes in which the Monster first experiences friendship in the film as he enters the hut of a blind man (Australian actor O. P. Heggie in his most famous role) who is playing "Ave Maria" on his violin.

The scenes with the blind hermit are some of the best beloved in horror cinema. Though they venture on the maudlin, they remain very effective and even moving. Karloff was against having the Monster talk, feeling it would detract from the mystique of the character, but he did a superb job with the Monster's vocalizations. As it turned out, the delight in having the Monster express his joy in good food, good music, and good fellowship outweigh the possible disadvantages. While he proves far from a consummate grammarian, the Monster's expression makes it clear that he has intelligence, reacts well to kindness and is not a brutish, unthinking thing.

The religious symbolism in *Bride of Frankenstein* has given many critics pause. With his resurrection and his being pilloried by the mob, the Monster does draw some parallels to Christ. Dr. Pretorius is openly contemptuous of religion, commenting in an aside that he is following the lead of nature, ". . . or of God, if you like your Bible stories. . . ." The Monster will later knock down the statue of a bishop and rail at an unkind creator in the heavens, while Frankenstein wonders if death is sacred and he has profaned it or if his discovery is part of God's divine plan.

While there are amusing religious jabs in the film, Whale is never contemptuous of the hermit's deeply religious faith nor of his following the commandment to love thy neighbor. Instead, he is portrayed as an extremely lonely man who gives thanks to God for the companionship of the Monster, moving the Monster himself to tears. Whale fades out on scene of the Monster comforting the hermit with an after-image of Christ on a crucifix lingering on momentarily after the rest of the scene has faded. Perhaps the point is that religion should not be used to excuse intolerance, something which Whale himself experienced in his own life, as did Colin Clive, who was an alcoholic bisexual married to a lesbian and a close friend of Whale's.

The point is further driven home when a pair of huntsmen, trying to help the old man, succeed merely in burning his

hut down and chasing his companion away. They are doing what they "know" is right, not stopping to inquire and learn about the situation, and the results are tragic. Alone again, the Monster realizes he has lost his only friend.

The "inhuman" Monster having achieved speech and humanity now meets up with the human but not humane Dr. Pretorius, who is delighted to have discovered the skeleton of a woman properly firm for his proposed artificial woman and is enjoying a macabre picnic in the crypt. Selling the Monster on the idea of persuading Frankenstein to make a friend and mate for him, Pretorius takes the Monster to Frankenstein's castle where he is preparing to leave for his belated honeymoon, having recovered from his bad fall.

While Pretorius cajoles him, the Monster has been instructed to kidnap Elizabeth, which he does successfully. The house is in an uproar, but Pretorius smashes a vase to get everyone's attention and announces that Elizabeth will be returned unharmed, so long as Henry cooperates. Pretorius will clearly do anything and use anyone to achieve his aims. When Frankenstein needs a heart, Pretorius has no compunctions about sending Karl out to murder someone. He even betrays the Monster by feeding him a drink with knock-out drops in it which he makes no effort to disguise.

The creation scene for the "Bride" is a vast improvement on the old one, as Whale builds up tension and makes use of more elaborate equipment. Frankenstein is depicted as suspicious of his "partner," but he gets caught up in the excitement of the experiment. Cameraman John Mescall, who did a superb job photographing the film although he was frequently reported to have been drunk, uses some dutch tilt angles very effectively to suggest that in performing the experiment, the scientists are out of kilter. This experiment requires two assistants, Karl and Ludwig, who release kites to catch the life-giving lightning that will be transferred to the Bride, who looks like a mummy swatched in bandages.

It has long been rumored that the original idea was for Elizabeth's heart to be placed within the Bride for the Monster, combining Frankenstein's and the Monster's bride into one, but there is no indication of this in the shooting script. Cut out of the film is a brief scene where Ludwig releases the kidnapped Elizabeth from her cave, explaining why she is able to run to the door of the watch tower just after the Bride is brought to life.

Franz Waxman's musical score, which even includes such amusing touches as wedding bells when the Bride first steps forth from her platform and expertly uses tympani to suggest the beating of the Bride's heart and to build tension, is a masterpiece, one of the best of his long and varied career, and was one of the first Hollywood scores to use leitmotifs for the characters. Waxman later sued Oscar Hammerstein for stealing his three-note, eerie "Bride's Theme" for the song "Bali Hai" in *South Pacific* and received a generous settlement.

Elsa Lanchester based her performance of the Bride on swans that she had seen while in England. Whale himself designed the Nefertiti hairstyle employed so memorably, made to stick up and out to suggest the electricity that had shocked her to life. Lanchester makes quick, darting, bird-like movements and easily conveys her preference for Frankenstein rather than her intended, whom she avoids and then screams and hisses at.

Originally when the Monster said, "We belong dead," his remarks were to have included Elizabeth and Frankenstein, as well as Pretorius, the Bride and himself. In the laboratory destruction sequence, the figure of Frankenstein can be briefly glimpsed standing next to the door after the Monster pulls the deadly switch, but at the last moment in filming, it was decided to let Frankenstein and Elizabeth live and let the Monster nobly spare their lives (though his reasons for doing so are unclear).

With its humor, whimsy, vivid characterizations, moving moments, and offbeat fairy-tale quality, **The Bride of Frankenstein** remains one of the best horror films ever made. Karloff gave unquestionably his best performance as the Monster, conveying a complexity in the creature as well as a soul. While the passage of over half a century has dated the film somewhat, in many ways the direction is still surprisingly modern with its quick cuts and artistic visual compositions.

How sad that **Bride** was a flop on initial release, that Whale's homosexuality caused him to be driven out of show business years later and he died a suicide in 1957. Like his Monster, Whale railed against a world that made no place for him.

FURTHER READING

Biography

Brosnan, John. "The Men Behind the Early Monsters: Karl Freund, Tod Browning and James Whale." In his *The Horror People*, pp 59-72. New York: St Martins Press, 1976.
A sketch of Whale's enigmatic life and career.

Clarens, Carlos. "Children of the Night: Hollywood, 1928-1947. In his *An Illustrated History of the Horror Films.*" New York: G.P. Putnams Sons, 1967, pp. 59-104.
Anecdotal account of the making of *Frankenstein, Bride of Frankenstein,* and *The Invisible Man.*

Curtis, James. *James Whale.* Metuchen, N.J. and London: The Scarecrow Press, 1982, 245 p.
First full-length study of Whale's life and work.

Karloff, Boris. "Memoirs of a Monster." *The Saturday Evening Post* 235, No. 39 (3 November 1962): 77-80.
Reminiscence of Karloff's experience acting in *Frankenstein.*

Thomaier, William, and Fink, Robert. "James Whale." *Films in Review* XIII, No. 5 (May 1962): 277-90.
A descriptive survey of Whale's career.

Whittemore, Don, and Cecchettini, Philip Alan. "James Whale." *In Passport to Hollywood: Film Immigrants Anthology,* pp. 271-324. New York: McGraw-Hill Book Co., 1976.
Biographical sketch highlighting Whale's early stage career in England and the circumstances under which he came to work in Hollywood.

Criticism

Anobile, Richard J., ed. *Frankenstein.* London: Pan Books, 1974, 256 p.
Reconstructs *Frankenstein* scene by scene through photographs and complete transcripted dialogue.

Arkadin. "Film Clips: *Hello Out There.*" *Sight and Sound* 37, No. 1, (Winter 1967-68): 47-9.
Recounts the discovery and restoration of a short film Whale directed in 1949.

Baxter, John. "Fantasy: Universal and Elsewhere." In *Hollywood in the Thirties,* pp. 70-87. London: A. Zwemmer, 1968.
Discusses Whale as well as other horror film directors who worked for Universal.

Bojarski, Richard, and Beale, Kenneth. "*Frankenstein, The Old Dark House,* and *Bride of Frankenstein.*" In *The Films of Boris Karloff,* pp. 55-63, 75-8, and 100-04. Secaucus, N.J.: The Citadel Press, 1974.
Analyzes the three Whale films starring Boris Karloff.

Butler, Ivan. "Dracula and Frankenstein." In *Horror in the Cinema,* pp. 27-42. Rev. ed. South Brunswick and New York: A.S. Barnes and Company, 1979.
Discusses Whale's two Frankenstein films as overcoming their limited production values, and also covers the many sequels that followed them.

Edwards, Roy. "Movie Gothick: A Tribute to James Whale." *Sight and Sound* 27, No. 2 (Autumn 1957): 95-8.
Appreciation of Whale's offbeat humor in his major horror films.

Ellis, Reed. *A Journey Into Darkness: The Art of James Whales Horror Films.* N.P.: University of Florida, 1979, 199 p.
Doctoral dissertation attempting to establish Whale as an auteur.

Glut, Donald F. "The Invisible Man and Co." In *Classic Movie Monsters,* pp. 130-61. Metuchen, N.J. & London: The Scarecrow Press, 1978.
Discussion of Whale's *The Invisible Man* and other films featuring invisible characters.

Steinbrunner, Chris, and Goldblatt, Burt. "*Bride of Frankenstein.*" In *Cinema of the Fantastic,* pp. 89-106. New York: Saturday Review Press, 1972.
Studies Whale's sequel to *Frankenstein.*

Review of *Bride of Frankenstein. Time* XXV, No. 17, (29 April 1935): 52-3.
Concludes that the sequel to *Frankenstein* suffers in comparison to the original.

Tropp, Martin. "Re-creation." In *Mary Shelley's Monster,* pp. 84-105. Boston: Houghton Mifflin, 1976.
Concludes that Whale's two Frankenstein films are artistically impressive but thematically nihilistic.

Twentieth-Century
Literary Criticism

Cumulative Indexes
Volumes 1-63

How to Use This Index

The main references

Calvino, Italo
1923-1985.....CLC 5, 8, 11, 22, 33, 39,
73; SSC 3

list all author entries in the following Gale Literary Criticism series:

BLC = *Black Literature Criticism*
CLC = *Contemporary Literary Criticism*
CLR = *Children's Literature Review*
CMLC = *Classical and Medieval Literature Criticism*
DA = *DISCovering Authors*
DC = *Drama Criticism*
HLC = *Hispanic Literature Criticism*
LC = *Literature Criticism from 1400 to 1800*
NCLC = *Nineteenth-Century Literature Criticism*
PC = *Poetry Criticism*
SSC = *Short Story Criticism*
TCLC = *Twentieth-Century Literary Criticism*
WLC = *World Literature Criticism, 1500 to the Present*

The cross-references

See also CANR 23; CA 85-88;
obituary CA 116

list all author entries in the following Gale biographical and literary sources:

AAYA = *Authors & Artists for Young Adults*
AITN = *Authors in the News*
BEST = *Bestsellers*
BW = *Black Writers*
CA = *Contemporary Authors*
CAAS = *Contemporary Authors Autobiography Series*
CABS = *Contemporary Authors Bibliographical Series*
CANR = *Contemporary Authors New Revision Series*
CAP = *Contemporary Authors Permanent Series*
CDALB = *Concise Dictionary of American Literary Biography*
CDBLB = *Concise Dictionary of British Literary Biography*
DLB = *Dictionary of Literary Biography*
DLBD = *Dictionary of Literary Biography Documentary Series*
DLBY = *Dictionary of Literary Biography Yearbook*
HW = *Hispanic Writers*
JRDA = *Junior DISCovering Authors*
MAICYA = *Major Authors and Illustrators for Children and Young Adults*
MTCW = *Major 20th-Century Writers*
NNAL = *Native North American Literature*
SAAS = *Something about the Author Autobiography Series*
SATA = *Something about the Author*
YABC = *Yesterday's Authors of Books for Children*

Literary Criticism Series
Cumulative Author Index

Alcott, Amos Bronson 1799-1888 .. **NCLC 1**
See also DLB 1

Alcott, Louisa May
1832-1888 .... **NCLC 6; DA; DAB;
DAC; WLC**
See also CDALB 1865-1917; CLR 1, 38;
DAM MST, NOV; DLB 1, 42, 79; JRDA;
MAICYA; YABC 1

Aldanov, M. A.
See Aldanov, Mark (Alexandrovich)

Aldanov, Mark (Alexandrovich)
1886(?)-1957 .... **TCLC 23**
See also CA 118

Aldington, Richard 1892-1962...... **CLC 49**
See also CA 85-88; CANR 45; DLB 20, 36,
100, 149

Aldiss, Brian W(ilson)
1925- .... **CLC 5, 14, 40**
See also CA 5-8R; CAAS 2; CANR 5, 28;
DAM NOV; DLB 14; MTCW; SATA 34

Alegria, Claribel 1924-........... **CLC 75**
See also CA 131; CAAS 15; DAM MULT;
DLB 145; HW

Alegria, Fernando 1918-........... **CLC 57**
See also CA 9-12R; CANR 5, 32; HW

Aleichem, Sholom .... **TCLC 1, 35**
See also Rabinovitch, Sholem

Aleixandre, Vicente
1898-1984 .... **CLC 9, 36; PC 15**
See also CA 85-88; 114; CANR 26;
DAM POET; DLB 108; HW; MTCW

Alepoudelis, Odysseus
See Elytis, Odysseus

Aleshkovsky, Joseph 1929-
See Aleshkovsky, Yuz
See also CA 121; 128

Aleshkovsky, Yuz .... **CLC 44**
See also Aleshkovsky, Joseph

Alexander, Lloyd (Chudley) 1924- .. **CLC 35**
See also AAYA 1; CA 1-4R; CANR 1, 24,
38; CLR 1, 5; DLB 52; JRDA; MAICYA;
MTCW; SAAS 19; SATA 3, 49, 81

Alfau, Felipe 1902-............... **CLC 66**
See also CA 137

Alger, Horatio, Jr. 1832-1899 ..... **NCLC 8**
See also DLB 42; SATA 16

Algren, Nelson 1909-1981 .... **CLC 4, 10, 33**
See also CA 13-16R; 103; CANR 20;
CDALB 1941-1968; DLB 9; DLBY 81,
82; MTCW

Ali, Ahmed 1910- .... **CLC 69**
See also CA 25-28R; CANR 15, 34

Alighieri, Dante 1265-1321 .... **CMLC 3**

Allan, John B.
See Westlake, Donald E(dwin)

Allen, Edward 1948-.............. **CLC 59**

Allen, Paula Gunn 1939-.......... **CLC 84**
See also CA 112; 143; DAM MULT;
NNAL

Allen, Roland
See Ayckbourn, Alan

Allen, Sarah A.
See Hopkins, Pauline Elizabeth

Allen, Woody 1935-.......... **CLC 16, 52**
See also AAYA 10; CA 33-36R; CANR 27,
38; DAM POP; DLB 44; MTCW

Allende, Isabel 1942-.... **CLC 39, 57; HLC**
See also CA 125; 130; CANR 51;
DAM MULT, NOV; DLB 145; HW;
INT 130; MTCW

Alleyn, Ellen
See Rossetti, Christina (Georgina)

Allingham, Margery (Louise)
1904-1966 .... **CLC 19**
See also CA 5-8R; 25-28R; CANR 4;
DLB 77; MTCW

Allingham, William 1824-1889 ... **NCLC 25**
See also DLB 35

Allison, Dorothy E. 1949- .... **CLC 78**
See also CA 140

Allston, Washington 1779-1843.... **NCLC 2**
See also DLB 1

Almedingen, E. M. .... **CLC 12**
See also Almedingen, Martha Edith von
See also SATA 3

Almedingen, Martha Edith von 1898-1971
See Almedingen, E. M.
See also CA 1-4R; CANR 1

Almqvist, Carl Jonas Love
1793-1866 .... **NCLC 42**

Alonso, Damaso 1898-1990 .... **CLC 14**
See also CA 110; 131; 130; DLB 108; HW

Alov
See Gogol, Nikolai (Vasilyevich)

Alta 1942-...................... **CLC 19**
See also CA 57-60

Alter, Robert B(ernard) 1935-...... **CLC 34**
See also CA 49-52; CANR 1, 47

Alther, Lisa 1944-............... **CLC 7, 41**
See also CA 65-68; CANR 12, 30, 51;
MTCW

Altman, Robert 1925-............. **CLC 16**
See also CA 73-76; CANR 43

Alvarez, A(lfred) 1929-......... **CLC 5, 13**
See also CA 1-4R; CANR 3, 33; DLB 14,
40

Alvarez, Alejandro Rodriguez 1903-1965
See Casona, Alejandro
See also CA 131; 93-96; HW

Alvaro, Corrado 1896-1956 .... **TCLC 60**

Amado, Jorge 1912-..... **CLC 13, 40; HLC**
See also CA 77-80; CANR 35;
DAM MULT, NOV; DLB 113; MTCW

Ambler, Eric 1909-............ **CLC 4, 6, 9**
See also CA 9-12R; CANR 7, 38; DLB 77;
MTCW

Amichai, Yehuda 1924- ...... **CLC 9, 22, 57**
See also CA 85-88; CANR 46; MTCW

Amiel, Henri Frederic 1821-1881 .. **NCLC 4**

Amis, Kingsley (William)
1922-1995 ..... **CLC 1, 2, 3, 5, 8, 13, 40,
44; DA; DAB; DAC**
See also AITN 2; CA 9-12R; 150; CANR 8,
28; CDBLB 1945-1960; DAM MST,
NOV; DLB 15, 27, 100, 139;
INT CANR-8; MTCW

Amis, Martin (Louis)
1949- .... **CLC 4, 9, 38, 62**
See also BEST 90:3; CA 65-68; CANR 8,
27; DLB 14; INT CANR-27

Ammons, A(rchie) R(andolph)
1926- .... **CLC 2, 3, 5, 8, 9, 25, 57**
See also AITN 1; CA 9-12R; CANR 6, 36,
51; DAM POET; DLB 5; MTCW

Amo, Tauraatua i
See Adams, Henry (Brooks)

Anand, Mulk Raj 1905-........... **CLC 23**
See also CA 65-68; CANR 32; DAM NOV;
MTCW

Anatol
See Schnitzler, Arthur

Anaya, Rudolfo A(lfonso)
1937- .... **CLC 23; HLC**
See also CA 45-48; CAAS 4; CANR 1, 32,
51; DAM MULT, NOV; DLB 82; HW 1;
MTCW

Andersen, Hans Christian
1805-1875 .... **NCLC 7; DA; DAB;
DAC; SSC 6; WLC**
See also CLR 6; DAM MST, POP;
MAICYA; YABC 1

Anderson, C. Farley
See Mencken, H(enry) L(ouis); Nathan,
George Jean

Anderson, Jessica (Margaret) Queale
.... **CLC 37**
See also CA 9-12R; CANR 4

Anderson, Jon (Victor) 1940- .... **CLC 9**
See also CA 25-28R; CANR 20;
DAM POET

Anderson, Lindsay (Gordon)
1923-1994 .... **CLC 20**
See also CA 125; 128; 146

Anderson, Maxwell 1888-1959 ..... **TCLC 2**
See also CA 105; DAM DRAM; DLB 7

Anderson, Poul (William) 1926- .... **CLC 15**
See also AAYA 5; CA 1-4R; CAAS 2;
CANR 2, 15, 34; DLB 8; INT CANR-15;
MTCW; SATA-Brief 39

Anderson, Robert (Woodruff)
1917- .... **CLC 23**
See also AITN 1; CA 21-24R; CANR 32;
DAM DRAM; DLB 7

Anderson, Sherwood
1876-1941 .... **TCLC 1, 10, 24; DA;
DAB; DAC; SSC 1; WLC**
See also CA 104; 121; CDALB 1917-1929;
DAM MST, NOV; DLB 4, 9, 86;
DLBD 1; MTCW

Andouard
See Giraudoux, (Hippolyte) Jean

Andrade, Carlos Drummond de ...... **CLC 18**
See also Drummond de Andrade, Carlos

Andrade, Mario de 1893-1945..... **TCLC 43**

Andreae, Johann V. 1586-1654 ...... **LC 32**

Andreas-Salome, Lou 1861-1937... **TCLC 56**
See also DLB 66

Andrewes, Lancelot 1555-1626 .... **LC 5**
See also DLB 151

Andrews, Cicily Fairfield
See West, Rebecca

Author Index

Asturias, Miguel Angel
1899-1974 .... **CLC 3, 8, 13; HLC**
See also CA 25-28; 49-52; CANR 32;
CAP 2; DAM MULT, NOV; DLB 113;
HW; MTCW

Atares, Carlos Saura
See Saura (Atares), Carlos

Atheling, William
See Pound, Ezra (Weston Loomis)

Atheling, William, Jr.
See Blish, James (Benjamin)

Atherton, Gertrude (Franklin Horn)
1857-1948 .... **TCLC 2**
See also CA 104; DLB 9, 78

Atherton, Lucius
See Masters, Edgar Lee

Atkins, Jack
See Harris, Mark

Attaway, William (Alexander)
1911-1986 .... **CLC 92; BLC**
See also BW 2; CA 143; DAM MULT;
DLB 76

Atticus
See Fleming, Ian (Lancaster)

Atwood, Margaret (Eleanor)
1939- ..... **CLC 2, 3, 4, 8, 13, 15, 25, 44,
84; DA; DAB; DAC; PC 8; SSC 2; WLC**
See also AAYA 12; BEST 89:2; CA 49-52;
CANR 3, 24, 33; DAM MST, NOV,
POET; DLB 53; INT CANR-24; MTCW;
SATA 50

Aubigny, Pierre d'
See Mencken, H(enry) L(ouis)

Aubin, Penelope 1685-1731(?) .... **LC 9**
See also DLB 39

Auchincloss, Louis (Stanton)
1917- .... **CLC 4, 6, 9, 18, 45**
See also CA 1-4R; CANR 6, 29;
DAM NOV; DLB 2; DLBY 80;
INT CANR-29; MTCW

Auden, W(ystan) H(ugh)
1907-1973 ..... **CLC 1, 2, 3, 4, 6, 9, 11,
14, 43; DA; DAB; DAC; PC 1; WLC**
See also CA 9-12R; 45-48; CANR 5;
CDBLB 1914-1945; DAM DRAM, MST,
POET; DLB 10, 20; MTCW

Audiberti, Jacques 1900-1965 ...... **CLC 38**
See also CA 25-28R; DAM DRAM

Audubon, John James
1785-1851 .... **NCLC 47**

Auel, Jean M(arie) 1936-......... **CLC 31**
See also AAYA 7; BEST 90:4; CA 103;
CANR 21; DAM POP; INT CANR-21

Auerbach, Erich 1892-1957 .... **TCLC 43**
See also CA 118

Augier, Emile 1820-1889 .... **NCLC 31**

August, John
See De Voto, Bernard (Augustine)

Augustine, St. 354-430 ...... **CMLC 6; DAB**

Aurelius
See Bourne, Randolph S(illiman)

Aurobindo, Sri 1872-1950 .... **TCLC 63**

Austen, Jane
1775-1817 ..... **NCLC 1, 13, 19, 33, 51;
DA; DAB; DAC; WLC**
See also CDBLB 1789-1832; DAM MST,
NOV; DLB 116

Auster, Paul 1947-.............. **CLC 47**
See also CA 69-72; CANR 23, 51

Austin, Frank
See Faust, Frederick (Schiller)

Austin, Mary (Hunter)
1868-1934 .... **TCLC 25**
See also CA 109; DLB 9, 78

Autran Dourado, Waldomiro
See Dourado, (Waldomiro Freitas) Autran

Averroes 1126-1198 .... **CMLC 7**
See also DLB 115

Avicenna 980-1037 .... **CMLC 16**
See also DLB 115

Avison, Margaret 1918-.... **CLC 2, 4; DAC**
See also CA 17-20R; DAM POET; DLB 53;
MTCW

Axton, David
See Koontz, Dean R(ay)

Ayckbourn, Alan
1939- .... **CLC 5, 8, 18, 33, 74; DAB**
See also CA 21-24R; CANR 31;
DAM DRAM; DLB 13; MTCW

Aydy, Catherine
See Tennant, Emma (Christina)

Ayme, Marcel (Andre) 1902-1967... **CLC 11**
See also CA 89-92; CLR 25; DLB 72

Ayrton, Michael 1921-1975 .... **CLC 7**
See also CA 5-8R; 61-64; CANR 9, 21

Azorin............................ **CLC 11**
See also Martinez Ruiz, Jose

Azuela, Mariano
1873-1952 .... **TCLC 3; HLC**
See also CA 104; 131; DAM MULT; HW;
MTCW

Baastad, Babbis Friis
See Friis-Baastad, Babbis Ellinor

Bab
See Gilbert, W(illiam) S(chwenck)

Babbis, Eleanor
See Friis-Baastad, Babbis Ellinor

Babel, Isaak (Emmanuilovich)
1894-1941(?) ...... **TCLC 2, 13; SSC 16**
See also CA 104

Babits, Mihaly 1883-1941 .... **TCLC 14**
See also CA 114

Babur 1483-1530 .... **LC 18**

Bacchelli, Riccardo 1891-1985 ..... **CLC 19**
See also CA 29-32R; 117

Bach, Richard (David) 1936-...... **CLC 14**
See also AITN 1; BEST 89:2; CA 9-12R;
CANR 18; DAM NOV, POP; MTCW;
SATA 13

Bachman, Richard
See King, Stephen (Edwin)

Bachmann, Ingeborg 1926-1973..... **CLC 69**
See also CA 93-96; 45-48; DLB 85

Bacon, Francis 1561-1626 .... **LC 18, 32**
See also CDBLB Before 1660; DLB 151

Bacon, Roger 1214(?)-1292 ...... **CMLC 14**
See also DLB 115

Bacovia, George.................. **TCLC 24**
See also Vasiliu, Gheorghe

Badanes, Jerome 1937-........... **CLC 59**

Bagehot, Walter 1826-1877 ...... **NCLC 10**
See also DLB 55

Bagnold, Enid 1889-1981......... **CLC 25**
See also CA 5-8R; 103; CANR 5, 40;
DAM DRAM; DLB 13, 160; MAICYA;
SATA 1, 25

Bagritsky, Eduard 1895-1934 ..... **TCLC 60**

Bagrjana, Elisaveta
See Belcheva, Elisaveta

Bagryana, Elisaveta................ **CLC 10**
See also Belcheva, Elisaveta
See also DLB 147

Bailey, Paul 1937-.............. **CLC 45**
See also CA 21-24R; CANR 16; DLB 14

Baillie, Joanna 1762-1851 .... **NCLC 2**
See also DLB 93

Bainbridge, Beryl (Margaret)
1933- .... **CLC 4, 5, 8, 10, 14, 18, 22, 62**
See also CA 21-24R; CANR 24;
DAM NOV; DLB 14; MTCW

Baker, Elliott 1922-.............. **CLC 8**
See also CA 45-48; CANR 2

Baker, Nicholson 1957-........... **CLC 61**
See also CA 135; DAM POP

Baker, Ray Stannard 1870-1946... **TCLC 47**
See also CA 118

Baker, Russell (Wayne) 1925-...... **CLC 31**
See also BEST 89:4; CA 57-60; CANR 11,
41; MTCW

Bakhtin, M.
See Bakhtin, Mikhail Mikhailovich

Bakhtin, M. M.
See Bakhtin, Mikhail Mikhailovich

Bakhtin, Mikhail
See Bakhtin, Mikhail Mikhailovich

Bakhtin, Mikhail Mikhailovich
1895-1975 .... **CLC 83**
See also CA 128; 113

Bakshi, Ralph 1938(?)-............ **CLC 26**
See also CA 112; 138

Bakunin, Mikhail (Alexandrovich)
1814-1876 .... **NCLC 25**

Baldwin, James (Arthur)
1924-1987 ...... **CLC 1, 2, 3, 4, 5, 8, 13,
15, 17, 42, 50, 67, 90; BLC; DA; DAB;
DAC; DC 1; SSC 10; WLC**
See also AAYA 4; BW 1; CA 1-4R; 124;
CABS 1; CANR 3, 24;
CDALB 1941-1968; DAM MST, MULT,
NOV, POP; DLB 2, 7, 33; DLBY 87;
MTCW; SATA 9; SATA-Obit 54

Ballard, J(ames) G(raham)
1930- .... **CLC 3, 6, 14, 36; SSC 1**
See also AAYA 3; CA 5-8R; CANR 15, 39;
DAM NOV, POP; DLB 14; MTCW

Balmont, Konstantin (Dmitriyevich)
1867-1943 .... **TCLC 11**
See also CA 109

Baxter, James K(eir) 1926-1972 .... **CLC 14**
See also CA 77-80

Baxter, John
See Hunt, E(verette) Howard, (Jr.)

Bayer, Sylvia
See Glassco, John

Baynton, Barbara 1857-1929 ..... **TCLC 57**

Beagle, Peter S(oyer) 1939- .... **CLC 7**
See also CA 9-12R; CANR 4, 51;
DLBY 80; INT CANR-4; SATA 60

Bean, Normal
See Burroughs, Edgar Rice

Beard, Charles A(ustin)
1874-1948 .... **TCLC 15**
See also CA 115; DLB 17; SATA 18

Beardsley, Aubrey 1872-1898 ..... **NCLC 6**

Beattie, Ann
1947- .... **CLC 8, 13, 18, 40, 63; SSC 11**
See also BEST 90:2; CA 81-84; DAM NOV,
POP; DLBY 82; MTCW

Beattie, James 1735-1803 .... **NCLC 25**
See also DLB 109

Beauchamp, Kathleen Mansfield 1888-1923
See Mansfield, Katherine
See also CA 104; 134; DA; DAC;
DAM MST

Beaumarchais, Pierre-Augustin Caron de
1732-1799 .... **DC 4**
See also DAM DRAM

Beaumont, Francis 1584(?)-1616 ...... **DC 6**
See also CDBLB Before 1660; DLB 58, 121

**Beauvoir, Simone (Lucie Ernestine Marie
Bertrand) de**
1908-1986 .... **CLC 1, 2, 4, 8, 14, 31, 44,
50, 71; DA; DAB; DAC; WLC**
See also CA 9-12R; 118; CANR 28;
DAM MST, NOV; DLB 72; DLBY 86;
MTCW

Becker, Carl 1873-1945 .... **TCLC 63**
See also DLB 17

Becker, Jurek 1937- .... **CLC 7, 19**
See also CA 85-88; DLB 75

Becker, Walter 1950- .... **CLC 26**

Beckett, Samuel (Barclay)
1906-1989 ...... **CLC 1, 2, 3, 4, 6, 9, 10,
11, 14, 18, 29, 57, 59, 83; DA; DAB;
DAC; SSC 16; WLC**
See also CA 5-8R; 130; CANR 33;
CDBLB 1945-1960; DAM DRAM, MST,
NOV; DLB 13, 15; DLBY 90; MTCW

Beckford, William 1760-1844 .... **NCLC 16**
See also DLB 39

Beckman, Gunnel 1910- .... **CLC 26**
See also CA 33-36R; CANR 15; CLR 25;
MAICYA; SAAS 9; SATA 6

Becque, Henri 1837-1899 .... **NCLC 3**

Beddoes, Thomas Lovell
1803-1849 .... **NCLC 3**
See also DLB 96

Bedford, Donald F.
See Fearing, Kenneth (Flexner)

Beecher, Catharine Esther
1800-1878 .... **NCLC 30**
See also DLB 1

Beecher, John 1904-1980 .... **CLC 6**
See also AITN 1; CA 5-8R; 105; CANR 8

Beer, Johann 1655-1700 .... **LC 5**

Beer, Patricia 1924- .... **CLC 58**
See also CA 61-64; CANR 13, 46; DLB 40

Beerbohm, Henry Maximilian
1872-1956 .... **TCLC 1, 24**
See also CA 104; DLB 34, 100

Beerbohm, Max
See Beerbohm, Henry Maximilian

Beer-Hofmann, Richard
1866-1945 .... **TCLC 60**
See also DLB 81

Begiebing, Robert J(ohn) 1946- ..... **CLC 70**
See also CA 122; CANR 40

Behan, Brendan
1923-1964 .... **CLC 1, 8, 11, 15, 79**
See also CA 73-76; CANR 33;
CDBLB 1945-1960; DAM DRAM;
DLB 13; MTCW

Behn, Aphra
1640(?)-1689 ...... **LC 1, 30; DA; DAB;
DAC; DC 4; PC 13; WLC**
See also DAM DRAM, MST, NOV, POET;
DLB 39, 80, 131

Behrman, S(amuel) N(athaniel)
1893-1973 .... **CLC 40**
See also CA 13-16; 45-48; CAP 1; DLB 7,
44

Belasco, David 1853-1931 .... **TCLC 3**
See also CA 104; DLB 7

Belcheva, Elisaveta 1893- .... **CLC 10**
See also Bagryana, Elisaveta

Beldone, Phil "Cheech"
See Ellison, Harlan (Jay)

Beleno
See Azuela, Mariano

Belinski, Vissarion Grigoryevich
1811-1848 .... **NCLC 5**

Belitt, Ben 1911- .... **CLC 22**
See also CA 13-16R; CAAS 4; CANR 7;
DLB 5

Bell, James Madison
1826-1902 .... **TCLC 43; BLC**
See also BW 1; CA 122; 124; DAM MULT;
DLB 50

Bell, Madison (Smartt) 1957- ...... **CLC 41**
See also CA 111; CANR 28

Bell, Marvin (Hartley) 1937- ..... **CLC 8, 31**
See also CA 21-24R; CAAS 14;
DAM POET; DLB 5; MTCW

Bell, W. L. D.
See Mencken, H(enry) L(ouis)

Bellamy, Atwood C.
See Mencken, H(enry) L(ouis)

Bellamy, Edward 1850-1898 ...... **NCLC 4**
See also DLB 12

Bellin, Edward J.
See Kuttner, Henry

Belloc, (Joseph) Hilaire (Pierre)
1870-1953 .... **TCLC 7, 18**
See also CA 106; DAM POET; DLB 19,
100, 141; YABC 1

Belloc, Joseph Peter Rene Hilaire
See Belloc, (Joseph) Hilaire (Pierre)

Belloc, Joseph Pierre Hilaire
See Belloc, (Joseph) Hilaire (Pierre)

Belloc, M. A.
See Lowndes, Marie Adelaide (Belloc)

Bellow, Saul
1915- ...... **CLC 1, 2, 3, 6, 8, 10, 13, 15,
25, 33, 34, 63, 79; DA; DAB; DAC;
SSC 14; WLC**
See also AITN 2; BEST 89:3; CA 5-8R;
CABS 1; CANR 29; CDALB 1941-1968;
DAM MST, NOV, POP; DLB 2, 28;
DLBD 3; DLBY 82; MTCW

Belser, Reimond Karel Maria de
See Ruyslinck, Ward

Bely, Andrey .... **TCLC 7; PC 11**
See also Bugayev, Boris Nikolayevich

Benary, Margot
See Benary-Isbert, Margot

Benary-Isbert, Margot 1889-1979 ... **CLC 12**
See also CA 5-8R; 89-92; CANR 4;
CLR 12; MAICYA; SATA 2;
SATA-Obit 21

Benavente (y Martinez), Jacinto
1866-1954 .... **TCLC 3**
See also CA 106; 131; DAM DRAM,
MULT; HW; MTCW

Benchley, Peter (Bradford)
1940- .... **CLC 4, 8**
See also AAYA 14; AITN 2; CA 17-20R;
CANR 12, 35; DAM NOV, POP;
MTCW; SATA 3

Benchley, Robert (Charles)
1889-1945 .... **TCLC 1, 55**
See also CA 105; DLB 11

Benda, Julien 1867-1956 .... **TCLC 60**
See also CA 120

Benedict, Ruth 1887-1948 .... **TCLC 60**

Benedikt, Michael 1935- .... **CLC 4, 14**
See also CA 13-16R; CANR 7; DLB 5

Benet, Juan 1927- .... **CLC 28**
See also CA 143

Benet, Stephen Vincent
1898-1943 .... **TCLC 7; SSC 10**
See also CA 104; DAM POET; DLB 4, 48,
102; YABC 1

Benet, William Rose 1886-1950 ... **TCLC 28**
See also CA 118; DAM POET; DLB 45

Benford, Gregory (Albert) 1941- .... **CLC 52**
See also CA 69-72; CANR 12, 24, 49;
DLBY 82

Bengtsson, Frans (Gunnar)
1894-1954 .... **TCLC 48**

Benjamin, David
See Slavitt, David R(ytman)

Benjamin, Lois
See Gould, Lois

Benjamin, Walter 1892-1940 ...... **TCLC 39**

Benn, Gottfried 1886-1956 .... **TCLC 3**
See also CA 106; DLB 56

Bennett, Alan 1934- ..... **CLC 45, 77; DAB**
See also CA 103; CANR 35; DAM MST;
MTCW

Bennett, (Enoch) Arnold
1867-1931 . . . . **TCLC 5, 20**
See also CA 106; CDBLB 1890-1914;
DLB 10, 34, 98, 135

Bennett, Elizabeth
See Mitchell, Margaret (Munnerlyn)

Bennett, George Harold 1930-
See Bennett, Hal
See also BW 1; CA 97-100

Bennett, Hal . . . . **CLC 5**
See also Bennett, George Harold
See also DLB 33

Bennett, Jay 1912- . . . . **CLC 35**
See also AAYA 10; CA 69-72; CANR 11,
42; JRDA; SAAS 4; SATA 41, 87;
SATA-Brief 27

Bennett, Louise (Simone)
1919- . . . . **CLC 28; BLC**
See also BW 2; DAM MULT; DLB 117

Benson, E(dward) F(rederic)
1867-1940 . . . . **TCLC 27**
See also CA 114; DLB 135, 153

Benson, Jackson J. 1930- . . . . **CLC 34**
See also CA 25-28R; DLB 111

Benson, Sally 1900-1972 . . . . **CLC 17**
See also CA 19-20; 37-40R; CAP 1;
SATA 1, 35; SATA-Obit 27

Benson, Stella 1892-1933 . . . . **TCLC 17**
See also CA 117; DLB 36, 162

Bentham, Jeremy 1748-1832 . . . . . **NCLC 38**
See also DLB 107, 158

Bentley, E(dmund) C(lerihew)
1875-1956 . . . . **TCLC 12**
See also CA 108; DLB 70

Bentley, Eric (Russell) 1916- . . . . . . **CLC 24**
See also CA 5-8R; CANR 6; INT CANR-6

Beranger, Pierre Jean de
1780-1857 . . . . **NCLC 34**

Berendt, John (Lawrence) 1939- . . . . **CLC 86**
See also CA 146

Berger, Colonel
See Malraux, (Georges-)Andre

Berger, John (Peter) 1926- . . . . . . **CLC 2, 19**
See also CA 81-84; CANR 51; DLB 14

Berger, Melvin H. 1927- . . . . **CLC 12**
See also CA 5-8R; CANR 4; CLR 32;
SAAS 2; SATA 5

Berger, Thomas (Louis)
1924- . . . . **CLC 3, 5, 8, 11, 18, 38**
See also CA 1-4R; CANR 5, 28, 51;
DAM NOV; DLB 2; DLBY 80;
INT CANR-28; MTCW

Bergman, (Ernst) Ingmar
1918- . . . . **CLC 16, 72**
See also CA 81-84; CANR 33

Bergson, Henri 1859-1941 . . . . **TCLC 32**

Bergstein, Eleanor 1938- . . . . **CLC 4**
See also CA 53-56; CANR 5

Berkoff, Steven 1937- . . . . **CLC 56**
See also CA 104

Bermant, Chaim (Icyk) 1929- . . . . . . **CLC 40**
See also CA 57-60; CANR 6, 31

Bern, Victoria
See Fisher, M(ary) F(rances) K(ennedy)

Bernanos, (Paul Louis) Georges
1888-1948 . . . . **TCLC 3**
See also CA 104; 130; DLB 72

Bernard, April 1956- . . . . **CLC 59**
See also CA 131

Berne, Victoria
See Fisher, M(ary) F(rances) K(ennedy)

Bernhard, Thomas
1931-1989 . . . . **CLC 3, 32, 61**
See also CA 85-88; 127; CANR 32;
DLB 85, 124; MTCW

Berriault, Gina 1926- . . . . **CLC 54**
See also CA 116; 129; DLB 130

Berrigan, Daniel 1921- . . . . **CLC 4**
See also CA 33-36R; CAAS 1; CANR 11,
43; DLB 5

Berrigan, Edmund Joseph Michael, Jr.
1934-1983
See Berrigan, Ted
See also CA 61-64; 110; CANR 14

Berrigan, Ted . . . . **CLC 37**
See also Berrigan, Edmund Joseph Michael,
Jr.
See also DLB 5

Berry, Charles Edward Anderson 1931-
See Berry, Chuck
See also CA 115

Berry, Chuck . . . . **CLC 17**
See also Berry, Charles Edward Anderson

Berry, Jonas
See Ashbery, John (Lawrence)

Berry, Wendell (Erdman)
1934- . . . . **CLC 4, 6, 8, 27, 46**
See also AITN 1; CA 73-76; CANR 50;
DAM POET; DLB 5, 6

Berryman, John
1914-1972 . . . . . . **CLC 1, 2, 3, 4, 6, 8, 10,
13, 25, 62**
See also CA 13-16; 33-36R; CABS 2;
CANR 35; CAP 1; CDALB 1941-1968;
DAM POET; DLB 48; MTCW

Bertolucci, Bernardo 1940- . . . . **CLC 16**
See also CA 106

Bertrand, Aloysius 1807-1841 . . . . **NCLC 31**

Bertran de Born c. 1140-1215 . . . . . **CMLC 5**

Besant, Annie (Wood) 1847-1933 . . . **TCLC 9**
See also CA 105

Bessie, Alvah 1904-1985 . . . . **CLC 23**
See also CA 5-8R; 116; CANR 2; DLB 26

Bethlen, T. D.
See Silverberg, Robert

Beti, Mongo . . . . **CLC 27; BLC**
See also Biyidi, Alexandre
See also DAM MULT

Betjeman, John
1906-1984 . . . **CLC 2, 6, 10, 34, 43; DAB**
See also CA 9-12R; 112; CANR 33;
CDBLB 1945-1960; DAM MST, POET;
DLB 20; DLBY 84; MTCW

Bettelheim, Bruno 1903-1990 . . . . . . **CLC 79**
See also CA 81-84; 131; CANR 23; MTCW

Betti, Ugo 1892-1953 . . . . **TCLC 5**
See also CA 104

Betts, Doris (Waugh) 1932- . . . . **CLC 3, 6, 28**
See also CA 13-16R; CANR 9; DLBY 82;
INT CANR-9

Bevan, Alistair
See Roberts, Keith (John Kingston)

Bialik, Chaim Nachman
1873-1934 . . . . **TCLC 25**

Bickerstaff, Isaac
See Swift, Jonathan

Bidart, Frank 1939- . . . . **CLC 33**
See also CA 140

Bienek, Horst 1930- . . . . **CLC 7, 11**
See also CA 73-76; DLB 75

Bierce, Ambrose (Gwinett)
1842-1914(?) . . . . **TCLC 1, 7, 44; DA;
DAC; SSC 9; WLC**
See also CA 104; 139; CDALB 1865-1917;
DAM MST; DLB 11, 12, 23, 71, 74

Billings, Josh
See Shaw, Henry Wheeler

Billington, (Lady) Rachel (Mary)
1942- . . . . **CLC 43**
See also AITN 2; CA 33-36R; CANR 44

Binyon, T(imothy) J(ohn) 1936- . . . . **CLC 34**
See also CA 111; CANR 28

Bioy Casares, Adolfo
1914- . . . **CLC 4, 8, 13, 88; HLC; SSC 17**
See also CA 29-32R; CANR 19, 43;
DAM MULT; DLB 113; HW; MTCW

Bird, Cordwainer
See Ellison, Harlan (Jay)

Bird, Robert Montgomery
1806-1854 . . . . **NCLC 1**

Birney, (Alfred) Earle
1904- . . . . **CLC 1, 4, 6, 11; DAC**
See also CA 1-4R; CANR 5, 20;
DAM MST, POET; DLB 88; MTCW

Bishop, Elizabeth
1911-1979 . . . . . . **CLC 1, 4, 9, 13, 15, 32;
DA; DAC; PC 3**
See also CA 5-8R; 89-92; CABS 2;
CANR 26; CDALB 1968-1988;
DAM MST, POET; DLB 5; MTCW;
SATA-Obit 24

Bishop, John 1935- . . . . **CLC 10**
See also CA 105

Bissett, Bill 1939- . . . . **CLC 18; PC 14**
See also CA 69-72; CAAS 19; CANR 15;
DLB 53; MTCW

Bitov, Andrei (Georgievich) 1937- . . . **CLC 57**
See also CA 142

Biyidi, Alexandre 1932-
See Beti, Mongo
See also BW 1; CA 114; 124; MTCW

Bjarme, Brynjolf
See Ibsen, Henrik (Johan)

Bjornson, Bjornstjerne (Martinius)
1832-1910 . . . . **TCLC 7, 37**
See also CA 104

Black, Robert
See Holdstock, Robert P.

Blackburn, Paul 1926-1971 . . . . . . **CLC 9, 43**
See also CA 81-84; 33-36R; CANR 34;
DLB 16; DLBY 81

Black Elk 1863-1950 . . . . TCLC **33**
See also CA 144; DAM MULT; NNAL

Black Hobart
See Sanders, (James) Ed(ward)

Blacklin, Malcolm
See Chambers, Aidan

Blackmore, R(ichard) D(oddridge)
1825-1900 . . . . TCLC **27**
See also CA 120; DLB 18

Blackmur, R(ichard) P(almer)
1904-1965 . . . . CLC **2, 24**
See also CA 11-12; 25-28R; CAP 1; DLB 63

Black Tarantula, The
See Acker, Kathy

Blackwood, Algernon (Henry)
1869-1951 . . . . TCLC **5**
See also CA 105; 150; DLB 153, 156

Blackwood, Caroline 1931- . . . . CLC **6, 9**
See also CA 85-88; CANR 32; DLB 14;
MTCW

Blade, Alexander
See Hamilton, Edmond; Silverberg, Robert

Blaga, Lucian 1895-1961 . . . . CLC **75**

Blair, Eric (Arthur) 1903-1950
See Orwell, George
See also CA 104; 132; DA; DAB; DAC;
DAM MST, NOV; MTCW; SATA 29

Blais, Marie-Claire
1939- . . . . CLC **2, 4, 6, 13, 22; DAC**
See also CA 21-24R; CAAS 4; CANR 38;
DAM MST; DLB 53; MTCW

Blaise, Clark 1940- . . . . CLC **29**
See also AITN 2; CA 53-56; CAAS 3;
CANR 5; DLB 53

Blake, Nicholas
See Day Lewis, C(ecil)
See also DLB 77

Blake, William
1757-1827 . . . . NCLC **13, 37; DA; DAB;
DAC; PC 12; WLC**
See also CDBLB 1789-1832; DAM MST,
POET; DLB 93, 163; MAICYA;
SATA 30

Blake, William J(ames) 1894-1969 . . . PC **12**
See also CA 5-8R; 25-28R

Blasco Ibanez, Vicente
1867-1928 . . . . TCLC **12**
See also CA 110; 131; DAM NOV; HW;
MTCW

Blatty, William Peter 1928- . . . . CLC **2**
See also CA 5-8R; CANR 9; DAM POP

Bleeck, Oliver
See Thomas, Ross (Elmore)

Blessing, Lee 1949- . . . . CLC **54**

Blish, James (Benjamin)
1921-1975 . . . . CLC **14**
See also CA 1-4R; 57-60; CANR 3; DLB 8;
MTCW; SATA 66

Bliss, Reginald
See Wells, H(erbert) G(eorge)

Blixen, Karen (Christentze Dinesen)
1885-1962
See Dinesen, Isak
See also CA 25-28; CANR 22, 50; CAP 2;
MTCW; SATA 44

Bloch, Robert (Albert) 1917-1994 . . . CLC **33**
See also CA 5-8R; 146; CAAS 20; CANR 5;
DLB 44; INT CANR-5; SATA 12;
SATA-Obit 82

Blok, Alexander (Alexandrovich)
1880-1921 . . . . TCLC **5**
See also CA 104

Blom, Jan
See Breytenbach, Breyten

Bloom, Harold 1930- . . . . CLC **24**
See also CA 13-16R; CANR 39; DLB 67

Bloomfield, Aurelius
See Bourne, Randolph S(illiman)

Blount, Roy (Alton), Jr. 1941- . . . . . CLC **38**
See also CA 53-56; CANR 10, 28;
INT CANR-28; MTCW

Bloy, Leon 1846-1917 . . . . TCLC **22**
See also CA 121; DLB 123

Blume, Judy (Sussman) 1938- . . . CLC **12, 30**
See also AAYA 3; CA 29-32R; CANR 13,
37; CLR 2, 15; DAM NOV, POP;
DLB 52; JRDA; MAICYA; MTCW;
SATA 2, 31, 79

Blunden, Edmund (Charles)
1896-1974 . . . . CLC **2, 56**
See also CA 17-18; 45-48; CAP 2; DLB 20,
100, 155; MTCW

Bly, Robert (Elwood)
1926- . . . . CLC **1, 2, 5, 10, 15, 38**
See also CA 5-8R; CANR 41; DAM POET;
DLB 5; MTCW

Boas, Franz 1858-1942 . . . . TCLC **56**
See also CA 115

Bobette
See Simenon, Georges (Jacques Christian)

Boccaccio, Giovanni
1313-1375 . . . . CMLC **13; SSC 10**

Bochco, Steven 1943- . . . . CLC **35**
See also AAYA 11; CA 124; 138

Bodenheim, Maxwell 1892-1954 . . . TCLC **44**
See also CA 110; DLB 9, 45

Bodker, Cecil 1927- . . . . CLC **21**
See also CA 73-76; CANR 13, 44; CLR 23;
MAICYA; SATA 14

Boell, Heinrich (Theodor)
1917-1985 . . . . CLC **2, 3, 6, 9, 11, 15, 27,
32, 72; DA; DAB; DAC; WLC**
See also CA 21-24R; 116; CANR 24;
DAM MST, NOV; DLB 69; DLBY 85;
MTCW

Boerne, Alfred
See Doeblin, Alfred

Boethius 480(?)-524(?) . . . . CMLC **15**
See also DLB 115

Bogan, Louise
1897-1970 . . . . . . CLC **4, 39, 46; PC 12**
See also CA 73-76; 25-28R; CANR 33;
DAM POET; DLB 45; MTCW

Bogarde, Dirk . . . . CLC **19**
See also Van Den Bogarde, Derek Jules
Gaspard Ulric Niven
See also DLB 14

Bogosian, Eric 1953- . . . . CLC **45**
See also CA 138

Bograd, Larry 1953- . . . . CLC **35**
See also CA 93-96; SAAS 21; SATA 33

Boiardo, Matteo Maria 1441-1494 . . . . LC **6**

Boileau-Despreaux, Nicolas
1636-1711 . . . . LC **3**

Boland, Eavan (Aisling) 1944- . . . CLC **40, 67**
See also CA 143; DAM POET; DLB 40

Bolt, Lee
See Faust, Frederick (Schiller)

Bolt, Robert (Oxton) 1924-1995 . . . . CLC **14**
See also CA 17-20R; 147; CANR 35;
DAM DRAM; DLB 13; MTCW

Bombet, Louis-Alexandre-Cesar
See Stendhal

Bomkauf
See Kaufman, Bob (Garnell)

Bonaventura . . . . NCLC **35**
See also DLB 90

Bond, Edward 1934- . . . . CLC **4, 6, 13, 23**
See also CA 25-28R; CANR 38;
DAM DRAM; DLB 13; MTCW

Bonham, Frank 1914-1989 . . . . CLC **12**
See also AAYA 1; CA 9-12R; CANR 4, 36;
JRDA; MAICYA; SAAS 3; SATA 1, 49;
SATA-Obit 62

Bonnefoy, Yves 1923- . . . . CLC **9, 15, 58**
See also CA 85-88; CANR 33; DAM MST,
POET; MTCW

Bontemps, Arna(ud Wendell)
1902-1973 . . . . CLC **1, 18; BLC**
See also BW 1; CA 1-4R; 41-44R; CANR 4,
35; CLR 6; DAM MULT, NOV, POET;
DLB 48, 51; JRDA; MAICYA; MTCW;
SATA 2, 44; SATA-Obit 24

Booth, Martin 1944- . . . . CLC **13**
See also CA 93-96; CAAS 2

Booth, Philip 1925- . . . . CLC **23**
See also CA 5-8R; CANR 5; DLBY 82

Booth, Wayne C(layson) 1921- . . . . . CLC **24**
See also CA 1-4R; CAAS 5; CANR 3, 43;
DLB 67

Borchert, Wolfgang 1921-1947 . . . . . TCLC **5**
See also CA 104; DLB 69, 124

Borel, Petrus 1809-1859 . . . . NCLC **41**

Borges, Jorge Luis
1899-1986 . . . CLC **1, 2, 3, 4, 6, 8, 9, 10,
13, 19, 44, 48, 83; DA; DAB; DAC;
HLC; SSC 4; WLC**
See also CA 21-24R; CANR 19, 33;
DAM MST, MULT; DLB 113; DLBY 86;
HW; MTCW

Borowski, Tadeusz 1922-1951 . . . . . . TCLC **9**
See also CA 106

Borrow, George (Henry)
1803-1881 . . . . NCLC **9**
See also DLB 21, 55

Bosman, Herman Charles
1905-1951 . . . . TCLC **49**

Bosschere, Jean de 1878(?)-1953 . . . TCLC **19**
See also CA 115

Boswell, James
1740-1795 . . . . . . LC **4; DA; DAB; DAC;
WLC**
See also CDBLB 1660-1789; DAM MST;
DLB 104, 142

Brink, Andre (Philippus)
1935- . . . . CLC 18, 36
See also CA 104; CANR 39; INT 103;
MTCW

Brinsmead, H(esba) F(ay) 1922- . . . . CLC 21
See also CA 21-24R; CANR 10; MAICYA;
SAAS 5; SATA 18, 78

Brittain, Vera (Mary)
1893(?)-1970 . . . . CLC 23
See also CA 13-16; 25-28R; CAP 1; MTCW

Broch, Hermann 1886-1951. . . . . . . TCLC 20
See also CA 117; DLB 85, 124

Brock, Rose
See Hansen, Joseph

Brodkey, Harold 1930-. . . . . CLC 56
See also CA 111; DLB 130

Brodsky, Iosif Alexandrovich 1940-
See Brodsky, Joseph
See also AITN 1; CA 41-44R; CANR 37;
DAM POET; MTCW

Brodsky, Joseph . . CLC 4, 6, 13, 36, 50; PC 9
See also Brodsky, Iosif Alexandrovich

Brodsky, Michael Mark 1948- . . . . . CLC 19
See also CA 102; CANR 18, 41

Bromell, Henry 1947-. . . . . CLC 5
See also CA 53-56; CANR 9

Bromfield, Louis (Brucker)
1896-1956 . . . . TCLC 11
See also CA 107; DLB 4, 9, 86

Broner, E(sther) M(asserman)
1930- . . . . CLC 19
See also CA 17-20R; CANR 8, 25; DLB 28

Bronk, William 1918-. . . . . CLC 10
See also CA 89-92; CANR 23

Bronstein, Lev Davidovich
See Trotsky, Leon

Bronte, Anne 1820-1849. . . . . NCLC 4
See also DLB 21

Bronte, Charlotte
1816-1855 . . . . NCLC 3, 8, 33; DA;
DAB; DAC; WLC
See also AAYA 17; CDBLB 1832-1890;
DAM MST, NOV; DLB 21, 159

Bronte, Emily (Jane)
1818-1848 . . . . NCLC 16, 35; DA; DAB;
DAC; PC 8; WLC
See also AAYA 17; CDBLB 1832-1890;
DAM MST, NOV, POET; DLB 21, 32

Brooke, Frances 1724-1789 . . . . LC 6
See also DLB 39, 99

Brooke, Henry 1703(?)-1783 . . . . LC 1
See also DLB 39

Brooke, Rupert (Chawner)
1887-1915 . . . . . . TCLC 2, 7; DA; DAB;
DAC; WLC
See also CA 104; 132; CDBLB 1914-1945;
DAM MST, POET; DLB 19; MTCW

Brooke-Haven, P.
See Wodehouse, P(elham) G(renville)

Brooke-Rose, Christine 1926- . . . . . . CLC 40
See also CA 13-16R; DLB 14

Brookner, Anita
1928- . . . . CLC 32, 34, 51; DAB
See also CA 114; 120; CANR 37;
DAM POP; DLBY 87; MTCW

Brooks, Cleanth 1906-1994 . . . . . CLC 24, 86
See also CA 17-20R; 145; CANR 33, 35;
DLB 63; DLBY 94; INT CANR-35;
MTCW

Brooks, George
See Baum, L(yman) Frank

Brooks, Gwendolyn
1917- . . . . . . CLC 1, 2, 4, 5, 15, 49; BLC;
DA; DAC; PC 7; WLC
See also AITN 1; BW 2; CA 1-4R;
CANR 1, 27; CDALB 1941-1968;
CLR 27; DAM MST, MULT, POET;
DLB 5, 76; MTCW; SATA 6

Brooks, Mel. CLC 12
See also Kaminsky, Melvin
See also AAYA 13; DLB 26

Brooks, Peter 1938-. . . . . CLC 34
See also CA 45-48; CANR 1

Brooks, Van Wyck 1886-1963. . . . . . CLC 29
See also CA 1-4R; CANR 6; DLB 45, 63,
103

Brophy, Brigid (Antonia)
1929-1995 . . . . CLC 6, 11, 29
See also CA 5-8R; 149; CAAS 4; CANR 25;
DLB 14; MTCW

Brosman, Catharine Savage 1934-. . . . CLC 9
See also CA 61-64; CANR 21, 46

Brother Antoninus
See Everson, William (Oliver)

Broughton, T(homas) Alan 1936- . . . CLC 19
See also CA 45-48; CANR 2, 23, 48

Broumas, Olga 1949-. . . . . CLC 10, 73
See also CA 85-88; CANR 20

Brown, Charles Brockden
1771-1810 . . . . NCLC 22
See also CDALB 1640-1865; DLB 37, 59,
73

Brown, Christy 1932-1981. . . . . CLC 63
See also CA 105; 104; DLB 14

Brown, Claude 1937- . . . . CLC 30; BLC
See also AAYA 7; BW 1; CA 73-76;
DAM MULT

Brown, Dee (Alexander) 1908- . . CLC 18, 47
See also CA 13-16R; CAAS 6; CANR 11,
45; DAM POP; DLBY 80; MTCW;
SATA 5

Brown, George
See Wertmueller, Lina

Brown, George Douglas
1869-1902 . . . . TCLC 28

Brown, George Mackay 1921-. . . . CLC 5, 48
See also CA 21-24R; CAAS 6; CANR 12,
37; DLB 14, 27, 139; MTCW; SATA 35

Brown, (William) Larry 1951-. . . . . . CLC 73
See also CA 130; 134; INT 133

Brown, Moses
See Barrett, William (Christopher)

Brown, Rita Mae 1944-. . . . . CLC 18, 43, 79
See also CA 45-48; CANR 2, 11, 35;
DAM NOV, POP; INT CANR-11;
MTCW

Brown, Roderick (Langmere) Haig-
See Haig-Brown, Roderick (Langmere)

Brown, Rosellen 1939-. . . . . CLC 32
See also CA 77-80; CAAS 10; CANR 14, 44

Brown, Sterling Allen
1901-1989 . . . . CLC 1, 23, 59; BLC
See also BW 1; CA 85-88; 127; CANR 26;
DAM MULT, POET; DLB 48, 51, 63;
MTCW

Brown, Will
See Ainsworth, William Harrison

Brown, William Wells
1813-1884 . . . . NCLC 2; BLC; DC 1
See also DAM MULT; DLB 3, 50

Browne, (Clyde) Jackson 1948(?)-. . . CLC 21
See also CA 120

Browning, Elizabeth Barrett
1806-1861 . . . . . NCLC 1, 16; DA; DAB;
DAC; PC 6; WLC
See also CDBLB 1832-1890; DAM MST,
POET; DLB 32

Browning, Robert
1812-1889 . . . . NCLC 19; DA; DAB;
DAC; PC 2
See also CDBLB 1832-1890; DAM MST,
POET; DLB 32, 163; YABC 1

Browning, Tod 1882-1962 . . . . CLC 16
See also CA 141; 117

Brownson, Orestes (Augustus)
1803-1876 . . . . NCLC 50

Bruccoli, Matthew J(oseph) 1931- . . CLC 34
See also CA 9-12R; CANR 7; DLB 103

Bruce, Lenny. . . . . CLC 21
See also Schneider, Leonard Alfred

Bruin, John
See Brutus, Dennis

Brulard, Henri
See Stendhal

Brulls, Christian
See Simenon, Georges (Jacques Christian)

Brunner, John (Kilian Houston)
1934-1995 . . . . CLC 8, 10
See also CA 1-4R; 149; CAAS 8; CANR 2,
37; DAM POP; MTCW

Bruno, Giordano 1548-1600. . . . . LC 27

Brutus, Dennis 1924- . . . . CLC 43; BLC
See also BW 2; CA 49-52; CAAS 14;
CANR 2, 27, 42; DAM MULT, POET;
DLB 117

Bryan, C(ourtlandt) D(ixon) B(arnes)
1936- . . . . CLC 29
See also CA 73-76; CANR 13;
INT CANR-13

Bryan, Michael
See Moore, Brian

Bryant, William Cullen
1794-1878 . . . . . NCLC 6, 46; DA; DAB;
DAC
See also CDALB 1640-1865; DAM MST,
POET; DLB 3, 43, 59

Bryusov, Valery Yakovlevich
1873-1924 . . . . TCLC 10
See also CA 107

Buchan, John 1875-1940 . . . TCLC 41; DAB
See also CA 108; 145; DAM POP; DLB 34,
70, 156; YABC 2

Buchanan, George 1506-1582 . . . . LC 4

Buchheim, Lothar-Guenther 1918- . . . CLC 6
See also CA 85-88

Buchner, (Karl) Georg
    1813-1837 . . . . NCLC 26

Buchwald, Art(hur)   1925- . . . . CLC 33
    See also AITN 1; CA 5-8R; CANR 21;
    MTCW; SATA 10

Buck, Pearl S(ydenstricker)
    1892-1973 . . . . CLC 7, 11, 18; DA; DAB;
                                         DAC
    See also AITN 1; CA 1-4R; 41-44R;
    CANR 1, 34; DAM MST, NOV; DLB 9,
    102; MTCW; SATA 1, 25

Buckler, Ernest   1908-1984. . . . CLC 13; DAC
    See also CA 11-12; 114; CAP 1;
    DAM MST; DLB 68; SATA 47

Buckley, Vincent (Thomas)
    1925-1988 . . . . CLC 57
    See also CA 101

Buckley, William F(rank), Jr.
    1925- . . . . CLC 7, 18, 37
    See also AITN 1; CA 1-4R; CANR 1, 24;
    DAM POP; DLB 137; DLBY 80;
    INT CANR-24; MTCW

Buechner, (Carl) Frederick
    1926- . . . . CLC 2, 4, 6, 9
    See also CA 13-16R; CANR 11, 39;
    DAM NOV; DLBY 80; INT CANR-11;
    MTCW

Buell, John (Edward)   1927- . . . . CLC 10
    See also CA 1-4R; DLB 53

Buero Vallejo, Antonio   1916- . . . CLC 15, 46
    See also CA 106; CANR 24, 49; HW;
    MTCW

Bufalino, Gesualdo   1920(?)- . . . . CLC 74

Bugayev, Boris Nikolayevich   1880-1934
    See Bely, Andrey
    See also CA 104

Bukowski, Charles
    1920-1994 . . . . CLC 2, 5, 9, 41, 82
    See also CA 17-20R; 144; CANR 40;
    DAM NOV, POET; DLB 5, 130; MTCW

Bulgakov, Mikhail (Afanas'evich)
    1891-1940 . . . . TCLC 2, 16; SSC 18
    See also CA 105; DAM DRAM, NOV

Bulgya, Alexander Alexandrovich
    1901-1956 . . . . TCLC 53
    See also Fadeyev, Alexander
    See also CA 117

Bullins, Ed   1935- . . CLC 1, 5, 7; BLC; DC 6
    See also BW 2; CA 49-52; CAAS 16;
    CANR 24, 46; DAM DRAM, MULT;
    DLB 7, 38; MTCW

Bulwer-Lytton, Edward (George Earle Lytton)
    1803-1873 . . . . NCLC 1, 45
    See also DLB 21

Bunin, Ivan Alexeyevich
    1870-1953 . . . . TCLC 6; SSC 5
    See also CA 104

Bunting, Basil   1900-1985. . . . CLC 10, 39, 47
    See also CA 53-56; 115; CANR 7;
    DAM POET; DLB 20

Bunuel, Luis   1900-1983 . . CLC 16, 80; HLC
    See also CA 101; 110; CANR 32;
    DAM MULT; HW

Bunyan, John
    1628-1688 . . . . . . LC 4; DA; DAB; DAC;
                                         WLC
    See also CDBLB 1660-1789; DAM MST;
    DLB 39

Burckhardt, Jacob (Christoph)
    1818-1897 . . . . NCLC 49

Burford, Eleanor
    See Hibbert, Eleanor Alice Burford

Burgess, Anthony
    . CLC 1, 2, 4, 5, 8, 10, 13, 15, 22, 40, 62,
                                     81; DAB
    See also Wilson, John (Anthony) Burgess
    See also AITN 1; CDBLB 1960 to Present;
    DLB 14

Burke, Edmund
    1729(?)-1797 . . . . LC 7; DA; DAB; DAC;
                                         WLC
    See also DAM MST; DLB 104

Burke, Kenneth (Duva)
    1897-1993 . . . . CLC 2, 24
    See also CA 5-8R; 143; CANR 39; DLB 45,
    63; MTCW

Burke, Leda
    See Garnett, David

Burke, Ralph
    See Silverberg, Robert

Burke, Thomas   1886-1945 . . . . TCLC 63
    See also CA 113

Burney, Fanny   1752-1840 . . . . NCLC 12, 54
    See also DLB 39

Burns, Robert   1759-1796. . . . . PC 6
    See also CDBLB 1789-1832; DA; DAB;
    DAC; DAM MST, POET; DLB 109;
    WLC

Burns, Tex
    See L'Amour, Louis (Dearborn)

Burnshaw, Stanley   1906- . . . . . CLC 3, 13, 44
    See also CA 9-12R; DLB 48

Burr, Anne   1937- . . . . CLC 6
    See also CA 25-28R

Burroughs, Edgar Rice
    1875-1950 . . . . TCLC 2, 32
    See also AAYA 11; CA 104; 132;
    DAM NOV; DLB 8; MTCW; SATA 41

Burroughs, William S(eward)
    1914- . . . . CLC 1, 2, 5, 15, 22, 42, 75;
                                 DA; DAB; DAC; WLC
    See also AITN 2; CA 9-12R; CANR 20;
    DAM MST, NOV, POP; DLB 2, 8, 16,
    152; DLBY 81; MTCW

Burton, Richard F.   1821-1890. . . . NCLC 42
    See also DLB 55

Busch, Frederick   1941- . . . CLC 7, 10, 18, 47
    See also CA 33-36R; CAAS 1; CANR 45;
    DLB 6

Bush, Ronald   1946- . . . . CLC 34
    See also CA 136

Bustos, F(rancisco)
    See Borges, Jorge Luis

Bustos Domecq, H(onorio)
    See Bioy Casares, Adolfo; Borges, Jorge
    Luis

Butler, Octavia E(stelle)   1947- . . . . . CLC 38
    See also BW 2; CA 73-76; CANR 12, 24,
    38; DAM MULT, POP; DLB 33;
    MTCW; SATA 84

Butler, Robert Olen (Jr.)   1945- . . . . . CLC 81
    See also CA 112; DAM POP; INT 112

Butler, Samuel   1612-1680 . . . . LC 16
    See also DLB 101, 126

Butler, Samuel
    1835-1902 . . . . . . TCLC 1, 33; DA; DAB;
                                     DAC; WLC
    See also CA 143; CDBLB 1890-1914;
    DAM MST, NOV; DLB 18, 57

Butler, Walter C.
    See Faust, Frederick (Schiller)

Butor, Michel (Marie Francois)
    1926- . . . . CLC 1, 3, 8, 11, 15
    See also CA 9-12R; CANR 33; DLB 83;
    MTCW

Buzo, Alexander (John)   1944- . . . . . . CLC 61
    See also CA 97-100; CANR 17, 39

Buzzati, Dino   1906-1972 . . . . CLC 36
    See also CA 33-36R

Byars, Betsy (Cromer)   1928- . . . . CLC 35
    See also CA 33-36R; CANR 18, 36; CLR 1,
    16; DLB 52; INT CANR-18; JRDA;
    MAICYA; MTCW; SAAS 1; SATA 4,
    46, 80

Byatt, A(ntonia) S(usan Drabble)
    1936- . . . . CLC 19, 65
    See also CA 13-16R; CANR 13, 33, 50;
    DAM NOV, POP; DLB 14; MTCW

Byrne, David   1952- . . . . CLC 26
    See also CA 127

Byrne, John Keyes   1926-
    See Leonard, Hugh
    See also CA 102; INT 102

Byron, George Gordon (Noel)
    1788-1824 . . . . . NCLC 2, 12; DA; DAB;
                                     DAC; WLC
    See also CDBLB 1789-1832; DAM MST,
    POET; DLB 96, 110

C. 3. 3.
    See Wilde, Oscar (Fingal O'Flahertie Wills)

Caballero, Fernan   1796-1877. . . . . NCLC 10

Cabell, James Branch   1879-1958 . . . TCLC 6
    See also CA 105; DLB 9, 78

Cable, George Washington
    1844-1925 . . . . TCLC 4; SSC 4
    See also CA 104; DLB 12, 74; DLBD 13

Cabral de Melo Neto, Joao   1920- . . . CLC 76
    See also DAM MULT

Cabrera Infante, G(uillermo)
    1929- . . . . CLC 5, 25, 45; HLC
    See also CA 85-88; CANR 29;
    DAM MULT; DLB 113; HW; MTCW

Cade, Toni
    See Bambara, Toni Cade

Cadmus and Harmonia
    See Buchan, John

Caedmon   fl. 658-680. . . . . CMLC 7
    See also DLB 146

Caeiro, Alberto
    See Pessoa, Fernando (Antonio Nogueira)

Cage, John (Milton, Jr.) 1912- ..... **CLC 41**
See also CA 13-16R; CANR 9;
INT CANR-9

Cain, G.
See Cabrera Infante, G(uillermo)

Cain, Guillermo
See Cabrera Infante, G(uillermo)

Cain, James M(allahan)
1892-1977 .... **CLC 3, 11, 28**
See also AITN 1; CA 17-20R; 73-76;
CANR 8, 34; MTCW

Caine, Mark
See Raphael, Frederic (Michael)

Calasso, Roberto 1941- .... **CLC 81**
See also CA 143

Calderon de la Barca, Pedro
1600-1681 .... **LC 23; DC 3**

Caldwell, Erskine (Preston)
1903-1987 .... **CLC 1, 8, 14, 50, 60;
SSC 19**
See also AITN 1; CA 1-4R; 121; CAAS 1;
CANR 2, 33; DAM NOV; DLB 9, 86;
MTCW

Caldwell, (Janet Miriam) Taylor (Holland)
1900-1985 .... **CLC 2, 28, 39**
See also CA 5-8R; 116; CANR 5;
DAM NOV, POP

Calhoun, John Caldwell
1782-1850 .... **NCLC 15**
See also DLB 3

Calisher, Hortense
1911- .... **CLC 2, 4, 8, 38; SSC 15**
See also CA 1-4R; CANR 1, 22;
DAM NOV; DLB 2; INT CANR-22;
MTCW

Callaghan, Morley Edward
1903-1990 ..... **CLC 3, 14, 41, 65; DAC**
See also CA 9-12R; 132; CANR 33;
DAM MST; DLB 68; MTCW

Calvino, Italo
1923-1985 ..... **CLC 5, 8, 11, 22, 33, 39,
73; SSC 3**
See also CA 85-88; 116; CANR 23;
DAM NOV; MTCW

Cameron, Carey 1952- .... **CLC 59**
See also CA 135

Cameron, Peter 1959-............. **CLC 44**
See also CA 125; CANR 50

Campana, Dino 1885-1932........ **TCLC 20**
See also CA 117; DLB 114

Campanella, Tommaso 1568-1639 .... **LC 32**

Campbell, John W(ood, Jr.)
1910-1971 .... **CLC 32**
See also CA 21-22; 29-32R; CANR 34;
CAP 2; DLB 8; MTCW

Campbell, Joseph 1904-1987 ...... **CLC 69**
See also AAYA 3; BEST 89:2; CA 1-4R;
124; CANR 3, 28; MTCW

Campbell, Maria 1940-....... **CLC 85; DAC**
See also CA 102; NNAL

Campbell, (John) Ramsey
1946- .... **CLC 42; SSC 19**
See also CA 57-60; CANR 7; INT CANR-7

Campbell, (Ignatius) Roy (Dunnachie)
1901-1957 .... **TCLC 5**
See also CA 104; DLB 20

Campbell, Thomas 1777-1844 .... **NCLC 19**
See also DLB 93; 144

Campbell, Wilfred................ **TCLC 9**
See also Campbell, William

Campbell, William 1858(?)-1918
See Campbell, Wilfred
See also CA 106; DLB 92

Campos, Alvaro de
See Pessoa, Fernando (Antonio Nogueira)

Camus, Albert
1913-1960 .... **CLC 1, 2, 4, 9, 11, 14, 32,
63, 69; DA; DAB; DAC; DC 2; SSC 9;
WLC**
See also CA 89-92; DAM DRAM, MST,
NOV; DLB 72; MTCW

Canby, Vincent 1924-............. **CLC 13**
See also CA 81-84

Cancale
See Desnos, Robert

Canetti, Elias
1905-1994 ...... **CLC 3, 14, 25, 75, 86**
See also CA 21-24R; 146; CANR 23;
DLB 85, 124; MTCW

Canin, Ethan 1960-............... **CLC 55**
See also CA 131; 135

Cannon, Curt
See Hunter, Evan

Cape, Judith
See Page, P(atricia) K(athleen)

Capek, Karel
1890-1938 ...... **TCLC 6, 37; DA; DAB;
DAC; DC 1; WLC**
See also CA 104; 140; DAM DRAM, MST,
NOV

Capote, Truman
1924-1984 ...... **CLC 1, 3, 8, 13, 19, 34,
38, 58; DA; DAB; DAC; SSC 2; WLC**
See also CA 5-8R; 113; CANR 18;
CDALB 1941-1968; DAM MST, NOV,
POP; DLB 2; DLBY 80, 84; MTCW

Capra, Frank 1897-1991.......... **CLC 16**
See also CA 61-64; 135

Caputo, Philip 1941-.............. **CLC 32**
See also CA 73-76; CANR 40

Card, Orson Scott 1951- .... **CLC 44, 47, 50**
See also AAYA 11; CA 102; CANR 27, 47;
DAM POP; INT CANR-27; MTCW;
SATA 83

Cardenal (Martinez), Ernesto
1925- .... **CLC 31; HLC**
See also CA 49-52; CANR 2, 32;
DAM MULT, POET; HW; MTCW

Carducci, Giosue 1835-1907...... **TCLC 32**

Carew, Thomas 1595(?)-1640........ **LC 13**
See also DLB 126

Carey, Ernestine Gilbreth 1908-.... **CLC 17**
See also CA 5-8R; SATA 2

Carey, Peter 1943-............ **CLC 40, 55**
See also CA 123; 127; INT 127; MTCW

Carleton, William 1794-1869...... **NCLC 3**
See also DLB 159

Carlisle, Henry (Coffin) 1926-...... **CLC 33**
See also CA 13-16R; CANR 15

Carlsen, Chris
See Holdstock, Robert P.

Carlson, Ron(ald F.) 1947-........ **CLC 54**
See also CA 105; CANR 27

Carlyle, Thomas
1795-1881 .. **NCLC 22; DA; DAB; DAC**
See also CDBLB 1789-1832; DAM MST;
DLB 55; 144

Carman, (William) Bliss
1861-1929 .... **TCLC 7; DAC**
See also CA 104; DLB 92

Carnegie, Dale 1888-1955 .... **TCLC 53**

Carossa, Hans 1878-1956........ **TCLC 48**
See also DLB 66

Carpenter, Don(ald Richard)
1931-1995 .... **CLC 41**
See also CA 45-48; 149; CANR 1

Carpentier (y Valmont), Alejo
1904-1980 .... **CLC 8, 11, 38; HLC**
See also CA 65-68; 97-100; CANR 11;
DAM MULT; DLB 113; HW

Carr, Caleb 1955(?)-.............. **CLC 86**
See also CA 147

Carr, Emily 1871-1945........... **TCLC 32**
See also DLB 68

Carr, John Dickson 1906-1977 ...... **CLC 3**
See also CA 49-52; 69-72; CANR 3, 33;
MTCW

Carr, Philippa
See Hibbert, Eleanor Alice Burford

Carr, Virginia Spencer 1929-....... **CLC 34**
See also CA 61-64; DLB 111

Carrere, Emmanuel 1957- .... **CLC 89**

Carrier, Roch 1937-..... **CLC 13, 78; DAC**
See also CA 130; DAM MST; DLB 53

Carroll, James P. 1943(?)-......... **CLC 38**
See also CA 81-84

Carroll, Jim 1951- .... **CLC 35**
See also AAYA 17; CA 45-48; CANR 42

Carroll, Lewis .... **NCLC 2, 53; WLC**
See also Dodgson, Charles Lutwidge
See also CDBLB 1832-1890; CLR 2, 18;
DLB 18, 163; JRDA

Carroll, Paul Vincent 1900-1968.... **CLC 10**
See also CA 9-12R; 25-28R; DLB 10

Carruth, Hayden
1921- ...... **CLC 4, 7, 10, 18, 84; PC 10**
See also CA 9-12R; CANR 4, 38; DLB 5;
INT CANR-4; MTCW; SATA 47

Carson, Rachel Louise 1907-1964... **CLC 71**
See also CA 77-80; CANR 35; DAM POP;
MTCW; SATA 23

Carter, Angela (Olive)
1940-1992 ...... **CLC 5, 41, 76; SSC 13**
See also CA 53-56; 136; CANR 12, 36;
DLB 14; MTCW; SATA 66;
SATA-Obit 70

Carter, Nick
See Smith, Martin Cruz

Carver, Raymond
  1938-1988 . . . **CLC 22, 36, 53, 55; SSC 8**
  See also CA 33-36R; 126; CANR 17, 34;
  DAM NOV; DLB 130; DLBY 84, 88;
  MTCW

Cary, Elizabeth, Lady Falkland
  1585-1639 . . . . **LC 30**

Cary, (Arthur) Joyce (Lunel)
  1888-1957 . . . . **TCLC 1, 29**
  See also CA 104; CDBLB 1914-1945;
  DLB 15, 100

Casanova de Seingalt, Giovanni Jacopo
  1725-1798 . . . . **LC 13**

Casares, Adolfo Bioy
  See Bioy Casares, Adolfo

Casely-Hayford, J(oseph) E(phraim)
  1866-1930 . . . . **TCLC 24; BLC**
  See also BW 2; CA 123; DAM MULT

Casey, John (Dudley) 1939- . . . . **CLC 59**
  See also BEST 90:2; CA 69-72; CANR 23

Casey, Michael 1947- . . . . **CLC 2**
  See also CA 65-68; DLB 5

Casey, Patrick
  See Thurman, Wallace (Henry)

Casey, Warren (Peter) 1935-1988 . . . **CLC 12**
  See also CA 101; 127; INT 101

Casona, Alejandro . . . . **CLC 49**
  See also Alvarez, Alejandro Rodriguez

Cassavetes, John 1929-1989 . . . . **CLC 20**
  See also CA 85-88; 127

Cassill, R(onald) V(erlin) 1919- . . . **CLC 4, 23**
  See also CA 9-12R; CAAS 1; CANR 7, 45;
  DLB 6

Cassirer, Ernst 1874-1945 . . . . **TCLC 61**

Cassity, (Allen) Turner 1929- . . . . **CLC 6, 42**
  See also CA 17-20R; CAAS 8; CANR 11;
  DLB 105

Castaneda, Carlos 1931(?)- . . . . **CLC 12**
  See also CA 25-28R; CANR 32; HW;
  MTCW

Castedo, Elena 1937- . . . . **CLC 65**
  See also CA 132

Castedo-Ellerman, Elena
  See Castedo, Elena

Castellanos, Rosario
  1925-1974 . . . . **CLC 66; HLC**
  See also CA 131; 53-56; DAM MULT;
  DLB 113; HW

Castelvetro, Lodovico 1505-1571 . . . . . **LC 12**

Castiglione, Baldassare 1478-1529 . . . **LC 12**

Castle, Robert
  See Hamilton, Edmond

Castro, Guillen de 1569-1631 . . . . **LC 19**

Castro, Rosalia de 1837-1885 . . . . . **NCLC 3**
  See also DAM MULT

Cather, Willa
  See Cather, Willa Sibert

Cather, Willa Sibert
  1873-1947 . . . . **TCLC 1, 11, 31; DA;**
                        DAB; DAC; SSC 2; WLC
  See also CA 104; 128; CDALB 1865-1917;
  DAM MST, NOV; DLB 9, 54, 78;
  DLBD 1; MTCW; SATA 30

Catton, (Charles) Bruce
  1899-1978 . . . . **CLC 35**
  See also AITN 1; CA 5-8R; 81-84;
  CANR 7; DLB 17; SATA 2;
  SATA-Obit 24

Cauldwell, Frank
  See King, Francis (Henry)

Caunitz, William J. 1933- . . . . **CLC 34**
  See also BEST 89:3; CA 125; 130; INT 130

Causley, Charles (Stanley) 1917- . . . . . **CLC 7**
  See also CA 9-12R; CANR 5, 35; CLR 30;
  DLB 27; MTCW; SATA 3, 66

Caute, David 1936- . . . . **CLC 29**
  See also CA 1-4R; CAAS 4; CANR 1, 33;
  DAM NOV; DLB 14

Cavafy, C(onstantine) P(eter)
  1863-1933 . . . . **TCLC 2, 7**
  See also Kavafis, Konstantinos Petrou
  See also CA 148; DAM POET

Cavallo, Evelyn
  See Spark, Muriel (Sarah)

Cavanna, Betty . . . . **CLC 12**
  See also Harrison, Elizabeth Cavanna
  See also JRDA; MAICYA; SAAS 4;
  SATA 1, 30

Cavendish, Margaret Lucas
  1623-1673 . . . . **LC 30**
  See also DLB 131

Caxton, William 1421(?)-1491(?) . . . . . **LC 17**

Cayrol, Jean 1911- . . . . **CLC 11**
  See also CA 89-92; DLB 83

Cela, Camilo Jose
  1916- . . . . **CLC 4, 13, 59; HLC**
  See also BEST 90:2; CA 21-24R; CAAS 10;
  CANR 21, 32; DAM MULT; DLBY 89;
  HW; MTCW

Celan, Paul . . . . . . **CLC 10, 19, 53, 82; PC 10**
  See also Antschel, Paul
  See also DLB 69

Celine, Louis-Ferdinand
  . . . . **CLC 1, 3, 4, 7, 9, 15, 47**
  See also Destouches, Louis-Ferdinand
  See also DLB 72

Cellini, Benvenuto 1500-1571 . . . . **LC 7**

Cendrars, Blaise . . . . **CLC 18**
  See also Sauser-Hall, Frederic

Cernuda (y Bidon), Luis
  1902-1963 . . . . **CLC 54**
  See also CA 131; 89-92; DAM POET;
  DLB 134; HW

Cervantes (Saavedra), Miguel de
  1547-1616 . . . . **LC 6, 23; DA; DAB;**
                          DAC; SSC 12; WLC
  See also DAM MST, NOV

Cesaire, Aime (Fernand)
  1913- . . . . **CLC 19, 32; BLC**
  See also BW 2; CA 65-68; CANR 24, 43;
  DAM MULT, POET; MTCW

Chabon, Michael 1965(?)- . . . . **CLC 55**
  See also CA 139

Chabrol, Claude 1930- . . . . **CLC 16**
  See also CA 110

Challans, Mary 1905-1983
  See Renault, Mary
  See also CA 81-84; 111; SATA 23;
  SATA-Obit 36

Challis, George
  See Faust, Frederick (Schiller)

Chambers, Aidan 1934- . . . . **CLC 35**
  See also CA 25-28R; CANR 12, 31; JRDA;
  MAICYA; SAAS 12; SATA 1, 69

Chambers, James 1948-
  See Cliff, Jimmy
  See also CA 124

Chambers, Jessie
  See Lawrence, D(avid) H(erbert Richards)

Chambers, Robert W. 1865-1933 . . . **TCLC 41**

Chandler, Raymond (Thornton)
  1888-1959 . . . . **TCLC 1, 7**
  See also CA 104; 129; CDALB 1929-1941;
  DLBD 6; MTCW

Chang, Jung 1952- . . . . **CLC 71**
  See also CA 142

Channing, William Ellery
  1780-1842 . . . . **NCLC 17**
  See also DLB 1, 59

Chaplin, Charles Spencer
  1889-1977 . . . . **CLC 16**
  See also Chaplin, Charlie
  See also CA 81-84; 73-76

Chaplin, Charlie
  See Chaplin, Charles Spencer
  See also DLB 44

Chapman, George 1559(?)-1634 . . . . . . **LC 22**
  See also DAM DRAM; DLB 62, 121

Chapman, Graham 1941-1989 . . . . . . **CLC 21**
  See also Monty Python
  See also CA 116; 129; CANR 35

Chapman, John Jay 1862-1933 . . . . . **TCLC 7**
  See also CA 104

Chapman, Walker
  See Silverberg, Robert

Chappell, Fred (Davis) 1936- . . . . **CLC 40, 78**
  See also CA 5-8R; CAAS 4; CANR 8, 33;
  DLB 6, 105

Char, Rene(-Emile)
  1907-1988 . . . . **CLC 9, 11, 14, 55**
  See also CA 13-16R; 124; CANR 32;
  DAM POET; MTCW

Charby, Jay
  See Ellison, Harlan (Jay)

Chardin, Pierre Teilhard de
  See Teilhard de Chardin, (Marie Joseph)
  Pierre

Charles I 1600-1649 . . . . **LC 13**

Charyn, Jerome 1937- . . . . **CLC 5, 8, 18**
  See also CA 5-8R; CAAS 1; CANR 7;
  DLBY 83; MTCW

Chase, Mary (Coyle) 1907-1981 . . . . . . **DC 1**
  See also CA 77-80; 105; SATA 17;
  SATA-Obit 29

Chase, Mary Ellen 1887-1973 . . . . **CLC 2**
  See also CA 13-16; 41-44R; CAP 1;
  SATA 10

Chase, Nicholas
  See Hyde, Anthony

Chateaubriand, Francois Rene de
   1768-1848 . . . . **NCLC 3**
   See also DLB 119

Chatterje, Sarat Chandra   1876-1936(?)
   See Chatterji, Saratchandra
   See also CA 109

Chatterji, Bankim Chandra
   1838-1894 . . . . **NCLC 19**

Chatterji, Saratchandra . . . . **TCLC 13**
   See also Chatterje, Sarat Chandra

Chatterton, Thomas   1752-1770 . . . . **LC 3**
   See also DAM POET; DLB 109

Chatwin, (Charles) Bruce
   1940-1989 . . . . **CLC 28, 57, 59**
   See also AAYA 4; BEST 90:1; CA 85-88;
   127; DAM POP

Chaucer, Daniel
   See Ford, Ford Madox

Chaucer, Geoffrey
   1340(?)-1400 . . . **LC 17; DA; DAB; DAC**
   See also CDBLB Before 1660; DAM MST,
   POET; DLB 146

Chaviaras, Strates   1935-
   See Haviaras, Stratis
   See also CA 105

Chayefsky, Paddy . . . . **CLC 23**
   See also Chayefsky, Sidney
   See also DLB 7, 44; DLBY 81

Chayefsky, Sidney   1923-1981
   See Chayefsky, Paddy
   See also CA 9-12R; 104; CANR 18;
   DAM DRAM

Chedid, Andree   1920- . . . . **CLC 47**
   See also CA 145

Cheever, John
   1912-1982 . . . . . . **CLC 3, 7, 8, 11, 15, 25,**
      64; DA; DAB; DAC; SSC 1; WLC
   See also CA 5-8R; 106; CABS 1; CANR 5,
   27; CDALB 1941-1968; DAM MST,
   NOV, POP; DLB 2, 102; DLBY 80, 82;
   INT CANR-5; MTCW

Cheever, Susan   1943- . . . . **CLC 18, 48**
   See also CA 103; CANR 27, 51; DLBY 82;
   INT CANR-27

Chekhonte, Antosha
   See Chekhov, Anton (Pavlovich)

Chekhov, Anton (Pavlovich)
   1860-1904 . . . . . **TCLC 3, 10, 31, 55; DA;**
      DAB; DAC; SSC 2; WLC
   See also CA 104; 124; DAM DRAM, MST

Chernyshevsky, Nikolay Gavrilovich
   1828-1889 . . . . **NCLC 1**

Cherry, Carolyn Janice   1942-
   See Cherryh, C. J.
   See also CA 65-68; CANR 10

Cherryh, C. J. . . . . **CLC 35**
   See also Cherry, Carolyn Janice
   See also DLBY 80

Chesnutt, Charles W(addell)
   1858-1932 . . . . **TCLC 5, 39; BLC; SSC 7**
   See also BW 1; CA 106; 125; DAM MULT;
   DLB 12, 50, 78; MTCW

Chester, Alfred   1929(?)-1971 . . . . **CLC 49**
   See also CA 33-36R; DLB 130

Chesterton, G(ilbert) K(eith)
   1874-1936 . . . . **TCLC 1, 6; SSC 1**
   See also CA 104; 132; CDBLB 1914-1945;
   DAM NOV, POET; DLB 10, 19, 34, 70,
   98, 149; MTCW; SATA 27

Chiang Pin-chin   1904-1986
   See Ding Ling
   See also CA 118

Ch'ien Chung-shu   1910- . . . . **CLC 22**
   See also CA 130; MTCW

Child, L. Maria
   See Child, Lydia Maria

Child, Lydia Maria   1802-1880 . . . . **NCLC 6**
   See also DLB 1, 74; SATA 67

Child, Mrs.
   See Child, Lydia Maria

Child, Philip   1898-1978 . . . . **CLC 19, 68**
   See also CA 13-14; CAP 1; SATA 47

Childress, Alice
   1920-1994 . . **CLC 12, 15, 86; BLC; DC 4**
   See also AAYA 8; BW 2; CA 45-48; 146;
   CANR 3, 27, 50; CLR 14; DAM DRAM,
   MULT, NOV; DLB 7, 38; JRDA;
   MAICYA; MTCW; SATA 7, 48, 81

Chislett, (Margaret) Anne   1943- . . . . **CLC 34**

Chitty, Thomas Willes   1926- . . . . **CLC 11**
   See also Hinde, Thomas
   See also CA 5-8R

Chivers, Thomas Holley
   1809-1858 . . . . **NCLC 49**
   See also DLB 3

Chomette, Rene Lucien   1898-1981
   See Clair, Rene
   See also CA 103

Chopin, Kate
   . . . . **TCLC 5, 14; DA; DAB; SSC 8**
   See also Chopin, Katherine
   See also CDALB 1865-1917; DLB 12, 78

Chopin, Katherine   1851-1904
   See Chopin, Kate
   See also CA 104; 122; DAC; DAM MST,
   NOV

Chretien de Troyes
   c. 12th cent. - . . . . **CMLC 10**

Christie
   See Ichikawa, Kon

Christie, Agatha (Mary Clarissa)
   1890-1976 . . . . . . **CLC 1, 6, 8, 12, 39, 48;**
                              DAB; DAC
   See also AAYA 9; AITN 1, 2; CA 17-20R;
   61-64; CANR 10, 37; CDBLB 1914-1945;
   DAM NOV; DLB 13, 77; MTCW;
   SATA 36

Christie, (Ann) Philippa
   See Pearce, Philippa
   See also CA 5-8R; CANR 4

Christine de Pizan   1365(?)-1431(?) . . . . **LC 9**

Chubb, Elmer
   See Masters, Edgar Lee

Chulkov, Mikhail Dmitrievich
   1743-1792 . . . . **LC 2**
   See also DLB 150

Churchill, Caryl   1938- . . . **CLC 31, 55; DC 5**
   See also CA 102; CANR 22, 46; DLB 13;
   MTCW

Churchill, Charles   1731-1764 . . . . **LC 3**
   See also DLB 109

Chute, Carolyn   1947- . . . . **CLC 39**
   See also CA 123

Ciardi, John (Anthony)
   1916-1986 . . . . **CLC 10, 40, 44**
   See also CA 5-8R; 118; CAAS 2; CANR 5,
   33; CLR 19; DAM POET; DLB 5;
   DLBY 86; INT CANR-5; MAICYA;
   MTCW; SATA 1, 65; SATA-Obit 46

Cicero, Marcus Tullius
   106B.C.-43B.C. . . . . **CMLC 3**

Cimino, Michael   1943- . . . . **CLC 16**
   See also CA 105

Cioran, E(mil) M.   1911-1995 . . . . . . **CLC 64**
   See also CA 25-28R; 149

Cisneros, Sandra   1954- . . . . . . **CLC 69; HLC**
   See also AAYA 9; CA 131; DAM MULT;
   DLB 122, 152; HW

Cixous, Helene   1937- . . . . **CLC 92**
   See also CA 126; DLB 83; MTCW

Clair, Rene . . . . **CLC 20**
   See also Chomette, Rene Lucien

Clampitt, Amy   1920-1994 . . . . **CLC 32**
   See also CA 110; 146; CANR 29; DLB 105

Clancy, Thomas L., Jr.   1947-
   See Clancy, Tom
   See also CA 125; 131; INT 131; MTCW

Clancy, Tom . . . . **CLC 45**
   See also Clancy, Thomas L., Jr.
   See also AAYA 9; BEST 89:1, 90:1;
   DAM NOV, POP

Clare, John   1793-1864 . . . . . . **NCLC 9; DAB**
   See also DAM POET; DLB 55, 96

Clarin
   See Alas (y Urena), Leopoldo (Enrique
   Garcia)

Clark, Al C.
   See Goines, Donald

Clark, (Robert) Brian   1932- . . . . **CLC 29**
   See also CA 41-44R

Clark, Curt
   See Westlake, Donald E(dwin)

Clark, Eleanor   1913- . . . . **CLC 5, 19**
   See also CA 9-12R; CANR 41; DLB 6

Clark, J. P.
   See Clark, John Pepper
   See also DLB 117

Clark, John Pepper
   1935- . . . . **CLC 38; BLC; DC 5**
   See also Clark, J. P.
   See also BW 1; CA 65-68; CANR 16;
   DAM DRAM, MULT

Clark, M. R.
   See Clark, Mavis Thorpe

Clark, Mavis Thorpe   1909- . . . . **CLC 12**
   See also CA 57-60; CANR 8, 37; CLR 30;
   MAICYA; SAAS 5; SATA 8, 74

Clark, Walter Van Tilburg
   1909-1971 . . . . **CLC 28**
   See also CA 9-12R; 33-36R; DLB 9;
   SATA 8

Clarke, Arthur C(harles)
1917- . . . . . . **CLC 1, 4, 13, 18, 35; SSC 3**
See also AAYA 4; CA 1-4R; CANR 2, 28;
DAM POP; JRDA; MAICYA; MTCW;
SATA 13, 70

Clarke, Austin 1896-1974. . . . . **CLC 6, 9**
See also CA 29-32; 49-52; CAP 2;
DAM POET; DLB 10, 20

Clarke, Austin C(hesterfield)
1934- . . . . **CLC 8, 53; BLC; DAC**
See also BW 1; CA 25-28R; CAAS 16;
CANR 14, 32; DAM MULT; DLB 53,
125

Clarke, Gillian 1937- . . . . **CLC 61**
See also CA 106; DLB 40

Clarke, Marcus (Andrew Hislop)
1846-1881 . . . . **NCLC 19**

Clarke, Shirley 1925- . . . . **CLC 16**

Clash, The
See Headon, (Nicky) Topper; Jones, Mick;
Simonon, Paul; Strummer, Joe

Claudel, Paul (Louis Charles Marie)
1868-1955 . . . . **TCLC 2, 10**
See also CA 104

Clavell, James (duMaresq)
1925-1994 . . . . **CLC 6, 25, 87**
See also CA 25-28R; 146; CANR 26, 48;
DAM NOV, POP; MTCW

Cleaver, (Leroy) Eldridge
1935- . . . . **CLC 30; BLC**
See also BW 1; CA 21-24R; CANR 16;
DAM MULT

Cleese, John (Marwood) 1939- . . . . . **CLC 21**
See also Monty Python
See also CA 112; 116; CANR 35; MTCW

Cleishbotham, Jebediah
See Scott, Walter

Cleland, John 1710-1789 . . . . **LC 2**
See also DLB 39

Clemens, Samuel Langhorne 1835-1910
See Twain, Mark
See also CA 104; 135; CDALB 1865-1917;
DA; DAB; DAC; DAM MST, NOV;
DLB 11, 12, 23, 64, 74; JRDA;
MAICYA; YABC 2

Cleophil
See Congreve, William

Clerihew, E.
See Bentley, E(dmund) C(lerihew)

Clerk, N. W.
See Lewis, C(live) S(taples)

Cliff, Jimmy . . . . **CLC 21**
See also Chambers, James

Clifton, (Thelma) Lucille
1936- . . . . **CLC 19, 66; BLC**
See also BW 2; CA 49-52; CANR 2, 24, 42;
CLR 5; DAM MULT, POET; DLB 5, 41;
MAICYA; MTCW; SATA 20, 69

Clinton, Dirk
See Silverberg, Robert

Clough, Arthur Hugh 1819-1861. . **NCLC 27**
See also DLB 32

Clutha, Janet Paterson Frame 1924-
See Frame, Janet
See also CA 1-4R; CANR 2, 36; MTCW

Clyne, Terence
See Blatty, William Peter

Cobalt, Martin
See Mayne, William (James Carter)

Cobbett, William 1763-1835 . . . . . **NCLC 49**
See also DLB 43, 107, 158

Coburn, D(onald) L(ee) 1938- . . . . . . **CLC 10**
See also CA 89-92

Cocteau, Jean (Maurice Eugene Clement)
1889-1963 . . . . **CLC 1, 8, 15, 16, 43; DA;**
DAB; DAC; WLC
See also CA 25-28; CANR 40; CAP 2;
DAM DRAM, MST, NOV; DLB 65;
MTCW

Codrescu, Andrei 1946- . . . . **CLC 46**
See also CA 33-36R; CAAS 19; CANR 13,
34; DAM POET

Coe, Max
See Bourne, Randolph S(illiman)

Coe, Tucker
See Westlake, Donald E(dwin)

Coetzee, J(ohn) M(ichael)
1940- . . . . **CLC 23, 33, 66**
See also CA 77-80; CANR 41; DAM NOV;
MTCW

Coffey, Brian
See Koontz, Dean R(ay)

Cohan, George M. 1878-1942 . . . . . **TCLC 60**

Cohen, Arthur A(llen)
1928-1986 . . . . **CLC 7, 31**
See also CA 1-4R; 120; CANR 1, 17, 42;
DLB 28

Cohen, Leonard (Norman)
1934- . . . . **CLC 3, 38; DAC**
See also CA 21-24R; CANR 14;
DAM MST; DLB 53; MTCW

Cohen, Matt 1942- . . . . **CLC 19; DAC**
See also CA 61-64; CAAS 18; CANR 40;
DLB 53

Cohen-Solal, Annie 19(?)- . . . . **CLC 50**

Colegate, Isabel 1931- . . . . **CLC 36**
See also CA 17-20R; CANR 8, 22; DLB 14;
INT CANR-22; MTCW

Coleman, Emmett
See Reed, Ishmael

Coleridge, Samuel Taylor
1772-1834 . . . . . **NCLC 9, 54; DA; DAB;**
DAC; PC 11; WLC
See also CDBLB 1789-1832; DAM MST,
POET; DLB 93, 107

Coleridge, Sara 1802-1852 . . . . . . **NCLC 31**

Coles, Don 1928- . . . . **CLC 46**
See also CA 115; CANR 38

Colette, (Sidonie-Gabrielle)
1873-1954 . . . . . . **TCLC 1, 5, 16; SSC 10**
See also CA 104; 131; DAM NOV; DLB 65;
MTCW

Collett, (Jacobine) Camilla (Wergeland)
1813-1895 . . . . **NCLC 22**

Collier, Christopher 1930- . . . . **CLC 30**
See also AAYA 13; CA 33-36R; CANR 13,
33; JRDA; MAICYA; SATA 16, 70

Collier, James L(incoln) 1928- . . . . . **CLC 30**
See also AAYA 13; CA 9-12R; CANR 4,
33; CLR 3; DAM POP; JRDA;
MAICYA; SAAS 21; SATA 8, 70

Collier, Jeremy 1650-1726 . . . . **LC 6**

Collier, John 1901-1980 . . . . **SSC 19**
See also CA 65-68; 97-100; CANR 10;
DLB 77

Collins, Hunt
See Hunter, Evan

Collins, Linda 1931- . . . . **CLC 44**
See also CA 125

Collins, (William) Wilkie
1824-1889 . . . . **NCLC 1, 18**
See also CDBLB 1832-1890; DLB 18, 70,
159

Collins, William 1721-1759 . . . . **LC 4**
See also DAM POET; DLB 109

Collodi, Carlo 1826-1890 . . . . **NCLC 54**
See also Lorenzini, Carlo
See also CLR 5

Colman, George
See Glassco, John

Colt, Winchester Remington
See Hubbard, L(afayette) Ron(ald)

Colter, Cyrus 1910- . . . . **CLC 58**
See also BW 1; CA 65-68; CANR 10;
DLB 33

Colton, James
See Hansen, Joseph

Colum, Padraic 1881-1972 . . . . **CLC 28**
See also CA 73-76; 33-36R; CANR 35;
CLR 36; MAICYA; MTCW; SATA 15

Colvin, James
See Moorcock, Michael (John)

Colwin, Laurie (E.)
1944-1992 . . . . **CLC 5, 13, 23, 84**
See also CA 89-92; 139; CANR 20, 46;
DLBY 80; MTCW

Comfort, Alex(ander) 1920- . . . . **CLC 7**
See also CA 1-4R; CANR 1, 45; DAM POP

Comfort, Montgomery
See Campbell, (John) Ramsey

Compton-Burnett, I(vy)
1884(?)-1969 . . . . . . **CLC 1, 3, 10, 15, 34**
See also CA 1-4R; 25-28R; CANR 4;
DAM NOV; DLB 36; MTCW

Comstock, Anthony 1844-1915 . . . . **TCLC 13**
See also CA 110

Comte, Auguste 1798-1857 . . . . **NCLC 54**

Conan Doyle, Arthur
See Doyle, Arthur Conan

Conde, Maryse 1937- . . . . **CLC 52, 92**
See also Boucolon, Maryse
See also BW 2; DAM MULT

Condillac, Etienne Bonnot de
1714-1780 . . . . **LC 26**

Condon, Richard (Thomas)
1915- . . . . **CLC 4, 6, 8, 10, 45**
See also BEST 90:3; CA 1-4R; CAAS 1;
CANR 2, 23; DAM NOV;
INT CANR-23; MTCW

Crane, Stephen (Townley)
1871-1900 . . . . . . TCLC **11, 17, 32;** DA;
DAB; DAC; SSC **7;** WLC
See also CA 109; 140; CDALB 1865-1917;
DAM MST, NOV, POET; DLB 12, 54,
78; YABC 2

Crase, Douglas 1944- . . . . CLC **58**
See also CA 106

Crashaw, Richard 1612(?)-1649 . . . . . . LC **24**
See also DLB 126

Craven, Margaret
1901-1980 . . . . CLC **17;** DAC
See also CA 103

Crawford, F(rancis) Marion
1854-1909 . . . . TCLC **10**
See also CA 107; DLB 71

Crawford, Isabella Valancy
1850-1887 . . . . NCLC **12**
See also DLB 92

Crayon, Geoffrey
See Irving, Washington

Creasey, John 1908-1973 . . . . CLC **11**
See also CA 5-8R; 41-44R; CANR 8;
DLB 77; MTCW

Crebillon, Claude Prosper Jolyot de (fils)
1707-1777 . . . . LC **28**

Credo
See Creasey, John

Creeley, Robert (White)
1926- . . . . . CLC **1, 2, 4, 8, 11, 15, 36, 78**
See also CA 1-4R; CAAS 10; CANR 23, 43;
DAM POET; DLB 5, 16; MTCW

Crews, Harry (Eugene)
1935- . . . . CLC **6, 23, 49**
See also AITN 1; CA 25-28R; CANR 20;
DLB 6, 143; MTCW

Crichton, (John) Michael
1942- . . . . CLC **2, 6, 54, 90**
See also AAYA 10; AITN 2; CA 25-28R;
CANR 13, 40; DAM NOV, POP;
DLBY 81; INT CANR-13; JRDA;
MTCW; SATA 9

Crispin, Edmund . . . . CLC **22**
See also Montgomery, (Robert) Bruce
See also DLB 87

Cristofer, Michael 1945(?)- . . . . CLC **28**
See also CA 110; DAM DRAM; DLB 7

Croce, Benedetto 1866-1952 . . . . . . TCLC **37**
See also CA 120

Crockett, David 1786-1836 . . . . NCLC **8**
See also DLB 3, 11

Crockett, Davy
See Crockett, David

Crofts, Freeman Wills
1879-1957 . . . . TCLC **55**
See also CA 115; DLB 77

Croker, John Wilson 1780-1857 . . NCLC **10**
See also DLB 110

Crommelynck, Fernand 1885-1970 . . CLC **75**
See also CA 89-92

Cronin, A(rchibald) J(oseph)
1896-1981 . . . . CLC **32**
See also CA 1-4R; 102; CANR 5; SATA 47;
SATA-Obit 25

Cross, Amanda
See Heilbrun, Carolyn G(old)

Crothers, Rachel 1878(?)-1958 . . . . . TCLC **19**
See also CA 113; DLB 7

Croves, Hal
See Traven, B.

Crowfield, Christopher
See Stowe, Harriet (Elizabeth) Beecher

Crowley, Aleister . . . . TCLC **7**
See also Crowley, Edward Alexander

Crowley, Edward Alexander 1875-1947
See Crowley, Aleister
See also CA 104

Crowley, John 1942- . . . . CLC **57**
See also CA 61-64; CANR 43; DLBY 82;
SATA 65

Crud
See Crumb, R(obert)

Crumarums
See Crumb, R(obert)

Crumb, R(obert) 1943- . . . . . . ,. . . . . CLC **17**
See also CA 106

Crumbum
See Crumb, R(obert)

Crumski
See Crumb, R(obert)

Crum the Bum
See Crumb, R(obert)

Crunk
See Crumb, R(obert)

Crustt
See Crumb, R(obert)

Cryer, Gretchen (Kiger) 1935- . . . . . . CLC **21**
See also CA 114; 123

Csath, Geza 1887-1919 . . . . TCLC **13**
See also CA 111

Cudlip, David 1933- . . . . CLC **34**

Cullen, Countee
1903-1946 . . . . . . TCLC **4, 37;** BLC; DA;
DAC
See also BW 1; CA 108; 124;
CDALB 1917-1929; DAM MST, MULT,
POET; DLB 4, 48, 51; MTCW; SATA 18

Cum, R.
See Crumb, R(obert)

Cummings, Bruce F(rederick) 1889-1919
See Barbellion, W. N. P.
See also CA 123

Cummings, E(dward) E(stlin)
1894-1962 . . . . . . CLC **1, 3, 8, 12, 15, 68;**
DA; DAB; DAC; PC **5;** WLC **2**
See also CA 73-76; CANR 31;
CDALB 1929-1941; DAM MST, POET;
DLB 4, 48; MTCW

Cunha, Euclides (Rodrigues Pimenta) da
1866-1909 . . . . TCLC **24**
See also CA 123

Cunningham, E. V.
See Fast, Howard (Melvin)

Cunningham, J(ames) V(incent)
1911-1985 . . . . CLC **3, 31**
See also CA 1-4R; 115; CANR 1; DLB 5

Cunningham, Julia (Woolfolk)
1916- . . . . CLC **12**
See also CA 9-12R; CANR 4, 19, 36;
JRDA; MAICYA; SAAS 2; SATA 1, 26

Cunningham, Michael 1952- . . . . CLC **34**
See also CA 136

Cunninghame Graham, R(obert) B(ontine)
1852-1936 . . . . TCLC **19**
See also Graham, R(obert) B(ontine)
Cunninghame
See also CA 119; DLB 98

Currie, Ellen 19(?)- . . . . CLC **44**

Curtin, Philip
See Lowndes, Marie Adelaide (Belloc)

Curtis, Price
See Ellison, Harlan (Jay)

Cutrate, Joe
See Spiegelman, Art

Czaczkes, Shmuel Yosef
See Agnon, S(hmuel) Y(osef Halevi)

Dabrowska, Maria (Szumska)
1889-1965 . . . . CLC **15**
See also CA 106

Dabydeen, David 1955- . . . . CLC **34**
See also BW 1; CA 125

Dacey, Philip 1939- . . . . CLC **51**
See also CA 37-40R; CAAS 17; CANR 14,
32; DLB 105

Dagerman, Stig (Halvard)
1923-1954 . . . . TCLC **17**
See also CA 117

Dahl, Roald
1916-1990 . . . . . . CLC **1, 6, 18, 79;** DAB;
DAC
See also AAYA 15; CA 1-4R; 133;
CANR 6, 32, 37; CLR 1, 7; DAM MST,
NOV, POP; DLB 139; JRDA; MAICYA;
MTCW; SATA 1, 26, 73; SATA-Obit 65

Dahlberg, Edward 1900-1977 . . . CLC **1, 7, 14**
See also CA 9-12R; 69-72; CANR 31;
DLB 48; MTCW

Dale, Colin . . . . TCLC **18**
See also Lawrence, T(homas) E(dward)

Dale, George E.
See Asimov, Isaac

Daly, Elizabeth 1878-1967 . . . . CLC **52**
See also CA 23-24; 25-28R; CAP 2

Daly, Maureen 1921- . . . . CLC **17**
See also AAYA 5; CANR 37; JRDA;
MAICYA; SAAS 1; SATA 2

Damas, Leon-Gontran 1912-1978 . . . CLC **84**
See also BW 1; CA 125; 73-76

Dana, Richard Henry Sr.
1787-1879 . . . . NCLC **53**

Daniel, Samuel 1562(?)-1619 . . . . LC **24**
See also DLB 62

Daniels, Brett
See Adler, Renata

Dannay, Frederic 1905-1982 . . . . CLC **11**
See also Queen, Ellery
See also CA 1-4R; 107; CANR 1, 39;
DAM POP; DLB 137; MTCW

D'Annunzio, Gabriele
1863-1938 . . . . TCLC **6, 40**
See also CA 104

Delibes Setien, Miguel 1920-
See Delibes, Miguel
See also CA 45-48; CANR 1, 32; HW;
MTCW

DeLillo, Don
1936- ..... **CLC 8, 10, 13, 27, 39, 54, 76**
See also BEST 89:1; CA 81-84; CANR 21;
DAM NOV, POP; DLB 6; MTCW

de Lisser, H. G.
See De Lisser, Herbert George
See also DLB 117

De Lisser, Herbert George
1878-1944 .... **TCLC 12**
See also de Lisser, H. G.
See also BW 2; CA 109

Deloria, Vine (Victor), Jr. 1933-.... **CLC 21**
See also CA 53-56; CANR 5, 20, 48;
DAM MULT; MTCW; NNAL; SATA 21

Del Vecchio, John M(ichael)
1947- .... **CLC 29**
See also CA 110; DLBD 9

de Man, Paul (Adolph Michel)
1919-1983 .... **CLC 55**
See also CA 128; 111; DLB 67; MTCW

De Marinis, Rick 1934-........... **CLC 54**
See also CA 57-60; CANR 9, 25, 50

Demby, William 1922-....... **CLC 53; BLC**
See also BW 1; CA 81-84; DAM MULT;
DLB 33

Demijohn, Thom
See Disch, Thomas M(ichael)

de Montherlant, Henry (Milon)
See Montherlant, Henry (Milon) de

Demosthenes 384B.C.-322B.C. ... **CMLC 13**

de Natale, Francine
See Malzberg, Barry N(athaniel)

Denby, Edwin (Orr) 1903-1983 ..... **CLC 48**
See also CA 138; 110

Denis, Julio
See Cortazar, Julio

Denmark, Harrison
See Zelazny, Roger (Joseph)

Dennis, John 1658-1734........... **LC 11**
See also DLB 101

Dennis, Nigel (Forbes) 1912-1989.... **CLC 8**
See also CA 25-28R; 129; DLB 13, 15;
MTCW

De Palma, Brian (Russell) 1940-.... **CLC 20**
See also CA 109

De Quincey, Thomas 1785-1859 ... **NCLC 4**
See also CDBLB 1789-1832; DLB 110; 144

Deren, Eleanora 1908(?)-1961
See Deren, Maya
See also CA 111

Deren, Maya .... **CLC 16**
See also Deren, Eleanora

Derleth, August (William)
1909-1971 .... **CLC 31**
See also CA 1-4R; 29-32R; CANR 4;
DLB 9; SATA 5

Der Nister 1884-1950........... **TCLC 56**

de Routisie, Albert
See Aragon, Louis

Derrida, Jacques 1930-........ **CLC 24, 87**
See also CA 124; 127

Derry Down Derry
See Lear, Edward

Dersonnes, Jacques
See Simenon, Georges (Jacques Christian)

Desai, Anita 1937- ...... **CLC 19, 37; DAB**
See also CA 81-84; CANR 33; DAM NOV;
MTCW; SATA 63

de Saint-Luc, Jean
See Glassco, John

de Saint Roman, Arnaud
See Aragon, Louis

Descartes, Rene 1596-1650 .... **LC 20**

De Sica, Vittorio 1901(?)-1974 ..... **CLC 20**
See also CA 117

Desnos, Robert 1900-1945........ **TCLC 22**
See also CA 121

Destouches, Louis-Ferdinand
1894-1961 .... **CLC 9, 15**
See also Celine, Louis-Ferdinand
See also CA 85-88; CANR 28; MTCW

Deutsch, Babette 1895-1982 .... **CLC 18**
See also CA 1-4R; 108; CANR 4; DLB 45;
SATA 1; SATA-Obit 33

Devenant, William 1606-1649 .... **LC 13**

Devkota, Laxmiprasad
1909-1959 .... **TCLC 23**
See also CA 123

De Voto, Bernard (Augustine)
1897-1955 .... **TCLC 29**
See also CA 113; DLB 9

De Vries, Peter
1910-1993 .... **CLC 1, 2, 3, 7, 10, 28, 46**
See also CA 17-20R; 142; CANR 41;
DAM NOV; DLB 6; DLBY 82; MTCW

Dexter, Martin
See Faust, Frederick (Schiller)

Dexter, Pete 1943-............ **CLC 34, 55**
See also BEST 89:2; CA 127; 131;
DAM POP; INT 131; MTCW

Diamano, Silmang
See Senghor, Leopold Sedar

Diamond, Neil 1941- .... **CLC 30**
See also CA 108

Diaz del Castillo, Bernal 1496-1584.. **LC 31**

di Bassetto, Corno
See Shaw, George Bernard

Dick, Philip K(indred)
1928-1982 .... **CLC 10, 30, 72**
See also CA 49-52; 106; CANR 2, 16;
DAM NOV, POP; DLB 8; MTCW

Dickens, Charles (John Huffam)
1812-1870 ...... **NCLC 3, 8, 18, 26, 37,
50; DA; DAB; DAC; SSC 17; WLC**
See also CDBLB 1832-1890; DAM MST,
NOV; DLB 21, 55, 70, 159; JRDA;
MAICYA; SATA 15

Dickey, James (Lafayette)
1923- .... **CLC 1, 2, 4, 7, 10, 15, 47**
See also AITN 1, 2; CA 9-12R; CABS 2;
CANR 10, 48; CDALB 1968-1988;
DAM NOV, POET, POP; DLB 5;
DLBD 7; DLBY 82, 93; INT CANR-10;
MTCW

Dickey, William 1928-1994 ...... **CLC 3, 28**
See also CA 9-12R; 145; CANR 24; DLB 5

Dickinson, Charles 1951-.......... **CLC 49**
See also CA 128

Dickinson, Emily (Elizabeth)
1830-1886 .... **NCLC 21; DA; DAB;
DAC; PC 1; WLC**
See also CDALB 1865-1917; DAM MST,
POET; DLB 1; SATA 29

Dickinson, Peter (Malcolm)
1927- .... **CLC 12, 35**
See also AAYA 9; CA 41-44R; CANR 31;
CLR 29; DLB 87, 161; JRDA; MAICYA;
SATA 5, 62

Dickson, Carr
See Carr, John Dickson

Dickson, Carter
See Carr, John Dickson

Diderot, Denis 1713-1784 .... **LC 26**

Didion, Joan 1934-..... **CLC 1, 3, 8, 14, 32**
See also AITN 1; CA 5-8R; CANR 14;
CDALB 1968-1988; DAM NOV; DLB 2;
DLBY 81, 86; MTCW

Dietrich, Robert
See Hunt, E(verette) Howard, (Jr.)

Dillard, Annie 1945-............ **CLC 9, 60**
See also AAYA 6; CA 49-52; CANR 3, 43;
DAM NOV; DLBY 80; MTCW;
SATA 10

Dillard, R(ichard) H(enry) W(ilde)
1937- .... **CLC 5**
See also CA 21-24R; CAAS 7; CANR 10;
DLB 5

Dillon, Eilis 1920-1994............ **CLC 17**
See also CA 9-12R; 147; CAAS 3; CANR 4,
38; CLR 26; MAICYA; SATA 2, 74;
SATA-Obit 83

Dimont, Penelope
See Mortimer, Penelope (Ruth)

Dinesen, Isak........... **CLC 10, 29; SSC 7**
See also Blixen, Karen (Christentze
Dinesen)

Ding Ling....................... **CLC 68**
See also Chiang Pin-chin

Disch, Thomas M(ichael) 1940-... **CLC 7, 36**
See also AAYA 17; CA 21-24R; CAAS 4;
CANR 17, 36; CLR 18; DLB 8;
MAICYA; MTCW; SAAS 15; SATA 54

Disch, Tom
See Disch, Thomas M(ichael)

d'Isly, Georges
See Simenon, Georges (Jacques Christian)

Disraeli, Benjamin 1804-1881 .. **NCLC 2, 39**
See also DLB 21, 55

Ditcum, Steve
See Crumb, R(obert)

Dixon, Paige
See Corcoran, Barbara

Dixon, Stephen 1936-..... **CLC 52; SSC 16**
See also CA 89-92; CANR 17, 40; DLB 130

Dobell, Sydney Thompson
1824-1874 .... **NCLC 43**
See also DLB 32

Doblin, Alfred .... **TCLC 13**
See also Doeblin, Alfred

Dubie, Norman (Evans) 1945-...... **CLC 36**
See also CA 69-72; CANR 12; DLB 120

Du Bois, W(illiam) E(dward) B(urghardt)
1868-1963 ...... **CLC 1, 2, 13, 64; BLC;**
DA; DAC; WLC
See also BW 1; CA 85-88; CANR 34;
CDALB 1865-1917; DAM MST, MULT,
NOV; DLB 47, 50, 91; MTCW; SATA 42

Dubus, Andre 1936-... **CLC 13, 36; SSC 15**
See also CA 21-24R; CANR 17; DLB 130;
INT CANR-17

Duca Minimo
See D'Annunzio, Gabriele

Ducharme, Rejean 1941-.......... **CLC 74**
See also DLB 60

Duclos, Charles Pinot 1704-1772 ..... **LC 1**

Dudek, Louis 1918- .... **CLC 11, 19**
See also CA 45-48; CAAS 14; CANR 1;
DLB 88

Duerrenmatt, Friedrich
1921-1990 ...... **CLC 1, 4, 8, 11, 15, 43**
See also CA 17-20R; CANR 33;
DAM DRAM; DLB 69, 124; MTCW

Duffy, Bruce (?)-................. **CLC 50**

Duffy, Maureen 1933- .... **CLC 37**
See also CA 25-28R; CANR 33; DLB 14;
MTCW

Dugan, Alan 1923- .... **CLC 2, 6**
See also CA 81-84; DLB 5

du Gard, Roger Martin
See Martin du Gard, Roger

Duhamel, Georges 1884-1966 .... **CLC 8**
See also CA 81-84; 25-28R; CANR 35;
DLB 65; MTCW

Dujardin, Edouard (Emile Louis)
1861-1949 .... **TCLC 13**
See also CA 109; DLB 123

Dumas, Alexandre (Davy de la Pailleterie)
1802-1870 .... **NCLC 11; DA; DAB;**
DAC; WLC
See also DAM MST, NOV; DLB 119;
SATA 18

Dumas, Alexandre
1824-1895 .... **NCLC 9; DC 1**

Dumas, Claudine
See Malzberg, Barry N(athaniel)

Dumas, Henry L. 1934-1968 ..... **CLC 6, 62**
See also BW 1; CA 85-88; DLB 41

du Maurier, Daphne
1907-1989 .... **CLC 6, 11, 59; DAB;**
DAC; SSC 18
See also CA 5-8R; 128; CANR 6;
DAM MST, POP; MTCW; SATA 27;
SATA-Obit 60

Dunbar, Paul Laurence
1872-1906 ...... **TCLC 2, 12; BLC; DA;**
DAC; PC 5; SSC 8; WLC
See also BW 1; CA 104; 124;
CDALB 1865-1917; DAM MST, MULT,
POET; DLB 50, 54, 78; SATA 34

Dunbar, William 1460(?)-1530(?) .... **LC 20**
See also DLB 132, 146

Duncan, Lois 1934-.............. **CLC 26**
See also AAYA 4; CA 1-4R; CANR 2, 23,
36; CLR 29; JRDA; MAICYA; SAAS 2;
SATA 1, 36, 75

Duncan, Robert (Edward)
1919-1988 .... **CLC 1, 2, 4, 7, 15, 41, 55;**
PC 2
See also CA 9-12R; 124; CANR 28;
DAM POET; DLB 5, 16; MTCW

Duncan, Sara Jeannette
1861-1922 .... **TCLC 60**
See also DLB 92

Dunlap, William 1766-1839....... **NCLC 2**
See also DLB 30, 37, 59

Dunn, Douglas (Eaglesham)
1942-..................... **CLC 6, 40**
See also CA 45-48; CANR 2, 33; DLB 40;
MTCW

Dunn, Katherine (Karen) 1945-..... **CLC 71**
See also CA 33-36R

Dunn, Stephen 1939- .... **CLC 36**
See also CA 33-36R; CANR 12, 48;
DLB 105

Dunne, Finley Peter 1867-1936.... **TCLC 28**
See also CA 108; DLB 11, 23

Dunne, John Gregory 1932-........ **CLC 28**
See also CA 25-28R; CANR 14, 50;
DLBY 80

Dunsany, Edward John Moreton Drax
Plunkett 1878-1957
See Dunsany, Lord
See also CA 104; 148; DLB 10

Dunsany, Lord................. **TCLC 2, 59**
See also Dunsany, Edward John Moreton
Drax Plunkett
See also DLB 77, 153, 156

du Perry, Jean
See Simenon, Georges (Jacques Christian)

Durang, Christopher (Ferdinand)
1949-.................... **CLC 27, 38**
See also CA 105; CANR 50

Duras, Marguerite
1914- ...... **CLC 3, 6, 11, 20, 34, 40, 68**
See also CA 25-28R; CANR 50; DLB 83;
MTCW

Durban, (Rosa) Pam 1947-........ **CLC 39**
See also CA 123

Durcan, Paul 1944-........... **CLC 43, 70**
See also CA 134; DAM POET

Durkheim, Emile 1858-1917 ..... **TCLC 55**

Durrell, Lawrence (George)
1912-1990 .... **CLC 1, 4, 6, 8, 13, 27, 41**
See also CA 9-12R; 132; CANR 40;
CDBLB 1945-1960; DAM NOV; DLB 15,
27; DLBY 90; MTCW

Durrenmatt, Friedrich
See Duerrenmatt, Friedrich

Dutt, Toru 1856-1877.......... **NCLC 29**

Dwight, Timothy 1752-1817...... **NCLC 13**
See also DLB 37

Dworkin, Andrea 1946- .... **CLC 43**
See also CA 77-80; CAAS 21; CANR 16,
39; INT CANR-16; MTCW

Dwyer, Deanna
See Koontz, Dean R(ay)

Dwyer, K. R.
See Koontz, Dean R(ay)

Dylan, Bob 1941-...... **CLC 3, 4, 6, 12, 77**
See also CA 41-44R; DLB 16

Eagleton, Terence (Francis) 1943-
See Eagleton, Terry
See also CA 57-60; CANR 7, 23; MTCW

Eagleton, Terry .... **CLC 63**
See also Eagleton, Terence (Francis)

Early, Jack
See Scoppettone, Sandra

East, Michael
See West, Morris L(anglo)

Eastaway, Edward
See Thomas, (Philip) Edward

Eastlake, William (Derry) 1917-..... **CLC 8**
See also CA 5-8R; CAAS 1; CANR 5;
DLB 6; INT CANR-5

Eastman, Charles A(lexander)
1858-1939 .... **TCLC 55**
See also DAM MULT; NNAL; YABC 1

Eberhart, Richard (Ghormley)
1904-............... **CLC 3, 11, 19, 56**
See also CA 1-4R; CANR 2;
CDALB 1941-1968; DAM POET;
DLB 48; MTCW

Eberstadt, Fernanda 1960-........ **CLC 39**
See also CA 136

Echegaray (y Eizaguirre), Jose (Maria Waldo)
1832-1916 .... **TCLC 4**
See also CA 104; CANR 32; HW; MTCW

Echeverria, (Jose) Esteban (Antonino)
1805-1851 .... **NCLC 18**

Echo
See Proust, (Valentin-Louis-George-Eugene-)
Marcel

Eckert, Allan W. 1931- .... **CLC 17**
See also CA 13-16R; CANR 14, 45;
INT CANR-14; SAAS 21; SATA 29;
SATA-Brief 27

Eckhart, Meister 1260(?)-1328(?) .. **CMLC 9**
See also DLB 115

Eckmar, F. R.
See de Hartog, Jan

Eco, Umberto 1932-........... **CLC 28, 60**
See also BEST 90:1; CA 77-80; CANR 12,
33; DAM NOV, POP; MTCW

Eddison, E(ric) R(ucker)
1882-1945 .... **TCLC 15**
See also CA 109

Edel, (Joseph) Leon 1907-...... **CLC 29, 34**
See also CA 1-4R; CANR 1, 22; DLB 103;
INT CANR-22

Eden, Emily 1797-1869 .... **NCLC 10**

Edgar, David 1948-............... **CLC 42**
See also CA 57-60; CANR 12;
DAM DRAM; DLB 13; MTCW

Edgerton, Clyde (Carlyle) 1944- .... **CLC 39**
See also AAYA 17; CA 118; 134; INT 134

Edgeworth, Maria 1768-1849... **NCLC 1, 51**
See also DLB 116, 159, 163; SATA 21

Edmonds, Paul
See Kuttner, Henry

Edmonds, Walter D(umaux) 1903- . . **CLC 35**
See also CA 5-8R; CANR 2; DLB 9;
MAICYA; SAAS 4; SATA 1, 27

Edmondson, Wallace
See Ellison, Harlan (Jay)

Edson, Russell . . . . **CLC 13**
See also CA 33-36R

Edwards, Bronwen Elizabeth
See Rose, Wendy

Edwards, G(erald) B(asil)
1899-1976 . . . . **CLC 25**
See also CA 110

Edwards, Gus 1939- . . . . **CLC 43**
See also CA 108; INT 108

Edwards, Jonathan
1703-1758 . . . . **LC 7; DA; DAC**
See also DAM MST; DLB 24

Efron, Marina Ivanovna Tsvetaeva
See Tsvetaeva (Efron), Marina (Ivanovna)

Ehle, John (Marsden, Jr.) 1925- . . . . **CLC 27**
See also CA 9-12R

Ehrenbourg, Ilya (Grigoryevich)
See Ehrenburg, Ilya (Grigoryevich)

Ehrenburg, Ilya (Grigoryevich)
1891-1967 . . . . **CLC 18, 34, 62**
See also CA 102; 25-28R

Ehrenburg, Ilyo (Grigoryevich)
See Ehrenburg, Ilya (Grigoryevich)

Eich, Guenter 1907-1972 . . . . **CLC 15**
See also CA 111; 93-96; DLB 69, 124

Eichendorff, Joseph Freiherr von
1788-1857 . . . . **NCLC 8**
See also DLB 90

Eigner, Larry . . . . **CLC 9**
See also Eigner, Laurence (Joel)
See also CAAS 23; DLB 5

Eigner, Laurence (Joel) 1927-1996
See Eigner, Larry
See also CA 9-12R; CANR 6

Eiseley, Loren Corey 1907-1977 . . . . . **CLC 7**
See also AAYA 5; CA 1-4R; 73-76;
CANR 6

Eisenstadt, Jill 1963- . . . . **CLC 50**
See also CA 140

Eisenstein, Sergei (Mikhailovich)
1898-1948 . . . . **TCLC 57**
See also CA 114; 149

Eisner, Simon
See Kornbluth, C(yril) M.

Ekeloef, (Bengt) Gunnar
1907-1968 . . . . **CLC 27**
See also CA 123; 25-28R; DAM POET

Ekelof, (Bengt) Gunnar
See Ekeloef, (Bengt) Gunnar

Ekwensi, C. O. D.
See Ekwensi, Cyprian (Odiatu Duaka)

Ekwensi, Cyprian (Odiatu Duaka)
1921- . . . . **CLC 4; BLC**
See also BW 2; CA 29-32R; CANR 18, 42;
DAM MULT; DLB 117; MTCW;
SATA 66

Elaine . . . . **TCLC 18**
See also Leverson, Ada

El Crummo
See Crumb, R(obert)

Elia
See Lamb, Charles

Eliade, Mircea 1907-1986 . . . . **CLC 19**
See also CA 65-68; 119; CANR 30; MTCW

Eliot, A. D.
See Jewett, (Theodora) Sarah Orne

Eliot, Alice
See Jewett, (Theodora) Sarah Orne

Eliot, Dan
See Silverberg, Robert

Eliot, George
1819-1880 . . . . . **NCLC 4, 13, 23, 41, 49;
DA; DAB; DAC; WLC**
See also CDBLB 1832-1890; DAM MST,
NOV; DLB 21, 35, 55

Eliot, John 1604-1690 . . . . **LC 5**
See also DLB 24

Eliot, T(homas) S(tearns)
1888-1965 . . . . . **CLC 1, 2, 3, 6, 9, 10, 13,
15, 24, 34, 41, 55, 57; DA; DAB; DAC;
PC 5; WLC 2**
See also CA 5-8R; 25-28R; CANR 41;
CDALB 1929-1941; DAM DRAM, MST,
POET; DLB 7, 10, 45, 63; DLBY 88;
MTCW

Elizabeth 1866-1941 . . . . **TCLC 41**

Elkin, Stanley L(awrence)
1930-1995 . . . . . . **CLC 4, 6, 9, 14, 27, 51,
91; SSC 12**
See also CA 9-12R; 148; CANR 8, 46;
DAM NOV, POP; DLB 2, 28; DLBY 80;
INT CANR-8; MTCW

Elledge, Scott . . . . **CLC 34**

Elliott, Don
See Silverberg, Robert

Elliott, George P(aul) 1918-1980 . . . . . **CLC 2**
See also CA 1-4R; 97-100; CANR 2

Elliott, Janice 1931- . . . . **CLC 47**
See also CA 13-16R; CANR 8, 29; DLB 14

Elliott, Sumner Locke 1917-1991 . . . **CLC 38**
See also CA 5-8R; 134; CANR 2, 21

Elliott, William
See Bradbury, Ray (Douglas)

Ellis, A. E. . . . . **CLC 7**

Ellis, Alice Thomas . . . . **CLC 40**
See also Haycraft, Anna

Ellis, Bret Easton 1964- . . . . **CLC 39, 71**
See also AAYA 2; CA 118; 123; CANR 51;
DAM POP; INT 123

Ellis, (Henry) Havelock
1859-1939 . . . . **TCLC 14**
See also CA 109

Ellis, Landon
See Ellison, Harlan (Jay)

Ellis, Trey 1962- . . . . **CLC 55**
See also CA 146

Ellison, Harlan (Jay)
1934- . . . . **CLC 1, 13, 42; SSC 14**
See also CA 5-8R; CANR 5, 46;
DAM POP; DLB 8; INT CANR-5;
MTCW

Ellison, Ralph (Waldo)
1914-1994 . . . . **CLC 1, 3, 11, 54, 86;
BLC; DA; DAB; DAC; WLC**
See also BW 1; CA 9-12R; 145; CANR 24;
CDALB 1941-1968; DAM MST, MULT,
NOV; DLB 2, 76; DLBY 94; MTCW

Ellmann, Lucy (Elizabeth) 1956- . . . . **CLC 61**
See also CA 128

Ellmann, Richard (David)
1918-1987 . . . . **CLC 50**
See also BEST 89:2; CA 1-4R; 122;
CANR 2, 28; DLB 103; DLBY 87;
MTCW

Elman, Richard 1934- . . . . **CLC 19**
See also CA 17-20R; CAAS 3; CANR 47

Elron
See Hubbard, L(afayette) Ron(ald)

Eluard, Paul . . . . **TCLC 7, 41**
See also Grindel, Eugene

Elyot, Sir Thomas 1490(?)-1546 . . . . . **LC 11**

Elytis, Odysseus 1911- . . . . **CLC 15, 49**
See also CA 102; DAM POET; MTCW

Emecheta, (Florence Onye) Buchi
1944- . . . . **CLC 14, 48; BLC**
See also BW 2; CA 81-84; CANR 27;
DAM MULT; DLB 117; MTCW;
SATA 66

Emerson, Ralph Waldo
1803-1882 . . . . . **NCLC 1, 38; DA; DAB;
DAC; WLC**
See also CDALB 1640-1865; DAM MST,
POET; DLB 1, 59, 73

Eminescu, Mihail 1850-1889 . . . . . **NCLC 33**

Empson, William
1906-1984 . . . . **CLC 3, 8, 19, 33, 34**
See also CA 17-20R; 112; CANR 31;
DLB 20; MTCW

Enchi Fumiko (Ueda) 1905-1986 . . . . **CLC 31**
See also CA 129; 121

Ende, Michael (Andreas Helmuth)
1929-1995 . . . . **CLC 31**
See also CA 118; 124; 149; CANR 36;
CLR 14; DLB 75; MAICYA; SATA 61;
SATA-Brief 42; SATA-Obit 86

Endo, Shusaku 1923- . . . . . **CLC 7, 14, 19, 54**
See also CA 29-32R; CANR 21;
DAM NOV; MTCW

Engel, Marian 1933-1985 . . . . **CLC 36**
See also CA 25-28R; CANR 12; DLB 53;
INT CANR-12

Engelhardt, Frederick
See Hubbard, L(afayette) Ron(ald)

Enright, D(ennis) J(oseph)
1920- . . . . **CLC 4, 8, 31**
See also CA 1-4R; CANR 1, 42; DLB 27;
SATA 25

Enzensberger, Hans Magnus
1929- . . . . **CLC 43**
See also CA 116; 119

Ephron, Nora 1941- . . . . **CLC 17, 31**
See also AITN 2; CA 65-68; CANR 12, 39

Epsilon
See Betjeman, John

Epstein, Daniel Mark 1948- . . . . **CLC 7**
See also CA 49-52; CANR 2

Foote, Shelby 1916- .... CLC **75**
See also CA 5-8R; CANR 3, 45;
DAM NOV, POP; DLB 2, 17

Forbes, Esther 1891-1967 .... CLC **12**
See also AAYA 17; CA 13-14; 25-28R;
CAP 1; CLR 27; DLB 22; JRDA;
MAICYA; SATA 2

Forche, Carolyn (Louise)
1950- .... CLC **25, 83, 86; PC 10**
See also CA 109; 117; CANR 50;
DAM POET; DLB 5; INT 117

Ford, Elbur
See Hibbert, Eleanor Alice Burford

Ford, Ford Madox
1873-1939 .... TCLC **1, 15, 39, 57**
See also CA 104; 132; CDBLB 1914-1945;
DAM NOV; DLB 162; MTCW

Ford, John 1895-1973 .... CLC **16**
See also CA 45-48

Ford, Richard 1944- .... CLC **46**
See also CA 69-72; CANR 11, 47

Ford, Webster
See Masters, Edgar Lee

Foreman, Richard 1937- .... CLC **50**
See also CA 65-68; CANR 32

Forester, C(ecil) S(cott)
1899-1966 .... CLC **35**
See also CA 73-76; 25-28R; SATA 13

Forez
See Mauriac, Francois (Charles)

Forman, James Douglas 1932- ...... CLC **21**
See also AAYA 17; CA 9-12R; CANR 4,
19, 42; JRDA; MAICYA; SATA 8, 70

Fornes, Maria Irene 1930- ...... CLC **39, 61**
See also CA 25-28R; CANR 28; DLB 7;
HW; INT CANR-28; MTCW

Forrest, Leon 1937- .... CLC **4**
See also BW 2; CA 89-92; CAAS 7;
CANR 25; DLB 33

Forster, E(dward) M(organ)
1879-1970 ..... CLC **1, 2, 3, 4, 9, 10, 13,
15, 22, 45, 77; DA; DAB; DAC; WLC**
See also AAYA 2; CA 13-14; 25-28R;
CANR 45; CAP 1; CDBLB 1914-1945;
DAM MST, NOV; DLB 34, 98, 162;
DLBD 10; MTCW; SATA 57

Forster, John 1812-1876 .... NCLC **11**
See also DLB 144

Forsyth, Frederick 1938- ...... CLC **2, 5, 36**
See also BEST 89:4; CA 85-88; CANR 38;
DAM NOV, POP; DLB 87; MTCW

Forten, Charlotte L. .... TCLC **16; BLC**
See also Grimke, Charlotte L(ottie) Forten
See also DLB 50

Foscolo, Ugo 1778-1827 .... NCLC **8**

Fosse, Bob .... CLC **20**
See also Fosse, Robert Louis

Fosse, Robert Louis 1927-1987
See Fosse, Bob
See also CA 110; 123

Foster, Stephen Collins
1826-1864 .... NCLC **26**

Foucault, Michel
1926-1984 .... CLC **31, 34, 69**
See also CA 105; 113; CANR 34; MTCW

Fouque, Friedrich (Heinrich Karl) de la Motte
1777-1843 .... NCLC **2**
See also DLB 90

Fourier, Charles 1772-1837 ...... NCLC **51**

Fournier, Henri Alban 1886-1914
See Alain-Fournier
See also CA 104

Fournier, Pierre 1916- .... CLC **11**
See also Gascar, Pierre
See also CA 89-92; CANR 16, 40

Fowles, John
1926- ...... CLC **1, 2, 3, 4, 6, 9, 10, 15,
33, 87; DAB; DAC**
See also CA 5-8R; CANR 25; CDBLB 1960
to Present; DAM MST; DLB 14, 139;
MTCW; SATA 22

Fox, Paula 1923- .... CLC **2, 8**
See also AAYA 3; CA 73-76; CANR 20,
36; CLR 1; DLB 52; JRDA; MAICYA;
MTCW; SATA 17, 60

Fox, William Price (Jr.) 1926- ..... CLC **22**
See also CA 17-20R; CAAS 19; CANR 11;
DLB 2; DLBY 81

Foxe, John 1516(?)-1587 .... LC **14**

Frame, Janet .... CLC **2, 3, 6, 22, 66**
See also Clutha, Janet Paterson Frame

France, Anatole .... TCLC **9**
See also Thibault, Jacques Anatole Francois
See also DLB 123

Francis, Claude 19(?)- .... CLC **50**

Francis, Dick 1920- .... CLC **2, 22, 42**
See also AAYA 5; BEST 89:3; CA 5-8R;
CANR 9, 42; CDBLB 1960 to Present;
DAM POP; DLB 87; INT CANR-9;
MTCW

Francis, Robert (Churchill)
1901-1987 .... CLC **15**
See also CA 1-4R; 123; CANR 1

Frank, Anne(lies Marie)
1929-1945 .... TCLC **17; DA; DAB;
DAC; WLC**
See also AAYA 12; CA 113; 133;
DAM MST; MTCW; SATA 87;
SATA-Brief 42

Frank, Elizabeth 1945- .... CLC **39**
See also CA 121; 126; INT 126

Franklin, Benjamin
See Hasek, Jaroslav (Matej Frantisek)

Franklin, Benjamin
1706-1790 ..... LC **25; DA; DAB; DAC**
See also CDALB 1640-1865; DAM MST;
DLB 24, 43, 73

Franklin, (Stella Maraia Sarah) Miles
1879-1954 .... TCLC **7**
See also CA 104

Fraser, (Lady) Antonia (Pakenham)
1932- .... CLC **32**
See also CA 85-88; CANR 44; MTCW;
SATA-Brief 32

Fraser, George MacDonald 1925- .... CLC **7**
See also CA 45-48; CANR 2, 48

Fraser, Sylvia 1935- .... CLC **64**
See also CA 45-48; CANR 1, 16

Frayn, Michael 1933- ...... CLC **3, 7, 31, 47**
See also CA 5-8R; CANR 30;
DAM DRAM, NOV; DLB 13, 14;
MTCW

Fraze, Candida (Merrill) 1945- ..... CLC **50**
See also CA 126

Frazer, J(ames) G(eorge)
1854-1941 .... TCLC **32**
See also CA 118

Frazer, Robert Caine
See Creasey, John

Frazer, Sir James George
See Frazer, J(ames) G(eorge)

Frazier, Ian 1951- .... CLC **46**
See also CA 130

Frederic, Harold 1856-1898 ...... NCLC **10**
See also DLB 12, 23; DLBD 13

Frederick, John
See Faust, Frederick (Schiller)

Frederick the Great 1712-1786 ...... LC **14**

Fredro, Aleksander 1793-1876 ..... NCLC **8**

Freeling, Nicolas 1927- .... CLC **38**
See also CA 49-52; CAAS 12; CANR 1, 17,
50; DLB 87

Freeman, Douglas Southall
1886-1953 .... TCLC **11**
See also CA 109; DLB 17

Freeman, Judith 1946- .... CLC **55**
See also CA 148

Freeman, Mary Eleanor Wilkins
1852-1930 .... TCLC **9; SSC 1**
See also CA 106; DLB 12, 78

Freeman, R(ichard) Austin
1862-1943 .... TCLC **21**
See also CA 113; DLB 70

French, Albert 1943- .... CLC **86**

French, Marilyn 1929- ...... CLC **10, 18, 60**
See also CA 69-72; CANR 3, 31;
DAM DRAM, NOV, POP;
INT CANR-31; MTCW

French, Paul
See Asimov, Isaac

Freneau, Philip Morin 1752-1832 .. NCLC **1**
See also DLB 37, 43

Freud, Sigmund 1856-1939 .... TCLC **52**
See also CA 115; 133; MTCW

Friedan, Betty (Naomi) 1921- ...... CLC **74**
See also CA 65-68; CANR 18, 45; MTCW

Friedlaender, Saul 1932- .... CLC **90**
See also CA 117; 130

Friedman, B(ernard) H(arper)
1926- .... CLC **7**
See also CA 1-4R; CANR 3, 48

Friedman, Bruce Jay 1930- .... CLC **3, 5, 56**
See also CA 9-12R; CANR 25; DLB 2, 28;
INT CANR-25

Friel, Brian 1929- .... CLC **5, 42, 59**
See also CA 21-24R; CANR 33; DLB 13;
MTCW

Friis-Baastad, Babbis Ellinor
1921-1970 .... CLC **12**
See also CA 17-20R; 134; SATA 7

Frisch, Max (Rudolf)
1911-1991 ..... **CLC 3, 9, 14, 18, 32, 44**
See also CA 85-88; 134; CANR 32;
DAM DRAM, NOV; DLB 69, 124;
MTCW

Fromentin, Eugene (Samuel Auguste)
1820-1876 .... **NCLC 10**
See also DLB 123

Frost, Frederick
See Faust, Frederick (Schiller)

Frost, Robert (Lee)
1874-1963 .... **CLC 1, 3, 4, 9, 10, 13, 15,**
26, 34, 44; DA; DAB; DAC; PC 1; WLC
See also CA 89-92; CANR 33;
CDALB 1917-1929; DAM MST, POET;
DLB 54; DLBD 7; MTCW; SATA 14

Froude, James Anthony
1818-1894 .... **NCLC 43**
See also DLB 18, 57, 144

Froy, Herald
See Waterhouse, Keith (Spencer)

Fry, Christopher 1907- ...... **CLC 2, 10, 14**
See also CA 17-20R; CAAS 23; CANR 9,
30; DAM DRAM; DLB 13; MTCW;
SATA 66

Frye, (Herman) Northrop
1912-1991 .... **CLC 24, 70**
See also CA 5-8R; 133; CANR 8, 37;
DLB 67, 68; MTCW

Fuchs, Daniel 1909-1993 .... **CLC 8, 22**
See also CA 81-84; 142; CAAS 5;
CANR 40; DLB 9, 26, 28; DLBY 93

Fuchs, Daniel 1934- .... **CLC 34**
See also CA 37-40R; CANR 14, 48

Fuentes, Carlos
1928- ...... **CLC 3, 8, 10, 13, 22, 41, 60;**
DA; DAB; DAC; HLC; WLC
See also AAYA 4; AITN 2; CA 69-72;
CANR 10, 32; DAM MST, MULT,
NOV; DLB 113; HW; MTCW

Fuentes, Gregorio Lopez y
See Lopez y Fuentes, Gregorio

Fugard, (Harold) Athol
1932- .... **CLC 5, 9, 14, 25, 40, 80; DC 3**
See also AAYA 17; CA 85-88; CANR 32;
DAM DRAM; MTCW

Fugard, Sheila 1932- .... **CLC 48**
See also CA 125

Fuller, Charles (H., Jr.)
1939- .... **CLC 25; BLC; DC 1**
See also BW 2; CA 108; 112;
DAM DRAM, MULT; DLB 38;
INT 112; MTCW

Fuller, John (Leopold) 1937- ...... **CLC 62**
See also CA 21-24R; CANR 9, 44; DLB 40

Fuller, Margaret .... **NCLC 5, 50**
See also Ossoli, Sarah Margaret (Fuller
marchesa d')

Fuller, Roy (Broadbent)
1912-1991 .... **CLC 4, 28**
See also CA 5-8R; 135; CAAS 10; DLB 15,
20; SATA 87

Fulton, Alice 1952- .... **CLC 52**
See also CA 116

Furphy, Joseph 1843-1912 .... **TCLC 25**

Fussell, Paul 1924- .... **CLC 74**
See also BEST 90:1; CA 17-20R; CANR 8,
21, 35; INT CANR-21; MTCW

Futabatei, Shimei 1864-1909 ..... **TCLC 44**

Futrelle, Jacques 1875-1912 ...... **TCLC 19**
See also CA 113

Gaboriau, Emile 1835-1873 ...... **NCLC 14**

Gadda, Carlo Emilio 1893-1973 .... **CLC 11**
See also CA 89-92

Gaddis, William
1922- ..... **CLC 1, 3, 6, 8, 10, 19, 43, 86**
See also CA 17-20R; CANR 21, 48; DLB 2;
MTCW

Gaines, Ernest J(ames)
1933- .... **CLC 3, 11, 18, 86; BLC**
See also AITN 1; BW 2; CA 9-12R;
CANR 6, 24, 42; CDALB 1968-1988;
DAM MULT; DLB 2, 33, 152; DLBY 80;
MTCW; SATA 86

Gaitskill, Mary 1954- .... **CLC 69**
See also CA 128

Galdos, Benito Perez
See Perez Galdos, Benito

Gale, Zona 1874-1938 .... **TCLC 7**
See also CA 105; DAM DRAM; DLB 9, 78

Galeano, Eduardo (Hughes) 1940- ... **CLC 72**
See also CA 29-32R; CANR 13, 32; HW

Galiano, Juan Valera y Alcala
See Valera y Alcala-Galiano, Juan

Gallagher, Tess 1943- .... **CLC 18, 63; PC 9**
See also CA 106; DAM POET; DLB 120

Gallant, Mavis
1922- ...... **CLC 7, 18, 38; DAC; SSC 5**
See also CA 69-72; CANR 29; DAM MST;
DLB 53; MTCW

Gallant, Roy A(rthur) 1924- .... **CLC 17**
See also CA 5-8R; CANR 4, 29; CLR 30;
MAICYA; SATA 4, 68

Gallico, Paul (William) 1897-1976 ... **CLC 2**
See also AITN 1; CA 5-8R; 69-72;
CANR 23; DLB 9; MAICYA; SATA 13

Gallup, Ralph
See Whitemore, Hugh (John)

Galsworthy, John
1867-1933 ...... **TCLC 1, 45; DA; DAB;**
DAC; WLC 2
See also CA 104; 141; CDBLB 1890-1914;
DAM DRAM, MST, NOV; DLB 10, 34,
98, 162

Galt, John 1779-1839 .... **NCLC 1**
See also DLB 99, 116, 159

Galvin, James 1951- .... **CLC 38**
See also CA 108; CANR 26

Gamboa, Federico 1864-1939 ..... **TCLC 36**

Gandhi, M. K.
See Gandhi, Mohandas Karamchand

Gandhi, Mahatma
See Gandhi, Mohandas Karamchand

Gandhi, Mohandas Karamchand
1869-1948 .... **TCLC 59**
See also CA 121; 132; DAM MULT;
MTCW

Gann, Ernest Kellogg 1910-1991 .... **CLC 23**
See also AITN 1; CA 1-4R; 136; CANR 1

Garcia, Cristina 1958- .... **CLC 76**
See also CA 141

Garcia Lorca, Federico
1898-1936 ... **TCLC 1, 7, 49; DA; DAB;**
DAC; DC 2; HLC; PC 3; WLC
See also CA 104; 131; DAM DRAM, MST,
MULT, POET; DLB 108; HW; MTCW

Garcia Marquez, Gabriel (Jose)
1928- .... **CLC 2, 3, 8, 10, 15, 27, 47, 55,**
68; DA; DAB; DAC; HLC; SSC 8; WLC
See also AAYA 3; BEST 89:1, 90:4;
CA 33-36R; CANR 10, 28, 50;
DAM MST, MULT, NOV, POP;
DLB 113; HW; MTCW

Gard, Janice
See Latham, Jean Lee

Gard, Roger Martin du
See Martin du Gard, Roger

Gardam, Jane 1928- .... **CLC 43**
See also CA 49-52; CANR 2, 18, 33;
CLR 12; DLB 14, 161; MAICYA;
MTCW; SAAS 9; SATA 39, 76;
SATA-Brief 28

Gardner, Herb(ert) 1934- .... **CLC 44**
See also CA 149

Gardner, John (Champlin), Jr.
1933-1982 ..... **CLC 2, 3, 5, 7, 8, 10, 18,**
28, 34; SSC 7
See also AITN 1; CA 65-68; 107;
CANR 33; DAM NOV, POP; DLB 2;
DLBY 82; MTCW; SATA 40;
SATA-Obit 31

Gardner, John (Edmund) 1926- ..... **CLC 30**
See also CA 103; CANR 15; DAM POP;
MTCW

Gardner, Noel
See Kuttner, Henry

Gardons, S. S.
See Snodgrass, W(illiam) D(e Witt)

Garfield, Leon 1921- .... **CLC 12**
See also AAYA 8; CA 17-20R; CANR 38,
41; CLR 21; DLB 161; JRDA; MAICYA;
SATA 1, 32, 76

Garland, (Hannibal) Hamlin
1860-1940 .... **TCLC 3; SSC 18**
See also CA 104; DLB 12, 71, 78

Garneau, (Hector de) Saint-Denys
1912-1943 .... **TCLC 13**
See also CA 111; DLB 88

Garner, Alan 1934- .... **CLC 17; DAB**
See also CA 73-76; CANR 15; CLR 20;
DAM POP; DLB 161; MAICYA;
MTCW; SATA 18, 69

Garner, Hugh 1913-1979 .... **CLC 13**
See also CA 69-72; CANR 31; DLB 68

Garnett, David 1892-1981 .... **CLC 3**
See also CA 5-8R; 103; CANR 17; DLB 34

Garos, Stephanie
See Katz, Steve

Garrett, George (Palmer)
1929- .... **CLC 3, 11, 51**
See also CA 1-4R; CAAS 5; CANR 1, 42;
DLB 2, 5, 130, 152; DLBY 83

Garrick, David 1717-1779 .... **LC 15**
See also DAM DRAM; DLB 84

Glanville, Brian (Lester) 1931- ...... **CLC 6**
See also CA 5-8R; CAAS 9; CANR 3;
DLB 15, 139; SATA 42

Glasgow, Ellen (Anderson Gholson)
1873(?)-1945 .... **TCLC 2, 7**
See also CA 104; DLB 9, 12

Glaspell, Susan (Keating)
1882(?)-1948 .... **TCLC 55**
See also CA 110; DLB 7, 9, 78; YABC 2

Glassco, John 1909-1981 .... **CLC 9**
See also CA 13-16R; 102; CANR 15;
DLB 68

Glasscock, Amnesia
See Steinbeck, John (Ernst)

Glasser, Ronald J. 1940(?)- .... **CLC 37**

Glassman, Joyce
See Johnson, Joyce

Glendinning, Victoria 1937- .... **CLC 50**
See also CA 120; 127; DLB 155

Glissant, Edouard 1928- .... **CLC 10, 68**
See also DAM MULT

Gloag, Julian 1930- .... **CLC 40**
See also AITN 1; CA 65-68; CANR 10

Glowacki, Aleksander
See Prus, Boleslaw

Glueck, Louise (Elisabeth)
1943- .... **CLC 7, 22, 44, 81**
See also CA 33-36R; CANR 40;
DAM POET; DLB 5

Gobineau, Joseph Arthur (Comte) de
1816-1882 .... **NCLC 17**
See also DLB 123

Godard, Jean-Luc 1930- .... **CLC 20**
See also CA 93-96

Godden, (Margaret) Rumer 1907- ... **CLC 53**
See also AAYA 6; CA 5-8R; CANR 4, 27,
36; CLR 20; DLB 161; MAICYA;
SAAS 12; SATA 3, 36

Godoy Alcayaga, Lucila 1889-1957
See Mistral, Gabriela
See also BW 2; CA 104; 131; DAM MULT;
HW; MTCW

Godwin, Gail (Kathleen)
1937- .... **CLC 5, 8, 22, 31, 69**
See also CA 29-32R; CANR 15, 43;
DAM POP; DLB 6; INT CANR-15;
MTCW

Godwin, William 1756-1836 ...... **NCLC 14**
See also CDBLB 1789-1832; DLB 39, 104,
142, 158, 163

Goethe, Johann Wolfgang von
1749-1832 .... **NCLC 4, 22, 34; DA;
DAB; DAC; PC 5; WLC 3**
See also DAM DRAM, MST, POET;
DLB 94

Gogarty, Oliver St. John
1878-1957 .... **TCLC 15**
See also CA 109; 150; DLB 15, 19

Gogol, Nikolai (Vasilyevich)
1809-1852 .... **NCLC 5, 15, 31; DA;
DAB; DAC; DC 1; SSC 4; WLC**
See also DAM DRAM, MST

Goines, Donald
1937(?)-1974 .... **CLC 80; BLC**
See also AITN 1; BW 1; CA 124; 114;
DAM MULT, POP; DLB 33

Gold, Herbert 1924- .... **CLC 4, 7, 14, 42**
See also CA 9-12R; CANR 17, 45; DLB 2;
DLBY 81

Goldbarth, Albert 1948- .... **CLC 5, 38**
See also CA 53-56; CANR 6, 40; DLB 120

Goldberg, Anatol 1910-1982 .... **CLC 34**
See also CA 131; 117

Goldemberg, Isaac 1945- .... **CLC 52**
See also CA 69-72; CAAS 12; CANR 11,
32; HW

Golding, William (Gerald)
1911-1993 .... **CLC 1, 2, 3, 8, 10, 17, 27,
58, 81; DA; DAB; DAC; WLC**
See also AAYA 5; CA 5-8R; 141;
CANR 13, 33; CDBLB 1945-1960;
DAM MST, NOV; DLB 15, 100; MTCW

Goldman, Emma 1869-1940 ...... **TCLC 13**
See also CA 110; 150

Goldman, Francisco 1955- .... **CLC 76**

Goldman, William (W.) 1931- ... **CLC 1, 48**
See also CA 9-12R; CANR 29; DLB 44

Goldmann, Lucien 1913-1970 ...... **CLC 24**
See also CA 25-28; CAP 2

Goldoni, Carlo 1707-1793 .... **LC 4**
See also DAM DRAM

Goldsberry, Steven 1949- .... **CLC 34**
See also CA 131

Goldsmith, Oliver
1728-1774 ...... **LC 2; DA; DAB; DAC;
WLC**
See also CDBLB 1660-1789; DAM DRAM,
MST, NOV, POET; DLB 39, 89, 104,
109, 142; SATA 26

Goldsmith, Peter
See Priestley, J(ohn) B(oynton)

Gombrowicz, Witold
1904-1969 .... **CLC 4, 7, 11, 49**
See also CA 19-20; 25-28R; CAP 2;
DAM DRAM

Gomez de la Serna, Ramon
1888-1963 .... **CLC 9**
See also CA 116; HW

Goncharov, Ivan Alexandrovich
1812-1891 .... **NCLC 1**

Goncourt, Edmond (Louis Antoine Huot) de
1822-1896 .... **NCLC 7**
See also DLB 123

Goncourt, Jules (Alfred Huot) de
1830-1870 .... **NCLC 7**
See also DLB 123

Gontier, Fernande 19(?)- .... **CLC 50**

Goodman, Paul 1911-1972 .... **CLC 1, 2, 4, 7**
See also CA 19-20; 37-40R; CANR 34;
CAP 2; DLB 130; MTCW

Gordimer, Nadine
1923- .... **CLC 3, 5, 7, 10, 18, 33, 51, 70;
DA; DAB; DAC; SSC 17**
See also CA 5-8R; CANR 3, 28;
DAM MST, NOV; INT CANR-28;
MTCW

Gordon, Adam Lindsay
1833-1870 .... **NCLC 21**

Gordon, Caroline
1895-1981 ... **CLC 6, 13, 29, 83; SSC 15**
See also CA 11-12; 103; CANR 36; CAP 1;
DLB 4, 9, 102; DLBY 81; MTCW

Gordon, Charles William 1860-1937
See Connor, Ralph
See also CA 109

Gordon, Mary (Catherine)
1949- .... **CLC 13, 22**
See also CA 102; CANR 44; DLB 6;
DLBY 81; INT 102; MTCW

Gordon, Sol 1923- .... **CLC 26**
See also CA 53-56; CANR 4; SATA 11

Gordone, Charles 1925-1995 ...... **CLC 1, 4**
See also BW 1; CA 93-96; 150;
DAM DRAM; DLB 7; INT 93-96;
MTCW

Gorenko, Anna Andreevna
See Akhmatova, Anna

Gorky, Maxim .... **TCLC 8; DAB; WLC**
See also Peshkov, Alexei Maximovich

Goryan, Sirak
See Saroyan, William

Gosse, Edmund (William)
1849-1928 .... **TCLC 28**
See also CA 117; DLB 57, 144

Gotlieb, Phyllis Fay (Bloom)
1926- .... **CLC 18**
See also CA 13-16R; CANR 7; DLB 88

Gottesman, S. D.
See Kornbluth, C(yril) M.; Pohl, Frederik

Gottfried von Strassburg
fl. c. 1210- .... **CMLC 10**
See also DLB 138

Gould, Lois .... **CLC 4, 10**
See also CA 77-80; CANR 29; MTCW

Gourmont, Remy (-Marie-Charles) de
1858-1915 .... **TCLC 17**
See also CA 109; 150

Govier, Katherine 1948- .... **CLC 51**
See also CA 101; CANR 18, 40

Goyen, (Charles) William
1915-1983 .... **CLC 5, 8, 14, 40**
See also AITN 2; CA 5-8R; 110; CANR 6;
DLB 2; DLBY 83; INT CANR-6

Goytisolo, Juan
1931- .... **CLC 5, 10, 23; HLC**
See also CA 85-88; CANR 32;
DAM MULT; HW; MTCW

Gozzano, Guido 1883-1916 .... **PC 10**
See also DLB 114

Gozzi, (Conte) Carlo 1720-1806 .. **NCLC 23**

Grabbe, Christian Dietrich
1801-1836 .... **NCLC 2**
See also DLB 133

Grace, Patricia 1937- .... **CLC 56**

Gracian y Morales, Baltasar
1601-1658 .... **LC 15**

Gracq, Julien .... **CLC 11, 48**
See also Poirier, Louis
See also DLB 83

Grade, Chaim 1910-1982 .... **CLC 10**
See also CA 93-96; 107

Graduate of Oxford, A
See Ruskin, John

Graham, John
See Phillips, David Graham

Graham, Jorie 1951- .... **CLC 48**
See also CA 111; DLB 120

Graham, R(obert) B(ontine) Cunninghame
See Cunninghame Graham, R(obert)
B(ontine)
See also DLB 98, 135

Graham, Robert
See Haldeman, Joe (William)

Graham, Tom
See Lewis, (Harry) Sinclair

Graham, W(illiam) S(ydney)
1918-1986 .... **CLC 29**
See also CA 73-76; 118; DLB 20

Graham, Winston (Mawdsley)
1910- .... **CLC 23**
See also CA 49-52; CANR 2, 22, 45;
DLB 77

Grant, Skeeter
See Spiegelman, Art

Granville-Barker, Harley
1877-1946 .... **TCLC 2**
See also Barker, Harley Granville
See also CA 104; DAM DRAM

Grass, Guenter (Wilhelm)
1927- ..... **CLC 1, 2, 4, 6, 11, 15, 22, 32,**
49, 88; DA; DAB; DAC; WLC
See also CA 13-16R; CANR 20;
DAM MST, NOV; DLB 75, 124; MTCW

Gratton, Thomas
See Hulme, T(homas) E(rnest)

Grau, Shirley Ann
1929- .... **CLC 4, 9; SSC 15**
See also CA 89-92; CANR 22; DLB 2;
INT CANR-22; MTCW

Gravel, Fern
See Hall, James Norman

Graver, Elizabeth 1964- .... **CLC 70**
See also CA 135

Graves, Richard Perceval 1945- .... **CLC 44**
See also CA 65-68; CANR 9, 26, 51

Graves, Robert (von Ranke)
1895-1985 ...... **CLC 1, 2, 6, 11, 39, 44,**
45; DAB; DAC; PC 6
See also CA 5-8R; 117; CANR 5, 36;
CDBLB 1914-1945; DAM MST, POET;
DLB 20, 100; DLBY 85; MTCW;
SATA 45

Gray, Alasdair (James) 1934- ...... **CLC 41**
See also CA 126; CANR 47; INT 126;
MTCW

Gray, Amlin 1946- .... **CLC 29**
See also CA 138

Gray, Francine du Plessix 1930-.... **CLC 22**
See also BEST 90:3; CA 61-64; CAAS 2;
CANR 11, 33; DAM NOV;
INT CANR-11; MTCW

Gray, John (Henry) 1866-1934 .... **TCLC 19**
See also CA 119

Gray, Simon (James Holliday)
1936- .... **CLC 9, 14, 36**
See also AITN 1; CA 21-24R; CAAS 3;
CANR 32; DLB 13; MTCW

Gray, Spalding 1941- .... **CLC 49**
See also CA 128; DAM POP

Gray, Thomas
1716-1771 ...... **LC 4; DA; DAB; DAC;**
PC 2; WLC
See also CDBLB 1660-1789; DAM MST;
DLB 109

Grayson, David
See Baker, Ray Stannard

Grayson, Richard (A.) 1951- .... **CLC 38**
See also CA 85-88; CANR 14, 31

Greeley, Andrew M(oran) 1928-.... **CLC 28**
See also CA 5-8R; CAAS 7; CANR 7, 43;
DAM POP; MTCW

Green, Anna Katharine
1846-1935 .... **TCLC 63**
See also CA 112

Green, Brian
See Card, Orson Scott

Green, Hannah
See Greenberg, Joanne (Goldenberg)

Green, Hannah .... **CLC 3**
See also CA 73-76

Green, Henry.................. **CLC 2, 13**
See also Yorke, Henry Vincent
See also DLB 15

Green, Julian (Hartridge) 1900-
See Green, Julien
See also CA 21-24R; CANR 33; DLB 4, 72;
MTCW

Green, Julien .... **CLC 3, 11, 77**
See also Green, Julian (Hartridge)

Green, Paul (Eliot) 1894-1981 ...... **CLC 25**
See also AITN 1; CA 5-8R; 103; CANR 3;
DAM DRAM; DLB 7, 9; DLBY 81

Greenberg, Ivan 1908-1973
See Rahv, Philip
See also CA 85-88

Greenberg, Joanne (Goldenberg)
1932- .... **CLC 7, 30**
See also AAYA 12; CA 5-8R; CANR 14,
32; SATA 25

Greenberg, Richard 1959(?)- .... **CLC 57**
See also CA 138

Greene, Bette 1934- .... **CLC 30**
See also AAYA 7; CA 53-56; CANR 4;
CLR 2; JRDA; MAICYA; SAAS 16;
SATA 8

Greene, Gael .... **CLC 8**
See also CA 13-16R; CANR 10

Greene, Graham
1904-1991 .... **CLC 1, 3, 6, 9, 14, 18, 27,**
37, 70, 72; DA; DAB; DAC; WLC
See also AITN 2; CA 13-16R; 133;
CANR 35; CDBLB 1945-1960;
DAM MST, NOV; DLB 13, 15, 77, 100,
162; DLBY 91; MTCW; SATA 20

Greer, Richard
See Silverberg, Robert

Gregor, Arthur 1923- .... **CLC 9**
See also CA 25-28R; CAAS 10; CANR 11;
SATA 36

Gregor, Lee
See Pohl, Frederik

Gregory, Isabella Augusta (Persse)
1852-1932 .... **TCLC 1**
See also CA 104; DLB 10

Gregory, J. Dennis
See Williams, John A(lfred)

Grendon, Stephen
See Derleth, August (William)

Grenville, Kate 1950- .... **CLC 61**
See also CA 118

Grenville, Pelham
See Wodehouse, P(elham) G(renville)

Greve, Felix Paul (Berthold Friedrich)
1879-1948
See Grove, Frederick Philip
See also CA 104; 141; DAC; DAM MST

Grey, Zane 1872-1939 .... **TCLC 6**
See also CA 104; 132; DAM POP; DLB 9;
MTCW

Grieg, (Johan) Nordahl (Brun)
1902-1943 .... **TCLC 10**
See also CA 107

Grieve, C(hristopher) M(urray)
1892-1978 .... **CLC 11, 19**
See also MacDiarmid, Hugh; Pteleon
See also CA 5-8R; 85-88; CANR 33;
DAM POET; MTCW

Griffin, Gerald 1803-1840 .... **NCLC 7**
See also DLB 159

Griffin, John Howard 1920-1980.... **CLC 68**
See also AITN 1; CA 1-4R; 101; CANR 2

Griffin, Peter 1942- .... **CLC 39**
See also CA 136

Griffiths, Trevor 1935-........... **CLC 13, 52**
See also CA 97-100; CANR 45; DLB 13

Grigson, Geoffrey (Edward Harvey)
1905-1985 .... **CLC 7, 39**
See also CA 25-28R; 118; CANR 20, 33;
DLB 27; MTCW

Grillparzer, Franz 1791-1872...... **NCLC 1**
See also DLB 133

Grimble, Reverend Charles James
See Eliot, T(homas) S(tearns)

Grimke, Charlotte L(ottie) Forten
1837(?)-1914
See Forten, Charlotte L.
See also BW 1; CA 117; 124; DAM MULT,
POET

Grimm, Jacob Ludwig Karl
1785-1863 .... **NCLC 3**
See also DLB 90; MAICYA; SATA 22

Grimm, Wilhelm Karl 1786-1859 .. **NCLC 3**
See also DLB 90; MAICYA; SATA 22

Grimmelshausen, Johann Jakob Christoffel
von 1621-1676 .... **LC 6**

Grindel, Eugene 1895-1952
See Eluard, Paul
See also CA 104

Grisham, John 1955- .... **CLC 84**
See also AAYA 14; CA 138; CANR 47;
DAM POP

Hamilton, Franklin
See Silverberg, Robert

Hamilton, Gail
See Corcoran, Barbara

Hamilton, Mollie
See Kaye, M(ary) M(argaret)

Hamilton, (Anthony Walter) Patrick
1904-1962 . . . . **CLC 51**
See also CA 113; DLB 10

Hamilton, Virginia 1936- . . . . **CLC 26**
See also AAYA 2; BW 2; CA 25-28R;
CANR 20, 37; CLR 1, 11, 40;
DAM MULT; DLB 33, 52;
INT CANR-20; JRDA; MAICYA;
MTCW; SATA 4, 56, 79

Hammett, (Samuel) Dashiell
1894-1961 . . . . **CLC 3, 5, 10, 19, 47;**
SSC 17
See also AITN 1; CA 81-84; CANR 42;
CDALB 1929-1941; DLBD 6; MTCW

Hammon, Jupiter
1711(?)-1800(?) . . . . **NCLC 5; BLC**
See also DAM MULT, POET; DLB 31, 50

Hammond, Keith
See Kuttner, Henry

Hamner, Earl (Henry), Jr. 1923- . . . **CLC 12**
See also AITN 2; CA 73-76; DLB 6

Hampton, Christopher (James)
1946- . . . . **CLC 4**
See also CA 25-28R; DLB 13; MTCW

Hamsun, Knut . . . . **TCLC 2, 14, 49**
See also Pedersen, Knut

Handke, Peter 1942- . . **CLC 5, 8, 10, 15, 38**
See also CA 77-80; CANR 33;
DAM DRAM, NOV; DLB 85, 124;
MTCW

Hanley, James 1901-1985 . . . **CLC 3, 5, 8, 13**
See also CA 73-76; 117; CANR 36; MTCW

Hannah, Barry 1942- . . . . **CLC 23, 38, 90**
See also CA 108; 110; CANR 43; DLB 6;
INT 110; MTCW

Hannon, Ezra
See Hunter, Evan

Hansberry, Lorraine (Vivian)
1930-1965 . . . . . . **CLC 17, 62; BLC; DA;**
DAB; DAC; DC 2
See also BW 1; CA 109; 25-28R; CABS 3;
CDALB 1941-1968; DAM DRAM, MST,
MULT; DLB 7, 38; MTCW

Hansen, Joseph 1923- . . . . **CLC 38**
See also CA 29-32R; CAAS 17; CANR 16,
44; INT CANR-16

Hansen, Martin A. 1909-1955 . . . . . **TCLC 32**

Hanson, Kenneth O(stlin) 1922- . . . . **CLC 13**
See also CA 53-56; CANR 7

Hardwick, Elizabeth 1916- . . . . **CLC 13**
See also CA 5-8R; CANR 3, 32;
DAM NOV; DLB 6; MTCW

Hardy, Thomas
1840-1928 . . . . . . **TCLC 4, 10, 18, 32, 48,**
53; DA; DAB; DAC; PC 8; SSC 2; WLC
See also CA 104; 123; CDBLB 1890-1914;
DAM MST, NOV, POET; DLB 18, 19,
135; MTCW

Hare, David 1947- . . . . **CLC 29, 58**
See also CA 97-100; CANR 39; DLB 13;
MTCW

Harford, Henry
See Hudson, W(illiam) H(enry)

Hargrave, Leonie
See Disch, Thomas M(ichael)

Harjo, Joy 1951- . . . . **CLC 83**
See also CA 114; CANR 35; DAM MULT;
DLB 120; NNAL

Harlan, Louis R(udolph) 1922- . . . . . **CLC 34**
See also CA 21-24R; CANR 25

Harling, Robert 1951(?)- . . . . **CLC 53**
See also CA 147

Harmon, William (Ruth) 1938- . . . . . **CLC 38**
See also CA 33-36R; CANR 14, 32, 35;
SATA 65

Harper, F. E. W.
See Harper, Frances Ellen Watkins

Harper, Frances E. W.
See Harper, Frances Ellen Watkins

Harper, Frances E. Watkins
See Harper, Frances Ellen Watkins

Harper, Frances Ellen
See Harper, Frances Ellen Watkins

Harper, Frances Ellen Watkins
1825-1911 . . . . **TCLC 14; BLC**
See also BW 1; CA 111; 125; DAM MULT,
POET; DLB 50

Harper, Michael S(teven) 1938- . . **CLC 7, 22**
See also BW 1; CA 33-36R; CANR 24;
DLB 41

Harper, Mrs. F. E. W.
See Harper, Frances Ellen Watkins

Harris, Christie (Lucy) Irwin
1907- . . . . **CLC 12**
See also CA 5-8R; CANR 6; DLB 88;
JRDA; MAICYA; SAAS 10; SATA 6, 74

Harris, Frank 1856-1931 . . . . **TCLC 24**
See also CA 109; 150; DLB 156

Harris, George Washington
1814-1869 . . . . **NCLC 23**
See also DLB 3, 11

Harris, Joel Chandler
1848-1908 . . . . **TCLC 2; SSC 19**
See also CA 104; 137; DLB 11, 23, 42, 78,
91; MAICYA; YABC 1

Harris, John (Wyndham Parkes Lucas)
Beynon 1903-1969
See Wyndham, John
See also CA 102; 89-92

Harris, MacDonald . . . . **CLC 9**
See also Heiney, Donald (William)

Harris, Mark 1922- . . . . **CLC 19**
See also CA 5-8R; CAAS 3; CANR 2;
DLB 2; DLBY 80

Harris, (Theodore) Wilson 1921- . . . . **CLC 25**
See also BW 2; CA 65-68; CAAS 16;
CANR 11, 27; DLB 117; MTCW

Harrison, Elizabeth Cavanna 1909-
See Cavanna, Betty
See also CA 9-12R; CANR 6, 27

Harrison, Harry (Max) 1925- . . . . . . **CLC 42**
See also CA 1-4R; CANR 5, 21; DLB 8;
SATA 4

Harrison, James (Thomas)
1937- . . . . **CLC 6, 14, 33, 66; SSC 19**
See also CA 13-16R; CANR 8, 51;
DLBY 82; INT CANR-8

Harrison, Jim
See Harrison, James (Thomas)

Harrison, Kathryn 1961- . . . . **CLC 70**
See also CA 144

Harrison, Tony 1937- . . . . **CLC 43**
See also CA 65-68; CANR 44; DLB 40;
MTCW

Harriss, Will(ard Irvin) 1922- . . . . . . **CLC 34**
See also CA 111

Harson, Sley
See Ellison, Harlan (Jay)

Hart, Ellis
See Ellison, Harlan (Jay)

Hart, Josephine 1942(?)- . . . . **CLC 70**
See also CA 138; DAM POP

Hart, Moss 1904-1961 . . . . **CLC 66**
See also CA 109; 89-92; DAM DRAM;
DLB 7

Harte, (Francis) Bret(t)
1836(?)-1902 . . . . **TCLC 1, 25; DA; DAC;**
SSC 8; WLC
See also CA 104; 140; CDALB 1865-1917;
DAM MST; DLB 12, 64, 74, 79;
SATA 26

Hartley, L(eslie) P(oles)
1895-1972 . . . . **CLC 2, 22**
See also CA 45-48; 37-40R; CANR 33;
DLB 15, 139; MTCW

Hartman, Geoffrey H. 1929- . . . . **CLC 27**
See also CA 117; 125; DLB 67

Hartmann von Aue
c. 1160-c. 1205 . . . . **CMLC 15**
See also DLB 138

Hartmann von Aue 1170-1210 . . . . **CMLC 15**

Haruf, Kent 1943- . . . . **CLC 34**
See also CA 149

Harwood, Ronald 1934- . . . . **CLC 32**
See also CA 1-4R; CANR 4; DAM DRAM,
MST; DLB 13

Hasek, Jaroslav (Matej Frantisek)
1883-1923 . . . . **TCLC 4**
See also CA 104; 129; MTCW

Hass, Robert 1941- . . . . **CLC 18, 39**
See also CA 111; CANR 30, 50; DLB 105

Hastings, Hudson
See Kuttner, Henry

Hastings, Selina . . . . **CLC 44**

Hatteras, Amelia
See Mencken, H(enry) L(ouis)

Hatteras, Owen . . . . **TCLC 18**
See also Mencken, H(enry) L(ouis); Nathan,
George Jean

Hauptmann, Gerhart (Johann Robert)
1862-1946 . . . . **TCLC 4**
See also CA 104; DAM DRAM; DLB 66,
118

Havel, Vaclav
1936- . . . . **CLC 25, 58, 65; DC 6**
See also CA 104; CANR 36; DAM DRAM;
MTCW

Haviaras, Stratis . . . . CLC 33
See also Chaviaras, Strates

Hawes, Stephen   1475(?)-1523(?) . . . . . LC 17

Hawkes, John (Clendennin Burne, Jr.)
1925- . . . . . . CLC 1, 2, 3, 4, 7, 9, 14, 15,
27, 49
See also CA 1-4R; CANR 2, 47; DLB 2, 7;
DLBY 80; MTCW

Hawking, S. W.
See Hawking, Stephen W(illiam)

Hawking, Stephen W(illiam)
1942- . . . . CLC 63
See also AAYA 13; BEST 89:1; CA 126;
129; CANR 48

Hawthorne, Julian   1846-1934 . . . . . TCLC 25

Hawthorne, Nathaniel
1804-1864 . . . . NCLC 39; DA; DAB;
DAC; SSC 3; WLC
See also CDALB 1640-1865; DAM MST,
NOV; DLB 1, 74; YABC 2

Haxton, Josephine Ayres   1921-
See Douglas, Ellen
See also CA 115; CANR 41

Hayaseca y Eizaguirre, Jorge
See Echegaray (y Eizaguirre), Jose (Maria
Waldo)

Hayashi Fumiko   1904-1951 . . . . . . TCLC 27

Haycraft, Anna
See Ellis, Alice Thomas
See also CA 122

Hayden, Robert E(arl)
1913-1980 . . . . . . CLC 5, 9, 14, 37; BLC;
DA; DAC; PC 6
See also BW 1; CA 69-72; 97-100; CABS 2;
CANR 24; CDALB 1941-1968;
DAM MST, MULT, POET; DLB 5, 76;
MTCW; SATA 19; SATA-Obit 26

Hayford, J(oseph) E(phraim) Casely
See Casely-Hayford, J(oseph) E(phraim)

Hayman, Ronald   1932- . . . . CLC 44
See also CA 25-28R; CANR 18, 50;
DLB 155

Haywood, Eliza (Fowler)
1693(?)-1756 . . . . LC 1

Hazlitt, William   1778-1830 . . . . . . NCLC 29
See also DLB 110, 158

Hazzard, Shirley   1931- . . . . CLC 18
See also CA 9-12R; CANR 4; DLBY 82;
MTCW

Head, Bessie   1937-1986 . . . CLC 25, 67; BLC
See also BW 2; CA 29-32R; 119; CANR 25;
DAM MULT; DLB 117; MTCW

Headon, (Nicky) Topper   1956(?)- . . . CLC 30

Heaney, Seamus (Justin)
1939- . . . . . . CLC 5, 7, 14, 25, 37, 74, 91;
DAB
See also CA 85-88; CANR 25, 48;
CDBLB 1960 to Present; DAM POET;
DLB 40; MTCW

Hearn, (Patricio) Lafcadio (Tessima Carlos)
1850-1904 . . . . TCLC 9
See also CA 105; DLB 12, 78

Hearne, Vicki   1946- . . . . CLC 56
See also CA 139

Hearon, Shelby   1931- . . . . CLC 63
See also AITN 2; CA 25-28R; CANR 18,
48

Heat-Moon, William Least . . . . CLC 29
See also Trogdon, William (Lewis)
See also AAYA 9

Hebbel, Friedrich   1813-1863 . . . . . NCLC 43
See also DAM DRAM; DLB 129

Hebert, Anne   1916- . . . CLC 4, 13, 29; DAC
See also CA 85-88; DAM MST, POET;
DLB 68; MTCW

Hecht, Anthony (Evan)
1923- . . . . CLC 8, 13, 19
See also CA 9-12R; CANR 6; DAM POET;
DLB 5

Hecht, Ben   1894-1964 . . . . CLC 8
See also CA 85-88; DLB 7, 9, 25, 26, 28, 86

Hedayat, Sadeq   1903-1951 . . . . TCLC 21
See also CA 120

Hegel, Georg Wilhelm Friedrich
1770-1831 . . . . NCLC 46
See also DLB 90

Heidegger, Martin   1889-1976 . . . . . . CLC 24
See also CA 81-84; 65-68; CANR 34;
MTCW

Heidenstam, (Carl Gustaf) Verner von
1859-1940 . . . . TCLC 5
See also CA 104

Heifner, Jack   1946- . . . . CLC 11
See also CA 105; CANR 47

Heijermans, Herman   1864-1924 . . . TCLC 24
See also CA 123

Heilbrun, Carolyn G(old)   1926- . . . . . CLC 25
See also CA 45-48; CANR 1, 28

Heine, Heinrich   1797-1856 . . . . NCLC 4, 54
See also DLB 90

Heinemann, Larry (Curtiss)   1944- . . CLC 50
See also CA 110; CAAS 21; CANR 31;
DLBD 9; INT CANR-31

Heiney, Donald (William)   1921-1993
See Harris, MacDonald
See also CA 1-4R; 142; CANR 3

Heinlein, Robert A(nson)
1907-1988 . . . . . . CLC 1, 3, 8, 14, 26, 55
See also AAYA 17; CA 1-4R; 125;
CANR 1, 20; DAM POP; DLB 8; JRDA;
MAICYA; MTCW; SATA 9, 69;
SATA-Obit 56

Helforth, John
See Doolittle, Hilda

Hellenhofferu, Vojtech Kapristian z
See Hasek, Jaroslav (Matej Frantisek)

Heller, Joseph
1923- . . . . CLC 1, 3, 5, 8, 11, 36, 63; DA;
DAB; DAC; WLC
See also AITN 1; CA 5-8R; CABS 1;
CANR 8, 42; DAM MST, NOV, POP;
DLB 2, 28; DLBY 80; INT CANR-8;
MTCW

Hellman, Lillian (Florence)
1906-1984 . . . . . . CLC 2, 4, 8, 14, 18, 34,
44, 52; DC 1
See also AITN 1, 2; CA 13-16R; 112;
CANR 33; DAM DRAM; DLB 7;
DLBY 84; MTCW

Helprin, Mark   1947- . . . . . CLC 7, 10, 22, 32
See also CA 81-84; CANR 47; DAM NOV,
POP; DLBY 85; MTCW

Helvetius, Claude-Adrien
1715-1771 . . . . LC 26

Helyar, Jane Penelope Josephine   1933-
See Poole, Josephine
See also CA 21-24R; CANR 10, 26;
SATA 82

Hemans, Felicia   1793-1835 . . . . . . NCLC 29
See also DLB 96

Hemingway, Ernest (Miller)
1899-1961 . . . . CLC 1, 3, 6, 8, 10, 13, 19,
30, 34, 39, 41, 44, 50, 61, 80; DA; DAB;
DAC; SSC 1; WLC
See also CA 77-80; CANR 34;
CDALB 1917-1929; DAM MST, NOV;
DLB 4, 9, 102; DLBD 1; DLBY 81, 87;
MTCW

Hempel, Amy   1951- . . . . CLC 39
See also CA 118; 137

Henderson, F. C.
See Mencken, H(enry) L(ouis)

Henderson, Sylvia
See Ashton-Warner, Sylvia (Constance)

Henley, Beth . . . . CLC 23; DC 6
See also Henley, Elizabeth Becker
See also CABS 3; DLBY 86

Henley, Elizabeth Becker   1952-
See Henley, Beth
See also CA 107; CANR 32; DAM DRAM,
MST; MTCW

Henley, William Ernest
1849-1903 . . . . TCLC 8
See also CA 105; DLB 19

Hennissart, Martha
See Lathen, Emma
See also CA 85-88

Henry, O. . . . . TCLC 1, 19; SSC 5; WLC
See also Porter, William Sydney

Henry, Patrick   1736-1799 . . . . LC 25

Henryson, Robert   1430(?)-1506(?). . . . LC 20
See also DLB 146

Henry VIII   1491-1547 . . . . LC 10

Henschke, Alfred
See Klabund

Hentoff, Nat(han Irving)   1925- . . . . . CLC 26
See also AAYA 4; CA 1-4R; CAAS 6;
CANR 5, 25; CLR 1; INT CANR-25;
JRDA; MAICYA; SATA 42, 69;
SATA-Brief 27

Heppenstall, (John) Rayner
1911-1981 . . . . CLC 10
See also CA 1-4R; 103; CANR 29

Herbert, Frank (Patrick)
1920-1986 . . . . . . CLC 12, 23, 35, 44, 85
See also CA 53-56; 118; CANR 5, 43;
DAM POP; DLB 8; INT CANR-5;
MTCW; SATA 9, 37; SATA-Obit 47

Herbert, George
1593-1633 . . . . LC 24; DAB; PC 4
See also CDBLB Before 1660; DAM POET;
DLB 126

Herbert, Zbigniew 1924- .... CLC 9, 43
See also CA 89-92; CANR 36;
DAM POET; MTCW

Herbst, Josephine (Frey)
1897-1969 .... CLC 34
See also CA 5-8R; 25-28R; DLB 9

Hergesheimer, Joseph
1880-1954 .... TCLC 11
See also CA 109; DLB 102, 9

Herlihy, James Leo 1927-1993 ..... CLC 6
See also CA 1-4R; 143; CANR 2

Hermogenes fl. c. 175- .... CMLC 6

Hernandez, Jose 1834-1886 ...... NCLC 17

Herodotus c. 484B.C.-429B.C. .... CMLC 17

Herrick, Robert
1591-1674 ..... LC 13; DA; DAB; DAC;
                                            PC 9
See also DAM MST, POP; DLB 126

Herring, Guilles
See Somerville, Edith

Herriot, James 1916-1995 .... CLC 12
See also Wight, James Alfred
See also AAYA 1; CA 148; CANR 40;
DAM POP; SATA 86

Herrmann, Dorothy 1941- .... CLC 44
See also CA 107

Herrmann, Taffy
See Herrmann, Dorothy

Hersey, John (Richard)
1914-1993 .... CLC 1, 2, 7, 9, 40, 81
See also CA 17-20R; 140; CANR 33;
DAM POP; DLB 6; MTCW; SATA 25;
SATA-Obit 76

Herzen, Aleksandr Ivanovich
1812-1870 .... NCLC 10

Herzl, Theodor 1860-1904 .... TCLC 36

Herzog, Werner 1942- .... CLC 16
See also CA 89-92

Hesiod c. 8th cent. B.C.- .... CMLC 5

Hesse, Hermann
1877-1962 .... CLC 1, 2, 3, 6, 11, 17, 25,
       69; DA; DAB; DAC; SSC 9; WLC
See also CA 17-18; CAP 2; DAM MST,
NOV; DLB 66; MTCW; SATA 50

Hewes, Cady
See De Voto, Bernard (Augustine)

Heyen, William 1940- .... CLC 13, 18
See also CA 33-36R; CAAS 9; DLB 5

Heyerdahl, Thor 1914- .... CLC 26
See also CA 5-8R; CANR 5, 22; MTCW;
SATA 2, 52

Heym, Georg (Theodor Franz Arthur)
1887-1912 .... TCLC 9
See also CA 106

Heym, Stefan 1913- .... CLC 41
See also CA 9-12R; CANR 4; DLB 69

Heyse, Paul (Johann Ludwig von)
1830-1914 .... TCLC 8
See also CA 104; DLB 129

Heyward, (Edwin) DuBose
1885-1940 .... TCLC 59
See also CA 108; DLB 7, 9, 45; SATA 21

Hibbert, Eleanor Alice Burford
1906-1993 .... CLC 7
See also BEST 90:4; CA 17-20R; 140;
CANR 9, 28; DAM POP; SATA 2;
SATA-Obit 74

Higgins, George V(incent)
1939- .... CLC 4, 7, 10, 18
See also CA 77-80; CAAS 5; CANR 17, 51;
DLB 2; DLBY 81; INT CANR-17;
MTCW

Higginson, Thomas Wentworth
1823-1911 .... TCLC 36
See also DLB 1, 64

Highet, Helen
See MacInnes, Helen (Clark)

Highsmith, (Mary) Patricia
1921-1995 .... CLC 2, 4, 14, 42
See also CA 1-4R; 147; CANR 1, 20, 48;
DAM NOV, POP; MTCW

Highwater, Jamake (Mamake)
1942(?)- .... CLC 12
See also AAYA 7; CA 65-68; CAAS 7;
CANR 10, 34; CLR 17; DLB 52;
DLBY 85; JRDA; MAICYA; SATA 32,
69; SATA-Brief 30

Highway, Tomson 1951- ...... CLC 92; DAC
See also DAM MULT; NNAL

Higuchi, Ichiyo 1872-1896 .... NCLC 49

Hijuelos, Oscar 1951- ...... CLC 65; HLC
See also BEST 90:1; CA 123; CANR 50;
DAM MULT, POP; DLB 145; HW

Hikmet, Nazim 1902(?)-1963 ...... CLC 40
See also CA 141; 93-96

Hildesheimer, Wolfgang
1916-1991 .... CLC 49
See also CA 101; 135; DLB 69, 124

Hill, Geoffrey (William)
1932- .... CLC 5, 8, 18, 45
See also CA 81-84; CANR 21;
CDBLB 1960 to Present; DAM POET;
DLB 40; MTCW

Hill, George Roy 1921- .... CLC 26
See also CA 110; 122

Hill, John
See Koontz, Dean R(ay)

Hill, Susan (Elizabeth)
1942- .... CLC 4; DAB
See also CA 33-36R; CANR 29;
DAM MST, NOV; DLB 14, 139; MTCW

Hillerman, Tony 1925- .... CLC 62
See also AAYA 6; BEST 89:1; CA 29-32R;
CANR 21, 42; DAM POP; SATA 6

Hillesum, Etty 1914-1943 .... TCLC 49
See also CA 137

Hilliard, Noel (Harvey) 1929- ...... CLC 15
See also CA 9-12R; CANR 7

Hillis, Rick 1956- .... CLC 66
See also CA 134

Hilton, James 1900-1954 .... TCLC 21
See also CA 108; DLB 34, 77; SATA 34

Himes, Chester (Bomar)
1909-1984 .... CLC 2, 4, 7, 18, 58; BLC
See also BW 2; CA 25-28R; 114; CANR 22;
DAM MULT; DLB 2, 76, 143; MTCW

Hinde, Thomas .... CLC 6, 11
See also Chitty, Thomas Willes

Hindin, Nathan
See Bloch, Robert (Albert)

Hine, (William) Daryl 1936- .... CLC 15
See also CA 1-4R; CAAS 15; CANR 1, 20;
DLB 60

Hinkson, Katharine Tynan
See Tynan, Katharine

Hinton, S(usan) E(loise)
1950- .... CLC 30; DA; DAB; DAC
See also AAYA 2; CA 81-84; CANR 32;
CLR 3, 23; DAM MST, NOV; JRDA;
MAICYA; MTCW; SATA 19, 58

Hippius, Zinaida .... TCLC 9
See also Gippius, Zinaida (Nikolayevna)

Hiraoka, Kimitake 1925-1970
See Mishima, Yukio
See also CA 97-100; 29-32R; DAM DRAM;
MTCW

Hirsch, E(ric) D(onald), Jr. 1928-... CLC 79
See also CA 25-28R; CANR 27, 51;
DLB 67; INT CANR-27; MTCW

Hirsch, Edward 1950- .... CLC 31, 50
See also CA 104; CANR 20, 42; DLB 120

Hitchcock, Alfred (Joseph)
1899-1980 .... CLC 16
See also CA 97-100; SATA 27;
SATA-Obit 24

Hitler, Adolf 1889-1945 .... TCLC 53
See also CA 117; 147

Hoagland, Edward 1932- .... CLC 28
See also CA 1-4R; CANR 2, 31; DLB 6;
SATA 51

Hoban, Russell (Conwell) 1925- .. CLC 7, 25
See also CA 5-8R; CANR 23, 37; CLR 3;
DAM NOV; DLB 52; MAICYA;
MTCW; SATA 1, 40, 78

Hobbs, Perry
See Blackmur, R(ichard) P(almer)

Hobson, Laura Z(ametkin)
1900-1986 .... CLC 7, 25
See also CA 17-20R; 118; DLB 28;
SATA 52

Hochhuth, Rolf 1931- .... CLC 4, 11, 18
See also CA 5-8R; CANR 33;
DAM DRAM; DLB 124; MTCW

Hochman, Sandra 1936- .... CLC 3, 8
See also CA 5-8R; DLB 5

Hochwaelder, Fritz 1911-1986 ...... CLC 36
See also CA 29-32R; 120; CANR 42;
DAM DRAM; MTCW

Hochwalder, Fritz
See Hochwaelder, Fritz

Hocking, Mary (Eunice) 1921- ..... CLC 13
See also CA 101; CANR 18, 40

Hodgins, Jack 1938- .... CLC 23
See also CA 93-96; DLB 60

Hodgson, William Hope
1877(?)-1918 .... TCLC 13
See also CA 111; DLB 70, 153, 156

Hoffman, Alice 1952- .... CLC 51
See also CA 77-80; CANR 34; DAM NOV;
MTCW

Hoffman, Daniel (Gerard)
1923- . . . . CLC 6, 13, 23
See also CA 1-4R; CANR 4; DLB 5

Hoffman, Stanley 1944- . . . . CLC 5
See also CA 77-80

Hoffman, William M(oses) 1939- . . . CLC 40
See also CA 57-60; CANR 11

Hoffmann, E(rnst) T(heodor) A(madeus)
1776-1822 . . . . NCLC 2; SSC 13
See also DLB 90; SATA 27

Hofmann, Gert 1931- . . . . CLC 54
See also CA 128

Hofmannsthal, Hugo von
1874-1929 . . . . TCLC 11; DC 4
See also CA 106; DAM DRAM; DLB 81,
118

Hogan, Linda 1947- . . . . CLC 73
See also CA 120; CANR 45; DAM MULT;
NNAL

Hogarth, Charles
See Creasey, John

Hogarth, Emmett
See Polonsky, Abraham (Lincoln)

Hogg, James 1770-1835 . . . . NCLC 4
See also DLB 93, 116, 159

Holbach, Paul Henri Thiry Baron
1723-1789 . . . . LC 14

Holberg, Ludvig 1684-1754 . . . . LC 6

Holden, Ursula 1921- . . . . CLC 18
See also CA 101; CAAS 8; CANR 22

Holderlin, (Johann Christian) Friedrich
1770-1843 . . . . NCLC 16; PC 4

Holdstock, Robert
See Holdstock, Robert P.

Holdstock, Robert P. 1948- . . . . CLC 39
See also CA 131

Holland, Isabelle 1920- . . . . CLC 21
See also AAYA 11; CA 21-24R; CANR 10,
25, 47; JRDA; MAICYA; SATA 8, 70

Holland, Marcus
See Caldwell, (Janet Miriam) Taylor
(Holland)

Hollander, John 1929- . . . . . . CLC 2, 5, 8, 14
See also CA 1-4R; CANR 1; DLB 5;
SATA 13

Hollander, Paul
See Silverberg, Robert

Holleran, Andrew 1943(?)- . . . . CLC 38
See also CA 144

Hollinghurst, Alan 1954- . . . . CLC 55, 91
See also CA 114

Hollis, Jim
See Summers, Hollis (Spurgeon, Jr.)

Holmes, John
See Souster, (Holmes) Raymond

Holmes, John Clellon 1926-1988 . . . . CLC 56
See also CA 9-12R; 125; CANR 4; DLB 16

Holmes, Oliver Wendell
1809-1894 . . . . NCLC 14
See also CDALB 1640-1865; DLB 1;
SATA 34

Holmes, Raymond
See Souster, (Holmes) Raymond

Holt, Victoria
See Hibbert, Eleanor Alice Burford

Holub, Miroslav 1923- . . . . CLC 4
See also CA 21-24R; CANR 10

Homer
c. 8th cent. B.C.- . . . . . CMLC 1, 16; DA;
DAB; DAC
See also DAM MST, POET

Honig, Edwin 1919- . . . . CLC 33
See also CA 5-8R; CAAS 8; CANR 4, 45;
DLB 5

Hood, Hugh (John Blagdon)
1928- . . . . CLC 15, 28
See also CA 49-52; CAAS 17; CANR 1, 33;
DLB 53

Hood, Thomas 1799-1845 . . . . NCLC 16
See also DLB 96

Hooker, (Peter) Jeremy 1941- . . . . . . CLC 43
See also CA 77-80; CANR 22; DLB 40

Hope, A(lec) D(erwent) 1907- . . . . CLC 3, 51
See also CA 21-24R; CANR 33; MTCW

Hope, Brian
See Creasey, John

Hope, Christopher (David Tully)
1944- . . . . CLC 52
See also CA 106; CANR 47; SATA 62

Hopkins, Gerard Manley
1844-1889 . . . . NCLC 17; DA; DAB;
DAC; PC 15; WLC
See also CDBLB 1890-1914; DAM MST,
POET; DLB 35, 57

Hopkins, John (Richard) 1931- . . . . . . CLC 4
See also CA 85-88

Hopkins, Pauline Elizabeth
1859-1930 . . . . TCLC 28; BLC
See also BW 2; CA 141; DAM MULT;
DLB 50

Hopkinson, Francis 1737-1791 . . . . . . LC 25
See also DLB 31

Hopley-Woolrich, Cornell George 1903-1968
See Woolrich, Cornell
See also CA 13-14; CAP 1

Horatio
See Proust, (Valentin-Louis-George-Eugene-)
Marcel

Horgan, Paul (George Vincent O'Shaughnessy)
1903-1995 . . . . CLC 9, 53
See also CA 13-16R; 147; CANR 9, 35;
DAM NOV; DLB 102; DLBY 85;
INT CANR-9; MTCW; SATA 13;
SATA-Obit 84

Horn, Peter
See Kuttner, Henry

Hornem, Horace Esq.
See Byron, George Gordon (Noel)

Hornung, E(rnest) W(illiam)
1866-1921 . . . . TCLC 59
See also CA 108; DLB 70

Horovitz, Israel (Arthur) 1939- . . . . . CLC 56
See also CA 33-36R; CANR 46;
DAM DRAM; DLB 7

Horvath, Odon von
See Horvath, Oedoen von
See also DLB 85, 124

Horvath, Oedoen von 1901-1938 . . . TCLC 45
See also Horvath, Odon von
See also CA 118

Horwitz, Julius 1920-1986 . . . . CLC 14
See also CA 9-12R; 119; CANR 12

Hospital, Janette Turner 1942- . . . . . CLC 42
See also CA 108; CANR 48

Hostos, E. M. de
See Hostos (y Bonilla), Eugenio Maria de

Hostos, Eugenio M. de
See Hostos (y Bonilla), Eugenio Maria de

Hostos, Eugenio Maria
See Hostos (y Bonilla), Eugenio Maria de

Hostos (y Bonilla), Eugenio Maria de
1839-1903 . . . . TCLC 24
See also CA 123; 131; HW

Houdini
See Lovecraft, H(oward) P(hillips)

Hougan, Carolyn 1943- . . . . CLC 34
See also CA 139

Household, Geoffrey (Edward West)
1900-1988 . . . . CLC 11
See also CA 77-80; 126; DLB 87; SATA 14;
SATA-Obit 59

Housman, A(lfred) E(dward)
1859-1936 . . . . . . TCLC 1, 10; DA; DAB;
DAC; PC 2
See also CA 104; 125; DAM MST, POET;
DLB 19; MTCW

Housman, Laurence 1865-1959 . . . . . TCLC 7
See also CA 106; DLB 10; SATA 25

Howard, Elizabeth Jane 1923- . . . CLC 7, 29
See also CA 5-8R; CANR 8

Howard, Maureen 1930- . . . . . CLC 5, 14, 46
See also CA 53-56; CANR 31; DLBY 83;
INT CANR-31; MTCW

Howard, Richard 1929- . . . . . . CLC 7, 10, 47
See also AITN 1; CA 85-88; CANR 25;
DLB 5; INT CANR-25

Howard, Robert Ervin 1906-1936 . . . TCLC 8
See also CA 105

Howard, Warren F.
See Pohl, Frederik

Howe, Fanny 1940- . . . . CLC 47
See also CA 117; SATA-Brief 52

Howe, Irving 1920-1993 . . . . CLC 85
See also CA 9-12R; 141; CANR 21, 50;
DLB 67; MTCW

Howe, Julia Ward 1819-1910 . . . . . TCLC 21
See also CA 117; DLB 1

Howe, Susan 1937- . . . . CLC 72
See also DLB 120

Howe, Tina 1937- . . . . CLC 48
See also CA 109

Howell, James 1594(?)-1666 . . . . LC 13
See also DLB 151

Howells, W. D.
See Howells, William Dean

Howells, William D.
See Howells, William Dean

Howells, William Dean
1837-1920 . . . . TCLC 7, 17, 41
See also CA 104; 134; CDALB 1865-1917;
DLB 12, 64, 74, 79

Ionesco, Eugene
1909-1994 .... **CLC 1, 4, 6, 9, 11, 15, 41,
86; DA; DAB; DAC; WLC**
See also CA 9-12R; 144; DAM DRAM,
MST; MTCW; SATA 7; SATA-Obit 79

Iqbal, Muhammad 1873-1938 ..... **TCLC 28**

Ireland, Patrick
See O'Doherty, Brian

Iron, Ralph
See Schreiner, Olive (Emilie Albertina)

Irving, John (Winslow)
1942- .... **CLC 13, 23, 38**
See also AAYA 8; BEST 89:3; CA 25-28R;
CANR 28; DAM NOV, POP; DLB 6;
DLBY 82; MTCW

Irving, Washington
1783-1859 ..... **NCLC 2, 19; DA; DAB;
SSC 2; WLC**
See also CDALB 1640-1865; DAM MST;
DLB 3, 11, 30, 59, 73, 74; YABC 2

Irwin, P. K.
See Page, P(atricia) K(athleen)

Isaacs, Susan 1943- .... **CLC 32**
See also BEST 89:1; CA 89-92; CANR 20,
41; DAM POP; INT CANR-20; MTCW

Isherwood, Christopher (William Bradshaw)
1904-1986 .... **CLC 1, 9, 11, 14, 44**
See also CA 13-16R; 117; CANR 35;
DAM DRAM, NOV; DLB 15; DLBY 86;
MTCW

Ishiguro, Kazuo 1954- ...... **CLC 27, 56, 59**
See also BEST 90:2; CA 120; CANR 49;
DAM NOV; MTCW

Ishikawa Takuboku
1886(?)-1912 .... **TCLC 15; PC 10**
See also CA 113; DAM POET

Iskander, Fazil 1929- .... **CLC 47**
See also CA 102

Isler, Alan .... **CLC 91**

Ivan IV 1530-1584 .... **LC 17**

Ivanov, Vyacheslav Ivanovich
1866-1949 .... **TCLC 33**
See also CA 122

Ivask, Ivar Vidrik 1927-1992 ...... **CLC 14**
See also CA 37-40R; 139; CANR 24

J. R. S.
See Gogarty, Oliver St. John

Jabran, Kahlil
See Gibran, Kahlil

Jabran, Khalil
See Gibran, Kahlil

Jackson, Daniel
See Wingrove, David (John)

Jackson, Jesse 1908-1983 .... **CLC 12**
See also BW 1; CA 25-28R; 109; CANR 27;
CLR 28; MAICYA; SATA 2, 29;
SATA-Obit 48

Jackson, Laura (Riding) 1901-1991
See Riding, Laura
See also CA 65-68; 135; CANR 28; DLB 48

Jackson, Sam
See Trumbo, Dalton

Jackson, Sara
See Wingrove, David (John)

Jackson, Shirley
1919-1965 .... **CLC 11, 60, 87; DA;
DAC; SSC 9; WLC**
See also AAYA 9; CA 1-4R; 25-28R;
CANR 4; CDALB 1941-1968;
DAM MST; DLB 6; SATA 2

Jacob, (Cyprien-)Max 1876-1944 ... **TCLC 6**
See also CA 104

Jacobs, Jim 1942- .... **CLC 12**
See also CA 97-100; INT 97-100

Jacobs, W(illiam) W(ymark)
1863-1943 .... **TCLC 22**
See also CA 121; DLB 135

Jacobsen, Jens Peter 1847-1885 .. **NCLC 34**

Jacobsen, Josephine 1908- .... **CLC 48**
See also CA 33-36R; CAAS 18; CANR 23,
48

Jacobson, Dan 1929- .... **CLC 4, 14**
See also CA 1-4R; CANR 2, 25; DLB 14;
MTCW

Jacqueline
See Carpentier (y Valmont), Alejo

Jagger, Mick 1944- .... **CLC 17**

Jakes, John (William) 1932- .... **CLC 29**
See also BEST 89:4; CA 57-60; CANR 10,
43; DAM NOV, POP; DLBY 83;
INT CANR-10; MTCW; SATA 62

James, Andrew
See Kirkup, James

James, C(yril) L(ionel) R(obert)
1901-1989 .... **CLC 33**
See also BW 2; CA 117; 125; 128; DLB 125;
MTCW

James, Daniel (Lewis) 1911-1988
See Santiago, Danny
See also CA 125

James, Dynely
See Mayne, William (James Carter)

James, Henry Sr. 1811-1882 ..... **NCLC 53**

James, Henry
1843-1916 ...... **TCLC 2, 11, 24, 40, 47;
DA; DAB; DAC; SSC 8; WLC**
See also CA 104; 132; CDALB 1865-1917;
DAM MST, NOV; DLB 12, 71, 74;
DLBD 13; MTCW

James, M. R.
See James, Montague (Rhodes)
See also DLB 156

James, Montague (Rhodes)
1862-1936 .... **TCLC 6; SSC 16**
See also CA 104

James, P. D. .... **CLC 18, 46**
See also White, Phyllis Dorothy James
See also BEST 90:2; CDBLB 1960 to
Present; DLB 87

James, Philip
See Moorcock, Michael (John)

James, William 1842-1910..... **TCLC 15, 32**
See also CA 109

James I 1394-1437 .... **LC 20**

Jameson, Anna 1794-1860 .... **NCLC 43**
See also DLB 99

Jami, Nur al-Din 'Abd al-Rahman
1414-1492 .... **LC 9**

Jandl, Ernst 1925- .... **CLC 34**

Janowitz, Tama 1957- .... **CLC 43**
See also CA 106; DAM POP

Japrisot, Sebastien 1931-......... **CLC 90**

Jarrell, Randall
1914-1965 .... **CLC 1, 2, 6, 9, 13, 49**
See also CA 5-8R; 25-28R; CABS 2;
CANR 6, 34; CDALB 1941-1968; CLR 6;
DAM POET; DLB 48, 52; MAICYA;
MTCW; SATA 7

Jarry, Alfred
1873-1907 .... **TCLC 2, 14; SSC 20**
See also CA 104; DAM DRAM

Jarvis, E. K.
See Bloch, Robert (Albert); Ellison, Harlan
(Jay); Silverberg, Robert

Jeake, Samuel, Jr.
See Aiken, Conrad (Potter)

Jean Paul 1763-1825 .... **NCLC 7**

Jefferies, (John) Richard
1848-1887 .... **NCLC 47**
See also DLB 98, 141; SATA 16

Jeffers, (John) Robinson
1887-1962 .... **CLC 2, 3, 11, 15, 54; DA;
DAC; WLC**
See also CA 85-88; CANR 35;
CDALB 1917-1929; DAM MST, POET;
DLB 45; MTCW

Jefferson, Janet
See Mencken, H(enry) L(ouis)

Jefferson, Thomas 1743-1826 .... **NCLC 11**
See also CDALB 1640-1865; DLB 31

Jeffrey, Francis 1773-1850....... **NCLC 33**
See also DLB 107

Jelakowitch, Ivan
See Heijermans, Herman

Jellicoe, (Patricia) Ann 1927-...... **CLC 27**
See also CA 85-88; DLB 13

Jen, Gish .... **CLC 70**
See also Jen, Lillian

Jen, Lillian 1956(?)-
See Jen, Gish
See also CA 135

Jenkins, (John) Robin 1912-....... **CLC 52**
See also CA 1-4R; CANR 1; DLB 14

Jennings, Elizabeth (Joan)
1926- .... **CLC 5, 14**
See also CA 61-64; CAAS 5; CANR 8, 39;
DLB 27; MTCW; SATA 66

Jennings, Waylon 1937-.......... **CLC 21**

Jensen, Johannes V. 1873-1950.... **TCLC 41**

Jensen, Laura (Linnea) 1948- ...... **CLC 37**
See also CA 103

Jerome, Jerome K(lapka)
1859-1927 .... **TCLC 23**
See also CA 119; DLB 10, 34, 135

Jerrold, Douglas William
1803-1857 .... **NCLC 2**
See also DLB 158, 159

Jewett, (Theodora) Sarah Orne
1849-1909 .... **TCLC 1, 22; SSC 6**
See also CA 108; 127; DLB 12, 74;
SATA 15

Jewsbury, Geraldine (Endsor)
1812-1880 . . . . NCLC **22**
See also DLB 21

Jhabvala, Ruth Prawer
1927- . . . . CLC **4, 8, 29; DAB**
See also CA 1-4R; CANR 2, 29, 51;
DAM NOV; DLB 139; INT CANR-29;
MTCW

Jibran, Kahlil
See Gibran, Kahlil

Jibran, Khalil
See Gibran, Kahlil

Jiles, Paulette 1943- . . . . CLC **13, 58**
See also CA 101

Jimenez (Mantecon), Juan Ramon
1881-1958 . . . . TCLC **4; HLC; PC 7**
See also CA 104; 131; DAM MULT,
POET; DLB 134; HW; MTCW

Jimenez, Ramon
See Jimenez (Mantecon), Juan Ramon

Jimenez Mantecon, Juan
See Jimenez (Mantecon), Juan Ramon

Joel, Billy . . . . CLC **26**
See also Joel, William Martin

Joel, William Martin 1949-
See Joel, Billy
See also CA 108

John of the Cross, St. 1542-1591 . . . . LC **18**

Johnson, B(ryan) S(tanley William)
1933-1973 . . . . CLC **6, 9**
See also CA 9-12R; 53-56; CANR 9;
DLB 14, 40

Johnson, Benj. F. of Boo
See Riley, James Whitcomb

Johnson, Benjamin F. of Boo
See Riley, James Whitcomb

Johnson, Charles (Richard)
1948- . . . . CLC **7, 51, 65; BLC**
See also BW 2; CA 116; CAAS 18;
CANR 42; DAM MULT; DLB 33

Johnson, Denis 1949- . . . . CLC **52**
See also CA 117; 121; DLB 120

Johnson, Diane 1934- . . . . CLC **5, 13, 48**
See also CA 41-44R; CANR 17, 40;
DLBY 80; INT CANR-17; MTCW

Johnson, Eyvind (Olof Verner)
1900-1976 . . . . CLC **14**
See also CA 73-76; 69-72; CANR 34

Johnson, J. R.
See James, C(yril) L(ionel) R(obert)

Johnson, James Weldon
1871-1938 . . . . TCLC **3, 19; BLC**
See also BW 1; CA 104; 125;
CDALB 1917-1929; CLR 32;
DAM MULT, POET; DLB 51; MTCW;
SATA 31

Johnson, Joyce 1935- . . . . CLC **58**
See also CA 125; 129

Johnson, Lionel (Pigot)
1867-1902 . . . . TCLC **19**
See also CA 117; DLB 19

Johnson, Mel
See Malzberg, Barry N(athaniel)

Johnson, Pamela Hansford
1912-1981 . . . . CLC **1, 7, 27**
See also CA 1-4R; 104; CANR 2, 28;
DLB 15; MTCW

Johnson, Samuel
1709-1784 . . . . . LC **15; DA; DAB; DAC;**
WLC
See also CDBLB 1660-1789; DAM MST;
DLB 39, 95, 104, 142

Johnson, Uwe
1934-1984 . . . . CLC **5, 10, 15, 40**
See also CA 1-4R; 112; CANR 1, 39;
DLB 75; MTCW

Johnston, George (Benson) 1913- . . . CLC **51**
See also CA 1-4R; CANR 5, 20; DLB 88

Johnston, Jennifer 1930- . . . . CLC **7**
See also CA 85-88; DLB 14

Jolley, (Monica) Elizabeth
1923- . . . . CLC **46; SSC 19**
See also CA 127; CAAS 13

Jones, Arthur Llewellyn 1863-1947
See Machen, Arthur
See also CA 104

Jones, D(ouglas) G(ordon) 1929- . . . . CLC **10**
See also CA 29-32R; CANR 13; DLB 53

Jones, David (Michael)
1895-1974 . . . . CLC **2, 4, 7, 13, 42**
See also CA 9-12R; 53-56; CANR 28;
CDBLB 1945-1960; DLB 20, 100; MTCW

Jones, David Robert 1947-
See Bowie, David
See also CA 103

Jones, Diana Wynne 1934- . . . . CLC **26**
See also AAYA 12; CA 49-52; CANR 4,
26; CLR 23; DLB 161; JRDA; MAICYA;
SAAS 7; SATA 9, 70

Jones, Edward P. 1950- . . . . CLC **76**
See also BW 2; CA 142

Jones, Gayl 1949- . . . . CLC **6, 9; BLC**
See also BW 2; CA 77-80; CANR 27;
DAM MULT; DLB 33; MTCW

Jones, James 1921-1977 . . . . CLC **1, 3, 10, 39**
See also AITN 1, 2; CA 1-4R; 69-72;
CANR 6; DLB 2, 143; MTCW

Jones, John J.
See Lovecraft, H(oward) P(hillips)

Jones, LeRoi . . . . CLC **1, 2, 3, 5, 10, 14**
See also Baraka, Amiri

Jones, Louis B. . . . . CLC **65**
See also CA 141

Jones, Madison (Percy, Jr.) 1925- . . . CLC **4**
See also CA 13-16R; CAAS 11; CANR 7;
DLB 152

Jones, Mervyn 1922- . . . . CLC **10, 52**
See also CA 45-48; CAAS 5; CANR 1;
MTCW

Jones, Mick 1956(?)- . . . . CLC **30**

Jones, Nettie (Pearl) 1941- . . . . CLC **34**
See also BW 2; CA 137; CAAS 20

Jones, Preston 1936-1979 . . . . CLC **10**
See also CA 73-76; 89-92; DLB 7

Jones, Robert F(rancis) 1934- . . . . . . CLC **7**
See also CA 49-52; CANR 2

Jones, Rod 1953- . . . . CLC **50**
See also CA 128

Jones, Terence Graham Parry
1942- . . . . CLC **21**
See also Jones, Terry; Monty Python
See also CA 112; 116; CANR 35; INT 116

Jones, Terry
See Jones, Terence Graham Parry
See also SATA 67; SATA-Brief 51

Jones, Thom 1945(?)- . . . . CLC **81**

Jong, Erica 1942- . . . . . . CLC **4, 6, 8, 18, 83**
See also AITN 1; BEST 90:2; CA 73-76;
CANR 26; DAM NOV, POP; DLB 2, 5,
28, 152; INT CANR-26; MTCW

Jonson, Ben(jamin)
1572(?)-1637 . . . . LC **6; DA; DAB; DAC;**
DC **4; WLC**
See also CDBLB Before 1660;
DAM DRAM, MST, POET; DLB 62,
121

Jordan, June 1936- . . . . CLC **5, 11, 23**
See also AAYA 2; BW 2; CA 33-36R;
CANR 25; CLR 10; DAM MULT,
POET; DLB 38; MAICYA; MTCW;
SATA 4

Jordan, Pat(rick M.) 1941- . . . . CLC **37**
See also CA 33-36R

Jorgensen, Ivar
See Ellison, Harlan (Jay)

Jorgenson, Ivar
See Silverberg, Robert

Josephus, Flavius c. 37-100 . . . . . . CMLC **13**

Josipovici, Gabriel 1940- . . . . CLC **6, 43**
See also CA 37-40R; CAAS 8; CANR 47;
DLB 14

Joubert, Joseph 1754-1824 . . . . NCLC **9**

Jouve, Pierre Jean 1887-1976 . . . . . . CLC **47**
See also CA 65-68

Joyce, James (Augustine Aloysius)
1882-1941 . . . . TCLC **3, 8, 16, 35, 52;**
DA; DAB; DAC; SSC **3; WLC**
See also CA 104; 126; CDBLB 1914-1945;
DAM MST, NOV, POET; DLB 10, 19,
36, 162; MTCW

Jozsef, Attila 1905-1937 . . . . TCLC **22**
See also CA 116

Juana Ines de la Cruz 1651(?)-1695 . . . LC **5**

Judd, Cyril
See Kornbluth, C(yril) M.; Pohl, Frederik

Julian of Norwich 1342(?)-1416(?) . . . . LC **6**
See also DLB 146

Juniper, Alex
See Hospital, Janette Turner

Junius
See Luxemburg, Rosa

Just, Ward (Swift) 1935- . . . . CLC **4, 27**
See also CA 25-28R; CANR 32;
INT CANR-32

Justice, Donald (Rodney) 1925- . . CLC **6, 19**
See also CA 5-8R; CANR 26; DAM POET;
DLBY 83; INT CANR-26

Juvenal c. 55-c. 127 . . . . CMLC **8**

Juvenis
See Bourne, Randolph S(illiman)

Kacew, Romain   1914-1980
See Gary, Romain
See also CA 108; 102

Kadare, Ismail   1936- . . . .   CLC 52

Kadohata, Cynthia. . . . .   CLC 59
See also CA 140

Kafka, Franz
1883-1924 . . . . TCLC 2, 6, 13, 29, 47, 53;
DA; DAB; DAC; SSC 5; WLC
See also CA 105; 126; DAM MST, NOV;
DLB 81; MTCW

Kahanovitsch, Pinkhes
See Der Nister

Kahn, Roger   1927- . . . .   CLC 30
See also CA 25-28R; CANR 44; SATA 37

Kain, Saul
See Sassoon, Siegfried (Lorraine)

Kaiser, Georg   1878-1945 . . . .   TCLC 9
See also CA 106; DLB 124

Kaletski, Alexander   1946- . . . .   CLC 39
See also CA 118; 143

Kalidasa   fl. c. 400- . . . .   CMLC 9

Kallman, Chester (Simon)
1921-1975 . . . .   CLC 2
See also CA 45-48; 53-56; CANR 3

Kaminsky, Melvin   1926-
See Brooks, Mel
See also CA 65-68; CANR 16

Kaminsky, Stuart M(elvin)   1934- . . .   CLC 59
See also CA 73-76; CANR 29

Kane, Paul
See Simon, Paul

Kane, Wilson
See Bloch, Robert (Albert)

Kanin, Garson   1912- . . . .   CLC 22
See also AITN 1; CA 5-8R; CANR 7;
DLB 7

Kaniuk, Yoram   1930- . . . .   CLC 19
See also CA 134

Kant, Immanuel   1724-1804 . . . . . .   NCLC 27
See also DLB 94

Kantor, MacKinlay   1904-1977 . . . . . .   CLC 7
See also CA 61-64; 73-76; DLB 9, 102

Kaplan, David Michael   1946- . . . . . .   CLC 50

Kaplan, James   1951- . . . .   CLC 59
See also CA 135

Karageorge, Michael
See Anderson, Poul (William)

Karamzin, Nikolai Mikhailovich
1766-1826 . . . .   NCLC 3
See also DLB 150

Karapanou, Margarita   1946- . . . .   CLC 13
See also CA 101

Karinthy, Frigyes   1887-1938 . . . . .   TCLC 47

Karl, Frederick R(obert)   1927- . . . . .   CLC 34
See also CA 5-8R; CANR 3, 44

Kastel, Warren
See Silverberg, Robert

Kataev, Evgeny Petrovich   1903-1942
See Petrov, Evgeny
See also CA 120

Kataphusin
See Ruskin, John

Katz, Steve   1935- . . . .   CLC 47
See also CA 25-28R; CAAS 14; CANR 12;
DLBY 83

Kauffman, Janet   1945- . . . .   CLC 42
See also CA 117; CANR 43; DLBY 86

Kaufman, Bob (Garnell)
1925-1986 . . . .   CLC 49
See also BW 1; CA 41-44R; 118; CANR 22;
DLB 16, 41

Kaufman, George S.   1889-1961 . . . . .   CLC 38
See also CA 108; 93-96; DAM DRAM;
DLB 7; INT 108

Kaufman, Sue . . . .   CLC 3, 8
See also Barondess, Sue K(aufman)

Kavafis, Konstantinos Petrou   1863-1933
See Cavafy, C(onstantine) P(eter)
See also CA 104

Kavan, Anna   1901-1968 . . . . . .   CLC 5, 13, 82
See also CA 5-8R; CANR 6; MTCW

Kavanagh, Dan
See Barnes, Julian

Kavanagh, Patrick (Joseph)
1904-1967 . . . .   CLC 22
See also CA 123; 25-28R; DLB 15, 20;
MTCW

Kawabata, Yasunari
1899-1972 . . . . . CLC 2, 5, 9, 18; SSC 17
See also CA 93-96; 33-36R; DAM MULT

Kaye, M(ary) M(argaret)   1909- . . . . .   CLC 28
See also CA 89-92; CANR 24; MTCW;
SATA 62

Kaye, Mollie
See Kaye, M(ary) M(argaret)

Kaye-Smith, Sheila   1887-1956. . . . .   TCLC 20
See also CA 118; DLB 36

Kaymor, Patrice Maguilene
See Senghor, Leopold Sedar

Kazan, Elia   1909- . . . .   CLC 6, 16, 63
See also CA 21-24R; CANR 32

Kazantzakis, Nikos
1883(?)-1957 . . . .   TCLC 2, 5, 33
See also CA 105; 132; MTCW

Kazin, Alfred   1915- . . . .   CLC 34, 38
See also CA 1-4R; CAAS 7; CANR 1, 45;
DLB 67

Keane, Mary Nesta (Skrine)   1904-
See Keane, Molly
See also CA 108; 114

Keane, Molly. . . . .   CLC 31
See also Keane, Mary Nesta (Skrine)
See also INT 114

Keates, Jonathan   19(?)- . . . .   CLC 34

Keaton, Buster   1895-1966 . . . .   CLC 20

Keats, John
1795-1821 . . . .   NCLC 8; DA; DAB;
DAC; PC 1; WLC
See also CDBLB 1789-1832; DAM MST,
POET; DLB 96, 110

Keene, Donald   1922- . . . .   CLC 34
See also CA 1-4R; CANR 5

Keillor, Garrison . . . .   CLC 40
See also Keillor, Gary (Edward)
See also AAYA 2; BEST 89:3; DLBY 87;
SATA 58

Keillor, Gary (Edward)   1942-
See Keillor, Garrison
See also CA 111; 117; CANR 36;
DAM POP; MTCW

Keith, Michael
See Hubbard, L(afayette) Ron(ald)

Keller, Gottfried   1819-1890 . . . . . .   NCLC 2
See also DLB 129

Kellerman, Jonathan   1949- . . . .   CLC 44
See also BEST 90:1; CA 106; CANR 29, 51;
DAM POP; INT CANR-29

Kelley, William Melvin   1937- . . . . . .   CLC 22
See also BW 1; CA 77-80; CANR 27;
DLB 33

Kellogg, Marjorie   1922- . . . .   CLC 2
See also CA 81-84

Kellow, Kathleen
See Hibbert, Eleanor Alice Burford

Kelly, M(ilton) T(erry)   1947- . . . .   CLC 55
See also CA 97-100; CAAS 22; CANR 19,
43

Kelman, James   1946- . . . .   CLC 58, 86
See also CA 148

Kemal, Yashar   1923- . . . .   CLC 14, 29
See also CA 89-92; CANR 44

Kemble, Fanny   1809-1893 . . . .   NCLC 18
See also DLB 32

Kemelman, Harry   1908- . . . .   CLC 2
See also AITN 1; CA 9-12R; CANR 6;
DLB 28

Kempe, Margery   1373(?)-1440(?) . . . . .   LC 6
See also DLB 146

Kempis, Thomas a   1380-1471 . . . .   LC 11

Kendall, Henry   1839-1882. . . . . . .   NCLC 12

Keneally, Thomas (Michael)
1935- . . . . . .   CLC 5, 8, 10, 14, 19, 27, 43
See also CA 85-88; CANR 10, 50;
DAM NOV; MTCW

Kennedy, Adrienne (Lita)
1931- . . . .   CLC 66; BLC; DC 5
See also BW 2; CA 103; CAAS 20; CABS 3;
CANR 26; DAM MULT; DLB 38

Kennedy, John Pendleton
1795-1870 . . . .   NCLC 2
See also DLB 3

Kennedy, Joseph Charles   1929-
See Kennedy, X. J.
See also CA 1-4R; CANR 4, 30, 40;
SATA 14, 86

Kennedy, William   1928- . . .   CLC 6, 28, 34, 53
See also AAYA 1; CA 85-88; CANR 14,
31; DAM NOV; DLB 143; DLBY 85;
INT CANR-31; MTCW; SATA 57

Kennedy, X. J.. . . . .   CLC 8, 42
See also Kennedy, Joseph Charles
See also CAAS 9; CLR 27; DLB 5;
SAAS 22

Kenny, Maurice (Francis)   1929- . . . .   CLC 87
See also CA 144; CAAS 22; DAM MULT;
NNAL

Kent, Kelvin
See Kuttner, Henry

Kenton, Maxwell
See Southern, Terry

Kenyon, Robert O.
 See Kuttner, Henry

Kerouac, Jack . . . . . **CLC 1, 2, 3, 5, 14, 29, 61**
 See also Kerouac, Jean-Louis Lebris de
 See also CDALB 1941-1968; DLB 2, 16;
 DLBD 3

Kerouac, Jean-Louis Lebris de 1922-1969
 See Kerouac, Jack
 See also AITN 1; CA 5-8R; 25-28R;
 CANR 26; DA; DAB; DAC; DAM MST,
 NOV, POET, POP; MTCW; WLC

Kerr, Jean 1923- . . . . **CLC 22**
 See also CA 5-8R; CANR 7; INT CANR-7

Kerr, M. E. . . . . **CLC 12, 35**
 See also Meaker, Marijane (Agnes)
 See also AAYA 2; CLR 29; SAAS 1

Kerr, Robert . . . . **CLC 55**

Kerrigan, (Thomas) Anthony
 1918- . . . . **CLC 4, 6**
 See also CA 49-52; CAAS 11; CANR 4

Kerry, Lois
 See Duncan, Lois

Kesey, Ken (Elton)
 1935- . . . . . . **CLC 1, 3, 6, 11, 46, 64; DA;**
 DAB; DAC; WLC
 See also CA 1-4R; CANR 22, 38;
 CDALB 1968-1988; DAM MST, NOV,
 POP; DLB 2, 16; MTCW; SATA 66

Kesselring, Joseph (Otto)
 1902-1967 . . . . **CLC 45**
 See also CA 150; DAM DRAM, MST

Kessler, Jascha (Frederick) 1929- . . . . **CLC 4**
 See also CA 17-20R; CANR 8, 48

Kettelkamp, Larry (Dale) 1933- . . . . **CLC 12**
 See also CA 29-32R; CANR 16; SAAS 3;
 SATA 2

Keyber, Conny
 See Fielding, Henry

Keyes, Daniel 1927- . . . . **CLC 80; DA; DAC**
 See also CA 17-20R; CANR 10, 26;
 DAM MST, NOV; SATA 37

Khanshendel, Chiron
 See Rose, Wendy

Khayyam, Omar
 1048-1131 . . . . **CMLC 11; PC 8**
 See also DAM POET

Kherdian, David 1931- . . . . **CLC 6, 9**
 See also CA 21-24R; CAAS 2; CANR 39;
 CLR 24; JRDA; MAICYA; SATA 16, 74

Khlebnikov, Velimir . . . . **TCLC 20**
 See also Khlebnikov, Viktor Vladimirovich

Khlebnikov, Viktor Vladimirovich 1885-1922
 See Khlebnikov, Velimir
 See also CA 117

Khodasevich, Vladislav (Felitsianovich)
 1886-1939 . . . . **TCLC 15**
 See also CA 115

Kielland, Alexander Lange
 1849-1906 . . . . **TCLC 5**
 See also CA 104

Kiely, Benedict 1919- . . . . **CLC 23, 43**
 See also CA 1-4R; CANR 2; DLB 15

Kienzle, William X(avier) 1928- . . . . **CLC 25**
 See also CA 93-96; CAAS 1; CANR 9, 31;
 DAM POP; INT CANR-31; MTCW

Kierkegaard, Soren 1813-1855 . . . . **NCLC 34**

Killens, John Oliver 1916-1987 . . . . . **CLC 10**
 See also BW 2; CA 77-80; 123; CAAS 2;
 CANR 26; DLB 33

Killigrew, Anne 1660-1685 . . . . **LC 4**
 See also DLB 131

Kim
 See Simenon, Georges (Jacques Christian)

Kincaid, Jamaica 1949- . . . **CLC 43, 68; BLC**
 See also AAYA 13; BW 2; CA 125;
 CANR 47; DAM MULT, NOV;
 DLB 157

King, Francis (Henry) 1923- . . . . . **CLC 8, 53**
 See also CA 1-4R; CANR 1, 33;
 DAM NOV; DLB 15, 139; MTCW

King, Martin Luther, Jr.
 1929-1968 . . . . **CLC 83; BLC; DA; DAB;**
 DAC
 See also BW 2; CA 25-28; CANR 27, 44;
 CAP 2; DAM MST, MULT; MTCW;
 SATA 14

King, Stephen (Edwin)
 1947- . . . . . . **CLC 12, 26, 37, 61; SSC 17**
 See also AAYA 1, 17; BEST 90:1;
 CA 61-64; CANR 1, 30; DAM NOV,
 POP; DLB 143; DLBY 80; JRDA;
 MTCW; SATA 9, 55

King, Steve
 See King, Stephen (Edwin)

King, Thomas 1943- . . . . **CLC 89; DAC**
 See also CA 144; DAM MULT; NNAL

Kingman, Lee . . . . **CLC 17**
 See also Natti, (Mary) Lee
 See also SAAS 3; SATA 1, 67

Kingsley, Charles 1819-1875 . . . . . **NCLC 35**
 See also DLB 21, 32, 163; YABC 2

Kingsley, Sidney 1906-1995 . . . . **CLC 44**
 See also CA 85-88; 147; DLB 7

Kingsolver, Barbara 1955- . . . . . . **CLC 55, 81**
 See also AAYA 15; CA 129; 134;
 DAM POP; INT 134

Kingston, Maxine (Ting Ting) Hong
 1940- . . . . **CLC 12, 19, 58**
 See also AAYA 8; CA 69-72; CANR 13,
 38; DAM MULT, NOV; DLBY 80;
 INT CANR-13; MTCW; SATA 53

Kinnell, Galway
 1927- . . . . **CLC 1, 2, 3, 5, 13, 29**
 See also CA 9-12R; CANR 10, 34; DLB 5;
 DLBY 87; INT CANR-34; MTCW

Kinsella, Thomas 1928- . . . . **CLC 4, 19**
 See also CA 17-20R; CANR 15; DLB 27;
 MTCW

Kinsella, W(illiam) P(atrick)
 1935- . . . . **CLC 27, 43; DAC**
 See also AAYA 7; CA 97-100; CAAS 7;
 CANR 21, 35; DAM NOV, POP;
 INT CANR-21; MTCW

Kipling, (Joseph) Rudyard
 1865-1936 . . . . . . **TCLC 8, 17; DA; DAB;**
 DAC; PC 3; SSC 5; WLC
 See also CA 105; 120; CANR 33;
 CDBLB 1890-1914; CLR 39; DAM MST,
 POET; DLB 19, 34, 141, 156; MAICYA;
 MTCW; YABC 2

Kirkup, James 1918- . . . . **CLC 1**
 See also CA 1-4R; CAAS 4; CANR 2;
 DLB 27; SATA 12

Kirkwood, James 1930(?)-1989 . . . . . . **CLC 9**
 See also AITN 2; CA 1-4R; 128; CANR 6,
 40

Kirshner, Sidney
 See Kingsley, Sidney

Kis, Danilo 1935-1989 . . . . **CLC 57**
 See also CA 109; 118; 129; MTCW

Kivi, Aleksis 1834-1872 . . . . **NCLC 30**

Kizer, Carolyn (Ashley)
 1925- . . . . **CLC 15, 39, 80**
 See also CA 65-68; CAAS 5; CANR 24;
 DAM POET; DLB 5

Klabund 1890-1928 . . . . **TCLC 44**
 See also DLB 66

Klappert, Peter 1942- . . . . **CLC 57**
 See also CA 33-36R; DLB 5

Klein, A(braham) M(oses)
 1909-1972 . . . . **CLC 19; DAB; DAC**
 See also CA 101; 37-40R; DAM MST;
 DLB 68

Klein, Norma 1938-1989 . . . . **CLC 30**
 See also AAYA 2; CA 41-44R; 128;
 CANR 15, 37; CLR 2, 19;
 INT CANR-15; JRDA; MAICYA;
 SAAS 1; SATA 7, 57

Klein, T(heodore) E(ibon) D(onald)
 1947- . . . . **CLC 34**
 See also CA 119; CANR 44

Kleist, Heinrich von
 1777-1811 . . . . **NCLC 2, 37**
 See also DAM DRAM; DLB 90

Klima, Ivan 1931- . . . . **CLC 56**
 See also CA 25-28R; CANR 17, 50;
 DAM NOV

Klimentov, Andrei Platonovich 1899-1951
 See Platonov, Andrei
 See also CA 108

Klinger, Friedrich Maximilian von
 1752-1831 . . . . **NCLC 1**
 See also DLB 94

Klopstock, Friedrich Gottlieb
 1724-1803 . . . . **NCLC 11**
 See also DLB 97

Knebel, Fletcher 1911-1993 . . . . **CLC 14**
 See also AITN 1; CA 1-4R; 140; CAAS 3;
 CANR 1, 36; SATA 36; SATA-Obit 75

Knickerbocker, Diedrich
 See Irving, Washington

Knight, Etheridge
 1931-1991 . . . . **CLC 40; BLC; PC 14**
 See also BW 1; CA 21-24R; 133; CANR 23;
 DAM POET; DLB 41

Knight, Sarah Kemble 1666-1727 . . . . . **LC 7**
 See also DLB 24

Knister, Raymond 1899-1932 . . . . . . **TCLC 56**
 See also DLB 68

Knowles, John
 1926- . . . . . . **CLC 1, 4, 10, 26; DA; DAC**
 See also AAYA 10; CA 17-20R; CANR 40;
 CDALB 1968-1988; DAM MST, NOV;
 DLB 6; MTCW; SATA 8

Knox, Calvin M.
See Silverberg, Robert

Knye, Cassandra
See Disch, Thomas M(ichael)

Koch, C(hristopher) J(ohn) 1932- . . . **CLC 42**
See also CA 127

Koch, Christopher
See Koch, C(hristopher) J(ohn)

Koch, Kenneth 1925- . . . . **CLC 5, 8, 44**
See also CA 1-4R; CANR 6, 36;
DAM POET; DLB 5; INT CANR-36;
SATA 65

Kochanowski, Jan 1530-1584. . . . . . . **LC 10**

Kock, Charles Paul de
1794-1871 . . . . **NCLC 16**

Koda Shigeyuki 1867-1947
See Rohan, Koda
See also CA 121

Koestler, Arthur
1905-1983 . . . . . . **CLC 1, 3, 6, 8, 15, 33**
See also CA 1-4R; 109; CANR 1, 33;
CDBLB 1945-1960; DLBY 83; MTCW

Kogawa, Joy Nozomi 1935- . . . **CLC 78; DAC**
See also CA 101; CANR 19; DAM MST,
MULT

Kohout, Pavel 1928- . . . . **CLC 13**
See also CA 45-48; CANR 3

Koizumi, Yakumo
See Hearn, (Patricio) Lafcadio (Tessima
Carlos)

Kolmar, Gertrud 1894-1943 . . . . . . **TCLC 40**

Komunyakaa, Yusef 1947- . . . . **CLC 86**
See also CA 147; DLB 120

Konrad, George
See Konrad, Gyoergy

Konrad, Gyoergy 1933- . . . . . . **CLC 4, 10, 73**
See also CA 85-88

Konwicki, Tadeusz 1926- . . . . . **CLC 8, 28, 54**
See also CA 101; CAAS 9; CANR 39;
MTCW

Koontz, Dean R(ay) 1945- . . . . **CLC 78**
See also AAYA 9; BEST 89:3, 90:2;
CA 108; CANR 19, 36; DAM NOV,
POP; MTCW

Kopit, Arthur (Lee) 1937- . . . . **CLC 1, 18, 33**
See also AITN 1; CA 81-84; CABS 3;
DAM DRAM; DLB 7; MTCW

Kops, Bernard 1926- . . . . **CLC 4**
See also CA 5-8R; DLB 13

Kornbluth, C(yril) M. 1923-1958. . . . **TCLC 8**
See also CA 105; DLB 8

Korolenko, V. G.
See Korolenko, Vladimir Galaktionovich

Korolenko, Vladimir
See Korolenko, Vladimir Galaktionovich

Korolenko, Vladimir G.
See Korolenko, Vladimir Galaktionovich

Korolenko, Vladimir Galaktionovich
1853-1921 . . . . **TCLC 22**
See also CA 121

Korzybski, Alfred (Habdank Skarbek)
1879-1950 . . . . **TCLC 61**
See also CA 123

Kosinski, Jerzy (Nikodem)
1933-1991 . . . . **CLC 1, 2, 3, 6, 10, 15, 53,
70**
See also CA 17-20R; 134; CANR 9, 46;
DAM NOV; DLB 2; DLBY 82; MTCW

Kostelanetz, Richard (Cory) 1940- . . **CLC 28**
See also CA 13-16R; CAAS 8; CANR 38

Kostrowitzki, Wilhelm Apollinaris de
1880-1918
See Apollinaire, Guillaume
See also CA 104

Kotlowitz, Robert 1924- . . . . **CLC 4**
See also CA 33-36R; CANR 36

Kotzebue, August (Friedrich Ferdinand) von
1761-1819 . . . . **NCLC 25**
See also DLB 94

Kotzwinkle, William 1938- . . . **CLC 5, 14, 35**
See also CA 45-48; CANR 3, 44; CLR 6;
MAICYA; SATA 24, 70

Kozol, Jonathan 1936- . . . . **CLC 17**
See also CA 61-64; CANR 16, 45

Kozoll, Michael 1940(?)- . . . . **CLC 35**

Kramer, Kathryn 19(?)- . . . . **CLC 34**

Kramer, Larry 1935- . . . . **CLC 42**
See also CA 124; 126; DAM POP

Krasicki, Ignacy 1735-1801 . . . . **NCLC 8**

Krasinski, Zygmunt 1812-1859 . . . . **NCLC 4**

Kraus, Karl 1874-1936. . . . . **TCLC 5**
See also CA 104; DLB 118

Kreve (Mickevicius), Vincas
1882-1954 . . . . **TCLC 27**

Kristeva, Julia 1941- . . . . **CLC 77**

Kristofferson, Kris 1936- . . . . **CLC 26**
See also CA 104

Krizanc, John 1956- . . . . **CLC 57**

Krleza, Miroslav 1893-1981. . . . . **CLC 8**
See also CA 97-100; 105; CANR 50;
DLB 147

Kroetsch, Robert
1927- . . . . **CLC 5, 23, 57; DAC**
See also CA 17-20R; CANR 8, 38;
DAM POET; DLB 53; MTCW

Kroetz, Franz
See Kroetz, Franz Xaver

Kroetz, Franz Xaver 1946- . . . . **CLC 41**
See also CA 130

Kroker, Arthur 1945- . . . . **CLC 77**

Kropotkin, Peter (Aleksieevich)
1842-1921 . . . . **TCLC 36**
See also CA 119

Krotkov, Yuri 1917- . . . . **CLC 19**
See also CA 102

Krumb
See Crumb, R(obert)

Krumgold, Joseph (Quincy)
1908-1980 . . . . **CLC 12**
See also CA 9-12R; 101; CANR 7;
MAICYA; SATA 1, 48; SATA-Obit 23

Krumwitz
See Crumb, R(obert)

Krutch, Joseph Wood 1893-1970. . . . **CLC 24**
See also CA 1-4R; 25-28R; CANR 4;
DLB 63

Krutzch, Gus
See Eliot, T(homas) S(tearns)

Krylov, Ivan Andreevich
1768(?)-1844 . . . . **NCLC 1**
See also DLB 150

Kubin, Alfred (Leopold Isidor)
1877-1959 . . . . **TCLC 23**
See also CA 112; 149; DLB 81

Kubrick, Stanley 1928- . . . . **CLC 16**
See also CA 81-84; CANR 33; DLB 26

Kumin, Maxine (Winokur)
1925- . . . . **CLC 5, 13, 28; PC 15**
See also AITN 2; CA 1-4R; CAAS 8;
CANR 1, 21; DAM POET; DLB 5;
MTCW; SATA 12

Kundera, Milan
1929- . . . . **CLC 4, 9, 19, 32, 68**
See also AAYA 2; CA 85-88; CANR 19;
DAM NOV; MTCW

Kunene, Mazisi (Raymond) 1930- . . . **CLC 85**
See also BW 1; CA 125; DLB 117

Kunitz, Stanley (Jasspon)
1905- . . . . **CLC 6, 11, 14**
See also CA 41-44R; CANR 26; DLB 48;
INT CANR-26; MTCW

Kunze, Reiner 1933- . . . . **CLC 10**
See also CA 93-96; DLB 75

Kuprin, Aleksandr Ivanovich
1870-1938 . . . . **TCLC 5**
See also CA 104

Kureishi, Hanif 1954(?)- . . . . **CLC 64**
See also CA 139

Kurosawa, Akira 1910- . . . . **CLC 16**
See also AAYA 11; CA 101; CANR 46;
DAM MULT

Kushner, Tony 1957(?)- . . . . **CLC 81**
See also CA 144; DAM DRAM

Kuttner, Henry 1915-1958. . . . . **TCLC 10**
See also CA 107; DLB 8

Kuzma, Greg 1944- . . . . **CLC 7**
See also CA 33-36R

Kuzmin, Mikhail 1872(?)-1936 . . . . **TCLC 40**

Kyd, Thomas 1558-1594. . . . . . . **LC 22; DC 3**
See also DAM DRAM; DLB 62

Kyprianos, Iossif
See Samarakis, Antonis

La Bruyere, Jean de 1645-1696. . . . . . **LC 17**

Lacan, Jacques (Marie Emile)
1901-1981 . . . . **CLC 75**
See also CA 121; 104

**Laclos, Pierre Ambroise Francois Choderlos
de** 1741-1803 . . . . **NCLC 4**

Lacolere, Francois
See Aragon, Louis

La Colere, Francois
See Aragon, Louis

La Deshabilleuse
See Simenon, Georges (Jacques Christian)

Lady Gregory
See Gregory, Isabella Augusta (Persse)

Lady of Quality, A
See Bagnold, Enid

**La Fayette, Marie (Madelaine Pioche de la
Vergne Comtes** 1634-1693. . . . . . **LC 2**

Lafayette, Rene
 See Hubbard, L(afayette) Ron(ald)

Laforgue, Jules
 1860-1887 . . . . **NCLC 5, 53; PC 14;**
            SSC 20

Lagerkvist, Paer (Fabian)
 1891-1974 . . . . **CLC 7, 10, 13, 54**
 See also Lagerkvist, Par
 See also CA 85-88; 49-52; DAM DRAM,
  NOV; MTCW

Lagerkvist, Par . . . . **SSC 12**
 See also Lagerkvist, Paer (Fabian)

Lagerloef, Selma (Ottiliana Lovisa)
 1858-1940 . . . . **TCLC 4, 36**
 See also Lagerlof, Selma (Ottiliana Lovisa)
 See also CA 108; SATA 15

Lagerlof, Selma (Ottiliana Lovisa)
 See Lagerloef, Selma (Ottiliana Lovisa)
 See also CLR 7; SATA 15

La Guma, (Justin) Alex(ander)
 1925-1985 . . . . **CLC 19**
 See also BW 1; CA 49-52; 118; CANR 25;
  DAM NOV; DLB 117; MTCW

Laidlaw, A. K.
 See Grieve, C(hristopher) M(urray)

Lainez, Manuel Mujica
 See Mujica Lainez, Manuel
 See also HW

Lamartine, Alphonse (Marie Louis Prat) de
 1790-1869 . . . . **NCLC 11; PC 15**
 See also DAM POET

Lamb, Charles
 1775-1834 . . . . **NCLC 10; DA; DAB;**
            DAC; WLC
 See also CDBLB 1789-1832; DAM MST;
  DLB 93, 107, 163; SATA 17

Lamb, Lady Caroline 1785-1828 . . **NCLC 38**
 See also DLB 116

Lamming, George (William)
 1927- . . . . **CLC 2, 4, 66; BLC**
 See also BW 2; CA 85-88; CANR 26;
  DAM MULT; DLB 125; MTCW

L'Amour, Louis (Dearborn)
 1908-1988 . . . . **CLC 25, 55**
 See also AAYA 16; AITN 2; BEST 89:2;
  CA 1-4R; 125; CANR 3, 25, 40;
  DAM NOV, POP; DLBY 80; MTCW

Lampedusa, Giuseppe (Tomasi) di . . . **TCLC 13**
 See also Tomasi di Lampedusa, Giuseppe

Lampman, Archibald 1861-1899 . . **NCLC 25**
 See also DLB 92

Lancaster, Bruce 1896-1963 . . . . **CLC 36**
 See also CA 9-10; CAP 1; SATA 9

Landau, Mark Alexandrovich
 See Aldanov, Mark (Alexandrovich)

Landau-Aldanov, Mark Alexandrovich
 See Aldanov, Mark (Alexandrovich)

Landis, John 1950- . . . . **CLC 26**
 See also CA 112; 122

Landolfi, Tommaso 1908-1979 . . . **CLC 11, 49**
 See also CA 127; 117

Landon, Letitia Elizabeth
 1802-1838 . . . . **NCLC 15**
 See also DLB 96

Landor, Walter Savage
 1775-1864 . . . . **NCLC 14**
 See also DLB 93, 107

Landwirth, Heinz 1927-
 See Lind, Jakov
 See also CA 9-12R; CANR 7

Lane, Patrick 1939- . . . . **CLC 25**
 See also CA 97-100; DAM POET; DLB 53;
  INT 97-100

Lang, Andrew 1844-1912 . . . . **TCLC 16**
 See also CA 114; 137; DLB 98, 141;
  MAICYA; SATA 16

Lang, Fritz 1890-1976 . . . . **CLC 20**
 See also CA 77-80; 69-72; CANR 30

Lange, John
 See Crichton, (John) Michael

Langer, Elinor 1939- . . . . **CLC 34**
 See also CA 121

Langland, William
 1330(?)-1400(?) . . . . . . **LC 19; DA; DAB;**
             DAC
 See also DAM MST, POET; DLB 146

Langstaff, Launcelot
 See Irving, Washington

Lanier, Sidney 1842-1881 . . . . **NCLC 6**
 See also DAM POET; DLB 64; DLBD 13;
  MAICYA; SATA 18

Lanyer, Aemilia 1569-1645 . . . . . . **LC 10, 30**
 See also DLB 121

Lao Tzu . . . . **CMLC 7**

Lapine, James (Elliot) 1949- . . . . **CLC 39**
 See also CA 123; 130; INT 130

Larbaud, Valery (Nicolas)
 1881-1957 . . . . **TCLC 9**
 See also CA 106

Lardner, Ring
 See Lardner, Ring(gold) W(ilmer)

Lardner, Ring W., Jr.
 See Lardner, Ring(gold) W(ilmer)

Lardner, Ring(gold) W(ilmer)
 1885-1933 . . . . **TCLC 2, 14**
 See also CA 104; 131; CDALB 1917-1929;
  DLB 11, 25, 86; MTCW

Laredo, Betty
 See Codrescu, Andrei

Larkin, Maia
 See Wojciechowska, Maia (Teresa)

Larkin, Philip (Arthur)
 1922-1985 . . . . **CLC 3, 5, 8, 9, 13, 18, 33,**
           39, 64; DAB
 See also CA 5-8R; 117; CANR 24;
  CDBLB 1960 to Present; DAM MST,
  POET; DLB 27; MTCW

Larra (y Sanchez de Castro), Mariano Jose de
 1809-1837 . . . . **NCLC 17**

Larsen, Eric 1941- . . . . **CLC 55**
 See also CA 132

Larsen, Nella 1891-1964 . . . . . **CLC 37; BLC**
 See also BW 1; CA 125; DAM MULT;
  DLB 51

Larson, Charles R(aymond) 1938- . . . **CLC 31**
 See also CA 53-56; CANR 4

Las Casas, Bartolome de 1474-1566 . . **LC 31**

Lasker-Schueler, Else 1869-1945 . . **TCLC 57**
 See also DLB 66, 124

Latham, Jean Lee 1902- . . . . **CLC 12**
 See also AITN 1; CA 5-8R; CANR 7;
  MAICYA; SATA 2, 68

Latham, Mavis
 See Clark, Mavis Thorpe

Lathen, Emma . . . . **CLC 2**
 See also Hennissart, Martha; Latsis, Mary
  J(ane)

Lathrop, Francis
 See Leiber, Fritz (Reuter, Jr.)

Latsis, Mary J(ane)
 See Lathen, Emma
 See also CA 85-88

Lattimore, Richmond (Alexander)
 1906-1984 . . . . **CLC 3**
 See also CA 1-4R; 112; CANR 1

Laughlin, James 1914- . . . . **CLC 49**
 See also CA 21-24R; CAAS 22; CANR 9,
  47; DLB 48

Laurence, (Jean) Margaret (Wemyss)
 1926-1987 . . . . **CLC 3, 6, 13, 50, 62;**
           DAC; SSC 7
 See also CA 5-8R; 121; CANR 33;
  DAM MST; DLB 53; MTCW;
  SATA-Obit 50

Laurent, Antoine 1952- . . . . **CLC 50**

Lauscher, Hermann
 See Hesse, Hermann

Lautreamont, Comte de
 1846-1870 . . . . **NCLC 12; SSC 14**

Laverty, Donald
 See Blish, James (Benjamin)

Lavin, Mary 1912- . . . . . . **CLC 4, 18; SSC 4**
 See also CA 9-12R; CANR 33; DLB 15;
  MTCW

Lavond, Paul Dennis
 See Kornbluth, C(yril) M.; Pohl, Frederik

Lawler, Raymond Evenor 1922- . . . . **CLC 58**
 See also CA 103

Lawrence, D(avid) H(erbert Richards)
 1885-1930 . . . . **TCLC 2, 9, 16, 33, 48, 61;**
      DA; DAB; DAC; SSC 4, 19; WLC
 See also CA 104; 121; CDBLB 1914-1945;
  DAM MST, NOV, POET; DLB 10, 19,
  36, 98, 162; MTCW

Lawrence, T(homas) E(dward)
 1888-1935 . . . . **TCLC 18**
 See also Dale, Colin
 See also CA 115

Lawrence of Arabia
 See Lawrence, T(homas) E(dward)

Lawson, Henry (Archibald Hertzberg)
 1867-1922 . . . . **TCLC 27; SSC 18**
 See also CA 120

Lawton, Dennis
 See Faust, Frederick (Schiller)

Laxness, Halldor . . . . **CLC 25**
 See also Gudjonsson, Halldor Kiljan

Layamon fl. c. 1200- . . . . **CMLC 10**
 See also DLB 146

Laye, Camara 1928-1980 . . . **CLC 4, 38; BLC**
 See also BW 1; CA 85-88; 97-100;
  CANR 25; DAM MULT; MTCW

Layton, Irving (Peter)
 1912- .... **CLC 2, 15; DAC**
 See also CA 1-4R; CANR 2, 33, 43;
 DAM MST, POET; DLB 88; MTCW

Lazarus, Emma 1849-1887........ **NCLC 8**

Lazarus, Felix
 See Cable, George Washington

Lazarus, Henry
 See Slavitt, David R(ytman)

Lea, Joan
 See Neufeld, John (Arthur)

Leacock, Stephen (Butler)
 1869-1944 .... **TCLC 2; DAC**
 See also CA 104; 141; DAM MST; DLB 92

Lear, Edward 1812-1888 .... **NCLC 3**
 See also CLR 1; DLB 32, 163; MAICYA;
 SATA 18

Lear, Norman (Milton) 1922- ...... **CLC 12**
 See also CA 73-76

Leavis, F(rank) R(aymond)
 1895-1978 .... **CLC 24**
 See also CA 21-24R; 77-80; CANR 44;
 MTCW

Leavitt, David 1961- .... **CLC 34**
 See also CA 116; 122; CANR 50;
 DAM POP; DLB 130; INT 122

Leblanc, Maurice (Marie Emile)
 1864-1941 .... **TCLC 49**
 See also CA 110

Lebowitz, Fran(ces Ann)
 1951(?)- .... **CLC 11, 36**
 See also CA 81-84; CANR 14;
 INT CANR-14; MTCW

Lebrecht, Peter
 See Tieck, (Johann) Ludwig

le Carre, John .... **CLC 3, 5, 9, 15, 28**
 See also Cornwell, David (John Moore)
 See also BEST 89:4; CDBLB 1960 to
 Present; DLB 87

Le Clezio, J(ean) M(arie) G(ustave)
 1940- .... **CLC 31**
 See also CA 116; 128; DLB 83

Leconte de Lisle, Charles-Marie-Rene
 1818-1894 .... **NCLC 29**

Le Coq, Monsieur
 See Simenon, Georges (Jacques Christian)

Leduc, Violette 1907-1972........ **CLC 22**
 See also CA 13-14; 33-36R; CAP 1

Ledwidge, Francis 1887(?)-1917 ... **TCLC 23**
 See also CA 123; DLB 20

Lee, Andrea 1953- .... **CLC 36; BLC**
 See also BW 1; CA 125; DAM MULT

Lee, Andrew
 See Auchincloss, Louis (Stanton)

Lee, Chang-rae 1965- .... **CLC 91**
 See also CA 148

Lee, Don L. .... **CLC 2**
 See also Madhubuti, Haki R.

Lee, George W(ashington)
 1894-1976 .... **CLC 52; BLC**
 See also BW 1; CA 125; DAM MULT;
 DLB 51

Lee, (Nelle) Harper
 1926- .... **CLC 12, 60; DA; DAB; DAC;
 WLC**
 See also AAYA 13; CA 13-16R; CANR 51;
 CDALB 1941-1968; DAM MST, NOV;
 DLB 6; MTCW; SATA 11

Lee, Helen Elaine 1959(?)- .... **CLC 86**
 See also CA 148

Lee, Julian
 See Latham, Jean Lee

Lee, Larry
 See Lee, Lawrence

Lee, Laurie 1914-........... **CLC 90; DAB**
 See also CA 77-80; CANR 33; DAM POP;
 DLB 27; MTCW

Lee, Lawrence 1941-1990......... **CLC 34**
 See also CA 131; CANR 43

Lee, Manfred B(ennington)
 1905-1971 .... **CLC 11**
 See also Queen, Ellery
 See also CA 1-4R; 29-32R; CANR 2;
 DLB 137

Lee, Stan 1922-................. **CLC 17**
 See also AAYA 5; CA 108; 111; INT 111

Lee, Tanith 1947- .... **CLC 46**
 See also AAYA 15; CA 37-40R; SATA 8

Lee, Vernon .... **TCLC 5**
 See also Paget, Violet
 See also DLB 57, 153, 156

Lee, William
 See Burroughs, William S(eward)

Lee, Willy
 See Burroughs, William S(eward)

Lee-Hamilton, Eugene (Jacob)
 1845-1907 .... **TCLC 22**
 See also CA 117

Leet, Judith 1935- .... **CLC 11**

Le Fanu, Joseph Sheridan
 1814-1873 .... **NCLC 9; SSC 14**
 See also DAM POP; DLB 21, 70, 159

Leffland, Ella 1931- .... **CLC 19**
 See also CA 29-32R; CANR 35; DLBY 84;
 INT CANR-35; SATA 65

Leger, Alexis
 See Leger, (Marie-Rene Auguste) Alexis
 Saint-Leger

**Leger, (Marie-Rene Auguste) Alexis
 Saint-Leger** 1887-1975........ **CLC 11**
 See also Perse, St.-John
 See also CA 13-16R; 61-64; CANR 43;
 DAM POET; MTCW

Leger, Saintleger
 See Leger, (Marie-Rene Auguste) Alexis
 Saint-Leger

Le Guin, Ursula K(roeber)
 1929- ...... **CLC 8, 13, 22, 45, 71; DAB;
 DAC; SSC 12**
 See also AAYA 9; AITN 1; CA 21-24R;
 CANR 9, 32; CDALB 1968-1988; CLR 3,
 28; DAM MST, POP; DLB 8, 52;
 INT CANR-32; JRDA; MAICYA;
 MTCW; SATA 4, 52

Lehmann, Rosamond (Nina)
 1901-1990 .... **CLC 5**
 See also CA 77-80; 131; CANR 8; DLB 15

Leiber, Fritz (Reuter, Jr.)
 1910-1992 .... **CLC 25**
 See also CA 45-48; 139; CANR 2, 40;
 DLB 8; MTCW; SATA 45;
 SATA-Obit 73

Leimbach, Martha 1963-
 See Leimbach, Marti
 See also CA 130

Leimbach, Marti .... **CLC 65**
 See also Leimbach, Martha

Leino, Eino .... **TCLC 24**
 See also Loennbohm, Armas Eino Leopold

Leiris, Michel (Julien) 1901-1990... **CLC 61**
 See also CA 119; 128; 132

Leithauser, Brad 1953-............ **CLC 27**
 See also CA 107; CANR 27; DLB 120

Lelchuk, Alan 1938-............... **CLC 5**
 See also CA 45-48; CAAS 20; CANR 1

Lem, Stanislaw 1921-........ **CLC 8, 15, 40**
 See also CA 105; CAAS 1; CANR 32;
 MTCW

Lemann, Nancy 1956-............. **CLC 39**
 See also CA 118; 136

Lemonnier, (Antoine Louis) Camille
 1844-1913 .... **TCLC 22**
 See also CA 121

Lenau, Nikolaus 1802-1850...... **NCLC 16**

L'Engle, Madeleine (Camp Franklin)
 1918- .... **CLC 12**
 See also AAYA 1; AITN 2; CA 1-4R;
 CANR 3, 21, 39; CLR 1, 14; DAM POP;
 DLB 52; JRDA; MAICYA; MTCW;
 SAAS 15; SATA 1, 27, 75

Lengyel, Jozsef 1896-1975.......... **CLC 7**
 See also CA 85-88; 57-60

Lennon, John (Ono)
 1940-1980 .... **CLC 12, 35**
 See also CA 102

Lennox, Charlotte Ramsay
 1729(?)-1804 .... **NCLC 23**
 See also DLB 39

Lentricchia, Frank (Jr.) 1940-...... **CLC 34**
 See also CA 25-28R; CANR 19

Lenz, Siegfried 1926-............. **CLC 27**
 See also CA 89-92; DLB 75

Leonard, Elmore (John, Jr.)
 1925- .... **CLC 28, 34, 71**
 See also AITN 1; BEST 89:1, 90:4;
 CA 81-84; CANR 12, 28; DAM POP;
 INT CANR-28; MTCW

Leonard, Hugh .... **CLC 19**
 See also Byrne, John Keyes
 See also DLB 13

Leonov, Leonid (Maximovich)
 1899-1994 .... **CLC 92**
 See also CA 129; DAM NOV; MTCW

Leopardi, (Conte) Giacomo
 1798-1837 .... **NCLC 22**

Le Reveler
 See Artaud, Antonin (Marie Joseph)

Lerman, Eleanor 1952-............ **CLC 9**
 See also CA 85-88

Lerman, Rhoda 1936-............. **CLC 56**
 See also CA 49-52

Author Index

Livesay, Dorothy (Kathleen)
1909- . . . . **CLC 4, 15, 79; DAC**
See also AITN 2; CA 25-28R; CAAS 8;
CANR 36; DAM MST, POET; DLB 68;
MTCW

Livy c. 59B.C.-c. 17 . . . . **CMLC 11**

Lizardi, Jose Joaquin Fernandez de
1776-1827 . . . . **NCLC 30**

Llewellyn, Richard
See Llewellyn Lloyd, Richard Dafydd
Vivian
See also DLB 15

Llewellyn Lloyd, Richard Dafydd Vivian
1906-1983 . . . . **CLC 7, 80**
See also Llewellyn, Richard
See also CA 53-56; 111; CANR 7;
SATA 11; SATA-Obit 37

Llosa, (Jorge) Mario (Pedro) Vargas
See Vargas Llosa, (Jorge) Mario (Pedro)

Lloyd Webber, Andrew 1948-
See Webber, Andrew Lloyd
See also AAYA 1; CA 116; 149;
DAM DRAM; SATA 56

Llull, Ramon c. 1235-c. 1316 . . . . . **CMLC 12**

Locke, Alain (Le Roy)
1886-1954 . . . . **TCLC 43**
See also BW 1; CA 106; 124; DLB 51

Locke, John 1632-1704 . . . . **LC 7**
See also DLB 101

Locke-Elliott, Sumner
See Elliott, Sumner Locke

Lockhart, John Gibson
1794-1854 . . . . **NCLC 6**
See also DLB 110, 116, 144

Lodge, David (John) 1935- . . . . **CLC 36**
See also BEST 90:1; CA 17-20R; CANR 19;
DAM POP; DLB 14; INT CANR-19;
MTCW

Loennbohm, Armas Eino Leopold 1878-1926
See Leino, Eino
See also CA 123

Loewinsohn, Ron(ald William)
1937- . . . . **CLC 52**
See also CA 25-28R

Logan, Jake
See Smith, Martin Cruz

Logan, John (Burton) 1923-1987 . . . . . **CLC 5**
See also CA 77-80; 124; CANR 45; DLB 5

Lo Kuan-chung 1330(?)-1400(?) . . . . . . **LC 12**

Lombard, Nap
See Johnson, Pamela Hansford

London, Jack . . **TCLC 9, 15, 39; SSC 4; WLC**
See also London, John Griffith
See also AAYA 13; AITN 2;
CDALB 1865-1917; DLB 8, 12, 78;
SATA 18

London, John Griffith 1876-1916
See London, Jack
See also CA 110; 119; DA; DAB; DAC;
DAM MST, NOV; JRDA; MAICYA;
MTCW

Long, Emmett
See Leonard, Elmore (John, Jr.)

Longbaugh, Harry
See Goldman, William (W.)

Longfellow, Henry Wadsworth
1807-1882 . . . . . **NCLC 2, 45; DA; DAB;
DAC**
See also CDALB 1640-1865; DAM MST,
POET; DLB 1, 59; SATA 19

Longley, Michael 1939- . . . . **CLC 29**
See also CA 102; DLB 40

Longus fl. c. 2nd cent. - . . . . **CMLC 7**

Longway, A. Hugh
See Lang, Andrew

Lonnrot, Elias 1802-1884 . . . . **NCLC 53**

Lopate, Phillip 1943- . . . . **CLC 29**
See also CA 97-100; DLBY 80; INT 97-100

Lopez Portillo (y Pacheco), Jose
1920- . . . . **CLC 46**
See also CA 129; HW

Lopez y Fuentes, Gregorio
1897(?)-1966 . . . . **CLC 32**
See also CA 131; HW

Lorca, Federico Garcia
See Garcia Lorca, Federico

Lord, Bette Bao 1938- . . . . **CLC 23**
See also BEST 90:3; CA 107; CANR 41;
INT 107; SATA 58

Lord Auch
See Bataille, Georges

Lord Byron
See Byron, George Gordon (Noel)

Lorde, Audre (Geraldine)
1934-1992 . . . . **CLC 18, 71; BLC; PC 12**
See also BW 1; CA 25-28R; 142; CANR 16,
26, 46; DAM MULT, POET; DLB 41;
MTCW

Lord Jeffrey
See Jeffrey, Francis

Lorenzini, Carlo 1826-1890
See Collodi, Carlo
See also MAICYA; SATA 29

Lorenzo, Heberto Padilla
See Padilla (Lorenzo), Heberto

Loris
See Hofmannsthal, Hugo von

Loti, Pierre . . . . **TCLC 11**
See also Viaud, (Louis Marie) Julien
See also DLB 123

Louie, David Wong 1954- . . . . **CLC 70**
See also CA 139

Louis, Father M.
See Merton, Thomas

Lovecraft, H(oward) P(hillips)
1890-1937 . . . . **TCLC 4, 22; SSC 3**
See also AAYA 14; CA 104; 133;
DAM POP; MTCW

Lovelace, Earl 1935- . . . . **CLC 51**
See also BW 2; CA 77-80; CANR 41;
DLB 125; MTCW

Lovelace, Richard 1618-1657 . . . . **LC 24**
See also DLB 131

Lowell, Amy 1874-1925 . . **TCLC 1, 8; PC 13**
See also CA 104; DAM POET; DLB 54,
140

Lowell, James Russell 1819-1891 . . **NCLC 2**
See also CDALB 1640-1865; DLB 1, 11, 64,
79

Lowell, Robert (Traill Spence, Jr.)
1917-1977 . . . **CLC 1, 2, 3, 4, 5, 8, 9, 11,
15, 37; DA; DAB; DAC; PC 3; WLC**
See also CA 9-12R; 73-76; CABS 2;
CANR 26; DAM MST, NOV; DLB 5;
MTCW

Lowndes, Marie Adelaide (Belloc)
1868-1947 . . . . **TCLC 12**
See also CA 107; DLB 70

Lowry, (Clarence) Malcolm
1909-1957 . . . . **TCLC 6, 40**
See also CA 105; 131; CDBLB 1945-1960;
DLB 15; MTCW

Lowry, Mina Gertrude 1882-1966
See Loy, Mina
See also CA 113

Loxsmith, John
See Brunner, John (Kilian Houston)

Loy, Mina . . . . **CLC 28**
See also Lowry, Mina Gertrude
See also DAM POET; DLB 4, 54

Loyson-Bridet
See Schwob, (Mayer Andre) Marcel

Lucas, Craig 1951- . . . . **CLC 64**
See also CA 137

Lucas, George 1944- . . . . **CLC 16**
See also AAYA 1; CA 77-80; CANR 30;
SATA 56

Lucas, Hans
See Godard, Jean-Luc

Lucas, Victoria
See Plath, Sylvia

Ludlam, Charles 1943-1987 . . . . . **CLC 46, 50**
See also CA 85-88; 122

Ludlum, Robert 1927- . . . . **CLC 22, 43**
See also AAYA 10; BEST 89:1, 90:3;
CA 33-36R; CANR 25, 41; DAM NOV,
POP; DLBY 82; MTCW

Ludwig, Ken . . . . **CLC 60**

Ludwig, Otto 1813-1865 . . . . **NCLC 4**
See also DLB 129

Lugones, Leopoldo 1874-1938 . . . . . **TCLC 15**
See also CA 116; 131; HW

Lu Hsun 1881-1936 . . . . . . **TCLC 3; SSC 20**
See also Shu-Jen, Chou

Lukacs, George . . . . **CLC 24**
See also Lukacs, Gyorgy (Szegeny von)

Lukacs, Gyorgy (Szegeny von) 1885-1971
See Lukacs, George
See also CA 101; 29-32R

Luke, Peter (Ambrose Cyprian)
1919-1995 . . . . **CLC 38**
See also CA 81-84; 147; DLB 13

Lunar, Dennis
See Mungo, Raymond

Lurie, Alison 1926- . . . . **CLC 4, 5, 18, 39**
See also CA 1-4R; CANR 2, 17, 50; DLB 2;
MTCW; SATA 46

Lustig, Arnost 1926- . . . . **CLC 56**
See also AAYA 3; CA 69-72; CANR 47;
SATA 56

Luther, Martin 1483-1546 . . . . **LC 9**

Luxemburg, Rosa 1870(?)-1919 . . . . **TCLC 63**
See also CA 118

Major, Clarence
  1936- .... CLC **3, 19, 48; BLC**
  See also BW 2; CA 21-24R; CAAS 6;
  CANR 13, 25; DAM MULT; DLB 33

Major, Kevin (Gerald)
  1949- .... CLC **26; DAC**
  See also AAYA 16; CA 97-100; CANR 21,
  38; CLR 11; DLB 60; INT CANR-21;
  JRDA; MAICYA; SATA 32, 82

Maki, James
  See Ozu, Yasujiro

Malabaila, Damiano
  See Levi, Primo

Malamud, Bernard
  1914-1986 ..... CLC **1, 2, 3, 5, 8, 9, 11,
  18, 27, 44, 78, 85; DA; DAB; DAC;
  SSC 15; WLC**
  See also AAYA 16; CA 5-8R; 118; CABS 1;
  CANR 28; CDALB 1941-1968;
  DAM MST, NOV, POP; DLB 2, 28, 152;
  DLBY 80, 86; MTCW

Malaparte, Curzio 1898-1957 ..... TCLC **52**

Malcolm, Dan
  See Silverberg, Robert

Malcolm X .... CLC **82; BLC**
  See also Little, Malcolm

Malherbe, Francois de 1555-1628 ..... LC **5**

Mallarme, Stephane
  1842-1898 .... NCLC **4, 41; PC 4**
  See also DAM POET

Mallet-Joris, Francoise 1930- ...... CLC **11**
  See also CA 65-68; CANR 17; DLB 83

Malley, Ern
  See McAuley, James Phillip

Mallowan, Agatha Christie
  See Christie, Agatha (Mary Clarissa)

Maloff, Saul 1922- .... CLC **5**
  See also CA 33-36R

Malone, Louis
  See MacNeice, (Frederick) Louis

Malone, Michael (Christopher)
  1942- .... CLC **43**
  See also CA 77-80; CANR 14, 32

Malory, (Sir) Thomas
  1410(?)-1471(?) ...... LC **11; DA; DAB;
  DAC**
  See also CDBLB Before 1660; DAM MST;
  DLB 146; SATA 59; SATA-Brief 33

Malouf, (George Joseph) David
  1934- .... CLC **28, 86**
  See also CA 124; CANR 50

Malraux, (Georges-)Andre
  1901-1976 ...... CLC **1, 4, 9, 13, 15, 57**
  See also CA 21-22; 69-72; CANR 34;
  CAP 2; DAM NOV; DLB 72; MTCW

Malzberg, Barry N(athaniel) 1939- ... CLC **7**
  See also CA 61-64; CAAS 4; CANR 16;
  DLB 8

Mamet, David (Alan)
  1947- ...... CLC **9, 15, 34, 46, 91; DC 4**
  See also AAYA 3; CA 81-84; CABS 3;
  CANR 15, 41; DAM DRAM; DLB 7;
  MTCW

Mamoulian, Rouben (Zachary)
  1897-1987 .... CLC **16**
  See also CA 25-28R; 124

Mandelstam, Osip (Emilievich)
  1891(?)-1938(?) ..... TCLC **2, 6; PC 14**
  See also CA 104; 150

Mander, (Mary) Jane 1877-1949... TCLC **31**

Mandiargues, Andre Pieyre de...... CLC **41**
  See also Pieyre de Mandiargues, Andre
  See also DLB 83

Mandrake, Ethel Belle
  See Thurman, Wallace (Henry)

Mangan, James Clarence
  1803-1849 .... NCLC **27**

Maniere, J.-E.
  See Giraudoux, (Hippolyte) Jean

Manley, (Mary) Delariviere
  1672(?)-1724 .... LC **1**
  See also DLB 39, 80

Mann, Abel
  See Creasey, John

Mann, (Luiz) Heinrich 1871-1950... TCLC **9**
  See also CA 106; DLB 66

Mann, (Paul) Thomas
  1875-1955 .... TCLC **2, 8, 14, 21, 35, 44,
  60; DA; DAB; DAC; SSC 5; WLC**
  See also CA 104; 128; DAM MST, NOV;
  DLB 66; MTCW

Manning, David
  See Faust, Frederick (Schiller)

Manning, Frederic 1887(?)-1935... TCLC **25**
  See also CA 124

Manning, Olivia 1915-1980 ...... CLC **5, 19**
  See also CA 5-8R; 101; CANR 29; MTCW

Mano, D. Keith 1942- .... CLC **2, 10**
  See also CA 25-28R; CAAS 6; CANR 26;
  DLB 6

Mansfield, Katherine
  ..... TCLC **2, 8, 39; DAB; SSC 9; WLC**
  See also Beauchamp, Kathleen Mansfield
  See also DLB 162

Manso, Peter 1940- .... CLC **39**
  See also CA 29-32R; CANR 44

Mantecon, Juan Jimenez
  See Jimenez (Mantecon), Juan Ramon

Manton, Peter
  See Creasey, John

Man Without a Spleen, A
  See Chekhov, Anton (Pavlovich)

Manzoni, Alessandro 1785-1873 .. NCLC **29**

Mapu, Abraham (ben Jekutiel)
  1808-1867 .... NCLC **18**

Mara, Sally
  See Queneau, Raymond

Marat, Jean Paul 1743-1793........ LC **10**

Marcel, Gabriel Honore
  1889-1973 .... CLC **15**
  See also CA 102; 45-48; MTCW

Marchbanks, Samuel
  See Davies, (William) Robertson

Marchi, Giacomo
  See Bassani, Giorgio

Margulies, Donald .... CLC **76**

Marie de France c. 12th cent. -.... CMLC **8**

Marie de l'Incarnation 1599-1672.... LC **10**

Mariner, Scott
  See Pohl, Frederik

Marinetti, Filippo Tommaso
  1876-1944 .... TCLC **10**
  See also CA 107; DLB 114

Marivaux, Pierre Carlet de Chamblain de
  1688-1763 .... LC **4**

Markandaya, Kamala .... CLC **8, 38**
  See also Taylor, Kamala (Purnaiya)

Markfield, Wallace 1926-.......... CLC **8**
  See also CA 69-72; CAAS 3; DLB 2, 28

Markham, Edwin 1852-1940 ...... TCLC **47**
  See also DLB 54

Markham, Robert
  See Amis, Kingsley (William)

Marks, J
  See Highwater, Jamake (Mamake)

Marks-Highwater, J
  See Highwater, Jamake (Mamake)

Markson, David M(errill) 1927- .... CLC **67**
  See also CA 49-52; CANR 1

Marley, Bob..................... CLC **17**
  See also Marley, Robert Nesta

Marley, Robert Nesta 1945-1981
  See Marley, Bob
  See also CA 107; 103

Marlowe, Christopher
  1564-1593 ..... LC **22; DA; DAB; DAC;
  DC 1; WLC**
  See also CDBLB Before 1660;
  DAM DRAM, MST; DLB 62

Marmontel, Jean-Francois
  1723-1799 .... LC **2**

Marquand, John P(hillips)
  1893-1960 .... CLC **2, 10**
  See also CA 85-88; DLB 9, 102

Marquez, Gabriel (Jose) Garcia
  See Garcia Marquez, Gabriel (Jose)

Marquis, Don(ald Robert Perry)
  1878-1937 .... TCLC **7**
  See also CA 104; DLB 11, 25

Marric, J. J.
  See Creasey, John

Marrow, Bernard
  See Moore, Brian

Marryat, Frederick 1792-1848 .... NCLC **3**
  See also DLB 21, 163

Marsden, James
  See Creasey, John

Marsh, (Edith) Ngaio
  1899-1982 .... CLC **7, 53**
  See also CA 9-12R; CANR 6; DAM POP;
  DLB 77; MTCW

Marshall, Garry 1934-............ CLC **17**
  See also AAYA 3; CA 111; SATA 60

Marshall, Paule
  1929- .... CLC **27, 72; BLC; SSC 3**
  See also BW 2; CA 77-80; CANR 25;
  DAM MULT; DLB 157; MTCW

Marsten, Richard
  See Hunter, Evan

Martha, Henry
See Harris, Mark

Martial c. 40-c. 104 .... **PC 10**

Martin, Ken
See Hubbard, L(afayette) Ron(ald)

Martin, Richard
See Creasey, John

Martin, Steve 1945- .... **CLC 30**
See also CA 97-100; CANR 30; MTCW

Martin, Valerie 1948-............ **CLC 89**
See also BEST 90:2; CA 85-88; CANR 49

Martin, Violet Florence
1862-1915 .... **TCLC 51**

Martin, Webber
See Silverberg, Robert

Martindale, Patrick Victor
See White, Patrick (Victor Martindale)

Martin du Gard, Roger
1881-1958 .... **TCLC 24**
See also CA 118; DLB 65

Martineau, Harriet 1802-1876.... **NCLC 26**
See also DLB 21, 55, 159, 163; YABC 2

Martines, Julia
See O'Faolain, Julia

Martinez, Jacinto Benavente y
See Benavente (y Martinez), Jacinto

Martinez Ruiz, Jose 1873-1967
See Azorin; Ruiz, Jose Martinez
See also CA 93-96; HW

Martinez Sierra, Gregorio
1881-1947 .... **TCLC 6**
See also CA 115

Martinez Sierra, Maria (de la O'LeJarraga)
1874-1974 .... **TCLC 6**
See also CA 115

Martinsen, Martin
See Follett, Ken(neth Martin)

Martinson, Harry (Edmund)
1904-1978 .... **CLC 14**
See also CA 77-80; CANR 34

Marut, Ret
See Traven, B.

Marut, Robert
See Traven, B.

Marvell, Andrew
1621-1678 ...... **LC 4; DA; DAB; DAC;**
PC 10; WLC
See also CDBLB 1660-1789; DAM MST,
POET; DLB 131

Marx, Karl (Heinrich)
1818-1883 .... **NCLC 17**
See also DLB 129

Masaoka Shiki.................. **TCLC 18**
See also Masaoka Tsunenori

Masaoka Tsunenori 1867-1902
See Masaoka Shiki
See also CA 117

Masefield, John (Edward)
1878-1967 .... **CLC 11, 47**
See also CA 19-20; 25-28R; CANR 33;
CAP 2; CDBLB 1890-1914; DAM POET;
DLB 10, 19, 153, 160; MTCW; SATA 19

Maso, Carole 19(?)- .... **CLC 44**

Mason, Bobbie Ann
1940- .... **CLC 28, 43, 82; SSC 4**
See also AAYA 5; CA 53-56; CANR 11,
31; DLBY 87; INT CANR-31; MTCW

Mason, Ernst
See Pohl, Frederik

Mason, Lee W.
See Malzberg, Barry N(athaniel)

Mason, Nick 1945-.............. **CLC 35**

Mason, Tally
See Derleth, August (William)

Mass, William
See Gibson, William

Masters, Edgar Lee
1868-1950 ...... **TCLC 2, 25; DA; DAC;**
PC 1
See also CA 104; 133; CDALB 1865-1917;
DAM MST, POET; DLB 54; MTCW

Masters, Hilary 1928- .... **CLC 48**
See also CA 25-28R; CANR 13, 47

Mastrosimone, William 19(?)-...... **CLC 36**

Mathe, Albert
See Camus, Albert

Matheson, Richard Burton 1926- ... **CLC 37**
See also CA 97-100; DLB 8, 44; INT 97-100

Mathews, Harry 1930-......... **CLC 6, 52**
See also CA 21-24R; CAAS 6; CANR 18,
40

Mathews, John Joseph 1894-1979... **CLC 84**
See also CA 19-20; 142; CANR 45; CAP 2;
DAM MULT; NNAL

Mathias, Roland (Glyn) 1915-...... **CLC 45**
See also CA 97-100; CANR 19, 41; DLB 27

Matsuo Basho 1644-1694........... **PC 3**
See also DAM POET

Mattheson, Rodney
See Creasey, John

Matthews, Greg 1949- .... **CLC 45**
See also CA 135

Matthews, William 1942-......... **CLC 40**
See also CA 29-32R; CAAS 18; CANR 12;
DLB 5

Matthias, John (Edward) 1941-...... **CLC 9**
See also CA 33-36R

Matthiessen, Peter
1927- .... **CLC 5, 7, 11, 32, 64**
See also AAYA 6; BEST 90:4; CA 9-12R;
CANR 21, 50; DAM NOV; DLB 6;
MTCW; SATA 27

Maturin, Charles Robert
1780(?)-1824 .... **NCLC 6**

Matute (Ausejo), Ana Maria
1925- .... **CLC 11**
See also CA 89-92; MTCW

Maugham, W. S.
See Maugham, W(illiam) Somerset

Maugham, W(illiam) Somerset
1874-1965 ...... **CLC 1, 11, 15, 67; DA;**
DAB; DAC; SSC 8; WLC
See also CA 5-8R; 25-28R; CANR 40;
CDBLB 1914-1945; DAM DRAM, MST,
NOV; DLB 10, 36, 77, 100, 162; MTCW;
SATA 54

Maugham, William Somerset
See Maugham, W(illiam) Somerset

Maupassant, (Henri Rene Albert) Guy de
1850-1893 ..... **NCLC 1, 42; DA; DAB;**
DAC; SSC 1; WLC
See also DAM MST; DLB 123

Maurhut, Richard
See Traven, B.

Mauriac, Claude 1914-............ **CLC 9**
See also CA 89-92; DLB 83

Mauriac, Francois (Charles)
1885-1970 .... **CLC 4, 9, 56**
See also CA 25-28; CAP 2; DLB 65;
MTCW

Mavor, Osborne Henry 1888-1951
See Bridie, James
See also CA 104

Maxwell, William (Keepers, Jr.)
1908- .... **CLC 19**
See also CA 93-96; DLBY 80; INT 93-96

May, Elaine 1932- .... **CLC 16**
See also CA 124; 142; DLB 44

Mayakovski, Vladimir (Vladimirovich)
1893-1930 .... **TCLC 4, 18**
See also CA 104

Mayhew, Henry 1812-1887...... **NCLC 31**
See also DLB 18, 55

Mayle, Peter 1939(?)-............ **CLC 89**
See also CA 139

Maynard, Joyce 1953-............ **CLC 23**
See also CA 111; 129

Mayne, William (James Carter)
1928- .... **CLC 12**
See also CA 9-12R; CANR 37; CLR 25;
JRDA; MAICYA; SAAS 11; SATA 6, 68

Mayo, Jim
See L'Amour, Louis (Dearborn)

Maysles, Albert 1926- .... **CLC 16**
See also CA 29-32R

Maysles, David 1932-............ **CLC 16**

Mazer, Norma Fox 1931- .... **CLC 26**
See also AAYA 5; CA 69-72; CANR 12,
32; CLR 23; JRDA; MAICYA; SAAS 1;
SATA 24, 67

Mazzini, Guiseppe 1805-1872 .... **NCLC 34**

McAuley, James Phillip
1917-1976 .... **CLC 45**
See also CA 97-100

McBain, Ed
See Hunter, Evan

McBrien, William Augustine
1930- .... **CLC 44**
See also CA 107

McCaffrey, Anne (Inez) 1926-...... **CLC 17**
See also AAYA 6; AITN 2; BEST 89:2;
CA 25-28R; CANR 15, 35; DAM NOV,
POP; DLB 8; JRDA; MAICYA; MTCW;
SAAS 11; SATA 8, 70

McCall, Nathan 1955(?)-.......... **CLC 86**
See also CA 146

McCann, Arthur
See Campbell, John W(ood, Jr.)

McCann, Edson
See Pohl, Frederik

McCarthy, Charles, Jr.   1933-
See McCarthy, Cormac
See also CANR 42; DAM POP

McCarthy, Cormac   1933- . . . . . **CLC 4, 57, 59**
See also McCarthy, Charles, Jr.
See also DLB 6, 143

McCarthy, Mary (Therese)
1912-1989 . . . **CLC 1, 3, 5, 14, 24, 39, 59**
See also CA 5-8R; 129; CANR 16, 50;
DLB 2; DLBY 81; INT CANR-16;
MTCW

McCartney, (James) Paul
1942- . . . . **CLC 12, 35**
See also CA 146

McCauley, Stephen (D.)   1955- . . . . . **CLC 50**
See also CA 141

McClure, Michael (Thomas)
1932- . . . . **CLC 6, 10**
See also CA 21-24R; CANR 17, 46;
DLB 16

McCorkle, Jill (Collins)   1958- . . . . . . **CLC 51**
See also CA 121; DLBY 87

McCourt, James   1941- . . . . **CLC 5**
See also CA 57-60

McCoy, Horace (Stanley)
1897-1955 . . . . **TCLC 28**
See also CA 108; DLB 9

McCrae, John   1872-1918 . . . . **TCLC 12**
See also CA 109; DLB 92

McCreigh, James
See Pohl, Frederik

McCullers, (Lula) Carson (Smith)
1917-1967 . . . . **CLC 1, 4, 10, 12, 48; DA;
DAB; DAC; SSC 9; WLC**
See also CA 5-8R; 25-28R; CABS 1, 3;
CANR 18; CDALB 1941-1968;
DAM MST, NOV; DLB 2, 7; MTCW;
SATA 27

McCulloch, John Tyler
See Burroughs, Edgar Rice

McCullough, Colleen   1938(?)- . . . . . . **CLC 27**
See also CA 81-84; CANR 17, 46;
DAM NOV, POP; MTCW

McDermott, Alice   1953- . . . . **CLC 90**
See also CA 109; CANR 40

McElroy, Joseph   1930- . . . . **CLC 5, 47**
See also CA 17-20R

McEwan, Ian (Russell)   1948- . . . **CLC 13, 66**
See also BEST 90:4; CA 61-64; CANR 14,
41; DAM NOV; DLB 14; MTCW

McFadden, David   1940- . . . . **CLC 48**
See also CA 104; DLB 60; INT 104

McFarland, Dennis   1950- . . . . **CLC 65**

McGahern, John
1934- . . . . **CLC 5, 9, 48; SSC 17**
See also CA 17-20R; CANR 29; DLB 14;
MTCW

McGinley, Patrick (Anthony)
1937- . . . . **CLC 41**
See also CA 120; 127; INT 127

McGinley, Phyllis   1905-1978 . . . . . . **CLC 14**
See also CA 9-12R; 77-80; CANR 19;
DLB 11, 48; SATA 2, 44; SATA-Obit 24

McGinniss, Joe   1942- . . . . **CLC 32**
See also AITN 2; BEST 89:2; CA 25-28R;
CANR 26; INT CANR-26

McGivern, Maureen Daly
See Daly, Maureen

McGrath, Patrick   1950- . . . . **CLC 55**
See also CA 136

McGrath, Thomas (Matthew)
1916-1990 . . . . **CLC 28, 59**
See also CA 9-12R; 132; CANR 6, 33;
DAM POET; MTCW; SATA 41;
SATA-Obit 66

McGuane, Thomas (Francis III)
1939- . . . . **CLC 3, 7, 18, 45**
See also AITN 2; CA 49-52; CANR 5, 24,
49; DLB 2; DLBY 80; INT CANR-24;
MTCW

McGuckian, Medbh   1950- . . . . **CLC 48**
See also CA 143; DAM POET; DLB 40

McHale, Tom   1942(?)-1982 . . . . **CLC 3, 5**
See also AITN 1; CA 77-80; 106

McIlvanney, William   1936- . . . . **CLC 42**
See also CA 25-28R; DLB 14

McIlwraith, Maureen Mollie Hunter
See Hunter, Mollie
See also SATA 2

McInerney, Jay   1955- . . . . **CLC 34**
See also CA 116; 123; CANR 45;
DAM POP; INT 123

McIntyre, Vonda N(eel)   1948- . . . . . **CLC 18**
See also CA 81-84; CANR 17, 34; MTCW

McKay, Claude
. . . . **TCLC 7, 41; BLC; DAB; PC 2**
See also McKay, Festus Claudius
See also DLB 4, 45, 51, 117

McKay, Festus Claudius   1889-1948
See McKay, Claude
See also BW 1; CA 104; 124; DA; DAC;
DAM MST, MULT, NOV, POET;
MTCW; WLC

McKuen, Rod   1933- . . . . **CLC 1, 3**
See also AITN 1; CA 41-44R; CANR 40

McLoughlin, R. B.
See Mencken, H(enry) L(ouis)

McLuhan, (Herbert) Marshall
1911-1980 . . . . **CLC 37, 83**
See also CA 9-12R; 102; CANR 12, 34;
DLB 88; INT CANR-12; MTCW

McMillan, Terry (L.)   1951- . . . . . **CLC 50, 61**
See also BW 2; CA 140; DAM MULT,
NOV, POP

McMurtry, Larry (Jeff)
1936- . . . . **CLC 2, 3, 7, 11, 27, 44**
See also AAYA 15; AITN 2; BEST 89:2;
CA 5-8R; CANR 19, 43;
CDALB 1968-1988; DAM NOV, POP;
DLB 2, 143; DLBY 80, 87; MTCW

McNally, T. M.   1961- . . . . **CLC 82**

McNally, Terrence   1939- . . . **CLC 4, 7, 41, 91**
See also CA 45-48; CANR 2;
DAM DRAM; DLB 7

McNamer, Deirdre   1950- . . . . **CLC 70**

McNeile, Herman Cyril   1888-1937
See Sapper
See also DLB 77

McNickle, (William) D'Arcy
1904-1977 . . . . **CLC 89**
See also CA 9-12R; 85-88; CANR 5, 45;
DAM MULT; NNAL; SATA-Obit 22

McPhee, John (Angus)   1931- . . . . . . **CLC 36**
See also BEST 90:1; CA 65-68; CANR 20,
46; MTCW

McPherson, James Alan
1943- . . . . **CLC 19, 77**
See also BW 1; CA 25-28R; CAAS 17;
CANR 24; DLB 38; MTCW

McPherson, William (Alexander)
1933- . . . . **CLC 34**
See also CA 69-72; CANR 28;
INT CANR-28

Mead, Margaret   1901-1978 . . . . **CLC 37**
See also AITN 1; CA 1-4R; 81-84;
CANR 4; MTCW; SATA-Obit 20

Meaker, Marijane (Agnes)   1927-
See Kerr, M. E.
See also CA 107; CANR 37; INT 107;
JRDA; MAICYA; MTCW; SATA 20, 61

Medoff, Mark (Howard)   1940- . . . **CLC 6, 23**
See also AITN 1; CA 53-56; CANR 5;
DAM DRAM; DLB 7; INT CANR-5

Medvedev, P. N.
See Bakhtin, Mikhail Mikhailovich

Meged, Aharon
See Megged, Aharon

Meged, Aron
See Megged, Aharon

Megged, Aharon   1920- . . . . **CLC 9**
See also CA 49-52; CAAS 13; CANR 1

Mehta, Ved (Parkash)   1934- . . . . **CLC 37**
See also CA 1-4R; CANR 2, 23; MTCW

Melanter
See Blackmore, R(ichard) D(oddridge)

Melikow, Loris
See Hofmannsthal, Hugo von

Melmoth, Sebastian
See Wilde, Oscar (Fingal O'Flahertie Wills)

Meltzer, Milton   1915- . . . . **CLC 26**
See also AAYA 8; CA 13-16R; CANR 38;
CLR 13; DLB 61; JRDA; MAICYA;
SAAS 1; SATA 1, 50, 80

Melville, Herman
1819-1891 . . . . . **NCLC 3, 12, 29, 45, 49;
DA; DAB; DAC; SSC 1, 17; WLC**
See also CDALB 1640-1865; DAM MST,
NOV; DLB 3, 74; SATA 59

Menander
c. 342B.C.-c. 292B.C. . . . . **CMLC 9; DC 3**
See also DAM DRAM

Mencken, H(enry) L(ouis)
1880-1956 . . . . **TCLC 13**
See also CA 105; 125; CDALB 1917-1929;
DLB 11, 29, 63, 137; MTCW

Mercer, David   1928-1980 . . . . **CLC 5**
See also CA 9-12R; 102; CANR 23;
DAM DRAM; DLB 13; MTCW

Merchant, Paul
See Ellison, Harlan (Jay)

Meredith, George   1828-1909 . . . **TCLC 17, 43**
See also CA 117; CDBLB 1832-1890;
DAM POET; DLB 18, 35, 57, 159

Meredith, William (Morris)
    1919- . . . . **CLC 4, 13, 22, 55**
    See also CA 9-12R; CAAS 14; CANR 6, 40;
    DAM POET; DLB 5

Merezhkovsky, Dmitry Sergeyevich
    1865-1941 . . . . **TCLC 29**

Merimee, Prosper
    1803-1870 . . . . **NCLC 6; SSC 7**
    See also DLB 119

Merkin, Daphne 1954- . . . . **CLC 44**
    See also CA 123

Merlin, Arthur
    See Blish, James (Benjamin)

Merrill, James (Ingram)
    1926-1995 . . . . **CLC 2, 3, 6, 8, 13, 18, 34,**
                                                    91
    See also CA 13-16R; 147; CANR 10, 49;
    DAM POET; DLB 5; DLBY 85;
    INT CANR-10; MTCW

Merriman, Alex
    See Silverberg, Robert

Merritt, E. B.
    See Waddington, Miriam

Merton, Thomas
    1915-1968 . . **CLC 1, 3, 11, 34, 83; PC 10**
    See also CA 5-8R; 25-28R; CANR 22;
    DLB 48; DLBY 81; MTCW

Merwin, W(illiam) S(tanley)
    1927- . . . **CLC 1, 2, 3, 5, 8, 13, 18, 45, 88**
    See also CA 13-16R; CANR 15, 51;
    DAM POET; DLB 5; INT CANR-15;
    MTCW

Metcalf, John 1938- . . . . **CLC 37**
    See also CA 113; DLB 60

Metcalf, Suzanne
    See Baum, L(yman) Frank

Mew, Charlotte (Mary)
    1870-1928 . . . . **TCLC 8**
    See also CA 105; DLB 19, 135

Mewshaw, Michael 1943- . . . . **CLC 9**
    See also CA 53-56; CANR 7, 47; DLBY 80

Meyer, June
    See Jordan, June

Meyer, Lynn
    See Slavitt, David R(ytman)

Meyer-Meyrink, Gustav 1868-1932
    See Meyrink, Gustav
    See also CA 117

Meyers, Jeffrey 1939- . . . . **CLC 39**
    See also CA 73-76; DLB 111

Meynell, Alice (Christina Gertrude Thompson)
    1847-1922 . . . . **TCLC 6**
    See also CA 104; DLB 19, 98

Meyrink, Gustav . . . . **TCLC 21**
    See also Meyer-Meyrink, Gustav
    See also DLB 81

Michaels, Leonard
    1933- . . . . **CLC 6, 25; SSC 16**
    See also CA 61-64; CANR 21; DLB 130;
    MTCW

Michaux, Henri 1899-1984 . . . . . . **CLC 8, 19**
    See also CA 85-88; 114

Michelangelo 1475-1564 . . . . **LC 12**

Michelet, Jules 1798-1874 . . . . **NCLC 31**

Michener, James A(lbert)
    1907(?)- . . . . **CLC 1, 5, 11, 29, 60**
    See also AITN 1; BEST 90:1; CA 5-8R;
    CANR 21, 45; DAM NOV, POP; DLB 6;
    MTCW

Mickiewicz, Adam 1798-1855 . . . . . **NCLC 3**

Middleton, Christopher 1926- . . . . . . **CLC 13**
    See also CA 13-16R; CANR 29; DLB 40

Middleton, Richard (Barham)
    1882-1911 . . . . **TCLC 56**
    See also DLB 156

Middleton, Stanley 1919- . . . . **CLC 7, 38**
    See also CA 25-28R; CAAS 23; CANR 21,
    46; DLB 14

Middleton, Thomas 1580-1627 . . . . **DC 5**
    See also DAM DRAM, MST; DLB 58

Migueis, Jose Rodrigues 1901- . . . . . **CLC 10**

Mikszath, Kalman 1847-1910 . . . . . **TCLC 31**

Miles, Josephine
    1911-1985 . . . . **CLC 1, 2, 14, 34, 39**
    See also CA 1-4R; 116; CANR 2;
    DAM POET; DLB 48

Militant
    See Sandburg, Carl (August)

Mill, John Stuart 1806-1873 . . . . . **NCLC 11**
    See also CDBLB 1832-1890; DLB 55

Millar, Kenneth 1915-1983 . . . . **CLC 14**
    See also Macdonald, Ross
    See also CA 9-12R; 110; CANR 16;
    DAM POP; DLB 2; DLBD 6; DLBY 83;
    MTCW

Millay, E. Vincent
    See Millay, Edna St. Vincent

Millay, Edna St. Vincent
    1892-1950 . . . . . . **TCLC 4, 49; DA; DAB;**
                                                DAC; PC 6
    See also CA 104; 130; CDALB 1917-1929;
    DAM MST, POET; DLB 45; MTCW

Miller, Arthur
    1915- . . . . **CLC 1, 2, 6, 10, 15, 26, 47, 78;**
                            DA; DAB; DAC; DC 1; WLC
    See also AAYA 15; AITN 1; CA 1-4R;
    CABS 3; CANR 2, 30;
    CDALB 1941-1968; DAM DRAM, MST;
    DLB 7; MTCW

Miller, Henry (Valentine)
    1891-1980 . . . . **CLC 1, 2, 4, 9, 14, 43, 84;**
                                    DA; DAB; DAC; WLC
    See also CA 9-12R; 97-100; CANR 33;
    CDALB 1929-1941; DAM MST, NOV;
    DLB 4, 9; DLBY 80; MTCW

Miller, Jason 1939(?)- . . . . **CLC 2**
    See also AITN 1; CA 73-76; DLB 7

Miller, Sue 1943- . . . . **CLC 44**
    See also BEST 90:3; CA 139; DAM POP;
    DLB 143

Miller, Walter M(ichael, Jr.)
    1923- . . . . **CLC 4, 30**
    See also CA 85-88; DLB 8

Millett, Kate 1934- . . . . **CLC 67**
    See also AITN 1; CA 73-76; CANR 32;
    MTCW

Millhauser, Steven 1943- . . . . **CLC 21, 54**
    See also CA 110; 111; DLB 2; INT 111

Millin, Sarah Gertrude 1889-1968 . . **CLC 49**
    See also CA 102; 93-96

Milne, A(lan) A(lexander)
    1882-1956 . . . . **TCLC 6; DAB; DAC**
    See also CA 104; 133; CLR 1, 26;
    DAM MST; DLB 10, 77, 100, 160;
    MAICYA; MTCW; YABC 1

Milner, Ron(ald) 1938- . . . . **CLC 56; BLC**
    See also AITN 1; BW 1; CA 73-76;
    CANR 24; DAM MULT; DLB 38;
    MTCW

Milosz, Czeslaw
    1911- . . . **CLC 5, 11, 22, 31, 56, 82; PC 8**
    See also CA 81-84; CANR 23, 51;
    DAM MST, POET; MTCW

Milton, John
    1608-1674 . . . . . . **LC 9; DA; DAB; DAC;**
                                                    WLC
    See also CDBLB 1660-1789; DAM MST,
    POET; DLB 131, 151

Min, Anchee 1957- . . . . **CLC 86**
    See also CA 146

Minehaha, Cornelius
    See Wedekind, (Benjamin) Frank(lin)

Miner, Valerie 1947- . . . . **CLC 40**
    See also CA 97-100

Minimo, Duca
    See D'Annunzio, Gabriele

Minot, Susan 1956- . . . . **CLC 44**
    See also CA 134

Minus, Ed 1938- . . . . **CLC 39**

Miranda, Javier
    See Bioy Casares, Adolfo

Mirbeau, Octave 1848-1917 . . . . . . **TCLC 55**
    See also DLB 123

Miro (Ferrer), Gabriel (Francisco Victor)
    1879-1930 . . . . **TCLC 5**
    See also CA 104

Mishima, Yukio
    . . . . **CLC 2, 4, 6, 9, 27; DC 1; SSC 4**
    See also Hiraoka, Kimitake

Mistral, Frederic 1830-1914 . . . . . . **TCLC 51**
    See also CA 122

Mistral, Gabriela . . . . **TCLC 2; HLC**
    See also Godoy Alcayaga, Lucila

Mistry, Rohinton 1952- . . . . . . **CLC 71; DAC**
    See also CA 141

Mitchell, Clyde
    See Ellison, Harlan (Jay); Silverberg, Robert

Mitchell, James Leslie 1901-1935
    See Gibbon, Lewis Grassic
    See also CA 104; DLB 15

Mitchell, Joni 1943- . . . . **CLC 12**
    See also CA 112

Mitchell, Margaret (Munnerlyn)
    1900-1949 . . . . **TCLC 11**
    See also CA 109; 125; DAM NOV, POP;
    DLB 9; MTCW

Mitchell, Peggy
    See Mitchell, Margaret (Munnerlyn)

Mitchell, S(ilas) Weir 1829-1914 . . **TCLC 36**

Mitchell, W(illiam) O(rmond)
1914- .... **CLC 25; DAC**
See also CA 77-80; CANR 15, 43;
DAM MST; DLB 88

Mitford, Mary Russell 1787-1855.. **NCLC 4**
See also DLB 110, 116

Mitford, Nancy 1904-1973......... **CLC 44**
See also CA 9-12R

Miyamoto, Yuriko 1899-1951 ..... **TCLC 37**

Mo, Timothy (Peter) 1950(?)- ...... **CLC 46**
See also CA 117; MTCW

Modarressi, Taghi (M.) 1931- ...... **CLC 44**
See also CA 121; 134; INT 134

Modiano, Patrick (Jean) 1945- ..... **CLC 18**
See also CA 85-88; CANR 17, 40; DLB 83

Moerck, Paal
See Roelvaag, O(le) E(dvart)

Mofolo, Thomas (Mokopu)
1875(?)-1948 .... **TCLC 22; BLC**
See also CA 121; DAM MULT

Mohr, Nicholasa 1935-...... **CLC 12; HLC**
See also AAYA 8; CA 49-52; CANR 1, 32;
CLR 22; DAM MULT; DLB 145; HW;
JRDA; SAAS 8; SATA 8

Mojtabai, A(nn) G(race)
1938- ....**CLC 5, 9, 15, 29**
See also CA 85-88

Moliere
1622-1673 ..... **LC 28; DA; DAB; DAC;**
WLC
See also DAM DRAM, MST

Molin, Charles
See Mayne, William (James Carter)

Molnar, Ferenc 1878-1952....... **TCLC 20**
See also CA 109; DAM DRAM

Momaday, N(avarre) Scott
1934- ... **CLC 2, 19, 85; DA; DAB; DAC**
See also AAYA 11; CA 25-28R; CANR 14,
34; DAM MST, MULT, NOV, POP;
DLB 143; INT CANR-14; MTCW;
NNAL; SATA 48; SATA-Brief 30

Monette, Paul 1945-1995.......... **CLC 82**
See also CA 139; 147

Monroe, Harriet 1860-1936....... **TCLC 12**
See also CA 109; DLB 54, 91

Monroe, Lyle
See Heinlein, Robert A(nson)

Montagu, Elizabeth 1917- .... **NCLC 7**
See also CA 9-12R

Montagu, Mary (Pierrepont) Wortley
1689-1762 .... **LC 9**
See also DLB 95, 101

Montagu, W. H.
See Coleridge, Samuel Taylor

Montague, John (Patrick)
1929- .... **CLC 13, 46**
See also CA 9-12R; CANR 9; DLB 40;
MTCW

Montaigne, Michel (Eyquem) de
1533-1592 ..... **LC 8; DA; DAB; DAC;**
WLC
See also DAM MST

Montale, Eugenio
1896-1981 .... **CLC 7, 9, 18; PC 13**
See also CA 17-20R; 104; CANR 30;
DLB 114; MTCW

Montesquieu, Charles-Louis de Secondat
1689-1755 .... **LC 7**

Montgomery, (Robert) Bruce 1921-1978
See Crispin, Edmund
See also CA 104

Montgomery, L(ucy) M(aud)
1874-1942 .... **TCLC 51; DAC**
See also AAYA 12; CA 108; 137; CLR 8;
DAM MST; DLB 92; JRDA; MAICYA;
YABC 1

Montgomery, Marion H., Jr. 1925- .. **CLC 7**
See also AITN 1; CA 1-4R; CANR 3, 48;
DLB 6

Montgomery, Max
See Davenport, Guy (Mattison, Jr.)

Montherlant, Henry (Milon) de
1896-1972 .... **CLC 8, 19**
See also CA 85-88; 37-40R; DAM DRAM;
DLB 72; MTCW

Monty Python
See Chapman, Graham; Cleese, John
(Marwood); Gilliam, Terry (Vance); Idle,
Eric; Jones, Terence Graham Parry; Palin,
Michael (Edward)
See also AAYA 7

Moodie, Susanna (Strickland)
1803-1885 .... **NCLC 14**
See also DLB 99

Mooney, Edward 1951-
See Mooney, Ted
See also CA 130

Mooney, Ted .... **CLC 25**
See also Mooney, Edward

Moorcock, Michael (John)
1939- .... **CLC 5, 27, 58**
See also CA 45-48; CAAS 5; CANR 2, 17,
38; DLB 14; MTCW

Moore, Brian
1921- ...... **CLC 1, 3, 5, 7, 8, 19, 32, 90;**
DAB; DAC
See also CA 1-4R; CANR 1, 25, 42;
DAM MST; MTCW

Moore, Edward
See Muir, Edwin

Moore, George Augustus
1852-1933 .... **TCLC 7; SSC 19**
See also CA 104; DLB 10, 18, 57, 135

Moore, Lorrie .... **CLC 39, 45, 68**
See also Moore, Marie Lorena

Moore, Marianne (Craig)
1887-1972 .... **CLC 1, 2, 4, 8, 10, 13, 19,**
47; DA; DAB; DAC; PC 4
See also CA 1-4R; 33-36R; CANR 3;
CDALB 1929-1941; DAM MST, POET;
DLB 45; DLBD 7; MTCW; SATA 20

Moore, Marie Lorena 1957-
See Moore, Lorrie
See also CA 116; CANR 39

Moore, Thomas 1779-1852....... **NCLC 6**
See also DLB 96, 144

Morand, Paul 1888-1976 .... **CLC 41**
See also CA 69-72; DLB 65

Morante, Elsa 1918-1985........ **CLC 8, 47**
See also CA 85-88; 117; CANR 35; MTCW

Moravia, Alberto ...... **CLC 2, 7, 11, 27, 46**
See also Pincherle, Alberto

More, Hannah 1745-1833 .... **NCLC 27**
See also DLB 107, 109, 116, 158

More, Henry 1614-1687............. **LC 9**
See also DLB 126

More, Sir Thomas 1478-1535 .... **LC 10, 32**

Moreas, Jean .... **TCLC 18**
See also Papadiamantopoulos, Johannes

Morgan, Berry 1919- .... **CLC 6**
See also CA 49-52; DLB 6

Morgan, Claire
See Highsmith, (Mary) Patricia

Morgan, Edwin (George) 1920- ..... **CLC 31**
See also CA 5-8R; CANR 3, 43; DLB 27

Morgan, (George) Frederick
1922- .... **CLC 23**
See also CA 17-20R; CANR 21

Morgan, Harriet
See Mencken, H(enry) L(ouis)

Morgan, Jane
See Cooper, James Fenimore

Morgan, Janet 1945- .... **CLC 39**
See also CA 65-68

Morgan, Lady 1776(?)-1859...... **NCLC 29**
See also DLB 116, 158

Morgan, Robin 1941-.............. **CLC 2**
See also CA 69-72; CANR 29; MTCW;
SATA 80

Morgan, Scott
See Kuttner, Henry

Morgan, Seth 1949(?)-1990 .... **CLC 65**
See also CA 132

Morgenstern, Christian
1871-1914 .... **TCLC 8**
See also CA 105

Morgenstern, S.
See Goldman, William (W.)

Moricz, Zsigmond 1879-1942 ..... **TCLC 33**

Morike, Eduard (Friedrich)
1804-1875 .... **NCLC 10**
See also DLB 133

Mori Ogai .... **TCLC 14**
See also Mori Rintaro

Mori Rintaro 1862-1922
See Mori Ogai
See also CA 110

Moritz, Karl Philipp 1756-1793 ...... **LC 2**
See also DLB 94

Morland, Peter Henry
See Faust, Frederick (Schiller)

Morren, Theophil
See Hofmannsthal, Hugo von

Morris, Bill 1952-............... **CLC 76**

Morris, Julian
See West, Morris L(anglo)

Morris, Steveland Judkins 1950(?)-
See Wonder, Stevie
See also CA 111

Morris, William 1834-1896 . . . . . . **NCLC 4**
See also CDBLB 1832-1890; DLB 18, 35,
57, 156

Morris, Wright 1910- . . . **CLC 1, 3, 7, 18, 37**
See also CA 9-12R; CANR 21; DLB 2;
DLBY 81; MTCW

Morrison, Chloe Anthony Wofford
See Morrison, Toni

Morrison, James Douglas 1943-1971
See Morrison, Jim
See also CA 73-76; CANR 40

Morrison, Jim . . . . **CLC 17**
See also Morrison, James Douglas

Morrison, Toni
1931- . . . . **CLC 4, 10, 22, 55, 81, 87;**
BLC; DA; DAB; DAC
See also AAYA 1; BW 2; CA 29-32R;
CANR 27, 42; CDALB 1968-1988;
DAM MST, MULT, NOV, POP; DLB 6,
33, 143; DLBY 81; MTCW; SATA 57

Morrison, Van 1945- . . . . **CLC 21**
See also CA 116

Mortimer, John (Clifford)
1923- . . . . **CLC 28, 43**
See also CA 13-16R; CANR 21;
CDBLB 1960 to Present; DAM DRAM,
POP; DLB 13; INT CANR-21; MTCW

Mortimer, Penelope (Ruth) 1918- . . . . **CLC 5**
See also CA 57-60; CANR 45

Morton, Anthony
See Creasey, John

Mosher, Howard Frank 1943- . . . . . . **CLC 62**
See also CA 139

Mosley, Nicholas 1923- . . . . **CLC 43, 70**
See also CA 69-72; CANR 41; DLB 14

Moss, Howard
1922-1987 . . . . **CLC 7, 14, 45, 50**
See also CA 1-4R; 123; CANR 1, 44;
DAM POET; DLB 5

Mossgiel, Rab
See Burns, Robert

Motion, Andrew (Peter) 1952- . . . . . . **CLC 47**
See also CA 146; DLB 40

Motley, Willard (Francis)
1909-1965 . . . . **CLC 18**
See also BW 1; CA 117; 106; DLB 76, 143

Motoori, Norinaga 1730-1801 . . . . **NCLC 45**

Mott, Michael (Charles Alston)
1930- . . . . **CLC 15, 34**
See also CA 5-8R; CAAS 7; CANR 7, 29

Mountain Wolf Woman
1884-1960 . . . . **CLC 92**
See also CA 144; NNAL

Moure, Erin 1955- . . . . **CLC 88**
See also CA 113; DLB 60

Mowat, Farley (McGill)
1921- . . . . **CLC 26; DAC**
See also AAYA 1; CA 1-4R; CANR 4, 24,
42; CLR 20; DAM MST; DLB 68;
INT CANAR-24; JRDA; MAICYA;
MTCW; SATA 3, 55

Moyers, Bill 1934- . . . . **CLC 74**
See also AITN 2; CA 61-64; CANR 31

Mphahlele, Es'kia
See Mphahlele, Ezekiel
See also DLB 125

Mphahlele, Ezekiel 1919- . . . . . **CLC 25; BLC**
See also Mphahlele, Es'kia
See also BW 2; CA 81-84; CANR 26;
DAM MULT

Mqhayi, S(amuel) E(dward) K(rune Loliwe)
1875-1945 . . . . **TCLC 25; BLC**
See also DAM MULT

Mr. Martin
See Burroughs, William S(eward)

Mrozek, Slawomir 1930- . . . . **CLC 3, 13**
See also CA 13-16R; CAAS 10; CANR 29;
MTCW

Mrs. Belloc-Lowndes
See Lowndes, Marie Adelaide (Belloc)

Mtwa, Percy (?)- . . . . **CLC 47**

Mueller, Lisel 1924- . . . . **CLC 13, 51**
See also CA 93-96; DLB 105

Muir, Edwin 1887-1959 . . . . **TCLC 2**
See also CA 104; DLB 20, 100

Muir, John 1838-1914 . . . . **TCLC 28**

Mujica Lainez, Manuel
1910-1984 . . . . **CLC 31**
See also Lainez, Manuel Mujica
See also CA 81-84; 112; CANR 32; HW

Mukherjee, Bharati 1940- . . . . **CLC 53**
See also BEST 89:2; CA 107; CANR 45;
DAM NOV; DLB 60; MTCW

Muldoon, Paul 1951- . . . . **CLC 32, 72**
See also CA 113; 129; DAM POET;
DLB 40; INT 129

Mulisch, Harry 1927- . . . . **CLC 42**
See also CA 9-12R; CANR 6, 26

Mull, Martin 1943- . . . . **CLC 17**
See also CA 105

Mulock, Dinah Maria
See Craik, Dinah Maria (Mulock)

Munford, Robert 1737(?)-1783 . . . . **LC 5**
See also DLB 31

Mungo, Raymond 1946- . . . . **CLC 72**
See also CA 49-52; CANR 2

Munro, Alice
1931- . . . **CLC 6, 10, 19, 50; DAC; SSC 3**
See also AITN 2; CA 33-36R; CANR 33;
DAM MST, NOV; DLB 53; MTCW;
SATA 29

Munro, H(ector) H(ugh) 1870-1916
See Saki
See also CA 104; 130; CDBLB 1890-1914;
DA; DAB; DAC; DAM MST, NOV;
DLB 34, 162; MTCW; WLC

Murasaki, Lady . . . . **CMLC 1**

Murdoch, (Jean) Iris
1919- . . . . . . **CLC 1, 2, 3, 4, 6, 8, 11, 15,**
22, 31, 51; DAB; DAC
See also CA 13-16R; CANR 8, 43;
CDBLB 1960 to Present; DAM MST,
NOV; DLB 14; INT CANR-8; MTCW

Murnau, Friedrich Wilhelm
See Plumpe, Friedrich Wilhelm

Murphy, Richard 1927- . . . . **CLC 41**
See also CA 29-32R; DLB 40

Murphy, Sylvia 1937- . . . . **CLC 34**
See also CA 121

Murphy, Thomas (Bernard) 1935- . . . **CLC 51**
See also CA 101

Murray, Albert L. 1916- . . . . **CLC 73**
See also BW 2; CA 49-52; CANR 26;
DLB 38

Murray, Les(lie) A(llan) 1938- . . . . . **CLC 40**
See also CA 21-24R; CANR 11, 27;
DAM POET

Murry, J. Middleton
See Murry, John Middleton

Murry, John Middleton
1889-1957 . . . . **TCLC 16**
See also CA 118; DLB 149

Musgrave, Susan 1951- . . . . **CLC 13, 54**
See also CA 69-72; CANR 45

Musil, Robert (Edler von)
1880-1942 . . . . **TCLC 12; SSC 18**
See also CA 109; DLB 81, 124

Muske, Carol 1945- . . . . **CLC 90**
See also Muske-Dukes, Carol (Anne)

Muske-Dukes, Carol (Anne) 1945-
See Muske, Carol
See also CA 65-68; CANR 32

Musset, (Louis Charles) Alfred de
1810-1857 . . . . **NCLC 7**

My Brother's Brother
See Chekhov, Anton (Pavlovich)

Myers, L. H. 1881-1944 . . . . **TCLC 59**
See also DLB 15

Myers, Walter Dean 1937- . . . **CLC 35; BLC**
See also AAYA 4; BW 2; CA 33-36R;
CANR 20, 42; CLR 4, 16, 35;
DAM MULT, NOV; DLB 33;
INT CANR-20; JRDA; MAICYA;
SAAS 2; SATA 41, 71; SATA-Brief 27

Myers, Walter M.
See Myers, Walter Dean

Myles, Symon
See Follett, Ken(neth Martin)

Nabokov, Vladimir (Vladimirovich)
1899-1977 . . . . . **CLC 1, 2, 3, 6, 8, 11, 15,**
23, 44, 46, 64; DA; DAB; DAC; SSC 11;
WLC
See also CA 5-8R; 69-72; CANR 20;
CDALB 1941-1968; DAM MST, NOV;
DLB 2; DLBD 3; DLBY 80, 91; MTCW

Nagai Kafu . . . . **TCLC 51**
See also Nagai Sokichi

Nagai Sokichi 1879-1959
See Nagai Kafu
See also CA 117

Nagy, Laszlo 1925-1978 . . . . **CLC 7**
See also CA 129; 112

Naipaul, Shiva(dhar Srinivasa)
1945-1985 . . . . **CLC 32, 39**
See also CA 110; 112; 116; CANR 33;
DAM NOV; DLB 157; DLBY 85;
MTCW

Naipaul, V(idiadhar) S(urajprasad)
1932- .... **CLC 4, 7, 9, 13, 18, 37; DAB;**
DAC
See also CA 1-4R; CANR 1, 33, 51;
CDBLB 1960 to Present; DAM MST,
NOV; DLB 125; DLBY 85; MTCW

Nakos, Lilika 1899(?)- .... **CLC 29**

Narayan, R(asipuram) K(rishnaswami)
1906- .... **CLC 7, 28, 47**
See also CA 81-84; CANR 33; DAM NOV;
MTCW; SATA 62

Nash, (Fredric) Ogden 1902-1971 .. **CLC 23**
See also CA 13-14; 29-32R; CANR 34;
CAP 1; DAM POET; DLB 11;
MAICYA; MTCW; SATA 2, 46

Nathan, Daniel
See Dannay, Frederic

Nathan, George Jean 1882-1958 ... **TCLC 18**
See also Hatteras, Owen
See also CA 114; DLB 137

Natsume, Kinnosuke 1867-1916
See Natsume, Soseki
See also CA 104

Natsume, Soseki .... **TCLC 2, 10**
See also Natsume, Kinnosuke

Natti, (Mary) Lee 1919-
See Kingman, Lee
See also CA 5-8R; CANR 2

Naylor, Gloria
1950- ..... **CLC 28, 52; BLC; DA; DAC**
See also AAYA 6; BW 2; CA 107;
CANR 27, 51; DAM MST, MULT,
NOV, POP; MTCW

Neihardt, John Gneisenau
1881-1973 .... **CLC 32**
See also CA 13-14; CAP 1; DLB 9, 54

Nekrasov, Nikolai Alekseevich
1821-1878 .... **NCLC 11**

Nelligan, Emile 1879-1941 .... **TCLC 14**
See also CA 114; DLB 92

Nelson, Willie 1933- .... **CLC 17**
See also CA 107

Nemerov, Howard (Stanley)
1920-1991 .... **CLC 2, 6, 9, 36**
See also CA 1-4R; 134; CABS 2; CANR 1,
27; DAM POET; DLB 5, 6; DLBY 83;
INT CANR-27; MTCW

Neruda, Pablo
1904-1973 ..... **CLC 1, 2, 5, 7, 9, 28, 62;**
DA; DAB; DAC; HLC; PC 4; WLC
See also CA 19-20; 45-48; CAP 2;
DAM MST, MULT, POET; HW; MTCW

Nerval, Gerard de
1808-1855 ..... **NCLC 1; PC 13; SSC 18**

Nervo, (Jose) Amado (Ruiz de)
1870-1919 .... **TCLC 11**
See also CA 109; 131; HW

Nessi, Pio Baroja y
See Baroja (y Nessi), Pio

Nestroy, Johann 1801-1862 ...... **NCLC 42**
See also DLB 133

Neufeld, John (Arthur) 1938- ...... **CLC 17**
See also AAYA 11; CA 25-28R; CANR 11,
37; MAICYA; SAAS 3; SATA 6, 81

Neville, Emily Cheney 1919- .... **CLC 12**
See also CA 5-8R; CANR 3, 37; JRDA;
MAICYA; SAAS 2; SATA 1

Newbound, Bernard Slade 1930-
See Slade, Bernard
See also CA 81-84; CANR 49;
DAM DRAM

Newby, P(ercy) H(oward)
1918- .... **CLC 2, 13**
See also CA 5-8R; CANR 32; DAM NOV;
DLB 15; MTCW

Newlove, Donald 1928- .... **CLC 6**
See also CA 29-32R; CANR 25

Newlove, John (Herbert) 1938- ..... **CLC 14**
See also CA 21-24R; CANR 9, 25

Newman, Charles 1938- .... **CLC 2, 8**
See also CA 21-24R

Newman, Edwin (Harold) 1919- .... **CLC 14**
See also AITN 1; CA 69-72; CANR 5

Newman, John Henry
1801-1890 .... **NCLC 38**
See also DLB 18, 32, 55

Newton, Suzanne 1936- .... **CLC 35**
See also CA 41-44R; CANR 14; JRDA;
SATA 5, 77

Nexo, Martin Andersen
1869-1954 .... **TCLC 43**

Nezval, Vitezslav 1900-1958 ...... **TCLC 44**
See also CA 123

Ng, Fae Myenne 1957(?)- .... **CLC 81**
See also CA 146

Ngema, Mbongeni 1955- .... **CLC 57**
See also BW 2; CA 143

Ngugi, James T(hiong'o) .... **CLC 3, 7, 13**
See also Ngugi wa Thiong'o

Ngugi wa Thiong'o 1938- ..... **CLC 36; BLC**
See also Ngugi, James T(hiong'o)
See also BW 2; CA 81-84; CANR 27;
DAM MULT, NOV; DLB 125; MTCW

Nichol, B(arrie) P(hillip)
1944-1988 .... **CLC 18**
See also CA 53-56; DLB 53; SATA 66

Nichols, John (Treadwell) 1940- .... **CLC 38**
See also CA 9-12R; CAAS 2; CANR 6;
DLBY 82

Nichols, Leigh
See Koontz, Dean R(ay)

Nichols, Peter (Richard)
1927- .... **CLC 5, 36, 65**
See also CA 104; CANR 33; DLB 13;
MTCW

Nicolas, F. R. E.
See Freeling, Nicolas

Niedecker, Lorine 1903-1970 .... **CLC 10, 42**
See also CA 25-28; CAP 2; DAM POET;
DLB 48

Nietzsche, Friedrich (Wilhelm)
1844-1900 .... **TCLC 10, 18, 55**
See also CA 107; 121; DLB 129

Nievo, Ippolito 1831-1861 .... **NCLC 22**

Nightingale, Anne Redmon 1943-
See Redmon, Anne
See also CA 103

Nik. T. O.
See Annensky, Innokenty Fyodorovich

Nin, Anais
1903-1977 ...... **CLC 1, 4, 8, 11, 14, 60;**
SSC 10
See also AITN 2; CA 13-16R; 69-72;
CANR 22; DAM NOV, POP; DLB 2, 4,
152; MTCW

Nishiwaki, Junzaburo 1894-1982 .... **PC 15**
See also CA 107

Nissenson, Hugh 1933- .... **CLC 4, 9**
See also CA 17-20R; CANR 27; DLB 28

Niven, Larry .... **CLC 8**
See also Niven, Laurence Van Cott
See also DLB 8

Niven, Laurence Van Cott 1938-
See Niven, Larry
See also CA 21-24R; CAAS 12; CANR 14,
44; DAM POP; MTCW

Nixon, Agnes Eckhardt 1927- ...... **CLC 21**
See also CA 110

Nizan, Paul 1905-1940 .... **TCLC 40**
See also DLB 72

Nkosi, Lewis 1936- .... **CLC 45; BLC**
See also BW 1; CA 65-68; CANR 27;
DAM MULT; DLB 157

Nodier, (Jean) Charles (Emmanuel)
1780-1844 .... **NCLC 19**
See also DLB 119

Nolan, Christopher 1965- .... **CLC 58**
See also CA 111

Noon, Jeff 1957- .... **CLC 91**
See also CA 148

Norden, Charles
See Durrell, Lawrence (George)

Nordhoff, Charles (Bernard)
1887-1947 .... **TCLC 23**
See also CA 108; DLB 9; SATA 23

Norfolk, Lawrence 1963- .... **CLC 76**
See also CA 144

Norman, Marsha 1947- .... **CLC 28**
See also CA 105; CABS 3; CANR 41;
DAM DRAM; DLBY 84

Norris, Benjamin Franklin, Jr.
1870-1902 .... **TCLC 24**
See also Norris, Frank
See also CA 110

Norris, Frank
See Norris, Benjamin Franklin, Jr.
See also CDALB 1865-1917; DLB 12, 71

Norris, Leslie 1921- .... **CLC 14**
See also CA 11-12; CANR 14; CAP 1;
DLB 27

North, Andrew
See Norton, Andre

North, Anthony
See Koontz, Dean R(ay)

North, Captain George
See Stevenson, Robert Louis (Balfour)

North, Milou
See Erdrich, Louise

Northrup, B. A.
See Hubbard, L(afayette) Ron(ald)

North Staffs
See Hulme, T(homas) E(rnest)

Norton, Alice Mary
See Norton, Andre
See also MAICYA; SATA 1, 43

Norton, Andre 1912- . . . . **CLC 12**
See also Norton, Alice Mary
See also AAYA 14; CA 1-4R; CANR 2, 31;
DLB 8, 52; JRDA; MTCW

Norton, Caroline 1808-1877. . . . . . **NCLC 47**
See also DLB 21, 159

Norway, Nevil Shute 1899-1960
See Shute, Nevil
See also CA 102; 93-96

Norwid, Cyprian Kamil
1821-1883 . . . . **NCLC 17**

Nosille, Nabrah
See Ellison, Harlan (Jay)

Nossack, Hans Erich 1901-1978 . . . . . **CLC 6**
See also CA 93-96; 85-88; DLB 69

Nostradamus 1503-1566. . . . . **LC 27**

Nosu, Chuji
See Ozu, Yasujiro

Notenburg, Eleanora (Genrikhovna) von
See Guro, Elena

Nova, Craig 1945-. . . . . **CLC 7, 31**
See also CA 45-48; CANR 2

Novak, Joseph
See Kosinski, Jerzy (Nikodem)

Novalis 1772-1801 . . . . **NCLC 13**
See also DLB 90

Nowlan, Alden (Albert)
1933-1983 . . . . **CLC 15; DAC**
See also CA 9-12R; CANR 5; DAM MST;
DLB 53

Noyes, Alfred 1880-1958 . . . . **TCLC 7**
See also CA 104; DLB 20

Nunn, Kem 19(?)- . . . . **CLC 34**

Nye, Robert 1939- . . . . **CLC 13, 42**
See also CA 33-36R; CANR 29;
DAM NOV; DLB 14; MTCW; SATA 6

Nyro, Laura 1947- . . . . **CLC 17**

Oates, Joyce Carol
1938- . . . . . . **CLC 1, 2, 3, 6, 9, 11, 15, 19,
33, 52; DA; DAB; DAC; SSC 6; WLC**
See also AAYA 15; AITN 1; BEST 89:2;
CA 5-8R; CANR 25, 45;
CDALB 1968-1988; DAM MST, NOV,
POP; DLB 2, 5, 130; DLBY 81;
INT CANR-25; MTCW

O'Brien, Darcy 1939- . . . . **CLC 11**
See also CA 21-24R; CANR 8

O'Brien, E. G.
See Clarke, Arthur C(harles)

O'Brien, Edna
1936- . . . **CLC 3, 5, 8, 13, 36, 65; SSC 10**
See also CA 1-4R; CANR 6, 41;
CDBLB 1960 to Present; DAM NOV;
DLB 14; MTCW

O'Brien, Fitz-James 1828-1862. . . **NCLC 21**
See also DLB 74

O'Brien, Flann. . . . . . . **CLC 1, 4, 5, 7, 10, 47**
See also O Nuallain, Brian

O'Brien, Richard 1942- . . . . **CLC 17**
See also CA 124

O'Brien, Tim 1946-. . . . . **CLC 7, 19, 40**
See also AAYA 16; CA 85-88; CANR 40;
DAM POP; DLB 152; DLBD 9;
DLBY 80

Obstfelder, Sigbjoern 1866-1900. . . **TCLC 23**
See also CA 123

O'Casey, Sean
1880-1964 . . . . . . **CLC 1, 5, 9, 11, 15, 88;
DAB; DAC**
See also CA 89-92; CDBLB 1914-1945;
DAM DRAM, MST; DLB 10; MTCW

O'Cathasaigh, Sean
See O'Casey, Sean

Ochs, Phil 1940-1976. . . . . **CLC 17**
See also CA 65-68

O'Connor, Edwin (Greene)
1918-1968 . . . . **CLC 14**
See also CA 93-96; 25-28R

O'Connor, (Mary) Flannery
1925-1964 . . . . **CLC 1, 2, 3, 6, 10, 13, 15,
21, 66; DA; DAB; DAC; SSC 1; WLC**
See also AAYA 7; CA 1-4R; CANR 3, 41;
CDALB 1941-1968; DAM MST, NOV;
DLB 2, 152; DLBD 12; DLBY 80;
MTCW

O'Connor, Frank. . . . . **CLC 23; SSC 5**
See also O'Donovan, Michael John
See also DLB 162

O'Dell, Scott 1898-1989. . . . . **CLC 30**
See also AAYA 3; CA 61-64; 129;
CANR 12, 30; CLR 1, 16; DLB 52;
JRDA; MAICYA; SATA 12, 60

Odets, Clifford
1906-1963 . . . . **CLC 2, 28; DC 6**
See also CA 85-88; DAM DRAM; DLB 7,
26; MTCW

O'Doherty, Brian 1934- . . . . **CLC 76**
See also CA 105

O'Donnell, K. M.
See Malzberg, Barry N(athaniel)

O'Donnell, Lawrence
See Kuttner, Henry

O'Donovan, Michael John
1903-1966 . . . . **CLC 14**
See also O'Connor, Frank
See also CA 93-96

Oe, Kenzaburo
1935- . . . . **CLC 10, 36, 86; SSC 20**
See also CA 97-100; CANR 36, 50;
DAM NOV; DLBY 94; MTCW

O'Faolain, Julia 1932- . . . . **CLC 6, 19, 47**
See also CA 81-84; CAAS 2; CANR 12;
DLB 14; MTCW

O'Faolain, Sean
1900-1991 . . . . **CLC 1, 7, 14, 32, 70;
SSC 13**
See also CA 61-64; 134; CANR 12;
DLB 15, 162; MTCW

O'Flaherty, Liam
1896-1984 . . . . **CLC 5, 34; SSC 6**
See also CA 101; 113; CANR 35; DLB 36,
162; DLBY 84; MTCW

Ogilvy, Gavin
See Barrie, J(ames) M(atthew)

O'Grady, Standish James
1846-1928 . . . . **TCLC 5**
See also CA 104

O'Grady, Timothy 1951- . . . . **CLC 59**
See also CA 138

O'Hara, Frank
1926-1966 . . . . **CLC 2, 5, 13, 78**
See also CA 9-12R; 25-28R; CANR 33;
DAM POET; DLB 5, 16; MTCW

O'Hara, John (Henry)
1905-1970 . . . . **CLC 1, 2, 3, 6, 11, 42;
SSC 15**
See also CA 5-8R; 25-28R; CANR 31;
CDALB 1929-1941; DAM NOV; DLB 9,
86; DLBD 2; MTCW

O Hehir, Diana 1922- . . . . **CLC 41**
See also CA 93-96

Okigbo, Christopher (Ifenayichukwu)
1932-1967 . . . . . **CLC 25, 84; BLC; PC 7**
See also BW 1; CA 77-80; DAM MULT,
POET; DLB 125; MTCW

Okri, Ben 1959- . . . . **CLC 87**
See also BW 2; CA 130; 138; DLB 157;
INT 138

Olds, Sharon 1942-. . . . . **CLC 32, 39, 85**
See also CA 101; CANR 18, 41;
DAM POET; DLB 120

Oldstyle, Jonathan
See Irving, Washington

Olesha, Yuri (Karlovich)
1899-1960 . . . . **CLC 8**
See also CA 85-88

Oliphant, Laurence
1829(?)-1888 . . . . **NCLC 47**
See also DLB 18

Oliphant, Margaret (Oliphant Wilson)
1828-1897 . . . . **NCLC 11**
See also DLB 18, 159

Oliver, Mary 1935-. . . . . **CLC 19, 34**
See also CA 21-24R; CANR 9, 43; DLB 5

Olivier, Laurence (Kerr)
1907-1989 . . . . **CLC 20**
See also CA 111; 150; 129

Olsen, Tillie
1913- . . . . . **CLC 4, 13; DA; DAB; DAC;
SSC 11**
See also CA 1-4R; CANR 1, 43;
DAM MST; DLB 28; DLBY 80; MTCW

Olson, Charles (John)
1910-1970 . . . . . **CLC 1, 2, 5, 6, 9, 11, 29**
See also CA 13-16; 25-28R; CABS 2;
CANR 35; CAP 1; DAM POET; DLB 5,
16; MTCW

Olson, Toby 1937- . . . . **CLC 28**
See also CA 65-68; CANR 9, 31

Olyesha, Yuri
See Olesha, Yuri (Karlovich)

Ondaatje, (Philip) Michael
1943- . . . **CLC 14, 29, 51, 76; DAB; DAC**
See also CA 77-80; CANR 42; DAM MST;
DLB 60

Oneal, Elizabeth 1934-
See Oneal, Zibby
See also CA 106; CANR 28; MAICYA;
SATA 30, 82

Oneal, Zibby . . . . CLC 30
  See also Oneal, Elizabeth
  See also AAYA 5; CLR 13; JRDA

O'Neill, Eugene (Gladstone)
  1888-1953 . . . . . . TCLC 1, 6, 27, 49; DA;
                               DAB; DAC; WLC
  See also AITN 1; CA 110; 132;
    CDALB 1929-1941; DAM DRAM, MST;
    DLB 7; MTCW

Onetti, Juan Carlos 1909-1994 . . . CLC 7, 10
  See also CA 85-88; 145; CANR 32;
    DAM MULT, NOV; DLB 113; HW;
    MTCW

O Nuallain, Brian 1911-1966
  See O'Brien, Flann
  See also CA 21-22; 25-28R; CAP 2

Oppen, George 1908-1984 . . . . CLC 7, 13, 34
  See also CA 13-16R; 113; CANR 8; DLB 5

Oppenheim, E(dward) Phillips
  1866-1946 . . . . TCLC 45
  See also CA 111; DLB 70

Orlovitz, Gil 1918-1973 . . . . CLC 22
  See also CA 77-80; 45-48; DLB 2, 5

Orris
  See Ingelow, Jean

Ortega y Gasset, Jose
  1883-1955 . . . . TCLC 9; HLC
  See also CA 106; 130; DAM MULT; HW;
    MTCW

Ortese, Anna Maria 1914- . . . . CLC 89

Ortiz, Simon J(oseph) 1941- . . . . CLC 45
  See also CA 134; DAM MULT, POET;
    DLB 120; NNAL

Orton, Joe . . . . CLC 4, 13, 43; DC 3
  See also Orton, John Kingsley
  See also CDBLB 1960 to Present; DLB 13

Orton, John Kingsley 1933-1967
  See Orton, Joe
  See also CA 85-88; CANR 35;
    DAM DRAM; MTCW

Orwell, George
  . . . . . TCLC 2, 6, 15, 31, 51; DAB; WLC
  See also Blair, Eric (Arthur)
  See also CDBLB 1945-1960; DLB 15, 98

Osborne, David
  See Silverberg, Robert

Osborne, George
  See Silverberg, Robert

Osborne, John (James)
  1929-1994 . . . . . CLC 1, 2, 5, 11, 45; DA;
                          DAB; DAC; WLC
  See also CA 13-16R; 147; CANR 21;
    CDBLB 1945-1960; DAM DRAM, MST;
    DLB 13; MTCW

Osborne, Lawrence 1958- . . . . CLC 50

Oshima, Nagisa 1932- . . . . CLC 20
  See also CA 116; 121

Oskison, John Milton
  1874-1947 . . . . TCLC 35
  See also CA 144; DAM MULT; NNAL

Ossoli, Sarah Margaret (Fuller marchesa d')
  1810-1850
  See Fuller, Margaret
  See also SATA 25

Ostrovsky, Alexander
  1823-1886 . . . . NCLC 30

Otero, Blas de 1916-1979 . . . . CLC 11
  See also CA 89-92; DLB 134

Otto, Whitney 1955- . . . . CLC 70
  See also CA 140

Ouida . . . . TCLC 43
  See also De La Ramee, (Marie) Louise
  See also DLB 18, 156

Ousmane, Sembene 1923- . . . . CLC 66; BLC
  See also BW 1; CA 117; 125; MTCW

Ovid 43B.C.-18(?) . . . . CMLC 7; PC 2
  See also DAM POET

Owen, Hugh
  See Faust, Frederick (Schiller)

Owen, Wilfred (Edward Salter)
  1893-1918 . . . . . . TCLC 5, 27; DA; DAB;
                               DAC; WLC
  See also CA 104; 141; CDBLB 1914-1945;
    DAM MST, POET; DLB 20

Owens, Rochelle 1936- . . . . CLC 8
  See also CA 17-20R; CAAS 2; CANR 39

Oz, Amos 1939- . . . CLC 5, 8, 11, 27, 33, 54
  See also CA 53-56; CANR 27, 47;
    DAM NOV; MTCW

Ozick, Cynthia
  1928- . . . . CLC 3, 7, 28, 62; SSC 15
  See also BEST 90:1; CA 17-20R; CANR 23;
    DAM NOV, POP; DLB 28, 152;
    DLBY 82; INT CANR-23; MTCW

Ozu, Yasujiro 1903-1963 . . . . CLC 16
  See also CA 112

Pacheco, C.
  See Pessoa, Fernando (Antonio Nogueira)

Pa Chin . . . . CLC 18
  See also Li Fei-kan

Pack, Robert 1929- . . . . CLC 13
  See also CA 1-4R; CANR 3, 44; DLB 5

Padgett, Lewis
  See Kuttner, Henry

Padilla (Lorenzo), Heberto 1932- . . . CLC 38
  See also AITN 1; CA 123; 131; HW

Page, Jimmy 1944- . . . . CLC 12

Page, Louise 1955- . . . . CLC 40
  See also CA 140

Page, P(atricia) K(athleen)
  1916- . . . . CLC 7, 18; DAC; PC 12
  See also CA 53-56; CANR 4, 22;
    DAM MST; DLB 68; MTCW

Paget, Violet 1856-1935
  See Lee, Vernon
  See also CA 104

Paget-Lowe, Henry
  See Lovecraft, H(oward) P(hillips)

Paglia, Camille (Anna) 1947- . . . . . . CLC 68
  See also CA 140

Paige, Richard
  See Koontz, Dean R(ay)

Pakenham, Antonia
  See Fraser, (Lady) Antonia (Pakenham)

Palamas, Kostes 1859-1943 . . . . TCLC 5
  See also CA 105

Palazzeschi, Aldo 1885-1974 . . . . CLC 11
  See also CA 89-92; 53-56; DLB 114

Paley, Grace 1922- . . . . CLC 4, 6, 37; SSC 8
  See also CA 25-28R; CANR 13, 46;
    DAM POP; DLB 28; INT CANR-13;
    MTCW

Palin, Michael (Edward) 1943- . . . . . CLC 21
  See also Monty Python
  See also CA 107; CANR 35; SATA 67

Palliser, Charles 1947- . . . . CLC 65
  See also CA 136

Palma, Ricardo 1833-1919 . . . . TCLC 29

Pancake, Breece Dexter 1952-1979
  See Pancake, Breece D'J
  See also CA 123; 109

Pancake, Breece D'J . . . . CLC 29
  See also Pancake, Breece Dexter
  See also DLB 130

Panko, Rudy
  See Gogol, Nikolai (Vasilyevich)

Papadiamantis, Alexandros
  1851-1911 . . . . TCLC 29

Papadiamantopoulos, Johannes 1856-1910
  See Moreas, Jean
  See also CA 117

Papini, Giovanni 1881-1956 . . . . TCLC 22
  See also CA 121

Paracelsus 1493-1541 . . . . LC 14

Parasol, Peter
  See Stevens, Wallace

Parfenie, Maria
  See Codrescu, Andrei

Parini, Jay (Lee) 1948- . . . . CLC 54
  See also CA 97-100; CAAS 16; CANR 32

Park, Jordan
  See Kornbluth, C(yril) M.; Pohl, Frederik

Parker, Bert
  See Ellison, Harlan (Jay)

Parker, Dorothy (Rothschild)
  1893-1967 . . . . CLC 15, 68; SSC 2
  See also CA 19-20; 25-28R; CAP 2;
    DAM POET; DLB 11, 45, 86; MTCW

Parker, Robert B(rown) 1932- . . . . . . CLC 27
  See also BEST 89:4; CA 49-52; CANR 1,
    26; DAM NOV, POP; INT CANR-26;
    MTCW

Parkin, Frank 1940- . . . . CLC 43
  See also CA 147

Parkman, Francis, Jr.
  1823-1893 . . . . NCLC 12
  See also DLB 1, 30

Parks, Gordon (Alexander Buchanan)
  1912- . . . . CLC 1, 16; BLC
  See also AITN 2; BW 2; CA 41-44R;
    CANR 26; DAM MULT; DLB 33;
    SATA 8

Parnell, Thomas 1679-1718 . . . . LC 3
  See also DLB 94

Parra, Nicanor 1914- . . . . CLC 2; HLC
  See also CA 85-88; CANR 32;
    DAM MULT; HW; MTCW

Parrish, Mary Frances
  See Fisher, M(ary) F(rances) K(ennedy)

Parson
  See Coleridge, Samuel Taylor

Parson Lot
See Kingsley, Charles

Partridge, Anthony
See Oppenheim, E(dward) Phillips

Pascoli, Giovanni 1855-1912 . . . . . . **TCLC 45**

Pasolini, Pier Paolo
1922-1975 . . . . **CLC 20, 37**
See also CA 93-96; 61-64; DLB 128;
MTCW

Pasquini
See Silone, Ignazio

Pastan, Linda (Olenik) 1932- . . . . . . **CLC 27**
See also CA 61-64; CANR 18, 40;
DAM POET; DLB 5

Pasternak, Boris (Leonidovich)
1890-1960 . . . . . . **CLC 7, 10, 18, 63; DA;**
DAB; DAC; PC 6; WLC
See also CA 127; 116; DAM MST, NOV,
POET; MTCW

Patchen, Kenneth 1911-1972 . . . **CLC 1, 2, 18**
See also CA 1-4R; 33-36R; CANR 3, 35;
DAM POET; DLB 16, 48; MTCW

Pater, Walter (Horatio)
1839-1894 . . . . **NCLC 7**
See also CDBLB 1832-1890; DLB 57, 156

Paterson, A(ndrew) B(arton)
1864-1941 . . . . **TCLC 32**

Paterson, Katherine (Womeldorf)
1932- . . . . **CLC 12, 30**
See also AAYA 1; CA 21-24R; CANR 28;
CLR 7; DLB 52; JRDA; MAICYA;
MTCW; SATA 13, 53

Patmore, Coventry Kersey Dighton
1823-1896 . . . . **NCLC 9**
See also DLB 35, 98

Paton, Alan (Stewart)
1903-1988 . . . . . . **CLC 4, 10, 25, 55; DA;**
DAB; DAC; WLC
See also CA 13-16; 125; CANR 22; CAP 1;
DAM MST, NOV; MTCW; SATA 11;
SATA-Obit 56

Paton Walsh, Gillian 1937-
See Walsh, Jill Paton
See also CANR 38; JRDA; MAICYA;
SAAS 3; SATA 4, 72

Paulding, James Kirke 1778-1860 . . **NCLC 2**
See also DLB 3, 59, 74

Paulin, Thomas Neilson 1949-
See Paulin, Tom
See also CA 123; 128

Paulin, Tom . . . . **CLC 37**
See also Paulin, Thomas Neilson
See also DLB 40

Paustovsky, Konstantin (Georgievich)
1892-1968 . . . . **CLC 40**
See also CA 93-96; 25-28R

Pavese, Cesare
1908-1950 . . . . . **TCLC 3; PC 13; SSC 19**
See also CA 104; DLB 128

Pavic, Milorad 1929- . . . . **CLC 60**
See also CA 136

Payne, Alan
See Jakes, John (William)

Paz, Gil
See Lugones, Leopoldo

Paz, Octavio
1914- . . . . . . **CLC 3, 4, 6, 10, 19, 51, 65;**
DA; DAB; DAC; HLC; PC 1; WLC
See also CA 73-76; CANR 32; DAM MST,
MULT, POET; DLBY 90; HW; MTCW

Peacock, Molly 1947- . . . . **CLC 60**
See also CA 103; CAAS 21; DLB 120

Peacock, Thomas Love
1785-1866 . . . . **NCLC 22**
See also DLB 96, 116

Peake, Mervyn 1911-1968 . . . . **CLC 7, 54**
See also CA 5-8R; 25-28R; CANR 3;
DLB 15, 160; MTCW; SATA 23

Pearce, Philippa . . . . **CLC 21**
See also Christie, (Ann) Philippa
See also CLR 9; DLB 161; MAICYA;
SATA 1, 67

Pearl, Eric
See Elman, Richard

Pearson, T(homas) R(eid) 1956- . . . . **CLC 39**
See also CA 120; 130; INT 130

Peck, Dale 1967- . . . . **CLC 81**
See also CA 146

Peck, John 1941- . . . . **CLC 3**
See also CA 49-52; CANR 3

Peck, Richard (Wayne) 1934- . . . . . . **CLC 21**
See also AAYA 1; CA 85-88; CANR 19,
38; CLR 15; INT CANR-19; JRDA;
MAICYA; SAAS 2; SATA 18, 55

Peck, Robert Newton
1928- . . . . **CLC 17; DA; DAC**
See also AAYA 3; CA 81-84; CANR 31;
DAM MST; JRDA; MAICYA; SAAS 1;
SATA 21, 62

Peckinpah, (David) Sam(uel)
1925-1984 . . . . **CLC 20**
See also CA 109; 114

Pedersen, Knut 1859-1952
See Hamsun, Knut
See also CA 104; 119; MTCW

Peeslake, Gaffer
See Durrell, Lawrence (George)

Peguy, Charles Pierre
1873-1914 . . . . **TCLC 10**
See also CA 107

Pena, Ramon del Valle y
See Valle-Inclan, Ramon (Maria) del

Pendennis, Arthur Esquir
See Thackeray, William Makepeace

Penn, William 1644-1718 . . . . **LC 25**
See also DLB 24

Pepys, Samuel
1633-1703 . . . . . **LC 11; DA; DAB; DAC;**
WLC
See also CDBLB 1660-1789; DAM MST;
DLB 101

Percy, Walker
1916-1990 . . . . **CLC 2, 3, 6, 8, 14, 18, 47,**
65
See also CA 1-4R; 131; CANR 1, 23;
DAM NOV, POP; DLB 2; DLBY 80, 90;
MTCW

Perec, Georges 1936-1982 . . . . **CLC 56**
See also CA 141; DLB 83

Pereda (y Sanchez de Porrua), Jose Maria de
1833-1906 . . . . **TCLC 16**
See also CA 117

Pereda y Porrua, Jose Maria de
See Pereda (y Sanchez de Porrua), Jose
Maria de

Peregoy, George Weems
See Mencken, H(enry) L(ouis)

Perelman, S(idney) J(oseph)
1904-1979 . . . **CLC 3, 5, 9, 15, 23, 44, 49**
See also AITN 1, 2; CA 73-76; 89-92;
CANR 18; DAM DRAM; DLB 11, 44;
MTCW

Peret, Benjamin 1899-1959 . . . . **TCLC 20**
See also CA 117

Peretz, Isaac Loeb 1851(?)-1915 . . . **TCLC 16**
See also CA 109

Peretz, Yitzkhok Leibush
See Peretz, Isaac Loeb

Perez Galdos, Benito 1843-1920 . . . **TCLC 27**
See also CA 125; HW

Perrault, Charles 1628-1703 . . . . **LC 2**
See also MAICYA; SATA 25

Perry, Brighton
See Sherwood, Robert E(mmet)

Perse, St.-John . . . . **CLC 4, 11, 46**
See also Leger, (Marie-Rene Auguste) Alexis
Saint-Leger

Perutz, Leo 1882-1957 . . . . **TCLC 60**
See also DLB 81

Peseenz, Tulio F.
See Lopez y Fuentes, Gregorio

Pesetsky, Bette 1932- . . . . **CLC 28**
See also CA 133; DLB 130

Peshkov, Alexei Maximovich 1868-1936
See Gorky, Maxim
See also CA 105; 141; DA; DAC;
DAM DRAM, MST, NOV

Pessoa, Fernando (Antonio Nogueira)
1888-1935 . . . . **TCLC 27; HLC**
See also CA 125

Peterkin, Julia Mood 1880-1961 . . . . **CLC 31**
See also CA 102; DLB 9

Peters, Joan K. 1945- . . . . **CLC 39**

Peters, Robert L(ouis) 1924- . . . . **CLC 7**
See also CA 13-16R; CAAS 8; DLB 105

Petofi, Sandor 1823-1849 . . . . **NCLC 21**

Petrakis, Harry Mark 1923- . . . . **CLC 3**
See also CA 9-12R; CANR 4, 30

Petrarch 1304-1374 . . . . **PC 8**
See also DAM POET

Petrov, Evgeny . . . . **TCLC 21**
See also Kataev, Evgeny Petrovich

Petry, Ann (Lane) 1908- . . . . . . **CLC 1, 7, 18**
See also BW 1; CA 5-8R; CAAS 6;
CANR 4, 46; CLR 12; DLB 76; JRDA;
MAICYA; MTCW; SATA 5

Petursson, Halligrimur 1614-1674 . . . . **LC 8**

Philips, Katherine 1632-1664 . . . . **LC 30**
See also DLB 131

Philipson, Morris H. 1926- . . . . **CLC 53**
See also CA 1-4R; CANR 4

Phillips, David Graham
1867-1911 . . . . TCLC 44
See also CA 108; DLB 9, 12

Phillips, Jack
See Sandburg, Carl (August)

Phillips, Jayne Anne
1952- . . . . CLC 15, 33; SSC 16
See also CA 101; CANR 24, 50; DLBY 80;
INT CANR-24; MTCW

Phillips, Richard
See Dick, Philip K(indred)

Phillips, Robert (Schaeffer) 1938-. . . CLC 28
See also CA 17-20R; CAAS 13; CANR 8;
DLB 105

Phillips, Ward
See Lovecraft, H(oward) P(hillips)

Piccolo, Lucio 1901-1969. . . . . CLC 13
See also CA 97-100; DLB 114

Pickthall, Marjorie L(owry) C(hristie)
1883-1922 . . . . TCLC 21
See also CA 107; DLB 92

Pico della Mirandola, Giovanni
1463-1494 . . . . LC 15

Piercy, Marge
1936- . . . . CLC 3, 6, 14, 18, 27, 62
See also CA 21-24R; CAAS 1; CANR 13,
43; DLB 120; MTCW

Piers, Robert
See Anthony, Piers

Pieyre de Mandiargues, Andre 1909-1991
See Mandiargues, Andre Pieyre de
See also CA 103; 136; CANR 22

Pilnyak, Boris . . . . TCLC 23
See also Vogau, Boris Andreyevich

Pincherle, Alberto 1907-1990 . . . CLC 11, 18
See also Moravia, Alberto
See also CA 25-28R; 132; CANR 33;
DAM NOV; MTCW

Pinckney, Darryl 1953- . . . . CLC 76
See also BW 2; CA 143

Pindar 518B.C.-446B.C. . . . . CMLC 12

Pineda, Cecile 1942-. . . . . CLC 39
See also CA 118

Pinero, Arthur Wing 1855-1934 . . . TCLC 32
See also CA 110; DAM DRAM; DLB 10

Pinero, Miguel (Antonio Gomez)
1946-1988 . . . . CLC 4, 55
See also CA 61-64; 125; CANR 29; HW

Pinget, Robert 1919- . . . . CLC 7, 13, 37
See also CA 85-88; DLB 83

Pink Floyd
See Barrett, (Roger) Syd; Gilmour, David;
Mason, Nick; Waters, Roger; Wright,
Rick

Pinkney, Edward 1802-1828 . . . . . NCLC 31

Pinkwater, Daniel Manus 1941-. . . . CLC 35
See also Pinkwater, Manus
See also AAYA 1; CA 29-32R; CANR 12,
38; CLR 4; JRDA; MAICYA; SAAS 3;
SATA 46, 76

Pinkwater, Manus
See Pinkwater, Daniel Manus
See also SATA 8

Pinsky, Robert 1940- . . . . . CLC 9, 19, 38, 91
See also CA 29-32R; CAAS 4;
DAM POET; DLBY 82

Pinta, Harold
See Pinter, Harold

Pinter, Harold
1930- . . . . . CLC 1, 3, 6, 9, 11, 15, 27, 58,
73; DA; DAB; DAC; WLC
See also CA 5-8R; CANR 33; CDBLB 1960
to Present; DAM DRAM, MST; DLB 13;
MTCW

Pirandello, Luigi
1867-1936 . . . . . . TCLC 4, 29; DA; DAB;
DAC; DC 5; WLC
See also CA 104; DAM DRAM, MST

Pirsig, Robert M(aynard)
1928- . . . . CLC 4, 6, 73
See also CA 53-56; CANR 42; DAM POP;
MTCW; SATA 39

Pisarev, Dmitry Ivanovich
1840-1868 . . . . NCLC 25

Pix, Mary (Griffith) 1666-1709 . . . . . . LC 8
See also DLB 80

Pixerecourt, Guilbert de
1773-1844 . . . . NCLC 39

Plaidy, Jean
See Hibbert, Eleanor Alice Burford

Planche, James Robinson
1796-1880 . . . . NCLC 42

Plant, Robert 1948- . . . . CLC 12

Plante, David (Robert)
1940- . . . . CLC 7, 23, 38
See also CA 37-40R; CANR 12, 36;
DAM NOV; DLBY 83; INT CANR-12;
MTCW

Plath, Sylvia
1932-1963 . . . . . CLC 1, 2, 3, 5, 9, 11, 14,
17, 50, 51, 62; DA; DAB; DAC; PC 1;
WLC
See also AAYA 13; CA 19-20; CANR 34;
CAP 2; CDALB 1941-1968; DAM MST,
POET; DLB 5, 6, 152; MTCW

Plato
428(?)B.C.-348(?)B.C. . . . . . CMLC 8; DA;
DAB; DAC
See also DAM MST

Platonov, Andrei . . . . TCLC 14
See also Klimentov, Andrei Platonovich

Platt, Kin 1911- . . . . CLC 26
See also AAYA 11; CA 17-20R; CANR 11;
JRDA; SAAS 17; SATA 21, 86

Plautus c. 251B.C.-184B.C. . . . . DC 6

Plick et Plock
See Simenon, Georges (Jacques Christian)

Plimpton, George (Ames) 1927-. . . . . CLC 36
See also AITN 1; CA 21-24R; CANR 32;
MTCW; SATA 10

Plomer, William Charles Franklin
1903-1973 . . . . CLC 4, 8
See also CA 21-22; CANR 34; CAP 2;
DLB 20, 162; MTCW; SATA 24

Plowman, Piers
See Kavanagh, Patrick (Joseph)

Plum, J.
See Wodehouse, P(elham) G(renville)

Plumly, Stanley (Ross) 1939- . . . . . . CLC 33
See also CA 108; 110; DLB 5; INT 110

Plumpe, Friedrich Wilhelm
1888-1931 . . . . TCLC 53
See also CA 112

Poe, Edgar Allan
1809-1849 . . . . NCLC 1, 16, 55; DA;
DAB; DAC; PC 1; SSC 1; WLC
See also AAYA 14; CDALB 1640-1865;
DAM MST, POET; DLB 3, 59, 73, 74;
SATA 23

Poet of Titchfield Street, The
See Pound, Ezra (Weston Loomis)

Pohl, Frederik 1919- . . . . CLC 18
See also CA 61-64; CAAS 1; CANR 11, 37;
DLB 8; INT CANR-11; MTCW;
SATA 24

Poirier, Louis 1910-
See Gracq, Julien
See also CA 122; 126

Poitier, Sidney 1927-. . . . . CLC 26
See also BW 1; CA 117

Polanski, Roman 1933- . . . . CLC 16
See also CA 77-80

Poliakoff, Stephen 1952- . . . . CLC 38
See also CA 106; DLB 13

Police, The
See Copeland, Stewart (Armstrong);
Summers, Andrew James; Sumner,
Gordon Matthew

Polidori, John William
1795-1821 . . . . NCLC 51
See also DLB 116

Pollitt, Katha 1949- . . . . CLC 28
See also CA 120; 122; MTCW

Pollock, (Mary) Sharon
1936-. . . . . CLC 50; DAC
See also CA 141; DAM DRAM, MST;
DLB 60

Polo, Marco 1254-1324 . . . . CMLC 15

Polonsky, Abraham (Lincoln)
1910- . . . . CLC 92
See also CA 104; DLB 26; INT 104

Polybius c. 200B.C.-c. 118B.C. . . . . CMLC 17

Pomerance, Bernard 1940-. . . . . CLC 13
See also CA 101; CANR 49; DAM DRAM

Ponge, Francis (Jean Gaston Alfred)
1899-1988 . . . . CLC 6, 18
See also CA 85-88; 126; CANR 40;
DAM POET

Pontoppidan, Henrik 1857-1943 . . . TCLC 29

Poole, Josephine . . . . CLC 17
See also Helyar, Jane Penelope Josephine
See also SAAS 2; SATA 5

Popa, Vasko 1922-1991 . . . . CLC 19
See also CA 112; 148

Pope, Alexander
1688-1744 . . . . . . LC 3; DA; DAB; DAC;
WLC
See also CDBLB 1660-1789; DAM MST,
POET; DLB 95, 101

Porter, Connie (Rose) 1959(?)- . . . . . CLC 70
See also BW 2; CA 142; SATA 81

Reid, Desmond
See Moorcock, Michael (John)

Reid Banks, Lynne 1929-
See Banks, Lynne Reid
See also CA 1-4R; CANR 6, 22, 38;
CLR 24; JRDA; MAICYA; SATA 22, 75

Reilly, William K.
See Creasey, John

Reiner, Max
See Caldwell, (Janet Miriam) Taylor
(Holland)

Reis, Ricardo
See Pessoa, Fernando (Antonio Nogueira)

Remarque, Erich Maria
1898-1970 . . . . **CLC 21; DA; DAB; DAC**
See also CA 77-80; 29-32R; DAM MST,
NOV; DLB 56; MTCW

Remizov, A.
See Remizov, Aleksei (Mikhailovich)

Remizov, A. M.
See Remizov, Aleksei (Mikhailovich)

Remizov, Aleksei (Mikhailovich)
1877-1957 . . . . **TCLC 27**
See also CA 125; 133

Renan, Joseph Ernest
1823-1892 . . . . **NCLC 26**

Renard, Jules 1864-1910 . . . . **TCLC 17**
See also CA 117

Renault, Mary . . . . **CLC 3, 11, 17**
See also Challans, Mary
See also DLBY 83

Rendell, Ruth (Barbara) 1930- . . **CLC 28, 48**
See also Vine, Barbara
See also CA 109; CANR 32; DAM POP;
DLB 87; INT CANR-32; MTCW

Renoir, Jean 1894-1979 . . . . **CLC 20**
See also CA 129; 85-88

Resnais, Alain 1922- . . . . **CLC 16**

Reverdy, Pierre 1889-1960 . . . . **CLC 53**
See also CA 97-100; 89-92

Rexroth, Kenneth
1905-1982 . . . . . **CLC 1, 2, 6, 11, 22, 49**
See also CA 5-8R; 107; CANR 14, 34;
CDALB 1941-1968; DAM POET;
DLB 16, 48; DLBY 82; INT CANR-14;
MTCW

Reyes, Alfonso 1889-1959 . . . . **TCLC 33**
See also CA 131; HW

Reyes y Basoalto, Ricardo Eliecer Neftali
See Neruda, Pablo

Reymont, Wladyslaw (Stanislaw)
1868(?)-1925 . . . . **TCLC 5**
See also CA 104

Reynolds, Jonathan 1942- . . . . **CLC 6, 38**
See also CA 65-68; CANR 28

Reynolds, Joshua 1723-1792 . . . . **LC 15**
See also DLB 104

Reynolds, Michael Shane 1937- . . . . **CLC 44**
See also CA 65-68; CANR 9

Reznikoff, Charles 1894-1976 . . . . **CLC 9**
See also CA 33-36; 61-64; CAP 2; DLB 28,
45

Rezzori (d'Arezzo), Gregor von
1914- . . . . **CLC 25**
See also CA 122; 136

Rhine, Richard
See Silverstein, Alvin

Rhodes, Eugene Manlove
1869-1934 . . . . **TCLC 53**

R'hoone
See Balzac, Honore de

Rhys, Jean
1890(?)-1979 . . . . **CLC 2, 4, 6, 14, 19, 51;
SSC 21**
See also CA 25-28R; 85-88; CANR 35;
CDBLB 1945-1960; DAM NOV; DLB 36,
117, 162; MTCW

Ribeiro, Darcy 1922- . . . . **CLC 34**
See also CA 33-36R

Ribeiro, Joao Ubaldo (Osorio Pimentel)
1941- . . . . **CLC 10, 67**
See also CA 81-84

Ribman, Ronald (Burt) 1932- . . . . **CLC 7**
See also CA 21-24R; CANR 46

Ricci, Nino 1959- . . . . **CLC 70**
See also CA 137

Rice, Anne 1941- . . . . **CLC 41**
See also AAYA 9; BEST 89:2; CA 65-68;
CANR 12, 36; DAM POP

Rice, Elmer (Leopold)
1892-1967 . . . . **CLC 7, 49**
See also CA 21-22; 25-28R; CAP 2;
DAM DRAM; DLB 4, 7; MTCW

Rice, Tim(othy Miles Bindon)
1944- . . . . **CLC 21**
See also CA 103; CANR 46

Rich, Adrienne (Cecile)
1929- . . . . **CLC 3, 6, 7, 11, 18, 36, 73, 76;
PC 5**
See also CA 9-12R; CANR 20;
DAM POET; DLB 5, 67; MTCW

Rich, Barbara
See Graves, Robert (von Ranke)

Rich, Robert
See Trumbo, Dalton

Richard, Keith . . . . **CLC 17**
See also Richards, Keith

Richards, David Adams
1950- . . . . **CLC 59; DAC**
See also CA 93-96; DLB 53

Richards, I(vor) A(rmstrong)
1893-1979 . . . . **CLC 14, 24**
See also CA 41-44R; 89-92; CANR 34;
DLB 27

Richards, Keith 1943-
See Richard, Keith
See also CA 107

Richardson, Anne
See Roiphe, Anne (Richardson)

Richardson, Dorothy Miller
1873-1957 . . . . **TCLC 3**
See also CA 104; DLB 36

Richardson, Ethel Florence (Lindesay)
1870-1946
See Richardson, Henry Handel
See also CA 105

Richardson, Henry Handel . . . . **TCLC 4**
See also Richardson, Ethel Florence
(Lindesay)

Richardson, John
1796-1852 . . . . **NCLC 55; DAC**
See also CA 140; DLB 99

Richardson, Samuel
1689-1761 . . . . . . **LC 1; DA; DAB; DAC;
WLC**
See also CDBLB 1660-1789; DAM MST,
NOV; DLB 39

Richler, Mordecai
1931- . . . . **CLC 3, 5, 9, 13, 18, 46, 70;
DAC**
See also AITN 1; CA 65-68; CANR 31;
CLR 17; DAM MST, NOV; DLB 53;
MAICYA; MTCW; SATA 44;
SATA-Brief 27

Richter, Conrad (Michael)
1890-1968 . . . . **CLC 30**
See also CA 5-8R; 25-28R; CANR 23;
DLB 9; MTCW; SATA 3

Ricostranza, Tom
See Ellis, Trey

Riddell, J. H. 1832-1906 . . . . **TCLC 40**

Riding, Laura . . . . **CLC 3, 7**
See also Jackson, Laura (Riding)

Riefenstahl, Berta Helene Amalia 1902-
See Riefenstahl, Leni
See also CA 108

Riefenstahl, Leni . . . . **CLC 16**
See also Riefenstahl, Berta Helene Amalia

Riffe, Ernest
See Bergman, (Ernst) Ingmar

Riggs, (Rolla) Lynn 1899-1954 . . . . **TCLC 56**
See also CA 144; DAM MULT; NNAL

Riley, James Whitcomb
1849-1916 . . . . **TCLC 51**
See also CA 118; 137; DAM POET;
MAICYA; SATA 17

Riley, Tex
See Creasey, John

Rilke, Rainer Maria
1875-1926 . . . . **TCLC 1, 6, 19; PC 2**
See also CA 104; 132; DAM POET;
DLB 81; MTCW

Rimbaud, (Jean Nicolas) Arthur
1854-1891 . . . . . **NCLC 4, 35; DA; DAB;
DAC; PC 3; WLC**
See also DAM MST, POET

Rinehart, Mary Roberts
1876-1958 . . . . **TCLC 52**
See also CA 108

Ringmaster, The
See Mencken, H(enry) L(ouis)

Ringwood, Gwen(dolyn Margaret) Pharis
1910-1984 . . . . **CLC 48**
See also CA 148; 112; DLB 88

Rio, Michel 19(?)- . . . . **CLC 43**

Ritsos, Giannes
See Ritsos, Yannis

Ritsos, Yannis 1909-1990 . . . . . **CLC 6, 13, 31**
See also CA 77-80; 133; CANR 39; MTCW

Ritter, Erika 1948(?)- . . . . **CLC 52**

Rivera, Jose Eustasio 1889-1928... **TCLC 35**
See also HW

Rivers, Conrad Kent 1933-1968...... **CLC 1**
See also BW 1; CA 85-88; DLB 41

Rivers, Elfrida
See Bradley, Marion Zimmer

Riverside, John
See Heinlein, Robert A(nson)

Rizal, Jose 1861-1896.......... **NCLC 27**

Roa Bastos, Augusto (Antonio)
1917-................... **CLC 45; HLC**
See also CA 131; DAM MULT; DLB 113;
HW

Robbe-Grillet, Alain
1922-...... **CLC 1, 2, 4, 6, 8, 10, 14, 43**
See also CA 9-12R; CANR 33; DLB 83;
MTCW

Robbins, Harold 1916-............. **CLC 5**
See also CA 73-76; CANR 26; DAM NOV;
MTCW

Robbins, Thomas Eugene 1936-
See Robbins, Tom
See also CA 81-84; CANR 29; DAM NOV,
POP; MTCW

Robbins, Tom............... **CLC 9, 32, 64**
See also Robbins, Thomas Eugene
See also BEST 90:3; DLBY 80

Robbins, Trina 1938-............. **CLC 21**
See also CA 128

Roberts, Charles G(eorge) D(ouglas)
1860-1943 .... **TCLC 8**
See also CA 105; CLR 33; DLB 92;
SATA-Brief 29

Roberts, Kate 1891-1985 .... **CLC 15**
See also CA 107; 116

Roberts, Keith (John Kingston)
1935-..................... **CLC 14**
See also CA 25-28R; CANR 46

Roberts, Kenneth (Lewis)
1885-1957 .... **TCLC 23**
See also CA 109; DLB 9

Roberts, Michele (B.) 1949-........ **CLC 48**
See also CA 115

Robertson, Ellis
See Ellison, Harlan (Jay); Silverberg, Robert

Robertson, Thomas William
1829-1871 .... **NCLC 35**
See also DAM DRAM

Robinson, Edwin Arlington
1869-1935 .... **TCLC 5; DA; DAC; PC 1**
See also CA 104; 133; CDALB 1865-1917;
DAM MST, POET; DLB 54; MTCW

Robinson, Henry Crabb
1775-1867 .... **NCLC 15**
See also DLB 107

Robinson, Jill 1936-.............. **CLC 10**
See also CA 102; INT 102

Robinson, Kim Stanley 1952-...... **CLC 34**
See also CA 126

Robinson, Lloyd
See Silverberg, Robert

Robinson, Marilynne 1944-........ **CLC 25**
See also CA 116

Robinson, Smokey................. **CLC 21**
See also Robinson, William, Jr.

Robinson, William, Jr. 1940-
See Robinson, Smokey
See also CA 116

Robison, Mary 1949-............. **CLC 42**
See also CA 113; 116; DLB 130; INT 116

Rod, Edouard 1857-1910 .... **TCLC 52**

Roddenberry, Eugene Wesley 1921-1991
See Roddenberry, Gene
See also CA 110; 135; CANR 37; SATA 45;
SATA-Obit 69

Roddenberry, Gene................ **CLC 17**
See also Roddenberry, Eugene Wesley
See also AAYA 5; SATA-Obit 69

Rodgers, Mary 1931-............. **CLC 12**
See also CA 49-52; CANR 8; CLR 20;
INT CANR-8; JRDA; MAICYA;
SATA 8

Rodgers, W(illiam) R(obert)
1909-1969 .... **CLC 7**
See also CA 85-88; DLB 20

Rodman, Eric
See Silverberg, Robert

Rodman, Howard 1920(?)-1985..... **CLC 65**
See also CA 118

Rodman, Maia
See Wojciechowska, Maia (Teresa)

Rodriguez, Claudio 1934-......... **CLC 10**
See also DLB 134

Roelvaag, O(le) E(dvart)
1876-1931 .... **TCLC 17**
See also CA 117; DLB 9

Roethke, Theodore (Huebner)
1908-1963 ...... **CLC 1, 3, 8, 11, 19, 46;
PC 15**
See also CA 81-84; CABS 2;
CDALB 1941-1968; DAM POET; DLB 5;
MTCW

Rogers, Thomas Hunton 1927-..... **CLC 57**
See also CA 89-92; INT 89-92

Rogers, Will(iam Penn Adair)
1879-1935 .... **TCLC 8**
See also CA 105; 144; DAM MULT;
DLB 11; NNAL

Rogin, Gilbert 1929-............. **CLC 18**
See also CA 65-68; CANR 15

Rohan, Koda................... **TCLC 22**
See also Koda Shigeyuki

Rohmer, Eric.................... **CLC 16**
See also Scherer, Jean-Marie Maurice

Rohmer, Sax.................... **TCLC 28**
See also Ward, Arthur Henry Sarsfield
See also DLB 70

Roiphe, Anne (Richardson)
1935-..................... **CLC 3, 9**
See also CA 89-92; CANR 45; DLBY 80;
INT 89-92

Rojas, Fernando de 1465-1541 ...... **LC 23**

**Rolfe, Frederick (William Serafino Austin
Lewis Mary)** 1860-1913..... **TCLC 12**
See also CA 107; DLB 34, 156

Rolland, Romain 1866-1944....... **TCLC 23**
See also CA 118; DLB 65

Rolvaag, O(le) E(dvart)
See Roelvaag, O(le) E(dvart)

Romain Arnaud, Saint
See Aragon, Louis

Romains, Jules 1885-1972.......... **CLC 7**
See also CA 85-88; CANR 34; DLB 65;
MTCW

Romero, Jose Ruben 1890-1952 ... **TCLC 14**
See also CA 114; 131; HW

Ronsard, Pierre de
1524-1585 .... **LC 6; PC 11**

Rooke, Leon 1934-............. **CLC 25, 34**
See also CA 25-28R; CANR 23; DAM POP

Roper, William 1498-1578 .... **LC 10**

Roquelaure, A. N.
See Rice, Anne

Rosa, Joao Guimaraes 1908-1967... **CLC 23**
See also CA 89-92; DLB 113

Rose, Wendy 1948-......... **CLC 85; PC 13**
See also CA 53-56; CANR 5, 51;
DAM MULT; NNAL; SATA 12

Rosen, Richard (Dean) 1949-...... **CLC 39**
See also CA 77-80; INT CANR-30

Rosenberg, Isaac 1890-1918....... **TCLC 12**
See also CA 107; DLB 20

Rosenblatt, Joe................... **CLC 15**
See also Rosenblatt, Joseph

Rosenblatt, Joseph 1933-
See Rosenblatt, Joe
See also CA 89-92; INT 89-92

Rosenfeld, Samuel 1896-1963
See Tzara, Tristan
See also CA 89-92

Rosenthal, M(acha) L(ouis) 1917-... **CLC 28**
See also CA 1-4R; CAAS 6; CANR 4, 51;
DLB 5; SATA 59

Ross, Barnaby
See Dannay, Frederic

Ross, Bernard L.
See Follett, Ken(neth Martin)

Ross, J. H.
See Lawrence, T(homas) E(dward)

Ross, Martin
See Martin, Violet Florence
See also DLB 135

Ross, (James) Sinclair
1908-................ **CLC 13; DAC**
See also CA 73-76; DAM MST; DLB 88

Rossetti, Christina (Georgina)
1830-1894 ..... **NCLC 2, 50; DA; DAB;
DAC; PC 7; WLC**
See also DAM MST, POET; DLB 35, 163;
MAICYA; SATA 20

Rossetti, Dante Gabriel
1828-1882 .... **NCLC 4; DA; DAB;
DAC; WLC**
See also CDBLB 1832-1890; DAM MST,
POET; DLB 35

Rossner, Judith (Perelman)
1935-................... **CLC 6, 9, 29**
See also AITN 2; BEST 90:3; CA 17-20R;
CANR 18, 51; DLB 6; INT CANR-18;
MTCW

Rostand, Edmond (Eugene Alexis)
1868-1918 . . . . . TCLC 6, 37; DA; DAB;
DAC
See also CA 104; 126; DAM DRAM, MST;
MTCW

Roth, Henry 1906-1995 . . . . . . CLC 2, 6, 11
See also CA 11-12; 149; CANR 38; CAP 1;
DLB 28; MTCW

Roth, Joseph 1894-1939 . . . . TCLC 33
See also DLB 85

Roth, Philip (Milton)
1933- . . . . . . CLC 1, 2, 3, 4, 6, 9, 15, 22,
31, 47, 66, 86; DA; DAB; DAC; WLC
See also BEST 90:3; CA 1-4R; CANR 1, 22,
36; CDALB 1968-1988; DAM MST,
NOV, POP; DLB 2, 28; DLBY 82;
MTCW

Rothenberg, Jerome 1931- . . . . CLC 6, 57
See also CA 45-48; CANR 1; DLB 5

Roumain, Jacques (Jean Baptiste)
1907-1944 . . . . TCLC 19; BLC
See also BW 1; CA 117; 125; DAM MULT

Rourke, Constance (Mayfield)
1885-1941 . . . . TCLC 12
See also CA 107; YABC 1

Rousseau, Jean-Baptiste 1671-1741 . . . LC 9

Rousseau, Jean-Jacques
1712-1778 . . . . . LC 14; DA; DAB; DAC;
WLC
See also DAM MST

Roussel, Raymond 1877-1933 . . . . . TCLC 20
See also CA 117

Rovit, Earl (Herbert) 1927- . . . . CLC 7
See also CA 5-8R; CANR 12

Rowe, Nicholas 1674-1718 . . . . LC 8
See also DLB 84

Rowley, Ames Dorrance
See Lovecraft, H(oward) P(hillips)

Rowson, Susanna Haswell
1762(?)-1824 . . . . NCLC 5
See also DLB 37

Roy, Gabrielle
1909-1983 . . . . . CLC 10, 14; DAB; DAC
See also CA 53-56; 110; CANR 5;
DAM MST; DLB 68; MTCW

Rozewicz, Tadeusz 1921- . . . . CLC 9, 23
See also CA 108; CANR 36; DAM POET;
MTCW

Ruark, Gibbons 1941- . . . . CLC 3
See also CA 33-36R; CAAS 23; CANR 14,
31; DLB 120

Rubens, Bernice (Ruth) 1923- . . . CLC 19, 31
See also CA 25-28R; CANR 33; DLB 14;
MTCW

Rudkin, (James) David 1936- . . . . . . CLC 14
See also CA 89-92; DLB 13

Rudnik, Raphael 1933- . . . . CLC 7
See also CA 29-32R

Ruffian, M.
See Hasek, Jaroslav (Matej Frantisek)

Ruiz, Jose Martinez . . . . CLC 11
See also Martinez Ruiz, Jose

Rukeyser, Muriel
1913-1980 . . . . CLC 6, 10, 15, 27; PC 12
See also CA 5-8R; 93-96; CANR 26;
DAM POET; DLB 48; MTCW;
SATA-Obit 22

Rule, Jane (Vance) 1931- . . . . CLC 27
See also CA 25-28R; CAAS 18; CANR 12;
DLB 60

Rulfo, Juan 1918-1986 . . . . CLC 8, 80; HLC
See also CA 85-88; 118; CANR 26;
DAM MULT; DLB 113; HW; MTCW

Runeberg, Johan 1804-1877 . . . . . NCLC 41

Runyon, (Alfred) Damon
1884(?)-1946 . . . . TCLC 10
See also CA 107; DLB 11, 86

Rush, Norman 1933- . . . . CLC 44
See also CA 121; 126; INT 126

Rushdie, (Ahmed) Salman
1947- . . . . . . CLC 23, 31, 55; DAB; DAC
See also BEST 89:3; CA 108; 111;
CANR 33; DAM MST, NOV, POP;
INT 111; MTCW

Rushforth, Peter (Scott) 1945- . . . . . CLC 19
See also CA 101

Ruskin, John 1819-1900 . . . . TCLC 63
See also CA 114; 129; CDBLB 1832-1890;
DLB 55, 163; SATA 24

Russ, Joanna 1937- . . . . CLC 15
See also CA 25-28R; CANR 11, 31; DLB 8;
MTCW

Russell, George William 1867-1935
See A. E.
See also CA 104; CDBLB 1890-1914;
DAM POET

Russell, (Henry) Ken(neth Alfred)
1927- . . . . CLC 16
See also CA 105

Russell, Willy 1947- . . . . CLC 60

Rutherford, Mark . . . . TCLC 25
See also White, William Hale
See also DLB 18

Ruyslinck, Ward 1929- . . . . CLC 14
See also Belser, Reimond Karel Maria de

Ryan, Cornelius (John) 1920-1974 . . . CLC 7
See also CA 69-72; 53-56; CANR 38

Ryan, Michael 1946- . . . . CLC 65
See also CA 49-52; DLBY 82

Rybakov, Anatoli (Naumovich)
1911- . . . . CLC 23, 53
See also CA 126; 135; SATA 79

Ryder, Jonathan
See Ludlum, Robert

Ryga, George 1932-1987 . . . . . CLC 14; DAC
See also CA 101; 124; CANR 43;
DAM MST; DLB 60

S. S.
See Sassoon, Siegfried (Lorraine)

Saba, Umberto 1883-1957 . . . . TCLC 33
See also CA 144; DLB 114

Sabatini, Rafael 1875-1950 . . . . TCLC 47

Sabato, Ernesto (R.)
1911- . . . . CLC 10, 23; HLC
See also CA 97-100; CANR 32;
DAM MULT; DLB 145; HW; MTCW

Sacastru, Martin
See Bioy Casares, Adolfo

Sacher-Masoch, Leopold von
1836(?)-1895 . . . . NCLC 31

Sachs, Marilyn (Stickle) 1927- . . . . . CLC 35
See also AAYA 2; CA 17-20R; CANR 13,
47; CLR 2; JRDA; MAICYA; SAAS 2;
SATA 3, 68

Sachs, Nelly 1891-1970 . . . . CLC 14
See also CA 17-18; 25-28R; CAP 2

Sackler, Howard (Oliver)
1929-1982 . . . . CLC 14
See also CA 61-64; 108; CANR 30; DLB 7

Sacks, Oliver (Wolf) 1933- . . . . CLC 67
See also CA 53-56; CANR 28, 50;
INT CANR-28; MTCW

Sade, Donatien Alphonse Francois Comte
1740-1814 . . . . NCLC 47

Sadoff, Ira 1945- . . . . CLC 9
See also CA 53-56; CANR 5, 21; DLB 120

Saetone
See Camus, Albert

Safire, William 1929- . . . . CLC 10
See also CA 17-20R; CANR 31

Sagan, Carl (Edward) 1934- . . . . CLC 30
See also AAYA 2; CA 25-28R; CANR 11,
36; MTCW; SATA 58

Sagan, Francoise . . . . CLC 3, 6, 9, 17, 36
See also Quoirez, Francoise
See also DLB 83

Sahgal, Nayantara (Pandit) 1927- . . . CLC 41
See also CA 9-12R; CANR 11

Saint, H(arry) F. 1941- . . . . CLC 50
See also CA 127

St. Aubin de Teran, Lisa 1953-
See Teran, Lisa St. Aubin de
See also CA 118; 126; INT 126

Sainte-Beuve, Charles Augustin
1804-1869 . . . . NCLC 5

Saint-Exupery, Antoine (Jean Baptiste Marie
Roger) de
1900-1944 . . . . TCLC 2, 56; WLC
See also CA 108; 132; CLR 10; DAM NOV;
DLB 72; MAICYA; MTCW; SATA 20

St. John, David
See Hunt, E(verette) Howard, (Jr.)

Saint-John Perse
See Leger, (Marie-Rene Auguste) Alexis
Saint-Leger

Saintsbury, George (Edward Bateman)
1845-1933 . . . . TCLC 31
See also DLB 57, 149

Sait Faik . . . . TCLC 23
See also Abasiyanik, Sait Faik

Saki . . . . TCLC 3; SSC 12
See also Munro, H(ector) H(ugh)

Sala, George Augustus . . . . NCLC 46

Salama, Hannu 1936- . . . . CLC 18

Salamanca, J(ack) R(ichard)
1922- . . . . CLC 4, 15
See also CA 25-28R

Sale, J. Kirkpatrick
See Sale, Kirkpatrick

453

Sale, Kirkpatrick 1937- .... **CLC 68**
See also CA 13-16R; CANR 10

Salinas, Luis Omar 1937- ... **CLC 90; HLC**
See also CA 131; DAM MULT; DLB 82;
HW

Salinas (y Serrano), Pedro
1891(?)-1951 .... **TCLC 17**
See also CA 117; DLB 134

Salinger, J(erome) D(avid)
1919- ...... **CLC 1, 3, 8, 12, 55, 56; DA;**
DAB; DAC; SSC 2; WLC
See also AAYA 2; CA 5-8R; CANR 39;
CDALB 1941-1968; CLR 18; DAM MST,
NOV, POP; DLB 2, 102; MAICYA;
MTCW; SATA 67

Salisbury, John
See Caute, David

Salter, James 1925- .... **CLC 7, 52, 59**
See also CA 73-76; DLB 130

Saltus, Edgar (Everton)
1855-1921 .... **TCLC 8**
See also CA 105

Saltykov, Mikhail Evgrafovich
1826-1889 .... **NCLC 16**

Samarakis, Antonis 1919- .... **CLC 5**
See also CA 25-28R; CAAS 16; CANR 36

Sanchez, Florencio 1875-1910..... **TCLC 37**
See also HW

Sanchez, Luis Rafael 1936-........ **CLC 23**
See also CA 128; DLB 145; HW

Sanchez, Sonia 1934- ... **CLC 5; BLC; PC 9**
See also BW 2; CA 33-36R; CANR 24, 49;
CLR 18; DAM MULT; DLB 41;
DLBD 8; MAICYA; MTCW; SATA 22

Sand, George
1804-1876 ..... **NCLC 2, 42; DA; DAB;**
DAC; WLC
See also DAM MST, NOV; DLB 119

Sandburg, Carl (August)
1878-1967 .... **CLC 1, 4, 10, 15, 35; DA;**
DAB; DAC; PC 2; WLC
See also CA 5-8R; 25-28R; CANR 35;
CDALB 1865-1917; DAM MST, POET;
DLB 17, 54; MAICYA; MTCW; SATA 8

Sandburg, Charles
See Sandburg, Carl (August)

Sandburg, Charles A.
See Sandburg, Carl (August)

Sanders, (James) Ed(ward) 1939- ... **CLC 53**
See also CA 13-16R; CAAS 21; CANR 13,
44; DLB 16

Sanders, Lawrence 1920-......... **CLC 41**
See also BEST 89:4; CA 81-84; CANR 33;
DAM POP; MTCW

Sanders, Noah
See Blount, Roy (Alton), Jr.

Sanders, Winston P.
See Anderson, Poul (William)

Sandoz, Mari(e Susette)
1896-1966 .... **CLC 28**
See also CA 1-4R; 25-28R; CANR 17;
DLB 9; MTCW; SATA 5

Saner, Reg(inald Anthony) 1931- .... **CLC 9**
See also CA 65-68

Sannazaro, Jacopo 1456(?)-1530...... **LC 8**

Sansom, William
1912-1976 .... **CLC 2, 6; SSC 21**
See also CA 5-8R; 65-68; CANR 42;
DAM NOV; DLB 139; MTCW

Santayana, George 1863-1952..... **TCLC 40**
See also CA 115; DLB 54, 71; DLBD 13

Santiago, Danny .... **CLC 33**
See also James, Daniel (Lewis)
See also DLB 122

Santmyer, Helen Hoover
1895-1986 .... **CLC 33**
See also CA 1-4R; 118; CANR 15, 33;
DLBY 84; MTCW

Santos, Bienvenido N(uqui) 1911-... **CLC 22**
See also CA 101; CANR 19, 46;
DAM MULT

Sapper .... **TCLC 44**
See also McNeile, Herman Cyril

Sappho fl. 6th cent. B.C.-.... **CMLC 3; PC 5**
See also DAM POET

Sarduy, Severo 1937-1993 .... **CLC 6**
See also CA 89-92; 142; DLB 113; HW

Sargeson, Frank 1903-1982........ **CLC 31**
See also CA 25-28R; 106; CANR 38

Sarmiento, Felix Ruben Garcia
See Dario, Ruben

Saroyan, William
1908-1981 ..... **CLC 1, 8, 10, 29, 34, 56;**
DA; DAB; DAC; SSC 21; WLC
See also CA 5-8R; 103; CANR 30;
DAM DRAM, MST, NOV; DLB 7, 9, 86;
DLBY 81; MTCW; SATA 23;
SATA-Obit 24

Sarraute, Nathalie
1900- .... **CLC 1, 2, 4, 8, 10, 31, 80**
See also CA 9-12R; CANR 23; DLB 83;
MTCW

Sarton, (Eleanor) May
1912-1995 .... **CLC 4, 14, 49, 91**
See also CA 1-4R; 149; CANR 1, 34;
DAM POET; DLB 48; DLBY 81;
INT CANR-34; MTCW; SATA 36;
SATA-Obit 86

Sartre, Jean-Paul
1905-1980 .... **CLC 1, 4, 7, 9, 13, 18, 24,**
44, 50, 52; DA; DAB; DAC; DC 3; WLC
See also CA 9-12R; 97-100; CANR 21;
DAM DRAM, MST, NOV; DLB 72;
MTCW

Sassoon, Siegfried (Lorraine)
1886-1967 .... **CLC 36; DAB; PC 12**
See also CA 104; 25-28R; CANR 36;
DAM MST, NOV, POET; DLB 20;
MTCW

Satterfield, Charles
See Pohl, Frederik

Saul, John (W. III) 1942- .... **CLC 46**
See also AAYA 10; BEST 90:4; CA 81-84;
CANR 16, 40; DAM NOV, POP

Saunders, Caleb
See Heinlein, Robert A(nson)

Saura (Atares), Carlos 1932-....... **CLC 20**
See also CA 114; 131; HW

Sauser-Hall, Frederic 1887-1961.... **CLC 18**
See also Cendrars, Blaise
See also CA 102; 93-96; CANR 36; MTCW

Saussure, Ferdinand de
1857-1913 .... **TCLC 49**

Savage, Catharine
See Brosman, Catharine Savage

Savage, Thomas 1915- .... **CLC 40**
See also CA 126; 132; CAAS 15; INT 132

Savan, Glenn 19(?)- .... **CLC 50**

Sayers, Dorothy L(eigh)
1893-1957 .... **TCLC 2, 15**
See also CA 104; 119; CDBLB 1914-1945;
DAM POP; DLB 10, 36, 77, 100; MTCW

Sayers, Valerie 1952-............. **CLC 50**
See also CA 134

Sayles, John (Thomas)
1950-.................. **CLC 7, 10, 14**
See also CA 57-60; CANR 41; DLB 44

Scammell, Michael .... **CLC 34**

Scannell, Vernon 1922- .... **CLC 49**
See also CA 5-8R; CANR 8, 24; DLB 27;
SATA 59

Scarlett, Susan
See Streatfeild, (Mary) Noel

Schaeffer, Susan Fromberg
1941- .... **CLC 6, 11, 22**
See also CA 49-52; CANR 18; DLB 28;
MTCW; SATA 22

Schary, Jill
See Robinson, Jill

Schell, Jonathan 1943-............ **CLC 35**
See also CA 73-76; CANR 12

Schelling, Friedrich Wilhelm Joseph von
1775-1854 .... **NCLC 30**
See also DLB 90

Schendel, Arthur van 1874-1946... **TCLC 56**

Scherer, Jean-Marie Maurice 1920-
See Rohmer, Eric
See also CA 110

Schevill, James (Erwin) 1920-....... **CLC 7**
See also CA 5-8R; CAAS 12

Schiller, Friedrich 1759-1805 .... **NCLC 39**
See also DAM DRAM; DLB 94

Schisgal, Murray (Joseph) 1926-..... **CLC 6**
See also CA 21-24R; CANR 48

Schlee, Ann 1934-................ **CLC 35**
See also CA 101; CANR 29; SATA 44;
SATA-Brief 36

Schlegel, August Wilhelm von
1767-1845 .... **NCLC 15**
See also DLB 94

Schlegel, Friedrich 1772-1829 .... **NCLC 45**
See also DLB 90

Schlegel, Johann Elias (von)
1719(?)-1749 .... **LC 5**

Schlesinger, Arthur M(eier), Jr.
1917- .... **CLC 84**
See also AITN 1; CA 1-4R; CANR 1, 28;
DLB 17; INT CANR-28; MTCW;
SATA 61

Schmidt, Arno (Otto) 1914-1979.... **CLC 56**
See also CA 128; 109; DLB 69

Schmitz, Aron Hector 1861-1928
See Svevo, Italo
See also CA 104; 122; MTCW

Schnackenberg, Gjertrud 1953-..... **CLC 40**
See also CA 116; DLB 120

Schneider, Leonard Alfred 1925-1966
See Bruce, Lenny
See also CA 89-92

Schnitzler, Arthur
1862-1931 .... **TCLC 4; SSC 15**
See also CA 104; DLB 81, 118

Schopenhauer, Arthur
1788-1860 .... **NCLC 51**
See also DLB 90

Schor, Sandra (M.) 1932(?)-1990 ... **CLC 65**
See also CA 132

Schorer, Mark 1908-1977 .... **CLC 9**
See also CA 5-8R; 73-76; CANR 7;
DLB 103

Schrader, Paul (Joseph) 1946-..... **CLC 26**
See also CA 37-40R; CANR 41; DLB 44

Schreiner, Olive (Emilie Albertina)
1855-1920 .... **TCLC 9**
See also CA 105; DLB 18, 156

Schulberg, Budd (Wilson)
1914-..................... **CLC 7, 48**
See also CA 25-28R; CANR 19; DLB 6, 26,
28; DLBY 81

Schulz, Bruno
1892-1942 .... **TCLC 5, 51; SSC 13**
See also CA 115; 123

Schulz, Charles M(onroe) 1922-.... **CLC 12**
See also CA 9-12R; CANR 6;
INT CANR-6; SATA 10

Schumacher, E(rnst) F(riedrich)
1911-1977 .... **CLC 80**
See also CA 81-84; 73-76; CANR 34

Schuyler, James Marcus
1923-1991 .... **CLC 5, 23**
See also CA 101; 134; DAM POET; DLB 5;
INT 101

Schwartz, Delmore (David)
1913-1966 ... **CLC 2, 4, 10, 45, 87; PC 8**
See also CA 17-18; 25-28R; CANR 35;
CAP 2; DLB 28, 48; MTCW

Schwartz, Ernst
See Ozu, Yasujiro

Schwartz, John Burnham 1965- .... **CLC 59**
See also CA 132

Schwartz, Lynne Sharon 1939-..... **CLC 31**
See also CA 103; CANR 44

Schwartz, Muriel A.
See Eliot, T(homas) S(tearns)

Schwarz-Bart, Andre 1928-....... **CLC 2, 4**
See also CA 89-92

Schwarz-Bart, Simone 1938-........ **CLC 7**
See also BW 2; CA 97-100

Schwob, (Mayer Andre) Marcel
1867-1905 .... **TCLC 20**
See also CA 117; DLB 123

Sciascia, Leonardo
1921-1989 .... **CLC 8, 9, 41**
See also CA 85-88; 130; CANR 35; MTCW

Scoppettone, Sandra 1936-........ **CLC 26**
See also AAYA 11; CA 5-8R; CANR 41;
SATA 9

Scorsese, Martin 1942- .... **CLC 20, 89**
See also CA 110; 114; CANR 46

Scotland, Jay
See Jakes, John (William)

Scott, Duncan Campbell
1862-1947 .... **TCLC 6; DAC**
See also CA 104; DLB 92

Scott, Evelyn 1893-1963........... **CLC 43**
See also CA 104; 112; DLB 9, 48

Scott, F(rancis) R(eginald)
1899-1985 .... **CLC 22**
See also CA 101; 114; DLB 88; INT 101

Scott, Frank
See Scott, F(rancis) R(eginald)

Scott, Joanna 1960- .... **CLC 50**
See also CA 126

Scott, Paul (Mark) 1920-1978.... **CLC 9, 60**
See also CA 81-84; 77-80; CANR 33;
DLB 14; MTCW

Scott, Walter
1771-1832 .... **NCLC 15; DA; DAB;**
DAC; PC 13; WLC
See also CDBLB 1789-1832; DAM MST,
NOV, POET; DLB 93, 107, 116, 144, 159;
YABC 2

Scribe, (Augustin) Eugene
1791-1861 .... **NCLC 16; DC 5**
See also DAM DRAM

Scrum, R.
See Crumb, R(obert)

Scudery, Madeleine de 1607-1701..... **LC 2**

Scum
See Crumb, R(obert)

Scumbag, Little Bobby
See Crumb, R(obert)

Seabrook, John
See Hubbard, L(afayette) Ron(ald)

Sealy, I. Allan 1951- .... **CLC 55**

Search, Alexander
See Pessoa, Fernando (Antonio Nogueira)

Sebastian, Lee
See Silverberg, Robert

Sebastian Owl
See Thompson, Hunter S(tockton)

Sebestyen, Ouida 1924-........... **CLC 30**
See also AAYA 8; CA 107; CANR 40;
CLR 17; JRDA; MAICYA; SAAS 10;
SATA 39

Secundus, H. Scriblerus
See Fielding, Henry

Sedges, John
See Buck, Pearl S(ydenstricker)

Sedgwick, Catharine Maria
1789-1867 .... **NCLC 19**
See also DLB 1, 74

Seelye, John 1931-............... **CLC 7**

Seferiades, Giorgos Stylianou 1900-1971
See Seferis, George
See also CA 5-8R; 33-36R; CANR 5, 36;
MTCW

Seferis, George .... **CLC 5, 11**
See also Seferiades, Giorgos Stylianou

Segal, Erich (Wolf) 1937- .... **CLC 3, 10**
See also BEST 89:1; CA 25-28R; CANR 20,
36; DAM POP; DLBY 86;
INT CANR-20; MTCW

Seger, Bob 1945-................. **CLC 35**

Seghers, Anna .... **CLC 7**
See also Radvanyi, Netty
See also DLB 69

Seidel, Frederick (Lewis) 1936-..... **CLC 18**
See also CA 13-16R; CANR 8; DLBY 84

Seifert, Jaroslav 1901-1986..... **CLC 34, 44**
See also CA 127; MTCW

Sei Shonagon c. 966-1017(?) ...... **CMLC 6**

Selby, Hubert, Jr.
1928-......... **CLC 1, 2, 4, 8; SSC 20**
See also CA 13-16R; CANR 33; DLB 2

Selzer, Richard 1928-............ **CLC 74**
See also CA 65-68; CANR 14

Sembene, Ousmane
See Ousmane, Sembene

Senancour, Etienne Pivert de
1770-1846 .... **NCLC 16**
See also DLB 119

Sender, Ramon (Jose)
1902-1982 .... **CLC 8; HLC**
See also CA 5-8R; 105; CANR 8;
DAM MULT; HW; MTCW

Seneca, Lucius Annaeus
4B.C.-65............. **CMLC 6; DC 5**
See also DAM DRAM

Senghor, Leopold Sedar
1906-................. **CLC 54; BLC**
See also BW 2; CA 116; 125; CANR 47;
DAM MULT, POET; MTCW

Serling, (Edward) Rod(man)
1924-1975 .... **CLC 30**
See also AAYA 14; AITN 1; CA 65-68;
57-60; DLB 26

Serna, Ramon Gomez de la
See Gomez de la Serna, Ramon

Serpieres
See Guillevic, (Eugene)

Service, Robert
See Service, Robert W(illiam)
See also DAB; DLB 92

Service, Robert W(illiam)
1874(?)-1958 ...... **TCLC 15; DA; DAC;**
WLC
See also Service, Robert
See also CA 115; 140; DAM MST, POET;
SATA 20

Seth, Vikram 1952-........... **CLC 43, 90**
See also CA 121; 127; CANR 50;
DAM MULT; DLB 120; INT 127

Seton, Cynthia Propper
1926-1982 .... **CLC 27**
See also CA 5-8R; 108; CANR 7

Seton, Ernest (Evan) Thompson
1860-1946................... **TCLC 31**
See also CA 109; DLB 92; DLBD 13;
JRDA; SATA 18

Seton-Thompson, Ernest
See Seton, Ernest (Evan) Thompson

Settle, Mary Lee 1918- .... **CLC 19, 61**
See also CA 89-92; CAAS 1; CANR 44;
DLB 6; INT 89-92

Seuphor, Michel
See Arp, Jean

Sevigne, Marie (de Rabutin-Chantal) Marquise de 1626-1696 .... LC 11

Sexton, Anne (Harvey)
1928-1974 .... CLC 2, 4, 6, 8, 10, 15, 53;
DA; DAB; DAC; PC 2; WLC
See also CA 1-4R; 53-56; CABS 2;
CANR 3, 36; CDALB 1941-1968;
DAM MST, POET; DLB 5; MTCW;
SATA 10

Shaara, Michael (Joseph, Jr.)
1929-1988 .... CLC 15
See also AITN 1; CA 102; 125; DAM POP;
DLBY 83

Shackleton, C. C.
See Aldiss, Brian W(ilson)

Shacochis, Bob .... CLC 39
See also Shacochis, Robert G.

Shacochis, Robert G. 1951-
See Shacochis, Bob
See also CA 119; 124; INT 124

Shaffer, Anthony (Joshua) 1926-.... CLC 19
See also CA 110; 116; DAM DRAM;
DLB 13

Shaffer, Peter (Levin)
1926- ...... CLC 5, 14, 18, 37, 60; DAB
See also CA 25-28R; CANR 25, 47;
CDBLB 1960 to Present; DAM DRAM,
MST; DLB 13; MTCW

Shakey, Bernard
See Young, Neil

Shalamov, Varlam (Tikhonovich)
1907(?)-1982 .... CLC 18
See also CA 129; 105

Shamlu, Ahmad 1925- .... CLC 10

Shammas, Anton 1951-........... CLC 55

Shange, Ntozake
1948- .... CLC 8, 25, 38, 74; BLC; DC 3
See also AAYA 9; BW 2; CA 85-88;
CABS 3; CANR 27, 48; DAM DRAM,
MULT; DLB 38; MTCW

Shanley, John Patrick 1950-....... CLC 75
See also CA 128; 133

Shapcott, Thomas W(illiam) 1935- .. CLC 38
See also CA 69-72; CANR 49

Shapiro, Jane.................... CLC 76

Shapiro, Karl (Jay) 1913- .. CLC 4, 8, 15, 53
See also CA 1-4R; CAAS 6; CANR 1, 36;
DLB 48; MTCW

Sharp, William 1855-1905 .... TCLC 39
See also DLB 156

Sharpe, Thomas Ridley 1928-
See Sharpe, Tom
See also CA 114; 122; INT 122

Sharpe, Tom.................... CLC 36
See also Sharpe, Thomas Ridley
See also DLB 14

Shaw, Bernard.................. TCLC 45
See also Shaw, George Bernard
See also BW 1

Shaw, G. Bernard
See Shaw, George Bernard

Shaw, George Bernard
1856-1950 ... TCLC 3, 9, 21; DA; DAB;
DAC; WLC
See also Shaw, Bernard
See also CA 104; 128; CDBLB 1914-1945;
DAM DRAM, MST; DLB 10, 57;
MTCW

Shaw, Henry Wheeler
1818-1885 .... NCLC 15
See also DLB 11

Shaw, Irwin 1913-1984...... CLC 7, 23, 34
See also AITN 1; CA 13-16R; 112;
CANR 21; CDALB 1941-1968;
DAM DRAM, POP; DLB 6, 102;
DLBY 84; MTCW

Shaw, Robert 1927-1978 .... CLC 5
See also AITN 1; CA 1-4R; 81-84;
CANR 4; DLB 13, 14

Shaw, T. E.
See Lawrence, T(homas) E(dward)

Shawn, Wallace 1943- .... CLC 41
See also CA 112

Shea, Lisa 1953-................. CLC 86
See also CA 147

Sheed, Wilfrid (John Joseph)
1930- .... CLC 2, 4, 10, 53
See also CA 65-68; CANR 30; DLB 6;
MTCW

Sheldon, Alice Hastings Bradley
1915(?)-1987
See Tiptree, James, Jr.
See also CA 108; 122; CANR 34; INT 108;
MTCW

Sheldon, John
See Bloch, Robert (Albert)

Shelley, Mary Wollstonecraft (Godwin)
1797-1851 .... NCLC 14; DA; DAB;
DAC; WLC
See also CDBLB 1789-1832; DAM MST,
NOV; DLB 110, 116, 159; SATA 29

Shelley, Percy Bysshe
1792-1822 .... NCLC 18; DA; DAB;
DAC; PC 14; WLC
See also CDBLB 1789-1832; DAM MST,
POET; DLB 96, 110, 158

Shepard, Jim 1956-............... CLC 36
See also CA 137

Shepard, Lucius 1947-........... CLC 34
See also CA 128; 141

Shepard, Sam
1943- .... CLC 4, 6, 17, 34, 41, 44; DC 5
See also AAYA 1; CA 69-72; CABS 3;
CANR 22; DAM DRAM; DLB 7;
MTCW

Shepherd, Michael
See Ludlum, Robert

Sherburne, Zoa (Morin) 1912-...... CLC 30
See also AAYA 13; CA 1-4R; CANR 3, 37;
MAICYA; SAAS 18; SATA 3

Sheridan, Frances 1724-1766........ LC 7
See also DLB 39, 84

Sheridan, Richard Brinsley
1751-1816 .... NCLC 5; DA; DAB;
DAC; DC 1; WLC
See also CDBLB 1660-1789; DAM DRAM,
MST; DLB 89

Sherman, Jonathan Marc .... CLC 55

Sherman, Martin 1941(?)-......... CLC 19
See also CA 116; 123

Sherwin, Judith Johnson 1936-... CLC 7, 15
See also CA 25-28R; CANR 34

Sherwood, Frances 1940-......... CLC 81
See also CA 146

Sherwood, Robert E(mmet)
1896-1955 .... TCLC 3
See also CA 104; DAM DRAM; DLB 7, 26

Shestov, Lev 1866-1938 .... TCLC 56

Shevchenko, Taras 1814-1861 .... NCLC 54

Shiel, M(atthew) P(hipps)
1865-1947 .... TCLC 8
See also CA 106; DLB 153

Shields, Carol 1935-......... CLC 91; DAC
See also CA 81-84; CANR 51

Shiga, Naoya 1883-1971.......... CLC 33
See also CA 101; 33-36R

Shilts, Randy 1951-1994 .... CLC 85
See also CA 115; 127; 144; CANR 45;
INT 127

Shimazaki Haruki 1872-1943
See Shimazaki Toson
See also CA 105; 134

Shimazaki Toson................. TCLC 5
See also Shimazaki Haruki

Sholokhov, Mikhail (Aleksandrovich)
1905-1984 .... CLC 7, 15
See also CA 101; 112; MTCW;
SATA-Obit 36

Shone, Patric
See Hanley, James

Shreve, Susan Richards 1939-...... CLC 23
See also CA 49-52; CAAS 5; CANR 5, 38;
MAICYA; SATA 46; SATA-Brief 41

Shue, Larry 1946-1985............ CLC 52
See also CA 145; 117; DAM DRAM

Shu-Jen, Chou 1881-1936
See Lu Hsun
See also CA 104

Shulman, Alix Kates 1932- ...... CLC 2, 10
See also CA 29-32R; CANR 43; SATA 7

Shuster, Joe 1914- .... CLC 21

Shute, Nevil.................... CLC 30
See also Norway, Nevil Shute

Shuttle, Penelope (Diane) 1947- ..... CLC 7
See also CA 93-96; CANR 39; DLB 14, 40

Sidney, Mary 1561-1621 .... LC 19

Sidney, Sir Philip
1554-1586 ..... LC 19; DA; DAB; DAC
See also CDBLB Before 1660; DAM MST,
POET

Siegel, Jerome 1914- .... CLC 21
See also CA 116

Siegel, Jerry
See Siegel, Jerome

Sienkiewicz, Henryk (Adam Alexander Pius)
1846-1916 .... TCLC 3
See also CA 104; 134

Sierra, Gregorio Martinez
See Martinez Sierra, Gregorio

Sierra, Maria (de la O'LeJarraga) Martinez
See Martinez Sierra, Maria (de la O'LeJarraga)

Sigal, Clancy 1926-.............. **CLC 7**
See also CA 1-4R

Sigourney, Lydia Howard (Huntley)
1791-1865 .... **NCLC 21**
See also DLB 1, 42, 73

Siguenza y Gongora, Carlos de
1645-1700 .... **LC 8**

Sigurjonsson, Johann 1880-1919... **TCLC 27**

Sikelianos, Angelos 1884-1951 .... **TCLC 39**

Silkin, Jon 1930- .... **CLC 2, 6, 43**
See also CA 5-8R; CAAS 5; DLB 27

Silko, Leslie (Marmon)
1948- .... **CLC 23, 74; DA; DAC**
See also AAYA 14; CA 115; 122;
CANR 45; DAM MST, MULT, POP;
DLB 143; NNAL

Sillanpaa, Frans Eemil 1888-1964... **CLC 19**
See also CA 129; 93-96; MTCW

Sillitoe, Alan
1928- .... **CLC 1, 3, 6, 10, 19, 57**
See also AITN 1; CA 9-12R; CAAS 2;
CANR 8, 26; CDBLB 1960 to Present;
DLB 14, 139; MTCW; SATA 61

Silone, Ignazio 1900-1978 .... **CLC 4**
See also CA 25-28; 81-84; CANR 34;
CAP 2; MTCW

Silver, Joan Micklin 1935- .... **CLC 20**
See also CA 114; 121; INT 121

Silver, Nicholas
See Faust, Frederick (Schiller)

Silverberg, Robert 1935- .... **CLC 7**
See also CA 1-4R; CAAS 3; CANR 1, 20,
36; DAM POP; DLB 8; INT CANR-20;
MAICYA; MTCW; SATA 13

Silverstein, Alvin 1933- .... **CLC 17**
See also CA 49-52; CANR 2; CLR 25;
JRDA; MAICYA; SATA 8, 69

Silverstein, Virginia B(arbara Opshelor)
1937- .... **CLC 17**
See also CA 49-52; CANR 2; CLR 25;
JRDA; MAICYA; SATA 8, 69

Sim, Georges
See Simenon, Georges (Jacques Christian)

Simak, Clifford D(onald)
1904-1988 .... **CLC 1, 55**
See also CA 1-4R; 125; CANR 1, 35;
DLB 8; MTCW; SATA-Obit 56

Simenon, Georges (Jacques Christian)
1903-1989 .... **CLC 1, 2, 3, 8, 18, 47**
See also CA 85-88; 129; CANR 35;
DAM POP; DLB 72; DLBY 89; MTCW

Simic, Charles 1938-... **CLC 6, 9, 22, 49, 68**
See also CA 29-32R; CAAS 4; CANR 12,
33; DAM POET; DLB 105

Simmons, Charles (Paul) 1924-..... **CLC 57**
See also CA 89-92; INT 89-92

Simmons, Dan 1948-.............. **CLC 44**
See also AAYA 16; CA 138; DAM POP

Simmons, James (Stewart Alexander)
1933- .... **CLC 43**
See also CA 105; CAAS 21; DLB 40

Simms, William Gilmore
1806-1870 .... **NCLC 3**
See also DLB 3, 30, 59, 73

Simon, Carly 1945-.............. **CLC 26**
See also CA 105

Simon, Claude 1913-....... **CLC 4, 9, 15, 39**
See also CA 89-92; CANR 33; DAM NOV;
DLB 83; MTCW

Simon, (Marvin) Neil
1927- .... **CLC 6, 11, 31, 39, 70**
See also AITN 1; CA 21-24R; CANR 26;
DAM DRAM; DLB 7; MTCW

Simon, Paul 1942(?)- .... **CLC 17**
See also CA 116

Simonon, Paul 1956(?)- .... **CLC 30**

Simpson, Harriette
See Arnow, Harriette (Louisa) Simpson

Simpson, Louis (Aston Marantz)
1923- .... **CLC 4, 7, 9, 32**
See also CA 1-4R; CAAS 4; CANR 1;
DAM POET; DLB 5; MTCW

Simpson, Mona (Elizabeth) 1957-... **CLC 44**
See also CA 122; 135

Simpson, N(orman) F(rederick)
1919- .... **CLC 29**
See also CA 13-16R; DLB 13

Sinclair, Andrew (Annandale)
1935- .... **CLC 2, 14**
See also CA 9-12R; CAAS 5; CANR 14, 38;
DLB 14; MTCW

Sinclair, Emil
See Hesse, Hermann

Sinclair, Iain 1943-.............. **CLC 76**
See also CA 132

Sinclair, Iain MacGregor
See Sinclair, Iain

Sinclair, Mary Amelia St. Clair 1865(?)-1946
See Sinclair, May
See also CA 104

Sinclair, May.................. **TCLC 3, 11**
See also Sinclair, Mary Amelia St. Clair
See also DLB 36, 135

Sinclair, Upton (Beall)
1878-1968 ...... **CLC 1, 11, 15, 63; DA;
DAB; DAC; WLC**
See also CA 5-8R; 25-28R; CANR 7;
CDALB 1929-1941; DAM MST, NOV;
DLB 9; INT CANR-7; MTCW; SATA 9

Singer, Isaac
See Singer, Isaac Bashevis

Singer, Isaac Bashevis
1904-1991 .... **CLC 1, 3, 6, 9, 11, 15, 23,
38, 69; DA; DAB; DAC; SSC 3; WLC**
See also AITN 1, 2; CA 1-4R; 134;
CANR 1, 39; CDALB 1941-1968; CLR 1;
DAM MST, NOV; DLB 6, 28, 52;
DLBY 91; JRDA; MAICYA; MTCW;
SATA 3, 27; SATA-Obit 68

Singer, Israel Joshua 1893-1944... **TCLC 33**

Singh, Khushwant 1915-........... **CLC 11**
See also CA 9-12R; CAAS 9; CANR 6

Sinjohn, John
See Galsworthy, John

Sinyavsky, Andrei (Donatevich)
1925-.................... **CLC 8**
See also CA 85-88

Sirin, V.
See Nabokov, Vladimir (Vladimirovich)

Sissman, L(ouis) E(dward)
1928-1976 .... **CLC 9, 18**
See also CA 21-24R; 65-68; CANR 13;
DLB 5

Sisson, C(harles) H(ubert) 1914-..... **CLC 8**
See also CA 1-4R; CAAS 3; CANR 3, 48;
DLB 27

Sitwell, Dame Edith
1887-1964 .... **CLC 2, 9, 67; PC 3**
See also CA 9-12R; CANR 35;
CDBLB 1945-1960; DAM POET;
DLB 20; MTCW

Sjoewall, Maj 1935-.............. **CLC 7**
See also CA 65-68

Sjowall, Maj
See Sjoewall, Maj

Skelton, Robin 1925-............. **CLC 13**
See also AITN 2; CA 5-8R; CAAS 5;
CANR 28; DLB 27, 53

Skolimowski, Jerzy 1938-......... **CLC 20**
See also CA 128

Skram, Amalie (Bertha)
1847-1905 .... **TCLC 25**

Skvorecky, Josef (Vaclav)
1924-........... **CLC 15, 39, 69; DAC**
See also CA 61-64; CAAS 1; CANR 10, 34;
DAM NOV; MTCW

Slade, Bernard................. **CLC 11, 46**
See also Newbound, Bernard Slade
See also CAAS 9; DLB 53

Slaughter, Carolyn 1946-.......... **CLC 56**
See also CA 85-88

Slaughter, Frank G(ill) 1908- ...... **CLC 29**
See also AITN 2; CA 5-8R; CANR 5;
INT CANR-5

Slavitt, David R(ytman) 1935-.... **CLC 5, 14**
See also CA 21-24R; CAAS 3; CANR 41;
DLB 5, 6

Slesinger, Tess 1905-1945 .... **TCLC 10**
See also CA 107; DLB 102

Slessor, Kenneth 1901-1971........ **CLC 14**
See also CA 102; 89-92

Slowacki, Juliusz 1809-1849 ..... **NCLC 15**

Smart, Christopher
1722-1771 .... **LC 3; PC 13**
See also DAM POET; DLB 109

Smart, Elizabeth 1913-1986........ **CLC 54**
See also CA 81-84; 118; DLB 88

Smiley, Jane (Graves) 1949- .... **CLC 53, 76**
See also CA 104; CANR 30, 50;
DAM POP; INT CANR-30

Smith, A(rthur) J(ames) M(arshall)
1902-1980 .... **CLC 15; DAC**
See also CA 1-4R; 102; CANR 4; DLB 88

Smith, Anna Deavere 1950-........ **CLC 86**
See also CA 133

Smith, Betty (Wehner) 1896-1972... **CLC 19**
See also CA 5-8R; 33-36R; DLBY 82;
SATA 6

Smith, Charlotte (Turner)
    1749-1806 .... **NCLC 23**
    See also DLB 39, 109

Smith, Clark Ashton 1893-1961 .... **CLC 43**
    See also CA 143

Smith, Dave .... **CLC 22, 42**
    See also Smith, David (Jeddie)
    See also CAAS 7; DLB 5

Smith, David (Jeddie) 1942-
    See Smith, Dave
    See also CA 49-52; CANR 1; DAM POET

Smith, Florence Margaret 1902-1971
    See Smith, Stevie
    See also CA 17-18; 29-32R; CANR 35;
    CAP 2; DAM POET; MTCW

Smith, Iain Crichton 1928- .... **CLC 64**
    See also CA 21-24R; DLB 40, 139

Smith, John 1580(?)-1631 .... **LC 9**

Smith, Johnston
    See Crane, Stephen (Townley)

Smith, Joseph, Jr. 1805-1844 .... **NCLC 53**

Smith, Lee 1944-............. **CLC 25, 73**
    See also CA 114; 119; CANR 46; DLB 143;
    DLBY 83; INT 119

Smith, Martin
    See Smith, Martin Cruz

Smith, Martin Cruz 1942-........ **CLC 25**
    See also BEST 89:4; CA 85-88; CANR 6,
    23, 43; DAM MULT, POP;
    INT CANR-23; NNAL

Smith, Mary-Ann Tirone 1944-..... **CLC 39**
    See also CA 118; 136

Smith, Patti 1946- .... **CLC 12**
    See also CA 93-96

Smith, Pauline (Urmson)
    1882-1959 .... **TCLC 25**

Smith, Rosamond
    See Oates, Joyce Carol

Smith, Sheila Kaye
    See Kaye-Smith, Sheila

Smith, Stevie .... **CLC 3, 8, 25, 44; PC 12**
    See also Smith, Florence Margaret
    See also DLB 20

Smith, Wilbur (Addison) 1933-..... **CLC 33**
    See also CA 13-16R; CANR 7, 46; MTCW

Smith, William Jay 1918- .... **CLC 6**
    See also CA 5-8R; CANR 44; DLB 5;
    MAICYA; SAAS 22; SATA 2, 68

Smith, Woodrow Wilson
    See Kuttner, Henry

Smolenskin, Peretz 1842-1885.... **NCLC 30**

Smollett, Tobias (George) 1721-1771 .. **LC 2**
    See also CDBLB 1660-1789; DLB 39, 104

Snodgrass, W(illiam) D(e Witt)
    1926- .... **CLC 2, 6, 10, 18, 68**
    See also CA 1-4R; CANR 6, 36;
    DAM POET; DLB 5; MTCW

Snow, C(harles) P(ercy)
    1905-1980 ...... **CLC 1, 4, 6, 9, 13, 19**
    See also CA 5-8R; 101; CANR 28;
    CDBLB 1945-1960; DAM NOV; DLB 15,
    77; MTCW

Snow, Frances Compton
    See Adams, Henry (Brooks)

Snyder, Gary (Sherman)
    1930- .... **CLC 1, 2, 5, 9, 32**
    See also CA 17-20R; CANR 30;
    DAM POET; DLB 5, 16

Snyder, Zilpha Keatley 1927- ...... **CLC 17**
    See also AAYA 15; CA 9-12R; CANR 38;
    CLR 31; JRDA; MAICYA; SAAS 2;
    SATA 1, 28, 75

Soares, Bernardo
    See Pessoa, Fernando (Antonio Nogueira)

Sobh, A.
    See Shamlu, Ahmad

Sobol, Joshua .... **CLC 60**

Soderberg, Hjalmar 1869-1941 .... **TCLC 39**

Sodergran, Edith (Irene)
    See Soedergran, Edith (Irene)

Soedergran, Edith (Irene)
    1892-1923 .... **TCLC 31**

Softly, Edgar
    See Lovecraft, H(oward) P(hillips)

Softly, Edward
    See Lovecraft, H(oward) P(hillips)

Sokolov, Raymond 1941-.......... **CLC 7**
    See also CA 85-88

Solo, Jay
    See Ellison, Harlan (Jay)

Sologub, Fyodor .... **TCLC 9**
    See also Teternikov, Fyodor Kuzmich

Solomons, Ikey Esquir
    See Thackeray, William Makepeace

Solomos, Dionysios 1798-1857 ... **NCLC 15**

Solwoska, Mara
    See French, Marilyn

Solzhenitsyn, Aleksandr I(sayevich)
    1918- ...... **CLC 1, 2, 4, 7, 9, 10, 18, 26,
        34, 78; DA; DAB; DAC; WLC**
    See also AITN 1; CA 69-72; CANR 40;
    DAM MST, NOV; MTCW

Somers, Jane
    See Lessing, Doris (May)

Somerville, Edith 1858-1949 ...... **TCLC 51**
    See also DLB 135

Somerville & Ross
    See Martin, Violet Florence; Somerville,
    Edith

Sommer, Scott 1951- .... **CLC 25**
    See also CA 106

Sondheim, Stephen (Joshua)
    1930- .... **CLC 30, 39**
    See also AAYA 11; CA 103; CANR 47;
    DAM DRAM

Sontag, Susan 1933-... **CLC 1, 2, 10, 13, 31**
    See also CA 17-20R; CANR 25, 51;
    DAM POP; DLB 2, 67; MTCW

Sophocles
    496(?)B.C.-406(?)B.C..... **CMLC 2; DA;
        DAB; DAC; DC 1**
    See also DAM DRAM, MST

Sordello 1189-1269............ **CMLC 15**

Sorel, Julia
    See Drexler, Rosalyn

Sorrentino, Gilbert
    1929- .... **CLC 3, 7, 14, 22, 40**
    See also CA 77-80; CANR 14, 33; DLB 5;
    DLBY 80; INT CANR-14

Soto, Gary 1952-........ **CLC 32, 80; HLC**
    See also AAYA 10; CA 119; 125;
    CANR 50; CLR 38; DAM MULT;
    DLB 82; HW; INT 125; JRDA; SATA 80

Soupault, Philippe 1897-1990 ...... **CLC 68**
    See also CA 116; 147; 131

Souster, (Holmes) Raymond
    1921- .... **CLC 5, 14; DAC**
    See also CA 13-16R; CAAS 14; CANR 13,
    29; DAM POET; DLB 88; SATA 63

Southern, Terry 1924(?)-1995 .... **CLC 7**
    See also CA 1-4R; 150; CANR 1; DLB 2

Southey, Robert 1774-1843 .... **NCLC 8**
    See also DLB 93, 107, 142; SATA 54

Southworth, Emma Dorothy Eliza Nevitte
    1819-1899 .... **NCLC 26**

Souza, Ernest
    See Scott, Evelyn

Soyinka, Wole
    1934- .... **CLC 3, 5, 14, 36, 44; BLC;
        DA; DAB; DAC; DC 2; WLC**
    See also BW 2; CA 13-16R; CANR 27, 39;
    DAM DRAM, MST, MULT; DLB 125;
    MTCW

Spackman, W(illiam) M(ode)
    1905-1990 .... **CLC 46**
    See also CA 81-84; 132

Spacks, Barry 1931-.............. **CLC 14**
    See also CA 29-32R; CANR 33; DLB 105

Spanidou, Irini 1946- .... **CLC 44**

Spark, Muriel (Sarah)
    1918- .... **CLC 2, 3, 5, 8, 13, 18, 40;
        DAB; DAC; SSC 10**
    See also CA 5-8R; CANR 12, 36;
    CDBLB 1945-1960; DAM MST, NOV;
    DLB 15, 139; INT CANR-12; MTCW

Spaulding, Douglas
    See Bradbury, Ray (Douglas)

Spaulding, Leonard
    See Bradbury, Ray (Douglas)

Spence, J. A. D.
    See Eliot, T(homas) S(tearns)

Spencer, Elizabeth 1921-.......... **CLC 22**
    See also CA 13-16R; CANR 32; DLB 6;
    MTCW; SATA 14

Spencer, Leonard G.
    See Silverberg, Robert

Spencer, Scott 1945-............. **CLC 30**
    See also CA 113; CANR 51; DLBY 86

Spender, Stephen (Harold)
    1909-1995 ...... **CLC 1, 2, 5, 10, 41, 91**
    See also CA 9-12R; 149; CANR 31;
    CDBLB 1945-1960; DAM POET;
    DLB 20; MTCW

Spengler, Oswald (Arnold Gottfried)
    1880-1936 .... **TCLC 25**
    See also CA 118

Spenser, Edmund
1552(?)-1599 .... **LC 5; DA; DAB; DAC;**
PC 8; WLC
See also CDBLB Before 1660; DAM MST,
POET

Spicer, Jack 1925-1965 ...... **CLC 8, 18, 72**
See also CA 85-88; DAM POET; DLB 5, 16

Spiegelman, Art 1948- .... **CLC 76**
See also AAYA 10; CA 125; CANR 41

Spielberg, Peter 1929- .... **CLC 6**
See also CA 5-8R; CANR 4, 48; DLBY 81

Spielberg, Steven 1947- .... **CLC 20**
See also AAYA 8; CA 77-80; CANR 32;
SATA 32

Spillane, Frank Morrison 1918-
See Spillane, Mickey
See also CA 25-28R; CANR 28; MTCW;
SATA 66

Spillane, Mickey .... **CLC 3, 13**
See also Spillane, Frank Morrison

Spinoza, Benedictus de 1632-1677 .... **LC 9**

Spinrad, Norman (Richard) 1940-... **CLC 46**
See also CA 37-40R; CAAS 19; CANR 20;
DLB 8; INT CANR-20

Spitteler, Carl (Friedrich Georg)
1845-1924 .... **TCLC 12**
See also CA 109; DLB 129

Spivack, Kathleen (Romola Drucker)
1938- .... **CLC 6**
See also CA 49-52

Spoto, Donald 1941- .... **CLC 39**
See also CA 65-68; CANR 11

Springsteen, Bruce (F.) 1949- ...... **CLC 17**
See also CA 111

Spurling, Hilary 1940- .... **CLC 34**
See also CA 104; CANR 25

Spyker, John Howland
See Elman, Richard

Squires, (James) Radcliffe
1917-1993 .... **CLC 51**
See also CA 1-4R; 140; CANR 6, 21

Srivastava, Dhanpat Rai 1880(?)-1936
See Premchand
See also CA 118

Stacy, Donald
See Pohl, Frederik

Stael, Germaine de
See Stael-Holstein, Anne Louise Germaine
Necker Baronn
See also DLB 119

Stael-Holstein, Anne Louise Germaine Necker
Baronn 1766-1817 .... **NCLC 3**
See also Stael, Germaine de

Stafford, Jean 1915-1979 ... **CLC 4, 7, 19, 68**
See also CA 1-4R; 85-88; CANR 3; DLB 2;
MTCW; SATA-Obit 22

Stafford, William (Edgar)
1914-1993 .... **CLC 4, 7, 29**
See also CA 5-8R; 142; CAAS 3; CANR 5,
22; DAM POET; DLB 5; INT CANR-22

Staines, Trevor
See Brunner, John (Kilian Houston)

Stairs, Gordon
See Austin, Mary (Hunter)

Stannard, Martin 1947- .... **CLC 44**
See also CA 142; DLB 155

Stanton, Maura 1946- .... **CLC 9**
See also CA 89-92; CANR 15; DLB 120

Stanton, Schuyler
See Baum, L(yman) Frank

Stapledon, (William) Olaf
1886-1950 .... **TCLC 22**
See also CA 111; DLB 15

Starbuck, George (Edwin) 1931-.... **CLC 53**
See also CA 21-24R; CANR 23;
DAM POET

Stark, Richard
See Westlake, Donald E(dwin)

Staunton, Schuyler
See Baum, L(yman) Frank

Stead, Christina (Ellen)
1902-1983 .... **CLC 2, 5, 8, 32, 80**
See also CA 13-16R; 109; CANR 33, 40;
MTCW

Stead, William Thomas
1849-1912 .... **TCLC 48**

Steele, Richard 1672-1729 .... **LC 18**
See also CDBLB 1660-1789; DLB 84, 101

Steele, Timothy (Reid) 1948-...... **CLC 45**
See also CA 93-96; CANR 16, 50; DLB 120

Steffens, (Joseph) Lincoln
1866-1936 .... **TCLC 20**
See also CA 117

Stegner, Wallace (Earle)
1909-1993 .... **CLC 9, 49, 81**
See also AITN 1; BEST 90:3; CA 1-4R;
141; CAAS 9; CANR 1, 21, 46;
DAM NOV; DLB 9; DLBY 93; MTCW

Stein, Gertrude
1874-1946 ...... **TCLC 1, 6, 28, 48; DA;**
DAB; DAC; WLC
See also CA 104; 132; CDALB 1917-1929;
DAM MST, NOV, POET; DLB 4, 54, 86;
MTCW

Steinbeck, John (Ernst)
1902-1968 ...... **CLC 1, 5, 9, 13, 21, 34,**
45, 75; DA; DAB; DAC; SSC 11; WLC
See also AAYA 12; CA 1-4R; 25-28R;
CANR 1, 35; CDALB 1929-1941;
DAM DRAM, MST, NOV; DLB 7, 9;
DLBD 2; MTCW; SATA 9

Steinem, Gloria 1934-............. **CLC 63**
See also CA 53-56; CANR 28, 51; MTCW

Steiner, George 1929-............. **CLC 24**
See also CA 73-76; CANR 31; DAM NOV;
DLB 67; MTCW; SATA 62

Steiner, K. Leslie
See Delany, Samuel R(ay, Jr.)

Steiner, Rudolf 1861-1925 .... **TCLC 13**
See also CA 107

Stendhal
1783-1842 .... **NCLC 23, 46; DA; DAB;**
DAC; WLC
See also DAM MST, NOV; DLB 119

Stephen, Leslie 1832-1904 .... **TCLC 23**
See also CA 123; DLB 57, 144

Stephen, Sir Leslie
See Stephen, Leslie

Stephen, Virginia
See Woolf, (Adeline) Virginia

Stephens, James 1882(?)-1950...... **TCLC 4**
See also CA 104; DLB 19, 153, 162

Stephens, Reed
See Donaldson, Stephen R.

Steptoe, Lydia
See Barnes, Djuna

Sterchi, Beat 1949-.............. **CLC 65**

Sterling, Brett
See Bradbury, Ray (Douglas); Hamilton,
Edmond

Sterling, Bruce 1954-............. **CLC 72**
See also CA 119; CANR 44

Sterling, George 1869-1926 .... **TCLC 20**
See also CA 117; DLB 54

Stern, Gerald 1925- .... **CLC 40**
See also CA 81-84; CANR 28; DLB 105

Stern, Richard (Gustave) 1928-... **CLC 4, 39**
See also CA 1-4R; CANR 1, 25; DLBY 87;
INT CANR-25

Sternberg, Josef von 1894-1969..... **CLC 20**
See also CA 81-84

Sterne, Laurence
1713-1768 ...... **LC 2; DA; DAB; DAC;**
WLC
See also CDBLB 1660-1789; DAM MST,
NOV; DLB 39

Sternheim, (William Adolf) Carl
1878-1942 .... **TCLC 8**
See also CA 105; DLB 56, 118

Stevens, Mark 1951- .... **CLC 34**
See also CA 122

Stevens, Wallace
1879-1955 .... **TCLC 3, 12, 45; DA;**
DAB; DAC; PC 6; WLC
See also CA 104; 124; CDALB 1929-1941;
DAM MST, POET; DLB 54; MTCW

Stevenson, Anne (Katharine)
1933- .... **CLC 7, 33**
See also CA 17-20R; CAAS 9; CANR 9, 33;
DLB 40; MTCW

Stevenson, Robert Louis (Balfour)
1850-1894 ..... **NCLC 5, 14; DA; DAB;**
DAC; SSC 11; WLC
See also CDBLB 1890-1914; CLR 10, 11;
DAM MST, NOV; DLB 18, 57, 141, 156;
DLBD 13; JRDA; MAICYA; YABC 2

Stewart, J(ohn) I(nnes) M(ackintosh)
1906-1994 .... **CLC 7, 14, 32**
See also CA 85-88; 147; CAAS 3;
CANR 47; MTCW

Stewart, Mary (Florence Elinor)
1916- .... **CLC 7, 35; DAB**
See also CA 1-4R; CANR 1; SATA 12

Stewart, Mary Rainbow
See Stewart, Mary (Florence Elinor)

Stifle, June
See Campbell, Maria

Stifter, Adalbert 1805-1868...... **NCLC 41**
See also DLB 133

Still, James 1906-................ **CLC 49**
See also CA 65-68; CAAS 17; CANR 10,
26; DLB 9; SATA 29

Sting
See Sumner, Gordon Matthew

Stirling, Arthur
See Sinclair, Upton (Beall)

Stitt, Milan 1941-............... **CLC 29**
See also CA 69-72

Stockton, Francis Richard 1834-1902
See Stockton, Frank R.
See also CA 108; 137; MAICYA; SATA 44

Stockton, Frank R.................**TCLC 47**
See also Stockton, Francis Richard
See also DLB 42, 74; DLBD 13;
SATA-Brief 32

Stoddard, Charles
See Kuttner, Henry

Stoker, Abraham 1847-1912
See Stoker, Bram
See also CA 105; DA; DAC; DAM MST,
NOV; SATA 29

Stoker, Bram
1847-1912 .... **TCLC 8; DAB; WLC**
See also Stoker, Abraham
See also CA 150; CDBLB 1890-1914;
DLB 36, 70

Stolz, Mary (Slattery) 1920-....... **CLC 12**
See also AAYA 8; AITN 1; CA 5-8R;
CANR 13, 41; JRDA; MAICYA;
SAAS 3; SATA 10, 71

Stone, Irving 1903-1989........... **CLC 7**
See also AITN 1; CA 1-4R; 129; CAAS 3;
CANR 1, 23; DAM POP;
INT CANR-23; MTCW; SATA 3;
SATA-Obit 64

Stone, Oliver 1946-............... **CLC 73**
See also AAYA 15; CA 110

Stone, Robert (Anthony)
1937-................ **CLC 5, 23, 42**
See also CA 85-88; CANR 23; DLB 152;
INT CANR-23; MTCW

Stone, Zachary
See Follett, Ken(neth Martin)

Stoppard, Tom
1937-...... **CLC 1, 3, 4, 5, 8, 15, 29, 34,
63, 91; DA; DAB; DAC; DC 6; WLC**
See also CA 81-84; CANR 39;
CDBLB 1960 to Present; DAM DRAM,
MST; DLB 13; DLBY 85; MTCW

Storey, David (Malcolm)
1933-................... **CLC 2, 4, 5, 8**
See also CA 81-84; CANR 36;
DAM DRAM; DLB 13, 14; MTCW

Storm, Hyemeyohsts 1935-......... **CLC 3**
See also CA 81-84; CANR 45;
DAM MULT; NNAL

Storm, (Hans) Theodor (Woldsen)
1817-1888 .... **NCLC 1**

Storni, Alfonsina
1892-1938 .... **TCLC 5; HLC**
See also CA 104; 131; DAM MULT; HW

Stout, Rex (Todhunter) 1886-1975 ... **CLC 3**
See also AITN 2; CA 61-64

Stow, (Julian) Randolph 1935-.. **CLC 23, 48**
See also CA 13-16R; CANR 33; MTCW

Stowe, Harriet (Elizabeth) Beecher
1811-1896 ..... **NCLC 3, 50; DA; DAB;
DAC; WLC**
See also CDALB 1865-1917; DAM MST,
NOV; DLB 1, 12, 42, 74; JRDA;
MAICYA; YABC 1

Strachey, (Giles) Lytton
1880-1932 .... **TCLC 12**
See also CA 110; DLB 149; DLBD 10

Strand, Mark 1934-...... **CLC 6, 18, 41, 71**
See also CA 21-24R; CANR 40;
DAM POET; DLB 5; SATA 41

Straub, Peter (Francis) 1943-...... **CLC 28**
See also BEST 89:1; CA 85-88; CANR 28;
DAM POP; DLBY 84; MTCW

Strauss, Botho 1944-............... **CLC 22**
See also DLB 124

Streatfeild, (Mary) Noel
1895(?)-1986 .... **CLC 21**
See also CA 81-84; 120; CANR 31;
CLR 17; DLB 160; MAICYA; SATA 20;
SATA-Obit 48

Stribling, T(homas) S(igismund)
1881-1965 .... **CLC 23**
See also CA 107; DLB 9

Strindberg, (Johan) August
1849-1912 ...... **TCLC 1, 8, 21, 47; DA;
DAB; DAC; WLC**
See also CA 104; 135; DAM DRAM, MST

Stringer, Arthur 1874-1950 ...... **TCLC 37**
See also DLB 92

Stringer, David
See Roberts, Keith (John Kingston)

Strugatskii, Arkadii (Natanovich)
1925-1991 .... **CLC 27**
See also CA 106; 135

Strugatskii, Boris (Natanovich)
1933-..................... **CLC 27**
See also CA 106

Strummer, Joe 1953(?)-........... **CLC 30**

Stuart, Don A.
See Campbell, John W(ood, Jr.)

Stuart, Ian
See MacLean, Alistair (Stuart)

Stuart, Jesse (Hilton)
1906-1984 .... **CLC 1, 8, 11, 14, 34**
See also CA 5-8R; 112; CANR 31; DLB 9,
48, 102; DLBY 84; SATA 2;
SATA-Obit 36

Sturgeon, Theodore (Hamilton)
1918-1985 .... **CLC 22, 39**
See also Queen, Ellery
See also CA 81-84; 116; CANR 32; DLB 8;
DLBY 85; MTCW

Sturges, Preston 1898-1959 ...... **TCLC 48**
See also CA 114; 149; DLB 26

Styron, William
1925-......... **CLC 1, 3, 5, 11, 15, 60**
See also BEST 90:4; CA 5-8R; CANR 6, 33;
CDALB 1968-1988; DAM NOV, POP;
DLB 2, 143; DLBY 80; INT CANR-6;
MTCW

Suarez Lynch, B.
See Bioy Casares, Adolfo; Borges, Jorge
Luis

Su Chien 1884-1918
See Su Man-shu
See also CA 123

Suckow, Ruth 1892-1960......... **SSC 18**
See also CA 113; DLB 9, 102

Sudermann, Hermann 1857-1928 .. **TCLC 15**
See also CA 107; DLB 118

Sue, Eugene 1804-1857 .... **NCLC 1**
See also DLB 119

Sueskind, Patrick 1949-........... **CLC 44**
See also Suskind, Patrick

Sukenick, Ronald 1932-..... **CLC 3, 4, 6, 48**
See also CA 25-28R; CAAS 8; CANR 32;
DLBY 81

Suknaski, Andrew 1942- .... **CLC 19**
See also CA 101; DLB 53

Sullivan, Vernon
See Vian, Boris

Sully Prudhomme 1839-1907...... **TCLC 31**

Su Man-shu .... **TCLC 24**
See also Su Chien

Summerforest, Ivy B.
See Kirkup, James

Summers, Andrew James 1942-..... **CLC 26**

Summers, Andy
See Summers, Andrew James

Summers, Hollis (Spurgeon, Jr.)
1916-...................... **CLC 10**
See also CA 5-8R; CANR 3; DLB 6

**Summers, (Alphonsus Joseph-Mary Augustus)
Montague** 1880-1948........ **TCLC 16**
See also CA 118

Sumner, Gordon Matthew 1951-.... **CLC 26**

Surtees, Robert Smith
1803-1864 .... **NCLC 14**
See also DLB 21

Susann, Jacqueline 1921-1974....... **CLC 3**
See also AITN 1; CA 65-68; 53-56; MTCW

Su Shih 1036-1101 .... **CMLC 15**

Suskind, Patrick
See Sueskind, Patrick
See also CA 145

Sutcliff, Rosemary
1920-1992 .... **CLC 26; DAB; DAC**
See also AAYA 10; CA 5-8R; 139;
CANR 37; CLR 1, 37; DAM MST, POP;
JRDA; MAICYA; SATA 6, 44, 78;
SATA-Obit 73

Sutro, Alfred 1863-1933.......... **TCLC 6**
See also CA 105; DLB 10

Sutton, Henry
See Slavitt, David R(ytman)

Svevo, Italo .... **TCLC 2, 35**
See also Schmitz, Aron Hector

Swados, Elizabeth (A.) 1951-....... **CLC 12**
See also CA 97-100; CANR 49; INT 97-100

Swados, Harvey 1920-1972 .... **CLC 5**
See also CA 5-8R; 37-40R; CANR 6;
DLB 2

Swan, Gladys 1934- .... **CLC 69**
See also CA 101; CANR 17, 39

Torsvan, Berwick Traven
See Traven, B.

Torsvan, Bruno Traven
See Traven, B.

Torsvan, Traven
See Traven, B.

Tournier, Michel (Edouard)
1924- . . . . **CLC 6, 23, 36**
See also CA 49-52; CANR 3, 36; DLB 83;
MTCW; SATA 23

Tournimparte, Alessandra
See Ginzburg, Natalia

Towers, Ivar
See Kornbluth, C(yril) M.

Towne, Robert (Burton) 1936(?)- . . . . **CLC 87**
See also CA 108; DLB 44

Townsend, Sue 1946- . . **CLC 61; DAB; DAC**
See also CA 119; 127; INT 127; MTCW;
SATA 55; SATA-Brief 48

Townshend, Peter (Dennis Blandford)
1945- . . . . **CLC 17, 42**
See also CA 107

Tozzi, Federigo 1883-1920. . . . . . . **TCLC 31**

Traill, Catharine Parr
1802-1899 . . . . **NCLC 31**
See also DLB 99

Trakl, Georg 1887-1914. . . . . **TCLC 5**
See also CA 104

Transtroemer, Tomas (Goesta)
1931- . . . . **CLC 52, 65**
See also CA 117; 129; CAAS 17;
DAM POET

Transtromer, Tomas Gosta
See Transtroemer, Tomas (Goesta)

Traven, B. (?)-1969. . . . . **CLC 8, 11**
See also CA 19-20; 25-28R; CAP 2; DLB 9,
56; MTCW

Treitel, Jonathan 1959- . . . . **CLC 70**

Tremain, Rose 1943-. . . . . **CLC 42**
See also CA 97-100; CANR 44; DLB 14

Tremblay, Michel 1942-. . . . . . **CLC 29; DAC**
See also CA 116; 128; DAM MST; DLB 60;
MTCW

Trevanian. . . . . **CLC 29**
See also Whitaker, Rod(ney)

Trevor, Glen
See Hilton, James

Trevor, William
1928- . . . . . **CLC 7, 9, 14, 25, 71; SSC 21**
See also Cox, William Trevor
See also DLB 14, 139

Trifonov, Yuri (Valentinovich)
1925-1981 . . . . **CLC 45**
See also CA 126; 103; MTCW

Trilling, Lionel 1905-1975 . . . . **CLC 9, 11, 24**
See also CA 9-12R; 61-64; CANR 10;
DLB 28, 63; INT CANR-10; MTCW

Trimball, W. H.
See Mencken, H(enry) L(ouis)

Tristan
See Gomez de la Serna, Ramon

Tristram
See Housman, A(lfred) E(dward)

Trogdon, William (Lewis) 1939-
See Heat-Moon, William Least
See also CA 115; 119; CANR 47; INT 119

Trollope, Anthony
1815-1882 . . . . . **NCLC 6, 33; DA; DAB;**
DAC; WLC
See also CDBLB 1832-1890; DAM MST,
NOV; DLB 21, 57, 159; SATA 22

Trollope, Frances 1779-1863 . . . . . **NCLC 30**
See also DLB 21

Trotsky, Leon 1879-1940. . . . . **TCLC 22**
See also CA 118

Trotter (Cockburn), Catharine
1679-1749 . . . . **LC 8**
See also DLB 84

Trout, Kilgore
See Farmer, Philip Jose

Trow, George W. S. 1943-. . . . . **CLC 52**
See also CA 126

Troyat, Henri 1911-. . . . . **CLC 23**
See also CA 45-48; CANR 2, 33; MTCW

Trudeau, G(arretson) B(eekman) 1948-
See Trudeau, Garry B.
See also CA 81-84; CANR 31; SATA 35

Trudeau, Garry B.. . . . . **CLC 12**
See also Trudeau, G(arretson) B(eekman)
See also AAYA 10; AITN 2

Truffaut, Francois 1932-1984. . . . . . **CLC 20**
See also CA 81-84; 113; CANR 34

Trumbo, Dalton 1905-1976 . . . . **CLC 19**
See also CA 21-24R; 69-72; CANR 10;
DLB 26

Trumbull, John 1750-1831. . . . . . **NCLC 30**
See also DLB 31

Trundlett, Helen B.
See Eliot, T(homas) S(tearns)

Tryon, Thomas 1926-1991 . . . . . . **CLC 3, 11**
See also AITN 1; CA 29-32R; 135;
CANR 32; DAM POP; MTCW

Tryon, Tom
See Tryon, Thomas

Ts'ao Hsueh-ch'in 1715(?)-1763. . . . . . **LC 1**

Tsushima, Shuji 1909-1948
See Dazai, Osamu
See also CA 107

Tsvetaeva (Efron), Marina (Ivanovna)
1892-1941 . . . . **TCLC 7, 35; PC 14**
See also CA 104; 128; MTCW

Tuck, Lily 1938-. . . . . **CLC 70**
See also CA 139

Tu Fu 712-770. . . . . **PC 9**
See also DAM MULT

Tunis, John R(oberts) 1889-1975 . . . **CLC 12**
See also CA 61-64; DLB 22; JRDA;
MAICYA; SATA 37; SATA-Brief 30

Tuohy, Frank. . . . . **CLC 37**
See also Tuohy, John Francis
See also DLB 14, 139

Tuohy, John Francis 1925-
See Tuohy, Frank
See also CA 5-8R; CANR 3, 47

Turco, Lewis (Putnam) 1934- . . . **CLC 11, 63**
See also CA 13-16R; CAAS 22; CANR 24,
51; DLBY 84

Turgenev, Ivan
1818-1883 . . . . **NCLC 21; DA; DAB;**
DAC; SSC 7; WLC
See also DAM MST, NOV

Turgot, Anne-Robert-Jacques
1727-1781 . . . . **LC 26**

Turner, Frederick 1943-. . . . . **CLC 48**
See also CA 73-76; CAAS 10; CANR 12,
30; DLB 40

Tutu, Desmond M(pilo)
1931- . . . . **CLC 80; BLC**
See also BW 1; CA 125; DAM MULT

Tutuola, Amos 1920- . . . **CLC 5, 14, 29; BLC**
See also BW 2; CA 9-12R; CANR 27;
DAM MULT; DLB 125; MTCW

Twain, Mark
. . . . . **TCLC 6, 12, 19, 36, 48, 59; SSC 6;**
WLC
See also Clemens, Samuel Langhorne
See also DLB 11, 12, 23, 64, 74

Tyler, Anne
1941- . . . . **CLC 7, 11, 18, 28, 44, 59**
See also BEST 89:1; CA 9-12R; CANR 11,
33; DAM NOV, POP; DLB 6, 143;
DLBY 82; MTCW; SATA 7

Tyler, Royall 1757-1826. . . . . **NCLC 3**
See also DLB 37

Tynan, Katharine 1861-1931 . . . . **TCLC 3**
See also CA 104; DLB 153

Tyutchev, Fyodor 1803-1873 . . . . . **NCLC 34**

Tzara, Tristan . . . . **CLC 47**
See also Rosenfeld, Samuel
See also DAM POET

Uhry, Alfred 1936-. . . . . **CLC 55**
See also CA 127; 133; DAM DRAM, POP;
INT 133

Ulf, Haerved
See Strindberg, (Johan) August

Ulf, Harved
See Strindberg, (Johan) August

Ulibarri, Sabine R(eyes) 1919- . . . . . **CLC 83**
See also CA 131; DAM MULT; DLB 82;
HW

Unamuno (y Jugo), Miguel de
1864-1936 . . . . **TCLC 2, 9; HLC; SSC 11**
See also CA 104; 131; DAM MULT, NOV;
DLB 108; HW; MTCW

Undercliffe, Errol
See Campbell, (John) Ramsey

Underwood, Miles
See Glassco, John

Undset, Sigrid
1882-1949 . . . . **TCLC 3; DA; DAB;**
DAC; WLC
See also CA 104; 129; DAM MST, NOV;
MTCW

Ungaretti, Giuseppe
1888-1970 . . . . **CLC 7, 11, 15**
See also CA 19-20; 25-28R; CAP 2;
DLB 114

Unger, Douglas 1952-. . . . . **CLC 34**
See also CA 130

Unsworth, Barry (Forster) 1930-. . . . **CLC 76**
See also CA 25-28R; CANR 30

Updike, John (Hoyer)
     1932- ...... **CLC 1, 2, 3, 5, 7, 9, 13, 15,**
     23, 34, 43, 70; DA; DAB; DAC; SSC 13;
                                                  WLC
     See also CA 1-4R; CABS 1; CANR 4, 33,
     51; CDALB 1968-1988; DAM MST,
     NOV, POET, POP; DLB 2, 5, 143;
     DLBD 3; DLBY 80, 82; MTCW

Upshaw, Margaret Mitchell
     See Mitchell, Margaret (Munnerlyn)

Upton, Mark
     See Sanders, Lawrence

Urdang, Constance (Henriette)
     1922- .... **CLC 47**
     See also CA 21-24R; CANR 9, 24

Uriel, Henry
     See Faust, Frederick (Schiller)

Uris, Leon (Marcus) 1924-...... **CLC 7, 32**
     See also AITN 1, 2; BEST 89:2; CA 1-4R;
     CANR 1, 40; DAM NOV, POP; MTCW;
     SATA 49

Urmuz
     See Codrescu, Andrei

Urquhart, Jane 1949-........ **CLC 90; DAC**
     See also CA 113; CANR 32

Ustinov, Peter (Alexander) 1921- .... **CLC 1**
     See also AITN 1; CA 13-16R; CANR 25,
     51; DLB 13

Vaculik, Ludvik 1926- .... **CLC 7**
     See also CA 53-56

Valdez, Luis (Miguel)
     1940- .... **CLC 84; HLC**
     See also CA 101; CANR 32; DAM MULT;
     DLB 122; HW

Valenzuela, Luisa 1938-... **CLC 31; SSC 14**
     See also CA 101; CANR 32; DAM MULT;
     DLB 113; HW

Valera y Alcala-Galiano, Juan
     1824-1905 .... **TCLC 10**
     See also CA 106

Valery, (Ambroise) Paul (Toussaint Jules)
     1871-1945 .... **TCLC 4, 15; PC 9**
     See also CA 104; 122; DAM POET; MTCW

Valle-Inclan, Ramon (Maria) del
     1866-1936 .... **TCLC 5; HLC**
     See also CA 106; DAM MULT; DLB 134

Vallejo, Antonio Buero
     See Buero Vallejo, Antonio

Vallejo, Cesar (Abraham)
     1892-1938 .... **TCLC 3, 56; HLC**
     See also CA 105; DAM MULT; HW

Valle Y Pena, Ramon del
     See Valle-Inclan, Ramon (Maria) del

Van Ash, Cay 1918- .... **CLC 34**

Vanbrugh, Sir John 1664-1726 ...... **LC 21**
     See also DAM DRAM; DLB 80

Van Campen, Karl
     See Campbell, John W(ood, Jr.)

Vance, Gerald
     See Silverberg, Robert

Vance, Jack .... **CLC 35**
     See also Vance, John Holbrook
     See also DLB 8

Vance, John Holbrook   1916-
     See Queen, Ellery; Vance, Jack
     See also CA 29-32R; CANR 17; MTCW

Van Den Bogarde, Derek Jules Gaspard Ulric
     Niven 1921-
     See Bogarde, Dirk
     See also CA 77-80

Vandenburgh, Jane .... **CLC 59**

Vanderhaeghe, Guy 1951- .... **CLC 41**
     See also CA 113

van der Post, Laurens (Jan) 1906- ... **CLC 5**
     See also CA 5-8R; CANR 35

van de Wetering, Janwillem 1931-.. **CLC 47**
     See also CA 49-52; CANR 4

Van Dine, S. S. .... **TCLC 23**
     See also Wright, Willard Huntington

Van Doren, Carl (Clinton)
     1885-1950 .... **TCLC 18**
     See also CA 111

Van Doren, Mark 1894-1972..... **CLC 6, 10**
     See also CA 1-4R; 37-40R; CANR 3;
     DLB 45; MTCW

Van Druten, John (William)
     1901-1957 .... **TCLC 2**
     See also CA 104; DLB 10

Van Duyn, Mona (Jane)
     1921- .... **CLC 3, 7, 63**
     See also CA 9-12R; CANR 7, 38;
     DAM POET; DLB 5

Van Dyne, Edith
     See Baum, L(yman) Frank

van Itallie, Jean-Claude 1936-....... **CLC 3**
     See also CA 45-48; CAAS 2; CANR 1, 48;
     DLB 7

van Ostaijen, Paul 1896-1928 ..... **TCLC 33**

Van Peebles, Melvin 1932- ...... **CLC 2, 20**
     See also BW 2; CA 85-88; CANR 27;
     DAM MULT

Vansittart, Peter 1920-............ **CLC 42**
     See also CA 1-4R; CANR 3, 49

Van Vechten, Carl 1880-1964 ...... **CLC 33**
     See also CA 89-92; DLB 4, 9, 51

Van Vogt, A(lfred) E(lton) 1912-..... **CLC 1**
     See also CA 21-24R; CANR 28; DLB 8;
     SATA 14

Varda, Agnes 1928- .... **CLC 16**
     See also CA 116; 122

Vargas Llosa, (Jorge) Mario (Pedro)
     1936- .... **CLC 3, 6, 9, 10, 15, 31, 42, 85;**
                            DA; DAB; DAC; HLC
     See also CA 73-76; CANR 18, 32, 42;
     DAM MST, MULT, NOV; DLB 145;
     HW; MTCW

Vasiliu, Gheorghe 1881-1957
     See Bacovia, George
     See also CA 123

Vassa, Gustavus
     See Equiano, Olaudah

Vassilikos, Vassilis 1933-........ **CLC 4, 8**
     See also CA 81-84

Vaughan, Henry 1621-1695 .... **LC 27**
     See also DLB 131

Vaughn, Stephanie .... **CLC 62**

Vazov, Ivan (Minchov)
     1850-1921 .... **TCLC 25**
     See also CA 121; DLB 147

Veblen, Thorstein (Bunde)
     1857-1929 .... **TCLC 31**
     See also CA 115

Vega, Lope de 1562-1635.......... **LC 23**

Venison, Alfred
     See Pound, Ezra (Weston Loomis)

Verdi, Marie de
     See Mencken, H(enry) L(ouis)

Verdu, Matilde
     See Cela, Camilo Jose

Verga, Giovanni (Carmelo)
     1840-1922 .... **TCLC 3; SSC 21**
     See also CA 104; 123

Vergil
     70B.C.-19B.C...... **CMLC 9; DA; DAB;**
                                      DAC; PC 12
     See also DAM MST, POET

Verhaeren, Emile (Adolphe Gustave)
     1855-1916 .... **TCLC 12**
     See also CA 109

Verlaine, Paul (Marie)
     1844-1896 .... **NCLC 2, 51; PC 2**
     See also DAM POET

Verne, Jules (Gabriel)
     1828-1905 .... **TCLC 6, 52**
     See also AAYA 16; CA 110; 131; DLB 123;
     JRDA; MAICYA; SATA 21

Very, Jones 1813-1880.......... **NCLC 9**
     See also DLB 1

Vesaas, Tarjei 1897-1970......... **CLC 48**
     See also CA 29-32R

Vialis, Gaston
     See Simenon, Georges (Jacques Christian)

Vian, Boris 1920-1959 .... **TCLC 9**
     See also CA 106; DLB 72

Viaud, (Louis Marie) Julien 1850-1923
     See Loti, Pierre
     See also CA 107

Vicar, Henry
     See Felsen, Henry Gregor

Vicker, Angus
     See Felsen, Henry Gregor

Vidal, Gore
     1925- ..... **CLC 2, 4, 6, 8, 10, 22, 33, 72**
     See also AITN 1; BEST 90:2; CA 5-8R;
     CANR 13, 45; DAM NOV, POP; DLB 6,
     152; INT CANR-13; MTCW

Viereck, Peter (Robert Edwin)
     1916- .... **CLC 4**
     See also CA 1-4R; CANR 1, 47; DLB 5

Vigny, Alfred (Victor) de
     1797-1863 .... **NCLC 7**
     See also DAM POET; DLB 119

Vilakazi, Benedict Wallet
     1906-1947 .... **TCLC 37**

Villiers de l'Isle Adam, Jean Marie Mathias
     Philippe Auguste Comte
     1838-1889 .... **NCLC 3; SSC 14**
     See also DLB 123

Villon, Francois 1431-1463(?) .... **PC 13**

Vinci, Leonardo da 1452-1519....... **LC 12**

Vine, Barbara .... CLC **50**
See also Rendell, Ruth (Barbara)
See also BEST 90:4

Vinge, Joan D(ennison) 1948- ...... CLC **30**
See also CA 93-96; SATA 36

Violis, G.
See Simenon, Georges (Jacques Christian)

Visconti, Luchino 1906-1976 .... CLC **16**
See also CA 81-84; 65-68; CANR 39

Vittorini, Elio 1908-1966 ...... CLC **6, 9, 14**
See also CA 133; 25-28R

Vizinczey, Stephen 1933- .... CLC **40**
See also CA 128; INT 128

Vliet, R(ussell) G(ordon)
1929-1984 .... CLC **22**
See also CA 37-40R; 112; CANR 18

Vogau, Boris Andreyevich 1894-1937(?)
See Pilnyak, Boris
See also CA 123

Vogel, Paula A(nne) 1951- .... CLC **76**
See also CA 108

Voight, Ellen Bryant 1943- .... CLC **54**
See also CA 69-72; CANR 11, 29; DLB 120

Voigt, Cynthia 1942- .... CLC **30**
See also AAYA 3; CA 106; CANR 18, 37, 40; CLR 13; INT CANR-18; JRDA; MAICYA; SATA 48, 79; SATA-Brief 33

Voinovich, Vladimir (Nikolaevich)
1932- .... CLC **10, 49**
See also CA 81-84; CAAS 12; CANR 33; MTCW

Vollmann, William T. 1959- .... CLC **89**
See also CA 134; DAM NOV, POP

Voloshinov, V. N.
See Bakhtin, Mikhail Mikhailovich

Voltaire
1694-1778 ..... LC **14**; DA; DAB; DAC; SSC **12**; WLC
See also DAM DRAM, MST

von Daeniken, Erich 1935- .... CLC **30**
See also AITN 1; CA 37-40R; CANR 17, 44

von Daniken, Erich
See von Daeniken, Erich

von Heidenstam, (Carl Gustaf) Verner
See Heidenstam, (Carl Gustaf) Verner von

von Heyse, Paul (Johann Ludwig)
See Heyse, Paul (Johann Ludwig von)

von Hofmannsthal, Hugo
See Hofmannsthal, Hugo von

von Horvath, Odon
See Horvath, Oedoen von

von Horvath, Oedoen
See Horvath, Oedoen von

von Liliencron, (Friedrich Adolf Axel) Detlev
See Liliencron, (Friedrich Adolf Axel) Detlev von

Vonnegut, Kurt, Jr.
1922- ...... CLC **1, 2, 3, 4, 5, 8, 12, 22, 40, 60**; DA; DAB; DAC; SSC **8**; WLC
See also AAYA 6; AITN 1; BEST 90:4; CA 1-4R; CANR 1, 25, 49; CDALB 1968-1988; DAM MST, NOV, POP; DLB 2, 8, 152; DLBD 3; DLBY 80; MTCW

Von Rachen, Kurt
See Hubbard, L(afayette) Ron(ald)

von Rezzori (d'Arezzo), Gregor
See Rezzori (d'Arezzo), Gregor von

von Sternberg, Josef
See Sternberg, Josef von

Vorster, Gordon 1924- .... CLC **34**
See also CA 133

Vosce, Trudie
See Ozick, Cynthia

Voznesensky, Andrei (Andreievich)
1933- .... CLC **1, 15, 57**
See also CA 89-92; CANR 37; DAM POET; MTCW

Waddington, Miriam 1917- .... CLC **28**
See also CA 21-24R; CANR 12, 30; DLB 68

Wagman, Fredrica 1937- .... CLC **7**
See also CA 97-100; INT 97-100

Wagner, Richard 1813-1883 .... NCLC **9**
See also DLB 129

Wagner-Martin, Linda 1936- .... CLC **50**

Wagoner, David (Russell)
1926- .... CLC **3, 5, 15**
See also CA 1-4R; CAAS 3; CANR 2; DLB 5; SATA 14

Wah, Fred(erick James) 1939- ...... CLC **44**
See also CA 107; 141; DLB 60

Wahloo, Per 1926-1975 .... CLC **7**
See also CA 61-64

Wahloo, Peter
See Wahloo, Per

Wain, John (Barrington)
1925-1994 .... CLC **2, 11, 15, 46**
See also CA 5-8R; 145; CAAS 4; CANR 23; CDBLB 1960 to Present; DLB 15, 27, 139, 155; MTCW

Wajda, Andrzej 1926- .... CLC **16**
See also CA 102

Wakefield, Dan 1932- .... CLC **7**
See also CA 21-24R; CAAS 7

Wakoski, Diane
1937- ..... CLC **2, 4, 7, 9, 11, 40**; PC **15**
See also CA 13-16R; CAAS 1; CANR 9; DAM POET; DLB 5; INT CANR-9

Wakoski-Sherbell, Diane
See Wakoski, Diane

Walcott, Derek (Alton)
1930- .... CLC **2, 4, 9, 14, 25, 42, 67, 76**; BLC; DAB; DAC
See also BW 2; CA 89-92; CANR 26, 47; DAM MST, MULT, POET; DLB 117; DLBY 81; MTCW

Waldman, Anne 1945- .... CLC **7**
See also CA 37-40R; CAAS 17; CANR 34; DLB 16

Waldo, E. Hunter
See Sturgeon, Theodore (Hamilton)

Waldo, Edward Hamilton
See Sturgeon, Theodore (Hamilton)

Walker, Alice (Malsenior)
1944- .... CLC **5, 6, 9, 19, 27, 46, 58**; BLC; DA; DAB; DAC; SSC **5**
See also AAYA 3; BEST 89:4; BW 2; CA 37-40R; CANR 9, 27, 49; CDALB 1968-1988; DAM MST, MULT, NOV, POET, POP; DLB 6, 33, 143; INT CANR-27; MTCW; SATA 31

Walker, David Harry 1911-1992 .... CLC **14**
See also CA 1-4R; 137; CANR 1; SATA 8; SATA-Obit 71

Walker, Edward Joseph 1934-
See Walker, Ted
See also CA 21-24R; CANR 12, 28

Walker, George F.
1947- .... CLC **44, 61**; DAB; DAC
See also CA 103; CANR 21, 43; DAM MST; DLB 60

Walker, Joseph A. 1935- .... CLC **19**
See also BW 1; CA 89-92; CANR 26; DAM DRAM, MST; DLB 38

Walker, Margaret (Abigail)
1915- .... CLC **1, 6**; BLC
See also BW 2; CA 73-76; CANR 26; DAM MULT; DLB 76, 152; MTCW

Walker, Ted .... CLC **13**
See also Walker, Edward Joseph
See also DLB 40

Wallace, David Foster 1962- .... CLC **50**
See also CA 132

Wallace, Dexter
See Masters, Edgar Lee

Wallace, (Richard Horatio) Edgar
1875-1932 .... TCLC **57**
See also CA 115; DLB 70

Wallace, Irving 1916-1990 .... CLC **7, 13**
See also AITN 1; CA 1-4R; 132; CAAS 1; CANR 1, 27; DAM NOV, POP; INT CANR-27; MTCW

Wallant, Edward Lewis
1926-1962 .... CLC **5, 10**
See also CA 1-4R; CANR 22; DLB 2, 28, 143; MTCW

Walley, Byron
See Card, Orson Scott

Walpole, Horace 1717-1797 .... LC **2**
See also DLB 39, 104

Walpole, Hugh (Seymour)
1884-1941 .... TCLC **5**
See also CA 104; DLB 34

Walser, Martin 1927- .... CLC **27**
See also CA 57-60; CANR 8, 46; DLB 75, 124

Walser, Robert
1878-1956 .... TCLC **18**; SSC **20**
See also CA 118; DLB 66

Walsh, Jill Paton .... CLC **35**
See also Paton Walsh, Gillian
See also AAYA 11; CLR 2; DLB 161; SAAS 3

Walter, Villiam Christian
See Andersen, Hans Christian

Wilbur, Richard (Purdy)
  1921- . . . **CLC 3, 6, 9, 14, 53; DA; DAB;**
                                        DAC
  See also CA 1-4R; CABS 2; CANR 2, 29;
  DAM MST, POET; DLB 5;
  INT CANR-29; MTCW; SATA 9

Wild, Peter 1940- . . . . **CLC 14**
  See also CA 37-40R; DLB 5

Wilde, Oscar (Fingal O'Flahertie Wills)
  1854(?)-1900 . . . . **TCLC 1, 8, 23, 41; DA;**
                        DAB; DAC; SSC 11; WLC
  See also CA 104; 119; CDBLB 1890-1914;
  DAM DRAM, MST, NOV; DLB 10, 19,
  34, 57, 141, 156; SATA 24

Wilder, Billy . . . . **CLC 20**
  See also Wilder, Samuel
  See also DLB 26

Wilder, Samuel 1906-
  See Wilder, Billy
  See also CA 89-92

Wilder, Thornton (Niven)
  1897-1975 . . . . . . **CLC 1, 5, 6, 10, 15, 35,**
              82; DA; DAB; DAC; DC 1; WLC
  See also AITN 2; CA 13-16R; 61-64;
  CANR 40; DAM DRAM, MST, NOV;
  DLB 4, 7, 9; MTCW

Wilding, Michael 1942- . . . . **CLC 73**
  See also CA 104; CANR 24, 49

Wiley, Richard 1944- . . . . **CLC 44**
  See also CA 121; 129

Wilhelm, Kate . . . . **CLC 7**
  See also Wilhelm, Katie Gertrude
  See also CAAS 5; DLB 8; INT CANR-17

Wilhelm, Katie Gertrude 1928-
  See Wilhelm, Kate
  See also CA 37-40R; CANR 17, 36; MTCW

Wilkins, Mary
  See Freeman, Mary Eleanor Wilkins

Willard, Nancy 1936- . . . . **CLC 7, 37**
  See also CA 89-92; CANR 10, 39; CLR 5;
  DLB 5, 52; MAICYA; MTCW;
  SATA 37, 71; SATA-Brief 30

Williams, C(harles) K(enneth)
  1936- . . . . **CLC 33, 56**
  See also CA 37-40R; DAM POET; DLB 5

Williams, Charles
  See Collier, James L(incoln)

Williams, Charles (Walter Stansby)
  1886-1945 . . . . **TCLC 1, 11**
  See also CA 104; DLB 100, 153

Williams, (George) Emlyn
  1905-1987 . . . . **CLC 15**
  See also CA 104; 123; CANR 36;
  DAM DRAM; DLB 10, 77; MTCW

Williams, Hugo 1942- . . . . **CLC 42**
  See also CA 17-20R; CANR 45; DLB 40

Williams, J. Walker
  See Wodehouse, P(elham) G(renville)

Williams, John A(lfred)
  1925- . . . . **CLC 5, 13; BLC**
  See also BW 2; CA 53-56; CAAS 3;
  CANR 6, 26, 51; DAM MULT; DLB 2,
  33; INT CANR-6

Williams, Jonathan (Chamberlain)
  1929- . . . . **CLC 13**
  See also CA 9-12R; CAAS 12; CANR 8;
  DLB 5

Williams, Joy 1944- . . . . **CLC 31**
  See also CA 41-44R; CANR 22, 48

Williams, Norman 1952- . . . . **CLC 39**
  See also CA 118

Williams, Sherley Anne
  1944- . . . . **CLC 89; BLC**
  See also BW 2; CA 73-76; CANR 25;
  DAM MULT, POET; DLB 41;
  INT CANR-25; SATA 78

Williams, Shirley
  See Williams, Sherley Anne

Williams, Tennessee
  1911-1983 . . . . . **CLC 1, 2, 5, 7, 8, 11, 15,**
    19, 30, 39, 45, 71; DA; DAB; DAC;
                                   DC 4; WLC
  See also AITN 1, 2; CA 5-8R; 108;
  CABS 3; CANR 31; CDALB 1941-1968;
  DAM DRAM, MST; DLB 7; DLBD 4;
  DLBY 83; MTCW

Williams, Thomas (Alonzo)
  1926-1990 . . . . **CLC 14**
  See also CA 1-4R; 132; CANR 2

Williams, William C.
  See Williams, William Carlos

Williams, William Carlos
  1883-1963 . . . . **CLC 1, 2, 5, 9, 13, 22, 42,**
                     67; DA; DAB; DAC; PC 7
  See also CA 89-92; CANR 34;
  CDALB 1917-1929; DAM MST, POET;
  DLB 4, 16, 54, 86; MTCW

Williamson, David (Keith) 1942- . . . . **CLC 56**
  See also CA 103; CANR 41

Williamson, Ellen Douglas 1905-1984
  See Douglas, Ellen
  See also CA 17-20R; 114; CANR 39

Williamson, Jack . . . . **CLC 29**
  See also Williamson, John Stewart
  See also CAAS 8; DLB 8

Williamson, John Stewart 1908-
  See Williamson, Jack
  See also CA 17-20R; CANR 23

Willie, Frederick
  See Lovecraft, H(oward) P(hillips)

Willingham, Calder (Baynard, Jr.)
  1922-1995 . . . . **CLC 5, 51**
  See also CA 5-8R; 147; CANR 3; DLB 2,
  44; MTCW

Willis, Charles
  See Clarke, Arthur C(harles)

Willy
  See Colette, (Sidonie-Gabrielle)

Willy, Colette
  See Colette, (Sidonie-Gabrielle)

Wilson, A(ndrew) N(orman) 1950- . . **CLC 33**
  See also CA 112; 122; DLB 14, 155

Wilson, Angus (Frank Johnstone)
  1913-1991 . . **CLC 2, 3, 5, 25, 34; SSC 21**
  See also CA 5-8R; 134; CANR 21; DLB 15,
  139, 155; MTCW

Wilson, August
  1945- . . . . **CLC 39, 50, 63; BLC; DA;**
                              DAB; DAC; DC 2
  See also AAYA 16; BW 2; CA 115; 122;
  CANR 42; DAM DRAM, MST, MULT;
  MTCW

Wilson, Brian 1942- . . . . **CLC 12**

Wilson, Colin 1931- . . . . **CLC 3, 14**
  See also CA 1-4R; CAAS 5; CANR 1, 22,
  33; DLB 14; MTCW

Wilson, Dirk
  See Pohl, Frederik

Wilson, Edmund
  1895-1972 . . . . **CLC 1, 2, 3, 8, 24**
  See also CA 1-4R; 37-40R; CANR 1, 46;
  DLB 63; MTCW

Wilson, Ethel Davis (Bryant)
  1888(?)-1980 . . . . **CLC 13; DAC**
  See also CA 102; DAM POET; DLB 68;
  MTCW

Wilson, John 1785-1854 . . . . **NCLC 5**

Wilson, John (Anthony) Burgess 1917-1993
  See Burgess, Anthony
  See also CA 1-4R; 143; CANR 2, 46; DAC;
  DAM NOV; MTCW

Wilson, Lanford 1937- . . . . **CLC 7, 14, 36**
  See also CA 17-20R; CABS 3; CANR 45;
  DAM DRAM; DLB 7

Wilson, Robert M. 1944- . . . . **CLC 7, 9**
  See also CA 49-52; CANR 2, 41; MTCW

Wilson, Robert McLiam 1964- . . . . . **CLC 59**
  See also CA 132

Wilson, Sloan 1920- . . . . **CLC 32**
  See also CA 1-4R; CANR 1, 44

Wilson, Snoo 1948- . . . . **CLC 33**
  See also CA 69-72

Wilson, William S(mith) 1932- . . . . . **CLC 49**
  See also CA 81-84

Winchilsea, Anne (Kingsmill) Finch Counte
  1661-1720 . . . . **LC 3**

Windham, Basil
  See Wodehouse, P(elham) G(renville)

Wingrove, David (John) 1954- . . . . . . **CLC 68**
  See also CA 133

Winters, Janet Lewis . . . . **CLC 41**
  See also Lewis, Janet
  See also DLBY 87

Winters, (Arthur) Yvor
  1900-1968 . . . . **CLC 4, 8, 32**
  See also CA 11-12; 25-28R; CAP 1;
  DLB 48; MTCW

Winterson, Jeanette 1959- . . . . **CLC 64**
  See also CA 136; DAM POP

Winthrop, John 1588-1649 . . . . **LC 31**
  See also DLB 24, 30

Wiseman, Frederick 1930- . . . . **CLC 20**

Wister, Owen 1860-1938 . . . . **TCLC 21**
  See also CA 108; DLB 9, 78; SATA 62

Witkacy
  See Witkiewicz, Stanislaw Ignacy

Witkiewicz, Stanislaw Ignacy
  1885-1939 . . . . **TCLC 8**
  See also CA 105

Wittgenstein, Ludwig (Josef Johann)
1889-1951 .... **TCLC 59**
See also CA 113

Wittig, Monique 1935(?)-.......... **CLC 22**
See also CA 116; 135; DLB 83

Wittlin, Jozef 1896-1976 .... **CLC 25**
See also CA 49-52; 65-68; CANR 3

Wodehouse, P(elham) G(renville)
1881-1975 ... **CLC 1, 2, 5, 10, 22; DAB;**
DAC; SSC 2
See also AITN 2; CA 45-48; 57-60;
CANR 3, 33; CDBLB 1914-1945;
DAM NOV; DLB 34, 162; MTCW;
SATA 22

Woiwode, L.
See Woiwode, Larry (Alfred)

Woiwode, Larry (Alfred) 1941- ... **CLC 6, 10**
See also CA 73-76; CANR 16; DLB 6;
INT CANR-16

Wojciechowska, Maia (Teresa)
1927- .... **CLC 26**
See also AAYA 8; CA 9-12R; CANR 4, 41;
CLR 1; JRDA; MAICYA; SAAS 1;
SATA 1, 28, 83

Wolf, Christa 1929- .... **CLC 14, 29, 58**
See also CA 85-88; CANR 45; DLB 75;
MTCW

Wolfe, Gene (Rodman) 1931-....... **CLC 25**
See also CA 57-60; CAAS 9; CANR 6, 32;
DAM POP; DLB 8

Wolfe, George C. 1954- .... **CLC 49**
See also CA 149

Wolfe, Thomas (Clayton)
1900-1938 ..... **TCLC 4, 13, 29, 61; DA;**
DAB; DAC; WLC
See also CA 104; 132; CDALB 1929-1941;
DAM MST, NOV; DLB 9, 102; DLBD 2;
DLBY 85; MTCW

Wolfe, Thomas Kennerly, Jr. 1931-
See Wolfe, Tom
See also CA 13-16R; CANR 9, 33;
DAM POP; INT CANR-9; MTCW

Wolfe, Tom .... **CLC 1, 2, 9, 15, 35, 51**
See also Wolfe, Thomas Kennerly, Jr.
See also AAYA 8; AITN 2; BEST 89:1;
DLB 152

Wolff, Geoffrey (Ansell) 1937- ..... **CLC 41**
See also CA 29-32R; CANR 29, 43

Wolff, Sonia
See Levitin, Sonia (Wolff)

Wolff, Tobias (Jonathan Ansell)
1945- .... **CLC 39, 64**
See also AAYA 16; BEST 90:2; CA 114;
117; CAAS 22; DLB 130; INT 117

Wolfram von Eschenbach
c. 1170-c. 1220 .... **CMLC 5**
See also DLB 138

Wolitzer, Hilma 1930-........... **CLC 17**
See also CA 65-68; CANR 18, 40;
INT CANR-18; SATA 31

Wollstonecraft, Mary 1759-1797...... **LC 5**
See also CDBLB 1789-1832; DLB 39, 104,
158

Wonder, Stevie .... **CLC 12**
See also Morris, Steveland Judkins

Wong, Jade Snow 1922-.......... **CLC 17**
See also CA 109

Woodcott, Keith
See Brunner, John (Kilian Houston)

Woodruff, Robert W.
See Mencken, H(enry) L(ouis)

Woolf, (Adeline) Virginia
1882-1941 .... **TCLC 1, 5, 20, 43, 56;**
DA; DAB; DAC; SSC 7; WLC
See also CA 104; 130; CDBLB 1914-1945;
DAM MST, NOV; DLB 36, 100, 162;
DLBD 10; MTCW

Woollcott, Alexander (Humphreys)
1887-1943 .... **TCLC 5**
See also CA 105; DLB 29

Woolrich, Cornell 1903-1968...... **CLC 77**
See also Hopley-Woolrich, Cornell George

Wordsworth, Dorothy
1771-1855 .... **NCLC 25**
See also DLB 107

Wordsworth, William
1770-1850 .... **NCLC 12, 38; DA; DAB;**
DAC; PC 4; WLC
See also CDBLB 1789-1832; DAM MST,
POET; DLB 93, 107

Wouk, Herman 1915-......... **CLC 1, 9, 38**
See also CA 5-8R; CANR 6, 33;
DAM NOV, POP; DLBY 82;
INT CANR-6; MTCW

Wright, Charles (Penzel, Jr.)
1935- .... **CLC 6, 13, 28**
See also CA 29-32R; CAAS 7; CANR 23,
36; DLBY 82; MTCW

Wright, Charles Stevenson
1932- .... **CLC 49; BLC 3**
See also BW 1; CA 9-12R; CANR 26;
DAM MULT, POET; DLB 33

Wright, Jack R.
See Harris, Mark

Wright, James (Arlington)
1927-1980 .... **CLC 3, 5, 10, 28**
See also AITN 2; CA 49-52; 97-100;
CANR 4, 34; DAM POET; DLB 5;
MTCW

Wright, Judith (Arandell)
1915- .... **CLC 11, 53; PC 14**
See also CA 13-16R; CANR 31; MTCW;
SATA 14

Wright, L(aurali) R. 1939-........ **CLC 44**
See also CA 138

Wright, Richard (Nathaniel)
1908-1960 .... **CLC 1, 3, 4, 9, 14, 21, 48,**
74; BLC; DA; DAB; DAC; SSC 2; WLC
See also AAYA 5; BW 1; CA 108;
CDALB 1929-1941; DAM MST, MULT,
NOV; DLB 76, 102; DLBD 2; MTCW

Wright, Richard B(ruce) 1937- ...... **CLC 6**
See also CA 85-88; DLB 53

Wright, Rick 1945-............... **CLC 35**

Wright, Rowland
See Wells, Carolyn

Wright, Stephen Caldwell 1946- .... **CLC 33**
See also BW 2

Wright, Willard Huntington 1888-1939
See Van Dine, S. S.
See also CA 115

Wright, William 1930-............ **CLC 44**
See also CA 53-56; CANR 7, 23

Wroth, LadyMary 1587-1653(?) ..... **LC 30**
See also DLB 121

Wu Ch'eng-en 1500(?)-1582(?)........ **LC 7**

Wu Ching-tzu 1701-1754 .... **LC 2**

Wurlitzer, Rudolph 1938(?)- ... **CLC 2, 4, 15**
See also CA 85-88

Wycherley, William 1641-1715.... **LC 8, 21**
See also CDBLB 1660-1789; DAM DRAM;
DLB 80

Wylie, Elinor (Morton Hoyt)
1885-1928 .... **TCLC 8**
See also CA 105; DLB 9, 45

Wylie, Philip (Gordon) 1902-1971... **CLC 43**
See also CA 21-22; 33-36R; CAP 2; DLB 9

Wyndham, John.................. **CLC 19**
See also Harris, John (Wyndham Parkes
Lucas) Beynon

Wyss, Johann David Von
1743-1818 .... **NCLC 10**
See also JRDA; MAICYA; SATA 29;
SATA-Brief 27

Xenophon
c. 430B.C.-c. 354B.C......... **CMLC 17**

Yakumo Koizumi
See Hearn, (Patricio) Lafcadio (Tessima
Carlos)

Yanez, Jose Donoso
See Donoso (Yanez), Jose

Yanovsky, Basile S.
See Yanovsky, V(assily) S(emenovich)

Yanovsky, V(assily) S(emenovich)
1906-1989 .... **CLC 2, 18**
See also CA 97-100; 129

Yates, Richard 1926-1992 ..... **CLC 7, 8, 23**
See also CA 5-8R; 139; CANR 10, 43;
DLB 2; DLBY 81, 92; INT CANR-10

Yeats, W. B.
See Yeats, William Butler

Yeats, William Butler
1865-1939 ..... **TCLC 1, 11, 18, 31; DA;**
DAB; DAC; WLC
See also CA 104; 127; CANR 45;
CDBLB 1890-1914; DAM DRAM, MST,
POET; DLB 10, 19, 98, 156; MTCW

Yehoshua, A(braham) B.
1936- .... **CLC 13, 31**
See also CA 33-36R; CANR 43

Yep, Laurence Michael 1948-....... **CLC 35**
See also AAYA 5; CA 49-52; CANR 1, 46;
CLR 3, 17; DLB 52; JRDA; MAICYA;
SATA 7, 69

Yerby, Frank G(arvin)
1916-1991 .... **CLC 1, 7, 22; BLC**
See also BW 1; CA 9-12R; 136; CANR 16;
DAM MULT; DLB 76; INT CANR-16;
MTCW

Yesenin, Sergei Alexandrovich
See Esenin, Sergei (Alexandrovich)

Yevtushenko, Yevgeny (Alexandrovich)
1933- .... **CLC 1, 3, 13, 26, 51**
See also CA 81-84; CANR 33;
DAM POET; MTCW

Literary Criticism Series
Cumulative Topic Index

This index lists all topic entries in Gale's *Classical and Medieval Literature Criticism, Contemporary Literary Criticism, Literature Criticism from 1400 to 1800, Nineteenth-Century Literature Criticism,* and *Twentieth-Century Literary Criticism.*

Topic Index

Topic Index

TCLC Cumulative Nationality Index

AMERICAN

Adams, Andy **56**
Adams, Henry (Brooks) **4, 52**
Agee, James (Rufus) **1, 19**
Anderson, Maxwell **2**
Anderson, Sherwood **1, 10, 24**
Atherton, Gertrude (Franklin Horn) **2**
Austin, Mary (Hunter) **25**
Baker, Ray Stannard **47**
Barry, Philip **11**
Baum, L(yman) Frank **7**
Beard, Charles A(ustin) **15**
Becker, Carl **63**
Belasco, David **3**
Bell, James Madison **43**
Benchley, Robert (Charles) **1, 55**
Benedict, Ruth **60**
Benet, Stephen Vincent **7**
Benet, William Rose **28**
Bierce, Ambrose (Gwinett) **1, 7, 44**
Black Elk **33**
Boas, Franz **56**
Bodenheim, Maxwell **44**
Bourne, Randolph S(illiman) **16**
Bradford, Gamaliel **36**
Brennan, Christopher John **17**
Bromfield, Louis (Brucker) **11**
Burroughs, Edgar Rice **2, 32**
Cabell, James Branch **6**
Cable, George Washington **4**
Carnegie, Dale **53**
Cather, Willa Sibert **1, 11, 31**
Chambers, Robert W. **41**
Chandler, Raymond (Thornton) **1, 7**
Chapman, John Jay **7**
Chesnutt, Charles W(addell) **5, 39**
Chopin, Kate **5, 14**
Cohan, George M. **60**
Comstock, Anthony **13**

Cotter, Joseph Seamon Sr. **28**
Cram, Ralph Adams **45**
Crane, (Harold) Hart **2, 5**
Crane, Stephen (Townley) **11, 17, 32**
Crawford, F(rancis) Marion **10**
Crothers, Rachel **19**
Cullen, Countee **4, 37**
Davis, Rebecca (Blaine) Harding **6**
Davis, Richard Harding **24**
Day, Clarence (Shepard Jr.) **25**
De Voto, Bernard (Augustine) **29**
Dreiser, Theodore (Herman Albert) **10, 18, 35**
Dunbar, Paul Laurence **2, 12**
Dunne, Finley Peter **28**
Eastman, Charles A(lexander) **55**
Faust, Frederick (Schiller) **49**
Fisher, Rudolph **11**
Fitzgerald, F(rancis) Scott (Key) **1, 6, 14, 28, 55**
Fitzgerald, Zelda (Sayre) **52**
Flecker, (Herman) James Elroy **43**
Fletcher, John Gould **35**
Forten, Charlotte L. **16**
Freeman, Douglas Southall **11**
Freeman, Mary Eleanor Wilkins **9**
Futrelle, Jacques **19**
Gale, Zona **7**
Garland, (Hannibal) Hamlin **3**
Gilman, Charlotte (Anna) Perkins (Stetson) **9, 37**
Glasgow, Ellen (Anderson Gholson) **2, 7**
Glaspell, Susan (Keating) **55**
Goldman, Emma **13**
Green, Anna Katharine **63**
Grey, Zane **6**
Guiney, Louise Imogen **41**
Hall, James Norman **23**
Harper, Frances Ellen Watkins **14**

Harris, Joel Chandler **2**
Harte, (Francis) Bret(t) **1, 25**
Hatteras, Owen **18**
Hawthorne, Julian **25**
Hearn, (Patricio) Lafcadio (Tessima Carlos) **9**
Henry, O. **1, 19**
Hergesheimer, Joseph **11**
Higginson, Thomas Wentworth **36**
Hopkins, Pauline Elizabeth **28**
Howard, Robert Ervin **8**
Howe, Julia Ward **21**
Howells, William Dean **7, 17, 41**
James, Henry **2, 11, 24, 40, 47**
James, William **15, 32**
Jewett, (Theodora) Sarah Orne **1, 22**
Johnson, James Weldon **3, 19**
Kornbluth, C(yril) M. **8**
Korzybski, Alfred (Habdank Skarbek) **61**
Kuttner, Henry **10**
Lardner, Ring(gold) W(ilmer) **2, 14**
Lewis, (Harry) Sinclair **4, 13, 23, 39**
Lewisohn, Ludwig **19**
Lindsay, (Nicholas) Vachel **17**
Locke, Alain (Le Roy) **43**
London, Jack **9, 15, 39**
Lovecraft, H(oward) P(hillips) **4, 22**
Lowell, Amy **1, 8**
Markham, Edwin **47**
Marquis, Don(ald Robert Perry) **7**
Masters, Edgar Lee **2, 25**
McCoy, Horace (Stanley) **28**
McKay, Claude **7, 41**
Mencken, H(enry) L(ouis) **13**
Millay, Edna St. Vincent **4, 49**
Mitchell, Margaret (Munnerlyn) **11**
Mitchell, S(ilas) Weir **36**
Monroe, Harriet **12**
Muir, John **28**

479